Baseball America®
2014 PROSPECT HANDBOOK

BASEBALL AMERICA INC. DURHAM, N.C.

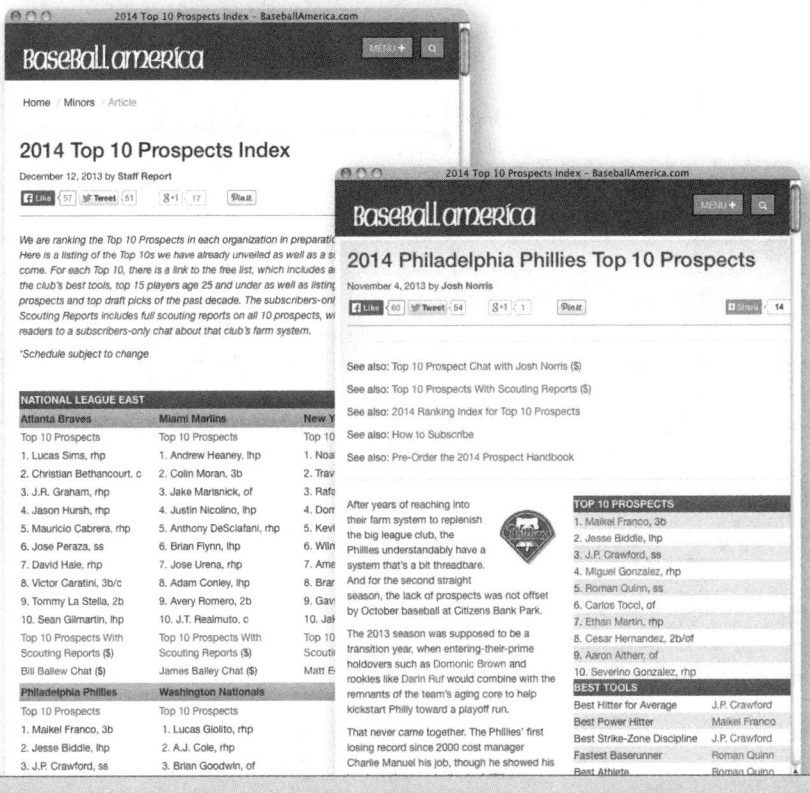

EDITOR'S NOTE: Transactions for this book go through Dec. 1. As always, you can find players even if they have changed organizations by using the handy index in the back. >> For the purposes of this book, a prospect is any player who has no more than 50 innings pitched, 30 relief appearances or 130 at-bats in the major leagues, regardless of service time. Finally, the grades you'll find for each team's drafts are based solely on the quality of the players signed, with no consideration for whom players were traded for or how many picks a team might have lost.

Baseball America 2014 Prospect Handbook

Editors

Matt Eddy, Will Lingo, John Manuel

Assistant Editors

Ben Badler, J.J. Cooper, Aaron Fitt, Vincent Lara-Cinisomo, Josh Leventhal, Clint Longenecker, Josh Norris, Jim Shonerd

Database and Application Development

Brent Lewis

Contributing Writers

Andy Baggarly, James Bailey, Bill Ballew, Mike Berardino, Jack Etkin, Derrick Goold, Tom Haudricourt, Steve Melewski, Bill Mitchell, John Perrotto, Alex Speier

Photo Editor

Jim Shonerd

Design & Production

Sara Hiatt McDaniel, Linwood Webb

Cover Photo

Miguel Sano by Mike Janes

For additional copies, visit our Website at BaseballAmerica.com or call 1-800-845-2726 to order. US $32.95, plus shipping and handling per order. Expedited shipping available.

Distributed by Simon & Schuster ISBN: 978-1-932391-50-3

Statistics provided by Major League Baseball Advanced Media and compiled by Baseball America

TABLE OF CONTENTS

The top two picks in the 2012 draft, Astros shorststop Carlos Correa (right) and Twins outfielder Byron Buxton (left), tore through the low Class A Midwest League during the 2013 season

INTRODUCTION

Our greatest hope with the 2014 Prospect Handbook is that it reads like the same old Prospect Handbook you have come to know and love.

That was a tall task, because the man who invented the Prospect Handbook, Jim Callis, left BA in 2013. The strength of the book, however, remained behind here at Baseball America's World Headquarters on the outskirts of Durham, N.C.

That strength is the process that everyone at BA has contributed to building in more than 30 years of Baseball America and now 14 years of Prospect Handbooks. When Allan Simpson created the magazine in 1981, he created a chronicle of the baseball world below the major league level. Over the years, he realized the best way to cover the sport at that level was through a scouting and player-development focus.

Editors and writers such as Danny Knobler, Ken Leiker, John Royster and Jon Scher honed that focus. Callis, who came aboard in the late 1980s and spent most of the next 25 years with BA, shaped it and helped define it. Writers such as Mike Berardino (who returns to the Handbook as a contributor this year) and Alan Schwarz proved we could deliver insider scouting and player development information with entertaining, lively prose while telling the stories behind these players, beyond their profiles.

The 21st century brought the Handbook and the Information Age, and it has brought changes to the BA staff, which usually come in waves. The last wave was in 2007-2008, and then 2013 brought another wave. Through these changes, Will Lingo (entering his 20th year at BA) and I have stuck around, becoming familiar with local restaurants for lunch and familiar to Handbook writers for badgering them to send their files and move this or that player up or down the list.

The writers have changed, but the process really hasn't. BA staffers such as Ben Badler and J.J. Cooper spearhead our minor league coverage during the season; veterans like me and Aaron Fitt cover the amateur game and draft, and our database of scouting reports from the games we attend and the scouts, managers and player-development personnel we talk to continues to grow.

This year, it was my task to marshall all those writers, with Associate Editor Matt Eddy stepping into the breech to provide his attention to detail and organizational chops. Mr. Lingo still comes in with a layer of editing to shape the book's final product with an ease of operation that we all envy.

We try to include the same basic tools information in all 900 scouting reports so they are readable both here in the Handbook and on the Player Cards for subscribers to BaseballAmerica.com, a challenge almost as great as compiling all the information for those 900 reports. We try to line up the players using the BA Grade Scale, found on Page 7, and profile players' future major league roles using the Minor League Depth Chart on Page 8. I strongly recommend reading those two pages first, to lay the foundation for the nearly 500 pages of reports that follow.

It takes a lot of passion—an audacity, really—to try to pull off such a task, and a lot of hard work by a lot of good people to make it so. The final result, we trust, is the same Prospect Handbook you've come to know and love over the years, the industry standard and BA's signature publication. We hope you enjoy it.

JOHN MANUEL
EDITOR IN CHIEF
BASEBALL AMERICA

BA GRADES

For the third year in a row, Baseball America has assigned Grades and Risk Factors for each and every one of the 900 prospects in the Prospect Handbook. For the BA Grade, we used a 20-to-80 scale, similar to the scale scouts use, to keep it familiar. However, most major league clubs put an overall numerical grade on players, called the Overall Future Potential or OFP. Often the OFP is merely an average of the player's tools.

The BA Grade is *not* an OFP. It's a measure of a prospect's value, and it attempts to gauge the player's realistic ceiling. We've continued to adjust our grades to try to be more realistic, and less optimistic, and keep refining the grade vetting process.

Because we're writing about prospects, the lowest grade given for a realistic ceiling is a 40. Bryce Harper remains the lone 80 grade we've given out, and Minor League Player of the Year Byron Buxton earned a 75 this year, highest in the book. He represents the ideal combination for prospects: prodigious, top-of-the-scale tools, success in the minor leagues, and a small gap between his potential and the "now" skills.

The realistic ceiling grade doesn't tell a prospect's entire story. How close that player is to reaching his ceiling matters just as much. The less we believe scouts have to project on the prospect, the less risky he is. That's why we also have assigned every player a Risk Factor to go with their BA Grade. That scale is fairly self-explanatory, ranging from Safe (least risk) to Extreme (riskiest). The closer a player is to reaching his realistic ceiling, the safer he rates.

Only players who have appeared in the major leagues can earn a Safe, while Low risk players have performed well in Double-A or Triple-A or need little projection. Most players are labeled High risk, which can incorporate a player's low level of experience, injury history or poor statistical profile, such as a lopsided strikeout-to-walk ratio for a hitter. The players with the largest gap between what they are and what they could be are labeled Extreme. We used that more liberally in this edition, particularly with players with injury history.

The goal of the Grade/Risk system is to allow readers to take a quick look at how strong their team's farm system is, and also how much immediate help the big league club can expect from its prospects. It should also help with our Organization Rankings, but those will not simply flow, in formulaic fashion, from the Grades/Risk Factor results. Some staff members favor star power in a farm system while others favor depth; that cannot be easily summed up in a spreadsheet.

The BA Grade has evolved in this third incarnation, just as the Prospect Handbook has evolved over the years. We keep trying to make the book better and believe the addition of the BA Grade system is the next step in making the Prospect Handbook more indispensable than ever to the game's fans and fantasy players.

BA Grade Scale

75-80: Franchise players and No. 1 starters, such as Miguel Cabrera, Clayton Kershaw, David Price and Mike Trout.

65-70: No. 2 starters and perennial all-stars in the mold of Adrian Beltre, Jon Lester and Yadier Molina.

55-60: First-division regulars and No. 3 starters and elite closers, such as Elvis Andrus, Jay Bruce, Craig Kimbrel and Justin Masterson would earn these grades.

BA GRADE
60
MEDIUM

45-50: The 50s profile as solid-average regulars with higher peaks, hard-throwing eighth-inning relievers and fourth starters on playoff teams such as Brett Gardner, Chris Iannetta and Mike Leake. The 45s are good utility players or semi-regulars, back-end starters and steady middle relievers such as Mike Aviles, Kevin Correia and Matt Guerrier.

40: Players with swingman or utility/backup catcher upside, or same-side relief specialists. This category includes the likes of Robert Andino, Joe Thatcher and P.J. Walters.

Risk Factors

SAFE: Has shown realistic ceiling in big leagues; ready to contribute in 2014.

LOW: Likely to reach realistic ceiling, certain big league career barring injury.

MEDIUM: Still some work to do to turn tools into major league-caliber skills.

HIGH: Most draft picks in their first seasons, players with plenty of projection left.

EXTREME: Teenagers in Rookie ball or players with significant injury histories.

MINOR LEAGUE DEPTH CHART

AN OVERVIEW

Another feature of the Prospect Handbook is a depth chart of every organization's minor league talent. This shows you at a glance what kind of talent a system has and provides even more prospects beyond the Top 30.

Players are usually listed on the depth charts where we think they'll ultimately end up. To help you better understand why players are slotted at particular positions, we show you here what scouts look for in the ideal candidate at each spot, with individual tools ranked in descending order.

LF
Power
Hitting
Fielding
Arm Strength
Speed

RF
Power
Hitting
Arm Strength
Fielding
Speed

3B
Power
Hitting
Fielding
Arm Strength
Speed

2B
Hitting
Fielding
Power
Speed
Arm Strength

1B
Power
Hitting
Fielding
Arm Strength
Speed

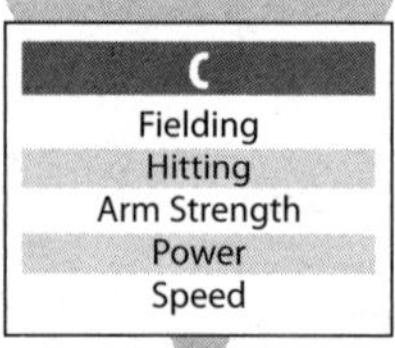

STARTING PITCHERS

No. 1 starter
- Two plus pitches
- Average third pitch
- Plus-plus command
- Plus makeup

No. 2 starter
- Two plus pitches
- Average third pitch
- Average command
- Average makeup

No. 3 starter
- One plus pitch
- Two average pitches
- Average command
- Average makeup

No. 4-5 starters
- Command of two major league pitches
- Average velocity
- Consistent breaking ball
- Decent changeup

CLOSER
- One dominant pitch
- Second plus pitch
- Plus command
- Plus-plus makeup

TOP 50 PROSPECTS

When Baseball America ranks prospects, there's almost always a byline attributing the ranking to the person who finally put the players in order, who decided, "OK, this guy's No. 6 and this guy's No. 7." But in truth, all of our rankings are more than one person's opinion. They are most often a reflection of the consensus of sources on the subject—managers, coaches, scouts, front-office personnel, the whole spectrum—filtered through the expertise of our writers and editors.

Except here, really. In this section of the Handbook, we get personal. Sifting through all of the information we've gathered to this point, four of our editors give their own personal takes on the game's top 50 prospects. This helps form the basis of the arguments that shape Baseball America's official Top 100 Prospects list, which is released each February. We consider it the definitive guide to the best talent in the minor leagues, and you can find it in our print edition or online at BaseballAmerica.com.

The rules for these lists are the same for any prospect who appears in the Handbook: no more than 130 at-bats, 50 innings or 30 relief appearances in the major leagues. We do not consider service time in our eligibility requirements.

As with any prospect list, these rankings represent how each person regarded the top minor league talent in the game at a moment in time. Ask us again in a few months—or even tomorrow—how these prospects stack up, and you'll get a different answer.

MIKE JANES

Raul A. Mondesi, 18, is the youngest hitter on a Top 50 list

JOHN MANUEL

1. Byron Buxton, of, Twins
2. Xander Bogaerts, ss/3b, Red Sox
3. Oscar Taveras, of, Cardinals
4. Miguel Sano, 3b, Twins
5. Javier Baez, ss, Cubs
6. Kris Bryant, 3b, Cubs
7. Carlos Correa, ss, Astros
8. Archie Bradley, rhp, Diamondbacks
9. Taijuan Walker, rhp, Mariners
10. Jonathan Gray, rhp, Rockies
11. Gregory Polanco, of, Pirates
12. Dylan Bundy, rhp, Orioles
13. Addison Russell, ss, Athletics
14. Francisco Lindor, ss, Indians
15. Noah Syndergaard, rhp, Mets
16. Eddie Butler, rhp, Rockies
17. Jameson Taillon, rhp, Pirates
18. Kevin Gausman, rhp, Orioles
19. George Springer, of, Astros
20. Robert Stephenson, rhp, Reds
21. Maikel Franco, 3b, Phillies
22. Nick Castellanos, 3b/of, Tigers
23. C.J. Edwards, rhp, Cubs
24. Kyle Crick, rhp, Giants
25. Austin Hedges, c, Padres
26. Kyle Zimmer, rhp, Royals
27. Andrew Heaney, lhp, Marlins
28. Gary Sanchez, c, Yankees
29. Yordano Ventura, rhp, Royals
30. Jorge Alfaro, c, Rangers
31. Clint Frazier, of, Indians
32. Austin Meadows, of, Pirates
33. Joc Pederson, of, Dodgers
34. Aaron Sanchez, rhp, Blue Jays
35. Henry Owens, lhp, Red Sox
36. Matt Wisler, rhp, Padres
37. Travis d'Arnaud, c, Mets
38. Corey Seager, ss, Dodgers
39. Lucas Giolito, rhp, Nationals
40. Jose Abreu, 1b, White Sox
41. Billy Hamilton, of, Reds
42. Julio Urias, lhp, Dodgers
43. Alex Meyer, rhp, Twins
44. Mark Appel, rhp, Astros
45. Edwin Escobar, lhp, Giants
46. Albert Almora, of, Cubs
47. Carlos Martinez, rhp, Cardinals
48. Rougned Odor, 2b, Rangers
49. Joey Gallo, 3b, Rangers
50. Raul A. Mondesi, ss, Royals

MATT EDDY

1. Byron Buxton, of, Twins
2. Xander Bogaerts, ss/3b, Red Sox
3. Oscar Taveras, of, Cardinals
4. Carlos Correa, ss, Astros
5. Jonathan Gray, rhp, Rockies
6. Archie Bradley, rhp, Diamondbacks
7. Javier Baez, ss, Cubs
8. Taijuan Walker, rhp, Mariners
9. Gregory Polanco, of, Pirates
10. Miguel Sano, 3b, Twins
11. Kris Bryant, 3b, Cubs
12. Francisco Lindor, ss, Indians
13. Maikel Franco, 3b, Phillies
14. Noah Syndergaard, rhp, Mets
15. Jameson Taillon, rhp, Pirates
16. Dylan Bundy, rhp, Orioles
17. Lucas Giolito, rhp, Nationals
18. Addison Russell, ss, Athletics
19. Eddie Butler, rhp, Rockies
20. Robert Stephenson, rhp, Reds
21. Nick Castellanos, 3b/of, Tigers
22. Kyle Zimmer, rhp, Royals
23. Kevin Gausman, rhp, Orioles
24. Austin Hedges, c, Padres
25. Kyle Crick, rhp, Giants
26. Rougned Odor, 2b, Rangers
27. George Springer, of, Astros
28. Andrew Heaney, lhp, Marlins
29. Matt Wisler, rhp, Padres
30. Gary Sanchez, c, Yankees
31. Jose Abreu, 1b, White Sox
32. Henry Owens, lhp, Red Sox
33. Joc Pederson, of, Dodgers
34. Clint Frazier, of, Indians
35. Mark Appel, rhp, Astros
36. Max Fried, lhp, Padres
37. Yordano Ventura, rhp, Royals
38. Carlos Martinez, rhp, Cardinals
39. C.J. Edwards, rhp, Cubs
40. Corey Seager, ss, Dodgers
41. Julio Urias, lhp, Dodgers
42. Jackie Bradley, of, Red Sox
43. Kolten Wong, 2b, Cardinals
44. Travis d'Arnaud, c, Mets
45. Tyler Glasnow, rhp, Pirates
46. Aaron Sanchez, rhp, Blue Jays
47. Marcus Stroman, rhp, Blue Jays
48. Jonathan Singleton, 1b, Astros
49. Chris Owings, ss, Diamondbacks
50. Raul A. Mondesi, ss, Royals

J. J. COOPER

1. Byron Buxton, of, Twins
2. Xander Bogaerts, ss/3b, Red Sox
3. Oscar Taveras, of, Cardinals
4. Javier Baez, ss, Cubs
5. Kris Bryant, 3b, Cubs
6. Miguel Sano, 3b, Twins
7. Addison Russell, ss, Athletics
8. Francisco Lindor, ss, Indians
9. Archie Bradley, rhp, Diamondbacks
10. Jonathan Gray, rhp, Rockies
11. Carlos Correa, ss, Astros
12. Taijuan Walker, rhp, Mariners
13. Gregory Polanco, of, Pirates
14. Carlos Martinez, rhp, Cardinals
15. Robert Stephenson, rhp, Reds
16. Dylan Bundy, rhp, Orioles
17. Kevin Gausman, rhp, Orioles
18. Eddie Butler, rhp, Rockies
19. Maikel Franco, 3b, Phillies
20. Noah Syndergaard, rhp, Mets
21. Kyle Zimmer, rhp, Royals
22. Yordano Ventura, rhp, Royals
23. Jameson Taillon, rhp, Pirates
24. Lucas Giolito, rhp, Nationals
25. George Springer, of, Astros
26. Kyle Crick, rhp, Giants
27. C.J. Edwards, rhp, Cubs
28. Jose Abreu, 1b, White Sox
29. Joc Pederson, of, Dodgers
30. Nick Castellanos, 3b/of, Tigers
31. Austin Hedges, c, Padres
32. Albert Almora, of, Cubs
33. Gary Sanchez, c, Yankees
34. Julio Urias, lhp, Dodgers
35. Corey Seager, ss, Dodgers
36. Billy Hamilton, of, Reds
37. Tyler Glasnow, rhp, Pirates
38. Aaron Sanchez, rhp, Blue Jays
39. Jorge Soler, of, Cubs
40. Jackie Bradley, of, Red Sox
41. Raul A. Mondesi, ss, Royals
42. Andrew Heaney, lhp, Marlins
43. Jorge Alfaro, c, Rangers
44. Erik Johnson, rhp, White Sox
45. Henry Owens, lhp, Red Sox
46. Travis d'Arnaud, c, Mets
47. Marcus Stroman, rhp, Blue Jays
48. Rougned Odor, 2b, Rangers
49. Chris Owings, ss, Diamondbacks
50. J.P. Crawford, ss, Phillies

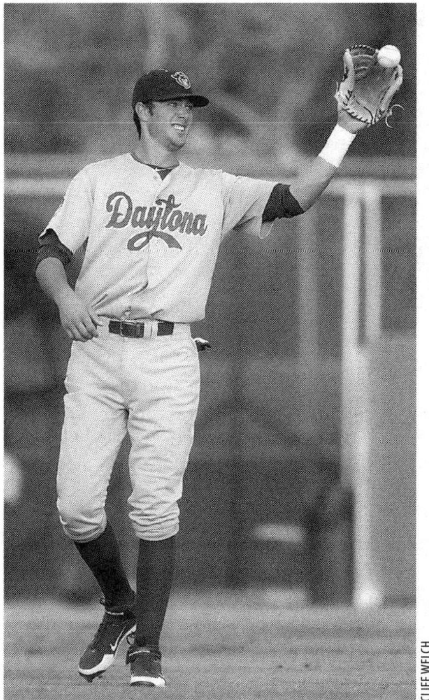

CLIFF WELCH

Kris Bryant won the Golden Spikes Award and the Florida State League championship

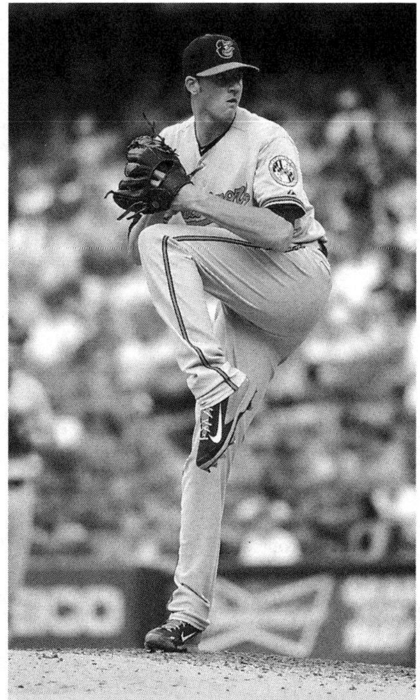

TOMASSO DeROSA

Kevin Gausman thrived while pitching in the Baltimore bullpen but profiles as a starter

BEN BADLER

1. Byron Buxton, of, Twins
2. Xander Bogaerts, ss/3b, Red Sox
3. Oscar Taveras, of, Cardinals
4. Addison Russell, ss, Athletics
5. Javier Baez, ss, Cubs
6. Carlos Correa, ss, Astros
7. Archie Bradley, rhp, Diamondbacks
8. Miguel Sano, 3b, Twins
9. Francisco Lindor, ss, Indians
10. Taijuan Walker, rhp, Mariners
11. Gregory Polanco, of, Pirates
12. Joc Pederson, of, Dodgers
13. Dylan Bundy, rhp, Orioles
14. Jonathan Gray, rhp, Rockies
15. Robert Stephenson, rhp, Reds
16. Travis d'Arnaud, c, Mets
17. Maikel Franco, 3b, Phillies
18. Jose Abreu, 1b, White Sox
19. Lucas Giolito, rhp, Nationals
20. Kyle Zimmer, rhp, Royals
21. Noah Syndergaard, rhp, Mets
22. Jorge Soler, of, Cubs
23. Kris Bryant, 3b, Cubs
24. Jackie Bradley, of, Red Sox
25. George Springer, of, Astros
26. Nick Castellanos, 3b/of, Tigers
27. Jameson Taillon, rhp, Pirates
28. Kohl Stewart, rhp, Twins
29. Garin Cecchini, 3b, Red Sox
30. Rougned Odor, 2b, Rangers
31. Albert Almora, of, Cubs
32. Corey Seager, ss, Dodgers
33. Julio Urias, lhp, Dodgers
34. Marcus Stroman, rhp, Blue Jays
35. Henry Owens, lhp, Red Sox
36. Mark Appel, rhp, Astros
37. Alex Meyer, rhp, Twins
38. Eddie Butler, rhp, Rockies
39. Tyler Glasnow, rhp, Pirates
40. Mookie Betts, 2b, Red Sox
41. Marcus Semien, ss/2b/3b, White Sox
42. Austin Meadows, of, Pirates
43. Allen Webster, rhp, Red Sox
44. Matt Wisler, rhp, Padres
45. Nick Kingham, rhp, Pirates
46. C.J. Edwards, rhp, Cubs
47. Carlos Martinez, rhp, Cardinals
48. David Dahl, of, Rockies
49. Jake Marisnick, of, Marlins
50. Jesse Winker, of, Reds

TALENT RANKINGS

		2013	2012	2011	2010	2009
01	**Pittsburgh Pirates**	8	13	19	16	18

Last year was first time Pirates cracked the top 10 organization rankings in Prospect Handbook history. Now they're No. 1 a year later. After ending their losing-seasons streak and playoff drought, the Pirates have brighter days ahead.

02	**Boston Red Sox**	6	10	17	6	13

Perennial playoff contender spends money but also builds from within. A playoff-proven shortstop, excellent up-the-middle depth and plenty of pitching prospects equal a top farm system once again for the World Series champs.

03	**Minnesota Twins**	10	19	13	7	22

The Twins have to build from within, so a recent dip in the farm system resulted in a corresponding drop in the big leagues. The Twins can't match a few other teams' depth of impact arms but Byron Buxton and Miguel Sano are a great equalizer.

04	**Chicago Cubs**	13	14	8	15	27

After building a very healthy farm system in Boston, Theo Epstein and company are doing the same in Chicago. It's a very top-heavy system that drops off in talent quickly, but championship teams are built on star power.

05	**Houston Astros**	9	17	26	30	30

What was once easily the worst system in baseball has gotten steadily better while the big league club has endured a disastrous stretch of futility. As good as the system is now, it could be even better in a year after drafting No. 1 again in June.

06	**San Diego Padres**	15	8	9	20	29

Pitchers love to pitch at Petco Park, and the Padres have plenty of pitchers who could end up there. The club stands out for its impressive depth of high-ceiling pitching prospects and top catcher Austin Hedges.

07	**St. Louis Cardinals**	1	12	24	29	8

Last year's top farm system graduated Michael Wacha, Shelby Miller, Trevor Rosenthal, Matt Adams and more. But the club still has one of the best pure hitters in the minors in Oscar Taveras and a 100 mph righthander in Carlos Martinez.

08	**Kansas City Royals**	18	3	1	17	11

The Royals have a second-wave of prospects nearing the big leagues. If Kansas City is going to take the final step to a playoff appearance, righthanders Yordano Ventura and Kyle Zimmer need to help fill the hole created when Ervin Santana left in free agency.

09	**Texas Rangers**	3	2	15	2	1

No farm system has been as consistently good as Texas' in the past five years. A decade from now, the Rangers could have produced the best or worst crop of prospects in this year's class—high ceilings, but they are oh so risky.

10	**New York Mets**	26	24	20	22	17

New CBA's draft spending rules have helped Mets, who rarely went over slot under old system. Some astute trades have butressed a steadily improving farm system that has several prospects ready to contribute.

11	**Colorado Rockies**	20	16	10	10	20

Rockies are another team with more potential impact talent than depth. The combination of Jonathan Gray and Eddie Butler lifts the Rockies from the late teens to the cusp of the top 10. A return to form from David Dahl after a lost season would help.

12	**Baltimore Orioles**	17	20	21	9	9

The Orioles are always a system built around a select few star prospects. It's worked quite well for Manny Machado, Matt Wieters and Adam Jones, and Kevin Gausman and Dylan Bundy look to continue the tradition in 2014 and beyond.

13	**Arizona Diamondbacks**	7	4	22	27	26

Even after trading Trevor Bauer and graduating Tyler Skaggs and Pat Corbin, the Diamondbacks still have power pitching, led by Archie Bradley and Braden Shipley. That, plus depth at shortstop, elevates an otherwise pretty run-of-the-mill farm system.

14	**Los Angeles Dodgers**	19	23	12	24	23

Dodgers' big-spending in recent years has helped bulk up a farm system once starved by Frank McCourt's miserly ways. A team that once spent almost nothing on international players has spent $100 million on Yasiel Puig, Hyun-Jin Ryu and Alex Guerrero in past two years.

15	**Toronto Blue Jays**	12	5	4	28	19

Think the Rangers have a high-risk, high-reward system? The Blue Jays took that approach and turned it up to 11. This system could be No. 1 next year if it all comes together, or No. 30 if high-ceiling, high-risk prospects crash and burn.

		2013	2012	2011	2010	2009
16	**Cincinnati Reds**	14	7	6	23	14
	Recent big league success and graduations have thinned a usually solid farm system. Reds have a number of interesting outfielders and a potential ace in Robert Stephenson, but lack infielders who profile as more than fringe big leaguers.					
17	**Cleveland Indians**	24	29	7	3	7
	After Danny Salazar helped spur a surprising playoff run, Francisco Lindor isn't far away from trying to build on that success. The system thins out pretty quickly, but a shift in draft philosophy has helped.					
18	**New York Yankees**	11	6	5	18	15
	It's hard to find a system that had a worse 2013, as many of New York's top prospects took a step backward, leaving the upper levels of the system quite thin. The steady development of catcher Gary Sanchez was a notable bright spot.					
19	**San Francisco Giants**	28	21	23	4	5
	After producing Buster Posey, Matt Cain and Madison Bumgarner, the Giants' pipeline slowed down. It's starting to improve again. San Francisco's strong track record at developing pitching bodes well for Kyle Crick and Edwin Escobar.					
20	**Tampa Bay Rays**	4	11	3	1	4
	Astute trading has made up for poor drafting in St. Petersburg. A David Price trade could replenish the system, but until then the Rays have depth with plenty of risky players. Injuries and drug suspensions plague potential impact talents.					
21	**Washington Nationals**	16	1	14	21	21
	The impressive return of Lucas Giolito from Tommy John surgery gave a much-needed boost to a farm system weakend by graduations and trades. But most of the prospects are still a few years from making it to D.C.					
22	**Philadelphia Phillies**	23	27	11	5	12
	What was once a model organization that succeeded because of homegrown talent has become one that is hanging on to an aging core. The overall health of the farm system isn't great, but Maikel Franco isn't far away from giving Phillies fans a new favorite slugger.					
23	**Oakland Athletics**	25	26	28	12	3
	No one has worked the big league trade market as astutely as the A's have in recent years, something that's not reflected in farm system talent rankings. Shortstop Addison Russell isn't all that far away from giving the big league club a homegrown cornerstone.					
24	**Chicago White Sox**	29	30	27	19	16
	Like the Mets, the White Sox farm system has started to improve with the new CBA's draft spending rules. A perennial bottom-five organization that rarely spent money in the draft has made some significant strides, but still has a ways to go					
25	**Seattle Mariners**	2	9	18	11	24
	Graduations of Brad Miller and Nick Franklin as well as Danny Hultzen's injury have quickly thinned a once-deep system. Taijuan Walker is in the running for title of game's best pitching prospect, but after that, the less said, the better.					
26	**Atlanta Braves**	21	15	2	13	6
	The graduations of players such as Alex Wood and Evan Gattis helped drop Atlanta to its lowest ranking in the Handbook era. The Braves' low Class A Rome club was pretty loaded last year, but rest of the system was lacking.					
27	**Miami Marlins**	5	28	29	8	2
	This ranking reflects the graduation of so many top prospects last year. Jose Fernandez would have bumped this club 10 spots if he wasn't good enough to skip Double-A and Triple-A. Having relievers as a system strength is a bad sign.					
28	**Detroit Tigers**	27	22	25	26	28
	Generally the Tigers have viewed the farm system as a piggy bank to supply materials to make big league trades. Nick Castellanos is a pure hitter, but the rest of the list is heavy on future relievers and backup catchers.					
29	**Milwaukee Brewers**	22	25	30	14	10
	The bad news is that the Brewers have few prospects who project as everyday regulars; the worse news is that three of the top seven farm systems in baseball are National League Central clubs, including the NL champs in St. Louis.					
30	**Los Angeles Angels**	30	18	16	25	25
	In the cellar for a second consecutive year, the Angels come by their ranking honestly—they have traded away multiple prospects and haven't spent significant money on the draft or internationally. The club is starting to invest more in Latin America.					

Arizona Diamondbacks

BY BILL MITCHELL

The 2013 season was supposed to be different for the Diamondbacks. An action-packed offseason saw general manager Kevin Towers trade star outfielder Justin Upton, outfielder Chris Young and 2011 first-round pick Trevor Bauer for a mix of prospects, gritty big leaguers—such as Martin Prado and Heath Bell—and shortstop Didi Gregorius.

The 2013 Diamondbacks were to be built around solid pitching, improved defense, a more balanced, contact-oriented offensive attack and better clubhouse chemistry.

Arizona led the National League West for 81 days, as deep into the season as July 21, but never really got hot, with its longest win streak lasting just five games. Meanwhile, the Dodgers became baseball's hottest team, going on a 40-12 run that included a June 11 game with the Diamondbacks with two brawls that seemed to spur on the Dodgers.

Righthander Ian Kennedy, who was the ace of the 2011 division-winning team, was at the center of the brawl, plunking both Yasiel Puig and opposing starter Zack Greinke. The Diamondbacks sent him packing to the Padres in July. Injuries already had thinned the lineup, including starting outfielders Adam Eaton (who was supposed to replace Young in center) and Cody Ross, catcher Miguel Montero and the keystone combo of Gregorius and second baseman Aaron Hill.

The injuries and underachievement left the team with the same 81-81 record that it registered in 2012. Pitching, considered to be the strength of the organization, also contributed to the disappointing season. Lefthander Pat Corbin provided a strong start and earned an All-Star Game berth, but he couldn't do it alone and wasn't as effective in the second half. Trevor Cahill, Brandon McCarthy and Wade Miley did not meet expectations, while last year's top prospect, lefthander Tyler Skaggs, failed to earn a regular rotation spot with an inconsistent performance. And the bullpen struggled to hold leads all season, cycling through several closers before settling on Brad Ziegler.

A monster performance by the new face of the franchise, first baseman Paul Goldschmidt, wasn't enough. Goldschmidt led the NL in home runs (36), RBIs (125), total bases (332), slugging (.551) and OPS (.952). He also led with 19 intentional walks, as the Upton-less lineup lacked punch around him.

While the major league team treaded water, the farm system provided a few success stories. Rookies Gregorius and A.J. Pollock, who put up a .730 OPS and played strong defense in center field, provided solid contributions. Double-A Mobile and low Class A South Bend reached their respective league finals, with South Bend buoyed in part by the organization's top two draft picks, college righthanders Braden Shipley and Aaron Blair. Triple-A Reno shortstop Chris Owings won both the MVP and top rookie honors in the Pacific Coast League before making his major league debut in September.

Reno manager Brett Butler, who joined the Marlins after the season, was one of several coaches to leave the organization, from third-base coach Matt Williams (now the Nationals manager) to pitching coach Charles Nagy and first-base coach Steve Sax, who were fired.

BILL MITCHELL

Shortstop Didi Gregorious provided a bright spot in an otherwise mediocre season

TOP PROSPECTS OF THE DECADE

Year	Player, Pos.	2013 Org
2004	Scott Hairston, 2b	Nationals
2005	Carlos Quentin, of	Padres
2006	Stephen Drew, ss	Red Sox
2007	Justin Upton, of	Braves
2008	Carlos Gonzalez, of	Rockies
2009	Jarrod Parker, rhp	Athletics
2010	Jarrod Parker, rhp	Athletics
2011	Jarrod Parker, rhp	Athletics
2012	Trevor Bauer, rhp	Indians
2013	Tyler Skaggs, lhp	Diamondbacks

ORGANIZATION OVERVIEW

General Manager: Kevin Towers. **Farm Director:** Mike Bell. **Scouting Director:** Ray Montgomery.

Class	Team	League	W	L	PCT	Finish	Manager
Majors	Arizona Diamondbacks	National	81	81	.500	7th (15)	Kirk Gibson
Triple-A	Reno Aces	Pacific Coast	60	84	.417	15th (16)	Brett Butler
Double-A	Mobile BayBears	Southern	79	60	.568	1st (10)	Andy Green
High Class A	Visalia Rawhide	California	77	63	.550	3rd (10)	Bill Plummer
Low Class A	South Bend Silver Hawks	Midwest	81	58	.583	4th (16)	Mark Haley
Short season	Hillsboro Hops	Northwest	34	42	.447	6th (8)	Audo Vicente
Rookie	Missoula Osprey	Pioneer	31	42	.425	7th (8)	Robby Hammock
Rookie	AZL Diamondbacks	Arizona	29	27	.518	6th (13)	Luis Urueta
Overall 2013 Minor League Record			**391**	**376**	**.510**	**9th (30)**	

THIS YEAR'S TOP 30

No.	Player, Pos.	Grade/Risk
1.	Archie Bradley, rhp	70/Medium
2.	Braden Shipley, rhp	60/High
3.	Chris Owings, ss	55/Medium
4.	Matt Davidson, 3b	55/Medium
5.	Aaron Blair, rhp	50/High
6.	Jose Martinez, rhp	55/Extreme
7.	David Holmberg, lhp	45/Low
8.	Stryker Trahan, c	50/High
9.	Matt Stites, rhp	45/Medium
10.	Brandon Drury, 3b	50/High
11.	Jake Barrett, rhp	50/High
12.	Jake Lamb, 3b	50/High
13.	Sergio Alcantara, ss	55/Extreme
14.	Justin Williams, of	55/Extreme
15.	Jimmie Sherfy, rhp	50/High
16.	Zeke Spruill, rhp	45/Medium
17.	Daniel Palka, 1b	50/High
18.	Nick Ahmed, ss	45/Medium
19.	Evan Marshall, rhp	45/Medium
20.	Michael Perez, c	50/Extreme
21.	Daniel Gibson, lhp	45/High
22.	Geordy Parra, rhp	45/High
23.	Chase Anderson, rhp	45/High
24.	Andrew Chafin, lhp	45/High
25.	Alfredo Marte, of	40/Low
26.	Joe Munoz, ss	45/High
27.	Jamie Westbrook, 2b	45/High
28.	Andrew Velazquez, ss/2b	45/High
29.	Bo Schultz, rhp	40/Medium
30.	Jose Herrera, c	50/Extreme

LAST YEAR'S TOP 30

No.	Player, Pos.	Status
1.	Tyler Skaggs, lhp	Majors
2.	Trevor Bauer, rhp	(Indians)
3.	Archie Bradley, rhp	No. 1
4.	Adam Eaton, of	Majors
5.	Matt Davidson, 3b	No. 4
6.	David Holmberg, lhp	No. 7
7.	Chris Owings, ss	No. 3
8.	Stryker Trahan, c	No. 8
9.	Andrew Chafin, lhp	No. 24
10.	A.J. Pollock, of	Majors
11.	Chase Anderson, rhp	No. 23
12.	Michael Perez, c	No. 20
13.	Anthony Meo, rhp	Dropped out
14.	Evan Marshall, rhp	No. 19
15.	Keon Broxton, of	Dropped out
16.	Jake Lamb, 3b	No. 12
17.	Jon Griffin, 1b	Dropped out
18.	Alfredo Marte, of	No. 25
19.	Jake Barrett, rhp	No. 11
20.	Felipe Perez, rhp	Dropped out
21.	Joe Munoz, ss	No. 26
22.	Ben Eckels, rhp	Dropped out
23.	Kyle Winkler, rhp	Dropped out
24.	Andrew Velasquez, 2b/ss	No. 28
25.	Jose Martinez, rhp	No. 6
26.	Starling Peralta, rhp	(Cubs)
27.	Tyler Green, rhp	Dropped out
28.	Kevin Munson, rhp	Dropped out
29.	Socrates Brito, of	Dropped out
30.	Evan Marzilli, of	Dropped out

BEST TOOLS

Best Hitter for Average	Chris Owings
Best Power Hitter	Matt Davidson
Best Strike-Zone Discipline	Jake Lamb
Fastest Baserunner	Ender Inciarte
Best Athlete	Socrates Brito
Best Fastball	Archie Bradley
Best Curveball	Jose Martinez
Best Slider	Jake Barrett
Best Changeup	Chase Anderson
Best Control	Matt Stites
Best Defensive Catcher	Michael Perez
Best Defensive Infielder	Nick Ahmed
Best Infield Arm	Sergio Alcantara
Best Defensive Outfielder	Evan Marzilli
Best Outfield Arm	Ender Inciarte

TOP 15 PLAYERS 25 AND UNDER

No.	Player, Pos. (Age)	Peak Level
1.	Archie Bradley, rhp (21)	Double-A
2.	Pat Corbin, lhp (24)	Majors
3.	Tyler Skaggs, lhp (22)	Majors
4.	Adam Eaton, of (25)	Majors
5.	Braden Shipley, rhp (22)	Low Class A
6.	Chris Owings, ss (22)	Majors
7.	Didi Gregorius, ss (24)	Majors
8.	Matt Davidson, 3b (23)	Majors
9.	Aaron Blair, rhp (21)	Low Class A
10.	Jose Martinez, rhp (19)	Short-season
11.	Randall Delgado, rhp (24)	Majors
12.	Stryker Trahan, c (19)	Rookie
13.	Matt Stites, rhp (23)	Double-A
14.	Brandon Drury, 3b (21)	Low Class A
15.	Jake Lamb, 3b (23)	High Class A

MINOR LEAGUE DEPTH CHART

ARIZONA DIAMONDBACKS

TOP 2014 ROOKIE: Archie Bradley, rhp. One of the top prospect righthanders in the game has the size and repertoire to be a frontline starter for many years.

BREAKOUT PROSPECT: Daniel Gibson, lhp. Florida southpaw has a power arm with a fastball up to 96 mph, and he could move quickly with just a little better command.

SLEEPER: Seth Simmons, rhp. 25-year-old undersized reliever with a big-time fastball and plus slider struck out more than 100 batters in relief in 2013.

SOURCE OF TOP 30 TALENT

Homegrown	**24**	**Acquired**	**6**
College	10	Trades	5
Junior college	0	Rule 5 draft	0
High school	9	Independent leagues	1
Nondrafted free agents	0	Free agents/waivers	0
International	5		

LF
- Justin Williams (14)
- Alex Glenn
- Francis Martinez
- David Peralta
- Yogey Perez-Ramos

CF
- Ender Inciarte
- Colin Bray
- Matt McPhearson
- Evan Marzilli
- Keon Broxton

RF
- Alfredo Marte (25)
- Socrates Brito
- Chuck Taylor
- Dane McFarland
- Yorman Garcia
- Ismael Penaf

3B
- Matt Davidson (4)
- Brandon Drury (10)
- Jake Lamb (12)
- Ryan Court

SS
- Chris Owings (3)
- Sergio Alcantara (13)
- Nick Ahmed (18)
- Joe Munoz (26)
- Kevin Medrano
- Jacob Cordero
- Sean Jamieson

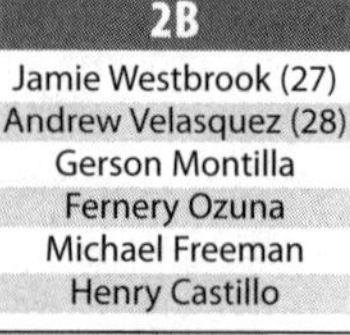

2B
- Jamie Westbrook (27)
- Andrew Velasquez (28)
- Gerson Montilla
- Fernery Ozuna
- Michael Freeman
- Henry Castillo

1B
- Daniel Palka (17)
- Rudy Flores

C
- Stryker Trahan (8)
- Michael Perez (20)
- Jose Herrera (30)
- Ronnie Freeman
- Yosbel Gutierrez
- Jose Queliz
- Fidel Pena
- Oswaldo Garcia

LHP

LHSP	LHRP
David Holmberg (7)	Daniel Gibson (21)
Andrew Chafin (24)	Will Locante
Anfernee Benitez	Eury de la Rosa
Cody Wheeler	Patrick Schuster
Andrew Barbosa	Henry Garcia
	Wagner Mateo

RHP

RHSP	RHRP
Archie Bradley (1)	Matt Stites (9)
Braden Shipley (2)	Jake Barrett (11)
Aaron Blair (5)	Jimmie Sherfy (15)
Jose Martinez (6)	Evan Marshall (19)
Zeke Spruill (16)	Geordy Parra (22)
Bo Schultz (29)	Chase Anderson (23)
Brad Keller	Kevin Munson
Felipe Perez	Tyler Green
Ben Eckels	Seth Simmons
Blake Perry	Charles Brewer
Carlos Hernandez	Michael Bolsinger
Jesse Darrah	Kyle Winkler
Brandon Sinnery	Anthony Meo
	Derek Eitel
	Kaleb Fleck
	Silvino Bracho

DRAFT ANALYSIS

2013

BONUSES: $7.1 MILLION

BEST PURE HITTER: He didn't see a ton of elite pitching in high school, but OF Justin Williams (2) adjusted quickly to pro ball, finishing up at low Class A South Bend after tearing through two Rookie levels. His present strength helps him drive the ball consistently.

BEST POWER HITTER: Some scouts thought Williams had the most raw power in the high school class, but 1B Daniel Palka (3) led the Atlantic Coast Conference in home runs (17) and slugging (.637) before hitting nine more homers and slugging .516 in 252 at-bats in his debut.

FASTEST RUNNER: Many scouts considered OF Matt McPhearson (4) the draft's fastest premium prospect, earning 80 grades on the 20-80 scale when he's healthy, with a 6.22-second 60-yard dash time. He was slowed by a hamstring injury this spring but stole 15 bases in 18 tries after signing despite a modest .200/.311/.238 start.

BEST DEFENSIVE PLAYER: OF Colin Bray (6) is a 70 runner and long strider in center field, and he has plenty of arm strength.

BEST FASTBALL: Arizona loaded up on big arms. Athletic RHP Braden Shipley (1) can sit in the 94-98 mph range. RHP Aaron Blair (1s) has heavy sinking life on an 88-94 mph heater that touches higher, while LHP Daniel Gibson (7) reaches 95 from the bullpen.

BEST SECONDARY PITCH: RHP Jimmy Sherfy (10) has a lot of effort in his low-slot delivery but produces plus sliders with mid-80s velocity.

BEST PRO DEBUT: Palka and Williams, who may have overachieved in batting .351/.397/.452 with 18 doubles in 208 at-bats over three levels. Sherfy had seven saves and 29 strikeouts in 17 innings, half of them at South Bend. Blair, Gibson and Shipley also pitched for the Silver Hawks in the Midwest League playoffs.

BEST ATHLETE: Shipley, who was recruited as a shortstop, is a fifth infielder after he delivers a pitch, and he ranks right with Bray and McPhearson.

MOST INTRIGUING BACKGROUND: OF Cory Hahn (34) was one of the nation's top freshman outfielders in 2011 when he injured his spine on a slide while playing for Arizona State, leaving him partially paralyzed from the neck down. He's remained an inspirational part of the Sun Devils community, which the hometown Diamondbacks honored by drafting him. Shipley's cousin Jordan was an NFL wide receiver. Four of McPhearson's brothers played college football, including Gerrick, who was an NFL draftee.

CLOSEST TO THE MAJORS: Sherfy and Gibson are quick-moving college relievers.

BEST LATE-ROUND PICK: OF Jacob Cordero (11) got $135,000 for his athleticism and bat speed.

THE ONE WHO GOT AWAY: RHP Andy Ravel (21) took his polished four-pitch mix and projectable upper-80s fastball to Kent State.

ASSESSMENT: Few teams had as many top picks perform as well as the Diamondbacks. If toolsy talents such as Williams, Bray and McPhearson come together, this class could go from good to great.

2012

BONUSES: $4.6 MILLION

High school catching is a rough demographic, and C Stryker Trahan (1) is off to a decent but not scintillating start. RHP Jake Barrett (3) and 3B Jake Lamb (6) just missed Arizona's Top 10.

GRADE: D

2011

BONUSES: $11.9 MILLION

Arizona had two of the top seven picks, yielding top prospect RHP Archie Bradley (1). No. 3 overall pick Trevor Bauer (1) was centerpiece of a trade with Cleveland. Other arms in this class have backed up.

GRADE: B+

2010

BONUSES: $4.4 MILLION

Arizona didn't sign RHP Barret Loux (1) when he failed his physical. OF Adam Eaton (19) exceeded expectations and became a regular; SS Zach Walters (9) was traded to Washington.

GRADE: C

TOP DRAFT PICKS OF THE DECADE

Year	Player, Pos.	2013 Org.
2004	Stephen, Drew, ss	Red Sox
2005	Justin Upton, of	Braves
2006	Max Scherzer, rhp	Tigers
2007	Jarrod Parker, rhp	Athletics
2008	Daniel Schlereth, lhp	Orioles
2009	Bobby Borchering, 3b	Astros
2010	*Barret Loux, rhp	Cubs
2011	Trevor Bauer, rhp	Indians
2012	Stryker Trahan, c	Diamondbacks
2013	Braden Shipley, rhp	Diamondbacks

*Did not sign

LARGEST BONUSES IN CLUB HISTORY

Travis Lee, 1996	$10,000,000
Justin Upton, 2005	$6,100,000
John Patterson, 1996	$6,075,000
Archie Bradley, 2011	$5,000,000
Stephen Drew, 2004	$4,000,000

1 ARCHIE BRADLEY, RHP

Born: Aug. 10, 1992. **B-T:** R-R. **Ht.:** 6-4 **Wt.:** 225.
Drafted: HS—Broken Arrow, Okla., 2011 (1st round).
Signed by: Kyle Denny.

BA GRADE
70
MEDIUM
SCOUTING GRADES
FASTBALL 70
CURVEBALL 60
CHANGEUP 50
COMMAND 45
DELIVERY 50

TONY FARLOW

Bradley arrived as Arizona's reward for failing to sign 2010 sixth overall pick Barret Loux. The Diamondbacks received the seventh pick in 2011 as compensation, selecting Bradley after taking Trevor Bauer third overall. It's the highest pair of picks by one team in draft history. The Diamondbacks offered a $5 million bonus just before the signing deadline to lure Bradley away from Oklahoma, where he would have played quarterback. He was one of two premium Oklahoma prep products in the 2011 draft, pairing with Dylan Bundy, whom Bradley beat in the state playoffs to conclude their senior seasons. After spending his first full year at low Class A South Bend, Bradley began the 2013 season with five dominating starts at high Class A Visalia before moving up to Double-A Mobile, where he helped lead the BayBears to a third consecutive trip to the Southern League finals. Bradley's combined 1.84 ERA ranked third in minors, and he placed fifth with 162 strikeouts. He even started a combined no-hitter against Huntsville on Aug. 14 with five innings, though he walked five and needed help from five relievers. Bradley ranked as the No. 2 prospect in the SL, behind only the Dodgers' Yasiel Puig.

With a solid, fairly athletic 6-foot-4 body and an electric arm, Bradley has the potential to be a frontline starter. The key to his repertoire is the overpowering, plus-plus fastball that he throws at 93-94 mph and up to 97 with good downhill plane and tailing life. Bradley's curveball gives him another plus pitch. His changeup is a slightly above-average pitch that he hasn't used enough to develop fully, though it could also be a plus pitch in time. Bradley throws with some effort, with an arm recoil to conclude his follow-through. He repeated his delivery more consistently in 2013, helping lower his walk rate from 5.6 to 4.1 per nine innings. That's still high for a starter, but the improvement encouraged the Diamondbacks, who believe maturity was a key to his improvement. He keeps the ball in the ballpark, allowing six homers in 26 starts.

The Diamondbacks might have brought Bradley to the big leagues had they remained in playoff contention, but because he does not yet have to be added to the 40-man roster he stayed in Mobile. The 2013 big league staff underachieved at times, and general manager Kevin Towers has indicated an interest in adding another starting pitcher. After an invitation to big league camp, Bradley will likely start the season at Triple-A Reno, a challenging assignment for any 21-year-old. A slow start or injury to a big league starter likely will result in his big league debut at some point in 2014.

Year	Club (League)	Class	W	L	ERA	G	GS	CG	SV	IP	H	HR	BB	SO	K/9	WHIP	AVG
2011	Missoula (PIO)	R	0	0	0.00	2	1	0	0	2	1	0	0	4	18.0	0.50	.143
2012	South Bend (MWL)	LoA	12	6	3.84	27	27	0	0	136	87	6	84	152	10.1	1.26	.181
2013	Visalia (CAL)	HiA	2	0	1.26	5	5	0	0	29	22	1	10	43	13.5	1.12	.218
	Mobile (SL)	AA	12	5	1.97	21	21	2	0	123	93	5	59	119	8.7	1.23	.214
Minor League Totals			26	11	2.76	55	54	2	0	290	203	12	153	318	9.9	1.23	.199

2 BRADEN SHIPLEY, RHP

MITCHELL DYER PHOTOGRAPHY

BA GRADE
60
HIGH

Born: Feb. 22, 1992. **B-T:** R-R. **Ht.:** 6-3. **Wt.:** 190. **Drafted:** Nevada, 2013 (1st round). **Signed by:** John Bartsch.

A potential top 10 selection in the 2013 draft, Shipley fell to the Diamondbacks at No. 15, and Arizona didn't hesitate to call his name. He signed soon after the draft for $2.25 million. Primarily a shortstop as a college freshman, Shipley's arm was too good to keep off the mound, and he thrived in his last two seasons to leap up draft boards. Shipley stands out for his athleticism, and he functions as a fifth infielder on the mound. His three pitches all could be plus offerings in time, and he pitches with confidence. His fastball ranges from 94-96 mph, and he has a good feel for an outstanding, late-tumbling changeup, his best secondary pitch, which he delivers with good arm speed. Shipley's hard curveball was already a good pitch and looked even better during instructional league action. His high three-quarters delivery is clean and repeatable. A tough competitor who has a resilient arm, Shipley was capable of going deep into games with Nevada. Despite his relatively short pitching résumé, Shipley has an advanced feel for pitching and profiles as a No. 3 starter. Shipley pitched effectively as low Class A South Bend advanced to the Midwest League finals, and he should head to high Class A Visalia in 2014.

Year	Club (League)	Class	W	L	ERA	G	GS	CG	SV	IP	H	HR	BB	SO	K/9	WHIP	AVG
2013	Hillsboro (NWL)	SS	0	2	7.58	8	8	0	0	19	30	1	6	24	11.4	1.89	.357
	South Bend (MWL)	LoA	0	1	2.61	4	4	0	0	21	14	2	8	16	7.0	1.06	.194
Minor League Totals			0	3	4.99	12	12	0	0	40	44	3	14	40	9.1	1.46	.282

3 CHRIS OWINGS, SS

BA GRADE
55
MEDIUM

Born: Aug. 12, 1991. **B-T:** R-R. **Ht.:** 5-10. **Wt.:** 180. **Drafted:** HS—Gilbert, S.C., 2009 (1st round supplemental). **Signed by:** George Swain.

The 40th overall pick in a strong 2009 draft class, Owings signed for $950,000 and reached the majors in September 2013. That followed his stellar season at Triple-A Reno, when the Pacific Coast League named him its MVP and top rookie. He led the PCL in hits (180), runs (104) and total bases (263). Owings is a gamer who is such a good athlete that his tools play up. He generates good bat speed with his strong hands and consistently squares up the ball. Never one to draw many walks, he cut down on the strikeouts that had long concerned scouts; he had struck out more than 130 times in each of his previous two full seasons. His low walk totals are still a concern, but Owings is a good fastball hitter who lays off nasty breaking balls. He is an average defender at short with enough range, solid infield actions and an average arm. He runs well and increased his basestealing after working with Reno manager Brett Butler. Owings played a combined 14 games at second base with Reno and Arizona, and he could handle second or short in Arizona soon. But with Aaron Hill locked in at second, Didi Gregorius at shortstop and Cliff Pennington in a utility role, there may not be room for Owings in 2014. He could be trade bait to acquire a starting pitcher or power bat.

Year	Club (League)	Class	AVG	G	AB	R	H	2B	3B	HR	RBI	BB	SO	SB	CS	OBP	SLG
2009	Missoula (PIO)	R	.306	24	108	20	33	5	1	2	10	3	25	3	0	.324	.426
2010	South Bend (MWL)	LoA	.298	62	255	39	76	19	2	5	28	9	50	1	3	.323	.447
2011	Visalia (CAL)	HiA	.246	121	521	67	128	29	6	11	50	15	130	10	4	.274	.388
2012	Visalia (CAL)	HiA	.324	59	241	51	78	16	2	11	24	13	63	8	3	.362	.544
	Mobile (SL)	AA	.263	69	297	35	78	10	3	6	28	11	69	4	3	.291	.377
2013	Reno (PCL)	AAA	.330	125	546	104	180	31	8	12	81	22	99	20	7	.359	.482
	Arizona (NL)	MAJ	.291	20	55	5	16	5	0	0	5	6	10	2	0	.361	.382
Major League Totals			.291	20	55	5	16	5	0	0	5	6	10	2	0	.361	.382
Minor League Totals			.291	460	1968	316	573	110	22	47	221	73	436	46	20	.320	.441

4 MATT DAVIDSON, 3B

Born: March 26, 1991. **B-T:** R-R. **Ht.:** 6-3. **Wt.:** 225. **Drafted:** HS—Yucaipa, Calif., 2009 (1st round supplemental). **Signed by:** Jeff Mousser.

Drafted five picks before Chris Owings in 2009, Davidson went 35th overall and signed for $900,000. He averaged nearly 20 home runs a year in his four full seasons in the organization and reached 20 last year with his first three big league homers. Davidson has big raw power and the ball jumps off his bat. He's got a bit of a long swing and struggles to make consistent contact, which will keep his average low, but he's selective enough to get to his power consistently. His walk rate dropped in his first Triple-A season, though he handled big league pitchers well after being promoted for two stints in Arizona. While he still needs to improve defensively, scouts project him to be an average defender in time, and he makes the routine play consistently. Davidson needs to improve his lateral movement, quickness and conditioning. He has well below-average speed. The Diamondbacks need another power bat to pair with Paul Goldschmidt, a role Davidson could fill if he can handle third base. He'll go to spring training with a good chance of earning a spot on the Opening Day roster.

Year	Club (League)	Class	AVG	G	AB	R	H	2B	3B	HR	RBI	BB	SO	SB	CS	OBP	SLG
2009	Yakima (NWL)	SS	.241	72	270	29	65	15	0	2	28	21	75	0	2	.312	.319
2010	South Bend (MWL)	LoA	.289	113	415	58	120	35	3	16	79	43	109	0	2	.371	.504
	Visalia (CAL)	HiA	.169	21	71	6	12	1	0	2	11	12	25	0	0	.298	.268
2011	Visalia (CAL)	HiA	.277	135	535	93	148	39	1	20	106	52	147	0	1	.348	.465
2012	Mobile (SL)	AA	.261	135	486	81	127	28	2	23	76	69	126	3	4	.367	.469
2013	Reno (PCL)	AAA	.280	115	443	55	124	32	3	17	74	46	134	1	0	.350	.481
	Arizona (NL)	MAJ	.237	31	76	8	18	6	0	3	12	10	24	0	1	.333	.434
Major League Totals			.237	31	76	8	18	6	0	3	12	10	24	0	1	.333	.434
Minor League Totals			.268	591	2220	322	596	150	9	80	374	243	616	4	9	.351	.452

5 AARON BLAIR, RHP

MITCHELL DYER PHOTOGRAPHY

Born: May 26, 1992. **B-T:** R-R. **Ht.:** 6-5. **Wt.:** 230. **Drafted:** Marshall, 2013 (1st round supplemental). **Signed by:** Rick Matsko.

Blair made an unlikely trip from his Las Vegas home all the way to West Virginia for his college career, after which he became Marshall's highest-drafted player ever—41st overall—and signed for $1.435 million. He finished his pro debut with 18 strikeouts in 16 innings in the low Class A Midwest League playoffs. Blair fits the profile of a mid-rotation starter thanks to his ability to pitch off his fastball, which gets up to 95 mph with late life, run and sink. He's a big-bodied innings eater with a plus changeup, and he knows how to pitch and makes adjustments on the mound. His delivery gives his pitches good life and allows him to induce weak contact. Blair's curveball and slider lag behind his other pitches, but both have average potential. His secondary pitches come out of the same plane as his fastball, and he repeats his high three-quarters delivery. Blair and first-rounder Braden Shipley are linked as the organization's top two picks from the 2013 draft, and they moved together after signing, piggybacking their outings in instructional league. Blair will try to keep pace in 2014, either back in the MWL or at high Class A Visalia.

Year	Club (League)	Class	W	L	ERA	G	GS	CG	SV	IP	H	HR	BB	SO	K/9	WHIP	AVG
2013	Hillsboro (NWL)	SS	1	1	2.90	8	8	0	0	31	25	2	13	28	8.1	1.23	.225
	South Bend (MWL)	LoA	0	2	3.57	3	3	0	0	18	19	0	4	13	6.6	1.30	.279
Minor League Totals			1	3	3.14	11	11	0	0	49	44	2	17	41	7.6	1.25	.246

6 JOSE MARTINEZ, RHP

MITCHELL DYER PHOTOGRAPHY

Born: April 14, 1994. **B-T:** R-R. **Ht.:** 6-1. **Wt.:** 160. **Signed:** Dominican Republic, 2011. **Signed by:** Junior Noboa.

The organization's pop-up prospect for 2013, Martinez signed for $55,000 under the name Jose Fermin in June 2011. The problem resulted from a name transcription mistake rather than any identity shenanigans, and Martinez made his U.S. debut with a pair of starts in the short-season Northwest League in late 2012 after dominating the Rookie-level Dominican Summer League. He returned to the NWL in 2013, and while his performance didn't stand out, he attracted plenty of attention for his electric arm and potential for two plus-plus pitches from a smallish frame. He has a quick arm, generating velocity up to 99 mph, and he works regularly in the 93-94 range. His curveball, the best in the organization, is outstanding because it's a hard pitch with late bite and tilt. Martinez's changeup still grades below-average, typical for a young power pitcher, though it has shown signs of improvement. He doesn't always repeat his three-quarters arm slot, a problem that could be solved by physical maturity. Martinez stands out in a system lacking high-end Latin American talent. Thanks to his slight frame and last name, he will draw comparisons with Pedro Martinez, much like the Cardinals' Carlos Martinez. He should be ready to move to low Class A South Bend in 2014 and has breakout potential.

Year	Club (League)	Class	W	L	ERA	G	GS	CG	SV	IP	H	HR	BB	SO	K/9	WHIP	AVG
2012	Diamondbacks (DSL)	R	5	2	1.72	14	14	0	0	73	57	0	22	71	8.7	1.08	.218
	Yakima (NWL)	SS	0	1	4.22	2	2	0	0	11	8	1	6	8	6.8	1.31	.205
2013	Hillsboro (NWL)	SS	2	3	4.03	10	10	0	0	38	20	3	25	30	7.1	1.18	.159
Minor League Totals			7	6	2.66	26	26	0	0	122	85	4	53	109	8.0	1.13	.199

7 DAVID HOLMBERG, LHP

Born: July 19, 1991. **B-T:** R-L. **Ht.:** 6-3. **Wt.:** 225. **Drafted:** HS—Port Charlotte, Fla., 2009 (2nd round). **Signed by:** Joe Siers (White Sox).

The 2009 draft has provided much of Arizona's young talent, from their own picks (Paul Goldschmidt, A.J. Pollock) to trade pickups such as Pat Corbin and Holmberg, acquired from the White Sox in the 2010 Edwin Jackson deal. Holmberg spent the entire 2013 season with Double-A Mobile, save for his major league debut on Aug. 27 against the Padres. He returned to the BayBears for the Southern League playoffs, losing both starts. Holmberg's scouting report has been consistent since his debut. He's polished, composed, mature and throws strikes. He shows excellent command and feel for pitching, and he's a good bet to reach his ceiling as a No. 4 starter. Holmberg has firmed up his body since starting pro ball and is more athletic than he appears. His fastball generally sits in the 89-91 mph range, touching 93 this year, but at times he pitches with below-average velocity, relying instead on run, sink and command. His changeup is his best pitch, and his curveball, which he throws for strikes at 73-75 mph, is close to an average pitch. His delivery has deception and he uses both sides of the plate well. Holmberg has drawn comparisons with Mark Buehrle, which would put him in line for a nice career if he reaches that ceiling. He's ready for Triple-A Reno and should be ready when an emergency starter is needed at the big league level in 2014.

Year	Club (League)	Class	W	L	ERA	G	GS	CG	SV	IP	H	HR	BB	SO	K/9	WHIP	AVG
2009	Bristol (APP)	R	2	2	4.73	14	7	0	0	40	40	5	18	37	8.3	1.45	.256
2010	Great Falls (PIO)	R	1	1	4.46	8	8	0	0	40	52	2	9	29	6.5	1.51	.315
	Missoula (PIO)	R	1	4	3.86	7	7	0	0	37	47	2	7	47	11.3	1.45	.294
2011	South Bend (MWL)	LoA	8	3	2.39	14	14	1	0	83	65	3	13	81	8.8	0.94	.212
	Visalia (CAL)	HiA	4	6	4.67	13	13	0	0	71	73	5	35	76	9.6	1.51	.263
2012	Visalia (CAL)	HiA	6	3	2.99	12	12	0	0	78	62	6	14	86	9.9	0.97	.214
	Mobile (SL)	AA	5	5	3.60	15	15	0	0	95	104	8	23	67	6.3	1.34	.281
2013	Arizona (NL)	MAJ	0	0	7.36	1	1	0	0	4	6	0	3	0	0.0	2.45	.375
	Mobile (SL)	AA	5	8	2.75	26	26	1	0	157	138	12	50	116	6.6	1.19	.239
Major League Totals			0	0	7.36	1	1	0	0	4	6	0	3	0	0.0	2.45	.375
Minor League Totals			32	32	3.40	109	102	2	0	603	581	43	169	539	8.0	1.24	.252

8 STRYKER TRAHAN, C

Born: April 25, 1994. **B-T:** L-R. **Ht.:** 6-0. **Wt.:** 232. **Drafted:** HS—Lafayette, La., 2012 (1st round). **Signed by:** Rusty Pendergrass.

Trahan, whose first name comes from a character in a Burt Reynolds movie, was the first high school catcher taken in the 2012 draft, when the Diamondbacks popped him at No. 26 overall. Signed for a $1.7 million bonus, Trahan advanced to the Rookie-level Pioneer League in 2013 after a stint in extended spring training. He missed a month when he returned home after the death of his mother. Scouts have differing opinions about whether Trahan can (or should) stay behind the plate. Some think his bat would develop faster without the strain of learning the intricacies of catching. But he continues to work hard, showing improvement with his blocking and footwork. His arm is well above-average, allowing him to throw out 40 percent of Pioneer League basestealers, but he sometimes loses focus behind the plate. Trahan is still finding his swing and struggled with pitches featuring good spin in 2013, but he showed plenty of pull power with Missoula, leading the team in home runs. He got bigger in his second pro season, probably the result of too much weight work, and will work to get into better baseball shape in the offseason. Arizona plans to keep Trahan behind the plate for now. He's ready for his full-season debut in 2014, which should come at low Class A South Bend.

Year	Club (League)	Class	AVG	G	AB	R	H	2B	3B	HR	RBI	BB	SO	SB	CS	OBP	SLG
2012	Diamondbacks (AZL)	R	.281	49	167	29	47	11	3	5	25	40	48	8	1	.422	.473
2013	Missoula (PIO)	R	.254	59	236	44	60	15	2	10	33	24	57	1	0	.328	.462
Minor League Totals			.266	108	403	73	107	26	5	15	58	64	105	9	1	.370	.467

9 MATT STITES, RHP

Born: May 28, 1990. **B-T:** R-R. **Ht.:** 5-11. **Wt.:** 170. **Drafted:** Missouri, 2011 (17th round). **Signed by:** Jeff Stewart (Padres).

First drafted by the Cubs in 2010 after pitching at Jefferson (Mo.) CC, Stites didn't sign and instead moved on to Missouri for his junior year. The Padres took Stites in the 17th round in 2011 and immediately moved him to a bullpen role. He opened 2013 as the closer at Double-A San Antonio before landing on the disabled list with an appendectomy. While he was laid up, the Padres traded him to the Diamondbacks in the Ian Kennedy deal. Stites is short and athletic, with a quick arm. He works with a fastball from 94-98 mph that gets on hitters quickly, as well as an effective slider. He throws his breaking ball with power, reaching 87 mph, and at times it has late, sharp action. He uses his lower half well, which gives him the plus velocity despite a smaller frame. Stites' changeup is a work in progress that he hopes to use against lefthanded batters. His best attribute is his strike-throwing ability, and he has the system's best control. Stites got back on the mound during instructional league and then spent six weeks in the Arizona Fall League, where he knocked off the rust and finished with nine scoreless outings, the last seven with no walks. The Diamondbacks will give Stites a chance to compete for a bullpen spot in spring training. He'll probably begin the year at Triple-A Reno, with a good chance for big league time before the year is out.

Year	Club (League)	Class	W	L	ERA	G	GS	CG	SV	IP	H	HR	BB	SO	K/9	WHIP	AVG
2011	Padres (AZL)	R	0	0	0.00	2	0	0	0	2	0	0	0	3	13.5	0.00	.000
	Eugene (NWL)	SS	4	0	1.93	24	0	0	5	33	14	1	8	36	9.9	0.67	.125
2012	Fort Wayne (MWL)	LoA	2	0	0.74	42	0	0	13	49	25	4	3	60	11.1	0.58	.148
2013	San Antonio (TL)	AA	2	2	2.08	46	0	0	14	52	37	6	8	51	8.8	0.87	.194
Minor League Totals			8	2	1.53	114	0	0	32	135	76	11	19	150	10.0	0.70	.159

10 BRANDON DRURY, 3B

Born: Aug. 21, 1992. **B-T:** R-R. **Ht.:** 6-2. **Wt.:** 190. **Drafted:** HS—Grants Pass, Ore., 2010 (13th round). **Signed by:** Brett Evert (Braves).

Drury came off a subpar 2012 season in his first try at low Class A when the Braves included him in the seven-player trade that sent Justin Upton to Atlanta. He repeated the level in his first season as a Diamondback and was a much different ballplayer, leading the Midwest League in doubles (51), games (134) and extra-base hits (70) while also improving significantly on defense. When Drury was with the Braves, many scouts expected him to have to move off the hot corner, but he now looks to be a solid-average defender with good hands and an above-average arm that allows him to play deep. He has an excellent frame and good athleticism for the position. As a hitter, Drury showed average power, good plate discipline and a swing with leverage last season, and scouts believe he hasn't yet tapped into his full power potential. He stood taller in his stance, which helped him get extended more consistently. He's a well below-average runner. Drury will have to keep hitting because the Diamondbacks have depth at third base with Matt Davidson ahead of him on the prospect list and Jake Lamb ahead of him developmentally. Drury's next big test will be an assignment to the high Class A California League, where his bat should play even better in more hitter-friendly environments.

Year	Club (League)	Class	AVG	G	AB	R	H	2B	3B	HR	RBI	BB	SO	SB	CS	OBP	SLG
2010	Braves (GCL)	R	.198	52	192	20	38	7	1	3	17	9	50	2	2	.248	.292
2011	Danville (APP)	R	.347	63	265	40	92	23	0	8	54	6	35	3	0	.367	.525
2012	Rome (SAL)	LoA	.229	123	445	47	102	22	3	6	51	20	73	3	4	.270	.333
2013	South Bend (MWL)	LoA	.302	134	526	78	159	51	4	15	85	47	92	1	1	.362	.500
Minor League Totals			.274	372	1428	185	391	103	8	32	207	82	250	9	7	.319	.424

11 JAKE BARRETT, RHP

Born: July 22, 1991. **B-T:** R-R Ht.: **6-2 Wt.:** 190 **Drafted:** Arizona State, 2012 (3rd round). **Signed by:** Matt Smith.

Barrett passed on a pro career as a Blue Jays third-round pick out of high school in 2009, instead choosing to stay home to play at Arizona State. The Diamondbacks popped him in the 2012 draft's third round and signed him for $392,900. After starting his college career as a starter, Barrett switched to closer as an ASU junior, and that could be his role moving forward. He broke out with dominating performances at both high Class A Visalia and Double-A Mobile in 2013, commanding three pitches, including a 94-98 mph fastball. He has the ability to use both sides of the plate. Barrett throws his plus slider, a pitch with tight, late break, in any count and gets plenty of swings and misses with it. His changeup has improved to fringe-average, if not better, and he continued to work on it in the Arizona Fall League. Barrett's delivery is a bit rough, with a lot of effort, but it doesn't keep him from commanding his pitches. With Arizona's closer situation in flux, he could become a key piece in the big league bullpen after more seasoning at Triple-A Reno.

Year	Club (League)	Class	W	L	ERA	G	GS	CG	SV	IP	H	HR	BB	SO	K/9	WHIP	AVG
2012	South Bend (MWL)	LoA	0	3	5.84	25	0	0	6	25	28	2	13	25	9.1	1.66	.283
2013	Visalia (CAL)	HiA	2	1	1.98	28	0	0	15	27	21	2	9	37	12.2	1.10	.198
	Mobile (SL)	AA	1	1	0.36	24	0	0	14	25	18	2	3	22	8.0	0.85	.196
Minor League Totals			3	5	2.70	77	0	0	35	77	67	6	25	84	9.9	1.20	.226

12 JAKE LAMB, 3B

BA GRADE **50** HIGH

Born: Oct. 9, 1990. **B-T:** L-R. **Ht.:** 6-2. **Wt.:** 200. **Drafted:** Washington, 2012 (6th round). **Signed by:** Donnie Reynolds.

The Diamondbacks gambled that they could iron out Lamb's swing when they selected him from Washington in the sixth round of the 2012 draft. So far, so good. After a strong 2012 debut at Rookie-level Missoula, Lamb jumped two levels to high Class A Visalia for 2013. He slammed eight homers in the first half while posting a .973 OPS to make the California League midseason all-star team, but he had to drop out when he broke the hamate bone in his right wrist in early June. He returned in early August and finished the year with a solid Arizona Fall League showing. Lamb's raw power began to emerge in 2013, and he offers a patient approach from the left side with the ability to go deep into counts, meaning he could hit for both solid average and power. He's a plus defender at third base with an above-average arm, though he can still be inconsistent on routine plays. Lamb projects as a big league third baseman, and he's ready to move to Double-A Mobile in 2014.

Year	Club (League)	Class	AVG	G	AB	R	H	2B	3B	HR	RBI	BB	SO	SB	CS	OBP	SLG
2012	Missoula (PIO)	R	.329	67	280	47	92	22	5	9	57	24	51	8	2	.390	.539
2013	Diamondbacks (AZL)	R	.294	5	17	4	5	2	0	0	5	2	5	0	0	.381	.412
	Visalia (CAL)	HiA	.303	64	231	44	70	20	0	13	47	48	70	0	0	.424	.558
Minor League Totals			.316	136	528	95	167	44	5	22	109	74	126	8	2	.405	.544

13 SERGIO ALCANTARA, SS

BA GRADE **55** EXTREME

Born: July 10, 1996. **B-T:** B-R. **Ht.:** 5-10. **Wt.:** 150. **Signed:** Dominican Republic, 2012. **Signed by:** Junior Noboa.

A nephew of former big league middle infielder Anderson Hernandez, Alcantara signed with the Diamondbacks for $700,000 in July 2012. Expected to spend his first pro season in the Dominican Summer League, he instead served as starting shortstop and leadoff hitter in the Rookie-level Arizona League following an eye-opening performance at the end of spring training. While he still has room to fill out, Alcantara more than held his own in the AZL, leading the league in walks (44) and turning on more fastballs later in the season. With good instincts and bat speed from both sides of the plate, he projects to develop gap power as he matures physically. He already has advanced skills in the field, with an accurate, double-plus throwing arm to pair with good hands and footwork. An average runner now, he could develop into a basestealer with experience and maturity. Alcantara probably will stay back in extended spring training in 2014 before reporting to short-season Hillsboro.

Year	Club (League)	Class	AVG	G	AB	R	H	2B	3B	HR	RBI	BB	SO	SB	CS	OBP	SLG
2013	Diamondbacks (AZL)	R	.243	48	169	31	41	5	4	0	16	44	36	3	2	.398	.320
Minor League Totals			.243	48	169	31	41	5	4	0	16	44	36	3	2	.398	.320

14 JUSTIN WILLIAMS, OF

BA GRADE **55** EXTREME

Born: Aug. 20, 1995. **B-T:** L-R. **Ht.:** 6-2. **Wt.:** 215. **Drafted:** HS—Houma, La., 2013 (2nd round). **Signed by:** Rusty Pendergrass.

The Diamondbacks kicked off the 2013 draft with a pair of advanced college pitchers—Braden Shipley (15th overall) and Aaron Blair (36th)—then in the second round went for a power bat in Williams. The Louisiana native was a shortstop in high school despite his physical frame. Converted to the outfield as a pro, Williams' inexperience in left field showed in his first year. He's a hard worker whom the organization believes will have the arm strength to handle right field once he improves his throwing technique. He had no trouble with the bat in his first year, showing power potential and the ability to hit the ball to all fields. Despite not turning 18 until late in the season, Williams was promoted twice in 2013, moving first to the Rookie-level Pioneer League and then to low Class A South Bend to finish the year. The ball jumps off his bat, which could lead to more over-the-fence power with experience. He's a below-average runner who runs a bit better underway. Since he's already seen the bright lights of South Bend, Williams may be challenged with a return assignment to the Midwest League.

Year	Club (League)	Class	AVG	G	AB	R	H	2B	3B	HR	RBI	BB	SO	SB	CS	OBP	SLG
2013	Diamondbacks (AZL)	R	.345	37	148	17	51	12	0	1	32	8	35	0	1	.398	.446
	Missoula (PIO)	R	.412	11	51	12	21	6	0	0	5	1	7	0	0	.423	.529
	South Bend (MWL)	LoA	.111	3	9	3	1	0	0	0	0	2	2	0	0	.273	.111
Minor League Totals			.351	51	208	32	73	18	0	1	37	11	44	0	1	.397	.452

15 JIMMIE SHERFY, RHP

BA GRADE 50 HIGH

Born: Dec. 27, 1991. **B-T:** R-R. **Ht.:** 5-10. **Wt.:** 160. **Drafted:** Oregon, 2013 (10th round). **Signed by:** Donnie Reynolds.

One of the most dominant closers in college baseball as an Oregon sophomore and junior, Sherfy dropped to the 10th round of the 2013 draft, where the Diamondbacks signed him for $100,000. His small stature and somewhat funky delivery must have scared off some teams, because his lightning-quick arm and electric stuff certainly play up in the bullpen. After pitching nine shutout innings with a 17/1 SO/BB ratio at short-season Hillsboro, Sherfy moved to low Class A South Bend to finish 2013. His low-three-quarters arm slot concerns some scouts in terms of its repeatability. His fastball sits at 95-96 mph and touches 98. His low-80s slider has the potential to be a wipeout pitch, along the lines of Giants closer Sergio Romo. Sherfy loves to pitch in pressure situations and could move quickly through the system, potentially following the path taken in 2012 by Jake Barrett, which means half the year at high Class A Visalia and half at Double-A Mobile.

Year	Club (League)	Class	W	L	ERA	G	GS	CG	SV	IP	H	HR	BB	SO	K/9	WHIP	AVG
2013	Hillsboro (NWL)	SS	0	0	0.00	9	0	0	5	9	3	0	1	17	17.0	0.44	.100
	South Bend (MWL)	LoA	1	1	2.16	9	0	0	2	8	10	0	3	12	13.0	1.56	.286
Minor League Totals			1	1	1.04	18	0	0	7	17	13	0	4	29	15.1	0.98	.200

16 ZEKE SPRUILL, RHP

BA GRADE 45 MEDIUM

Born: Sept. 11, 1989. **B-T:** R-R. **Ht.:** 6-5. **Wt.:** 190. **Drafted:** HS—Marietta, Ga., 2008 (2nd round). **Signed by:** Brian Bridges (Braves).

A 2008 second-round pick, Spruill pitched for five seasons in the Braves organization, spending the last season and a half at the Double-A level. The Diamondbacks acquired Spruill, a Georgia native, along with Martin Prado and Randall Delgado in the deal that shipped Justin Upton and Chris Johnson to Atlanta. Spruill returned to the Southern League for five starts before moving up to Triple-A Reno, where his performance varied in 16 starts. He made his big league debut by making two starts and four relief appearances during callups in June and August. Big league opponents hit .354 against Spruill as he struggled to mix his pitches effectively. He's a groundball pitcher with a good sinker whose stuff should play well at Chase Field. He works his two-seam fastball in the 90-94 mph range and it has plus movement. His changeup is a solid-average pitch with sink complementing the fastball. Spruill's best breaking ball is his slider, which showed improvement in 2013 and projects to average. He'll contend for a roster spot in spring training but could spend another year on the Reno-to-Phoenix shuttle.

Year	Club (League)	Class	W	L	ERA	G	GS	CG	SV	IP	H	HR	BB	SO	K/9	WHIP	AVG
2008	Braves (GCL)	R	7	0	2.93	10	3	0	0	40	42	1	8	32	7.2	1.25	.268
2009	Braves (GCL)	R	1	0	4.58	4	4	0	0	20	24	2	5	23	10.5	1.47	.289
	Rome (SAL)	LoA	8	6	3.03	20	19	0	1	116	120	9	24	95	7.4	1.24	.261
2010	Braves (GCL)	R	0	0	3.00	2	2	0	0	3	4	0	1	1	3.0	1.67	.333
	Myrtle Beach (CAR)	HiA	3	5	5.54	14	13	1	0	65	83	4	13	41	5.7	1.48	.310
2011	Lynchburg (CAR)	HiA	7	9	3.19	20	20	5	0	130	108	7	23	92	6.4	1.01	.227
	Mississippi (SL)	AA	3	2	3.20	7	7	1	0	45	45	3	17	16	3.2	1.38	.266
2012	Mississippi (SL)	AA	9	11	3.67	27	27	1	0	162	158	8	46	106	5.9	1.26	.260
2013	Mobile (SL)	AA	0	3	1.42	5	5	0	0	32	24	0	12	20	5.7	1.14	.224
	Arizona (NL)	MAJ	0	2	5.56	6	2	0	0	11	17	3	5	9	7.1	1.94	.354
	Reno (PCL)	AAA	6	5	4.21	16	16	1	0	92	98	8	33	48	4.7	1.42	.277
Major League Totals			0	2	5.56	6	2	0	0	11	17	3	5	9	7.1	1.94	.354
Minor League Totals			44	41	3.57	125	116	9	1	704	706	42	182	474	6.1	1.26	.262

17 DANIEL PALKA, 1B

BA GRADE 50 HIGH

Born: Oct. 28, 1991. **B-T:** L-L. **Ht.:** 6-2. **Wt.:** 220. **Drafted:** Georgia Tech, 2013 (3rd round). **Signed by:** T.R. Lewis.

Arizona shifted its focus from power pitchers to power bats for their second- and third-round picks in the 2013 draft, taking Justin Williams in the third, followed by Palka, the Atlantic Coast Conference home run champ, in the fourth. Palka started his pro career at Rookie-level Missoula after signing for $550,000. He played mostly right field and pitched at Georgia Tech because of his strong left arm, but his lack of athleticism resulted in a move to first base in pro ball. Palka hit well at both Missoula and then short-season Hillsboro, though a hitch in his swing results in plenty of whiffs. He's got strong hands and plenty of bat speed, so the raw power should play when he solidifies his approach and gets used to seeing better breaking stuff. Palka is still very raw at first base but made improvements with footwork and positioning during instructional league. He'll make his full-season debut in 2014 with a probable assignment to low Class A South Bend.

Year	Club (League)	Class	AVG	G	AB	R	H	2B	3B	HR	RBI	BB	SO	SB	CS	OBP	SLG
2013	Missoula (PIO)	R	.302	56	205	36	62	20	0	7	38	29	45	2	2	.386	.502
	Hillsboro (NWL)	SS	.340	12	47	10	16	1	2	2	10	7	16	1	0	.418	.574
Minor League Totals			.310	68	252	46	78	21	2	9	48	36	61	3	2	.392	.516

18 NICK AHMED, SS

BA GRADE
45
MEDIUM

Born: March 15, 1990. **B-T:** R-R. **Ht.:** 6-3. **Wt.:** 205. **Drafted:** Connecticut, 2011 (2nd round). **Signed by:** Kevin Barry (Braves).

A Braves second-round pick in 2011, Ahmed is another in the bundle of players received by the Diamondbacks in the January 2013 Justin Upton trade. Regarded as one of the best defensive shortstops in the minors, he struggled mightily with the bat at Double-A Mobile over the first two months of 2013 before righting the ship and hitting .284/.326/.404 in the final three months. Scouts who believe in Ahmed think he'll hit enough to contribute at the big league level because he's athletic, drives the ball with his hips and has good bat speed. Others see too much weak contact to project his bat as anything but well below-average. Ahmed is a plus defender at shortstop with soft hands, a strong, accurate arm and a quick release. He's an above-average runner with plenty of first-step quickness. He also shows good instincts on the bases, having swiped 26 bags in 2013 and 40 the year before. Ahmed has good makeup and draws comparisons with former Diamondbacks shortstop John McDonald, who carved out a long career with a similar skillset. Ahmed will move to Triple-A Reno for 2014, but with a lot of shortstops ahead of him in the organization he'll likely spend the whole season there.

Year	Club (League)	Class	AVG	G	AB	R	H	2B	3B	HR	RBI	BB	SO	SB	CS	OBP	SLG
2011	Danville (APP)	R	.262	59	248	46	65	13	2	4	24	30	46	18	6	.346	.379
2012	Lynchburg (CAR)	HiA	.269	130	506	84	136	36	4	6	49	49	102	40	10	.337	.391
2013	Mobile (SL)	AA	.236	136	487	58	115	21	5	4	46	33	72	26	7	.288	.324
Minor League Totals			.255	325	1241	188	316	70	11	14	119	112	220	84	23	.320	.363

19 EVAN MARSHALL, RHP

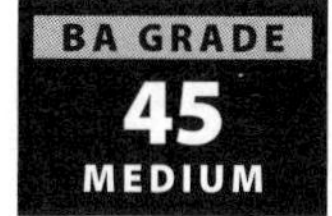

Born: April 18, 1990. **B-T:** R-R. **Ht.:** 6-2. **Wt.:** 220. **Drafted:** Kansas State, 2011 (4th round). **Signed by:** Joe Robinson.

A starter at Kansas State before moving to the bullpen as a junior in 2011, Marshall signed for $232,500 as a fourth-round pick and has moved quickly through the system, reaching Triple-A Reno in 2013. Scouts project him to have enough stuff to pitch at the back of a bullpen. Marshall throws a big, 92-96 mph fastball with heavy sink and a hard, true curveball. His funky delivery features a deceptive body turn and a three-quarters arm slot. When Marshall fails to execute his pitch, he often misses down because of the natural sink, so his mistakes tend to stay in the ballpark. He's allowed two home runs in each of the past two seasons. What's holding him back right now is a lack of fastball command and control, because without improvement in that area he's probably more middle reliever than impact set-up man. Marshall will be one of an army of pitchers battling for a big league bullpen job in 2014, and he could rack up plenty of frequent-flyer miles traveling between Reno and Phoenix.

Year	Club (League)	Class	W	L	ERA	G	GS	CG	SV	IP	H	HR	BB	SO	K/9	WHIP	AVG
2011	Yakima (NWL)	SS	0	0	0.75	11	0	0	2	12	10	0	2	13	9.8	1.00	.213
	Visalia (CAL)	HiA	0	1	1.59	15	0	0	4	17	14	2	5	18	9.5	1.12	.212
	Mobile (SL)	AA	0	0	0.00	1	0	0	0	2	2	0	0	0	0.0	1.00	.286
2012	Mobile (SL)	AA	6	3	3.51	42	0	0	16	49	55	2	16	27	5.0	1.46	.284
2013	Reno (PCL)	AAA	3	6	4.34	54	0	0	3	58	75	2	30	59	9.2	1.81	.322
Minor League Totals			9	10	3.33	123	0	0	25	138	156	6	53	117	7.6	1.52	.285

20 MICHAEL PEREZ, C

BA GRADE
50
EXTREME

Born: Aug. 7, 1992. **B-T:** L-R. **Ht.:** 5-11. **Wt.:** 180. **Drafted:** HS—San Juan, P.R., 2011 (5th round). **Signed by:** Frankie Thon Jr.

Perez signed for $235,000 after being selected in the fifth round of the 2011 draft, making rapid progress by jumping from Rookie-level Missoula in 2012 to high Class A Visalia in 2013. He wound up having a lost season, missing time in spring training with a fractured hamate bone in his wrist and then missing three weeks in May after getting hit in the face by a bat. Perez's aggressive hitting approach got exposed by the better pitching in the California League even when he was healthy. He was taking longer and loopier swings with Visalia and hit just .173 before being demoted to low Class A South Bend. Perez hit better there, but still struggled to maintain consistency. He remains the best defensive catcher in the system, and he improved his blocking of pitches in 2013. Despite his offensive struggles at Visalia, he threw out 43 percent of basestealers thanks to an above-average arm and good footwork behind the plate. Most notably, he improved his command of the English language, enhancing his ability to work with the pitchers. Perez learned from his adversity and ought to be ready for a repeat trip to Visalia in 2014.

Year	Club (League)	Class	AVG	G	AB	R	H	2B	3B	HR	RBI	BB	SO	SB	CS	OBP	SLG
2011	Diamondbacks (AZL)	R	.217	7	23	5	5	2	0	2	3	2	10	1	0	.280	.565
2012	Missoula (PIO)	R	.293	58	225	43	66	16	5	10	60	20	72	0	1	.358	.542
2013	Visalia (CAL)	HiA	.173	47	179	21	31	9	0	5	24	11	78	1	1	.223	.307
	South Bend (MWL)	LoA	.247	46	162	20	40	12	2	2	14	14	55	0	0	.303	.383
Minor League Totals			.241	158	589	89	142	39	7	19	101	47	215	2	2	.300	.428

21 DANIEL GIBSON, LHP

BA GRADE
45
HIGH

Born: Oct. 16, 1991. **B-T:** R-L. **Ht.:** 6-2. **Wt.:** 219. **Drafted:** Florida, 2013 (7th round). **Signed by:** Luke Wrenn.

Gibson joins the University of Florida parade of lefty power relievers to march from Gainesville through the pro ranks. The Angels' Nick Maronde and the Dodgers' Paco Rodriguez, former Gators both, reached the big leagues in 2012. A seventh-round pick in 2013, Gibson signed for $178,600 before reporting first to short-season Hillsboro and then low Class A South Bend. He pitched well at both stops, with a cumulative 0.64 ERA and 27/10 SO/BB ratio in 28 innings. If Gibson's command improves, he could project as a quality set-up man. Otherwise he can function as a situational lefty because he creates terrific angle against same-side hitters. His hard fastball is a plus pitch, ranging from 92-96 mph and sitting at 94. His slider and curveball are both average pitches. Gibson gets the ball across the plate, but not without some funkiness to his across-the-body delivery. Power lefthanders tend to move quickly, so Gibson could begin 2014 at high Class A Visalia.

Year	Club (League)	Class	W	L	ERA	G	GS	CG	SV	IP	H	HR	BB	SO	K/9	WHIP	AVG
2013	Hillsboro (NWL)	SS	1	0	0.45	14	0	0	3	20	17	0	8	22	9.9	1.25	.227
	South Bend (MWL)	LoA	0	1	1.08	6	0	0	0	8	6	0	2	5	5.4	0.96	.214
Minor League Totals			1	1	0.64	20	0	0	3	28	23	0	10	27	8.6	1.16	.223

22 GEORDY PARRA, RHP

BA GRADE
45
HIGH

Born: Sept. 6, 1993. **B-T:** R-R. **Ht.:** 6-2. **Wt.:** 208. **Signed:** Venezuela, 2011. **Signed by:** Marlon Urdaneta.

More famous for being the younger brother of Diamondbacks outfielder Gerardo Parra, Geordy began gaining attention for his pitching in 2013. He has gained about 40 pounds since signing out of Venezuela in 2011 and has added a splitter to his arsenal to now look like a late-inning reliever in the making. Parra dominated the Rookie-level Pioneer League in 2013 with a 0.40 ERA and 35 strikeouts in 23 innings. After working with a high-80s fastball in 2012, Parra now commands a 92-97 mph heater and at times shows a plus splitter at 84-86. He's also got good command of a curveball that at times flashes average potential. Parra is a strike-throwing machine who repeats his delivery and uses a high three-quarters arm slot. He's a hard worker who takes his side sessions and bullpen work seriously. Parra will be just 20 as 2014 opens, so a return to low Class A South Bend is his most likely destination.

Year	Club (League)	Class	W	L	ERA	G	GS	CG	SV	IP	H	HR	BB	SO	K/9	WHIP	AVG
2011	Diamondbacks (DSL)	R	0	0	1.13	6	2	0	0	16	12	0	6	18	10.1	1.13	.218
2012	Diamondbacks (DSL)	R	1	0	4.50	3	3	0	0	16	19	3	2	17	9.6	1.31	.279
	Diamondbacks (AZL)	R	1	4	5.45	12	7	0	0	40	52	3	19	37	8.4	1.79	.311
2013	Missoula (PIO)	R	4	1	0.40	19	0	0	0	23	14	0	11	35	13.9	1.10	.167
	South Bend (MWL)	LoA	0	0	0.00	4	0	0	0	4	3	0	1	4	8.3	0.92	.200
Minor League Totals			6	5	3.19	44	12	0	0	99	100	6	39	111	10.1	1.41	.257

23 CHASE ANDERSON, RHP

BA GRADE
45
HIGH

Born: Nov. 30, 1987. **B-T:** R-R. **Ht.:** 6-1. **Wt.:** 175. **Drafted:** Oklahoma, 2009 (9th round). **Signed by:** Jason Karegeannes.

A reliever at Oklahoma prior to signing with the Diamondbacks for $85,000 as a ninth-round round pick in 2009, Anderson joined the Arizona 40-man roster after a strong Arizona Fall League showing in 2012. He struggled as a starter at Triple-A Reno in 2013 before being shut down for six weeks at midseason with a triceps strain. Anderson returned as a reliever, and that may be his role moving forward in order to keep him healthy after a series of arm problems, including a forearm strain that caused him to miss nearly all of 2011. He has the repertoire to start but perhaps not the durability. The highlight of Anderson's arsenal is a double-plus changeup, perennially rated as the best in the organization, which plays well off his fastball. His heater sits in the 87-92 mph range, though it tends to get flat when he worked in the rotation. Anderson also has a curveball with good depth and a useable slider. He repeats his delivery and throws from a high-three-quarters arm slot, throwing enough strikes to profile as a middle reliever. He heads to camp in 2014 looking for a bullpen job in Arizona.

Year	Club (League)	Class	W	L	ERA	G	GS	CG	SV	IP	H	HR	BB	SO	K/9	WHIP	AVG
2009	Missoula (PIO)	R	3	1	2.38	18	4	0	0	45	35	1	13	48	9.5	1.06	.206
2010	South Bend (MWL)	LoA	2	4	2.82	7	7	1	0	38	36	1	9	31	7.3	1.17	.238
	Visalia (CAL)	HiA	5	3	3.60	19	4	0	3	70	58	7	16	83	10.7	1.06	.227
2011	Visalia (CAL)	HiA	1	1	5.40	3	3	0	0	13	14	1	1	20	13.5	1.13	.259
2012	Mobile (SL)	AA	5	4	2.86	21	21	0	0	104	91	9	25	97	8.4	1.12	.238
2013	Reno (PCL)	AAA	4	7	5.73	26	13	0	0	88	107	11	33	80	8.2	1.59	.301
Minor League Totals			20	20	3.74	94	52	1	3	359	341	30	97	359	9.0	1.22	.249

24 ANDREW CHAFIN, LHP

BA GRADE **45** HIGH

Born: June 17, 1990. **B-T:** R-L. **Ht.:** 6-2. **Wt.:** 205. **Drafted:** Kent State, 2011 (1st round supplemental). **Signed by:** Nate Birtwell.

Chafin made his full-season debut in 2012 at high Class A Visalia after signing with the Diamondbacks for $875,000 as the 43rd overall pick the previous year. After striking out 11.0 batters per nine innings in 2012, Chafin showed diminished velocity in his return to the California League in 2013. His fastball, which previously sat in the 90-94 mph range, dipped into the 89-91 range and sometimes lower. Chafin's slider at times lacked the depth and tilt that made it a plus pitch in the past, but he improved his changeup enough to the point where it's now an above-average pitch. After a six-start encore in Visalia, Chafin moved up to Double-A Mobile, where he worked more on pitching to contact. A lower walk rate at Mobile also was a positive sign that Chafin was more aggressive in the zone. His funky delivery provides deception and helps him get the ball on batters more quickly. Considering that he might recover velocity in short relief outings, that might be his best role. Assigned to the Arizona Fall League to work as a reliever, Chafin was shut down with a dead arm after two outings.

Year	Club (League)	Class	W	L	ERA	G	GS	CG	SV	IP	H	HR	BB	SO	K/9	WHIP	AVG
2011	Diamondbacks (AZL)	R	0	0	0.00	1	1	0	0	1	1	0	0	2	18.0	1.00	.250
2012	Visalia (CAL)	HiA	6	6	4.93	30	22	0	0	122	112	12	69	150	11.0	1.48	.241
2013	Visalia (CAL)	HiA	3	1	4.65	6	6	0	0	31	32	1	14	32	9.3	1.48	.262
	Mobile (SL)	AA	10	7	2.85	21	21	2	0	126	118	5	41	87	6.2	1.26	.252
Minor League Totals			19	14	3.94	58	50	2	0	281	263	18	124	271	8.7	1.38	.248

25 ALFREDO MARTE, OF

BA GRADE **40** LOW

Born: March 31, 1989. **B-T:** R-R. **Ht.:** 6-0. **Wt.:** 190. **Signed:** Dominican Republic, 2005. **Signed by:** Junior Noboa.

Marte took six years before breaking out with a strong season at Double-A Mobile during the 2011 season, which included an appearance at the Futures Game. Sent down to minor league camp during 2013 spring training, Marte reappeared after injuries struck down outfielders Adam Eaton and Cody Ross, and he wound up making the Opening Day roster. Demoted to Triple-A Reno in mid-May, Marte was hit in the face by a pitch and missed about a month. He had modest success at Triple-A and didn't return to Arizona when rosters expanded in September. He shows flashes of turning the corner but frustrates by never quite putting it all together. He's athletic and has plenty of pull power, but he went deep just seven times in Triple-A after hitting 20 homers with Mobile in 2012. He showed improvement in the outfield and with an average arm is capable of handling right field. Marte profiles best as an extra outfielder with close-to-average tools across the board, but he could earn regular playing time if it all comes together. He appears ticketed for Reno to begin 2014, waiting there for another opportunity.

Year	Club (League)	Class	AVG	G	AB	R	H	2B	3B	HR	RBI	BB	SO	SB	CS	OBP	SLG
2006	Diamondbacks (DSL)	R	.250	19	68	9	17	4	0	1	10	5	10	0	1	.316	.353
2007	Diamondbacks (DSL)	R	.328	67	265	30	87	19	4	4	45	17	37	3	1	.377	.475
2008	Yakima (NWL)	SS	.251	70	267	37	67	18	0	1	27	24	44	19	5	.324	.330
2009	South Bend (MWL)	LoA	.251	120	475	49	119	27	3	7	71	25	78	5	2	.294	.364
2010	Visalia (CAL)	HiA	.260	130	516	76	134	26	3	9	61	34	107	9	5	.314	.374
2011	Mobile (SL)	AA	.233	17	43	4	10	1	0	1	6	4	10	1	0	.306	.326
	Visalia (CAL)	HiA	.299	59	234	35	70	15	3	7	33	14	43	5	0	.344	.479
2012	Mobile (SL)	AA	.294	113	398	68	117	25	3	20	75	34	72	6	6	.363	.523
2013	Arizona (NL)	MAJ	.186	22	43	4	8	3	0	0	4	4	12	0	0	.271	.256
	Reno (PCL)	AAA	.280	86	311	37	87	24	1	7	48	22	63	2	1	.335	.431
Major League Totals			.186	22	43	4	8	3	0	0	4	4	12	0	0	.271	.256
Minor League Totals			.275	681	2577	345	708	159	17	57	376	179	464	50	21	.331	.416

26 JOE MUNOZ, SS

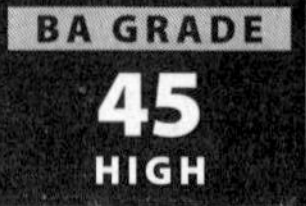

Born: Dec. 28,1993. **B-T:** R-R. **Ht.:** 6-3. **Wt.:** 195. **Drafted:** HS—Hacienda Heights, Calif., 2012 (2nd round). **Signed by:** Jeff Mousser.

Munoz made strides on both sides of the ball as the everyday shortstop at Rookie-level Missoula in 2013. A second-round pick the year before, he hit .360/.433/.663 with five homers in July but managed a .625 OPS the rest of the way. Munoz's power is slowly developing, but scouts ding him for below-average bat speed that makes him vulnerable to good fastballs. He split time at both shortstop and third base during instructional league, and at a physical 6-foot-3 he could eventually outgrow shortstop and need to move to the hot corner, where his bat could be a tough sell. Defensively, Munoz's footwork and hands improved in 2013. He has average range at shortstop but needs to better learn game situations and pre-pitch positioning. His above-average arm will play at either spot on the left side of the infield. Munoz will be 20 in 2014 so he could use another year of development in short-season ball, though a move to low Class A South Bend is most likely.

Year	Club (League)	Class	AVG	G	AB	R	H	2B	3B	HR	RBI	BB	SO	SB	CS	OBP	SLG
2012	Diamondbacks (AZL)	R	.260	47	173	25	45	4	2	2	20	16	53	4	4	.326	.341
2013	Missoula (PIO)	R	.263	54	194	32	51	12	3	6	30	20	61	5	0	.342	.448
Minor League Totals			.262	101	367	57	96	16	5	8	50	36	114	9	4	.335	.398

27 JAMIE WESTBROOK, 2B

Born: June 18, 1995. **B-T:** R-R. **Ht.:** 5-9. **Wt.:** 170. **Drafted:** HS—Chandler, Ariz., 2013 (5th round). **Signed by:** Doyle Wilson.

A product of Basha High in Chandler, Ariz., Westbrook stuck close to home when he began his pro career in the Rookie-level Arizona League after signing for $450,000 as a Diamondbacks fifth-round pick. He's a gamer and coach's favorite who loves to play and improve. The prep shortstop didn't have the arm strength to stay at the position in pro ball, but he handled the move to second base, where he could be an average defender if he improves his arm strength, footwork and hands. Westbrook swings the bat well with a compact, righthanded swing, good bat speed and power for his size. One observer compared him with Dan Uggla for his squat body type and pop in his bat. Westbrook's average speed plays up on the bases because of his aggressive nature and the way he studies pitcher tendencies. He'll get another year in short-season ball in 2014, possibly at short-season Hillsboro.

Year	Club (League)	Class	AVG	G	AB	R	H	2B	3B	HR	RBI	BB	SO	SB	CS	OBP	SLG
2013	Diamondbacks (AZL)	R	.292	40	154	31	45	8	8	1	20	17	21	3	3	.373	.468
	Missoula (PIO)	R	.254	17	67	12	17	3	0	1	13	6	20	1	0	.315	.343
Minor League Totals			.281	57	221	43	62	11	8	2	33	23	41	4	3	.356	.430

28 ANDREW VELAZQUEZ, SS/2B

Born: July 14, 1994. **B-T:** B-R. **Ht.:** 5-8. **Wt.:** 175. **Drafted:** HS—New York, 2012 (7th round). **Signed by:** Todd Donovan.

The Bronx, N.Y., native turned pro rather than attend Virginia Tech when the Diamondbacks offered him $200,000 as a seventh-round pick in 2012. After a successful debut in the Rookie-level Arizona League, he played so well in 2013 extended spring training that Arizona assigned him to low Class A South Bend in early June. A diminutive switch-hitter, Velazquez had his ups and downs in full-season ball, but he finished strong by batting .303/.404/.360 over the final month after gaining a better understanding of the strike zone. While he doesn't hit for power, he generates above-average bat speed owing to strong hands. He's a plus runner with good instincts on the bases, but he needs to learn better basestealing techniques. Primarily a second baseman in 2012, Velasquez actually spent more time at shortstop with South Bend. He has the arm strength for the position but needs to learn how to go to his backhand and throw from different angles. Velazquez may return to South Bend for more seasoning, and he profiles best as a utility infielder.

Year	Club (League)	Class	AVG	G	AB	R	H	2B	3B	HR	RBI	BB	SO	SB	CS	OBP	SLG
2012	Diamondbacks (AZL)	R	.319	29	116	33	37	8	5	1	20	18	35	20	3	.406	.500
	Missoula (PIO)	R	.220	14	50	9	11	0	2	0	4	5	12	2	0	.286	.300
2013	South Bend (MWL)	LoA	.260	65	235	23	61	10	4	0	16	21	59	7	2	.319	.336
Minor League Totals			.272	108	401	65	109	18	11	1	40	44	106	29	5	.341	.379

29 BO SCHULTZ, RHP

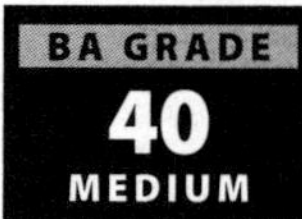

Born: Sept. 25, 1985. **B-T:** R-R. **Ht.:** 6-3. **Wt.:** 215. **Signed:** Northwestern, 2008 (NDFA). **Signed by:** Gil Patterson (Athletics).

The feel good story of 2013 for the Diamondbacks, Schultz originally signed with the Athletics as a nondrafted free agent from Northwestern in 2008. He pitched parts of four seasons in the Oakland organization, topping out at high Class A, before being released and landing in the independent American Association in 2011. Previously a sidearm pitcher who sat in the high 80s, Schultz raised his arm slot to high-three-quarters with Arizona in 2012, which had the effect of adding velocity and improving his secondary pitches. The D-backs used him as a reliever at two levels in 2012 but put him in the rotation at Double-A Mobile in 2013. While Schultz's two-seam fastball has sink and some movement, he doesn't offer much deception. He pitched regularly in the low 90s as a starter, and Arizona says he even hit triple digits at Mobile while also improving his cutter-type slider, his most trusted secondary pitch. The changeup is still a work in progress. Schultz has plus makeup, so after raising eyebrows with a strong performance in the Arizona Fall League, he earned a spot on the 40-man roster and a chance to win a job with the big club in 2014.

Year	Club (League)	Class	W	L	ERA	G	GS	CG	SV	IP	H	HR	BB	SO	K/9	WHIP	AVG
2008	Athletics (AZL)	R	4	3	5.24	14	7	0	0	45	43	0	25	30	6.0	1.52	.250
2009	Vancouver (NWL)	SS	2	3	2.66	26	0	0	0	44	29	0	19	48	9.8	1.09	.185
2010	Kane County (MWL)	LoA	6	1	2.87	41	0	0	0	75	57	2	34	65	7.8	1.21	.208
2011	Stockton (CAL)	HiA	0	0	14.85	7	0	0	1	7	11	0	5	4	5.4	2.40	.367
	Grand Prairie (A-A)	IND	4	3	4.13	37	4	0	1	72	80	2	24	54	6.8	1.44	—
2012	Visalia (CAL)	HiA	4	2	4.50	29	0	0	11	34	41	3	10	36	9.5	1.50	.295
	Mobile (SL)	AA	2	3	2.11	17	0	0	0	21	20	0	7	13	5.5	1.27	.244
2013	Reno (PCL)	AAA	0	2	5.49	17	0	0	0	20	29	4	7	23	10.5	1.83	.345
	Mobile (SL)	AA	5	4	2.86	20	16	0	1	85	62	3	29	52	5.5	1.07	.205
Minor League Totals			23	18	3.67	171	23	0	13	331	292	12	136	271	7.4	1.29	.235

30 JOSE HERRERA, C

BA GRADE
50
EXTREME

Born: Feb. 24, 1997. **B-T:** B-R. **Ht.:** 5-10. **Wt.:** 180. **Signed:** Venezuela, 2013. **Signed by:** Marlon Urdaneta.

The top catcher on the 2013 international market, Herrera tried out with the Diamondbacks during extended spring training. The relationship that developed convinced the native Venezuelan to sign with Arizona for $1,060,000 on July 2, when 16-year-old international amateurs became eligible to sign. Herrera played for Venezuela's 15U World Championship team in 2012, making the all-tournament team not long after converting to catcher from third base. He's relatively new to switch-hitting but already shows the potential to hit for power from both sides because he has strength and the lift in his swing. He also has a good batting eye at the plate. Defensively, Herrera shows quickness behind the plate, good hands and a solid arm that could project to be above-average. While he needs a lot of experience, he's already ahead of other catchers his age. Herrera will turn 17 just before the start of spring training. Considering that the Diamondbacks brought him to the States for instructional league, they could choose to have him begin his pro career in the Rookie-level Arizona League.

Year	Club (League)	Class	AVG	G	AB	R	H	2B	3B	HR	RBI	BB	SO	SB	CS	OBP	SLG
2013	Did not play—Signed 2014 contract																

Atlanta Braves

BY BILL BALLEW

Disappointment reigned in October, when the Braves failed to build on a remarkable regular season. In the process of overcoming numerous ailments, including seven season-ending injuries, Atlanta led the National League East for all but one day of the 2013 campaign and captured its first division crown since 2005. The team also won 96 games, paced the majors with a 3.18 ERA and topped the NL with 181 home runs. Still, the Braves dropped their NL Division Series to the Dodgers, their eighth straight playoff series loss, dating back to 2001.

The team overachieved for much of 2013, incorporating more young talent. Shortstop Andrelton Simmons solidified his spot as part of the team's future foundation, and rookie Evan Gattis provided power and run production while seeing action at catcher and left field. Third baseman Chris Johnson, an extra piece in the Justin Upton deal with the Diamondbacks, ranked second in the NL in batting (.321) and replaced the retired Chipper Jones admirably.

The farm system also contributed righthander Julio Teheran, who established himself as one of Atlanta's most dependable starters, and lefty Alex Wood, who made his big league debut a year after being drafted in the second round out of Georgia.

In other words, the Braves keep producing talent, both stars like Simmons and complementary pieces. With Brian McCann gone for free agent megabucks, Panamanian catcher Christian Bethancourt is on the verge of filling the next lineup vacancy behind the plate, and second baseman Tommy La Stella should get a long look despite the $26 million still owed Dan Uggla over the next two years.

Scouting director Tony DeMacio has filled voids by dipping into the college ranks for low-mileage arms while building a deeper base with high school players. Righthander Lucas Sims, a local product drafted in the first round in 2012, blossomed in his first full season. Former Oklahoma State righty Jason Hursh brought a power repertoire as 2013's first-rounder.

Reliever Shae Simmons made the jump to Double-A Mississippi in his first full season and could take his high-90s heat to Atlanta in 2014. Another late-round sign, righthander Tyler Brosius, generated excitement, as did nondrafted free agent righty Wes Parsons, who made 19 starts at low Class A Rome.

The Braves' international efforts are also paying dividends. Shortstop Jose Peraza made strides at Rome, and righthander Mauricio Cabrera displayed impressive arm strength in the South Atlantic League despite struggling with his control. Outfielder Victor Reyes is blossoming in Rookie ball and could emerge as a premier prospect in the near future.

Even though the two Braves affiliates to make the playoffs—high Class A Lynchburg and Mississippi—did so as wild-card entries, the only team to struggle for much of 2013 was Triple-A Gwinnett. The G-Braves will have a new manager in 2014, with Randy Ready fired after one season. Taking his place will be Brian Snitker, who has served as Atlanta's third-base coach for the past seven years and has been in the organization as a player, coach or manager since 1977. In fact, Snitker's last managerial gig came with the Braves' Triple-A affiliate (then in Richmond) in 2006.

BILL NICHOLS

Julio Teheran quickly established himself as one of the Braves' most dependable starters

TOP PROSPECTS OF THE DECADE

Year	Player, Pos.	2013 Org.
2004	Andy Marte, 3b	Angels
2005	Jeff Francoeur, of	Giants
2006	Jarrod Saltalamacchia, c	Red Sox
2007	Jarrod Saltalamacchia, c	Red Sox
2008	Jordan Schafer, of	Braves
2009	Tommy Hanson, rhp	Angels
2010	Jason Heyward, of	Braves
2011	Julio Teheran, rhp	Braves
2012	Julio Teheran, rhp	Braves
2013	Julio Teheran, rhp	Braves

ORGANIZATION OVERVIEW

General Manager: Frank Wren. **Farm Director:** Ronnie Richardson. **Scouting Director:** Tony DeMacio.

Class	Team	League	W	L	PCT	Finish	Manager
Majors	Atlanta Braves	National	96	66	.593	2nd (15)	Fredi Gonzalez
Triple-A	Gwinnett Braves	International	60	84	.417	14th (14)	Randy Ready
Double-A	Mississippi Braves	Southern	76	63	.547	4th (10)	Aaron Holbert
High Class A	Lynchburg Hillcats	Carolina	69	70	.496	5th (8)	Luis Salazar
Low Class A	Rome Braves	South Atlantic	73	66	.525	7th (14)	Randy Ingle
Rookie	Danville Braves	Appalachian	29	36	.446	7th (10)	Jonathan Schuerholz
Rookie	GCL Braves	Gulf Coast	26	34	.433	13th (16)	Rocket Wheeler
Overall 2013 Minor League Record			**333**	**353**	**.485**	**22nd (30)**	

THIS YEAR'S TOP 30

No.	Player, Pos.	Grade/Risk
1.	Lucas Sims, rhp	60/High
2.	Christian Bethancourt, c	55/Medium
3.	J.R. Graham, rhp	60/High
4.	Jason Hursh, rhp	55/High
5.	Mauricio Cabrera, rhp	55/High
6.	Jose Peraza, ss	55/High
7.	David Hale, rhp	45/Low
8.	Victor Caratini, 3b/c	50/High
9.	Tommy La Stella, 2b	45/Medium
10.	Sean Gilmartin, lhp	45/Medium
11.	Cody Martin, rhp	45/Medium
12.	Edward Salcedo, 3b	50/High
13.	Josh Elander, of	45/Medium
14.	Victor Reyes, of	55/Extreme
15.	Joey Terdoslavich, of/1b	45/Medium
16.	Shae Simmons, rhp	45/Medium
17.	Carlos Salazar, rhp	50/High
18.	Kyle Wren, of	50/High
19.	Johan Camargo, ss	50/High
20.	Wes Parsons, rhp	50/High
21.	Tanner Murphy, c	50/Extreme
22.	Kyle Kubitza, 3b	45/High
23.	Todd Cunningham, of	40/Low
24.	Matt Lipka, of	45/High
25.	Aaron Northcraft, rhp	45/High
26.	Luis Merejo, lhp	50/Extreme
27.	Juan Jaime, rhp	45/High
28.	Tyler Brosius, rhp	45/High
29.	Robby Hefflinger, of	45/High
30.	James Hoyt, rhp	45/High

LAST YEAR'S TOP 30

No.	Player, Pos.	Status
1.	Julio Teheran, rhp	Majors
2.	J.R. Graham, rhp	No. 3
3.	Christian Bethancourt, c	No. 2
4.	Sean Gilmartin, lhp	No. 10
5.	Lucas Sims, rhp	No. 1
6.	Mauricio Cabrera, rhp	No. 5
7.	Alex Wood, lhp	Majors
8.	Evan Gattis, of/c	Majors
9.	Zeke Spruill, rhp	(Diamondbacks)
10.	Jose Peraza, ss	No. 6
11.	Nick Ahmed, ss	(Diamondbacks)
12.	Todd Cunningham, of	No. 23
13.	Cody Martin, rhp	No. 11
14.	Matt Lipka, of	No. 24
15.	Navery Moore, rhp	Dropped out
16.	David Hale, rhp	No. 7
17.	Edward Salcedo, 3b	No. 12
18.	Joey Terdoslavich, 1b/3b	No. 15
19.	Josh Elander, c	No. 13
20.	Juan Jaime, rhp	No. 27
21.	Carlos Franco, 3b	Dropped out
22.	Luis Merejo, rhp	No. 26
23.	Bryan De La Rosa, c	Dropped out
24.	Billy Bullock, rhp	(Released)
25.	Kyle Kubitza, 3b	No. 22
26.	Nathan Hyatt, rhp	Dropped out
27.	Brandon Drury, 1b/3b	(Diamondbacks)
28.	Carlos Perez, lhp	Dropped out
29.	Robby Hefflinger, of	No. 29
30.	Aaron Northcraft, rhp	No. 25

BEST TOOLS

Best Hitter for Average	Tommy La Stella
Best Power Hitter	Robby Hefflinger
Best Strike-Zone Discipline	Tommy La Stella
Fastest Baserunner	Matt Lipka
Best Athlete	Matt Lipka
Best Fastball	Shae Simmons
Best Curveball	Lucas Sims
Best Slider	Cody Martin
Best Changeup	Sean Gilmartin
Best Control	J.R. Graham
Best Defensive Catcher	Christian Bethancourt
Best Defensive Infielder	Johan Camargo
Best Infield Arm	Kyle Kubitza
Best Defensive Outfielder	Kyle Wren
Best Outfield Arm	Alejandro Piloto

TOP 15 PLAYERS 25 AND UNDER

No.	Player, Pos. (Age)	Peak Level
1.	Freddie Freeman, 1b (24)	Majors
2.	Andrelton Simmons, ss (24)	Majors
3.	Jason Heyward, of (24)	Majors
4.	Craig Kimbrel, rhp (25)	Majors
5.	Julio Teheran, rhp (23)	Majors
6.	Lucas Sims, rhp (19)	Low Class A
7.	Christian Bethancourt, c (22)	Majors
8.	Alex Wood, lhp (23)	Majors
9.	J.R. Graham, rhp (24)	Double-A
10.	Jason Hursh, rhp (22)	Low Class A
11.	Mauricio Cabrera, rhp (20)	Low Class A
12.	Jose Peraza, ss (19)	Low Class A
13.	Victor Caratini, 3b/c (20)	Rookie
14.	Tommy La Stella, 2b (25)	Double-A
15.	Sean Gilmartin, lhp (23)	Triple-A

MINOR LEAGUE DEPTH CHART

ATLANTA BRAVES

TOP 2014 ROOKIE: Tommy La Stella, 2b. With Dan Uggla struggling to make contact, the Braves may opt for the former Coastal Carolina product who has hit .327/.412/.496 as a pro.

BREAKOUT PROSPECT: Victor Reyes, of. After hitting an organization-best .342 in 2013, Reyes evidently has the tools to emerge as a top-shelf outfield prospect at low Class A Rome.

SOURCE OF TOP 30 TALENT			
Homegrown	**28**	**Acquired**	**2**
College	12	Trades	0
Junior college	3	Rule 5 draft	0
High school	5	Independent leagues	1
Nondrafted free agents	1	Free agents/waivers	1
International	7		

SLEEPER: Patrick Scoggin, rhp. The Virginia Tech product was Rome's best starter in the first half of 2013 and could take his game to another level as he gains more consistency with his offspeed pitches.

LF
- Josh Elander (13)
- Joey Terdoslavich (15)
- Robby Hefflinger (29)

CF
- Kyle Wren (18)
- Todd Cunningham (23)
- Matt Lipka (24)
- Mycal Jones
- Connor Lien

RF
- Victor Reyes (14)
- Alejandro Piloto
- David Rohm
- Felix Marte
- Fernelys Sanchez

3B
- Edward Salcedo (12)
- Kyle Kubitza (22)
- Joe Leonard
- Carlos Franco

SS
- Jose Peraza (6)
- Elmer Reyes
- Mikey Reynolds

2B
- Tommy La Stella (9)
- Johan Camargo (19)
- Levi Hyams
- Phil Gosselin
- Ross Heffley
- Ronald Luna

1B
- Ernesto Mejia
- William Beckwith

C
- Christian Bethancourt (2)
- Victor Caratini (8)
- Tanner Murphy (21)
- Bryan de la Rosa

LHP

LHSP	LHRP
Sean Gilmartin (10)	Ryan Buchter
Luis Merejo (26)	Carlos Perez
Ryan Hinson	Ian Thomas
	Ronan Pacheco
	Matt Chaffee
	Eric Pfisterer
	Blaine Sims
	Robert Fish
	Chasen Shreve

RHP

RHSP	RHRP
Lucas Sims (1)	Shea Simmons (16)
J.R. Graham (3)	Wes Parsons (20)
Jason Hursh (4)	Juan Jaime (27)
Mauricio Cabrera (5)	Tyler Brosius (28)
David Hale (7)	James Hoyt (30)
Cody Martin (11)	Luis Vasquez
Carlos Salazar (17)	Patrick Scoggin
Aaron Northcraft (25)	John Cornely
Gus Schlosser	Wirfin Obispo
Stephen Janas	Navery Moore
Ian Stifflen	Mark Lamm
Alec Grosser	Nathan Hyatt
	Zach Jadofsky
	Alex Wilson
	Jeremy Fitzgerald
	Williams Perez

DRAFT ANALYSIS

2013

BONUSES: $4.7 MILLION

BEST PURE HITTER: Victor Caratini (2) hit .377 in the spring at Miami-Dade CC, then rapped 23 doubles and hit .290/.415/.430 in his pro debut. He has a polished approach and compact, line-drive swing. He's converting from third base to catcher.

BEST POWER HITTER: The Braves believe Caratini will translate some of his doubles into home runs with more experience against pro pitching. Scouts outside the organization aren't as sure due to a flat bat path.

FASTEST RUNNER: Scouts thought OF Kyle Wren (8) slowed down in 2012 as an eligible sophomore, but his explosive speed was back in 2013. It plays on the bases and in center field.

BEST DEFENSIVE PLAYER: C Tanner Murphy (4) will trail Caratini developmentally, but he has better raw tools defensively, with good hands and arm strength.

BEST FASTBALL: RHP Jason Hursh (1) is a Tommy John survivor who can pitch from 92-98 mph with his fastball as a starter, with heavy life at times. RHP Carlos Salazar (3) has reached 97 mph as a starter and has a strong build to maintain his velocity.

BEST SECONDARY PITCH: RHP Tyler Brosius (21) hadn't pitched in two years but picked up a cutter/slider at Walters State (Tenn.) JC this spring. By the end of the year, he was throwing it with power at up to 87 mph with a solid, hard curveball.

BEST PRO DEBUT: Wren was too good for Rookie-level Danville (9-for-22), then hit .328/.382/.456 for low Class A Rome. He ranked third in the organization with 35 steals despite playing just 53 games. Brosius struck out 35 in 27 innings and joined Wren in Rome. Hursh didn't give up a run in his first 18 innings.

BEST ATHLETE: RHP Alec Grosser (11) has excellent athleticism for a pitcher. He was a prep quarterback and throws plenty of strikes from a low three-quarters slot. He also has the hand speed to improve his below-average breaking ball. OF Connor Oliver (23) is the best athlete among position players.

MOST INTRIGUING BACKGROUND: Wren's father Frank is the Braves' general manager. Brosius originally attended North Carolina State as a quarterback, where he sat behind current NFL quarterbacks Mike Glennon and Russell Wilson. After he quit football in August 2012, he turned to baseball after a two-year hiatus and finished his debut in full-season ball. 3B Dylan Manwaring (9) is the son of former big league C Kirt. Unsigned OF Jacob Heyward (38) is the younger brother of Braves OF Jason.

CLOSEST TO THE MAJORS: Hursh and Wren.

BEST LATE-ROUND PICK: Brosius and Grosser, who signed for $400,000.

THE ONE WHO GOT AWAY: The Braves made a hard run at 1B Tyler Kuresa (14), who returned to UC Santa Barbara. Prep OF Stephen Wrenn (28) took his intriguing speed to Georgia.

ASSESSMENT: Atlanta has sped players to the majors in recent years, and Hursh, Wren and Caratini could join that parade. Considering their track record with junior-college products, keep an eye on Brosius and Oliver as well.

2012

BONUSES: $4.8 MILLION

LHP Alex Wood (2) rocketed to the majors and contributed in Atlanta's playoff run. RHP Lucas Sims (1) is the system's top prospect.

GRADE: B+

2011

BONUSES: $3.7 MILLION

RHP J.R. Graham (4) and 2B Tommy La Stella (8) shine when healthy. Top picks LHP Sean Gilmartin (1) and since-traded SS Nick Ahmed (2) have low ceilings.

GRADE: C

2010

BONUSES: $3.9 MILLION

Tony DeMacio's first draft with Atlanta provided a bonanza, led by SS Andrelton Simmons (2). C/OF Evan Gattis (23) is one of four other big leaguers so far.

GRADE: A

TOP DRAFT PICKS OF THE DECADE

Year	Player, Pos.	2013 Org.
2004	Eric Campbell, 3b (2nd round)	Out of baseball
2005	Joey Devine, rhp	Out of baseball
2006	Cody Johnson, of	York (Can-Am)
2007	Jason Heyward, of	Braves
2008	Brett DeVall (1st round supp.)	Out of baseball
2009	Mike Minor, lhp	Braves
2010	Matt Lipka, ss (1st round supp.)	Braves
2011	Sean Gilmartin, lhp	Braves
2012	Lucas Sims, rhp	Braves
2013	Jason Hursh, rhp	Braves

LARGEST BONUSES IN CLUB HISTORY

Player	Bonus
Mike Minor, 2009	$2,420,000
Jeff Francoeur, 2002	$2,200,000
Matt Belisle, 1998	$1,750,000
Jason Hursh, 2013	$1,704,200
Jason Heyward, 2007	$1,700,000

1 LUCAS SIMS, RHP

Born: May 10, 1994. **B-T:** R-R. **Ht.:** 6-2. **Wt.:** 195.
Drafted: HS—Snellville, Ga., 2012 (1st round).
Signed by: Brian Bridges.

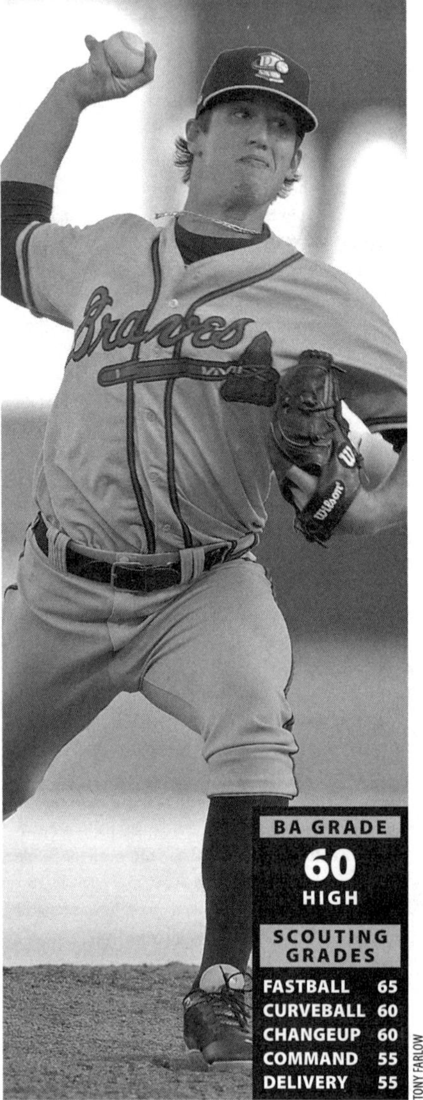

Braves
BA GRADE
60
HIGH
SCOUTING GRADES
FASTBALL 65
CURVEBALL 60
CHANGEUP 60
COMMAND 55
DELIVERY 55

TONY FARLOW

The Braves returned to their roots in 2012 when they drafted Sims, a local high school product with the 21st overall pick. After seeing the Clemson recruit endure a relatively heavy workload during the latter part of his high school career, the Braves were cautious with the righthander after signing him for $1.65 million by limiting him to 34 innings between two Rookie leagues in 2012. The organization continued to err on the side of caution by controlling Sims' innings and relegating him to 10 relief outings for the first six weeks of 2013 at low Class A Rome. He joined the rotation in May and got stronger as he added experience and honed his mechanics. In his last eight starts, beginning on July 23, Sims went 8-0, 1.60, allowing 34 hits and striking out 57 batters in 45 innings. Ranked as the South Atlantic League's No. 9 prospect, he led the loop in opponent average (.203), placed second in wins (12) and ERA (2.62) and finished fourth in strikeouts (134).

A shortstop as well as pitcher at Brookwood High, Sims has plus athleticism that allows him to repeat his delivery with relative ease. He struggled shortly after signing with his mechanics and finding a consistent release point, but he has fine-tuned those after working with the organization's pitching coaches. Sims challenges hitters and works off his fastball, which he spots on both sides of the plate. The pitch resides at 93-95 mph with good run, leading to many swings and misses in the SAL. The consistency of his slurvy, mid-70s curveball tends to come and go, but it has a tight spin and sharp break and was deemed the best breaking ball in the SAL by league managers. The biggest step Sims took in 2013 centered on the development of his changeup, which has the makings of a plus pitch. He learned early in the season about the importance of maintaining control of all his pitches and did an excellent job of improving as the season progressed. He has a great presence on the mound and follows in the footsteps of longtime Braves star (and 1990 first-rounder) Chipper Jones with his "necessary arrogance" and confidence on the field.

Rumors have persisted that the Braves would move Sims to the bullpen, rumors that spread like a crush in a middle school lunchroom when he opened the 2013 season in the Rome bullpen. His successful second-half shift to the rotation should put those whispers to rest, as he finished strong and accomplished the organization's goals. The Braves would prefer him to put in full seasons at high Class A Lynchburg and Double-A Mississippi over the next two years as he continues his development as a potential No. 2 starter in an Atlanta rotation that already features many homegrown arms.

Year	Club (League)	Class	W	L	ERA	G	GS	CG	SV	IP	H	HR	BB	SO	K/9	WHIP	AVG
2012	Braves (GCL)	R	0	0	1.29	3	3	0	0	7	2	1	1	10	12.9	0.43	.091
	Danville (APP)	R	2	4	4.33	8	8	0	0	27	26	2	12	29	9.7	1.41	.243
2013	Rome (SAL)	LoA	12	4	2.62	28	18	1	0	117	83	3	46	134	10.3	1.11	.203
Minor League Totals			14	8	2.87	39	29	1	0	151	111	6	59	173	10.3	1.13	.206

2 CHRISTIAN BETHANCOURT, C

Born: Sept. 2, 1991. **B-T:** R-R. **Ht.:** 6-2. **Wt.:** 215. **Signed:** Panama, 2008. **Signed by:** Luis Ortiz.

Bethancourt starred for Panama in the 2004 Little League World Series as a 12-year-old, and the Braves signed him for $600,000 four years later. He had his best all-around season in 2013, hitting a career-best 12 home runs and making his major league debut. Bethancourt has everything scouts want in a defensive-oriented receiver. His plus arm strength stands out most, paired with a quick release and excellent accuracy and carry on his throws. He has impressive quickness behind the plate with nimble feet. His rapport with pitchers has improved considerably as he has become more fluent in English. He can get lackadaisical at times, particularly in his willingness to block balls in the dirt, leading to 12 passed balls and 13 errors last season. While he rarely walks, Bethancourt has good hand-eye coordination, solid-average power and puts the ball in play despite his tendency to swing at breaking balls outside the zone. The Braves envisioned Bethancourt as their long-term answer behind the plate almost as soon as they signed him, and now they appear to be on the verge of turning over the keys following Brian McCann's departure in free agency. Even with Gerald Laird and Evan Gattis expected back, he should have the opportunity to work his way into the starting lineup and could be the full-time receiver by the second half.

Year	Club (League)	Class	AVG	G	AB	R	H	2B	3B	HR	RBI	BB	SO	SB	CS	OBP	SLG
2008	Braves (DSL)	R	.267	34	116	12	31	6	3	0	17	11	25	1	0	.328	.371
2009	Braves (GCL)	R	.284	32	116	22	33	9	1	2	19	11	22	7	0	.344	.431
	Danville (APP)	R	.260	14	50	10	13	5	0	2	8	6	16	1	1	.339	.480
2010	Rome (SAL)	LoA	.251	108	399	31	100	19	2	3	34	14	62	11	3	.276	.331
2011	Rome (SAL)	LoA	.303	54	221	25	67	10	3	4	33	8	27	6	3	.323	.430
	Lynchburg (CAR)	HiA	.271	45	166	11	45	6	0	1	20	3	35	3	2	.277	.325
2012	Mississippi (SL)	AA	.243	71	268	30	65	5	1	2	26	11	45	8	6	.275	.291
2013	Mississippi (SL)	AA	.277	90	358	42	99	21	0	12	45	16	57	11	7	.305	.436
	Atlanta (NL)	MAJ	.000	1	1	0	0	0	0	0	0	0	1	0	0	.000	.000
Major League Totals			.000	1	1	0	0	0	0	0	0	0	1	0	0	.000	.000
Minor League Totals			.267	448	1694	183	453	81	10	26	202	80	289	48	22	.299	.373

3 J.R. GRAHAM, RHP

Born: Jan. 14, 1990. **B-T:** R-R. **Ht.:** 6-0. **Wt.:** 185. **Drafted:** Santa Clara, 2011 (4th round). **Signed by:** Tim Moore.

A two-way player in college, Graham had emerged as a fast-track pitcher as a pro before a strained shoulder suffered in May limited him to eight games with Double-A Mississippi in 2013. Since focusing on pitching full-time, he has led the Appalachian League with a 1.72 ERA in 2011 and posted a combined 12-2, 2.80 season in 2012 between high Class A Lynchburg and Mississippi. Graham's success stems from his ability to work down in the zone and force batters to hit groundballs. His four-seam fastball sits in the mid-90s and has been clocked as high as 97 mph, while his two-seamer is a heavy pitch with great sinking action. He employs the same motion to throw his 82-85 mph slider, thereby keeping hitters off-balance. His changeup is also an effective offering, giving him four above-average pitches. Graham repeats his clean delivery well and has the best command in the organization. Graham's shoulder injury, which kept him from throwing during instructional league, and his smaller frame raise questions about his durability. Had he not been sidetracked in 2013, then he probably would have ranked as the system's top prospect. If healthy, Graham should return to Mississippi to open the 2014 season to see if he can get back on track as a future rotation piece.

Year	Club (League)	Class	W	L	ERA	G	GS	CG	SV	IP	H	HR	BB	SO	K/9	WHIP	AVG
2011	Danville (APP)	R	5	2	1.72	13	8	0	0	58	52	0	13	52	8.1	1.13	.245
2012	Lynchburg (CAR)	HiA	9	1	2.63	17	17	1	0	103	88	6	17	68	6.0	1.02	.236
	Mississippi (SL)	AA	3	1	3.18	9	9	0	0	45	35	2	17	42	8.3	1.15	.210
2013	Mississippi (SL)	AA	1	3	4.04	8	8	0	0	36	39	0	10	28	7.1	1.37	.283
Minor League Totals			18	7	2.72	47	42	1	0	241	214	8	57	190	7.1	1.12	.240

4 JASON HURSH, RHP

Born: Oct. 2, 1991. **B-T:** R-R. **Ht.:** 6-3. **Wt.:** 190. **Drafted:** Oklahoma State, 2013 (1st round). **Signed by:** Gerald Turner.

The Braves scouted Hursh heavily as a Dallas-area prep but correctly gauged that he was not signable. The Pirates took him in the sixth round in 2010 but didn't sign him. After pitching 30 innings as a freshman at Oklahoma State, Hursh missed 2012 after having Tommy John surgery, returning to the mound as a redshirt sophomore and going 6-5, 2.79 for the Cowboys. The Braves picked him 31st overall in 2013 and signed him for just more than $1.7 million. Hursh's best offering is a mid-90s fastball with heavy life and a late tail that made it one of the most intriguing pitches in the 2013 draft. He has touched 98 mph and generates easy heat after improving his delivery and arm action in college and fine-tuning his mechanics with Braves coaches. His secondary pitches need work, though he shows a decent feel for both his slider and changeup. He commands the strike zone well, works fast, and coaxes plenty of groundball outs, as evidenced by his near 2-to-1 groundout-airout ratio in nine starts at low Class A Rome. The Braves believe Hursh has a low-mileage arm with tremendous upside once he improves his secondary pitches. Some scouts consider him a potential high-leverage reliever, but Atlanta's plans center on keeping him in the rotation. He will likely start 2014 at high Class A Lynchburg but could make the jump to Double-A Mississippi early in the season.

Year	Club (League)	Class	W	L	ERA	G	GS	CG	SV	IP	H	HR	BB	SO	K/9	WHIP	AVG
2013	Rome (SAL)	LoA	1	1	0.67	9	9	0	0	27	20	1	10	15	5.0	1.11	.206
Minor League Totals			1	1	0.67	9	9	0	0	27	20	1	10	15	5.0	1.11	.206

5 MAURICIO CABRERA, RHP

Born: Sept. 22, 1993. **B-T:** R-R. **Ht.:** 6-2. **Wt.:** 180. **Signed:** Dominican Republic, 2010. **Signed by:** Roberto Aquino.

The younger brother of Cubs righthander Alberto Cabrera, Mauricio signed with Atlanta for $400,000 in 2010. He made his U.S. debut two years later in the Rookie-level Appalachian League and led the circuit with a .213 opponent average. A jump to low Class A Rome followed in 2013, and he ranked as the No. 10 prospect in the South Atlantic League. Cabrera has a live arm that generates pure heat. His fastball sits at 93-97 mph, touches 100, and has good movement given its speed. He throws it with an easy delivery but an unusual path in which he swings his arm wide before throwing across his body. Control is the biggest hurdle Cabrera faces. He worked around a lot of traffic at Rome, walking 4.9 batters per nine innings while giving up 118 hits in 131 innings. He has a decent changeup and is working on a curveball that flashed plus potential during the second half of last season. He pitched under control more consistently after getting rattled on the mound during the first three months of the season. Some scouts project Cabrera as a reliever, but the Braves believe his secondary offerings hold promise and his delivery can handle the workload. He has the fastball to be a frontline starter in the major leagues. Spring training will determine whether he returns to Rome or joins high Class A Lynchburg.

Year	Club (League)	Class	W	L	ERA	G	GS	CG	SV	IP	H	HR	BB	SO	K/9	WHIP	AVG
2011	Braves (DSL)	R	1	5	4.30	19	9	0	0	52	51	3	24	36	6.2	1.43	.251
2012	Danville (APP)	R	2	2	2.97	12	12	0	0	58	45	2	23	48	7.5	1.18	.213
2013	Rome (SAL)	LoA	3	8	4.18	24	24	1	0	131	118	3	71	107	7.3	1.44	.243
Minor League Totals			6	15	3.92	55	45	1	0	241	214	8	118	191	7.1	1.38	.238

6 JOSE PERAZA, SS

Born: April 30, 1994. **B-T:** R-R. **Ht.:** 6-0. **Wt.:** 165. **Signed:** Venezuela, 2010. **Signed by:** Rolando Petit.

Signed out of Venezuela for $350,000 in 2010, Peraza made his U.S. debut two years later as the No. 10 prospect in the Rookie-level Gulf Coast League. He impressed with his all-around improvements at low Class A Rome in 2013, when he was tabbed as the South Atlantic League's No. 16 prospect after hitting .288 and ranking second in the SAL with 64 steals. Peraza's game is centered on tremendous body control. He gets great jumps on the bases as well as in the field and has the ability to go from full speed to immediate standstill. His plus baseball instincts make his above-average range and plus speed even better. His hands are soft and consistent, and he has a quick release that makes up for average arm strength. At the plate, he has quick hands and outstanding hand-eye coordination that allows him to hit virtually any pitch, though he has little in the way of home-run power. He succeeded in 2013 as both a leadoff and No. 2 hitter with his ability to hit behind the runner and bunt. Peraza has exceeded the expectations of many scouts. While he needs to play a little more under control, his aggressiveness is an asset and makes him a pesky, dangerous player for opponents. He should be able to remain up the middle at either shortstop or second base. His next stop will be high Class A Lynchburg.

Year	Club (League)	Class	AVG	G	AB	R	H	2B	3B	HR	RBI	BB	SO	SB	CS	OBP	SLG
2011	Braves (DSL)	R	.281	66	235	29	66	5	3	1	22	15	27	28	7	.346	.340
2012	Braves (GCL)	R	.318	21	85	17	27	3	3	0	10	4	6	10	3	.348	.424
	Danville (APP)	R	.281	32	121	21	34	4	0	1	18	9	18	15	2	.351	.339
2013	Rome (SAL)	LoA	.288	114	448	72	129	18	8	1	47	34	64	64	15	.341	.371
Minor League Totals			.288	233	889	139	256	30	14	3	97	62	115	117	27	.345	.363

7 DAVID HALE, RHP

Born: Sept. 27, 1987. **B-T:** R-R. **Ht.:** 6-2. **Wt.:** 205. **Drafted:** Princeton, 2009 (3rd round). **Signed by:** Kevin Barry.

Hale fits the Braves' new profile for the draft as a power arm with low mileage. He was a two-way player at Princeton who threw fewer than 130 innings in college and did not become a full-time pitcher until he signed with Atlanta in 2009. He moved into the rotation full-time at Double-A Mississippi in 2012. The Marietta, Ga., resident established a Braves debut record with nine strikeouts over five scoreless innings versus the Padres on Sept. 13. The Braves drafted Hale for his lightning-quick arm that generates heavy action on most of his pitches. He works off a 92-94 mph fastball with good sinking action. The righthander also has improved his sharp slider and his solid changeup with above-average depth and fade. He was more effective against lefthanders (.701 OPS) than righthanders (.799) at Triple-A Gwinnett in 2013. Hale struggled with his control in 2012 but made significant strides in that area by improving his mechanics. He is a very good athlete who fields his position well and has a good pickoff move for a righthander. With four pitches he can throw for strikes, Hale prefers starting and profiles as a rotation piece in the near future. However, Atlanta's short-term need could land him in a relief role, where his velocity will tick up. His versatility should allow him to help the big league club in 2014.

Year	Club (League)	Class	W	L	ERA	G	GS	CG	SV	IP	H	HR	BB	SO	K/9	WHIP	AVG
2009	Danville (APP)	R	2	1	1.13	7	1	0	1	16	7	0	5	12	6.8	0.75	.130
2010	Rome (SAL)	LoA	5	8	4.13	28	7	0	5	94	97	1	44	69	6.6	1.51	.268
2011	Lynchburg (CAR)	HiA	4	6	4.10	28	13	1	0	101	106	9	30	86	7.7	1.35	.275
2012	Mississippi (SL)	AA	8	4	3.77	27	27	0	0	146	121	11	67	124	7.7	1.29	.228
2013	Gwinnett (IL)	AAA	6	9	3.22	22	20	0	0	115	123	8	36	77	6.0	1.39	.279
	Atlanta (NL)	MAJ	1	0	0.82	2	2	0	0	11	11	0	1	14	11.5	1.09	.244
Major League Totals			1	0	0.82	2	2	0	0	11	11	0	1	14	11.5	1.09	.244
Minor League Totals			25	28	3.69	112	68	1	6	471	454	29	182	368	7.0	1.35	.256

8 VICTOR CARATINI, 3B/C

Born: Aug. 17, 1993. **B-T:** B-R. **Ht.:** 6-0. **Wt.:** 190. **Drafted:** Miami Dade JC, 2013 (2nd round). **Signed by:** Buddy Hernandez.

Caratini attended the Puerto Rico Baseball Academy before going to Southern, where he was ineligible as a freshman. He transferred to Miami Dade JC, played third base with some catcher mixed in, and helped guide the team to the Florida state junior-college tournament before becoming the 65th overall pick in the 2013 draft. After signing for $800,000, he continued to impress in pro ball and was ranked as the No. 3 prospect in the Rookie-level Appalachian League. Caratini is an advanced hitter with a line-drive swing, a gap-to-gap approach from both sides of the plate and an excellent feel for the strike zone. He stroked 25 extra-base hits at Rookie-level Danville and can drive the ball to the opposite field, but scouts are mixed regarding his power potential at higher levels. He's a below-average runner who lacks quickness and agility at third base, which could lead to a full-time shift to catcher, a position he played at times at Miami Dade. Caratini has plus arm strength and enough quickness to handle the job behind the plate. Realizing his plus arm strength as well as his limitations as an infielder, the Braves worked Caratini at catcher during instructional league and would love to see him develop there. Should he make the transition, he could open 2014 in extended spring training with a return trip to Danville.

Year	Club (League)	Class	AVG	G	AB	R	H	2B	3B	HR	RBI	BB	SO	SB	CS	OBP	SLG
2013	Danville (APP)	R	.290	58	200	29	58	23	1	1	25	39	49	0	2	.415	.430
Minor League Totals			.290	58	200	29	58	23	1	1	25	39	49	0	2	.415	.430

9 TOMMY LA STELLA, 2B

Born: Jan. 31, 1989. **B-T:** L-R. **Ht.:** 5-11. **Wt.:** 185. **Drafted:** Coastal Carolina, 2011 (8th round). **Signed by:** Billy Best.

La Stella transferred from St. John's to Coastal Carolina and emerged as a second-team All-American and the Big South Conference player of the year in 2011. Injuries slowed him in 2012 before La Stella put together an impressive season in the Double-A Southern League, where he was ranked as the circuit's No. 16 prospect. La Stella has hit at every level thanks to great hand-eye coordination and above-average bat speed. He has an excellent approach and exceptional feel for the strike zone, which helps him rack up more walks than strikeouts. La Stella also shines as a situational hitter with his ability to advance runners via the hit-and-run or by bunting. He runs the bases well and with intelligence despite not being blessed with great quick-twitch athleticism. Defensively, he makes all of the routine plays at the keystone and has an average arm. Nagging injuries, including an elbow issue this season, have kept him from playing even 100 games in a season. Braves fans are begging for La Stella to get an opportunity to unseat Dan Uggla at second base. Finances could play a role, but his bat appears to be near big league ready if needed.

Year	Club (League)	Class	AVG	G	AB	R	H	2B	3B	HR	RBI	BB	SO	SB	CS	OBP	SLG
2011	Rome (SAL)	LoA	.328	63	232	46	76	13	5	9	40	26	28	2	2	.401	.543
2012	Braves (GCL)	R	.231	5	13	4	3	0	1	1	3	4	1	0	0	.444	.615
	Lynchburg (CAR)	HiA	.302	85	298	43	90	22	5	5	56	36	24	13	2	.386	.460
2013	Lynchburg (CAR)	HiA	.550	7	20	7	11	1	0	1	4	8	1	1	1	.690	.750
	Mississippi (SL)	AA	.343	81	283	32	97	21	2	4	41	37	34	7	1	.422	.473
Minor League Totals			.327	241	846	132	277	57	13	20	144	111	88	23	6	.412	.496

10 SEAN GILMARTIN, LHP

Born: May 8, 1990. **B-T:** L-L. **Ht.:** 6-2. **Wt.:** 190. **Drafted:** Florida State, 2011 (1st round). **Signed by:** Hugh Buchanan.

Gilmartin reached Triple-A in his first full season, 2012, but struggled in his follow-up while battling a shoulder injury that cost him two months at midseason. Florida State's Friday night starter throughout his three years in Tallahassee, he went 28th overall in the 2011 draft. Gilmartin is a finesse pitcher who knows how to set up hitters and pitch to his strengths. His fastball has good movement while sitting in the 89-91 mph range, and he mixes it well with a plus changeup and a low-80s slider with a sharp, late break. He uses the same arm slot with all of his offerings, creating deception. Gilmartin does a good job of pounding the lower half of the strike zone, and his excellent command allows him to paint the black. He doesn't have the velocity to get away with mistakes, though. A former two-way player, Gilmartin repeats his delivery well and is a good fielder who controls the running game. The Braves are confident Gilmartin will bounce back from his injury-plagued 2013 season, projecting him as a No. 4 starter. The lefthander should to return to Triple-A Gwinnett but could be among the first promoted should Atlanta need assistance.

Year	Club (League)	Class	W	L	ERA	G	GS	CG	SV	IP	H	HR	BB	SO	K/9	WHIP	AVG
2011	Braves (GCL)	R	0	1	9.00	1	1	0	0	2	3	0	0	1	4.5	1.50	.333
	Rome (SAL)	LoA	2	1	2.53	5	5	0	0	21	18	3	2	30	12.7	0.94	.217
2012	Mississippi (SL)	AA	5	8	3.54	20	20	3	0	119	111	9	26	86	6.5	1.15	.248
	Gwinnett (IL)	AAA	1	2	4.78	7	7	0	0	38	41	6	13	25	6.0	1.43	.273
2013	Braves (GCL)	R	0	0	0.00	3	2	0	0	9	1	0	0	11	11.0	0.11	.034
	Rome (SAL)	LoA	1	0	1.80	1	1	0	0	5	4	0	0	5	9.0	0.80	.222
	Gwinnett (IL)	AAA	3	8	5.74	17	17	0	0	91	112	12	33	65	6.4	1.59	.304
Minor League Totals			12	20	4.23	54	53	3	0	285	290	30	74	223	7.0	1.28	.262

11 CODY MARTIN, RHP

Born: Sept. 4, 1989. **B-T:** R-R. **Ht.:** 6-2. **Wt.:** 225. **Drafted:** Gonzaga, 2011 (7th round). **Signed by:** Brett Evert.

Martin's father Chuck pitched in the Braves system in 1984-85 after being a 24th-round pick in 1984. The son already has exceeded the father's career, splitting the 2013 campaign between Double-A Mississippi and Triple-A Gwinnett. The Braves believe Martin, a former All-America closer at Gonzaga, could help in Atlanta as either a starter or reliever in the near future. He allowed two earned runs or fewer in 10 of his 11 starts in the Southern League and had a strong start to his Triple-A debut before the league caught up to him. Martin led the organization in strikeouts (137) for the second straight season by throwing four pitches for strikes, though none grades as plus. He pounds the zone with a low-90s fastball that has good late movement and mixes it well with a mid-80s slider, which serves as his strikeout pitch. His curveball and changeup are both solid-average, and he mixed in a two-seam fastball in 2013 for the first time since college. Having led NCAA Division I with a 0.86 ERA as a senior reliever, Martin has proven effective in any role and draws comparisons with Kris Medlen from the Braves for his versatility. While his long-term future could be determined by the needs of the big club, Martin should reach Atlanta during the 2014 season.

Year	Club (League)	Class	W	L	ERA	G	GS	CG	SV	IP	H	HR	BB	SO	K/9	WHIP	AVG
2011	Danville (APP)	R	0	0	0.00	8	0	0	3	9	2	0	1	14	14.0	0.33	.069
	Rome (SAL)	LoA	1	0	1.48	14	0	0	6	24	18	2	4	35	12.9	0.90	.212
2012	Lynchburg (CAR)	HiA	12	7	2.93	22	19	1	0	107	93	7	34	123	10.3	1.18	.235
2013	Mississippi (SL)	AA	3	3	2.82	16	11	0	0	67	63	3	27	71	9.5	1.34	.250
	Gwinnett (IL)	AAA	3	4	3.49	13	11	1	1	70	59	6	31	66	8.5	1.29	.232
Minor League Totals			19	14	2.82	73	41	2	10	277	235	18	97	309	10.0	1.20	.232

12 EDWARD SALCEDO, 3B

Born: July 30, 1991. **B-T:** R-R. **Ht.:** 6-3. **Wt.:** 205. **Signed:** Dominican Republic, 2010. **Signed by:** Roberto Aquino.

The Braves have been aggressive in promoting Salcedo since signing him for $1.6 million in 2010 after he missed nearly two years due to an age discrepancy. His performance has yet to match his prodigious tools, however. Still raw in many aspects of the game, Salcedo showed signs of settling in at third base last year after moving from shortstop at the beginning of the 2011 campaign. He has fringe-average hands but a strong, accurate arm and good range. He also moves his feet well and can make the spectacular play when he does not rush, but his lack of consistency contributed to an SL-high 29 errors. Salcedo's aggressiveness also is evident at the plate, where he has made improvements with his pitch selection, even though he continues to fall victim to breaking balls. He has plus power potential and the bat speed to catch up to good fastballs. He's an average runner and aggressive basestealer. The Braves point out Salcedo's tools, work ethic and relative youth and believe he is on the verge of a breakout season in 2014. Spring training will determine whether he starts back in Mississippi or graduates to Triple-A Gwinnett.

Year	Club (League)	Class	AVG	G	AB	R	H	2B	3B	HR	RBI	BB	SO	SB	CS	OBP	SLG
2010	Braves (DSL)	R	.297	23	74	16	22	5	1	1	11	18	19	8	1	.453	.432
	Rome (SAL)	LoA	.197	54	193	23	38	5	4	2	16	11	56	6	5	.239	.295
2011	Rome (SAL)	LoA	.248	132	508	83	126	27	6	12	68	41	105	23	10	.315	.396
2012	Lynchburg (CAR)	HiA	.240	130	471	65	113	26	2	17	61	33	130	23	14	.295	.412
2013	Mississippi (SL)	AA	.239	132	468	52	112	22	2	12	55	44	111	20	10	.304	.372
Minor League Totals			.240	471	1714	239	411	85	15	44	211	147	421	80	40	.305	.384

13 JOSH ELANDER, OF

Born: March 19, 1991. **B-T:** R-R. **Ht.:** 6-1. **Wt.:** 220. **Drafted:** Texas Christian, 2012 (6th round). **Signed by:** Gerald Turner.

Drafted as a catcher out of Texas Christian, Elander made his professional debut behind the plate at Rookie-level Danville in 2012. The Braves shifted him to left field during spring training 2013 and were pleased with the rapid adjustments he made to his new position. Elander moved well in the garden, showed acceptable range and displayed a strong arm for left field. His routes improved as the season progressed, and he demonstrated the potential to develop into an average defender. Elander's ceiling will be determined by his bat, which earned him a midseason promotion to the high Class A Carolina League. He has a quick hands and a compact righthanded swing with good bat speed. He had a consistent season as a run-producer, showing solid pull power, and he could add more pop to all fields as he gains experience. Elander controls the strike zone and runs the bases well, with an overall intelligence that enhances his feel for the game. Elander ought to make the jump to Double-A Mississippi in 2014.

Year	Club (League)	Class	AVG	G	AB	R	H	2B	3B	HR	RBI	BB	SO	SB	CS	OBP	SLG
2012	Danville (APP)	R	.260	36	123	19	32	6	2	4	19	16	19	3	1	.366	.439
2013	Rome (SAL)	LoA	.318	74	280	47	89	22	3	11	61	29	61	6	2	.381	.536
	Lynchburg (CAR)	HiA	.262	61	221	28	58	12	0	4	32	26	48	3	1	.345	.371
Minor League Totals			.287	171	624	94	179	40	5	19	112	71	128	12	4	.365	.458

14 VICTOR REYES, OF

BA GRADE
55
EXTREME

Born: Oct. 5, 1994. **B-T:** L-R. **Ht.:** 6-3. **Wt.:** 190. **Signed:** Venezuela, 2011. **Signed by:** Rolando Petit.

The Braves' top international signing in 2011, Reyes agreed to a $365,000 bonus. Since then he has made quick adjustments and emerged as a sleeper who could blossom into one of the system's top outfield prospects. After toiling in the Dominican Summer League in 2012, Reyes made his U.S. debut the following year and wound up splitting time between the Rookie-level Gulf Coast and

Appalachian leagues, hitting a combined .342/.387/.409 in 49 games and ranking as the No. 14 prospect in the GCL. Reyes has an ideal athletic frame that could easily add another 20 pounds of muscle as he matures. While his power has yet to emerge, Reyes generates above-average bat speed from the left side and can drive the ball when he keeps his hands and weight back. He has an advanced approach for a young player, displaying good patience while covering the plate well and rarely expanding the strike zone. He runs well for his size and has enough carry on his throws to play right field, though he has been limited to left thus far in pro ball. The Braves want to see what Reyes can achieve in a full-season league and will assign him to low Class A Rome to open 2014.

Year	Club (League)	Class	AVG	G	AB	R	H	2B	3B	HR	RBI	BB	SO	SB	CS	OBP	SLG
2012	Braves (DSL)	R	.296	52	162	40	48	3	0	0	33	31	39	12	6	.418	.315
2013	Braves (GCL)	R	.357	31	112	22	40	8	1	0	21	12	20	5	1	.414	.446
	Danville (APP)	R	.321	18	81	12	26	3	0	0	4	3	9	0	0	.345	.358
Minor League Totals			.321	101	355	74	114	14	1	0	58	46	68	17	7	.402	.366

15 JOEY TERDOSLAVICH, OF/1B

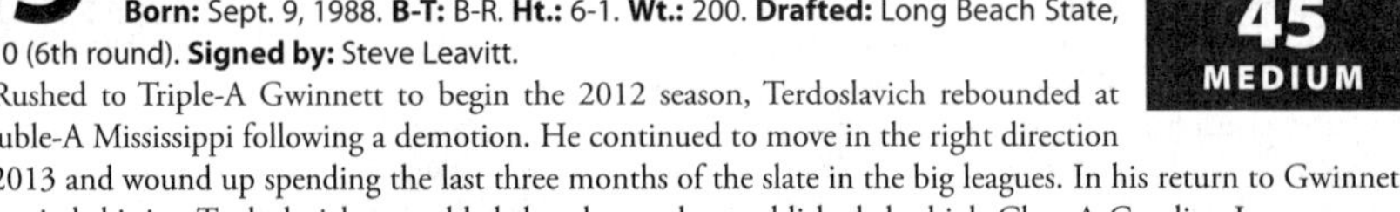

BA GRADE
45
MEDIUM

Born: Sept. 9, 1988. **B-T:** B-R. **Ht.:** 6-1. **Wt.:** 200. **Drafted:** Long Beach State, 2010 (6th round). **Signed by:** Steve Leavitt.

Rushed to Triple-A Gwinnett to begin the 2012 season, Terdoslavich rebounded at Double-A Mississippi following a demotion. He continued to move in the right direction in 2013 and wound up spending the last three months of the slate in the big leagues. In his return to Gwinnett, the switch-hitting Terdoslavich resembled the player who established the high Class A Carolina League record with 52 doubles and garnered organization player of the year honors in 2011. Most of Terdoslavich's above-average raw power comes from the left side, and he dominated Triple-A righthanders by hitting .340/.375/.617 with 17 of his 18 home runs. Though he has an uppercut swing from both sides of the plate, which can be exploited by pitchers with above-average offspeed pitches, he gets good backspin on the ball and excellent carry. He also makes consistent contact and does not strike out much despite his aggressive approach. Terdoslavich bounced between first and third base during his first two pro seasons and wound up in right field much of the time at Gwinnett. An average defender on both outfield corners, he could provide serviceable glove work at the infielder corners as well, though he lacks ideal agility to play third on an everyday basis. His versatility and switch-hit stick make Terdoslavich an attractive option on a big league bench, and he could return to Atlanta in 2014 and contribute as a part-timer.

Year	Club (League)	Class	AVG	G	AB	R	H	2B	3B	HR	RBI	BB	SO	SB	CS	OBP	SLG
2010	Danville (APP)	R	.296	49	189	27	56	10	2	2	24	15	27	3	3	.351	.402
	Rome (SAL)	LoA	.316	21	79	7	25	9	0	0	10	5	18	0	0	.365	.430
2011	Lynchburg (CAR)	HiA	.286	131	483	72	138	52	2	20	82	41	107	2	0	.341	.526
2012	Gwinnett (IL)	AAA	.180	53	194	19	35	4	0	4	20	19	50	3	0	.252	.263
	Mississippi (SL)	AA	.315	78	298	43	94	24	5	5	51	27	62	4	0	.372	.480
2013	Gwinnett (IL)	AAA	.318	85	321	48	102	24	1	18	58	23	65	3	6	.359	.567
	Atlanta (NL)	MAJ	.215	55	79	11	17	4	0	0	4	12	24	1	0	.315	.266
Major League Totals			.215	55	79	11	17	4	0	0	4	12	24	1	0	.315	.266
Minor League Totals			.288	417	1564	216	450	123	10	49	245	130	329	15	9	.342	.473

16 SHAE SIMMONS, RHP

BA GRADE
45
MEDIUM

Born: Sept. 3, 1990. **B-T:** R-R. **Ht.:** 5-9. **Wt.:** 180. **Drafted:** Southeast Missouri State, 2012 (22nd round). **Signed by:** Terry Tripp.

A reliever his first two years at Southeast Missouri State, Simmons became a starter during his final year at Southeast Missouri State with ex-big leaguer Steve Bieser as his pitching coach. Simmons returned to the bullpen to open the 2013 campaign at low Class A Rome and proceeded to dominate the South Atlantic League by saving 24 games in 25 opportunities and averaging 14 strikeouts per nine innings. He continued to perform in a set-up role at Double-A Mississippi following a two-step promotion in early August. An undersized righthander, Simmons is a power pitcher whose heavy fastball hit 100 mph on several occasions last season and sat in the 95-97 mph range. He also throws an above-average slider that can be unhittable when he generates proper tilt, and he keeps hitters honest with a 12-to-6 curveball that works as his change of pace. Simmons' mechanics require some effort, and his frame does not resemble the fire-breathing reliever prototype. Most scouts believe he can be an effective situational option late in games against righthanders, who batted just .148 against him in 2013. Simmons could be pitching in Atlanta at some point in 2014 provided he picks up where he left off.

Year	Club (League)	Class	W	L	ERA	G	GS	CG	SV	IP	H	HR	BB	SO	K/9	WHIP	AVG
2012	Braves (GCL)	R	2	0	0.00	7	1	0	0	14	5	0	8	15	9.4	0.91	.109
	Danville (APP)	R	0	2	3.48	9	0	0	2	10	11	0	8	21	18.3	1.84	.256
2013	Rome (SAL)	LoA	1	1	1.49	39	0	0	24	42	26	0	15	66	14.0	0.97	.169
	Mississippi (SL)	AA	0	0	2.45	11	0	0	0	11	5	0	7	16	13.1	1.09	.139
Minor League Totals			3	3	1.62	66	1	0	26	78	47	0	38	118	13.6	1.09	.168

17 CARLOS SALAZAR, RHP

Born: Nov. 23, 1994. **B-T:** R-R. **Ht.:** 6-0. **Wt.:** 200. **Drafted:** HS—Kerman, Calif., 2013 (3rd round). **Signed by:** Brett Evert.

The Braves lured 2013 third-rounder Salazar away from a Fresno State commitment with a $625,000 bonus. The organization knew that the stocky righthander would require work and patience, but given Atlanta's track record in developing young pitchers, they felt he was worth the risk. The Braves spoon-fed Salazar during his pro debut in the Rookie-level Gulf Coast League, where he showed better-than-advertised control but was hittable due to a tendency to be too fine with his pitches. Salazar's busy, unconventional mechanics have drawn comparisons with Braves reliever Jordan Walden, and he generated one of the best fastballs among prep pitchers in the 2013 draft. His heater features good, late life, sits at 92-94 mph and has touched 97. His changeup has potential, and the Braves are working on adding to his repertoire a curveball that is in early development. Salazar has strong, thick legs and a barrel chest, and from a physical standpoint, he does not have much projection remaining. He's is a prime candidate to spend 2014 at Rookie-level Danville.

Year	Club (League)	Class	W	L	ERA	G	GS	CG	SV	IP	H	HR	BB	SO	K/9	WHIP	AVG
2013	Braves (GCL)	R	0	3	6.92	8	4	0	0	13	18	0	5	14	9.7	1.77	.321
Minor League Totals			0	3	6.92	8	4	0	0	13	18	0	5	14	9.7	1.77	.321

18 KYLE WREN, OF

BA GRADE
50
HIGH

Born: April 23, 1991. **B-T:** L-L. **Ht.:** 5-10. **Wt.:** 175. **Drafted:** Georgia Tech, 2013 (8th round). **Signed by:** Brian Bridges.

The son of Braves general manager Frank Wren, Kyle may prove to be a steal as an eighth-round pick. A first-team all-Atlantic Coast Conference selection as a Georgia Tech freshman in 2011, Wren struggled as a draft-eligible sophomore the following year, yet the Reds took a 30th-round flier on him. He returned to school for his junior year and thrived, pacing the ACC in hits while scoring 50 runs in 64 games. A prototype leadoff hitter who can play left and center field, Wren continued to wreak havoc in his first taste of pro ball by stealing 35 bases in 53 games across three levels, ranking third in the organization. Wren's speed has been graded as high as 70 on the 20-80 scouting scale. He has explosive first-step quickness on the bases and in the field, and he has learned to steal third base with relative ease. His routes have improved in the outfield, and while his arm strength is below-average, his throws are accurate. An intelligent player, Wren has a good eye at the plate and drives the ball from gap to gap after adding 15 pounds of muscle prior to his junior year. He also is a proficient drag bunter. Wren may open 2014 at Double-A Mississippi and could be fast-tracked to Atlanta if he continues to reach base and steal efficiently.

Year	Club (League)	Class	AVG	G	AB	R	H	2B	3B	HR	RBI	BB	SO	SB	CS	OBP	SLG
2013	Danville (APP)	R	.409	5	22	6	9	3	1	0	4	2	3	3	0	.458	.636
	Rome (SAL)	LoA	.328	47	195	36	64	11	4	2	20	16	21	32	6	.382	.456
	Lynchburg (CAR)	HiA	.000	1	1	0	0	0	0	0	0	1	0	0	1	.500	.000
Minor League Totals			.335	53	218	42	73	14	5	2	24	19	24	35	7	.391	.472

19 JOHAN CAMARGO, SS

BA GRADE
50
HIGH

Born: Dec. 13, 1993. **B-T:** B-R. **Ht.:** 6-0. **Wt.:** 160. **Signed:** Panama, 2010. **Signed by:** Luis Ortiz.

The Braves' latest find from Panama, Camargo built on an impressive showing in the Dominican Summer League in 2012 with a solid U.S. debut in the Rookie-level Appalachian League in 2013, ranking as the circuit's No. 11 prospect. He made positive impressions with his steady defense and plus hand-eye coordination, allowing him to both make plays at shortstop and consistent contact at the plate. Camargo is a disciplined hitter who rarely strikes out. He has a mature approach at the plate and an outstanding feel for the strike zone for a young hitter. The switch-hitter must add strength and size in order to drive the ball more consistently. Defensively, Camargo has above-average arm strength, soft hands and smooth actions. He does not have exceptional speed or quickness, but because he does an excellent job of anticipating plays, he may be rangy enough to stick at shortstop. Camargo showed leadership skills on the infield at Danville and has solid baseball instincts. A promotion to low Class A Rome awaits in 2014. Year

	Club (League)	Class	AVG	G	AB	R	H	2B	3B	HR	RBI	BB	SO	SB	CS	OBP	SLG
2012	Braves (DSL)	R	.343	59	198	38	68	14	1	2	26	25	27	6	3	.433	.455
2013	Danville (APP)	R	.294	57	228	28	67	7	4	0	14	18	31	3	3	.359	.360
Minor League Totals			.317	116	426	66	135	21	5	2	40	43	58	9	6	.394	.404

20 WES PARSONS, RHP

Born: Sept. 9, 1992. **B-T:** R-R. **Ht.:** 6-5. **Wt.:** 190. **Signed:** NDFA—Jackson State (Tenn.) CC, 2012. **Signed by:** Terry Tripp Jr.

Parsons made impressive progress in 2013, his first season in the organization. After giving up baseball early in his high school career to concentrate on golf, the tall right-hander returned to the mound as a junior and later pitched at Jackson State (Tenn.) CC. He then joined Thunder Bay in the summer-collegiate Northwoods League, earning a place in the circuit's all-star game. Parsons posted a 2.61 ERA in 55 innings over 12 games, including six starts, and tossed a scoreless inning in the all-star game, where he hit 95 mph with his fastball. Signed by the Braves for $200,000 in late-July 2012, he pitched in instructional league and joined the low Class A Rome rotation in May 2013. Parsons has a free-and-easy delivery with a projectable frame. His fastball has good movement and he pitches downhill well by using his height to his advantage. He mixes the fastball well with his low-80s slider, which has a chance to be a plus offering, and an improving changeup. Parsons also has excellent command that allows him to pitch ahead in the count. While his future may be in the bullpen, Parsons will continue to start at high Class A Lynchburg in 2014.

Year	Club (League)	Class	W	L	ERA	G	GS	CG	SV	IP	H	HR	BB	SO	K/9	WHIP	AVG
2013	Rome (SAL)	LoA	7	7	2.63	19	19	1	0	110	91	5	21	101	8.3	1.02	.224
Minor League Totals			7	7	2.63	19	19	1	0	110	91	5	21	101	8.3	1.02	.224

21 TANNER MURPHY, C

BA GRADE
50
EXTREME

Born: Feb. 27, 1995. **B-T:** R-R. **Ht.:** 6-2. **Wt.:** 215. **Drafted:** HS—Malden, Mo., 2013 (4th round). **Signed by:** Terry Tripp Jr.

Murphy signed with the Braves for $250,000 to bypass a Southern Illinois commitment. Some scouts questioned the talent level faced by Murphy as an amateur but liked the raw skills he displayed behind the plate and on the mound. Clocked in the low 90s as a pitcher, he attracted some teams as a potential hurler, but the Braves were intrigued with his physical tools. In addition to his plus arm strength, Murphy has a strong, solid frame with impressive power in his forearms and hands. While his footwork behind the plate needs work, he moves well for his size and shows the ability to take charge of a pitching staff. Murphy's frame suggests he should hit for above-average power as he gains experience, but he needs to cut down his long swing and level out his tendency to uppercut pitches. That will help him make more consistent contact. A high-risk/high-reward type of player, Murphy likely will open 2014 in extended spring training before reporting to Rookie-level Danville in mid-June.

Year	Club (League)	Class	AVG	G	AB	R	H	2B	3B	HR	RBI	BB	SO	SB	CS	OBP	SLG
2013	Braves (GCL)	R	.227	32	97	7	22	3	0	0	8	12	34	5	0	.313	.258
Minor League Totals			.227	32	97	7	22	3	0	0	8	12	34	5	0	.313	.258

22 KYLE KUBITZA, 3B

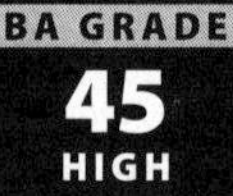

Born: July 15, 1990. **B-T:** L-R. **Ht.:** 6-3. **Wt.:** 190. **Drafted:** Texas State, 2011 (3rd round). **Signed by:** John Barron.

Kubitza improved his consistency at high Class A Lynchburg in 2013, just as the Braves envisioned he would in his second full season, and he wound up earning a trip to the Arizona Fall League. His batting average climbed by more than 20 points over his 2012 showing at low Class Rome, and Kubitza continued to display one of the best batting eyes in the organization. At times he can be too patient, causing him to fall behind in the count and be subject to the varying strike zones of minor league umpires. He struck out in a quarter of his plate appearances in 2013, yet also walked 80 times, leading to a system-best .380 on-base percentage. Kubitza has a sweet swing from the left side, though it tends to get long. His hands work well, he sprays line drives to the gaps, and his power is continuing to increase as he gains experience, resulting in 46 extra-base hits in 2013. At third base, he has soft hands, adequate range and plus-plus arm strength, which runs in the family—his brother Austin pitched at Rice and now is in the Tigers system. While he made numerous spectacular plays in 2013, many of his 25 errors came on routine plays, so he needs to improve the consistency of his footwork. A fiery player who is driven to succeed, Kubitza is making steady progress and will advance to Double-A Mississippi in 2014.

Year	Club (League)	Class	AVG	G	AB	R	H	2B	3B	HR	RBI	BB	SO	SB	CS	OBP	SLG
2011	Danville (APP)	R	.321	44	162	36	52	16	3	1	34	24	38	9	3	.407	.475
2012	Rome (SAL)	LoA	.239	128	448	68	107	24	9	9	59	73	127	18	11	.349	.393
2013	Lynchburg (CAR)	HiA	.260	132	435	75	113	28	6	12	57	80	132	8	16	.380	.434
Minor League Totals			.260	304	1045	179	272	68	18	22	150	177	297	35	30	.371	.423

23 TODD CUNNINGHAM, OF

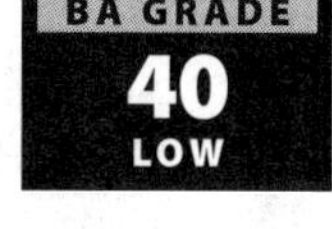

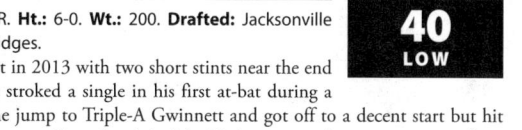

Born: March 20, 1989. **B-T:** B-R. **Ht.:** 6-0. **Wt.:** 200. **Drafted:** Jacksonville State, 2010 (2nd round). **Signed by:** Brian Bridges.

Cunningham made his major league debut in 2013 with two short stints near the end of his fourth season in the organization. He stroked a single in his first at-bat during a pinch-hit appearance. Cunningham made the jump to Triple-A Gwinnett and got off to a decent start but hit just .198/.274/.250 after the International League all-star break in July. He has a smooth, compact swing from both sides of the plate and makes consistent contact, which helps him limit strikeouts. He is also an effective bunter and can execute the hit-and-run as the No. 2 hitter. His on-base percentage lags due to relatively low walk totals, though he showed more patience during the first half of 2013. Cunningham has strong hands and quick wrists, and he hits hard line drives from gap to gap despite possessing limited power. An above-average runner with good first-step quickness, he is nevertheless only an average basestealer. He's a plus defender in center field who could easily handle left but lacks the arm strength to play right. Cunningham's tools do not lend themselves to an everyday role in the big leagues, but he could be a solid fourth outfielder once he gains more consistency at the plate. A return to Gwinnett appears most likely in 2014.

Year	Club (League)	Class	AVG	G	AB	R	H	2B	3B	HR	RBI	BB	SO	SB	CS	OBP	SLG
2010	Rome (SAL)	LoA	.260	65	231	32	60	9	3	1	20	14	30	7	4	.341	.338
2011	Braves (GCL)	R	.182	4	11	2	2	0	1	0	4	1	5	1	0	.286	.364
	Lynchburg (CAR)	HiA	.257	87	334	59	86	12	4	4	20	33	47	14	6	.348	.353
2012	Mississippi (SL)	AA	.309	120	466	77	144	23	6	3	51	38	51	24	8	.364	.403
2013	Atlanta (NL)	MAJ	.250	8	8	2	2	0	0	0	0	0	3	0	0	.250	.250
	Gwinnett (IL)	AAA	.265	116	427	60	113	13	5	2	38	41	62	20	7	.342	.333
Major League Totals			.250	8	8	2	2	0	0	0	0	0	3	0	0	.250	.250
Minor League Totals			.276	392	1469	230	405	57	19	10	133	127	195	66	25	.350	.361

24 MATT LIPKA, OF

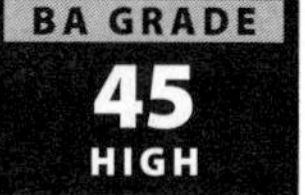

Born: April 15, 1992. **B-T:** R-R. **Ht.:** 6-1. **Wt.:** 200. **Drafted:** HS—McKinney, Texas, 2010 (1st round supplemental). **Signed by:** Gerald Turner.

Having missed more than half of the 2012 season after having surgery that essentially reattached his hamstring, Lipka returned to high Class A Lynchburg in 2013 and showed he had not lost a step of his plus-plus speed. A two-sport standout in high school who attracted collegiate attention as a football wide receiver, the former shortstop continued to go all-out on every play while taking his performance to another level during his second season in center field. One of the most aggressive outfielders in the minors, Lipka gets great reads on balls off the bat and has improved his routes to flyballs. His arm strength is below-average, and despite a funky throwing motion he makes accurate throws. Offensively, Lipka has struggled to find an approach. He does not walk enough to utilize his speed on the basepaths, and he strikes out too often for a player with such limited power potential. He must increase his paltry .305 on-base percentage in order to take advantage of his skill set. The 2010 supplemental first-rounder pick should make the move to Double-A Mississippi in 2014.

Year	Club (League)	Class	AVG	G	AB	R	H	2B	3B	HR	RBI	BB	SO	SB	CS	OBP	SLG
2010	Braves (GCL)	R	.302	48	192	33	58	8	4	1	24	14	22	20	3	.357	.401
	Danville (APP)	R	.125	4	16	1	2	0	0	0	1	1	2	1	0	.176	.125
2011	Rome (SAL)	LoA	.247	127	530	78	131	21	3	1	37	42	83	28	14	.305	.304
2012	Lynchburg (CAR)	HiA	.271	51	199	32	54	5	1	2	13	20	32	12	6	.335	.337
2013	Lynchburg (CAR)	HiA	.251	131	525	76	132	29	7	5	40	29	107	37	14	.305	.362
Minor League Totals			.258	361	1462	220	377	63	15	9	115	106	246	98	37	.315	.340

25 AARON NORTHCRAFT, RHP

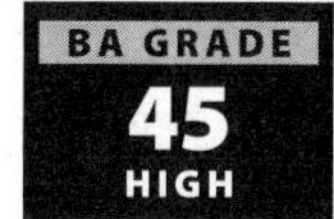

Born: May 28, 1990. **B-T:** R-R. **Ht.:** 6-4. **Wt.:** 225. **Drafted:** HS—Santa Ana, Calif., 2009 (10th round). **Signed by:** Tom Battista.

Northcraft struggled in the first half of 2013 while making the jump to Double-A Mississippi before putting together an outstanding final two months that included a 2.31 ERA and 2.3 SO/BB ratio over 11 starts. With good size and excellent mound presence, Northcraft has steadily climbed the organizational ladder since signing out of Mater Dei High and opting to bypass Southern California. He works quickly using a low three-quarters arm slot that generates a sinking fastball in the 88-90 mph range as well as a solid changeup and inconsistent curveball. His fastball and changeup have good movement and depth, and he challenges hitters with his aggressive approach in hopes of coaxing groundball outs. Northcraft has the makings of a workhorse but continues to draw some concerns from scouts regarding his long arm action and stiff front leg in his delivery. He has shown an uncanny ability to make adjustments to his delivery. Northcraft fared poorly in the Arizona Fall League, more evidence he's not quite ready for prime time. He projects as a back-end starter in the big leagues, and he will move to Triple-A Gwinnett in 2014.

Year	Club (League)	Class	W	L	ERA	G	GS	CG	SV	IP	H	HR	BB	SO	K/9	WHIP	AVG
2009	Braves (GCL)	R	1	2	4.50	11	10	0	0	40	33	2	21	31	7.0	1.35	.229
2010	Danville (APP)	R	6	1	2.73	10	9	0	0	53	44	1	9	38	6.5	1.01	.228
	Rome (SAL)	LoA	1	3	8.16	4	3	0	0	14	21	1	15	8	5.0	2.51	.328
2011	Rome (SAL)	LoA	7	8	3.34	23	19	0	0	113	108	8	41	88	7.0	1.31	.254
2012	Lynchburg (CAR)	HiA	10	11	3.98	27	27	2	0	152	143	4	53	160	9.5	1.29	.247
2013	Mississippi (SL)	AA	8	8	3.42	26	26	0	0	137	124	7	51	121	7.9	1.28	.241
Minor League Totals			33	33	3.71	101	94	2	0	509	473	23	190	446	7.9	1.30	.246

26 LUIS MEREJO, LHP

BA GRADE
50
EXTREME

Born: Oct. 8, 1994. **B-T:** L-L. **Ht.:** 6-0. **Wt.:** 170. **Signed:** Dominican Republic, 2011. **Signed by:** Matias Laureano Fortunato.

Having put together a solid debut in the Rookie-level Gulf Coast League in 2012, Merejo appeared poised to break through in 2013. After tossing 10 shutout innings at Rookie-level Danville, however, the undersized lefty's campaign was over before it began. Placed on the 60-day disabled list following his July 20 appearance, he had Tommy John surgery in August. The Braves were cautious with Merejo prior to his injury and will continue to be conservative with his rehab. Signed for a modest $65,000, he has shown advanced feel, three potentially plus pitches and an ability to throw strikes on a consistent basis. The athletic Merejo works fast, mixes his pitches and stays ahead in the count. His 89-91 mph fastball has good movement and touches 94. He also has a quality curveball with tight spin and a changeup that continues to improve in its fade and depth. While the first concern centers on getting Merejo healthy, he is expected to bounce back and possibly open the 2015 season as a 20-year-old at low Class A Rome.

Year	Club (League)	Class	W	L	ERA	G	GS	CG	SV	IP	H	HR	BB	SO	K/9	WHIP	AVG
2012	Braves (GCL)	R	0	5	4.61	10	8	0	0	41	38	1	9	53	11.6	1.15	.245
2013	Braves (GCL)	R	0	0	0.00	2	0	0	0	6	4	0	4	1	1.5	1.33	.182
	Danville (APP)	R	1	0	0.00	3	1	0	0	10	8	0	5	11	9.9	1.30	.222
Minor League Totals			1	5	3.32	15	9	0	0	57	50	1	18	65	10.3	1.19	.235

27 JUAN JAIME, RHP

BA GRADE
45
HIGH

Born: Aug. 2, 1987. **B-T:** R-R. **Ht.:** 6-1. **Wt.:** 180. **Signed:** Dominican Republic, 2004. **Signed by:** Ismael Cruz (Expos).

While staying healthy has been an issue for Jaime since he signed with the Expos as a 17-year-old, his power arm earned him a spot on the Braves' 40-man roster and a potential role in the big league bullpen. The righthander missed nearly two years after having Tommy John surgery, passing through the Diamondbacks organization on his way to signing with the Braves in August 2011. He blossomed at high Class A Lynchburg in 2012, ranking second in the Carolina League with 18 saves. He made the jump to Double-A Mississippi in 2013 after spending the first six weeks on the disabled list with right forearm tightness. Jaime has a classic power arm and challenges hitters with his upper-90s fastball that touches triple digits. While his average changeup has potential, his slurvy curveball is little more than a show-me pitch. Overall, Jaime's control is below-average, and he struggled to close games in Double-A. He has the potential to be an overpowering set-up man if everything falls into place, but with a career walk rate of 5.8 per nine innings, he has always struggled to throw strikes consistently. Jaime should move to Triple-A Gwinnett in 2014.

Year	Club (League)	Class	W	L	ERA	G	GS	CG	SV	IP	H	HR	BB	SO	K/9	WHIP	AVG
2005	Nationals (DSL)	R	1	0	2.51	9	0	0	0	14	9	1	11	14	8.8	1.40	.176
2006	Nationals2 (DSL)	R	0	0	2.61	6	0	0	1	10	5	0	8	13	11.3	1.26	.135
2007	Nationals1 (DSL)	R	3	0	1.35	14	0	0	0	27	11	0	14	34	11.5	0.94	.121
2008	Nationals (GCL)	R	2	1	4.74	8	2	1	0	19	16	1	18	23	10.9	1.79	.232
2009	Vermont (NYP)	SS	2	1	1.88	6	5	0	0	24	15	0	15	36	13.5	1.25	.183
	Hagerstown (SAL)	LoA	3	1	2.27	8	7	0	0	32	22	2	16	40	11.4	1.20	.193
2010	Did not play—Injured																
2011	Did not play—Injured																
2012	Lynchburg (CAR)	HiA	1	3	3.16	42	0	0	18	51	31	4	33	73	12.8	1.25	.173
2013	Mississippi (SL)	AA	2	5	4.07	35	0	0	0	42	30	1	28	70	15.0	1.38	.201
Minor League Totals			14	11	2.91	128	14	1	19	219	139	9	143	303	12.4	1.29	.180

28 TYLER BROSIUS, RHP

Born: Jan. 7, 1992. **B-T:** R-R. **Ht.:** 6-4. **Wt.:** 230. **Drafted:** Walters State (Tenn.) CC, 2013 (21st round). **Signed by:** Billy Best.

After turning pro as a 21st-rounder out of junior college, Brosius worked his way through three levels of the system as a reliever. He spent two years as a backup quarterback at North Carolina State before deciding to transfer to Walters State (Tenn.) CC in 2013 and return to the diamond. In a private workout with the Braves, he hit four of 10 pitches over the fence and sat in the low 90s with his fastball. After one juco season, Brosius turned down offers to play baseball and football at Appalachian State to sign with Atlanta. A big-bodied righthander with above-average strength and athleticism, Brosius throws a heavy fastball in the 90-93 mph range. He mixes it with a hard curveball and a power slider/cutter that touches 87 mph. He does a good job of working down in the zone, which results in numerous groundouts. Brosius could move quickly once he gains a firmer foundation after being away from the game for two years. He will open 2014 at either low Class A Rome or high Class A Lynchburg, based on the progress he shows in spring training.

Year	Club (League)	Class	W	L	ERA	G	GS	CG	SV	IP	H	HR	BB	SO	K/9	WHIP	AVG
2013	Braves (GCL)	R	1	1	4.91	6	0	0	0	7	6	0	4	9	11.0	1.36	.214
	Danville (APP)	R	2	1	1.76	7	0	0	0	15	7	0	6	17	10.0	0.85	.135
	Rome (SAL)	LoA	0	1	1.93	4	0	0	0	5	2	0	4	9	17.4	1.29	.125
Minor League Totals			3	3	2.63	17	0	0	0	27	15	0	14	35	11.5	1.06	.156

29 ROBBY HEFFLINGER, OF

BA GRADE **45** HIGH

Born: Jan. 3, 1990. **B-T:** R-R. **Ht.:** 6-4. **Wt.:** 220. **Drafted:** Georgia Perimeter JC, 2009 (7th round). **Signed by:** Brian Bridges.

Hefflinger finally cleared the Carolina League hurdle on his third try at high Class A Lynchburg, ranking second in the league with 21 homers in just 74 games. He made a midseason jump to Double-A Mississippi and discovered more adjustments need to be made. Across both stops, he hit a career-high 27 home runs, one shy of the organization lead. Hefflinger has as much raw power as anyone in the Braves system and has learned how to use it over the past two years by working extensively with hitting coordinator Don Long. He now goes to right-center field more often and has become more aggressive early in the count. While his overall approach continues to improve, Hefflinger remains susceptible to chasing breaking balls and tends to swing and miss frequently due to a hole in his swing. He struck out in 17 of the 20 games he played in the Arizona Fall League. A good athlete for his large frame, he runs well but is continuing to work on improving his routes in the outfield. He has above-average arm strength with consistent accuracy that is more of an advantage in right field than left. He will likely return to Mississippi to open the 2014 slate.

Year	Club (League)	Class	AVG	G	AB	R	H	2B	3B	HR	RBI	BB	SO	SB	CS	OBP	SLG
2009	Danville (APP)	R	.242	61	240	23	58	11	1	7	37	16	76	1	0	.288	.383
2010	Rome (SAL)	LoA	.245	77	282	28	69	19	0	6	53	25	85	2	5	.302	.376
2011	Lynchburg (CAR)	HiA	.114	12	44	2	5	2	0	0	2	3	19	0	0	.170	.159
	Rome (SAL)	LoA	.256	112	425	55	109	34	3	8	56	24	123	1	1	.296	.407
2012	Lynchburg (CAR)	HiA	.228	37	123	14	28	8	0	4	11	18	47	1	1	.336	.390
	Rome (SAL)	LoA	.284	84	296	44	84	21	1	12	58	38	81	7	1	.362	.483
2013	Lynchburg (CAR)	HiA	.286	74	280	44	80	17	1	21	52	22	71	1	1	.339	.579
	Mississippi (SL)	AA	.170	53	188	19	32	8	1	6	25	15	64	2	1	.227	.319
Minor League Totals			.248	510	1878	229	465	120	7	64	294	161	566	15	10	.306	.421

30 JAMES HOYT, RHP

BA GRADE **45** HIGH

Born: Sept. 30, 1986. **B-T:** R-R. **Ht.:** 6-5. **Wt.:** 220. **Signed:** Tabasco (Mexican League), 2012. **Signed by:** Manuel Samaniego.

Hoyt has overcome long odds to become a potential bullpen contributor in the big leagues. The Boise, Idaho, native attended Palomar (Calif.) JC and Centenary College in Louisiana before he started working on sailboats, returning to baseball only after attending a tryout to play for Yuma in the independent North American League in 2011. After that team folded, Hoyt spent 2012 with Edinburg in the same circuit prior to being traded to Wichita in the American Association and then signing with Tabasco in the Mexican League. After averaging 11.9 strikeouts per nine innings in his two seasons of indy ball and posting a 1.76 ERA with 54 strikeouts in 41 innings in 2012, he signed his first contract in affiliated ball with the Braves in November 2012. He pitched in long relief with three spot starts at high Class A Lynchburg in 2013 before putting together an impressive second half at Double-A Mississippi. Hoyt has tremendous size and presence on the mound. He has an above-average fastball that sits in the 94-96 mph range and a slider that has a chance to develop into a plus offering. Deemed raw in spring training, Hoyt went from trying to blow the ball past hitters early in the season to learning how to get outs. He needs more consistency with his mechanics out of the stretch. He is also working on controlling the running game by improving his pickoff move and ability to hold runners. Having made great progress in a short period, Hoyt should see time at Triple-A Gwinnett in 2014.

Year	Club (League)	Class	W	L	ERA	G	GS	CG	SV	IP	H	HR	BB	SO	K/9	WHIP	AVG
2011	Yuma (NAL)	IND	2	0	4.34	19	1	0	1	37	34	4	24	50	12.1	1.55	—
2012	Edinburg (NAL)	IND	0	0	1.04	12	0	0	1	17	13	0	10	19	9.9	1.33	—
	Wichita (A-A)	IND	2	0	2.61	11	0	0	1	10	9	0	5	15	13.1	1.35	—
	Tabasco (MEX)	AAA	0	2	2.03	11	0	0	1	13	12	1	7	20	13.5	1.43	—
2013	Lynchburg (CAR)	HiA	3	2	4.89	17	3	0	0	50	39	3	25	72	13.0	1.29	.213
	Mississippi (SL)	AA	0	1	2.48	22	0	0	1	33	17	1	13	33	9.1	0.92	.147
Minor League Totals			3	5	3.67	50	3	0	2	96	68	5	45	125	11.8	1.18	.187

Baltimore Orioles

BY STEVE MELEWSKI

The Orioles have returned winning baseball to Baltimore. A year after winning 93 games and the American League Wild Card game, they came up short of a second straight playoff berth, but did finish 85-77 and in third place in the AL East.

The Orioles will look for a third straight winning season in 2014, something they have not done since 1992-94, and they have bigger goals of returning to the playoffs in the rugged AL East. Baltimore ended 14 years of losing baseball in 2012. Now they begin to find out if they've come far enough to compete year in and year out.

Unlike in 2012, the Orioles faded down the stretch in 2013, and a late six-game losing streak ended any fleeting playoff hopes. Their record in one-run games, an amazing 29-9 in 2012, slipped to 20-31.

The great Orioles teams of the past were built on pitching and defense, and the 2013 version had half of that equation covered. The Orioles set major league records for fielding percentage (.991), fewest errors in a 162-game season (54) and most errorless games (119). But the club fell from sixth in the AL in ERA to 10th, and their starters' ERA of 4.57 ranked 12th in the league, while the bullpen ERA increased from 3.02 to 3.52. Closer Jim Johnson became the first AL pitcher to record consecutive 50-save seasons, but he also had nine blown opportunities (and was traded after the season).

The Orioles now face several key questions, most notably whether they can keep Chris Davis, who led the majors with 53 homers and 138 RBIs, and catcher Matt Wieters long-term. Both Scott Boras clients are two years from free agency. Two of the people who will answer that question for the Orioles—general manager Dan Duquette and manager Buck Showalter—are signed through 2018 and have proven a formidable one-two punch atop the club's baseball operations.

Duquette has said often the Orioles need to produce their core players, and trades in 2013 thinned an already shallow farm system. But the Orioles do have young pitching, and a lot will ride on the club's production in that department. In recent years, young arms like Jake Arrieta and Zach Britton have failed to reach their potential, and now the O's find out if the next wave will come through.

The Orioles feel confident their young pitchers are in good hands. Rick Peterson completed his second season as the club's director of pitching development, and his program, which features the use of biomechanical analysis, has led to both improvements in mechanics and velocity gains throughout the system. Nevertheless, top prospect Bundy missed the 2013 season with Tommy John surgery and likely is out until at least June 2014.

The player-development operation is in capable hands with farm director Brian Graham, while Gary Rajsich completed his second draft as scouting director, taking Gausman and Harvey with his two first-round picks. The club also is making gains on the international front, pursuing Cubans such as outfielder Henry Urrutia and giving the largest bonus in franchise history in September to a Dominican amateur, righthander Ofelky Peralta.

Buck Showalter (left) and Dan Duquette have restored a winning attitude in Baltimore

TOP PROSPECTS OF THE DECADE

Year	Player, Pos.	2013 Org.
2004	Adam Loewen, lhp	Blue Jays
2005	Nick Markakis, of	Orioles
2006	Nick Markakis, of	Orioles
2007	Billy Rowell, 3b	Out of baseball
2008	Matt Wieters, c	Orioles
2009	Matt Wieters, c	Orioles
2010	Brian Matusz, lhp	Orioles
2011	Manny Machado, ss	Orioles
2012	Dylan Bundy, rhp	Orioles
2013	Dylan Bundy, rhp	Orioles

ORGANIZATION OVERVIEW

General Manager: Dan Duquette. **Farm Director:** Brian Graham. **Scouting Director:** Gary Rajsich.

Class	Team	League	W	L	PCT	Finish	Manager
Majors	Baltimore Orioles	American	85	77	.525	8th (15)	Buck Showalter
Triple-A	Norfolk Tides	International	77	67	.535	t-4th (14)	Ron Johnson
Double-A	Bowie Baysox	Eastern	71	71	.500	5th (12)	Gary Kendall
High A	Frederick Keys	Carolina	61	78	.439	7th (8)	Ryan Minor
Low A	Delmarva Shorebirds	South Atlantic	54	82	.397	13th (14)	Luis Pujols
Short-season	Aberdeen Ironbirds	New York-Penn	40	32	.556	4th (14)	Matt Merullo
Rookie	GCL Orioles	Gulf Coast	30	30	.500	6th (16)	Orlando Gomez
Overall 2013 Minor League Record			**333**	**360**	**.481**	**25th (30)**	

THIS YEAR'S TOP 30

No.	Player, Pos.	Grade/Risk
1.	Dylan Bundy, rhp	70/High
2.	Kevin Gausman, rhp	65/Medium
3.	Eduardo Rodriguez, lhp	55/Medium
4.	Hunter Harvey, rhp	60/Extreme
5.	Jonathan Schoop, 2b/ss	50/Medium
6.	Tim Berry, lhp	50/High
7.	Henry Urrutia, of	45/Low
8.	Mike Wright, rhp	50/High
9.	Michael Ohlman, c	50/High
10.	Chance Sisco, c	55/Extreme
11.	Zach Davies, rhp	50/High
12.	Adrian Marin, ss	50/High
13.	Josh Hart, of	45/High
14.	Steven Brault, lhp	50/High
15.	Dariel Alvarez, of	45/High
16.	Travis Seabrooke, lhp	45/High
17.	Jon Keller, rhp	50/Extreme
18.	Christian Walker, 1b	45/High
19.	Parker Bridwell, rhp	45/High
20.	Branden Kline, rhp	50/Extreme
21.	Stephen Tarpley, lhp	50/Extreme
22.	Ofelky Peralta, rhp	50/Extreme
23.	Mychal Givens, rhp	50/Extreme
24.	Oliver Drake, rhp	45/High
25.	Trey Mancini, 1b	45/High
26.	Jonah Heim, c	45/Extreme
27.	Chris Jones, lhp	40/Low
28.	Josh Stinson, rhp	40/Low
29.	Glynn Davis, of	45/Extreme
30.	Jason Gurka, lhp	40/Medium

LAST YEAR'S TOP 30

No.	Player, Pos.	Status
1.	Dylan Bundy, rhp	No. 1
2.	Kevin Gausman, rhp	No. 2
3.	Jonathan Schoop. 2b	No. 5
4.	Nick Delmonico, 3b	(Brewers)
5.	Eduardo Rodriguez, lhp	No. 3
6.	L.J. Hoes, of	(Astros)
7.	Xavier Avery, of	(Mariners)
8.	Mike Wright, rhp	No. 8
9.	Branden Kline, rhp	No. 20
10.	Adrian Marin, ss	No. 12
11.	Tim Berry, lhp	No. 6
12.	Christian Walker, 1b	No. 18
13.	Henry Urrutia, of	No. 7
14.	Glynn Davis, of	No. 29
15.	Torsten Boss, 2b	Dropped out
16.	Steve Johnson, rhp	Majors
17.	Clay Schrader, rhp	Dropped out
18.	Devin Jones, rhp	(Padres)
19.	Josh Hader, lhp	(Astros)
20.	Zach Davies, rhp	No. 11
21.	Tsuyoshi Wada, lhp	(Free Agent)
22.	T.J. McFarland, lhp	Majors
23.	Parker Bridwell, rhp	No. 19
24.	Mike Belfiore, lhp	Dropped out
25.	Lex Rutledge, lhp	Dropped out
26.	Tyler Wilson, rhp	Dropped out
27.	Brenden Webb, of	Dropped out
28.	Oliver Drake, rhp	No. 24
29.	Greg Lorenzo, of	Dropped out
30.	Ty Kelly, 2b	(Mariners)

BEST TOOLS

Best Hitter for Average	Henry Urrutia
Best Power Hitter	Jonathan Schoop
Best Strike-Zone Discipline	Michael Ohlman
Fastest Baserunner	Glynn Davis
Best Athlete	Josh Hart
Best Fastball	Kevin Gausman
Best Curveball	Dylan Bundy
Best Slider	Mike Wright
Best Changeup	Kevin Gausman
Best Control	Zach Davies
Best Defensive Catcher	Brian Ward
Best Defensive Infielder	Adrian Marin
Best Infield Arm	Jonathan Schoop
Best Defensive Outfielder	Josh Hart
Best Outfield Arm	Dariel Alvarez

TOP 15 PLAYERS 25 AND UNDER

No.	Player, Pos. (Age)	Peak Level
1.	Manny Machado, 3b (21)	Majors
2.	Dylan Bundy, rhp (21)	Majors
3.	Kevin Gausman, rhp (23)	Majors
4.	Chris Tillman, rhp (25)	Majors
5.	Eduardo Rodriguez, lhp (20)	Double-A
6.	Hunter Harvey, rhp (19)	Short-season
7.	Jonathan Schoop, 2b (22)	Majors
8.	Tim Berry, lhp (23)	High Class A
9.	Mike Wright, rhp (24)	Triple-A
10.	Michael Ohlman, c (23)	High Class A
11.	Chance Sisco, c (19)	Short-Season
12.	Zach Davies, rhp (21)	High Class A
13.	Adrian Marin, ss (20)	Low Class A
14.	T.J. McFarland, lhp (24)	Majors
15.	Steven Brault, lhp (21)	Short-Season

MINOR LEAGUE DEPTH CHART

BALTIMORE ORIOLES

TOP 2014 ROOKIE: Kevin Gausman, rhp. Gained valuable experience in 2013 and looks to win rotation spot in 2014.

BREAKOUT PROSPECT: Mychal Givens, rhp. After solid second half and strong instructional league, converted shortstop could take a big leap forward.

SLEEPER: Matt Hobgood, rhp. 2009 first-rounder returned to health and saw some velocity come back in 2013.

SOURCE OF TOP 30 TALENT

Homegrown	**29**	**Acquired**	**1**
College	9	Trades	1
Junior college	2	Rule 5 draft	0
High school	12	Independent leagues	0
Nondrafted free agents	1	Free agents/waivers	0
International	5		

LF
Henry Urrutia (7)
Mike Yastrzemski
John Ruettiger
K.D. Kang

CF
Josh Hart (13)
Glynn Davis (29)
Trent Mummey
Greg Lorenzo

RF
Dariel Alvarez (15)
Conor Bierfeldt
Brendan Webb

3B
Drew Dosch
Jason Esposito
Hector Veloz

SS
Adrian Marin (12)
Jared Breen
Justin Viele

2B
Jonathan Schoop (5)
Garabez Rosa
Jeff Kemp
Buck Britton

1B
Christian Walker (18)
Trey Mancini (25)
Randolph Gassaway

C
Michael Ohlman (9)
Chance Sisco (10)
Jonah Heim (26)
Alex Murphy
Caleb Joseph
Brian Ward

LHP

LHSP	LHRP
Eduardo Rodriguez (3)	Chris Jones (27)
Tim Berry (6)	Jason Gurka (30)
Steven Brault (14)	Mike Belfiore
Travis Seabrooke (16)	Kelvin de la Cruz
Stephen Tarpley (21)	Lex Rutledge
Matt Taylor	
Mitch Horacek	

RHP

RHSP	RHRP
Dylan Bundy (1)	Branden Kline (20)
Kevin Gausman (2)	Mychal Givens (23)
Hunter Harvey (4)	Oliver Drake (24)
Mike Wright (8)	Josh Stinson (28)
Zach Davies (11)	Miguel Chalas
Jon Keller (17)	Edgmer Escalona
Parker Bridwell (19)	Jimmy Yacabonis
Ofelky Peralta (22)	Matt Hobgood
Brady Wager	Nik Nowottnick
Eddie Gamboa	
Garrett Cortright	
Mark Blackmar	

DRAFT ANALYSIS

2013

BONUSES: $6.4 MILLION

BEST PURE HITTER: The Orioles are excited about C Chance Sisco (2), mostly because of his bat. He has tremendous plate discipline for his age, natural rhythm and a feel for the barrel of the bat with some strength from the left side.

BEST POWER HITTER: OF Conor Bierfeldt (12) was a Division III stud as a two-way player, and he has the Orioles intrigued with his well above-average raw power. The 6-foot-2, 220-pounder does a lot right in the batter's box, from a short swing with strength and leverage to getting plenty of extension and using the opposite field.

FASTEST RUNNER: OF Josh Hart (1s) earns 70 grades on the 20-80 scale for his 3.98-second times to first base.

BEST DEFENSIVE PLAYER: OF Mike Yastrzemski (14) has solid defensive tools, with an average, accurate arm and slightly above-average speed. He layers on tremendous instincts and skilled footwork and routes in center.

BEST FASTBALL: RHP Hunter Harvey (1) has a fresh, lively arm with a fastball that sits in the low 90s and has touched 97, and it's easy to project more consistent premium velocity. RHP Jon Keller (22) was expected to get drafted higher thanks to a 90-95 mph fastball that comes out easy. He has also touched 97.

BEST SECONDARY PITCH: Harvey's curveball flashes plus; the Orioles describe it as "electric" thanks to his good hand speed. LHP Stephen Tarpley (3) also flashes plus with his curve.

BEST PRO DEBUT: Sisco fell short of the playing time to qualify for the batting title (.371/.475/.464 in 97 at-bats) but dominated the Rookie-level Gulf Coast League before a promotion to short-season Aberdeen. Bierfeldt led Aberdeen to its first-ever playoff berth, ranking second in the New York-Penn League with 12 homers and leading it in slugging while hitting .264/.351/.511. 1B Trey Mancini (8), who also has plus raw power, set Aberdeen's single-season hits record (84) while batting .328/.382/.449.

BEST ATHLETE: Hart.

MOST INTRIGUING BACKGROUND: Yastrzemski is the grandson of Hall of Famer Carl. Harvey's father Bryan was a two-time all-star closer with the Angels and Marlins. 3B Federico Castagnini (30) was born and raised in Italy before moving to Colorado in high school and then playing at Creighton. LHP Travis Seabrooke (5) is the son of former NHL player Glen.

CLOSEST TO THE MAJORS: The Orioles see Harvey moving quickly, but Keller could beat him if he relieves.

BEST LATE-ROUND PICK: Keller, Bierfeldt and LHP Steven Brault (11), a polished Colorado product who is a good enough singer to have performed the national anthem prior to a Northwoods League game last summer.

THE ONE WHO GOT AWAY: The new coaching staff at Georgia successfully re-recruited projectable RHP Robert Tyler (28).

ASSESSMENT: Baltimore had a young draft focused on high-upside preps, but still found potential college contributors in Bierfeldt, Brault and Keller. A farm system in need of depth got an infusion of it.

2012

BONUSES: $7.4 MILLION

RHP Kevin Gausman (1) looks like a potential star. SS Adrian Marin (3) offers middle infield tools. Late find LHP Josh Hader (19) was traded for Bud Norris.

GRADE: B

2011

BONUSES: $8.4 MILLION

The Orioles are counting on a healthy return by RHP Dylan Bundy (1). RHPs Mike Wright (3) and Zach Davies (26) provide depth to the system.

GRADE: B

2010

BONUSES: $9.2 MILLION

This draft class began with SS Manny Machado (1), since shifted to 3B. It basically ends there too other than RHP Parker Bridwell (9).

GRADE: A

TOP DRAFT PICKS OF THE DECADE

Year	Player, Pos.	2013 Org.
2004	*Wade Townsend, rhp	Out of baseball
2005	Brandon Snyder, c	Red Sox
2006	Billy Rowell, 3b	Out of baseball
2007	Matt Wieters, c	Orioles
2008	Brian Matusz, lhp	Orioles
2009	Matt Hobgood, rhp	Orioles
2010	Manny Machado, ss	Orioles
2011	Dylan Bundy, rhp	Orioles
2012	Kevin Gausman, rhp	Orioles
2013	Hunter Harvey, rhp	Orioles

*Did not sign

LARGEST BONUSES IN CLUB HISTORY

Matt Wieters, 2007	$6,000,000
Manny Machado, 2010	$5,250,000
Kevin Gausman, 2012	$4,320,000
Dylan Bundy, 2011	$4,000,000
Adam Loewen, 2002	$3,200,000

1 DYLAN BUNDY, RHP

Born: Nov. 15, 1992. **B-T:** R-R. **Ht.:** 6-1. **Wt.:** 195.
Drafted: HS—Owasso, Okla., 2011 (1st round).
Signed by: Ernie Jacobs

BA GRADE
70
HIGH
SCOUTING GRADES
FASTBALL 70
CURVEBALL 65
CHANGEUP 60
COMMAND 65
DELIVERY 65

MIKE JANES

Considered among the most advanced prep pitchers in years, Bundy went fourth overall in a deep 2011 draft and signed a $6.225 million major league contract that included a $4 million bonus. He then lived up to that by going 9-3, 2.08 at three levels of the minors in 2012, fanning 119 batters in 104 innings and reaching Double-A Bowie. Bundy became the fourth player from his draft class to reach the big leagues, as well as the fourth 19-year-old to pitch in the majors in the last decade when he made two September relief appearances for the Orioles. He became the first Baltimore player to debut before age 20 since righthander Mike Adamson on July 1, 1967. Ticketed to begin the 2013 season at Bowie, Bundy saw his velocity dip during a spring training start, and late in March he was shut down with elbow soreness. After rest and rehab didn't alleviate the issue, Bundy had Tommy John surgery performed by Dr. James Andrews on June 27. He continued his rehab over the winter at the Orioles' spring training facilities in Sarasota, Fla.

Bundy showed the expected high-end velocity throughout 2012, pitching in the mid-90s and at times touching 98 mph. The Orioles asked him to not throw his cut fastball during the minor league season to get more work on his secondary pitches, and he showed a plus curveball with sharp break and a changeup that made dramatic improvement through the season and was often a plus pitch by the end of the year. Despite his 6-foot-1 build, Bundy has tremendous strength, creates good plane on his pitches and is very athletic. What truly makes him special, with No. 1 starter potential, is the talent in combination with tremendous work ethic and makeup.

Bundy was the first prep pitcher from the deep 2011 draft to reach the majors, but now he has a long way to go to match Jose Fernandez as the best high school arm from that class, and fellow Oklahoman and friend Archie Bradley of the Diamondbacks is catching up. Bundy's rehab schedule called for him to begin throwing six months after surgery, around Jan. 1. He likely won't throw off a mound until April. Bundy's strong drive and work ethic have him on schedule, if not ahead a bit, in his recovery. It may be a couple of months into the season before he is game ready, and the Orioles figure to be cautious and conservative with such a young talent. He likely will start 2014 at extended spring training and may begin pitching in games there with the hope that he could eventually settle in at Bowie to get the bulk of his innings. Can he make an impact at the big league level in 2014? That seems ambitious, yet no one will rule it out with Bundy.

Year	Club (League)	Class	W	L	ERA	G	GS	CG	SV	IP	H	HR	BB	SO	K/9	WHIP	AVG
2012	Delmarva (SAL)	LoA	1	0	0.00	8	8	0	0	30	5	0	2	40	12.0	0.23	.053
	Frederick (CAR)	HiA	6	3	2.84	12	12	0	0	57	48	5	18	66	10.4	1.16	.233
	Bowie (EL)	AA	2	0	3.24	3	3	0	0	17	14	1	8	13	7.0	1.32	.230
	Baltimore (AL)	MAJ	0	0	0.00	2	0	0	0	2	1	0	1	0	0.0	1.20	.200
2013	Did not play—Injured																
Major League Totals			0	0	0.00	2	0	0	0	2	1	0	1	0	0.0	1.20	.200
Minor League Totals			9	3	2.08	23	23	0	0	104	67	6	28	119	10.3	0.92	.186

2 KEVIN GAUSMAN, RHP

BA GRADE
65
MEDIUM

Born: Jan. 6, 1991. **B-T:** R-R. **Ht.:** 6-3. **Wt.:** 190. **Drafted:** Louisiana State, 2012 (1st round). **Signed by:** Dave Jennings.

A sixth-round pick out of a Colorado high school in 2010, Gausman went to Louisiana State before the Orioles took him with the fourth overall pick in 2012 and he signed for $4.32 million. Eight starts into his 2013 season at Double-A Bowie, the Orioles summoned him to make his big league debut in May against the Blue Jays. He shifted to the bullpen in subsequent recalls to the majors. Gausman has pitched with more velocity than he'd shown at LSU, sitting in the mid-90s with his fastball and touching 99 mph. He throws a lot of strikes with his fastball and now does with his changeup as well. He added a get-me-over circle change, thrown harder than his original plus split-changeup, around midseason. The Orioles decided Gausman's slider would become his primary breaking pitch, and it shows good depth and bite but lacks consistency. Gausman wants to add bulk to his slender frame, and maintaining his control and improved slider will be crucial for him to fulfill his No. 2 starter potential. He could open the season in the Baltimore rotation.

Year	Club (League)	Class	W	L	ERA	G	GS	CG	SV	IP	H	HR	BB	SO	K/9	WHIP	AVG
2012	Aberdeen (NYP)	SS	0	0	0.00	2	2	0	0	6	1	0	0	5	7.5	0.17	.053
	Frederick (CAR)	HiA	0	1	6.00	3	3	0	0	9	10	3	1	8	8.0	1.22	.278
2013	Bowie (EL)	AA	2	4	3.11	8	8	0	0	46	44	3	5	49	9.5	1.06	.246
	Norfolk (IL)	AAA	1	2	4.04	8	7	0	0	36	36	1	9	33	8.3	1.26	.271
	Baltimore (AL)	MAJ	3	5	5.66	20	5	0	0	48	51	8	13	49	9.3	1.34	.276
Major League Totals			3	5	5.66	20	5	0	0	48	51	8	13	49	9.3	1.34	.276
Minor League Totals			3	7	3.53	21	20	0	0	97	91	7	15	95	8.8	1.09	.248

3 EDUARDO RODRIGUEZ, LHP

BA GRADE
55
MEDIUM

Born: April 7, 1993. **B-T:** L-L. **Ht.:** 6-2. **Wt.:** 200. **Signed:** Venezuela, 2010. **Signed by:** Calvin Maduro.

The Orioles signed Rodriguez for $175,000 as a 17-year-old, and they invited him to big league spring training in 2013 and he jumped on the fast track, finishing the year with three scoreless innings in the Arizona Fall League championship game. Rodriguez works off a fastball with natural cut to the glove side. He pitches mostly at 92-93 mph, touching 95, and showed the ability to work to both sides of the plate. His slider is his best secondary pitch and has made nice gains in the last year. So too has his changeup, which he even threw to some lefthanded hitters. He still has some issues repeating his delivery, but he made improvement there while showing durability in a long season. Rodriguez is close to big league ready and ought to begin 2014 in the Double-A Bowie rotation and finish at Triple-A Norfolk—or possibly Baltimore. He has a No. 3 starter ceiling, with a chance to become an Orioles rarity as a player signed by the organization from Venezuela.

Year	Club (League)	Class	W	L	ERA	G	GS	CG	SV	IP	H	HR	BB	SO	K/9	WHIP	AVG
2010	Orioles1 (DSL)	R	3	4	2.33	12	12	1	0	66	49	0	28	62	8.5	1.17	.213
2011	Orioles (GCL)	R	1	1	1.81	11	10	0	1	45	28	0	17	46	9.3	1.01	.177
	Aberdeen (NYP)	SS	0	0	6.75	1	1	0	0	4	6	1	1	4	9.0	1.75	.333
2012	Delmarva (SAL)	LoA	5	7	3.70	22	22	1	0	107	103	4	30	73	6.1	1.24	.251
2013	Frederick (CAR)	HiA	6	4	2.85	14	14	0	0	85	78	4	25	66	7.0	1.21	.245
	Bowie (EL)	AA	4	3	4.22	11	11	1	0	60	53	5	24	59	8.9	1.29	.237
Minor League Totals			19	19	3.14	71	70	3	1	366	317	14	125	310	7.6	1.21	.233

4 HUNTER HARVEY, RHP

BA GRADE
60
EXTREME

Born: Dec. 9, 1994. **B-T:** R-R. **Ht.:** 6-4. **Wt.:** 178. **Drafted:** HS—Catawba, N.C., 2013 (1st round). **Signed by:** Chris Gale.

For the third year in a row the Orioles took a righthander with their top draft pick when they selected Harvey 22nd overall last June. About two weeks later he agreed to a $1,947,600 bonus. Hunter's father Bryan saved 177 games over a nine-year big league career, and Baltimore considered Hunter to have advanced mechanics and knowledge of pitching. He impressed at short-season Aberdeen, then was at his best in the New York-Penn League playoffs, when he threw five no-hit innings against Tri-City. His fastball sat 93-94 mph and touched 95 in that start, and peaked at 97 early in the spring. He has smooth mechanics that ought to allow him to maintain premium velocity as he fills out. His sharp curveball earns plus grades at its best. Aberdeen manager Matt Merullo described him as "intimidating, not intimidated." Harvey seldom threw changeups in high school but has shown potential with that pitch. He showed the poise and mound presence of a much more experienced pitcher. The Orioles expect Harvey to begin 2014 at low Class A Delmarva, where he'll work on developing his changeup. He has shown the potential to be a top-of-the-rotation pitcher.

Year	Club (League)	Class	W	L	ERA	G	GS	CG	SV	IP	H	HR	BB	SO	K/9	WHIP	AVG
2013	Orioles (GCL)	R	0	0	1.35	5	5	0	0	13	10	0	2	18	12.2	0.90	.208
	Aberdeen (NYP)	SS	0	1	2.25	3	3	0	0	12	11	0	4	15	11.3	1.25	.239
Minor League Totals			0	1	1.78	8	8	0	0	25	21	0	6	33	11.7	1.07	.223

5 JONATHAN SCHOOP, 2B/SS

BA GRADE **50** MEDIUM

Born: Oct. 16, 1991. **B-T:** R-R. **Ht.:** 6-2. **Wt.:** 212. **Signed:** Curacao, 2008. **Signed by:** Ernst Meyer.

Schoop's brother Sharlon preceded him in pro ball with the Giants and signed as a minor league free agent with Baltimore in November. The younger Schoop was the Orioles' 2011 minor league player of the year and has become a stalwart on Dutch national teams. A stress fracture in his lower back limited him to 70 games at Triple-A Norfolk, but he was healthy enough to make his major league debut Sept. 25, homering off Kyle Drabek in his third at-bat. Schoop is a solid hitter who can use the whole field and shows good bat speed with average plate discipline. His middle-of-the-field approach allows him to stay square a long time, but sometimes his timing becomes inconsistent. The Orioles expect the leverage in his swing to grow into solid-average power. He projects to hit .270-.280 with 10-15 home runs a year. He needs to work on hitting offspeed pitches. A below-average runner, Schoop has first-step quickness to go with good hands and a plus arm. He's capable of playing second base, shortstop and third and appears best suited for second. Schoop could be the future second baseman for the Orioles, but he's not ready for Opening Day 2014. He ought to begin the year at Triple-A, but his day as a potential offensive second baseman is coming.

Year	Club (League)	Class	AVG	G	AB	R	H	2B	3B	HR	RBI	BB	SO	SB	CS	OBP	SLG
2009	Orioles (DSL)	R	.239	68	247	28	59	7	3	0	35	24	39	11	3	.320	.291
2010	Orioles (GCL)	R	.250	17	60	11	15	4	0	3	16	7	7	0	0	.329	.467
	Bluefield (APP)	R	.316	39	133	16	42	11	1	2	16	12	14	1	1	.372	.459
	Frederick (CAR)	HiA	.238	6	21	5	5	3	0	0	3	1	4	0	0	.273	.381
2011	Delmarva (SAL)	LoA	.316	51	212	45	67	12	3	8	34	20	32	6	4	.376	.514
	Frederick (CAR)	HiA	.271	77	299	37	81	12	2	5	37	22	44	6	3	.329	.375
2012	Bowie (EL)	AA	.245	124	485	68	119	24	1	14	56	50	103	5	3	.324	.386
2013	Orioles (GCL)	R	.360	8	25	9	9	2	0	3	9	6	6	0	0	.469	.800
	Aberdeen (NYP)	SS	.571	3	14	3	8	1	0	2	9	1	1	0	1	.600	1.071
	Norfolk (IL)	AAA	.256	70	270	30	69	11	0	9	34	13	55	1	2	.301	.396
	Baltimore (AL)	MAJ	.286	5	14	5	4	0	0	1	1	1	2	0	0	.333	.500
Major League Totals			.286	5	14	5	4	0	0	1	1	1	2	0	0	.333	.500
Minor League Totals			.268	463	1766	252	474	87	10	46	249	156	305	30	17	.335	.407

6 TIM BERRY, LHP

BA GRADE **50** HIGH

Born: March 18, 1991. **B-T:** L-L. **Ht.:** 6-3. **Wt.:** 180. **Drafted:** HS—San Marcos, Calif., 2009 (50th round). **Signed by:** Mark Ralston.

Berry received a $125,000 bonus as a 50th-round pick in 2009 after having Tommy John surgery as a prep senior. He showed he was healthy in his first two seasons before breaking out in 2013 and finishing with a strong effort in the Arizona Fall League. The wiry, athletic Berry has a loose arm and attacks hitters with three average pitches, beginning with a fastball that earns occasional above-average grades. He pitched last season at 91-92 mph, touching 94, with improved command. His hard curveball has good downward action with tight spin, helping him neutralize lefthanded hitters, who hit .217/.275/.286 against him in 2013. Berry's firm changeup has improved, but he's still vulnerable against righthanders, who slugged .452 against him. The Orioles were impressed with the strides Berry made with his focus and the mental side of the game. He earned a spot on the 40-man roster and ought to spend 2014 at Double-A Bowie. He'll have to figure out how to combat righthanders to fulfill his potential as a mid-rotation starter.

Year	Club (League)	Class	W	L	ERA	G	GS	CG	SV	IP	H	HR	BB	SO	K/9	WHIP	AVG
2010	Orioles (GCL)	R	0	1	1.35	14	0	0	0	20	13	0	14	23	10.4	1.35	.181
2011	Delmarva (SAL)	LoA	3	7	5.17	26	26	0	0	117	107	11	61	96	7.4	1.44	.251
2012	Delmarva (SAL)	LoA	2	7	5.02	10	10	0	0	52	60	3	17	44	7.6	1.48	.282
	Frederick (CAR)	HiA	5	5	4.32	15	13	0	0	75	83	6	20	61	7.3	1.37	.285
	Bowie (EL)	AA	0	1	37.80	1	1	0	0	2	7	0	2	4	21.6	5.40	.583
2013	Frederick (CAR)	HiA	11	7	3.85	27	27	0	0	152	156	13	40	119	7.0	1.29	.265
Minor League Totals			21	28	4.46	93	77	0	0	417	426	33	154	347	7.5	1.39	.266

7 HENRY URRUTIA, OF

BA GRADE
45
LOW

Born: Feb. 13, 1987. **B-T:** L-R. **Ht.:** 6-5. **Wt.:** 200. **Signed:** Cuba, 2012. **Signed by:** Fred Ferreira.

Urrutia played in Cuba's Serie Nacional from 2006-10, hitting .397/.461/.579 with 12 home runs in his final season. Suspended in 2011 after a failed defection, he left Cuba in 2012 and signed that July with the Orioles for $778,500. After trouble securing a visa, Urrutia did not play until joining Double-A Bowie last April. He played in the Futures Game and made his big league debut on July 20. The Orioles say Urrutia has a lean, long frame like Bernie Williams in his prime. Previously a switch-hitter, Urrutia has batted lefthanded only with the Orioles. He has a level, line-drive swing with solid contact and plate-discipline skills. He has below-average home run power and is more comfortable using the opposite field, spraying line drives to the gaps. He's a below-average runner and fringy defender who fits best in left field. He has an average arm. Urrutia will compete for an outfield job in Baltimore with Steve Pearce and Nolan Reimold. He'll have to defend better to earn manager Buck Showalter's trust and avoid a return to Triple-A. At age 27, the time is now.

Year	Club (League)	Class	AVG	G	AB	R	H	2B	3B	HR	RBI	BB	SO	SB	CS	OBP	SLG
2013	Bowie (EL)	AA	.365	52	200	33	73	16	0	7	37	24	36	1	1	.433	.550
	Norfolk (IL)	AAA	.316	29	114	16	36	5	1	2	13	8	15	0	0	.358	.430
	Baltimore (AL)	MAJ	.276	24	58	5	16	0	1	0	2	0	11	0	0	.276	.310
Major League Totals			.276	24	58	5	16	0	1	0	2	0	11	0	0	.276	.310
Minor League Totals			.347	81	314	49	109	21	1	9	50	32	51	1	1	.406	.506

8 MIKE WRIGHT, RHP

BILL VAUGHAN PHOTOGRAPHY

BA GRADE
50
HIGH

Born: Jan. 3, 1990. **B-T:** R-R. **Ht.:** 6-6. **Wt.:** 215. **Drafted:** East Carolina, 2011 (3rd round). **Signed by:** Chris Gale.

Wright nearly won the organization's pitching triple crown in 2013, leading in wins (11) and ERA (3.11) and finishing a close second in strikeouts to Parker Bridwell. He made his Triple-A Norfolk debut on Sept. 2, with a scoreless start for a team still in the playoff hunt. Wright throws a fastball, slider, curve and changeup. He pitches at 92-93 mph with sink, touching 95. He has an aggressive tempo and fills up the strike zone with all four pitches when he's going well. He also keeps the same arm slot with all his pitches, including a hard cutter-type slider around 85 mph and a changeup with good sink and life. His curveball is his fourth pitch, and more of a surprise-attack option. None of his pitches grade as a true plus, so he has to be fine with his command. While he doesn't have a true out pitch, Wright has a good feel for pitching and profiles as a durable No. 4 starter. His stuff could play up if he's pressed into bullpen service. He should begin the 2014 season in Norfolk's rotation as he tries earn a spot on the 40-man roster.

Year	Club (League)	Class	W	L	ERA	G	GS	CG	SV	IP	H	HR	BB	SO	K/9	WHIP	AVG
2011	Orioles (GCL)	R	0	0	0.00	1	0	0	0	1	0	0	0	1	9.0	0.00	.000
	Aberdeen (NYP)	SS	2	1	3.77	7	7	0	0	31	29	3	6	29	8.4	1.13	.248
	Delmarva (SAL)	LoA	1	1	10.54	4	1	0	0	14	21	3	4	12	7.9	1.83	.356
2012	Frederick (CAR)	HiA	5	2	2.91	8	8	0	0	46	47	3	5	35	6.8	1.12	.266
	Bowie (EL)	AA	5	3	4.91	12	12	0	0	62	71	7	17	45	6.5	1.41	.289
2013	Bowie (EL)	AA	11	3	3.26	26	26	0	0	144	152	9	39	136	8.5	1.33	.267
	Norfolk (IL)	AAA	0	0	0.00	1	1	0	0	7	6	0	0	2	2.7	0.90	.231
Minor League Totals			24	10	3.84	59	55	0	0	305	326	25	71	260	7.7	1.30	.272

9 MICHAEL OHLMAN, C

BA GRADE
50
HIGH

Born: Dec. 14, 1990. **B-T:** R-R. **Ht.:** 6-5. **Wt.:** 215. **Drafted:** HS—Bradenton, Fla., 2009 (11th round). **Signed by:** John Martin.

The Orioles signed Ohlman to an over-slot bonus of $995,000 as part of an expensive, draft class in 2009 that quickly went awry. He seemed to bottom out in 2012 when he injured his shoulder in a spring-training car accident, then was suspended 50 games for a second positive test for a recreational drug. He started to hit in 2012 and had his best season in 2013, winning the high Class A Carolina League batting (.313) and slugging (.524) titles. His bat has blossomed as he has polished his approach, improving his pitch selection and getting to his above-average power more frequently. His swing can get long, and because he's not afraid to go deep in counts, he's prone to strikeouts. However, he repeats his hitting mechanics, staying with a middle-of-the-field approach and has excellent timing. At 6-foot-5, Ohlman is tall for a catcher, and while he has solid-average arm strength, he's unlikely to be more than an average receiver, and he struggles with his blocking. The Orioles like his feel for calling a game. Ohlman earned a spot on the 40-man roster and will head to Double-A Bowie in 2014, where he could play some first base. If his glove improves, he could be a long-term replacement for Matt Wieters.

Year	Club (League)	Class	AVG	G	AB	R	H	2B	3B	HR	RBI	BB	SO	SB	CS	OBP	SLG
2009	Orioles (GCL)	R	.182	4	11	1	2	1	0	0	1	1	3	1	0	.250	.273
2010	Delmarva (SAL)	LoA	.174	34	109	14	19	6	0	2	17	16	34	1	0	.285	.284
	Bluefield (APP)	R	.233	50	150	11	35	8	1	0	20	17	52	2	0	.315	.300
2011	Delmarva (SAL)	LoA	.224	105	375	38	84	15	2	4	51	48	96	1	2	.320	.307
2012	Orioles (GCL)	R	.276	8	29	5	8	3	0	1	3	2	10	1	0	.323	.483
	Delmarva (SAL)	LoA	.304	51	171	27	52	16	2	2	28	33	27	0	1	.411	.456
2013	Frederick (CAR)	HiA	.313	100	361	61	113	29	4	13	53	56	93	5	0	.410	.524
Minor League Totals			.260	352	1206	157	313	78	9	22	173	173	315	11	3	.357	.394

10 CHANCE SISCO, C

Born: Feb. 24, 1995. **B-T:** L-R. **Ht.:** 6-2. **Wt.:** 190. **Drafted:** HS—Lake Elsinore, Calif., 2013 (2nd round). **Signed by:** Mark Ralston.

Sisco's older brother Leland played Division II college ball, and Chance thrived in high school as a pitcher, third baseman and shortstop. But his pro stock took off when he started catching, and he shined last February at a Major League Scouting Bureau workout. The Orioles took Sisco 61st overall in 2013 and signed him for $785,000. The first of three high school catchers the Orioles took in the first six rounds, they drafted him for his bat, so if he can catch that will be a bonus. He showed an impressive, smooth lefthanded swing after the draft with a mature approach and good natural timing. He works the count well, uses the whole field and already has a decent two-strike approach. He has modest home run power for now and will have to get stronger to help offensively and to handle the grind defensively. Sisco showed a solid-average arm and good athleticism behind the plate, as well as solid receiving and blocking skills, which was impressive because he did not regularly catch until his senior year. He needs more experience catching at higher levels. Sisco ought to begin the 2014 season as the regular catcher at low Class A Delmarva, where he'll get reps and likely catch 70-90 games. The Orioles are optimistic about his offensive upside at a premium defensive position.

Year	Club (League)	Class	AVG	G	AB	R	H	2B	3B	HR	RBI	BB	SO	SB	CS	OBP	SLG
2013	Orioles (GCL)	R	.371	31	97	15	36	4	1	1	11	17	21	1	1	.475	.464
	Aberdeen (NYP)	SS	.200	2	5	1	1	0	0	0	0	1	2	0	0	.333	.200
Minor League Totals			.363	33	102	16	37	4	1	1	11	18	23	1	1	.468	.451

11 ZACH DAVIES, RHP

BA GRADE
50
HIGH

Born: Feb. 7, 1993. **B-T:** R-R. **Ht.:** 6-0. **Wt.:** 155. **Drafted:** HS—Gilbert, Ariz., 2011 (26th round). **Signed by:** John Gillette.

Davies signed for an over-slot bonus of $575,000 out of the 2011 draft, and so far he has lived up to it. He ranked 10th in the low Class A South Atlantic League in ERA in 2012 (3.86) and 10th in the high Class A Carolina League (3.69) last year. He also ranked second in strikeouts (132) and fourth among starters in walk rate (2.3 per nine innings). Scouts long have compared Davies with Reds righthander Mike Leake for his slight build, plus athleticism and command of four pitches. He impressed the Orioles with a strong pitching IQ and his ability to read opponents' swings. His fastball sits in the 87-91 mph range with solid-average life. He uses it to set up an advanced arsenal of offspeed stuff, starting with a plus changeup that he sells with excellent arm speed. Davies throws both a slider and a curveball, with the curve flashing above-average. The Orioles hope he adds velocity as he fills out, but he never figures to pitch with a plus fastball. Davies proved durable in 2013, taking every turn and logging nearly 150 innings. He'll head to the Double-A Bowie rotation for 2014.

Year	Club (League)	Class	W	L	ERA	G	GS	CG	SV	IP	H	HR	BB	SO	K/9	WHIP	AVG
2012	Delmarva (SAL)	LoA	5	7	3.86	25	17	0	1	114	109	11	46	91	7.2	1.36	.255
2013	Frederick (CAR)	HiA	7	9	3.69	26	26	0	0	149	145	10	38	132	8.0	1.23	.256
Minor League Totals			12	16	3.76	51	43	0	1	263	254	21	84	223	7.6	1.29	.256

12 ADRIAN MARIN, SS

Born: March 8, 1994. **B-T:** R-R. **Ht.:** 5-10. **Wt.:** 180. **Drafted:** HS—Miami, 2012 (3rd round). **Signed by:** Juan Alvarez.

The Orioles selected Marin 99th overall in 2012 and signed him to a slot bonus of $481,100. He shows advanced feel for the game and had a solid 2013 season at age 19 playing shortstop every day at low Class A Delmarva. The righthanded-hitting Marin showed the ability to grind through a season, hitting for more pop in the second half, adding nearly 50 points to his slugging percentage in virtually the same number of at-bats. To relieve pressure, the Orioles batted him eighth most of the season. Right now Marin's defense is ahead of his offense, but scouts can foresee his bat developing, even if the power likely will never be there. He possesses a strong baseball IQ and a handful of solid-average tools, though none profile as plus. He has shown solid fundamentals and the ability to carry out bat-handling tasks, such as bunting, serving the ball the other way and executing the hit-and-run. A slightly above-average runner, Marin has a chance to play a major league average shortstop, though his average arm may prove merely adequate for the position. Scouts expect him stay in the middle of the diamond because he moves well and shows good body control. The development of Marin's bat will determine if he's a regular or fills a utility role. The system's lack of middle-infield depth means he's headed for high Class A Frederick as a 20-year-old.

Year	Club (League)	Class	AVG	G	AB	R	H	2B	3B	HR	RBI	BB	SO	SB	CS	OBP	SLG
2012	Orioles (GCL)	R	.287	47	178	24	51	7	3	0	13	11	34	6	1	.339	.360
	Delmarva (SAL)	LoA	.286	6	21	5	6	0	0	0	2	1	2	2	0	.348	.286
2013	Delmarva (SAL)	LoA	.265	108	388	30	103	19	2	4	48	23	90	11	4	.311	.356
Minor League Totals			.273	161	587	59	160	26	5	4	63	35	126	19	5	.321	.354

13 JOSH HART, OF

BA GRADE
50
HIGH

Born: Oct. 2, 1994. **B-T:** L-L. **Ht.:** 6-2. **Wt.:** 180. **Drafted:** HS—Lilburn, Ga., 2013 (1st round supplemental). **Signed by:** Arthur McConnehead.

The Orioles drafted Hart 37th overall in 2013 and signed the Georgia prep outfielder for $1.45 million. He reported to the Rookie-level Gulf Coast League before moving to short-season Aberdeen for a few games late in the season. Hart missed a couple of weeks with a hamstring injury, one reason why he struggled a bit in his debut, though he kept grinding and had five hits in his final two games. Hart profiles as a speedy, top-of-the-order hitter with little power. He has been timed at 3.98 seconds to first base from the left side and was 11 of 14 in stolen-base attempts in the GCL. Hart needs to improve his plate discipline. He chases too many pitches and at times gets out on his front foot too much, and some scouts who saw him as an amateur lamented his inability to incorporate his lower half into his swing. Others cited his loose hands and gave him a chance to hit for a high average, even without having much power. He needs to work the count better and draw walks to fulfill his leadoff profile. Hart projects as a plus defender in center field with a below-average arm. He gets good jumps and can really get the ball in the gaps, and he is aggressive on groundballs. Hart played for a pair of Georgia state champions at Parkview High, and scouts like his makeup. He'll try to earn the everyday center-fielder job at low Class A Delmarva in 2014.

Year	Club (League)	Class	AVG	G	AB	R	H	2B	3B	HR	RBI	BB	SO	SB	CS	OBP	SLG
2013	Orioles (GCL)	R	.228	33	123	14	28	5	2	0	9	13	23	11	3	.312	.301
	Aberdeen (NYP)	SS	.100	3	10	0	1	0	0	0	0	1	4	0	0	.182	.100
Minor League Totals			.218	36	133	14	29	5	2	0	9	14	27	11	3	.302	.286

14 STEVEN BRAULT, LHP

BA GRADE
50
HIGH

Born: April 29, 1992. **B-T:** L-L. **Ht.:** 6-1. **Wt.:** 185. **Drafted:** Regis (Colo.), 2013 (11th round). **Signed by:** John Gillette.

Division II Regis in Denver never has produced a single-digit draft pick, but Brault came close. A two-way player in college, he had a tremendous junior season, ranking among the D-II leaders in doubles (20) as a hitter and strikeouts (103, ninth in the country) on the mound. All-conference as both a hitter and pitcher, he signed as a lefthander with the Orioles and had a strong debut in the short-season New York-Penn League, helping Aberdeen to its first-ever playoff berth. Also a talented vocalist, he sang the national anthem before an Ironbirds playoff game in September. The Orioles were careful with Brault's workload after he threw 78 innings in college, and he tossed more than four innings just three times. He showed a four-pitch mix, using a fastball, curve, slider and changeup. He pitches at 89-90 mph, touching 92, and uses an aggressive tempo. He pitched ahead in the count, kept the ball down and showed good sink. He repeats his delivery, which includes some deception because he hides the ball behind his body. His secondary pitches are fringe-average, with his slider being the best of the bunch. He likes to expand the zone with it. Brault's stuff could improve as he concentrates on pitching full-time, and he has solid athleticism. He fields his position and holds runners well and should begin 2014 in the low Class A Delmarva rotation. With solid command and a four-pitch mix, his ceiling is as a back-end starter.

Year	Club (League)	Class	W	L	ERA	G	GS	CG	SV	IP	H	HR	BB	SO	K/9	WHIP	AVG
2013	Aberdeen (NYP)	SS	1	2	2.09	12	12	0	0	43	35	1	12	38	8.0	1.09	.227
Minor League Totals			1	2	2.09	12	12	0	0	43	35	1	12	38	8.0	1.09	.227

15 DARIEL ALVAREZ, OF

Born: Nov. 7, 1988. **B-T:** R-R. **Ht.:** 6-0. **Wt.:** 195. **Signed:** Cuba, 2013. **Signed by:** Fred Ferreira.

One year after signing Henry Urrutia in July 2012, the Orioles added fellow Cuban outfielder Alvarez, signing him for $800,000. He played for Camaguey in Serie Nacional, Cuba's major league, from 2007-11, batting .297 with 37 home runs. After defecting in 2012, but before Major League Baseball had declared him a free agent, Alvarez played for Tuxpan of the Northwestern Mexican League, a six-team minor league affiliated with the Mexican League. He began playing in the Orioles system less than a month after signing, joining the Rookie-level Gulf Coast League club and earning a quick promotion to high Class A Frederick. In his first six games in the U.S., Alvarez went 13-for-24 (.542) with seven extra-base hits. His bat finally cooled when he advanced to Double-A Bowie, as he struggled against offspeed pitches. Some scouts expressed concern about Alvarez's uppercut swing, which they say doesn't stay in the hitting zone long enough. He has shown good bat speed and modest power potential, as well as a willingness to use the whole field, but his pitch recognition faltered against higher-level competition. Alvarez is an average runner and should be an above-average right fielder with an easy plus arm. (He even showcased for teams on the mound, but decided to remain a position player.) Alvarez has his skeptics and will try to answer them in 2014 at Double-A Bowie.

Year	Club (League)	Class	AVG	G	AB	R	H	2B	3B	HR	RBI	BB	SO	SB	CS	OBP	SLG
2013	Orioles (GCL)	R	.444	3	9	2	4	2	1	1	2	1	1	0	0	.500	1.222
	Frederick (CAR)	HiA	.436	10	39	5	17	2	0	2	7	2	1	1	2	.463	.641
	Bowie (EL)	AA	.194	9	31	2	6	0	0	1	1	1	9	0	0	.219	.290
Minor League Totals			.342	22	79	9	27	4	1	4	10	4	11	1	2	.373	.570

16 TRAVIS SEABROOKE, LHP

BA GRADE
45
HIGH

Born: Sept. 16, 1995. **B-T:** R-L. **Ht.:** 6-5. **Wt.:** 197. **Drafted:** HS—North Monaghan, Ontario, 2013 (5th round). **Signed by:** Tyler Moe.

Seabrooke's father Glen was a first-round pick in the 1985 NHL draft and spent three seasons with the Philadelphia Flyers. The second player drafted out of Canada in 2013, Travis signed for $291,800. He pitched briefly in the Rookie-level Gulf Coast League before the Orioles allowed him to join Canada's junior national team for the World Junior Championship in Taiwan in September. He lost in his lone outing to the host country. Seabrooke was one of the youngest players in the 2013 draft, and the Orioles see a lot of projection in him. He has a big frame and throws a fastball, curve and changeup, all of which have plus potential. His fastball sits around 88-91 mph and touches 93, and he should add velocity as he matures. His two secondary pitches are close, but he appears to have more confidence in the changeup. He worked with director of pitching development Rick Peterson to clean up his delivery and make it more fluid. The ability to repeat that delivery will prove key to his future success. Seabrooke will likely start 2014 in extended spring training, with an assignment to short-season Aberdeen thereafter.

Year	Club (League)	Class	W	L	ERA	G	GS	CG	SV	IP	H	HR	BB	SO	K/9	WHIP	AVG
2013	Orioles (GCL)	R	0	0	1.13	3	2	0	0	8	5	1	5	7	7.9	1.25	.185
Minor League Totals			0	0	1.13	3	2	0	0	8	5	1	5	7	7.9	1.25	.185

17 JON KELLER, RHP

Born: Aug. 8, 1992. **B-T:** R-R. **Ht.:** 6-4. **Wt.:** 220. **Drafted:** Tampa, 2013 (22nd round). **Signed by:** Jim Thrift.

The Mariners drafted Keller in the 11th round out of an Iowa high school in 2010, but opted to attend Nebraska instead. He transferred to Tampa after two seasons and led the Spartans to the Division II College World Series in 2013. He fell to the Orioles in the 22nd round due to medical questions and signability, though he ultimately signed for $100,000. He had surgery for thoracic outlet syndrome in spring 2012 and has dealt with an elbow strain in the past, but he made all his college starts in 2013 and finished the year healthy in instructional league. A strong-bodied power pitcher, Keller throws a fastball, slider and changeup and had one of the better fastballs in the 2013 draft class among college starters. He pitched often at 92-93 mph and touched 97 in a late-season outing at short-season Aberdeen. The Orioles believe in his slider, which has above-average potential. He has a good delivery, throws downhill and gets movement to spare on his fastball. Despite his stuff, however, he has never posted big strikeout numbers. Some see his future in the bullpen, and he would move faster in that role, but one scout compared him to Brandon Morrow and thought he had the potential to pitch toward the front of a rotation. Keller probably will begin 2014 in the low Class A Delmarva rotation to continue to refine his pitches.

Year	Club (League)	Class	W	L	ERA	G	GS	CG	SV	IP	H	HR	BB	SO	K/9	WHIP	AVG
2013	Orioles (GCL)	R	1	2	4.11	6	5	0	0	15	17	0	2	18	10.6	1.24	.274
	Aberdeen (NYP)	SS	1	0	3.00	1	0	0	0	3	1	0	1	2	6.0	0.67	.100
Minor League Totals			2	2	3.93	7	5	0	0	18	18	0	3	20	9.8	1.15	.250

18 CHRISTIAN WALKER, 1B

BA GRADE **45** HIGH

Born: March 28, 1991. **B-T:** R-R. **Ht.:** 6-0. **Wt.:** 220. **Drafted:** South Carolina, 2012 (4th round). **Signed by:** Chris Gale.

After playing a key role on three College World Series teams at South Carolina, Walker turned pro with the Orioles as a fourth-rounder in 2012. He spent his first full season in 2013 at three levels and batted .300 over 103 games to rank fourth among Orioles minor leaguers despite leveling off at Double-A. His two pro seasons ended in August with lower-back soreness, and he rehabbed during instructional league and is expected to be healthy for spring training. Walker is a solid righthanded hitter with gap-to-gap power right now. He keeps his bat in the zone a long time, recognizes pitches well and has good bat speed. He has a consistent approach and competes well from at-bat to at-bat. He can drive the ball to right and right-center field, but many scouts doubt that he'll hit for the power associated with the first-base profile. He needs to work on looking for particular pitches and better understanding counts and how pitchers are working him. Walker's defense at first needs work, though he made footwork improvements in 2013 and has average hands. He doesn't have the speed to move to the outfield and isn't a great athlete. Walker will go as far as his bat takes him, and in 2014 it will take him back to Bowie.

Year	Club (League)	Class	AVG	G	AB	R	H	2B	3B	HR	RBI	BB	SO	SB	CS	OBP	SLG
2012	Aberdeen (NYP)	SS	.284	22	81	12	23	5	0	2	9	10	14	2	1	.376	.420
2013	Delmarva (SAL)	LoA	.353	31	116	19	41	5	0	3	20	11	16	0	3	.420	.474
	Frederick (CAR)	HiA	.288	55	215	25	62	17	0	8	35	17	41	2	0	.343	.479
	Bowie (EL)	AA	.242	17	62	7	15	5	0	0	1	6	10	0	0	.319	.323
Minor League Totals			.297	125	474	63	141	32	0	13	65	44	81	4	4	.365	.447

19 PARKER BRIDWELL, RHP

BA GRADE **45** HIGH

Born: Aug. 2, 1991. **B-T:** R-R. **Ht.:** 6-4. **Wt.:** 207. **Drafted:** HS—Hereford, Texas, 2010 (9th round). **Signed by:** Ernie Jacobs.

A three-sport prep athlete, Bridwell drew interest from college football programs as a quarterback before the Orioles drafted him. He has lacked consistency since signing out of high school in 2010, and if he finds it he could rocket up this list. He repeated low Class A Delmarva in 2013 and improved his performance, leading the organization with 144 strikeouts in 143 innings. One scout said some nights Bridwell looks like he can pitch in Baltimore, citing an August start when he threw eight shutout innings of two-hit ball with no walks and 14 strikeouts. It was the most strikeouts by a Shorebirds starter since Erik Bedard fanned 14 in 2000. In the two starts before that outing, however, Bridwell gave up 12 runs with just 10 strikeouts. He works primarily off an 89-93 mph fastball that touches 95 and parks around 90 with life and sink. His changeup is solid-average, and his curveball has been below-average but has improved. His arm is quick, helping him get through a stab in his backswing that inhibits the consistency of his breaking ball. Sometimes he rushes and gets underneath the ball, and his lower half can be an issue. Bridwell's modest control and live arm portend a future move to the bullpen, but he has shown the durability to start. He'll move up to high Class A Frederick in 2014.

Year	Club (League)	Class	W	L	ERA	G	GS	CG	SV	IP	H	HR	BB	SO	K/9	WHIP	AVG
2010	Orioles (GCL)	R	0	0	5.40	2	2	0	0	2	1	0	3	4	21.6	2.40	.167
	Aberdeen (NYP)	SS	0	0	0.00	2	0	0	0	4	3	0	1	2	4.5	1.00	.214
2011	Aberdeen (NYP)	SS	2	5	4.53	12	11	0	0	54	56	2	22	57	9.6	1.45	.271
	Delmarva (SAL)	LoA	0	3	7.06	5	5	0	0	22	23	0	13	13	5.4	1.66	.271
2012	Delmarva (SAL)	LoA	5	9	5.98	23	22	1	0	114	122	15	63	71	5.6	1.62	.281
2013	Delmarva (SAL)	LoA	8	9	4.73	26	26	0	0	143	141	9	59	144	9.1	1.40	.255
Minor League Totals			15	26	5.22	70	66	1	0	338	346	26	161	291	7.7	1.50	.266

20 BRANDEN KLINE, RHP

BA GRADE **50** EXTREME

Born: Sept. 29, 1991. **B-T:** R-R. **Ht.:** 6-3. **Wt.:** 205. **Drafted:** Virginia, 2012 (2nd round). **Signed by:** Chris Gale.

The Red Sox drafted Kline out of a Frederick, Md., high school, but he held to his Virginia commitment and became an all-Atlantic Coast Conference closer in 2011. He started for the Cavaliers in 2012 and became the 65th overall pick in that year's draft, signing with the Orioles for $793,700. Kline could return to Frederick in 2014 with the Orioles' high Class A affiliate—if he's healthy. His 2013 season ended in May when he was injured during conditioning drills at low Class A Delmarva, and he had surgery in late May to repair a broken right ankle. He pitched in the Arizona Fall League to get more work, though he was hammered for 23 hits in 14 innings. Kline throws a fastball, slider and changeup. He has pitched at 88-92 mph as a starter, but his velocity plays up in shorter outings at 91-95, hinting at a return to his old college role. His fastball can be too straight from his high overhand arm slot, and his command right now is below-average. A good athlete who repeats his delivery, Kline has a strong slider and has shown aptitude since signing. He'll go home to Frederick for 2014 to get as many innings as possible.

Year	Club (League)	Class	W	L	ERA	G	GS	CG	SV	IP	H	HR	BB	SO	K/9	WHIP	AVG
2012	Aberdeen (NYP)	SS	0	0	4.50	4	4	0	0	12	12	1	4	12	9.0	1.33	.273
2013	Delmarva (SAL)	LoA	1	2	5.86	7	7	0	0	35	41	4	14	32	8.2	1.56	.289
Minor League Totals			1	2	5.51	11	11	0	0	47	53	5	18	44	8.4	1.50	.285

21 STEPHEN TARPLEY, LHP

BA GRADE **50** EXTREME

Born: Feb. 17, 1993. **B-T:** R-L. **Ht.:** 6-2. **Wt.:** 195. **Drafted:** Scottsdale (Ariz.) CC, 2013 (3rd round). **Signed by:** Jim Gillette.

An eighth-round pick of the Indians out of an Arizona high school in 2011, Tarpley chose to go to Southern California and made 13 starts as a freshman, going 5-3, 3.22 in 78 innings. He transferred to Scottsdale (Ariz.) CC so he would be eligible for the 2013 draft and posted a 2.35 ERA and 108 strikeouts (fourth-best in NJCAA) in 92 innings in a wood-bat junior college league. Tarpley signed for $525,000 as a third-round pick (98th overall) in the 2013 draft. He pitched mostly at 90-92 mph with a fastball that showed good life in the zone and touched 96. He also throws a curveball and changeup, but the Orioles took away his slider for now so he can improve his curveball. At times Tarpley needed several innings of work before his fastball velocity would rise to accustomed levels. With better extension in his delivery, he would have more consistent velocity and finish his breaking ball. Orioles officials want to see him cut loose more often and improve the tempo in his delivery. Tarpley has the stuff to start and should begin 2014 in the low Class A Delmarva rotation.

Year	Club (League)	Class	W	L	ERA	G	GS	CG	SV	IP	H	HR	BB	SO	K/9	WHIP	AVG
2013	Orioles (GCL)	R	0	1	2.14	7	7	0	0	21	20	0	3	25	10.7	1.10	.256
Minor League Totals			0	1	2.14	7	7	0	0	21	20	0	3	25	10.7	1.10	.256

22 OFELKY PERALTA, RHP

BA GRADE **50** EXTREME

Born: April 20, 1997. **B-T:** R-R. **Ht.:** 6-5. **Wt.:** 195. **Signed:** Dominican Republic, 2013. **Signed by:** Fred Ferreira.

The Orioles rarely have gotten as excited about a Dominican signing as they are about Peralta, and several club officials consider him one of the organization's top dozen or so prospects. He signed for $325,000 on Sept. 7, the same day veteran international scout Fred Ferreira saw him throw for the first time during a showcase at the Arias-Goodman academy in San Pedro de Macoris. Peralta had a dominant three-inning outing, throwing 93-95 mph and touching 97, and Ferreira didn't wait to see more. It's the largest bonus the organization ever has given a Dominican-born amateur, topping the $300,000 bonus received by Hector Veloz in July 2010. The Orioles had Peralta take his physical in Baltimore, something they also do with their top draft picks. After that he went to instructional league and impressed club personnel with his bullpen sessions. He showed a free-and-easy delivery, generating plus velocity with minimal effort. Peralta's secondary stuff is rudimentary, but he showed enough ability to spin a breaking ball to dream on its future potential. Scouts outside the organization are less enthused about Peralta, but the Orioles are excited about his live arm. He probably will begin his pro career in the Dominican Summer League in 2014.

Year	Club (League)	Class	W	L	ERA	G	GS	CG	SV	IP	H	HR	BB	SO	K/9	WHIP	AVG
2013	Did not play—Signed 2014 contract																

23 MYCHAL GIVENS, RHP

BA GRADE **45** HIGH

Born: May 13, 1990. **B-T:** R-R. **Ht.:** 6-1. **Wt.:** 210. **Drafted:** HS—Tampa, 2009 (2nd round). **Signed by:** John Martin.

When the Orioles drafted Givens in the second round (54th pick) in 2009 and signed him for $800,000, they saw the potential to develop a strong, athletic shortstop who could grow into some power. But Givens didn't develop as a hitter, batting just .247 with a .311 slugging percentage in three seasons, mostly at low Class A Delmarva. He had pitched a bit in high school, so the Orioles moved him to the mound in 2013. The conversion went well, though he experienced some tenderness early on, missed a month and was limited to 16 innings at Delmarva through June. The Orioles were conservative with Givens, giving him time between bullpen outings, and in the second half his stuff improved. Throwing from the low three-quarters slot he used in high school, he pitched off an upper-80s fastball that ultimately sat 92 mph later in the year and touched 94 in instructional league. His low slot gives his fastball heavy sink. He throws his flat slider hard in the 84-86 mph range, and his changeup progressed as well. Givens has taken to the switch and has a great desire to be a success on the mound. He'll work in a relief role and could move quickly now that he's made the conversion, with time at Double-A Bowie likely in 2014.

Year	Club (League)	Class	W	L	ERA	G	GS	CG	SV	IP	H	HR	BB	SO	K/9	WHIP	AVG
2013	Delmarva (SAL)	LoA	2	3	4.22	28	0	0	3	43	34	1	19	36	7.6	1.24	.219
Minor League Totals			2	3	4.22	28	0	0	3	43	34	1	19	36	7.6	1.24	.219

Year	Club (League)	Class	AVG	G	AB	R	H	2B	3B	HR	RBI	BB	SO	SB	CS	OBP	SLG
2010	Delmarva (SAL)	LoA	.222	7	18	2	4	0	0	0	4	5	4	1	1	.444	.222
	Orioles (GCL)	R	.207	7	29	2	6	2	0	0	2	0	4	0	0	.207	.276
	Aberdeen (NYP)	SS	.364	8	33	8	12	3	0	3	5	6	2	2	1	.488	.727
	Frederick (CAR)	HiA	.500	1	4	2	2	0	0	0	1	0	0	0	1	.600	.500
2011	Delmarva (SAL)	LoA	.195	57	210	21	41	7	0	0	15	11	35	6	6	.260	.229
	Aberdeen (NYP)	SS	.279	74	276	30	77	9	2	1	30	30	40	14	5	.361	.337
2012	Delmarva (SAL)	LoA	.243	100	337	43	82	15	0	2	27	39	49	13	8	.330	.306
Minor League Totals			.247	254	907	108	224	36	2	6	84	91	134	36	22	.331	.311

24 OLIVER DRAKE, RHP

BA GRADE
45
HIGH

Born: Jan. 13, 1987. **B-T:** R-R. **Ht.:** 6-4. **Wt.:** 230. **Drafted:** Navy, 2008 (43rd round). **Signed by:** Dean Albany.

An organization veteran, Drake earned a spot on the 40-man roster after the 2011 season. He began the 2012 season on the disabled list, pitched just 18 innings and had surgery in August to clean up the labrum and shrink a capsule in his shoulder. Outrighted off the 40-man in November 2012, Drake began 2013 in extended spring training before heading to Double-A Bowie in June. He pitched well in short stints, as the Orioles meticulously planned his outings and made sure he had plenty of rest. Proving he was healthy, Drake pitched with a 90-93 mph fastball that peaked at 94. He threw his second-best pitch, his split-finger fastball, but no breaking balls after the surgery. Unlike many pitchers who use the split as a chase pitch, Drake sometimes throws it for strikes. Still working to develop a third pitch, probably a slider, he projects as a reliever. He has excellent makeup and pitched aggressively in his return. Drake probably will begin 2014 in Triple-A Norfolk's bullpen.

Year	Club (League)	Class	W	L	ERA	G	GS	CG	SV	IP	H	HR	BB	SO	K/9	WHIP	AVG
2008	Bluefield (APP)	R	1	0	0.77	7	0	0	0	12	7	1	2	11	8.5	0.77	.167
	Aberdeen (NYP)	SS	0	0	0.87	5	0	0	1	10	9	0	1	13	11.3	0.97	.214
2009	Delmarva (SAL)	LoA	8	9	4.34	25	24	0	0	131	138	6	42	104	7.2	1.38	.277
2010	Frederick (CAR)	HiA	6	6	4.36	24	21	0	0	128	135	19	37	100	7.0	1.34	.272
2011	Norfolk (IL)	AAA	0	0	0.00	1	0	0	0	2	1	0	1	2	9.0	1.00	.143
	Frederick (CAR)	HiA	8	3	2.14	14	13	2	0	97	78	1	18	80	7.4	0.99	.224
	Bowie (EL)	AA	3	5	5.20	12	12	2	0	64	77	8	24	47	6.6	1.58	.292
2012	Bowie (EL)	AA	1	1	1.50	3	3	0	0	18	8	1	4	15	7.5	0.67	.125
2013	Bowie (EL)	AA	3	0	1.74	19	0	0	8	31	19	1	13	38	11.0	1.03	.173
Minor League Totals			30	24	3.58	110	73	4	9	492	472	37	142	410	7.5	1.25	.252

25 TREY MANCINI, 1B

Born: March 18, 1992. **B-T:** R-R. **Ht.:** 6-4. **Wt.:** 215. **Drafted:** Notre Dame, 2013 (8th round). **Signed by:** Kirk Fredriksson.

Mancini had a strong 2013, starting in the spring at Notre Dame. He led the Big East Conference in batting (.389) and total bases (138) while ranking second in slugging (.603) en route to being an eighth-round pick. After signing, he was short-season Aberdeen's best hitter, setting a franchise record for hits (84), ranking second in the New York-Penn League in batting (.328) and fourth in on-base percentage (.382). Mancini uses the whole field well with a righthanded, line-drive swing that produced gap-to-gap power. Sometimes he got too aggressive at the plate and got himself out. The Orioles asked him to stride into the pitch, something he had not been doing, and it created better balance and timing. He showed home run power in batting practice and now needs to carry that into the game more consistently. He was a clubhouse leader for an Aberdeen team that made the playoffs for the first time. He played average defense with good footwork and hands at first base. With below-average speed and a slightly-below-average arm, he is locked in at first. A first shot at full-season ball begins at low Class A Delmarva in 2014.

Year	Club (League)	Class	AVG	G	AB	R	H	2B	3B	HR	RBI	BB	SO	SB	CS	OBP	SLG
2013	Aberdeen (NYP)	SS	.328	68	256	43	84	18	2	3	35	20	43	3	1	.382	.449
Minor League Totals			.328	68	256	43	84	18	2	3	35	20	43	3	1	.382	.449

26 JONAH HEIM, C

BA GRADE
45
EXTREME

Born: June 27, 1995. **B-T:** B-R. **Ht.:** 6-3. **Wt.:** 198. **Drafted:** HS—Amherst, N.Y, 2013 (4th round). **Signed by:** Kirk Fredriksson.

The Orioles consider the long, lean, switch-hitting Heim a sleeper after making him a fourth-round pick in 2013, taking him from a high school in the Buffalo suburb of Amherst, N.Y. He received a slot bonus of $389,700 to forgo his Michigan State commitment and reported to the Rookie-level Gulf Coast League, where he was a bit overmatched offensively. Heim is solid defensively but scouts have some questions about his bat, and he needs to add strength. He receives well with strong hands and flashed pop times of 1.92 seconds on throws to second base, showing a potential plus arm with accuracy as he gets on top of the ball well. Heim has a quiet setup and decent blocking skills. Right now he shows little differentiation from either side at the plate, though scouts liked his power more from the right side as an amateur. He has average bat speed with a swing that he needs to shorten. Heim has a solid body and room to fill out, though he's already a below-average runner. He encouraged the Orioles in instructional league by making hard contact at the plate. With 2013 second-rounder Chance Sisco ahead of him, Heim will compete for a spot at low Class A Delmarva in 2014 but probably will be held back in extended spring training for a short-season Aberdeen assignment.

Year	Club (League)	Class	AVG	G	AB	R	H	2B	3B	HR	RBI	BB	SO	SB	CS	OBP	SLG
2013	Orioles (GCL)	R	.185	27	81	8	15	5	0	0	4	10	13	1	1	.275	.247
Minor League Totals			.185	27	81	8	15	5	0	0	4	10	13	1	1	.275	.247

27 CHRIS JONES, LHP

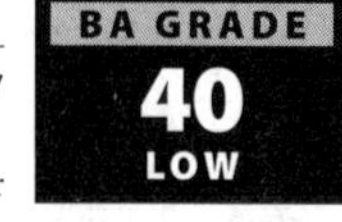

Born: Sept. 19, 1988. **B-T:** L-L. **Ht.:** 6-2. **Wt.:** 205. **Drafted:** HS—Tampa, 2007 (15th round). **Signed by:** Mike Soper (Indians).

The Orioles acquired Jones from the Braves in an April 2013 deal involving reliever Luis Ayala. Jones has had success against lefthanders in his career, and he did so again in 2013, holding them to a .205 average with zero homers in 123 at-bats at Double-A and Triple-A, though he'll have to throw more strikes versus lefties after walking 12 percent of them. The Orioles see him as more than just a lefty specialist, as he's shown durability in the form of successful multi-inning outings. Jones has some effort in his delivery but also some deception. His fastball touches 92 mph and sits 89-90 to go with a curveball and changeup. None of the three stands out, but Jones has learned to mix and match, and he earned a spot on the Orioles 40-man roster. He'll have the chance to win a bullpen job in spring training but likely will begin 2014 back at Triple-A Norfolk.

Year	Club (League)	Class	W	L	ERA	G	GS	CG	SV	IP	H	HR	BB	SO	K/9	WHIP	AVG
2007	Indians (GCL)	R	0	0	2.45	1	1	0	0	4	4	0	2	5	12.3	1.64	.267
	Lake County (SAL)	LoA	0	1	6.75	1	1	0	0	4	4	1	3	2	4.5	1.75	.286
2008	Indians (GCL)	R	3	4	3.10	11	10	0	0	52	44	4	20	36	6.2	1.22	.229
2009	Lake County (SAL)	LoA	5	3	4.07	12	7	0	0	55	60	1	19	50	8.1	1.43	.276
	Kinston (CAR)	HiA	1	1	7.50	4	4	0	0	18	22	5	8	21	10.5	1.67	.306
2010	Lake County (MWL)	LoA	2	2	2.86	7	1	0	1	22	16	2	2	20	8.2	0.82	—
	Kinston (CAR)	HiA	4	3	2.39	31	0	0	2	68	60	2	27	65	8.6	1.29	.234
2011	Kinston (CAR)	HiA	7	1	3.36	43	0	0	0	72	65	6	30	66	8.2	1.31	.240
2012	Mississippi (SL)	AA	2	5	3.90	45	0	0	2	60	69	1	19	61	9.2	1.47	.285
2013	Mississippi (SL)	AA	0	0	13.50	1	0	0	0	1	2	0	2	1	6.8	3.00	.333
	Bowie (EL)	AA	0	0	2.57	4	0	0	1	7	8	0	0	6	7.7	1.14	.286
	Norfolk (IL)	AAA	4	4	2.67	31	2	0	1	71	72	3	34	47	6.0	1.50	.268
Minor League Totals			28	24	3.42	191	26	0	7	434	426	25	166	380	7.9	1.36	.256

28 JOSH STINSON, RHP

Born: March 14, 1988. **B-T:** R-R. **Ht.:** 6-4. **Wt.:** 210. **Drafted:** HS—Shreveport, La., 2006 (37th round). **Signed by:** Benny Latino (Mets).

Stinson has made cameo appearances in the major leagues in each of the last three seasons, with three different clubs. The Mets signed him for $125,000 as a 37th-round pick in 2006, and while he was far from an immediate hit, he reached the majors with them in 2011. The Mets lost him on a waiver claim to the Brewers in April 2012, and he had his best year as a starter at Double-A Huntsville, earning a September callup to Milwaukee. Again the next spring, teams tried to sneak him off the 40-man roster and lost him on waiver claims. It happened twice, as the Athletics claimed him from Milwaukee on March 29 and the Orioles claimed him from the A's a week later. He led Triple-A Norfolk in innings in 2013, then pitched well again during a big league callup in September. Stinson throws hard, with a sinker in the 89-93 mph range, and he reaches 95 out of the bullpen with his four-seamer. He uses a hard curveball as his out-pitch that reaches 80 mph even as a starter, but his firm, fringy changeup leaves him vulnerable to lefthanders. He's developed a hard, moderately effective cutter to try to combat them. His fastball and cutter tend to be flat when elevated, leaving him homer prone, as was the case in his lone big league start in 2013, a four-homer outing against the Blue Jays. He'll try to shed the 4-A label in spring training with the Orioles.

Year	Club (League)	Class	W	L	ERA	G	GS	CG	SV	IP	H	HR	BB	SO	K/9	WHIP	AVG
2006	Mets (GCL)	R	1	2	2.00	9	4	0	0	27	27	0	5	14	4.7	1.19	.273
	Hagerstown (SAL)	LoA	0	1	1.35	3	3	0	0	13	11	0	4	5	3.4	1.13	.239
2007	Savannah (SAL)	LoA	3	11	4.86	26	21	0	0	109	131	13	33	52	4.3	1.50	.294
2008	Savannah (SAL)	LoA	3	6	3.52	21	6	0	3	72	78	7	32	46	5.8	1.53	.280
	St. Lucie (FSL)	HiA	0	2	6.14	7	2	0	0	15	17	0	5	14	8.6	1.50	.293
2009	Savannah (SAL)	LoA	2	2	3.61	25	1	0	2	42	45	1	10	49	10.4	1.30	.287
	St. Lucie (FSL)	HiA	3	1	1.98	25	0	0	6	36	22	0	19	35	8.7	1.13	.168

2010	Binghamton (EL)	AA	9	3	4.24	32	14	0	1	110	108	7	50	68	5.5	1.43	.260
	Buffalo (IL)	AAA	2	2	2.57	4	4	1	0	28	22	5	8	21	6.8	1.07	.212
2011	Buffalo (IL)	AAA	3	7	7.44	13	13	0	0	62	77	7	33	32	4.7	1.78	.312
	Binghamton (EL)	AA	4	3	3.99	27	2	0	6	47	46	1	16	39	7.4	1.31	.257
	New York (NL)	MAJ	0	2	6.92	14	0	0	1	13	14	1	7	8	5.5	1.62	.286
2012	Huntsville (SL)	AA	11	9	3.16	29	24	1	1	145	167	7	71	91	5.6	1.64	.291
	Milwaukee (NL)	MAJ	0	0	0.96	6	1	0	0	9	7	1	5	3	2.9	1.29	.212
2013	Frederick (CAR)	HiA	0	0	4.50	1	0	0	0	2	4	0	0	1	4.5	2.00	.400
	Norfolk (IL)	AAA	7	6	3.78	23	23	0	0	131	126	11	54	87	6.0	1.37	.257
	Baltimore (AL)	MAJ	0	0	3.18	11	1	0	0	17	10	4	3	12	6.4	0.76	.169
Major League Totals			0	2	3.89	31	2	0	1	39	31	6	15	23	5.3	1.17	.220
Minor League Totals			48	55	3.95	245	117	2	19	840	881	59	340	554	5.9	1.45	.272

29 GLYNN DAVIS, OF

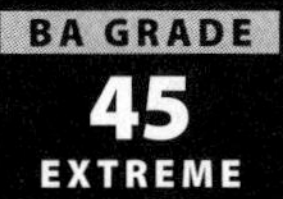

Born: Dec. 7, 1991. **B-T:** R-R. **Ht.:** 6-3. **Wt.:** 185. **Signed:** CC of Baltimore County-Catonsville (Md.), 2010 (NDFA). **Signed by:** Dean Albany/Chris Gale.

The Orioles signed Davis as a nondrafted free agent in August 2010 after he had played junior-college ball near Baltimore and after he had a big summer with their Youse's Orioles scout team. Davis was hardly scouted as an amateur, but still the Orioles followed him. When he led the Youse's team to a national championship, he began popping up on other teams' radars, but the Orioles got to him first, and they felt like they were getting a top-10 rounds talent. Davis has yet to produce as a pro, however. Bothered at times by a hamstring injury in the first half of the 2013 season, he regressed across the board at high Class A Frederick. A clear plus-plus runner, Davis chased too many breaking balls in the dirt and needs to work on his pitch recognition skills and staying more square to the ball. Showing very little power, he will need to become a high on-base guy to realize his potential. With good range and a solid-average arm, he can stay in center field and is a solid defender. One scout questioned if he worked hard enough, so 2014 will be a big year for Davis as he takes another stab at Frederick.

Year	Club (League)	Class	AVG	G	AB	R	H	2B	3B	HR	RBI	BB	SO	SB	CS	OBP	SLG
2011	Orioles (GCL)	R	.435	6	23	4	10	2	0	1	2	4	3	1	1	.519	.652
	Aberdeen (NYP)	SS	.271	62	255	34	69	14	0	1	14	25	53	23	9	.337	.337
	Frederick (CAR)	HiA	.250	1	4	0	1	0	0	0	0	0	1	0	0	.250	.250
2012	Delmarva (SAL)	LoA	.252	101	397	53	100	16	2	0	25	51	91	29	9	.342	.302
	Frederick (CAR)	HiA	.256	22	82	11	21	1	1	0	4	12	25	8	1	.358	.293
2013	Frederick (CAR)	HiA	.234	97	364	42	85	17	3	2	32	43	74	19	7	.316	.313
Minor League Totals			.254	289	1125	144	286	50	6	4	77	135	247	80	27	.337	.320

30 JASON GURKA, LHP

BA GRADE
40
MEDIUM

Born: Jan. 10, 1988. **B-T:** L-L. **Ht.:** 6-0. **Wt.:** 170. **Drafted:** Angelina (Texas) JC, 2008 (15th round). **Signed by:** Ralph Garr Jr.

A 15th-round pick out of Angelina (Texas) JC in 2008, Gurka has made 109 career pro appearances, all but one out of the bullpen. He has gotten on the Orioles radar with three straight sub-3.00 ERA seasons, the most recent in 2013 at Double-A Bowie. Baltimore considered him for a 40-man roster spot in November after he pitched in the Arizona Fall League, but ultimately the club did not add him. Gurka has averaged 10.3 strikeouts per nine innings in his career with a solid, high-spin curve as a putaway pitch, but he has walked 30 over 60 innings at the Double-A level. Gurka throws a 90-91 mph fastball to go with the mid-70s curve and decent changeup. His arm speed on his change is solid, and that pitch made strides in 2013. He works with easy arm action but sometimes flies open a bit, and the inconsistent mechanics can lead to high pitch counts and too many walks. A hamstring strain ended his regular season in mid-July but he showed he was healthy in the AFL. He'll have a shot at the Triple-A Norfolk bullpen in 2014.

Year	Club (League)	Class	W	L	ERA	G	GS	CG	SV	IP	H	HR	BB	SO	K/9	WHIP	AVG
2008	Bluefield (APP)	R	0	0	9.00	2	0	0	0	3	5	1	0	5	15.0	1.67	.357
2009	Did not play—Injured																
2010	Aberdeen (NYP)	SS	2	2	4.93	22	0	0	0	38	27	4	19	46	10.8	1.20	.200
2011	Delmarva (SAL)	LoA	2	0	2.52	13	0	0	0	25	28	4	2	33	11.9	1.20	.277
	Frederick (CAR)	HiA	1	1	3.18	20	0	0	1	28	19	2	9	34	10.8	0.99	.192
2012	Frederick (CAR)	HiA	1	2	2.18	20	1	0	1	45	30	1	12	43	8.5	0.93	.191
	Bowie (EL)	AA	2	3	3.60	12	0	0	1	20	19	3	12	22	9.9	1.55	.250
2013	Bowie (EL)	AA	2	2	2.95	20	0	0	4	40	35	2	18	46	10.4	1.34	.243
Minor League Totals			10	10	3.29	109	1	0	7	200	163	17	72	229	10.3	1.18	.225

Boston Red Sox

BY ALEX SPEIER

As the Red Sox tried to emerge from the wreckage of a last-place finish in 2012, they did so with a mission of building a contender for 2013 in a fashion that did nothing to jeopardize what appeared to be a promising future.

With a talented ensemble of minor leaguers reaching the upper levels, the team signed seven free agents—none of whom required the sacrifice of a draft pick—to compete at a time when those prospects were expected to be in the finishing stages of their development. The idea was to construct a competitive team for 2013 while buying time for the arrival of what general manager Ben Cherington described as "the next great Red Sox team."

Rather unexpectedly, the 2013 Red Sox ended up being a great team. The return to form of a core that included David Ortiz, Dustin Pedroia, Jon Lester, Jacoby Ellsbury and Clay Buchholz was buttressed by strong performances by virtually every player the Red Sox added.

The result was a team whose strong performances ran more than 25 deep, a versatile and deep roster that ultimately proved the best team in baseball, winning 97 games and marching through October for a World Series championship, the franchise's third in a decade.

Yet as captivating a run as the major league squad offered, the activity beneath that surface proved nearly as compelling. The Red Sox enjoyed a year of striking progress in their farm system, with top prospects taking steps forward in lockstep.

Both shortstop Xander Bogaerts and righthander Brandon Workman assumed significant postseason roles, but behind them, Boston's top prospects produced a wealth of all-star seasons across levels that suggested the possibility of homegrown depth in the coming years.

The emergence of Bogaerts (with 2012 first-rounder Deven Marrero not far behind) rendered Jose Iglesias expendable at the trade deadline. Third baseman Garin Cecchini led the minors with a .443 on-base percentage, giving the Red Sox a depth of talent on the left side of the infield that few can rival.

Center fielder Jackie Bradley joins Bogaerts as a player who could be ready to assume an everyday big league role as soon as Opening Day. Behind Workman, the organization featured three potential big league starters (righthanders Allen Webster, Matt Barnes and Anthony Ranaudo) in the Triple-A Pawtucket rotation by season's end.

The strength of the system runs far deeper than just Triple-A, however. High Class A Salem had a loaded roster all season. Top pitching prospect Henry Owens, a southpaw, thrived there before moving up to Double-A, while up-the-middle players such as catcher Blake Swihart and second baseman Mookie Betts helped Salem win the Carolina League title.

The organization also added high-ceiling amateurs in 2013, taking lefthander Trey Ball with the No. 7 overall pick in the draft and a potentially elite bat in Dominican third baseman Rafael Devers.

The Red Sox system is deep in many areas but does lack a prototype corner bat, but beyond that, athletic, well-rounded players abound. Led by Bogaerts, the next wave of Boston prospects is impressive enough to keep the club close to its 2013 perch for some time.

KEN BABBITT

A homegrown core, led by Dustin Pedroia, helped lead the Red Sox to another title

TOP PROSPECTS OF THE DECADE

Year	Player, Pos.	2013 Org.
2004	Hanley Ramirez, ss	Dodgers
2005	Hanley Ramirez, ss	Dodgers
2006	Andy Marte, 3b	Angels
2007	Daisuke Matsuzaka, rhp	Mets
2008	Clay Buchholz, rhp	Red Sox
2009	Lars Anderson, 1b	White Sox
2010	Ryan Westmoreland, of	Out of baseball
2011	Jose Iglesias, ss	Tigers
2012	Will Middlebrooks, 3b	Red Sox
2013	Xander Bogaerts, ss	Red Sox

ORGANIZATION OVERVIEW

General Manager: Ben Cherington. **Farm Director:** Ben Crockett. **Scouting Director:** Amiel Sawdaye.

Class	Team	League	W	L	PCT	Finish	Manager
Majors	Boston Red Sox	American	97	65	.599	1st (15)	John Farrell
Triple-A	Pawtucket Red Sox	International	80	63	.559	2nd (14)	Gary DiSarcina
Double-A	Portland Sea Dogs	Eastern	68	73	.472	t-8th (12)	Kevin Boles
High A	Salem Red Sox	Carolina	76	64	.543	3rd (8)	Billy McMillon
Low A	Greenville Drive	South Atlantic	51	87	.370	14th (14)	Carlos Febles
Short-season	Lowell Spinners	New York-Penn	40	33	.548	5th (14)	Bruce Crabbe
Rookie	GCL Red Sox	Gulf Coast	35	25	.583	3rd (16)	Darren Fenster
Overall 2013 Minor League Record			**350**	**345**	**.504**	**t-10 (30)**	

THIS YEAR'S TOP 30

No.	Player, Pos.	Grade
1.	Xander Bogaerts, ss/3b	70/Low
2.	Henry Owens, lhp	60/High
3.	Jackie Bradley, of	55/Medium
4.	Allen Webster, rhp	55/High
5.	Blake Swihart, c	55/High
6.	Garin Cecchini, 3b	55/High
7.	Mookie Betts, 2b	55/High
8.	Brandon Workman, rhp	50/Safe
9.	Matt Barnes, rhp	55/High
10.	Trey Ball, lhp	65/Extreme
11.	Anthony Ranaudo, rhp	55/High
12.	Christian Vazquez, c	50/High
13.	Manuel Margot, of	55/Extreme
14.	Brian Johnson, lhp	50/High
15.	Deven Marrero, ss	50/High
16.	Bryce Brentz, of	50/High
17.	Drake Britton, lhp	45/Low
18.	Wendell Rijo, 2b	50/High
19.	Teddy Stankiewicz, rhp	50/High
20.	Rafael Devers, 3b	55/Extreme
21.	Cody Kukuk, lhp	50/High
22.	Jamie Callahan, rhp	50/High
23.	Daniel McGrath, lhp	45/High
24.	Simon Mercedes, rhp	50/Extreme
25.	Dan Butler, c	40/Low
26.	Travis Shaw, 1b	45/High
27.	Javier Guerra, ss	50/Extreme
28.	Tzu-Wei Lin, ss	50/Extreme
29.	Alex Wilson, rhp	40/Low
30.	Sean Coyle, 2b	50/Extreme

LAST YEAR'S TOP 30

No.	Player, Pos.	Status
1.	Xander Bogaerts, ss	No. 1
2.	Jackie Bradley, of	No. 3
3.	Matt Barnes, rhp	No. 9
4.	Allen Webster, rhp	No. 4
5.	Henry Owens, lhp	No. 2
6.	Blake Swihart, c	No. 5
7.	Garin Cecchini, 3b	No. 6
8.	Bryce Brentz, of	No. 16
9.	Jose Iglesias, ss	(Tigers)
10.	Deven Marrero, ss	No. 15
11.	Drake Britton, lhp	No. 17
12.	Brandon Workman, rhp	No. 8
13.	Brandon Jacobs, of	(White Sox)
14.	Anthony Ranaudo, rhp	No. 11
15.	Brian Johnson, lhp	No. 14
16.	Tzu-Wei Lin, ss	No. 28
17.	Jose Vinicio, ss	Dropped out
18.	Alex Wilson, rhp	No. 29
19.	Christian Vazquez, c	No. 12
20.	Manuel Margot, of	No. 13
21.	Pat Light, rhp	Dropped out
22.	Frank Montas, rhp	(White Sox)
23.	Travis Shaw, 1b/3b	No. 26
24.	Sean Coyle, 2b	No. 30
25.	Keury de la Cruz, of	Dropped out
26.	Ty Buttrey, rhp	Dropped out
27.	Cody Kukuk, lhp	No. 21
28.	Simon Mercedes, rhp	No. 24
29.	Stolmy Pimentel, rhp	(Pirates)
30.	Miguel Pena, lhp	Dropped out

BEST TOOLS

Best Hitter for Average	Garin Cecchini
Best Power Hitter	Xander Bogaerts
Best Strike-Zone Discipline	Garin Cecchini
Fastest Baserunner	Bryan Hudson
Best Athlete	Mookie Betts
Best Fastball	Matt Barnes
Best Curveball	Brandon Workman
Best Slider	Allen Webster
Best Changeup	Henry Owens
Best Control	Brandon Workman
Best Defensive Catcher	Christian Vazquez
Best Defensive Infielder	Deven Marrero
Best Infield Arm	Deven Marrero
Best Defensive Outfielder	Jackie Bradley
Best Outfield Arm	Jackie Bradley

TOP 15 PLAYERS 25 AND UNDER

No.	Player, Pos. (Age)	Peak Level
1.	Xander Bogaerts, ss/3b (21)	Majors
2.	Henry Owens, lhp (21)	Double-A
3.	Jackie Bradley, of (23)	Majors
4.	Allen Webster, rhp (24)	Majors
5.	Blake Swihart, c (21)	High Class A
6.	Will Middlebrooks, 3b (25)	Majors
7.	Garin Cecchini, 3b (22)	Double-A
8.	Mookie Betts, 2b (21)	High Class A
9.	Rubby de la Rosa, rhp (25)	Majors
10.	Brandon Workman, rhp (25)	Majors
11.	Matt Barnes, rhp (23)	Double-A
12.	Trey Ball, lhp (19)	Rookie
13.	Anthony Ranaudo, rhp (24)	Triple-A
14.	Christian Vazquez, c (23)	Triple-A
15.	Manuel Margot, of (19)	Short-season

MINOR LEAGUE DEPTH CHART

BOSTON RED SOX

TOP 2014 ROOKIE: Xander Bogaerts, ss. Expect growing pains at some point, but expect them to be brief for one of game's brightest prospects.

BREAKOUT PROSPECT: Rafael Devers, 3b. A scintillating instructional league showing in 2013 could vault him to the Rookie-level Gulf Coast League in 2014.

SLEEPER: Pat Light, rhp. The 2012 sandwich pick had a year lost to injury in 2013, but he impressed in instructional league, retaining his mid- to high-90s fastball with sink.

SOURCE OF TOP 30 TALENT			
Homegrown	**29**	**Acquired**	**1**
College	10	Trades	1
Junior college	1	Rule 5 draft	0
High school	9	Independent leagues	0
Nondrafted free agents	1	Free agents/waivers	0
International	8		

LF
Garin Cecchini (6)
Bryce Brentz (16)
Alex Hassan
Keury de la Cruz
Nick Longhi
Kolbrin Vitek

CF
Jackie Bradley (3)
Manuel Margot (13)
Henry Ramos
Luis Alejandro Basabe
Jordon Austin

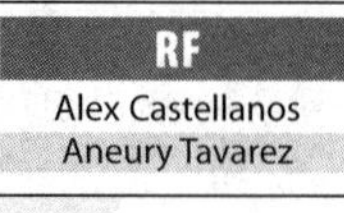

RF
Alex Castellanos
Aneury Tavarez

3B
Rafael Devers (20)
Victor Acosta

SS
Xander Bogaerts (1)
Deven Marrero (15)
Javier Guerra (27)
Tzu-Wei Lin (28)
Jose Vinicio

2B
Mookie Betts (7)
Wendell Rijo (18)
Sean Coyle (30)
Brock Holt
Heiker Meneses

1B
Travis Shaw (26)
Michael Almanzar
Jon Denney

C
Blake Swihart (5)
Christian Vazquez (12)
Dan Butler (25)

LHP	
LHSP	**LHRP**
Henry Owens (2)	Drake Britton (17)
Trey Ball (10)	Cody Kukuk (21)
Brian Johnson (14)	Chris Hernandez
Daniel McGrath (23)	
Corey Littrell	
Miguel Pena	

RHP	
RHSP	**RHRP**
Allen Webster (4)	Jamie Callahan (22)
Brandon Workman (8)	Simon Mercedes (24)
Matt Barnes (9)	Alex Wilson (29)
Anthony Ranaudo (11)	Joe Gunkel
Teddy Stankiewicz (19)	Pat Light
Ty Buttrey	Rafael Hinojosa
Sergio Gomez	Myles Smith
Dioscar Romero	Chris Martin
	Noe Ramirez
	Kyle Martin
	Matt Price
	Madison Younginer

DRAFT ANALYSIS

2013

BONUSES: $6.2 MILLION

BEST PURE HITTER: OF Nick Longhi (30) could become an above-average hitter, with an easy swing, quick bat and an ability to use the whole field. He faces questions about his ability to hit for power in games but has above-average raw power.

BEST POWER HITTER: C Jonathan Denney (3) has natural strength in his 6-foot-2, 205-pound frame and plus raw power, especially to his pull side. His hitting approach remains raw, as he is still learning to hit and adjusting to quality breaking stuff.

FASTEST RUNNER: OF Bryan Hudson (15) did not get many looks this spring but is a well above-average runner with a quick first step. He is working on getting out of the box quicker. NDFA OF Jervenski Johnson from Louisiana can run the 60-yard dash in 6.4 seconds.

BEST DEFENSIVE PLAYER: SS Mauricio Dubon (26) is a former soccer player who grew up in Honduras and moved to California during high school. He has great body control and feet, soft hands and the ability to throw from all angles.

BEST FASTBALL: Physical 6-foot-5, 225-pound RHP Joe Gunkel (18) was the talk of instructional league after showing a 90-94 mph fastball with life and command from a low arm slot. RHP Myles Smith (4) can touch 97 mph, and RHP Teddy Stankiewicz (2) can touch 96.

BEST SECONDARY PITCH: LHP Corey Littrell (5) has a plus changeup that flashes even better. Stankiewicz can get caught between two breaking balls at times, but his slider has plus potential. LHP Trey Ball (1) has the makings of a plus curveball.

BEST PRO DEBUT: Gunkel struck out 43 percent of the New York-Penn League hitters he faced, with a nearly 11-1 strikeout-walk ratio and 1.29 ERA in 20 innings. RHP Kyle Martin (9) had an inconsistent arm slot and velocity at Texas A&M. Boston raised his slot, and the 6-foot-6 Martin's velocity returned to 91-95 mph, and he registered a 1.25 ERA at two stops.

BEST ATHLETE: A lean 6-foot-6, 185-pound athlete, Ball is a plus runner and can dunk a basketball. RHP Jalen Williams (16) has a low-90s fastball and was committed to Nicholls State as a wide receiver. At 6-foot-5, 190 pounds, Johnson has rare athleticism and was committed to Southeast Louisiana as a football/baseball athlete.

MOST INTRIGUING BACKGROUND: OF Jeff Driskel (29) was Florida's starting quarterback this fall but was lost for the season to a leg injury. LHP Gabe Speier (19) is the nephew of Reds bench coach and former major leaguer Chris. Littrell's father Jack played in the minors and his grandfather played in the majors.

CLOSEST TO THE MAJORS: Gunkel as a reliever and Littrell as a starter.

BEST LATE-ROUND PICK: Longhi netted $400,000, the most of four over-slot signings after the 10th round; Gunkel for under slot.

THE ONE WHO GOT AWAY: A knee injury pushed OF Ryan Boldt (22) out of first-round consideration. He's now at Nebraska.

ASSESSMENT: Boston invested heavily in building pitching depth in this draft, taking Ball as the first high school lefthander in the draft, and Denney, who looked like a first-round pick heading into the spring.

2012

BONUSES: $7.9 MILLION

SS Deven Marrero (1). LHP Brian Johnson (1) and RHP Jamie Callahan (2) had solid first full seasons. The Sox may rue not signing SS Alex Bregman (29).

GRADE: C

2011

BONUSES: $11.0 MILLION

OF Jackie Bradley (1s) reached MLB first from this deep class, leading four other Top 10 prospects such as LHP Henry Owens (1s) and 2B Mookie Betts (5).

GRADE: B+

2010

BONUSES: $10.7 MILLION

RHP Brandon Workman (2) was a key arm for the 2013 World Series champs. RHP Anthony Ranaudo (1s), 3B Garin Cecchini (4) have promise.

GRADE: B

TOP DRAFT PICKS OF THE DECADE

Year	Player, Pos.	2013 Org.
2004	Dustin Pedroia, ss (2nd round)	Red Sox
2005	Jacoby Ellsbury, of	Red Sox
2006	Jason Place, of	Out of baseball
2007	Nick Hagadone, lhp (1st round supp.)	Indians
2008	Casey Kelly, rhp	Padres
2009	Reymond Fuentes, of	Padres
2010	Kolbrin Vitek, 3b	Red Sox
2011	Matt Barnes, rhp	Red Sox
2012	Deven Marrero, ss	Red Sox
2013	Trey Ball, lhp	Red Sox

LARGEST BONUSES IN CLUB HISTORY

Jose Iglesias, 2009	$6,250,000
Casey Kelly, 2008	$3,000,000
Trey Ball, 2013	$2,750,000
Anthony Ranaudo, 2010	$2,550,000
Blake Swihart, 2011	$2,500,000

1 XANDER BOGAERTS, SS/3B

Born: Oct. 1, 1992. **B-T:** R-R. **Ht.:** 6-3. **Wt.:** 205.
Signed: Aruba, 2009. **Signed by:** Mike Lord.

As Mike Lord wrapped up his scouting trip to Aruba in early 2009, he'd identified only one player—catcher Jair Bogaerts—who represented a strong candidate to sign. But before leaving, the Red Sox international crosschecker made his standard inquiry: Anyone else to see? Most emphatically yes. Lord learned that Jair's twin brother Xander had to be seen despite being bedridden with chicken pox. The scout then persuaded Bogaerts' family to let the young shortstop come to a workout, and it was love at first sight when Boston signed Bogaerts for $410,000. In four years, Bogaerts has rocketed to the big leagues, spending no more than 104 games at any level. He has been a standout performer at every stop since then despite being one of the youngest players at each level. The Red Sox emphasized their desire to see him improve his plate discipline in spring training 2013, and improve he did. Bogaerts posted a .388 on-base percentage between Double-A and Triple-A, then drew critical walks both in the American League Division Series against the Rays and the AL Championship Series against the Tigers' Max Scherzer. He became the youngest Red Sox position player in four decades when he made his debut as a 20-year-old in August and the team's youngest postseason starter since Babe Ruth.

BA GRADE
70
LOW
SCOUTING GRADES
BATTING 60
POWER 70
SPEED 50
DEFENSE 55
ARM 60

KEN BABBITT

Bogaerts has already shown the ability to excel against top pitching in the playoffs, with game-changing patience and power. With a simple, balanced swing, impressive bat speed and strength, he demonstrated shocking maturity and advancement at the plate in his year-ending exposure to the majors. He has home run power from left field to right-center, resulting in the confidence to stay back on pitches, swing at strikes and drive them. Defensively, he continued to make strides, showing the athleticism, hands, arm and mechanical efficiency (despite his size) to play shortstop, a position most evaluators believe he can play at a major league level. After playing the hot corner for the Netherlands in the World Baseball Classic, he adapted quickly to his crash course at third. Bogaerts made considerable defensive progress at both positions, to the point where he gives Boston the flexibility to let him play either position, depending on the team's offseason. He has average speed, and stolen bases won't be part of his game.

October may not have been so much Bogaerts' coming-out party as a tantalizing scratching of the surface. "They may end up making a statue of this guy," one evaluator said. He's major league ready as a shortstop or third baseman, one who will hit lower in the order to begin 2014, with a likely peak of 25-plus homers a year in the middle of the lineup.

Year	Club (League)	Class	AVG	G	AB	R	H	2B	3B	HR	RBI	BB	SO	SB	CS	OBP	SLG
2010	Red Sox (DSL)	R	.314	63	239	39	75	7	5	3	42	30	37	4	5	.396	.423
2011	Greenville (SAL)	LoA	.260	72	265	38	69	14	2	16	45	25	71	1	3	.324	.509
2012	Salem (CAR)	HiA	.302	104	384	59	116	27	3	15	64	43	85	4	4	.378	.505
	Portland (EL)	AA	.326	23	92	12	30	10	0	5	17	1	21	1	1	.351	.598
2013	Portland (EL)	AA	.311	56	219	40	68	12	6	6	35	35	51	5	1	.407	.502
	Pawtucket (IL)	AAA	.284	60	225	32	64	11	0	9	32	28	44	2	2	.369	.453
	Boston (AL)	MAJ	.250	18	44	7	11	2	0	1	5	5	13	1	0	.320	.364
Major League Totals			.250	18	44	7	11	2	0	1	5	5	13	1	0	.320	.364
Minor League Totals			.296	378	1424	220	422	81	16	54	235	162	309	17	16	.373	.489

2 HENRY OWENS, LHP

Born: July 21, 1992. **B-T:** L-L. **Ht.:** 6-7. **Wt.:** 210. **Drafted:** HS—Huntington Beach, Calif., 2011 (1st round supplemental). **Signed by:** Tom Battista.

Owens backed up a 2012 season when he had one of the top strikeout rates in the minors with an even better year in 2013. He topped all minor league ERA qualifiers in opponent average (.177), ranked second in strikeouts (169) and dropped his ERA from 4.87 in 2012 to 2.67. At one point, he had a streak of 19 ⅓ straight no-hit innings at Salem. Owens has added roughly 25 pounds of muscle since signing, resulting in better velocity and an increased ability to repeat his delivery. He works mostly at 88-92 mph, but has touched 95, and hitters struggle to pick up the ball out of his hand, resulting in swings and misses on his fastball and excellent changeup. His curveball has been on and off, but when it's effective, he dominates. Owens also shows an advanced feel for pitching. The Red Sox believe his command and control will improve, but his walk rate was 4.5 per nine innings and got worse over the course of the season. Owens should be at least a No. 4 starter with the upside of a very good No. 3 or perhaps a No. 2. He'll open 2014 in Double-A.

Year	Club (League)	Class	W	L	ERA	G	GS	CG	SV	IP	H	HR	BB	SO	K/9	WHIP	AVG
2012	Greenville (SAL)	LoA	12	5	4.87	23	22	0	0	102	100	10	47	130	11.5	1.45	.256
2013	Salem (CAR)	HiA	8	5	2.92	20	20	0	0	105	66	6	53	123	10.6	1.14	.180
	Portland (EL)	AA	3	1	1.78	6	6	0	0	30	18	3	15	46	13.6	1.09	.167
Minor League Totals			23	11	3.61	49	48	0	0	237	184	19	115	299	11.4	1.26	.213

3 JACKIE BRADLEY, OF

Born: April 19,1990. **B-T:** L-R. **Ht.:** 5-10. **Wt.:** 190. **Drafted:** South Carolina, 2011 (1st round supplemental). **Signed by:** Quincy Boyd.

After a stellar first full season in 2012, Bradley dazzled in 2013 spring training and opened the year in the big league lineup. He struggled there but rebounded at Triple-A Pawtucket to show a leadoff hitter's skills and impact defense in center field, which translated to improvement in his subsequent two big league callups. While he showed pull power in 2013, Bradley does so at the expense of his plate discipline and line-to-line hitting approach. After being beaten by inside fastballs in his first big league callup, he showed signs during 2013 of addressing that deficiency. Evaluators are convinced his aptitude, pitch recognition and strike-zone awareness will permit him to make the necessary adjustments. Though not a burner, Bradley's instincts permit him to get great breaks while taking strong routes to the ball, resulting in outstanding defense in center field. Bradley is capable of replacing Jacoby Ellsbury as the everyday center fielder in 2014 and could grow into an above-average regular. At worst, his defense suggests a floor of a valuable part-time outfielder.

Year	Club (League)	Class	AVG	G	AB	R	H	2B	3B	HR	RBI	BB	SO	SB	CS	OBP	SLG
2011	Lowell (NYP)	SS	.190	6	21	5	4	0	0	0	0	4	5	0	2	.320	.190
	Greenville (SAL)	LoA	.333	4	15	2	5	1	0	1	3	0	3	0	0	.333	.600
2012	Salem (CAR)	HiA	.359	67	234	53	84	26	2	3	34	52	40	16	6	.480	.526
	Portland (EL)	AA	.271	61	229	37	62	16	2	6	29	35	49	8	3	.373	.437
2013	Pawtucket (IL)	AAA	.275	80	320	57	88	26	3	10	35	41	75	7	7	.374	.469
	Boston (AL)	MAJ	.189	37	95	18	18	5	0	3	10	10	31	2	0	.280	.337
Major League Totals			.189	37	95	18	18	5	0	3	10	10	31	2	0	.280	.337
Minor League Totals			.297	218	819	154	243	69	7	20	101	132	172	31	18	.404	.471

4 ALLEN WEBSTER, RHP

Born: Feb. 10, 1990. **B-T:** R-R. **Ht.:** 6-2. **Wt.:** 190. **Drafted:** HS—Mayodan, N.C., 2008 (18th round). **Signed by:** Lon Joyce (Dodgers).

A shortstop until the end of his prep career, Webster enticed Dodgers scout Lon Joyce to turn him in as a pitcher after showcasing a low-90s heater, promising curveball and sound delivery. Signed for $20,000 as an 18th-round pick, Webster added velocity and became a key trade chip for the Dodgers, who traded him to Boston in the August 2012 Adrian Gonzalez-Carl Crawford-Josh Beckett blockbuster. Webster showed the best pure stuff in the Red Sox system, though inconsistent command and trust in his fastball resulted in him getting roughed up in the big leagues. Webster features a 93-98 mph fastball that he can sink for bad contact or swings and misses, and he can also get whiffs with his plus changeup—his best secondary pitch—and slider. His athletic delivery suggests that he should be able to control his stuff, but there are times when he can't harness his two-seamer, as evidenced by his surprisingly high home run yield in the big leagues (2.1 per nine innings) and 16 hit batters in 105 innings at Triple-A Pawtucket. Webster's stuff is outrageous, suggesting top-of-the-rotation potential, but his inability to command his fastball and questions about his confidence raise real concerns about whether he'll reach his ceiling. A floor as a middle reliever is possible, but he'll try to aim higher as he returns to Pawtucket's rotation in 2014.

Year	Club (League)	Class	W	L	ERA	G	GS	CG	SV	IP	H	HR	BB	SO	K/9	WHIP	AVG
2008	Dodgers (GCL)	R	1	1	3.44	12	0	0	1	18	12	1	17	13	6.4	1.58	.197
2009	Dodgers (AZL)	R	2	1	2.08	12	8	0	0	48	35	0	14	56	10.6	1.03	.197
	Ogden (PIO)	R	2	0	3.00	4	3	0	0	21	23	1	4	21	9.0	1.29	.277
2010	Great Lakes (MWL)	LoA	12	9	2.88	26	23	0	0	131	119	6	53	114	7.8	1.31	.239
2011	R. Cucamonga (CAL)	HiA	5	2	2.33	9	9	0	0	54	46	2	21	62	10.3	1.24	.228
	Chattanooga (SL)	AA	6	3	5.04	18	17	1	0	91	101	7	36	73	7.2	1.51	.286
2012	Chattanooga (SL)	AA	6	8	3.55	27	22	0	0	122	120	1	57	117	8.7	1.45	.260
	Portland (EL)	AA	0	1	8.00	2	2	0	0	9	13	1	4	12	12.0	1.89	.325
2013	Pawtucket (IL)	AAA	8	4	3.60	21	21	0	0	105	71	9	43	116	9.9	1.09	.190
	Boston (AL)	MAJ	1	2	8.60	8	7	0	0	30	37	7	18	23	6.8	1.81	.308
Major League Totals			1	2	8.60	8	7	0	0	30	37	7	18	23	6.8	1.81	.308
Minor League Totals			42	29	3.46	131	105	1	1	599	540	28	249	584	8.8	1.32	.240

5 BLAKE SWIHART, C

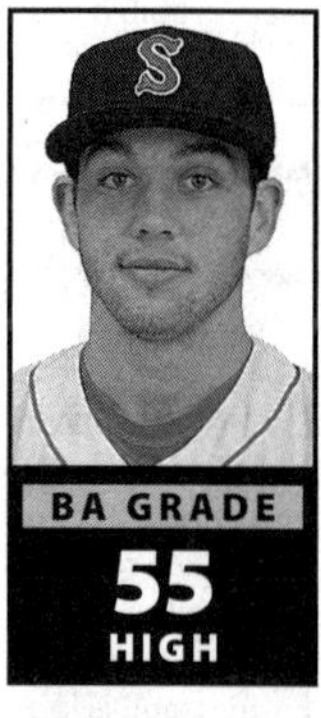

BA GRADE 55 HIGH

Born: April 3, 1992. **B-T:** B-R. **Ht.:** 6-1. **Wt.:** 185. **Drafted:** HS—Rio Rancho, N.M., 2011 (1st round). **Signed by:** Matt Mahoney.

In what proved to be a wise decision, Swihart took up both catching and switch-hitting in high school to improve his draft stock. Though somewhat raw when he turned pro, he made considerable strides offensively and defensively in 2013 for a high Class A Salem team that won the Carolina League championship. He showed steady offensive improvement throughout the year. Though his swing from both sides is geared for line drives, Swihart makes consistently loud, hard contact, and could go from hitting for average with solid on-base skills to a catcher with the potential for 15-20 homers in his prime. His swing is fluid from both sides of the plate. He's an unusually-athletic catcher who moves well and can control the running game with above-average arm strength, while possessing tremendous intangibles that suggest an ability to lead a pitching staff. He moves well for a catcher, showing average baserunning ability. Swihart ought to open 2014 at Double-A Portland, and with a system that has a number of solid catching options in the upper levels, the Red Sox need not rush his development. Still, the team believes development of his present tools would make him an above-average catcher. If, as team officials believe, he develops more power as he matures, he has the ceiling of an all-star.

Year	Club (League)	Class	AVG	G	AB	R	H	2B	3B	HR	RBI	BB	SO	SB	CS	OBP	SLG
2011	Red Sox (GCL)	R	.000	2	6	0	0	0	0	0	0	0	2	0	0	.000	.000
2012	Greenville (SAL)	LoA	.262	92	344	44	90	17	4	7	53	26	68	6	2	.307	.395
2013	Salem (CAR)	HiA	.298	103	376	45	112	29	7	2	42	41	63	7	8	.366	.428
Minor League Totals			.278	197	726	89	202	46	11	9	95	67	133	13	10	.335	.409

6 GARIN CECCHINI, 3B

BA GRADE 55 HIGH

Born: April 20, 1991. **B-T:** L-R. **Ht.:** 6-2. **Wt.:** 210. **Drafted:** HS—Lake Charles, La., 2010 (4th round). **Signed by:** Matt Dorey.

Brought up in a family of baseball rats that included Mets 2012 first-rounder Gavin Cecchini, Garin slipped to the fourth round in 2010 over signability concerns at a time when he was recovering from a torn ACL. In his pro career, he's been a study in offensive consistency, an on-base machine who led full-season minor leaguers in OBP (.443) in 2013 while spending the season's second half at Double-A Portland. Cecchini has what one evaluator called a "magic barrel" that allows him to send liners up the middle and to left-center field, a trait amplified by tremendous strike-zone judgment. Though he's strong, scouts question whether he will (or should) sell out his approach to generate prototype power for a corner. He has at best average speed, yet his feel for the game permits him to steal bases. At third base, some feel he could be an average defender, while others wonder whether his subpar range may result in a move to left field or first base. Cecchini's ability to hit for average and get on base is unquestioned, suggesting a future as a big league regular. Given that the Red Sox have superior defenders on the left side of the infield—Xander Bogaerts, Deven Marrero and Will Middlebrooks—he may shift positions. Cecchini's spring will determine if he graduates to Triple-A Pawtucket.

Year	Club (League)	Class	AVG	G	AB	R	H	2B	3B	HR	RBI	BB	SO	SB	CS	OBP	SLG
2011	Lowell (NYP)	SS	.298	32	114	21	34	12	1	3	23	17	19	12	2	.398	.500
2012	Greenville (SAL)	LoA	.305	118	455	84	139	38	4	4	62	61	90	51	6	.394	.433
2013	Salem (CAR)	HiA	.350	63	214	44	75	19	4	5	33	43	34	15	7	.469	.547
	Portland (EL)	AA	.296	66	240	36	71	14	3	2	28	51	52	8	2	.420	.404
Minor League Totals			.312	279	1023	185	319	83	12	14	146	172	195	86	17	.417	.457

7 MOOKIE BETTS, 2B

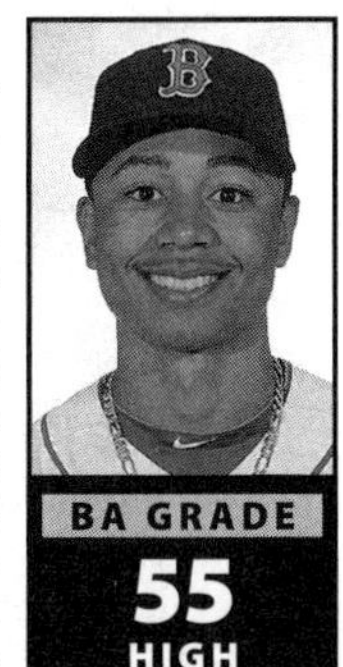

BA GRADE
55
HIGH

Born: Oct. 7, 1992. **B-T:** R-R. **Ht.:** 5-9. **Wt.:** 170. **Drafted:** HS—Brentwood, Tenn., 2011 (5th round). **Signed by:** Danny Watkins.

No one more significantly redefined his prospect status in the system in 2013 quite like Betts. Drafted as a multi-sport athlete (baseball, basketball, bowling), he showed a line-drive swing, good strike-zone judgment, speed and no power (zero homers) at short-season Lowell in 2012. That changed in 2013, when he showed improved patience and drove the ball for extra bases with startling frequency, first at low Class A Greenville then at high Class A Salem. Betts joined eight other minor leaguers with at least 15 homers and 30 steals in 2013. Though he has a sizable leg kick, Betts has the body control and athleticism to maintain balance, the quick hands to let the ball travel and the hand-eye coordination and bat speed to produce extra-base power. He shows a penchant for highlight-reel defensive plays at second base, and he has the athleticism and range for the Red Sox to consider shortstop and center field as possibilities. Betts' arm is better suited for the right side of the infield. He pairs above-average speed with good reads to steal bases at an excellent rate. With Dustin Pedroia signed for eight years, Betts' future with organization, barring a trade, is most likely at any position but the one he's playing. He appears headed for Double-A Portland in 2014.

Year	Club (League)	Class	AVG	G	AB	R	H	2B	3B	HR	RBI	BB	SO	SB	CS	OBP	SLG
2011	Red Sox (GCL)	R	.500	1	4	0	2	0	0	0	2	0	0	1	0	.500	.500
2012	Lowell (NYP)	SS	.267	71	251	34	67	8	1	0	31	32	30	20	4	.352	.307
2013	Greenville (SAL)	LoA	.296	76	277	63	82	24	1	8	26	58	40	18	2	.418	.477
	Salem (CAR)	HiA	.341	51	185	30	63	12	3	7	39	23	17	20	2	.414	.551
Minor League Totals			.298	199	717	127	214	44	5	15	98	113	87	59	8	.395	.437

8 BRANDON WORKMAN, RHP

BA GRADE
50
SAFE

Born: Aug. 13, 1988. **B-T:** R-R. **Ht.:** 6-5. **Wt.:** 235. **Drafted:** Texas, 2010 (2nd round). **Signed by:** Jim Robinson.

Most scouts viewed Workman as a future bullpen arm when he was drafted in 2010. Yet the development of his curveball and changeup in 2011 along with fearlessness about throwing strikes has forced many to reconsider. Workman opened 2013 at Double-A Portland but was in the big leagues by July, making three impressive starts before moving to the bullpen. He gained the trust of manager John Farrell to the point of pitching the eighth inning of the final game of the World Series. Workman's delivery has always shown sufficient effort to raise questions about his ability to start, but his professional track record suggests he has no problems repeating his motion or sustaining power through 100 pitches. He's the most consistent strike-thrower in the Red Sox system, with a career 4.0 SO/BB ratio in the minors. As a starter, Workman sits at 92-94 mph with an average curve that can get swings and misses, a cutter that elicits groundballs and an occasional changeup. As a reliever, he typically sticks to his fastball and curve. He's willing to challenge opponents with his four-seamer, sometimes proving vulnerable to homers but getting swings and misses as well. Workman represents a big league-ready reliever (with closer potential) or depth starting option. Needs at the big league level likely will dictate 2014 big league role.

Year	Club (League)	Class	W	L	ERA	G	GS	CG	SV	IP	H	HR	BB	SO	K/9	WHIP	AVG
2011	Greenville (SAL)	LoA	6	7	3.71	26	26	0	0	131	128	10	33	115	7.9	1.23	.260
2012	Salem (CAR)	HiA	7	7	3.40	20	20	0	0	114	104	10	20	107	8.5	1.09	.244
	Portland (EL)	AA	3	1	3.96	5	5	0	0	25	23	2	5	23	8.3	1.12	.247
2013	Portland (EL)	AA	5	1	3.43	11	10	0	0	66	51	6	17	74	10.1	1.04	.216
	Pawtucket (IL)	AAA	3	1	2.80	6	6	0	0	35	39	6	13	34	8.7	1.47	.289
	Boston (AL)	MAJ	6	3	4.97	20	3	0	0	42	44	5	15	47	10.2	1.42	.272
Major League Totals			6	3	4.97	20	3	0	0	42	44	5	15	47	10.2	1.42	.272
Minor League Totals			24	17	3.50	68	67	0	0	371	345	34	88	353	8.6	1.17	.249

9 MATT BARNES, RHP

Born: June 17, 1990. **B-T:** R-R. **Ht.:** 6-4. **Wt.:** 205. **Drafted:** Connecticut, 2011 (1st round). **Signed by:** Ray Fagnant.

Barnes generated unrealistic expectations with five overpowering starts at low Class A Greenville to begin his pro career in 2012, but he hit a wall in the second half of that year at high Class A Salem. He then saw his walk rate and vulnerability to hard contact increase at Double-A Portland in 2013. Still, his strikeout rate of 11.3 per nine innings topped Eastern Leaguers with at least 100 innings. Barnes is a big, durable pitcher who works at 93-96 mph and has touched 98 with the ability to command his fastball to both sides and get swings and misses in the strike zone. He's developed a solid changeup. His curveball has some potential but is inconsistent to the point of being mostly a non-factor. Barnes' long arm action makes it difficult to project the breaking ball to be more than average. The power, life and command he shows with his fastball, in combination with a changeup to get opponents off the heat, are sufficiently impressive to suggest a future big league starter. Whether Barnes fits best as a back-end starter or closer—or his ultimate ceiling of first-division No. 3—will depend on the development of his curveball. He'll open 2014 at Triple-A Pawtucket, but Boston's rotation depth suggests he need not be rushed in 2014.

Year	Club (League)	Class	W	L	ERA	G	GS	CG	SV	IP	H	HR	BB	SO	K/9	WHIP	AVG
2012	Greenville (SAL)	LoA	2	0	0.34	5	5	0	0	27	12	0	4	42	14.2	0.60	.130
	Salem (CAR)	HiA	5	5	3.58	20	20	1	0	93	85	6	25	91	8.8	1.18	.250
2013	Portland (EL)	AA	5	10	4.33	24	24	0	0	108	112	11	46	135	11.3	1.46	.265
	Pawtucket (IL)	AAA	1	0	0.00	1	1	0	0	5	3	0	2	7	11.8	0.94	.167
Minor League Totals			13	15	3.48	50	50	1	0	233	212	17	77	275	10.6	1.24	.243

10 TREY BALL, LHP

MIKE JANES

Born: June 27, 1994. **B-T:** L-L. **Ht.:** 6-6. **Wt.:** 175. **Drafted:** HS—New Castle, Ind., 2013 (1st round). **Signed by:** John Pyle.

Ball entered the 2013 draft as perhaps the top two-way prospect, but when he opened the year sitting comfortably at 92-94 mph, the question about whether his upside was greater as a pitcher or center fielder evaporated. The possibility of an athletic lefthander with three above-average pitches convinced the Red Sox to take Ball with the seventh overall pick, the club's highest draft position in nearly half a century. Boston signed him for $2.75 million, the second-highest in Red Sox draft history. Ball is one of the top athletes in the system, underscoring the idea that he can have the body control and strength to repeat his delivery as well as command three solid to plus offerings. His fastball sat 88-94 mph in high school, with more velocity possible as he fills out. His plus changeup pairs nicely with a curve that Ball began throwing as a high school junior. His curve already has the makings of a solid to plus pitch. Scouts admire his clean arm action. Ball likely will begin 2014 at low Class A Greenville. With the potential for three plus pitches, he may represent the greatest potential for a true No. 1 in the Sox system, possessing what one evaluator called "serious wow factor," albeit with a mountain of variables that come with any high school pitching prospect.

Year	Club (League)	Class	W	L	ERA	G	GS	CG	SV	IP	H	HR	BB	SO	K/9	WHIP	AVG
2013	Red Sox (GCL)	R	0	1	6.43	5	5	0	0	7	10	1	6	5	6.4	2.29	.357
Minor League Totals			0	1	6.43	5	5	0	0	7	10	1	6	5	6.4	2.29	.357

11 ANTHONY RANAUDO, RHP

BA GRADE
55
HIGH

Born: Sept. 9, 1989. **B-T:** R-R. **Ht.:** 6-7. **Wt.:** 245. **Drafted:** Louisiana State, 2010 (1st round supplemental). **Signed by:** Matt Dorey.

The year after leading Louisiana State to the 2009 College World Series championship, Ranaudo signed with the Red Sox for $2.55 million as a supplemental pick out of the 2010 draft. As a pro, he's mixed healthy seasons with unhealthy ones, struggling to post consistent results prior to 2013, when he started the Double-A Eastern League all-star game, appeared in the Futures Game and made two playoff starts for Triple-A Pawtucket. Ranaudo shows the ability to overpower opponents with a 91-95 mph fastball, which tops out at 97, and a solid curveball while mixing in an effective changeup with some sink. The curve flashes plus with power at up to 82 mph, but he struggles to locate it. Some evaluators said Ranaudo flashes the stuff of a potential No. 2 starter, while others note his inconsistent secondary stuff and peg his upside as that of a mid-rotation arm. The latter group cautions that he may not get the swings and misses on the high fastballs he favored at Double-A Portland. That certainly was the case in Triple-A, where his strikeout rate dipped to a career-low 6.2 per nine innings. With Boston's crowded big league rotation, Ranaudo will return to Pawtucket to start 2014, with a chance to position himself for a callup if he performs well in his first big league camp.

Year	Club (League)	Class	W	L	ERA	G	GS	CG	SV	IP	H	HR	BB	SO	K/9	WHIP	AVG
2011	Greenville (SAL)	LoA	4	1	3.33	10	10	0	0	46	35	4	16	50	9.8	1.11	.211
	Salem (CAR)	HiA	5	5	4.33	16	16	0	0	81	80	6	30	67	7.4	1.36	.262
2012	Portland (EL)	AA	1	3	6.69	9	9	0	0	38	41	4	27	27	6.5	1.81	.283
2013	Portland (EL)	AA	8	4	2.95	19	19	0	0	110	80	9	40	106	8.7	1.09	.204
	Pawtucket (IL)	AAA	3	1	2.97	6	5	0	0	30	32	1	7	21	6.2	1.29	.271
Minor League Totals			21	14	3.84	60	59	0	0	305	268	24	120	271	8.0	1.27	.238

12 CHRISTIAN VAZQUEZ, C

BA GRADE
50
HIGH

Born: Aug. 21, 1990. **B-T:** R-R. **Ht.:** 5-9. **Wt.:** 205. **Drafted:** HS—Gurabo, P.R., 2008 (9th round). **Signed by:** Edgar Perez.

Vazquez grew up in Puerto Rico watching Ivan Rodriguez's catching instruction video, and the lessons evidently took, as he shows above-average defensive ability behind the plate. Pitchers love throwing to him, and swear by his judgment when it comes to understanding their strengths and reading hitters' swings. Vazquez routinely records pop times between 1.7 and 1.8 seconds on throws to second base. "He can be a difference-maker," one evaluator said. "He's going to be so good defensively that he won't have to hit a ton." However, his aggressiveness on defense resulted in a bit of a regression in 2013. While Vazquez led the Double-A Eastern League in assists (80) and total chances (871), he also led the way in errors (10) and passed balls (23). At the plate, he cut his strikeout rate nearly in half while hitting .289/.376/.395 at Portland, finishing eighth in the EL batting race. Evaluators feel that, despite Vazquez's five homers, he possesses sneaky pop that could permit double-digit home run totals in tandem with an ability to swing at strikes and get on base at a respectable rate. That package suggests a ceiling as a big league starter, with his defense being a separator that will buy him time to develop his bat in the majors. A return to Triple-A Pawtucket awaits in 2014.

Year	Club (League)	Class	AVG	G	AB	R	H	2B	3B	HR	RBI	BB	SO	SB	CS	OBP	SLG
2008	Red Sox (GCL)	R	.190	21	58	7	11	1	0	0	5	6	17	0	0	.266	.207
2009	Red Sox (GCL)	R	.278	10	36	5	10	5	0	0	7	4	7	0	0	.366	.417
	Lowell (NYP)	SS	.123	21	65	4	8	2	0	2	9	11	16	0	0	.250	.246
2010	Greenville (SAL)	LoA	.263	79	270	34	71	11	0	3	32	23	62	3	1	.328	.337
2011	Greenville (SAL)	LoA	.283	105	392	71	111	27	3	18	84	43	84	1	1	.358	.505
2012	Salem (CAR)	HiA	.266	81	293	43	78	17	0	7	41	40	70	2	2	.360	.396
	Portland (EL)	AA	.205	20	73	11	15	4	0	0	5	8	9	0	0	.280	.260
2013	Portland (EL)	AA	.289	96	342	48	99	19	1	5	48	47	44	7	5	.376	.395
	Pawtucket (IL)	AAA	.000	1	3	0	0	0	0	0	0	1	0	0	0	.250	.000
Minor League Totals			.263	434	1532	223	403	86	4	35	231	183	309	13	9	.346	.393

13 MANUEL MARGOT, OF

Born: Sept. 28, 1994. **B-T:** R-R. **Ht.:** 5-11. **Wt.:** 175. **Signed:** Dominican Republic, 2011. **Signed by:** Manny Nanita/Craig Shipley.

Margot is the preeminent five-tool prospect in the system, with a combination of tools and maturity to allow him to compete against much older competition. He signed for $800,000 out of the Dominican Republic in 2011. The Red Sox discussed the possibility of assigning Margot to low Class A Greenville in 2013, but the 18-year-old instead made his U.S. debut in the short-season New York-Penn League, holding his own with a .270/.346/.351 batting line and 18 steals. While his well above-average bat speed didn't produce loud results in 2013, Margot showed energy and impact on the bases and in the field, with a No. 2 hitter's mix of above-average hitting and and on-base skills. Scouts who like him see a ceiling of perhaps 12-15 homers and 25-plus steals, all while contributing above-average defense in center field. Margot needs to show that he can hit breaking balls and not chase them outside of the zone, but such concerns came as little surprise for the youngest position player in the Penn League. He'll make his full-season debut at Greenville in 2014.

Year	Club (League)	Class	AVG	G	AB	R	H	2B	3B	HR	RBI	BB	SO	SB	CS	OBP	SLG
2012	Red Sox (DSL)	R	.285	68	260	49	74	10	7	4	45	36	25	33	9	.382	.423
2013	Lowell (NYP)	SS	.270	49	185	29	50	8	2	1	21	22	40	18	8	.346	.351
Minor League Totals			.279	117	445	78	124	18	9	5	66	58	65	51	17	.367	.393

14 BRIAN JOHNSON, LHP

BA GRADE
50
HIGH

Born: Dec. 7, 1990. **B-T:** L-L. **Ht.:** 6-3. **Wt.:** 240. **Drafted:** Florida, 2012 (1st round). **Signed by:** Anthony Turco.

Drafted 31st overall in 2012 and signed for $1.575 million, Johnson's pro debut season came to a terrifying halt when he was struck in the face by a line drive. Unable to eat solid food for months, he lost significant weight and strength, resulting in unimpressive stuff and performance to begin the 2013 season at low Class A Greenville. The Red Sox shut Johnson down for six weeks with shoulder tendinitis, and when he returned, so did his stuff. He showed the ability to throw a low-90s fastball down in the zone, while getting swings and misses with a solid curveball (better than what Boston saw from him as an amateur) and changeup. In his final eight starts at Greenville and high Class A Salem, Johnson logged a 1.50 ERA with 38 strikeouts in 42 innings. With a healthy offseason, he should come to camp in 2014 with the four-pitch mix—fastball, curve, changeup and cutter/slider—he showed at Florida, and he has the pitchability to suggest a No. 5 starter floor and a mid-rotation ceiling. Though he'll open in Salem after spending almost all of 2013 in Greenville, Johnson's ability to throw strikes could allow him to move quickly.

Year	Club (League)	Class	W	L	ERA	G	GS	CG	SV	IP	H	HR	BB	SO	K/9	WHIP	AVG
2012	Lowell (NYP)	SS	0	0	0.00	4	4	0	0	6	2	0	1	4	6.4	0.53	.111
2013	Red Sox (GCL)	R	0	0	0.00	2	2	0	0	5	1	0	2	7	12.6	0.60	.067
	Greenville (SAL)	LoA	1	6	2.87	15	15	0	0	69	50	4	28	69	9.0	1.13	.197
	Salem (CAR)	HiA	1	0	1.64	2	2	0	0	11	9	0	5	8	6.5	1.27	.225
Minor League Totals			2	6	2.38	23	23	0	0	91	62	4	36	88	8.7	1.08	.190

15 DEVEN MARRERO, SS

BA GRADE **50** HIGH

Born: Aug. 25, 1990. **B-T:** R-R. **Ht.:** 6-1. **Wt.:** 185. **Drafted:** Arizona State, 2012 (1st round). **Signed by:** Vaughn Williams.

College shortstops who project as big league regulars are rarely available in the draft, and so the Red Sox jumped at the chance to select Marrero in the 2012 draft after a modest offensive performance as a junior left him available at No. 24. He projects as a bottom-of-the-order hitter who can serve as the defensive anchor of an infield. His instincts and intelligence permit him to have above-average range with great hands and a strong, reliable arm. It's a defensive package that compares favorably with what the Red Sox received from Stephen Drew in 2013. Marrero's offense was modest in 2013, when he hit .252/.338/.317 between high Class A Salem and Double-A Portland. He shows good strike-zone judgment and keeps the bat head in the zone with a clean swing that yields liners up the middle with some doubles. His baseball acumen, meanwhile, permits him to be an above-average runner, and he went 27-for-29 in stolen base attempts in 2013 despite average speed. Marrero is a solid bet to be a big league regular, even if one with second-division potential. He will return to Double-A in 2014.

Year	Club (League)	Class	AVG	G	AB	R	H	2B	3B	HR	RBI	BB	SO	SB	CS	OBP	SLG
2012	Lowell (NYP)	SS	.268	64	246	45	66	14	3	2	24	34	48	24	6	.358	.374
2013	Salem (CAR)	HiA	.256	85	332	50	85	20	0	2	21	42	60	21	2	.341	.334
	Portland (EL)	AA	.236	19	72	7	17	0	0	0	5	10	16	6	0	.321	.236
Minor League Totals			.258	168	650	102	168	34	3	4	50	86	124	51	8	.345	.338

16 BRYCE BRENTZ, OF

BA GRADE **50** HIGH

Born: Dec. 30, 1988. **B-T:** R-R. **Ht.:** 6-0. **Wt.:** 200. **Drafted:** Middle Tennessee State, 2010 (1st round supplemental). **Signed by:** Danny Watkins.

The Red Sox drafted Brentz after he followed a spectacular sophomore year in which he displayed substantial raw power with an injury-impaired struggle as a Middle Tennessee State junior. The boom or bust pattern has followed him into the professional ranks, with a particularly forgettable 2013. On the cusp of his first big league camp, Brentz accidentally shot himself in the left leg, he said, while cleaning his handgun. The Red Sox subsequently revoked his spring training invitation. Though he led Boston minor leaguers with 19 home runs in 2013, Brentz played in just 88 games after suffering a torn meniscus in his right knee that required surgery in July. Offensively, his aggressiveness and penchant to chase breaking balls led to streakiness and a .262/.313/.487 batting line at Triple-A Pawtucket. Still, he possesses considerable upside as a righthanded hitter with "rare double-plus power," according to one scout with an American League club. Brentz has regressed defensively since college, and looks increasingly like a left fielder, but there's still a chance that he could emerge as a run-producer who can bat in the lower third of the order.

Year	Club (League)	Class	AVG	G	AB	R	H	2B	3B	HR	RBI	BB	SO	SB	CS	OBP	SLG
2010	Lowell (NYP)	SS	.198	69	262	28	52	14	4	5	39	21	76	5	4	.259	.340
2011	Greenville (SAL)	LoA	.359	40	170	43	61	10	3	11	36	14	35	2	2	.414	.647
	Salem (CAR)	HiA	.274	75	288	48	79	15	1	19	58	26	80	1	1	.336	.531
2012	Portland (EL)	AA	.296	122	456	62	135	30	1	17	76	40	130	7	5	.355	.478
	Pawtucket (IL)	AAA	.118	5	17	0	2	0	0	0	0	1	6	0	0	.167	.118
2013	Red Sox (GCL)	R	.235	6	17	3	4	2	0	2	8	1	4	0	0	.316	.706
	Pawtucket (IL)	AAA	.264	82	326	36	86	16	1	17	56	20	86	1	0	.312	.475
Minor League Totals			.273	399	1536	220	419	87	10	71	273	123	417	16	12	.330	.481

17 DRAKE BRITTON, LHP

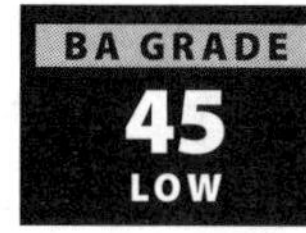

Born: May 22, 1989. **B-T:** L-L. **Ht.:** 6-2. **Wt.:** 208. **Drafted:** HS—Tomball, Texas, 2007 (23rd round). **Signed by:** Jim Robinson.

Bryce Brentz wasn't the only Red Sox prospect to gain notoriety during spring training 2013. While Brentz shot himself in the leg in February, Britton's brush with infamy came when he was arrested and charged with a DUI and reckless driving in Fort Myers, Fla., in early March. But after a slow start, the lefthander showed an improved slider that, in tandem with a 91-95 mph fastball, allowed him to start dominating in Double-A to earn a July promotion to Triple-A. That stop proved brief, as a need for lefty bullpen help resulted in Britton's on-the-fly conversion to the bullpen in Boston. He opened his big league career with seven scoreless appearances, spanning nine innings, but he subsequently tailed. Still, Britton showed the ability to get swings and misses in the big leagues with two pitches. The Red Sox haven't abandoned the idea of moving the strong southpaw back into the rotation, given that he also can spin a curveball and has made progress with his changeup. At the least, Britton looks like an impact bullpen arm after making strides as a strike-thrower.

Year	Club (League)	Class	W	L	ERA	G	GS	CG	SV	IP	H	HR	BB	SO	K/9	WHIP	AVG
2008	Lowell (NYP)	SS	1	2	4.28	8	7	0	0	34	30	3	16	26	7.0	1.37	.234
2009	Red Sox (GCL)	R	0	0	0.00	4	4	0	0	7	2	0	4	11	14.1	0.86	.080
	Lowell (NYP)	SS	0	0	1.93	3	3	0	0	5	4	0	3	8	15.4	1.50	.235
2010	Greenville (SAL)	LoA	2	3	2.97	21	21	0	0	76	69	5	23	78	9.3	1.22	.240
2011	Salem (CAR)	HiA	1	13	6.91	26	26	0	0	98	111	12	55	89	8.2	1.70	.285
2012	Salem (CAR)	HiA	3	5	5.80	10	8	0	0	45	42	5	19	42	8.4	1.36	.246
	Portland (EL)	AA	4	7	3.72	16	16	0	0	85	86	3	38	76	8.1	1.46	.266
2013	Portland (EL)	AA	7	6	3.51	17	16	1	0	97	94	5	36	80	7.4	1.34	.254
	Pawtucket (IL)	AAA	0	1	8.44	1	1	0	0	5	10	0	1	5	8.4	2.06	.385
	Boston (AL)	MAJ	1	1	3.86	18	0	0	0	21	21	1	7	17	7.3	1.33	.280
Major League Totals			1	1	3.86	18	0	0	0	21	21	1	7	17	7.3	1.33	.280
Minor League Totals			18	37	4.47	106	102	1	0	451	448	33	195	415	8.3	1.43	.258

18 WENDELL RIJO, 2B

BA GRADE
50
HIGH

Born: Sept. 4, 1995. **B-T:** R-R. **Ht.:** 5-11. **Wt.:** 170. **Signed:** Dominican Republic, 2012. **Signed by:** Victor Rodriguez Jr.

The son of Dodgers Dominican scout Rafael Rijo, Wendell signed for $575,000 in July 2012 and showed considerable polish in his 2013 pro debut. He skipped the Dominican Summer League and played in the Rookie-level Gulf Coast League before reaching short-season Lowell at the tail end of the season. Rijo hit .277/.368/.359 in 184 at-bats across his two stops, while showing a good feel for the strike zone (22 walks, 32 strikeouts) and the hint of gap power (15 doubles). His combination of feel for the barrel, on-base skills, solid defense and slightly above-average speed offer a straightforward projection—if everything breaks right—as a regular second baseman. Some scouts think Rijo could move around the field as well, particularly as he gains quickness when further removed from a torn ACL in his knee he suffered in 2012. He may end up being one of the youngest players in the low Class A South Atlantic League in 2014.

Year	Club (League)	Class	AVG	G	AB	R	H	2B	3B	HR	RBI	BB	SO	SB	CS	OBP	SLG
2013	Red Sox (GCL)	R	.271	49	170	28	46	15	0	0	20	22	29	15	5	.368	.359
	Lowell (NYP)	SS	.357	3	14	1	5	1	1	0	1	0	3	0	1	.357	.571
Minor League Totals			.277	52	184	29	51	16	1	0	21	22	32	15	6	.367	.375

19 TEDDY STANKIEWICZ, RHP

Born: Nov. 25, 1993. **B-T:** R-R. **Ht.:** 6-4. **Wt.:** 190. **Drafted:** Seminole State (Okla.) JC, 2013 (2nd round). **Signed by:** Chris Mears.

The Mets failed to sign Stankiewicz as a second-round pick out of high school in 2012, offering him an under-slot bonus, so he enrolled at Seminole State (Okla.) JC. His velocity improved in one year there, resulting in his selection with the 45th pick in the 2013 draft, 30 places higher than he went in 2012, though both times he went in the second round. Stankiewicz's signing delayed by a minor physical issue, the Red Sox reduced of his bonus from $1.1 million to $915,000. At Seminole State, he upped his velocity to 90-94 mph, touching 96, and he gained greater feel for his secondary arsenal, which helped him perform well at short-season Lowell. Not all scouts like Stankiewicz's drop-and-drive delivery, but the athletic righthander repeats his motion and throws strikes. While he didn't make much use of his secondary arsenal during short stints in his pro debut, Stankiewicz showed an above-average slider as an amateur, though his slider has farther to go. His combination of power and strike-throwing ability allows some in the organization to dream on a No. 3 starter ceiling, and he likely will begin 2014 in the low Class A Greenville rotation.

Year	Club (League)	Class	W	L	ERA	G	GS	CG	SV	IP	H	HR	BB	SO	K/9	WHIP	AVG
2013	Lowell (NYP)	SS	0	0	2.29	9	9	0	0	20	17	1	2	15	6.9	0.97	.227
Minor League Totals			0	0	2.29	9	9	0	0	20	17	1	2	15	6.9	0.97	.227

20 RAFAEL DEVERS, 3B

BA GRADE **55** EXTREME

Born: Oct. 24, 1996. **B-T:** L-R. **Ht.:** 6-0. **Wt.:** 200. **Signed:** Dominican Republic, 2013. **Signed by:** Manny Nanita.

Signed for $1.5 million in August 2013, Devers has yet to play a game in the organization, but he was a head-turning performer as a 16-year-old in instructional league. One evaluator gave Devers' power a present grade of 60 on the 20-80 scouting scale, with a future forecast of double-plus being a possibility. Others are more reserved in assessing his power potential, but Devers was considered by many to be the best pure hitter in the 2013 international amateur class. The rare Dominican lefthanded hitter, he shows the ability to hit line drives to left-center field and to pulverize pitches on the inner half with outstanding bat speed, resulting in middle-of-the-order potential. Defensively, Devers shows decent, if unexceptional, hands, actions and arm strength at third base, though he'll have to stay on top of his conditioning if he wants to avoid a move to first base. He may bypass the Dominican Summer League to make his pro debut in the Rookie-level Gulf Coast League in 2014, when he'll be 17.

Year	Club (League)	Class	AVG	G	AB	R	H	2B	3B	HR	RBI	BB	SO	SB	CS	OBP	SLG
2013	Did not play—Signed 2014 contract																

21 CODY KUKUK, LHP

BA GRADE **50** HIGH

Born: April 10, 1993. **B-T:** L-L. **Ht.:** 6-4. **Wt.:** 212. **Drafted:** HS—Lawrence, Kan., 2011 (7th round). **Signed by:** Chris Mears.

A big, powerful, athletic lefthander who draws physical comparisons with Jon Lester, Kukuk threw just 10 innings in 2012 following an arrest on suspicion of DUI and subsequent team suspension. He got back on the field in 2013, spending the year in the low Class A Greenville rotation, where he showed one of the more substantial ceiling/floor chasms in the system. Kukuk's fastball played up during the year, as he bumped up from 90-92 mph to sit at 93, while registering as high as 97 in the season's final months. His hard slider continues to evade bats, and even his changeup was a swing-and-miss offering by season's end. Opponents could do little against him when he threw strikes, hitting .197 with a .274 slugging percentage, and he struck out 9.5 per nine innings. However, Kukuk endured several outings where he had little control, which is reflected in a walk rate of 6.8 per nine innings. If he can harness his stuff, his future probably fits best as a late-innings bullpen weapon. However, because of his athleticism and power stuff, Kukuk might make a breakthrough and emerge as a starter—or he might stall in the minors. Either way, he's headed to high Class A Salem in 2014.

Year	Club (League)	Class	W	L	ERA	G	GS	CG	SV	IP	H	HR	BB	SO	K/9	WHIP	AVG
2012	Red Sox (GCL)	R	2	0	0.90	5	0	0	0	10	3	0	3	16	14.4	0.60	.086
2013	Greenville (SAL)	LoA	4	13	4.63	26	24	0	1	107	77	5	81	113	9.5	1.48	.197
Minor League Totals			6	13	4.31	31	24	0	1	117	80	5	84	129	9.9	1.40	.188

22 JAMIE CALLAHAN, RHP

BA GRADE **50** HIGH

Born: Aug. 24, 1994. **B-T:** R-R. **Ht.:** 6-2. **Wt.:** 215. **Drafted:** HS—Dillon, S.C., 2012 (2nd round). **Signed by:** Quincy Boyd.

Though Callahan features a high-effort delivery with a long arm swing, he also brings a heavy fastball to the table that has what one evaluator called "serious giddy-up." At times with short-season Lowell, he could bulldoze his way through opposing lineups primarily on the strength of that pitch, as when he allowed one hit and no walks while punching out 17 in 12 innings over a two-start stretch. Callahan showed a good deal of inconsistency en route to going 5-1, 3.92 at Lowell while notching 8.1 strikeouts and 2.6 walks per nine innings. Put in perspective, Callahan was the youngest starter (minimum 10 starts) in the New York-Penn League. His size, aggressiveness in the strike zone with his fastball/curveball combination and demeanor have been likened to Brandon Workman. Callahan sits at 91-93 mph and touches 95, while mixing in a quality, high-70s slider. His changeup needs a lot of work. Some see a potential late-innings reliever, while others see a pitcher who could be a back-end starter. Callahan likely will open 2014 at low Class A Greenville.

Year	Club (League)	Class	W	L	ERA	G	GS	CG	SV	IP	H	HR	BB	SO	K/9	WHIP	AVG
2012	Red Sox (GCL)	R	1	0	5.19	5	4	0	0	9	8	0	3	7	7.3	1.27	.258
2013	Lowell (NYP)	SS	5	1	3.92	13	12	0	0	60	48	4	17	54	8.1	1.09	.221
Minor League Totals			6	1	4.08	18	16	0	0	68	56	4	20	61	8.0	1.11	.226

23 DANIEL McGRATH, LHP

BA GRADE **45** HIGH

Born: July 7, 1994. **B-T:** R-L. **Ht.:** 6-3. **Wt.:** 205. **Signed:** Australia, 2012. **Signed by:** Jon Deeble.

McGrath's mother hails from New England, and the family racehorse is named Schilling, factors that help explain why the then-18-year-old Australian lefthander took less money ($400,000) to sign with the Red Sox in 2012. McGrath made a revelatory pro debut in 2013, making short work of Rookie-level hitters and advancing to the short-season New York-Penn League, in part because he dramatically improved his conditioning in the offseason. Now he features a leaner frame that allows him to throw strikes with a surprisingly advanced three-pitch mix: a mid- to high-80s fastball, a solid changeup and a fringe curveball. McGrath recorded half of his outs in the GCL via strikeout, and after a promotion to Lowell, he struck out more than a batter per inning, though he relies more on command than pure stuff. McGrath's lefthandedness and pitchability present a mid-rotation ceiling that will be tested at low Class A Greenville in 2014.

Year	Club (League)	Class	W	L	ERA	G	GS	CG	SV	IP	H	HR	BB	SO	K/9	WHIP	AVG
2013	Red Sox (GCL)	R	0	1	1.35	4	4	0	0	20	8	2	6	30	13.5	0.70	.129
	Lowell (NYP)	SS	3	3	4.86	8	7	0	0	33	29	2	13	35	9.5	1.26	.242
Minor League Totals			3	4	3.54	12	11	0	0	53	37	4	19	65	11.0	1.05	.203

24 SIMON MERCEDES, RHP

BA GRADE **50** EXTREME

Born: Feb. 17, 1992. **B-T:** R-R. **Ht.:** 6-4. **Wt.:** 240. **Signed:** Dominican Republic, 2012. **Signed by:** Manny Nanita/Eddie Romero.

The Red Sox signed Mercedes for $800,000 in March 2012, after he had agreed to a $400,000 deal with the Giants in March 2011, only to have Major League Baseball kill it and declare him ineligible to sign for one year. He used the same name and birthdate on both contracts, and he finally received a U.S. visa in August 2012. As a piggyback starter at short-season Lowell in 2013, Mercedes posted a 3.13 ERA with a fine 3.4 SO/BB ratio in 63 innings. He pitched with aggressiveness with a heavy, mid-90s fastball, deploying a pair of secondary pitches that need further refinement. His low-80s breaking ball flashes solid-average potential but also morphs into a mid-70s slurve when he gets around the ball. His changeup has a long way to go, and without one he probably fits best in the bullpen. Given that Mercedes will be 22 in 2014, the Red Sox may push him from Lowell to high Class A Salem.

Year	Club (League)	Class	W	L	ERA	G	GS	CG	SV	IP	H	HR	BB	SO	K/9	WHIP	AVG
2012	Red Sox (DSL)	R	0	0	0.00	1	1	0	0	4	4	0	2	4	9.0	1.50	.250
2013	Lowell (NYP)	SS	2	2	3.13	13	3	0	1	63	62	2	17	57	8.1	1.25	.263
Minor League Totals			2	2	2.94	14	4	0	1	67	66	2	19	61	8.2	1.26	.262

25 DAN BUTLER, C

Born: Oct. 17, 1986. **B-T:** R-R. **Ht.:** 5-10. **Wt.:** 210. **Signed:** Arizona, 2009 (NDFA). **Signed by:** Matt Mahoney.

Butler's career began in relative obscurity, when he signed for $10,000 as a nondrafted free agent in 2009, with the Red Sox intrigued by his strong performance in the Cape Cod League. Butler logged little playing time at Arizona, where he missed a year with Tommy John surgery, redshirted a year and returned as a backup. He has shown strong leadership and solid defensive tools at catcher while delivering respectable offense, as he hit .262/.350/.479 with 14 homers in 84 games at Triple-A Pawtucket in 2013. Added to the 40-man roster following the 2012 season, Butler has found himself behind or astride other catchers in the system, such as Ryan Lavarnway and Christian Vazquez. Given an everyday role at Pawtucket in June 2013, however, Butler made a significant impression, chasing fewer pitches above the zone and bashing 12 homers in 55 games. He lacks standout tools, but scouts from multiple organizations feel he has the potential to spend several years as at least a backup catcher and someone who may get a starting opportunity in the right situation.

Year	Club (League)	Class	AVG	G	AB	R	H	2B	3B	HR	RBI	BB	SO	SB	CS	OBP	SLG
2009	Lowell (NYP)	SS	.179	22	78	7	14	3	1	1	10	4	14	0	1	.261	.282
	Salem (CAR)	HiA	.000	2	3	0	0	0	0	0	0	0	1	0	0	.000	.000
2010	Pawtucket (IL)	AAA	.000	2	5	0	0	0	0	0	0	0	1	0	0	.000	.000
	Greenville (SAL)	LoA	.327	61	214	37	70	18	3	6	31	20	44	0	0	.406	.523
	Salem (CAR)	HiA	.292	35	113	16	33	12	0	1	17	23	21	1	0	.434	.425
2011	Salem (CAR)	HiA	.247	91	312	39	77	20	0	11	66	45	56	4	1	.350	.417
	Portland (EL)	AA	.212	21	66	4	14	5	0	0	2	9	11	0	0	.316	.288
	Pawtucket (IL)	AAA	.333	1	3	1	1	0	0	1	3	0	2	0	0	.333	1.333
2012	Portland (EL)	AA	.251	73	247	29	62	14	2	6	26	31	42	0	0	.351	.397
	Pawtucket (IL)	AAA	.233	22	73	8	17	5	0	3	11	9	20	0	0	.313	.425
2013	Pawtucket (IL)	AAA	.262	84	282	32	74	19	0	14	45	34	59	1	1	.350	.479
Minor League Totals			.259	414	1396	173	362	96	6	43	211	175	271	6	3	.356	.429

26 TRAVIS SHAW, 1B

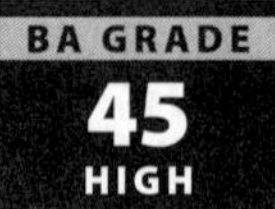

Born: April 16, 1990. **B-T:** L-R. **Ht.:** 6-4. **Wt.:** 235. **Drafted:** Kent State, 2011 (9th round). **Signed by:** Jon Adkins.

The son of former all-star closer Jeff Shaw, Travis excelled at high Class A Salem in 2012 and earned a second-half promotion to Double-A Portland on the strength of terrific strike-zone judgment and rock-steady power production in the form of 19 homers and 44 doubles. At his best, Shaw mixes the ability to drive the ball to left-center field—something that bodes well for any hitter who calls Fenway Park home—with flashes of pull power. But he became too pull-conscious while struggling at Portland in 2013, batting .221/.342/.394 and losing 25 extra-base hits from his ledger. Shaw reestablished his credentials with a standout performance in the 2013 Arizona Fall League—five homers and a .705 slugging percentage in 17 games—after he incorporated a leg kick to force him to stay back on the ball. That AFL showing rekindled the notion that he has a chance to be a first baseman with solid on-base skills, gap power and solid-average defense. The likelihood of becoming a big league regular depends on his ability to add more power without selling out his approach, something he'll work on at Triple-A Pawtucket in 2014.

Year	Club (League)	Class	AVG	G	AB	R	H	2B	3B	HR	RBI	BB	SO	SB	CS	OBP	SLG
2011	Lowell (NYP)	SS	.262	57	202	33	53	13	0	8	36	34	47	3	0	.371	.446
	Greenville (SAL)	LoA	.333	2	9	1	3	1	0	0	1	1	0	0	0	.400	.444
2012	Salem (CAR)	HiA	.305	99	354	69	108	31	3	16	73	59	81	11	2	.411	.545
	Portland (EL)	AA	.227	31	110	13	25	13	0	3	12	21	34	1	1	.353	.427
2013	Portland (EL)	AA	.221	127	444	57	98	21	4	16	50	78	117	7	3	.342	.394
Minor League Totals			.256	316	1119	173	287	79	7	43	172	193	279	22	6	.371	.455

27 JAVIER GUERRA, SS

BA GRADE
50
EXTREME

Born: Sept. 29, 1995. **B-T:** L-R. **Ht.:** 5-11. **Wt.:** 155. **Signed:** Panama, 2012. **Signed by:** Eddie Romero.

The Red Sox loved Guerra's upside when they signed him as a 16-year-old out of Panama for $250,000 in 2012. They saw a player with the athleticism, the internal clock and arm strength to play shortstop, plus a line-drive, lefthanded stroke that works against both lefties and righties. Guerra's performance in his pro debut in the Dominican Summer League in 2013 was modest, however, as he hit .248/.356/.290 with just nine extra-base hits (all doubles). He carried a strong DSL finish into an impressive performance in instructional league, validating impressions of his maturity for his age. "He opened some eyes in instructional league," said one evaluator. As he fills out, Guerra's upside is that of a shortstop who can contribute on both sides of the ball, though amateur scouts pegged him as a a player with below-average speed and average arm strength, attributes that could signal a move to second base one day. If he adds a bit more power to his arsenal and continues to counteract fringe run times with strong baserunning instincts, he might make it at the keystone. The Red Sox probably will send Guerra to the Rookie-level Gulf Coast League in 2014.

Year	Club (League)	Class	AVG	G	AB	R	H	2B	3B	HR	RBI	BB	SO	SB	CS	OBP	SLG
2013	Red Sox (DSL)	R	.248	60	210	27	52	9	0	0	23	33	40	7	4	.356	.290
Minor League Totals			.248	60	210	27	52	9	0	0	23	33	40	7	4	.356	.290

28 TZU-WEI LIN, SS

BA GRADE
50
EXTREME

Born: Feb. 15, 1994. **B-T:** L-R. **Ht.:** 5-9. **Wt.:** 162. **Signed:** Taiwan, 2012. **Signed by:** Louie Lin/Jon Deeble/Eddie Romero.

The Red Sox signed Lin for $2.05 million in June 2012, just before the imposition of the new international bonus rules took effect. He has generated mixed impressions from his early career performance in the Rookie-level Gulf Coast League in 2012 and at short-season Lowell in 2013. Many evaluators feel Lin has the defensive tools to be a shortstop, while simultaneously offering a line-drive, lefthanded swing geared toward the opposite field, paired with the plate discipline to hit for average and get on base. He also has the well above-average speed to make an impact once on base. Others see a player who hit .226/.312/.296 and stole just 12 bases in the New York-Penn League and appeared worn out by the end of the season. The latter group wonders whether Lin will ever be physical enough to withstand the physical grind of a full season. Thus his transition to full-season ball in 2014 at low Class A Greenville will offer an important indicator of his impact potential.

Year	Club (League)	Class	AVG	G	AB	R	H	2B	3B	HR	RBI	BB	SO	SB	CS	OBP	SLG
2012	Red Sox (GCL)	R	.255	29	110	21	28	5	1	0	16	16	28	4	2	.341	.318
2013	Lowell (NYP)	SS	.226	60	230	34	52	9	2	1	20	28	59	12	4	.312	.296
Minor League Totals			.235	89	340	55	80	14	3	1	36	44	87	16	6	.321	.303

29 ALEX WILSON, RHP

Born: Nov. 3, 1986. **B-T:** R-R. **Ht.:** 6-0. **Wt.:** 225. **Drafted:** Texas A&M, 2009 (2nd round). **Signed by:** Jim Robinson.

A second-round pick in 2009, Wilson spent his first two and a half pro seasons as a starter before the Red Sox moved him to the bullpen in 2012. They anticipated that his fastball/slider combination would play up in short stints. But his velocity—mostly 92-93 mph—and overall stuff have yet to receive a late-inning bump. Wilson, however, now works more with a two-seamer than a four-seamer, and in his big league debut in 2013, he induced enough bad contact to become a viable seventh-inning option. That lasted through the end of June, by which point Wilson had posted a 3.33 ERA and strikeout rate of 7.0 per nine innings, but then a thumb injury led to a couple of ERA-inflating outings in early July. The injury ultimately proved the end of his season, requiring surgery. Despite the modest profile, Wilson is a major league-ready bullpen option who could step in and contribute in the sixth or seventh inning to begin 2014, with the possibility that his stuff could tick up a bit with his thumb issue behind him.

Year	Club (League)	Class	W	L	ERA	G	GS	CG	SV	IP	H	HR	BB	SO	K/9	WHIP	AVG
2009	Lowell (NYP)	SS	0	1	0.50	13	13	0	0	36	10	0	7	33	8.3	0.47	.085
2010	Salem (CAR)	HiA	2	1	3.40	11	11	0	0	56	43	4	15	50	8.1	1.04	.212
	Portland (EL)	AA	4	5	6.66	16	16	0	0	78	95	15	34	56	6.4	1.65	.302
2011	Portland (EL)	AA	9	4	3.05	21	21	0	0	112	103	8	37	99	8.0	1.25	.246
	Pawtucket (IL)	AAA	1	0	3.43	4	4	0	0	21	19	2	7	24	10.3	1.24	.235
2012	Pawtucket (IL)	AAA	5	3	3.72	40	3	0	1	73	76	3	33	78	9.7	1.50	.270
2013	Boston (AL)	MAJ	1	1	4.88	26	0	0	0	28	34	0	14	22	7.2	1.73	.306
	Pawtucket (IL)	AAA	3	1	3.71	14	0	0	0	17	17	2	5	16	8.5	1.29	.262
Major League Totals			1	1	4.88	26	0	0	0	28	34	0	14	22	7.2	1.73	.306
Minor League Totals			24	15	3.76	119	68	0	1	393	363	34	138	356	8.2	1.28	.245

30 SEAN COYLE, 2B

BA GRADE
50
EXTREME

Born: Jan. 17, 1992. **B-T:** R-R. **Ht.:** 5-8. **Wt.:** 180. **Drafted:** HS—Fort Washington, Pa., 2010 (3rd round). **Signed by:** Chris Calciano.

The Red Sox signed Coyle, a 2010 third-rounder, away from a scholarship to North Carolina with a $1.3 million bonus. If he hadn't signed, he would have joined brother Tommy, now a second basemen in the Rays system, on the Tar Heels infield. Boston believed Sean Coyle had the potential for 25 homers, with a chance to develop into an average defender at second base and provide excess baserunning value. He's a perfect 27-for-27 in stolen base attempts in two seasons at high Class A Salem. Coyle has lived up to that potential at times—foremost in the early stages of 2013, when he hit nine homers in 17 games at Salem—but from that point forward, his season unraveled due to ongoing challenges staying healthy and over-aggressiveness at the plate. He missed two months with a knee injury, then had an elbow issue at the end of the year that cost him an assignment to the Arizona Fall League. Some wonder if his makeup will permit him to accept the game's inherent failure. He spent his second straight season in the Carolina League in 2013, but given Coyle's plus speed, average glove and chance to unlock at least average power, he could be a late-bloomer. The Red Sox must decide how to divvy up playing time at the keystone for Coyle and Mookie Betts at Double-A Portland in 2014, and it's a crossroads season for the former.

Year	Club (League)	Class	AVG	G	AB	R	H	2B	3B	HR	RBI	BB	SO	SB	CS	OBP	SLG
2010	Red Sox (GCL)	R	.200	3	10	5	2	1	0	0	0	1	1	0	0	.333	.300
2011	Greenville (SAL)	LoA	.247	106	384	77	95	27	7	14	64	60	110	20	6	.362	.464
2012	Salem (CAR)	HiA	.249	116	437	60	109	31	2	9	63	29	116	16	0	.316	.391
2013	Red Sox (GCL)	R	.150	6	20	3	3	0	0	1	3	3	6	1	1	.292	.300
	Greenville (SAL)	LoA	.320	6	25	4	8	3	0	1	4	3	9	0	1	.393	.560
	Salem (CAR)	HiA	.241	48	195	41	47	9	1	14	28	24	65	11	0	.321	.513
Minor League Totals			.246	285	1071	190	264	71	10	39	162	120	307	48	8	.336	.441

Chicago Cubs

BY JOHN MANUEL

Expectations for the 2013 edition of the Cubs remained low entering the season. The North Siders did their best to live down to them.

Not only did the Cubs improve by just five games over the 101-loss 2012 campaign, but the perceived stalwarts of the team stalled significantly on their way to being first-division starters for a contender.

First baseman Anthony Rizzo played in 160 games but hit .233/.323/.419, and his inability to hit lefthanders (.617 OPS in 320 career at-bats) remains alarming. Righthander Jeff Samardzija had his moments but also allowed 25 home runs, and veteran Edwin Jackson, brought in on a four-year deal to provide stability, lost 18 games with an ugly 4.98 ERA. Most concerning was 23-year-old shortstop Starlin Castro, who frequently lost focus and became an out machine during a disastrous .245/.284/.347 season.

Poor seasons by those core Cubs contributed to manager Dale Sveum being let go after two seasons, though communication issues and 197 losses helped grease the skids. Team president Theo Epstein and general manager Jed Hoyer selected Padres bench coach Rick Renteria as Sveum's replacement in November.

Getting the best out of the likes of Castro, Rizzo and Samardzija will be crucial for Renteria, and Castro's 2014 performance also will affect the farm system. The Cubs quickly have built farm depth and boast an impressive array of talent, particularly among their young hitters.

Shortstop Javier Baez ranked second in the minors with 37 home runs, and the 2011 first-round pick hit 20 of them in 54 games at Double-A Tennessee. The system's top prospect could move off short if Castro, signed through 2019 for $60 million, bounces back. But if Castro doesn't and Baez tones down his errors, the Cubs will have a crunch on their hands.

Baez could move to second, though the Cubs like Arismendy Alcantara, a power/speed middle infielder who moved to second in 2013. Baez could shift to third, but that's also where 2013 first-rounder Kris Bryant, the No. 2 overall pick and BA College Player of the Year, plays.

Bryant could move to right, but that's where Cuban import Jorge Soler, signed for $30 million in June 2012, profiles best. Baez, Bryant and Soler will have to work out where to play, but the trio gives the Cubs a unique collection of 80-power righthanded bats that other organizations envy.

Developing pitchers has been harder for Chicago, but 2012 supplemental first-rounder Pierce Johnson had a strong season, finishing at high Class A Daytona. He was joined in the second-half rotation by three trade imports, chief among them righthander C.J. Edwards, the centerpiece of the Matt Garza deal with the Rangers. Edwards and Bryant helped Daytona earn Minor League Team of the Year honors.

Chicago added more talent in the July 2 international signing period, signing the top two prospects available, Dominican outfielder Eloy Jimenez and Venezuelan shortstop Gleyber Torres, for a combined $4.5 million. The organization spent more than $7.6 million on its top five international signings, blowing past its international bonus pool of more than $5.5 million.

GEORGE GOJKOVICH

The Cubs want to build around Starlin Castro but he had a disastrous 2013 season

TOP PROSPECTS OF THE DECADE

Year	Player, Pos.	2013 Org.
2004	Angel Guzman, rhp	Out of baseball
2005	Brian Dopirak, 1b	Out of baseball
2006	Felix Pie, of	Pirates
2007	Felix Pie, of	Pirates
2008	Josh Vitters, 3b	Cubs
2009	Josh Vitters, 3b	Cubs
2010	Starlin Castro, ss	Cubs
2011	Chris Archer, rhp	Rays
2012	Brett Jackson, of	Cubs
2013	Javier Baez, ss	Cubs

ORGANIZATION OVERVIEW

General Manager: Jed Hoyer. **Farm Director:** Jaron Madison. **Scouting Director:** Matt Dorey.

Class	Team	League	W	L	PCT	Finish	Manager
Majors	Chicago Cubs	National	66	96	.407	14th (15)	Dale Sveum
Triple-A	Iowa Cubs	Pacific Coast	66	78	.458	14th (16)	Marty Pevey
Double-A	Tennessee Smokies	Southern	76	62	.571	2nd (10)	Buddy Bailey
High Class A	Daytona Cubs	Florida State	35	31	.530	1st (12)	Dave Keller
Low Class A	Kane County Cougars	Midwest	55	80	.407	15th (16)	Mark Johnson
Short-season	Boise Hawks	Northwest	41	35	.539	3rd (8)	Gary Van Tol
Rookie	AZL Cubs	Arizona	27	28	.491	8th (13)	Bobby Mitchell
Overall 2013 Minor League Record			**340**	**334**	**.504**	**t-10th (30)**	

THIS YEAR'S TOP 30

No.	Player, Pos.	Grade/Risk
1.	Javier Baez, ss	70/Medium
2.	Kris Bryant, 3b	70/Medium
3.	C.J. Edwards, rhp	65/High
4.	Albert Almora, of	60/Medium
5.	Jorge Soler, of	65/Extreme
6.	Pierce Johnson, rhp	55/High
7.	Arismendy Alcantara, 2b/ss	55/High
8.	Jeimer Candelario, 3b	50/High
9.	Dan Vogelbach, 1b	50/High
10.	Arodys Vizcaino, rhp	55/Extreme
11.	Kyle Hendricks, rhp	45/Low
12.	Paul Blackburn, rhp	50/High
13.	Christian Villanueva, 3b	45/Medium
14.	Mike Olt, 3b	55/Extreme
15.	Corey Black, rhp	50/High
16.	Eloy Jimenez, of	55/Extreme
17.	Jacob Hannemann, of	55/Extreme
18.	Dillon Maples, rhp	55/Extreme
19.	Tyler Skulina, rhp	50/High
20.	Rob Zastryzny, lhp	50/High
21.	Ivan Pineyro, rhp	45/Medium
22.	Kyuji Fujikawa, rhp	45/Medium
23.	Gleyber Torres, ss	55/Extreme
24.	Dallas Beeler, rhp	45/High
25.	Armando Rivero, rhp	45/High
26.	Matt Szczur, of	45/High
27.	Zach Cates, rhp	45/High
28.	Ben Wells, rhp	45/High
29.	Rubi Silva, of	50/Extreme
30.	Danny Lockhart, 2b	45/High

LAST YEAR'S TOP 30

No.	Player, Pos.	Status
1.	Javier Baez, ss	No. 1
2.	Albert Almora, of	No. 4
3.	Jorge Soler, of	No. 5
4.	Arodys Vizcaino, rhp	No. 10
5.	Brett Jackson, of	Dropped out
6.	Pierce Johnson, rhp	No. 6
7.	Dan Vogelbach, 1b	No. 9
8.	Jeimer Candelario, 3b	No. 8
9.	Kyuji Fujikawa, rhp	No. 22
10.	Arismendy Alcantara, 2b	No. 7
11.	Juan Carlos Paniagua, rhp	Dropped out
12.	Christian Villanueva, 3b	No. 13
13.	Alberto Cabrera, rhp	Majors
14.	Matt Szczur, of	No. 26
15.	Junior Lake, ss/3b	Majors
16.	Paul Blackburn, rhp	No. 12
17.	Duane Underwood, rhp	Dropped out
18.	Dillon Maples, rhp	No. 18
19.	Logan Watkins, 2b/ss/of	Dropped out
20.	Marco Hernandez, ss	Dropped out
21.	Gioskar Amaya, 2b	Dropped out
22.	Tony Zych, rhp	Dropped out
23.	Robert Whitenack, rhp	(Indians)
24.	Trey McNutt, rhp	Dropped out
25.	Josh Vitters, 3b/of	Dropped out
26.	Barret Loux, rhp	Dropped out
27.	Matt Loosen, rhp	Dropped out
28.	Lendy Castillo, rhp	Dropped out
29.	Marcus Hatley, rhp	Dropped out
30.	Trey Martin, of	Dropped out

BEST TOOLS

Best Hitter for Average	Albert Almora
Best Power Hitter	Javier Baez
Best Strike-Zone Discipline	Jeimer Candelario
Fastest Baserunner	Jacob Hannemann
Best Athlete	Jacob Hannemann
Best Fastball	C.J. Edwards
Best Curveball	C.J. Edwards
Best Slider	Pierce Johnson
Best Changeup	Kyle Hendricks
Best Control	Kyle Hendricks
Best Defensive Catcher	Will Remillard
Best Defensive Infielder	Christian Villanueva
Best Infield Arm	Kris Bryant
Best Defensive Outfielder	Albert Almora
Best Outfield Arm	Jorge Soler

TOP 15 PLAYERS 25 AND UNDER

No.	Player, Pos. (Age)	Peak Level
1.	Javier Baez, ss (21)	Double-A
2.	Kris Bryant, 3b (22)	High Class A
3.	Starlin Castro, ss (24)	Majors
4.	Anthony Rizzo, 1b (24)	Majors
5.	C.J. Edwards, rhp (22)	High Class A
6.	Albert Almora, of (19)	Low Class A
7.	Jorge Soler, of (22)	High Class A
8.	Pierce Johnson, rhp (22)	High Class A
9.	Arismendy Alcantara, 2b/ss (22)	Double-A
10.	Jeimer Candelario, 3b (20)	Low Class A
11.	Dan Vogelbach, 1b (21)	High Class A
12.	Arodys Vizcaino, rhp (23)	Majors
13.	Junior Lake, of (24)	Majors
14.	Justin Grimm, rhp (25)	Majors
15.	Kyle Hendricks, rhp (24)	Triple-A

MINOR LEAGUE DEPTH CHART

CHICAGO CUBS

TOP 2014 ROOKIE: Kyle Hendricks, rhp. The big league rotation will have opportunity, which Hendricks is savvy enough to exploit.

BREAKOUT PROSPECT: Corey Black, rhp. Acquired in the 2013 Alfonso Soriano trade with the Yankees, he may have the stuff to stay in the rotation.

SLEEPER: Stephen Bruno, 2b. The Cubs' infield picture is crowded, but (when healthy) Bruno hits.

SOURCE OF TOP 30 TALENT

Homegrown	**23**	**Acquired**	**7**
College	7	Trades	7
Junior college	0	Rule 5 draft	0
High school	7	Independent leagues	0
Nondrafted free agents	0	Free agents/waivers	0
International	9		

LF

Josh Vitters
Trevor Gretzky
John Andrioli
Zeke DeVoss

CF

Albert Almora (4)
Jacob Hannemann (17)
Matt Szczur (26)
Brett Jackson
Shawon Dunston Jr.
Trey Martin
Jae-Hoon Ha
Pin-Chieh Chen

RF

Jorge Soler (5)
Eloy Jimenez (16)
Rubi Silva (29)
Bijan Rademacher

3B

Kris Bryant (2)
Jeimer Candelario (8)
Christian Villanueva (13)
Mike Olt (14)
Wes Darvill

SS

Javier Baez (1)
Marco Hernandez
Tim Saunders

2B

Arismendy Alcantara (7)
Gleyber Torres (23)
Daniel Lockhart (30)
Stephen Bruno
Logan Watkins
Gioskar Amaya

1B

Dan Vogelbach (9)
Dustin Geiger
Rock Shoulders

C

Willson Contreras
Chadd Krist
Ben Carhart
Jordan Hankins

LHP

LHSP	LHRP
Rob Zastryzny (20)	Sam Wilson
Brooks Raley	

RHP

RHSP	RHRP
C.J. Edwards (3)	Arodys Vizcaino (10)
Pierce Johnson (6)	Kyuji Fujikawa (22)
Kyle Hendricks (11)	Armando Rivero (25)
Paul Blackburn (12)	Zach Cates (27)
Corey Black (15)	Marcus Hatley
Dillon Maples (18)	Juan Carlos Paniagua
Tyler Skulina (19)	Scott Frazier
Ivan Pineyro (21)	
Dallas Beeler (24)	
Ben Wells (28)	
Tayler Scott	
Matt Loosen	
Duane Underwood	
Trey Masek	
Erick Leal	

DRAFT ANALYSIS

2013

BONUSES: $11.1 MILLION

BEST PURE HITTER: 3B Kris Bryant (1) spread out at the plate this spring, keeping his head still and lower while reducing his overall pre-swing movement. That cut down on his swing-and-miss tendencies, and he hit .336 in 128 at-bats in his pro debut.

BEST POWER HITTER: Bryant showed his top-of-the-scale raw power all spring, hitting 31 homers to earn BA's College Player of the Year award, and as a pro, when he hit nine homers and slugged .688.

FASTEST RUNNER: OF Carcer Burks (9) turned in 6.5-second 60-yard times in a predraft workout. OF Jacob Hannemann (3) isn't as fast out of the batter's box but flies once under way.

BEST DEFENSIVE PLAYER: Hannemann could stand to add polish, but he outruns his mistakes in center field. C Will Remillard (19) got a $150,000 bonus mostly for his catch-and-throw skills, with his arm being his best tool.

BEST FASTBALL: Six-foot-7 RHP Scott Frazier (6) tops out at 97 mph and sits in the 94-96 range, but right now he doesn't generate many swings and misses. LHP Rob Zastryzny (2) sits at 90-91 but adds and subtracts, throws strikes and gets many more swings and misses in the strike zone with his heater. RHP Trey Masek (5) has touched 95 with life.

BEST SECONDARY PITCH: RHP Tyler Skulina (4) stands out for his hard, late power slider in the low 80s.

BEST PRO DEBUT: Bryant helped Daytona win the high Class A Florida State League title, hitting .350 in the playoffs. RHP Zack Godley (10) helped Boise reach the short-season Northwest League finals, going 2-0, 2.03 overall with 28 strikeouts in 27 innings.

BEST ATHLETE: Hannemann redshirted for Brigham Young's football team as a 6-foot-1, 195-pound defensive back, then raked in the spring for BYU's baseball team after having missed two years while serving on his Mormon mission.

MOST INTRIGUING BACKGROUND: Hannemann, who is distantly related to assistant general manager for scouting/player development Jason McLeod. RHP Daniel Poncedeleon (14) signed a term sheet but failed his physical. He has been ruled ineligible to return to his college team, though Houston is appealing the NCAA's decision.

CLOSEST TO THE MAJORS: Bryant won't need long at all with the bat; the only question is if he'll play third base or move to an outfield corner.

BEST LATE-ROUND PICK: RHP Trevor Clifton (12) signed for $375,000. He fell thanks to a raw delivery and his green makeup, but his arm strength produces 91-94 mph fastballs and he flashes plus secondary stuff. He needs a lot of polish.

THE ONE WHO GOT AWAY: Poncedeleon, as well as C Jeremy Martinez (37), a physically mature, strong-bodied centerpiece of Southern California's recruiting class.

ASSESSMENT: Bryant was too good for the pitching-starved Cubs to pass up. They went for volume with their pitchers thereafter, with Zastryzny likely to help soon and Clifton the biggest wild card.

2012

BONUSES: $9.2 MILLION

Albert Almora (1) had an injury-plagued debut. RHPs Pierce Johnson (1s) and Paul Blackburn (1s) may be more important to a pitching-needy system.

GRADE: B

2011

BONUSES: $12.0 MILLION

SS Javier Baez (1) has exceeded expectations thus far. Signed for $2.5 million, raw RHP Dillon Maples (14) is the best arm in a hitter-heavy group.

GRADE: B+

2010

BONUSES: $4.7 MILLION

RHP Hayden Simpson (1) backfired almost immediately. There's hope for OF Matt Szczur (5) and RHPs Ben Wells (7) and Dallas Beeler (41).

GRADE: D

TOP DRAFT PICKS OF THE DECADE

Year	Player, Pos.	2013 Org.
2004	Grant Johnson, rhp (2nd round)	Out of baseball
2005	Mark Pawelek, lhp	Out of baseball
2006	Tyler Colvin, of	Rockies
2007	Josh Vitters, 3b	Cubs
2008	Andrew Cashner, rhp	Padres
2009	Brett Jackson, of	Cubs
2010	Hayden Simpson, rhp	Southern Illinois (Frontier)
2011	Javier Baez, ss	Cubs
2012	Albert Almora, of	Cubs
2013	Kris Bryant, 3b	Cubs

LARGEST BONUSES IN CLUB HISTORY

Kris Bryant, 2013	$6,708,400
Jorge Soler, 2012	$6,000,000
Mark Prior, 2001	$4,000,000
Kosuke Fukudome, 2007	$4,000,000
Albert Almora, 2012	$3,900,000

1 JAVIER BAEZ, SS

Born: Dec. 1, 1992. **B-T:** R-R. **Ht.:** 6-0. **Wt.:** 195.
Drafted: HS—Jacksonville, 2011 (1st round).
Signed by: Tom Clark.

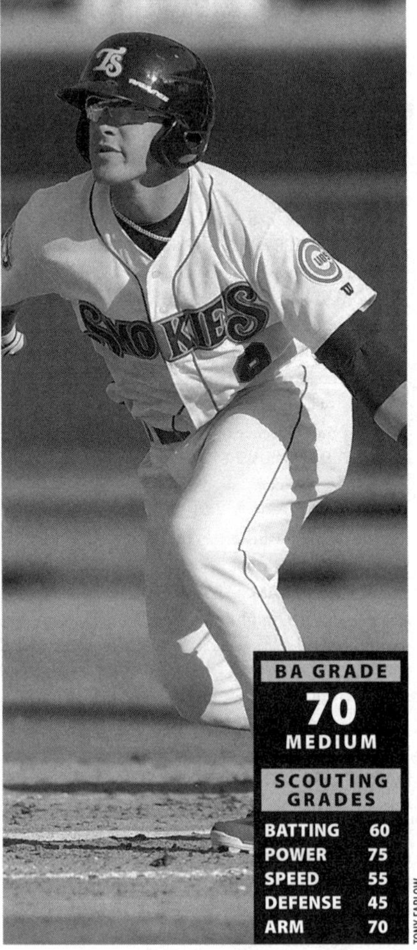

BA GRADE
70
MEDIUM
SCOUTING GRADES
BATTING 60
POWER 75
SPEED 55
DEFENSE 45
ARM 70

TONY FARLOW

Tom Clark coached at Lake City (Fla.) CC for more than 20 years and had a history of recruiting and coaching Puerto Rican players. When the school changed its name and dropped athletics, Clark latched on with the Cubs as an area scout, and his experience came in handy scouting Baez, who was born in Puerto Rico and moved to Florida when he was 12. Baez's aggressive style had boiled over at times in his amateur career, even prompting a near-brawl at a 2010 showcase in Jupiter, Fla., but Clark got to know Baez and his family. The Cubs were confident enough to draft him ninth overall in 2011, signing him for a $2.625 bonus. After ending 2012 with a broken left thumb, Baez showed no ill effects in 2013, with a torrid finish at Double-A Tennessee pushing him to 37 home runs, tied for second in the minors. He led all minor leaguers with 111 RBIs and 75 extra-base hits.

Baez has special bat speed and produces top-of-the-scale power with an exceptionally aggressive approach and swing. He has tremendous plate coverage and really has no true holes in his swing, which takes a direct and violent path to the ball. Baez has work to do with pitch recognition and can drift at times thanks to his leg kick, but he hits the ball so hard, he doesn't have to square it up to hit it out of the park. His patience and pitch recognition improved against better competition, and some scouts see him as an above-average hitter despite his propensity to chase. Baez's defensive tools suit him for shortstop, while his aggressiveness does not. He has average speed and solid range to go with solid actions and a 70-grade arm, but he needs to slow the game down and consistently make the routine play. He committed 44 errors on the season. His baseball instincts suit him well at the plate and on the basepaths, and his competitiveness, which at times comes across as over-the-top swagger, has helped him rise to big moments, such as a walk-off homer against Japan's World Baseball Classic team during a spring training exhibition game.

Baez hit 41 homers in 2013 between big league spring training and the regular season—plus 10 more in minor league camp—and his power should make Wrigley Field look small sooner than later. With Starlin Castro signed through 2019 but coming off a poor season, Baez presents the Cubs with a fascinating option. If his defense improves with maturity and experience—reasonable, given his tools—he could force Castro to second or third base. More likely, Baez shifts to second or third, causing a logjam with other Cubs prospects such as 2013 first-rounder Kris Bryant and Baez's Tennessee double-play partner Arismendy Alcantara. Spring training will help decide Baez's 2014 assignment and position, but he profiles as an all-star-caliber, 30-homer infielder wherever he lands.

Year	Club (League)	Class	AVG	G	AB	R	H	2B	3B	HR	RBI	BB	SO	SB	CS	OBP	SLG
2011	Cubs (AZL)	R	.333	3	12	2	4	2	0	0	0	0	2	2	0	.333	.500
	Boise (NWL)	SS	.167	2	6	0	1	0	0	0	1	0	2	0	0	.167	.167
2012	Peoria (MWL)	LoA	.333	57	213	41	71	10	5	12	33	9	48	20	3	.383	.596
	Daytona (FSL)	HiA	.188	23	80	9	15	3	1	4	13	5	21	4	2	.244	.400
2013	Daytona (FSL)	HiA	.274	76	299	59	82	19	4	17	57	21	78	12	2	.338	.535
	Tennessee (SL)	AA	.294	54	218	39	64	15	0	20	54	19	69	8	2	.346	.638
Minor League Totals			.286	215	828	150	237	49	10	53	158	54	220	46	9	.342	.562

2 KRIS BRYANT, 3B

Born: Jan. 4, 1992. **B-T:** R-R. **Ht.:** 6-5. **Wt.:** 215. **Drafted:** San Diego, 2013 (1st round). **Signed by:** Alex Lontayo.

Bryant was an 18th-round pick out of Las Vegas' Bonanza High in 2010 but attended San Diego instead. After hitting 23 home runs in his first two seasons, Bryant was BA's College Player of the Year as a junior, leading the nation in home runs (31), walks, total bases and slugging. The Cubs drafted him No. 2 overall, and he got the largest signing bonus in franchise history and in the 2013 draft, $6,708,400. He hit nine homers in his debut and helped high Class A Daytona win the Florida State League title. Tall, lean and athletic, Bryant has all-star tools. He adjusted as a junior by spreading out in the batter's box, lowering his head and eliminating pre-swing movement. He can still get a bit uphill with his swing but now punishes the low ball. He has the leverage and loft in his swing to produce 40 homers annually while being an above-average hitter. Bryant's easy arm strength fits well at third base, and he has solid infield actions, but he's tall for the position and some scouts consider him a better fit for right field. He played some right and even center field in college thanks to his average speed and long strides. Bryant's torrid Arizona Fall League tour indicates he is on the fast track to Wrigley Field. If he moves quickly, he likely will shift to an outfield corner.

Year	Club (League)	Class	AVG	G	AB	R	H	2B	3B	HR	RBI	BB	SO	SB	CS	OBP	SLG
2013	Cubs (AZL)	R	.167	2	6	0	1	1	0	0	2	0	1	0	0	.143	.333
	Boise (NWL)	SS	.354	18	65	13	23	8	1	4	16	8	17	0	0	.416	.692
	Daytona (FSL)	HiA	.333	16	57	9	19	5	1	5	14	3	17	1	0	.387	.719
Minor League Totals			.336	36	128	22	43	14	2	9	32	11	35	1	0	.390	.688

3 C.J. EDWARDS, RHP

Born: Sept. 3, 1991. **B-T:** R-R. **Ht.:** 6-2. **Wt.:** 155. **Drafted:** HS—Prosperity, S.C., 2011 (48th round). **Signed by:** Chris Kemp (Rangers).

Rangers area scout Chris Kemp found Edwards in a South Carolina adult league playing with other members of his baseball-steeped family. The Rangers waited until the 48th round to draft him and signed him for $50,000, then watched him emerge as the top prospect on their loaded 2013 low Class A Hickory team. He became the key piece in the package of prospects the Cubs received in the Matt Garza trade. Edwards misses barrels and bats, combining great stuff with tremendous work ethic and makeup. His thin frame evokes comparisons with Oil Can Boyd and prompts questions about his durability, but his stuff was at its best in September during the Florida State League playoffs. He locates his 93-95 mph fastball with excellent riding life and has allowed only one pro homer. His curveball gives him a second plus pitch, and he throws a hard slider that earns average grades. He uses his changeup sparingly but locked up lefthanded hitters anyway (.175, five extra-base hits in 166 at-bats). He needs more strength to maintain his stuff and keep his long arms and delivery on time. If he can hold up physically over the long term, Edwards has front-of-the-rotation potential. He's headed to Double-A for 2014.

Year	Club (League)	Class	W	L	ERA	G	GS	CG	SV	IP	H	HR	BB	SO	K/9	WHIP	AVG
2012	Rangers (AZL)	R	3	0	0.00	4	3	0	0	20	6	0	6	25	11.3	0.60	.094
	Spokane (NWL)	SS	2	3	2.11	10	10	0	0	47	26	0	19	60	11.5	0.96	.160
2013	Hickory (SAL)	LoA	8	2	1.83	18	18	1	0	93	62	0	34	122	11.8	1.03	.186
	Daytona (FSL)	HiA	0	0	1.96	6	6	0	0	23	14	1	7	33	12.9	0.91	.169
Minor League Totals			13	5	1.72	38	37	1	0	183	108	1	66	240	11.8	0.95	.168

4 ALBERT ALMORA, OF

Born: April 16, 1994. **B-T:** R-R. **Ht.:** 6-2. **Wt.:** 180. **Drafted:** HS—Hialeah Gardens, Fla., 2012 (1st round). **Signed by:** John Koronka/Laz Llanos.

USA Baseball turned to Almora frequently during his amateur career. He tied A.J. Hinch's record by playing on six national teams, though Hinch had the advantage of a four-year college career. The sixth overall pick in the 2012 draft signed for a $3.9 million bonus. His first full season was delayed until late May by a broken hamate in his left hand and ended in early August due to a groin pull. Almora has good tools and maximizes them with tremendous baseball instincts. His best tool is his bat, which scouts project as above-average or better. He has a loose swing, present strength and good hand-eye coordination. He uses the whole field, using what one club official calls a "no-ego approach" at the plate. Almora employs a leg kick and has to be on time but has good natural hitting rhythm, and had 24 multi-hit games in 61 Midwest League starts. He projects to have average or better home run power. Almora is just an average runner, if not a tick below, but he has premium range in center field thanks to his impeccable breaks on the ball, first-step reactions and passion for playing defense. He has a plus, accurate arm as well. A natural leader, the bilingual Almora bridges the cultural gap for Cubs farmhands from Jorge Soler to Kris Bryant. Almora has taken system-mate Jorge Soler under his wing, and they played together in the Arizona Fall League to make up for time lost to injuries. A healthy Almora should move quickly and settle in as a talented glue guy in a lineup with plenty of explosive bats such as Javier Baez, Bryant and Soler.

Year	Club (League)	Class	AVG	G	AB	R	H	2B	3B	HR	RBI	BB	SO	SB	CS	OBP	SLG
2012	Cubs (AZL)	R	.347	18	75	18	26	5	1	1	13	2	8	5	1	.363	.480
	Boise (NWL)	SS	.292	15	65	9	19	7	0	1	6	0	5	0	1	.292	.446
2013	Kane County (MWL)	LoA	.329	61	249	39	82	17	4	3	23	17	30	4	4	.376	.466
Minor League Totals			.326	94	389	66	127	29	5	5	42	19	43	9	6	.361	.465

5 JORGE SOLER, OF

BA GRADE
65
EXTREME

Born: Feb. 25, 1992. **B-T:** R-R. **Ht.:** 6-4. **Wt.:** 215. **Signed:** Cuba, 2012. **Signed by:** Louie Eljaua/Jose Serra/Alex Suarez.

Soler burst on the scene in 2010 while playing for Cuba's national team in the World Junior Championship, with current Cubs farmhand Yasiel Balaguert as a teammate. He left the island in 2011, and the Cubs signed him in 2012 to a nine-year, $30 million deal that included a $6 million bonus. Soler missed games in the first half due to two suspensions, then played his last game on June 13, going down with a stress fracture in his left tibia. Soler is what a right fielder is supposed to look like. High Class A Daytona manager Dave Keller said he has never seen a hitter impart backspin to the ball like Soler does, and his swing, strength and sound plate approach give him top-shelf hitting ability and power. Some scouts give Soler 80 raw power on the 20-80 scale, and his arm earns 70 grades from some scouts. His defense is average. While Soler wasn't fully healthy all spring, he also didn't always give a full effort, and at times he appeared uninspired about playing in the minors. He charged the opposing dugout wielding a bat in an April 10 game against Clearwater that prompted a five-game suspension. The Cubs insist Soler is a good teammate who just needs maturity to handle the cultural adjustment and attention his contract brings. Heavier after his leg injury, Soler knocked off some rust in the Arizona Fall League, but his inactivity showed. A healthy, motivated Soler has special offensive potential, and he'll likely return to Daytona to team with Albert Almora to start 2014.

Year	Club (League)	Class	AVG	G	AB	R	H	2B	3B	HR	RBI	BB	SO	SB	CS	OBP	SLG
2012	Cubs (AZL)	R	.241	14	54	14	13	2	0	2	10	6	13	8	0	.328	.389
	Peoria (MWL)	LoA	.338	20	80	14	27	5	0	3	15	6	6	4	1	.398	.513
2013	Daytona (FSL)	HiA	.281	55	210	38	59	13	1	8	35	21	38	5	1	.343	.467
Minor League Totals			.288	89	344	66	99	20	1	13	60	33	57	17	2	.353	.465

6 PIERCE JOHNSON, RHP

BA GRADE
55
HIGH

Born: May 10, 1991. **B-T:** R-R. **Ht.:** 6-3. **Wt.:** 170. **Drafted:** Missouri State, 2012 (1st round supplemental). **Signed by:** Stan Zielinski.

The lineage of lanky Colorado pitching products since Roy Halladay emerged in 1995 inspires confidence for Johnson. Big leaguers of recent vintage from the Rocky Mountain state include Brad Lidge, Scott Elarton, Luke Hochevar, Mark Melancon and Kevin Gausman. Johnson went from the Denver area to Missouri State, signing for $1.196 million as the 43rd overall pick in 2012. He finished his first full season in the high Class A Daytona playoff rotation. Blessed with a lean, athletic pitcher's frame, Johnson attacks hitters with two plus pitches. His fastball sits in the 90-94 mph range, touching 96. His breaking ball, a power curve in the low 80s, is one of the best in the system, and he has a feel for using it. The Cubs thought Johnson improved at using his inconsistent, but at times solid-average, changeup to both lefties and righties. He also excelled at locating his fastball to both sides of the plate. Johnson had health issues as an amateur but stayed healthy in 2013. Some scouts retain concern about his arm action, which may have contributed to forearm issues he had as a prep senior, but most scouts project him to have average to above-average control. Johnson and C.J. Edwards are the best pitching prospects in the Cubs system. They'll head to Double-A Tennessee in 2014 to see which one gets to Chicago first. Health likely will be the biggest factor in who wins the race.

Year	Club (League)	Class	W	L	ERA	G	GS	CG	SV	IP	H	HR	BB	SO	K/9	WHIP	AVG
2012	Cubs (AZL)	R	0	0	0.00	2	2	0	0	3	4	0	0	2	6.0	1.33	.364
	Boise (NWL)	SS	0	0	4.50	4	4	0	0	8	10	0	3	12	13.5	1.63	.323
2013	Kane County (MWL)	LoA	5	5	3.10	13	13	0	0	70	68	4	22	74	9.6	1.29	.255
	Daytona (FSL)	HiA	6	1	2.22	10	8	0	0	49	41	1	21	50	9.2	1.27	.240
Minor League Totals			11	6	2.78	29	27	0	0	129	123	5	46	138	9.6	1.31	.256

7 ARISMENDY ALCANTARA, 2B/SS

Born: Oct. 29, 1991. **B-T:** B-R. **Ht.:** 5-10. **Wt.:** 170. **Signed:** Dominican Republic, 2008. **Signed by:** Jose Serra/Marino Encarnacion/Carlos Reyes.

Alcantara has the longest tenure in the organization of any of the system's Top 10 Prospects, and holdovers and newcomers alike admire his combination of aptitude and athleticism, which began to come together in 2012 and resulted in a 2013 Futures Game spot. Alcantara played shortstop in the first half for Double-A Tennessee, then moved to second base in deference to Javier Baez. He has a plus arm that plays at short but is a true weapon at second base, especially when it comes to turning the double play. His hands are a bit hard and fit better at second, where he has above-average potential. A plus runner with first-step quickness, Alcantara is an adept basestealer, and an improved approach at the plate helped him triple his walk rate, meaning more chances to steal. Deeper counts meant more strikeouts but also more hitter's counts, unleashing the solid-average power in Alcantara's short, compact swing. He ranked second in the Southern League in doubles and extra-base hits (55). With all the Cubs' infield options, Alcantara may be the most versatile piece. He'd fit as a super-utility player and has the tools to play center field well. He played second base for Licey in the Dominican League and heads to Triple-A for 2014 to consolidate the gains made last season.

Year	Club (League)	Class	AVG	G	AB	R	H	2B	3B	HR	RBI	BB	SO	SB	CS	OBP	SLG
2009	Cubs 1 (DSL)	R	.275	65	258	44	71	11	8	3	32	30	47	20	2	.349	.415
2010	Boise (NWL)	SS	.283	59	219	29	62	5	6	3	24	10	53	7	3	.315	.402
2011	Peoria (MWL)	LoA	.271	99	369	45	100	14	5	2	37	16	76	8	8	.303	.352
2012	Daytona (FSL)	HiA	.302	85	331	47	100	13	7	7	51	19	61	25	4	.339	.447
2013	Tennessee (SL)	AA	.271	133	494	69	134	36	4	15	69	62	125	31	6	.352	.451
Minor League Totals			.279	441	1671	234	467	79	30	30	213	137	362	91	23	.334	.417

8 JEIMER CANDELARIO, 3B

Born: Nov. 24, 1993. **B-T:** B-R. **Ht.:** 6-1. **Wt.:** 180. **Signed:** Dominican Republic, 2010. **Signed by:** Jose Serra/Marino Encarnacion.

The Cubs pushed Candelario in 2013 with an Opening Day assignment in the low Class A Midwest League as a 19-year-old. In his first full season since signing for $500,000 in 2010, he grinded out a productive season, leading Kane County in games and walks while ranking third in the MWL in doubles. Though as a switch-hitter he has to put in twice the work, Candelario has one of the more polished swings in the organization. He stays balanced in the box with a little knee tuck to get his swing started, then stays in the strike zone well with his line-drive swing plane. He started realizing his own hot zones as a hitter and hit eight of his 11 homers after July 1. Club officials project him to hit for above-average power, with average or slightly better hitting ability. He's a grinder defensively as well, with modest first-step quickness and below-average speed, but enough arm strength for third and solid hands. With added strength and continued defensive polish, Candelario can fit the third-base profile. If he doesn't stay at third, however, he'll be limited to first base, so the Cubs will give him time. He's headed to high Class A Daytona for 2014.

Year	Club (League)	Class	AVG	G	AB	R	H	2B	3B	HR	RBI	BB	SO	SB	CS	OBP	SLG
2011	Cubs 2 (DSL)	R	.337	72	249	50	84	16	2	5	53	50	42	4	4	.443	.478
2012	Boise (NWL)	SS	.281	71	278	34	78	14	0	6	47	26	55	2	1	.345	.396
2013	Kane County (MWL)	LoA	.256	130	500	71	128	35	1	11	57	68	88	1	0	.346	.396
Minor League Totals			.282	273	1027	155	290	65	3	22	157	144	185	7	5	.371	.416

9 DAN VOGELBACH, 1B

Born: Dec. 17, 1992. **B-T:** L-R. **Ht.:** 6-0. **Wt.:** 260. **Drafted:** HS—Fort Myers, Fla., 2011 (2nd round). **Signed by:** Lukas McKnight.

Vogelbach teamed with fellow meaty prospect Hudson Boyd in high school and faced Boyd (now with the Twins) in the low Class A Midwest League in 2013, twice hitting home runs against him. Since signing for $1.6 million in August 2011, Vogelbach has done what he was paid to do: hit. His polish helped him join Daytona late in the season as the DH for its playoff run. Thick and strong, Vogelbach cherishes the one-on-one competition with pitchers and comes out on top more often than not. He trusts his approach, works counts and has the strength to punish pitches he's looking for. He's consistent and doesn't give away at-bats. His strength and short swing give him plus power from left-center to the right-field pole. Until he changes his shape, however, he's going to contend with questions about his future role. He's a poor defender at first with minimal range, though his speed is merely below-average. He sought out his high school track coach to help him with running technique. Vogelbach's future may come down to his weight, and Cubs officials contend he is motivated to prove doubters wrong. If he can keep it under control, he can hit enough to overcome his defensive shortcomings. He'll go through a full high Class A Florida State League season, where the heat and humidity could help him.

Year	Club (League)	Class	AVG	G	AB	R	H	2B	3B	HR	RBI	BB	SO	SB	CS	OBP	SLG
2011	Cubs (AZL)	R	.292	6	24	4	7	3	0	1	6	2	2	1	0	.370	.542
2012	Cubs (AZL)	R	.324	24	102	16	33	12	2	7	31	12	14	1	0	.391	.686
	Boise (NWL)	SS	.322	37	143	23	46	9	1	10	31	23	34	0	1	.423	.608
2013	Kane County (MWL)	LoA	.284	114	433	55	123	21	0	17	71	57	76	4	4	.364	.450
	Daytona (FSL)	HiA	.280	17	50	13	14	2	0	2	5	16	13	1	0	.455	.440
Minor League Totals			.297	198	752	111	223	47	3	37	144	110	139	7	5	.386	.515

10 ARODYS VIZCAINO, RHP

BA GRADE **55** EXTREME

Born: Nov. 13, 1990. **B-T:** R-R. **Ht.:** 6-0. **Wt.:** 190. **Signed:** Dominican Republic, 2007. **Signed by:** Alfredo Dominguez (Yankees).

A veteran prospect, Vizcaino ranked in the Yankees' Top 10 after the 2009 season, which was cut short by a muscle strain in his back. The Yankees traded him to the Braves in the Javier Vazquez deal, and after two years—including his big league debut in 2011—he joined the Cubs in a trade that sent Paul Maholm and Reed Johnson to Atlanta. He had Tommy John surgery in March 2012 and had a long recovery, including a setback in May (surgery to remove debris in his elbow) that essentially wiped out his 2013 season as well. Vizcaino returned to the mound in August and was slated to pick up innings in the Arizona Fall League but instead threw in instructional league, both in Arizona and in the Dominican Republic. The zip on his mid-90s fastball has returned, and Vizcaino hasn't lost the snap on his plus curveball either. Before his injury, he had average control, though his fastball command needs to improve. He has a fast arm and tremendous hand speed, and both his heater and curve can elicit swings and misses thanks to their power and late action. Vizcaino remains a wild card that the Cubs believe in, even though he has yet to throw an official pitch for the organization. Scouts say he can be an impact reliever if he ever stays healthy.

Year	Club (League)	Class	W	L	ERA	G	GS	CG	SV	IP	H	HR	BB	SO	K/9	WHIP	AVG
2008	Yankees (GCL)	R	3	2	3.68	12	6	0	0	44	38	5	13	48	9.8	1.16	.222
2009	Staten Island (NYP)	SS	2	4	2.13	10	10	0	0	42	34	2	15	52	11.1	1.16	.211
2010	Myrtle Beach (CAR)	HiA	0	0	4.61	3	3	0	0	14	16	1	3	11	7.2	1.39	.296
	Rome (SAL)	LoA	9	4	2.39	14	14	0	0	72	63	1	9	68	8.5	1.00	.229
2011	Lynchburg (CAR)	HiA	2	2	2.45	9	9	0	0	40	31	3	10	37	8.3	1.02	.207
	Mississippi (SL)	AA	2	3	3.81	11	8	0	0	50	44	3	18	55	10.0	1.25	.234
	Gwinnett (IL)	AAA	1	0	1.29	6	0	0	0	7	7	1	0	8	10.3	1.00	.259
	Atlanta (NL)	MAJ	1	1	4.67	17	0	0	0	17	16	1	9	17	8.8	1.44	.239
2012	Did not play—Injured																
2013	Did not play—Injured																
Major League Totals			1	1	4.67	17	0	0	0	17	16	1	9	17	8.8	1.44	.239
Minor League Totals			19	15	2.91	65	50	0	0	269	233	16	68	279	9.3	1.12	.227

11 KYLE HENDRICKS, RHP

BA GRADE **45** LOW

Born: Dec. 7, 1989. **B-T:** R-R. **Ht.:** 6-3. **Wt.:** 190. **Drafted:** Dartmouth, 2011 (8th round). **Signed by:** Jay Heafner (Rangers).

Hendricks came to the Cubs with third baseman Christian Villanueva in the 2012 Ryan Dempster trade. Hendricks' fastball touched 95 mph in his Ivy League days, but as a pro he's settled in as a command-oriented starter who relies on his feel for pitching, a good changeup and ability to locate his fastball. He mostly pitches in the 85-92 mph range, reading hitters' swings and disrupting their timing. Hendricks throws his changeup to all hitters and has shown the ability to pitch to the inside and outside corners and down with both his fastball and change. He limited righthanders to a .197 average while leading the organization in wins (13), innings (166) and ERA (2.00). He throws both a slider and a curve, both fringe-average, and most scouts prefer the curve, which he throws with some power in the upper 70s. Some scouts give Hendricks 70 control grades. He's not on the 40-man roster yet and should start 2014 at Triple-A Iowa.

Year	Club (League)	Class	W	L	ERA	G	GS	CG	SV	IP	H	HR	BB	SO	K/9	WHIP	AVG
2011	Spokane (NWL)	SS	2	2	1.93	20	0	0	3	33	20	0	4	36	9.9	0.73	.169
	Frisco (TL)	AA	0	0	3.00	1	1	0	0	3	4	0	2	2	6.0	2.00	.308
2012	Myrtle Beach (CAR)	HiA	5	8	2.82	20	20	2	0	131	123	8	15	112	7.7	1.06	.253
	Daytona (FSL)	HiA	1	0	4.24	5	4	0	0	17	17	3	3	11	5.8	1.18	.254
2013	Tennessee (SL)	AA	10	3	1.85	21	21	1	0	126	107	3	26	101	7.2	1.05	.227
	Iowa (PCL)	AAA	3	1	2.48	6	6	0	0	40	35	2	8	27	6.1	1.08	.235
Minor League Totals			21	14	2.42	73	52	3	3	350	306	16	58	289	7.4	1.04	.234

12 PAUL BLACKBURN, RHP

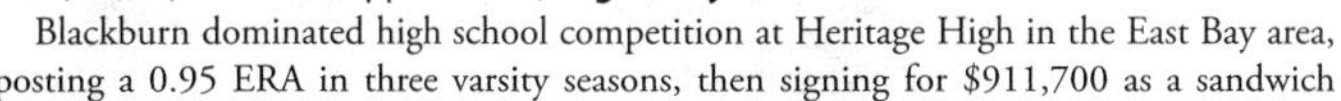

Born: Dec. 4, 1993. **B-T:** R-R. **Ht.:** 6-2. **Wt.:** 185. **Drafted:** HS—Brentwood, Calif., 2012 (1st round supplemental). **Signed by:** Scott Fairbanks.

Blackburn dominated high school competition at Heritage High in the East Bay area, posting a 0.95 ERA in three varsity seasons, then signing for $911,700 as a sandwich pick. The Cubs took it slow with Blackburn, sending him to short-season Boise in 2013, where he started the campaign with 17 innings without giving up an earned run. But his command faltered after that start, and he walked 27 in his final 31 innings, mostly as he struggled to locate his fastball. Blackburn has the stuff to start, with a three-pitch mix that includes increased fastball velocity. He touches 95 mph and sits in the 90-93 range, while his curveball has the proper spin and shape, and he flashes an above-average changeup as well. Despite his bouts of wildness, he pitches with poise and has mound presence to spare. A solid athlete, he has gained 35 pounds since signing and is still learning to tame his bigger frame. Blackburn's control issues surprised the Cubs, who see him as a pitchability guy with above-average stuff. He's headed for low Class A Kane County for his first shot at full-season ball in 2014.

Year	Club (League)	Class	W	L	ERA	G	GS	CG	SV	IP	H	HR	BB	SO	K/9	WHIP	AVG
2012	Cubs (AZL)	R	2	0	3.48	9	6	0	0	21	23	2	7	13	5.7	1.45	.284
2013	Boise (NWL)	SS	2	3	3.33	13	12	0	0	46	41	3	29	38	7.4	1.52	.241
Minor League Totals			4	3	3.38	22	18	0	0	67	64	5	36	51	6.9	1.50	.255

13 CHRISTIAN VILLANUEVA, 3B

Born: June 19, 1991. **B-T:** R-R. **Ht.:** 5-11. **Wt.:** 160. **Signed:** Mexico, 2008. **Signed by:** Mike Daly/Bill McLaughlin (Rangers).

Villanueva was acquired from Texas in the 2012 Ryan Dempster trade. He broke onto the prospect map in 2011 with low Class A Hickory and had a similar season with Double-A Tennessee in his first full Cubs campaign. He's an aggressive hitter with a somewhat stiff swing that he makes up for with solid bat-to-ball skills. Villanueva thrived in the second half, hitting 14 of his 19 home runs after he became less pull-conscious and used the whole field. He adopts a swing-first mentality when he's ahead in the count and could use a bit more selectivity, but he also has solid-average power that helped him lead the Southern League in doubles (41), total bases (230) extra-base hits (62). Defensively, Villanueva stands out at third with soft hands, good instincts and the agility and body control to make the play on slow rollers and throw on the move. He's a hard worker who loves to play and was getting more reps as an everyday player for Obregon in his native Mexico's Pacific League this winter. Villanueva is in a position crunch in the system but is on the 40-man roster and ought to have a chance to compete for the big league job in 2014, though a step up to Triple-A Iowa is much more likely.

Year	Club (League)	Class	AVG	G	AB	R	H	2B	3B	HR	RBI	BB	SO	SB	CS	OBP	SLG
2009	Rangers 2 (DSL)	R	.208	8	24	2	5	1	0	0	3	6	5	1	0	.375	.250
2010	Rangers (AZL)	R	.314	51	188	30	59	14	1	2	35	13	42	6	2	.365	.431
2011	Hickory (SAL)	LoA	.278	126	467	78	130	30	3	17	84	37	86	32	6	.338	.465
2012	Myrtle Beach (CAR)	HiA	.285	100	375	45	107	19	1	10	59	24	83	9	9	.356	.421
	Daytona (FSL)	HiA	.250	25	84	14	21	5	0	4	9	10	24	5	2	.337	.452
2013	Tennessee (SL)	AA	.261	133	490	60	128	41	2	19	72	34	117	5	7	.317	.469
Minor League Totals			.276	443	1628	229	450	110	7	52	262	124	357	58	26	.340	.448

14 MIKE OLT, 3B

BA GRADE
55
EXTREME

Born: Aug. 27, 1988. **B-T:** R-R. **Ht.:** 6-2. **Wt.:** 210. **Drafted:** Connecticut, 2010 (1st round supplemental). **Signed by:** Jay Heafner (Rangers).

Olt led the Double-A Texas League with 28 home runs in 2012, playing in the Futures Game and making his major league debut with Texas. Injuries had slowed him in the past, such as a broken collarbone in 2011 and plantar fasciitis in 2012. But none of that prepared Olt for 2013, which was an unmitigated disaster. In November 2012, Olt was hit in the head by a Francisco Samuel pitch while playing for Licey in the Dominican League. He missed a week with a concussion but returned to the field and participated in big league camp in 2013, then opened the season with Triple-A Round Rock. He went on the disabled list with blurred vision in late April but seemed to return to normal in June and July, hitting 10 home runs in a 45-game stretch prior to being traded to the Cubs in the Matt Garza deal. He struggled mightily after the move as his vision issues persisted. Olt has changed prescriptions on his eye drops, which the Cubs hope will solve the problem. Concussions and beanings have felled many players in baseball's history, and the Cubs hope Olt doesn't join their ranks. Even when he's at his best, his swing tends to get uphill, making some scouts believe he'll have trouble tapping into his plus power while being a below-average hitter for average. Olt has the actions, arm strength and agility to be an above-average defender at third. If the 2012 version of Olt shows up, he could seize the everyday job in Chicago.

Year	Club (League)	Class	AVG	G	AB	R	H	2B	3B	HR	RBI	BB	SO	SB	CS	OBP	SLG
2010	Spokane (NWL)	SS	.293	69	263	57	77	16	1	9	43	40	77	6	0	.390	.464
2011	Rangers (AZL)	R	.214	4	14	2	3	0	0	1	4	1	5	0	0	.267	.429
	Myrtle Beach (CAR)	HiA	.267	69	240	39	64	15	0	14	42	48	70	0	1	.387	.504
2012	Frisco (TL)	AA	.288	95	354	65	102	17	1	28	82	61	101	4	0	.398	.579
	Texas (AL)	MAJ	.152	16	33	2	5	1	0	0	5	5	13	1	1	.250	.182
2013	Frisco (TL)	AA	.333	3	12	1	4	2	0	1	2	0	6	0	0	.333	.750
	Round Rock (PCL)	AAA	.213	65	230	37	49	15	0	11	32	35	89	0	0	.317	.422
	Iowa (PCL)	AAA	.168	39	131	11	22	3	1	3	8	20	37	0	0	.276	.275
Major League Totals			.152	16	33	2	5	1	0	0	5	5	13	1	1	.250	.182
Minor League Totals			.258	344	1244	212	321	68	3	67	213	205	385	10	1	.365	.479

15 COREY BLACK, RHP

BA GRADE
50
HIGH

Born: Aug. 4, 1991. **B-T:** R-R. **Ht.:** 5-11. **Wt.:** 175. **Drafted:** Faulkner (Ala.), 2012 (4th round). **Signed by:** D.J. Svihlik (Yankees).

Black was forced to transfer out of San Diego State and wound up at NAIA Faulkner (Ala.), where the Yankees drafted him in the fourth round in 2012 and signed him for $215,000. Black started his first full season at high Class A Tampa and lost six decisions in a row at one point before the Cubs acquired him in a trade for Alfonso Soriano. Yankees general manager Brian Cashman said publicly he didn't want to give up Black, and the smallish but athletic righty made the Yankees regret it by beating Tampa in two of his five starts after being acquired by Daytona, running his fastball up to 96 mph in both starts, as well as in the playoffs. He also throws a curveball, changeup and slider, and his curve has made significant progress, going from a show-me pitch to a potential above-average offering. Black has a good feel for his solid-average changeup and limited lefthanders to a .164/.289/.212 line with no home runs in 173 plate appearances. His improved feel for pitching and power stuff helped him lead the Florida State League with 116 strikeouts. He's done a good job to this point of maintaining some plane on his fastball and staying tall in his delivery, essential at his height. It's easier to find scouts who believe Black has a chance to remain a starter now than it was a year ago, especially after he continued to show firm stuff in the FSL playoffs. He's headed for Double-A Tennessee in 2014.

Year	Club (League)	Class	W	L	ERA	G	GS	CG	SV	IP	H	HR	BB	SO	K/9	WHIP	AVG
2012	Yankees (GCL)	R	0	0	6.75	1	1	0	0	1	2	0	2	0	0.0	3.00	.333
	Staten Island (NYP)	SS	0	0	2.28	6	6	0	0	28	22	1	8	21	6.8	1.08	.222
	Charleston, SC (SAL)	LoA	2	2	3.80	5	5	0	0	24	18	0	5	29	11.0	0.97	.214
2013	Tampa (FSL)	HiA	3	8	4.25	19	19	0	0	83	79	2	45	88	9.6	1.50	.243
	Daytona (FSL)	HiA	4	0	2.88	5	5	0	0	25	22	3	10	28	10.1	1.28	.237
Minor League Totals			9	10	3.65	36	36	0	0	160	143	6	70	166	9.3	1.33	.236

16 ELOY JIMENEZ, OF

BA GRADE
55
EXTREME

Born: Nov. 27, 1996. **B-T:** R-R. **Ht.:** 6-4. **Wt.:** 200. **Signed:** Dominican Republic, 2013. **Signed by:** Louie Eljaua/Jose Serra/Carlos Reyes.

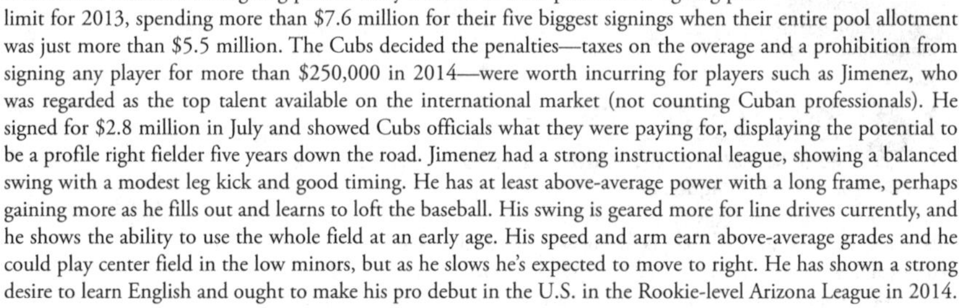

Led by special assistant to the general manager Louie Eljaua, the Cubs were aggressive in the 2013 international signing period. They decided to blow past MLB's signing pool limit for 2013, spending more than $7.6 million for their five biggest signings when their entire pool allotment was just more than $5.5 million. The Cubs decided the penalties—taxes on the overage and a prohibition from signing any player for more than $250,000 in 2014—were worth incurring for players such as Jimenez, who was regarded as the top talent available on the international market (not counting Cuban professionals). He signed for $2.8 million in July and showed Cubs officials what they were paying for, displaying the potential to be a profile right fielder five years down the road. Jimenez had a strong instructional league, showing a balanced swing with a modest leg kick and good timing. He has at least above-average power with a long frame, perhaps gaining more as he fills out and learns to loft the baseball. His swing is geared more for line drives currently, and he shows the ability to use the whole field at an early age. His speed and arm earn above-average grades and he could play center field in the low minors, but as he slows he's expected to move to right. He has shown a strong desire to learn English and ought to make his pro debut in the U.S. in the Rookie-level Arizona League in 2014.

Year	Club (League)	Class	AVG	G	AB	R	H	2B	3B	HR	RBI	BB	SO	SB	CS	OBP	SLG
2013	Did not play—Signed 2014 contract																

17 JACOB HANNEMANN, OF

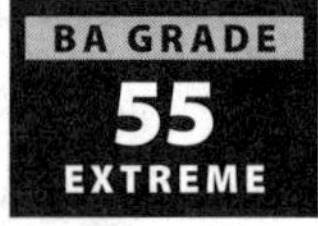

Born: April 29, 1991. **B-T:** L-L. **Ht.:** 6-1. **Wt.:** 190. **Drafted:** Brigham Young, 2013 (3rd round). **Signed by:** Steve McFarland.

Hannemann was drafted out of high school by the Royals (48th round) in 2010 and turned down pro ball to accept a two-sport scholarship to Brigham Young. He then took his two-year Mormon mission, which took him to exotic Little Rock, Ark., before returning to BYU. He redshirted in football as a cornerback in the fall of 2012 and got into shape, then exploded on the scene for the Cougars baseball team, being named West Coast Conference freshman of the year. Already 22, Hannemann gave up his football career when the Cubs signed him for $1 million in 2013. His pro debut started well before being cut short by a partially torn elbow ligament in his right (non-throwing) elbow, which didn't require surgery. Hannemann was one of the best athletes in the draft, strong and explosive with an overall tools package that reminds Cubs officials of Jacoby Ellsbury. He's not an experienced basestealer yet but is a plus runner who reaches top speed quickly, and he outruns his at-times ragged routes in center field. His arm strength is his weakest tool, earning some 20 grades. Hannemann's offensive game is strong. He's aggressive at the plate but repeats his simple, strong swing and has natural timing, giving him average power potential with plus raw power to his pull side. As long as his elbow doesn't interrupt him, Hannemann will get much-needed at-bats at low Class A Kane County in 2014.

Year	Club (League)	Class	AVG	G	AB	R	H	2B	3B	HR	RBI	BB	SO	SB	CS	OBP	SLG
2013	Cubs (AZL)	R	.111	3	9	1	1	1	0	0	2	0	1	1	0	.111	.222
	Boise (NWL)	SS	.290	14	62	8	18	4	2	1	5	2	11	3	1	.313	.468
Minor League Totals			.268	17	71	9	19	5	2	1	7	2	12	4	1	.288	.437

18 DILLON MAPLES, RHP

BA GRADE
55
EXTREME

Born: May 9, 1992. **B-T:** R-R. **Ht.:** 6-2. **Wt.:** 195. **Drafted:** HS—Southern Pines, N.C., 2011 (14th round). **Signed by:** Billy Swoope.

The Cubs invested $2.5 million to lure Maples away from North Carolina, where he was expected to play football (as a placekicker) and baseball. He signed just before the mid-August deadline in 2011 and didn't make his pro debut until 2012. He made his full-season debut in 2013 at low Class A Kane County but had a disastrous stint, showing no ability to throw consistent strikes. His confidence flagging, Maples reported to short-season Boise for the second half and turned his season around with the help of pitching coach David Rosario, improving his delivery, particularly its tempo, and his consistency. While he still has a ways to go commanding his stuff, Maples threw two plus pitches while with the Hawks. His fastball reaches 97 mph and sits 92-95, and he has shown life down with his two-seamer and up in the zone with his four-seamer. Maples adds an upper-70s curveball, which has downer action and helps him change hitters' eye levels. The Cubs haven't done much with Maples' changeup yet, focusing on fastball command. Adding one will be an integral part of his spring to-do list as he works to earn a return trip to Kane County in 2014.

Year	Club (League)	Class	W	L	ERA	G	GS	CG	SV	IP	H	HR	BB	SO	K/9	WHIP	AVG
2012	Cubs (AZL)	R	0	1	4.35	6	4	0	0	10	6	0	10	12	10.5	1.55	.162
2013	Kane County (MWL)	LoA	0	2	8.31	11	7	0	1	35	33	1	31	34	8.8	1.85	.248
	Boise (NWL)	SS	5	2	2.14	10	9	0	0	42	37	0	19	41	8.8	1.33	.242
Minor League Totals			5	5	4.86	27	20	0	1	87	76	1	60	87	9.0	1.56	.235

19 TYLER SKULINA, RHP

Born: Sept. 18, 1991. **B-T:** R-R. **Ht.:** 6-5. **Wt.:** 252. **Drafted:** Kent State, 2013 (4th round). **Signed by:** Tim Adkins.

Skulina originally started his college career at Virginia but left after a semester, sat out 2011, then helped the Golden Flashes to a surprise College World Series run in 2012. He has a power arm and the best breaking ball in the Cubs' draft class, a hard slider that he uses for strikeouts and to get groundball outs. He throws the slider with power, up to 84 mph as an amateur. He has a good feel for using the pitch and has a strong body that allows him to hold the velocity on his 91-94 mph fastball, which peaks at 96. Skulina also throws a curveball and decent changeup, which is definitely his fourth-best pitch. He threw well in his pro debut before tiring after a promotion to low Class A Kane County. He'll head back there for 2014 to see if he can adjust to the five-day professional rotation while maintaining his power stuff.

Year	Club (League)	Class	W	L	ERA	G	GS	CG	SV	IP	H	HR	BB	SO	K/9	WHIP	AVG
2013	Boise (NWL)	SS	0	0	1.20	8	2	0	0	15	9	0	3	10	6.0	0.80	.170
	Kane County (MWL)	LoA	0	2	9.31	4	4	0	0	10	14	1	6	9	8.4	2.07	.341
Minor League Totals			0	2	4.38	12	6	0	0	25	23	1	9	19	6.9	1.30	.245

20 ROB ZASTRYZNY, LHP

BA GRADE
50
HIGH

Born: March 26, 1992. **B-T:** R-L. **Ht.:** 6-3. **Wt.:** 205. **Drafted:** Missouri, 2013 (2nd round). **Signed by:** Ty Nichols.

Zastryzny could be the next Mizzou ace in the Max Scherzer/Aaron Crow/Kyle Gibson line to reach the majors. He enjoyed less success than his predecessors in college, going just 9-19, including 2-9 as a junior. Nevertheless, he was the first pitcher the Cubs drafted in 2013 and signed for $1.1 million as the 41st overall pick. Zastryzny had less velocity after signing than he showed as an amateur, but he was still able to pitch off his fastball anyway. It was effective in the 86-91 mph range because of his ability to locate it to all four quadrants of the plate and his willingness to use the pitch, as well as some deception. He was firmer in college, sitting at 91-92 mph and touching 94, and he gets swings and misses in the strike zone with his fastball, a must for a starting pitcher. He throws a curveball that has average potential and has some touch with his curve and slurvy slider. His above-average changeup is his best secondary offering. Zastryzny's delivery can get out of whack, causing him to lose the plane on his fastball and become homer-prone. He has the strength and fastball to be a mid-rotation power pitcher if it all comes together. Zastryzny will begin 2014 where he finished his pro debut, with low Class A Kane County.

Year	Club (League)	Class	W	L	ERA	G	GS	CG	SV	IP	H	HR	BB	SO	K/9	WHIP	AVG
2013	Boise (NWL)	SS	0	0	3.14	8	7	0	0	14	15	0	4	16	10.0	1.33	.268
	Kane County (MWL)	LoA	1	0	0.93	3	0	0	0	10	9	0	4	6	5.6	1.34	.257
Minor League Totals			1	0	2.25	11	7	0	0	24	24	0	8	22	8.3	1.33	.264

21 IVAN PINEYRO, RHP

BA GRADE **45** MEDIUM

Born: Sept. 29, 1991. **B-T:** R-R. **Ht.:** 6-1. **Wt.:** 200. **Signed:** Dominican Republic, 2010. **Signed by:** Johnny DiPuglia (Nationals).

Pineyro has had an eventful pro career already. He signed late for an international amateur, as he was 18 when the Nationals inked him in July 2010. A line drive that broke his jaw delayed his 2012 U.S. debut, but he recovered from the injury well enough to jump to short-season Auburn in late July. The Nats gave him his first taste of full-season ball in 2013, and he had just earned a promotion to high Class A when they traded him to the Cubs for platoon outfielder Scott Hairston. Pineyro finished the year in the high Class A Daytona rotation, tossing seven scoreless innings in one of the team's four playoff shutouts as it won the Florida State League title. Short but with long arms, Pineyro fills up the strike zone with a 90-93 mph fastball that touches 94. He held his velocity well in 2013 while surpassing 130 innings, including his playoff start. Pineyro uses his changeup as his top secondary pitch, an above-average offering at times that he trusts in any count. His curveball flashes average at 73-77 mph, though its break is fairly short. Pineyro and the rest of Daytona's Class of 2013 rotation are Chicago's best combination of upside and depth on the mound in the system. A potential No. 4 starter, Pineyro will ascend a level to Double-A Tennessee.

Year	Club (League)	Class	W	L	ERA	G	GS	CG	SV	IP	H	HR	BB	SO	K/9	WHIP	AVG
2011	Nationals (DSL)	R	4	6	2.20	14	14	1	0	70	63	2	20	73	9.4	1.19	.237
2012	Nationals (GCL)	R	0	0	2.38	5	5	0	0	23	13	2	7	23	9.1	0.88	.163
	Auburn (NYP)	SS	3	2	5.50	8	8	0	0	34	49	2	8	27	7.1	1.66	.345
2013	Hagerstown (SAL)	LoA	5	3	3.14	13	13	0	0	66	57	4	17	65	8.9	1.12	.237
	Potomac (CAR)	HiA	1	0	3.68	3	3	0	0	15	14	1	5	8	4.9	1.30	.255
	Daytona (FSL)	HiA	3	1	3.40	8	8	0	0	45	44	2	9	38	7.6	1.18	.259
Minor League Totals			16	12	3.21	51	51	1	0	252	240	13	66	234	8.3	1.21	.252

22 KYUJI FUJIKAWA, RHP

BA GRADE **45** MEDIUM

Born: July 21, 1980. **B-T:** L-R. **Ht.:** 6-0. **Wt.:** 190. **Signed:** Japan, 2012. **Signed by:** Paul Weaver.

Fujikawa was one of Japan's top closers for the Hanshin Tigers from 2005-2012, and also pitched on Japan's 2006 and 2009 World Baseball Classic winners. He had to wait until he became a free agent to come to the U.S., signing with the Cubs on a two-year, $9.5 million contract in December 2012. He made the Opening Day roster in Chicago and saved a win against the Pirates in his big league debut. But Fujikawa missed a month with a strained right forearm, and after returning in May, he felt pain in his elbow in an outing against the Reds. A June exam with Dr. James Andrews revealed ligament damage in his elbow, and he had Tommy John surgery on June 11. Fujikawa was throwing off flat ground in Arizona in November, and the plan was for him to be game-ready in May 2014. When healthy, the veteran has a fastball that reached 95 mph and sat 91-94 with cut action. He relies on a split-finger fastball as his primary secondary pitch, so command of the fastball will be key if he wants to become the Cubs' closer in 2014.

Year	Club (League)	Class	W	L	ERA	G	GS	CG	SV	IP	H	HR	BB	SO	K/9	WHIP	AVG
2000	Hanshin (CL)	JPN	0	0	4.76	19	0	0	0	23	25	1	18	25	9.9	1.90	—
2001	Played in Japanese minors																
2002	Hanshin (CL)	JPN	1	5	3.71	12	12	0	0	68	56	6	30	64	8.5	1.26	—
2003	Hanshin (CL)	JPN	1	1	3.38	17	2	0	0	29	28	4	12	19	5.8	1.36	—
2004	Hanshin (CL)	JPN	2	0	2.61	26	0	0	0	31	26	3	11	35	10.2	1.19	—
2005	Hanshin (CL)	JPN	7	1	1.36	80	0	0	1	92	57	5	20	139	13.5	0.83	—
2006	Hanshin (CL)	JPN	5	0	0.68	63	0	0	17	79	46	3	22	122	13.8	0.86	—
2007	Hanshin (CL)	JPN	5	5	1.63	71	0	0	46	83	50	2	18	115	12.5	0.82	—
2008	Hanshin (CL)	JPN	8	1	0.67	63	0	0	38	68	34	2	13	90	12.0	0.69	—
2009	Hanshin (CL)	JPN	5	3	1.25	49	0	0	25	58	32	4	15	86	13.4	0.82	—
2010	Hanshin (CL)	JPN	3	4	2.01	58	0	0	28	63	47	7	20	81	11.6	1.07	—
2011	Hanshin (CL)	JPN	3	3	1.24	56	0	0	41	51	25	2	13	80	14.1	0.75	—
2012	Hanshin (CL)	JPN	2	2	1.32	48	0	0	24	48	34	1	15	58	11.0	1.03	—

2013	Iowa (PCL)	AAA	0	0	0.00	1	0	0	0	1	0	0	1	2	18.0	1.00	.000
	Tennessee (SL)	AA	0	0	0.00	1	0	0	0	2	1	0	0	0	0.0	0.50	.167
	Chicago (NL)	MAJ	1	1	5.25	12	0	0	2	12	11	1	2	14	10.5	1.08	.239
Major League Totals			1	1	5.25	12	0	0	2	12	11	1	2	14	10.5	1.08	.239
Minor League Totals			0	0	0.00	2	0	0	0	3	1	0	1	2	6.0	0.67	.111
Japanese League Totals			42	25	1.77	562	14	0	220	692	460	40	207	914	11.9	0.96	—

23 GLEYBER TORRES, SS

BA GRADE 55 EXTREME

Born: Dec. 13, 1996. **B-T:** R-R. **Ht.:** 5-11. **Wt.:** 185. **Signed:** Venezuela, 2013. **Signed by:** Louie Eljaua/Hector Ortega.

The Cubs blew past the international bonus pool limit in part because they signed both the Nos. 1 and 2 prospects during the July 2 signing period. Dominican outfielder Eloy Jimenez ranked first, and Venezuelan shortstop Gleyber Torres ranked second and signed for $1.7 million. The Cubs had been linked to Torres for a while. He has a compact infielder's build and offers present strength and tools with less long-term projection. Cubs officials like Torres' swing from the right side. He has strength in his legs and could develop solid-average power as he learns his hot zones and adjusts to professional pitching. Scouts like his bat speed and hand-eye coordination, and he might hit enough to be a third baseman down the road. Other scouts like him better at second base, and some see him as a shortstop. Scouts like his infield actions, solid hands and above-average arm strength, but he doesn't have a prototypical fluid, athletic shortstop's body. He should be advanced enough to make his U.S. debut in the Rookie-level Arizona League in 2014.

Year	Club (League)	Class	AVG	G	AB	R	H	2B	3B	HR	RBI	BB	SO	SB	CS	OBP	SLG
2013	Did not play—Signed 2014 contract																

24 DALLAS BEELER, RHP

BA GRADE 45 HIGH

Born: June 12, 1989. **B-T:** R-R. **Ht.:** 6-5. **Wt.:** 210. **Drafted:** Oral Roberts, 2010 (41st round). **Signed by:** Ty Nichols.

Beeler, whose brother Chase was an all-America center for Stanford's football team, didn't pitch after mid-May due to a torn tendon in his right middle finger. He made up for lost time by throwing well in the Arizona Fall League, earning a 40-man-roster spot. He admires Roy Halladay and has adopted the same knee-tuck mechanics and similar arm slot, working to make his 89-92 mph fastball sink, cut and run away from the middle of the plate. He can touch 94 mph with the fastball and has a slurvy slider as his main breaking ball, working to get early contact with both pitches. He uses both forkball-type of splitter that he can use in the strike zone and a more conventional split-finger pitch that he tries to bury out of the zone. Beeler added a cutter in the AFL to help him get inside on lefthanders, and it showed promise in the high 80s with late cut. His Fall League showing was that of a back-end starter—if he can stay healthy (he also had Tommy John surgery in 2009). He should graduate to Triple-A Iowa for the first time.

Year	Club (League)	Class	W	L	ERA	G	GS	CG	SV	IP	H	HR	BB	SO	K/9	WHIP	AVG
2010	Cubs (AZL)	R	0	3	3.31	8	2	0	0	16	20	0	2	16	8.8	1.35	.303
	Boise (NWL)	SS	0	0	0.00	1	0	0	0	2	2	0	0	2	9.0	1.00	.250
2011	Tennessee (SL)	AA	1	5	4.53	9	9	0	0	52	68	7	7	33	5.7	1.45	.315
	Peoria (MWL)	LoA	1	1	1.66	12	11	0	0	43	35	1	6	35	7.3	0.95	.222
2012	Tennessee (SL)	AA	6	7	4.24	27	27	1	0	136	166	11	48	70	4.6	1.57	.305
2013	Tennessee (SL)	AA	4	2	3.13	9	9	0	0	55	43	3	17	35	5.8	1.10	.214
Minor League Totals			12	18	3.64	66	58	1	0	304	334	22	80	191	5.7	1.36	.280

25 ARMANDO RIVERO, RHP

BA GRADE 45 HIGH

Born: Feb. 1, 1988. **B-T:** R-R. **Ht.:** 6-4. **Wt.:** 190. **Signed:** Cuba, 2013. **Signed by:** Louie Eljaua

The Cubs have nine players who have left Cuba in recent years in their farm system, five more than any other farm system. Most of them haven't provided must production, most notably lefthander Gerardo Concepcion, who signed a $6 million major league contract and hardly lasted a year on the 40-man roster before being outrighted. Rivero and Concepcion were teammates for Industriales in Cuba's Serie Nacional, and Rivero signed with the Cubs in March 2013 for $3.1 million but had a problem getting a visa to get to the U.S. to make his pro debut. By the time he reported to Arizona it was extended spring training, and he didn't get into a game that counted until June 22, getting in a little extra work in the Arizona Fall League. Rivero has an athletic pitcher's body and quick arm that produces one of the system's best fastballs, sitting 94-97 mph at times. He has focused on a hard slider as his go-to secondary pitch, varying the release point by design. It's not a great pitch and needs to be tightened but can be effective with his varied looks and power in the mid-80s. He also throws split-changeup and attacks hitters fearlessly with all three pitches. A healthy Rivero ought to be able to reach Chicago in 2014 as long as he throws strikes, likely settling into a set-up role. Some scouts think he has the moxie to close.

Year	Club (League)	Class	W	L	ERA	G	GS	CG	SV	IP	H	HR	BB	SO	K/9	WHIP	AVG
2013	Kane County (MWL)	LoA	0	0	5.40	11	0	0	1	18	19	4	9	28	13.7	1.53	.264
	Daytona (FSL)	HiA	0	0	2.70	3	0	0	1	3	3	0	0	5	13.5	0.90	.200
	Tennessee (SL)	AA	0	1	2.08	6	0	0	0	9	8	0	3	12	12.5	1.27	.242
Minor League Totals			0	1	4.15	20	0	0	2	30	30	4	12	45	13.4	1.38	.250

26 MATT SZCZUR, OF

BA GRADE
45
HIGH

Born: July 20, 1989. **B-T:** R-R. **Ht.:** 6-1. **Wt.:** 195. **Drafted:** Villanova, 2010 (5th round). **Signed by:** Tim Adkins.

Szczur's athleticism wowed the Cubs when he played football at Villanova, and they paid him $100,000 to sign and then $1.4 million to choose baseball over a possible football career. He remains a top athlete and speedster, but he also remains the owner of a somewhat ugly swing that makes it hard for scouts to project him as a regular. Szczur's swing simply doesn't stay in the strike zone long enough for him to drive the ball with any consistency. He has plus raw power but struggles when every pitch isn't straight. Szczur draws walks and grinds through a season without giving up too many at-bats, but he just doesn't have the offensive impact needed from a regular. His speed remains plus but his baserunning instincts lag behind. He's a strong defender in center field, a leader for the other outfielders, and has improved his throwing arm, earning solid-average grades. His energy, work ethic and grinder mentality will make managers want to have him in their clubhouse as a useful fourth outfielder, his likely ceiling now. He's headed to Triple-A Iowa in 2014.

Year	Club (League)	Class	AVG	G	AB	R	H	2B	3B	HR	RBI	BB	SO	SB	CS	OBP	SLG
2010	Cubs (AZL)	R	.500	1	2	1	1	0	0	0	0	1	0	1	0	.750	.500
	Boise (NWL)	SS	.397	18	73	17	29	9	0	0	8	6	11	1	0	.439	.521
	Peoria (MWL)	LoA	.192	6	26	6	5	1	1	0	2	3	5	0	0	.300	.308
2011	Peoria (MWL)	LoA	.314	66	274	55	86	15	1	5	27	21	28	17	5	.366	.431
	Daytona (FSL)	HiA	.260	43	173	20	45	7	2	5	19	5	20	7	0	.283	.410
2012	Daytona (FSL)	HiA	.295	78	295	68	87	19	4	2	34	47	50	38	12	.394	.407
	Tennessee (SL)	AA	.210	35	143	24	30	7	4	2	6	14	29	4	2	.285	.357
2013	Tennessee (SL)	AA	.281	128	512	78	144	27	4	3	44	50	75	22	12	.350	.367
Minor League Totals			.285	375	1498	269	427	85	16	17	140	147	218	90	31	.353	.397

27 ZACH CATES, RHP

BA GRADE
45
HIGH

Born: Dec. 17, 1989. **B-T:** R-R. **Ht.:** 6-3. **Wt.:** 200. **Drafted:** Northeast Texas CC, 2010 (3rd round). **Signed by:** Jeff Curtis (Padres).

Scouts have fingered Cates as a future reliever since he converted from catching to pitching at Northeast Texas CC in 2010. The Padres signed him for $765,000 that year and used him as a starter to get him experience, then sent him the Cubs as part of the 2012 trade highlighted by Andrew Cashner and Anthony Rizzo. Cates had an unsightly 0-9, 7.16 season in 2012 that included a trip back to extended spring training, and the Cubs sent him back to high Class A Daytona for 2013. He returned to the rotation for the bulk of the season but finally shifted to a relief role in August and thrived, as he no longer felt pressure to pace himself and was able to pitch more aggressively. His fastball sat at 92-95 mph as a starter and reached 97 as a reliever with good downhill plane that makes him tough to elevate. He has lost the feel for a changeup he threw with aplomb as an amateur and has focused on a slider, which sits in the low 80s, in the bullpen. He'll need to locate better to challenge lefthanders more effectively if he wants to be a closer. More likely, he has a chance to be an effective set-up man. Cates is headed to Double-A Tennessee for the first time in 2014.

Year	Club (League)	Class	W	L	ERA	G	GS	CG	SV	IP	H	HR	BB	SO	K/9	WHIP	AVG
2011	Fort Wayne (MWL)	LoA	4	10	4.73	25	25	0	0	118	107	4	53	111	8.5	1.36	.244
2012	Daytona (FSL)	HiA	0	6	10.50	7	7	0	0	24	42	0	13	10	3.8	2.29	.389
	Cubs (AZL)	R	0	0	2.70	1	1	0	0	3	4	0	1	5	13.5	1.50	.308
	Peoria (MWL)	LoA	0	3	5.45	9	9	0	0	38	49	1	13	31	7.3	1.63	.314
2013	Daytona (FSL)	HiA	9	9	4.12	28	20	0	3	109	107	3	48	87	7.2	1.42	.258
Minor League Totals			13	28	5.04	70	62	0	3	293	309	8	128	244	7.5	1.49	.273

28 BEN WELLS, RHP

BA GRADE
45
HIGH

Born: Sept. 19, 1992. **B-T:** R-R. **Ht.:** 6-3. **Wt.:** 230. **Drafted:** HS—Bryant, Ark., 2010 (7th round). **Signed by:** Jim Crawford.

Wells had a strong bounceback year in 2013, pitching as one of the most consistent starters for high Class A Daytona, which was honored as the BA Minor League Team of the Year. Signed out of an Arkansas high school for $530,000 in 2010, Wells had his progress interrupted by an elbow injury that limited him to 45 innings in 2012. He didn't need surgery, however, and returned to full duty in 2013 and led Daytona with 112 innings. That's even though the Cubs tapered his workload in the second half, using him for just four outings in August and shutting him down during the Florida State League playoffs. Wells had gotten his work in, focusing on fastball location and throwing his changeup at least 10 percent of the time. His fastball runs up to 91-93 mph at times, but he mostly pitched at 89-90 in 2013 with plus sink. He generated 2.3 groundouts for every out in the air, the ninth-best ratio among minor league ERA title qualifiers. Wells' fringe-average changeup has similar sinking action to his fastball, and his fringe-average slider also helps him get early-count soft contact. He has a big frame, though his arm action makes some scouts doubt his potential for durability. He has to monitor his conditioning and could develop more consistent low-90s velocity if he does. He will either be the fifth starter at Double-A Tennessee in 2014 or return to Daytona to anchor the FSL rotation.

Year	Club (League)	Class	W	L	ERA	G	GS	CG	SV	IP	H	HR	BB	SO	K/9	WHIP	AVG
2011	Boise (NWL)	SS	4	4	4.66	16	15	0	0	77	83	4	19	53	6.2	1.32	.265
2012	Cubs (AZL)	R	0	0	0.00	1	0	0	0	1	0	0	1	3	27.0	1.00	.000
	Peoria (MWL)	LoA	3	2	3.27	12	8	0	1	44	48	0	12	36	7.4	1.36	.274
2013	Daytona (FSL)	HiA	9	6	3.28	23	21	0	0	112	96	7	40	69	5.5	1.21	.232
Minor League Totals			16	12	3.72	52	44	0	1	235	227	11	72	161	6.2	1.27	.251

29 RUBI SILVA, OF

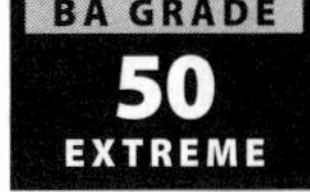

Born: June 25, 1989. **B-T:** L-R. **Ht.:** 5-11. **Wt.:** 180. **Signed:** Cuba, 2010. **Signed by:** Louie Eljaua.

The Cubs have become a haven for Cuban expatriates such as Silva, who has better tools than other Cuban outfielders in the system who merit Top 30 consideration such as Yasiel Balaguert. A former shortstop, Silva played on Cuba's 18-and-under national team with players such as Jose Iglesias and Adeiny Hechevarria, but they were better defensively, which forced Silva to the outfield. He left the island in 2010, and the Cubs signed him for $1 million in 2011. They gave him some reps at second base initially, but he's being groomed for a fourth outfielder role. Silva played virtually every day at Double-A Tennessee in 2013 and showed first-division tools, with a quick bat that helps him overcome a slight wrap in his swing and surprising, solid-average power. He's a plus runner when he smells a hit or needs to run a ball down in the outfield, and his solid-average arm helps him slide from center field to right when needed. He led the Southern League with 16 outfield assists. Silva appears allergic to walks with a hyper-aggressive approach, and he expands his zone even more with runners on base, hitting just .208 with runners in scoring position. He fits best as an extra outfielder if his makeup will allow it. He doesn't need to be on the 40-man roster until after the 2014 season and will move up to Triple-A Iowa.

Year	Club (League)	Class	AVG	G	AB	R	H	2B	3B	HR	RBI	BB	SO	SB	CS	OBP	SLG
2011	Daytona (FSL)	HiA	.229	29	105	13	24	6	1	2	7	3	22	0	0	.250	.362
	Peoria (MWL)	LoA	.300	93	390	59	117	16	7	3	37	13	73	6	6	.319	.400
2012	Daytona (FSL)	HiA	.302	111	420	48	127	15	11	3	61	13	75	7	18	.322	.412
	Tennessee (SL)	AA	.263	20	80	8	21	0	3	2	13	2	17	3	0	.277	.413
2013	Tennessee (SL)	AA	.284	126	468	56	133	30	9	15	52	18	99	13	7	.310	.483
Minor League Totals			.288	379	1463	184	422	67	31	25	170	49	286	29	31	.310	.428

30 DANNY LOCKHART, 2B

BA GRADE
45
HIGH

Born: Nov. 4, 1992. **B-T:** L-R. **Ht.:** 5-11. **Wt.:** 165. **Drafted:** HS—Dacula, Ga., 2011 (10th round). **Signed by:** Keith Lockhart.

Lockhart's father Keith is more than just his signing scout. He's also an ex-major leaguer who played nearly 1,000 games for three teams. The elder Lockhart didn't make his major league debut until he was 29 but still played parts of 10 seasons. Danny has gotten off to a faster start since signing for $395,000 as a 10th-rounder in 2011, but he has a similar overall profile to his father. He has a solid lefthanded bat with natural rhythm and feel for hitting. He lacks power presently but has consistent quality at-bats and competes at the plate. When Triple-A Iowa was on the road at Tacoma and Logan Watkins got a big league callup, the I-Cubs needed a middle infielder and looked to Lockhart, who was playing nearby with short-season Boise. Not only did the logistics work out, but Lockhart actually had to play and went 4-for-9 with a strikeout. His best tool besides his bat is his speed, which also is above-average. He's a reliable but not flashy defender at second base who also has enough arm strength to fill in at shortstop and third base. Lockhart ought to fit into the infield picture in 2014 at low Class A Kane County.

Year	Club (League)	Class	AVG	G	AB	R	H	2B	3B	HR	RBI	BB	SO	SB	CS	OBP	SLG
2011	Cubs (AZL)	R	.219	7	32	1	7	0	0	0	3	2	7	2	1	.265	.219
2012	Cubs (AZL)	R	.221	45	190	31	42	5	4	1	20	18	27	11	3	.302	.305
2013	Iowa (PCL)	AAA	.444	2	9	1	4	1	0	0	0	0	1	1	1	.444	.556
	Boise (NWL)	SS	.290	67	248	29	72	8	1	0	23	18	39	7	1	.346	.331
Minor League Totals			.261	121	479	62	125	14	5	1	46	38	74	21	6	.324	.317

Chicago White Sox

BY JOHN MANUEL

The White Sox, who contended for most of the 2012 season, opened 2013 expecting to contend again, with a payroll approaching $120 million. Instead, Chicago began a rebuilding project under first-year general manager Rick Hahn, Kenny Williams' longtime lieutenant who ascended to the GM role when Williams was promoted to team president.

Hahn inherited an offense that collapsed despite a veteran presence. The White Sox ranked last in the American League in runs in 2013, en route to their worst record (63-99) since 1970.

With the team out of contention, Hahn started selling some of those veterans, with righthander Jake Peavy and outfielder Alex Rios as his chief bargaining chips. He turned two trades with the Red Sox, sending lefty Matt Thornton and Peavy to Boston in separate deals, and sent Rios to the Rangers for speedy utilityman Leury Garcia. The Peavy trade, a three-team transaction involving the Tigers, netted an impressive haul led by outfielder Avisail Garcia.

The process also brought several White Sox farmhands to Chicago. Catcher Josh Phegley, fully healthy for the first time since being a supplemental first-round pick in 2009, dominated Triple-A before struggling for a half-season in the majors. Righty Andre Rienzo, who started for Brazil in the World Baseball Classic in March, finished a long season as the first Brazilian pitcher to reach the majors. Former University of California teammates Marcus Semien, a second baseman, and Erik Johnson, a righthander, sped from Double-A Birmingham to the South Side.

More prospects are behind them. For the first time since at least 2000, when the White Sox had the game's No. 2 farm system, their system has depth. Birmingham, celebrating a new downtown ballpark, won the Southern League title behind playoff MVP Micah Johnson, who led the minors with 84 stolen bases and ranked sixth with 167 hits. The White Sox also liked what they saw in 2013 first-rounder Tim Anderson, who jumped to low Class A from a Mississippi junior college.

Chicago doesn't intend to be rebuilding for long, as it spent $68 million on its top prospect, Cuban first baseman Jose Abreu. The plan is for him to replace franchise icon Paul Konerko, who will be back for at least one more season of DH, first base and mentoring duty. With pitching coach Don Cooper still in the majors, and with organization veterans Curt Hasler as roving pitching instructor and Kirk Champion as field coordinator, the White Sox are confident in their ability to develop pitching to go with Abreu and potential igniters Anderson and Johnson.

A major reason for the improved talent and depth in the farm system is the White Sox's decision to spend on scouting and player development, which is directly related to the current labor agreement. Owner Jerry Reinsdorf disdained the old draft rules and restricted his club's spending on amateurs, and from 2007-11, Chicago spent just $18.3 million on signing bonuses, barely half the league average. Under the new rules, however, the White Sox have spent every penny of their signing bonus pools, and under assistant to the GM Marco Paddy, they are working hard to be a factor in Latin America.

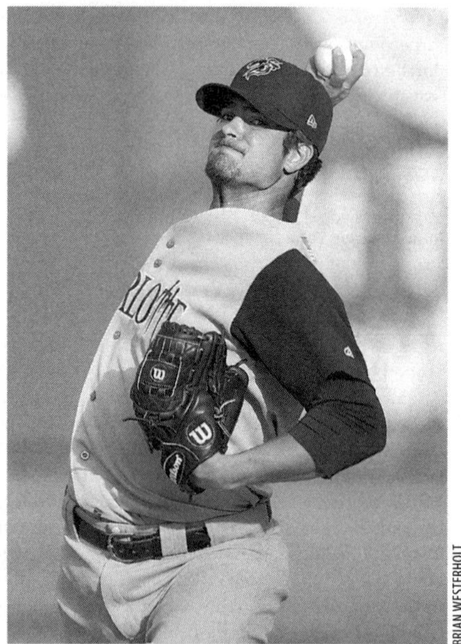

BRIAN WESTERHOLT

Armed with a good curveball, Andre Rienzo became MLB's first Brazilian-born pitcher

TOP PROSPECTS OF THE DECADE

Year	Player, Pos.	2013 Org.
2004	Joe Borchard, of	Out of baseball
2005	Brian Anderson, of	Out of baseball
2006	Bobby Jenks, rhp	Out of baseball
2007	Ryan Sweeney, of	Cubs
2008	Aaron Poreda, lhp	Out of baseball
2009	Gordon Beckham, ss	White Sox
2010	Jared Mitchell, of	White Sox
2011	Chris Sale, lhp	White Sox
2012	Addison Reed, rhp	White Sox
2013	Courtney Hawkins, of	White Sox

ORGANIZATION OVERVIEW

General Manager: Rick Hahn. **Farm Director:** Nick Capra. **Scouting Director:** Doug Laumann.

Class	Team	League	W	L	PCT	Finish	Manager
Majors	Chicago White Sox	American	63	99	.389	14th (15)	Robin Ventura
Triple-A	Charlotte Knights	International	65	78	.455	12th (14)	Joel Skinner
Double-A	Birmingham Barons	Southern	77	63	.550	3rd (10)	Julio Vinas
High A	Winston-Salem Dash	Carolina	71	69	.507	4th (8)	Ryan Newman
Low A	Kannapolis Intimidators	South Atlantic	61	76	.445	11th (14)	Tommy Thompson
Rookie	Great Falls Voyagers	Pioneer	48	28	.632	1st (8)	Pete Rose Jr.
Rookie	Bristol White Sox	Appalachian	20	45	.308	10th (10)	Mike Gellinger
Overall 2013 Minor League Record			**342**	**359**	**.488**	**20th (30)**	

THIS YEAR'S TOP 30

No.	Player, Pos.	Grade/Risk
1.	Jose Abreu, 1b	60/Medium
2.	Erik Johnson, rhp	55/Low
3.	Tim Anderson, ss	60/High
4.	Marcus Semien, ss/2b/3b	50/Medium
5.	Micah Johnson, 2b	55/High
6.	Courtney Hawkins, of	55/Extreme
7.	Trayce Thompson, of	50/High
8.	Chris Beck, rhp	50/High
9.	Jacob May, of	50/High
10.	Tyler Danish, rhp	50/High
11.	Daniel Webb, rhp	45/Medium
12.	Carlos Sanchez, ss/2b	45/Medium
13.	Jared Mitchell, of	50/High
14.	Keon Barnum, 1b	50/High
15.	Chris Bassitt, rhp	45/Medium
16.	Scott Snodgress, lhp	50/High
17.	Leury Garcia, ss/of	45/Medium
18.	Micker Zapata, of	55/Extreme
19.	Trey Michalczewski, 3b	50/High
20.	Braulio Ortiz, rhp	50/Extreme
21.	Jake Petricka, rhp	45/High
22.	Adam Engel, of	50/Extreme
23.	Keenyn Walker, of	45/High
24.	Myles Jaye, rhp	45/High
25.	Brandon Jacobs, of	45/High
26.	Cleuluis Rondon, ss	45/High
27.	Andrew Mitchell, rhp	45/High
28.	Brad Goldberg, rhp	45/High
29.	Francellis Montas, rhp	45/High
30.	Rangel Ravelo, 1b	45/High

LAST YEAR'S TOP 30

No.	Player, Pos.	Status
1.	Courtney Hawkins, of	No. 6
2.	Trayce Thompson, of	No. 7
3.	Carlos Sanchez, 2b	No. 12
4.	Erik Johnson, rhp	No. 2
5.	Keenyn Walker, of	No. 23
6.	Scott Snodgress, lhp	No. 16
7.	Andre Rienzo, rhp	Majors
8.	Keon Barnum, 1b	No. 14
9.	Jered Mitchell, of	No. 13
10.	Chris Beck, rhp	No. 8
11.	Charlie Leesman, lhp	Dropped out
12.	Andy Wilkins, 1b	Dropped out
13.	Jhan Marinez, rhp	(Tigers)
14.	Marcus Semien, ss/2b	No. 4
15.	Blake Tekotte, of	Dropped out
16.	Jake Petricka, rhp	No. 21
17.	Brian Omogrosso, rhp	Dropped out
18.	Josh Phegley, c	Majors
19.	Kevin Vance, rhp	Dropped out
20.	Simon Castro, rhp	(Free agent)
21.	Santos Rodriguez, lhp	Dropped out
22.	Sammy Ayala, c	Dropped out
23.	Brandon Brennan, rhp	Dropped out
24.	Joey DeMichele, 2b	Dropped out
25.	Micah Johnson, 2b	No. 5
26.	Tyler Saladino, 2b/ss	Dropped out
27.	Kevan Smith, c	Dropped out
28.	Nestor Molina, rhp	Dropped out
29.	Jeff Soptic, rhp	(Giants)
30.	Jefferson Olacio, lhp	Dropped out

BEST TOOLS

Best Hitter for Average	Micah Johnson
Best Power Hitter	Jose Abreu
Best Strike-Zone Discipline	Marcus Semien
Fastest Baserunner	Micah Johnson
Best Athlete	Trayce Thompson
Best Fastball	Daniel Webb
Best Curveball	Scott Snodgress
Best Slider	Erik Johnson
Best Changeup	Chris Beck
Best Control	Erik Johnson
Best Defensive Catcher	Miguel Gonzalez
Best Defensive Infielder	Cleuluis Rondon
Best Infield Arm	Cleuluis Rondon
Best Defensive Outfielder	Trayce Thompson
Best Outfield Arm	Keenyn Walker

TOP 15 PLAYERS 25 AND UNDER

No.	Player, Pos. (Age)	Peak Level
1.	Chris Sale, lhp (25)	Majors
2.	Avisail Garcia, of (22)	Majors
3.	Jose Quintana, lhp (25)	Majors
4.	Erik Johnson, rhp (24)	Majors
5.	Dayan Viciedo, of (25)	Majors
6.	Addison Reed, rhp (25)	Majors
7.	Tim Anderson, ss (20)	Low Class A
8.	Andre Rienzo, rhp (25)	Majors
9.	Marcus Semien, ss/2b/3b (23)	Majors
10.	Micah Johnson, 2b (23)	Double-A
11.	Courtney Hawkins, of (20)	High Class A
12.	Trayce Thompson, of (23)	Double-A
13.	Chris Beck, rhp (23)	Double-A
14.	Jacob May, of (22)	Low Class A
15.	Tyler Danish, rhp (19)	Low Class A

MINOR LEAGUE DEPTH CHART

CHICAGO WHITE SOX

TOP 2014 ROOKIE: Erik Johnson, rhp. The White Sox got Johnson's feet wet last year, and he's ready to stick in the 2014 rotation.

BREAKOUT PROSPECT: Adam Engel, of. If Engel hits at all, he has the other tools to make an impact.

SLEEPER: Kevan Smith, c. He's not terribly agile, but the strong-bodied Smith has toughness and can hit a little.

SOURCE OF TOP 30 TALENT

Homegrown	25	Acquired	5
College	12	Trades	5
Junior college	2	Rule 5 draft	0
High school	6	Independent leagues	0
Nondrafted free agents	0	Free agents/waivers	0
International	5		

LF
- Jared Mitchell (13)
- Brandon Jacobs (25)
- Jason Coats

CF
- Trayce Thompson (7)
- Jacob May (9)
- Adam Engel (22)
- Keenyn Walker (23)
- Blake Tekotte

RF
- Courtney Hawkins (6)
- Micker Zapata (18)

3B
- Marcus Semien (4)
- Trey Michalczewski (19)
- Chris Curley
- Nick Basto

SS
- Tim Anderson (3)
- Leury Garcia (17)
- Cleulius Rondon (26)

2B
- Micah Johnson (5)
- Carlos Sanchez (12)
- Joey DiMichele

1B
- Jose Abreu (1)
- Keon Barnum (14)
- Rangel Ravelo (30)
- Andy Wilkins
- Mike McDade
- Dan Black

C
- Kevan Smith
- Miguel Gonzalez
- Sammy Ayala

LHP

LHSP	LHRP
Scott Snodgress (16)	Frank de los Santos
Jefferson Olacio	Santos Rodriguez
Chris Freudenberg	Charlie Leesman
	Andrew Wheeler

RHP

RHSP	RHRP
Erik Johnson (2)	Daniel Webb (11)
Chris Beck (8)	Braulio Ortiz (20)
Tyler Danish (10)	Jake Petricka (21)
Chris Bassitt (15)	Andrew Mitchell (27)
Myles Jaye (24)	Brad Goldberg (28)
Thaddius Lowry	Francellis Montas (29)
Kyle Hansen	J.B. Wendelken
Stephen McCray	Nestor Molina
James Dykstra	Jose Ascanio
	Matt Ball
	Kevin Vance

DRAFT ANALYSIS

2013 BONUSES: $5.3 MILLION

BEST PURE HITTER: From a wiry build with strong wrists and forearms, SS Tim Anderson (1) has an easy and simple swing, compact path and above-average bat speed.

BEST POWER HITTER: The athletic, switch-hitting 3B Trey Michalczewski (7) has natural strength, bat speed and leverage in his swing, and could eventually hit at least 20 home runs a season.

FASTEST RUNNER: Chicago prioritized athleticism, and came away with three runners who grade as 70 or better on the 20-80 scale: Anderson, OF Adam Engel (19) and OF Jacob May (3). May doesn't maximize his speed out of the box because of a big hack and is learning to use his speed, but he ran the 60-yard dash in 6.3 seconds at his predraft workout.

BEST DEFENSIVE PLAYER: Engel has first-step quickness and gets good reads in center and a fringy but accurate arm.

BEST FASTBALL: Physical 6-foot-4, 228-pound RHP Brad Goldberg (10) sat 94-96 mph out of the bullpen with above-average sink. RHP Thaddius Lowry (5) can touch 96. RHP Tyler Danish (2) sits in the low 90s from a low arm slot with plus-plus movement at his best and plus command.

BEST SECONDARY PITCH: Danish has a plus slider and an emerging changeup that flashes plus.

BEST PRO DEBUT: SS Toby Thomas (21) hit .319/.329/.462 for Rookie-level Bristol, May hit .286/.346/.461 at low Class A Kannapolis and Engel hit .301/.379/.414 at Rookie-level Great Falls and led the Pioneer League with 31 steals. Goldberg posted a 1.54 ERA across three levels, and Danish had a 1.38 ERA in 26 Appy League innings.

BEST ATHLETE: A standout high school basketball player, Anderson is an outstanding athlete with speed, quickness and natural strength.

MOST INTRIGUING BACKGROUND: May's father (Lee Jr.) was a 1986 first-rounder and is the Mariners hitting coordinator, his grandfather (Lee Sr.) was a three time all-star outfielder and his uncle Carlos played 10 seasons in the majors. RHP James Dykstra (6), whose fastball touches 94 mph, is the brother of 2006 first-rounder Allan. 1B Cody Yount (37) is the nephew of Hall of Famer Robin and the son of former big league pitcher Larry.

CLOSEST TO THE MAJORS: Goldberg, who finished at high Class A, has a chance to move swiftly in the bullpen if his slider continues to develop. Danish could move as quickly as any high school pitcher because of his advanced stuff, command and bulldog mentality.

BEST LATE-ROUND PICK: Engel at slot. RHP Matt Ball (11), a projectable 6-foot-5, 195 pounder who touches the low 90s, was the only over-slot selection after the 10th round, signing for $150,000.

THE ONE WHO GOT AWAY: Chicago signed all but four of its picks. LHP Tavo Rodriguez (33), who had inconsistent velocity but was up to 93 mph at times, will attend Oklahoma.

ASSESSMENT: Chicago loaded up on power arms like RHP Andrew Mitchell (4), Lowry and Danish, and focused on athletic up-the-middle position players, getting one of the draft's best athletes in Anderson.

2012 BONUSES: $6.5 MILLION

OF Courtney Hawkins (1) took a big step back in 2013, but 2B Micah Johnson (9) broke through. RHP Chris Beck (2) is one of the system's top starting arms.

GRADE: C

2011 BONUSES: $2.8 MILLION

Top pick Keenyn Walker (1s) struggled in Double-A and may not make it, but RHP Erik Johnson (2) and SS/2B Marcus Semien (5) already have.

GRADE: B

2010 BONUSES: $3.9 MILLION

LHP Chris Sale (1) gives the White Sox a rotation ace, while RHP Addison Reed (3) gives them a closer. RHP Jake Petricka (2) also has reached the majors.

GRADE: A

TOP DRAFT PICKS OF THE DECADE

Year	Player, Pos.	2013 Org.
2004	Josh Fields, 3b	Phillies
2005	Lance Broadway, rhp	Out of baseball
2006	Kyle McCulloch, rhp	Out of baseball
2007	Aaron Poreda, lhp	Out of baseball
2008	Gordon Beckham, ss	White Sox
2009	Jared Mitchell, of	White Sox
2010	Chris Sale, lhp	White Sox
2011	Keenyn Walker, of (1st round supp.)	White Sox
2012	Courtney Hawkins, of	White Sox
2013	Tim Anderson, ss	White Sox

LARGEST BONUSES IN CLUB HISTORY

Jose Abreu, 2013	$10,000,000
Joe Borchard, 2000	$5,300,000
Dayan Vicideo, 2008	$4,000,000
Gordon Beckham, 2008	$2,600,000
Courtney Hawkins, 2012	$2,475,000

1 JOSE ABREU, 1B

Born: Jan. 29, 1987. **B-T:** R-R. **Ht.:** 6-2. **Wt.:** 258.
Signed: Cuba, 2013. **Signed by:** Marco Paddy.

Abreu started playing in Cuba's top league, Serie Nacional, when he was 16 and was one of its best hitters by 2007-08, when he hit .295. As the league's offense spiked, Abreu matured, and he began to put up almost comedic offensive numbers. His best year was 2010-11, when he was the league's MVP and broke Yoenis Cespedes' single-season home run record by batting .453/.597/.986 with 33 homers in 66 games. In his last full season, 2011-12, he hit .394/.542/.837 with 35 home runs and led the league in batting, on-base, slugging and OPS. Abreu also became a stalwart on Cuban national teams, and BA ranked him as the No. 4 prospect in the 2013 World Baseball Classic. He joined the exodus of talent from the island in August 2013, was declared a free agent shortly thereafter by Major League Baseball and worked out for teams in the Dominican Republic. The White Sox signed him to a six-year, $64 million contract in October that included a $10 million signing bonus, the largest in franchise history.

Physically, Abreu fits right in with the Chicago's recent string of all-star first basemen and DHs, from Frank Thomas in the 1990s to Paul Konerko, Jim Thome and Adam Dunn. He derives massive raw power from his physicality and strength, with strong hands and forearms and the ability to hit balls out to any part of the ballpark. He wowed team president Kenny Williams in a private workout with his feel for hitting, not just his pure power. He has a simple line-drive swing without too many moving parts, at least in his upper half. His swing lacks much of a trigger and his hands come from a dead start, but his bat stays in the hitting zone a long time, and he has the strength to compensate. Some scouts worry about his double toe-tap stride and average bat speed, fearing they will inhibit his ability to catch up to premium velocity on the inner half. Abreu is just a fair athlete and well below-average runner who is tied to first base defensively. He should be an adequate defender there as long as he maintains his fitness.

The White Sox have had success with Cubans, from Minnie Minoso in the 1950s to 2005 World Series hero Jose Contreras to current lineup stalwarts Alexei Ramirez and Dayan Vicideo. They see Abreu as the best of the recent lot and as a middle-of-the-order force to replace the production, if not the leadership, of the 38-year-old Konerko. Ideally, he would hit fifth or sixth in the lineup as a rookie, as the team doesn't want to put too much pressure on him. If Abreu sees time in the minor leagues in 2014, the White Sox will be disappointed.

BA GRADE
60
MEDIUM

SCOUTING GRADES

BATTING	60
POWER	70
SPEED	30
DEFENSE	45
ARM	40

EZIO RATTI/IBAF

Year	Club (League)	Class	AVG	G	AB	R	H	2B	3B	HR	RBI	BB	SO	SB	CS	OBP	SLG
Did not play—Signed 2014 contract																	

2 ERIK JOHNSON, RHP

Born: Dec. 30, 1989. **B-T:** R-R. **Ht.:** 6-3. **Wt.:** 225. **Drafted:** California, 2011 (2nd round). **Signed by:** Adam Virchis.

A key starter on California's 2010 College World Series team, Johnson was a workhorse the following season as a junior, pitching his way into the second round. After signing for $450,000, he had his full-season debut delayed by shoulder fatigue then was limited to 17 starts in 2012. He showed he was fully healthy in 2013, wrapping the season with a five-game big league trial. Projected as a rotation workhorse, Johnson has a classic power pitcher's body and repertoire, as well as demeanor. His fastball isn't a pure dominator, and he sits at 92 mph and brushes 95 with his four-seamer while sitting around 90 mph with a two-seamer. He thrives with above-average control of both fastballs as well as his hard, upper-80s slider, a plus pitch that helped him shackle righthanded hitters to the tune of a .173 average and just two home runs in 324 at-bats last year. His show-me curveball and fringe-average changeup aren't where they need to be, though the changeup plays off his fastball well and has promise. His September trial taught Johnson that he needs to throw his changeup more. A potential No. 3 starter, his power righthanded profile fits in well Chicago's lefty-heavy big league rotation.

Year	Club (League)	Class	W	L	ERA	G	GS	CG	SV	IP	H	HR	BB	SO	K/9	WHIP	AVG
2011	Great Falls (PIO)	R	0	0	4.50	2	0	0	0	2	4	0	1	2	9.0	2.50	.444
2012	Kannapolis (SAL)	LoA	2	2	2.30	9	9	0	0	43	39	3	19	39	8.2	1.35	.235
	Winston-Salem (CAR)	HiA	4	3	2.74	8	8	0	0	49	43	0	10	48	8.8	1.07	.230
2013	Birmingham (SL)	AA	8	2	2.23	14	14	3	0	85	57	6	21	74	7.9	0.92	.189
	Charlotte (IL)	AAA	4	1	1.57	10	10	0	0	57	43	1	19	57	8.9	1.08	.209
	Chicago (AL)	MAJ	3	2	3.25	5	5	0	0	28	32	5	11	18	5.9	1.55	.281
Major League Totals			3	2	3.25	5	5	0	0	28	32	5	11	18	5.9	1.55	.281
Minor League Totals			18	8	2.21	43	41	3	0	236	186	10	70	220	8.4	1.08	.214

3 TIM ANDERSON, SS

RAY MARSDEN

Born: June 23, 1993. **B-T:** R-R. **Ht.:** 6-1. **Wt.:** 180. **Drafted:** East Central (Miss.) CC, 2013 (1st round). **Signed by:** Warren Hughes.

A prep basketball point guard who led his team to an Alabama state championship, Anderson also played baseball but lost playing time to a knee injury and basketball. Undrafted out of high school, he went to East Central CC to focus on baseball and started to come on in the summer Jayhawk League in 2012. He steadily climbed draft boards all spring in 2013 before the White Sox drafted him 17th overall. A potential top-of-the-order shortstop, Anderson has explosive raw tools and is adding skills to match. He's a well above-average runner and accomplished basestealer with a tremendous first step. That plays well in the infield as well, and Anderson has made strides by better positioning himself and learning to anticipate balls off the bat. His average arm strength has improved a bit since signing and should be enough for shortstop if he stays on his throwing program. He has an easy swing with below-average power, showing enough juice to keep pitchers honest. His pitch recognition remains understandably modest, but scouts in and out of the organization laud his aptitude and calm, confident demeanor. The White Sox hope Anderson can be ready by the time Alexei Ramirez's contract expires after the 2015 season and will push him to high Class A Winston-Salem in 2014.

Year	Club (League)	Class	AVG	G	AB	R	H	2B	3B	HR	RBI	BB	SO	SB	CS	OBP	SLG
2013	Kannapolis (SAL)	LoA	.277	68	267	45	74	10	5	1	21	23	78	24	4	.348	.363
Minor League Totals			.277	68	267	45	74	10	5	1	21	23	78	24	4	.348	.363

4 MARCUS SEMIEN, SS/2B/3B

Born: Sept. 17, 1990. **B-T:** R-R. **Ht.:** 6-1. **Wt.:** 190. **Drafted:** California, 2011 (6th round). **Signed by:** Adam Virchis.

Semien's father Eric played football at California, and Marcus followed him to the school and helped the Bears on a Cinderella 2010 College World Series run. He fell to the sixth round after a mediocre junior season in 2011 but hasn't stopped hitting as a pro, reaching the major leagues in 2013 with a two-hit game at Yankee Stadium in September. Semien is an average athlete who can make the routine play at any infield position while being a productive hitter. He repeats his simple swing with good strength and bat speed, and he's disciplined enough to get himself into hitter's counts. Semien's power is more to the gaps, and scouts don't expect him to repeat his 21-homer 2013 campaign. Still, he can punish mistakes and is a smart basestealer whose average speed will play. He has played mostly shortstop in the minors and can fill in there at the big league level, and he has solid infield actions. He fits better at second base or third long term due to modest arm strength and fair first-step quickness. His offensive showing as a pro has pushed Semien beyond his original utility profile. He could push for playing time in Chicago at second, short or third in 2014, and he fits best at third long-term alongside Tim Anderson and Micah Johnson in a future White Sox infield.

Year	Club (League)	Class	AVG	G	AB	R	H	2B	3B	HR	RBI	BB	SO	SB	CS	OBP	SLG
2011	Kannapolis (SAL)	LoA	.253	60	229	35	58	15	2	3	26	22	53	3	4	.320	.376
2012	Winston-Salem (CAR)	HiA	.273	107	418	80	114	31	5	14	59	55	97	11	5	.362	.471
2013	Birmingham (SL)	AA	.290	105	393	90	114	21	5	15	49	84	66	20	5	.420	.483
	Charlotte (IL)	AAA	.264	32	125	20	33	11	1	4	17	14	24	4	0	.338	.464
	Chicago (AL)	MAJ	.261	21	69	7	18	4	0	2	7	1	22	2	2	.268	.406
Major League Totals			.261	21	69	7	18	4	0	2	7	1	22	2	2	.268	.406
Minor League Totals			.274	304	1165	225	319	78	13	36	151	175	240	38	14	.372	.456

5 MICAH JOHNSON, 2B

Born: Dec. 18, 1990. **B-T:** B-R. **Ht.:** 5-11. **Wt.:** 190. **Drafted:** Indiana, 2012 (9th round). **Signed by:** Mike Shirley.

An arm injury that required surgery limited Johnson to 80 at-bats as an Indiana junior, allowing the White Sox to snap him up in the ninth round of the 2012 draft and sign him for $127,600. His first full season exceeded expectations, as he led the minors with 84 stolen bases and dominated the Southern League playoffs. He led Double-A Birmingham to a championship, hitting .368 with seven steals in 10 playoff games. Johnson showed up to spring training with just 6 percent body fat and showed explosive tools, including top-of-the-scale speed with sub-4.0-second times to first base. Once a slap-and-dash switch-hitter, he now hangs in to drive the ball more often, especially from the left side, and isn't afraid to go deep in counts and draw a walk. Johnson's hard hands contributed to 29 errors in the regular season. He has improved with the help of infield coordinator Ever Magallanes, and the organization thinks he'll be an adequate defender. If not, he'll move to center field. The White Sox believe his leadership and offensive upside will help him and Tim Anderson form a dynamic tandem in their middle infield and at the top of future lineups, with Johnson arriving first.

Year	Club (League)	Class	AVG	G	AB	R	H	2B	3B	HR	RBI	BB	SO	SB	CS	OBP	SLG
2012	Great Falls (PIO)	R	.273	69	271	49	74	10	5	4	25	43	74	19	6	.375	.391
2013	Kannapolis (SAL)	LoA	.342	77	304	76	104	17	11	6	42	40	67	61	19	.422	.530
	Winston-Salem (CAR)	HiA	.275	49	211	28	58	7	4	1	15	10	27	22	7	.309	.360
	Birmingham (SL)	AA	.238	5	21	2	5	0	0	0	1	0	4	1	0	.227	.238
Minor League Totals			.299	200	807	155	241	34	20	11	83	93	172	103	32	.373	.431

6 COURTNEY HAWKINS, OF

Born: Nov. 12, 1993. **B-T:** R-R. **Ht.:** 6-3. **Wt.:** 220. **Drafted:** HS—Corpus Christi, Texas, 2012 (1st round). **Signed by:** Keith Staab.

Hawkins back-flipped his way into draft lore in 2012 when he attended the draft at MLB Network's studios and celebrated his selection by the White Sox. The former high school cheerleader then hit 10 home runs (including the playoffs) in his pro debut before a dismal first full season. Hawkins ended 2012 in the high Class A Carolina League playoffs but wasn't ready for a full season with Winston-Salem. Familiarity bred contempt in the eight-team league, as opposing coaches picked him apart. As his confidence waned and Hawkins failed to adjust his aggressive, swing-for-the-fences approach, anything other than a fastball over the plate proved very challenging. Still, the organization kept him in Winston-Salem, further exposing his immature approach. Hawkins missed a month with a left shoulder strain but showed his above-average speed and arm strength all season despite his struggles. He has plus power, especially to his pull side. He played center last season but profiles better defensively on a corner. While he fits the right-field profile, Hawkins struck out in more than 37 percent of his plate appearances, so his hitting approach needs an overhaul. Scouts outside the organization were impressed with how Hawkins kept smiling and playing hard despite his struggles, and the White Sox say the season didn't crush his spirit. He'll head back to Winston-Salem for 2014.

Year	Club (League)	Class	AVG	G	AB	R	H	2B	3B	HR	RBI	BB	SO	SB	CS	OBP	SLG
2012	Bristol (APP)	R	.272	38	147	25	40	8	1	3	16	7	37	8	2	.314	.401
	Kannapolis (SAL)	LoA	.308	16	65	11	20	5	2	4	15	4	17	3	2	.352	.631
	Winston-Salem (CAR)	HiA	.294	5	17	3	5	2	0	1	2	0	2	0	1	.294	.588
2013	Winston-Salem (CAR)	HiA	.178	103	383	48	68	16	3	19	62	29	160	10	5	.249	.384
Minor League Totals			.217	162	612	87	133	31	6	27	95	40	216	21	10	.277	.420

7 TRAYCE THOMPSON, OF

BA GRADE 50 HIGH

Born: March 15, 1991. **B-T:** R-R. **Ht.:** 6-3. **Wt.:** 215. **Drafted:** HS—Santa Margarita, Calif., 2009 (2nd round). **Signed by:** George Kashigian.

Thompson's brother Klay is a sweet-shooting guard for the Golden State Warriors, while his father Mychal played 14 seasons after being the No. 1 overall pick in the 1978 NBA draft. Trayce chose baseball and was a stalwart for Birmingham's Double-A Southern League champions, hitting two postseason home runs. He has a Jermaine Dye look and similar tools, with more athleticism and speed. He lacks Dye's all-around savvy, however, and struggles to make consistent contact. His swing remains too long, which leads to plenty of strikeouts and modest batting averages, and he hasn't realized he can still hit for power with a shorter swing. Thompson can blast tape-measure shots thanks to his leverage, strength and loft-oriented swing. He has improved at recognizing breaking balls but still struggles with them. He's an average runner and effective basestealer who can handle center field, thanks to graceful, long strides and good instincts. His accurate, average arm helped him rank second in the SL with 13 assists. Thompson should head to Triple-A for the first time in 2014.

Year	Club (League)	Class	AVG	G	AB	R	H	2B	3B	HR	RBI	BB	SO	SB	CS	OBP	SLG
2009	Bristol (APP)	R	.188	25	85	8	16	3	1	0	10	4	33	2	0	.247	.247
	Great Falls (PIO)	R	.238	7	21	2	5	0	0	0	0	3	8	1	0	.333	.238
2010	Kannapolis (SAL)	LoA	.229	58	210	28	48	13	3	8	31	21	69	6	4	.302	.433
2011	Kannapolis (SAL)	LoA	.241	136	519	95	125	36	2	24	87	60	172	8	4	.329	.457
2012	Winston-Salem (CAR)	HiA	.254	116	449	77	114	28	5	22	90	45	144	18	3	.325	.486
	Birmingham (SL)	AA	.280	14	50	10	14	1	1	3	6	8	16	2	0	.379	.520
	Charlotte (IL)	AAA	.167	6	18	1	3	2	0	0	0	2	6	1	0	.250	.278
2013	Birmingham (SL)	AA	.229	135	507	78	116	23	5	15	73	60	139	25	8	.321	.383
Minor League Totals			.237	497	1859	299	441	106	17	72	297	203	587	63	19	.320	.429

8 CHRIS BECK, RHP

BA GRADE 50 HIGH

Born: Sept. 4, 1990. **B-T:** R-R. **Ht.:** 6-3. **Wt.:** 225. **Drafted:** Georgia Southern, 2012 (2nd round). **Signed by:** Kevin Burrell.

Beck was the ace for two seasons at Georgia Southern, and coming off a strong Cape Cod League he was positioned to go in the top 10 picks of the 2012 draft. He had a dreadful spring, though, losing velocity and crispness, and fell to the 76th overall pick. The White Sox signed him for $600,000. Beck still flashes two plus pitches and an average third pitch. His fastball touches 95 mph and sits 89-93 with good life down in the zone. His slider, once a premium power pitch, now is shorter and shallower, but even in the mid-80s it helps him get groundballs. His changeup has become a weapon, and he can throw strikes with a show-me curve. Some scouts think he could rediscover his wipeout slider if he were to ditch his curve. Beck finished his first full season with a strong Double-A Southern League playoff performance, reinforcing the organization's belief in his competitiveness and big-game ability. If he doesn't get his old slider back, he could still be a back-end starter or middle reliever. If the old depth and power return, though, Beck could be a No. 2 starter.

Year	Club (League)	Class	W	L	ERA	G	GS	CG	SV	IP	H	HR	BB	SO	K/9	WHIP	AVG
2012	Great Falls (PIO)	R	4	3	4.69	15	6	0	0	40	51	3	12	36	8.0	1.56	.319
2013	Winston-Salem (CAR)	HiA	11	8	3.11	21	21	1	0	119	117	11	42	57	4.3	1.34	.262
	Birmingham (SL)	AA	2	2	2.89	5	5	0	0	28	26	0	3	22	7.1	1.04	.250
Minor League Totals			17	13	3.42	41	32	1	0	187	194	14	57	115	5.5	1.34	.273

9 JACOB MAY, OF

RAY MARSDEN

BA GRADE 50 HIGH

Born: Jan. 23, 1992. **B-T:** B-R. **Ht.:** 5-10. **Wt.:** 180. **Drafted:** Coastal Carolina, 2013 (3rd round). **Signed by:** Kevin Burrell.

May's baseball bloodlines are hard to beat. His father Lee Jr. was a first-round pick in 1986 and reached Triple-A with the Mets, while his grandfather Lee Sr. hit 354 home runs in an 18-year major league career for the Reds, Astros, Orioles and Royals. His uncle Carlos, a first-round pick in 1966, also had a 10-year big league career. May had an unremarkable college career at Coastal Carolina but has hit better with wood bats, both in summer ball and as a pro. After being criticized for complacent play in college, May showed scintillating center field tools in his pro debut and played with energy and the White Sox love his maturity and leadership ability. The ball jumped off his bat, with eight home runs in 206 at-bats at low Class A Kannapolis after hitting just nine in college. In the past scouts said he had enough power to get him in trouble, but he's a legitimate hitter from both sides of the plate. May has plate discipline and could be a top-of-the-order presence thanks to top-of-the-scale speed that exceeds even that of 2013 first-rounder Tim Anderson. He has rough edges to iron out on the bases, where he could improve his jumps, and in center field, where his routes need work. He has modest arm strength that is playable in center. May's debut startled scouts who had not been impressed by him in college, and he likely will push Courtney Hawkins to right field in the high Class A Winston-Salem outfield to begin 2014.

Year	Club (League)	Class	AVG	G	AB	R	H	2B	3B	HR	RBI	BB	SO	SB	CS	OBP	SLG
2013	Great Falls (PIO)	R	.378	12	45	5	17	1	1	0	7	7	6	5	1	.481	.444
	Kannapolis (SAL)	LoA	.286	54	206	36	59	6	3	8	28	16	43	19	5	.346	.461
Minor League Totals			.303	66	251	41	76	7	4	8	35	23	49	24	6	.372	.458

10 TYLER DANISH, RHP

BRIAN WESTERHOLT

Born: Sept. 12, 1994. **B-T:** R-R. **Ht.:** 6-2. **Wt.:** 190. **Drafted:** HS—Plant City, Fla., 2013 (2nd round). **Signed by:** Joe Siers.

A first-team BA High School All-American, Danish had one of the best campaigns of any prep player in 2013, pitching 94 innings in Florida's highest classification without giving up an earned run. He signed for $1,001,800 as the 55th overall pick. Danish has overcome the loss of his father Mike, who died of cancer just after Christmas in 2010 while serving a prison sentence for fraud. Scouts love how Danish pitches with purpose and never gives in, often comparing him with Jake Peavy for his toughness, size and low release point. The White Sox compare him more with a pitcher they drafted, Daniel Hudson, because of the low three-quarters arm slot and sinker/slider repertoire. Danish's low-90s fastball features heavy sink, and his plus slider has late break. He got plenty of groundballs in his debut at Rookie-level Bristol, even at times with his developing changeup, which is below-average for now. Danish has enough athleticism to repeat his high-maintenance, energetic delivery, though some scouts say it features too much effort for him to remain in the rotation. Danish's slot may evoke Daniel Hudson, but his stuff says Tim Hudson, if he can hold up physically. The White Sox will put him on the fast track, starting him back at low Class A Kannapolis in 2014, but likely getting him to Double-A Birmingham by the end of the year if he pitches well.

Year	Club (League)	Class	W	L	ERA	G	GS	CG	SV	IP	H	HR	BB	SO	K/9	WHIP	AVG
2013	Bristol (APP)	R	1	0	1.38	13	1	0	0	26	15	1	5	22	7.6	0.77	.165
	Kannapolis (SAL)	LoA	0	0	0.00	2	0	0	0	4	2	0	0	6	13.5	0.50	.143
Minor League Totals			1	0	1.20	15	1	0	0	30	17	1	5	28	8.4	0.73	.162

11 DANIEL WEBB, RHP

Born: Aug. 18, 1989. **B-T:** R-R. **Ht.:** 6-3. **Wt.:** 210. **Drafted:** Northwest Florida State JC, 2009 (18th round). **Signed by:** Joel Grampietro (Blue Jays).

Barely more than five months after first acquiring Jason Frasor, the White Sox traded him back to Toronto, from whence he came, for minor league righthanders Miles Jaye and Webb. Webb had entered the 2008 draft as part of a loaded Kentucky prep pitching class that included future big leaguers Robbie Ross and Nick Maronde. Webb had a spotty spring and his signability proved difficult to gauge, and he fell to the 12th round. He spurned the Diamondbacks and went to Northwest Florida State JC, where he struggled and went to the 18th round in 2009, where the Jays signed him for $450,000. He struggled as a starter in the minors, as evidenced by his 8-21 overall record, but he took off as a reliever in 2013, finishing the season in the major leagues. Webb attacks hitters with three pitches, including an explosive fastball that has late hard sink at 93-94 mph while touching 96. He has focused on a slider to combat righthanded hitters, scraping 85 mph with depth and hard, late bite when it's on. He doesn't use his changeup often, but the White Sox consider it one of the system's best, a swing-and-miss pitch he sells with good arm speed. Consistency on and off the mound has been an issue with Webb for years, but Chicago pitching coaches have a history of getting the most out of power arms. He has a line on a role on the 2014 big league bullpen.

Year	Club (League)	Class	W	L	ERA	G	GS	CG	SV	IP	H	HR	BB	SO	K/9	WHIP	AVG
2010	Auburn (NYP)	SS	0	6	5.24	13	13	0	0	57	69	4	26	39	6.2	1.68	.299
	Lansing (MWL)	LoA	1	1	2.31	2	2	0	0	12	8	0	6	4	3.1	1.20	.195
2011	Blue Jays (GCL)	R	0	0	0.00	1	0	0	0	1	2	0	0	0	0.0	1.50	.333
	Lansing (MWL)	LoA	4	5	5.59	18	12	0	2	66	80	7	24	51	7.0	1.58	.303
2012	Kannapolis (SAL)	LoA	1	8	5.81	31	4	0	3	62	73	2	27	50	7.3	1.61	.293
2013	Winston-Salem (CAR)	HiA	1	0	0.00	8	0	0	2	15	10	0	5	19	11.4	1.00	.182
	Birmingham (SL)	AA	0	0	1.77	13	0	0	4	20	11	0	5	21	9.3	0.79	.155
	Charlotte (IL)	AAA	1	1	2.96	21	0	0	4	27	24	1	17	38	12.5	1.50	.226
	Chicago (AL)	MAJ	0	0	3.18	9	0	0	0	11	9	0	4	10	7.9	1.15	.220
Major League Totals			0	0	3.18	9	0	0	0	11	9	0	4	10	7.9	1.15	.220
Minor League Totals			8	21	4.49	107	31	0	15	260	277	14	110	222	7.7	1.49	.271

12 CARLOS SANCHEZ, SS/2B

Born: June 29, 1992. **B-T:** B-R. **Ht.:** 5-11. **Wt.:** 195. **Signed:** Venezuela, 2009. **Signed by:** Amador Arias.

While Chicago's big league team has a strong Latin American presence, much of it comes from Cuba (Jose Abreu, Alexei Ramirez, Dayan Viciedo) or other organizations. Sanchez, signed out of Venezuela as a 16-year-old, remains the best recent in-house product of the organization's international efforts. He finished 2012 in Triple-A Charlotte after starting in high Class A Winston-Salem, with a stop in the Futures Game along the way. Sanchez was pegged to play shortstop every day as a 20-year-old in Triple-A in 2014, and it proved too much. Offseason weight gain cost him a bit of first-step burst that had separated him in the past. Sanchez wound up playing more at second base than short, where he made 13 errors in just 52 games. He still has an above-average arm and soft hands and was playing well as a second baseman for La Guaira in winter ball back in Venezuela. Sanchez has little power to speak of and is a plus runner at his best, so he'll need to keep refining his short game and defense. He could wind up serving a utility infielder role unless he regains the zip he showed in 2012, but the organization still sees him as a potential regular at second. He's ticketed for a trip back to Charlotte in 2014, barring a big spring.

Year	Club (League)	Class	AVG	G	AB	R	H	2B	3B	HR	RBI	BB	SO	SB	CS	OBP	SLG
2009	White Sox (DSL)	R	.156	22	32	7	5	0	0	0	3	8	10	1	0	.341	.156
2010	White Sox (DSL)	R	.269	52	156	26	42	5	2	1	18	41	26	7	3	.431	.346
2011	Bristol (APP)	R	.250	5	16	4	4	1	0	0	3	5	2	1	2	.500	.313
	Kannapolis (SAL)	LoA	.288	63	264	44	76	10	1	1	27	15	49	7	8	.341	.345
2012	Winston-Salem (CAR)	HiA	.315	92	365	58	115	14	6	1	42	31	64	19	10	.374	.395
	Birmingham (SL)	AA	.370	30	119	17	44	9	1	0	13	10	22	7	5	.424	.462
	Charlotte (IL)	AAA	.256	11	39	4	10	2	0	0	1	0	6	0	0	.256	.308
2013	Charlotte (IL)	AAA	.241	112	432	50	104	20	2	0	28	29	76	16	7	.293	.296
Minor League Totals			.281	387	1423	210	400	61	12	3	135	139	255	58	35	.354	.347

13 JARED MITCHELL, OF

BA GRADE
50
HIGH

Born: Oct. 13, 1988. **B-T:** L-L. **Ht.:** 6-0. **Wt.:** 205. **Drafted:** Louisiana State, 2009 (1st round). **Signed by:** Warren Hughes.

Mitchell has had an eventful athletic career, winning national titles in baseball and football at Louisiana State. His pro baseball career has two key points: his 2010 spring-training collision with an outfield wall that tore a tendon in his left ankle and cost him the season, and his swing-and-miss tendencies since then as he's tried to catch up. He has struck out in 33 percent of his professional plate appearances. Mitchell had a strong 2013 spring in big league camp but an awful season that included two disabled list stints, a .550 OPS, a demotion and finally a Southern League championship with Double-A Birmingham. Mitchell then hit five home runs to tie for second in the Arizona Fall League. Mitchell remains an above-average, explosive athlete with well-above-average power potential. He has an average arm but his reads off the bat make him best suited for left field. His future all depends on his ability to make adjustments at the plate. He tinkers with his hitting mechanics, goes deep in counts without an effective two-strike approach, expands his strike zone and gets out of synch with his swing. Mitchell's AFL stint gave the White Sox hope he will be more flexible with his hitting approach. He'll take his third shot at Charlotte, in the Knights' new downtown ballpark, in 2014.

Year	Club (League)	Class	AVG	G	AB	R	H	2B	3B	HR	RBI	BB	SO	SB	CS	OBP	SLG
2009	Kannapolis (SAL)	LoA	.296	34	115	13	34	12	2	0	10	23	40	5	3	.417	.435
2010	Did not play—Injured																
2011	Winston-Salem (CAR)	HiA	.222	129	477	74	106	31	8	9	58	52	183	14	6	.304	.377
2012	Birmingham (SL)	AA	.240	94	334	51	80	13	12	10	54	62	126	20	5	.368	.440
	Charlotte (IL)	AAA	.231	36	121	18	28	11	1	1	13	16	53	1	1	.329	.364
2013	Charlotte (IL)	AAA	.132	14	53	7	7	2	0	0	3	10	27	4	1	.277	.170
	Birmingham (SL)	AA	.174	76	247	23	43	6	2	5	20	41	96	13	5	.297	.275
Minor League Totals			.221	383	1347	186	298	75	25	25	158	204	525	57	21	.330	.370

14 KEON BARNUM, 1B

BA GRADE
50
HIGH

Born: Jan. 16, 1993. **B-T:** L-L. **Ht.:** 6-5. **Wt.:** 225. **Drafted:** HS—Tampa, 2012 (1st round supplemental). **Signed by:** Joe Siers.

Barnum, who signed for $950,000 as the 48th overall pick in 2012, hasn't stayed on the field enough for the White Sox to fully evaluate him. He has solid athleticism, but his limited speed makes him a first baseman all the way. He does have soft hands around the bag and shouldn't be a liability defensively. Barnum's value is all in his bat and 80 grade raw power. His swing is naturally geared toward left-center field, and he still hasn't really learned how to incorporate his lower half into his swing and pull the ball consistently with authority. Barnum has had trouble staying healthy, with a shoulder injury limiting him in

2012, then a hamate injury in March 2013, followed by a left knee problem in May that combined to delay his low Class A Kannapolis debut until June. The White Sox gave him extra at-bats in instructional league and were encouraged by his increased ability to use his legs and turn on inside pitches. If he can stay healthy, he's likely to start 2014 back at Kannapolis but could earn a quick promotion.

Year	Club (League)	Class	AVG	G	AB	R	H	2B	3B	HR	RBI	BB	SO	SB	CS	OBP	SLG
2012	Bristol (APP)	R	.279	13	43	6	12	1	0	3	8	5	13	0	0	.347	.512
2013	Kannapolis (SAL)	LoA	.254	56	201	22	51	13	1	5	26	19	65	0	0	.315	.403
Minor League Totals			.258	69	244	28	63	14	1	8	34	24	78	0	0	.321	.422

15 CHRIS BASSITT, RHP

BA GRADE **45** MEDIUM

Born: Feb. 22, 1989. **B-T:** R-R. **Ht.:** 6-5. **Wt.:** 205. **Drafted:** Akron, 2011 (16th round). **Signed by:** Phil Gulley.

The White Sox scouted Bassitt somewhat by accident, seeing him as Akron's closer when he was pitching against Pittsburgh, where they were scouting Kevan Smith—who has been his catcher for most of the last two seasons at high Class A Winston-Salem. Bassitt never started in college, but the White Sox shifted him into the role in 2012 and he threw 149 innings in 2013. His loose arm and competitiveness helped, as did his ability to throw four pitches for strikes. His fastball reaches 93-95 mph in short bursts and more often sits at 90-93 with sink, though at times it flattens out when he loses his low-three-quarters arm slot. Bassitt lacks a wipeout secondary pitch. He throws both a slider and a curveball, though usually only one is working on a given night, and his changeup is fringe-average. His ability to make big pitches in big situations showed in minor league playoffs in the last two seasons, when he won all three of his starts and yielded one earned run in 19 innings with 19 strikeouts. Bassitt could be a back-end starter but more likely will return to his relief roots when he reaches Chicago. He's slated for the Double-A Birmingham rotation to open 2014.

Year	Club (League)	Class	W	L	ERA	G	GS	CG	SV	IP	H	HR	BB	SO	K/9	WHIP	AVG
2011	Bristol (APP)	R	0	0	1.08	6	0	0	0	8	9	0	2	11	11.9	1.32	.273
	Winston-Salem (CAR)	HiA	0	0	5.40	1	0	0	0	2	2	0	0	1	5.4	1.20	.286
	Kannapolis (SAL)	LoA	3	1	1.82	16	0	0	1	25	18	1	6	29	10.6	0.97	.202
2012	Winston-Salem (CAR)	HiA	5	4	3.66	38	10	0	4	91	74	6	54	75	7.4	1.41	.218
2013	Winston-Salem (CAR)	HiA	7	2	3.46	18	18	0	0	101	90	9	42	101	9.0	1.30	.231
	Birmingham (SL)	AA	4	2	2.27	8	8	0	0	48	35	2	17	37	7.0	1.09	.213
Minor League Totals			19	9	3.11	87	36	0	5	275	228	18	121	254	8.3	1.27	.223

16 SCOTT SNODGRESS, LHP

BA GRADE **50** HIGH

Born: Sept. 20, 1989. **B-T:** L-L. **Ht.:** 6-6. **Wt.:** 225. **Drafted:** Stanford, 2011 (5th round). **Signed by:** Adam Virchis.

The White Sox have moved Snodgress aggressively, especially considering that he threw just 100 innings in three seasons in Stanford's bullpen. Chicago immediately placed him in the rotation and he rewarded the club with 27 starts in 2012, finishing the year at high Class A Winston-Salem, helping the Dash reach the playoffs. He was starting for Double-A Birmingham in the Southern League playoffs in 2013, losing both starts to sum up a disappointing season. Snodgress has the mix of pitches to start, with a fringe-average fastball in the 87-91 mph range that plays up thanks to some deception, a hard cutter up to 87, and both his curveball and changeup flash plus. His curve, the best in the system now that Andre Rienzo has graduated to the big leagues, has tight rotation and good shape when it's on, and his change shows fade and 10 mph separation from his fastball. Snodgress struggled to repeat his slightly crossfire delivery in 2013, overthrowing and getting out of synch with his delivery whenever he got in trouble. Scouts didn't like his mound presence or body language, with some questioning his competitiveness. The White Sox still like him as a starter but likely will slow him down in 2014, scheduling a return trip to Birmingham.

Year	Club (League)	Class	W	L	ERA	G	GS	CG	SV	IP	H	HR	BB	SO	K/9	WHIP	AVG
2011	Great Falls (PIO)	R	3	3	3.34	16	12	0	0	59	61	5	17	68	10.3	1.31	.262
2012	Kannapolis (SAL)	LoA	3	3	3.64	19	19	0	0	99	86	4	49	84	7.6	1.36	.233
	Winston-Salem (CAR)	HiA	4	0	1.50	8	8	0	0	42	26	2	15	44	9.4	0.98	.176
2013	Birmingham (SL)	AA	11	11	4.70	26	26	2	0	144	146	9	59	90	5.6	1.43	.269
Minor League Totals			21	17	3.77	69	65	2	0	344	319	20	140	286	7.5	1.33	.247

17 LEURY GARCIA, SS/OF

Born: March 18, 1991. **B-T:** B-R. **Ht.:** 5-7. **Wt.:** 160. **Signed:** Dominican Republic, 2007. **Signed by:** Jesus Ovalle (Rangers).

Garcia played for five teams in 2013, starting with a bit role as a utility player on the Dominican Republic's title-winning roster for the World Baseball Classic. Despite the interruption of his spring training and the fact that he got only one at-bat in the WBC, Garcia made the Rangers'

Opening Day roster as a utility infielder and extra outfielder. He played sparingly, however, and was demoted to Triple-A in mid-June before being traded in August for Alex Rios. After a short stint at Triple-A Charlotte, Garcia returned to the majors with the White Sox. He has exciting tools for the middle infield, with premium range to his right and left, an easy plus arm and explosive first-step quickness. That would play on the bases as well, but the switch-hitting Garcia can't steal first. For all his tools, his bat remains light, with an approach better suited to a bigger man that leads to long swing paths. A free swinger, Garcia has bottom-of-the-lineup skills and needs to be more efficient at bunting, moving runners and stealing bases. He's also more erratic defensively at short than the White Sox were expecting, with 11 errors in 44 Triple-A games at the position due to shaky hands. His bat is a bigger question mark and will determine whether Garcia can be a future regular or is set for a super-utility role, the latter of which appears to be the case for 2014.

Year	Club (League)	Class	AVG	G	AB	R	H	2B	3B	HR	RBI	BB	SO	SB	CS	OBP	SLG
2008	Rangers (AZL)	R	.209	41	129	17	27	3	3	0	14	8	40	12	3	.250	.279
2009	Hickory (SAL)	LoA	.232	83	276	28	64	6	3	1	18	18	64	19	6	.288	.286
2010	Rangers (AZL)	R	.500	6	18	5	9	2	0	0	2	4	4	4	2	.591	.611
	Hickory (SAL)	LoA	.262	89	359	57	94	5	4	3	22	23	57	47	9	.307	.323
2011	Myrtle Beach (CAR)	HiA	.256	109	442	65	113	19	5	3	38	28	100	30	12	.306	.342
2012	Frisco (TL)	AA	.292	100	377	55	110	12	11	2	30	22	79	31	7	.337	.398
2013	Texas (AL)	MAJ	.192	25	52	8	10	0	1	0	1	3	16	1	0	.236	.231
	Round Rock (PCL)	AAA	.264	47	193	31	51	8	4	4	19	14	53	12	4	.314	.409
	Charlotte (IL)	AAA	.267	8	30	3	8	1	0	0	1	1	8	3	0	.313	.300
	Chicago (AL)	MAJ	.204	20	49	2	10	1	0	0	1	4	18	6	2	.259	.224
Major League Totals			.198	45	101	10	20	1	1	0	2	7	34	7	2	.248	.228
Minor League Totals			.261	483	1824	261	476	56	30	13	144	118	405	158	43	.310	.346

18 MICKER ZAPATA, OF

BA GRADE
55
EXTREME

Born: Sept. 11, 1996. **B-T:** R-R. **Ht.:** 6-3. **Wt.:** 225. **Signed:** Dominican Republic, 2013. **Signed by:** Marco Paddy.

The White Sox badly want to resuscitate their presence internationally, particularly in the Dominican Republic, and aggressively pursued Zapata, who also has been known by the surname Adolfo. They were tied to him before the July 2 signing period began and eventually inked him for a $1.6 million bonus, the largest in franchise history for a Latin American amateur. He has an unusual background for a Dominican prospect, having been born in the U.S. Virgin Islands; White Sox officials say his English is better than his Spanish. At age 14, Zapata moved to the D.R. to train and practice at La Academia and work with Moreno Tejada, the trainer who handled Twins prospect Miguel Sano. Like Sano, Zapata stands out for his size and precocious raw power. He's athletic enough to be an average runner despite his size, and he got a Michael Jordan physical comparison from one club official. Zapata has five-tool ability if he hits, though most scouts see his power ahead of his feel for hitting. His swing can be undisciplined and too geared for power, while the White Sox see a hitter who has time to learn that he's strong enough to punish the ball without trying too hard. The organization hopes Zapata will be ready to begin his pro career in the Rookie-level Arizona League in 2014, though a Dominican Summer League start is possible as well.

Year	Club (League)	Class	AVG	G	AB	R	H	2B	3B	HR	RBI	BB	SO	SB	CS	OBP	SLG
2013	Did not play—Signed 2014 contract																

19 TREY MICHALCZEWSKI, 3B

BA GRADE
50
HIGH

Born: Feb. 27, 1995. **B-T:** B-R. **Ht.:** 6-3. **Wt.:** 210. **Drafted:** HS—Jenks, Okla., 2013 (7th round). **Signed by:** Clay Overcash.

Michalczewski may be the greatest sign that with the change in draft rules, the White Sox have changed their scouting and player-development approach. Usually, the high school players the White Sox have drafted and signed are toolsy outfielders such as Courtney Hawkins or 2001 pick Chris Young. Michalczewski does have a football background, which fits Chicago's usual preference, as he played tight end at Jenks (Okla.) High, helping the team win a state championship. Despite his two-sport pedigree, Michalczewski has a fairly mature hitting approach and a sound swing from both sides of the plate. Scouts consider his hitting ability more advanced than his present power, a trait they prefer, especially in a physical, athletic player. He was a little raw at third base after playing shortstop in high school but has the arm strength and actions for the position, and he runs well for his size. He had to catch up a bit to the speed of the game in the Rookie-level Appalachian League, but managers there liked his feel for the game and considered his $500,000 signing bonus money well spent. He should earn a spot on the low Class A Kannapolis roster in 2014.

Year	Club (League)	Class	AVG	G	AB	R	H	2B	3B	HR	RBI	BB	SO	SB	CS	OBP	SLG
2013	Bristol (APP)	R	.236	56	195	25	46	5	2	3	21	23	56	2	0	.324	.328
Minor League Totals			.236	56	195	25	46	5	2	3	21	23	56	2	0	.324	.328

20 BRAULIO ORTIZ, RHP

BA GRADE
50
EXTREME

Born: Dec. 20, 1991. **B-T:** R-R. **Ht.:** 6-5. **Wt.:** 205. **Signed:** Dominican Republic, 2011. **Signed by:** Pablo Cruz.

Ortiz made his U.S. debut in 2013 and broke out, finishing the year in high Class A. He has a good pitcher's frame and has started filling out physically. When he maintains his delivery and repeats it, he can pump his fastball up to 97-98 mph at times, usually sitting more in the mid-90s. Signed as a 19-year-old, Ortiz was making his U.S. debut in 2013 and began in the low Class A Kannapolis bullpen. By June he was ready for the rotation and he earned a promotion to high Class A Winston-Salem thanks to his velocity and sink on his fastball. He also throws a slider that flashes average. The White Sox are eager to get him more innings even though he profiles more as a reliever. He doesn't throw consistent strikes because he doesn't repeat his delivery well, and he also is yet to throw a changeup. Ortiz's arm strength is tantalizing, but even the White Sox don't plan to rush him. He's headed back to Winston-Salem to start 2014.

Year	Club (League)	Class	W	L	ERA	G	GS	CG	SV	IP	H	HR	BB	SO	K/9	WHIP	AVG
2011	White Sox (DSL)	R	0	1	8.31	6	1	0	0	9	9	0	11	7	7.3	2.31	.265
2012	White Sox (DSL)	R	3	3	3.93	16	8	0	1	50	54	1	20	37	6.6	1.47	.276
2013	Kannapolis (SAL)	LoA	0	4	3.45	22	8	0	3	63	43	3	39	74	10.6	1.31	.196
	Winston-Salem (CAR)	HiA	1	3	6.91	6	6	0	0	27	28	2	24	29	9.5	1.90	.252
Minor League Totals			4	11	4.53	50	23	0	4	149	134	6	94	147	8.9	1.53	.239

21 JAKE PETRICKA, RHP

BA GRADE
45
HIGH

Born: June 5, 1988. **B-T:** R-R. **Ht.:** 6-5. **Wt.:** 200. **Drafted:** Indiana State, 2010 (2nd round). **Signed by:** Mike Shirley.

Petricka has teased scouts with his stuff for years, finally putting it all together in 2013 after a move to the bullpen. Drafted out of high school in 2006, he had Tommy John surgery in 2007 and went to Iowa Western CC before emerging at Indiana State. After signing for $540,000 as a 2010 second-rounder, Petricka threw more than 250 innings over two full seasons as a starter, reaching Double-A Birmingham. More thrower than pitcher, he shifted to relief in 2013 and finished the season in the major leagues, finding confidence in the role and becoming more consistently aggressive. Petricka's fastball velocity fluctuates. On good days, his fastball features heavy sink from 92-96 mph, and he complements it with a hard slider that has cutter action and scrapes the upper 80s. He'll mix in a changeup from time to time. In some outings, his velocity backed up, sitting at 91-92 mph, and his slider lacked consistency as well. Petricka threw a few more strikes in 2013 but will never have fine command, and his control likely limits him to a set-up role rather than a future closer potential. He'll have to have a good spring to earn a return trip to Chicago.

Year	Club (League)	Class	W	L	ERA	G	GS	CG	SV	IP	H	HR	BB	SO	K/9	WHIP	AVG
2010	Bristol (APP)	R	2	4	2.86	8	8	0	0	35	25	1	7	38	9.9	0.92	.197
	Kannapolis (SAL)	LoA	0	1	3.72	9	0	0	0	10	13	0	8	10	9.3	2.17	.295
2011	Kannapolis (SAL)	LoA	3	1	2.81	8	8	0	0	42	39	0	13	48	10.4	1.25	.255
	Bristol (APP)	R	0	0	0.00	2	1	0	0	4	4	0	0	5	11.3	1.00	.286
	Winston-Salem (CAR)	HiA	4	7	4.39	13	13	0	0	68	71	3	26	46	6.1	1.43	.265
2012	Winston-Salem (CAR)	HiA	5	5	5.33	19	19	0	0	83	93	2	46	84	9.1	1.68	.284
	Birmingham (SL)	AA	3	3	5.46	10	10	0	0	58	63	7	35	27	4.2	1.70	.290
2013	Birmingham (SL)	AA	3	0	2.06	21	1	0	0	39	36	1	18	41	9.4	1.37	.255
	Charlotte (IL)	AAA	2	0	1.17	10	0	0	1	15	9	0	7	17	10.0	1.04	.167
	Chicago (AL)	MAJ	1	1	3.26	16	0	0	0	19	20	0	10	10	4.7	1.55	.278
Major League Totals			1	1	3.26	16	0	0	0	19	20	0	10	10	4.7	1.55	.278
Minor League Totals			22	21	3.98	100	60	0	1	353	353	14	160	316	8.1	1.45	.262

22 ADAM ENGEL, OF

BA GRADE
50
EXTREME

Born: Dec. 9, 1991. **B-T:** R-R. **Ht.:** 6-1. **Wt.:** 215. **Drafted:** Louisville, 2013 (19th round). **Signed by:** Phil Gulley.

No one in NCAA Division I stole more bases in 2012-13 than Engel (88). That's despite the fact that Engel hit just .236/.367/.301 as a junior at Louisville, with 20 hit-by-pitches accounting for a good portion of the on-base percentage. Scouts knew Engel was an elite athlete, an 80 runner who can cover 60 yards in 6.4 seconds. He combines that with physicality, with one scout comparing his body to that of an NFL safety. Engel just didn't hit in college, and the White Sox (with help from the Louisville coaches) set about adjusting his swing after he signed for $100,000. An adjustment to his hand positioning in his setup helped Engel get to pitches middle-in, and once he began seeing results, his confidence took off. Engel, who led the Rookie-level Pioneer League in steals, has the strength to hit for average power but the White Sox just want him to keep focusing on making consistent, hard contact. If he hits, Engel has the speed to be a factor as a leadoff man and defender in center field, with a fringe-average arm and good instincts. With a good spring training in 2014, Engel could make good on his Peter Bourjos comparisons, starting at low Class A Kannapolis.

Year	Club (League)	Class	AVG	G	AB	R	H	2B	3B	HR	RBI	BB	SO	SB	CS	OBP	SLG
2013	Great Falls (PIO)	R	.301	56	239	44	72	12	3	3	30	21	34	31	8	.379	.414
Minor League Totals			.301	56	239	44	72	12	3	3	30	21	34	31	8	.379	.414

23 KEENYN WALKER, OF

BA GRADE 45 HIGH

Born: Aug. 12, 1990. **B-T:** B-R. **Ht.:** 6-3. **Wt.:** 190. **Drafted:** Central Arizona JC, 2011 (1st round supplemental). **Signed by:** John Kazanas.

Drafted out of high school in 2009 (Cubs) and again in 2010 out of Central Arizona JC (Phillies), Walker finally signed with the White Sox as their top pick in 2011, receiving a $795,000 bonus as a sandwich pick. He was a regular in Birmingham's outfield playing all three spots but wasn't ready for the jump, posting the second-lowest batting average (.201) by a qualifier in the Southern League while leading it in strikeouts (153), caught stealing (15) and errors by an outfielder (11). Walker packs speed and strength into his 6-foot-3, 190-pound frame, though he has little power to speak of with his present slap-and-dash approach. He will draw a walk but doesn't fare well with two strikes and could stand to be more aggressive with fastballs. He's a potentially outstanding defender in center field, with plus speed, excellent range thanks to good reads off the bat and a solid-average arm. As at the plate, he can get sloppy in the field, and Walker needs polish even to reach a fourth-outfielder ceiling, which seems more reasonable at this stage. He could return to Birmingham, at least to begin 2014.

Year	Club (League)	Class	AVG	G	AB	R	H	2B	3B	HR	RBI	BB	SO	SB	CS	OBP	SLG
2011	Great Falls (PIO)	R	.333	15	60	16	20	7	1	0	9	7	17	11	5	.431	.483
	Kannapolis (SAL)	LoA	.228	39	162	25	37	1	2	0	15	14	64	10	4	.296	.259
2012	Kannapolis (SAL)	LoA	.282	74	266	53	75	15	5	1	39	50	93	39	11	.395	.387
	Winston-Salem (CAR)	HiA	.238	37	143	31	34	7	1	3	16	24	50	17	4	.345	.364
2013	Birmingham (SL)	AA	.201	130	462	77	93	16	5	3	32	69	153	38	15	.319	.277
Minor League Totals			.237	295	1093	202	259	46	14	7	111	164	377	115	39	.345	.324

24 MYLES JAYE, RHP

BA GRADE 45 HIGH

Born: Dec. 28, 1991. **B-T:** B-R. **Ht.:** 6-3. **Wt.:** 170. **Drafted:** HS—Fayetteville, Ga., 2010 (17th round). **Signed by:** Eric McQueen (Blue Jays).

Jaye came to the White Sox with Daniel Webb in the January 2012 Jason Frasor trade. The Blue Jays had given the 2010 17th-rounder $250,000 to pry the projectable right-hander away from a commitment to Kennesaw State. The White Sox pushed him to low Class A Kannapolis in his first full season, before he was ready, and he was hammered most of the season. He started 2013 back there but finished at Double-A Birmingham, earning the clinching victory in the Southern League championship series. Jaye's thin frame hasn't added much muscle, but he is stronger than he used to be and his stuff has improved from fringy to solid-average, with an 89-93 mph fastball at his best. He pitches with a quick tempo and flashes an above-average changeup with sink. His slider is surprisingly hard at up to 82 mph, and at times it's an average pitch with some late tilt. Jaye's playoff outing likely clinched a return to the Birmingham rotation for 2014.

Year	Club (League)	Class	W	L	ERA	G	GS	CG	SV	IP	H	HR	BB	SO	K/9	WHIP	AVG
2011	Bluefield (APP)	R	3	3	3.00	13	9	1	1	54	48	7	18	49	8.2	1.22	.239
2012	Kannapolis (SAL)	LoA	4	7	6.04	17	17	0	0	79	102	6	39	65	7.4	1.78	.318
2013	Kannapolis (SAL)	LoA	4	1	2.20	7	7	0	0	41	36	2	17	37	8.1	1.29	.238
	Winston-Salem (CAR)	HiA	9	6	4.11	20	20	1	0	118	122	8	44	89	6.8	1.40	.266
	Birmingham (SL)	AA	0	1	17.18	1	1	0	0	4	8	0	2	3	7.4	2.73	.400
Minor League Totals			20	18	4.32	58	54	2	1	296	316	23	120	243	7.4	1.47	.275

25 BRANDON JACOBS, OF

BA GRADE 45 HIGH

Born: Dec. 8, 1990. **B-T:** R-R. **Ht.:** 5-11. **Wt.:** 240. **Drafted:** HS—Lilburn, Ga., 2009 (10th round). **Signed by:** Tim Hyers (Red Sox).

The Red Sox gave Jacobs $750,000 to steer him away from an Auburn football scholarship, and he surprised scouts with how polished his offensive game was for a two-spot player. His 2011 season at low Class A Greenville appeared to be a revelation, as he combined extra-base power with 30 stolen bases while showing premium bat speed and surprising pitch recognition. But Jacobs' Greenville season now looks like the outlier rather than the harbinger of things to come. He's a .247 hitter in more than 1,100 at-bats outside of that year, and the White Sox picked him up in a July 2013 trade for lefty reliever Matt Thornton. He didn't wow his new employers after his arrival, particularly in struggling to hit for power. While he showed some ability to lay off breaking balls earlier in his career, he's struggled to do so against more advanced pitching, keeping his plus power more in the "raw" category instead of "usable." Jacobs has slowed down as he's matured physically and is just an average runner with a below-average arm, which limits him to left field. A return engagement with Double-A Birmingham in 2014 is most likely.

Year	Club (League)	Class	AVG	G	AB	R	H	2B	3B	HR	RBI	BB	SO	SB	CS	OBP	SLG
2009	Red Sox (GCL)	R	.250	8	24	1	6	2	0	0	0	2	8	0	0	.333	.333
2010	Lowell (NYP)	SS	.242	64	236	30	57	18	2	6	31	21	59	4	1	.308	.411
2011	Greenville (SAL)	LoA	.303	115	442	75	134	32	3	17	80	43	123	30	7	.376	.505
2012	Salem (CAR)	HiA	.252	114	437	62	110	30	0	13	61	39	128	17	9	.322	.410
2013	Salem (CAR)	HiA	.244	81	291	44	71	24	0	11	44	33	88	10	4	.334	.440
	Portland (EL)	AA	.375	3	8	2	3	1	1	0	0	0	2	0	0	.375	.750
	Birmingham (SL)	AA	.237	43	156	13	37	8	0	2	22	11	50	2	3	.291	.327
Minor League Totals			.262	428	1594	227	418	115	6	49	238	149	458	63	24	.335	.434

26 CLEULUIS RONDON, SS

BA GRADE **45** HIGH

Born: April 13, 1994. **B-T:** R-R. **Ht.:** 6-0. **Wt.:** 155. **Signed:** Venezuela, 2010. **Signed by:** Angel Escobar (Red Sox).

In a year when middle infielders Micah Johnson and Marcus Semien made huge strides and jumped into the organization's top five prospects, the White Sox nevertheless added significant middle-infield depth in 2013. They drafted Tim Anderson 17th overall, then traded for a pair of potentially dynamic defenders in Leury Garcia and Rondon, who came from the Red Sox in the three-team Jake Peavy trade. Rondon signed with the Red Sox in 2010 and had moved slowly before beginning to hit a bit at short-season Lowell when the trade occurred. Naturally, the White Sox accelerated him to low Class A Kannapolis and he struggled, with only one extra-base hit. Defense is Rondon's claim to fame, thanks to very soft, nimble hands. Assistant general manager Buddy Bell, part of a family with three generations of major leaguers, went so far as to say Rondon's hands were as good as any he's ever seen. His defense could get even better as he becomes more proficient fundamentally, but already he has an above-average and accurate arm, a tremendous internal clock and the mustard necessary to make the spectacular play. An average runner, Rondon was a below-average hitter when he signed and he remains so, lacking strength and getting the bat knocked out of his hands. He has the hand-eye coordination to survive offensively if he gains strength. He's slated to be Kannapolis' shortstop again when the 2014 season opens.

Year	Club (League)	Class	AVG	G	AB	R	H	2B	3B	HR	RBI	BB	SO	SB	CS	OBP	SLG
2011	Red Sox (DSL)	R	.171	62	205	39	35	6	1	2	27	43	50	14	1	.348	.239
2012	Red Sox (GCL)	R	.231	47	182	19	42	10	6	0	16	9	42	2	2	.270	.352
	Lowell (NYP)	SS	.000	2	4	0	0	0	0	0	0	0	1	0	0	.000	.000
2013	Lowell (NYP)	SS	.276	37	123	13	34	4	1	1	10	7	26	6	1	.326	.350
	Kannapolis (SAL)	LoA	.202	29	94	11	19	0	0	1	6	7	24	1	0	.279	.234
Minor League Totals			.214	177	608	82	130	20	8	4	59	66	143	23	4	.310	.293

27 ANDREW MITCHELL, RHP

Born: Nov. 9, 1991. **B-T:** R-R. **Ht.:** 6-3. **Wt.:** 205. **Drafted:** Texas Christian, 2013 (4th round). **Signed by:** Keith Staab.

Mitchell opened 2013 as Texas Christian's closer, but its poor offense prompted his midseason move to the rotation. Mitchell struggled a bit with the shift, helping contribute to him dropping to the fourth round of the 2013 draft. He signed for $413,000. Mitchell offers two plus pitches in his fastball and curve. His 80-81 mph curve ranked as the best available in the draft among college pitchers, and if he proves he can throw it for strikes as a pro, he'll have a potential 70 pitch on his hands. Mitchell's fastball can reach 98 mph in a relief role and touched 95-96 as a starter after signing. If he commanded either pitch, he'd be a starter for sure, but he walked 110 in 202 college innings, almost exactly the same walk rate of 4.8 per nine innings he had as a pro. He tends to rush through his delivery and lose his release point. Mitchell's nascent changeup remains inconsistent and will be another development focus for 2014, when he will get another chance to start. He has a durable frame and should skip to high Class A Winston-Salem with a good spring performance.

Year	Club (League)	Class	W	L	ERA	G	GS	CG	SV	IP	H	HR	BB	SO	K/9	WHIP	AVG
2013	Great Falls (PIO)	R	1	3	4.50	14	14	1	0	56	57	6	30	47	7.6	1.55	.273
Minor League Totals			1	3	4.50	14	14	1	0	56	57	6	30	47	7.6	1.55	.273

28 BRAD GOLDBERG, RHP

BA GRADE **45** HIGH

Born: Feb. 21, 1990. **B-T:** R-R. **Ht.:** 6-4. **Wt.:** 228. **Drafted:** Ohio State, 2013 (10th round). **Signed by:** Phil Gulley.

Goldberg spent the 2013 season making up for lost time. The Ohio native started his college career at Coastal Carolina before a grandfather's bout with cancer prompted him to transfer to Ohio State. He had to sit out two years, one for NCAA rules and another due to a credit mishap that left him ineligible in 2012. He finally got his spot in the Buckeyes rotation in 2013 and went 6-1, 2.99. Goldberg's fastball peaked at 95-96 mph as an amateur with good movement, especially down in the zone, and the White Sox signed him for $10,000 as a budget-minded 10th-round pick. His power sinker played up in relief, sitting 94 mph and flashing 96, helping him get more strikeouts than he ever did as a college starter. The White Sox jumped him up to high Class A Winston-Salem to finish the season. Goldberg used both a slider and curveball as an amateur, both with power. The curve could sit in the 75-78 mph range, while his slider sat 82-84 mph at the Big Ten Conference tournament with some tilt. He also threw a changeup rarely as an amateur, which he'll need more if he starts as a pro. Goldberg has a chance to move quickly if he repeats his 2013 success and projects as a middle reliever in the Nate Jones mold.

Year	Club (League)	Class	W	L	ERA	G	GS	CG	SV	IP	H	HR	BB	SO	K/9	WHIP	AVG
2013	Great Falls (PIO)	R	0	0	0.00	2	0	0	0	4	2	0	0	7	15.8	0.50	.133
	Kannapolis (SAL)	LoA	3	0	1.42	12	0	0	2	25	10	0	6	37	13.1	0.63	.120
	Winston-Salem (CAR)	HiA	0	0	3.18	2	0	0	1	6	5	1	3	5	7.9	1.41	.238
Minor League Totals			3	0	1.54	16	0	0	3	35	17	1	9	49	12.6	0.74	.143

29 FRANCELLIS MONTAS, RHP

BA GRADE
45
HIGH

Born: March 21, 1993. **B-T:** R-R. **Ht.:** 6-2. **Wt.:** 185. **Signed:** Dominican Republic, 2009. **Signed by:** Manny Nanita (Red Sox).

Montas was yet another former Red Sox prospect who came to the White Sox as part of the three-team Jake Peavy trade at the 2013 trade deadline. Boston signed him for $75,000 in 2009, then saw his fastball hit 100 mph. Montas has learned to dial back his fastball and pace himself as a starter, and he showed good durability by making 23 starts in 2013 between two stops. He struggled to minimize damage at times thanks to spotty command, which was worse after the trade, while sitting 91-95 mph and still touching 97 regularly. Montas throws both a slider and curveball, and he'll flash an average breaker with mid-80s velocity and bite, but neither pitch is consistent. He throws a changeup but lacks conviction in it and allowed a .276/.369/.529 line to lefthanded hitters. One club official compared Montas' wide-hipped body to that of Livan Hernandez, implying he will have to work hard to stay in shape. Montas' iffy secondary stuff could push him to the bullpen. For now, he remains a starter and likely moves up to high Class A Winston-Salem in 2014.

Year	Club (League)	Class	W	L	ERA	G	GS	CG	SV	IP	H	HR	BB	SO	K/9	WHIP	AVG
2010	Red Sox (DSL)	R	0	3	9.55	12	4	0	0	22	28	2	18	18	7.5	2.12	.322
2011	Red Sox (DSL)	R	0	1	4.26	5	5	0	0	13	7	0	12	12	8.5	1.50	.159
2012	Red Sox (GCL)	R	1	5	3.98	12	9	0	0	41	34	0	12	41	9.1	1.13	.228
	Lowell (NYP)	SS	0	0	0.00	1	1	0	0	4	5	0	1	4	9.8	1.64	.357
2013	Greenville (SAL)	LoA	2	9	5.70	19	18	1	0	85	94	10	32	96	10.1	1.48	.276
	Kannapolis (SAL)	LoA	3	2	4.56	5	5	0	0	26	20	1	18	31	10.9	1.48	.215
Minor League Totals			6	20	5.41	54	42	1	0	190	188	13	93	202	9.6	1.48	.258

30 RANGEL RAVELO, 1B

BA GRADE
45
HIGH

Born: April 24, 1992. **B-T:** R-R. **Ht.:** 6-2. **Wt.:** 210. **Drafted:** HS—Hialeah, Fla., 2010 (6th round). **Signed by:** Jose Ortega.

The Cuban-born Ravelo signed for $125,000 in 2010 and finally surpassed 100 games or 400 plate appearances for the first time in 2013. He missed part of the 2012 season on the restricted list, then had a lacerated thumb on his left hand in April and an elbow injury in August that cut into his playing time in 2013. When healthy, Ravelo showed a feel for the barrel, gap power and a discerning eye at the plate. Ravelo showed the ability to make adjustments to offspeed stuff. He struggled more against lefthanders with pitchability than with hard-throwing righthanders and likes using the opposite field. Ravelo shows raw power in batting practice but has yet to translate that into over-the-fence power. He's big-bodied and has moved from third base to first. He's a below-average runner on his way to being a baseclogger if he's not careful. If he's the kind of bat-first, power-second hitter who comes into his power later in his career, Ravelo could get interesting. He'll graduate to Double-A Birmingham for 2014.

Year	Club (League)	Class	AVG	G	AB	R	H	2B	3B	HR	RBI	BB	SO	SB	CS	OBP	SLG
2010	Bristol (APP)	R	.254	48	173	17	44	9	1	1	21	9	25	0	2	.291	.335
2011	Bristol (APP)	R	.384	20	73	10	28	7	1	0	13	2	12	2	0	.410	.507
	Kannapolis (SAL)	LoA	.317	43	161	11	51	9	0	0	21	12	19	0	1	.368	.373
2012	Kannapolis (SAL)	LoA	.290	76	290	32	84	19	3	2	39	20	38	6	1	.343	.397
2013	Kannapolis (SAL)	LoA	.226	17	53	9	12	4	0	0	9	11	11	1	1	.364	.302
	Winston-Salem (CAR)	HiA	.312	84	301	43	94	27	2	4	53	40	46	4	1	.393	.455
Minor League Totals			.298	288	1051	122	313	75	7	7	156	94	151	13	6	.359	.402

Cincinnati Reds

BY J.J. COOPER

In the middle of the club's longest run of success since the Big Red Machine of the 1970s, Reds fans are still understandably asking, "Is that all there is?"

Cincinnati has built a consistent winner in a mid-revenue market. Largely thanks to developing talent through their farm system, the Reds have topped 90 wins in three of the past four seasons, after winning 90 or more games just three times in the previous 30 years.

But what they don't have during this recent run of success is a playoff series victory. Cincinnati was swept by the Phillies in the National League Division Series in 2010, then lost the last three games of the NLDS to the Giants in 2012. The 2013 season ended poorly and abruptly with a five-game losing streak and a decisive loss to the Pirates in the winner-takes-all wild card game. That cost Dusty Baker his job after six years as the team's skipper, with pitching coach Bryan Price named as his replacement.

The firing of Baker fits into a larger theme for the Reds—the window of success may be closing quicker than they would like. As successful as Cincinnati has been recently, it plays in what suddenly has become baseball's best division. The Cardinals won the NL Central in 2013 and claimed their fourth pennant in a decade with a younger team (and deeper farm system) than the Reds. Cincinnati also now finds itself chasing the Pirates, who also have a deeper farm system, and at least for now, a younger, less expensive big league club. And while the Cubs have been a disaster at the big league level, they have financial resources and a farm system loaded with impact bats that could mark them as a contender in years to come.

While much of the rest of the division seems to be on the rise, Cincinnati is largely trying to hang on, maintaining success while the big league roster gets significantly more expensive. The Reds spent big to lock up first baseman Joey Votto, second baseman Brandon Phillips, outfielder Jay Bruce and righthander Johnny Cueto. Those deals keep the core of the current team together but make it harder to re-sign free agents such as outfielder Shin-Shoo Choo or righthander Bronson Arroyo. Righthander Homer Bailey is set to hit free agency after the 2014 season.

The farm system has produced players commensurate with upcoming needs. Lefthander Tony Cingrani, a success as a fill-in starter in 2013, looks ready to replace Arroyo in the Reds rotation. If Choo leaves, speedster Billy Hamilton will replace him in center field as soon as Opening Day. And No. 1 prospect Robert Stephenson should follow Bailey as the team's next homegrown frontline starter.

But beyond that group, the next wave of Reds prospects is significantly thinner than the group that preceded it, which is partly an artifact of picking later in recent drafts. One sign of the organization's waning farm talent: a .426 winning percentage for its domestic minor league affiliates, worst in baseball.

When the Reds won 91 games in 2010, their young core made them a team on the rise in a downtrodden NL Central. Now they are fighting to keep the window of opportunity open in a division full of teams built for the long haul.

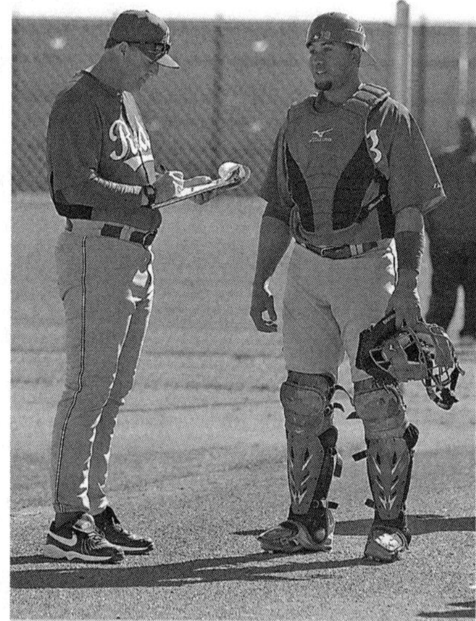

BILL MITCHELL

The Reds replaced fired manager Dusty Baker with pitching coach Bryan Price

TOP PROSPECTS OF THE DECADE

Year	Player, Pos.	2013 Org
2004	Ryan Wagner, rhp	Out of baseball
2005	Homer Bailey, rhp	Reds
2006	Homer Bailey, rhp	Reds
2007	Homer Bailey, rhp	Reds
2008	Jay Bruce, of	Reds
2009	Yonder Alonso, 1b	Padres
2010	Todd Frazier, 3b/of	Reds
2011	Aroldis Chapman, lhp	Reds
2012	Devin Mesoraco, c	Reds
2013	Billy Hamilton, ss	Reds

ORGANIZATION OVERVIEW

General Manager: Walt Jocketty. **Farm Director:** Jeff Graupe. **Scouting Director:** Chris Buckley.

Class	Team	League	W	L	PCT	Finish	Manager
Majors	Cincinnati Reds	National	90	72	.556	5th (15)	Dusty Baker
Triple-A	Louisville Bats	International	69	75	.479	9th (14)	Jim Riggleman
Double-A	Pensacola Blue Wahoos	Southern	59	79	.428	t-8th (10)	Delino Deshields
High Class A	Bakersfield Blaze	California	55	85	.392	10th (10)	Ken Griffey
Low Class A	Dayton Dragons	Midwest	65	74	.468	11th (16)	Jose Nieves
Rookie	Billings Mustangs	Pioneer	28	46	.378	8th (8)	Pat Kelly
Rookie	AZL Reds	Arizona	18	37	.327	13th (13)	Eli Marrero
Overall 2013 Minor League Record			**294**	**396**	**.426**	**30th (30)**	

THIS YEAR'S TOP 30

No.	Player, Pos.	Grade/Risk
1.	Robert Stephenson, rhp	65/High
2.	Billy Hamilton, of	60/Medium
3.	Phillip Ervin, of	55/High
4.	Jesse Winker, of	55/High
5.	Yorman Rodriguez, of	55/High
6.	Michael Lorenzen, rhp	50/High
7.	Carlos Contreras, rhp	50/High
8.	Nick Travieso, rhp	50/High
9.	Ben Lively, rhp	50/High
10.	Tucker Barnhart, c	45/Medium
11.	Jeremy Kivel, rhp	55/Extreme
12.	Ismael Guillon, lhp	50/High
13.	Daniel Corcino, rhp	50/High
14.	Junior Arias, of	50/High
15.	Chad Rogers, rhp	45/Medium
16.	Donald Lutz, of	45/Medium
17.	Jacob Constante, lhp	50/Extreme
18.	Amir Garrett, lhp	50/Extreme
19.	Jackson Stephens, rhp	50/Extreme
20.	Jonathan Reynoso, of	50/Extreme
21.	Seth Mejias-Brean, 3b	45/High
22.	K.J. Franklin, 3b	50/Extreme
23.	Jon Moscot, rhp	45/High
24.	Aristides Aquino, of	45/High
25.	Sal Romano, rhp	50/Extreme
26.	Sebastian Elizalde, of	50/Extreme
27.	Tanner Rahier, 3b	45/High
28.	Curtis Partch, rhp	40/Medium
29.	Reydel Medina, of	50/Extreme
30.	Dan Langfield, rhp	50/Extreme

LAST YEAR'S TOP 30

No.	Player, Pos.	Status
1.	Billy Hamilton, of/ss	No. 2
2.	Robert Stephenson, rhp	No. 1
3.	Tony Cingrani, lhp	Majors
4.	Daniel Corcino, rhp	No. 13
5.	Didi Gregorius, ss	(Diamondbacks)
6.	Nick Travieso, rhp	No. 8
7.	Jesse Winker, of	No. 4
8.	J.J. Hoover, rhp	Majors
9.	Ismael Guillon, lhp	No. 12
10.	Jonathan Reynoso, of	No. 20
11.	Dan Langfield, rhp	No. 30
12.	Kyle Lotzkar, rhp	(Rangers)
13.	Carlos Contreras, rhp	No. 7
14.	Jeff Gelalich, of	Dropped out
15.	Amir Garrett, lhp	No. 18
16.	Yorman Rodriguez, of	No. 5
17.	Pedro Diaz, rhp	Dropped out
18.	Donald Lutz, of/1b	No. 16
19.	Seth Mejias-Brean, 3b	No. 21
20.	Tanner Rahier, 3b	No. 27
21.	Ryan LaMarre, of	Dropped out
22.	Kyle Waldrop, of	Dropped out
23.	Tucker Barnhart, c	No. 10
24.	Henry Rodriguez, 3b/2b	Dropped out
25.	Devin Lohman, 2b/ss	Dropped out
26.	Neftali Soto, 1b	Dropped out
27.	Curtis Partch, rhp	No. 28
28.	Chad Rogers, rhp	No. 15
29.	Gabriel Rosa, 3b	Dropped out
30.	Sal Romano, rhp	No. 25

BEST TOOLS

Best Hitter for Average	Phillip Ervin
Best Power Hitter	Jesse Winker
Best Strike-Zone Discipline	Jesse Winker
Fastest Baserunner	Billy Hamilton
Best Athlete	Billy Hamilton
Best Fastball	Robert Stephenson
Best Curveball	Robert Stephenson
Best Slider	Curtis Partch
Best Changeup	Ismael Guillon
Best Control	Drew Cisco
Best Defensive Catcher	Tucker Barnhart
Best Defensive Infielder	Tanner Rahier
Best Infield Arm	Cory Thompson
Best Defensive Outfielder	Ryan LaMarre
Best Outfield Arm	Yorman Rodriguez

TOP 15 PLAYERS 25 AND UNDER

No.	Player, Pos. (Age)	Peak Level
1.	Tony Cingrani, lhp (24)	Majors
2.	Robert Stephenson, rhp (21)	Double-A
3.	Billy Hamilton, of (23)	Majors
4.	Devin Mesoraco, c (25)	Majors
5.	Phillip Ervin, of (21)	Low Class A
6.	Jesse Winker, of (20)	Low Class A
7.	Yorman Rodriguez, of (21)	Double-A
8.	Michael Lorenzen, rhp (22)	Double-A
9.	Carlos Contreras, rhp (23)	Double-A
10.	Nick Travieso, rhp (20)	Low Class A
11.	Tucker Barnhart, c (23)	Double-A
12.	Ben Lively, rhp (22)	Low Class A
13.	Jeremy Kivel, rhp (20)	Rookie
14.	Ismael Guillon, lhp (22)	Low Class A
15.	Daniel Corcino, rhp (23)	Triple-A

MINOR LEAGUE DEPTH CHART

CINCINNATI REDS

TOP 2014 ROOKIE: Billy Hamilton, of. His bat may limit his initial impact, but his speed and glove will buy him time for his bat to catch up.

BREAKOUT PROSPECT: Jacob Constante, lhp. After a year toying with DSL hitters, Constante could move quickly to full season ball.

SLEEPER: Hector Vargas, ss. The Reds had a pair of intriguing shortstops in the DSL in 2013, Vargas combines an athletic frame with plenty of tools.

SOURCE OF TOP 30 TALENT

Homegrown	30	Acquired	0
College	6	Trades	0
Junior college	2	Rule 5 draft	0
High school	11	Independent leagues	0
Nondrafted free agents	0	Free agents/waivers	0
International	11		

LF

- Jesse Winker (4)
- Raydel Medina (29)
- Bryson Smith
- Gabriel Rosa
- Josh Fellhauer
- Narciso Cook
- Steve Selsky

CF

- Billy Hamilton (2)
- Phillip Ervin (3)
- Junior Arias (14)
- Jonathan Reynoso (19)
- Sebastian Elizalde (26)
- Ryan LaMarre
- Jose Siri
- Beau Amaral
- Juan Silva
- Felix Perez

RF

- Yorman Rodriguez (5)
- Aristides Aquino (24)
- Jeff Gelalich

3B

- Seth Mejias-Bream (20)
- K.J. Franklin (21)
- Tanner Rahier (27)
- Neftali Soto
- Travis Mattair
- David Vidal

SS

- Hector Vargas
- Luis Gonzalez
- Cory Thompson
- Carlton Daal
- Devin Lohman
- Ronald Bueno
- Zach Vincej

2B

- Henry Rodriguez
- Francis Azcona
- Brodie Greene
- Juan Perez
- Rob Ramirez
- Ryan Wright

1B

- Donald Lutz (16)
- Juan Duran
- Kyle Waldrop
- Sean Buckley

C

- Tucker Barnhart (10)
- Jose Ortiz
- Joe Hudson
- Morgan Lofstrom

LHP

LHSP	LHRP
Ismael Guillon (12)	Chad Jones
Jacob Constante (17)	Wandy Peralta
Amir Garrett (18)	
Manuel Aybar	

RHP

RHSP	RHRP
Robert Stephenson (1)	Michael Lorenzen (6)
Carlos Contreras (7)	Chad Rogers (15)
Nick Travieso (8)	Curtis Partch (28)
Ben Lively (9)	Pedro Diaz
Jeremy Kivel (11)	Nick Christiani
Daniel Corcino (13)	Justin Freeman
Jackson Stephens (19)	Kyle McMyne
Jon Moscot (23)	Drew Hayes
Sal Romano (25)	
Dan Langfield (30)	
Mark Armstrong	
Jarrett Freeland	
Drew Cisco	

DRAFT ANALYSIS

2013 — BONUSES: $6.0 MILLION

BEST PURE HITTER: OF Phillip Ervin (1) has hit wherever he has played. He hit better than .300 in his first pro season, after doing the same in the Cape Cod League and in all three seasons at Samford. He has the bat speed and eye to continue doing it.

BEST POWER HITTER: 3B K.J. Franklin (2) has plenty of raw power, but he still needs work to bring it into games. A pull-heavy approach makes him vulnerable to pitches on the outer half.

FASTEST RUNNER: RHP Michael Lorenzen (1s) will be a pitcher for the Reds, but he was also a center fielder at Cal State Fullerton and is a plus runner. Among those who will remain position players, Ervin and SS Cory Thompson (5) are fastest.

BEST DEFENSIVE PLAYER: The Reds didn't draft many standout defenders, though here too Lorenzen could be one if he were a position player. Ervin and Thompson both could be a tick above-average defenders.

BEST FASTBALL: Lorenzen consistently showed a 96-99 mph fastball out of the bullpen after signing, and his stuff didn't drop off when he worked back-to-back outings.

BEST SECONDARY PITCH: RHP Ben Lively (4) gets a lot of swings and misses thanks to a deceptive delivery that allows his 91-95 mph fastball to play up, but he also has an above-average slider with good depth. He showed he can bury it or throw it for strikes depending on the situation.

BEST PRO DEBUT: Ervin posted a .331/.416/.597 line at Rookie-level Billings. Lively was equally impressive with his 0-4, 0.88 record with 56 strikeouts in 41 innings between Billings and low Class A Dayton.

BEST ATHLETE: As noted above, Lorenzen would be a legitimate prospect as a center fielder.

MOST INTRIGUING BACKGROUND: LHP Chad Jones (9) was a 2010 third-round pick of the NFL's New York Giants as a safety after a two-sport career at Louisiana State. A car wreck nearly killed him, and he spent the past three years working his way back from severe leg injuries. When football was no longer an option he started pitching again. He has flashed a 90-92 mph fastball and good slider but is still regaining his stamina.

CLOSEST TO THE MAJORS: Lorenzen jumped all the way to Double-A in his pro debut. He could pitch in Cincinnati in 2014 as a reliever, but he's more likely to take a slower track as a starter. Lively could also move quickly if he ends up in the bullpen.

BEST LATE-ROUND PICK: C/RHP Jarrett Freeland (15) missed most of his senior high school season due to Tommy John surgery. The 6-foot-7 righthander showed a 92-94 mph fastball before the injury.

THE ONE WHO GOT AWAY: The Reds made a run at OF Willie Abreu (14), a lefthanded hitter with excellent raw power and a solid arm, but he opted to head to Miami.

ASSESSMENT: The Reds targeted Ervin and were happy he fell to the 29th pick, and Lorenzen should at least become a useful reliever. That allowed bigger risks with later picks like Thompson and Franklin.

2012 — BONUSES: $7.5 MILLION

Florida preps OF Jesse Winker (1s) and RHP Nick Travieso (1) remains the class of this crop, especially after an arm injury felled RHP Dan Langfield (2).

GRADE: C

2011 — BONUSES: $6.4 MILLION

Top pick RHP Robert Stephenson (1) is the Reds' top prospect, but LHP Tony Cingrani (3) passed him on his quick trip to the majors.

GRADE: B+

2010 — BONUSES: $5.7 MILLION

The Reds traded C Yasmani Grandal (1) to San Diego for Mat Latos. No one else from the class ranks in the Top 30.

GRADE: D

TOP DRAFT PICKS OF THE DECADE

Year	Player, Pos.	2013 Org
2004	Homer Bailey, rhp	Reds
2005	Jay Bruce, of	Reds
2006	Drew Stubbs, of	Indians
2007	Devin Mesoraco, c	Reds
2008	Yonder Alonso, 1b	Padres
2009	Mike Leake, rhp	Reds
2010	Yasmani Grandal, c	Padres
2011	Robert Stephenson, rhp	Reds
2012	Nick Travieso, rhp	Reds
2013	Phillip Ervin, of	Reds

LARGEST BONUSES IN CLUB HISTORY

Aroldis Chapman, 2010	$16,250,000
Chris Gruler, 2002	$2,500,000
Yorman Rodriguez, 2008	$2,500,000
Homer Bailey, 2004	$2,300,000
Mike Leake, 2009	$2,270,000

1 ROBERT STEPHENSON, RHP

Born: Feb. 24, 1993. **Ht.:** 6-2. **Wt.:** 190. **B-T:** R-R.
Drafted: HS—Martinez, Calif., 2011 (1st round).
Signed by: Rich Bordi.

MIKE JANES

Hindsight confirms what scouts thought at the time—the 2011 class of high school righthanders was one of the best in years. Jose Fernandez pitched like an ace for the Marlins in 2013. The Orioles' Dylan Bundy had Tommy John surgery, but not before reaching the big leagues in 2012, and the Diamondbacks' Archie Bradley isn't far away. And then there's Stephenson, who fell to the 27th pick in part because of the large number of talented high school pitchers in his class. The righthander sometimes gets lost in the shuffle but has some of the best pure stuff in the minors. After a rocky April, Stephenson settled down to allow four earned runs in his next eight starts, including a May 30 gem where he carried a perfect game into the sixth inning with Reds general manager Walt Jocketty in attendance. A hamstring injury kept him out of the Midwest League all-star game and kept him off the mound for most of June, but he quickly recovered to earn a mid-July promotion to high Class A Bakersfield. Just four starts later, he was pitching for Double-A Pensacola.

Stephenson's fastball seems to gain a tick each year, going from a 92-95 mph pitch fresh out of the draft to the 94-99 fireball he throws now. He's done it while toning down a delivery that had some effort in high school but is now relatively free and easy. He has a stab in the back of his delivery, but it has not interfered with his ability to throw strikes. Stephenson added a two-seamer back to his repertoire this year, though his season took off when he went back to pitching more off his four-seamer. His four-seam fastball lacks much life, but because he generally locates it well, it's still a plus-plus pitch. His 76-80 mph curveball gives Stephenson a second potential 70 pitch on the 20-80 scouting scale. He can bury it or throw it for strikes, and it is an excellent two-strike weapon with a big 12-to-6 break. Stephenson has improved his 86-88 mph changeup to the point where it's an average offering and could end up as a third plus pitch. Stephenson threw a split-finger fastball in high school, but the Reds shelved it. With the quality of his three present offerings, there's no real pressure to bring it back. He has present average control, but needs to improve his command to be ready for Cincinnati.

Barring a trade, the Reds' rotation is set for 2014, but Stephenson could be ready to help as a midseason injury replacement. By 2015, the Reds will be making room for him at the front of its rotation if everything progresses as planned.

Year	Club (League)	Class	W	L	ERA	G	GS	CG	SV	IP	H	HR	BB	SO	K/9	WHIP	AVG
2012	Billings (PIO)	R	1	0	2.05	7	7	0	0	31	22	2	8	37	10.9	0.98	.195
	Dayton (MWL)	LoA	2	4	4.19	8	8	0	0	34	32	4	15	35	9.2	1.37	.246
2013	Dayton (MWL)	LoA	5	3	2.57	14	14	0	0	77	56	5	20	96	11.2	0.99	.200
	Bakersfield (CAL)	HiA	2	2	3.05	4	4	0	0	21	19	3	2	22	9.6	1.02	.235
	Pensacola (SL)	AA	0	2	4.86	4	4	0	0	17	17	2	13	18	9.7	1.80	.274
Minor League Totals			10	11	3.06	37	37	0	0	179	146	16	58	208	10.4	1.14	.217

2 BILLY HAMILTON, OF

Born: Sept. 9, 1990. **B-T:** B-R. **Ht.:** 6-1. **Wt.:** 160. **Drafted:** HS—Taylorsville, Miss., 2009 (2nd round). **Signed by:** Tyler Jennings.

A year after he set the pro stolen base record with 155 steals, Hamilton finished second in the minors with 75 (nine behind leader Micah Johnson of the White Sox). Hamilton made his big league debut as a September callup and quickly became the story of baseball with 13 steals in just 13 games. Hamilton's speed is the stuff of legend. Multiple scouts describe him as the fastest player they've ever seen, with one noting that he and others have timed Hamilton at just under three seconds from first to second base on steals, faster than Rickey Henderson was in his prime. Hamilton made a quick transition from shortstop to center field. While his jumps and routes can continue to improve, he has the speed to outrun mistakes. He has an average arm. The questions about Hamilton revolve around his hitting. He will never have more than 30-grade power. Hamilton's game centers on slapping line drives and dropping bunts, though Triple-A pitchers were able to overpower him at times last year, especially when he hit lefthanded. If Shin-Soo Choo doesn't re-sign with the Reds, Hamilton is the heir apparent in center field. He's ready for the job defensively and on the basepaths, but his bat has not convinced scouts he is ready for the leadoff spot.

Year	Club (League)	Class	AVG	G	AB	R	H	2B	3B	HR	RBI	BB	SO	SB	CS	OBP	SLG
2009	Reds (GCL)	R	.205	43	166	19	34	6	3	0	11	11	47	14	3	.253	.277
2010	Billings (PIO)	R	.318	69	283	61	90	13	10	2	24	28	56	48	9	.383	.456
2011	Dayton (MWL)	LoA	.278	135	550	99	153	18	9	3	50	52	133	103	20	.340	.360
2012	Bakersfield (CAL)	HiA	.323	82	337	79	109	18	9	1	30	50	70	104	21	.413	.439
	Pensacola (SL)	AA	.286	50	175	33	50	4	5	1	15	36	43	51	16	.406	.383
2013	Louisville (IL)	AAA	.256	123	504	75	129	18	4	6	41	38	102	75	15	.308	.343
	Cincinnati (NL)	MAJ	.368	13	19	9	7	2	0	0	1	2	4	13	1	.429	.474
Major League Totals			.368	13	19	9	7	2	0	0	1	2	4	13	1	.429	.474
Minor League Totals			.280	502	2015	366	565	77	40	13	171	215	451	395	84	.350	.378

3 PHILLIP ERVIN, OF

NICHOLAS FALZERANO

Born: July 17, 1992. **B-T:** R-R. **Ht.:** 5-11. **Wt. 190. Drafted:** Samford, 2013 (1st round). **Signed by:** Ben Jones.

Ervin has hit .300 everywhere he's played. He did it in in college at Samford (.344 career mark) and with wood bats in the summer collegiate Northwoods (2011) and Cape Cod (2012) leagues. And he did it with the Reds, hitting .331 between stops at Rookie-level Billings and low Class A Dayton. Ervin may not have a plus-plus tool, but his scouting report has plenty of 60s on the 20-80 scale. He's an above-average hitter thanks to a simple short stroke that allows him to square up pitches consistently. He has 60 raw power and is translating that into productive power already. He's a 60 runner when healthy. Ervin has battled minor injuries since high school, starting with a knee injury as a prep senior. He's had hand and hamstring injuries (summer after freshman year), a sprained ankle (junior year) and a wrist injury that cut his pro debut short. He has enough speed to play center, but his routes aren't ideal. He has plenty of arm (he was clocked at 92 mph off the mound at Samford) to play right. Ervin was one of the safer bats in the 2013 draft. He may lack star potential, but he should advance quickly. High Class A Bakersfield is a likely starting point, but he could reach Double-A Pensacola in 2014.

Year	Club (League)	Class	AVG	G	AB	R	H	2B	3B	HR	RBI	BB	SO	SB	CS	OBP	SLG
2013	Billings (PIO)	R	.326	34	129	27	42	9	1	8	29	17	24	12	0	.416	.597
	Dayton (MWL)	LoA	.349	12	43	7	15	2	0	1	6	8	10	2	1	.451	.465
Minor League Totals			.331	46	172	34	57	11	1	9	35	25	34	14	1	.425	.564

4 JESSE WINKER, OF

NICHOLAS FALZERANO

BA GRADE
55
HIGH

Born: Aug. 17, 1993. **B-T:** L-L. **Ht.:** 6-3. **Wt.:** 195. **Drafted:** HS—Orlando, 2012 (1st round supplemental). **Signed by:** Greg Zunino.

Winker joined his older brother Joey, who plays in the Dodgers organization, in the low Class A Midwest League this season. The Winkers helped add to a recent run for the baseball program at Olympia High, the Orlando school that also produced Mariners shortstop Brad Miller, Yankees outfield prospect Mason Williams and Padres righthander Walker Wieckel. Winker pitched and played center field for Olympia as it won 29 straight at in his senior season, then signed for $1 million. Winker is a pure hitter with a short, simple stroke. He's toned down what was once a picturesque, one-handed, high finish to a more conventional two-handed finish. He projects as a potential plus hitter with plus power. Winker works counts into his favor and uses the whole field. He pulled 10 of his 16 home runs, but hit four the other way and two to straight center field. His modest athleticism, below-average speed, range and arm strength limits him to left field defensively and he projects as likely below-average there. In a different organization, Winker would potentially end up as a first baseman, but with Joey Votto in Cincinnati, he'll stay in left. Scouts are sold on Winker's hitting ability but question about how athletic he'll be by the time he reaches the big leagues. He's ready for the offensive environment of high Class A Bakersfield.

Year	Club (League)	Class	AVG	G	AB	R	H	2B	3B	HR	RBI	BB	SO	SB	CS	OBP	SLG
2012	Billings (PIO)	R	.338	62	228	42	77	16	3	5	35	40	50	1	3	.443	.500
2013	Dayton (MWL)	LoA	.281	112	417	73	117	18	5	16	76	63	75	6	1	.379	.463
Minor League Totals			.301	174	645	115	194	34	8	21	111	103	125	7	4	.402	.476

5 YORMAN RODRIGUEZ, OF

BA GRADE
55
HIGH

Born: Aug. 15, 1992. **B-T:** R-R. **Ht.:** 6-3. **Wt.:** 197. **Signed:** Venezuela, 2008. **Signed by:** Tony Arias.

It's been a wild ride for Rodriguez, who set a then-Venezuelan amateur record with a $2.5 million bonus in 2008. Since then, he's had to grow up on and off the field. He disappointed scouts with inconsistent effort through the first few years of his career. When the Reds sent him back to low Class A Dayton from high Class A Bakersfield in 2012, it served as a wakeup call. Now married and a father, Rodriguez appears to have turned a corner in his maturity. Rodriguez remains still somewhat raw, but he has two present plus tools and three others that project as potentially average. Rodriguez is a 60 runner, has a 60-65 arm that is the system's best and has improved into an average defender in right field. He's not as comfortable in center. Rodriguez has above-average raw power, but his difficulties making contact have limited his production. The biggest question facing him is how much contact he will make. Rodriguez uses the whole field well, but he doesn't barrel the ball consistently, and his pitch recognition needs to improve. Rodriguez justified his place on the 40-man roster with his improvement in 2013. Still just 21, he likely will return to Pensacola, but he could be ready for a September callup. He projects as at least a useful fourth outfielder with the potential to be much more.

Year	Club (League)	Class	AVG	G	AB	R	H	2B	3B	HR	RBI	BB	SO	SB	CS	OBP	SLG
2009	Reds (GCL)	R	.274	22	84	9	23	2	1	0	2	10	23	5	0	.347	.321
	Billings (PIO)	R	.219	46	183	21	40	10	2	3	17	9	61	5	2	.259	.344
2010	Billings (PIO)	R	.339	43	171	25	58	8	3	2	39	8	30	12	2	.361	.456
2011	Dayton (MWL)	LoA	.254	79	280	38	71	10	4	7	40	25	84	20	8	.318	.393
2012	Bakersfield (CAL)	HiA	.156	23	90	7	14	4	0	0	7	3	39	4	0	.181	.200
	Dayton (MWL)	LoA	.271	65	258	35	70	17	3	6	44	12	61	7	5	.307	.430
2013	Bakersfield (CAL)	HiA	.251	63	251	41	63	20	4	9	35	22	77	6	3	.319	.470
	Pensacola (SL)	AA	.267	66	262	30	70	15	2	4	31	25	76	4	0	.329	.385
Minor League Totals			.259	407	1579	206	409	86	19	31	215	114	451	63	20	.310	.396

6 MICHAEL LORENZEN, RHP

NICHOLAS FALZERANO

BA GRADE
50
HIGH

Born: Jan. 4, 1992. **B-T:** R-R. **Ht.:** 6-3. **Wt.:** 180. **Drafted:** Cal State Fullerton, 2013 (1st round supplemental). **Signed by:** Mike Misuraca.

Lorenzen threw just 45 innings in college, mainly because he was also a center fielder. But whenever he did pitch the game was likely on the line. Lorenzen appeared as a pitcher 42 times, recording 35 saves (a school record) while going 5-0. Lorenzen was draftable as a center fielder, but he faced concerns about his ability to hit for average, which made him more appealing as a strong-armed righthander. A $1.5 million signing bonus persuaded him to give up hitting. Lorenzen is understandably raw on the mound, but he could move very quickly as a reliever. His 95-99 mph fastball has surprising life considering its velocity. It's a plus-plus pitch, and his 80-83 mph slurve projects as plus as well. While that repertoire has served him well in a relief role, Lorenzen has athleticism, competitiveness and a fresh arm, so the Reds want to see if he can start. For the switch to take, he must improve his below-average changeup, the consistency of his slurve and his command. Lorenzen never threw more than two innings in a game in college, so developing stamina is another issue The Reds sent Lorenzen to the Arizona Fall League to get more innings as a starter. If they stick with the plan to start him, he'll likely need to drop back down to high Class A. Long-term, his most likely role is late-game reliever, potentially as a closer.

Year	Club (League)	Class	W	L	ERA	G	GS	CG	SV	IP	H	HR	BB	SO	K/9	WHIP	AVG
2013	Reds (AZL)	R	0	0	0.00	1	1	0	0	1	1	0	0	1	9.0	1.00	.200
	Dayton (MWL)	LoA	1	0	0.00	9	0	0	2	8	7	0	2	7	7.6	1.08	.233
	Bakersfield (CAL)	HiA	0	1	6.35	5	0	0	2	6	6	1	5	6	9.5	1.94	.273
	Pensacola (SL)	AA	0	0	4.50	7	0	0	0	6	6	1	6	5	7.5	2.00	.286
Minor League Totals			1	1	3.00	22	1	0	4	21	20	2	13	19	8.1	1.57	.256

7 CARLOS CONTRERAS, RHP

BA GRADE
50
HIGH

Born: Jan. 8, 1991. B-**T:** R-R. **Ht.:** 5-11. **Wt.:** 205. **Signed:** Dominican Republic, 2008. **Signed by:** Richard Jimenez.

Another of a growing line of intriguing short Dominican righthanders the Reds have signed in Johnny Cueto's wake, Contreras' ERA stood at 5.98 four years into his pro career. He's a reminder that it pays to be patient with pitchers with good stuff and poor results, as he's jumped four levels the last two years while posting a 3.36 ERA. He successfully transitioned back to starting this year, allowing two runs or less while working at least five innings in his last seven starts for Double-A Pensacola. Contreras has a plus fastball that generally sits at 92-93 mph as a starter. He's complemented that with a plus changeup for several years, but this year, he also significantly sharpened his breaking ball, which enabled him to finally neutralize righthanded hitters, who had previously had their way with him. Like several other Reds starters, Contreras' arm travels a long way to get to the release point, which has hindered his control. Contreras' future is perched precariously on the edge between the rotation and the bullpen. His improved breaking ball makes a case for a future as a starter, but his shaky control makes it more likely he ends up as a power reliever, albeit one with a brighter future now that his slider is sharper.

Year	Club (League)	Class	W	L	ERA	G	GS	CG	SV	IP	H	HR	BB	SO	K/9	WHIP	AVG
2008	Reds (DSL)	R	0	1	8.64	17	0	0	0	17	14	0	30	17	9.2	2.64	.241
2009	Reds (DSL)	R	4	4	5.60	14	12	0	0	72	65	6	30	58	7.2	1.31	.242
2010	Reds (AZL)	R	2	4	6.45	10	6	0	2	38	44	8	16	30	7.2	1.59	.288
2011	Billings (PIO)	R	2	1	5.00	18	0	0	0	36	35	5	23	38	9.5	1.61	.259
2012	Dayton (MWL)	LoA	0	1	3.20	40	0	0	16	51	29	6	19	51	9.1	0.95	.158
	Bakersfield (CAL)	HiA	1	0	2.70	9	0	0	4	10	9	1	5	12	10.8	1.40	.225
2013	Bakersfield (CAL)	HiA	5	7	3.80	18	18	0	0	90	70	9	41	96	9.6	1.23	.215
	Pensacola (SL)	AA	3	2	2.76	8	8	0	0	42	36	2	21	26	5.5	1.35	.238
Minor League Totals			17	20	4.55	134	44	0	22	356	302	37	185	328	8.3	1.37	.230

8 NICK TRAVIESO, RHP

NICHOLAS FALZERANO

BA GRADE **50** HIGH

Born: Jan. 31, 1994. **B-T:** R-R. **Ht.:** 6-2. **Wt.:** 215. **Drafted:** HS—Southwest Ranches, Fla., 2012 (1st round). **Signed by:** Tony Arias/Miguel Machado.

As a high school junior, Travieso threw 18 innings as a middle reliever as Archbishop McCarthy High finished No. 1 in the nation. He stepped into the rotation as a senior, helping his team to a fifth-place national finish. The Reds signed him for $2 million, which was $375,000 under the recommended slot. When high school or college pitchers transition to the five-man rotation, the quality of their stuff can suffer under the increased workload, and that has happened to Travieso. He generally has shown solid but unspectacular stuff as a pro. After touching 98 mph and sitting 92-95 in high school, he sat at 92 in 2013, pitching anywhere from 89-95 depending on the day. His slider, which pushed the mid-80s in high school, has suffered a little as well. It's a potentially average pitch, but it sometimes flattens out and lacks the depth it needs. His changeup has improved but still is below-average. His command is advanced for his age, and he does a good job of pitching up and down in the zone to change hitters' eye levels. Though he won't get to make use of his bat for a few years, Travieso is an excellent hitter for a pitcher with surprising power. Unless his stuff picks back up, Travieso is on a trajectory to be a back-end starter or a reliever. He should be ready for high Class A Bakersfield in 2014.

Year	Club (League)	Class	W	L	ERA	G	GS	CG	SV	IP	H	HR	BB	SO	K/9	WHIP	AVG
2012	Reds (AZL)	R	0	2	4.71	8	8	0	0	21	20	3	5	14	6.0	1.19	.250
2013	Dayton (MWL)	LoA	7	4	4.63	17	17	0	0	82	83	7	27	61	6.7	1.35	.263
Minor League Totals			7	6	4.65	25	25	0	0	103	103	10	32	75	6.6	1.31	.261

9 BEN LIVELY, RHP

BA GRADE **50** HIGH

Born: March 5, 1992. **B-T:** R-R. **Ht.:** 6-4. **Wt.:** 190. **Drafted:** Central Florida, 2013 (4th round). **Signed by:** Greg Zunino.

Lively turned down a six-figure bonus as an Indians 26th-round pick in 2010. That was Central Florida's gain, for Lively was a key member of the Knights' rotation all three years. It worked out for Lively as well, when he signed in 2013 for $350,000 as a fourth-round pick. Lively's ability to mix and locate four average or better pitches simply overmatched hitters in the short stints he threw in his first pro season at Rookie-level Billings. The Reds generally limited him to three innings, allowing Lively's 90-95 mph fastball to sit 92-93 with good movement. He keeps the ball down in the zone and keeps hitters off-balance, using an average changeup and curveball and a potentially above-average slider. Part of Lively's success comes from his delivery, which also concerns some scouts. He hides the ball until late in his delivery, but he does so with a long arm stroke and some effort. While Lively had control issues early in his college career, he's thrown strikes consistently as a pro. The Reds found a steal in Tony Cingrani, a lefthander whose less-than-ideal delivery caused him to fall in the 2011 draft but hasn't affected him as a pro. If Lively charts a similar path, the Reds will be thrilled. He's advanced enough to potentially jump to high Class A Bakersfield.

Year	Club (League)	Class	W	L	ERA	G	GS	CG	SV	IP	H	HR	BB	SO	K/9	WHIP	AVG
2013	Billings (PIO)	R	0	3	0.73	12	12	0	0	37	21	0	12	49	11.9	0.89	.163
	Dayton (MWL)	LoA	0	1	2.25	1	1	0	0	4	2	0	1	7	15.8	0.75	.143
Minor League Totals			0	4	0.88	13	13	0	0	41	23	0	13	56	12.3	0.88	.161

10 TUCKER BARNHART, C

BA GRADE **45** MEDIUM

Born: Jan. 7, 1991. **B-T:** B-R. **Ht.:** 5-10. **Wt.:** 185. **Drafted:** HS—Brownsburg, Ind., 2009 (10th round). **Signed by:** Rick Sellers.

Barnhart's defensive prowess has been noted for years. Scouts first noticed him when he caught Nationals righthander Drew Storen during Barnhart's sophomore year. He developed into one of the nation's best prep defensive catchers thanks in part to his high school coach Patrick O'Neil, a former Rays scout. Barnhart's defense is big league caliber right now. He blocks pitches well, calls a good game and has excellent agility. Thanks to a quick release and a strong arm, he turns in sub-1.9-seconds pop times regularly. He threw out 37 percent of basestealers this year at Double-A Pensacola, which actually is a dip from the 41 percent he has thrown out in his career. At the plate, Barnhart showed better bat control after switching to a shorter, lighter bat, but he's a bottom-of-the-order spray hitter with well-below-average power. Unlike many switch-hitters, Barnhart is a natural lefthanded hitter, and it shows. He's never hit well from the right side, and his career average as a lefthanded hitter is more than 100 points higher. He has yet to hit a hit a home run batting righty.

Barnhart is ready for Triple-A Louisville and is a likely candidate to be added to the 40-man roster this winter. His catch-and-throw skills and contact bat profile him as a second-division regular who could have a long career at a valuable defensive spot.

Year	Club (League)	Class	AVG	G	AB	R	H	2B	3B	HR	RBI	BB	SO	SB	CS	OBP	SLG
2009	Reds (GCL)	R	.208	14	48	5	10	2	0	0	6	6	9	0	0	.291	.250
2010	Billings (PIO)	R	.306	35	111	17	34	9	0	0	12	18	25	4	1	.412	.387
2011	Dayton (MWL)	LoA	.273	97	326	47	89	24	2	3	43	37	59	2	1	.344	.387
2012	Bakersfield (CAL)	HiA	.278	59	198	26	55	12	1	4	22	29	45	0	2	.371	.409
	Pensacola (SL)	AA	.200	41	130	10	26	4	1	2	12	11	22	1	1	.262	.292
2013	Pensacola (SL)	AA	.260	98	339	31	88	19	1	3	44	45	57	1	0	.348	.348
Minor League Totals			.262	344	1152	136	302	70	5	12	139	146	217	8	5	.346	.363

11 JEREMY KIVEL, RHP

BA GRADE
55
EXTREME

Born: Oct. 16, 1993. **B-T:** R-R. **Ht.:** 6-1. **Wt.:** 200. **Drafted:** HS—Spring, Texas, 2012 (10th round). **Signed by:** Bryan Ewing.

Hitters need to think twice before rushing the mound against Kivel. A mixed-martial arts aficionado in high school, he had much more mat time than mound time when the Reds went well above slot to sign him for $500,000 in 2012, using money they had saved by signing first-rounder Nick Travieso to a discounted deal. Kivel blew out his knee as a high school senior, his first year playing baseball, so he had just six innings of experience when he signed. Not surprisingly, the Reds had plenty of work to do to refine his delivery. He had a tendency to drop his arm slot, but he's now throwing more consistently from a three-quarters delivery. Kivel's stuff ranks among the best in the organization. His fastball sits at 93-94 mph and touches 99. His 80-82 mph slider projects as an average pitch. His changeup has improved, but it's still a long way from being even average. An intriguing lottery ticket, Kivel has the arm to be a front-end starter or a late-inning power reliever. He could begin 2014 in extended spring training or possibly jump to low Class A Dayton.

Year	Club (League)	Class	W	L	ERA	G	GS	CG	SV	IP	H	HR	BB	SO	K/9	WHIP	AVG
2013	Reds (AZL)	R	0	2	3.91	13	12	0	0	51	50	4	23	56	9.9	1.44	.249
Minor League Totals			0	2	3.91	13	12	0	0	51	50	4	23	56	9.9	1.44	.249

12 ISMAEL GUILLON, LHP

Born: Feb. 13, 1992. **B-T:** L-L. **Ht.:** 6-2. **Wt.:** 218. **Signed:** Venezuela, 2009. **Signed by:** Tony Arias.

The Reds added Guillon to the 40-man roster following the 2012 season after he lit up instructional league with a plus fastball and changeup. At the time, they feared some team might take a Rule 5 chance on the southpaw despite his inexperience (just 25 innings in full-season ball). Fast-forward a year and Guillon is the same baffling combination of promise and pratfalls. In one early-season start, he threw 12 balls in his first 13 pitches, bouncing four of them. In another stretch, he walked 15 batters in five innings, showing 20 command and a below-average, mid-80s fastball. Guillon, however, closed the season by going 3-1, 1.34 over his last six starts with vastly improved control, and when he's maintaining his delivery, he works with a 91-96 mph fastball. Guillon's changeup is the best in the system with excellent deception and good late fade. His 11-to-5 curveball improved significantly this year to flash average. His control problems stem in part from a long arm action and a wrap in his takeaway. Guillon will advance to the high Class A Bakersfield rotation in 2014, though ultimately he may settle as a power reliever, where his fastball will play up and his poor control will be mitigated.

Year	Club (League)	Class	W	L	ERA	G	GS	CG	SV	IP	H	HR	BB	SO	K/9	WHIP	AVG
2009	Did not play—Injured																
2010	Reds (AZL)	R	3	3	3.32	12	10	0	0	57	39	1	23	73	11.5	1.09	.193
2011	Billings (PIO)	R	3	6	6.57	15	15	0	0	63	78	11	46	61	8.7	1.97	.305
2012	Billings (PIO)	R	4	1	2.29	11	10	0	0	51	39	1	24	63	11.1	1.24	.210
	Dayton (MWL)	LoA	2	0	2.55	4	4	0	0	25	22	2	7	27	9.9	1.18	.247
2013	Dayton (MWL)	LoA	7	8	4.75	27	26	0	0	121	95	14	95	134	9.9	1.57	.220
Minor League Totals			19	18	4.29	69	65	0	0	317	273	29	195	358	10.2	1.48	.234

13 DANIEL CORCINO, RHP

BA GRADE
50
HIGH

Born: Aug. 26, 1990. **B-T:** R-R. **Ht.:** 5-11. **Wt.:** 205. **Signed:** Dominican Republic, 2008. **Signed by:** Richard Jimenez.

Heading into the 2013 season, Corcino appeared to be just a call away at Triple-A Louisville. The Reds thought he might be able to help as a power reliever or emergency starter, thanks to a plus fastball he could cut, run or sink as well as an average slider and changeup. But that possibility seemed to weigh on Corcino. He had a terrible spring as he consistently overthrew and saw his velocity dip from the low 90s to 88-91 mph. That carried over to the season, where Corcino eventually lost his spot in the Louisville rotation. He tinkered with his arm slot, dropping down from the low three-quarters he had used at his best, before eventually bringing his arm back up. That helped his slider regain some depth. Late in the season Corcino started relying more on his sinker than the four-seamer. He at times seemed to forget about using his average changeup as he struggled to throw strikes. Based solely on what he showed in 2013, Corcino is barely a prospect, but pitchers can reverse their fortunes in a hurry with slight changes. The Reds believe Corcino still could be a useful mid-rotation starter or power reliever, though to do so he must demonstrate better control, better velocity and better secondary stuff in his return to Louisville in 2014.

Year	Club (League)	Class	W	L	ERA	G	GS	CG	SV	IP	H	HR	BB	SO	K/9	WHIP	AVG
2008	Reds (DSL)	R	6	2	5.29	23	0	0	0	34	37	2	14	26	6.9	1.50	.280
2009	Reds (GCL)	R	0	1	0.00	2	0	0	0	3	5	0	1	2	6.8	2.25	.455
	Billings (PIO)	R	1	4	4.91	20	0	0	3	26	23	2	15	30	10.5	1.48	.245
2010	Billings (PIO)	R	1	3	3.40	9	9	0	0	40	38	2	17	31	7.0	1.39	.255
	Dayton (MWL)	LoA	1	1	4.31	6	6	0	0	31	31	1	15	29	8.3	1.47	.254
2011	Dayton (MWL)	LoA	11	7	3.42	26	26	1	0	139	128	10	34	156	10.1	1.16	.238
2012	Pensacola (SL)	AA	8	8	3.01	26	26	0	0	143	111	9	65	126	7.9	1.23	.216
2013	Louisville (IL)	AAA	7	14	5.86	28	23	0	0	129	141	17	73	90	6.3	1.66	.279
Minor League Totals			35	40	4.11	140	90	1	3	545	514	43	234	490	8.1	1.37	.249

14 JUNIOR ARIAS, OF

BA GRADE
50
HIGH

Born: Jan. 9, 1992. **B-T:** R-R. **Ht.:** 6-1. **Wt.:** 200. **Signed:** Dominican Republic, 2008. **Signed by:** Richard Jimenez.

When the Reds moved Arias from third base to center field in 2013, everybody benefitted, from Arias to Reds pitchers to fans sitting behind first base at low Class A Dayton games. That's because he committed 36 errors in 95 games at the hot corner in 2012, 20 of which came on errant throws. Arias never was comfortable in the dirt, and his speed fits much better in the outfield. He's a solid defender in center with a chance to be above-average as he gets more fly balls under his belt. His arm is a tick above-average. Tools-wise, few in the organization can compare with Arias. A 70 runner, he has the ability to turn ground balls into infield hits. At the plate, he has above-average raw power, but he expands his zone too often and can look helpless against a pitcher who can locate his secondary stuff. Even though the move to the outfield jumpstarted Arias' development, the Reds left him off the 40-man roster and thus eligible for selection in the Rule 5 draft. Thanks to an elevated strikeout rate, his most likely role may be reserve outfielder with the arm for right and the speed for center.

Year	Club (League)	Class	AVG	G	AB	R	H	2B	3B	HR	RBI	BB	SO	SB	CS	OBP	SLG
2009	Reds (DSL)	R	.231	55	208	33	48	11	2	6	27	19	66	10	6	.304	.389
2010	Reds (AZL)	R	.287	47	195	44	56	10	5	6	25	12	58	4	3	.336	.482
2011	Billings (PIO)	R	.251	61	219	47	55	14	3	8	30	19	74	7	5	.320	.452
2012	Dayton (MWL)	LoA	.208	97	361	52	75	11	3	7	35	20	96	28	7	.255	.313
2013	Dayton (MWL)	LoA	.284	72	271	45	77	12	4	10	33	13	72	40	10	.323	.469
	Bakersfield (CAL)	HiA	.257	53	222	30	57	12	2	5	20	5	60	20	10	.283	.396
Minor League Totals			.249	385	1476	251	368	70	19	42	170	88	426	109	41	.299	.408

15 CHAD ROGERS, RHP

BA GRADE
45
MEDIUM

Born: Aug. 3, 1989. **B-T:** R-R. **Ht.:** 5-11. **Wt.:** 205. **Drafted:** Galveston (Texas) CC, 2010 (28th round). **Signed by:** Jerry Flowers.

Bitten by a shark while surfing off the coast of Galveston, Texas, just before he was supposed to sign his contract with the Reds, Rogers has paid back the organization's decision to sign him while he recovered from the 60-stitch wound to his foot. Much like fellow Texas righthander Sam LeCure before him, Rogers has steadily climbed the ladder with solid but unspectacular stuff and plus command. Like LeCure, Rogers' ultimate destination likely is low-leverage relief, in part because his stuff will play up in shorter stints but also because he lacks a quality changeup. He pitches at 88-92 mph, sitting 91 with an average fastball that he can sink, cut or run. He also can manipulate an average slider, throwing it harder or softer depending on the situation. Rogers' changeup clearly is his third-best pitch, a below-average offering he doesn't trust, which makes him vulnerable to lefthanders. Rogers will return to Triple-A Louisville to begin 2014, but he ought to make his big league debut at some point during the season.

Year	Club (League)	Class	W	L	ERA	G	GS	CG	SV	IP	H	HR	BB	SO	K/9	WHIP	AVG
2011	Dayton (MWL)	LoA	6	4	2.99	37	1	0	1	69	57	3	24	72	9.3	1.17	.227
2012	Bakersfield (CAL)	HiA	6	4	3.15	21	21	0	0	111	113	11	29	88	7.1	1.28	.263
	Pensacola (SL)	AA	3	1	1.99	6	6	0	0	32	27	3	6	23	6.5	1.04	.241
2013	Pensacola (SL)	AA	3	2	2.20	13	13	0	0	70	47	5	26	55	7.1	1.05	.193
	Louisville (IL)	AAA	5	5	4.22	12	12	0	0	70	66	9	19	48	6.1	1.21	.247
Minor League Totals			23	16	3.04	89	53	0	1	352	310	31	104	286	7.3	1.18	.238

16 DONALD LUTZ, OF

BA GRADE
45
MEDIUM

Born: Feb. 6, 1989. **B-T:** L-R. **Ht.:** 6-3. **Wt.:** 235. **Signed:** Germany, 2007. **Signed by:** Jim Stoeckel.

Thanks in part to the fact that he was already on the 40-man roster, Lutz made it to Cincinnati in 2013, becoming one of the first German citizens to make it to the big leagues. Lutz's swing, like that of many power hitters, is somewhat high-maintenance. After playing sparingly with the Reds, the rust showed upon his return to Double-A Pensacola, and he missed further time with a broken finger. Lutz's swing has a pronounced waggle as he prepares for the load, but he generates excellent bat speed, which helps make up for the mechanical flaw. He's turned high-90s fastballs into home runs with plus raw power. Lutz always has struggled to hit lefthanders and projects as a slightly below-average hitter at best. He's an average runner even at 250 pounds but below-average in left field and at first base, with a below-average arm. He's ready for Triple-A Louisville but would be better off not spending too much of 2014 on the Cincinnati bench.

Year	Club (League)	Class	AVG	G	AB	R	H	2B	3B	HR	RBI	BB	SO	SB	CS	OBP	SLG
2008	Reds (GCL)	R	.250	34	108	22	27	9	0	1	19	9	21	4	1	.317	.361
2009	Reds (GCL)	R	.169	16	59	9	10	1	2	1	10	5	14	2	1	.246	.305
2010	Billings (PIO)	R	.286	55	203	36	58	10	4	7	28	21	45	6	2	.356	.478
2011	Dayton (MWL)	LoA	.301	123	465	85	140	23	3	20	75	34	125	5	4	.358	.492
2012	Reds (AZL)	R	.643	4	14	3	9	2	2	0	5	3	4	0	0	.706	1.071
	Bakersfield (CAL)	HiA	.265	63	253	42	67	18	3	17	51	19	71	7	2	.325	.561
	Pensacola (SL)	AA	.242	40	149	17	36	5	1	5	15	13	32	1	3	.315	.389
2013	Cincinnati (NL)	MAJ	.241	34	58	5	14	1	0	1	8	1	14	2	0	.254	.310
	Pensacola (SL)	AA	.245	65	229	35	56	12	4	7	30	19	56	4	1	.318	.424
Major League Totals			.241	34	58	5	14	1	0	1	8	1	14	2	0	.254	.310
Minor League Totals			.272	400	1480	249	403	80	19	58	233	123	368	29	14	.338	.470

17 JACOB CONSTANTE, LHP

BA GRADE
50
EXTREME

Born: March 22, 1994. **B-T:** L-L. **Ht.:** 6-4. **Wt.:** 215. **Signed:** Dominican Republic, 2013. **Signed by:** Tony Arias.

Signed for $730,000 after he impressed scouts at the International Prospect League all-star game in January 2013, Constante isn't the typical big-money Dominican signee, namely because he was about to turn 19 at the time he signed. By signing in February, Constante didn't count against the Reds' tiny international bonus-pool allocation for 2013. Constante's contract carried an assurance that he would spend the season in the Dominican Summer League, so he spent his time toying with younger, less advanced hitters. With a 91-94 mph fastball with excellent life and a biting slider that could end up as a plus pitch, Constante rarely was squared up in the DSL. He throws a rudimentary, low-80s changeup that he doesn't locate yet, partly because he hasn't had a need to use it much. Constante struggled to throw strikes in 2013 in part because of the life on his fastball, though his loose, quick arm and clean delivery don't foretell significant control problems. He'll be ready to make his U.S. debut in 2014.

Year	Club (League)	Class	W	L	ERA	G	GS	CG	SV	IP	H	HR	BB	SO	K/9	WHIP	AVG
2013	Reds (DSL)	R	0	1	1.86	12	11	0	0	39	28	0	22	55	12.8	1.29	.197
Minor League Totals			0	1	1.86	12	11	0	0	39	28	0	22	55	12.8	1.29	.197

18 AMIR GARRETT, LHP

BA GRADE
50
EXTREME

Born: May 3, 1992. **B-T:** L-L. **Ht.:** 6-5. **Wt. 210. Drafted:** HS—Henderson, Nev., 2011 (22nd round). **Signed by:** Clark Crist.

The scouting report on Garrett hasn't changed much since he signed for $1 million out of high school in 2011. He's a long-limbed lefty with a great arm who needs a lot of innings. Garrett didn't even play baseball as a senior, as he focused primarily on his basketball career, which has taken him to Cal State Northridge after two years at St. John's. His hoops career has limited his time on the mound to short bursts, which is evident in Garrett's inconsistent control. He'll paint the corner on one pitch, then bounce his next two fastballs. His velocity also wavers as he struggles to repeat his delivery. His fastball ranges from 89-95 mph and plays as plus when he locates it. His breaking ball has morphed from a slider into a curveball. It can be an average pitch when he throws it for strikes, but he doesn't control it well. Garrett's changeup has promise as he throws it with good arm speed, but he has no feel for locating it yet. His chance to advance depends on him giving up his basketball career, but until he does that, he'll be on the slow track through Class A.

Year	Club (League)	Class	W	L	ERA	G	GS	CG	SV	IP	H	HR	BB	SO	K/9	WHIP	AVG
2012	Reds (AZL)	R	0	2	5.79	7	5	0	0	14	14	1	12	13	8.4	1.86	.255
	Billings (PIO)	R	0	0	0.00	2	2	0	0	6	4	0	1	5	7.5	0.83	.211
2013	Billings (PIO)	R	1	1	2.66	5	5	0	0	24	22	0	10	17	6.5	1.35	.250
	Dayton (MWL)	LoA	1	3	6.88	8	8	0	0	34	40	4	16	15	4.0	1.65	.294
Minor League Totals			2	6	4.87	22	20	0	0	78	80	5	39	50	5.8	1.53	.268

19 JACKSON STEPHENS, RHP

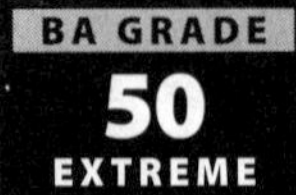

Born: May 11, 1994. **B-T:** R-R. **Ht.:** 6-3. **Wt.:** 205. **Drafted:** HS—Oxford, Ala., 2012 (18th round). **Signed by:** Ben Jones.

A fine high school quarterback, Stephens led the Oxford High baseball team to the Alabama 6A state title with his bat as much as his pitching. He decided to put away his third baseman's mitt after being drafted, turning down a scholarship to play both ways at Alabama to sign with the Reds for $100,000. Held back in extended spring until June, Stephens quickly has established himself as one of the more polished young pitchers in the organization, but one who also has solid stuff. His fastball has gained a tick since he signed. He now sits 91-92 mph and touches 95, pairing his fastball with an average curveball and slider. He can throw all three for strikes, though sometimes he catches more of the zone than he should. Stephens' biggest weakness is a below-average changeup, which explains why he struggles mightily against lefties—they hit .379/.434/.558 at low Class A Dayton in 2013. If Stephens can improve his changeup, he projects as a useful No. 4 or 5 starter. He'll try to earn a trip to Bakersfield in 2014.

Year	Club (League)	Class	W	L	ERA	G	GS	CG	SV	IP	H	HR	BB	SO	K/9	WHIP	AVG
2012	Reds (AZL)	R	1	1	4.64	20	0	0	2	21	23	2	3	22	9.3	1.22	.274
2013	Dayton (MWL)	LoA	3	7	4.59	14	6	0	1	65	79	6	18	55	7.7	1.50	.312
Minor League Totals			4	8	4.60	34	6	0	3	86	102	8	21	77	8.1	1.43	.303

20 JONATHAN REYNOSO, OF

Born: Jan. 7, 1993. **B-T:** R-R. **Ht.:** 6-3. **Wt.:** 177. **Signed:** Dominican Republic, 2010. **Signed by:** Richard Jimenez.

One of the toolsier players in the Reds system, Reynoso appeared set to leap into prospect prominence after a solid season in the Rookie-level Arizona League in 2012. Instead, he struggled at the plate in an injury-shortened stint with Rookie-level Billings before being shut down to have minor knee surgery to repair cartilage damage. Reynoso still has very loud tools. He's a plus runner who showed off his speed in 2013 with a sub-15-seconds inside-the-park home run. He's quickened his release, allowing his above-average arm to become more of a factor in the outfield. Defensively, he's solid in center field or right, though his ultimate position likely will depend on how much more weight he adds to his large frame. Reynoso has a picture-perfect swing that is simple and direct to the ball, but it hasn't mattered because he consistently sets his hands to hit too late. In instructional league, the Reds tweaked Reynoso's flat-footed stance, opening him up so he has to incorporate a small step as part of his setup. He will head to low Class A Dayton in 2014.

Year	Club (League)	Class	AVG	G	AB	R	H	2B	3B	HR	RBI	BB	SO	SB	CS	OBP	SLG
2010	Reds (DSL)	R	.202	35	104	16	21	3	2	0	7	9	20	9	0	.272	.269
2011	Reds (DSL)	R	.236	56	178	27	42	8	4	0	24	19	38	22	5	.340	.326
2012	Reds (AZL)	R	.311	50	190	37	59	7	3	2	16	6	23	30	9	.328	.411
2013	Billings (PIO)	R	.238	38	160	16	38	5	0	2	12	5	29	9	5	.259	.306
Minor League Totals			.253	179	632	96	160	23	9	4	59	39	110	70	19	.306	.337

21 SETH MEJIAS-BREAN, 3B/1B

BA GRADE
45
HIGH

Born: April 5, 1991. **B-T:** R-R. **Ht.:** 6-2. **Wt.:** 210. **Drafted:** Arizona, 2012 (8th round). **Signed by:** Clark Crist.

One of the stars of Arizona's 2012 College World Series championship team, Mejias-Brean always has impressed with his defense at third base and his ability to hit. Scouts, however, were turned off by his lack of power production in college; he hit two home runs in three seasons. That hasn't been a problem as a pro. Mejias-Brean is now taller at the plate than he was in college, and as a result he uses his legs more, turning from a spray hitter into someone who can drive the ball to all fields. Some scouts still worry that his rock-lean-and-waggle set-up won't allow him to hit for average. Because he played at low Class A Dayton with Tanner Rahier, Mejias-Brean played a good bit of first base, but he's solid-average at third with a solid-average arm. Cincinnati tried him behind the plate in instructional league, but they quickly scrapped that plan. With Rahier ticketed to return to Dayton, Mejias-Brean ought to play third more consistently at high Class A Bakersfield in 2014. In the long term, he projects as a useful backup corner infielder who provides solid defense.

Year	Club (League)	Class	AVG	G	AB	R	H	2B	3B	HR	RBI	BB	SO	SB	CS	OBP	SLG
2012	Billings (PIO)	R	.313	46	179	35	56	12	2	8	40	21	29	6	0	.389	.536
2013	Dayton (MWL)	LoA	.305	127	479	70	146	35	3	10	79	55	83	3	2	.381	.453
	Bakersfield (CAL)	HiA	.308	3	13	3	4	1	0	1	3	0	0	1	0	.308	.615
Minor League Totals			.307	176	671	108	206	48	5	19	122	76	112	10	2	.382	.478

22 K.J. FRANKLIN, 3B

BA GRADE **50** EXTREME

Born: Nov. 24, 1994. **B-T:** R-R. **Ht.:** 6-1. **Wt.:** 220. **Drafted:** HS—Cerritos, Calif., 2013 (2nd round). **Signed by:** Mike Misuraca.

With power becoming harder and harder to find, the Reds were willing to pay a premium to land Franklin, one of the better prep power hitters in the 2013 draft. Despite hitting only one home run in his pro debut, Franklin has above-average power potential thanks to strength in his swing. AZL pitchers quickly discovered that he was helpless against fastballs just off the outer half or any breaking ball. Defensively, he moves pretty well for a 220-pounder, but he will have to work hard if he wants to stay at third. His hands are soft on the balls he gets to and his arm has above-average strength, though it lacks accuracy. He had 20 errors in 46 games. In another organization, Franklin most likely would end up at first base, but Joey Votto's presence means that, despite below-average speed, a corner-outfield position is the fallback option. Franklin probably will stay back in extended spring training before heading to Rookie-level Billings in 2014.

Year	Club (League)	Class	AVG	G	AB	R	H	2B	3B	HR	RBI	BB	SO	SB	CS	OBP	SLG
2013	Reds (AZL)	R	.260	45	173	17	45	15	0	1	25	13	53	1	1	.326	.364
Minor League Totals			.260	45	173	17	45	15	0	1	25	13	53	1	1	.326	.364

23 JON MOSCOT, RHP

BA GRADE **45** HIGH

Born: Aug. 15, 1991. **B-T:** R-R. **Ht.:** 6-4. **Wt.:** 205. **Drafted:** Pepperdine, 2012 (4th round). **Signed by:** Rex de la Nuez.

If one sought the unluckiest pitcher in the minors in 2013, Moscot would have a compelling case. Pitching for a woeful high Class A Bakersfield team, he earned an 0-3 start with a 7.36 ERA in April. But from the start of May to the end of July, Moscot was very reliable, posting a 4.27 ERA while working at least five innings in 15 of 18 starts. His reward: A 2-14 record at the time of his promotion to Double-A Pensacola. Moscot improved his pitch sequences as the season progressed, learning when to double up on his breaking ball and when to mix his pitches. He works with three average pitches—a 91-93 mph fastball, a slider and a changeup. Moscot finishes his delivery with an arm recoil, but he's proven to be durable. Even if he returns to Pensacola in April, Moscot could reach Triple-A Louisville at some point this year.

Year	Club (League)	Class	W	L	ERA	G	GS	CG	SV	IP	H	HR	BB	SO	K/9	WHIP	AVG
2012	Reds (AZL)	R	0	1	0.00	2	1	0	0	2	3	0	5	1	3.9	3.43	.273
	Billings (PIO)	R	0	1	2.88	10	10	0	0	25	19	2	6	26	9.4	1.00	.213
2013	Bakersfield (CAL)	HiA	2	14	4.59	22	22	0	0	116	109	17	36	112	8.7	1.25	.247
	Pensacola (SL)	AA	2	1	3.19	6	6	0	0	31	34	3	12	28	8.1	1.48	.281
Minor League Totals			4	17	4.03	40	39	0	0	174	165	22	59	167	8.6	1.29	.249

24 ARISTIDES AQUINO, OF

BA GRADE **45** HIGH

Born: April 22, 1994. **B-T:** R-R. **Ht.:** 6-4. **Wt.:** 190. **Signed:** Dominican Republic, 2011. **Signed by:** Richard Jimenez.

Signed for $110,000 in January 2011, Aquino was the story of extended spring training last year as he launched home run after home run. The same power didn't show didn't show up in games at first, but after a slow start, Aquino wound up leading the Rookie-level Arizona League with 25 extra-base hits. At the plate, he has significant power potential. He chases too many breaking balls, but the Reds are impressed with how he studies the game. He analyzes not only his own at-bats, showing the ability to make in-game adjustments, but also those of his teammates. A long-legged outfielder who has the frame to carry plenty of good weight once he matures, Aquino is an average defender in right field with a well above-average arm. He led the AZL with 10 assists. He's an average runner who likely will slow as he gets bigger. Aquino likely will return to Rookie-level Billings in 2014, though a jump to low Class A Dayton isn't out of the question.

Year	Club (League)	Class	AVG	G	AB	R	H	2B	3B	HR	RBI	BB	SO	SB	CS	OBP	SLG
2011	Reds (DSL)	R	.188	60	202	27	38	4	4	3	21	21	63	4	10	.284	.292
2012	Reds (DSL)	R	.197	65	239	28	47	11	0	3	26	24	65	5	8	.277	.280
2013	Reds (AZL)	R	.278	46	194	37	54	15	6	4	38	10	40	4	3	.325	.479
	Billings (PIO)	R	.212	15	66	13	14	1	1	3	10	2	22	1	1	.229	.394
Minor League Totals			.218	186	701	105	153	31	11	13	95	57	190	14	22	.288	.350

25 SAL ROMANO, RHP

BA GRADE **50** EXTREME

Born: Oct. 12, 1993. **B-T:** L-R. **Ht.:** 6-5. **Wt.:** 220. **Drafted:** HS—Southington, Conn., 2011 (23rd round). **Signed by:** Lee Seras.

Romano has spent his pro career trying to catch up. The Connecticut native, like many Northeastern pitchers, had fewer innings under his belt when he signed with the Reds for $450,000. His delivery also has him playing catch up, as Romano's tendency to break his hands late leaves his arm trailing behind his lower half, forcing him to hurry his arm to get it to his release point on time. That has led to problems locating his stuff. Romano needs to firm up his big frame and clean up his delivery, but at his best he can pound the zone with a 90-93 mph fastball that has excellent downhill plane and good life. He also throws a promising curveball that could end up as an average pitch. His changeup is much too firm currently, which helps explain why lefties hit .318/.397/.453 against him at low Class A Dayton in 2013. Romano's big frame and strong legs are what scouts look for in a durable pitcher who can eat innings. He made every scheduled start in 2013, and he will look to do the same at high Class A Bakersfield in 2014.

Year	Club (League)	Class	W	L	ERA	G	GS	CG	SV	IP	H	HR	BB	SO	K/9	WHIP	AVG
2012	Billings (PIO)	R	5	6	5.32	15	15	0	0	64	74	1	23	52	7.3	1.51	.288
2013	Dayton (MWL)	LoA	7	11	4.86	25	25	0	0	120	134	10	57	89	6.7	1.59	.291
Minor League Totals			12	17	5.02	40	40	0	0	185	208	11	80	141	6.9	1.56	.290

26 SEBASTIAN ELIZALDE, OF

BA GRADE **50** EXTREME

Born: Nov. 20, 1991. **B-T:** L-R. **Ht.:** 6-0. **Wt.:** 175. **Signed:** Mexico, 2013. **Signed by:** Tony Arias.

As an organization that generally has stuck to slot recommendations for first-round picks, the Reds have been willing to get creative to acquire talent. That includes trading for Rule 5 pick Josh Hamilton in 2006, spending big for Cuban flame-thrower Aroldis Chapman in 2010 and taking a flier on former New York Giants safety Chad Jones in the 2013 draft. The Reds opened up another avenue by going south of the border to sign Elizalde, whom they spotted during a summer scouting trip to Mexico. He had little trouble keeping his head above water in the Mexican League, as the 22-year-old had played parts of four seasons with Monterrey, hitting .301 as a part-timer. Soon after signing, though, he had Tommy John surgery, which sidelined him for 2013. Elizalde is a plus runner (6.6 seconds in the 60-yard dash) and solid center fielder. It's hard to project his arm until he's throwing again post-surgery. He projects as a lefty-hitting leadoff hitter with an average or better feel to hit and below-average power, though like many young players, he'll need to improve his plate discipline. Elizalde will start his Reds career at Class A, either at Dayton or Bakersfield.

Year	Club (League)	Class	AVG	G	AB	R	H	2B	3B	HR	RBI	BB	SO	SB	CS	OBP	SLG
2010	Monterrey (MEX)	AAA	.333	11	3	1	1	0	0	0	0	0	0	0	0	.333	.333
2011	Monterrey (MEX)	AAA	.306	26	36	8	11	3	0	1	5	2	6	0	0	.341	.472
2012	Monterrey (MEX)	AAA	.276	74	134	25	37	9	4	2	14	15	37	7	3	.351	.448
2013	Monterrey (MEX)	AAA	.328	36	116	24	38	5	0	3	10	5	22	5	3	.361	.448
Minor League Totals			.301	147	289	58	87	17	4	6	29	22	65	12	6	.353	.450

27 TANNER RAHIER, 3B

BA GRADE **45** HIGH

Born: Oct. 12, 1993. **B-T:** R-R. **Ht.:** 6-2. **Wt.:** 205. **Drafted:** HS—Palm Desert, Calif., 2012 (2nd round). **Signed by:** Mike Misuraca.

A 2013 season that began poorly ended in equally awful form for Rahier. He posted a sub-.200 on-base percentage in both April and August, ruining a season where he showed flashes of competence at the plate and plenty of promise in the field. A high school shortstop, Rahier is an above-average defender with excellent range at third base and an accurate arm with above-average arm strength. The Reds felt comfortable enough with his defense to slide him back to shortstop as an emergency fill-in. A tick-below-average runner, Rahier has much more work to do at the plate. He has yet to tone down a pull-happy approach that leaves him vulnerable to pitches away. Only one extra-base hit in 2013—and zero of seven homers—went to right field. Rahier also struggles with his timing, which leads to difficulty squaring up the ball. He has average power potential with leverage in his swing, but he needs a better plan at the plate to have a chance to unlock it. Rahier needs to repeat low Class A Dayton to prove he can hit.

Year	Club (League)	Class	AVG	G	AB	R	H	2B	3B	HR	RBI	BB	SO	SB	CS	OBP	SLG
2012	Reds (AZL)	R	.192	51	193	21	37	9	1	4	30	21	43	5	2	.266	.311
2013	Dayton (MWL)	LoA	.222	106	410	31	91	15	2	7	61	12	81	0	5	.252	.320
Minor League Totals			.212	157	603	52	128	24	3	11	91	33	124	5	7	.256	.317

28 CURTIS PARTCH, RHP

BA GRADE **40** MEDIUM

Born: Feb. 13, 1987. **B-T:** R-R. **Ht.:** 6-2. **Wt.:** 230. **Drafted:** Merced (Calif.) JC, 2007 (26th round). **Signed by:** Tom Wheeler.

Yet another example of a starter who turned into a prospect after a move to the bullpen, Partch, along with fellow hard-throwing righthander Josh Ravin, earned himself a spot on the 40-man roster following the 2012 season after showcasing a plus-plus fastball in the Arizona Fall League. Ravin's control problems led the Reds to waive him during the 2013 season, but Partch parlayed his new status into his big league debut, though a lack of command led to some rough mop-up outings. With a 94-97 mph fastball, Partch doesn't have to paint the black, but he'll have to improve his ability to work down in the zone. He gave up six home runs over the course of four straight big league outings because he kept missing up in the zone. Considering his 6-foot-2 height, he needs to get more downhill plane on his fastball. At his best, Partch mixes a plus fastball and slider that flashes plus. When he stays on top of his slider, it shows good tilt and bite, handcuffing hitters. He has toyed with adding a cutter, because his changeup isn't good enough to keep lefthanders honest. Partch has the stuff to pitch the seventh or eighth inning in the big leagues, but he'll need to fine-tune his command at Triple-A Louisville first.

Year	Club (League)	Class	W	L	ERA	G	GS	CG	SV	IP	H	HR	BB	SO	K/9	WHIP	AVG
2007	Reds (GCL)	R	0	0	1.29	5	0	0	2	7	2	0	7	4	5.1	1.29	.083
	Billings (PIO)	R	1	0	3.29	12	1	0	1	27	21	3	21	22	7.2	1.54	.221
2008	Dayton (MWL)	LoA	5	11	5.00	33	17	0	1	112	118	6	42	74	6.0	1.43	.267
2009	Carolina (SL)	AA	1	0	1.80	1	1	0	0	5	5	0	2	2	3.6	1.40	.238
	Dayton (MWL)	LoA	8	7	4.67	19	19	0	0	104	107	11	39	77	6.7	1.40	.270
	Sarasota (FSL)	HiA	3	2	4.35	7	7	0	0	39	38	0	18	25	5.7	1.42	.257
2010	Carolina (SL)	AA	0	1	21.00	1	1	0	0	3	7	2	2	1	3.0	3.00	.467
	Lynchburg (CAR)	HiA	7	11	4.98	28	24	0	0	132	165	11	45	96	6.5	1.59	.308
2011	Bakersfield (CAL)	HiA	6	11	5.25	21	21	2	0	122	161	14	28	93	6.9	1.55	.317
	Carolina (SL)	AA	2	2	6.92	7	7	0	0	39	55	3	13	33	7.6	1.74	.337
2012	Bakersfield (CAL)	HiA	0	0	1.50	7	0	0	2	12	7	1	3	15	11.3	0.83	.167
	Pensacola (SL)	AA	7	4	4.73	45	4	0	6	70	75	7	33	64	8.2	1.54	.274
2013	Pensacola (SL)	AA	0	0	2.16	8	0	0	4	8	6	0	2	14	15.1	0.96	.200
	Louisville (IL)	AAA	1	2	4.13	24	0	0	2	28	27	2	12	31	9.8	1.38	.250
	Cincinnati (NL)	MAJ	0	1	6.17	14	0	0	0	23	17	8	17	16	6.2	1.46	.210
Major League Totals			0	1	6.17	14	0	0	0	23	17	8	17	16	6.2	1.46	.210
Minor League Totals			41	51	4.85	218	102	2	18	709	794	60	267	551	7.0	1.50	.283

29 REYDEL MEDINA, OF

BA GRADE **50** EXTREME

Born: February 14, 1993. **B-T:** L-L. **Ht.:** 6-2. **Wt.:** 198. **Signed:** Cuba, 2013. **Signed by:** Tony Arias.

The Reds have scouted the Cuban-defector market extensively, signing Aroldis Chapman to a massive deal and landing complementary pieces such as outfielder Felix Perez, who finished 2013 at Triple-A Louisville. Medina more resembles Perez than Chapman in both the size of his deal ($400,000) and his impact potential. Before leaving Cuba in 2011, he played for the Cuba youth national team, including the 16U squad that went to the World Championships in Taiwan in 2009. Medina performed well there, hitting .444/.516/.852. If it all comes together, he's an above-average runner with above-average power from the left side of the plate. His swing is simple and leveraged, featuring a quiet setup and a closed front foot, but it also has some length to go with solid bat speed. Like many young hitters, Medina must improve his pitch selection. Defensively, he has the tools to be a solid-average corner outfielder, though his average arm always will be stretched in right. He could join a crowded outfield rotation at low Class A Dayton in 2014.

Year	Club (League)	Class	AVG	G	AB	R	H	2B	3B	HR	RBI	BB	SO	SB	CS	OBP	SLG
Did not play—Signed 2014 contract																	

30 DAN LANGFIELD, RHP

BA GRADE **50** EXTREME

Born: Jan. 21, 1991. **B-T:** R-R. **Ht.:** 6-2. **Wt.:** 196. **Drafted:** Memphis, 2012 (3rd round). **Signed by:** Joe Katuska.

A year ago, Langfield seemed to be following a somewhat similar trajectory as lefthander Tony Cingrani. Like Cingrani, he was a college pitcher the Reds drafted in the third round after falling because of concerns about his delivery. Langfield had a loud pro debut, going 3-0, 2.68 with 54 strikeouts in 37 innings while showing plus stuff at Rookie-level Billing in 2012. The similarities with Cingrani ended in 2013 when Langfield battled a shoulder injury that required surgery and sidelined him for the entire season. He had not recovered enough to pitch in instructional league, so the Reds won't really know until 2014 if he can regain his pre-surgery stuff. Before the injury, Langfield had a 93-97 mph fastball, a hard slider that could end up as a second plus pitch and a fringy changeup and curveball that flash average at times. His delivery through college involved effort and recoil, and while he had toned down his motion with the Reds, it will remain a concern until he once again throws free and easy off the mound.

Year	Club (League)	Class	W	L	ERA	G	GS	CG	SV	IP	H	HR	BB	SO	K/9	WHIP	AVG
2012	Billings (PIO)	R	3	0	2.68	15	5	0	0	37	27	1	17	54	13.1	1.19	.197
2013	Did not play—Injured																
Minor League Totals			3	0	2.68	15	5	0	0	37	27	1	17	54	13.1	1.19	.197

Cleveland Indians

BY JIM SHONERD

After five years out of the limelight, the Indians were an attraction again in 2013. With World Series-winning manager Terry Francona installed at the helm, the Tribe charged to a 21-6 record in September and snagged a wild-card berth, their first playoff appearance since 2007, though the season came to a disappointing end in a home loss to the Rays in the American League Wild Card game.

While the Indians have become relevant again, their improvement was largely thanks to veteran acquisitions rather than youth. In addition to putting Francona in the dugout, the Indians signed free agents Nick Swisher, Jason Giambi and Michael Bourn. It helped also that Ubaldo Jimenez, largely a disappointment for most of his tenure in Cleveland since coming over in a blockbuster trade in 2011, reinvigorated his career by going 13-9, 3.30 for the season and 4-0, 1.09 in September.

The farm system played a relatively minor part in the Indians' reversal of fortunes. Just four players who made meaningful contributions were fully homegrown, led by second baseman Jason Kipnis, who became an all-star in his second full season in the majors.

Dominican rookie righthander Danny Salazar was the only homegrown pitcher to start a game for Cleveland in 2013, though he was instrumental to the Tribe's September run. But outside of Salazar, rookie reliever Cody Allen was the only other homegrown pitcher to see significant action.

The Indians struggled to get good returns when they traded Cy Young Award-winning southpaws C.C. Sabathia and Cliff Lee in 2008 and 2009, which set back their rebuilding process. They sold off another productive veteran prior to the 2013 season when they gave up Shin-Soo Choo in a three-team deal with the Reds and Diamondbacks, landing righthanders Trevor Bauer and Bryan Shaw from Arizona. Shaw contributed 70 appearances and a 3.24 ERA out of the bullpen, but Bauer was a disappointment.

The No. 3 overall pick in the 2011 draft, Bauer rarely got on track at Triple-A Columbus and put up an uninspiring 4.15 ERA. He made just four big league starts during the season, and the club didn't bother calling him up in September.

As was the case in past trades for Choo, Carlos Santana and Asdrubal Cabrera, the Indians score better on the margins. For example, they got catcher Yan Gomes along with utilityman Mike Aviles from the Blue Jays for Esmil Rogers. The first Brazilian to ever play in the majors, Gomes hit .294/.345/.481 for the Indians to force his way into the lineup, leading to Santana spending more time at DH.

Other than an imminent changing of the guard at shortstop from Cabrera to top prospect Francisco Lindor, the Indians will have to lean heavily on their current core in the immediate future. The system has few true impact players outside of Lindor and 2013 first-rounder Clint Frazier, the BA High School Player of the Year in 2013. Whatever contributions the team gets from young players in 2014 will probably be from relievers such as righthanders Austin Adams and C.C. Lee, along with a hoped-for rebound from Bauer.

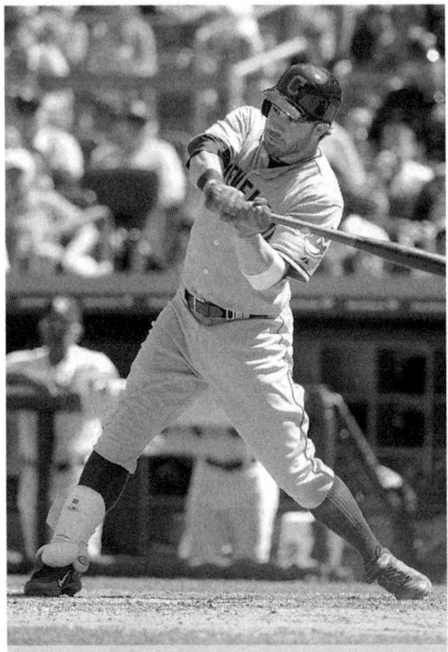

TOMASSO DEROSA

Second baseman Jason Kipnis blossomed into a homegrown all-star for the Indians

TOP PROSPECTS OF THE DECADE

Year	Player, Pos.	2013 Org.
2004	Grady Sizemore, of	Did not play
2005	Adam Miller, rhp	Sugar Land (Atlantic)
2006	Adam Miller, rhp	Sugar Land (Atlantic)
2007	Adam Miller, rhp	Sugar Land (Atlantic)
2008	Adam Miller, rhp	Sugar Land (Atlantic)
2009	Carlos Santana, c	Indians
2010	Carlos Santana, c	Indians
2011	Lonnie Chisenhall, 3b	Indians
2012	Francisco Lindor, ss	Indians
2013	Francisco Lindor, ss	Indians

ORGANIZATION OVERVIEW

General Manager: Chris Antonetti. **Farm Director:** Ross Atkins. **Scouting Director:** Brad Grant.

Class	Team	League	W	L	PCT	Finish	Manager
Majors	Cleveland Indians	American	92	70	.568	4th (15)	Terry Francona
Triple-A	Columbus Clippers	International	71	73	.493	8th (14)	Chris Tremie
Double-A	Akron Aeros	Eastern	68	73	.482	t-8th (12)	Edwin Rodriguez
High Class A	Carolina Mudcats	Carolina	57	83	.411	8th (8)	David Wallace
Low Class A	Lake County Captains	Midwest	54	83	.394	16th (16)	Scooter Tucker
Short-season	Mahoning Valley Scrappers	New York-Penn	30	44	.405	13th (14)	Ted Kubiak
Rookie	AZL Indians	Arizona	28	28	.500	7th (13)	Anthony Medrano
Overall 2013 Minor League Record			**308**	**384**	**.445**	**29th (30)**	

THIS YEAR'S TOP 30

No.	Player, Pos.	Grade/Risk
1.	Francisco Lindor, ss	65/Medium
2.	Clint Frazier, of	65/High
3.	Trevor Bauer, rhp	60/High
4.	Tyler Naquin, of	50/Medium
5.	Cody Anderson, rhp	50/Medium
6.	Dorssys Paulino, ss	55/Extreme
7.	Ronny Rodriguez, ss/2b	50/High
8.	C.C. Lee, rhp	45/Low
9.	Jose Ramirez, 2b/ss	45/Medium
10.	Austin Adams, rhp	45/Medium
11.	Kyle Crockett, lhp	45/Medium
12.	Francisco Mejia, c	55/Extreme
13.	Luigi Rodriguez, of	50/High
14.	Carlos Moncrief, of	50/High
15.	Jesus Aguilar, 1b	45/Medium
16.	Dace Kime, rhp	50/High
17.	Joe Wendle, 2b	45/Medium
18.	Adam Plutko, rhp	45/Medium
19.	Erik Gonzalez, ss	50/High
20.	Anthony Santander, of	45/High
21.	Luis Lugo, lhp	45/High
22.	Shawn Morimando, lhp	45/High
23.	Casey Shane, rhp	50/Extreme
24.	Mitch Brown, rhp	45/High
25.	Tony Wolters, c	45/High
26.	Scott Barnes, lhp	40/Medium
27.	Nelson Rodriguez, 1b	45/High
28.	Trey Haley, rhp	45/High
29.	Shawn Armstrong, rhp	45/High
30.	Sean Brady, lhp	45/High

LAST YEAR'S TOP 30

No.	Player, Pos.	Status
1.	Francisco Lindor, ss	No. 1
2.	Dorssys Paulino, ss	No. 6
3.	Tyler Naquin, of	No. 4
4.	Cody Allen, rhp	Majors
5.	Mitch Brown, rhp	No. 24
6.	Danny Salazar, rhp	Majors
7.	Luigi Rodriguez, of	No. 13
8.	Ronny Rodriguez, ss/2b	No. 7
9.	Jesus Aguilar, 1b	No. 15
10.	C.C. Lee, rhp	No. 8
11.	Scott Barnes, lhp	No. 26
12.	Luis Lugo, lhp	No. 21
13.	Anthony Santander, of	No. 20
14.	Trey Haley, rhp	No. 28
15.	D'vone McClure	Dropped out
16.	Dylan Baker, rhp	Dropped out
17.	Tony Wolters, 2b/ss	No. 25
18.	Chris McGuiness, 1b	(Rangers)
19.	Tim Fedroff, of	Dropped out
20.	Shawn Armstrong, rhp	No. 29
21.	Kieran Lovegrove, rhp	Dropped out
22.	Giovanny Urshela, 3b	Dropped out
23.	Jose Ramirez, 2b	No. 9
24.	Austin Adams, rhp	No. 10
25.	Dillon Howard, rhp	Dropped out
26.	Elvis Araujo, lhp	Dropped out
27.	Yan Gomes, c/1b/3b	Majors
28.	Thomas Neal, of	(Cubs)
29.	Cody Anderson, rhp	No. 5
30.	Jordan Smith, of	Dropped out

BEST TOOLS

Best Hitter for Average	Francisco Lindor
Best Power Hitter	Clint Frazier
Best Strike-Zone Discipline	Francisco Lindor
Fastest Baserunner	Jose Ramirez
Best Athlete	D'vone McClure
Best Fastball	Trey Haley
Best Curveball	Trevor Bauer
Best Slider	C.C. Lee
Best Changeup	Trevor Bauer
Best Control	Kyle Crockett
Best Defensive Catcher	Roberto Perez
Best Defensive Infielder	Francisco Lindor
Best Infield Arm	Erik Gonzalez
Best Defensive Outfielder	Tyler Naquin
Best Outfield Arm	Tyler Naquin

TOP 15 PLAYERS 25 AND UNDER

No.	Player, Pos. (Age)	Peak Level
1.	Francisco Lindor, ss (20)	Double-A
2.	Danny Salazar, rhp (24)	Majors
3.	Clint Frazier, of (19)	Rookie
4.	Lonnie Chisenhall, 3b (25)	Majors
5.	Trevor Bauer, rhp (23)	Majors
6.	Tyler Naquin, of (22)	Double-A
7.	Cody Allen, rhp (25)	Majors
8.	Cody Anderson, rhp (23)	Double-A
9.	Dorssys Paulino, ss (19)	Low Class A
10.	Ronny Rodriguez (21)	Double-A
11.	Jose Ramirez, 2b/ss (21)	Majors
12.	Kyle Crockett, lhp (22)	Double-A
13.	Francisco Mejia, c (18)	Rookie
14.	Luigi Rodriguz, of (21)	High Class A
15.	Carlos Moncrief, of (25)	Double-A

MINOR LEAGUE DEPTH CHART

CLEVELAND INDIANS

TOP 2014 ROOKIE: Trevor Bauer, rhp. If he rediscovers his old form, Bauer still has the stuff to be a quality big league starter.

BREAKOUT PROSPECT: Kyle Crockett, lhp. A lefty reliever with plus command, he could be one of the first 2013 draftees to reach the majors

SLEEPER: Silento Sayles, of. He's extremely raw, but the 2013 14th-round pick has elite speed and shows promising signs with the bat.

SOURCE OF TOP 30 TALENT

Homegrown	**28**	**Acquired**	**2**
College	7	Trades	2
Junior college	2	Rule 5 draft	0
High school	9	Independent leagues	0
Nondrafted free agents	0	Free agents/waivers	0
International	10		

LF

Bryson Myles
Tim Fedroff

CF

Clint Frazier (2)
Tyler Naquin (4)
Luigi Rodriguez (13)
D'vone McClure
LeVon Washington
Silento Sayles

RF

Carlos Moncrief (14)
Anthony Santander (20)
Jordan Smith

3B

Giovanny Urshela
Robel Garcia

SS

Francisco Lindor (1)
Ronny Rodriguez (7)
Erik Gonzalez (19)
James Roberts

2B

Dorssys Paulino (6)
Jose Ramirez (9)
Joe Wendle (17)
Claudio Bautista
Paul Hendrix

1B

Jesus Aguilar (15)
Nelson Rodriguez (27)
Chun Chen

C

Francisco Mejia (12)
Tony Wolters (25)
Roberto Perez
Alex Monsalve
Eric Haase
Jake Lowery
Sicnarf Loopstok

LHP

LHSP	LHRP
Luis Lugo (21)	Kyle Crockett (11)
Shawn Morimando (22)	Scott Barnes (26)
Shawn Brady (30)	Thomas Pannone
T.J. House	Elvis Araujo
Matt Packer	
Kenny Mathews	
Matt Whitehouse	
Ryan Merritt	

RHP

RHSP	RHRP
Trevor Bauer (3)	C.C. Lee (8)
Cody Anderson (5)	Austin Adams (10)
Dace Kime (16)	Trey Haley (28)
Adam Plutko (18)	Shawn Armstrong (29)
Casey Shane (23)	Bryan Price
Mitch Brown (24)	Preston Guilmet
Dylan Baker	Francisco Valera
Leandro Linares	Ben Heller
Kieran Lovegrove	Cortland Cox
Robert Whitenack	Jeff Johnson
Nick Pasquale	
Dillon Howard	

DRAFT ANALYSIS

2013

BONUSES: $5.9 MILLION

BEST PURE HITTER: OF Clint Frazier (1) had the best bat speed in the 2013 draft class, with tremendous strength in his forearms and wrists and an aggressive approach. Grant Fink (23), who hit .263/.355/.425 this summer, has a strong hit tool for a late-round pick.

BEST POWER HITTER: Frazier uses his bat speed to produce well above-average raw power from a 6-foot, 190-pound frame. The Indians believe he can hit 25-30 home runs a year at the major league level.

FASTEST RUNNER: OF Silento Sayles (14) stole 103 bases this spring, which is believed to be a national high school record, thanks to speed that grades a legitimate 80 on the 20-80 scale.

BEST DEFENSIVE PLAYER: James Roberts (15) saw time at shortstop and third base and has an above-average arm, good actions and steady hands. He could also play second base or the outfield as well because of his speed. He'll need to improve his reads off the bat.

BEST FASTBALL: RHP Ben Heller (22) sat 92-95 mph and touched 96 after signing. RHPs Jordan Milbrath (35) and Trevor Frank (8) can touch 95. RHP Casey Shane (6) has pitched at 90-94 mph with great sink but was more in the upper 80s this spring.

BEST SECONDARY PITCH: LHP Kyle Crockett (4) has a plus slider. RHP Dace Kime (3) has a plus curveball. LHP Sean Brady (5) has advanced feel, and both his curveball and changeup have plus potential.

BEST PRO DEBUT: Frazier was the top prospect in the Rookie-level Arizona League after batting .297/.362/.506 with 21 extra-base hits in 44 games. Brady had a 5-1 strikeout-walk ratio and 1.97 ERA in 32 AZL innings.

BEST ATHLETE: Frazier and Sayles have loud tools and athleticism. LHP Thomas Pannone (9), who has a fastball up to 93 mph, was drafted last year as an outfielder.

MOST INTRIGUING BACKGROUND: C Sicnarf Loopstok (13), who grew up in Aruba and moved to Pennsylvania during high school, speaks seven languages. His first name comes from spelling his father's name backward.

CLOSEST TO THE MAJORS: Crockett reached Double-A, and has the command, fastball and breaking ball to be a tough left-on-left reliever.

BEST LATE-ROUND PICK: Cleveland spent $300,000 on RHP Adam Plutko (11) who has feel for pitching, control and solid-average stuff. Sayles showed a surprisingly advanced offensive approach and made strides defensively this summer.

THE ONE WHO GOT AWAY: 2B Ross Kivett (10) was an offensive force for Kansas State and decided to return to Manhattan for his senior season. The Indians made a late run at RHP Paul Young (21), but he's at Mississippi.

ASSESSMENT: Cleveland took the draft's first high school position player, Frazier, a potential impact hitter with a well-rounded tool set. The organization then focused on the mound, as its next eight picks were pitchers.

2012

BONUSES: $5.3 MILLION

As it usually does, Cleveland played it safe with a college bat, OF Tyler Naquin (1). The other best hope in the class is 2B Joe Wendle (6). Prep RHPs Matt Brown (2) and Kieran Lovegrove (3) started slowly.

GRADE: C

2011

BONUSES: $8.2 MILLION

The Tribe stepped out with prep SS Francisco Lindor (1), who has star potential. RHP Cody Allen (23) was one of the first 2011 draftees to reach the majors and could be the team's closer soon.

GRADE: B+

2010

BONUSES: $9.4 MILLION

LHP Drew Pomeranz (1) hasn't lived up to his promise but was used in the Ubaldo Jimenez deal. Only OF LeVon Washington (2) offers hope among the rest of the class.

GRADE: D

TOP DRAFT PICKS OF THE DECADE

Year	Player, Pos.	2013 Org.
2004	Jeremy Sowers, lhp	Out of baseball
2005	Trevor Crowe, of	Astros
2006	David Huff, lhp (1st round supp.)	Yankees
2007	Beau Mills, 3b/1b	Out of baseball
2008	Lonnie Chisenhall, 3b	Indians
2009	Alex White, rhp	Astros
2010	Drew Pomeranz, lhp	Rockies
2011	Francisco Lindor, ss	Indians
2012	Tyler Naquin, of	Indians
2013	Clint Frazier, of	Indians

LARGEST BONUSES IN CLUB HISTORY

Danys Baez, 1999	$4,500,000
Clint Frazier, 2013	$3,500,000
Jeremy Guthrie, 2002	$3,000,000
Francisco Lindor, 2011	$2,650,000
Drew Pomeranz, 2004	$2,650,000

1 FRANCISCO LINDOR, SS

Born: Nov. 14, 1993. **B-T:** B-R. **Ht.:** 5-11. **Wt.:** 175.
Drafted: HS—Montverde, Fla., 2011 (1st round).
Signed by: Mike Soper.

Lindor gained minor fame as a youth in Puerto Rico, where his local all-star teams won 8- and 9-year-old national championships, and the mayor of his hometown of Caguas honored him as the town's player of the year. Seeking better competition than he could find on the island, Lindor's family enrolled him at Montverde (Fla.) Academy at age 12. He went on to star on the high school showcase circuit and for USA Baseball's 16U national team, for which he served as captain and won a gold medal at the 2009 World Youth Championships in Taiwan. Lindor even scored the winning run in the ninth inning of the gold-medal game as Team USA rallied back from a 5-1 deficit to beat Cuba 7-6. The Indians made Lindor the first high schooler they'd taken in the first round since 2001 when they snagged him No. 8 overall in 2011, signing him for $2.9 million. A precocious talent, he wasn't out of his element as the second-youngest everyday player in the high Class A Carolina League in 2013. After hitting .306/.373/.410 for Carolina, Lindor moved up to Double-A Akron in July and was the youngest position player to play in the Eastern League.

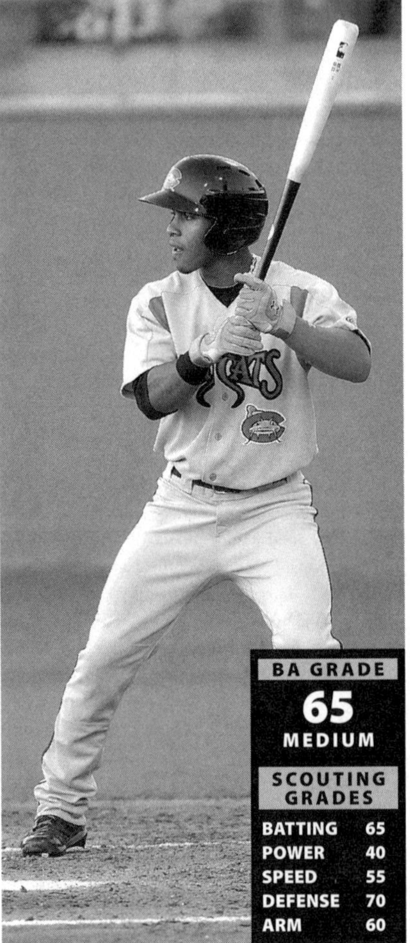

BA GRADE
65
MEDIUM
SCOUTING GRADES
BATTING 65
POWER 40
SPEED 55
DEFENSE 70
ARM 60

TOM PRIDDY

Lindor brings everything to the table with his tools, instincts and makeup. He'll fit more as a No. 1 or 2 hitter in a future big league lineup rather than as a run-producer, but there's very little he can't do. He has a compact swing from both sides of the plate and drives balls to all fields. Raw power is the only tool where he's not above-average, but he could still be a threat to hit 15 homers once he fills out. He does have a little more power from the right side that would sometimes cause his righthanded swing to get bigger, but he did a better job of keeping it more consistent in 2013. Lindor has an uncanny feel for the strike zone, especially for his age. He rarely chases bad pitches or gives away at-bats, drawing more walks than he had strikeouts across two levels last year. Though he's still polishing the small-ball aspects of his game, such as bunting and stealing, he's an intelligent baserunner with above-average speed. Lindor shines even brighter on defense, where he has the potential to be a Gold Glove shortstop. Beyond just his soft hands and above-average arm, Lindor has an advanced feel for anticipating plays. He slows the game down and always plays under control. His work ethic is second to none as well, as he doesn't just settle with getting by on talent and is driven to be a complete player.

The only areas for improvement for Lindor at this stage are adding a bit more strength and gaining more experience against upper-level pitchers. With Asdrubal Cabrera's contract expiring after the 2014 season, Lindor is right on schedule to be the Indians' Opening Day shortstop in 2015. He'll begin the 2014 season back in Akron, but if he shows he's ready, Cleveland may ring in the Lindor era sooner than later.

Year	Club (League)	Class	AVG	G	AB	R	H	2B	3B	HR	RBI	BB	SO	SB	CS	OBP	SLG
2011	Mahoning Valley (NYP)	SS	.316	5	19	4	6	0	0	0	2	1	5	1	0	.350	.316
2012	Lake County (MWL)	LoA	.257	122	490	83	126	24	3	6	42	61	78	27	12	.352	.355
2013	Carolina (CAR)	HiA	.306	83	327	51	100	19	6	1	27	35	39	20	5	.373	.410
	Akron (EL)	AA	.289	21	76	14	22	3	1	1	7	14	7	5	2	.407	.395
Minor League Totals			.279	231	912	152	254	46	10	8	78	111	129	53	19	.364	.377

2 CLINT FRAZIER, OF

Born: Sept. 6, 1994. **B-T:** R-R. **Ht.:** 5-11. **Wt.:** 185. **Drafted:** HS—Loganville, Ga., 2013 (1st round). **Signed by:** Brad Tyler.

BILL MITCHELL

Frazier cemented his star prospect status when he belted two home runs in a March 2013 game for Loganville (Ga.) High against crosstown rival Grayson High, which was led by Frazier's friend and fellow first-rounder Austin Meadows. The audience that night included more than 1,300 fans, hordes of scouts and scouting directors—and a few general mangers. Frazier went on to win the Baseball America High School Player of the Year award after hitting .485 with 17 homers for Loganville and signed for $3.5 million, the largest bonus Cleveland ever has given a drafted player, as the fifth overall pick. Frazier comes loaded with tools. He can put on shows in batting practice, with his raw power rating a 70 on the 20-80 scouting scale. He generates lightning-quick bat speed and takes short, quick swings. Like most teenage hitters, Frazier will swing and miss too much at times. He'll have to get accustomed to pitchers throwing him a steady diet of breaking balls as he moves up, but the Indians believe he'll be able to make the adjustment and will hit for solid averages. An infielder until his junior year in high school, Frazier impressed the team with how quickly his outfield play progressed. His routes and angles need to get better, but he has the above-average speed to play center field. Some scouts believe he'll eventually outgrow center, though his above-average arm would fit fine in right if he does move. Between Frazier and Francisco Lindor, the Indians boast two elite prospects at up-the-middle positions, with Frazier having the most offensive impact potential of any hitter in the system. After a successful showing in the Rookie-level Arizona League in his pro debut, he'll go to low Class A Lake County as a 19-year-old in 2014.

Year	Club (League)	Class	AVG	G	AB	R	H	2B	3B	HR	RBI	BB	SO	SB	CS	OBP	SLG
2013	Indians (AZL)	R	.297	44	172	32	51	11	5	5	28	17	61	3	2	.362	.506
Minor League Totals			.297	44	172	32	51	11	5	5	28	17	61	3	2	.362	.506

3 TREVOR BAUER, RHP

Born: Jan. 17, 1991. **B-T:** R-R. **Ht.:** 6-1. **Wt.:** 190. **Drafted:** UCLA, 2011 (1st round). **Signed by:** Hal Kurtzman (Diamondbacks).

Bauer came into pro ball fresh off winning the Baseball America College Player of the Year Award and the Golden Spikes Award when the Diamondbacks made him the third overall pick in 2011. However, his pro career hasn't gone the way most envisioned. He wore out his welcome in Arizona, which parted with him in a three-team deal in December 2012, with Bauer going to the Indians. He languished at Triple-A Columbus in 2013, his numbers and stuff declining across the board from the year before, and he made a scant four appearances in Cleveland. Bauer takes an intellectual approach, studying biomechanics to carefully craft his delivery, but it got out of whack last season as he tried to compensate for a groin injury. His stride got shorter, his finish was more upright and he wasn't able to get the same depth and leverage on his pitches. His fastball has some slight tailing movement, sitting in the low 90s and hitting 95 mph when he needs it to. Bauer still shows wipeout secondary stuff. He has two plus pitches in his curveball with late downward break and his sinking changeup. He can mix in a usable slider as well. However, Bauer relied too heavily on his breaking stuff last season, struggled to command his fastball and constantly fell behind in counts. He needs to trust his fastball more and get his delivery back in order so he can command it down in the zone. At times Bauer still looks like a frontline arm, but skeptics who doubted he could hold up with his diligent throwing program at the professional level had some vindication in 2013. He likely will begin 2014 back in Triple-A Columbus, barring a spectacular spring training.

Year	Club (League)	Class	W	L	ERA	G	GS	CG	SV	IP	H	HR	BB	SO	K/9	WHIP	AVG
2011	Visalia (CAL)	HiA	0	1	3.00	3	3	0	0	9	7	1	4	17	17.0	1.22	.200
	Mobile (SL)	AA	1	1	7.56	4	4	0	0	17	20	2	8	26	14.0	1.68	.286
2012	Mobile (SL)	AA	7	1	1.68	8	8	0	0	48	33	1	26	60	11.2	1.22	.192
	Arizona (NL)	MAJ	1	2	6.06	4	4	0	0	16	14	2	13	17	9.4	1.65	.230
	Reno (PCL)	AAA	5	1	2.85	14	14	1	0	82	74	8	35	97	10.6	1.33	.241
2013	Cleveland (AL)	MAJ	1	2	5.29	4	4	0	0	17	15	3	16	11	5.8	1.82	.238
	Columbus (IL)	AAA	6	7	4.15	22	22	1	0	121	119	14	73	106	7.9	1.58	.266
Major League Totals			2	4	5.67	8	8	0	0	33	29	5	29	28	7.6	1.74	.234
Minor League Totals			19	11	3.50	51	51	2	0	277	253	26	146	306	9.9	1.44	.245

4 TYLER NAQUIN, OF

BA GRADE
50
MEDIUM

Born: April 24, 1991. **B-T:** L-R. **Ht.:** 6-2. **Wt.:** 175. **Drafted:** Texas A&M, 2012 (1st round). **Signed by:** Kyle Van Hook.

Naquin claimed back-to-back Big 12 Conference batting titles as a sophomore and junior before landing a $1.75 million bonus as the 15th overall pick in 2012. Going to high Class A Carolina for his first full season, Naquin came out of the gates strong and hit .311/.375/.468 in the first half before wearing down. Hailed as the best pure hitter in the 2012 draft class, Naquin has quick hands and exceptional bat control, allowing him to spray line drives all over the field. He spread out his stance in 2013 to give himself a stronger base and allow him to use his legs better. However, scouts would like to see him turn on inside pitches with more authority rather than looking to flick them the other way. He has below-average power but he can accumulate extra bases with his above-average speed and aggressiveness. That lack of home run pop makes it essential Naquin stay in center field. He was a right fielder in college, but he has the range and instincts to make a go of it center. His arm is also well-above-average. Naquin's doubters see him as a future fourth outfielder, which would likely be his fate if he doesn't make it in center field. If everything comes together, he'll be a top-of-the-order table-setter and everyday center fielder. He'll start 2014 at Double-A Akron.

Year	Club (League)	Class	AVG	G	AB	R	H	2B	3B	HR	RBI	BB	SO	SB	CS	OBP	SLG
2012	Mahoning Valley (NYP)	SS	.270	36	137	22	37	11	2	0	13	17	26	4	3	.379	.380
2013	Carolina (CAR)	HiA	.277	108	448	69	124	27	6	9	42	41	112	14	7	.345	.424
	Akron (EL)	AA	.225	18	80	9	18	3	0	1	6	5	22	1	3	.271	.300
Minor League Totals			.269	162	665	100	179	41	8	10	61	63	160	19	13	.344	.400

5 CODY ANDERSON, RHP

BA GRADE
50
MEDIUM

Born: Sept. 14, 1990. **B-T:** R-R. **Ht.:** 6-4. **Wt.:** 220. **Drafted:** Feather River (Calif.) JC, 2011 (14th round). **Signed by:** Don Lyle.

Anderson dabbled in pitching in high school but spent most of his time in the outfield, along with playing football and basketball. He eventually moved to the mound full-time at Feather River (Calif.) JC, though only as a reliever. His career took off in 2013, when he won pitcher of the year awards for both the high Class A Carolina League and the Indians' organization. From the beginning, the Indians believed in Anderson's ability to be a starter thanks to his easy, repeatable delivery and variety of pitches. He generates nice downhill plane on his plus fastball that reaches 95 mph and sits in the low 90s. His slider and curveball are solid if unspectacular. The slider stepped forward last season once Anderson stopped trying to guide it into the strike zone and used it more aggressively, improving its bite and making it a swing-and-miss offering. His changeup needs the most work, but he does show some feel for it and has good arm speed with it. He doesn't have any issues with his delivery and already has solid command. Anderson looked tired by the time he got a late season promotion to Double-A Akron in 2013, and he'll go back there to open 2014. The Indians have watched his innings carefully, and he should top 150 for the first time as he attempts to fulfill his potential as a mid-rotation starter.

Year	Club (League)	Class	W	L	ERA	G	GS	CG	SV	IP	H	HR	BB	SO	K/9	WHIP	AVG
2011	Mahoning Valley (NYP)	SS	0	0	1.80	3	1	0	0	5	4	0	4	3	5.4	1.60	.235
2012	Lake County (MWL)	LoA	4	7	3.20	24	23	0	0	98	92	8	29	72	6.6	1.23	.249
2013	Carolina (CAR)	HiA	9	4	2.34	23	23	0	0	123	105	6	31	112	8.2	1.10	.236
	Akron (EL)	AA	0	0	5.68	3	3	0	0	13	16	2	9	10	7.1	1.97	.320
Minor League Totals			13	11	2.86	53	50	0	0	239	217	16	73	197	7.4	1.21	.246

6 DORSSYS PAULINO, SS

BA GRADE
55
EXTREME

Born: Nov. 21, 1994. **B-T:** R-R. **Ht.:** 6-0. **Wt.:** 175. **Signed:** Dominican Republic, 2011. **Signed by:** Ramon Pena/Claudio Brito/Felix Nivar.

One of the most sought-after bats on the 2011 international market, Paulino landed with the Indians for $1.1 million. He was among the youngest players in the low Class A Midwest League in 2013 at age 18 and struggled to adjust to the cold weather early in the season. His numbers fell into a hole, though he did recover to hit .281 in August. Despite Paulino's down year, the Indians remain excited about his upside. He has strong hands and can whip the bat through the zone. His hands are quick enough that he can let balls travel deep and smash line drives to all fields. He has some raw power though it's mainly to the gaps. When he's going well, Paulino does a good job of staying inside the ball, but last season he pressed too much to get out of his funk and got over-aggressive. He's a solid runner underway, but he lacks a quick first step. Paulino probably will face a move to second base at some point, though the Indians will keep him at shortstop for the time being. His arm is playable there but his range is fringy. He made 39 errors in 2013, the most among MWL shortstops, as he struggled with his footwork and internal clock. Even if Paulino does have to move over to second base, he has the tools to be an offensive asset. He still has to conquer the MWL though, and he'll go back to Lake County to open 2014.

Year	Club (League)	Class	AVG	G	AB	R	H	2B	3B	HR	RBI	BB	SO	SB	CS	OBP	SLG
2012	Indians (AZL)	R	.355	41	172	42	61	14	6	6	30	15	31	9	1	.404	.610
	Mahoning Valley (NYP)	SS	.271	15	59	5	16	5	0	1	8	3	14	2	1	.306	.407
2013	Lake County (MWL)	LoA	.246	120	476	56	117	28	3	5	46	30	91	12	7	.297	.349
Minor League Totals			.274	176	707	103	194	47	9	12	84	48	136	23	9	.324	.417

7 RONNY RODRIGUEZ, SS/2B

Born: April 17, 1992. **B-T:** R-R. **Ht.:** 6-0. **Wt.:** 170. **Signed:** Dominican Republic, 2010. **Signed by:** Ramon Pena/Miguel Valdez.

Growing up, Rodriguez spent several years living in the U.S., and he even attended high school in the States. He eventually relocated back to his native Dominican Republic and signed with the Indians for $375,000 in 2010. Rodriguez came straight to the U.S. for his pro debut in 2011, and he's been young for his league at each stop in the system. He has as much or more pure athleticism as any Indians middle-infield prospect, including Francisco Lindor, but he lacks polish. He has quick-twitch ability and generates plenty of bat speed. His home run output dropped markedly from 2012, though Cleveland chalks this up at least partly to Double-A Akron's stingy Canal Park. Rodriguez is wiry strong and leverages balls well, and he should be capable of solid-average power. His inexperience shows up in his overly aggressive plate approach. He has the bat-to-ball skills to make consistent contact to all fields, but he's tough to walk and doesn't show much ability to adjust with two strikes. Rodriguez played shortstop until moving over to second base upon Lindor's arrival in Akron. He has the pure tools for shortstop, with plus range, quick hands and a strong-enough arm. While he's unlikely to beat out Lindor for the shortstop's job, Rodriguez has the athleticism to shift to several other positions. His ultimate defensive home remains in question as he heads to Triple-A Columbus in 2014.

Year	Club (League)	Class	AVG	G	AB	R	H	2B	3B	HR	RBI	BB	SO	SB	CS	OBP	SLG
2011	Lake County (MWL)	LoA	.246	98	370	41	91	28	7	11	42	13	83	10	7	.274	.449
2012	Carolina (CAR)	HiA	.264	126	454	67	120	20	4	19	66	19	88	7	7	.300	.452
2013	Akron (EL)	AA	.265	116	468	62	124	25	6	5	52	16	76	12	3	.291	.376
Minor League Totals			.259	340	1292	170	335	73	17	35	160	48	247	29	17	.289	.423

8 C.C. LEE, RHP

Born: Oct. 21, 1986. **B-T:** R-R. **Ht.:** 5-11. **Wt.:** 190. **Signed:** Taiwan, 2008. **Signed by:** Jason Lee.

Lee finally made his long-awaited major league debut in 2013 at age 26. Cleveland signed him for $400,000 in 2008 and he made his way through the system smoothly until 2012, when he went down early in the season and needed Tommy John surgery. After getting back on the mound in May, Lee received two big league callups in 2013. A sinker/slider reliever, he throws from a low three-quarters slot with deception. He has plus velocity on his fastball, ranging from 92-96 mph with late sinking and running life. His slider doesn't have a ton of depth but its good, late bite makes it tough for righthanders to handle. Coming off T.J. surgery, Lee was a bit tentative with his slider early in the year but it looked impressive by the end. He does have a little splitter he can use against lefties, but he's primarily a two-pitch pitcher. Control isn't a problem, but he does need to tighten his fastball command to give himself a better chance against lefthanders. Lee should pitch in the majors again in 2014, though he'll have to compete for a job in the bullpen in spring training. He has good stuff but may end up filling a situational role if he doesn't hone his command.

Year	Club (League)	Class	W	L	ERA	G	GS	CG	SV	IP	H	HR	BB	SO	K/9	WHIP	AVG
2009	Kinston (CAR)	HiA	4	6	3.35	45	0	0	2	83	67	5	28	97	10.5	1.14	.220
2010	Akron (EL)	AA	5	4	3.22	44	0	0	0	73	59	6	22	82	10.2	1.11	.219
2011	Akron (EL)	AA	2	1	2.50	23	0	0	0	40	27	1	11	56	12.7	0.96	.196
	Columbus (IL)	AAA	4	0	2.27	21	0	0	1	32	26	2	12	43	12.2	1.20	.228
2012	Columbus (IL)	AAA	2	0	2.57	5	0	0	0	7	5	1	1	8	10.3	0.86	.208
2013	Lake County (MWL)	LoA	0	0	0.00	2	0	0	0	2	1	0	1	4	18.0	1.00	.167
	Akron (EL)	AA	0	0	3.38	8	0	0	0	8	3	0	4	9	10.1	0.88	.111
	Columbus (IL)	AAA	1	0	2.37	19	0	0	0	19	14	1	5	24	11.4	1.00	.212
	Cleveland (AL)	MAJ	0	0	4.15	8	0	0	0	4	4	0	3	4	8.3	1.62	.250
Major League Totals			0	0	4.15	8	0	0	0	4	4	0	3	4	8.3	1.62	.250
Minor League Totals			18	11	2.94	167	0	0	3	263	202	16	84	323	11.0	1.09	.213

9 JOSE RAMIREZ, 2B/SS

BA GRADE
45
MEDIUM

Born: Sept. 17, 1992. **B-T:** B-R. **Ht.:** 5-9. **Wt.:** 165. **Signed:** Dominican Republic, 2009. **Signed by:** Lino Diaz/Omar Rogers.

Ramirez has made a rapid ascent through the system, going from the Midwest League to the majors in the span of a year. After he finished 2012 strong with low Class A Lake County, Ramirez went on to hit .312 over the winter in the Dominican League, which spurred the Indians to skip him over high Class A. He held his own as a 20-year-old in Double-A, and Cleveland gave him a September callup in the heat of the playoff race. Ramirez's speed and on-base skills are his biggest assets. He has a smooth swing from both sides of the plate and sprays line drives to all fields. He does have some pull-side power, more so as a righthanded hitter, but home runs aren't part of his game. Ramirez excels at working counts and rarely chases. Though Ramirez has plus speed and led the Eastern League in steals (38), he wasn't particularly efficient and tended to be too aggressive. Ramirez has the athleticism and versatility to play second base, third base or shortstop, but second is the only spot where he profiles as a regular. His hands work well and he has smooth actions, but he lacks the arm for shortstop or power for third. The game never speeds up on Ramirez, and the major league staff raved about his energy. A left thumb injury in winter ball could slow him in spring training, so after getting a taste of the majors, he'll begin 2014 at Triple-A Columbus to add more polish.

Year	Club (League)	Class	AVG	G	AB	R	H	2B	3B	HR	RBI	BB	SO	SB	CS	OBP	SLG
2010	Did not play																
2011	Indians (AZL)	R	.325	48	194	30	63	13	4	1	20	7	17	12	6	.351	.448
2012	Mahoning Valley (NYP)	SS	.364	3	11	2	4	2	0	0	0	1	0	2	1	.417	.545
	Lake County (MWL)	LoA	.354	67	277	54	98	13	4	3	27	24	26	15	6	.403	.462
2013	Akron (EL)	AA	.272	113	482	78	131	16	6	3	38	39	41	38	16	.325	.349
	Cleveland (AL)	MAJ	.333	15	12	5	4	0	1	0	0	2	2	0	1	.429	.500
Major League Totals			.333	15	12	5	4	0	1	0	0	2	2	0	1	.429	.500
Minor League Totals			.307	231	964	164	296	44	14	7	85	71	84	67	29	.354	.404

10 AUSTIN ADAMS, RHP

BA GRADE
45
MEDIUM

Born: Aug. 19, 1986. **B-T:** R-R. **Ht.:** 5-11. **Wt.:** 190. **Drafted:** Faulkner (Ala.), 2009 (5th round). **Signed by:** Chuck Bartlett.

The Brewers liked Adams enough as a shortstop prospect to take him in the 27th round in 2008, but he passed on signing to continue playing both ways at NAIA Faulkner (Ala.). Cleveland's fifth-round pick in 2009, this time as a pitcher, he rated as one of the Indians' best pitching prospects after the 2011 season, but shoulder surgery cost him all of 2012 and his road to the majors has been rerouted to the bullpen. The high-90s velocity he showed before his injury has come all the way back, as he pitched with his fastball at 95-97 mph with cutting action. Adams also still has the depth to his repertoire from his days as a starter. His curveball and changeup have the best chances to be quality offerings from among his secondary pitches, and he can mix in an early-count slider as well. He's a good athlete but isn't overly physical. The Indians believe Adams will have better command than his walk figures from last season suggest (4.7 per nine), but he has effort to his delivery and his ability to locate is unlikely to ever be more than average. Adams has the power arm to be a late-inning option, and he joined the 40-man roster after the 2013 season. He'll begin 2014 at Triple-A Columbus.

Year	Club (League)	Class	W	L	ERA	G	GS	CG	SV	IP	H	HR	BB	SO	K/9	WHIP	AVG
2009	Mahoning Valley (NYP)	SS	3	1	4.86	17	0	0	1	37	39	4	15	29	7.1	1.46	.269
2010	Lake County (MWL)	LoA	2	4	3.54	13	8	0	1	53	40	7	21	61	10.3	1.14	—
	Kinston (CAR)	HiA	6	1	1.53	13	12	0	0	59	50	5	15	51	7.8	1.11	.228
2011	Akron (EL)	AA	11	10	3.77	26	26	0	0	136	147	6	63	131	8.7	1.54	.280
2013	Akron (EL)	AA	3	2	2.62	45	0	0	4	55	44	3	29	76	12.4	1.33	.215
Minor League Totals			25	18	3.28	114	46	0	6	340	320	25	143	348	9.2	1.36	.248

11 KYLE CROCKETT, LHP

BA GRADE
45
MEDIUM

Born: Dec. 15, 1991. **B-T:** L-L. **Ht.:** 6-2. **Wt.:** 170. **Drafted:** Virginia, 2013 (4th round). **Signed by:** Bob Mayer.

Crockett enjoyed a sterling three-year run at Virginia, posting the second-best career ERA (1.98) in school history. He assumed the closer's role as a junior and racked up 12 saves. The Indians signed him for $463,600 as their 2013 fourth-round pick. Pegged as one of the players closest to the big leagues in the entire draft class, Crockett lived up to his billing, reaching Double-A Akron just two months after the draft. He doesn't have overwhelming velocity, working at 88-89 mph and topping out at 92, but what he has plays up because of the life and deception he gets on his fastball. He hides the ball well, and he can locate his fastball with sink wherever he wants. He goes to a late-breaking slider as his second pitch. The Indians moved him towards the first base side of the rubber after he signed, which helped him get a better angle on the slider against lefthanders. If he commands the fastball to both sides of the plate, Crockett can be more than a left-on-left reliever because he also has a changeup he can use on occasion. He might go back to Akron to start 2014 but is the clear favorite to be the first of the Indians' 2013 draft class to reach the majors.

Year	Club (League)	Class	W	L	ERA	G	GS	CG	SV	IP	H	HR	BB	SO	K/9	WHIP	AVG
2013	Mahoning Valley (NYP)	SS	0	0	0.00	8	0	0	0	9	5	0	2	16	15.4	0.75	.152
	Lake County (MWL)	LoA	0	0	1.80	4	0	0	0	5	4	1	1	7	12.6	1.00	.211
	Akron (EL)	AA	1	0	0.00	9	0	0	0	10	7	0	2	9	7.8	0.87	.200
Minor League Totals			1	0	0.36	21	0	0	0	25	16	1	5	32	11.7	0.85	.184

12 FRANCISCO MEJIA, C

BA GRADE 55 EXTREME

Born: Oct. 27, 1995. **B-T:** B-R. **Ht.:** 5-10. **Wt.:** 175. **Signed:** Dominican Republic, 2012. **Signed by:** Ramon Pena.

The Indians haven't shied away from skipping their high-profile Latin American prospects over the Dominican Summer League, and Mejia is another example. Cleveland brought him to the Rookie-level Arizona League in 2013, and he quickly showed why Cleveland spent $350,000 to sign him. A natural hitter, he already has a good idea at the plate and a quality swing with few moving parts that allows him to stay inside the ball consistently. He has decent raw power, though it shows up more often in batting practice and he focuses on an up-the-middle approach in games. While Mejia has plenty of promise at the plate, he's extremely raw behind it. His greatest strength is a throwing arm that receives a few 70 grades on the 20-80 scouting scale, but he allowed 11 passed balls in 25 games at catcher in his debut. He often played second base as an amateur and his technique as a catcher needs plenty of development. To his credit, he's embraced the position and doesn't take bad at-bats with him into the field. He shows some leadership qualities and his work ethic won over pitchers despite his struggles. Mejia will stay in extended spring training in 2014 to keep working on his catching before going to the short-season New York-Penn League.

Year	Club (League)	Class	AVG	G	AB	R	H	2B	3B	HR	RBI	BB	SO	SB	CS	OBP	SLG
2013	Indians (AZL)	R	.305	30	105	16	32	9	1	4	24	5	18	3	1	.348	.524
Minor League Totals			.305	30	105	16	32	9	1	4	24	5	18	3	1	.348	.524

13 LUIGI RODRIGUEZ, OF

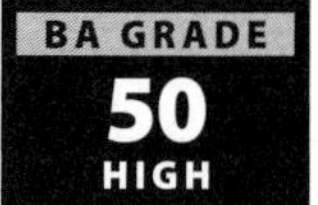

Born: Nov. 13, 1992. **B-T:** B-R. **Ht.:** 5-11. **Wt.:** 160. **Signed:** Dominican Republic, 2009. **Signed by:** Lino Diaz.

After three stints in low Class A, Rodriguez made it to high Class A Carolina at the end of April 2013, but his stay lasted just 34 games. A left (non-throwing) shoulder problem nagged him, and the Indians shut him down in the second half. When he's going well, he shows a smooth, compact swing with a nice bat path. Home runs won't be his forte, but he does have surprising pop for his size and lashes balls into both gaps. Plate discipline has been an issue, however, and the switch-hitter battles a tendency to get out on his front foot, particularly in his lefthanded swing. Rodriguez played center field at low Class A Lake County but shifted to left with Carolina due to Tyler Naquin's presence. Despite the move, Rodriguez can be a quality center fielder in his own right. His routes need some improvement but his plus speed allows him to make up for mistakes. He has a strong arm as well. Rodriguez was able to get back on the field in instructional league and should be good to go in 2014, which he'll open back in Carolina.

Year	Club (League)	Class	AVG	G	AB	R	H	2B	3B	HR	RBI	BB	SO	SB	CS	OBP	SLG
2010	Indians (DSL)	R	.301	63	206	43	62	7	10	2	27	36	35	31	9	.403	.461
2011	Indians (AZL)	R	.379	25	95	18	36	6	2	3	14	5	19	12	5	.408	.579
	Lake County (MWL)	LoA	.250	34	132	10	33	4	2	0	5	14	36	6	5	.320	.311
2012	Lake County (MWL)	LoA	.268	117	463	75	124	21	5	11	48	50	133	24	9	.338	.406
2013	Lake County (MWL)	LoA	.263	22	76	14	20	2	0	1	9	10	25	5	3	.345	.329
	Carolina (CAR)	HiA	.283	34	113	16	32	11	1	0	11	18	36	3	4	.383	.398
Minor League Totals			.283	295	1085	176	307	51	20	17	114	133	284	81	35	.360	.414

14 CARLOS MONCRIEF, OF

BA GRADE 50 HIGH

Born: Nov. 3, 1988. **B-T:** L-R. **Ht.:** 6-0. **Wt.:** 219. **Drafted:** Chipola (Fla.) JC, 2008 (14th round). **Signed by:** Chuck Bartlett.

Moncrief's stock took off in 2013, eventually landing him a spot on Cleveland's 40-man roster. A two-way player at Chipola (Fla.) JC, he began his pro career on the mound but posted a 7.75 ERA over two seasons in Rookie ball. He shifted to the outfield in 2010 and has hit at least 15 homers in each of his three years in full-season ball. He tied for the organizational home run lead in 2013 with 17. Moncrief has the strength to hit home runs and a feel for the barrel, though most of his power comes to his pull side. His increased power came with increased contact, as he cut his strikeout rate from 31 percent of plate appearances in 2012 to 18 percent last season. Moncrief had a better plan at the plate and more experience under his belt, though he does need to show he can handle lefthanders after he hit just .215 against them in 2013. Scouts worry about a wrap in his swing, and he tends to open up early against lefties. He's at least an average runner and takes good routes in the outfield. He could throw 96 mph in his pitching days and his arm is a weapon in right field. The Indians will send him to Triple-A Columbus to open 2014.

Year	Club (League)	Class	W	L	ERA	G	GS	CG	SV	IP	H	HR	BB	SO	K/9	WHIP	AVG
2008	Indians (GCL)	R	0	0	13.50	9	0	0	0	6	9	1	10	4	6.0	3.17	.346
2009	Indians (AZL)	R	1	2	6.51	19	0	0	0	28	30	0	12	39	12.7	1.52	.275
Minor League Totals			1	2	7.75	28	0	0	0	34	39	1	22	43	11.5	1.81	.289

Year	Club (League)	Class	AVG	G	AB	R	H	2B	3B	HR	RBI	BB	SO	SB	CS	OBP	SLG
2010	Mahoning Valley (NYP)	SS	.241	66	245	30	59	11	4	5	21	27	56	7	5	.324	.380
	Kinston (CAR)	HiA	.111	5	9	1	1	1	0	0	0	1	4	0	0	.200	.222
2011	Lake County (MWL)	LoA	.233	122	464	73	108	26	7	16	53	76	158	20	7	.346	.422
2012	Carolina (CAR)	HiA	.249	101	353	57	88	23	4	15	53	46	126	17	2	.339	.465
2013	Akron (EL)	AA	.284	129	489	77	139	26	7	17	75	55	98	15	7	.354	.470
Minor League Totals			.253	423	1560	238	395	87	22	53	202	205	442	59	21	.343	.439

15 JESUS AGUILAR, 1B

BA GRADE **45** MEDIUM

Born: June 30, 1990. **B-T:** R-R. **Ht.:** 6-3. **Wt.:** 250. **Signed:** Venezuela, 2007. **Signed by:** Jesus Mendoza.

Aguilar signed with the Indians at age 17 and took three years to get out of short-season ball, but he's made steady progress since 2011, when he broke out with 23 homers between two Class A levels. The Indians left him exposed to the Rule 5 draft after the 2012 season but didn't take that chance again and added him to the 40-man roster in 2013. Aguilar's future depends entirely on his bat. He has a hulking frame and well-above-average power, with the bat speed to handle velocity. He posted the lowest strikeout rate of his career in 2013 as he did a better job of getting into favorable counts and of staying back on offspeed pitches. Club officials also noted his ability to bear down with men on base. He led the Eastern League with 105 RBIs, hitting .229 with the bases empty versus .339 with runners in scoring position. Aguilar has good hands and is a better athlete than he looks, though unsurprisingly his speed still rates below-average, as does his throwing arm. He led EL first basemen with 14 errors. Aguilar sticks out as the best power bat the Indians have in the upper levels of the system. He'll have to overcome the tough profile of being a righthanded-hitting first baseman, so he'll need to put up big numbers at Triple-A Columbus in 2014.

Year	Club (League)	Class	AVG	G	AB	R	H	2B	3B	HR	RBI	BB	SO	SB	CS	OBP	SLG
2008	Indians (DSL)	R	.209	68	235	23	49	12	0	4	45	23	29	4	3	.286	.311
2009	Indians (DSL)	R	.305	55	200	33	61	16	0	5	46	31	24	5	1	.412	.460
2010	Indians (AZL)	R	.259	29	112	15	29	2	1	7	22	5	33	1	1	.293	.482
	Mahoning Valley (NYP)	SS	.244	32	123	8	30	9	0	2	17	11	28	2	0	.301	.366
2011	Lake County (MWL)	LoA	.292	95	349	58	102	27	2	19	69	35	98	1	0	.370	.544
	Kinston (CAR)	HiA	.257	31	113	12	29	3	0	4	13	11	28	1	0	.323	.389
2012	Carolina (CAR)	HiA	.277	107	368	63	102	25	2	12	58	45	91	0	1	.365	.454
	Akron (EL)	AA	.292	20	72	12	21	6	0	3	13	13	24	0	0	.402	.500
2013	Akron (EL)	AA	.275	130	499	66	137	28	0	16	105	56	107	0	1	.349	.427
Minor League Totals			.270	567	2071	290	560	128	5	72	388	230	462	14	7	.349	.441

16 DACE KIME, RHP

BA GRADE **50** HIGH

Born: March 6, 1992. **B-T:** R-R. **Ht.:** 6-4. **Wt.:** 200. **Drafted:** Louisville, 2013 (3rd round). **Signed by:** Junie Melendez.

Kime had been on the Indians' radar since his high school days in the northwestern Ohio town of Defiance. He wound up being taken in the eighth round by the Pirates in 2010 but opted to attend Louisville. Kime was in and out of the Cardinals' rotation as a junior but had his best season, going 6-1, 2.99 to help Louisville reach the College World Series and net himself a $525,000 bonus in the third round from the Indians. Cleveland saw a potential starter in Kime thanks to his four-pitch mix, clean delivery and durable frame. His fastball reached 95 mph as a reliever and sat 90-92 in a starting role. The heater doesn't have much movement, which puts a premium on his fringy command. He does command his curveball well and it has the makings of a plus pitch with 12-to-6 bite. He also has a hard slider that acts similarly to a cutter—and sometimes gets labeled as one—along with a work-in-progress changeup. The changeup shows some fading movement, but it atrophied a bit when he was a reliever. Kime has the tools to be a mid-rotation starter and should open 2014 in the low Class A Lake County rotation.

Year	Club (League)	Class	W	L	ERA	G	GS	CG	SV	IP	H	HR	BB	SO	K/9	WHIP	AVG
2013	Mahoning Valley (NYP)	SS	0	2	2.92	9	9	0	0	25	19	0	16	26	9.5	1.42	.224
Minor League Totals			0	2	2.92	9	9	0	0	25	19	0	16	26	9.5	1.42	.224

17 JOE WENDLE, 2B

BA GRADE **45** MEDIUM

Born: April 26, 1990. **B-T:** L-R. **Ht.:** 5-11. **Wt.:** 190. **Drafted:** West Chester (Pa.), 2012 (6th round). **Signed by:** Brent Urcheck.

Wendle finished his college career by leading West Chester (Pa.) to its first-ever NCAA Division II national championship in 2012. He cost the Indians just $10,000 as a sixth-round senior sign after batting .366 over four years in college, and he hasn't skipped a beat since turning pro. Wendle's hit tool might be the only one that's plus, but that could be enough to get him to the majors. He has a short, compact swing, an advanced feel for hitting and solid control of the strike zone. He probably will settle in around 10-12 homers per year at the upper levels, with more of his sock coming to his pull side. He has good hands and agility at second base to go with adequate range and arm strength. His speed rates as merely fringe-average. The organization loves Wendle's blue-collar mentality and top-shelf makeup. He finished 2013 by handling himself well in the Arizona Fall League and will move up to Double-A Akron in 2014. With Jason Kipnis in the majors and the Indians' depth of middle-infield prospects, he may have more luck as a utility player or trade bait.

Year	Club (League)	Class	AVG	G	AB	R	H	2B	3B	HR	RBI	BB	SO	SB	CS	OBP	SLG
2012	Mahoning Valley (NYP)	SS	.327	61	245	32	80	15	4	4	37	15	25	4	1	.375	.469
2013	Carolina (CAR)	HiA	.295	107	413	73	122	32	5	16	64	44	79	10	2	.372	.513
Minor League Totals			.307	168	658	105	202	47	9	20	101	59	104	14	3	.373	.497

18 ADAM PLUTKO, RHP

BA GRADE **45** MEDIUM

Born: Dec. 13, 1990. **B-T:** R-R. **Ht.:** 6-2. **Wt.:** 205. **Drafted:** UCLA, 2013 (11th round). **Signed by:** Carlos Muniz.

Plutko stepped out of the shadows of Gerrit Cole and Trevor Bauer to lead the UCLA program to even greater heights than did the two more ballyhooed top-three picks. Taking over as the Bruins' No. 1 starter in 2012, Plutko established himself as a dominant big-game pitcher while helping UCLA to its first national championship in 2013. Shortly after being named Most Outstanding Player at the College World Series, Plutko collected a $300,000 bonus from the Indians, the fourth-largest in Cleveland's draft class. He had already thrown 124 innings during the college season, so the Indians chose to shut him down after signing him. Plutko gets by without plus velocity, but he offers four average pitches and the moxie to get his stuff to play up. He works at 87-91 mph, though the Indians do think he could add some velocity once he gets on a professional throwing program. His changeup gets the highest marks of his three secondary pitches, which also include a curveball and slider. He doesn't rely on any one pitch though. He has superb command, an intelligent pitching mind and a repeatable delivery. Plutko's stuff may not make him more than a No. 4 starter at the major league level, but he has a good chance to move through the system quickly.

Year	Club (League)	Class	W	L	ERA	G	GS	CG	SV	IP	H	HR	BB	SO	K/9	WHIP	AVG
2013	Did not play																

19 ERIK GONZALEZ, SS

BA GRADE **50** HIGH

Born: Aug. 31, 1991. **B-T:** R-R. **Ht.:** 6-1. **Wt.:** 165. **Signed:** Dominican Republic, 2008. **Signed by:** Andres Garcia.

With the Indians' glut of middle-infield prospects, Gonzalez flew under the radar until 2013. Part of that is because he simply hadn't played shortstop since 2010 in the Dominican Summer League, instead seeing time at third base, first base and the outfield. He played third again in 2013 at low Class A Lake County before finally getting his chance at shortstop following a promotion to high Class A Carolina in July, taking over the spot vacated by Francisco Lindor's move to Double-A. The Indians had always liked Gonzalez's athleticism, but he took time to grow into his gangly body. He has the tools to stick at shortstop with his good hands, lateral agility and above-average arm. Gonzalez's defensive abilities prompted Cleveland to add him to its 40-man roster, but his bat has a long way to go. He has a balanced stroke with line-drive power, but he uses a high leg kick that disrupts his timing. He can hit a fastball, though he cheats at times, leaving him vulnerable to breaking pitches which he struggles to recognize. He's a slightly-above-average runner underway, but his speed doesn't translate into stolen bases. He tore up winter ball in the Dominican and should move quickly if he keeps progressing, but he'll begin 2014 back at Carolina.

Year	Club (League)	Class	AVG	G	AB	R	H	2B	3B	HR	RBI	BB	SO	SB	CS	OBP	SLG
2009	Indians (DSL)	R	.248	61	234	33	58	9	3	0	27	15	36	14	2	.307	.312
2010	Indians (DSL)	R	.346	64	240	38	83	18	1	1	27	14	19	9	4	.384	.442
2011	Indians (AZL)	R	.258	41	159	28	41	2	3	2	14	12	31	5	1	.316	.346
2012	Mahoning Valley (NYP)	SS	.220	60	214	30	47	9	1	2	18	11	50	9	1	.264	.299
2013	Lake County (MWL)	LoA	.259	93	355	59	92	23	7	9	49	24	71	10	4	.307	.439
	Carolina (CAR)	HiA	.242	39	153	16	37	9	5	0	27	5	38	1	2	.259	.366
Minor League Totals			.264	358	1355	204	358	70	20	14	162	81	245	48	14	.310	.376

20 ANTHONY SANTANDER, OF

Born: Oct. 19, 1994. **B-T:** B-R. **Ht.:** 6-2. **Wt.:** 187. **Signed:** Venezuela, 2011. **Signed by:** Ramon Pena/Antonio Caballero.

Santander landed one of the Indians' largest international signing bonuses in 2011 at $385,000. The team wasn't surprised by his early-season struggles in 2013 in the cold weather of the low Class A Midwest League, a tough assignment for the 18-year-old, and his bat had started coming around before a right elbow injury cut his season short. Santander's body type and swing draw comparisons with current Indians outfielder Michael Brantley. He has similar raw power as well but should have a better chance to get to it in games. He does show some feel for hitting, along with quiet hands at the plate and a naturally powerful stroke, giving him the potential for average raw power. Santander didn't take up switch-hitting until about a year before he turned pro, and his lefthanded swing looks further ahead than his righty swing. He's played on an outfield corner exclusively as a pro. He's a decent athlete and his slightly above-average arm gives him a shot to stick in right field. Santander has a chance to earn a spot on high Class A Carolina's roster, but he most likely will open 2014 back in the MWL, where he'd still be young for the level as a 19-year-old.

Year	Club (League)	Class	AVG	G	AB	R	H	2B	3B	HR	RBI	BB	SO	SB	CS	OBP	SLG
2012	Indians (AZL)	R	.305	43	154	27	47	15	1	4	32	13	37	6	3	.381	.494
2013	Lake County (MWL)	LoA	.242	61	219	27	53	13	0	5	31	13	43	6	3	.303	.370
Minor League Totals			.268	104	373	54	100	28	1	9	63	26	80	12	6	.336	.421

21 LUIS LUGO, LHP

Born: March 5, 1994. **B-T:** L-L. **Ht.:** 6-5. **Wt.:** 200. **Signed:** Venezuela, 2011. **Signed by:** Ramon Pena/Antonio Caballero.

Lugo took some extra time to find a landing spot after becoming eligible to sign with clubs in July 2010, eventually netting a $415,000 bonus from the Indians in February 2011. He was the youngest member of short-season Mahoning Valley's pitching staff in 2013 at age 19, yet he pitched like its ace, allowing one earned run or fewer in nine of 11 starts for the Scrappers. Something of a late bloomer, Lugo has physicality in his 6-foot-5 frame that sets him apart from most teenagers. He works mainly at 89-91 mph and tops out at 93 with his fastball, and his size and strength allow for projection, especially as he learns to use his lower half. He throws downhill and doesn't have any trouble throwing strikes. Lugo should have the repertoire to remain a starter. He needs to firm up his curveball, as he tends to just flip it up to the plate at times, but he flashes a 12-to-6 downer. He gets good arm speed on his changeup and shows some feel for using it. The Indians laud Lugo's pitching aptitude, and his English has come along well. After making a cameo with low Class A Lake County at the end of 2013, he'll head back there to open 2014.

Year	Club (League)	Class	W	L	ERA	G	GS	CG	SV	IP	H	HR	BB	SO	K/9	WHIP	AVG
2011	Indians (DSL)	R	0	3	3.38	9	7	0	0	29	21	3	16	36	11.0	1.26	.194
	Indians (AZL)	R	0	2	6.14	3	2	0	0	7	10	1	8	8	9.8	2.45	.303
2012	Indians (AZL)	R	2	4	4.50	11	10	0	0	42	38	4	21	51	10.9	1.40	.242
2013	Mahoning Valley (NYP)	SS	1	4	1.97	11	11	0	0	50	39	1	11	30	5.4	0.99	.222
	Lake County (MWL)	LoA	0	1	3.77	3	3	0	0	14	14	1	5	14	8.8	1.33	.250
Minor League Totals			3	14	3.39	37	33	0	0	143	122	10	61	139	8.7	1.28	.230

22 SHAWN MORIMANDO, LHP

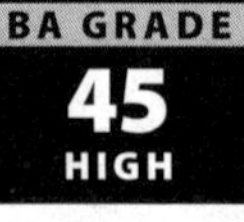

Born: Nov. 11, 1992. **B-T:** L-L. **Ht.:** 5-11. **Wt.:** 170. **Drafted:** HS—Virginia Beach, 2011 (19th round). **Signed by:** Bob Mayer.

Given his wiry frame and fastball that operated in the 87-91 mph range as a high school senior, Morimando lasted until the 19th round of the 2011 draft. Cleveland convinced him to give up an East Carolina commitment with a $350,000 bonus, and he's done nothing but perform as a pro. Morimando was the second-youngest player on high Class A Carolina's Opening Day roster last season, older than only Francisco Lindor, yet he posted a 2.71 ERA in the first half before tailing off. Embracing the organization's strength and conditioning programs, Morimando has added a few ticks to his fastball, now getting it up to 94 mph and sitting at 90-92. He spins a tight curveball with depth that looks like it has the makings of an average pitch, and he made strides with his changeup. He can also mix in a short slider. Morimando's 76 walks were the second-most in the Carolina League, as his control needs tightening and he tends to nibble. He's athletic with a low-effort delivery, though, and his command should be solid in time. Morimando lacks a plus pitch but has a chance to have four average pitches. He'll reach Double-A Akron as a 21-year-old in 2014.

Year	Club (League)	Class	W	L	ERA	G	GS	CG	SV	IP	H	HR	BB	SO	K/9	WHIP	AVG
2011	Indians (AZL)	R	0	0	3.00	3	0	0	0	6	5	0	2	8	12.0	1.17	.227
2012	Lake County (MWL)	LoA	7	6	3.59	22	22	1	0	110	96	11	52	69	5.6	1.34	.239
2013	Carolina (CAR)	HiA	8	13	3.73	27	27	1	0	135	115	8	76	102	6.8	1.41	.231
Minor League Totals			15	19	3.65	52	49	2	0	251	216	19	130	179	6.4	1.38	.235

23 CASEY SHANE, RHP

Born: Aug. 23, 1995. **B-T:** R-R. **Ht.:** 6-4. **Wt.:** 200. **Drafted:** HS—Burleson, Texas, 2013 (6th round). **Signed by:** Mark Allen.

Shane attracted crowds of scouts at the 2012 World Wood Bat Championship and ranked as the second-best high school pitcher in Texas going into 2013. However, he fell out of shape over the winter and his stuff wasn't the same during his senior season at Centennial High. He fell to the sixth round of the draft, but the Indians believed enough in his ability to bounce back to spend $150,000 to buy him out of a Texas A&M commitment. When going well, Shane showed 92-94 mph velocity with sinking life, though his fastball dropped into the 87-91 range last spring. His changeup and slider both show promise when he has them working, and he has a feel for using them. He doesn't always get the right shape on the slider, but it can be a swing-and-miss pitch at times. He can also throw an early-count curveball to give hitters a different look. Shane has a smooth, repeatable delivery that portends a future as a solid strike-thrower once he learns to repeat his delivery. Getting back in shape takes precedent over anything else for 2014, when he'll stay in extended spring training before embarking on an assignment to short-season Mahoning Valley.

Year	Club (League)	Class	W	L	ERA	G	GS	CG	SV	IP	H	HR	BB	SO	K/9	WHIP	AVG
2013	Indians (AZL)	R	1	1	6.52	11	3	0	1	29	33	1	16	22	6.8	1.69	.282
Minor League Totals			1	1	6.52	11	3	0	1	29	33	1	16	22	6.8	1.69	.282

24 MITCH BROWN, RHP

Born: April 13, 1994. **B-T:** R-R. **Ht.:** 6-1. **Wt.:** 195. **Drafted:** HS—Rochester, Minn., 2012 (2nd round). **Signed by:** Les Pajari.

The Indians signed Brown for $800,000 in 2012 after making him one of just two Minnesota high schoolers to go in the top two rounds of the draft since Joe Mauer went first overall in 2001. Cleveland believed he was ready to compete at the low Class A level in his first full year, but Brown was hit hard for five starts before going down with a biceps injury. In high school, Brown showed a solid four-pitch mix and topped out at 95 mph, but his stuff in 2013 was inconsistent as he struggled with his mechanics. Brown could still hit 93-94 mph at times but would pitch at 90-91 as he focused more on throwing strikes. When his delivery got out of sync, he would overcompensate and search to find a consistent release point. He tended to get too far out front and have his arm drag, which led to many fastballs missing high to his arm side. Unable to throw enough strikes with his fastball, Brown couldn't get to his secondary stuff. His three-quarters curveball has plus potential. He shows feel for using his changeup, and he also features a slider/cutter hybrid that's shown promise. In high school, Brown threw with a sound, repeatable delivery, and he appeared to get back to it in instructional league. He'll get another crack at the Midwest League in 2014.

Year	Club (League)	Class	W	L	ERA	G	GS	CG	SV	IP	H	HR	BB	SO	K/9	WHIP	AVG
2012	Indians (AZL)	R	2	0	3.58	8	8	0	0	28	20	3	10	26	8.5	1.08	.204
2013	Lake County (MWL)	LoA	1	1	11.49	5	5	0	0	16	21	4	11	18	10.3	2.04	.328
	Indians (AZL)	R	2	4	5.37	12	10	0	0	52	57	2	29	48	8.3	1.65	.284
Minor League Totals			5	5	5.85	25	23	0	0	95	98	9	50	92	8.7	1.55	.270

25 TONY WOLTERS, C

Born: June 9, 1992. **B-T:** L-R. **Ht.:** 5-10. **Wt.:** 177. **Drafted:** HS—Vista, Calif., 2010 (3rd round). **Signed by:** Jason Smith.

Wolters made a strong impression on Indians manager Terry Francona when he got to play in a few big league spring training games in 2013. Francona noted the then-second baseman Wolters' feel for hitting and physical similarity to Tigers catcher Alex Avila. Given Cleveland's surplus of middle infield prospects, the team decided to have Wolters make the move behind the plate. The recipient of a $1.35 million bonus in 2010, Wolters benefitted from working with Sandy Alomar Jr. in spring training and with high Class A Carolina manager Dave Wallace, another former catcher. Predictably, the transition wasn't easy, and scouts outside the organization were skeptical of his future, but the Indians believed by the end of the season that he played an acceptable catcher at the minor league level. Wolters is a good athlete who has quick hands and a strong arm that plays up thanks to a quick transfer. He still has much to learn, but he's embraced the move and the Indians love his work ethic and leadership qualities. He's a line-drive, gap-to-gap hitter who does a good job of controlling the strike zone. He'll run into some home runs but has below-average power. His profile as a lefty-hitting catcher would give him great value and reduces demands on his bat. He'll start 2014 at Double-A Akron.

Year	Club (League)	Class	AVG	G	AB	R	H	2B	3B	HR	RBI	BB	SO	SB	CS	OBP	SLG
2010	Indians (AZL)	R	.211	5	19	2	4	0	0	0	3	2	5	2	0	.286	.211
2011	Mahoning Valley (NYP)	SS	.292	69	267	50	78	10	3	1	20	30	49	19	4	.385	.363
2012	Carolina (CAR)	HiA	.260	125	485	66	126	30	8	8	58	36	104	5	9	.320	.404
2013	Carolina (CAR)	HiA	.277	80	289	36	80	13	0	3	33	41	58	3	6	.369	.353
Minor League Totals			.272	279	1060	154	288	53	11	12	114	109	216	29	19	.350	.376

26 SCOTT BARNES, LHP

BA GRADE 40 MEDIUM

Born: Sept. 5, 1987. **B-T:** L-L. **Ht.:** 6-4. **Wt.:** 200. **Drafted:** St. John's, 2008 (8th round). **Signed by:** John DiCarlo (Giants).

Barnes looked poised to be a key piece in the Indians' bullpen in 2013, but his season went off the rails at Triple-A Columbus. Barnes had pitched well in Cactus League games but was one of the last cuts from the big league roster. His confidence suffered and his delivery got out of whack, leading to a 7.81 ERA at Columbus before a left wrist sprain cost him most of the second half. A former starter the Indians acquired from the Giants for Ryan Garko in July 2009, Barnes has a reliever's delivery and converted to the bullpen in 2012 when he was coming off a torn left anterior cruciate ligament. When he's going well, Barnes' crossfire delivery can be hard for hitters to pick up, but it's complicated with a lot of moving parts, and his command fell apart last season. His fastball is a plus pitch from the left side, working at 91-93 mph with life and peaking as high as 95. He didn't always trust his fastball in 2013, though, while his delivery issues made it hard for him to work down in the zone. Barnes can show an 84-86 mph slider with plus, late bite at times, giving him a knockout weapon against lefthanders. He also has a seldom-used straight changeup. The Indians believe in Barnes' potential as a seventh- or eighth-inning reliever enough to keep him on the 40-man roster. He'll go back to spring training with another shot at the big league club.

Year	Club (League)	Class	W	L	ERA	G	GS	CG	SV	IP	H	HR	BB	SO	K/9	WHIP	AVG
2008	Giants (AZL)	R	0	1	3.38	3	0	0	0	5	3	0	4	11	18.6	1.31	.167
	Salem-Keizer (NWL)	SS	0	0	4.76	2	1	0	0	6	6	0	1	11	17.5	1.24	.250
	Augusta (SAL)	LoA	3	2	1.38	6	6	0	0	33	15	0	7	41	11.3	0.67	.133
2009	San Jose (CAL)	HiA	12	3	2.85	18	18	0	0	98	82	7	29	99	9.1	1.13	.227
	Kinston (CAR)	HiA	0	0	2.13	3	3	0	0	13	14	1	6	10	7.1	1.58	.280
	Akron (EL)	AA	2	2	5.68	6	6	0	0	32	35	7	14	29	8.2	1.55	.292
2010	Akron (EL)	AA	6	11	5.22	26	26	0	0	138	126	15	58	127	8.3	1.33	.241
2011	Akron (EL)	AA	1	0	1.64	2	2	0	0	11	5	0	2	17	13.9	0.64	.139
	Columbus (IL)	AAA	7	4	3.68	16	15	0	0	88	80	12	34	90	9.2	1.30	.240
2012	Columbus (IL)	AAA	2	3	3.98	31	3	0	2	52	37	1	23	67	11.6	1.15	.196
	Cleveland (AL)	MAJ	0	0	4.26	16	0	0	0	19	17	1	7	16	7.6	1.26	.236
2013	Cleveland (AL)	MAJ	0	1	7.27	6	0	0	1	9	8	3	3	10	10.4	1.27	.242
	Columbus (IL)	AAA	3	3	7.81	23	0	0	0	28	30	4	20	35	11.4	1.81	.286
	Indians (AZL)	R	0	0	27.00	1	1	0	0	1	3	1	0	0	0.0	3.00	.500
Major League Totals			0	1	5.20	22	0	0	1	28	25	4	10	26	8.5	1.27	.238
Minor League Totals			36	29	4.15	137	81	0	2	504	436	48	198	537	9.6	1.26	.232

27 NELSON RODRIGUEZ, 1B

BA GRADE 45 HIGH

Born: June 12, 1994. **B-T:** R-R. **Ht.:** 6-3. **Wt.:** 245. **Drafted:** HS—New York, 2012 (15th round). **Signed by:** Brent Urcheck.

An alum of George Washington High, the same New York high school that produced Manny Ramirez, Rodriguez signed for $100,000 in the 15th round in 2012. He did some catching as an amateur but quickly converted to first base full-time after signing. Rodriguez garners comparisons with Jesus Aguilar and faces the same challenges as a hefty, righthanded-hitting first baseman. He struggled to handle low Class A Lake County early in 2013 but rebounded to lead short-season Mahoning Valley with nine home runs. Nicknamed "Rhino," Rodriguez has plenty of raw power and the bat speed and strength to get around on good fastballs, though there's some length to his swing as well. His approach improved over the course of the season as he stopped trying to pull everything. The team was encouraged with his ability to hit breaking pitches the other way, and he also showed a willingness to take his walks once teams started pitching around him. Rodriguez impressed with his work ethic and intelligence, and he'll return to Lake County for another go in 2014.

Year	Club (League)	Class	AVG	G	AB	R	H	2B	3B	HR	RBI	BB	SO	SB	CS	OBP	SLG
2012	Indians (AZL)	R	.229	32	109	19	25	7	3	4	17	24	41	0	0	.375	.459
2013	Lake County (MWL)	LoA	.194	47	160	18	31	7	0	1	13	26	53	0	0	.305	.256
	Mahoning Valley (NYP)	SS	.287	73	261	32	75	16	0	9	37	29	61	0	2	.366	.452
Minor League Totals			.247	152	530	69	131	30	3	14	67	79	155	0	2	.350	.394

28 TREY HALEY, RHP

BA GRADE 45 HIGH

Born: June 21, 1990. **B-T:** R-R. **Ht.:** 6-4. **Wt.:** 205. **Drafted:** HS—Nacogdoches, Texas, 2008 (2nd round). **Signed by:** Kevin Cullen.

After receiving the largest bonus in the Indians' 2008 draft class at $1.25 million, Haley has been a tease. He may have the best pure stuff of any pitcher in the system, but he frustrates evaluators with an inability to stay healthy or throw the ball over the plate. His velocity picked up when the Indians moved him to relief in 2011. He can touch triple digits and sits easily in the mid-90s with late sinking action. He has a second plus pitch in his true curveball, a swing-and-miss pitch when he's able to set it up, and he can mix in some tight sliders as well. The Indians had Haley ditch throwing from the windup and go exclusively from the stretch at Double-A Akron in 2013 in an effort to help him throw strikes, yet his control issues were as bad as ever with a walk rate of nearly eight batters per nine innings. Haley throws with a violent delivery, landing hard on his front foot and finishing with a head whack. He doesn't help himself by often trying to overpower every hitter, and the Indians have encouraged him to throw more curveballs even early in counts. Haley has a laundry list of injuries in his past, including a sports hernia operation in 2012, but thus far he has avoided anything major. The Indians won't give up on his potential as an impact reliever until his time runs out.

Year	Club (League)	Class	W	L	ERA	G	GS	CG	SV	IP	H	HR	BB	SO	K/9	WHIP	AVG
2008	Indians (GCL)	R	0	0	0.00	1	1	0	0	1	0	0	1	1	9.0	1.00	.000
	Mahoning Valley (NYP)	SS	0	1	54.00	2	1	0	0	1	4	0	6	1	6.8	7.50	.571
2009	Lake County (SAL)	LoA	4	8	5.56	19	16	0	0	78	70	6	65	57	6.6	1.74	.241
2010	Lake County (MWL)	LoA	5	11	5.97	27	26	0	0	116	122	13	86	97	7.5	1.79	—
2011	Lake County (MWL)	LoA	0	0	2.84	8	2	0	1	13	5	0	8	17	12.1	1.03	.125
	Indians (AZL)	R	0	0	0.00	2	1	0	0	3	0	0	0	4	12.0	0.00	.000
	Kinston (CAR)	HiA	1	1	3.77	19	0	0	1	29	25	1	17	27	8.5	1.47	.240
2012	Indians (AZL)	R	1	0	7.50	4	0	0	0	6	8	0	2	10	15.0	1.67	.320
	Carolina (CAR)	HiA	0	0	1.04	12	0	0	2	17	8	0	6	16	8.3	0.81	.133
	Akron (EL)	AA	3	1	1.76	9	0	0	0	15	10	0	11	23	13.5	1.37	.189
2013	Akron (EL)	AA	1	4	4.70	39	0	0	7	44	37	0	39	46	9.4	1.73	.239
Minor League Totals			15	26	5.07	142	47	0	11	323	289	20	241	299	8.3	1.64	.243

29 SHAWN ARMSTRONG, RHP

Born: Sept. 11, 1990. **B-T:** R-R. **Ht.:** 6-2. **Wt.:** 210. **Drafted:** East Carolina, 2011 (18th round). **Signed by:** Bob Mayer.

Armstrong went into the spring of 2008 as the top high school pitcher in North Carolina, but a sore arm diminished his velocity and he turned down the Astros as a 33rd-round pick to go to East Carolina. An up-and-down junior season for the Pirates saw his draft stock fall again, and he lasted until the 18th round in 2011 when Cleveland snagged him. Armstrong finally seemed to put it all together in 2012, but a hand injury set him back in 2013. He tried to return too quickly and his velocity didn't come all the way back until the end of the year. After pitching at 88-91 mph early on, he was back up to the low 90s with sink in the fall, touching 96. Armstrong has a usable hard slider that rates as his best secondary pitch, and he can also throw a cutter and a changeup to attack lefthanded hitters. He's got a physical frame, and he tweaked his delivery to incorporate his lower half and stay more on line to the plate, helping his velocity pick up. Armstrong throws slightly across his body, and he needs to repeat his delivery more consistently. After posting a 1.59 ERA in the Arizona Fall League, he'll try to keep that momentum going as he returns to Double-A Akron in 2014. Armstrong could be a middle relief option for Cleveland in the near future if things come together.

Year	Club (League)	Class	W	L	ERA	G	GS	CG	SV	IP	H	HR	BB	SO	K/9	WHIP	AVG
2011	Mahoning Valley (NYP)	SS	0	0	0.00	1	0	0	0	2	1	0	0	2	9.0	0.50	.167
2012	Lake County (MWL)	LoA	0	0	0.00	2	0	0	0	4	1	0	2	4	9.8	0.82	.091
	Carolina (CAR)	HiA	1	3	2.06	26	0	0	1	44	31	0	23	52	10.7	1.24	.205
	Akron (EL)	AA	1	0	0.89	17	0	0	3	20	12	0	12	22	9.7	1.18	.176
2013	Indians (AZL)	R	0	0	4.50	3	0	0	0	4	3	1	0	5	11.3	0.75	.200
	Akron (EL)	AA	2	3	4.09	30	0	0	0	33	32	2	21	43	11.7	1.61	.252
Minor League Totals			4	6	2.45	79	0	0	4	107	80	3	58	128	10.8	1.29	.212

30 SEAN BRADY, LHP

BA GRADE
45
HIGH

Born: June 9, 1994. **B-T:** L-L. **Ht.:** 5-11. **Wt.:** 185. **Drafted:** HS—Cape Coral, Fla., 2013 (5th round). **Signed by:** Mike Soper.

Brady was one of the few standouts in a weak high school pitching crop in the state of Florida in 2013. Despite staying on the board until the fifth round, he landed the second-largest bonus in Cleveland's draft class at $800,000. He dominated in the Rookie-level Arizona League after signing, allowing two earned runs or fewer in all 10 of his starts. For a high school pitcher, Brady is less about projection and more about present stuff. He'll touch 92 mph with his fastball but pitches at 88-91. While he lacks plus velocity, he gets the most out of his tailing fastball thanks to his ability to command it to both sides of the plate. His curveball has the better chance to be a plus pitch. It has top-to-bottom break and he can use it as a chase pitch or for an early-count strike. His changeup is his third option and shows promising fade and sink. Coming into the draft, the Indians loved Brady's clean delivery and arm action, along with his advanced feel for pitching. He's a fierce competitor, and he took a leadership role on the staff with the AZL team. His upside may only be that of a mid-rotation starter, but he could move quickly for a high school arm. He'll open his first full season at low Class A Lake County.

Year	Club (League)	Class	W	L	ERA	G	GS	CG	SV	IP	H	HR	BB	SO	K/9	WHIP	AVG
2013	Indians (AZL)	R	0	1	1.97	10	10	0	0	32	24	2	6	30	8.4	0.94	.205
Minor League Totals			0	1	1.97	10	10	0	0	32	24	2	6	30	8.4	0.94	.205

Colorado Rockies

BY JACK ETKIN

For the first time in their 21-year history, the Rockies finished last in consecutive seasons, albeit with a 10-game improvement to 74-88 in 2013 under first-year manager Walt Weiss.

Weiss had never managed professionally before taking the Rockies job with a one-year contract. He now has earned the stability of a three-year deal after showing the requisite leadership, communication and decision-making skills to manage in the big leagues.

After successive losing seasons at home, Weiss wanted the Rockies to re-establish their dominance at Coors Field and approach .500 on the road, where Colorado has had only one winning record (41-40 in 2009). The Rockies did go 45-36 at Coors Field but were 29-52 on the road, losing 23 of their final 32 away games.

Pitching is typically a Rockies shortcoming, in part because of the challenges Coors Field presents. While Colorado starters had a 4.57 ERA, the third-lowest in franchise history, they still ranked last in the National League due to trouble at the back end of the rotation.

The Rockies found three reliable starters in righthander Tyler Chatwood, who began the year at Triple-A Colorado Springs, righty Jhoulys Chacin and lefty Jorge de la Rosa. Top prospects Jonathan Gray and Eddie Butler, a pair of righthanders who throw in the upper 90s, project to be front-of-the-rotation starters and aren't far away.

The Rockies have continued to develop solid role players around star shortstop Troy Tulowitzki and left fielder Carlos Gonzalez. In 2013, Nolan Arenado led the way as he became the first NL rookie third baseman to win a Gold Glove award.

Injuries in the final two months provided playing time for outfielders Charlie Blackmon, who hit .309/.336/.467 in his longest stint in the majors, and rookie Corey Dickerson, who played with hustle and posted a 1.003 OPS at Coors Field. Rookie righthander Chad Bettis also showed a power arm over the final two months and likely will fill a late-inning role in the 2014 bullpen.

The Rockies have rebuilt their depth in recent drafts, though highly regarded 2012 first-round outfielder David Dahl essentially had a lost year due to disciplinary issues and injuries.

The Rockies made some significant changes to their farm system to try to become more productive, and beginning in August 2012 general manager Dan O'Dowd and assistant GM Bill Geivett essentially switched positions, with Geivett becoming the director of major league operations. While retaining his GM title, O'Dowd began to focus on player development and scouting. The minor league field staff has been energized by O'Dowd's increased involvement.

The Rockies created the role of development supervisor, who assists the minor league manager and coaching staff and works daily with them and the players. The position was never filled at Colorado Springs, and at high Class A Modesto, development supervisor Fred Nelson assumed managerial duties when Lenn Sakata, who was at odds with this change, was fired during the season. Only one Colorado affiliate posted a winning record in 2013, yet the organization believes the new position proved to be beneficial.

LARRY GOREN

Rookie third baseman Nolan Arenado won a Gold Glove and held his own at the plate

TOP PROSPECTS OF THE DECADE

Year	Player, Pos.	2013 Org
2004	Chin-Hui Tsao, rhp	Out of baseball
2005	Ian Stewart, 3b	Dodgers
2006	Ian Stewart, 3b	Dodgers
2007	Troy Tulowitzki, ss	Rockies
2008	Franklin Morales, lhp	Red Sox
2009	Dexter Fowler, of	Rockies
2010	Tyler Matzek, lhp	Rockies
2011	Drew Pomeranz, lhp	Rockies
2012	Drew Pomeranz, lhp	Rockies
2013	Nolan Arenado, 3b	Rockies

ORGANIZATION OVERVIEW

General Manager: Dan O'Dowd. **Farm Director:** Jeff Bridich. **Scouting Director:** Bill Schmidt.

Class	Team	League	W	L	PCT	Finish	Manager
Majors	Colorado Rockies	National	74	88	.457	t-10th (15)	Walt Weiss
Triple-A	Colorado Springs Sky Sox	Pacific Coast	67	76	.469	13th (16)	Glenallen Hill
Double-A	Tulsa Drillers	Texas	68	70	.493	5th (8)	Kevin Riggs
High Class A	Modesto Nuts	California	75	65	.536	4th (10)	Lenn Sakata/Fred Nelson
Low Class A	Asheville Tourists	South Atlantic	63	73	.463	10th (14)	Fred Ocasio
Short-season	Tri-City Dust Devils	Northwest	34	42	.447	7th (8)	Drew Saylor
Rookie	Grand Junction Rockies	Pioneer	35	41	.461	6th (8)	Anthony Sanders
Overall 2013 Minor League Record			**342**	**367**	**.482**	**24th (30)**	

THIS YEAR'S TOP 30

No.	Player, Pos.	Grade/Risk
1.	Jonathan Gray, rhp	70/High
2.	Eddie Butler, rhp	65/Medium
3.	Rosell Herrera, ss	55/High
4.	Kyle Parker, 1b/of	50/Medium
5.	Chad Bettis, rhp	50/Medium
6.	David Dahl, of	60/Extreme
7.	Tom Murphy, c	50/High
8.	Ryan McMahon, 3b	50/High
9.	Trevor Story, ss	50/High
10.	Raimel Tapia, of	55/Extreme
11.	Tyler Anderson, lhp	45/High
12.	Tyler Matzek, lhp	45/High
13.	Scott Oberg, rhp	45/High
14.	Rayan Gonzalez, rhp	45/High
15.	Sam Moll, lhp	45/High
16.	Charlie Culberson, 2b/ss/of	40/Medium
17.	Rob Scahill, rhp	45/High
18.	Taylor Featherston, 2b	45/High
19.	Chris Jensen, rhp	45/High
20.	Emerson Jimenez, ss	50/Extreme
21.	Cristhian Adames, ss	45/High
22.	Raul Fernandez, rhp	50/Extreme
23.	Francisco Sosa, of	50/Extreme
24.	Antonio Senzatela, rhp	50/Extreme
25.	Dan Houston, rhp	45/High
26.	Max White, of	50/Extreme
27.	Johendi Jiminian, rhp	45/High
28.	Jayson Aquino, lhp	50/Extreme
29.	Jose Briceno, c	50/Extreme
30.	Ryan Warner, rhp	50/Extreme

LAST YEAR'S TOP 30

No.	Player, Pos.	Status
1.	Nolan Arenado, 3b	Majors
2.	David Dahl, of	No. 6
3.	Trevor Story, ss/3b	No. 9
4.	Kyle Parker, of	No. 4
5.	Chad Bettis, rhp	No. 5
6.	Eddie Butler, rhp	No. 2
7.	Tyler Anderson, lhp	No. 11
8.	Tyler Matzek, lhp	No. 12
9.	Jayson Aquino, lhp	No. 28
10.	Ryan Wheeler, 3b/1b/of	Majors
11.	Tim Wheeler, of	Dropped out
12.	Rob Scahill, rhp	No. 17
13.	Corey Dickerson, of	Majors
14.	Tom Murphy, c	No. 7
15.	Rafael Ortega, of	(Rangers)
16.	Kent Matthes, of	Dropped out
17.	Edwar Cabrera, lhp	(Rangers)
18.	Josh Sullivan, rhp	Dropped out
19.	Cristhian Adames, ss	No. 21
20.	Julian Yan, of	Dropped out
21.	Will Swanner, c	Dropped out
22.	Danny Rosenbaum, lhp	(Nationals)
23.	Harold Riggins, 1b	Dropped out
24.	Seth Willoughby, rhp	Dropped out
25.	Max White, of	No. 26
26.	Ryan Warner, rhp	No. 30
27.	Wilfredo Rodriguez, c	Dropped out
28.	Christian Bergman, rhp	Dropped out
29.	Peter Tago, rhp	Dropped out
30.	Parker Frazier, rhp	(White Sox)

BEST TOOLS

Best Hitter for Average	David Dahl
Best Power Hitter	Kyle Parker
Best Strike-Zone Discipline	Rosell Herrera
Fastest Baserunner	Max White
Best Athlete	Rosell Herrera
Best Fastball	Jonathan Gray
Best Curveball	Scott Oberg
Best Slider	Eddie Butler
Best Changeup	Eddie Butler
Best Command	Christian Bergman
Best Defensive Catcher	Dustin Garneau
Best Defensive Infielder	Trevor Story
Best Infield Arm	Trevor Story
Best Defensive Outfielder	Wilson Soriano
Best Outfield Arm	Jared Simon

TOP 15 PLAYERS 25 AND UNDER

	Player, Pos. (Age)	Peak Level
1.	Jonathan Gray, rhp (22)	High Class A
2.	Eddie Butler, rhp (23)	Double-A
3.	Nolan Arenado, 3b (22)	Majors
4.	Tyler Chatwood, rhp (24)	Majors
5.	Wilin Rosario, c (25)	Majors
6.	Rosell Herrera, ss (21)	Low Class A
7.	Kyle Parker, 1b/of (24)	Double-A
8.	Chad Bettis, rhp (24)	Majors
9.	David Dahl, of (20)	Low Class A
10.	Tom Murphy, c (22)	Double-A
11.	Ryan McMahon, 3b (19)	Rookie
12.	Josh Rutledge, 2b/ss (24)	Majors
13.	Drew Pomeranz, lhp (25)	Majors
14.	Corey Dickerson, of (24)	Majors
15.	D.J. LeMahieu, 2b/3b (25)	Majors

MINOR LEAGUE DEPTH CHART

COLORADO ROCKIES

TOP 2014 ROOKIE: Eddie Butler, rhp. He's a power pitcher with great movement on three plus offerings and could be in the rotation early in the season.

BREAKOUT PROSPECT: Rayan Gonzalez, rhp. He throws hard, controls the strike zone and his cutter is a double-plus, knockout pitch.

SLEEPER: Bruce Kern, rhp. He came back from Tommy John surgery in 2013 and was up to 95 mph with a hard, sharp curveball.

SOURCE OF TOP 30 TALENT

Homegrown	**29**	**Acquired**	**1**
College	13	Trades	1
Junior college	0	Rule 5 draft	0
High school	6	Independent leagues	0
Nondrafted free agents	0	Free agents/waivers	0
International	10		

LF
Francisco Sosa (23)
Brian Humphries
David Kandilas
Dillon Thomas
Mike Tauchman

CF
David Dahl (6)
Raimel Tapia (10)
Max White (26)
Tyler Massey
Wilson Soriano
Terry McClure
Kyle VonTungeln

RF
Tim Wheeler
Kent Matthes
Julian Yan
Jared Simon
Derek Jones

3B
Ryan McMahon (8)
Sam Mende
Brett Tanos
Matt Wessinger
Jayson Langfels

SS
Rosell Herrera (3)
Trevor Story (9)
Emerson Jimenez (20)
Cristhian Adames (21)

2B
Charlie Culberson (16)
Taylor Featherston (18)
Angelys Nina
Miguel Dilone
Pat Valaika
Joey Wong

1B
Kyle Parker (4)
Ryan Wheeler
Harold Riggins
Corelle Prime

C
Tom Murphy (7)
Jose Briceno (29)
Dustin Garneau
Wilfredo Rodriguez
Will Swanner
Dom Nunez
Ryan Casteel

LHP

LHSP	LHRP
Tyler Anderson (11)	Tyler Matzek (12)
Jayson Aquino (28)	Sam Moll (15)
	Kraig Sitton
	Kenny Roberts

RHP

RHSP	RHRP
Jonathan Gray (1)	Chad Bettis (5)
Eddie Butler (2)	Scott Oberg (13)
Chris Jensen (19)	Rayan Gonzalez (14)
Antonio Senzatela (24)	Rob Scahill (17)
Johendi Jiminian (27)	Raul Fernandez (22)
Ryan Warner (30)	Dan Houston (25)
Dan Winkler	Burce Kern
Christian Bergman	Nelson Gonzalez
Konner Wade	Seth Willoughby
Zach Jemiola	Dylan Stamey
Matt Flemer	Trent Daniel
Alex Balog	Jacob Newberry

DRAFT ANALYSIS

2013

BONUSES: $9.8 MILLION

BEST PURE HITTER: The Rockies love football quarterbacks and got a good one in 3B Ryan McMahon (2), who starred at California prep powerhouse Mater Dei. His two-sport prowess makes his polish more impressive. He has good hitting instincts, stays inside the ball and uses the whole field like an older hitter. OF Jordan Patterson (4) has a line-drive swing.

BEST POWER HITTER: McMahon has leverage in his swing and crushed the ball in the Rookie-level Pioneer League, batting .321/.402/.583 and ranking second in the league in slugging. OF Sean Dwyer (11) won the short-season Northwest League home run derby but hasn't consistently hit for power in games.

FASTEST RUNNER: This class lacks a burner, but OF Terry McClure (8) turns in plus times over 60 yards in workouts. His speed plays more average in games, as does Patterson's.

BEST DEFENSIVE PLAYER: McMahon has profile third-base tools. SS Pat Valaika (9) is the consummate college shortstop, with fair range but good hands, arm strength and a steady, reliable glove.

BEST FASTBALL: RHP Jonathan Gray (1) had the best fastball in the draft, sitting at 96-97 mph as a starter and hitting 100 regularly. He's country strong and has a loose arm but generates that velocity through a sound, powerful delivery.

BEST SECONDARY PITCH: Gray's slider is well above-average, and his changeup grades out as average but plays up thanks to the quality of his other pitches. The combination helped him strike out 51 in 37 innings of his debut. LHP Sam Moll (3) tops the mere mortals with an above-average slider.

BEST PRO DEBUT: Gray went 4-0, 1.93 overall and finished with a torrid five-start stretch with high Class A Modesto. McMahon ranked as the Pioneer League's No. 4 prospect. Patterson hit .291/.389/.495 with 10 homers as his Grand Junction teammate. RHP Dylan Stamey (14), Grand Junction's closer, went 4-1, 1.26 with 29 strikeouts in 29 innings.

BEST ATHLETE: McClure has strength to go with his speed and should stick in center field.

MOST INTRIGUING BACKGROUND: Unsigned RHP Kyle Serrano (29) is the son of Tennessee head coach Dave. Unsigned SS Brody Weiss (22) is the son of Rockies manager and former major league shortstop Walt. 3B Mike Benjamin Jr. (13) is the son of the ex-big leaguer of the same name. Valaika has two brothers who've been drafted, including big leaguer Chris.

CLOSEST TO THE MAJORS: Gray, whose biggest adjustment will be throwing every five days and maintaining the command of his high-voltage stuff.

BEST LATE-ROUND PICK: Stamey could move quickly as a reliever who has touched 95 mph. Valaika also has a chance to fill a role.

THE ONE WHO GOT AWAY: Serrano had first-round talent but decided to pitch for his father with the Volunteers. Weiss was less of a priority and headed to UC Santa Barbara.

ASSESSMENT: Gray and McMahon both could be impact players at their positions. A breakthrough by other arms such as Moll or RHPs Alex Balog (2s), Blake Shouse (5) or Konner Wade (7) would help a pitching-thirsty franchise.

2012

BONUSES: $7.0 MILLION

OF David Dahl (1) had a lost year in 2013 but RHP Eddie Butler (1s) plowed through three levels. C Tommy Murphy (3) already has reached Double-A.

GRADE: B

2011

BONUSES: $4.0 MILLION

LHP Tyler Anderson (1) has a low ceiling, while SS Trevor Story (1s) had a difficult 2013. RHP Danny Winkler (20) led the minors in strikeouts.

GRADE: D

2010

BONUSES: $4.8 MILLION

RHP Chad Bettis (2), SS Josh Rutledge (3) and OF Corey Dickerson (8) already have reached Denver. 1B Kyle Parker (1) should join them soon.

GRADE: B+

TOP DRAFT PICKS OF THE DECADE

Year	Player, Pos.	2013 Org
2004	Chris Nelson, ss	Angels
2005	Troy Tulowitzki, ss	Rockies
2006	Greg Reynolds, rhp	Reds
2007	Casey Weathers, rhp	Cubs
2008	Christian Friedrich, lhp	Rockies
2009	Tyler Matzek, lhp	Rockies
2010	Kyle Parker, of	Rockies
2011	Tyler Anderson, lhp	Rockies
2012	David Dahl, of	Rockies
2013	Jonathan Gray, rhp	Rockies

LARGEST BONUSES IN CLUB HISTORY

Jonathan Gray, 2013	$4,800,000
Tyler Matzek, 2009	$3,900,000
Greg Reynolds, 2006	$3,200,000
Jason Young, 2000	$2,750,000
David Dahl, 2012	$2,600,000

1 JONATHAN GRAY, RHP

Born: Nov. 5, 1991. **B-T:** R-R. **Ht.:** 6-4. **Wt.:** 250.
Drafted: Oklahoma, 2013 (1st round).
Signed by: Jesse Retzlaff.

The Rockies had Gray ranked atop their draft board in 2013 and were ecstatic when the Astros chose Mark Appel and the Cubs selected Kris Bryant, allowing Colorado to take Gray with the third overall pick. He signed for a franchise-record $4.8 million, well above the previous mark of $3.9 million given to 2009 first-rounder Tyler Matzek. Gray had been drafted twice previously. The Royals took him in the 13th round in 2010 out of Chandler (Okla.) High. He went to Eastern Oklahoma State JC, where the Yankees took him in the 10th round in 2011. He rejected New York's $500,000 offer and transferred to Oklahoma, where he got in better shape. In his junior season at OU, Gray went 10-3, 1.64 in 17 starts with 147 strikeouts and 24 walks in 126 innings. In the pre-draft drug testing, he tested positive for the prescription drug Adderall, a stimulant that cannot be used without a waiver under the Major League Baseball policy on performance-enhancing substances. As a result, he will be subject to additional testing during his professional career. Gray is the fourth college righthander drafted by the Rockies in the first round, following John Burke (Florida, 1992), Jason Jennings (Baylor, 1999) and Greg Reynolds (Stanford, 2006). Because of his college workload, the Rockies limited him to no more than five innings in any start, and after accumulating 163 innings between college and pro ball, the Rockies scratched him from his final start at high Class A Modesto.

The Rockies have never had a power pitcher with command as sharp as Gray's. Ubaldo Jimenez threw nearly as hard but didn't have Gray's command. Gray sits at 95-96 mph with his four-seam fastball that ranges from 93-100 and on multiple occasions hit 102. His heater has good finish with a small amount of run and little, if any, sink. The pitch has only a bit of movement, understandable given the high velocity. Because Gray had thrown his slider excessively at Oklahoma, the Rockies limited him to throwing one slider per batter at Rookie-level Grand Junction. That restriction was removed at Modesto, where he was virtually unhittable. Gray has an 85-88 mph slider with tight, late break when thrown properly, but it can get big at times and needs more consistency. He has a good feel for a straight changeup that needs more work, not surprising since it wasn't a necessary pitch in college. But when he keeps it down, his changeup is 83-87 mph with slight fade.

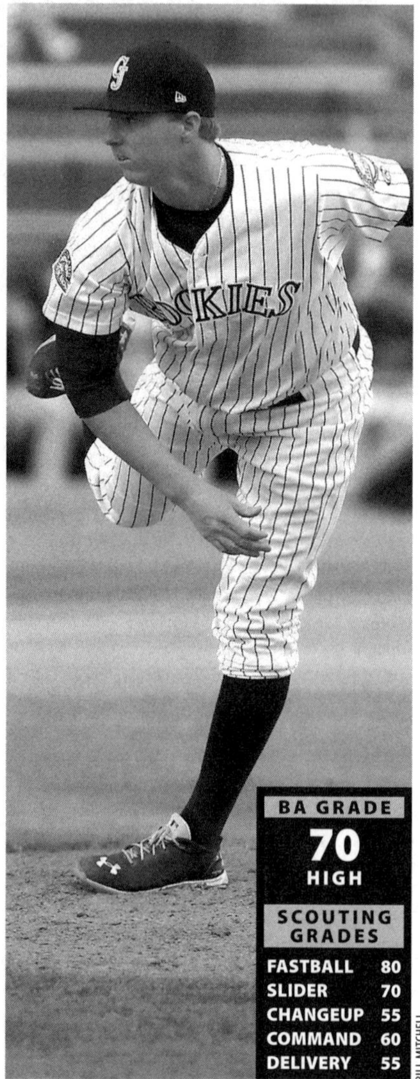

ROCKIES
BA GRADE
70
HIGH
SCOUTING GRADES
FASTBALL 80
SLIDER 70
CHANGEUP 55
COMMAND 60
DELIVERY 55

BILL MITCHELL

Gray has three very good pitches, and the Rockies expect that all will be above-average offerings. Power pitchers are often burdened by walks, which shouldn't be the case with Gray, whose command is good thanks to an efficient delivery. He'll start at Double-A Tulsa and could reach the majors at some point during the 2014 season. His combination of power and efficiency makes him a potential No. 1 starter.

Year	Club (League)	Class	W	L	ERA	G	GS	CG	SV	IP	H	HR	BB	SO	K/9	WHIP	AVG
2013	Grand Junction (PIO)	R	0	0	4.05	4	4	0	0	13	15	0	2	15	10.1	1.28	.278
	Modesto (CAL)	HiA	4	0	0.75	5	5	0	0	24	10	0	6	36	13.5	0.67	.128
Minor League Totals			4	0	1.93	9	9	0	0	37	25	0	8	51	12.3	0.88	.189

2 EDDIE BUTLER, RHP

BA GRADE
65
MEDIUM

Born: March 13, 1991. **B-T:** S-R. **Ht.:** 6-2. **Wt.:** 180. **Drafted:** Radford, 2012 (1st round supplemental). **Signed by:** Jay Matthews.

The Rockies signed Butler for $1 million after taking him 46th overall in the 2012 draft as compensation for the loss of free agent Mark Ellis to the Dodgers. He began his career by leading the Rookie-level Pioneer League in ERA (2.13), WHIP (1.06) and opponent average (.230), but his encore was even more impressive. He began 2013 at low Class A Asheville but worked his way through three levels, throwing an eye-opening inning at the Futures Game, and finishing 9-5, 1.80 overall, ranking second in the minors in ERA and opponent average (.180). Butler's fastball, slider and changeup are plus pitches with exceptional movement, and his hard curveball is solid-average. He touches 99 mph with a fastball that sits at 95-96. With its life and his ability to spot it, Butler earns 70 grades or higher from scouts for his heater. His changeup is extraordinary, a finished pitch he throws at 88 mph that bottoms out like a split and is thrown with great arm speed. He used it to thoroughly vex Red Sox prospect Xander Bogaerts in the Futures Game. Butler's slider is 85-88 mph and features tight, late break. He shows good feel for his craft, as he can add and subtract and vary the break on his secondary stuff. In addition to a power sinker, Butler throws a four-seamer that he worked hard at Double-A Tulsa to make more consistent to his arm side. He was much improved last season at not letting his emotions affect him when encountering adversity. Butler could be in the Rockies rotation by May. He figures to begin the season with several starts in the high minors, with the weather possibly dictating a return to Double-A Tulsa. His front-of-the-rotation starter upside rivals that of Gray.

Year	Club (League)	Class	W	L	ERA	G	GS	CG	SV	IP	H	HR	BB	SO	K/9	WHIP	AVG
2012	Grand Junction (PIO)	R	7	1	2.13	13	12	0	0	68	59	1	13	55	7.3	1.06	.230
2013	Asheville (SAL)	LoA	5	1	1.66	9	9	0	0	54	25	2	25	51	8.4	0.92	.137
	Modesto (CAL)	HiA	3	4	2.39	13	13	0	0	68	58	7	21	67	8.9	1.17	.227
	Tulsa (TL)	AA	1	0	0.65	6	6	0	0	28	13	0	6	25	8.1	0.69	.138
Minor League Totals			16	6	1.90	41	40	0	0	217	155	10	65	198	8.2	1.01	.196

3 ROSELL HERRERA, SS

TONY FARLOW

BA GRADE
55
HIGH

Born: Oct. 16, 1992. **B-T:** B-R. **Ht.:** 6-3. **Wt.:** 180. **Signed:** Dominican Republic, 2009. **Signed by:** Rolando Fernandez/Jhonathan Leyba.

Herrera, who signed for $550,000 in 2009, came from the Dominican Republic to the United States in 2011 and played well in the Rookie-level Pioneer League. He clearly was overwhelmed at low Class A Asheville in 2012 (.543 OPS), but a more confident, mature and aggressive Herrera returned to Asheville in 2013. He earned South Atlantic League MVP honors after leading the circuit in average (.343) and hits (162) while ranking second in total bases (242). The key for the switch-hitting Herrera was an improved swing. He still has a leg kick but now gets his front foot down on time and is more under control. He has learned to stay back and let the ball travel, and has much better balance and improved strike-zone management. He has much more power and aggressiveness from the left side but is driving the ball from the right side more than in the past. The lanky Herrera could develop more power as he fills out. An average runner, he might lose some of the quickness necessary for shortstop, where he has better range to his glove side than backhand and solid arm strength. He made too many errors by laying back on balls. However, after committing 24 miscues in his first 77 games, Herrera got more aggressive defensively and made just four in his final 49 games. Herrera will move up to high Class A Modesto in 2014. If a position change is needed, Herrera has the arm, hands and actions to play second or third base, though he also took fly balls in center field during instructional league, opening another possibility.

Year	Club (League)	Class	AVG	G	AB	R	H	2B	3B	HR	RBI	BB	SO	SB	CS	OBP	SLG
2010	Rockies (DSL)	R	.237	67	232	27	55	6	1	1	26	24	24	17	8	.323	.284
2011	Casper (PIO)	R	.284	63	243	38	69	6	8	6	34	27	62	5	4	.361	.449
2012	Asheville (SAL)	LoA	.202	63	213	22	43	8	2	1	26	21	49	6	3	.271	.272
	Tri-City (NWL)	SS	.284	47	194	30	55	6	2	1	30	14	34	7	3	.332	.351
2013	Asheville (SAL)	LoA	.343	126	472	83	162	33	0	16	76	61	96	21	8	.419	.515
Minor League Totals			.284	366	1354	200	384	59	13	25	192	147	265	56	26	.357	.402

4 KYLE PARKER, 1B/OF

BA GRADE 50 MEDIUM

Born: Sept. 30, 1989. **B-T:** R-R. **Ht.:** 6-0. **Wt.:** 200. **Drafted:** Clemson, 2010 (1st round). **Signed by:** Jay Matthews.

Parker also played quarterback at Clemson and turned down a $2.2 million offer from the Rockies that would have forced him to give up football, choosing to sign for $1.4 million and play a final season on the gridiron. Parker is the only player in NCAA Division I history to throw 20 touchdown passes and hit 20 homers in the same school year. Parker's contact rate has improved each season, with his strikeout rate falling to just shy of 19 percent of plate appearances at Double-A Tulsa in 2013—a career best. When he makes contact, Parker's strength and bat speed generate good power, particularly to right-center field, and he has gotten much better at staying on the ball longer and using the entire field more consistently. He has gained a much better understanding of his swing and can afford to wait due to his quick wrists and quiet approach. A below-average runner, Parker was introduced to first base at Tulsa and played the position exclusively in the Arizona Fall League. A former college third baseman, he improved greatly at being able to read balls off the bat and correctly incorporating his feet. Parker has a solid, accurate arm. With Todd Helton retiring, right fielder Michael Cuddyer is expected to move to first base in 2014, the final year of his contract. Parker should begin 2014 at Triple-A Colorado Springs and join the Rockies during the season before taking over at first base in 2015.

Year	Club (League)	Class	AVG	G	AB	R	H	2B	3B	HR	RBI	BB	SO	SB	CS	OBP	SLG
2011	Asheville (SAL)	LoA	.285	117	445	75	127	23	1	21	95	48	133	2	0	.367	.483
2012	Modesto (CAL)	HiA	.308	102	390	86	120	18	6	23	73	66	88	1	2	.415	.562
2013	Tulsa (TL)	AA	.288	123	480	70	138	23	3	23	74	40	99	6	6	.345	.492
Minor League Totals			.293	342	1315	231	385	64	10	67	242	154	320	9	8	.374	.510

5 CHAD BETTIS, RHP

BA GRADE 50 MEDIUM

Born: April 26, 1989. **B-T:** R-R. **Ht.:** 6-1. **Wt.:** 200. **Drafted:** Texas Tech, 2010 (2nd round). **Signed by:** Dar Cox.

After being named high Class A California League pitcher of the year in 2011, Bettis missed the entire 2012 season. He strained a muscle behind his shoulder in his second spring-training outing and was out until instructional league. He resumed his career at Double-A Tulsa in 2013, missing two months with an oblique strain, then earned a promotion to the Rockies on Aug. 1. After making eight starts, Bettis moved to the bullpen as Colorado wanted to limit his workload after a year off and see how he handled relieving. Before his shoulder injury, Bettis reached 97-98 mph with his fastball. Last season, he hit 96 and pitched at 92-93. The Rockies hope he'll regain velocity as he gains more distance from his injury. His vastly improved changeup is a plus pitch with sink and serves as his best secondary pitch. His slider has turned into more of a cutter, an 86-89 mph pitch that can be too hard and close in velocity to his fastball. At times he threw his curveball more than his cutter in relief, but it's his fourth-best pitch. Bettis can control the strike zone but doesn't command it yet. Like a lot of rookie pitchers, he resorted to a faster/harder mentality when the game sped up on him, but it was in keeping with his fierce competitiveness. Bettis' fast-action delivery may not allow him to hold up physically as a starter, and a permanent move to the bullpen is likely. He could begin 2014 relieving in the majors.

Year	Club (League)	Class	W	L	ERA	G	GS	CG	SV	IP	H	HR	BB	SO	K/9	WHIP	AVG
2010	Tri-City (NWL)	SS	4	1	1.12	10	9	0	0	48	44	0	10	39	7.3	1.12	.227
	Asheville (SAL)	LoA	2	0	0.96	3	3	0	0	19	14	1	3	17	8.2	0.91	.209
2011	Modesto (CAL)	HiA	12	5	3.34	27	27	0	0	170	142	10	45	184	9.8	1.10	.225
2012	Did not play—Injured																
2013	Tulsa (TL)	AA	3	4	3.71	12	12	0	0	63	60	9	13	68	9.7	1.16	.255
	Colorado (NL)	MAJ	1	3	5.64	16	8	0	0	45	55	6	20	30	6.0	1.68	.302
Major League Totals			1	3	5.64	16	8	0	0	45	55	6	20	30	6.0	1.68	.302
Minor League Totals			21	10	2.91	52	51	0	0	300	260	20	71	308	9.3	1.10	.231

6 DAVID DAHL, OF

BA GRADE
60
EXTREME

Born: April 1, 1994. **B-T:** L-R. **Ht.:** 6-2. **Wt.:** 185. **Drafted:** HS—Birmingham, 2012 (1st round). **Signed by:** Damon Iannelli.

Drafted 10th overall in 2012, Dahl is the first high school outfielder the Rockies ever selected with their first pick. After signing for $2.6 million, he won MVP honors in the 2012 Rookie-level Pioneer League, where he had a 27-game hitting streak and batted a league-leading .379. But 2013 was a lost season. He played Opening Night at low Class A Asheville, but afterward the Rockies sent him to extended spring training, a disciplinary measure for making his own airline reservation out of spring training. Dahl returned to Asheville on April 29, but a week later he tore his right hamstring running to first base and didn't play the rest of the season. Lower back soreness developed during his rehab, keeping him from participating in instructional league. Dahl is a pure hitter with exceptional hand-eye coordination and the ability to make adjustments from at-bat to at-bat and even pitch to pitch, which is rare for a young player. He has extra-base power that should yield 15-20 homers annually in the big leagues, and his above-average speed will yield leg hits, further raising his average. He has five-tool ability and profiles as a No. 3 hitter. Dahl has a plus arm and covers a lot of ground in center field, where he has plus potential. Chastened, humbled and presumably more mature, he'll return to Asheville to begin 2014 but could reach high Class A Modesto during the season.

Year	Club (League)	Class	AVG	G	AB	R	H	2B	3B	HR	RBI	BB	SO	SB	CS	OBP	SLG
2012	Grand Junction (PIO)	R	.379	67	280	62	106	22	10	9	57	21	42	12	7	.423	.625
2013	Asheville (SAL)	LoA	.275	10	40	9	11	4	1	0	7	2	8	2	0	.310	.425
Minor League Totals			.366	77	320	71	117	26	11	9	64	23	50	14	7	.409	.600

7 TOM MURPHY, C

BA GRADE
50
HIGH

Born: Jan. 3, 1991. **B-T:** R-R. **Ht.:** 6-1. **Wt.:** 220. **Drafted:** Buffalo, 2012 (3rd round). **Signed by:** Ed Santa.

Murphy signed for $454,000 after becoming the fifth catcher the Rockies have taken as high as the third round since they began drafting in 1992, a group that includes Ben Petrick (second round, 1995), Jeff Winchester (supplemental first, 1998) and third-rounders Josh Bard (1999), Lars Davis (2007) and Pete O'Brien (2011), who didn't sign. Murphy began his first full season at low Class A Asheville and earned a promotion in August to Double-A Tulsa. He generates a lot of power with a short, simple swing and good strength. He has solid plate discipline for a young power hitter but doesn't run well enough or have enough feel to project for a high average. He's a bulwark behind the plate and has an above-average arm and soft hands. He threw out 28 percent of basestealers on the season. Murphy receives and blocks the ball well, provides a low target and sets up well. He needs to experience game situations to grow in subtle areas such as implementing a scouting report and altering it as needed during a game. Murphy will likely return to Double-A to start the season but could reach the big leagues as quickly as 2014. The Rockies project him as an everyday catcher who could help them push incumbent Wilin Rosario, who has defensive shortcomings, to an outfield corner.

Year	Club (League)	Class	AVG	G	AB	R	H	2B	3B	HR	RBI	BB	SO	SB	CS	OBP	SLG
2012	Tri-City (NWL)	SS	.288	55	212	26	61	13	3	6	38	14	52	1	1	.349	.462
2013	Asheville (SAL)	LoA	.288	80	288	55	83	26	2	19	74	37	87	4	5	.385	.590
	Tulsa (TL)	AA	.290	20	69	9	20	5	0	3	9	4	16	0	0	.338	.493
Minor League Totals			.288	155	569	90	164	44	5	28	121	55	155	5	6	.366	.531

8 RYAN McMAHON, 3B

BA GRADE
50
HIGH

Born: Dec. 14, 1994. **B-T:** L-R. **Ht.:** 6-2. **Wt.:** 185. **Drafted:** HS—Santa Ana, Calif., 2013 (2nd round). **Signed by:** Jon Lukens.

The Rockies have a history of drafting and signing quarterbacks, including Todd Helton, Seth Smith and Russell Wilson, each of whom played the position in college. McMahon played quarterback at perennial California power Mater Dei High, but rather than follow through with his commitment to play baseball at Southern California, he signed with the Rockies for $1,327,600. In his debut, McMahon ranked second in the Rookie-level Pioneer League in slugging (.583) despite being one of the league's youngest regulars. McMahon has a fluid lefty swing and a middle-of-the-field approach that is impressive for a young player and helps him make steady contact. Already possessing present strength and solid athleticism, he projects to have plus power and the ability to hit for a high average. He has a solid arm that is plus at times, average range and is a tick-below-average runner. Despite his youth, McMahon, drawing on his days as a quarterback, was a leader on the field and a presence in the middle of the lineup for a Grand Junction team that made the playoffs. McMahon was the best pure hitter and power hitter in the Rockies' draft class and plays like a veteran despite his youth and two-sport background. He will advance to low Class A Asheville in 2014 and could move quickly.

Year	Club (League)	Class	AVG	G	AB	R	H	2B	3B	HR	RBI	BB	SO	SB	CS	OBP	SLG
2013	Grand Junction (PIO)	R	.321	59	218	42	70	18	3	11	52	28	59	4	6	.402	.583
Minor League Totals			.321	59	218	42	70	18	3	11	52	28	59	4	6	.402	.583

9 TREVOR STORY, SS

Born: Nov. 15, 1992. **B-T:** R-R. **Ht.:** 6-1. **Wt.:** 175. **Drafted:** HS—Irving, Texas, 2011 (1st round supplemental). **Signed by:** Dar Cox.

The Rockies took Story 45th overall as a compensation pick in the 2011 draft for the loss of free agent righthander Octavio Dotel, who pitched in just eight games for them in 2010. He signed for $915,000 and has advanced one level yearly. After a big season in 2012, when he played both third base and shortstop, he experienced plenty of growing pains in 2013 at high Class A Modesto. Story was hitting .204 at the end of June before making a few adjustments for the final two months. He has good bat speed, power and arm strength, but he fell into an early trap of trying to pull the ball too much and chasing bad pitches. He did a better job of going up the middle and using the off gap as the season went on. Story can be overly aggressive and finished second in the Cal League with 183 strikeouts, or once every third trip to the plate. Defensively, Story has good range and arm strength for the left side and plays with calmness. Some scouts believe the average runner is better suited for third than short. The Rockies laud him for continuing to play hard and with energy through instructional league. Story likely will return to Modesto in 2014. That could mean more time at third base if he's sharing shortstop with Rosell Herrera, as he did in 2011 and '12.

Year	Club (League)	Class	AVG	G	AB	R	H	2B	3B	HR	RBI	BB	SO	SB	CS	OBP	SLG
2011	Casper (PIO)	R	.268	47	179	37	48	8	2	6	28	26	41	13	1	.364	.436
2012	Asheville (SAL)	LoA	.277	122	477	96	132	43	6	18	63	60	121	15	3	.367	.505
2013	Modesto (CAL)	HiA	.233	130	497	71	116	34	5	12	65	45	183	23	1	.305	.394
Minor League Totals			.257	299	1153	204	296	85	13	36	156	131	345	51	5	.340	.447

10 RAIMEL TAPIA, OF

Born: Feb. 4, 1994. **B-T:** L-L. **Ht.:** 6-2. **Wt.:** 160. **Signed:** Dominican Republic, 2010. **Signed by:** Rolando Fernandez/Jhonathan Leyba/Hector Roa.

After hitting well at the Rockies' Dominican complex in a workout against Juan Nicasio and Esmil Rogers, Tapia signed with Colorado for $175,000 in November 2010. He played two seasons in the Dominican Summer League before the Rockies pushed him in 2013 by bringing him to minor league camp, and he earned a ticket to the Rookie-level Pioneer League, where he led the league in batting (.357) and hits (92), ranked second in total bases (145) and third in extra-base hits (33). His 29-game hitting streak fell three short of the league record. Tapia has exceptional hand-eye coordination and doesn't strike out often. He keeps his hands back and has a knack for putting his barrel on the ball, even on pitches out of the strike zone, with a short, lefthanded stroke. He has a loose, wiry frame with plenty of room for added strength and should be able to hit 20 home runs a season. An above-average runner, he played all three outfield spots at Grand Junction and could stay in center field, depending on how much he grows. He has enough range to stay up the middle and a plus arm that will play well in right. Tapia will start 2014 at low Class A Asheville, where he will play at age 20.

Year	Club (League)	Class	AVG	G	AB	R	H	2B	3B	HR	RBI	BB	SO	SB	CS	OBP	SLG
2011	Rockies (DSL)	R	.262	67	248	29	65	6	3	1	35	26	41	15	8	.336	.323
2012	Rockies (DSL)	R	.316	63	237	31	75	9	1	0	35	20	35	13	11	.383	.363
2013	Grand Junction (PIO)	R	.357	66	258	53	92	20	6	7	47	15	31	10	9	.399	.562
Minor League Totals			.312	196	743	113	232	35	10	8	117	61	107	38	28	.372	.419

11 TYLER ANDERSON, LHP

Born: Dec. 30, 1989. **B-T:** L-L. **Ht.:** 6-4. **Wt.:** 215. **Drafted:** Oregon, 2011 (1st round). **Signed by:** Jesse Retzlaff.

Injuries have become a growing concern with Anderson, who signed for $1.4 million as the 20th overall pick in the 2011 draft. He coped with a sports hernia while having a successful season at low Class A Asheville in 2012 and missed nine weeks at high Class A Modesto in 2013 due to shoulder soreness, finishing with 90 innings. Anderson returned in August and was scheduled to pitch in the Arizona Fall League but was scratched because of a stress fracture in his left elbow that may put him behind in 2014. Anderson pitches at 89-90 mph with his fastball and tops out at 93. Some scouts consider his average 86-87 mph cutter his best secondary pitch, one he uses to get in on righthanders, but he tends to throw it too often. Others prefer his changeup, which can flash plus with fade and sink. His 76-77 mph curveball is more fringy. Anderson's anything-but-fluid delivery features a leg kick and slight pause, but his mechanics help him hide the ball. Despite not having a pitch that stands out, his command and deception enhance his repertoire. Anderson is more effective against righthanded hitters (.649 OPS) than lefthanded hitters (.805), so he profiles better as a starter than a relief lefty. When he's ready, he'll pitch at Double-A Tulsa in 2014. He projects as a No. 5 starter.

Year	Club (League)	Class	W	L	ERA	G	GS	CG	SV	IP	H	HR	BB	SO	K/9	WHIP	AVG
2012	Asheville (SAL)	LoA	12	3	2.47	20	20	2	0	120	102	5	28	81	6.1	1.08	.232
2013	Tri-City (NWL)	SS	1	1	0.60	3	3	0	0	15	9	0	3	13	7.8	0.80	.164
	Modesto (CAL)	HiA	3	2	3.25	13	13	0	0	75	62	10	24	63	7.6	1.15	.224
Minor League Totals			16	6	2.61	36	36	2	0	210	173	15	55	157	6.7	1.09	.224

12 TYLER MATZEK, LHP

BA GRADE **45** HIGH

Born: Oct. 19, 1990. **B-T:** L-L. **Ht.:** 6-3. **Wt.:** 210. **Drafted:** HS—Mission Viejo, Calif., 2009 (1st round). **Signed by:** Jon Lukens.

The 11th overall pick in the 2009 draft, Matzek signed for $3.9 million and has made slow progress. His franchise bonus record stood until Jonathan Gray received $4.8 million in 2013. Matzek entered pro baseball adhering to the unorthodox Mike Marshall warm-up routine and even went home for three weeks during the 2011 season to work with his youth pitching coach, a Marshall disciple. He scrapped that routine during the 2012 season and has become far less analytical and a good deal more receptive to instruction. However, control and command remain issues for Matzek, mostly with his fastball. For the second successive season, he led his league in free passes (75), this time at Double-A Tulsa, though he did manage to lower his walk rate from 6 per nine innings to 4.8. The Rockies sent Matzek to the Arizona Fall League in 2013 to pitch in relief. His fastball ranged from 87-94 mph during the season but sat 93 and touched 95 in the AFL. Matzek's average curveball and fringy slider have gotten a little better, but his below-average changeup, which he tends to throw too hard, still isn't where it needs to be. He seems destined for the bullpen, given that his walk totals build up his pitch counts, making it difficult for him to go five innings as a starter. He ought to pitch at Triple-A in 2014.

Year	Club (League)	Class	W	L	ERA	G	GS	CG	SV	IP	H	HR	BB	SO	K/9	WHIP	AVG
2010	Asheville (SAL)	LoA	5	1	2.92	18	18	0	0	89	62	6	62	88	8.9	1.39	.204
2011	Modesto (CAL)	HiA	0	3	9.82	10	10	0	0	33	34	5	46	37	10.1	2.42	.266
	Asheville (SAL)	LoA	5	4	4.36	12	12	0	0	64	45	3	50	74	10.4	1.48	.202
2012	Modesto (CAL)	HiA	6	8	4.62	28	28	0	0	142	134	7	95	153	9.7	1.61	.246
2013	Tulsa (TL)	AA	8	9	3.79	26	26	0	0	142	147	13	76	95	6.0	1.57	.276
Minor League Totals			24	25	4.38	94	94	0	0	471	422	34	329	447	8.5	1.59	.244

13 SCOTT OBERG, RHP

BA GRADE **45** HIGH

Born: March 13, 1990. **B-T:** R-R. **Ht.:** 6-2. **Wt.:** 205. **Drafted:** Connecticut, 2012 (15th round). **Signed by:** Mike Garlatti.

Oberg had Tommy John surgery in college and missed his junior year at Connecticut, but he returned to record nine saves in 2012, prompting the Rockies to make him a 15th-round pick. He began his pro career as closer at Rookie-level Grand Junction, then jumped to high Class A Modesto in 2013 and led the California League with 33 saves. Oberg throws a fastball, curveball and changeup, using an aggressive, fearless temperament that is ideal for a closer. He sits 94-95 mph with his fastball but has below-average command of the pitch, a reason his 10.3 strikeouts per nine innings were offset by 4.6 walks in 2013. His plus curveball is a put-away pitch, and it's a hard breaking ball with true 12-to-6 action. Oberg also throws an above-average changeup that he used more in the second half of 2013. He has the weapons to combat lefthanders, who batted .190 against him. Oberg will begin 2014 at Double-A Tulsa and could move quickly, particularly if he refines his fastball command.

Year	Club (League)	Class	W	L	ERA	G	GS	CG	SV	IP	H	HR	BB	SO	K/9	WHIP	AVG
2012	Grand Junction (PIO)	R	0	2	2.33	25	0	0	13	27	20	2	6	29	9.7	0.96	.196
2013	Modesto (CAL)	HiA	1	6	1.86	56	0	0	33	53	34	4	27	61	10.3	1.14	.178
Minor League Totals			1	8	2.02	81	0	0	46	80	54	6	33	90	10.1	1.08	.184

14 RAYAN GONZALEZ, RHP

Born: Oct. 18, 1990. **B-T:** R-R. **Ht.:** 6-3. **Wt.:** 175. **Drafted:** Bethune-Cookman, 2012 (21st round). **Signed by:** John Cedarburg.

Gonzalez attended high school in Arecibo, Puerto Rico, but did not sign with the Athletics as an 18th-rounder in 2008. Instead he attended Bethune-Cookman, a historically black college in Daytona Beach, Fla., whose baseball coach Jason Beverlin recruits Puerto Rico. Gonzalez began his career with 22 relief appearances at Rookie-level Grand Junction in 2012, then posted a 3.3 SO/BB ratio in 49 relief appearances at low Class A Asheville, logging 12 saves when he filled in for injured closer Raul Fernandez. Gonzalez throws a hard sinker and a devastating cutter and doesn't throw anything straight. His heavy sinker ranges from 92-95 mph and is consistently 93-94. Gonzalez also has an above-average changeup. He can control the strike zone but doesn't yet command it and can get into stretches of missing the strike zone entirely. Gonzalez is an extreme groundball pitcher, posting a 2.5 groundout/airout ratio in 2013, and is intriguing because of his stuff. He will pitch at high Class A Modesto in 2014 and has a chance to progress quickly.

Year	Club (League)	Class	W	L	ERA	G	GS	CG	SV	IP	H	HR	BB	SO	K/9	WHIP	AVG
2012	Grand Junction (PIO)	R	0	3	6.75	22	0	0	0	24	33	3	15	27	10.1	2.00	.308
2013	Asheville (SAL)	LoA	2	3	2.68	49	0	0	12	54	51	0	21	70	11.7	1.34	.243
Minor League Totals			2	6	3.94	71	0	0	12	78	84	3	36	97	11.2	1.55	.265

15 SAM MOLL, LHP

BA GRADE
45
HIGH

Born: Jan. 3, 1992. **B-T:** L-L. **Ht.:** 5-10. **Wt.:** 185. **Drafted:** Memphis, 2013 (3rd round). **Signed by:** Scott Corman.

When they drafted Moll, a starter in college, the Rockies said he could end up in the bullpen. After he signed for $600,000 as a 2013 third-rounder, he began his pro career at short-season Tri-City. He made six starts and then missed a month with a broken left pinkie toe, an injury that occurred when he stubbed it against a dresser in the middle of the night in a hotel room. Moll returned on Aug. 24 and eased back into action by making four relief appearances and pitching six scoreless innings. As a starter, his fastball sat 90-91 mph, though he could reach back for 94 when needed. He sits at 93 mph out of the bullpen and touches 96. Moll's breaking pitch is a plus slurve that has two-plane movement and late action up to 87 mph. His developing changeup remains below par, and if it improves, he could remain a starter despite his longer arm action. Moll's tenacity played well in the bullpen, where he has the makings of another Rex Brothers. He should begin 2014 at low Class A Asheville but has a chance to move fast.

Year	Club (League)	Class	W	L	ERA	G	GS	CG	SV	IP	H	HR	BB	SO	K/9	WHIP	AVG
2013	Tri-City (NWL)	SS	3	1	1.80	10	6	0	0	30	20	0	10	29	8.7	1.00	.182
Minor League Totals			3	1	1.80	10	6	0	0	30	20	0	10	29	8.7	1.00	.182

16 CHARLIE CULBERSON, 2B/SS/OF

Born: April 10, 1989. **B-T:** R-R. **Ht.:** 6-1. **Wt.:** 200. **Drafted:** HS—Calhoun, Ga., 2007 (1st round supplemental). **Signed by:** Sean O'Connor (Giants).

Culberson has baseball bloodlines. His father Charles was the Giants' 16th-round pick in 1984 and coached in the White Sox system, and his grandfather Leon was an outfielder who spent six seasons with the Red Sox and Senators. The Giants drafted Charlie as a sandwich pick in 2007, then traded him to the Rockies for second baseman Marco Scutaro in July 2012. He began 2013 at Triple-A Colorado Springs and made his Rockies debut on July 29. He played more shortstop than second base for the Sky Sox, and he further enhanced his versatility by logging time in center field. He played just four games at second base with the Rockies and 27 in left field, where his inexperience showed on his reads and routes. The athletic Culberson runs and throws well, feasts on fastballs down and in and has surprising power to right-center field. At Triple-A, he improved at staying back and letting the ball travel, which opened up the whole field. With one option remaining, Culberson will compete for a utility role in 2014, which is likely his ceiling at this point.

Year	Club (League)	Class	AVG	G	AB	R	H	2B	3B	HR	RBI	BB	SO	SB	CS	OBP	SLG
2007	Giants (AZL)	R	.286	46	161	32	46	8	5	1	16	19	38	19	1	.374	.416
2008	Augusta (SAL)	LoA	.234	81	282	31	66	11	2	3	27	18	57	6	6	.290	.319
2009	Augusta (SAL)	LoA	.246	132	509	71	125	19	3	2	36	33	110	15	4	.303	.306
2010	San Jose (CAL)	HiA	.290	128	503	80	146	28	4	16	71	33	99	25	7	.340	.457
2011	Richmond (EL)	AA	.259	137	553	69	143	34	2	10	56	22	129	14	4	.293	.382
2012	San Francisco (NL)	MAJ	.136	6	22	0	3	0	0	0	1	0	7	0	0	.136	.136
	Fresno (PCL)	AAA	.236	91	351	53	83	14	6	10	53	20	76	8	2	.283	.396
	Colorado Springs (PCL)	AAA	.336	30	125	17	42	11	1	2	12	1	18	6	2	.344	.488
2013	Colorado Springs (PCL)	AAA	.310	97	397	63	123	27	8	14	64	17	74	13	9	.338	.524
	Colorado (NL)	MAJ	.293	47	99	12	29	5	0	2	12	4	23	5	1	.317	.404
Major League Totals			.264	53	121	12	32	5	0	2	13	4	30	5	1	.286	.355
Minor League Totals			.269	742	2881	416	774	152	31	58	335	163	601	106	35	.315	.403

17 ROB SCAHILL, RHP

BA GRADE 45 HIGH

Born: Feb. 15, 1987. **B-T:** L-R. **Ht.:** 6-2. **Wt.:** 220. **Drafted:** Bradley, 2009 (8th round). **Signed by:** Mark Germann.

The proverbial up-and-down reliever in 2013, Scahill began the season at Triple-A Colorado Springs but was recalled on April 21 for what proved to be the first of four stints with the Rockies. He pitched in 23 big league games, working two innings or more eight times and pitching three innings three times. Scahill stranded 11 of 12 inherited runners and retired 17 of 23 first batters. He struggled toward the end by allowing eight runs in his final five outings. A starter until the Rockies called him up in September 2012, Scahill has plenty of stuff. And while his command improved from 2012, it needs to be better. He sits at 93-94 mph with his fastball, which touches 96. His average 86-87 mph slider can be flat at times but is effective when thrown with depth. Scahill's fringy changeup is his weakest pitch. It's good enough to get outs and get him back in counts, but he doesn't have confidence in it and rarely throws it. A trustworthy changeup would give Scahill another weapon against lefthanders, who in the big leagues hit .344 in 64 at-bats against him. He'll vie for a middle-relief role with the Rockies in spring training, but he has two minor league options remaining.

Year	Club (League)	Class	W	L	ERA	G	GS	CG	SV	IP	H	HR	BB	SO	K/9	WHIP	AVG
2009	Tri-City (NWL)	SS	1	4	3.14	15	15	0	0	63	58	2	20	58	8.3	1.24	.245
2010	Modesto (CAL)	HiA	10	7	4.73	27	27	1	0	156	173	9	59	140	8.1	1.49	.284
2011	Tulsa (TL)	AA	12	11	3.92	27	26	1	0	161	164	12	60	104	5.8	1.39	.266
2012	Colorado Springs (PCL)	AAA	9	11	5.68	29	29	1	0	152	168	11	74	159	9.4	1.59	.280
	Colorado (NL)	MAJ	0	0	1.04	6	0	0	0	9	7	0	3	4	4.2	1.15	.233
2013	Colorado Springs (PCL)	AAA	5	1	4.50	23	0	0	1	46	53	6	11	45	8.8	1.39	.294
	Colorado (NL)	MAJ	1	0	5.13	23	0	0	0	33	40	5	9	20	5.4	1.47	.301
Major League Totals			1	0	4.29	29	0	0	0	42	47	5	12	24	5.1	1.40	.288
Minor League Totals			37	34	4.56	121	97	3	1	578	616	40	224	506	7.9	1.45	.275

18 TAYLOR FEATHERSTON, 2B

BA GRADE 45 HIGH

Born: Oct. 8, 1989. **B-T:** R-R. **Ht.:** 6-1. **Wt.:** 185. **Drafted:** Texas Christian, 2011 (5th round). **Signed by:** Dar Cox.

Featherston played shortstop at Texas Christian and helped lead the team to the College World Series in 2010. The following year, the Rockies drafted him in the fifth round and signed him for $144,900. Featherston played shortstop exclusively at short-season Tri-City in 2011, but he shifted to primarily second base in 2012 with Trevor Story and Rosell Herrera at low Class A Asheville. He continued to play mostly second in high Class A in 2013 after missing the first couple weeks of the season with an oblique strain. Featherston grinds out at-bats and can consistently get the barrel to the ball, as evidenced by his 54 extra-base hits in 2013, including 13 homers. He's a savvy baserunner with average speed, he plays hard and has leadership skills. Featherston has above-average range at second base, where his shortstop's arm is a plus. He needs work on turning the double play to have utility potential. Featherston ought to play at Double-A Tulsa in 2014.

Year	Club (League)	Class	AVG	G	AB	R	H	2B	3B	HR	RBI	BB	SO	SB	CS	OBP	SLG
2011	Tri-City (NWL)	SS	.231	49	169	19	39	8	3	2	20	17	38	3	1	.312	.349
2012	Asheville (SAL)	LoA	.299	105	378	75	113	30	4	12	53	53	87	15	4	.393	.495
2013	Modesto (CAL)	HiA	.292	116	469	87	137	31	10	13	81	30	110	17	4	.342	.484
Minor League Totals			.284	270	1016	181	289	69	17	27	154	100	235	35	9	.357	.466

19 CHRIS JENSEN, RHP

BA GRADE 45 HIGH

Born: Sept. 30, 1990. **B-T:** R-R. **Ht.:** 6-4. **Wt.:** 200. **Drafted:** San Diego, 2011 (6th round). **Signed by:** Jon Lukens.

Jensen signed for $135,000 in 2011 after being taken in the sixth round out of San Diego, where he primarily relieved before starting in 12 of 18 appearances as a junior. He has proven to be a durable starter in pro ball, logging 145 innings at low Class A Asheville in 2012 and 152 at high Class A Modesto in 2013. He has above-average command of a fastball that ranges from 92-95 mph and sits at 93. Because he doesn't have a great feel for his secondary stuff, he regularly throws at least 70 percent fastballs. Jensen throws a hard, sharp curveball that grades average when he throw it for strikes, which isn't often enough. He adds a fringy changeup and needs a pitch to rely on besides his fastball. The Rockies want that pitch to be a slider, and Jensen is receptive to learning to throw one, though he preferred to wait until the offseason to begin his crash course. He ought to pitch at Double-A Tulsa in 2014. Whether he develops a feel for his secondary stuff will determine whether Jensen moves to the bullpen, where he had ample experience in college.

Year	Club (League)	Class	W	L	ERA	G	GS	CG	SV	IP	H	HR	BB	SO	K/9	WHIP	AVG
2011	Tri-City (NWL)	SS	2	1	2.65	8	8	0	0	37	27	1	10	28	6.8	0.99	.206
2012	Asheville (SAL)	LoA	12	3	4.28	25	25	0	0	145	148	14	50	95	5.9	1.37	.262
2013	Modesto (CAL)	HiA	5	8	4.55	28	28	0	0	152	161	15	39	136	8.0	1.31	.264
Minor League Totals			19	12	4.22	61	61	0	0	335	336	30	99	259	7.0	1.30	.257

20 EMERSON JIMENEZ, SS

Born: Dec. 16, 1994. **B-T:** L-R. **Ht.:** 6-1. **Wt.:** 160. **Signed:** Dominican Republic, 2011. **Signed by:** Rolando Fernandez/Jhonathan Leyba/Martin Cabrera.

Jimenez began his career in the Dominican Summer League in 2012 after he signed for $275,000 a year earlier. The Rockies like to give their Latin players two years in the DSL, meaning for the most part that they'll be 19 when they come to the U.S., typically with an assignment to the Rookie-level Pioneer League. With Jimenez's instincts for the game, and the organization's lack of superior shortstop options at Grand Junction, the Rockies correctly assessed that he could handle the jump at 18 after one season in the DSL. The wiry Jimenez needs to gain strength, which given his youth isn't surprising. His package of tools is exciting, including a plus arm, plus range and plus speed. He has a loose, quick swing from the left side and generates good bat speed. He needs to become a better bunter. Jimenez will chase out of the zone, particularly against lefthanders, but he will develop more plate discipline as he gains experience. Jimenez should move up to low Class A Asheville and play his first full professional season in 2014 at age 19.

Year	Club (League)	Class	AVG	G	AB	R	H	2B	3B	HR	RBI	BB	SO	SB	CS	OBP	SLG
2012	Rockies (DSL)	R	.261	65	238	23	62	9	1	0	16	9	42	13	4	.289	.307
2013	Rockies (DSL)	R	.222	8	36	3	8	1	0	0	4	1	4	1	2	.243	.250
	Grand Junction (PIO)	R	.309	46	181	32	56	8	1	3	20	9	42	6	3	.344	.414
Minor League Totals			.277	119	455	58	126	18	2	3	40	19	88	20	9	.308	.345

21 CRISTHIAN ADAMES, SS

BA GRADE
45
HIGH

Born: July 26, 1991. **B-T:** B-R. **Ht.:** 6-0. **Wt.:** 160. **Signed:** Dominican Republic, 2007. **Signed by:** Rolando Fernandez/Felix Feliz.

Adames has moved steadily through the system, advancing one level annually since he came from the Dominican Summer League to Rookie-level Casper in 2010. He played at Double-A Tulsa in 2013, then went to the Arizona Fall League. Adames' bat likely will not carry him to everyday status in the big leagues, but he could be valuable in a utility role. The switch-hitter swings with more authority from the right side, with more of a slap swing lefthanded. Strikeouts have never been an issue for Adames, who makes steady contact. He has shown gap power in the past, but his three home runs in 2013 are indicative of 20 power on the 20-80 scouting scale. His below-average speed further reduces his offensive ceiling. Adames' strength is his defense. He's an instinctive shortstop with very good hands, solid range and plenty of arm strength with a quick release. Save for seven games at second base in 2013, Adames has played exclusively shortstop—but he ought to adapt easily if called upon to move around the diamond. Adames will play at Triple-A Colorado Springs in 2014.

Year	Club (League)	Class	AVG	G	AB	R	H	2B	3B	HR	RBI	BB	SO	SB	CS	OBP	SLG
2008	Rockies (DSL)	R	.262	51	168	22	44	5	0	0	8	18	26	7	8	.339	.292
2009	Rockies (DSL)	R	.231	36	121	17	28	6	0	1	19	18	24	8	3	.340	.306
2010	Casper (PIO)	R	.290	37	145	30	42	9	0	1	15	14	24	4	5	.356	.372
2011	Asheville (SAL)	LoA	.273	108	399	63	109	17	2	8	44	42	74	2	0	.350	.386
2012	Modesto (CAL)	HiA	.280	115	418	59	117	21	7	2	54	47	82	4	2	.352	.378
2013	Tulsa (TL)	AA	.267	107	389	45	104	19	2	3	36	34	78	13	7	.331	.350
Minor League Totals			.271	454	1640	236	444	77	11	15	176	173	308	38	25	.345	.359

22 RAUL FERNANDEZ, RHP

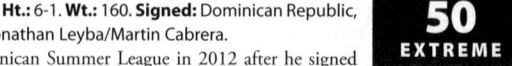

BA GRADE
50
EXTREME

Born: June 22, 1990. **B-T:** R-R. **Ht.:** 6-2. **Wt.:** 180. **Signed:** Dominican Republic, 2007. **Signed by:** Rolando Fernandez/Jhonathan Leyba.

Fernandez played catcher when he signed for $50,000 in November 2007. The Rockies saw him as a pitcher, but he wanted to continue to catch. The Rockies let Fernandez do so in the Dominican Summer League in 2008 before beginning the conversion to pitcher. He spent two more years in the DSL as a reliever before advancing to Rookie-level Casper in 2011 and repeating the Pioneer League in 2012. He advanced to low Class A Asheville in 2013, serving as closer for the Tourists. Fernandez remains raw with little feel for pitching, but has a power arm. His fastball touches 98-99 mph and sits at 96. He often leaves it up in the zone, and he lacks pitchability. He can control the strike zone but doesn't command it and is unable to pitch to the corners. Fernandez throws an average split-changeup and a slider that is getting better. He was throwing the latter at 79-81 mph in 2012, but in instructional league that year worked on throwing it harder. Before missing about six weeks in 2013 with a strained elbow ligament, Fernandez's slider sat in the mid-80s. Even though he pitched just 34 innings in 2013, Fernandez figures to advance to high Class A Modesto in 2014.

Year	Club (League)	Class	W	L	ERA	G	GS	CG	SV	IP	H	HR	BB	SO	K/9	WHIP	AVG
2009	Rockies (DSL)	R	2	1	3.29	25	0	0	2	41	39	0	10	27	5.9	1.20	.245
2010	Rockies (DSL)	R	4	3	1.52	12	11	0	0	65	55	0	21	46	6.4	1.17	.232
2011	Casper (PIO)	R	4	7	8.20	14	14	0	0	64	91	11	18	50	7.1	1.71	.330
2012	Grand Junction (PIO)	R	1	1	3.52	30	0	0	2	31	28	3	6	27	7.9	1.11	.231
2013	Asheville (SAL)	LoA	2	2	6.29	35	0	0	16	34	40	6	11	55	14.4	1.49	.284
Minor League Totals			13	14	4.60	116	25	0	20	235	253	20	66	205	7.9	1.36	.271

Year	Club (League)	Class	AVG	G	AB	R	H	2B	3B	HR	RBI	BB	SO	SB	CS	OBP	SLG
2008	Rockies (DSL)	R	.221	21	68	5	15	3	0	0	6	4	12	2	0	.264	.265
Minor League Totals			.221	21	68	5	15	3	0	0	6	4	12	2	0	.264	.265

23 FRANCISCO SOSA, OF

BA GRADE **50** EXTREME

Born: Feb. 27, 1990. **B-T:** R-R. **Ht.:** 6-4. **Wt.:** 180. **Signed:** Dominican Republic, 2007. **Signed by:** Rolando Fernandez/Frank Roa.

Sosa is a potential late-bloomer. Signed for $400,000 in 2007, he spent 2008-09 in the Dominican Summer League. Following the '09 season, Sosa was involved in a car accident that resulted in a rod being surgically inserted into his left arm. He played sparingly in 2010, finishing the season with 78 at-bats, and didn't pick up the pace until joining low Class A Asheville in 2013. Sosa led the South Atlantic League in RBIs (89) and total bases (244), showing well-rounded tools. However, away from Asheville's hitter-friendly ballpark, he hit just .256/.326/.355 with five homers. Still, Sosa has developed better separation in his swing, enabling him to get his hands involved and let the ball travel. He has strength and above-average power, but recognizing offspeed pitches earlier will be his biggest challenge to hit for average against better pitchers. His strike-zone discipline improved during 2013 as he chased fewer sliders in the dirt late in the season. Sosa has become a capable outfielder and can play all three positions adequately. His arm is fringe-average. Sosa runs well, knows how to steal and is not afraid to try. He will play at high Class A Modesto in 2014.

Year	Club (League)	Class	AVG	G	AB	R	H	2B	3B	HR	RBI	BB	SO	SB	CS	OBP	SLG
2008	Rockies (DSL)	R	.203	57	182	18	37	6	1	3	13	15	55	10	9	.288	.297
2009	Rockies (DSL)	R	.291	57	199	23	58	8	1	2	29	22	54	16	6	.381	.372
2010	Casper (PIO)	R	.176	5	17	3	3	0	0	0	1	1	5	0	1	.222	.176
	Rockies (DSL)	R	.148	23	61	8	9	3	0	0	1	9	21	4	5	.288	.197
2011	Casper (PIO)	R	.254	50	185	21	47	10	3	6	28	13	57	7	4	.305	.438
2012	Tri-City (NWL)	SS	.275	68	251	35	69	14	2	4	36	24	57	21	2	.354	.394
2013	Asheville (SAL)	LoA	.315	127	461	85	145	35	2	20	89	57	125	30	10	.397	.529
Minor League Totals			.271	387	1356	193	368	76	9	35	197	141	374	88	37	.353	.418

24 ANTONIO SENZATELA, RHP

BA GRADE **50** EXTREME

Born: Jan. 21, 1995. **B-T:** R-R. **Ht.:** 6-1. **Wt.:** 180. **Signed:** Venezuela, 2011. **Signed by:** Rolando Fernandez/Orlando Medina/Carlos Gomez.

Senzatela signed for $250,000 in 2011 and began his career in the Dominican Summer League the following season. He made eight dominant starts in the DSL in 2013 to earn an in-season promotion to short-season Tri-City, where he allowed three or fewer earned runs in seven of his eight starts for the Dust Devils. He tops out at 95 mph without looking like he's throwing that hard. He pitches consistently at 92-93 mph with late life and throws downhill. His youth suggests the potential for velocity gains, but Senzatela has a mature body with little projection. He has a curveball that showed some improvement in instructional league, but the pitch still needs work. His splitter has depth and he can throw it for strikes. Senzatela prompts comparisons with Rockies starter Jhoulys Chacin, a fellow Venezuelan, though he lacks the breaking ball and changeup that Chacin had at the same stage. Senzatela throws harder, however, and likely will head to low Class A Asheville in 2014.

Year	Club (League)	Class	W	L	ERA	G	GS	CG	SV	IP	H	HR	BB	SO	K/9	WHIP	AVG
2012	Rockies (DSL)	R	5	2	0.72	13	12	0	0	63	40	0	14	35	5.0	0.86	.179
2013	Rockies (DSL)	R	6	1	1.76	8	8	1	0	51	32	1	3	46	8.1	0.69	.179
	Tri-City (NWL)	SS	2	4	3.83	8	8	0	0	42	48	1	13	20	4.3	1.44	.282
Minor League Totals			13	7	1.90	29	28	1	0	156	120	2	30	101	5.8	0.96	.209

25 DAN HOUSTON, RHP

BA GRADE **45** HIGH

Born: Oct. 24, 1986. **B-T:** R-R. **Ht.:** 6-3. **Wt.:** 205. **Drafted:** Boston College, 2008 (7th round). **Signed by:** Ed Santa.

A move to the bullpen jumpstarted Houston's career, which appeared stalled at Double-A Tulsa, where he had spent all of 2012 and the second half of 2011. Back for a third tour in 2013, he moved to the bullpen when Roy Oswalt joined the Drillers rotation, and he hasn't looked back. He threw three hitless innings in his first outing, made 20 relief appearances at Tulsa and Triple-A Colorado

Springs and then earned a trip to the Arizona Fall League. As a starter, Houston's fastball topped out at 92 mph and was generally around 88 mph. Out of the bullpen, he sits at 92 mph and has ticked up to 94-95 occasionally. His straight changeup has a little fade and has also become much more effective. It's an above-average pitch with the potential to further improve. Houston also developed a true cutter in 2013, a good weapon against lefthanders. He will contend for a middle-relief role in big league camp and likely begin 2014 in Triple-A.

Year	Club (League)	Class	W	L	ERA	G	GS	CG	SV	IP	H	HR	BB	SO	K/9	WHIP	AVG
2008	Casper (PIO)	R	6	4	4.17	14	14	1	0	69	61	10	20	68	8.9	1.17	.229
2009	Asheville (SAL)	LoA	8	9	3.63	26	26	0	0	149	141	11	63	121	7.3	1.37	.250
2010	Modesto (CAL)	HiA	5	7	5.92	21	20	0	0	114	157	9	43	80	6.3	1.75	.333
2011	Modesto (CAL)	HiA	7	1	2.53	13	13	1	0	85	71	7	22	67	7.1	1.09	.224
	Tulsa (TL)	AA	4	4	4.27	13	13	1	0	78	89	6	18	51	5.9	1.37	.288
2012	Tulsa (TL)	AA	10	10	3.74	27	27	0	0	161	174	16	38	96	5.4	1.31	.279
2013	Tulsa (TL)	AA	4	6	3.36	31	13	0	2	102	97	7	30	67	5.9	1.25	.249
	Colorado Springs (PCL)	AAA	0	0	4.91	2	0	0	0	4	4	0	3	5	12.3	1.91	.250
Minor League Totals			44	41	3.96	147	126	3	2	762	794	66	237	555	6.6	1.35	.269

26 MAX WHITE, OF

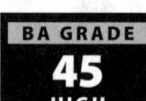

BA GRADE **50** EXTREME

Born: Oct. 10, 1993. **B-T:** L-L. **Ht.:** 6-2. **Wt.:** 175. **Drafted:** HS—Williston, Fla., 2012 (2nd round). **Signed by:** Alan Matthews.

The Rockies drafted White 73rd overall in 2012 and signed him for $1 million to steer him away from his commitment to Florida. His debut season at Rookie-level Grand Junction presented myriad challenges as he struggled to hit, particularly at the outset, though he did improve as the season unfolded. He began 2013 in extended spring training before heading to low Class A Asheville in May when the team had an outfield opening. The lean, wiry White needs to gain strength and be more aggressive at the plate with his smooth, easy swing from the left side. His pitch recognition needs improvement as well, particularly against breaking pitches from lefthanders. He has good hand speed and balance and plenty of bat speed. As he grows into his body, he could develop enough power to hit 15 homers a year. He runs well but needs to bunt more often to capitalize on his speed. He is a pure center fielder with above-average range. His arm strength was above-average when he got to Asheville but tailed off later in the season. Shoulder surgery in high school diminished White's status as a professional pitching prospect, but he has plenty of arm to play center. He likely will return to Asheville in 2014.

Year	Club (League)	Class	AVG	G	AB	R	H	2B	3B	HR	RBI	BB	SO	SB	CS	OBP	SLG
2012	Grand Junction (PIO)	R	.200	50	170	30	34	5	3	4	18	29	72	6	5	.322	.335
2013	Asheville (SAL)	LoA	.226	72	243	25	55	16	1	3	21	20	79	11	8	.288	.337
Minor League Totals			.215	122	413	55	89	21	4	7	39	49	151	17	13	.303	.337

27 JOHENDI JIMINIAN, RHP

BA GRADE **45** HIGH

Born: Oct. 14, 1992. **B-T:** R-R. **Ht.:** 6-3. **Wt.:** 170. **Signed:** Dominican Republic, 2010. **Signed by:** Rolando Fernandez/Jhonathan Leyba/Frank Roa.

Jiminian signed for $350,000 and pitched in the Dominican Summer League in 2010-11 before coming to the U.S. He has a live arm and a chance to throw with above-average velocity, particularly when he irons out a raw delivery. Jiminian can get his fastball up to 93-94 mph with life. His breaking ball has the makings of a power slurve that eventually should be average to a tick above. He throws it up to 81 mph with tight, late break despite a tendency to release it too early. His changeup is below-average and a pitch that he'll have to develop. Jiminian throws a lot of secondary pitches in the dirt, as evidenced by 14 wild pitches in 83 innings at short-season Tri-City in 2013. He will probably move up to low Class A Asheville for 2014.

Year	Club (League)	Class	W	L	ERA	G	GS	CG	SV	IP	H	HR	BB	SO	K/9	WHIP	AVG
2010	Rockies (DSL)	R	3	5	4.40	12	11	0	0	47	46	1	17	31	5.9	1.34	.256
2011	Rockies (DSL)	R	6	3	3.18	14	14	0	0	68	57	4	23	47	6.2	1.18	.230
2012	Grand Junction (PIO)	R	2	4	7.71	14	13	0	0	47	60	5	33	28	5.4	1.99	.311
2013	Tri-City (NWL)	SS	3	5	3.38	15	14	0	0	83	79	3	24	57	6.2	1.25	.256
Minor League Totals			14	17	4.35	55	52	0	0	244	242	13	97	163	6.0	1.39	.260

28 JAYSON AQUINO, LHP

Born: Nov. 22, 1992. **B-T:** L-L. **Ht.:** 6-1. **Wt.:** 170. **Signed:** Dominican Republic, 2009. **Signed by:** Rolando Fernandez/Jhonathan Leyba/Frank Roa.

Aquino, who signed for $175,000 in 2009, pitched well in 2010-11 in the Dominican Summer League. The Rockies sent him back to the DSL in 2012 after he reported to spring training overweight. He made it to Rookie-level Grand Junction in August 2012 and pitched well, but 2013 was a difficult year for Aquino—and not just because he went winless in 10 decisions, most of them at low Class A Asheville. He can touch 92 mph with his fastball and pitches at 88-89, but he doesn't throw it often enough or command it, particularly to his glove side. When he throws fastball strikes, it's to his arm side, though there the pitch tends to run off the plate. Aquino has a well above-average changeup that he throws too often and a sharp curveball that is a solid-average pitch. He's too emotional and must learn to ignore umpires' calls that he disagrees with, and he also needs to develop better tempo in his delivery. He doesn't field his position or hold runners well. Added to the 40-man roster after the season, Aquino is scheduled for a return to Asheville in 2014.

Year	Club (League)	Class	W	L	ERA	G	GS	CG	SV	IP	H	HR	BB	SO	K/9	WHIP	AVG
2010	Rockies (DSL)	R	4	3	1.02	12	12	2	0	62	35	0	9	59	8.6	0.71	.161
2011	Rockies (DSL)	R	8	2	1.30	14	14	3	0	90	55	1	22	80	8.0	0.86	.175
2012	Rockies (DSL)	R	6	1	1.52	9	9	2	0	65	45	1	9	74	10.2	0.83	.191
	Grand Junction (PIO)	R	4	0	1.87	7	7	0	0	43	32	2	11	36	7.5	0.99	.203
2013	Tri-City (NWL)	SS	0	1	3.13	4	4	0	0	23	21	1	5	16	6.3	1.13	.244
	Asheville (SAL)	LoA	0	9	4.78	11	10	0	0	64	66	4	21	57	8.0	1.36	.275
Minor League Totals			22	16	2.13	57	56	7	0	347	254	9	77	322	8.4	0.95	.203

29 JOSE BRICENO, C

BA GRADE
50
EXTREME

Born: Sept. 19, 1992. **B-T:** R-R. **Ht.:** 6-0. **Wt.:** 195. **Signed:** Venezuela, 2009. **Signed by:** Rolando Fernandez/Francisco Cartaya.

Briceno signed for $250,000 in 2009 and played his first two seasons in the Dominican Summer League. He began 2013 at Rookie-level Grand Junction, where he hit .333/.356/.614 with nine homers in 153 at-bats to earn a promotion to low Class A Asheville in early August. At the conclusion of the Tourists' season, Briceno returned to Grand Junction for the Pioneer League playoffs. His best tools are his above-average power and arm strength. The raw catching tools, with solid feet and good hands, are evident, so now it's a matter of repetition and refinement. He struggles to block pitches in the dirt because he doesn't anticipate the ball well. Briceno has an inside-out swing with some length and is a low-ball hitter. He struggled to hit breaking pitches at Asheville, but worked to tone down his leg kick in instructional league, develop a better hitting base and slow the game down. Briceno is mature in the hips and legs, prompting concern about diminished speed (currently average) and flexibility his down the road. A move to first base might ultimately result. Regardless, Briceno has a chance to wield an impact bat. He will probably return to Asheville to begin 2014 but could earn another midseason promotion.

Year	Club (League)	Class	AVG	G	AB	R	H	2B	3B	HR	RBI	BB	SO	SB	CS	OBP	SLG
2010	Rockies (DSL)	R	.205	52	151	12	31	6	0	0	17	17	28	9	5	.295	.245
2011	Rockies (DSL)	R	.288	47	160	26	46	10	1	0	18	23	22	12	3	.389	.363
2012	Grand Junction (PIO)	R	.391	7	23	5	9	0	0	2	5	2	2	0	0	.462	.652
2013	Asheville (SAL)	LoA	.264	26	91	12	24	6	0	1	8	5	20	1	0	.302	.363
	Grand Junction (PIO)	R	.333	36	153	32	51	16	0	9	30	5	30	8	2	.356	.614
Minor League Totals			.279	168	578	87	161	38	1	12	78	52	102	30	10	.346	.410

30 RYAN WARNER, RHP

BA GRADE
50
EXTREME

Born: Jan. 21, 1994. **B-T:** L-R. **Ht.:** 6-7. **Wt.:** 195. **Drafted:** HS—Colorado Springs, 2012 (3rd round supplemental). **Signed by:** Marc Gustafson.

The Rockies lured Warner, a Colorado Springs native, away from a North Carolina State commitment, possibly the only organization that could have done so. He grew up a Rockies fan and wanted the opportunity to play for the organization. Warner signed for a $363,700 bonus as a supplemental third-round pick in 2012. He worked on a 60-pitch limit that summer as he began his career at Rookie-level Grand Junction. then pitched a team-leading 88 innings at short-season Tri-City in 2013. The 6-foot-7 Warner is a good athlete who played quarterback and wide receiver in high school. He shows maturity on the mound, a feel for his craft and can make adjustments more quickly than most young pitchers. His size enables him to create a downhill angle on his fastball, though he needs to locate it down better. His curveball improved notably as the 2013 season progressed and has the makings of an above-average pitch. His changeup is a work in progress. He tired late in the season, causing his arm slot to drop. That reduced his velocity slightly to 88-89 mph and took away the bite on his curveball. As he learns to work his stuff lower in the zone and keep his arm slot up, Warner should regain the sharp break on his curveball and get his fastball back to 90 mph. He's still very projectable and will pitch at low Class A Asheville in 2014.

Year	Club (League)	Class	W	L	ERA	G	GS	CG	SV	IP	H	HR	BB	SO	K/9	WHIP	AVG
2012	Grand Junction (PIO)	R	3	0	7.00	14	10	0	0	45	63	9	13	36	7.2	1.69	.333
2013	Tri-City (NWL)	SS	3	4	3.36	15	15	0	0	88	79	4	23	46	4.7	1.15	.239
Minor League Totals			6	4	4.59	29	25	0	0	133	142	13	36	82	5.5	1.34	.273

Detroit Tigers

BY BEN BADLER

With one of baseball's best offenses and a dominant starting rotation, the Tigers won the American League Central and reached the AL Championship Series for the third straight season.

While the Tigers couldn't get back to the World Series after falling to the Red Sox in six games in the ALCS, general manager Dave Dombrowski has built the Tigers into the perennial favorite in the AL Central with a series of savvy trades and free agent signings with the financial backing to make it work.

The Tigers' track record in trades and free agency

speaks both to the organization's ability to forecast performance for other teams' major leaguers and to properly evaluate their own prospect inventory. While some teams fall too much in love with the prospects they signed as amateurs and have spent time developing, the Tigers have done well selling off their minor league prospects at the peak of their value.

They did it to acquire Miguel Cabrera after the 2007 season, parting with 2005 and 2006 first-rounders Cameron Maybin and Andrew Miller as headliners in the deal.

Dombrowski added Max Scherzer from the Diamondbacks along with Austin Jackson and Phil Coke from the Yankees after the 2009 season. The Tigers had to give up Curtis Granderson and Edwin Jackson in the three-team exchange, but Austin Jackson gave the Tigers a younger everyday center fielder with more years of control than Granderson, and Scherzer won the 2013 AL Cy Young Award.

At the 2011 trade deadline, the Tigers sent third baseman Francisco Martinez (the team's No. 4 prospect entering the season), outfielder Casper Wells and lefthander Charlie Furbush to the Mariners for Doug Fister. The Tigers astutely sold high on Martinez and got an above-average starter in return.

The book is still out on righthander Jacob Turner, the 2009 first-rounder who ranked as Detroit's No. 1 prospect from 2009-11, but including him in the 2012 midseason trade to acquire righthander Anibal Sanchez and second baseman Omar Infante was a win.

When the Tigers lost Jhonny Peralta to a 50-game suspension in 2013 for his involvement with Biogenesis, the Tigers again dipped into their farm system, trading toolsy outfielder Avisail Garcia to the White Sox in the midst of his breakout season in a three-team deal that imported shortstop Jose Iglesias from the Red Sox.

TOMASSO DEROSA

Max Scherzer is the product of one of several trades that turned out favorably for Detroit

TOP PROSPECTS OF THE DECADE

Year	Player, Pos.	2013 Org.
2004	Kyle Sleeth, rhp	Out of baseball
2005	Curtis Granderson, of	Yankees
2006	Justin Verlander, rhp	Tigers
2007	Cameron Maybin, of	Padres
2008	Rick Porcello, rhp	Tigers
2009	Rick Porecello, rhp	Tigers
2010	Jacob Turner, rhp	Marlins
2011	Jacob Turner, rhp	Marlins
2012	Jacob Turner, rhp	Marlins
2013	Nick Castellanos, 3b/of	Tigers

Dombrowski executed a blockbuster after the season, moving Prince Fielder to Texas for second baseman Ian Kinsler, a move that allowed Cabrera to move back to first base and No. 1 prospect Nick Castellanos to return to third.

The Tigers' farm system isn't the strongest and it hasn't been for several years. Sacrificing first-round picks from 2010-12 to sign free agents hasn't helped them there, but the Tigers have held on to homegrown players who have been productive, including catcher Alex Avila. The Tigers are betting on Castellanos to emerge as their third baseman after playing all of 2013 at left field, and for Bruce Rondon, one of several prospects from Venezuela, to pitch high-leverage innings in front of free agent signing Joe Nathan.

ORGANIZATION OVERVIEW

General Manager: Dave Dombrowski. **Farm Director:** Dan Lunetta. **Scouting Director:** Scott Pleis.

Class	Team	League	W	L	PCT	Finish	Manager
Majors	Detroit Tigers	American	93	69	.574	3rd (15)	Jim Leyland
Triple-A	Toledo Mud Hens	International	61	83	.424	13th (14)	Phil Nevin
Double-A	Erie SeaWolves	Eastern	76	66	.535	3rd (12)	Chris Cron
High Class A	Lakeland Flying Tigers	Florida State	64	68	.485	8th (12)	Dave Huppert
Low Class A	West Michigan Whitecaps	Midwest	69	70	.496	t-7th (16)	Larry Parrish
Short-season	Connecticut Tigers	New York-Penn	33	42	.440	11th (14)	Andrew Graham
Rookie	GCL Tigers	Gulf Coast	32	28	.533	5th (16)	Basilio Cabrera
Overall 2013 Minor League Record			**335**	**357**	**.484**	**23rd (30)**	

THIS YEAR'S TOP 30

No.	Player, Pos.	Grade/Risk
1.	Nick Castellanos, 3b/of	60/Medium
2.	Devon Travis, 2b	55/High
3.	Bruce Rondon, rhp	50/Low
4.	Jake Thompson, rhp	55/High
5.	Jonathon Crawford, rhp	55/High
6.	Corey Knebel, rhp	50/High
7.	Eugenio Suarez, ss/2b	50/High
8.	Domingo Leyba, ss/2b	55/Extreme
9.	Hernan Perez, 2b/ss	45/Low
10.	Kevin Ziomek, lhp	50/High
11.	James McCann, c	45/Medium
12.	Drew VerHagen, rhp	45/Medium
13.	Jose Ortega, rhp	45/Medium
14.	Javier Betancourt, ss	50/Extreme
15.	Steven Moya, of	50/Extreme
16.	Melvin Mercedes, rhp	45/High
17.	Casey Crosby, lhp	40/Medium
18.	Jose Valdez, rhp	45/High
19.	Jordan Lennerton, 1b	40/Low
20.	Tyler Collins, of	45/High
21.	Jose Alvarez, lhp	40/Low
22.	Daniel Fields, of	45/High
23.	Kyle Lobstein, lhp	40/Medium
24.	Jeff Thompson, rhp	45/High
25.	Zac Reininger, rhp	45/High
26.	Bryan Holaday, c	40/Low
27.	Ramon Cabrera, c	40/Medium
28.	Steven Fuentes, 3b	50/Extreme
29.	Calvin Drummond, rhp	45/Extreme
30.	Willy Adames, ss/3b	45/Extreme

LAST YEAR'S TOP 30

No.	Player, Pos.	Status
1.	Nick Castellanos, 3b/of	No. 1
2.	Avisail Garcia, of	(White Sox)
3.	Bruce Rondon, rhp	No. 3
4.	Jake Thompson, rhp	No. 4
5.	Austin Schotts, of	Dropped out
6.	Danry Vasquez, of	(Astros)
7.	Tyler Collins, of	No. 20
8.	Casey Crosby, lhp	No. 17
9.	Eugenio Suarez, ss/2b	No. 7
10.	Adam Wilk, lhp	(Korea)
11.	James McCann, c	No. 11
12.	Tyler Clark, rhp	Dropped out
13.	Melvin Mercedes, rhp	No. 16
14.	Drew VerHagen, rhp	No. 12
15.	Steven Moya, of	No. 15
16.	Jose Ortega, rhp	No. 13
17.	Harold Castro, 2b	Dropped out
18.	Montreal Robertson, rhp	Dropped out
19.	Kyle Lobstein, lhp	No. 23
20.	Jeff Kobernus, 2b	(Nationals)
21.	Brenny Paulino, rhp	Dropped out
22.	Endrys Briceno, rhp	Dropped out
23.	Curt Casali, c	(Rays)
24.	Bryan Holaday, c	No. 26
25.	Luke Putkonen, rhp	Majors
26.	Ramon Cabrera, c	No. 27
27.	Dixon Machado, ss	Dropped out
28.	Hernan Perez, 2b/ss	No. 9
29.	Edgar de la Rosa, rhp	Dropped out
30.	Daniel Fields, of	No. 22

BEST TOOLS

Best Hitter for Average	Nick Castellanos
Best Power Hitter	Steven Moya
Best Strike-Zone Discipline	Devon Travis
Fastest Baserunner	Austin Schotts
Best Athlete	Austin Schotts
Best Fastball	Bruce Rondon
Best Curveball	Corey Knebel
Best Slider	Jonathon Crawford
Best Changeup	Jose Alvarez
Best Control	Jose Alvarez
Best Defensive Catcher	James McCann
Best Defensive Infielder	Dixon Machado
Best Infield Arm	Dixon Machado
Best Defensive Outfielder	Daniel Fields
Best Outfield Arm	Steven Moya

TOP 15 PLAYERS 25 AND UNDER

No.	Player, Pos (Age)	Peak Level
1.	Nick Castellanos, 3b/of (22)	Majors
2.	Jose Iglesias, ss (24)	Majors
3.	Rick Porcello, rhp (25)	Majors
4.	Drew Smyly, lhp (24)	Majors
5.	Devon Travis, 2b (23)	High Class A
6.	Bruce Rondon, rhp (23)	Majors
7.	Jonathon Crawford, rhp (22)	Short-season
8.	Jake Thompson, rhp (20)	Low Class A
9.	Corey Knebel, rhp (22)	Low Class A
10.	Eugenio Suarez, ss (22)	Double-A
11.	Domingo Leyba, ss (18)	Rookie
12.	Hernan Perez, ss (23)	Majors
13.	Kevin Ziomek, lhp (22)	Short-season
14.	James McCann, c (23)	Double-A
15.	Jose Ortega, rhp (25)	Majors

MINOR LEAGUE DEPTH CHART

DETROIT TIGERS

TOP 2014 ROOKIE: Nick Castellanos, 3b. The transition back to third base could be bumpy, but he has the offensive upside to contend for American League top rookie honors.

BREAKOUT PROSPECT: Javier Betancourt, ss. He has a knack for squaring up the ball with advanced instincts for a teenager.

SLEEPER: Wilsen Palacios, rhp. His stuff is ordinary as a starter, but he fills up the strike zone and his fastball/splitter combo could play up in relief.

SOURCE OF TOP 30 TALENT

Homegrown	27	Acquired	3
College	10	Trades	2
Junior college	2	Rule 5 draft	0
High school	4	Independent leagues	0
Nondrafted free agents	0	Free agents/waivers	1
International	11		

LF

Tyler Collins (20)
Daniel Fields (22)

CF

Austin Schotts
Jeff McVaney

RF

Steven Moya (15)
Ben Guez
Jeff McVaney
Samuel Crafort

3B

Nick Castellanos (1)
Steven Fuentes (28)
Francisco Martinez
Wade Gaynor
Jason King

SS

Eugenio Suarez (7)
Domingo Leyba (8)
Willy Adames (30)
Dixon Machado
Hector Martinez
Adrian Alfaro

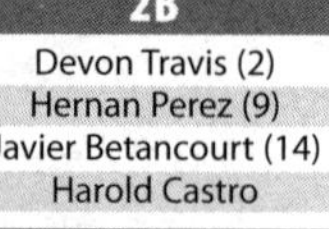

2B

Devon Travis (2)
Hernan Perez (9)
Javier Betancourt (14)
Harold Castro

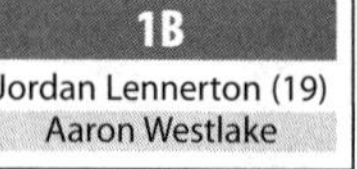

1B

Jordan Lennerton (19)
Aaron Westlake

C

James McCann (11)
Bryan Holaday (26)
Ramon Cabrera (27)
Elys Escobar
Franklin Navarro

LHP

LHSP	LHRP
Kevin Ziomek (10)	Casey Crosby (17)
Jose Alvarez (21)	Kyle Lobstein (23)
Kyle Ryan	Blaine Hardy
Jordan John	

RHP

RHSP	RHRP
Jake Thompson (4)	Bruce Rondon (3)
Jonathon Crawford (5)	Corey Knebel (6)
Drew VerHagen (12)	Jose Ortega (13)
Jeff Thompson (24)	Melvin Mercedes (16)
Zach Reininger (25)	Jose Valdez (18)
Calvin Drummond (29)	Will Clinard
Wilsen Palacios	Austin Kubitza
Endrys Briceno	Guido Knudson
Buck Farmer	Angel Nesbitt
Warwick Saupold	Tyler Clark

DRAFT ANALYSIS

2013 — BONUSES: $6.2 MILLION

BEST PURE HITTER: Despite switch-hitting 2B Dominic Ficociello's (12) flagging production each year at Arkansas, the Tigers say he should be a productive hitter and could grow into average power as well. OF Raph Rhymes (15) led NCAA Division I in batting (.431/.489/.530) in 2012, finished his Louisiana State career with a .373 average and posted a .296/.412/.379 line this summer.

BEST POWER HITTER: OF Connor Harrell (7) is susceptible to breaking stuff and has strikeout tendencies, but he led Vanderbilt in home runs the past two years and has the natural strength to develop average power.

FASTEST RUNNER: Harrell is an above-average runner with good instincts on the bases. OF Kasey Coffman (10) also has above-average speed.

BEST DEFENSIVE PLAYER: Harrell played center field at Vanderbilt and this summer with an average arm and athleticism.

BEST FASTBALL: Detroit netted a collection of power arms. RHP Jonathan Crawford (1) can sit 92-95 mph with his fastball, featuring above-average life through the zone. RHP Corey Knebel (1s) touches 98 out of the bullpen.

BEST SECONDARY PITCH: Knebel's curveball is a true out pitch with power and late bite. Crawford also has a plus slider.

BEST PRO DEBUT: Knebel had 41 strikeouts and 10 walks along with a 0.87 ERA in 31 innings at low Class A West Michigan. Oft-injured but talented RHP Calvin Drummond (6), whose fastball touches 97 mph, struck out 10.6 per nine in 38 MWL innings with a 2.35 ERA. RHPs Zac Reininger (8), who had a 1.00 ERA and 32 SO/6 BB in 27 IP, and Scott Sitz (28), who had a 2.16 ERA and 23 SO/4 BB in 25 IP, both dominated in the New York-Penn League.

BEST ATHLETE: At 6-foot-3, 205 pounds, Harrell has a rare combination of tools and athleticism for a senior sign.

MOST INTRIGUING BACKGROUND: OF Ben Verlander (14) is the younger brother of Justin, who also attended Old Dominion. The Tigers did not sign OF Torii Hunter Jr. (36), the son of their right fielder. He headed to Notre Dame to play wide receiver but sat out last fall because of a broken leg. RHP Austin Kubitza (4) is the brother of Braves third base prospect Kyle. This was the fourth time Drummond, 24, was drafted, and he attended four different colleges.

CLOSEST TO THE MAJORS: Many of the power arms the Tigers drafted could move quickly as bullpen candidates. Knebel's two-pitch mix make him the strongest candidate to be fast-tracked.

BEST LATE-ROUND PICK: Rhymes provides organizational depth and contact ability.

THE ONE WHO GOT AWAY: Athletic LHP Tyler Alexander (23), the Tigers' highest-drafted high schooler, had an inconsistent spring and headed to Texas Christian.

ASSESSMENT: The Tigers' first seven picks were all college pitchers, and 20 of the 30 players they signed were college arms. The emphasis was on power arms, highlighted by Crawford and Knebel.

2012 — BONUSES: $3.2 MILLION

RHP Jake Thompson (2), the club's top pick, is trending in the right direction. RHP Drew VerHagen (4) has moved quickly, reaching Double-A.

GRADE: D

2011 — BONUSES: $2.9 MILLION

With no first-round pick, the Tigers aimed low with a college-heavy class. LHP Brian Flynn (6) was traded; C James McCann (2) is the best of what's left.

GRADE: D

2010 — BONUSES: $7.3 MILLION

Nick Castellanos (1s) will join LHP Drew Smyly (2) as a key part of the 2014 Tigers. RHP Chance Ruffin (1s) and Cs Rob Brantly (3) and Bryan Holaday (6) have reached the majors.

GRADE: B+

TOP DRAFT PICKS OF THE DECADE

Year	Player, Pos.	2013 Org.
2004	Justin Verlander, rhp	Tigers
2005	Cameron Maybin, of	Padres
2006	Andrew Miller, lhp	Red Sox
2007	Rick Porcello, rhp	Tigers
2008	Ryan Perry, rhp	Nationals
2009	Jacob Turner, rhp	Marlins
2010	Nick Castellanos, 3b (1st round supp.)	Tigers
2011	James McCann, c (2nd round)	Tigers
2012	Jake Thompson, rhp (2nd round)	Tigers
2013	Jonathon Crawford, rhp	Tigers

LARGEST BONUSES IN CLUB HISTORY

Jacob Turner, 2009	$4,700,000
Rick Porcello, 2007	$3,580,000
Andrew Miller, 2006	$3,550,000
Eric Munson, 1999	$3,500,000
Nick Castellanos, 2010	$3,450,000

1 NICK CASTELLANOS, 3B/OF

Born: March 4, 1992. **B-T:** R-R. **Ht.:** 6-4. **Wt.:** 210. **Drafted:** HS—Southwest Ranches, Fla., 2010 (1st round supplemental). **Signed by:** Rolando Casanova.

BA GRADE
60
MEDIUM
SCOUTING GRADES
BATTING 65
POWER 55
SPEED 40
DEFENSE 45
ARM 50

MIKE JANES

The Tigers surrendered their 2010 first-round pick after signing free-agent reliever Jose Valverde the previous offseason, so they didn't pick until the supplemental first round at 44th overall. When Castellanos slid in the draft amidst reports he was demanding $6 million to sign, the Tigers were elated when he was still available with their first pick and signed him for $3.45 million. After an outstanding pro debut in the low Class A Midwest League in 2011, he opened the 2012 season by hitting over .400 through his first 55 games in the high Class A Florida State League. Castellanos struggled the second half of the season at Double-A Erie, but the Tigers pushed him to Triple-A Toledo to open 2013, where he had a solid season despite a slow start and made his major league debut as a September callup.

Castellanos' bat is his calling card. He's a natural, instinctive hitter with strong wrists who eschews batting gloves and unleashes a loose, righthanded swing. He lets the ball travel deep and the bat head stays in the zone a long time, which helps him hit to all fields and wear out right-center field. He finishes his slight uppercut stroke with a high finish and generates plenty of loft with good feel for the barrel. He starts his swing by dropping his hands but his above-average bat speed and compact stroke allow him to catch up to good velocity. He has solid plate patience, makes in-game adjustments and has trimmed his strikeout rate, leading scouts to project him as a potential .300 hitter. The split among scouts centers around Castellanos' power potential. He has average raw power and some scouts think there isn't much more size for him to put on, so they see him as a 15-20 home run guy, whereas others look at his long frame and see 25-plus longball potential. He faces the difficult task of breaking into the majors while manning a position he didn't play in 2013. Castellanos started his pro career at third base, but the Tigers shifted him to left field midway through 2012. With the offseason trade of Prince Fielder, shifting Miguel Cabrera to first base, Castellanos will return to third, where he projects as a fringy but playable defender. He's a below-average runner with limited range, decent hands and an average arm, but at the very least he should give Detroit better defense than Cabrera.

The Tigers are counting on Castellanos to be their Opening Day third baseman. While he'll need a refresher course on defense, his bat is good enough to make a run at the American League Rookie of the Year award. He could be a perennial all-star depending on how much power he develops.

Year	Club (League)	Class	AVG	G	AB	R	H	2B	3B	HR	RBI	BB	SO	SB	CS	OBP	SLG
2010	Tigers (GCL)	R	.333	7	24	5	8	2	0	0	3	4	5	0	1	.414	.417
2011	West Michigan (MWL)	LoA	.312	135	507	65	158	36	3	7	76	45	130	3	2	.367	.436
2012	Lakeland (FSL)	HiA	.405	55	215	37	87	17	3	3	32	22	42	3	2	.461	.553
	Erie (EL)	AA	.264	79	322	35	85	15	1	7	25	14	76	5	4	.296	.382
2013	Toledo (IL)	AAA	.276	134	533	81	147	37	1	18	76	54	100	4	1	.343	.450
	Detroit (AL)	MAJ	.278	11	18	1	5	0	0	0	0	0	1	0	0	.278	.278
Major League Totals			.278	11	18	1	5	0	0	0	0	0	1	0	0	.278	.278
Minor League Totals			.303	410	1601	223	485	107	8	35	212	139	353	15	10	.359	.445

2 DEVON TRAVIS, 2B

Born: Feb. 21, 1991. **B-T:** R-R. **Ht.:** 5-9. **Wt.:** 183. **Drafted:** Florida State, 2012 (13th round). **Signed by:** Jim Rough.

Travis was a three-year starter an Florida State and a strong offensive performer his final two seasons, but with his small stature he lasted until the 13th round of the 2012 draft and signed for $200,000. He already looks like a steal after ranking 13th among full-season minor leaguers in on-base percentage (.418) and second in average (.351) in 2013. Travis has a short, line-drive swing, good plate coverage and he goes with the pitch to use the whole field. He's a patient, disciplined hitter who draws his walks and waits for a good pitch to hit. After having a more spread-out stance in college, Travis is now more upright and has lowered his hands, with a shorter load to help him get to good velocity on the inner-third and stay inside the ball. He is strong and has surprising sock for his size, though he'll max out with average power at best, mostly to his pull side. His plus speed and quick-twitch athleticism gives him good range at second, where he has solid actions, an average arm and a smooth double-play pivot. He's a smart player and a grinder who gets the most from his tools. Travis still has his skeptics, but scouts highest on him believe he can be an everyday second baseman who hits at the top of a big league lineup. He'll graduate to Double-A Erie in 2014.

Year	Club (League)	Class	AVG	G	AB	R	H	2B	3B	HR	RBI	BB	SO	SB	CS	OBP	SLG
2012	Connecticut (NYP)	SS	.280	25	93	17	26	2	2	3	11	8	10	3	1	.352	.441
2013	West Michigan (MWL)	LoA	.352	77	290	55	102	17	2	6	42	35	32	14	3	.430	.486
	Lakeland (FSL)	HiA	.350	55	214	38	75	11	2	10	34	18	32	8	1	.401	.561
Minor League Totals			.340	157	597	110	203	30	6	19	87	61	74	25	5	.408	.506

3 BRUCE RONDON, RHP

Born: Dec. 9, 1990. **B-T:** R-R. **Ht.:** 6-3. **Wt.:** 275. **Signed:** Venezuela, 2007. **Signed by:** German Robles/Pedro Chavez/Miguel Garcia.

Had Rondon made one more relief appearance in Detroit, he would no longer be eligible for this prospect list. He would have easily surpassed that cutoff had he been more effective early in the 2013 season. After a sluggish spring training, Rondon opened at Triple-A Erie, got to Detroit in late April but scuffled in three appearances before getting sent back down. He returned for good in late June, pitching just once after Sept. 2 with what the club termed a tender elbow. Rondon is a jumbo-sized reliever with one of the game's best fastballs. He pushes 300 pounds on the scale and 103 mph off the mound. Rondon's fastball sits at 97-100 mph and bores in on the hands of righthanders, making him proficient at getting swinging strikes and groundouts. His high-80s slider was at its best late in the season but still gets slurvy and inconsistent on him. He made strides with his changeup and started using it more frequently when his slider wasn't working, but it's also inconsistent. His fastball gives him more margin for error with his below-average command, which he's steadily improved the last two seasons. Tigers officials believe Rondon may have put too much pressure on himself to win the closer job in 2013, but with the signing of Joe Nathan to a two-year deal he should be able to settle in as a set-up man in 2014, with the potential to close at some point in the future.

Year	Club (League)	Class	W	L	ERA	G	GS	CG	SV	IP	H	HR	BB	SO	K/9	WHIP	AVG
2008	Tigers (VSL)	R	2	6	3.58	13	13	1	0	55	48	0	20	34	5.5	1.23	.225
2009	Tigers (GCL)	R	0	1	4.76	3	3	0	0	11	12	0	8	15	11.9	1.76	.267
	Tigers (VSL)	R	0	0	13.50	3	0	0	0	4	5	0	7	4	9.0	3.00	.313
2010	Tigers (GCL)	R	0	0	0.70	24	0	0	15	26	11	1	14	26	9.1	0.97	.133
	Lakeland (FSL)	HiA	0	0	1.35	4	0	0	2	7	2	1	2	7	9.5	0.60	.095
2011	West Michigan (MWL)	LoA	2	2	2.03	41	0	0	19	40	22	0	34	61	13.7	1.40	.164
2012	Lakeland (FSL)	HiA	1	0	1.93	22	0	0	15	23	12	1	10	34	13.1	0.94	.152
	Erie (EL)	AA	0	1	0.83	21	0	0	12	22	15	1	9	23	9.6	1.11	.195
	Toledo (IL)	AAA	1	0	2.25	9	0	0	2	8	5	1	7	9	10.1	1.50	.167
2013	Toledo (IL)	AAA	1	1	1.52	30	0	0	14	30	14	1	13	40	12.1	0.91	.139
	Detroit (AL)	MAJ	1	2	3.45	30	0	0	1	29	28	2	11	30	9.4	1.36	.259
Major League Totals			1	2	3.45	30	0	0	1	29	28	2	11	30	9.4	1.36	.259
Minor League Totals			7	11	2.39	170	16	1	79	226	146	6	124	253	10.1	1.20	.183

4 JAKE THOMPSON, RHP

Born: Jan. 31, 1994. **B-T:** R-R. **Ht.:** 6-4. **Wt.:** 235. **Drafted:** HS—Heath, Texas, 2012 (2nd round). **Signed by:** Tim Grieve.

The Tigers forfeited their first-round draft pick in 2012 for signing Prince Fielder, so they had to wait until pick No. 91 for their first selection, which they used on Thompson. After staying back in extended spring training the first two months of 2013, Thompson reported to low Class A West Michigan and had a solid season. Thompson throws three average or better pitches, operating off a low-90s fastball that can touch 95 mph. He delivers the ball with a steep downhill plane, mixing a harder four-seamer with a livelier two-seamer that has solid sink and tail. Thompson's low-80s slider has tight bite when it's on, though it can flatten out on him. It's a potential plus pitch that he commands well. Thompson has shown feel for an average circle-changeup that could tick up higher, but he hasn't used it much yet. He also introduced a mid- to high-70s curveball in 2013 that improved as the season progressed, but it's still a new pitch. Thompson wore down after his high school season in 2012 and the Tigers let him throw just 83 innings in 2013, so he'll have to prove he can handle a larger workload. If he can, he's a potential mid-rotation starter whose next stop is high Class A Lakeland.

Year	Club (League)	Class	W	L	ERA	G	GS	CG	SV	IP	H	HR	BB	SO	K/9	WHIP	AVG
2012	Tigers (GCL)	R	1	2	1.91	7	7	0	0	28	14	1	10	31	9.8	0.85	.149
2013	West Michigan (MWL)	LoA	3	3	3.13	17	16	0	0	83	79	4	32	91	9.8	1.33	.244
Minor League Totals			4	5	2.82	24	23	0	0	112	93	5	42	122	9.8	1.21	.222

5 JONATHON CRAWFORD, RHP

Born: Nov. 1, 1991. **B-T:** R-R. **Ht.:** 6-2. **Wt.:** 205. **Drafted:** Florida, 2013 (1st round). **Signed by:** Jimmy Rough.

After being the ace of USA Baseball's Collegiate National Team in 2012, Crawford struggled to a 3-6, 3.84 mark as a junior at Florida, but in a 2013 draft thin on college starters, the Tigers picked Crawford with the 20th overall pick and signed him for $2,001,700. He was Detroit's first first-round pick since 2009. Between his fastball and his breaking ball, Crawford has two plus pitches. He throws 92-96 mph sinkers with heavy life that makes it difficult for hitters to lift, and he maintains his velocity deep into his starts. He adds and subtracts from his plus slider, cranking it up to the high 80s at times. His changeup is better than it was when he got to Florida but remains a below-average pitch. Crawford tends to fight his delivery and has trouble repeating his release point due to a wrist wrap, which causes inconsistent command. Scouts are split on whether Crawford fits best as a starter or as a two-pitch power reliever. He should head to one of Detroit's Class A affiliates in 2014.

Year	Club (League)	Class	W	L	ERA	G	GS	CG	SV	IP	H	HR	BB	SO	K/9	WHIP	AVG
2013	Connecticut (NYP)	SS	0	2	1.89	8	8	0	0	19	15	0	9	21	9.9	1.26	.205
Minor League Totals			0	2	1.89	8	8	0	0	19	15	0	9	21	9.9	1.26	.205

6 COREY KNEBEL, RHP

Born: Nov. 26, 1991. **B-T:** R-R. **Ht.:** 6-3. **Wt.:** 195. **Drafted:** Texas, 2013 (1st round supplemental). **Signed by:** Tim Grieve.

Knebel followed the Huston Street career path, going from undrafted high schooler to immediate success at Texas, where he ranked second in NCAA Division I with 19 saves as a freshman in 2011. After two more seasons as one of the best closers in the nation, Knebel went to the Tigers with the No. 39 pick in the 2013 draft and signed for $1,433,400. He then looked electric for short-season Connecticut in his pro debut and pitched in the Arizona Fall League. Knebel has high-octane stuff, firing 91-98 mph fastballs for strikes with downhill plane and explosive late life. His low-80s hammer curveball has power, tight spin and late break, earning a few 70 grades and plenty of swings and misses. Knebel doesn't have much need for a changeup, but he's shown feel for that pitch too. He has a max-effort delivery with a short, funky arm stroke and head tilt, but he throws strikes. Deception in his delivery helps hide his release point from hitters. Given his stuff and ability to throw strikes, Knebel could move quickly through the system as a potential closer, though some Tigers officials want to try him in the rotation. He appears destined for high Class A Lakeland in 2014.

Year	Club (League)	Class	W	L	ERA	G	GS	CG	SV	IP	H	HR	BB	SO	K/9	WHIP	AVG
2013	West Michigan (MWL)	LoA	2	1	0.87	31	0	0	15	31	14	0	10	41	11.9	0.77	.133
Minor League Totals			2	1	0.87	31	0	0	15	31	14	0	10	41	11.9	0.77	.133

7 EUGENIO SUAREZ, SS/2B

BA GRADE **50** HIGH

Born: July 18, 1991. **B-T:** B-R. **Ht.:** 5-11. **Wt.:** 180. **Signed:** Venezuela, 2008. **Signed by:** Alejandro Rodriguez.

When the Tigers signed Suarez out of Venezuela in 2008, they were taking a flier on a low-level player who was 5-foot-9 but had good feel for the game. After signing, he grew taller, gained muscle and his stock jumped. Suarez started 2013 at high Class A Lakeland but after a hot start the Tigers promoted him to Double-A Erie, where he held his own. Suarez has a quiet approach with a short, flat swing from both sides of the plate that allows him to keep the bat head in the zone a long time. He makes frequent contact but also shows solid plate patience, though his swing got inconsistent in Double-A when he would get too uphill trying to launch the ball. Suarez has below-average power, so he's at his best staying inside the ball and working the gaps. Some scouts see him as an offensive-oriented utility man, but others think he made significant strides on defense and consider him a potential above-average defender at shortstop. He has a plus arm, a quick release, good footwork and soft hands, though he can still get careless at times. He's a below-average runner, however, and some scouts question his range, preferring him at second base. Suarez continues to surpass expectations each year, and he has a chance to be an everyday shortstop in the majors.

Year	Club (League)	Class	AVG	G	AB	R	H	2B	3B	HR	RBI	BB	SO	SB	CS	OBP	SLG
2009	Tigers (VSL)	R	.262	57	206	29	54	9	3	1	15	17	32	8	4	.360	.350
2010	Tigers (VSL)	R	.311	61	225	32	70	12	2	1	18	23	44	8	6	.389	.396
2011	Tigers (GCL)	R	.341	12	44	11	15	7	0	2	9	3	4	2	0	.408	.636
	Connecticut (NYP)	SS	.250	58	204	37	51	11	5	5	24	18	43	9	5	.323	.426
2012	West Michigan (MWL)	LoA	.288	135	511	82	147	34	5	6	67	65	116	21	9	.380	.409
2013	Lakeland (FSL)	HiA	.311	25	103	17	32	6	2	1	12	14	25	2	3	.410	.437
	Erie (EL)	AA	.253	111	442	53	112	24	4	9	45	46	98	9	11	.332	.387
Minor League Totals			.277	459	1735	261	481	103	21	25	190	186	362	59	38	.363	.404

8 DOMINGO LEYBA, SS/2B

BA GRADE **55** EXTREME

Born: Sept. 11, 1995. **B-T:** B-R. **Ht.:** 5-11. **Wt.:** 160. **Signed:** Dominican Republic, 2012. **Signed by:** Miguel Rodriguez/Carlos Santana/Ramon Perez/Miguel Garcia.

Leyba played for the Reviving Baseball in Inner Cities (RBI) program that won the junior division championship in 2011 in Minneapolis before signing with the Tigers for $400,000 the next year on July 2. Leyba proved more advanced than expected in his pro debut in 2013, leading the Rookie-level Dominican Summer League in OPS (1.023) as a 17-year-old. Leyba stands out more in games than he did in a tryout setting. He has a polished hitting approach for his age, controls the strike zone and hits line drives to all fields. He showed surprising power, though he'll probably be more of a doubles threat who maxes out around 10 home runs. Leyba split time between second base and shortstop with Willy Adames, a more athletic Dominican shortstop, but the former's speed, range and arm all grade out around average, with a quick release, good footwork and smooth hands. Leyba could end up at second base, but he's a sound enough defender to be given every opportunity to stay at shortstop. Leyba's next test will be the Rookie-level Gulf Coast League.

Year	Club (League)	Class	AVG	G	AB	R	H	2B	3B	HR	RBI	BB	SO	SB	CS	OBP	SLG
2013	Tigers (DSL)	R	.348	57	201	51	70	15	8	5	36	34	26	16	8	.446	.577
Minor League Totals			.348	57	201	51	70	15	8	5	36	34	26	16	8	.446	.577

9 HERNAN PEREZ, 2B/SS

BA GRADE **45** LOW

Born: March 26, 1991. **B-T:** R-R. **Ht.:** 6-1. **Wt.:** 185. **Signed:** Venezuela, 2007. **Signed by:** Jesus Garces/Pedro Chavez.

Perez signed with the Tigers for $237,000 when the 2007 international signing period opened, then never hit above .270 in any of his first five minor league seasons. Nevertheless, the Tigers summoned him to Detroit in 2012 when Jhonny Peralta went on paternity leave, and he got his first big league hit off Alfredo Simon. Perez broke out in 2013, hitting .300 in the upper minors and spending most of the second half of the season with the big league club. He's a grinder and an instinctive player who endears himself to managers. He has good bat speed with a short, line-drive stroke and keeps the barrel in the zone a long time. He has good plate coverage and uses the whole field. Perez doesn't have much power, expands his strike zone early in the count and doesn't walk much, though he has a good two-strike approach. He's an average runner and an efficient basestealer because he gets good jumps. Perez has split time between second base and shortstop, and most scouts feel he's a better fit at the keystone. He's an athletic player with an average arm, solid range, good actions and is generally sure-handed. The Tigers' offseason trade for second baseman Ian Kinsler puts Perez's role in doubt for 2014. He could play every day at Triple-A Toledo, serve as a utility man or be traded to a team that sees him as an everyday player.

Year	Club (League)	Class	AVG	G	AB	R	H	2B	3B	HR	RBI	BB	SO	SB	CS	OBP	SLG
2008	Tigers (VSL)	R	.226	68	265	38	60	8	4	1	22	16	35	4	4	.278	.298
2009	West Michigan (MWL)	LoA	.227	12	44	0	10	0	1	0	5	0	8	2	1	.227	.273
	Tigers (GCL)	R	.222	21	81	9	18	9	1	1	9	3	14	2	0	.259	.395
	Lakeland (FSL)	HiA	.264	21	72	7	19	4	1	0	10	3	21	0	0	.289	.347
2010	West Michigan (MWL)	LoA	.235	124	473	45	111	15	0	5	50	25	98	5	1	.273	.298
2011	West Michigan (MWL)	LoA	.258	129	503	69	130	23	3	8	42	38	87	23	6	.314	.364
2012	Detroit (AL)	MAJ	.500	2	2	1	1	0	0	0	0	0	0	0	0	.500	.500
	Lakeland (FSL)	HiA	.261	124	441	50	115	11	4	5	44	24	70	27	4	.298	.338
2013	Erie (EL)	AA	.301	87	362	45	109	28	2	4	35	12	48	24	7	.325	.423
	Toledo (IL)	AAA	.299	16	67	3	20	3	0	0	4	5	7	4	0	.356	.343
	Detroit (AL)	MAJ	.197	34	66	13	13	0	1	0	5	2	15	1	0	.217	.227
Major League Totals			.206	36	68	14	14	0	1	0	5	2	15	1	0	.225	.235
Minor League Totals			.256	602	2308	266	592	101	16	24	221	126	388	91	23	.297	.345

10 KEVIN ZIOMEK, LHP

BA GRADE **50** HIGH

Born: March 21, 1992. **B-T:** R-L. **Ht.:** 6-3. **Wt.:** 190. **Drafted:** Vanderbilt, 2013 (2nd round). **Signed by:** Harold Zonder.

Vanderbilt has become a factory for lefthanders over the past decade, most notably for 2012 American League Cy Young Award winner David Price and the Braves' Mike Minor. Ziomek became the school's eighth lefty drafted in the top three rounds since 2004 when the Tigers selected him in the second round in 2013 and signed him for $956,600. He pitched briefly in the short-season New York-Penn League, with all four of his starts limited to two innings to keep his workload down. Ziomek doesn't have one put-away pitch but his stuff is steady across the board, including a fastball that parks at 88-92 mph and hits 94. He showed an above-average changeup in 2012 in the Cape Cod League, where he pitched well after a down year as a sophomore, but it was an inconsistent pitch his junior year. His slider can be an average pitch, with more sweep than bite. Ziomek is an athletic pitcher with some mechanical hickeys, including a wrap in his arm action and a crossfire delivery, which may contribute to inconsistent command, but it does enhance deception. Ziomek doesn't wow scouts with stuff but has the potential to fit into the back of a rotation. He could be ticketed for high Class A Lakeland in 2014.

Year	Club (League)	Class	W	L	ERA	G	GS	CG	SV	IP	H	HR	BB	SO	K/9	WHIP	AVG
2013	Connecticut (NYP)	SS	0	1	4.50	4	4	0	0	8	5	0	5	3	3.4	1.25	.200
Minor League Totals			0	1	4.50	4	4	0	0	8	5	0	5	3	3.4	1.25	.200

11 JAMES McCANN, C

BA GRADE **45** MEDIUM

Born: June 13, 1990. **B-T:** R-R. **Ht.:** 6-2. **Wt.:** 210. **Drafted:** Arkansas, 2011 (2nd round). **Signed by:** Chris Wimmer.

When the Tigers signed Victor Martinez as a free agent following the 2010 season, they surrendered their 2011 first-round pick as compensation. They used their top pick, No. 76 overall and in the second round, on McCann, who signed for $577,900. McCann reached Double-A Erie in 2012 and spent the entire 2013 season repeating the level, showing steady skills with a defensive-oriented profile and durability. Intelligent behind the plate, he earns high marks both inside and outside the organization for his ability to handle a pitching staff. His speed is well-below-average, but he moves well behind the plate, is a good receiver and does a nice job framing pitches. He has an average arm and controls the running game, throwing out 37 percent of basestealers in 2013. McCann's bat hasn't progressed as quickly as the Tigers had hoped, but he had his best season in 2013. He doesn't swing and miss excessively, but he has a bat wrap that creates length to his stroke, and his power is below-average. McCann's defense will have to carry him to the big leagues, with perhaps enough skill at the plate to carve out a career as a second-division catcher.

Year	Club (League)	Class	AVG	G	AB	R	H	2B	3B	HR	RBI	BB	SO	SB	CS	OBP	SLG
2011	Tigers (GCL)	R	.357	5	14	1	5	1	0	1	6	1	1	0	0	.438	.643
	West Michigan (MWL)	LoA	.059	9	34	0	2	1	0	0	1	2	12	0	0	.132	.088
2012	Lakeland (FSL)	HiA	.288	45	160	24	46	10	0	0	20	10	29	3	0	.345	.350
	Erie (EL)	AA	.200	64	220	15	44	12	0	2	19	8	44	2	2	.227	.282
2013	Erie (EL)	AA	.277	119	441	50	122	30	1	8	54	30	85	3	3	.328	.404
Minor League Totals			.252	242	869	90	219	54	1	11	100	51	171	8	5	.301	.354

12 DREW VERHAGEN, RHP

BA GRADE **45** MEDIUM

Born: Oct. 22, 1990. **B-T:** R-R. **Ht.:** 6-6. **Wt.:** 230. **Drafted:** Vanderbilt, 2012 (4th round). **Signed by:** Harold Zonder.

After having Tommy John surgery as a senior in high school, VerHagen went undrafted and spent his freshman year at Oklahoma before transferring to Navarro (Texas) JC and helping the school win its first Junior College World Series. He ended up at Vanderbilt in 2012, when the Tigers drafted him in the fourth round. He had a solid 2013 season and reached Double-A Erie in June. He delivers his stuff with downhill angle and good extension from an extra-large, 6-foot-6 frame. His best pitch by far is his fastball, which parks at 91-95 mph and can reach 97. VerHagen's fastball has late, heavy sink, and he can add cutting action or tailing life to it. His fastball produces a wave of groundballs, but his lack of secondary weapons explains his low strikeout rate. The Tigers see promise in his curveball, but it's below-average and he tends to get around the ball rather than stay on top of the pitch, while his changeup is also below-average. He throws slightly across his body but generally is around the strike zone, though a wrist wrap and stiffness in his long arm action concern some scouts. VerHagen is the team's best upper-level starter, but his fastball could play up in the bullpen.

Year	Club (League)	Class	W	L	ERA	G	GS	CG	SV	IP	H	HR	BB	SO	K/9	WHIP	AVG
2012	Tigers (GCL)	R	0	0	2.25	2	0	0	0	4	5	0	0	2	4.5	1.25	.313
	Lakeland (FSL)	HiA	0	3	3.67	8	6	0	0	27	20	0	14	17	5.7	1.26	.206
2013	Lakeland (FSL)	HiA	5	3	2.81	12	11	0	0	67	49	1	27	35	4.7	1.13	.207
	Erie (EL)	AA	2	5	3.00	12	12	1	0	60	53	3	17	40	6.0	1.17	.240
Minor League Totals			7	11	3.01	34	29	1	0	158	127	4	58	94	5.3	1.17	.222

13 JOSE ORTEGA, RHP

BA GRADE **45** MEDIUM

Born: Oct. 12, 1988. **B-T:** R-R. **Ht.:** 5-11. **Wt.:** 185. **Signed:** Venezuela, 2006. **Signed by:** German Robles.

The Tigers have developed Ortega as a pure relief prospect since the day he signed in 2006. He has progressed slowly with an explosive fastball and erratic control. After getting to the major leagues for the first time in 2012, he began 2013 at Triple-A Toledo before getting back to Detroit in May, staying there for a month but finishing the year in Triple-A. His money pitch is his fastball, which comes out of his hand at 94-98 mph and crosses the plate with vicious life. It's a hard, heavy pitch with late movement through the zone, enabling him to blow it by hitters or get weak groundballs. When it's on, his 84-88 mph slider gives him another plus pitch with late tilt. His problem continues to be that he's more thrower than pitcher. He has trouble repeating his violent, max-effort mechanics and crossfire delivery, making it difficult to find the strike zone. Ortega has the pure stuff to be a high-leverage reliever, but he must find control first.

Year	Club (League)	Class	W	L	ERA	G	GS	CG	SV	IP	H	HR	BB	SO	K/9	WHIP	AVG
2007	Tigers (VSL)	R	0	0	2.45	10	0	0	0	11	9	1	3	11	9.0	1.09	.209
2008	Tigers (VSL)	R	1	1	2.20	23	0	0	5	45	43	5	15	27	5.4	1.29	.256
2009	Oneonta (NYP)	SS	2	2	3.97	25	0	0	1	34	28	2	23	32	8.5	1.50	.220
2010	West Michigan (MWL)	LoA	0	3	4.56	18	0	0	1	26	28	1	17	22	7.7	1.75	.275
	Lakeland (FSL)	HiA	2	1	0.95	10	0	0	0	19	14	0	7	20	9.5	1.11	.212
	Erie (EL)	AA	1	0	3.04	15	1	0	0	24	22	2	7	19	7.2	1.23	.242
2011	Toledo (IL)	AAA	1	3	6.30	33	0	0	0	50	61	7	27	44	7.9	1.76	.310
2012	Detroit (AL)	MAJ	0	0	3.38	2	0	0	0	3	3	1	1	4	13.5	1.50	.250
	Toledo (IL)	AAA	5	8	5.74	45	0	0	1	63	76	4	51	68	9.8	2.03	.311
2013	Detroit (AL)	MAJ	0	2	3.86	11	0	0	0	12	10	2	6	10	7.7	1.37	.227
	Toledo (IL)	AAA	4	3	1.86	40	0	0	4	48	28	2	33	56	10.4	1.26	.169
Major League Totals			0	2	3.77	13	0	0	0	14	13	3	7	14	8.8	1.40	.232
Minor League Totals			16	21	3.86	219	1	0	12	319	309	24	183	299	8.4	1.54	.257

14 JAVIER BETANCOURT, SS

BA GRADE **50** EXTREME

Born: May 8, 1995. **B-T:** R-R. **Ht.:** 5-10. **Wt.:** 173. **Signed:** Venezuela, 2011. **Signed by:** Oscar Garcia/Pedro Chavez.

Betancourt's polish can be traced to his upbringing. His uncle, Edgardo Alfonzo, played 12 seasons in the big leagues from 1995-2006, mostly as a Mets third baseman. Betancourt trained with Roberto Alfonzo, Edgardo's brother and a former Mets scout, before signing with the Tigers for $200,000 in August 2011. He hit well in his pro debut in the Rookie-level Venezuelan Summer League in 2012 before making a strong impression in the Rookie-level Gulf Coast League in 2013. Betancourt doesn't swing and miss often—he had the GCL's second-lowest strikeout rate—thanks to his hand-eye coordination and feel for the barrel. He stays within his swing and maintains a line-drive, middle-of-the-field approach. He puts a lot of balls on the ground, doesn't have much pop now and doesn't project to be a big power threat, so his game will center around putting the ball in play and getting on base. Betancourt is a fundamentally sound defender who makes good decisions in the field, understands where he needs to be and has a good sense of timing along with an adequate arm. He's a fringy runner and isn't a quick-twitch, rangy shortstop, so there's a chance he slides over to second base. He's advanced enough to head to low Class A West Michigan in 2014.

Year	Club (League)	Class	AVG	G	AB	R	H	2B	3B	HR	RBI	BB	SO	SB	CS	OBP	SLG
2012	Tigers (VSL)	R	.333	32	123	24	41	6	0	3	15	10	16	4	5	.391	.455
2013	Tigers (GCL)	R	.333	50	177	28	59	9	2	2	22	12	14	5	3	.379	.441
Minor League Totals			.333	82	300	52	100	15	2	5	37	22	30	9	8	.384	.447

15 STEVEN MOYA, OF

Born: Sept. 8, 1991. **B-T:** R-R. **Ht.:** 6-6. **Wt.:** 230. **Signed:** Dominican Republic, 2008. **Signed by:** Miguel Rodriguez/Ramon Perez/Miguel Garcia.

Born in Puerto Rico, Moya grew up in the Dominican Republic and signed as an international free agent in 2008. Moya, who missed six weeks early in 2013 with a separated left shoulder, has an enormous frame with long arms and plenty of lift in his swing. He has plus raw power and can drive the ball over the fence to any part of the park when he gets his arms extended. Moya has trouble tapping into his power in games because of his free-swinging approach and long swing with plenty of holes. His 6-foot-6 frame gives pitchers a large strike zone, and he doesn't help himself by chasing pitches, leading to few walks and high strikeouts. Moya is athletic for his size and surprises people with average speed. Even after Tommy John surgery ended his 2012 season in June, Moya still has a plus arm. He has the tools to be a solid right fielder, but he gets poor reads off the bat. The Tigers love Moya's upside if everything clicks, so they put him on the 40-man roster in November to protect him from the Rule 5 draft, but everything about his game remains raw.

Year	Club (League)	Class	AVG	G	AB	R	H	2B	3B	HR	RBI	BB	SO	SB	CS	OBP	SLG
2009	Tigers (DSL)	R	.252	60	218	36	55	8	0	6	33	33	58	4	2	.361	.372
2010	Tigers (GCL)	R	.190	40	137	12	26	5	2	2	11	6	64	0	0	.229	.299
2011	West Michigan (MWL)	LoA	.204	86	323	38	66	10	1	13	39	12	127	1	1	.234	.362
2012	West Michigan (MWL)	LoA	.288	59	243	28	70	14	3	9	47	11	59	5	3	.319	.481
2013	Lakeland (FSL)	HiA	.255	93	365	52	93	19	5	12	55	18	106	6	0	.296	.433
Minor League Totals			.241	338	1286	166	310	56	11	42	185	80	414	16	6	.290	.400

16 MELVIN MERCEDES, RHP

BA GRADE
45
HIGH

Born: Nov. 2, 1990. **B-T:** R-R. **Ht.:** 6-1. **Wt.:** 250. **Signed:** Dominican Republic, 2008. **Signed by:** Miguel Rodriguez/Ramon Perez.

Mercedes hasn't started a game since the Tigers signed him for $200,000 out of the Dominican Republic in March 2008. He ran his fastball up to 94 mph as a 17-year-old, and he has seen his velocity jump since then to 93-99 with plus life. His high-80s slider usually is an average pitch with short break, though it will show flashes of being a plus pitch. He still needs to sharpen his fastball command, but his control has been improving, and he walked just 2.4 batters per nine innings in 2013. In spite of his fastball, Mercedes doesn't strike out many hitters. Improving his slider would help, but his long arm action allows hitters to pick up the ball out of his hand early. He had Tommy John surgery in 2010 and has a lot of effort in his delivery, recoiling after he delivers the ball, which puts extra stress on his arm. He has a hefty build, so some scouts would like to see him improve his conditioning. After a strong 2013 campaign, Mercedes should make his major league debut in 2014. He has high-leverage potential if he can figure out a way to miss more bats.

Year	Club (League)	Class	W	L	ERA	G	GS	CG	SV	IP	H	HR	BB	SO	K/9	WHIP	AVG
2008	Tigers (DSL)	R	2	2	3.19	24	0	0	6	37	28	1	24	33	8.1	1.42	.207
2009	Tigers (GCL)	R	1	1	1.82	26	0	0	16	25	19	0	14	20	7.3	1.34	.221
	West Michigan (MWL)	LoA	0	1	11.57	3	0	0	0	2	1	0	3	1	3.9	1.71	.125
2010	West Michigan (MWL)	LoA	1	2	5.03	15	0	0	3	20	16	0	19	12	5.5	1.78	.225
2011	West Michigan (MWL)	LoA	0	0	10.80	2	0	0	0	2	3	0	1	1	5.4	2.40	.375
	Connecticut (NYP)	SS	3	1	2.67	21	0	0	3	34	32	0	16	21	5.6	1.43	.246
2012	West Michigan (MWL)	LoA	0	3	2.80	37	0	0	9	64	54	3	23	43	6.0	1.20	.230
	Lakeland (FSL)	HiA	0	0	0.00	1	0	0	0	1	1	0	1	0	0.0	2.00	.250
2013	Lakeland (FSL)	HiA	3	1	0.96	24	0	0	11	28	23	1	5	17	5.5	1.00	.221
	Erie (EL)	AA	2	1	1.44	26	0	0	12	25	23	3	9	19	6.8	1.28	.237
Minor League Totals			12	12	2.70	179	0	0	60	237	200	8	115	167	6.3	1.33	.228

17 CASEY CROSBY, LHP

Born: Sept. 17, 1988. **B-T:** R-L. **Ht.:** 6-5. **Wt.:** 225. **Drafted:** HS—Maple Park, Ill., 2007 (5th round). **Signed by:** Marty Miller.

For years, Crosby has tantalized with his stuff but been equally frustrating for his inability to harness it or stay healthy. Shortly after the Tigers signed him for $748,500 as a fifth-round pick out of high school in 2007, Crosby hurt his elbow at instructional league and missed nearly all of 2008 following Tommy John surgery. He barely pitched in 2010 due to swelling in the joint. In May

2013, Crosby missed two weeks with a left shoulder impingement but didn't pitch after June 17 after more shoulder soreness and to have a bone spur removed from his left elbow. At his best, he throws 91-94 mph and touches 96 with heavy life. He changes speeds on his power curveball, dialing it up to the low 80s at times for his out-pitch. He's shown some feel for a changeup, but it's mostly a fringe-average offering. Crosby can miss bats and get groundballs, but aside from health his biggest impediment has been an inability to throw strikes. He has tinkered with his delivery to try to improve his control, but he walked a career-worst 6.2 batters per nine innings at Triple-A Toledo in 2013 and has a career mark of 4.88 BB/9 in the minors. A shift to the bullpen appears imminent in 2014.

Year	Club (League)	Class	W	L	ERA	G	GS	CG	SV	IP	H	HR	BB	SO	K/9	WHIP	AVG
2008	Tigers (GCL)	R	0	0	0.00	3	3	0	0	5	4	0	3	2	3.9	1.50	.211
2009	West Michigan (MWL)	LoA	10	4	2.41	24	24	0	0	105	70	3	48	117	10.1	1.13	.195
2010	Tigers (GCL)	R	0	1	8.76	3	3	0	0	12	21	1	4	10	7.3	2.03	.382
2011	Erie (EL)	AA	9	7	4.10	25	25	0	0	132	122	11	77	121	8.3	1.51	.253
2012	Detroit (AL)	MAJ	1	1	9.49	3	3	0	0	12	15	2	11	9	6.6	2.11	.313
	Toledo (IL)	AAA	7	9	4.01	22	22	2	0	126	112	12	65	112	8.0	1.41	.238
2013	Toledo (IL)	AAA	2	5	4.84	13	13	0	0	58	55	3	40	61	9.5	1.65	.258
Major League Totals			1	1	9.49	3	3	0	0	12	15	2	11	9	6.6	2.11	.312
Minor League Totals			28	26	3.85	90	90	2	0	437	384	30	237	423	8.7	1.42	.240

18 JOSE VALDEZ, RHP

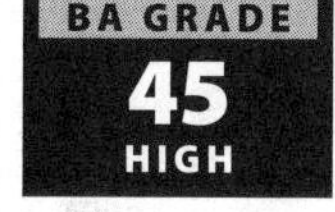

Born: March 1, 1990. **B-T:** R-R. **Ht.:** 6-1. **Wt.:** 200. **Signed:** Dominican Republic, 2009. **Signed by:** Carlos Santana/Ramon Perez/Miguel Garcia.

Catch him on the right night and Valdez will look like he should be pitching in the back of a big league bullpen. He has good arm speed, is extremely strong and has wipeout stuff, including a 93-98 mph fastball with plus life. He has a plus slider, a pitch he'll throw in the mid-80s at times or zip it up to 87-89 mph at others. Between two Class A stops in 2013, Valdez struck out 12.2 batters per nine innings, but he also walked 6.2 per nine. His lack of control and advanced age (23) in Class A can be partially attributed to his development path. He signed at an older age than most Dominican pitchers (19) in 2009, then at the end of July 2010 he was suspended for 50 games after testing positive for Boldenone while he was in the Rookie-level Dominican Summer League. Valdez has sound arm action and a solid delivery, which might help him turn the corner with his control. He could pitch in high-leverage situations if he ever figures it out.

Year	Club (League)	Class	W	L	ERA	G	GS	CG	SV	IP	H	HR	BB	SO	K/9	WHIP	AVG
2009	Tigers (DSL)	R	4	5	5.23	26	0	0	4	31	25	2	23	30	8.7	1.55	.231
2010	Tigers (DSL)	R	1	1	2.18	17	0	0	11	21	11	0	13	21	9.1	1.16	.159
2011	Tigers (DSL)	R	1	1	2.29	18	0	0	9	20	13	0	10	27	12.4	1.17	.191
2012	Tigers (GCL)	R	0	1	0.82	23	0	0	15	22	15	0	10	28	11.5	1.14	.188
2013	West Michigan (MWL)	LoA	1	1	2.73	27	0	0	16	26	16	0	20	35	12.0	1.37	.178
	Lakeland (FSL)	HiA	1	1	2.74	23	0	0	17	23	16	1	14	32	12.5	1.30	.195
Minor League Totals			8	10	2.84	134	0	0	72	143	96	3	90	173	10.9	1.30	.193

19 JORDAN LENNERTON, 1B

BA GRADE
40
LOW

Born: Feb. 16, 1986. **B-T:** L-L. **Ht.:** 6-2. **Wt.:** 220. **Drafted:** Oregon State, 2008 (33rd round). **Signed by:** Ryan Johnson.

Entering his age-28 season in 2014, Lennerton doesn't have much gap between his present and future ability. He starred for Oregon State at the 2007 College World Series, was a 33rd-round pick in 2008 and didn't begin his pro career until he was 23. Lennerton has made slow, steady progress since then, improving his hitting approach, adding power and becoming a smooth defender. Lennerton is a smart, patient hitter who walks frequently. His lefty swing has good balance, and he rarely mis-hits a ball. He keeps the bat head in the zone a long time, which helps him hit the ball over the fence to all fields despite having only average raw power. Lennerton doesn't have much speed but he has worked his way into a plus defender at first, with sure hands, good actions and reads off the bat along with an average arm. He finished his first season at Triple-A Toledo in 2013 and the Tigers placed him on the 40-man roster to avoid exposing him to the Rule 5 draft. With Miguel Cabrera at first base and Victor Martinez at DH, Lennerton's path is blocked for now.

Year	Club (League)	Class	AVG	G	AB	R	H	2B	3B	HR	RBI	BB	SO	SB	CS	OBP	SLG
2008	Tigers (GCL)	R	.243	36	115	11	28	9	1	1	22	18	36	2	1	.348	.365
	Lakeland (FSL)	HiA	.179	18	56	9	10	2	0	1	8	14	18	0	0	.338	.268
2009	West Michigan (MWL)	LoA	.282	119	433	56	122	30	0	12	71	64	127	1	2	.370	.434
2010	West Michigan (MWL)	LoA	.290	59	214	21	62	15	0	3	23	31	65	0	0	.386	.402
	Lakeland (FSL)	HiA	.301	57	206	25	62	15	0	9	33	30	54	1	0	.393	.505
2011	Lakeland (FSL)	HiA	.285	136	484	75	138	33	1	14	75	92	125	0	0	.397	.444
2012	Erie (EL)	AA	.269	139	495	73	133	34	1	21	82	79	141	2	4	.368	.469
2013	Toledo (IL)	AAA	.278	139	514	68	143	25	1	17	57	84	133	0	3	.382	.430
Minor League Totals			.277	703	2517	338	698	163	4	78	371	412	699	6	10	.379	.438

20 TYLER COLLINS, OF

BA GRADE **45** HIGH

Born: June 6, 1990. **B-T:** L-L. **Ht.:** 5-11. **Wt.:** 215. **Drafted:** Howard (Texas) JC, 2011 (6th round). **Signed by:** Tim Grieve.

Collins was one of the biggest disappointments for the Tigers in 2013, especially after he hit so well in spring training and nearly made the big league team. Instead, the Tigers assigned him to Double-A Erie and he struggled, seemingly trying to hit his way to Detroit with every swing. Normally lauded for his mature hitting approach, Collins' swing got longer and more uphill as he tried swinging for the fences, flying open early and going into pull mode. He ended up hitting 21 home runs after just seven in 2012, but his strikeout rate nearly doubled from the previous season, going from 12 percent to 23 percent, as his overall production slipped. Collins still takes his walks, but he needs to find a better blend of hitting for average and power that's more conducive to the former, because his power is average at best and won't carry him. He has a strong, stocky frame with below-average speed and an average arm that could play in either corner-outfield spot. Collins' stock is down from a year ago, but he's an intriguing candidate for a bounce back year at Triple-A Toledo.

Year	Club (League)	Class	AVG	G	AB	R	H	2B	3B	HR	RBI	BB	SO	SB	CS	OBP	SLG
2011	Tigers (GCL)	R	.333	1	3	2	1	1	0	0	1	2	0	0	0	.600	.667
	Connecticut (NYP)	SS	.313	42	163	28	51	10	1	8	31	10	17	6	1	.360	.534
2012	Lakeland (FSL)	HiA	.290	126	473	68	137	35	5	7	66	58	64	20	3	.371	.429
2013	Erie (EL)	AA	.240	129	466	67	112	29	0	21	79	51	122	4	5	.323	.438
Minor League Totals			.272	298	1105	165	301	75	6	36	177	121	203	30	9	.350	.449

21 JOSE ALVAREZ, LHP

BA GRADE **40** LOW

Born: May 6, 1989. **B-T:** L-L. **Ht.:** 5-11. **Wt.:** 180. **Signed:** Venezuela, 2005. **Signed by:** Alejandro Rodriguez (Red Sox).

Alvarez turned pro in 2005 when he signed with the Red Sox out of Venezuela. Boston traded him to the Marlins following the 2009 season to acquire outfielder Jeremy Hermida. Alvarez pitched well for the Marlins in the low minors, but his strikeout rate dipped at Double-A in 2011, and he signed with the Tigers as a minor league free agent at age 23 after the 2012 season. Detroit made a shrewd signing, as Alvarez jumped to Triple-A Toledo and performed better than ever and made his major league debut in June 2013. Sitting at 88-90 mph and touching 92, Alvarez lacks plus velocity, so he needs to command his fastball down and keep the ball on the ground. He keeps hitters honest with a plus changeup, which he throws with the same arm speed and release point as his fastball. His best breaking ball is a fringy low-80s slider with sweepy action, and he'll sprinkle in a below-average curve on occasion. Alvarez could be a No. 5 starter or a swingman, though with the Tigers' rotation depth, his best chance to stay in Detroit might be as a reliever.

Year	Club (League)	Class	W	L	ERA	G	GS	CG	SV	IP	H	HR	BB	SO	K/9	WHIP	AVG
2006	Red Sox (DSL)	R	2	1	1.61	15	8	0	0	62	46	1	19	64	9.3	1.05	.205
2007	Red Sox (GCL)	R	4	1	1.84	11	9	0	0	49	36	4	14	38	7.0	1.02	.202
2008	Greenville (SAL)	LoA	8	9	5.70	24	19	0	0	107	118	15	37	86	7.2	1.44	.281
2009	Salem (CAR)	HiA	1	1	4.74	12	0	0	0	25	32	1	6	11	4.0	1.54	.308
	Lowell (NYP)	SS	8	3	1.52	14	12	2	0	83	60	4	10	63	6.8	0.84	.203
2010	Greensboro (SAL)	LoA	10	3	3.58	26	13	0	0	108	114	9	32	113	9.4	1.35	.273
2011	Jupiter (FSL)	HiA	6	5	2.96	15	14	0	0	82	79	2	19	73	8.0	1.20	.258
	Jacksonville (SL)	AA	2	6	5.35	12	12	0	0	66	80	9	22	45	6.2	1.55	.308
2012	Jacksonville (SL)	AA	6	9	4.22	25	24	3	0	136	141	8	26	70	4.6	1.22	.274
2013	Toledo (IL)	AAA	8	6	2.80	21	20	1	1	129	114	11	25	115	8.0	1.08	.235
	Detroit (AL)	MAJ	1	5	5.82	14	6	0	0	39	42	7	16	31	7.2	1.50	.280
Major League Totals			1	5	5.82	14	6	0	0	39	42	7	16	31	7.2	1.50	.280
Minor League Totals			55	44	3.50	175	131	6	1	846	820	64	210	678	7.2	1.22	.256

22 DANIEL FIELDS, OF

BA GRADE **45** HIGH

Born: Jan. 3, 1991. **B-T:** L-R. **Ht.:** 6-2. **Wt.:** 215. **Drafted:** HS—Detroit, 2009 (6th round). **Signed by:** Tom Osowski.

When Fields signed for $1.625 million out of high school as a sixth-round pick in 2009, he was athletic but raw. Yet Detroit skipped Fields over the low Class A Midwest League and sent him straight to high Class A Lakeland in 2010 as a 19-year-old, where he understandably looked over his head. After three straight seasons in Lakeland, Fields went to Double-A Erie and put together the best season of his career. Adding size and strength over the last few years has helped, giving him more quickness to his swing. While Fields' offensive production improved, his strikeout rate went up, as his uppercut stroke leaves him with holes. He uses the whole field, with a tick above-average raw power. Fields, whose father Bruce returned to the organization in 2013 as roving hitting instructor, is a fringy runner whose basestealing acumen has improved. He gets good reads off the bat, but he has a fringy arm and isn't a true center fielder. His best defensive fit might be left field, but he doesn't have the bat to be an everyday player. Triple-A Toledo will be the next step.

Year	Club (League)	Class	AVG	G	AB	R	H	2B	3B	HR	RBI	BB	SO	SB	CS	OBP	SLG
2010	Lakeland (FSL)	HiA	.240	109	375	33	90	13	6	8	47	55	119	8	9	.343	.371
2011	Lakeland (FSL)	HiA	.220	124	432	57	95	14	4	8	46	49	133	4	4	.308	.326
2012	Lakeland (FSL)	HiA	.266	62	244	31	65	11	4	1	26	19	55	14	7	.318	.357
	Erie (EL)	AA	.264	29	106	13	28	4	0	2	7	13	21	9	1	.352	.358
2013	Erie (EL)	AA	.284	118	457	71	130	27	6	10	58	45	130	24	7	.356	.435
Minor League Totals			.253	442	1614	205	408	69	20	29	184	181	458	59	28	.334	.374

23 KYLE LOBSTEIN, LHP

BA GRADE 40 MEDIUM

Born: Aug. 12, 1989. **B-T:** L-L. **Ht.:** 6-3. **Wt.:** 200. **Drafted:** HS—Flagstaff, Ariz., 2008 (2nd round). **Signed by:** Jayson Durocher (Rays).

The Rays had high hopes for Lobstein when they drafted him out of high school in the second round of the 2008 draft and signed him for $1.5 million. His stuff never ticked up like Tampa Bay hoped, however, and they chose not to protect him on the 40-man roster after the 2012 season. The Mets took Lobstein in the Rule 5 draft and sold him to the Tigers, who worked out a trade with the Rays just before the 2013 season to retain him, sending catcher Curt Casali to Tampa Bay. Lobstein has easy mechanics, a loose arm action and the ball comes out of his hand cleanly, but he lacks the arm speed for an average fastball, settling in at 85-90 mph. He doesn't have an out pitch, so scouts are split on his best secondary offering, but most prefer his changeup, an average pitch with solid fade. He throws a slider and a curveball, but they're fringy. Lobstein's lack of velocity gives him little margin for error, so he has to work down, keep the ball away and spot his fastball to have success. Like Jose Alvarez, Lobstein could be a No. 5 starter or a swingman, though some scouts think he'd have more success as a reliever if he doesn't have to go through a lineup multiple times.

Year	Club (League)	Class	W	L	ERA	G	GS	CG	SV	IP	H	HR	BB	SO	K/9	WHIP	AVG
2009	Hudson Valley (NYP)	SS	3	5	2.58	14	14	0	0	73	55	4	23	74	9.1	1.06	.204
2010	Bowling Green (MWL)	LoA	9	8	4.14	27	27	1	0	148	140	14	54	128	7.8	1.31	–
2011	Charlotte (FSL)	HiA	9	9	3.71	22	21	1	0	121	120	11	30	85	6.3	1.24	.257
	Montgomery (SL)	AA	1	1	7.36	2	2	0	0	11	14	4	6	11	9.0	1.82	.318
2012	Montgomery (SL)	AA	8	7	4.06	27	27	0	0	144	140	12	69	129	8.1	1.45	.260
2013	Erie (EL)	AA	7	4	3.12	15	15	2	0	95	92	6	27	83	7.8	1.25	.262
	Toledo (IL)	AAA	6	3	3.48	13	13	0	0	72	73	2	25	65	8.1	1.35	.267
Minor League Totals			43	37	3.71	120	119	4	0	665	634	53	234	575	7.8	1.30	.254

24 JEFF THOMPSON, RHP

BA GRADE 45 HIGH

Born: Sept. 23, 1991. **B-T:** R-R. **Ht.:** 6-6. **Wt.:** 245. **Drafted:** Louisville, 2013 (3rd round). **Signed by:** Harold Zonder.

An Indiana all-state tight end and defensive end in high school, Thompson's size and athleticism made him attractive to some college football programs, but he chose to play baseball at Louisville instead. He led the Cardinals to the 2013 College World Series, then signed for $549,400 as the fourth of seven consecutive college pitchers the Tigers selected to start their draft. Thompson uses his behemoth size and long arms to produce downhill plane on a fastball that camps at 90-93 mph and can hit 95 with occasional cutting action, though it can get straight. His low-80s slider has slurvy action. It's an average pitch that low-level hitters will chase out of the zone, though more discerning hitters will hold back. His changeup is a below-average pitch that he doesn't use much. Thompson has a good delivery with smooth arm action and hides the ball well behind a high leg lift to add deception. The Tigers view him as a starter and will develop him that way, though some scouts have him pegged for bullpen. He should be ready for high Class A Lakeland.

Year	Club (League)	Class	W	L	ERA	G	GS	CG	SV	IP	H	HR	BB	SO	K/9	WHIP	AVG
2013	West Michigan (MWL)	LoA	2	2	3.80	14	6	0	1	45	41	3	19	42	8.4	1.33	.240
Minor League Totals			2	2	3.80	14	6	0	1	45	41	3	19	42	8.4	1.33	.240

25 ZAC REININGER, RHP

BA GRADE 45 HIGH

Born: Jan. 28, 1993. **B-T:** B-R. **Ht.:** 6-3. **Wt.:** 170. **Drafted:** Hill (Texas) JC, 2013 (8th round). **Signed by:** Tim Grieve.

Reininger's brother J.D. played seven years as a professional, much of it in indy ball. The younger Reininger went undrafted out of high school, but his velocity jumped as a Hill (Texas) JC sophomore, and he starting touching 93 mph. The Tigers signed him for $153,000 out of the eighth round in 2013. Reininger had a stellar pro debut at short-season Connecticut, where he pounded the bottom of the zone with heavy low-90s fastballs. With a skinny frame and a loose arm, Reininger could throw even harder in the future once he gets stronger. A two-way player in junior college, he's a good athlete who repeats his delivery and doesn't walk many batters. His ability to throw strikes and keep the ball on the ground creates a lot of quick, efficient innings. With a solid-average slider, a serviceable changeup that could be a future average pitch and a get-me-over curveball, Reininger's repertoire is deep enough that he could move into a starting role next year, though some scouts like him better as a reliever who could move quickly. He's ready for low Class A West Michigan in 2014, with the polish for an early-season promotion to high Class A Lakeland if he gets off to a strong start.

Year	Club (League)	Class	W	L	ERA	G	GS	CG	SV	IP	H	HR	BB	SO	K/9	WHIP	AVG
2013	Connecticut (NYP)	SS	1	2	1.00	22	1	0	10	27	17	0	6	32	10.7	0.85	.172
Minor League Totals			1	2	1.00	22	1	0	10	27	17	0	6	32	10.7	0.85	.172

26 BRYAN HOLADAY, C

Born: Nov. 19, 1987. **B-T:** R-R. **Ht.:** 6-0. **Wt.:** 205. **Drafted:** Texas Christian, 2010 (6th round). **Signed by:** Tim Grieve.

At Texas Christian, Holaday helped the Horned Frogs make their first College World Series appearance in 2010, when the Tigers drafted him in the sixth round and signed him for $115,000. After making his major league debut in June 2012 when Alex Avila strained a hamstring, Holaday opened 2013 at Triple-A Toledo but again found himself in the big leagues in June when Avila went on the disabled list. The Tigers sent Holaday back to Toledo after he appeared in four games, then brought him back up in August and used him sporadically as a September callup. Holaday's defense is ahead of his hitting. He's a smart catcher with an average arm who controlled the running game in Triple-A, throwing out 41 percent of basestealers. He's a dependable receiver with the solid hands and footwork. Holaday doesn't have the bat to be an everyday catcher. He has a long, slow swing with an uppercut path and a pull-oriented approach with below-average power. He also needs to tighten his strike-zone discipline. Like most catchers, he's a well-below-average runner. If Holaday could bring a little more to the table at the plate, he could stick around as a backup, a role he's expected to fill behind Avila in the big leagues in 2014.

Year	Club (League)	Class	AVG	G	AB	R	H	2B	3B	HR	RBI	BB	SO	SB	CS	OBP	SLG
2010	Lakeland (FSL)	HiA	.220	44	159	14	35	8	0	3	12	21	43	0	0	.335	.327
2011	Erie (EL)	AA	.242	95	330	35	80	18	0	7	42	27	76	6	1	.304	.361
2012	Toledo (IL)	AAA	.240	75	250	18	60	12	1	2	25	22	43	2	0	.312	.320
	Detroit (AL)	MAJ	.250	6	12	3	3	1	0	0	0	0	2	0	0	.250	.333
2013	Toledo (IL)	AAA	.260	80	288	28	75	18	1	4	24	18	57	0	1	.312	.372
	Detroit (AL)	MAJ	.296	16	27	8	8	1	0	1	2	2	3	0	0	.367	.444
Major League Totals			.282	22	39	11	11	2	0	1	2	2	5	0	0	.333	.410
Minor League Totals			.243	294	1027	95	250	56	2	16	103	88	219	8	2	.313	.349

27 RAMON CABRERA, C

Born: Nov. 5, 1989. **B-T:** B-R. **Ht.:** 5-8. **Wt.:** 197. **Signed:** Venezuela, 2008. **Signed by:** Rene Gayo/Rodolfo Petit (Pirates).

Cabrera's father Alex played for the Diamondbacks in 2000 before becoming a big power hitter in Japan. Father and son were able to play against each other in the 2013 Venezuelan League, where 41-year-old Alex posted monster numbers for La Guaira while Ramon caught for Caracas. Ramon originally signed with the Pirates for $100,000 in 2008, then joined the Tigers in December 2012 when Pittsburgh traded him for lefthander Andy Oliver. Cabrera yo-yoed between Double-A Erie and Triple-A Toledo in 2013, settling in at the former with a solid offensive performance. He seldom swings and misses, with a contact-oriented swing that helps him hit for a high batting average. Cabrera improved his walk rate last year but has just 20 power and is a slow runner. With a swing path lacking loft, along with his maxed out body, he'll never have a double-digit home run season. Cabrera caught just 50 games in 2013 and his defense remains below-average, especially controlling the running game, as he caught 26 percent of basestealers. While their body types are different, Cabrera has the upside to contribute a performance along the lines of Josh Thole.

Year	Club (League)	Class	AVG	G	AB	R	H	2B	3B	HR	RBI	BB	SO	SB	CS	OBP	SLG
2008	Pirates (VSL)	R	.264	56	178	24	47	16	0	3	22	28	27	5	0	.367	.404
2009	Pirates (VSL)	R	.312	20	77	10	24	6	0	2	19	12	11	1	2	.400	.468
	Pirates (GCL)	R	.291	37	127	15	37	11	1	1	16	16	16	2	1	.372	.417
2010	West Virginia (SAL)	LoA	.269	90	342	49	92	14	4	1	40	22	42	3	4	.312	.342
2011	Bradenton (FSL)	HiA	.343	92	327	46	112	25	4	3	53	38	29	5	1	.410	.471
2012	Altoona (EL)	AA	.276	112	384	47	106	22	2	3	50	39	44	0	3	.342	.367
	Indianapolis (IL)	AAA	.400	1	5	1	2	1	0	0	0	0	0	0	0	.400	.600
2013	Toledo (IL)	AAA	.242	39	149	13	36	9	1	1	15	14	21	0	1	.311	.336
	Erie (EL)	AA	.304	84	312	44	95	22	2	0	54	44	34	4	0	.392	.388
Minor League Totals			.290	531	1901	249	551	126	14	14	269	213	224	20	12	.362	.393

28 STEVEN FUENTES, 3B

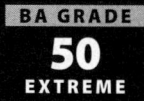

BA GRADE 50 EXTREME

Born: Oct. 21, 1994. **B-T:** B-R. **Ht.:** 5-11. **Wt.:** 180. **Signed:** Venezuela, 2011. **Signed by:** Oscar Garcia/Pedro Chavez.

The Tigers are one of the active teams when it comes to signing Venezuelan players, as they're one of the few organizations with an academy remaining in the country. In 2011, they signed a shortstop Javier Betancourt for $200,000 and Fuentes for $210,000, then put them together the next season in the Rookie-level Venezuelan Summer League, with Fuentes splitting time between shortstop, second base and third base. The two came over to the Rookie-level Gulf Coast League in 2013, with Fuentes playing exclusively third base. He doesn't have the smoothness or advanced baseball sense of Betancourt, but his tools are louder. Fuentes is athletic, has good bat speed and had a solid U.S. debut. He does use the middle of the field, but he needs to improve his plate discipline to get himself better pitches to hit. He'll flash gap power that should grow with more strength, but it's not a big part of his game. Fuentes' home-to-first times are average and he's an above-average runner underway. He has the arm strength and quick release to play on the left side of the field, but the game speeds up on him defensively. The Tigers tend to push their players, so Fuentes could head to low Class A West Michigan in 2014.

Year	Club (League)	Class	AVG	G	AB	R	H	2B	3B	HR	RBI	BB	SO	SB	CS	OBP	SLG
2012	Tigers (VSL)	R	.257	59	226	23	58	8	4	2	25	18	47	8	8	.317	.354
2013	Tigers (GCL)	R	.272	46	151	26	41	10	2	2	24	12	41	5	0	.353	.404
Minor League Totals			.263	105	377	49	99	18	6	4	49	30	88	13	8	.332	.374

29 CALVIN DRUMMOND, RHP

BA GRADE 45 EXTREME

Born: Sept. 22, 1989. **B-T:** R-R. **Ht.:** 6-3. **Wt.:** 200. **Drafted:** Arizona Christian, 2013 (6th round). **Signed by:** Brian Reid.

Drummond took an unorthodox path to pro ball, going unsigned three times after being drafted and attending four colleges before landing with the Tigers. An unsigned Brewers 34th-round pick out of high school in 2008, Drummond went to Arizona State but transferred to Orange Coast (Calif.) JC before the 2009 season even started. He transferred to San Diego in 2010, where he redshirted. He pitched two seasons for the Toreros, going unsigned as a Nationals 34th-round pick in 2011 and an Athletics 38th-rounder in 2012. When he became ineligible at San Diego, he transferred to NAIA Arizona Christian as a senior, but he couldn't get eligible there either, so major league teams had to evaluate him throwing bullpens. The Tigers jumped on Drummond in the sixth round of the 2013 draft, signing him for $60,000. He throws 92-96 mph with sink, tail and downhill angle that helps him generate groundballs. When it's on, his plus slider is an out-pitch, though it sometimes flattens out on him. He has a below-average curveball and shows some feel for changeup, but he'll mostly need the fastball and slider out of the bullpen. He's generally around the plate with some funkiness and effort in his delivery, hiding the ball well behind a high leg lift. As a reliever entering his age-24 season, Drummond should open at high Class A Lakeland in 2014.

Year	Club (League)	Class	W	L	ERA	G	GS	CG	SV	IP	H	HR	BB	SO	K/9	WHIP	AVG
2013	Tigers (GCL)	R	1	0	0.00	2	0	0	0	2	1	0	0	2	9.0	0.50	.167
	West Michigan (MWL)	LoA	3	2	2.23	23	2	0	1	40	23	1	16	47	10.5	0.97	.167
Minor League Totals			4	2	2.13	25	2	0	1	42	24	1	16	49	10.4	0.94	.167

30 WILLY ADAMES, SS/3B

BA GRADE 45 EXTREME

Born: Sept. 2, 1995. **B-T:** R-R. **Ht.:** 6-1. **Wt.:** 180. **Signed:** Dominican Republic, 2012. **Signed by:** Aldo Perez/Ramon Perez/Miguel Garcia.

Detroit's two big signings from the 2012 international signing period were Adames and fellow Dominican shortstop Domingo Leyba. Signed for $420,000, Adames was the Tigers' most expensive international signing that year, and while he didn't match Leyba's sparkling 2013 debut in the Rookie-level Dominican Summer League, there were plenty of promising signs in his first season. Adames lacks Leyba's all-around baseball instincts and knack for making contact, but Adames is a better athlete and a more physical player. He still is ironing out his swing to hit for a higher average, but he has a very patient approach, evidenced by him drawing the second-most walks (56) in the DSL. He has gap power presently, with the size and bat speed to project for more once he adds size and strength. He's around an average runner and is raw as a baserunner. Adames got most of his repetitions at shortstop, occasionally playing third base, and showed good hands and a strong arm, though like many young infielders he still needs to cut down on mistakes. Adding size could be a double-edged sword for Adames, as it should help his power but could push him to third base. He should head to the Rookie-level Gulf Coast League in 2014.

Year	Club (League)	Class	AVG	G	AB	R	H	2B	3B	HR	RBI	BB	SO	SB	CS	OBP	SLG
2013	Tigers (DSL)	R	.245	60	200	48	49	12	5	1	21	56	44	9	12	.419	.370
Minor League Totals			.245	60	200	48	49	12	5	1	21	56	44	9	12	.419	.370

Houston Astros

BY J.J. COOPER

Another year, another disastrous record for the Astros.

After Houston won fewer than 60 games for the first and second time in franchise history in 2011 and 2012, they shifted to the American League and got even worse. The 2013 Astros went 51-111 for the worst record in club history and the worst in the majors since the 2004 Diamondbacks also lost 111.

Fans stayed away. The Astros in 2013 drew 1.65 million fans, up slightly from the 1.6 million they drew the year before, but that's roughly half of what the club drew at its peak in the middle of the 2000s.

In fact, a September game drew a 0.0 rating, as the Nielsen company could not statistically prove that anyone in the Houston market actually watched the game. And the Astros' local TV deal is so bad—about 40 percent of Houston-area homes receive Comcast Sports Houston—that owner Jim Crane (who also owns 40 percent of the network) filed suit against former owner Drayton McLane for misleading him about the deal.

The 2013 season was an unmitigated disaster. But by being a disaster, the Astros also got a step closer to the playoffs.

Since trading Michael Bourn and Hunter Pence in July 2011, the Astros have conducted a fascinating experiment. They have torn down the big league roster to a level rarely seen from a non-expansion team.

Since inheriting a woebegone farm system and little big league talent in December 2011, general manager Jeff Luhnow and his staff dismantled the big league club with an eye on future success. The organization's overhaul came at a time when the latest Collective Bargaining Agreement has placed much stricter restrictions on team spending for amateurs, both domestic and international. The amount teams are allowed to spend is tied to the previous year's record, so it gives significant advantages to the teams at the bottom of the standings.

As the worst team in baseball each of the past three seasons, the Astros have benefited. They have had the No. 1 overall pick, and the largest bonus-pool allotment, in each of the past two drafts. The same is true for the 2014 draft. No team before has had three straight No. 1 overall picks.

Houston selected shortstop Carlos Correa, one of the top prospects in baseball, with the No. 1 pick in 2012, then used some of the money they saved in signing Correa to also sign sandwich pick Lance McCullers Jr. and fourth-rounder Rio Ruiz.

In 2013, the Astros took righthander Mark Appel with the No. 1 pick, and he joined an already enviable group of young pitching prospects. Jarred Cosart, acquired from the Phillies in the Pence trade, was first-year manager Bo Porter's best starter after Cosart's July promotion. Fellow rookie Brett Oberholtzer, acquired from the Braves in the Bourn deal, also grabbed and held a rotation spot.

By 2015 or 2016, Houston may be once again contending for a playoff spot, at which point another data point in this experiment will reveal itself:

Will the fans return or will they feel too neglected to care?

CLIFF WELCH

Jarred Cosart quickly became the Astros' best starter after getting called up in July

TOP PROSPECTS OF THE DECADE

Year	Player, Pos.	2013 Org.
2004	Taylor Buchholz, rhp	Out of baseball
2005	Chris Burke, 2b	Out of baseball
2006	Jason Hirsh, rhp	Amarillo (American Assoc.)
2007	Hunter Pence, of	Giants
2008	J.R. Towles, c	Dodgers
2009	Jason Castro, c	Astros
2010	Jason Castro, c	Astros
2011	Jordan Lyles, rhp	Astros
2012	Jonathan Singleton, rhp	Astros
2013	Carlos Correa, ss	Astros

ORGANIZATION OVERVIEW

General Manager: Jeff Luhnow. **Farm Director:** Quinton McCracken. **Scouting Director:** Mike Elias.

Class	Team	League	W	L	PCT	Finish	Manager
Majors	Houston Astros	American	51	111	.315	15th (15)	Bo Porter
Triple-A	Oklahoma City RedHawks	Pacific Coast	82	62	.569	1st (16)	Tony DeFrancesco
Double-A	Corpus Christi Hooks	Texas	83	57	.593	1st (8)	Keith Bodie
High Class A	Lancaster JetHawks	California	82	58	.586	2nd (10)	Rodney Linares
Low Class A	Quad Cities River Bandits	Midwest	81	57	.587	3rd (16)	Omar Lopez
Short-season	Tri-City ValleyCats	New York-Penn	44	32	.579	2nd (14)	Ed Romero
Rookie	Greeneville Astros	Appalachian	38	30	.559	4th (10)	Josh Bonifay
Rookie	GCL Astros	Gulf Coast	27	33	.450	11th (16)	Ed Alfonzo
Overall 2013 Minor League Record			**437**	**329**	**.570**	**1st (30)**	

THIS YEAR'S TOP 30

No.	Player, Pos.	Grade/Risk
1.	Carlos Correa, ss	70/Medium
2.	George Springer, of	65/Medium
3.	Mark Appel, rhp	60/High
4.	Mike Foltynewicz, rhp	60/High
5.	Lance McCullers Jr., rhp	55/High
6.	Vince Velasquez, rhp	55/High
7.	Jonathan Singleton, 1b	55/High
8.	Domingo Santana, of	55/High
9.	Michael Feliz, rhp	55/Extreme
10.	Asher Wojciechowski, rhp	50/Medium
11.	Rio Ruiz, 3b	50/High
12.	Max Stassi, c	50/High
13.	Delino DeShields Jr., of	50/High
14.	Josh Hader, lhp	50/High
15.	Andrew Thurman, rhp	50/High
16.	Teoscar Hernandez, of	50/High
17.	Kevin Chapman, lhp	45/Medium
18.	Nick Tropeano, rhp	45/Medium
19.	Andrew Aplin, of	45/Medium
20.	Nolan Fontana, ss	45/Medium
21.	Jake Buchanan, rhp	45/Medium
22.	Kyle Smith, rhp	45/Medium
23.	Kent Emanuel, lhp	45/Medium
24.	Chris Lee, rhp	50/Extreme
25.	Leo Heras, of	45/High
26.	Gonzalo Sanudo, rhp	45/High
27.	Jandel Gustave, rhp	50/Extreme
28.	Reymin Guduan, lhp	50/Extreme
29.	Danry Vasquez, of	45/High
30.	Brett Phillips, of	50/Extreme

LAST YEAR'S TOP 30

No.	Player, Pos.	Status
1.	Carlos Correa, ss	No. 1
2.	Jonathan Singleton, 1b	No. 7
3.	George Springer, of	No. 2
4.	Lance McCullers Jr., rhp	No. 5
5.	Mike Foltynewicz, rhp	No. 4
6.	Delino DeShields Jr., of	No. 13
7.	Jarred Cosart, rhp	Majors
8.	Rio Ruiz, 3b	No. 11
9.	Nick Tropeano, rhp	No. 18
10.	Nolan Fontana, ss	No. 20
11.	Domingo Santana, of	No. 8
12.	Jonathan Villar, ss	Majors
13.	Vince Velasquez, rhp	No. 6
14.	Asher Wojciechowski, rhp	No. 10
15.	Jose Cisnero, rhp	Dropped out
16.	Adrian Houser, rhp	Dropped out
17.	Robbie Grossman, of	Majors
18.	Brett Phillips, of	No. 30
19.	Rob Rasmussen, lhp	(Phillies)
20.	Brett Oberholtzer, lhp	Majors
21.	Ross Seaton, rhp	Dropped out
22.	Chia-Jen Lo, rhp	Dropped out
23.	Brady Rodgers, rhp	Dropped out
24.	Andrew Aplin, of	No. 19
25.	Josh Fields, rhp	Majors
26.	Austin Wates, of	Dropped out
27.	Paul Clemens, rhp	Majors
28.	Carlos Perez, c	Dropped out
29.	Aaron West, rhp	Dropped out
30.	Tyler Heineman, c	Dropped out

BEST TOOLS

Best Hitter for Average	Carlos Correa
Best Power Hitter	George Springer
Best Strike-Zone Discipline	Nolan Fontana
Fastest Baserunner	Delino DeShields Jr.
Best Athlete	George Springer
Best Fastball	Mike Foltynewicz
Best Curveball	Lance McCullers Jr.
Best Slider	Mark Appel
Best Changeup	Vince Velasquez
Best Control	Jake Buchanan
Best Defensive Catcher	Roberto Pena
Best Defensive Infielder	Carlos Correa
Best Infield Arm	Carlos Correa
Best Defensive Outfielder	George Springer
Best Outfield Arm	Brett Phillips

TOP 15 PLAYERS 25 AND UNDER

No.	Player, Pos (Age)	Peak Level
1.	Carlos Correa, ss (19)	Low Class A
2.	George Springer, of (24)	Triple-A
3.	Jarred Cosart, rhp (23)	Majors
4.	Mark Appel, rhp (22)	Low Class A
5.	Mike Foltynewicz, rhp (22)	Double-A
6.	Lance McCullers Jr., rhp (20)	Low Class A
7.	Vince Velasquez, rhp (21)	High Class A
8.	Jonathan Singleton, 1b (22)	Triple-A
9.	Domingo Santana, of (21)	Double-A
10.	Michael Feliz, rhp (20)	Short-season
11.	Jose Altuve, 2b (23)	Majors
12.	Brett Oberholtzer, rhp (24)	Majors
13.	Jonathan Villar, ss (22)	Majors
14.	Asher Wojciechowski, rhp (25)	Triple-A
15.	Matt Dominguez, 3b (24)	Majors

MINOR LEAGUE DEPTH CHART

HOUSTON ASTROS

TOP 2014 ROOKIE: George Springer, of. He may strike out excessively, but he also will give the Astros lineup a much-needed jolt with his power and speed.

BREAKOUT PROSPECT: Chris Lee, lhp. Lee took big strides towards refining his control, and he could show flashes of dominance at low Class A in 2014.

SLEEPER: Juan Minaya, rhp. At 23, he's a little older than one would like for a pitcher who has just pitched in low Class A, but with a 95 mph fastball and a solid breaking ball, his development could speed up.

SOURCE OF TOP 30 TALENT			
Homegrown	**21**	**Acquired**	**9**
College	8	Trades	9
Junior college	1	Rule 5 draft	0
High school	7	Independent leagues	0
Nondrafted free agents	0	Free agents/waivers	0
International	5		

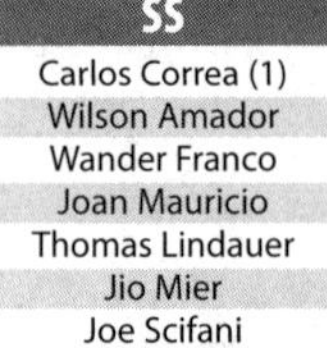

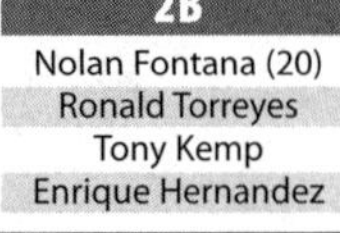

LF
- Teoscar Hernandez (16)
- Leonardo Heras (25)
- Danry Vasquez (29)
- Preston Tucker
- Marc Krauss
- Austin Wates
- Brandon Meredith

CF
- George Springer (2)
- Delino DeShields Jr. (13)
- Andrew Aplin (19)
- Brett Phillips (30)
- James Ramsay
- Jason Martin
- Nestor Tejada

RF
- Domingo Santana (8)
- Ariel Ovando
- Dan Gulbransen
- Felix Lucas

3B
- Rio Ruiz (11)
- Jonathan Meyer
- Tyler White
- Matt Duffy

SS
- Carlos Correa (1)
- Wilson Amador
- Wander Franco
- Joan Mauricio
- Thomas Lindauer
- Jio Mier
- Joe Scifani

2B
- Nolan Fontana (20)
- Ronald Torreyes
- Tony Kemp
- Enrique Hernandez

1B
- Jonathan Singleton (7)
- Conrad Gregor
- Japhey Amador
- Telvin Nash
- Bobby Borchering

C
- Max Stassi (12)
- Carlos Perez
- Tyler Heineman
- Rene Garcia
- Roberto Pena
- Jacob Nottingham
- Alfredo Gonzalez
- Brian Holberton

LHP

LHSP	LHRP
Josh Hader (14)	Kevin Chapman (17)
Kent Emanuel (23)	Reymin Guduan (28)
Chris Lee (24)	Alex Sogard
Luis Cruz	Kenny Long
Rudy Owens	
Austin Nicely	
Randall Fant	

RHP

RHSP	RHRP
Mark Appel (3)	Gonzalo Sanudo (26)
Mike Foltynewicz (4)	Jandel Gustave (27)
Lance McCullers Jr. (5)	Jose Cisnero
Vince Velasquez (6)	Chia-Jen Lo
Michael Feliz (9)	David Martinez
Asher Wojciechowski (10)	Adrian Houser
Andrew Thurman (15)	Juan Minaya
Nick Tropeano (18)	Kyle Westwood
Jake Buchanan (21)	Francis Ramirez
Kyle Smith (22)	
Brady Rogers	
Aaron West	
Devonte German	

DRAFT ANALYSIS

2013

BONUSES: $10.8 MILLION

BEST PURE HITTER: The Astros say that 1B Conrad Gregor (4) will be an above-average hitter with excellent on-base skills. He does a good job of drawing walks and using the whole field.

BEST POWER HITTER: C Jacob Nottingham (6) has shown plus raw power in batting practice and workouts. Like many young hitters, he didn't translate that into home runs in the difficult conditions of the Rookie-level Gulf Coast League, with one home run in 44 games.

FASTEST RUNNER: 2B Tony Kemp (5) is a 65 runner on the 20-80 scouting scale at his best, and he's aggressive on the basepaths. He can still improve on some of the finer points of getting a good jump.

BEST DEFENSIVE PLAYER: OF James Ramsey (7) is at least a solid-average center fielder, with a tick above-average speed to go with excellent routes.

BEST FASTBALL: RHP Mark Appel (1) sits at 93-96 mph and will run it up to 99 on a regular basis. He generates that velocity while throwing primarily two-seamers with good movement. The Astros are working on adding more four-seamers as well.

BEST SECONDARY PITCH: Scouts differ over whether Appel's changeup or slider is the better pitch, and the Astros say both could end up being plus or even plus-plus pitches at their best.

BEST PRO DEBUT: 3B Tyler White (33) hit .322/.406/.456 at three different stops while walking (27) more than he struck out (24). RHP Kyle Westwood (13) anchored the New York-Penn League champion Tri-City club, going 2-2, 0.81 in 45 innings.

BEST ATHLETE: Kemp is 5-foot-6, but he packs a lot of strength into his small frame to go with excellent speed. His leaping ability has come in handy at second base, as he can climb the ladder to snag line drives.

MOST INTRIGUING BACKGROUND: Appel was a high-profile Stanford senior after turning down the Pirates as a first-round pick in 2012. Unsigned RHP Kacy Clemens (35) is the son of Roger.

CLOSEST TO THE MAJORS: When a polished pitcher like Appel goes No. 1 overall, fans start counting the days until he arrives in the big leagues. Appel won't be expected to start the 2014 season in Houston, but he could be there by the end of the year if everything goes well.

BEST LATE-ROUND PICK: Westwood, a senior sign out of Jacksonville, generates a lot of ground balls with a heavy 91-95 mph fastball and a solid curveball. He has enough stuff to be a potentially useful starting pitcher.

THE ONE WHO GOT AWAY: RHP Alex Schick (17) was an intriguing sleeper as a 6-foot-6 righthander who generates excellent angle on his 90 mph fastball, and he has a useful curveball. His skinny frame gives him the potential to add velocity, and teams will see how he develops after three years at California.

ASSESSMENT: With the first pick and a $11.7 million bonus pool, the Astros made another significant talent infusion through the draft. After going high school heavy in 2012, Houston went the college route in each of the first five rounds this year.

2012

BONUSES: $12.1 MILLION

Houston gambled, passing on Byron Buxton to sign SS Carlos Correa (1) for $4.8 million and also get RHP Lance McCullers Jr. (1s) and 3B Rio Ruiz (4). Correa has been worth it so far.

GRADE: B+

2011

BONUSES: $5.5 MILLION

OF George Springer (1) nearly went 40-40 in the minors, but the rest of this class is much more vanilla.

GRADE: C

2010

BONUSES: $7.3 MILLION

A prep-heavy class looks better as RHPs Mike Foltynewicz (1) and Vince Velasquez (2) progress. Delino DeShields Jr. (1) moved to center field.

GRADE: B

TOP DRAFT PICKS OF THE DECADE

Year	Player, Pos.	2013 Org.
2004	Hunter Pence, of (2nd)	Giants
2005	Brian Bogusevic, lhp	Cubs
2006	Max Sapp, c	Out of baseball
2007	*Derek Dietrich, 3b (3rd round)	Marlins
2008	Jason Castro, c	Astros
2009	Jio Mier, ss	Astros
2010	Delino DeShields Jr., 2b	Astros
2011	George Springer, of	Astros
2012	Carlos Correa, ss	Astros
2013	Mark Appel, rhp	Astros

*Did not sign.

LARGEST BONUSES IN CLUB HISTORY

Mark Appel, 2013	$6,350,000
Carlos Correa, 2012	$4,800,000
Ariel Ovando, 2010	$2,600,000
George Springer, 2011	$2,525,000
Lance McCullers Jr., 2012	$2,500,000

1 CARLOS CORREA, SS

Born: Sept. 22, 1994. **B-T:** R-R. **Ht.:** 6-4. **Wt.:** 190.
Drafted: HS—Gurabo, P.R., 2012 (1st round).
Signed by: Larry Pardo/Joey Sola.

The Astros had several good options with the No. 1 pick in the 2012 draft. They could have taken Byron Buxton, considered the top position player in the draft. They could have taken one of a trio of college righthanders—Mark Appel, Kyle Zimmer or Kevin Gausman—or they could be a little more creative. By choosing Correa, the Astros were able to sign the No. 1 overall pick for $4.8 million, less than it would have taken to sign Buxton or Appel, freeing up money to sign sandwich-rounder Lance McCullers Jr. and fourth-rounder Rio Ruiz to above-slot deals. While Buxton was considered the superior prospect, Correa wasn't a signability pick. He starred at the Puerto Rico Baseball Academy and on the showcase circuit in 2011, and as a shortstop, he filled a glaring need in the organization in a way that Buxton, a center fielder, did not. Since signing, Correa has lived up to, and arguably exceeded, expectations. As one of the youngest players in the low Class A Midwest League in 2013, he finished third in batting (.320) and top five in on-base percentage (.405) while leading league shortstops in fielding percentage (.973) and finishing second in total chances (551). He also participated in the Futures Game, where he was the exhibition's youngest player.

Correa combines exceptional tools and outstanding knowledge and feel for the game. Some scouts worry that he'll have to move to third base eventually because of his size and speed. He's an average runner at best right now and likely will slow down. At 6-foot-4 and pushing 200 pounds, he's already one of the bigger shortstops around. But others note that Correa makes all the plays expected of a front-line shortstop. He can make plays in the hole thanks in part to a 70 arm, and he also goes to his left well. Correa is more sure-handed than most young shortstops, with soft hands and a refined internal clock that lets him know when to charge a ball, when to stay back and when to put the ball in his back pocket. At the plate, he should hit for above-average power and average. He has the bat speed to rip fastballs, but his advanced pitch recognition means he also has excellent plate coverage and lays off breaking balls out of the zone. While he hangs in against righthanders, he hit .432/.523/.550 against southpaws in 111 at-bats for Quad Cities in 2013. Though he hit just nine home runs in his first full season, he has 20-25 potential.

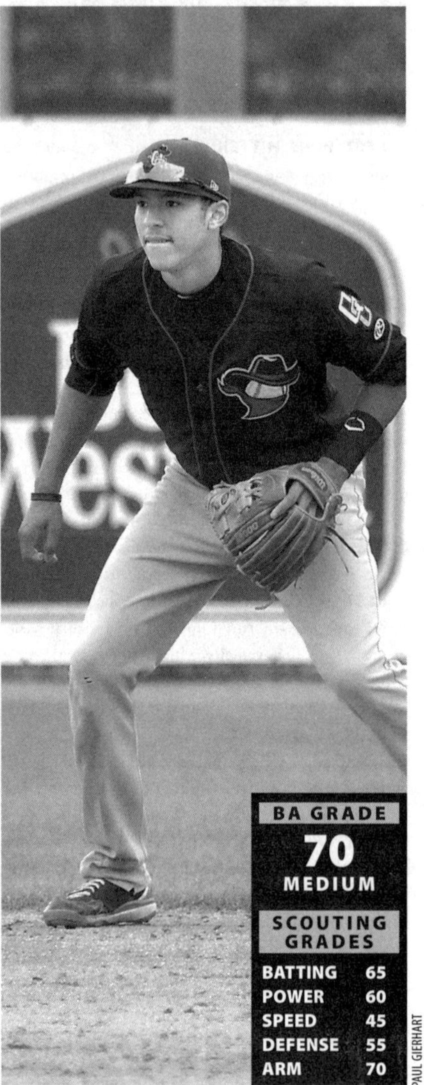

BA GRADE
70
MEDIUM
SCOUTING GRADES
BATTING 65
POWER 60
SPEED 45
DEFENSE 55
ARM 70

PAUL GIERHART

Correa is one of those rare players who could hit in the middle of the lineup while playing a solid shortstop. Even if he ends up moving to third base, he has the power to be an impact player. After posting loud numbers in 2013, he could take those numbers to a new stratosphere at the hitter's paradise that is high Class A Lancaster in 2014.

Year	Club (League)	Class	AVG	G	AB	R	H	2B	3B	HR	RBI	BB	SO	SB	CS	OBP	SLG
2012	Astros (GCL)	R	.232	39	155	23	36	11	1	2	9	7	36	5	1	.270	.355
	Greeneville (APP)	R	.371	11	35	5	13	3	1	1	3	5	8	1	0	.450	.600
2013	Quad Cities (MWL)	LoA	.320	117	450	73	144	33	3	9	86	58	83	10	10	.405	.467
Minor League Totals			.302	167	640	101	193	47	5	12	98	70	127	16	11	.377	.447

2 GEORGE SPRINGER, OF

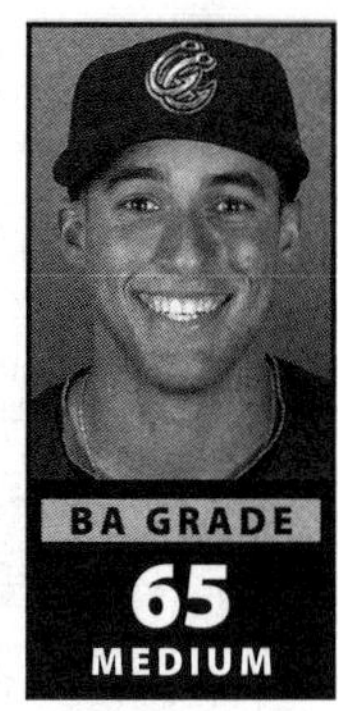

Born: Sept. 19, 1989. **B-T:** R-R. **Ht.:** 6-3. **Wt.:** 200. **Drafted:** Connecticut, 2011 (1st round). **Signed by:** John Kosciak/Bobby Heck.

Springer has a fascinating family history, but since signing for $2.525 million as the 11th pick in the 2011 draft, he's made his own name, including a strong run at a 40-40 season in 2013 in which he fell three home runs short of the feat. He goes to the plate looking for a pitch on the inner half that he can drive, and he succeeded frequently in doing so in 2013 as he advanced to Triple-A Oklahoma City. His outstanding bat speed allows him to catch up to most anything, but his aggressive approach often leaves him out on his front foot when he faces quality offspeed stuff. Because his arm, speed, power and defense all rate as at least plus tools, Springer can be productive even as he strikes out excessively. A .299 career minor league hitter, he won't approach that in the majors unless he starts lining pitches on the outer half to right field more often. Though he's not on the 40-man roster, Springer should earn a big league spot in Houston's woeful outfield at some point in 2014. If he makes enough contact to hit .270 in the big leagues, he's a perennial all-star. He has enough other tools to help a team win even if his swing-and-miss tendencies turn him into a .240 hitter.

Year	Club (League)	Class	AVG	G	AB	R	H	2B	3B	HR	RBI	BB	SO	SB	CS	OBP	SLG
2011	Tri-City (NYP)	SS	.179	8	28	8	5	3	0	1	3	2	2	4	0	.303	.393
2012	Lancaster (CAL)	HiA	.316	106	433	101	137	18	10	22	82	56	131	28	6	.398	.557
	Corpus Christi (TL)	AA	.219	22	73	8	16	3	0	2	5	6	25	4	2	.288	.342
2013	Corpus Christi (TL)	AA	.297	73	273	56	81	20	0	19	55	42	96	23	5	.399	.579
	Oklahoma City (PCL)	AAA	.311	62	219	50	68	7	4	18	53	41	65	22	3	.425	.626
Minor League Totals			.299	271	1026	223	307	51	14	62	198	147	319	81	16	.394	.558

3 MARK APPEL, RHP

Born: July 15, 1991. **B-T:** R-R. **Ht.:** 6-5. **Wt.:** 190. **Drafted:** Stanford, 2013 (1st round). **Signed by:** Brian Byrne.

The Astros flirted with taking Appel, who lived in Houston until he was 12, with the first pick in the 2012 draft, but they weren't sure he'd sign for the $6 million they were offering, so they passed. The move ended up paying off—on and off the field—for Appel. He was able to finish his Management Science and Engineering degree at Stanford, while on the field, he dominated more consistently as a senior and ended up signing a $6.35 million bonus as the No. 1 overall pick in 2013. Appel can't match the pure gas of fellow first-rounder Jonathan Gray, but he does have one of the best fastballs in his draft class. He sits 93-96 mph and will touch 99 from a clean delivery. Appel pairs his fastball with a potentially plus slider and an average to plus changeup. His stuff was crisper and firmer as an amateur than in his pro debut. He would tip his changeup by slowing his arm, and he struggled to locate his slider. Amateur scouts saw a potential front-line starter, but pro scouts saw a middle-of-the-rotation candidate. The latter group also was less impressed with his athleticism. Appel should move quickly, but the Astros have no need to rush him. He'll start the 2014 season at high Class A Lancaster or Double-A Corpus Christi, depending on how spring training goes. No one would be surprised to see him in Houston by the end of the year.

Year	Club (League)	Class	W	L	ERA	G	GS	CG	SV	IP	H	HR	BB	SO	K/9	WHIP	AVG
2013	Tri-City (NYP)	SS	0	0	3.60	2	2	0	0	5	6	0	0	6	10.8	1.20	.300
	Quad Cities (MWL)	LoA	3	1	3.82	8	8	0	0	33	30	2	9	27	7.4	1.18	.236
Minor League Totals			3	1	3.79	10	10	0	0	38	36	2	9	33	7.8	1.18	.245

4 MIKE FOLTYNEWICZ, RHP

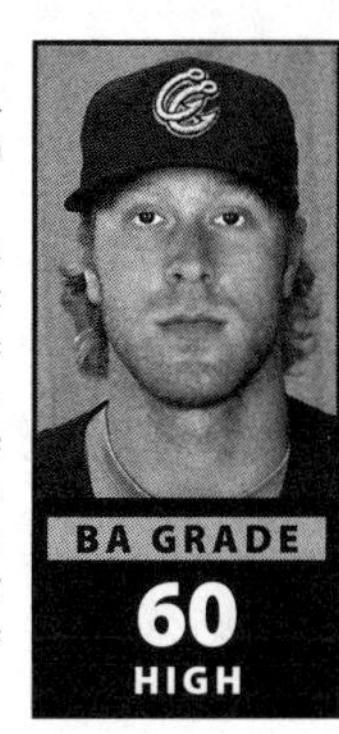

Born: Oct. 7, 1991. **B-T:** R-R. **Ht.:** 6-4. **Wt.:** 200. **Drafted:** HS—Minooka, Ill., 2010 (1st round). **Signed by:** Troy Hoerner.

Foltynewicz wasn't a consensus first-round pick when the Astros picked him 19th overall in 2010, making him the first Illinois high school pitcher to be selected in the first round since Kris Honel in 2001. He's developed into one of the top power arms in the minors and reached Double-A Corpus Christi for the first time in his third full season. No minor league starter touched 100 mph more often in 2013 than Foltynewicz, and he hit 101 and 102 on occasion. He doesn't locate his fastball with precision, so even when he's sitting 96-98 mph, it flattens out, making it a hittable pitch. When he locates down in the zone, it's a wipeout pitch with good sink. The Astros let him work on both his slider and curveball again after emphasizing the slider in 2012. While both breaking balls can be plus, he throws as many below-average offerings as above-average ones.

His changeup will probably always be his fourth pitch, but he flashes average with it. Some scouts think Foltynewicz will end up as an elite reliever because of his control issues—he walked 4.6 batters per nine innings in 2013—but his frame, stamina and delivery all point to him being at least a mid-rotation starter if he can throw more strikes.

Year	Club (League)	Class	W	L	ERA	G	GS	CG	SV	IP	H	HR	BB	SO	K/9	WHIP	AVG
2010	Greeneville (APP)	R	0	3	4.03	12	12	0	0	45	46	3	15	39	7.9	1.37	.272
2011	Lexington (SAL)	LoA	5	11	4.97	26	26	0	0	134	149	10	51	88	5.9	1.49	.289
2012	Lexington (SAL)	LoA	14	4	3.14	27	27	0	0	152	145	11	62	125	7.4	1.36	.250
2013	Lancaster (CAL)	HiA	1	0	3.81	7	5	0	0	26	31	4	14	29	10.0	1.73	.290
	Corpus Christi (TL)	AA	5	3	2.87	23	16	0	3	103	75	8	52	95	8.3	1.23	.207
Minor League Totals			25	21	3.74	95	86	0	3	460	446	36	194	376	7.4	1.39	.257

5 LANCE McCULLERS JR., RHP

Born: Oct. 2, 1993. **B-T:** L-R. **Ht.:** 6-1. **Wt.:** 190. **Drafted:** HS—Tampa, 2012 (1st round supplemental). **Signed by:** John Martin.

The number 41 fits the McCullers family. The Phillies selected Lance Sr. 41st overall in the 1982 draft, and he wore No. 41 at the peak of his seven-year major league career. The Astros drafted Lance Jr. 41st overall in 2012 and signed him for $2.5 million, more than his father earned in his big league career. McCullers has two potential 70 pitches on the 20-80 scouting scale. He fires a 93-98 mph fastball that sometimes he struggles to keep in the zone because of its excellent life. His breaking ball can be described as either a curveball or slider, but either way it has 11-to-5 downward movement. At 81-85 mph it's harder than the average curveball. He's equally effective against lefties and righties because of the power and bite on his breaking ball. Scouts wonder if McCullers will wind up in the bullpen, because his changeup is well below average now. He throws it because he knows he has to develop it, but it lacks deception, separation or movement. Teams don't usually send top pitching prospects to a hitter's haven like high Class A Lancaster—at least not for long—but McCullers, Vince Velasquez, Andrew Thurman and maybe Mark Appel could be headed there in 2014. Long-term, McCullers could end up as a front-line starter if his changeup develops. If not, he could be a closer, like his father.

Year	Club (League)	Class	W	L	ERA	G	GS	CG	SV	IP	H	HR	BB	SO	K/9	WHIP	AVG
2012	Astros (GCL)	R	0	1	1.64	4	4	0	0	11	10	0	2	12	9.8	1.09	.227
	Greeneville (APP)	R	0	3	4.80	4	4	0	0	15	10	2	10	17	10.2	1.33	.182
2013	Quad Cities (MWL)	LoA	6	5	3.18	25	19	0	0	105	92	3	49	117	10.1	1.35	.239
Minor League Totals			6	9	3.24	33	27	0	0	131	112	5	61	146	10.1	1.32	.231

6 VINCE VELASQUEZ, RHP

Born: June 7, 1992. **B-T:** B-R. **Ht.:** 6-3. **Wt.:** 185. **Drafted:** HS—Pomona, Calif., 2010 (2nd round). **Signed by:** Tim Costic/Bobby Heck.

When he's been healthy, Velasquez has been an effective pitcher, but staying healthy has been a battle. He didn't pitch as a high school junior because of a strained elbow ligament and stress fracture in his arm. After impressing scouts as both a pitcher and shortstop as a senior, he further damaged the elbow ligament in his pro debut at Rookie-level Greeneville in 2010, requiring Tommy John surgery that forced him to miss the entire 2011 season. The Astros have been cautious since then, limiting Velasquez to nine starts in 2012 before letting him take a larger role in 2013. On a low Class A Quad Cities staff that included Lance McCullers Jr., Mark Appel and Josh Hader, he convinced some scouts he'll be the best of the group. Velasquez has two plus pitches now and the chance to have a third average pitch. His fastball is an easy 92-95 mph and his changeup is extremely advanced for an inexperienced pitcher. He needs to tighten his below-average, loopy curveball, but he does show the feel to spin it. Velasquez's delivery has a slight crossfire aspect to it, but otherwise he throws free and easy. He's in the picture for a crowded high Class A Lancaster rotation in 2014.

Year	Club (League)	Class	W	L	ERA	G	GS	CG	SV	IP	H	HR	BB	SO	K/9	WHIP	AVG
2010	Greeneville (APP)	R	2	2	3.07	8	6	0	0	29	24	4	5	25	7.7	0.99	.216
2011	Did not play—Injured																
2012	Tri-City (NYP)	SS	4	1	3.35	9	9	0	0	46	37	2	17	51	10.1	1.18	.223
2013	Quad Cities (MWL)	LoA	9	4	3.19	25	16	0	3	110	90	7	33	123	10.1	1.12	.221
	Lancaster (CAL)	HiA	0	2	6.14	3	3	0	0	15	14	2	8	19	11.7	1.50	.259
Minor League Totals			15	9	3.43	45	34	0	3	200	165	15	63	218	9.8	1.14	.223

7 JONATHAN SINGLETON, 1B

Born: Sept. 18, 1991. **B-T:** L-L. **Ht.:** 6-2. **Wt.:** 235. **Drafted:** HS—Long Beach, 2009 (8th round). **Signed by:** Demetrius Pittman (Phillies).

Acquired from the Phillies in the 2011 Hunter Pence trade, Singleton got in on the ground floor of the Astros' rebuilding effort. By the time 2012 ended, he appeared to be on track to be Houston's everyday first baseman at some point in 2013. Instead, Singleton drew a 50-game suspension following a second positive test for marijuana. He was out of shape when he returned from his suspension at the end of May, struggled at Triple-A Oklahoma City and was pointedly not included among the club's September callups. While Singleton may have had a disastrous 2013 season, he still ranks among the best first-base prospects in the game. He shows excellent bat speed, draws walks and has plus raw power. While he struggled to make contact in 2013, he did show more willingness to pull the ball when he got pitches to drive. He needs to do a better job of hanging in versus lefthanders, but when he's locked in, he hits screaming line drives to all fields. He's an average first baseman with solid hands but a poor arm. He's a below-average runner. The Astros added Singleton to the 40-man roster on Oct. 2, nearly two months before they needed to for Rule 5 draft purposes, and he no longer will be tested for recreational drugs. A powerful performance in the Puerto Rican League helped him make up for lost time. Singleton will return to Triple-A to begin 2014, but he should be in Houston at some point in 2014. He still has middle-of-the-order potential.

Year	Club (League)	Class	AVG	G	AB	R	H	2B	3B	HR	RBI	BB	SO	SB	CS	OBP	SLG
2009	Phillies (GCL)	R	.290	31	100	12	29	9	0	2	12	18	13	1	0	.395	.440
2010	Lakewood (SAL)	LoA	.290	104	376	64	109	25	2	14	77	62	74	9	7	.393	.479
2011	Clearwater (FSL)	HiA	.284	93	320	48	91	14	0	9	47	56	83	3	3	.387	.413
	Lancaster (CAL)	HiA	.333	35	129	20	43	9	1	4	16	14	40	0	0	.405	.512
2012	Corpus Christi (TL)	AA	.284	131	461	94	131	27	4	21	79	88	131	7	2	.396	.497
2013	Quad Cities (MWL)	LoA	.286	6	21	6	6	2	0	3	5	4	5	0	0	.400	.810
	Corpus Christi (TL)	AA	.263	11	38	5	10	2	1	2	8	9	16	0	0	.396	.526
	Oklahoma City (PCL)	AAA	.220	73	245	31	54	13	0	6	31	46	89	1	0	.340	.347
Minor League Totals			.280	484	1690	280	473	101	8	61	275	297	451	21	12	.386	.457

8 DOMINGO SANTANA, OF

Born: Aug. 5, 1992. **B-T:** R-R. **Ht.:** 6-5. **Wt.:** 228. **Signed:** Dominican Republic, 2009. **Signed by:** Sal Agostinelli (Phillies).

Former general manager Ed Wade kicked off the Astros rebuild in July 2011 with the Hunter Pence trade, which brought back two 2013 big league rookies, righthanders Jarred Cosart and Josh Zeid, plus Jonathan Singleton and Santana, the Nos. 7 and 8 prospects. Signed for $330,000 in 2009, Santana jumped straight to the Rookie-level Gulf Coast League as a 16-year-old, which helps explain how he has more than 1,750 at-bats even though he'll play most of the 2013 season at age 21. He fits the prototype of what scouts look for in a power-hitting right fielder, combining strength with athleticism. He's average defensively with an above-average arm, and while he's a physical 6-foot-5, he's an average runner who even filled in as a center fielder at times in 2013. At the plate, Santana's long arms ensure that he'll always strike out some, something he exacerbates with a high hand position, which forces his the bat to travel a long way to get through the zone. But when he gets his arms extended, he can hit the ball out of the park to all fields. At Double-A Corpus Christi in 2013, 11 of his 25 home runs went to right or center field. Ready for Triple-A and added to the 40-man roster, Santana is ahead of schedule, but he needs further refinement before he's ready to be a power threat in the middle of the Astros lineup.

Year	Club (League)	Class	AVG	G	AB	R	H	2B	3B	HR	RBI	BB	SO	SB	CS	OBP	SLG
2009	Phillies (GCL)	R	.288	37	118	17	34	6	1	6	28	15	44	3	1	.388	.508
2010	Lakewood (SAL)	LoA	.182	49	165	27	30	10	0	3	16	29	76	5	6	.322	.297
	Williamsport (NYP)	SS	.237	54	186	28	44	9	0	5	20	23	73	4	4	.336	.366
2011	Lakewood (SAL)	LoA	.269	96	350	45	94	29	4	7	32	26	120	4	1	.345	.434
	Lexington (SAL)	LoA	.382	17	68	13	26	4	0	5	21	6	15	1	0	.447	.662
2012	Lancaster (CAL)	HiA	.302	119	457	87	138	26	6	23	97	55	148	7	1	.385	.536
2013	Corpus Christi (TL)	AA	.252	112	416	72	105	23	2	25	64	46	139	12	5	.345	.498
Minor League Totals			.268	484	1760	289	471	107	13	74	278	200	615	36	18	.359	.469

9 MICHAEL FELIZ, RHP

BA GRADE
55
EXTREME

Born: June 28, 1993. **B-T:** R-R. **Ht.:** 6-4. **Wt.:** 211. **Signed:** Dominican Republic, 2010. **Signed by:** Felix Francisco/Rafael Belen/Jose Lima.

If not for a positive drug test, Feliz likely would be positioned on the Athletics prospect list right now. He originally signed with Oakland for $800,000 in 2010, but that contract was voided after he tested positive for an anabolic steroid. Feliz then signed with the Astros for half of his initial bonus. Suspended for 50 games in 2010, he made it to the U.S. in 2011 and took a big step forward in 2013 at short-season Tri-City. He gave up just 10 extra-base hits in 69 innings while leading the New York-Penn League ERA title at 1.96. Feliz, like many Astros pitchers, has benefited from the organization's emphasis on athletic deliveries that help develop velocity. He sat at 88-92 mph when he signed, but now he sits 93-96 and touches 98 from a lightning-quick arm. His command sometimes wavers because his arm trails his lower body, but he already has above-average control and doesn't miss the zone much. His slider flashes average to plus, and he can throws it for strikes or bury it. Feliz is a long way from the big leagues, but he has the makings of a three-pitch mix and he's more than ready for low Class A Quad Cities in 2014.

Year	Club (League)	Class	W	L	ERA	G	GS	CG	SV	IP	H	HR	BB	SO	K/9	WHIP	AVG
2010	Astros (DSL)	R	0	1	4.26	3	3	0	0	13	9	1	3	13	9.2	0.95	.196
2011	Astros (GCL)	R	0	3	4.32	12	10	0	0	50	53	2	21	44	7.9	1.48	.270
2012	Astros (GCL)	R	5	0	1.64	7	3	0	0	38	25	2	9	35	8.2	0.89	.185
	Greeneville (APP)	R	1	1	5.13	6	6	0	0	26	28	1	14	28	9.6	1.59	.269
2013	Tri-City (NYP)	SS	4	2	1.96	14	10	0	1	69	53	2	13	78	10.2	0.96	.209
Minor League Totals			10	7	3.07	42	32	0	1	196	168	8	60	198	9.1	1.16	.229

10 ASHER WOJCIECHOWSKI, RHP

BA GRADE
50
MEDIUM

Born: Dec. 21, 1988. **B-T:** R-R. **Ht.:** 6-4. **Wt.:** 235. **Drafted:** The Citadel, 2010 (1st round supplemental). **Signed by:** John Hendricks (Blue Jays).

Timing may be everything for Wojciechowski. Selected as part of the Blue Jays' pitching-rich 2010 draft that also included the likes of Aaron Sanchez and Noah Syndergaard, he joined the Astros along with six other players at the 2012 trade deadline in the deal that sent J.A. Happ and Brandon Lyon to Toronto. Wojciechowski gets outs by locating an average 90-93 mph fastball to both sides of the plate and mixing in an average slider and changeup with a tick-above-average control. Since joining the Astros, he's learned to get more downward plane on his fastball, in part because he made tweaks to lead more with his hips in his delivery. Wojciechowski does a good job of helping himself by controlling the running game, and just two of seven basestealers succeeded against him in 134 innings at Triple-A Oklahoma City in 2013. While he doesn't have the high ceiling of other pitchers in the system, Wojciechowski is a relatively polished candidate to contribute to the rotation, and he has the advantage of reaching Houston before the next pitching wave crashes. Now a member of the 40-man roster, he could reach his ceiling as a reliable, durable No. 4 starter beginning in 2014.

Year	Club (League)	Class	W	L	ERA	G	GS	CG	SV	IP	H	HR	BB	SO	K/9	WHIP	AVG
2010	Auburn (NYP)	SS	0	0	0.75	3	3	0	0	12	6	0	4	11	8.3	0.83	.146
2011	Dunedin (FSL)	HiA	11	9	4.70	25	22	0	0	130	156	15	31	96	6.6	1.43	.292
2012	Dunedin (FSL)	HiA	7	3	3.57	18	18	0	0	93	91	3	22	76	7.3	1.21	.261
	Corpus Christi (TL)	AA	2	2	2.06	8	8	0	0	44	30	0	14	34	7.0	1.01	.190
2013	Corpus Christi (TL)	AA	2	1	2.08	6	3	0	1	26	17	1	7	27	9.3	0.92	.189
	Oklahoma City (PCL)	AAA	9	7	3.56	22	21	2	0	134	116	10	44	104	7.0	1.19	.229
Minor League Totals			31	22	3.58	82	75	2	1	439	416	29	122	348	7.1	1.22	.248

11 RIO RUIZ, 3B

BA GRADE
50
HIGH

Born: May 22, 1994. **B-T:** L-R. **Ht.:** 6-1. **Wt.:** 180. **Drafted:** HS—La Puente, Calif., 2012 (4th round). **Signed by:** Tim Costic.

A football and baseball star as a prep junior at Bishop Amat High, Ruiz had a senior year to forget. He missed much of the football season with a knee injury, while a blood clot in his arm forced him to miss most of the baseball season as well. The 2012 fourth-rounder proved to be surprisingly raw in 2013. Ruiz always has had a sweet, lefty swing, but he addressed mechanical flaws during his time at low Class A Quad Cities. Early in the season he was collapsing his front side in his swing, so that he'd land on the edge of his front foot, leading to an unstable base that often left him dragging the bat through the zone. Once he cleaned that up, Ruiz's tick-above-average power started to appear. Thanks to strong hands and wrists, he has above-average bat speed and should be at least an average hitter. Defensively, Ruiz has an average arm, but he had trouble fielding balls cleanly and was sometimes caught in-between hops on grounders. Scouts give him a chance to be average defensively, but he must clean up his footwork to get there. He impressed scouts with his aptitude and improvement as the season went along. Ruiz looks like a solid everyday third baseman if he can make mechanical adjustments on both sides of the ball, though the hard, fast infields at high Class A Lancaster might impede his defensive progress in 2014.

Year	Club (League)	Class	AVG	G	AB	R	H	2B	3B	HR	RBI	BB	SO	SB	CS	OBP	SLG
2012	Astros (GCL)	R	.271	23	85	13	23	8	2	0	11	12	22	2	0	.361	.412
	Greeneville (APP)	R	.220	15	50	8	11	3	1	1	7	4	10	0	0	.291	.380
2013	Quad Cities (MWL)	LoA	.260	114	416	46	108	33	1	12	63	50	92	12	3	.335	.430
Minor League Totals			.258	152	551	67	142	44	4	13	81	66	124	14	3	.335	.423

12 MAX STASSI, C

Born: March 15, 1991. **B-T:** R-R. **Ht.:** 5-10. **Wt.:** 205. **Drafted:** HS—Yuba City, Calif., 2009 (4th round). **Signed by:** Jermaine Clark (Athletics).

Stassi has rarely been healthy since signing for $1.5 million as an Athletics fourth-round pick in 2009. A shoulder injury limited him to being a DH for part of his senior year of high school, and the same malady forced him to have surgery that cost him much of his 2011 season. Stassi missed time in 2012 with ankle and oblique problems. The Astros acquired him when they dealt Jed Lowrie to Oakland in February 2013, then found he had a detached muscle in his hip that was repaired surgically. They believe that was the root of his injury problems. Upon his return, Stassi hit 10 home runs in a 15-game stretch at Double-A Corpus Christi in July. His poor injury luck continued, however. Called up to Houston, he suffered a concussion in his big league debut after being hit by a pitch. Stassi's injury history is frightening, but his above-average power potential is rare for a catcher, especially one who is a solid-average receiver behind the plate. His arm is average despite the shoulder problems in the past. Stassi isn't picky enough at the plate—he had neary as many home runs as walks in 2013—but he has a chance to be an everyday catcher thanks to his power. In 2014, he'll try to earn the job as backup to Jason Castro and could get his first time at Triple-A Oklahoma City.

Year	Club (League)	Class	AVG	G	AB	R	H	2B	3B	HR	RBI	BB	SO	SB	CS	OBP	SLG
2009	Athletics (AZL)	R	.000	1	1	0	0	0	0	0	0	1	1	0	0	.500	.000
	Vancouver (NWL)	SS	.286	13	49	3	14	4	0	0	8	2	11	0	0	.340	.367
2010	Kane County (MWL)	LoA	.229	110	411	54	94	21	1	13	51	45	141	3	3	.310	.380
2011	Stockton (CAL)	HiA	.231	31	121	22	28	6	0	2	19	16	22	1	1	.331	.331
2012	Stockton (CAL)	HiA	.268	84	314	48	84	18	0	15	45	27	83	3	1	.331	.468
2013	Corpus Christi (TL)	AA	.277	76	289	40	80	20	1	17	60	19	68	1	1	.333	.529
	Houston (AL)	MAJ	.286	3	7	0	2	0	0	0	1	0	2	0	0	.375	.286
Major League Totals			.286	3	7	0	2	0	0	0	1	0	2	0	0	.375	.286
Minor League Totals			.253	315	1185	167	300	69	2	47	183	110	326	8	6	.325	.434

13 DELINO DESHIELDS JR., OF/2B

Born: Aug. 16, 1992. **B-T:** R-R. **Ht.:** 5-9. **Wt.:** 190. **Drafted:** HS—College Park, Ga., 2010 (1st round). **Signed by:** Lincoln Martin.

With 12 home runs and 101 stolen bases in 2012, DeShields became the first player in minor league history to reach double digits in homers and triple digits in steals in the same season. Moving to the hitter's paradise of high Class A Lancaster in 2013, he seemed poised for a loud encore, but instead he turned in a solid, but not spectacular, effort. After the season, the Astros looked at DeShields' limitations at second base—where his father Delino Sr. spent the bulk of his 13-year big league career—and decided to move him to center field, his position in high school. While DeShields had worked hard to become a fringy defender at the keystone, he looks like a better fit in center, where 80 speed gives him excellent range and a below-average arm is less of a liability. He still has work to do on his jumps and reads. At the plate, DeShields was susceptible to being busted inside early in the season, but he developed the ability to pull the ball more consistently as the season developed. With a compact stroke and a solid feel for the strike zone, he projects as a potentially disruptive leadoff hitter with on-base skills and the speed to wreak havoc once he reaches. Surprisingly stocky and strong for a speedster, DeShields has average power potential as well. Disappointed not to be assigned to Double-A Corpus Christi in 2013, he will get his shot to go there in 2014.

Year	Club (League)	Class	AVG	G	AB	R	H	2B	3B	HR	RBI	BB	SO	SB	CS	OBP	SLG
2010	Astros (GCL)	R	.111	2	9	3	1	0	0	0	0	1	2	0	0	.200	.111
	Greeneville (APP)	R	.313	16	67	11	21	6	1	0	8	5	18	5	1	.356	.433
2011	Lexington (SAL)	LoA	.220	119	469	73	103	17	2	9	48	52	118	30	11	.305	.322
2012	Lexington (SAL)	LoA	.298	111	440	96	131	22	5	10	52	70	108	83	14	.401	.439
	Lancaster (CAL)	HiA	.237	24	97	17	23	2	3	2	9	13	23	18	5	.336	.381
2013	Lancaster (CAL)	HiA	.317	111	451	100	143	25	14	5	54	57	91	51	18	.405	.468
Minor League Totals			.275	383	1533	300	422	72	25	26	171	198	360	187	49	.366	.406

14 JOSH HADER, LHP

Born: April 7, 1994. **B-T:** L-L. **Ht.:** 6-3. **Wt.:** 160. **Drafted:** HS—Millersville, Md., 2012 (19th round). **Signed by:** Dean Albany (Orioles).

A skinny southpaw who sat 84-87 mph during much of his senior season of high school, Hader signed with the Orioles for $40,000 as a 19th-rounder, then went on long-toss and weight-training programs that quickly developed him into a much more interesting low-90s slinger. The Astros acquired Hader, along with L.J. Hoes, for Bud Norris in July 2013. He sets up with his body pointed at a 45-degree angle to home plate. He then winds with a big leg kick and fires from a crossfire, nearly sidearm delivery. It's one of the more unconventional deliveries a starter could use, but because Hader has an extremely loose arm, it generally works for him. His 90-94 mph fastball grades as an above-average pitch, but few hitters ever seem to get a good swing because of how well he hides the ball. Because of his arm slot, Hader throws a slurvy 75-78 mph curveball that will flash average. The Astros believe Hader will continue getting stronger and will improve his control, giving him a chance to be a mid-rotation starter. But other scouts see him as a future lefty reliever where his low angle will make life difficult for lefthanders. He'll be battling in spring training to be part of a crowded high Class A Lancaster rotation in 2014.

Year	Club (League)	Class	W	L	ERA	G	GS	CG	SV	IP	H	HR	BB	SO	K/9	WHIP	AVG
2012	Orioles (GCL)	R	2	0	2.66	12	0	0	2	20	12	2	7	35	15.5	0.93	.174
	Aberdeen (NYP)	SS	0	0	0.00	5	0	0	0	8	2	0	2	13	14.0	0.48	.074
2013	Delmarva (SAL)	LoA	3	6	2.65	17	17	0	0	85	67	4	42	79	8.4	1.28	.215
	Quad Cities (MWL)	LoA	2	0	3.22	5	5	0	0	22	14	0	12	16	6.4	1.16	.182
Minor League Totals			7	6	2.58	39	22	0	2	136	95	6	63	143	9.5	1.16	.196

15 ANDREW THURMAN, RHP

Born: Dec. 10, 1991. **B-T:** R-R. **Ht.:** 6-3. **Wt.:** 200. **Drafted:** UC Irvine, 2013 (2nd round). **Signed by:** Brad Budzinski

After spending big on Mark Appel in the first round, the Astros used the rest of the 2013 draft to acquire polished, lower-ceiling prospects who should be able to move quickly through the system. Thurman, a second-round pick, is a perfect example, because he lacks a true plus pitch, but he has a long track record of success because of his above-average control and ability to read batters' swings. He spent his first two years at UC Irvine handcuffing hitters (he no-hit Long Beach State in 2012) even though he had a fringy fastball. In 2013, Thurman's fastball jumped to average velocity, and he now sits 90-92 mph and touches 95. He throws both a slider and curveball. Both are average at best, but they are less destructive than his tick-above-average changeup, which he uses with equal effectiveness against lefthanders and righthanders. Thurman has a solid pitcher's frame, a clean delivery and a long track record of durability. He projects as a back-end starter, and he should move quickly with an assignment to high Class A Lancaster in 2014, if there's room in the rotation.

Year	Club (League)	Class	W	L	ERA	G	GS	CG	SV	IP	H	HR	BB	SO	K/9	WHIP	AVG
2013	Tri-City (NYP)	SS	4	2	3.86	12	5	0	1	40	43	5	11	43	9.8	1.36	.277
Minor League Totals			4	2	3.86	12	5	0	1	40	43	5	11	43	9.8	1.36	.277

16 TEOSCAR HERNANDEZ, OF

BA GRADE
50
HIGH

Born: Oct. 15, 1992. **B-T:** R-R. **Ht.:** 6-2. **Wt.:** 180. **Signed:** Dominican Republic, 2011. **Signed by:** Felix Francisco/Rafael Belen/Francis Mojica.

Hernandez may not have a plus tool on his scouting report, but with average grades across the board he fits the description some scouts use as a "cheap five-tool player." A potentially average hitter with average power, Hernandez can pull the ball for home runs, but he is equally comfortable spraying the ball around the field. As he's filled out, he's lost some of his once above-average speed, but he's gained strength in return. Hernandez has solid bat speed, but he struck out nearly a quarter of the time at low Class A Quad Cities in 2013, in part because he took too many called strike threes. His arm is a tick-above-average and could work in right field, though he's better suited for left. As a solid-if-unspectacular, righthanded hitter who doesn't have enough glove to project in center, Hernandez doesn't fit the prototype for the corner outfielder, but his hitting ability and feel for the game give him a chance to exceed expectations. He'll head to high Class A Lancaster in 2014.

Year	Club (League)	Class	AVG	G	AB	R	H	2B	3B	HR	RBI	BB	SO	SB	CS	OBP	SLG
2011	Astros (DSL)	R	.274	65	226	41	62	13	7	7	35	28	42	16	4	.360	.487
2012	Astros (GCL)	R	.243	51	177	25	43	11	2	4	18	19	54	10	1	.325	.395
	Lexington (SAL)	LoA	.240	8	25	2	6	2	0	1	5	3	12	1	0	.310	.440
2013	Quad Cities (MWL)	LoA	.271	123	499	97	135	25	9	13	55	41	135	24	11	.328	.435
Minor League Totals			.265	247	927	165	246	51	18	25	113	91	243	51	16	.335	.440

17 KEVIN CHAPMAN, LHP

BA GRADE **45** MEDIUM

Born: Feb. 19, 1988. **B-T:** L-L. **Ht.:** 6-3. **Wt.:** 220. **Drafted:** Florida, 2010 (4th round). **Signed by:** Colin Gonzales (Royals).

When the Royals suffered a series of catching injuries during spring training 2012, they found themselves desperate for a fill-in, which led them to explore the trade market. The Astros were more than happy to send veteran backstop Humberto Quintero to Kansas City to acquire Chapman and outfielder D'Andre Toney. In 2013, Chapman was one of the few bright spots in the worst bullpen in the big leagues. He quickly moved from being a situational lefty to pitching the eighth inning, but whether Chapman can keep that job will depend on his control. He straddles the line between effectively wild and just plain wild, with a career walk rate of 5.0 batters per nine innings in the minors. Chapman always will have below-average control and poor command, thanks to a effortful delivery in which he spins over a stiff front leg. But his 92-93 mph fastball gets in on lefties, setting up a plus, wipeout 80 mph slider. Chapman has the potential to pitch high-leverage innings in Houston in 2014, but Astros fans will always have reason to be nervous when he's on the mound.

Year	Club (League)	Class	W	L	ERA	G	GS	CG	SV	IP	H	HR	BB	SO	K/9	WHIP	AVG
2010	Wilmington (CAR)	HiA	1	1	5.50	14	0	0	1	18	20	1	8	20	10.0	1.56	.267
2011	Wilmington (CAR)	HiA	0	2	4.84	15	0	0	7	22	24	1	7	40	16.1	1.39	.264
	NW Arkansas (TL)	AA	1	2	4.99	25	0	0	3	40	37	5	21	50	11.3	1.46	.255
2012	Corpus Christi (TL)	AA	6	3	2.64	49	0	0	2	58	49	2	32	59	9.2	1.40	.226
2013	Oklahoma City (PCL)	AAA	1	2	3.20	45	0	0	2	51	42	2	36	61	10.8	1.54	.223
	Houston (AL)	MAJ	1	1	1.77	25	0	0	1	20	13	1	13	15	6.6	1.28	.183
Major League Totals			1	1	1.77	25	0	0	1	20	13	1	13	15	6.6	1.28	.183
Minor League Totals			9	10	3.82	148	0	0	15	189	172	11	104	230	11.0	1.46	.240

18 NICK TROPEANO, RHP

BA GRADE **45** MEDIUM

Born: Aug. 27, 1990. **B-T:** R-R. **Ht.:** 6-4. **Wt.:** 205. **Drafted:** Stony Brook, 2011 (5th round). **Signed by:** John Kosciak.

Because of an overabundance of starters in the minors, the Astros went to a tandem-starter system at all four of their full-season clubs during the first half of 2013, with pitchers alternating starting and relieving every four days. It worked well for some pitchers, but it didn't seem to suit Tropeano, who seemed to wear down and wasn't as precise without the side sessions that come more regularly in a five-man rotation. His fastball still sits 90-92 mph, better than the 86-90 he worked with in college, but as he tired, Tropeano had a tendency to leave pitches up too often. He has a plus changeup that he throws early and late in the count to both righties and lefties, but he still has work do to stay on top of his fringy slider rather than getting on the side of it. Tropeano still has a chance to be a solid back-end starter, and maybe a little more. He heads to spring training looking to earn a spot at Triple-A Oklahoma City in 2014.

Year	Club (League)	Class	W	L	ERA	G	GS	CG	SV	IP	H	HR	BB	SO	K/9	WHIP	AVG
2011	Tri-City (NYP)	SS	3	2	2.36	12	12	0	0	53	42	1	21	63	10.6	1.18	.212
2012	Lexington (SAL)	LoA	6	4	2.78	15	14	0	0	87	77	3	26	97	10.0	1.18	.238
	Lancaster (CAL)	HiA	6	3	3.31	12	12	0	0	71	72	8	21	69	8.8	1.32	.265
2013	Corpus Christi (TL)	AA	7	10	4.11	28	20	1	5	134	140	15	39	130	8.8	1.34	.275
Minor League Totals			22	19	3.34	67	58	1	5	345	331	27	107	359	9.4	1.27	.254

19 ANDREW APLIN, OF

BA GRADE **45** MEDIUM

Born: March 21, 1991. **B-T:** L-L. **Ht.:** 6-0. **Wt.:** 190. **Drafted:** Arizona State, 2012 (5th round). **Signed by:** Mike Brown.

Some players pass the eye test with pretty swings and an abundance of tools, even if they never develop into productive baseball players. Then there's a player like Aplin, a 2012 fifth-rounder, who doesn't do anything all that conventionally but is quite productive nevertheless. He has a high-maintenance, lefthanded swing that starts with a pronounced leg kick. That leg kick means he has to get everything started a little quicker than is ideal, and he's not direct to the ball. But he has enough feel for hitting and good enough hands to generally time his swings properly, and he has excellent barrel control that keeps him from striking out. Aplin's numbers got a boost from the hitting environment at high Class A Lancaster—his OPS was 233 points higher at home—but he might profile as a useful top-of-the-order hitter because of his contact and on-base skills. Defensively he's an above-average center fielder, despite average speed, thanks to great reads and jumps. He has an average arm. Aplin could wind up as a regular center fielder on a second-division team, but his tools seem to fit better as a versatile extra outfielder.

Year	Club (League)	Class	AVG	G	AB	R	H	2B	3B	HR	RBI	BB	SO	SB	CS	OBP	SLG
2012	Tri-City (NYP)	SS	.348	44	164	38	57	9	5	4	25	24	22	20	7	.441	.537
	Lancaster (CAL)	HiA	.260	24	104	19	27	4	2	3	13	4	16	4	3	.287	.423
2013	Lancaster (CAL)	HiA	.278	128	500	102	139	32	7	9	107	83	63	24	6	.376	.424
Minor League Totals			.290	196	768	159	223	45	14	16	145	111	101	48	16	.380	.448

20 NOLAN FONTANA, SS

BA GRADE **45** MEDIUM

Born: June 6, 1991. **B-T:** L-R. **Ht.:** 5-11. **Wt.:** 190. **Drafted:** Florida, 2012 (2nd round). **Signed by:** John Martin.

The minors are filled with heady college shortstops who make up for their less-than-ideal range with excellent positioning, reliable hands and a grinder's intensity. Fontana, grandson of former Braves star Lew Burdette, filled that role for three years at Florida, helping the Gators to three straight appearances in the College World Series. He's done the same with the Astros, showing less-than-ideal tools but a heady approach that leads scouts to think he can be a big league contributor. Scouts doubt that Fontana will ever be a regular big league shortstop with his fringy range and tick-below-average arm, but he's sure-handed enough to play shortstop on occasion. With average speed, he doesn't run as well as one would ideally like for a utility infielder, but he does have manifest on-base skills thanks to a patient approach that approaches passivity at times. The Astros are looking to spot Fontana at second base in 2014 to add to his versatility as he moves up to Double-A Corpus Christi.

Year	Club (League)	Class	AVG	G	AB	R	H	2B	3B	HR	RBI	BB	SO	SB	CS	OBP	SLG
2012	Lexington (SAL)	LoA	.225	49	151	37	34	9	1	2	25	65	44	12	2	.464	.338
2013	Lancaster (CAL)	HiA	.259	104	386	88	100	18	6	8	60	102	100	16	5	.415	.399
Minor League Totals			.250	153	537	125	134	27	7	10	85	167	144	28	7	.430	.382

21 JAKE BUCHANAN, RHP

BA GRADE **45** MEDIUM

Born: Sept. 24, 1989. **B-T:** R-R. **Ht.:** 6-0. **Wt.:** 242. **Drafted:** North Carolina State, 2010 (8th round). **Signed by:** J.D. Alleva.

Buchanan is the type of pitcher who performs more effectively in pro ball than in college. A solid starter for North Carolina State, he impressed scouts even more with his dominant work (3-1, 0.84) in the Cape Cod League in 2009, the summer before his junior year. Because he relies on a sinker-heavy approach, Buchanan's stuff works better against wood bats than metal, especially with the NCAA's older, springier bats where a jam-job could land as a bloop single. He pounds the bottom half of the strike zone pitch after pitch with an 88-90 mph sinker. Buchanan has to work the inside and outside corners, because if he ventures into the top half of the zone, he's out of his comfort zone. He'll throw a cutter to keep lefties from getting comfortable and every now and then he mixes in a short, fringe-average curveball. Buchanan relies on above-average control and command to get weak contact and stay out of big innings. He doesn't profile as anything more than a No. 5 starter or useful middle reliever, but he's ready to compete for those jobs in 2014.

Year	Club (League)	Class	W	L	ERA	G	GS	CG	SV	IP	H	HR	BB	SO	K/9	WHIP	AVG
2010	Tri-City (NYP)	SS	4	5	4.28	14	14	0	0	61	69	3	11	42	6.2	1.31	.286
2011	Lancaster (CAL)	HiA	5	10	3.91	25	25	1	0	159	157	10	35	102	5.8	1.21	.256
	Corpus Christi (TL)	AA	0	0	1.29	1	1	0	0	7	6	0	1	2	2.6	1.00	.231
2012	Oklahoma City (PCL)	AAA	0	1	10.13	3	1	0	0	8	17	1	5	5	5.6	2.75	.459
	Corpus Christi (TL)	AA	5	9	4.96	27	19	0	0	134	171	11	33	83	5.6	1.52	.310
2013	Corpus Christi (TL)	AA	7	2	2.09	18	13	0	1	82	67	4	9	44	4.8	0.93	.226
	Oklahoma City (PCL)	AAA	5	5	3.89	12	12	0	0	76	85	6	13	55	6.5	1.28	.285
Minor League Totals			26	32	3.99	100	85	1	1	527	572	35	107	333	5.7	1.29	.277

22 KYLE SMITH, RHP

BA GRADE **45** MEDIUM

Born: Sept. 10, 1992. **B-T:** R-R. **Ht.:** 5-11. **Wt.:** 175. **Drafted:** HS—Lantana, Fla., 2011 (4th round). **Signed by:** Alex Mesa (Royals).

To watch Smith pitch is to respect him. Not many short righthanders have as much success as he does with a below-average fastball—he generally sits 89-90 mph—thanks to a fearless approach, a compact, clean delivery and an ability to stay a step ahead of the hitter. Scouts love his aggressive approach. Smith attacks hitters with his fastball, a plus curveball and a fringy changeup. Acquired from the Royals for outfielder Justin Maxwell at the 2013 trade deadline, Smith impressed the Astros when, after he was knocked out of the game in the first inning of his high Class A Lancaster debut, he bounced back to throw a complete-game shutout at High Desert in his encore appearance. Smith has flashed 95 mph briefly in the past, but he now touches 92 at his best. His body is nearly maxed out, so he's not likely to gain the velocity that scouts once thought was possible. The track record for finesse righthanders who pitch off their changeup isn't a great one, but scouts see Smith as a potential No. 5 starter because of his excellent feel for pitching. He'll have to prove it every step up the ladder, including in 2014 at Double-A Corpus Christi.

Year	Club (League)	Class	W	L	ERA	G	GS	CG	SV	IP	H	HR	BB	SO	K/9	WHIP	AVG
2012	Idaho Falls (PIO)	R	1	0	1.80	1	1	0	0	5	3	0	1	11	19.8	0.80	.167
	Kane County (MWL)	LoA	4	3	2.94	13	13	0	0	67	62	3	20	87	11.6	1.22	.241
2013	Wilmington (CAR)	HiA	5	4	2.85	19	19	0	0	104	93	9	29	96	8.3	1.17	.238
	Lancaster (CAL)	HiA	1	1	7.33	5	5	1	0	23	26	4	9	21	8.1	1.50	.289
Minor League Totals			11	8	3.38	38	38	1	0	200	184	16	59	215	9.7	1.22	.243

23 KENT EMANUEL, LHP

Born: June 4, 1992. **B-T:** L-L. **Ht.:** 6-3. **Wt.:** 190. **Drafted:** North Carolina, 2013 (3rd round). **Signed by:** Tim Bittner.

Emanuel became a college ace as a freshman, throwing a complete-game shutout against Texas in the 2011 College World Series. He helped North Carolina reach Omaha again in 2013 as its Friday starter but wore out late in the season. He ranked fourth in NCAA Division I with 132 innings and was gassed after being used in relief in a regional final, on one day of rest after a 124-pitch outing. The Astros were extremely careful with Emanuel, their third-rounder, after signing him for $747,000. They shut him down after four brief appearances in the Rookie-level Gulf Coast League, except for a few sessions in instructional league. Emanuel has an ideal, broad-shouldered, high-waisted pitcher's frame, present strength and underrated athleticism, but he outsmarts more than he overpowers hitters due to a funky, rather than fluid, delivery. He pitches off an 87-89 mph fastball that touches 90, though it plays up because of his size, angle to the plate and ability to command it. He's a mature competitor with excellent makeup. His ceiling is that of a No. 5 starter because he lacks plus stuff, but he can move quickly because of his polish.

Year	Club (League)	Class	W	L	ERA	G	GS	CG	SV	IP	H	HR	BB	SO	K/9	WHIP	AVG
2013	Astros (GCL)	R	0	0	0.00	4	4	0	0	9	6	0	2	8	8.0	0.89	.188
Minor League Totals			0	0	0.00	4	4	0	0	9	6	0	2	8	8.0	0.89	.188

24 CHRIS LEE, LHP

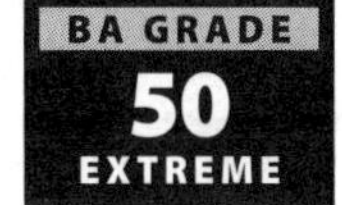

Born: Aug. 17, 1992. **B-T:** L-L. **Ht.:** 6-3. **Wt.:** 176. **Drafted:** Santa Fe (Fla.) CC, 2011 (4th round). **Signed by:** Larry Pardo.

When Lee joined the Astros as a fourth-rounder in 2011, he was a hard-thrower with no real idea of the strike zone. After missing much of the 2012 season as he dealt with complications after having his wisdom teeth removed, Lee developed into a much more refined, though still erratic, pitcher in 2013. At his best, he showed nearly untouchable stuff at Rookie-level Greeneville by sitting 92-95 mph with his four-seam fastball, mixing in a useful two-seamer and pairing them with a potentially plus curveball. Lee still needs to add some weight to his slight frame. His control, which has improved from well-below-average to merely below-average, needs to continue to trend up. Lee sometimes has trouble with the tempo of his delivery to the plate, and he needs to learn how to read swings and set up hitters, but as he puts more innings on his résumé, he has a chance to develop into a solid mid-rotation starter. He'll join a talented low Class A Quad Cities staff in 2014.

Year	Club (League)	Class	W	L	ERA	G	GS	CG	SV	IP	H	HR	BB	SO	K/9	WHIP	AVG
2011	Greeneville (APP)	R	1	5	5.18	13	13	0	0	49	53	4	34	47	8.7	1.79	.279
2012	Greeneville (APP)	R	1	2	11.42	5	3	0	0	9	13	1	9	9	9.3	2.54	.361
2013	Greeneville (APP)	R	2	2	3.10	11	10	0	0	49	37	3	17	54	9.9	1.09	.207
Minor League Totals			4	9	4.73	29	26	0	0	107	103	8	60	110	9.3	1.53	.254

25 LEONARDO HERAS, OF

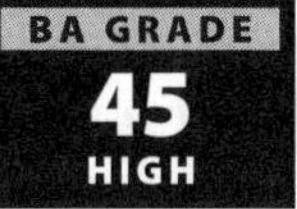

Born: May 29, 1990. **B-T:** L-R. **Ht.:** 5-9. **Wt.:** 190. **Signed:** Mexico, 2013. **Signed by:** Kevin Goldstein.

Mexico is one of the few remaining places where teams can spend money unfettered by MLB-mandated spending restrictions that affect draft picks and international amateurs. On a scouting trip through Mexico City in August 2013, the Astros purchased the contracts of a pair of Red Devils players, Heras and mammoth first baseman Japhet Amador. The 23-year-old Heras, who debuted in the Mexican League at age 17 in 2007, has a better shot at the big leagues as a potentially above-average hitter with below-average power. He has a long track record for hitting, having posted a .900-plus OPS in Mexico in each of the past three seasons. He's a solid left fielder defensively and could play center sporadically as a fourth outfielder. He has the hand-eye coordination and the lefthanded swing to potentially fit in that role, but his excellent plate discipline and ability to hit righties and lefties may allow him sneak into a larger role. Heras doesn't need a whole lot of seasoning to be ready for a shot in Houston, but he probably will begin 2014 at Triple-A Oklahoma City.

Year	Club (League)	Class	AVG	G	AB	R	H	2B	3B	HR	RBI	BB	SO	SB	CS	OBP	SLG
2007	Tijuana (MEX)	AAA	.190	11	21	7	4	0	0	0	0	1	6	0	0	.227	.190
2008	Tijuana (MEX)	AAA	.271	78	280	50	76	20	7	2	27	21	51	9	5	.322	.414
2009	Reynosa (MEX)	AAA	.330	105	442	89	146	21	10	1	46	30	57	13	10	.376	.430
2010	Reynosa (MEX)	AAA	.316	96	399	58	126	15	8	4	55	42	45	11	5	.379	.424
2011	Mexico City (MEX)	AAA	.342	102	444	100	152	16	8	18	60	38	48	25	9	.399	.536
2012	Mexico City (MEX)	AAA	.323	112	455	111	147	18	8	24	64	53	83	17	7	.398	.556
2013	Mexico City (MEX)	AAA	.310	91	335	81	104	19	9	11	42	48	73	14	6	.398	.519
	Corpus Christi (TL)	AA	.205	10	39	7	8	2	1	1	5	8	11	1	0	.354	.385
Minor League Totals			.316	605	2415	503	763	111	51	61	299	241	374	90	42	.380	.480

26 GONZALO SANUDO, RHP

BA GRADE **45** HIGH

Born: Jan. 10, 1992. **B-T:** L-R. **Ht.:** 6-3. **Wt.:** 235. **Signed:** Mexico, 2011. **Signed by:** Hector Otero (Twins).

The Astros picked up Sanudo for 2010 supplemental first-round bust Mike Kvasnicka in a spring training trade with the Twins. Signed out of Mexico in 2011, Sanudo is a control specialist with a good body, but he sat at 86-89 mph and had not made it out of the Rookie-level Gulf Coast League. The Astros worked with his delivery to get his legs more involved and increased his extension and coaxed 3-4 mph of velocity out of him without impeding his already above-average control. Sanudo now sits 91-92 mph and touches 95. After a brief emergency stint in Double-A, he dominated the Rookie-level Appalachian and short-season New York-Penn leagues while working out of the bullpen. He struck out 41 in his final 27 innings, all scoreless, while allowing just five hits and one walk. Owing to his body control and repertoire, the Astros will consider moving Sanudo to the rotation as he moves up to low Class A Quad Cities in 2014.

Year	Club (League)	Class	W	L	ERA	G	GS	CG	SV	IP	H	HR	BB	SO	K/9	WHIP	AVG
2011	Twins (GCL)	R	0	1	5.66	12	0	0	1	21	19	0	7	22	9.6	1.26	.244
2012	Twins (GCL)	R	2	0	2.00	15	2	0	4	36	34	0	2	33	8.3	1.00	.252
2013	Corpus Christi (TL)	AA	0	0	3.86	3	0	0	0	5	6	1	2	1	1.9	1.71	.316
	Greeneville (APP)	R	1	2	1.29	18	0	0	11	21	11	1	1	30	12.9	0.57	.153
	Tri-City (NYP)	SS	0	0	0.00	9	0	0	8	13	3	0	1	20	13.8	0.31	.070
Minor League Totals			3	3	2.45	57	2	0	24	95	73	2	13	106	10.0	0.90	.210

27 JANDEL GUSTAVE, RHP

BA GRADE **50** EXTREME

Born: Oct. 12, 1992. **B-T:** R-R. **Ht.:** 6-2. **Wt.:** 160. **Signed:** Dominican Republic, 2010. **Signed by:** Felix Francisco/Rafael Belen.

Scouts who caught a day of Astros instructional league in 2013 left amazed at the number of lower-level power arms the organization is developing. But in a system that has multiple pitchers who can tickle triple digits, Gustave reaches that lofty realm more than almost anyone. Gustave took a significant step forward in 2013, as his control went from a shotgun spread to more of a rifle with a bad sight. He still misses his target, but now it's more likely to be by inches rather than feet. Gustave sits at 95-98 mph from a relatively easy delivery. He throws a below-average 87-88 mph slider with excellent velocity, but he needs to develop more tilt. His firm, below-average changeup needs more separation from his fastball. His extreme rawness, shaky secondary stuff and poor control could present challenges when it comes to retiring low Class A hitters at Quad Cities in 2014. But with an 80 fastball and no clear delivery flaws that will prevent him improving his control, the Astros will be happy to be patient with him.

Year	Club (League)	Class	W	L	ERA	G	GS	CG	SV	IP	H	HR	BB	SO	K/9	WHIP	AVG
2010	Astros (DSL)	R	0	5	8.20	14	5	0	0	26	24	0	33	27	9.2	2.16	.245
2011	Astros (DSL)	R	0	4	12.10	14	1	0	0	19	24	2	34	19	8.8	3.00	.320
2012	Astros (GCL)	R	2	1	5.79	10	4	0	0	28	24	0	27	22	7.1	1.82	.224
2013	Greeneville (APP)	R	2	3	2.68	10	10	0	0	44	38	2	23	49	10.1	1.40	.235
Minor League Totals			4	13	6.21	48	20	0	0	117	110	4	117	117	9.0	1.93	.249

28 REYMIN GUDUAN, LHP

BA GRADE **50** EXTREME

Born: March 16, 1992. **B-T:** L-L. **Ht.:** 6-4. **Wt.:** 185. **Signed:** Dominican Republic, 2009. **Signed by:** Felix Francisco/Rafael Belen.

When the Astros needed an emergency reliever to fill in at Triple-A Oklahoma City at the end of the 2013 season, they promoted Guduan from the Rookie-level Gulf Coast League. Making his RedHawks debut, the lanky 6-foot-4 lefty not only hadn't pitched in a ballpark with a second deck, he had never pitched in a game where they charge for admission. Jumping straight from the backfields to the Pacific Coast League, Guduan didn't seem awed. He struck out four batters in 2 1/3 innings, allowing one run. The Astros were comfortable with him making the massive jump because few lefties in baseball have a better one-two punch with a 94-97 mph fastball that touches 99 to go with a slider that flashes plus thanks to a two-plane break and good bite. Guduan has an amazingly quick arm, and like many Astros pitchers, he gets excellent extension in his delivery. His control is scattershot, but his delivery doesn't have excessive effort, so many believe he will eventually find the strike zone. Guduan is a long way from his ceiling, but he has the potential to be a closer if his control improves. He's ready to join a high-octane low Class A Quad Cities bullpen in 2014.

Year	Club (League)	Class	W	L	ERA	G	GS	CG	SV	IP	H	HR	BB	SO	K/9	WHIP	AVG
2010	Astros (DSL)	R	1	2	11.95	15	4	0	0	20	38	0	31	19	8.4	3.39	.384
2011	Astros (DSL)	R	1	3	2.17	13	13	0	0	46	31	0	42	61	12.0	1.60	.193
2012	Astros (GCL)	R	1	1	5.40	8	3	0	0	18	26	1	16	16	7.9	2.29	.342
2013	Astros (GCL)	R	0	1	4.35	10	2	0	0	21	19	3	10	28	12.2	1.40	.235
	Oklahoma City (PCL)	AAA	0	0	3.86	1	0	0	0	2	1	0	3	4	15.4	1.71	.143
Minor League Totals			3	7	5.03	47	22	0	0	107	115	4	102	128	10.7	2.02	.271

29 DANRY VASQUEZ, OF

BA GRADE **45** HIGH

Born: Jan. 8, 1994. **B-T:** L-R. **Ht.:** 6-3. **Wt.:** 177. **Signed:** Venezuela, 2010. **Signed by:** Oscar Garcia/Pedro Chavez (Tigers).

The Tigers are not a team that typically spends big money on any one prospect in Latin America, but they made an exception for Vasquez. He signed for $1.4 million, setting a team record for an international bonus. Because of Vasquez's simple swing and feel for hitting, the Tigers moved him aggressively through the system. That helped the Astros get a good look at him in time for the 2013 trade deadline, when they acquired him for righthander Jose Veras. Vasquez always has shown an ability to hit for average because he has a short, lefthanded swing that can spray line drives. But because he can put the bat on the ball so well, he hasn't learned to be selective yet. Vasquez doesn't have much present strength, another obstacle to hitting for power. Scouts who like him see him as a bat-first outfielder who will develop average to a tick above pop as he fills out. He faces pressure to do so, as his below-average speed and below-average arm limit him to left field, where he's a poor defender now. On the bases, Vasquez is aggressive at times but probably not a factor when it comes to stealing bases. His bat will have to get him to the big leagues, because he doesn't add value to a team in other ways. He should find the exceptional hitting conditions at high Class A Lancaster to his liking in 2014.

Year	Club (League)	Class	AVG	G	AB	R	H	2B	3B	HR	RBI	BB	SO	SB	CS	OBP	SLG
2011	Tigers (GCL)	R	.272	54	206	25	56	8	1	2	30	7	34	3	2	.306	.350
2012	West Michigan (MWL)	LoA	.162	29	99	5	16	3	0	1	7	7	20	0	0	.218	.222
	Connecticut (NYP)	SS	.311	72	289	36	90	16	2	2	35	13	45	6	4	.341	.401
2013	West Michigan (MWL)	LoA	.283	97	375	47	106	16	5	6	40	31	56	9	8	.334	.400
	Quad Cities (MWL)	LoA	.288	32	118	12	34	2	1	3	20	6	15	2	0	.323	.398
Minor League Totals			.278	284	1087	125	302	45	9	14	132	64	170	20	14	.319	.374

30 BRETT PHILLIPS, OF

BA GRADE **50** EXTREME

Born: May 30, 1994. **B-T:** L-R. **Ht.:** 6-0. **Wt.:** 175. **Drafted:** HS—Seminole, Fla., 2012 (6th round). **Signed by:** John Martin.

A teammate of Angels minor league reliever Joe Krehbiel at Seminole High, Phillips was a good enough athlete that when he decided to play football for the first time as a senior, he earned honorable mention on the all-county team. An Astros sixth-round pick in 2012, Phillips opened 2013 in extended spring training but got a taste of full-season ball at low Class A Quad Cities before being reassigned to Rookie-level Greeneville. He is a potentially above-average center fielder thanks to his solid routes, and he has an above-average arm. At the plate, he has work to do. Phillips has a fringe-average raw power that he shows in batting practice, but in games, he has a more contact-oriented approach, even though his swing has some length to it. He draws walks against lower-level competition because he's comfortable working deep counts. However, scouts aren't convinced he has the contact skills to make that approach work against more advanced pitchers, and he may never be more than an average hitter. Phillips is a tick-above-average runner, but he doesn't fully understand how to get a good lead and when to steal. Scouts like his high-energy approach, and he should return to Quad Cities in 2014.

Year	Club (League)	Class	AVG	G	AB	R	H	2B	3B	HR	RBI	BB	SO	SB	CS	OBP	SLG
2012	Astros (GCL)	R	.251	54	175	26	44	7	6	0	13	28	48	7	5	.360	.360
2013	Quad Cities (MWL)	LoA	.231	12	39	4	9	2	0	0	3	3	10	1	1	.286	.282
	Greeneville (APP)	R	.247	29	85	9	21	7	1	0	9	17	21	4	3	.371	.353
Minor League Totals			.247	95	299	39	74	16	7	0	25	48	79	12	9	.355	.348

Kansas City Royals

BY J.J. COOPER

For any Royals fan under the age of 30, the 2013 season provided a new experience—September games that actually mattered.

With 86 wins, Kansas City won more games than it had in any season since the 1980s. Thanks to the two wild card system, the Royals sat on at least the periphery of the playoff chase until the final week of the season.

It was a more thrilling season than any in Kansas City in years. But a repeat in 2014 won't come close to being enough.

If 2013 was the year the Royals returned to respectability, then 2014 is the time for October baseball in Kansas City. The front office ensured as much when it dealt away Wil Myers and Jake Odorizzi in a December 2012 trade that brought righthanders James Shields and Wade Davis to the Royals.

Shields gave the Royals the first ace they've had since Zack Greinke left town. But he arrived with two years remaining on his current deal. In trading away six-plus cost-controlled years of Myers, the 2013 American League Rookie of the Year, and Jake Odorizzi, the Rays' No. 1 prospect, for two years of Shields, the Royals explicitly traded away the long term for the short term.

The short term now has one year remaining. Shields did everything the Royals could have expected in 2013, going 13-9, 3.15 and leading the AL with 34 starts and 229 innings, to help the club climb from the basement to third place in the division. But if he leaves in free agency after the 2014 season without a Royals playoff appearance on his résumé, it's fair for fans to consider the trade a short-sighted failure.

Kansas City actually disappeared from the playoff race in May thanks to a brutal 6-22 stretch that included an eight-game losing streak. But the streaky club rallied back into contention, getting a boost from rookie right fielder David Lough, who proved a significant improvement on veteran Jeff Francoeur, as well as franchise icon George Brett. The Hall of Famer became an interim hitting coach and helped spur a bounceback season from first baseman Eric Hosmer.

The Royals built their best pitching staff in years, thanks in part to the acquisition of Shields and the trade for righthander Ervin Santana, but even more so because of the best bullpen in baseball. Greg Holland developed into one of the game's best closers and he was well supported by Tim Collins, Aaron Crow, Will Smith and Luke Hochevar, revitalized by a move to the bullpen.

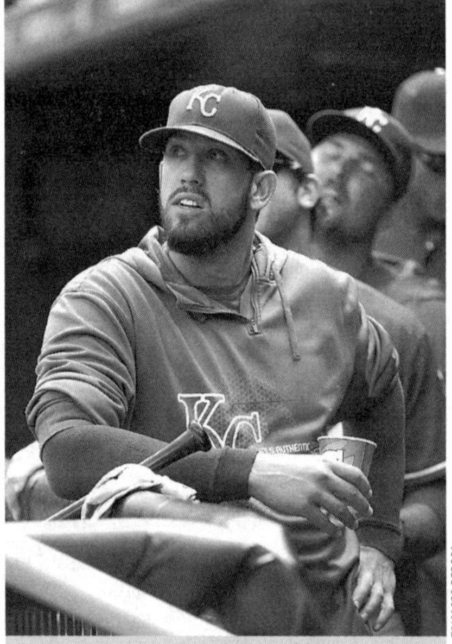

TOMASSO DEROSA

James Shields came at a steep price but finally gave the Royals a legitimate ace

TOP PROSPECTS OF THE DECADE

Year	Player, Pos.	2013 Org.
2004	Zack Greinke, rhp	Dodgers
2005	Billy Butler, 1b	Royals
2006	Alex Gordon, 3b	Royals
2007	Alex Gordon, 3b	Royals
2008	Mike Moustakas, 3b	Royals
2009	Mike Moustakas, 3b	Royals
2010	Mike Montgomery, lhp	Rays
2011	Eric Hosmer, 1b	Royals
2012	Mike Montgomery, lhp	Rays
2013	Kyle Zimmer, rhp	Royals

The next step for the Royals is to develop homegrown starters, so they don't have to continue trading players such as Myers for pitchers. Their top two prospects are starters in 2012 first-rounder Kyle Zimmer and diminutive righty Yordano Ventura, who was the majors' hardest-throwing starter in September. And they got one of the draft's top arms in lefty Sean Manaea, whom they signed for $3.55 million with the 34th overall pick.

The Royals may have other complementary pieces ready to help soon, as their Triple-A Omaha team won the Pacific Coast League, despite a 70-74 record, and then the one-game Triple-A National Championship.

ORGANIZATION OVERVIEW

General Manager: Dayton Moore. **Farm Director:** Scott Sharp. **Scouting Director:** Lonnie Goldberg.

Class	Team	League	W	L	PCT	Finish	Manager
Majors	Kansas City Royals	American	86	76	.531	7th (15)	Ned Yost
Triple-A	Omaha Stormchasers	Pacific Coast	70	74	.486	10th (16)	Mike Jirschele
Double-A	NW Arkansas Naturals	Texas	59	81	.421	8th (8)	Brian Poldberg
High A	Wilmington Blue Rocks	Carolina	63	77	.450	6th (8)	Vance Wilson
Low A	Lexington Legends	South Atlantic	68	70	.493	8th (14)	Brian Buchanan
Rookie	Idaho Falls Chukars	Pioneer	41	35	.539	3rd (8)	Omar Ramirez
Rookie	Burlington Royals	Appalachian	29	38	.433	8th (10)	Tommy Shields
Rookie	AZL Royals	Arizona	22	33	.400	12th (13)	Daryl Kennedy
Overall 2013 Minor League Record			**352**	**408**	**.463**	**27th (30)**	

THIS YEAR'S TOP 30

No.	Player, Pos.	Grade
1.	Kyle Zimmer, rhp	65/Medium
2.	Yordano Ventura, rhp	65/Medium
3.	Raul A. Mondesi, ss	60/High
4.	Jorge Bonifacio, of	55/High
5.	Miguel Almonte, rhp	55/High
6.	Sean Manaea, lhp	60/Extreme
7.	Hunter Dozier, 3b	55/High
8.	Bubba Starling, of	60/Extreme
9.	Jason Adam, rhp	50/High
10.	Christian Binford, rhp	50/High
11.	Elier Hernandez, of	55/Extreme
12.	Sam Selman, lhp	50/High
13.	Orlando Calixte, ss	50/High
14.	Cheslor Cuthbert, 3b	50/High
15.	Michael Mariot, rhp	45/Low
16.	Pedro Fernandez, rhp	55/Extreme
17.	Brett Eibner, of	50/High
18.	Lane Adams, of	45/Medium
19.	Samir Duenez, 1b/of	50/Extreme
20.	Marten Gasparini, ss	50/Extreme
21.	Chris Dwyer, lhp	40/Low
22.	Donnie Joseph, lhp	45/Medium
23.	Cam Gallagher, c	50/High
24.	Zane Evans, c	45/High
25.	Christian Colon, 2b/ss	40/Low
26.	Bryan Brickhouse, rhp	50/Extreme
27.	Angel Baez, rhp	45/High
28.	Cody Reed, lhp	45/High
29.	Christhian Vasquez, of	50/Extreme
30.	Terrance Gore, of	45/High

LAST YEAR'S TOP 30

No.	Player, Pos.	Status
1.	Kyle Zimmer, rhp	No. 1
2.	Bubba Starling, of	No. 8
3.	Yordano Ventura, rhp	No. 2
4.	Jorge Bonifaco, of	No. 4
5.	Raul A. Mondesi, ss	No. 3
6.	Sam Selman, lhp	No. 12
7.	Orlando Calixte, ss	No. 13
8.	Jason Adam, rhp	No. 9
9.	Cheslor Cuthbert, 3b	No. 14
10.	Miguel Almonte, rhp	No. 5
11.	John Lamb, lhp	Dropped out
12.	Kyle Smith, rhp	(Astros)
13.	Christian Colon, ss/2b	No. 25
14.	Donnie Joseph, lhp	No. 22
15.	Cam Gallagher, c	No. 23
16.	Elier Hernandez, of	No. 11
17.	Bryan Brickhouse, rhp	No. 26
18.	Angel Baez, rhp	No. 27
19.	Jack Lopez, ss	Dropped out
20.	Humberto Arteaga, ss	Dropped out
21.	Chris Dwyer, lhp	No. 21
22.	Ramon Torres, ss/2b	Dropped out
23.	Fred Ford, of	Dropped out
24.	David Lough, of	Majors
25.	Colin Rodgers, lhp	Dropped out
26.	Christian Binford, rhp	No. 10
27.	Jake Junis, rhp	Dropped out
28.	Robinson Yambati, rhp	Dropped out
29.	Brett Eibner, of	No. 17
30.	Brian Fletcher, 1b/of	Dropped out

BEST TOOLS

Best Hitter for Average	Hunter Dozier
Best Power Hitter	Bubba Starling
Best Strike-Zone Discipline	Hunter Dozier
Fastest Baserunner	Terrence Gore
Best Athlete	Bubba Starling
Best Fastball	Yordano Ventura
Best Curveball	Kyle Zimmer
Best Slider	Kyle Zimmer
Best Changeup	Miguel Almonte
Best Control	Christian Binford
Best Defensive Catcher	Parker Morin
Best Defensive Infielder	Raul A. Mondesi
Best Infield Arm	Jack Lopez
Best Defensive Outfielder	Bubba Starling
Best Outfield Arm	Brett Eibner

TOP 15 PLAYERS 25 AND UNDER

No.	Player, Pos. (Age)	Peak Level
1.	Salvador Perez, c (23)	Majors
2.	Eric Hosmer, 1b (24)	Majors
3.	Kyle Zimmer, rhp (22)	Double-A
4.	Yordano Ventura, rhp (22)	Majors
5.	Raul A. Mondesi, ss (18)	Low Class A
6.	Mike Moustakas, 3b (25)	Majors
7.	Danny Duffy, lhp (25)	Majors
8.	Jorge Bonifaco, of (20)	Double-A
9.	Miguel Almonte, rhp (20)	Low Class A
10.	Sean Manaea, lhp (22)	Did not play
11.	Hunter Dozier, 3b (22)	Low Class A
12.	Kelvin Herrera, rhp (24)	Majors
13.	Bubba Starling, of (21)	Low Class A
14.	Tim Collins, lhp (24)	Majors
15.	Jason Adam, rhp (22)	Double-A

MINOR LEAGUE DEPTH CHART

KANSAS CITY ROYALS

TOP 2014 ROOKIE: Yordano Ventura, rhp. After some excellent work in September, it will be hard to keep him out of the rotation.

BREAKOUT PROSPECT: Samir Duenez, 1b/of: Duenez is one of the best hitters in the organization with bat speed, hand-eye coordination and a feel for the strike zone.

SLEEPER: Jack Lopez, ss: He's been pushed because of organizational need, but a chance to repeat high Class A Wilmington should get his bat going.

SOURCE OF TOP 30 TALENT

Homegrown	**29**	**Acquired**	**1**
College	9	Trades	1
Junior college	2	Rule 5 draft	0
High school	6	Independent leagues	0
Nondrafted free agents	0	Free agents/waivers	0
International	12		

LF
Cristhian Vasquez (29)
Brian Fletcher
Alfred Escalera-Maldonado
Alexis Rivera

CF
Bubba Starling (8)
Brett Eibner (17)
Lane Adams (18)
Terrance Gore (30)
Daniel Rockett
Amalani Fukofuka
Yem Prades
Dominique Taylor

RF
Jorge Bonifacio (4)
Elier Hernandez (11)

3B
Hunter Dozier (7)
Cheslor Cuthbert (14)
Mike Antonio

SS
Raul A. Mondesi (3)
Orlando Calixte (13)
Marten Gasparini (20)
Humberto Arteaga
Jack Lopez
Ramon Torres

2B
Christian Colon (25)
Justin Trapp

1B
Samir Duenez (19)
Cody Stubbs
Fred Ford
Matt Fields

C
Cam Gallagher (23)
Zane Evans (24)
Chad Johnson
Xavier Fernandez
Julio Rodriguez
Beau Maggi

LHP

LHSP	LHRP
Sean Manaea (6)	Sam Selman (12)
Chris Dwyer (21)	Donnie Joseph (22)
Crawford Simmons	Cody Reed (28)
Justin Marks	Buddy Baumann
Daniel Stumpf	Jon Keck
Colin Rodgers	Scott Alexander
	Jon Dziedzic

RHP

RHSP	RHRP
Kyle Zimmer (1)	Michael Mariot (15)
Yordano Ventura (2)	Angel Baez (27)
Miguel Almonte (5)	Robinson Yambati
Jason Adam (9)	Alec Mills
Christian Binford (10)	Greg Billo
Pedro Fernandez (16)	Malcom Culver
Bryan Brickhouse (26)	Andrew Triggs
Carter Hope	Spencer Patton
Aaron Brooks	J.C. Sulbaran
Luke Farrell	Jake Junis

DRAFT ANALYSIS

2013 BONUSES: $8.4 MILLION

BEST PURE HITTER: 3B Hunter Dozier (1) recognizes pitches early, doesn't often chase out of the strike zone and works counts to get a pitch he can drive. He walked more than he struck out in his pro debut.

Best power hitter: 1B Brandon Dulin (12) has the best raw power, as he'll show above-average raw power consistently in batting practice. Dozier already has excellent gap power, as evidenced by his 30 doubles in a half-season, and could have the ability to hit 20-25 home runs a year at the big league level.

FASTEST RUNNER: The Royals love 80 runners but had to be content with OF Dominique Taylor (15), who is merely above-average.

BEST DEFENSIVE PLAYER: OF Daniel Rockett (9) could have been drafted based solely on the highlight reel of catches. The center fielder is an average runner, but he takes outstanding routes and has a knack for the sensational play.

BEST FASTBALL: LHP Sean Manaea (1s) dominated the Cape Cod League in the summer of 2012 with a 91-93 mph fastball that touched 96 and played up because of its late life and his deceptive delivery. A torn labrum in his hip bothered him during his junior season at Indiana State and sapped his velocity, especially in later innings, but after surgery he's expected to make a full recovery.

BEST SECONDARY PITCH: LHP Cody Reed (2) can snap off an above-average slider, though the pitch is wildly inconsistent.

BEST PRO DEBUT: Dozier hit .308/.397/.495 between Rookie-level Idaho Falls and low Class A Lexington. His 30 doubles were second-most among all Royals minor leaguers.

BEST ATHLETE: OF Amalani Fukofuka (5) hasn't played a lot of baseball, but he is an excellent athlete. He had 1,100 yards receiving as a high school senior as he helped his team to the California North Coast Section Division I championship game.

MOST INTRIGUING BACKGROUND: RHP Luke Farrell (6) is the son of Red Sox manager John. He has also overcome multiple benign tumors in his neck that required surgery in 2009 and 2011. He bounced back to finish second in the Big 10 Conference this summer with a 2.13 ERA.

CLOSEST TO THE MAJORS: Dozier has the advanced approach that should allow him to move quickly. It wouldn't be surprising to see him begin his first full season in high Class A Wilmington.

BEST LATE-ROUND PICK: LHP Jonathan Dziedzic (13) doesn't have a particularly high ceiling, but thanks to an average fastball, curveball and changeup, he could end up as a solid back-end starter who throws strikes.

THE ONE WHO GOT AWAY: The Royals liked 1B Shane Conlon (21) and thought they had a good chance to sign the Kansas State junior, but Conlon decided to return for his senior season.

ASSESSMENT: The Royals said they considered Dozier a legitimate choice at eighth overall, but as the first pick in a two-part plan that saw the Royals nab Manaea with a supplemental pick, he could be part of a draft day coup.

2012 BONUSES: $7.6 MILLION

After RHP Kyle Zimmer (1), the system's top prospect, and LHP Sam Selman (2), this class drops off precipitously.

GRADE: B

2011 BONUSES: $14.1 MILLION

While this crop provided depth and RHP Kyle Smith (5, traded for Justin Maxwell), it comes down to the $7.5 million gamble on OF Bubba Starling (1).

GRADE: C

2010 BONUSES: $6.7 MILLION

LHP Kevin Chapman (4) has reached the majors with Houston, and OF Brett Eibner (2), RHP Jason Adam (5) remain prospects. No. 4 overall pick 2B Christian Colon (1) has to be considered a bust.

GRADE: D

TOP DRAFT PICKS OF THE DECADE

Year	Player, Pos.	2013 Org.
2004	Billy Butler	Royals
2005	Alex Gordon, 3b	Royals
2006	Luke Hochevar, rhp	Royals
2007	Mike Moustakas, ss	Royals
2008	Eric Hosmer, 1b	Royals
2009	Aaron Crow, rhp	Royals
2010	Christian Colon, ss	Royals
2011	Bubba Starling, of	Royals
2012	Kyle Zimmer, rhp	Royals
2013	Hunter Dozier, 3b	Royals

LARGEST BONUSES IN CLUB HISTORY

Bubba Starling, 2011	$7,500,000
Eric Hosmer, 2008	$6,000,000
Alex Gordon, 2005	$4,000,000
Mike Moustkas, 2007	$4,000,000
Sean Manaea, 2013	$3,550,000

1 KYLE ZIMMER, RHP

Born: Sept. 13, 1991. **B-T:** R-R. **Ht.:** 6-3. **Wt.:** 215.
Drafted: San Francisco, 2012 (1st round).
Signed by: Max Valencia.

When the University of San Francisco's coaching staff watched Zimmer play third base as a senior at La Jolla (Calif.) High, they noticed his strong arm more than his bat. In fact, his arm impressed them enough that they asked Zimmer to walk on to the club. He moved to the mound as a freshman, joined the Dons rotation as a sophomore and pulled down $3 million as a first-round pick as a junior, going fifth overall to the Royals in the 2012 draft. Zimmer's younger brother Bradley is a junior outfielder for San Francisco, who projects to be a first-round pick in 2014. After a rocky start in 2013—Zimmer logged a 5.98 ERA in 13 first-half starts at high Class A Wilmington—he settled down to dominate over the second half. Shut down right before the season ended with a tight throwing shoulder, he isn't expected to have any long-term problems.

Depending on the night, Zimmer can have three above-average pitches, including a fastball that rates near the top of the scale. He sits at 92-96 mph and has touched 100. He'll sometimes start the night throwing 92-94 mph, then steadily add velocity as the game goes along, then add another few ticks on top of that in a key situation. His slider and curveball alternate in effectiveness, with Zimmer often relying more on whichever one he has a better feel for on that night. He's alternated between a conventional and a spike grip on the curveball. Both are above-average at their best, with the slider earning some 70 grades. He showed an improved ability to throw the curve for an early-count strike as the season progressed. Zimmer's changeup is a step behind his breaking pitches. It has some deception because hitters have to gear up for his fastball, but it doesn't have much life. His first-half problems stemmed a bit of bad luck as well as ineffective pitching from the stretch. More than half of all baserunners he allowed scored in his first 14 starts compared to a quarter of baserunners in his final eight starts. A few tweaks to how he broke his hands from the stretch seemed to fix the issue.

Even when he was getting knocked out of starts early, scouts pegged Zimmer as one of the best pitching prospects in the minors. He had surgery during the 2012 offseason to remove bone chips in his elbow, so he has some durability questions, but Zimmer has ace potential. He could reach Kansas City at some point in 2014.

BA GRADE
65
MEDIUM

SCOUTING GRADES

FASTBALL	70
SLIDER	60
CURVEBALL	60
CHANGEUP	45
COMMAND	50
DELIVERY	50

BRIAN WESTERHOLT

Year	Club (League)	Class	W	L	ERA	G	GS	CG	SV	IP	H	HR	BB	SO	K/9	WHIP	AVG
2012	Royals (AZL)	R	1	0	0.90	3	3	1	0	10	5	0	0	13	11.7	0.50	.152
	Kane County (MWL)	LoA	2	3	2.43	6	6	0	0	30	34	1	8	29	8.8	1.42	.301
2013	Wilmington (CAR)	HiA	4	8	4.82	18	18	1	0	90	80	9	31	113	11.3	1.24	.237
	NW Arkansas (TL)	AA	2	1	1.93	4	4	0	0	19	11	2	5	27	13.0	0.86	.162
Minor League Totals			9	12	3.71	31	31	2	0	148	130	12	44	182	11.1	1.18	.236

2 YORDANO VENTURA, RHP

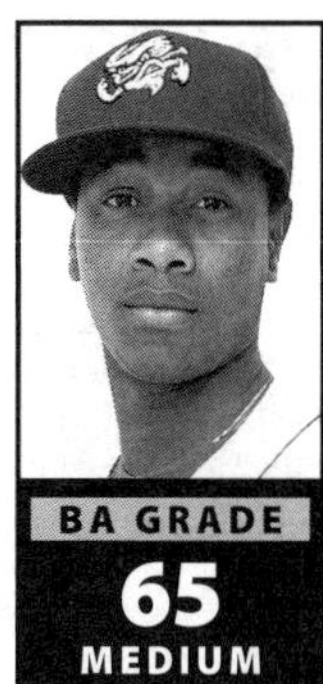

BA GRADE
65
MEDIUM

Born: June 3, 1991. **B-T:** R-R. **Ht.:** 5-11. **Wt.:** 180. **Signed:** Dominican Republic, 2008. **Signed by:** Pedro Silverio.

Signed for just $28,000 as a short 17-year-old with a high-80s fastball but excellent arm speed, Ventura was touching 100 mph just two years later. His fastball hasn't gained velocity since then, but it comes easier now. Where he once threw with a max-effort delivery, now he tickles triple digits with a natural, easy motion. As Ventura showed in three late-season big league starts, he has one of the best arms in baseball. His fastball sat at 97 mph in those three starts, topping out at 102. Ventura's fastball is a true 80 pitch, but his development as a starter has taken off now that he's refined his curveball into a second plus pitch. It's a tight 12-to-6 breaking ball that he can throw for strikes or bury. Ventura has improved the movement on his changeup to the point where it's an average pitch now that it has late fade. He pitches with a speedy tempo that fits his power approach and does a good job of holding runners. The only remaining red flags with Ventura are his command and his short stature. Ventura throws strikes, but he doesn't always hit his spots. His lack of size leads some scouts to be concerned about his durability, but Ventura threw 150 innings in 2013, and he's been healthy throughout his minor league career. He's ready to battle for a job in the Royals rotation.

Year	Club (League)	Class	W	L	ERA	G	GS	CG	SV	IP	H	HR	BB	SO	K/9	WHIP	AVG
2009	Royals (DSL)	R	0	1	2.78	10	5	0	3	23	28	0	5	11	4.4	1.46	.304
2010	Royals (DSL)	R	0	1	2.31	3	3	0	0	12	9	0	1	13	10.0	0.86	.209
	Royals (AZL)	R	4	2	3.25	14	6	0	0	53	49	3	17	58	9.9	1.25	.236
2011	Kane County (MWL)	LoA	4	6	4.27	19	19	0	0	84	82	8	24	88	9.4	1.26	.258
2012	Wilmington (CAR)	HiA	3	5	3.30	16	16	0	0	76	66	7	28	98	11.6	1.23	.229
	Royals (AZL)	R	0	0	2.45	1	1	0	0	4	3	0	1	7	17.2	1.09	.214
	NW Arkansas (TL)	AA	1	2	4.60	6	6	0	0	29	23	1	13	25	7.7	1.23	.221
2013	NW Arkansas (TL)	AA	3	2	2.34	11	11	0	0	58	39	3	20	74	11.5	1.02	.189
	Omaha (PCL)	AAA	5	4	3.74	15	14	0	0	77	80	4	33	81	9.5	1.47	.271
	Kansas City (AL)	MAJ	0	1	3.52	3	3	0	0	15	13	3	6	11	6.5	1.24	.224
Major League Totals			0	1	3.52	3	3	0	0	15	13	3	6	11	6.5	1.24	.224
Minor League Totals			20	23	3.47	95	81	0	3	415	379	26	142	455	9.9	1.25	.242

3 RAUL A. MONDESI, SS

BA GRADE
60
HIGH

Born: July 27, 1995. **B-T:** B-R. **Ht.:** 6-1. **Wt.:** 165. **Signed:** Dominican Republic, 2011. **Signed by:** Edis Perez/Alvin Cuevas.

The son of longtime big league outfielder Raul Mondesi, Raul Adalberto has grown up around the game and it shows. (His brother Raul Jr. is an outfielder who spent time in the Rays and Brewers systems.) Rarely overwhelmed despite playing against much older competition, Mondesi signed for $2 million in 2011 and has been matching or exceeding expectations ever since. He made his pro debut as the youngest player in the Rookie-level Pioneer League and was the second-youngest player in the low Class A South Atlantic League in 2013. Mondesi combines flashes of present brilliance with enticing projection. He will chase pitches out of the zone, but at times he shows solid pitch recognition. He has a pretty simple swing from both sides of the plate and shows no pronounced difference when hitting against lefthanders or righthanders. Long-term, he projects as an above-average hitter with average power. He's gained speed since signing to become a 60 runner. Defensively, Mondesi has fluid actions, above-average range and an above-average arm and is especially good coming in on balls. He committed 30 errors in 2013, split almost evenly between fielding and throwing miscues, but scouts expect him to improve his efficiency. Slated to be that rare 18-year-old in the high Class A Carolina League in 2014, Mondesi is moving fast enough to reach the big leagues just in time to supplant Alcides Escobar in 2017 at the latest.

Year	Club (League)	Class	AVG	G	AB	R	H	2B	3B	HR	RBI	BB	SO	SB	CS	OBP	SLG
2012	Idaho Falls (PIO)	R	.290	50	207	35	60	7	2	3	30	19	65	11	2	.346	.386
2013	Lexington (SAL)	LoA	.261	125	482	61	126	13	7	7	47	34	118	24	10	.311	.361
Minor League Totals			.270	175	689	96	186	20	9	10	77	53	183	35	12	.322	.369

4 JORGE BONIFACIO, OF

Born: June 4, 1993. **B-T:** R-R. **Ht.:** 6-1. **Wt.:** 216. **Signed:** Dominican Republic, 2009. **Signed by:** Edis Perez.

From the moment the Royals traded away Wil Myers, Bonifacio became the club's best hope for a long-term right fielder. His older brother Emilio joined the Royals in a midseason trade. Jorge's climb was slowed in 2013 by a broken hamate bone he suffered in mid-May, though he showed few ill effects upon returning, earning a quick promotion to Double-A Northwest Arkansas. Bonifacio is one of the best pure hitters in the organization. He has a significant hand waggle to start his trigger, but he gets into hitting position quickly, taking a small step for timing, followed by a short, direct swing. He uses the entire field. While Bonifacio projects as an above-average hitter, he may never have more than average power because of his approach. The Royals shortened his stance a few inches during the Arizona Fall League to help him get more leverage in his swing to see if that will lead to more home runs. Bonifacio is a 40 runner who neither helps nor hurts on the basepaths. He's an average right fielder, with his range limited by his speed, but he takes good routes, throws to the right base and has an above-average arm. Bonifacio is expected to start 2014 back at Double-A, but he could see Triple-A Omaha by the middle of the season.

Year	Club (League)	Class	AVG	G	AB	R	H	2B	3B	HR	RBI	BB	SO	SB	CS	OBP	SLG
2010	Royals (DSL)	R	.335	48	164	22	55	16	2	1	28	26	27	13	5	.429	.476
	Royals (AZL)	R	.211	21	76	9	16	0	5	0	6	6	31	1	2	.271	.342
2011	Burlington (APP)	R	.284	62	236	26	67	20	4	7	30	16	58	5	6	.333	.492
2012	Kane County (MWL)	LoA	.282	105	412	54	116	20	6	10	61	30	84	6	3	.336	.432
2013	Royals (AZL)	R	.300	9	30	4	9	3	2	0	6	4	6	1	0	.400	.533
	Wilmington (CAR)	HiA	.296	54	206	32	61	11	3	2	29	23	40	0	2	.368	.408
	NW Arkansas (TL)	AA	.301	25	93	15	28	7	0	2	19	11	23	2	1	.371	.441
Minor League Totals			.289	324	1217	162	352	77	22	22	179	116	269	28	19	.355	.443

5 MIGUEL ALMONTE, RHP

Born: April 4, 1993. **B-T:** R-R. **Ht.:** 6-2. **Wt.:** 180. **Signed:** Dominican Republic, 2010. **Signed by:** Fausto Morel/Alvin Cuevas.

The Royals have developed a pipeline of young Dominican pitchers, starting with Kelvin Herrera and followed by Yordano Ventura and now Almonte, who like his predecessors signed for a bargain price, in his case $25,000. Almonte made the jump to low Class A Lexington just nine months after he was pitching in the Dominican Summer League and performed so well that he earned a spot in the Futures Game. Polished for a 20-year-old with little more than 200 pro innings, he has a smooth, clean delivery, though he is prone to overthrowing. Almonte locates his 90-94 mph fastball, which will touch 97. His mid-80s changeup is above-average as well. Those two pitches were enough to carve up South Atlantic League lineups. He led qualified league starters with 9.1 strikeouts per nine innings. He's still working on the feel for his breaking ball and has a tendency to shelve it. Almonte split a fingernail late in spring training, which played a role with him going back and forth between a spike-curve and a more conventional curveball grip. Almonte doesn't have the ceiling of Kyle Zimmer or Ventura, but he could eventually slot behind them as a No. 3 starter. His ability to throw strikes and his advanced understanding of pitching could earn him a challenging assignment to Double-A Northwest Arkansas to begin 2014.

Year	Club (League)	Class	W	L	ERA	G	GS	CG	SV	IP	H	HR	BB	SO	K/9	WHIP	AVG
2011	Royals (DSL)	R	0	0	5.40	5	1	0	0	12	11	0	7	9	6.9	1.54	.256
2012	Royals (DSL)	R	6	1	1.44	10	10	0	0	50	34	2	8	46	8.3	0.84	.194
	Royals (AZL)	R	2	1	2.33	6	2	0	0	27	22	0	5	28	9.3	1.00	.212
2013	Lexington (SAL)	LoA	6	9	3.10	25	25	1	0	131	115	6	36	132	9.1	1.16	.237
Minor League Totals			14	11	2.75	46	38	1	0	219	182	8	56	215	8.8	1.09	.226

6 SEAN MANAEA, LHP

BA GRADE
60
EXTREME

Born: Feb. 1, 1992. **B-T:** R-L. **Ht.:** 6-5. **Wt.:** 235. **Drafted:** Indiana State, 2013 (1st round supplemental). **Signed by:** Jason Bryans

The Royals pulled off the surprise of the 2013 draft when they selected Hunter Dozier, a late-first-round talent, with the eighth overall pick. Their intentions became clear later when they selected Manaea with the 34th pick. He had projected as a potential top-five choice before an injury ruined his junior season at Indiana State. The Royals were confident that the torn labrum in Manaea's hip would not be a long-term problem—it's an injury Jason Vargas and Brett Myers returned from with no issues—so they were willing to spend $3.55 million, using the bonus-pool surplus they built by drafting Dozier. As a junior Manaea went 5-4, 1.47 while ranking fourth in NCAA Division I in strikeouts per nine innings (11.4). In the Cape Cod League in 2012, he threw his fastball at 94-96 mph with an above-average slider, but he was effective as Sycamores ace at 88-92, still managing to deceive hitters because of his fastball's deception and late life. Manaea throws from a low-three quarters arm slot that makes it hard for lefties to pick him up. His changeup is his No. 3 pitch, but it shows potential to be average. His control was above-average. Manaea got on the mound at the end of instructional league and should be ready for spring training. He probably will begin 2014 at high Class A Wilmington.

Year	Club (League)	Class	W	L	ERA	G	GS	CG	SV	IP	H	HR	BB	SO	K/9	WHIP	AVG
2013	Did not play—Injured																

7 HUNTER DOZIER, 3B

BA GRADE
55
HIGH

Born: Aug. 22, 1991. **B-T:** R-R. **Ht.:** 6-4. **Wt.:** 220. **Drafted:** Stephen F. Austin State, 2013 (1st round). **Signed by:** Mitch Thompson.

Thanks in part to a broken collarbone that ruined his junior season, Dozier was lightly recruited coming out of high school. He left Stephen F. Austin after three years as the school's first first-round pick, all-time leader in hits and doubles as well as the highest drafted player in Southland Conference history. The Royals liked Dozier enough to take him eighth overall, believing he wouldn't last until their second pick at No. 34. They signed him for $1 million under slot, freeing money to pursue sandwich pick Sean Manaea. Dozier has an advanced feel for hitting, sorting out pitches early in the count to get into favorable situations, but he's equally comfortable hitting with two strikes. He walked (38) more than he struck out (37) while hitting 30 doubles in just 69 games at Rookie-level Idaho Falls and low Class A Lexington in his debut. Dozier has an above-average hit tool and the potential to have at least solid-average power as well, if some of those doubles begin clearing the fence as he matures. While Dozier was too big to stick at shortstop as a pro, he has plenty of lateral range and an above-average arm that fits well at third base. He's an average runner. Dozier is advanced enough to jump right to high Class A Wilmington in 2014. He could be in Double-A Northwest Arkansas by the end of the year and challenge Mike Moustakas for the third base job shortly thereafter.

Year	Club (League)	Class	AVG	G	AB	R	H	2B	3B	HR	RBI	BB	SO	SB	CS	OBP	SLG
2013	Lexington (SAL)	LoA	.327	15	55	6	18	6	0	0	9	3	5	0	0	.373	.436
	Idaho Falls (PIO)	R	.303	54	218	43	66	24	0	7	43	35	32	3	1	.403	.509
Minor League Totals			.308	69	273	49	84	30	0	7	52	38	37	3	1	.397	.495

8 BUBBA STARLING, OF

BA GRADE
60
EXTREME

Born: Aug. 3, 1992. **B-T:** R-R. **Ht.:** 6-4. **Wt.:** 205. **Drafted:** HS—Gardner, Kan., 2011 (1st round). **Signed by:** Blake Davis.

As a high school star in Gardner, Kan., everything came easy to Starling. He showed NCAA Division I ability in football, basketball and baseball. He turned down a chance to be Nebraska's quarterback to sign with the Royals for $7.5 million as the fifth overall pick in 2011. Professional baseball has proven more of a challenge, though Starling did improve his contact rate significantly after mid-May laser eye surgery. He has above-average speed, is a plus center fielder and has an above-average arm. But none of that will matter if he doesn't improve his feel for hitting. The Royals spread out Starling's stance early in his pro career, but have now moved his feet back together to improve his timing. With the wide stance and a small toe tap, he struggled to get his legs involved in his swing, and a torso-turn as part of his load made it hard to properly time pitches. Starling has enough bat speed that he is rarely late on pitches, but when he doesn't get the timing of his front foot and hands in sync, he often rushes the bat through the zone, rolling over outside pitches. He has decent pitch recognition skills and draws walks, so if he can get his timing issues corrected, he could unlock his plus power potential. Starling needs to prove that a solid second half—.269/.359/.434 in 65 games—is a sign of good things to come. He'll face the difficult hitting environment of high Class A Wilmington in 2014.

Year	Club (League)	Class	AVG	G	AB	R	H	2B	3B	HR	RBI	BB	SO	SB	CS	OBP	SLG
2012	Burlington (APP)	R	.275	53	200	35	55	8	2	10	33	28	70	10	1	.371	.485
2013	Lexington (SAL)	LoA	.241	125	435	51	105	21	4	13	63	53	128	22	3	.329	.398
Minor League Totals			.252	178	635	86	160	29	6	23	96	81	198	32	4	.342	.425

9 JASON ADAM, RHP

Born: Aug. 4, 1991. **B-T:** R-R. **Ht.:** 6-4. **Wt.:** 225. **Drafted:** HS—Overland Park, Kan., 2010 (5th round). **Signed by:** Steve Gossett.

Adam's durability with solid stuff had been his calling card through much of his pro career, but then he regained the plus velocity that intrigued the Royals when they signed him for $800,000 out of the fifth round in 2010. His overall numbers look bad for 2013, but he was solid at Double-A Northwest Arkansas after a brutal April when he posted a 12.84 ERA. He went 8-9, 3.93 for the rest of the year. Adam's fastball gained a full grade in 2013 as he went from sitting 90-92 mph, touching 94, to sitting 92-94 and touching 97. His improved stuff came from better tempo and incorporating his legs into his delivery. He also added an average slider midway through the season, finding that it generated swings and misses better than his fringy curveball. His changeup also is fringy because he can't consistently throw it with the same arm speed as his fastball. Either the curveball or changeup will have to improve to give him something to better combat lefthanded hitters. Adam heads to spring training in 2014 with at least a chance to earn a spot on the Triple-A Omaha roster. Whether he breaks with Omaha or not, he should be ready to compete for a big league job in 2015.

Year	Club (League)	Class	W	L	ERA	G	GS	CG	SV	IP	H	HR	BB	SO	K/9	WHIP	AVG
2011	Kane County (MWL)	LoA	6	9	4.23	21	21	0	0	104	94	9	25	76	6.6	1.14	.235
2012	Wilmington (CAR)	HiA	7	12	3.53	27	27	0	0	158	148	18	36	123	7.0	1.16	.251
2013	NW Arkansas (TL)	AA	8	11	5.19	26	26	0	0	144	153	12	54	126	7.9	1.44	.277
Minor League Totals			21	32	4.30	74	74	0	0	406	395	39	115	325	7.2	1.26	.256

10 CHRISTIAN BINFORD, RHP

Born: Dec. 20, 1992. **B-T:** R-R. **Ht.:** 6-7. **Wt.:** 215. **Drafted:** HS—Mercersburg, Pa., 2011 (30th round). **Signed by:** Jim Farr.

The Royals spent aggressively under the draft rules of the previous Collective Bargaining Agreement, and Binford was one of the final beneficiaries. A $575,000 bonus swayed the Tommy John surgery alumnus and 30th-round pick in 2011 away from a Virginia commitment, and so far the Royals have seen a return on their investment. He allowed two earned runs or fewer in 20 of 23 starts at low Class A Lexington in 2013. Binford shows excellent command and feel for a young pitcher with his size. He doesn't throw especially hard, but he generates excellent downhill angle on his naturally heavy 88-93 mph fastball, and he locates it with precision. Binford's delivery isn't picture-perfect—he has a wrap in his takeaway and his delivery ends with his momentum carrying him toward first base—but he repeats his motion consistently. His changeup has developed into an average pitch that generates weak contact. His fringy breaking ball is on the line between curveball and slurve. He can throw it for strikes but needs to tighten it up. Binford projects as a back-end starter if he maintains his present velocity with a chance for more if he adds a little more. He will pitch at high Class A Wilmington in 2014.

Year	Club (League)	Class	W	L	ERA	G	GS	CG	SV	IP	H	HR	BB	SO	K/9	WHIP	AVG
2012	Burlington (APP)	R	2	3	2.03	8	8	0	0	40	40	1	4	31	7.0	1.10	.252
2013	Lexington (SAL)	LoA	8	7	2.67	23	23	0	0	135	129	7	25	130	8.7	1.14	.253
Minor League Totals			10	10	2.52	31	31	0	0	175	169	8	29	161	8.3	1.13	.253

11 ELIER HERNANDEZ, OF

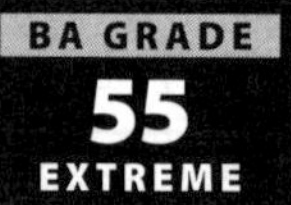

Born: Nov. 21, 1994. **B-T:** R-R. **Ht.:** 6-3. **Wt.:** 200. **Signed:** Dominican Republic, 2011. **Signed by:** Rene Francisco.

When the Royals hit the Dominican Republic showcase circuit to prepare for the 2011 international signing period, they discovered that Hernandez, and not shortstop Raul A. Mondesi, was the focus of an intense bidding war. Hernandez signed for $3 million, then joined Mondesi in the Rookie-level Pioneer League to make his pro debut in 2012 and looked overwhelmed, struggling to put together competitive at-bats. While Mondesi advanced to low Class A Lexington in 2013, Hernandez went back to Idaho Falls. His second stint went much better than the first. Where Hernandez was often simply trying to make contact in 2012, he drove the ball in 2013, which allowed him to lead the PL in triples (eight) despite being only an average runner. A center fielder as an amateur, Hernandez is shaky defensively in right field now, as he seemed to struggle to read balls at night and in the higher altitude parks of the PL. His 10 errors ranked second in the league. He has an above-average arm and has the tools to be at least an average outfielder, appearing more confident in day games. Hernandez is ready for low Class A Lexington in 2014, and he could grow to be an above-average hitter with at least average power, but he's years away from reaching that ceiling.

Year	Club (League)	Class	AVG	G	AB	R	H	2B	3B	HR	RBI	BB	SO	SB	CS	OBP	SLG
2012	Idaho Falls (PIO)	R	.208	60	250	30	52	10	4	0	34	14	66	2	0	.256	.280
2013	Idaho Falls (PIO)	R	.301	66	289	44	87	15	8	3	44	18	62	9	2	.350	.439
Minor League Totals			.258	126	539	74	139	25	12	3	78	32	128	11	2	.307	.365

12 SAM SELMAN, LHP

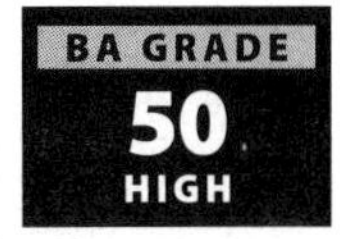

Born: Nov. 14, 1990. **B-T:** R-L. **Ht.:** 6-3. **Wt.:** 195. **Drafted:** Vanderbilt, 2012 (2nd round). **Signed by:** Sean Gibbs.

After an excellent 2012 pro debut, the ghost of Sam Selman past returned in large part in 2013. He showed many of the same control and delivery issues that affected much of his career at Vanderbilt. Even when he was missing his spots repeatedly, Selman proved very hard to square up—he held opponents to a .197 average and .268 slugging percentage. On the other hand, he led the high Class A Carolina League in walks (85) and ranked second with 14 hit batters. His poor command stems from an inability to consistently stay back over the rubber and a wrist wrap that makes his long arm action hard to repeat. Too often Selman's arm is trying to catch up to his body, which also affects how much break he gets on his curveball and slider. The curveball is fringe-average at best, while the slider flashes above-average when he's maintaining his delivery. After sitting 90-95 mph and touching 98 in 2012, Selman backed off his velocity to 88-93 as he tried to throw strikes. His heater still is an above-average pitch when he locates because it's hard to lift. His changeup has improved significantly since signing to become a fringe-average pitch. Everything about Selman's potential revolves around his control and his delivery. He'll try to sort it out at Double-A Northwest Arkansas in 2014.

Year	Club (League)	Class	W	L	ERA	G	GS	CG	SV	IP	H	HR	BB	SO	K/9	WHIP	AVG
2012	Idaho Falls (PIO)	R	5	4	2.09	13	12	0	0	60	45	1	22	89	13.3	1.11	.204
2013	Wilmington (CAR)	HiA	11	9	3.38	27	27	0	0	125	88	3	85	128	9.2	1.38	.197
Minor League Totals			16	13	2.96	40	39	0	0	186	133	4	107	217	10.5	1.29	.199

13 ORLANDO CALIXTE, SS

BA GRADE
50
HIGH

Born: Feb. 3, 1992. **B-T:** R-R. **Ht.:** 6-0. **Wt.:** 174. **Signed:** Dominican Republic, 2010. **Signed by:** Alvin Cuevas/Hector Pineda.

Calixte hasn't met a fastball he can't hit. Signed for $1 million in 2010, he has proven he can turn around velocity and he has more power than most middle infielders. But while he can hit anything straight, Calixte has yet to prove he can lay off breaking balls in or out of the strike zone. His aggressiveness has proven to be his undoing, as it limits the projection of his hit tool and keeps him from fully unleashing his average power. Defensively, Calixte was more reliable in 2013 and he showed his versatility by playing some second and third base. He looked reasonably comfortable at both, with an above-average arm and plus range. He has average range at shortstop with fluid actions and is an average runner. With Raul A. Mondesi breathing down his neck, Calixte could wind up as a super-sub with enough pop to play anywhere in the infield as well as the outfield corners. At the least, his versatility and track record versus lefthanders (.296/.368/.543 over the past two seasons) could make him a quality reserve. Calixte will return to Double-A Northwest Arkansas to try to learn to temper his aggressiveness.

Year	Club (League)	Class	AVG	G	AB	R	H	2B	3B	HR	RBI	BB	SO	SB	CS	OBP	SLG
2010	Royals (DSL)	R	.227	20	66	10	15	6	0	0	12	13	13	3	1	.350	.318
2011	Kane County (MWL)	LoA	.208	81	289	19	60	5	1	3	31	20	70	11	4	.256	.263
2012	Kane County (MWL)	LoA	.241	62	228	31	55	13	4	10	34	21	44	2	5	.303	.465
	Wilmington (CAR)	HiA	.281	63	256	38	72	17	4	4	28	15	65	8	3	.326	.426
2013	NW Arkansas (TL)	AA	.250	123	484	59	121	25	4	8	36	42	131	14	11	.312	.368
Minor League Totals			.244	349	1323	157	323	66	13	25	141	111	323	38	24	.303	.370

14 CHESLOR CUTHBERT, 3B

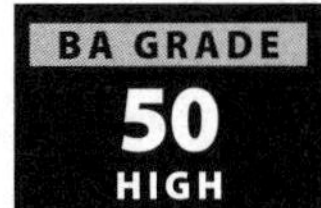

Born: Nov. 16, 1992. **B-T:** R-R. **Ht.:** 6-0. **Wt.:** 193. **Signed:** Nicaragua, 2009. **Signed by:** Orlando Esteves/Juan Lopez.

Halfway through the 2011 season, Cuthbert was outhitting the more highly touted members of a stacked 2009 international signing class that included Gary Sanchez and Miguel Sano. At the time, he was hitting .289/.350/.467 as an 18-year-old at low Class A Kane County. Scouts have been waiting to see Cuthbert recreate that production ever since. As one scout explained, "Two years ago, I expected to see him in the big leagues by now." Cuthbert had a solid first half while repeating high Class A Wilmington in 2013, but he was exposed after a promotion to Double-A Northwest Arkansas, with a lack of selectivity leaving him prone to chasing breaking balls out of the zone and negating his above-average raw power. He has a relatively simple swing but often tries to do too much instead of letting his above-average power come naturally. Scouts are not enamored of Cuthbert's body, as he has a thick lower half that makes him a baseclogger. Despite his lack of speed, he has good first-step quickness and an above-average arm that has allowed him to stick at third base. He will play the entire 2014 season as a 21-year-old, so he's still young enough to fix his selectivity issues, and the club added him to their 40-man roster in the offseason. Now he needs to pick up the production in a return to Double-A.

Year	Club (League)	Class	AVG	G	AB	R	H	2B	3B	HR	RBI	BB	SO	SB	CS	OBP	SLG
2010	Royals (AZL)	R	.265	18	68	14	18	3	2	1	5	6	19	1	1	.342	.412
	Idaho Falls (PIO)	R	.233	14	60	10	14	4	1	2	10	3	16	1	0	.281	.433
2011	Kane County (MWL)	LoA	.267	81	300	33	80	13	1	8	51	36	65	2	0	.345	.397
2012	Wilmington (CAR)	HiA	.240	124	475	47	114	18	0	7	59	37	80	6	3	.296	.322
2013	Wilmington (CAR)	HiA	.280	60	225	32	63	21	2	2	31	27	37	1	2	.354	.418
	NW Arkansas (TL)	AA	.215	64	237	25	51	16	0	6	28	20	51	5	2	.279	.359
Minor League Totals			.249	361	1365	161	340	75	6	26	184	129	268	16	8	.316	.370

15 MICHAEL MARIOT, RHP

BA GRADE 45 LOW

Born: Oct. 20, 1988. **B-T:** R-R. **Ht.:** 5-11. **Wt.:** 197. **Drafted:** Nebraska, 2010 (8th round). **Signed by:** Steve Gossett.

As the Royals watched Mariot's stuff get better and better, it's been hard for them not to flash back to the development of current closer Greg Holland. Like Holland, Mariot is a short righthander drafted out of college. And like Holland, Mariot's stuff has improved as he's climbed the ladder. Mariot sat at 89-93 mph early in the 2013 season, but by the end he was consistently touching 98 with his fastball while also aggressively using his average slider. He mixes in a fringy curveball and a tick-below-average changeup. Mariot's control, an asset previously, wavered a little as he adjusted to his newfound velocity. He finished the year by giving up one unearned run in his final 21 innings and finished fifth among Triple-A Pacific Coast League relievers in strikeout rate (9.8 per nine innings). The former starter shared the Omaha closer job, but he worked two or more innings 11 different times. Added to the 40-man roster in November, Mariot will begin 2014 back at Triple-A but could work his way into a crowded Royals bullpen at some point.

Year	Club (League)	Class	W	L	ERA	G	GS	CG	SV	IP	H	HR	BB	SO	K/9	WHIP	AVG
2010	Idaho Falls (PIO)	R	2	2	3.54	15	7	0	0	56	50	4	16	64	10.3	1.18	.237
2011	Wilmington (CAR)	HiA	8	4	3.41	28	9	0	5	100	99	7	21	80	7.2	1.20	.248
2012	NW Arkansas (TL)	AA	6	3	3.40	31	14	0	1	114	111	12	30	81	6.4	1.24	.258
	Omaha (PCL)	AAA	0	0	2.25	2	0	0	0	8	6	0	3	3	3.4	1.13	.214
2013	Omaha (PCL)	AAA	4	5	3.56	47	1	0	11	61	59	4	25	66	9.8	1.38	.258
Minor League Totals			20	14	3.43	123	31	0	17	339	325	27	95	294	7.8	1.24	.250

16 PEDRO FERNANDEZ, RHP

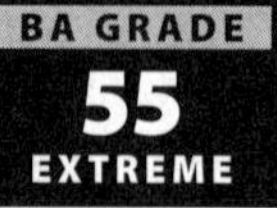

Born: May 25, 1994. **B-T:** R-R. **Ht.:** 6-0. **Wt.:** 175. **Signed:** Dominican Republic, 2011. **Signed by:** Edis Perez/Alvin Cuevas.

International scouting director Rene Francisco and his staff have had success signing short Dominican righthanders to reasonable contracts. Examples include Kelvin Herrera and Yordano Ventura. They snagged Fernandez for $45,000 in 2011 and watched him pitch his way out of the Dominican Summer League in 2012 by allowing just five hits in 12 innings. After arriving in the Rookie-level Arizona League, he similarly dominated with a 90-94 mph fastball that could develop into a consistent plus pitch, an average slider that shows tilt and bite and a decent changeup. If he continues to get stronger, Fernandez has the makings of three average or better pitches to go with a clean delivery. He hasn't worked deep in games yet, but he has shown an ability to maintain his velocity for all five innings start after start. Fernandez's control and feel is significantly more advanced than the average 19-year-old, which opens up the possibility that he could jump to low Class A Lexington in 2014.

Year	Club (League)	Class	W	L	ERA	G	GS	CG	SV	IP	H	HR	BB	SO	K/9	WHIP	AVG
2012	Royals (DSL)	R	3	2	1.93	12	10	0	0	51	44	0	14	49	8.6	1.13	.237
2013	Royals (DSL)	R	0	0	0.75	4	2	0	0	12	5	0	3	15	11.3	0.67	.128
	Royals (AZL)	R	0	1	1.82	8	7	0	0	35	28	3	8	38	9.9	1.04	.215
Minor League Totals			3	3	1.74	24	19	0	0	98	77	3	25	102	9.4	1.04	.217

17 BRETT EIBNER, OF

Born: Dec. 2, 1988. **B-T:** R-R. **Ht.:** 6-4. **Wt.:** 210. **Drafted:** Arkansas, 2010 (2nd round). **Signed by:** Lloyd Simmons.

For the first time since he signed with the Royals as a second-round pick in 2010, Eibner quieted some of the voices calling for him to move to the mound. He produced the best season of his pro career at Double-A Northwest Arkansas, improving his power production and showing a modest improvement in his always-outsized strikeout rate. Much like a lesser version of Drew Stubbs, Eibner provides power and above-average defense in center field, but it comes with a well-below-average hit tool. As you would expect for a former pitcher with a low- to mid-90s fastball, his arm is above-average, and Eibner has a tick-above-average speed that gets better once he's underway. But his power comes from a big, righthanded swing that has never been conducive to making consistent contact. Adopting a more closed stance in 2013 helped him stop pulling off as many balls, improving his plate coverage and triggering an .854 OPS in the second half. Eibner can drive the ball for extra bases to all fields and crushed lefthanders in 2013, batting .341/.442/.635. His defensive chops and power give him a chance to at least be a reserve outfielder and possible platoon player, and if his second-half improvements stick, he could end up being even more. He's expected to join Triple-A Omaha in 2014.

Year	Club (League)	Class	AVG	G	AB	R	H	2B	3B	HR	RBI	BB	SO	SB	CS	OBP	SLG
2011	Kane County (MWL)	LoA	.213	76	272	46	58	13	2	12	31	48	90	2	3	.340	.408
2012	Wilmington (CAR)	HiA	.196	120	423	60	83	26	5	15	53	57	165	5	2	.299	.388
2013	NW Arkansas (TL)	AA	.243	114	441	74	107	17	9	19	41	53	149	7	3	.330	.451
Minor League Totals			.218	310	1136	180	248	56	16	46	125	158	404	14	8	.321	.417

18 LANE ADAMS, OF

BA GRADE
45
MEDIUM

Born: Nov. 13, 1989. **B-T:** R-R. **Ht.:** 6-2. **Wt.:** 204. **Drafted:** HS—Red Oak (Okla.), 2009 (13th round). **Signed by:** Steve Gossett.

Much like David Lough, a football/baseball player at Mercyhurst (Pa.) College who blossomed after focusing on baseball full-time, Adams is an athletic two-sport star who has improved significantly once he chose baseball as his vocation. A Missouri State basketball recruit as a shooting guard with an excellent three-point shot, Adams spent two years in Rookie ball and parts of three seasons in Class A before finally reaching Double-A Northwest Arkansas in 2013. He joined Triple-A Omaha for the playoffs, hitting a pair of triples and stealing two bases as the Storm Chasers won the Triple-A national championship game. Adams was an above-average runner when he signed with the Royals, but he's steadily gained speed to become a double-plus runner. He's also started to unleash his plus raw power. Adams can play all three outfield positions, though his fringe-average arm is a poor fit in right field and he's better as a fill-in than a regular in center. He projects as a potential fourth outfielder who could be more if his bat continues to improve. Even after a brutal Arizona Fall League stint—he hit .146 with 20 strikeouts in 46 at-bats—the Royals added Adams to the 40-man roster.

Year	Club (League)	Class	AVG	G	AB	R	H	2B	3B	HR	RBI	BB	SO	SB	CS	OBP	SLG
2009	Royals (AZL)	R	.233	29	103	18	24	2	2	0	10	16	32	14	1	.339	.291
2010	Idaho Falls (PIO)	R	.282	41	170	31	48	8	3	2	18	18	38	8	0	.347	.400
2011	Kane County (MWL)	LoA	.230	43	152	22	35	7	2	1	11	14	44	7	2	.300	.322
	Royals (AZL)	R	.357	4	14	5	5	3	0	0	1	3	4	0	1	.500	.571
	Burlington (APP)	R	.281	43	167	31	47	9	3	5	20	17	45	9	1	.353	.461
2012	Kane County (MWL)	LoA	.298	67	262	40	78	13	4	5	44	21	48	11	1	.349	.435
	Wilmington (CAR)	HiA	.240	68	262	37	63	10	1	6	25	21	64	8	4	.302	.355
2013	Wilmington (CAR)	HiA	.276	87	323	56	89	23	2	7	39	43	66	23	6	.362	.424
	NW Arkansas (TL)	AA	.244	44	156	30	38	7	1	5	26	18	45	15	0	.333	.397
Minor League Totals			.265	426	1609	270	427	82	18	31	194	171	386	95	16	.339	.397

19 SAMIR DUENEZ, 1B/OF

BA GRADE
50
EXTREME

Born: June 11, 1995. **B-T:** L-R. **Ht.:** 6-1. **Wt.:** 195. **Signed:** Venezuela, 2012. **Signed by:** Alberto Garcia/Richard Castro/Orlando Estevez.

When Duenez toured the workout circuit, most scouts wondered where he'd play. He doesn't run well, so that narrowed his positional possibilities to first base or possibly the corner outfield. In a Latin America amateur market where most of the prized position prospects play shortstop or center field, that was a red flag. The Royals focused instead on his ability to hit after they saw him square up baseballs time after time, signing him for $425,000 in 2012. He quickly made the jump to the Rookie-level Arizona League for his pro debut in 2013, showing the same all-field approach with good bat speed and excellent barrel control. Duenez will have to hit because he's a tick-below-average runner who will slow as he matures, and his power is all projection. He primarily played first base in 2013, leading the AZL with eight errors, though the Royals also want to try him in left field. He does have a potentially above-average arm. Duenez is one of the best pure hitters in the organization and polished enough that he has a shot at making the jump to low Class A Lexington in 2014.

Year	Club (League)	Class	AVG	G	AB	R	H	2B	3B	HR	RBI	BB	SO	SB	CS	OBP	SLG
2013	Royals (AZL)	R	.294	47	187	26	55	12	2	0	19	12	27	6	4	.337	.380
Minor League Totals			.294	47	187	26	55	12	2	0	19	12	27	6	4	.337	.380

20 MARTEN GASPARINI, SS

BA GRADE
50
EXTREME

Born: May 24, 1997. **B-T:** B-R. **Ht.:** 6-0. **Wt.:** 175. **Signed:** Italy, 2013. **Signed by:** Nick Leto.

Gasparini signed the richest contract ever for a European amateur when he inked his $1.3 million deal with the Royals in July 2013. That's understandable seeing as scouts regarded him as arguably the finest amateur prospect ever from Europe. His bonus easily topped the Twins' 2009 deal with German outfielder Max Kepler for $800,000. Gasparini moved 300 miles to train at the Italian Baseball Academy as a 14-year-old, which means he's more advanced than the average European prospect, and his knowledge of the English language helps ease his cultural transition. But he still has faced less advanced competition than the average U.S. or Latin American prospect. Gasparini is an excellent athlete with easy actions and speed that grades as a 65 on the 20-80 scouting scale. His arm is a tick-below-average with an unconventional action that leads many scouts to think he'll move to center field eventually. At the plate, Gasparini has plenty of bat speed and a reasonably smooth swing from both sides of the plate. He projects as a top-of-the-order hitter with below-average power for now, but he's young enough to exceed that power projection if he fills out. For now, Gasparini will continue to work out at the Royals complex with an eye on his first pro action in the second half of 2014.

Year	Club (League)	Class	AVG	G	AB	R	H	2B	3B	HR	RBI	BB	SO	SB	CS	OBP	SLG
2013	Did not play—Signed 2014 contract																

21 CHRIS DWYER, LHP

BA GRADE
40
LOW

Born: April 10, 1988. **B-T:** R-L. **Ht.:** 6-2. **Wt.:** 210. **Drafted:** Clemson, 2009 (4th round). **Signed by:** Steve Connelly.

It's been quite an up-and-down path through the minors for Dwyer. Signed for an above-slot $1.45 million in 2009 as a draft-eligible freshman after one year at Clemson, Dwyer arrived as a power pitcher with a 90-94 mph fastball and plus curveball but without much feel for setting up hitters and below-average control. After a thyroid condition sapped his strength in 2012, however, Dwyer bounced back in 2013 as more of a touch-and-feel lefty who retired hitters at Triple-A Omaha with average stuff. He pitched anywhere from 86-92 mph with his fastball, working backwards at times by getting ahead with a now above-average changeup that he throws with good arm speed and excellent late fade. His curveball has diminished in stature, and he struggles to throw it for strikes at times, but it's an average pitch. He still issues too many walks (4.1 per nine innings in 2013) even with his diminished velocity, nibbling around the strike zone's edges. Dwyer started and won the Triple-A national championship game and made his big league debut in 2013. Unless his old plus fastball and curve return, he profiles as a reliever or spot starter rather than as a rotation stalwart.

Year	Club (League)	Class	W	L	ERA	G	GS	CG	SV	IP	H	HR	BB	SO	K/9	WHIP	AVG
2009	Idaho Falls (PIO)	R	0	0	4.15	4	4	0	0	9	12	1	8	15	15.6	2.31	.324
2010	Wilmington (CAR)	HiA	6	3	2.99	15	15	1	0	84	79	3	33	93	9.9	1.33	.246
	NW Arkansas (TL)	AA	2	1	3.06	4	4	0	0	18	11	2	10	20	10.2	1.19	.175
2011	NW Arkansas (TL)	AA	8	10	5.60	27	27	2	0	141	124	14	78	126	8.0	1.43	.238
2012	NW Arkansas (TL)	AA	5	8	5.25	17	16	0	0	86	79	13	44	71	7.5	1.44	.242
	Omaha (PCL)	AAA	3	4	6.97	9	9	1	0	50	73	10	24	33	5.9	1.93	.349
2013	Omaha (PCL)	AAA	10	11	3.55	29	28	0	0	160	140	15	72	112	6.3	1.33	.234
	Kansas City (AL)	MAJ	0	0	0.00	2	0	0	0	3	2	0	1	2	6.0	1.00	.200
Major League Totals			0	0	0.00	2	0	0	0	3	2	0	1	2	6.0	1.00	.200
Minor League Totals			34	37	4.57	105	103	4	0	548	518	58	269	470	7.7	1.44	.249

22 DONNIE JOSEPH, LHP

Born: Nov. 1, 1987. **B-T:** L-L. **Ht.:** 6-3. **Wt.:** 190. **Drafted:** Houston, 2009 (3rd round). **Signed by:** Jerry Flowers (Reds).

With Joseph, you get the good with the bad. He's got a fastball/slider pairing that is devastating to lefthanders and can be a tough look for righthanders as well. That repertoire comes with a delivery that makes it hard to throw strikes consistently, however. Joseph's pitching motion is the antithesis of direct to the plate. He stands with his back turned to the batter, his front foot pointing somewhere between home plate and first base. He hangs over the rubber at this cocked angle, then sweeps his front foot to the plate at the last moment, ensuring that his momentum is carrying him toward third base as he delivers the pitch. Acquired from the Reds in a July 2012 trade that sent Jonathan Broxton to Cincinnati, Joseph's delivery may be beyond repair, but its funkiness provides deception. He must do a better job of throwing strike one to set up his plus slider. At times he tries to take velocity off to throw his slider for strikes, but it's more of a chase pitch, so it's only effective when paired with his 88-92 mph fastball in the zone. If Joseph threw more strikes, he could be a solid late-inning reliever, but for now, he looks more like a second lefty in the pen.

Year	Club (League)	Class	W	L	ERA	G	GS	CG	SV	IP	H	HR	BB	SO	K/9	WHIP	AVG
2009	Billings (PIO)	R	2	1	0.77	8	0	0	0	12	6	0	4	11	8.5	0.86	.146
	Dayton (MWL)	LoA	2	2	4.35	16	0	0	4	21	13	0	10	31	13.5	1.11	.176
2010	Dayton (MWL)	LoA	2	1	0.78	19	0	0	6	23	13	0	7	40	15.7	0.87	.160
	Lynchburg (CAR)	HiA	0	4	2.31	31	0	0	17	35	23	2	16	56	14.4	1.11	.181
	Carolina (SL)	AA	1	0	5.14	7	0	0	1	7	7	0	2	7	9.0	1.29	.250
2011	Carolina (SL)	AA	1	3	6.94	57	0	0	8	58	67	8	30	66	10.2	1.66	.286
2012	Pensacola (SL)	AA	4	2	0.89	26	0	0	13	30	13	1	8	46	13.6	0.69	.129
	Louisville (IL)	AAA	4	1	2.86	18	0	0	5	22	22	0	9	22	9.0	1.41	.259
	Omaha (PCL)	AAA	1	0	4.15	11	0	0	2	17	21	1	13	19	9.9	1.96	.296
2013	Omaha (PCL)	AAA	4	3	3.95	47	0	0	6	55	39	5	40	84	13.8	1.45	.199
	Kansas City (AL)	MAJ	0	0	0.00	6	0	0	0	6	4	0	4	7	11.1	1.41	.200
Major League Totals			0	0	0.00	6	0	0	0	6	4	0	4	7	11.1	1.41	.200
Minor League Totals			21	17	3.63	240	0	0	62	280	224	17	139	382	12.3	1.30	.216

23 CAM GALLAGHER, C

BA GRADE **50** HIGH

Born: Dec. 6, 1992. **B-T:** R-R. **Ht.:** 6-3. **Wt.:** 215. **Drafted:** HS—Lancaster, Pa., 2011 (2nd round). **Signed by:** Jim Farr.

The life of a catcher is never easy, but Gallagher has already had more than his share of bumps, bruises and broken bones that come with being a backstop. Part of a baseball family that has seen his father Glenn and brother Austin both play in the minor leagues, Cam is looking for his first injury-free season. In 2012, he was accidentally hit on the hand by a backswing and also endured a shoulder injury. In 2013, he missed a month and a half when he broke his hand when hit by a pitch and missed 10 days in August after a foul tip nipped him. In three seasons, he has accrued fewer than 500 total at-bats. Gallagher's timing at the plate never recovered from his broken hand—he hit .268 before the injury and .193 afterwards. He has soft hands, calls a solid game and has a solid-average arm. Gallagher has shortened his swing since high school. He makes contact, draws walks and doesn't strike out excessively, but so far, he's yet to show the above-average power that the Royals forecasted when they drafted him in the second round in 2011. Gallagher still has the ceiling of a regular catcher, but he needs to stay on the field to develop his game. He may head back to low Class A Lexington to start 2014.

Year	Club (League)	Class	AVG	G	AB	R	H	2B	3B	HR	RBI	BB	SO	SB	CS	OBP	SLG
2011	Royals (AZL)	R	.141	20	78	6	11	0	0	1	7	7	15	0	0	.209	.179
	Idaho Falls (PIO)	R	.200	8	30	2	6	0	0	1	2	3	4	0	0	.273	.300
2012	Burlington (APP)	R	.276	36	127	13	35	10	0	3	15	10	16	1	3	.331	.425
2013	Lexington (SAL)	LoA	.212	66	222	19	47	15	0	2	18	24	28	0	0	.302	.306
Minor League Totals			.217	130	457	40	99	25	0	7	42	44	63	1	3	.292	.317

24 ZANE EVANS, C

BA GRADE **50** HIGH

Born: Nov. 29, 1991. **B-T:** R-R. **Ht.:** 6-2. **Wt.:** 209. **Drafted:** Georgia Tech, 2013 (4th round). **Signed by:** Sean Gibbs.

When Evans arrived at Georgia Tech in 2011, he became the first freshman to serve as the Yellow Jackets regular catcher since Jason Varitek in 1991. A two-way player as a catcher/reliever at Georgia Tech, much like Orioles catcher Matt Wieters, Evans combines at least average power potential at the plate with a chance to develop into at least an average receiver. His 2013 debut ended early when he broke his hand on a foul tip at Rookie-level Idaho Falls. A large-framed catcher, Evans has an excellent arm, which has been clocked at 94-96 mph off the mound, but he needs to improve his footwork. His hands also could get quieter as he receives pitches. Evans has a solid approach at the plate for a power hitter. He's looking for something to pull, but he recognizes pitches well enough to work counts to get himself in situations to zone pitches. The Royals have all-star Salvador Perez signed through 2019, but Evans and Cam Gallagher stand out as the two in-house backstops who have a chance to develop into everyday regulars. Evans could jump over Gallagher to high Class A Wilmington for his first full season.

Year	Club (League)	Class	AVG	G	AB	R	H	2B	3B	HR	RBI	BB	SO	SB	CS	OBP	SLG
2013	Idaho Falls (PIO)	R	.352	41	162	26	57	18	0	4	31	11	25	1	0	.394	.537
Minor League Totals			.352	41	162	26	57	18	0	4	31	11	25	1	0	.394	.537

25 CHRISTIAN COLON, 2B/SS

Born: May 14, 1989. **B-T:** R-R. **Ht.:** 6-1. **Wt.:** 180. **Drafted:** Cal State Fullerton, 2010 (1st round). **Signed by:** Scott Groot.

At this point, it's highly unlikely that Colon ever will live up to the expectations that come with being the fourth overall pick in the 2010 draft, but he should make it to the big leagues for the first time in 2014. It's been a slow climb for the middle infielder, who was expected to move quickly when he was drafted as a heady shortstop whose feel for the game made his average tools play up. Instead, his heady approach is all that has kept his below-average tools from sinking his big league chances. A teammate of future Athletics first-round pick Grant Green in high school and Giants 2010 first-rounder Gary Brown at Cal State Fullerton, Colon has proven to have a lot more 40 grades on his scouting report than 50s. He has below-average power and is a below-average runner with below-average range and a below-average arm at shortstop, though those limitations are diminished when he slides over to second base. He's a sure-handed infielder at any spot. He did steal 15 bases thanks to his baseball intelligence. He's an average hitter, with strong contact ability his best attribute. The Royals spent the first two-thirds of the 2013 season looking for a second baseman without calling up Colon. He will head to spring training with a chance to make the big league team as a utility infielder.

Year	Club (League)	Class	AVG	G	AB	R	H	2B	3B	HR	RBI	BB	SO	SB	CS	OBP	SLG
2010	Wilmington (CAR)	HiA	.278	60	245	38	68	12	2	3	30	13	33	2	4	.326	.380
2011	NW Arkansas (TL)	AA	.257	127	491	69	126	14	2	8	61	46	51	17	7	.325	.342
2012	Royals (AZL)	R	.364	7	22	6	8	3	0	0	4	4	0	1	1	.481	.500
	NW Arkansas (TL)	AA	.289	73	273	33	79	9	2	5	27	31	27	12	6	.364	.392
	Omaha (PCL)	AAA	.412	5	17	4	7	1	0	1	5	2	1	0	0	.429	.647
2013	Omaha (PCL)	AAA	.273	131	512	72	140	12	3	12	58	41	57	15	4	.335	.379
Minor League Totals			.274	403	1560	222	428	51	9	29	185	137	169	47	22	.339	.374

26 BRYAN BRICKHOUSE, RHP

BA GRADE
50
EXTREME

Born: June 6, 1992. **B-T:** R-R. **Ht.:** 6-0. **Wt:** 209. **Drafted:** HS—The Woodlands, Texas, 2011 (3rd round). **Signed by:** Brian Rhees.

When The Woodlands' baseball program holds an alumni get-together, first-rounders Jameson Taillon and Kyle Drabek and 2013 MVP candidate Paul Goldschmidt should be the first to offer to pay for dinner, but Brickhouse can chip in as well. In the Royals' final spending spree under the old draft rules, Brickhouse signed for $1.5 million, nearly $1.2 million above slot for the third round. After a rough debut in 2012, he took significant steps forward in a second try at low Class A before elbow problems sidelined him in early June. One of a number of Royals pitchers to have Tommy John surgery in 2013, Brickhouse is expected to be sidelined until roughly the middle of 2014. Before the injury, Brickhouse was getting groundballs with a heavy 90-95 mph fastball that shows natural sink and late movement, especially when he's getting on top of his two-seamer. His breaking ball is less consistent, and he struggles to maintain his arm speed when throwing his changeup. Brickhouse did a good job of refining his delivery and improving his ability to repeat it, but the stocky righthander still shows some effort. Now he'll be effectively starting over as he works back from a lengthy rehab.

Year	Club (League)	Class	W	L	ERA	G	GS	CG	SV	IP	H	HR	BB	SO	K/9	WHIP	AVG
2012	Idaho Falls (PIO)	R	0	0	37.80	1	1	0	0	2	5	1	3	1	5.4	4.80	.500
	Kane County (MWL)	LoA	3	3	5.61	10	10	0	0	51	50	3	23	40	7.0	1.42	.249
2013	Lexington (SAL)	LoA	4	4	2.25	11	11	0	0	60	54	3	21	49	7.4	1.25	.238
Minor League Totals			7	7	4.30	22	22	0	0	113	109	7	47	90	7.2	1.38	.249

27 ANGEL BAEZ, RHP

BA GRADE
45
HIGH

Born: Feb. 14, 1991. **B-T:** R-R. **Ht.:** 6-3. **Wt.:** 226. **Signed:** Dominican Republic, 2008. **Signed by:** Edis Perez.

Baez was supposed to be next in line among the Royals' Dominican pitching pipeline before he took a step back in 2013. Blessed with one of the best arms in the system, he lost the feel for the strike zone, then lost his control, breaking his pitching hand in a fit of anger. He returned in time to show the same electric, erratic stuff in a late-season return to high Class A Wilmington and a stint in the Arizona Fall League. He struck out 19 batters in the AFL in just 13 innings, but he also walked nine and gave up 14 hits. Baez's fastball will vary from 88-98 mph depending on how well he's maintaining his delivery. His curveball and changeup both show flashes of being average, but they are inconsistent because of his control and delivery issues. After five years as a starter, Baez likely will move to the bullpen in 2014 to see if his control can improve. The Royals left him off the 40-man roster, figuring that teams will pass on his great arm in the Rule 5 draft because he hasn't proven he can throw strikes. Baez's ultimate ceiling could be late-inning reliever.

Year	Club (League)	Class	W	L	ERA	G	GS	CG	SV	IP	H	HR	BB	SO	K/9	WHIP	AVG
2009	Royals (DSL)	R	0	6	3.88	14	11	0	0	49	54	0	19	45	8.3	1.50	.280
2010	Royals (DSL)	R	0	1	2.93	8	7	0	0	31	29	1	14	25	7.3	1.40	.257
	Royals (AZL)	R	0	2	5.40	7	4	0	0	15	9	1	10	14	8.4	1.27	.167
2011	Burlington (APP)	R	0	6	7.09	14	14	0	0	47	67	3	30	41	7.9	2.06	.321
2012	Kane County (MWL)	LoA	6	5	3.17	16	15	1	0	77	65	5	31	83	9.7	1.25	.220
2013	Royals (AZL)	R	1	0	2.51	6	3	0	0	14	17	0	3	17	10.7	1.40	.293
	Wilmington (CAR)	HiA	3	1	4.38	8	8	0	0	37	34	3	28	35	8.5	1.68	.248
Minor League Totals			10	21	4.21	73	62	1	0	269	275	13	135	260	8.7	1.52	.260

28 CODY REED, LHP

Born: April 15, 1993. **B-T:** L-L. **Ht.:** 6-5. **Wt.:** 220. **Drafted:** Northwest Mississppi CC, 2013 (2nd round). **Signed by:** Travis Ezi.

Two years at Northwest Mississippi CC served Reed well. He went from an unnoticed high school arm to a power lefty who signed with the Royals for $1.2 million as a second-round pick in 2013. Reed didn't throw particularly hard coming out of high school, but his velocity jumped from 86-90 mph to 92-93 mph (touching 96) as a juco sophomore. The Royals didn't see the same Reed in his first pro exposure and shut him down for nearly two weeks in the middle of the Rookie-level Idaho Falls season because he was throwing with more effort and less stuff, and his fastball sat at 88-92 mph. At his best, he had toned down his formerly high-effort delivery. He flashes an above-average slider, though it's inconsistent. His changeup is fringy at best. Reed's biggest problem is he has yet to demonstrate that he can consistently throw strikes. He walked 4.7 batters per nine innings in junior college and was even worse in Idaho Falls (7.0 BB/9). Scouts see Reed ending up in a relief role. Though he's raw, he should open with low Class A Lexington to start 2014.

Year	Club (League)	Class	W	L	ERA	G	GS	CG	SV	IP	H	HR	BB	SO	K/9	WHIP	AVG
2013	Idaho Falls (PIO)	R	0	1	6.07	15	6	0	0	30	31	0	23	25	7.6	1.82	.270
Minor League Totals			0	1	6.07	15	6	0	0	30	31	0	23	25	7.6	1.82	.270

29 CHRISTHIAN VASQUEZ, OF

BA GRADE
50
EXTREME

Born: Sept. 11, 1996. **Ht.:** 5-11. **Wt.:** 180. **B-T:** L-L. **Signed:** Venezuela, 2013. **Signed by:** Juan Gualdron/Richard Castro.

The Royals have put an emphasis in recent years on signing Latin American prospects who can square up the ball, emphasizing hitting ability over athleticism. Like Samir Duenez, Vasquez's best attribute as an amateur was his simple lefthanded swing and all-fields, line-drive hitting approach. Kansas City made him one of its top targets for 2013, signing him for $750,000. The Royals believe Vasquez can stick in center field, but scouts for other teams note his average speed and expect he'll end up moving to a corner outfield spot, likely left field because of his below-average arm. If he does have to move to a corner, some question whether his gap power will profile. Vasquez will either open 2014 with Rookie-level Burlington or play in the Dominican Summer League.

Year	Club (League)	Class	AVG	G	AB	R	H	2B	3B	HR	RBI	BB	SO	SB	CS	OBP	SLG
2013	Did not play—Signed 2014 contract																

30 TERRANCE GORE, OF

BA GRADE
45
HIGH

Born: June 8, 1991. **B-T:** R-R. **Ht.:** 5-7. **Wt.:** 165. **Drafted:** Gulf Coast (Fla.) CC, 2011 (20th round). **Signed by:** Colin Gonzales.

Gore's .215 average at low Class A Lexington and absolute lack of power don't stamp him as a prospect. A closer look reveals a few reasons to believe that he has big league potential, at least as an extra outfielder or pinch-runner. Gore has absolute top-of-the-scale speed, and he's one of the best basestealers in the minors. His 89 percent success rate was easily the best among minor leaguers with 50 or more steals in 2013. He can go from first to second in three seconds flat at his best. Like the Reds' Billy Hamilton, Gore can't be thrown out at second base when he gets a good jump, even on a pitchout. He improved his reads defensively to become an above-average left fielder and average center fielder, though he doesn't throw well. At the plate, Gore drew 62 walks in 2013, and his on-base percentage was nearly 120 points higher than his batting average. In instructional league, the Royals told Gore to bunt in nearly every at-bat, turning a weakness into a potential strength. Even with infielders in, he bunted his way to a .458 average, suggesting that if he can improve his average to about .270—a tick above the major league average—he could be a useful contributor.

Year	Club (League)	Class	AVG	G	AB	R	H	2B	3B	HR	RBI	BB	SO	SB	CS	OBP	SLG
2011	Royals (AZL)	R	.340	35	94	22	32	2	2	0	16	15	21	17	0	.447	.404
2012	Burlington (APP)	R	.256	61	227	50	58	4	2	0	13	36	52	36	2	.379	.291
2013	Lexington (SAL)	LoA	.215	128	455	76	98	6	3	0	24	62	120	68	8	.334	.242
Minor League Totals			.242	224	776	148	188	12	7	0	53	113	193	121	10	.361	.276

Los Angeles Angels

BY J.J. COOPER

The best player in baseball has been playing for an also-ran.

The Angels haven't been bad in either of Mike Trout's first two epic seasons as the club's star of the present and future. But they haven't been good either, finishing as also-rans in the American League West. And in the new world of baseball economics, that may be the worst possible place to be.

The Angels have won between 78-89 games in each of the past four years. They hang around the fringes of playoff races, enough to often be buyers around the trade deadline, but the run of six playoff appearances and a World Series title in an eight-year run from 2002-09 seems long ago.

The Angels at some point will have to empty their coffers to sign Trout long-term, and they have spared no expense when trying to help the big league club by signing free agents. A year after signing Albert Pujols to a 10-year, $240 million contract, Los Angeles splurged again, spending $125 million prior to the 2013 season to lock up outfielder Josh Hamilton for five years. Lefthander C.J. Wilson and righty Jered Weaver also are making more than $15 million a year.

At the minor league level, no team is more parsimonious. Thanks to the signings of Pujols and Hamilton, the Angels have not had a first-round pick in either of the past two drafts. The farm system has been even more depleted by prospects-for-big leaguer trades.

The Angels have traded away lefthanders Pat Corbin and Tyler Skaggs, shortstop Jean Segura, outfielder Randal Grichuk and righthanders Ariel Pena and Johnny Hellweg in recent years.

In many ways, the Angels are among the worst-served by the new Collective Bargaining Agreement. They never are bad enough to have first-round picks protected from free-agent compensation rules and they spend enough to frequently lose first-round picks. And because they are a middle-of-the-pack team at the big league level, their international allotment is also never particularly large. The result is the thinnest farm system in baseball.

The Angels have gotten what they have paid for. They spent less on their 2011-13 drafts combined then the Pirates did to sign 2011 No. 1 overall pick Gerrit Cole. The Angels have also spent very little internationally. This year's signing of Venezuelan lefthander Ricardo Sanchez for $580,000 was the first time the club had spent more than $250,000 on an international amateur in the past four years.

CLIFF WELCH

With little help on the farm, the Angels have spent millions to build around Mike Trout

TOP PROSPECTS OF THE DECADE

Year	Player, Pos.	2013 Org.
2004	Casey Kotchman, 1b	Marlins
2005	Casey Kotchman, 1b	Marlins
2006	Brandon Wood, ss	Orioles
2007	Brandon Wood, ss	Orioles
2008	Brandon Wood, ss	Orioles
2009	Nick Adenhart, rhp	Deceased
2010	Hank Conger, c	Angels
2011	Mike Trout, of	Angels
2012	Mike Trout, of	Angels
2013	Kaleb Cowart, 3b	Angels

There is a realization in the Angels braintrust that things have to change. The club has moved into a new Dominican Republic facility that signifies an increased emphasis on international development. For the first time in three years, it looks like Los Angeles will have a first-round pick when the 2014 draft comes around.

In the long term, those moves should revitalize a farm system in need of an infusion of talent. But the new CBA does not make it easy for teams to execute rapid turnarounds of the farm system, especially for teams stuck in the middle. So for now, Trout may shine brightly from April to September, but he's not going to get much homegrown help anytime soon.

ORGANIZATION OVERVIEW

General Manager: Jerry Dipoto. **Farm Director:** Bobby Scales. **Scouting Director:** Ric Wilson.

Class	Team	League	W	L	PCT	Finish	Manager
Majors	Los Angeles Angels	American	78	84	.481	10th (15)	Mike Scioscia
Triple-A	Salt Lake Bees	Pacific Coast	78	66	.542	4th (16)	Keith Johnson
Double-A	Arkansas Travelers	Texas	73	66	.525	3rd (8)	Tim Bogar
High Class A	Inland Empire 66ers	California	69	71	.493	t-5th (10)	Bill Haselman
Low Class A	Burlington Bees	Midwest	56	78	.418	14th (14)	Jamie Burke
Rookie	Orem Owlz	Pioneer	39	36	.520	4th (8)	Bill Richardson
Rookie	AZL Angels	Arizona	30	26	.536	4th (13)	Denny Hocking
Overall 2013 Minor League Record			**345**	**343**	**.501**	**12th (30)**	

THIS YEAR'S TOP 30

No.	Player, Pos.	Grade/Risk
1.	Taylor Lindsey, 2b	55/Medium
2.	C.J. Cron, 1b	50/Medium
3.	Kaleb Cowart, 3b	50/High
4.	R.J. Alvarez, rhp	50/High
5.	Mark Sappington, rhp	45/Medium
6.	Hunter Green, lhp	50/Extreme
7.	Ricardo Sanchez, rhp	50/Extreme
8.	Alex Yarbrough, 2b	45/Medium
9.	Zach Borenstein, of	45/Medium
10.	Cam Bedrosian, rhp	45/High
11.	Ryan Brasier, rhp	45/High
12.	Jose Rondon, ss	50/Extreme
13.	Eric Stamets, ss	40/Low
14.	Mike Morin, rhp	45/Medium
15.	Victor Alcantara, rhp	50/Extreme
16.	Natanael Delgado, of	50/Extreme
17.	Mike Clevinger, rhp	45/High
18.	Mike Fish, of	45/High
19.	Cal Towey, 3b/c	45/High
20.	A.J. Schugel, rhp	40/Medium
21.	Buddy Boshers, lhp	40/Medium
22.	Nick Maronde, lhp	40/Medium
23.	Joe Krehbiel, rhp	45/High
24.	Eduar Lopez, rhp	50/Extreme
25.	Jett Bandy, c	40/Medium
26.	Keynan Middleton, rhp	50/Extreme
27.	Erick Salcedo, ss	45/High
28.	Andrew Ray, of	45/High
29.	Kyle McGowin, rhp	45/High
30.	Reid Scoggins, rhp	45/Extreme

LAST YEAR'S TOP 30

No.	Player, Pos.	Status
1.	Kaleb Cowart, 3b	No. 3
2.	Nick Maronde, lhp	No. 22
3.	C.J. Cron, 1b	No. 2
4.	Mike Clevenger, rhp	No. 17
5.	Austin Wood, rhp	Dropped out
6.	Randal Grichuk, of	(Cardinals)
7.	Taylor Lindsey, 2b	No. 1
8.	R.J. Alvarez, rhp	No. 4
9.	Mark Sappington, rhp	No. 5
10.	Alex Yarbrough, 2b	No. 8
11.	Kole Calhoun, of	Majors
12.	A.J. Schugel, rhp	No. 20
13.	Ryan Chaffee, rhp	Dropped out
14.	Eric Stamets, ss	No. 13
15.	Reid Scoggins, rhp	No. 30
16.	Yency Almonte, rhp	Dropped out
17.	Luis Jimenez, 3b	Dropped out
18.	Victor Alcantara, rhp	No. 15
19.	Jose Rondon, ss	No. 12
20.	Daniel Tillman, rhp	Dropped out
21.	Andrew Romine, ss	Majors
22.	Arjenis Fernandez, rhp	Dropped out
23.	Eduar Lopez, rhp	No. 24
24.	Travis Witherspoon, of	(Mariners)
25.	Ryan Brasier, rhp	No. 11
26.	Steve Geltz, rhp	(Rays)
27.	Drew Taylor, lhp	Dropped out
28.	Cam Bedrosian, rhp	No. 10
29.	Kevin Johnson, rhp	Dropped out
30.	Michael Roth, lhp	Dropped out

BEST TOOLS

Best Hitter for Average	Alex Yarbrough
Best Power Hitter	C.J. Cron
Best Strike-Zone Discipline	Cal Towey
Fastest Baserunner	Eric Stamets
Best Athlete	Eric Stamets
Best Fastball	Victor Alcantara
Best Curveball	Buddy Boshers
Best Slider	Mike Clevinger
Best Changeup	Mike Morin
Best Control	Mike Morin
Best Defensive Catcher	Jett Bandy
Best Defensive Infielder	Eric Stamets
Best Infield Arm	Kaleb Cowart
Best Defensive Outfielder	Chevy Clarke
Best Outfield Arm	Chevy Clarke

TOP 15 PLAYERS 25 AND UNDER

No.	Player, Pos. (Age)	Peak Level
1.	Mike Trout, of (22)	Majors
2.	Garrett Richards, rhp (25)	Majors
3.	Taylor Lindsey, 2b (23)	Double-A
4.	C.J. Cron, 1b (24)	Double-A
5.	Kaleb Cowart, 3b (21)	High Class A
6.	R.J. Alvarez, rhp (22)	High Class A
7.	Mark Sappington, rhp (23)	Double-A
8.	Hunter Green, lhp (18)	Rookie
9.	Ricardo Sanchez, rhp (16)	Did not play
10.	Alex Yarbrough, 2b (22)	High Class A
11.	Zach Borenstein, of (23)	High Class A
12.	Cam Bedrosian, rhp (22)	High Class A
13.	Jose Rondon, ss (20)	Rookie
14.	Eric Stamets, ss (22)	High Class A
15.	Mike Morin, rhp (22)	Double-A

MINOR LEAGUE DEPTH CHART

LOS ANGELES ANGELS

TOP 2014 ROOKIE: R.J. Alvarez, rhp. Alvarez is the best of the Angels' power bullpen arms, and the club isn't shy about rushing relievers.

BREAKOUT PROSPECT: Eduar Lopez, lhp. It's time for Lopez to make his U.S. debut. If he can add a changeup, he'll quickly become one of the club's top pitching prospects.

SLEEPER: Mike Monster, rhp. A one-time elite prospect from Canada who hasn't pitched in a couple of years, he showed a 95-97 mph fastball in a workout. He's a complete wild card.

SOURCE OF TOP 30 TALENT			
Homegrown	**30**	**Acquired**	**0**
College	13	Trades	0
Junior college	6	Rule 5 draft	0
High school	5	Independent leagues	0
Nondrafted free agents	0	Free agents/waivers	0
International	6		

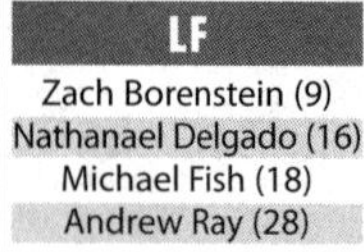

LF
Zach Borenstein (9)
Nathanael Delgado (16)
Michael Fish (18)
Andrew Ray (28)

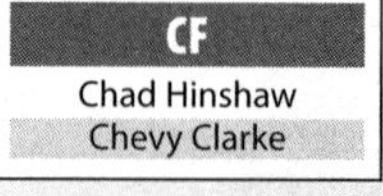

CF
Chad Hinshaw
Chevy Clarke

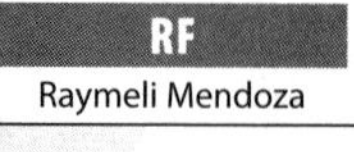

RF
Raymeli Mendoza

3B
Kaleb Cowart (3)
Cal Towey (19)

SS
Jose Rondon (12)
Eric Stamets (13)
Erick Salcedo (27)
Wendell Soto

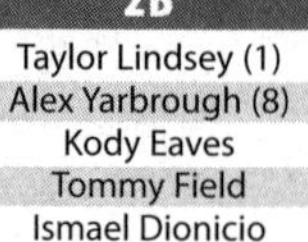

2B
Taylor Lindsey (1)
Alex Yarbrough (8)
Kody Eaves
Tommy Field
Ismael Dionicio

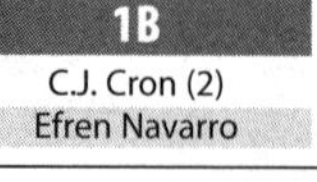

1B
C.J. Cron (2)
Efren Navarro

C
Jett Bandy (25)
Mario Martinez
Stephen McGee
Cambric Moye
Brad Guenther

LHP

LHSP	LHRP
Hunter Green (6)	Buddy Boshers (21)
Eduar Lopez (24)	Nick Maronde (22)
Nathanael Rodriguez	Michael Roth
Nate Smith	Kramer Sneed
Tyler DeLoach	Cole Swanson
Ryan Crowley	

RHP

RHSP	RHRP
Ricardo Sanchez (7)	R.J. Alvarez (4)
Keynan Middleton (26)	Mark Sappington (5)
Kyle McGowin (29)	Cam Bedrosian (10)
Matt Shoemaker	Ryan Brasier (11)
Elliot Morris	Mike Morin (14)
Garrett Nuss	Victor Alcantara (15)
	Mike Clevinger (17)
	A.J. Schugel (20)
	Joe Krehbiel (23)
	Reid Scoggins (30)
	Austin Wood
	Ryan Chaffee
	Mike Monster
	Austin Adams
	Josh Wall
	Cory Rasmus
	Arjenis Fernandez
	Harrison Cooney
	Yency Almonte
	Eduard Santos
	Daniel Tillman

2013 BONUSES: $2.6 MILLION

BEST PURE HITTER: 3B Cal Towey (17) has an excellent batting eye that gets him into lots of hitter's counts. He can drive the ball, but he's best at getting on base. He posted on-base percentages north of .400 in all three years at Baylor and led the minor leagues with an astronomical .492 on-base percentage last summer.

BEST POWER HITTER: OF Eric Aguilera (34) projects to have slightly above-average power eventually, thanks to an easy swing that creates leverage.

FASTEST RUNNER: OF Chad Hinshaw (15), a college teammate of Aguilera's at Illinois State, is an above-average runner with a knack for stealing bases. He was 33-for-37 as a college senior, then added nine in 10 tries with the Angels' Rookie-level Orem club.

BEST DEFENSIVE PLAYER: Hinshaw is still working on getting better reads and taking better routes, but his speed gives him a chance to be at least an average center fielder with an average arm.

BEST FASTBALL: RHPs Elliot Morris (4), Harrison Cooney (6) and Garrett Nuss (7) all sit in the 90-92 mph range, touching 95. Morris has the best life on his fastball, while Nuss and Cooney have better command.

BEST SECONDARY PITCH: LHP Nate Smith (8) throws an above-average changeup with conviction. He will use it at any point in the count and will double-up with it because of its effectiveness. RHP Trevor Foss (22) throws an above-average curveball at its best.

BEST PRO DEBUT: OF Michael Fish (32) hit .366/.422/.689 with nine home runs between stops in the Rookie-level Arizona League and Orem. Towey posted a .492 on-base percentage that was easily the best among Angels minor leaguers.

BEST ATHLETE: LHP Hunter Green (2) brings a lot of athleticism to the mound, as does RHP Keynan Middleton (3), who was a shooting guard at Lane (Ore.) CC in addition to playing baseball.

MOST INTRIGUING BACKGROUND: RHP Kyle McGowin (5) has an aunt who is Ty Cobb's granddaughter.

CLOSEST TO THE MAJORS: LHP Cole Swanson (19) was a late-round pick, but like Michael Roth from the Angels' 2012 draft class, he could move to the majors quickly because of his success in a specialized role. Swanson's short arm action, deceptive delivery and adequate 88-92 mph stuff should make it hard for lefties to square him up, although they posted a .941 OPS against him in his professional debut.

BEST LATE-ROUND PICK: Fish's tools won't wow scouts, but he can hit and he succeeds with a heady, all-out approach. The Angels will keep sending him up the ladder to see if he can continue his early success.

THE ONE WHO GOT AWAY: RHP Blake Goins (12) showed plus stuff at times leading up to the draft. The Angels would have been thrilled to add him to their long list of pitching draftees, but he headed to Texas instead.

ASSESSMENT: Los Angeles had a miniscule $3 million bonus pool. Scouting director Ric Wilson went for long-term pitching help.

2012 BONUSES: $2.3 MILLION

RHPs R.J. Alvarez (3) and Mark Sappington (5) have power arms destined for the bullpen. LHP Michael Roth (9) zipped to Anaheim but hasn't stuck. 2B Alex Yarbrough (4) can hit, but that may be it.

GRADE: C

2011 BONUSES: $3.3 MILLION

1B/DH C.J. Cron (1) can hit but is limited with the glove. LHP Nick Maronde (2) reached MLB quickly but also hasn't stuck.

GRADE: D

2010 BONUSES: $8.1 MILLION

The Angels squandered extra picks on prep OFs Chevy Clarke (1) and Ryan Bolden (1s). Top prospect Taylor Lindsey (1s), 3B Kaleb Cowart (1) and big league OF Kole Calhoun (8) may save the class yet.

GRADE: C

TOP DRAFT PICKS OF THE DECADE

Year	Player, Pos.	2013 Org.
2004	Jered Weaver, rhp	Angels
2005	Trevor Bell, rhp (1st round supp.)	Reds
2006	Hank Conger, c	Angels
2007	Jon Bachanov, rhp (1st round supp.)	Out of baseball
2008	Tyler Chatwood, rhp (2nd round)	Rockies
2009	Randal Grichuk, of	Angels
2010	Kaleb Cowart, 3b	Angels
2011	C.J. Cron, 1b	Angels
2012	R.J. Alvarez, rhp (3rd round)	Angels
2013	Hunter Green, lhp (2nd round)	Angels

LARGEST BONUSES IN CLUB HISTORY

Jered Weaver, 2004	$4,000,000
Kendrys Morales, 2004	$3,000,000
Kaleb Cowart, 2010	$2,300,000
Troy Glaus, 1997	$2,250,000
Joe Torres, 2000	$2,080,000

1 TAYLOR LINDSEY, 2B

Born: Dec. 2, 1991. **B-T:** L-R. **Ht.:** 6-0. **Wt:** 195. **Drafted:** HS—Scottsdale, Ariz., 2010 (1st round supplemental). **Signed by:** John Gracio.

When Eddie Bane was Angels scouting director, he was quite willing to buck consensus when he and his scouts believed in a player. It worked out well with Mark Trumbo, who signed for $1.425 million as an 18th-rounder out of high school in 2004, but not so well with players like outfielders Chevy Clarke and Ryan Bolden. The Angels liked Lindsey more than most clubs, taking him in the supplemental first round in the 2010 draft, in between Clarke and Bolden, and they signed him for $873,000 as the 37th overall pick. The fourth of Los Angeles' five picks before the second round that year, Lindsey so far has been best of the bunch. Clarke and Bolden have flamed out, while first-rounders Kaleb Cowart and Cam Bedrosian have struggled but remain prospects. Lindsey won Rookie-level Pioneer League MVP honors in 2011, and after a slow start in 2013, he rallied to hit .274/.339/.441 at Double-A Arkansas and finish fourth in the Texas League with 224 total bases.

Lindsey always has been a controversial prospect for some scouts because of his unconventional lefthanded swing. He uses a pronounced step to trigger his swing. He almost rests the bat on his shoulder as he begins his hand pump, bringing his front foot back into his body from his already narrow stance. As he reads the pitch, nearly all his weight rests on his back foot while his front foot hangs in the air. He then uncoils into the pitch. It's the kind of stance that should leave him caught leaning on offspeed pitches or behind fastballs, but Lindsey has quick enough hands and balance to make it work. Because the rhythm of his swing is so important, he will go through stretches where he looks lost at the plate, but those difficulties are matched by stretches where he's locked in and hitting everything. Lindsey can turn on any fastball, something he proved by pulling a 95 mph fastball from Carlos Martinez for a home run in late April. He will hit to the opposite field for singles, but his tick-below-average power is all to his pull side. His six triples and 17 home runs all went to right field. Defensively, Lindsey has improved significantly as a pro, especially at turning the double play, where his pivot has transformed from liability to asset. He makes up for a below-average arm by getting rid of the ball quickly. He has reliable hands, but his range will never be more than average. Lindsey is an average runner at best who doesn't hurt or help the club on the bases.

BA GRADE
55
MEDIUM

SCOUTING GRADES

BATTING	60
POWER	45
SPEED	50
DEFENSE	50
ARM	40

JOHN WILLIAMSON

Lindsey profiles as an offensive-oriented second baseman whose hitting ability makes up for any liabilities he brings to the field. He's headed to Triple-A Salt Lake in 2014 as a 22-year-old and could make big league incumbent Howie Kendrick, signed through 2015, trade bait.

Year	Club (League)	Class	AVG	G	AB	R	H	2B	3B	HR	RBI	BB	SO	SB	CS	OBP	SLG
2010	Angels (AZL)	R	.284	45	194	26	55	12	6	0	18	12	33	8	3	.325	.407
2011	Orem (PIO)	R	.362	63	290	64	105	28	6	9	46	13	46	10	4	.394	.593
2012	Inland Empire (CAL)	HiA	.289	134	547	79	158	26	6	9	58	29	66	8	6	.328	.408
2013	Arkansas (TL)	AA	.274	134	508	68	139	22	6	17	56	48	91	4	4	.339	.441
Minor League Totals			.297	376	1539	237	457	88	24	35	178	102	236	30	17	.344	.454

2 C.J. CRON, 1B

Born: Jan. 5, 1990. **B-T:** R-R. **Ht.:** 6-4. **Wt.:** 235. **Drafted:** Utah, 2011 (1st round). **Signed by:** John Gracio.

Some players are born to play baseball. C.J.'s father Chris reached the majors and has spent years as a minor league coach and manager, piloting Double-A Erie in the Tigers system in 2013. His younger brother Kevin, drafted by the Mariners out of high school in 2011, plays at Texas Christian. Cron's righthanded power potential made it a little easier for the Angels to consider trading Mark Trumbo. While he isn't the athlete Trumbo is, Cron has nearly as much raw pull power and the bat speed to catch up to fastballs. He never has walked much, but he also has the hand-eye coordination to make consistent hard contact. Scouts liked his aggressiveness in the Arizona Fall League, where he hit .413 to win the batting title. Cron has to hit, because his value is entirely tied to his bat. He's a below-average defender at first base. Cron is headed to Triple-A Salt Lake, and could reach Anaheim sometime in 2014.

Year	Club (League)	Class	AVG	G	AB	R	H	2B	3B	HR	RBI	BB	SO	SB	CS	OBP	SLG
2011	Orem (PIO)	R	.308	34	143	30	44	5	1	13	41	10	34	0	0	.371	.629
2012	Inland Empire (CAL)	HiA	.293	129	525	73	154	32	2	27	123	17	72	3	4	.327	.516
2013	Arkansas (TL)	AA	.274	134	519	56	142	36	1	14	83	23	83	8	4	.319	.428
Minor League Totals			.286	297	1187	159	340	73	4	54	247	50	189	11	8	.329	.491

3 KALEB COWART, 3B

Born: June 2, 1992. **B-T:** R-R. **Ht.:** 6-3. **Wt.:** 190. **Drafted:** HS—Adel, Ga., 2010 (1st round). **Signed by:** Chris McAlpin.

The Baseball America High School Player of the Year in 2010, Cowart was generally viewed as a better pitching prospect than hitter. But he wanted to hit, and the Angels signed him for $2.3 million as a third baseman. Cowart stumbled in 2013, when he was the fourth-youngest player in the Double-A Texas League when the season began. The switch-hitter completely lost the timing of his lefthanded swing in 2013, getting his foot down too early and leaving him with no real trigger for his load. Cowart's righthanded swing has fewer issues, but he needs more selectivity from both sides. His power disappeared in 2013, but he has above-average raw power if he straightens out his swing. Defensively, Cowart plays a good third base with a plus arm and good range. He will repeat Double-A Arkansas in 2014, which will determine if 2013 was merely a speed bump or his true level as a hitter.

Year	Club (League)	Class	AVG	G	AB	R	H	2B	3B	HR	RBI	BB	SO	SB	CS	OBP	SLG
2011	Orem (PIO)	R	.283	72	283	49	80	12	3	7	40	25	81	11	4	.345	.420
2012	Cedar Rapids (MWL)	LoA	.293	66	263	42	77	16	3	9	54	22	44	9	4	.348	.479
	Inland Empire (CAL)	HiA	.259	69	263	48	68	15	4	7	49	45	67	5	3	.366	.426
2013	Arkansas (TL)	AA	.221	132	498	48	110	20	1	6	42	38	124	14	5	.279	.301
Minor League Totals			.255	346	1333	188	340	63	11	30	192	131	324	39	16	.324	.386

4 R.J. ALVAREZ, RHP

Born: June 8, 1991. **B-T:** R-R. **Ht.:** 6-1. **Wt.:** 180. **Drafted:** Florida Atlantic, 2012 (3rd round). **Signed by:** Ralph Reyes.

The Angels have moved a number of future relievers to the rotation to get them additional innings. But in the case of Alvarez, they aren't messing with a good thing. He struggled to a 5.17 ERA in two years as a starter at Florida Atlantic, then took off as a reliever as a junior, posting a 0.53 ERA. Alvarez's approach suits a bullpen role, seeing as he dishes pure power from a high-effort delivery. The Angels worked to improve his direction to the plate in 2013. Alvarez throws a plus 93-99 mph fastball and now pairs it with a high-80s slider that flashes plus. The slider is a new addition, as it largely replaces a bigger overhand curveball that he struggled to throw for strikes. His violent delivery leads some scouts to see him as an injury risk, but he also has some of the best stuff in the system. Alvarez isn't too far away from being ready to help the Angels as a set-up man, and he could one day close.

Year	Club (League)	Class	W	L	ERA	G	GS	CG	SV	IP	H	HR	BB	SO	K/9	WHIP	AVG
2012	Cedar Rapids (MWL)	LoA	3	2	3.29	23	0	0	0	27	22	2	11	38	12.5	1.21	.216
2013	Inland Empire (CAL)	HiA	4	2	2.96	37	2	0	4	49	34	2	27	79	14.6	1.25	.191
Minor League Totals			7	4	3.08	60	2	0	4	76	56	4	38	117	13.9	1.24	.200

5 MARK SAPPINGTON, RHP

BA GRADE 45 MEDIUM

Born: Nov. 17, 1990. **B-T:** R-R. **Ht.:** 6-5. **Wt.:** 209. **Drafted:** Rockhurst (Mo.), 2012 (5th round). **Signed by:** Joel Murrie.

Sappington entered pro ball with no real feel for a changeup, but after graduating from Wise University, it's now his second-best pitch. Ex-big league righthander Matt Wise teaches the changeup to Angels prospects in the Rookie-level Arizona League. Sappington's main weapon, however, remains his plus fastball, which sits 92-95 mph and will touch 97. His two-seamer has good movement and excellent sink, but he struggles to locate it, so he relies primarily on a four-seamer. Sappington's changeup has turned into an average pitch that flashes plus, and he kept lefthanders at bay in 2013. Sappington's biggest problem is a somewhat-rotational delivery. He struggles with flying open too early, which hinders his control and causes him to overthrow. The delivery and breaking ball issues may conspire to send Sappington to the bullpen long-term, but the Angels will keep him in the Double-A rotation in 2014.

Year	Club (League)	Class	W	L	ERA	G	GS	CG	SV	IP	H	HR	BB	SO	K/9	WHIP	AVG
2012	Orem (PIO)	R	1	1	5.15	15	12	0	0	37	31	3	16	34	8.3	1.28	.231
2013	Inland Empire (CAL)	HiA	11	4	3.38	22	22	0	0	131	103	10	62	110	7.6	1.26	.220
	Arkansas (TL)	AA	1	1	3.86	5	5	0	0	26	23	1	20	26	9.1	1.68	.240
Minor League Totals			13	6	3.78	42	39	0	0	193	157	14	98	170	7.9	1.32	.225

6 HUNTER GREEN, LHP

BILL MITCHELL

BA GRADE 50 EXTREME

Born: July 12, 1995. **B-T:** L-L. **Ht.:** 6-4. **Wt.:** 175. **Drafted:** HS—Bowling Green, Ky., 2013 (2nd round). **Signed by:** John Burden.

One of the youngest players in the 2013 draft, Green dominated as a senior at Warren East High, going 3-1, 0.14 with 110 strikeouts in 52 innings. He allowed an earned run in his first start, then didn't allow another in nine more appearances. Projected as a potential late first-rounder, Green fell to the Angels at their first pick, No. 59 overall in the second round. He signed for $942,000. Green has an easy delivery and it looks like he's playing catch at 90-93 mph, but he struggles to maintain his arm slot. As he tires, he starts dropping his arm lower from its low-three-quarters position, which leads to bouts of wildness. Green walked a high number of batters in high school, and that carried over to his pro debut in the Rookie-level Arizona League. His arm angle gives him excellent arm-side run on his fastball. Green could begin 2014 in extended spring training before embarking on an assignment to low Class A Burlington.

Year	Club (League)	Class	W	L	ERA	G	GS	CG	SV	IP	H	HR	BB	SO	K/9	WHIP	AVG
2013	Angels (AZL)	R	0	1	4.32	8	7	0	0	17	16	0	16	11	5.9	1.92	.254
Minor League Totals			0	1	4.32	8	7	0	0	17	16	0	16	11	5.9	1.92	.254

7 RICARDO SANCHEZ, LHP

BILL MITCHELL

BA GRADE 50 EXTREME

Born: April 11, 1997. **B-T:** L-L. **Ht.:** 5-10. **Wt.:** 160. **Signed:** Venezuela, 2013. **Signed By:** Lebi Ochoa/Carlos Ramirez.

While many pitchers signed out of the Dominican Republic are scouted largely on the basis of workouts, the Angels in 2013 had a chance to see how Sanchez, a Venezuela native, handles the pressure of a game. Pitching in the gold-medal game of the 15U World Championship, Sanchez held Cuba to two runs in seven innings to pick up the win. Signed by the Angels for $580,000—more than a quarter of the club's international signing allotment for 2013—he immediately becomes one of the club's top pitching prospects. In a system full of future relievers, Sanchez stands out for his feel, delivery and easy arm action. Like most 16-year-olds, his curveball is erratic, but it flashes plus. Sanchez will have to prove he can keep his delivery under control. He and 2013 top pick Hunter Green are key cogs to improving the farm system as pitchers with starter traits. Sanchez is advanced enough to possibly jump straight to the Rookie-level Arizona League in 2014.

Year	Club (League)	Class	W	L	ERA	G	GS	CG	SV	IP	H	HR	BB	SO	K/9	WHIP	AVG
2013	Did not play—Signed 2014 contract																

8 ALEX YARBROUGH, 2B

Born: Aug. 3, 1991. **B-T:** B-R. **Ht.:** 5-11. **Wt.:** 180. **Drafted:** Mississippi, 2012 (4th round). **Signed by:** J.T. Zink.

A first-team All-American in 2012 at Mississippi, where he hit .380 while committing just three errors as a junior, Yarbrough has been similarly productive as a pro, hitting .313 in 2013 while leading high Class A California League second basemen in fielding percentage. He's a natural switch-hitter who has been hitting from both sides since he was nine, showing nearly identical swings. Yarbrough has excellent barrel control, which allows him to hit comfortably at any point in the count. He can spoil pitches when he's working with two strikes, but he too often swings until he puts the ball in play rather than taking ball four. Yarbrough's hitting ability is his only plus tool. He's unlikely to hit more than 10 home runs a year in the big leagues. Defensively, he's sure-handed but below-average at second, lacking fluid actions and range. He has a below-average arm that's challenged even at second. He's aggressive on the bases and picks his spots well, which allows him to swipe bases even though he's a below-average runner. Yarbrough edges C.J. Cron as the best pure hitter in the organization, and he exceeds expectations because he gets the most out of his tools. He only profiles as a regular if he can handle second base, because he isn't athletic enough to be a utility man. Yarbrough will move up to Double-A Arkansas in 2014.

Year	Club (League)	Class	AVG	G	AB	R	H	2B	3B	HR	RBI	BB	SO	SB	CS	OBP	SLG
2012	Cedar Rapids (MWL)	LoA	.287	58	244	35	70	12	9	0	27	10	20	9	2	.320	.410
	Arkansas (TL)	AA	.111	5	18	1	2	1	0	0	0	0	3	0	0	.111	.167
2013	Inland Empire (CAL)	HiA	.313	136	582	77	182	32	10	11	80	27	106	14	4	.341	.459
Minor League Totals			.301	199	844	113	254	45	19	11	107	37	129	23	6	.331	.438

9 ZACH BORENSTEIN, OF

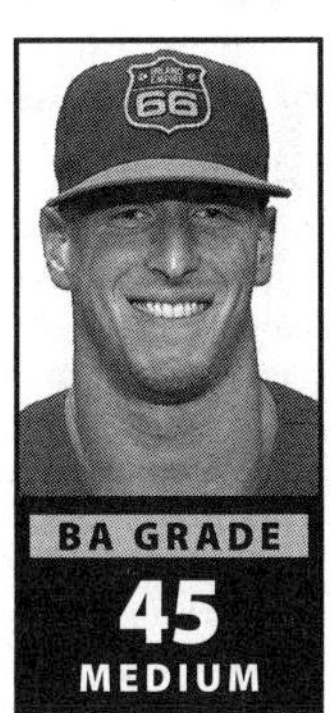

Born: July 23, 1990. **B-T:** L-R. **Ht.:** 6-0. **Wt.:** 205. **Drafted:** Eastern Illinois, 2011 (23rd round). **Signed by:** Joel Murrie.

Borenstein played first, second and third base as well as outfield in college while batting .362 over three seasons at Eastern Illinois. Throughout his travels around the diamond, his best position was in the batter's box. That's proven true as a pro as well. He led the high Class A California League in batting (.337), home runs (28) and slugging percentage (.631) in 2013 despite missing a month with a hip flexor injury. He also sang an excellent rendition of the national anthem before an Inland Empire game in the final weeks of the season. Borenstein has a very valuable carrying tool in that he's a lefthanded hitter with plus power potential. He hits from an open stance, though he has straightened up more when he plants his front foot, giving him plate coverage on the outer half he once lacked. Observers knock his swing's uppercut path. Borenstein has solid bat speed and quick hands but sometimes appears to be guessing, leading to some bad swings. Some Cal League managers also felt he could be beaten by premium velocity. A modest athlete, Borenstein is a below-average runner and thrower who is playable in left field. He heads into 2014 trying to prove he's not just a Cal League creation, and his 6-for-44 (.136) showing in the Arizona Fall League didn't help. The Angels' lack of outfield depth gives Borenstein a chance to move quickly, so it's not out of the realm of possibility that he could spend significant time at Triple-A Salt Lake in 2014.

Year	Club (League)	Class	AVG	G	AB	R	H	2B	3B	HR	RBI	BB	SO	SB	CS	OBP	SLG
2011	Angels (AZL)	R	.274	31	113	21	31	6	4	2	21	17	21	12	1	.397	.451
2012	Cedar Rapids (MWL)	LoA	.266	79	293	42	78	25	3	11	50	27	60	13	5	.339	.485
2013	Inland Empire (CAL)	HiA	.337	112	407	76	137	22	7	28	95	43	88	5	5	.403	.631
Minor League Totals			.303	222	813	139	246	53	14	41	166	87	169	30	11	.380	.554

10 CAM BEDROSIAN, RHP

Born: Oct. 2, 1991. **B-T:** R-R. **Ht.:** 6-0. **Wt.** 205. **Drafted:** HS—Sharpsburg, Ga., 2010 (1st round). **Signed by:** Chris McAlpin.

The son of 1987 Cy Young Award-winning closer Steve Bedrosian, Cam found that he also is a better fit in the bullpen. Signed for $1.116 million as a 2010 first-rounder, Bedrosian initially saw work as a starter, but he blew out his elbow just 12 innings into his pro career. After a 2011 season lost recovering from Tommy John surgery, he nibbled his way through an unimpressive year as a starter in low Class A Cedar Rapids in 2012 and gave up 14 runs in five innings over his first two starts in 2013. Mercifully, the Angels shifted him to the pen, scrapped his loopy curveball, de-emphasized his changeup and told him adopt a power approach, using his fastball and the power slider he threw in high school. Bedrosian's velocity picked back up from the high 80s to where he was once again a 92-95 mph pitcher with flashes of an average slider. He'll mix in a below-average changeup every now and then against lefthanders. He still doesn't locate as well as he needs to, and scouts think he nibbles too much, but he had a 3.28 ERA and 4.0 SO/BB ratio out of the bullpen at high Class A Inland Empire in 2013. Bedrosian finished with a strong effort in the Arizona Fall League. He's ready for a return to the Cal League in 2014, with a shot at making it to Double-A Arkansas.

Year	Club (League)	Class	W	L	ERA	G	GS	CG	SV	IP	H	HR	BB	SO	K/9	WHIP	AVG
2010	Angels (AZL)	R	0	2	4.50	5	4	0	0	12	13	0	7	10	7.5	1.67	.283
2011	Did not play—Injured																
2012	Cedar Rapids (MWL)	LoA	3	11	6.31	21	21	0	0	83	91	5	52	48	5.2	1.73	.286
2013	Burlington (MWL)	LoA	1	5	5.30	37	2	0	7	54	55	4	22	69	11.4	1.42	.258
	Inland Empire (CAL)	HiA	0	0	0.00	7	0	0	0	9	4	0	7	9	9.3	1.27	.143
Minor League Totals			4	18	5.48	70	27	0	7	158	163	9	88	136	7.8	1.59	.269

11 RYAN BRASIER, RHP

BA GRADE
45
HIGH

Born: Aug. 26, 1987. **B-T:** R-R. **Ht.:** 6-0. **Wt.:** 205. **Drafted:** Weatherford (Texas) JC, 2007 (6th round). **Signed by:** Arnold Brathwaite.

It's been a slow climb for Brasier, a high school catcher turned junior college pitcher who joined the system in 2007, when Bill Stoneman was still the general manager. He entered the system as a reliever but moved to a starting role in 2009 to see if he would develop his secondary pitches. Even though Brasier threw a no-hitter in 2010, the move to the rotation never really took, and his secondary stuff didn't get much better. But he did make the big leagues for the first time in 2013. Brasier's success is based on his 93-97 mph four-seam fastball, a true 70 pitch that seems to take off as it nears the plate. He throws a fringy 86-88 mph slider that is better as a surprise pitch early in the count than something he can use to generate a strikeout with two strikes. He'll also throw a below-average changeup to lefthanders every now and then. Brasier has never dominated, but his double-plus fastball makes him a potentially useful low-leverage reliever. He'll head to spring training with a shot at the big league bullpen.

Year	Club (League)	Class	W	L	ERA	G	GS	CG	SV	IP	H	HR	BB	SO	K/9	WHIP	AVG
2007	Orem (PIO)	R	1	2	2.08	26	0	0	9	30	22	2	7	26	7.7	0.96	.212
2008	Cedar Rapids (MWL)	LoA	1	3	1.59	23	0	0	9	28	22	0	14	24	7.6	1.27	.210
	Angels (AZL)	R	1	0	3.86	4	0	0	1	5	3	0	1	2	3.9	0.86	.188
	R. Cucamonga (CAL)	HiA	0	0	2.70	3	0	0	1	3	3	0	2	0	0.0	1.50	.300
2009	Arkansas (TL)	AA	2	1	5.56	8	0	0	2	11	13	1	7	6	4.8	1.76	.283
	R. Cucamonga (CAL)	HiA	5	4	5.23	27	14	0	0	98	103	17	32	93	8.5	1.38	.270
2010	Arkansas (TL)	AA	7	12	5.07	28	23	1	0	142	127	28	68	94	6.0	1.37	.242
2011	Arkansas (TL)	AA	0	1	0.71	25	0	0	16	25	18	1	14	26	9.2	1.26	.198
	Salt Lake (PCL)	AAA	2	1	5.00	25	0	0	3	27	26	2	9	26	8.7	1.30	.257
2012	Salt Lake (PCL)	AAA	7	3	4.37	55	0	0	13	60	66	1	24	54	8.1	1.51	.286
2013	Salt Lake (PCL)	AAA	5	2	4.13	38	0	0	10	57	69	6	16	57	9.1	1.50	.295
	Los Angeles (AL)	MAJ	0	0	2.00	7	0	0	0	9	7	1	4	7	7.0	1.22	.233
Major League Totals			0	0	2.00	7	0	0	0	9	7	1	4	7	7.0	1.22	.233
Minor League Totals			31	29	4.27	262	37	1	64	487	472	58	194	408	7.5	1.37	.256

12 JOSE RONDON, SS

Born: March 3, 1994. **B-T:** R-R. **Ht.:** 6-1. **Wt.:** 185. **Signed:** Venezuela, 2011. **Signed by:** Lebi Ochoa/Carlos Ramirez.

Rondon was an athletic 16-year-old with a skinny frame when the Angels signed him for $70,000 in 2011. Due to natural maturation, plus plenty of work in the weight room, he has added nearly 25 pounds since he signed, which has paid off with line drives that carry farther, though he still has 20 power on the 20-80 scouting scale at this point. While Eric Stamets is the best defensive shortstop in the system, Rondon gives the club a more well-rounded shortstop, albeit one with less defensive ability. He has excellent bat-to-ball skills and a very workable, simple stroke with a good swing path. He was the fifth-toughest player in the Rookie-level Pioneer League to strike out in 2013. Rondon has walked more than he has struck out in two of his three pro seasons, which could serve him well as a top-of-the-order hitter. He's a tick-above-average runner, though he has yet to show he can pick his spots to steal. Rondon has a solid-average arm and makes the routine play at shortstop very reliably—he led the PL with a .955 fielding percentage—but he lacks ideal first-step quickness for the position. That might force a move to second base or more of a utility role. He's ready for low Class A Burlington in 2014.

Year	Club (League)	Class	AVG	G	AB	R	H	2B	3B	HR	RBI	BB	SO	SB	CS	OBP	SLG
2011	Angels (DSL)	R	.315	49	165	28	52	11	2	0	21	17	16	9	4	.378	.406
2012	Angels (AZL)	R	.260	48	192	26	50	13	2	1	20	14	24	5	5	.314	.365
	Orem (PIO)	R	.300	6	20	4	6	1	1	0	1	2	3	1	0	.348	.450
2013	Orem (PIO)	R	.293	68	276	45	81	22	2	1	50	30	31	13	8	.359	.399
Minor League Totals			.289	171	653	103	189	47	7	2	92	63	74	28	17	.351	.392

13 ERIC STAMETS, SS

BA GRADE
40
LOW

Born: Sept. 25, 1991. **B-R:** R-R. **Ht.:** 6-0. **Wt.:** 185. **Drafted:** Evansville, 2012 (6th round). **Signed by:** John Burden.

The rare glove-first, speedy, athletic shortstop out of college, Stamets made the Cape Cod League all-star team in 2011 and set the Evansville record for assists in a single season as well as the school's single-season stolen base record. He was the highest-drafted Purple Aces hitter in 24 years, yet because hitting is Stamets' weakest tool, he lasted until the sixth round of the 2012 draft. Scouts always have had skepticism about his bat, with 20 power and a swing that leaves him largely cut off from his lower half. While he makes plenty of contact, it's rarely hard contact. His best offensive attribute is 70 speed, which he needs to put to use more as a basestealer instead of just turning infield outs into hits. His defensive strengths include excellent hands, easy lateral movement and the requisite arm strength to make the play in the hole. Stamets projects at best as a bottom-of-the-order hitter whose defense and speed help cover for his deficiencies with the bat. More likely, he's a useful utility infielder whose bat falls well short of acceptable for a regular. He'll continue to team with second baseman Alex Yarbrough at Double-A Arkansas in 2014.

Year	Club (League)	Class	AVG	G	AB	R	H	2B	3B	HR	RBI	BB	SO	SB	CS	OBP	SLG
2012	Cedar Rapids (MWL)	LoA	.274	62	248	34	68	13	1	1	20	15	35	7	2	.323	.347
2013	Inland Empire (CAL)	HiA	.281	126	506	80	142	28	4	4	53	34	66	16	4	.335	.375
Minor League Totals			.279	188	754	114	210	41	5	5	73	49	101	23	6	.331	.366

14 MIKE MORIN, RHP

Born: May 3, 1991. **B-T:** R-R. **Ht.:** 6-4. **Wt.:** 175. **Drafted:** North Carolina, 2012 (13th round). **Signed by:** Brandon McArthur.

Morin appeared to be destined for success when he was named the top prospect in the summer-college MINK League the summer before he began his North Carolina career. He lived up to those expectations by setting a UNC and Atlantic Coast Conference single-season saves record with 19 as a junior. Morin added 27 more in just a season and a half as a pro, reaching Double-A Arkansas for the second half of 2013. When batters dig in against him, they have a pretty good idea of what's coming. But knowing Morin's changeup is coming is not the same as being able to hit it. His plus changeup is essentially two different pitches, as he can make it break away from both lefthanders and righthanders depending on how he cuts it or lets it run. In 2013, he started to do a better job of throwing his below-average slider as a surprise pitch early in counts. Morin's 90-94 mph fastball has enough velocity, but it's his ability to throw strikes—he doles out a walk or two per month—that makes it even better. The combination of Morin's plus changeup, average fastball and excellent location should be enough to carve out a useful career as a late-inning reliever, and his competitiveness means he might end up exceeding expectations.

Year	Club (League)	Class	W	L	ERA	G	GS	CG	SV	IP	H	HR	BB	SO	K/9	WHIP	AVG
2012	Orem (PIO)	R	2	2	4.93	24	0	0	4	35	34	2	14	29	7.5	1.38	.262
2013	Inland Empire (CAL)	HiA	3	1	1.85	30	0	0	13	39	30	2	5	43	9.9	0.90	.221
	Arkansas (TL)	AA	0	2	2.03	26	0	0	10	31	26	2	5	33	9.6	1.00	.230
Minor League Totals			5	5	2.92	80	0	0	27	105	90	6	24	105	9.0	1.09	.237

15 VICTOR ALCANTARA, RHP

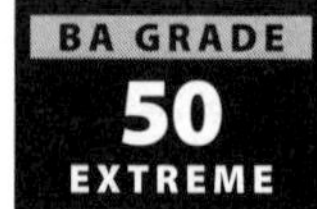

Born: April 3, 1993. **B-T:** R-R. **Ht.:** 6-2. **Wt.:** 188. **Signed:** Dominican Republic, 2011. **Signed by:** Roman Ocumarez.

With Alcantara, catchers don't yet know what they're going to get from pitch to pitch. He may bounce a fastball and follow it with another that forces the catcher to come out of his crouch to nab it. But in those instances where Alcantara delivers his pitch with proper tempo through his delivery, he has some of the best stuff in the organization. He tends to rush his motion, forcing his arm to try to catch up to his delivery. At other times, he'll stay back on the rubber too long, with his arm racing off ahead of his weight transfer. When he's in sync, Alcantara will run his fastball anywhere from 94-97 mph, and he's touched 100. His below-average slider is improving, and at it's best it's a tight pitch with late tilt that flashes average. Long-term, Alcantara projects as a late-inning power reliever, but he'll likely remain in the rotation for a while to get innings. He'll have to earn a full-season assignment in 2014 with a strong spring training.

Year	Club (League)	Class	W	L	ERA	G	GS	CG	SV	IP	H	HR	BB	SO	K/9	WHIP	AVG
2012	Angels (DSL)	R	5	4	2.13	14	14	0	0	72	51	0	40	77	9.6	1.26	.199
2013	Orem (PIO)	R	2	5	7.47	17	12	0	0	59	73	10	35	48	7.3	1.83	.304
Minor League Totals			7	9	4.53	31	26	0	0	131	124	10	75	125	8.6	1.52	.250

16 NATANAEL DELGADO, OF

BA GRADE
50
EXTREME

Born: Oct. 23, 1995. **B-T:** L-L. **Ht.:** 6-1. **Wt.:** 170. **Signed:** Dominican Republic, 2012. **Signed by:** Roman Ocumarez.

A good scout can project, but it's hard to say with any certainty what a 16-year-old's body will look like once he has grown up. In Delgado's case, he's turned from a skinny right fielder to a thicker left fielder, but he still looks like the Angels could get a return on their $280,000 investment. The switch from right to left has happened because, while he's gotten physically stronger, Delgado's arm has gotten weaker. What once was a plus arm now grades average. He's a below-average runner who runs better once he gets going. The added weight and strength has paid off at the plate however, as Delgado's power has developed to go with an advanced approach and strong lefthanded swing that attracted the Angels. He shows pull power, and he's just as comfortable lining balls to the opposite-field power alley. Delgado has a simple stroke and good balance at the plate. He's advanced enough to compete for an assignment at low Class A Burlington for 2014.

Year	Club (League)	Class	AVG	G	AB	R	H	2B	3B	HR	RBI	BB	SO	SB	CS	OBP	SLG
2013	Angels (AZL)	R	.271	51	192	23	52	16	2	3	33	11	43	4	0	.311	.422
Minor League Totals			.271	51	192	23	52	16	2	3	33	11	43	4	0	.311	.422

17 MIKE CLEVINGER, RHP

Born: Dec. 21, 1990. **B-T:** R-R. **Ht.:** 6-2. **Wt.** 202. **Drafted:** Seminole State (Fla.) JC, 2011 (4th round). **Signed by:** Tom Kotchman.

The Angels mined Florida junior colleges successfully for years—see Pat Corbin, Howie Kendrick and Will Smith, among others—and Clevinger could be the latest. He also might be the last, now that Tom Kotchman, signing scout for the aforementioned trio, has left the organization to work for the Red Sox. Clevinger had emerged as the top starter prospect in the Angels system before he went down with an elbow injury in 2012 that required Tommy John surgery. He returned to the mound late in 2013 and remains one of the system's few prospective starters. Clevinger has shown four potential average pitches with a 91-93 mph fastball and potentially solid-average changeup, curveball and slider. He also has shown the ability to cut his fastball. Clevinger's control was shaky in his brief return to the mound in 2013 in part because he struggled to repeat his landing point as he struggled to stay direct to the plate. His delivery has some effort to it, leading some scouts to see him as a future reliever, but in a system in need of starters, he'll get every chance to remain in the rotation. He should get a second try at the low Class A Midwest League in 2014.

Year	Club (League)	Class	W	L	ERA	G	GS	CG	SV	IP	H	HR	BB	SO	K/9	WHIP	AVG
2011	Orem (PIO)	R	0	0	2.25	3	0	0	0	4	3	0	2	5	11.3	1.25	.200
2012	Cedar Rapids (MWL)	LoA	1	1	3.73	8	8	0	0	41	37	3	13	34	7.5	1.22	.243
2013	Angels (AZL)	R	0	0	3.00	2	2	0	0	3	2	0	2	3	9.0	1.33	.200
	Orem (PIO)	R	0	1	16.88	1	1	0	0	3	6	0	2	2	6.8	3.00	.429
Minor League Totals			1	2	4.26	14	11	0	0	51	48	3	19	44	7.8	1.32	.251

18 MIKE FISH, OF

Born: Jan. 3, 1991. **B-T:** R-R. **Ht:** 6-1. **Wt.:** 190. **Drafted:** Siena, 2013 (32nd round). **Signed by:** Nick Gorneault.

Two of the Angels' all-time best players are outfielders Tim Salmon and Mike Trout, so the organization is perhaps the perfect landing spot for a player named Fish. Few 2013 draft picks had a better pro debut than Fish, an unheralded senior sign out of Siena. The Metro Atlantic Athletic Conference player of the year, he hit a home run every 18 at-bats in Rookie ball, hitting nine despite missing time with a hamstring injury. Fish looks like a grinder but has solid tools, beginning with tick-above-average speed and solid-average arm strength. He's also average defensively in left field and doesn't look completely overmatched at his college position of center field, making a few highlight plays. In fact, two such attempts set Fish back in college. He tore the labrum in his right shoulder as a sophomore and broke his left wrist as a junior, both times while trying to make circus catches. He has quick hands and does a decent job of recognizing breaking balls. Fish will have to prove that his success is more than just an experienced player taking advantage of younger pitchers, but he'll get that chance at low Class A Burlington in 2014.

Year	Club (League)	Class	AVG	G	AB	R	H	2B	3B	HR	RBI	BB	SO	SB	CS	OBP	SLG
2013	Angels (AZL)	R	.409	20	66	19	27	10	2	2	9	5	14	6	0	.451	.712
	Orem (PIO)	R	.337	26	98	27	33	8	2	7	33	7	16	1	2	.404	.673
Minor League Totals			.366	46	164	46	60	18	4	9	42	12	30	7	2	.422	.689

19 CAL TOWEY, 3B/C

BA GRADE
45
HIGH

Born: Feb. 6, 1990. **B-T:** L-R. **Ht.:** 6-1. **Wt.:** 215. **Drafted:** Baylor, 2013 (17th round). **Signed by:** Rudy Vasquez.

A four-year starter at Baylor, Towey was a solid college player, hitting .287 with 17 homers while striking out more than he walked and earning first-team all-Big 12 Conference honors as a senior. Facing younger, less experienced pitchers in his pro debut at Rookie-level Orem, Towey was the toughest out in the Pioneer League, leading domestic professional leagues in on-base percentage (.492). The son of an ex-pro pitcher who also coached him in high school, Towey uses a gap-to-gap approach from the left side that should allow him to continue to hit for average as he climbs the ladder. The Angels are interested to see how Towey looks behind the plate, and will experiment with him catching in 2014. His arm should be at least adequate, with a short, clean stroke and good hands. He has limited range at third base and iffy hands. He made 17 errors in 53 games for an ugly .899 fielding percentage. He's also played left field, but he's a below-average runner. Towey's bat profiles much better if he can handle catching. Offensively, he could be ready for high Class A Inland Empire, but if he's catching, he'll move more slowly.

Year	Club (League)	Class	AVG	G	AB	R	H	2B	3B	HR	RBI	BB	SO	SB	CS	OBP	SLG
2013	Orem (PIO)	R	.317	70	230	69	73	16	6	8	53	67	59	13	3	.492	.543
Minor League Totals			.317	70	230	69	73	16	6	8	53	67	59	13	3	.492	.543

20 A.J. SCHUGEL, RHP

BA GRADE
40
MEDIUM

Born: June 27, 1989. **B-T:** R-R. **Ht.:** 6-1. **Wt.:** 190. **Drafted:** Central Arizona JC, 2010 (25th round). **Signed by:** John Gracio.

The Angels have a history of taking talented arms who spent more time as position players as amateurs and converting them to full-time pitchers. The son of Angels major league scout Jeff Schugel, A.J. was a prime example. He played the infield almost exclusively at Central Arizona JC but hasn't picked up a bat since being selected in the 25th round in 2010. One of the system's standouts in 2012, Schugel struggled mightily in a jump to Triple-A Salt Lake in 2013. He primarily works with a 90-92 mph fastball with good sink and a solid-average changeup. He still is working to improve his slurvy curveball. It's generally only effective as a get-me-over surprise pitch early in counts, but he needs to do a better job of burying it later in counts for swings and misses. Because of the lack of a consistent breaking ball, righthanders feasted on Schugel's fastball, and he allowed righthanders to hit .370/.415/.579 in 2013. Schugel throws from a crossfire delivery that generally has added deception, but he fooled no one in the Pacific Coast League. Shut down with a toe injury in July, Schugel should be fine for spring training. He has started in the minors, but he projects more as a sixth- or seventh-inning reliever if he can improve his breaking ball.

Year	Club (League)	Class	W	L	ERA	G	GS	CG	SV	IP	H	HR	BB	SO	K/9	WHIP	AVG
2010	Angels (AZL)	R	0	0	1.72	11	0	0	2	16	15	0	5	12	6.9	1.28	.259
	Orem (PIO)	R	2	2	8.59	6	0	0	1	7	8	0	6	9	11.0	1.91	.267
2011	Cedar Rapids (MWL)	LoA	4	3	2.59	25	12	0	1	90	73	2	39	80	8.0	1.24	.220
	Inland Empire (CAL)	HiA	1	2	5.03	4	4	0	0	20	22	1	6	15	6.9	1.42	.278
2012	Arkansas (TL)	AA	6	8	2.89	27	27	0	0	140	117	9	55	109	7.0	1.23	.232
2013	Salt Lake (PCL)	AAA	4	6	7.05	19	19	0	0	89	121	12	33	76	7.7	1.72	.324
Minor League Totals			17	21	4.02	92	62	0	4	363	356	24	144	301	7.5	1.38	.259

21 BUDDY BOSHERS, LHP

BA GRADE 40 MEDIUM

Born: May 9, 1988. **B-T:** L-L. **Ht.:** 6-3. **Wt.:** 205. **Drafted:** Calhoun (Ala.) CC, 2008 (4th round). **Signed by:** Jim Bryant.

If Boshers winds up as the second-best reliever from his high school team, he'll be doing well. That's because he was teammates with Braves closer Craig Kimbrel at Lee High in Huntsville, Ala. In 2013, Boshers joined Kimbrel in the big leagues on Aug. 10. The Angels don't have a lot of immediate help coming up from the system, but when it comes to lefthanded relievers, a trio of arms might be battling for one job. Boshers, Nick Maronde and Michael Roth all bring different strengths to the table, with Boshers featuring the best curveball of the trio. He also had the most success in the majors, albeit in a limited stint. His stuff improved a tick in 2013, as his fastball improved from being an average 88-91 mph offering to a more lethal 91-94 pitch. He falls in love with his plus breaking ball, though, and often doesn't throw his fastball enough. Boshers' long-armed delivery inhibits his below-average control and likely will limit his upside, but it also adds to his deception, limiting him to a likely role as second lefty out of the pen. He may be ready to do that at some point in 2014.

Year	Club (League)	Class	W	L	ERA	G	GS	CG	SV	IP	H	HR	BB	SO	K/9	WHIP	AVG
2008	Orem (PIO)	R	5	0	2.68	13	12	0	0	50	43	1	22	43	7.7	1.29	.221
2009	Salt Lake (PCL)	AAA	0	0	0.00	2	0	0	0	1	1	0	0	1	6.8	0.75	.200
	Orem (PIO)	R	2	1	2.55	5	5	0	0	25	24	2	8	23	8.4	1.30	.247
	Cedar Rapids (MWL)	LoA	3	1	5.97	6	6	1	0	32	31	5	7	27	7.7	1.20	.254
2010	Cedar Rapids (MWL)	LoA	3	0	4.31	36	7	1	0	77	84	5	20	75	8.7	1.34	.270
2011	Inland Empire (CAL)	HiA	2	5	4.30	43	4	0	1	75	88	7	41	61	7.3	1.71	.299
2012	Inland Empire (CAL)	HiA	4	2	2.52	26	0	0	1	39	30	4	16	48	11.0	1.17	.201
	Arkansas (TL)	AA	1	0	3.75	19	0	0	0	24	28	3	5	27	10.1	1.38	.292
2013	Arkansas (TL)	AA	3	2	3.14	28	0	0	1	29	20	1	13	35	11.0	1.15	.196
	Salt Lake (PCL)	AAA	1	0	3.66	16	0	0	1	20	18	1	12	26	11.9	1.53	.247
	Los Angeles (AL)	MAJ	0	0	4.70	25	0	0	0	15	13	0	8	13	7.6	1.37	.241
Major League Totals			0	0	4.70	25	0	0	0	15	13	0	8	13	7.6	1.37	.241
Minor League Totals			24	11	3.75	194	34	2	4	372	367	29	144	366	8.8	1.37	.254

22 NICK MARONDE, LHP

BA GRADE 40 MEDIUM

Born: Sept. 5, 1989. **B-T:** B-L. **Ht.:** 6-3. **Wt.:** 205. **Drafted:** Florida, 2011 (3rd round). **Signed by:** Tom Kotchman.

A little success might have been the worst thing to happen to Maronde, who made it to the big leagues in 2012, his first full pro season after being a third-rounder in 2011. He didn't look out of place in the Angels bullpen, so the club toyed with the idea of developing him as a starter. They abandoned the idea before the 2013 season began, however, because the bullpen clearly meshed with Maronde's temperament. He didn't use the same aggressive approach that had suited him in 2012. He's better off letting it rip early in counts with an above-average, 91-94 mph fastball. Nibbling too often left Maronde behind in counts, leading to situations where hitters could sit on his fastball or draw a walk. He reshaped his inconsistent slider in 2013. It doesn't have as much depth, but it's a harder pitch with late tilt. As a reliever, Maronde's fringy straight changeup is the secondary pitch he uses almost exclusively against righthanders to give them something to worry about on the outer half of the plate. His control problems—he walked 5.9 batters per nine innings at Double-A Arkansas in 2013—leave him at least a step away from the big leagues, probably at Triple-A Salt Lake to begin 2014.

Year	Club (League)	Class	W	L	ERA	G	GS	CG	SV	IP	H	HR	BB	SO	K/9	WHIP	AVG
2011	Orem (PIO)	R	5	0	2.14	11	11	0	0	46	36	5	15	50	9.7	1.10	.217
2012	Angels (AZL)	R	0	1	1.13	3	3	0	0	8	3	0	2	9	10.1	0.63	.107
	Inland Empire (CAL)	HiA	3	1	1.82	10	10	0	0	59	40	4	14	60	9.1	0.91	.187
	Arkansas (TL)	AA	3	2	3.34	7	5	0	0	32	39	1	3	21	5.8	1.30	.300
	Los Angeles (AL)	MAJ	0	0	1.50	12	0	0	0	6	6	0	3	7	10.5	1.50	.261
2013	Los Angeles (AL)	MAJ	0	0	6.75	10	0	0	0	5	4	1	8	5	8.4	2.25	.200
	Arkansas (TL)	AA	2	4	3.51	41	0	0	0	56	41	4	37	63	10.1	1.38	.203
Major League Totals			0	0	3.97	22	0	0	0	11	10	1	11	12	9.5	1.85	.233
Minor League Totals			13	8	2.58	72	29	0	0	202	159	14	71	203	9.0	1.14	.215

23 JOE KREHBIEL, RHP

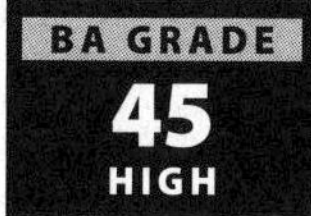

Born: Dec. 20, 1992. **B-T:** R-R. **Ht.:** 6-2. **Wt.:** 185. **Drafted:** HS—Seminole, Fla., 2011 (12th round). **Signed by:** Tom Kotchman.

Krehbiel's signing scout, Tom Kotchman, knows the Seminole (Fla.) High program well, seeing as that's where his son Casey played prior to being the Angels' first-round pick in 2001. Krehbiel won Pinellas County's player of the year award as a junior shortstop in 2010 and then its pitcher of the year honor in 2011. Signed for $125,000 as a 12th-rounder in 2011, he initially believed he was going to play third base, but he's been a pitcher throughout his pro career. An elbow injury sidelined Krehbiel for much of 2011, but he seems to have put that behind him. He has been used as a set-up man as an Angels farmhand, so he isn't exactly a priority prospect, but he's shown a 91-93 mph fastball that touches 95 from a low-three-quarters arm slot that makes him a very rough look for righthanders (.454 OPS at low Class A Burlington in 2013) but a relatively easy one for lefties (.806 OPS). Krehbiel has a solid-average breaking ball and a tick-below-average changeup. He's ready to try to survive the hitting environments of the high Class A California League in 2014.

Year	Club (League)	Class	W	L	ERA	G	GS	CG	SV	IP	H	HR	BB	SO	K/9	WHIP	AVG
2011	Angels (AZL)	R	0	0	14.21	5	3	0	0	6	12	0	2	6	8.5	2.21	.400
2012	Orem (PIO)	R	2	2	5.12	22	0	0	0	32	38	2	10	34	9.7	1.52	.292
2013	Burlington (MWL)	LoA	6	5	2.74	48	1	0	1	66	49	3	28	70	9.6	1.17	.204
Minor League Totals			8	7	4.17	75	4	0	1	104	99	5	40	110	9.5	1.34	.248

24 EDUAR LOPEZ, RHP

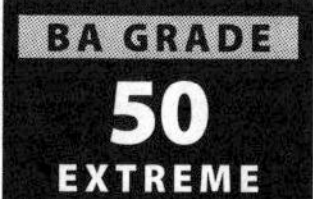

Born: Feb. 21, 1995. **B-T:** R-R. **Ht.:** 6-0. **Wt.:** 180. **Signed:** Dominican Republic, 2012. **Signed by:** Roman Ocumarez.

The Angels decided Lopez would be better served by a second year in the Dominican Summer League in 2013, and he responded by putting together a similar year, striking out the same number of batters, walking more but but allowing fewer hits. Right now, Lopez can dominate DSL hitters with a two-pitch mix consisting of a 90-94 mph fastball and a promising breaking ball that handcuffs young hitters. The next step is to work with Rookie-level Arizona League pitching coach Matt Wise when he comes to the U.S. in 2014 to develop a changeup. Lopez's control took a step back in his second year in the DSL. His delivery is relatively clean, but he'll have to improve his ability to hit his spots if he's going to stay in the rotation. Lopez is more than ready to make the jump to the AZL and try his luck against more experienced hitters.

Year	Club (League)	Class	W	L	ERA	G	GS	CG	SV	IP	H	HR	BB	SO	K/9	WHIP	AVG
2012	Angels (DSL)	R	2	1	3.54	12	11	0	0	53	42	5	23	83	14.0	1.22	.212
2013	Angels (DSL)	R	6	3	1.88	14	13	0	0	62	27	0	42	83	12.0	1.11	.132
Minor League Totals			8	4	2.65	26	24	0	0	116	69	5	65	166	12.9	1.16	.171

25 JETT BANDY, C

BA GRADE
40
MEDIUM

Born: March 26, 1990. **B-R:** R-R. **Ht.:** 6-4. **Wt.:** 210. **Drafted:** Arizona, 2011 (31st round). **Signed by:** John Gracio.

In a system that's thin on catchers, Bandy stands out because of his reliability. Pitchers like throwing to him because he's a big catcher who calls a good game and does a solid job of receiving. He has a tick-above-average arm, but his slow release and less-than-ideal footwork means he can be run on. He did throw out 32 percent of basestealers at Double-A Arkansas in 2013, but opponents attempted nearly a steal a game against him. At the plate, Bandy's lack of bat speed concerns scouts. He has a long swing that leaves him vulnerable to good velocity. When he tries to gear up for fastballs, he's susceptible to pitchers who pitch backwards and throw him off-balance. Though he has yet to show it as a pro, Bandy possesses some pull power in his swing, and he might be able to hit 10 home runs eventually. Like most catchers, he's a well-below-average runner. He's never hit into many double plays, in part because he often hits the ball in the air. Bandy projects as a backup catcher at best, but in a system that lacks receivers, he could get a big league shot at some point.

Year	Club (League)	Class	AVG	G	AB	R	H	2B	3B	HR	RBI	BB	SO	SB	CS	OBP	SLG
2011	Salt Lake (PCL)	AAA	.000	1	1	0	0	0	0	0	0	0	0	0	0	.000	.000
	Angels (AZL)	R	.307	46	176	32	54	18	0	4	29	10	23	2	0	.394	.477
	Arkansas (TL)	AA	.500	1	2	1	1	0	0	1	1	0	0	0	0	.500	2.000
	Orem (PIO)	R	.333	2	6	2	2	1	0	0	2	0	0	0	0	.333	.500
2012	Inland Empire (CAL)	HiA	.247	94	324	42	80	22	1	7	46	20	51	1	1	.318	.386
2013	Arkansas (TL)	AA	.241	78	245	26	59	17	2	4	28	14	39	0	1	.303	.376
Minor League Totals			.260	222	754	103	196	58	3	16	106	44	113	3	2	.332	.408

26 KEYNAN MIDDLETON, RHP

Born: Sept. 12, 1993. **B-T:** R-R. **Ht.:** 6-2. **Wt.:** 185. **Drafted:** Lane (Ore.) CC, 2013 (3rd round). **Signed by:** Jason Ellison.

If Middleton was looking for immediate success, he would have stuck with basketball. On the court, the shooting guard averaged 11 points, 4.6 rebounds and 1.5 steals per game for Lane (Ore.) CC as a freshman, and he had mid-major NCAA Division I interest if he had focused on hoops. But Middleton focused on the long game, opting to sign with the Angels as a third-round pick in 2013. He's a better pro prospect as a pitcher, but he's also much further away from the big leagues because he's extremely raw, and he will likely need several years to iron out delivery issues. Middleton has excellent athleticism and a clean arm stroke, but he can't come close to repeating his delivery yet, as he'll throw one pitch from a crossfire delivery and follow it by opening up too soon. His fastball will vary from 88-95 mph as a result. He throws a fringy slider that sometimes turns into more of a curveball, but he's shown some ability to spin a breaking ball. His changeup, like everything else, needs lots of work. Middleton has plenty of potential to go with an athletic 6-foot-2 frame that should handle plenty of innings, but for now, he's got to accept that there will be lots of growing pains along the way. He'll be trying to pitch his way to low Class A Burlington in 2014.

Year	Club (League)	Class	W	L	ERA	G	GS	CG	SV	IP	H	HR	BB	SO	K/9	WHIP	AVG
2013	Orem (PIO)	R	1	3	8.10	6	6	0	0	23	29	4	15	15	5.8	1.89	.319
	Angels (AZL)	R	0	0	6.35	4	1	0	0	6	3	0	3	5	7.9	1.06	.143
Minor League Totals			1	3	7.76	10	7	0	0	29	32	4	18	20	6.2	1.72	.286

27 ERICK SALCEDO, SS

BA GRADE
45
HIGH

Born: June 28, 1993. **B-T:** B-R. **Ht.:** 5-10. **Wt.:** 155. **Signed:** Venezuela, 2010. **Signed by:** Lebi Ochoa.

Recently retired shortstop Omar Vizquel already has moved on to become the Tigers' first-base coach, but in his one year working with Angels minor league infielders, he made an impact with Salcedo. Vizquel was one of the coaches pushing the speedy shortstop to take up switch-hitting again. After batting righthanded exclusively in 2013 extended spring training, Salcedo started swinging lefthanded in workouts, and before long brought it into games, showing a solid gap-to-gap swing in the Rookie-level Arizona League. Defensively, Salcedo is an average but generally reliable defender at shortstop, though he does have a tendency to take bad at-bats into the field with him. He shows an average arm most of the time, but he can unleash a rocket every now and then when he gets his feet set properly before he throws. Salcedo has a chance to be a solid utility infielder if he continues to develop and will try to earn a full-season job in 2014.

Year	Club (League)	Class	AVG	G	AB	R	H	2B	3B	HR	RBI	BB	SO	SB	CS	OBP	SLG
2010	Angels (DSL)	R	.226	29	62	14	14	3	2	0	5	8	17	1	0	.310	.339
2011	Angels (DSL)	R	.241	38	108	19	26	4	2	0	16	25	14	4	4	.396	.315
2012	Angels (DSL)	R	.240	56	175	30	42	5	0	0	22	33	25	7	4	.362	.269
2013	Angels (AZL)	R	.270	48	189	27	51	8	5	0	22	16	32	10	3	.325	.365
Minor League Totals			.249	171	534	90	133	20	9	0	65	82	88	22	11	.351	.320

28 ANDREW RAY, OF

Born: May 1, 1991. **B-T:** R-R. **Ht.:** 6-1. **Wt.:** 195. **Drafted:** Northeast Texas CC, 2011 (5th round). **Signed by:** Rudy Vasquez.

Six weeks into the 2013 season, Ray went on the disabled list. The DL in the minor leagues is a little more free-wheeling than the big league version, and if you were looking for an explanation for Ray's DL trip, it would be most accurately be diagnosed as a sick bat. He was hitting .193/.239/.355 at the time with 46 strikeouts in 105 at-bats at low Class A Burlington. Ray tended to pull everything foul, so the Angels shut him down for a few weeks to retool his swing. He came back with a simple trigger of a hand pump that allowed him to stay back on pitches more consistently, and he worked to stop opening up so much, which had left him vulnerable to anything outside or offspeed. Once he returned, Ray hit nine home runs in June, which included a stretch of five consecutive games with a homer. He has to hit for power because that's his only above-average tool. His speed, defense in left field and throwing arm all grade below-average. Ray's contact skills improved with his mechanical tweak, but he still strikes out a lot and seldom walks, in part because he struggles with pitch recognition. His power gives him a long leash and should carry him to high Class A Inland Empire in 2014.

Year	Club (League)	Class	AVG	G	AB	R	H	2B	3B	HR	RBI	BB	SO	SB	CS	OBP	SLG
2011	Orem (PIO)	R	.175	43	126	18	22	4	0	2	13	14	44	3	0	.259	.254
2012	Orem (PIO)	R	.283	46	180	23	51	18	3	6	36	5	43	0	0	.301	.517
2013	Burlington (MWL)	LoA	.275	75	287	40	79	27	1	15	52	9	93	0	1	.300	.533
Minor League Totals			.256	164	593	81	152	49	4	23	101	28	180	3	1	.291	.469

29 KYLE McGOWIN, RHP

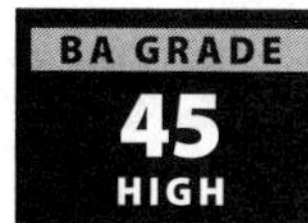

Born: Nov. 27, 1991. **B-T:** R-R. **Ht.:** 6-3. **Wt.:** 180. **Drafted:** Savannah State, 2013 (5th round). **Signed by:** Todd Hogan.

The Angels have plenty of high-velocity arms with shaky command and high-effort deliveries. As a group, they may help as relievers, but not many arms in the system project as starters. In a course correction, Los Angeles drafted 10 pitchers in their first 11 picks in 2013 with an emphasis on those with clean deliveries and feel for setting up hitters. McGowin, a fifth-round pick, is a prime example of the organization's new approach. He showed durability and stuff at Savannah State, leading the club to its first-ever Mid-Eastern Athletic Conference title. Along the way, he finished second in NCAA Division I with 128 strikeouts. The heavy workload did wear McGowin down, as he threw 121 innings as a junior, including a 144-pitch shutout in the MEAC championship game where he pitched with three days of rest. The Angels kept him on a tight leash at Rookie-level Orem, but they'll expand his role in 2014. McGowin throws an 86-89 mph two-seam fastball and a 90-93 mph four-seamer as well as a promising slider and a potentially average changeup. McGowin's best-case scenario is as a back-end starter, one that could move quickly through the system. The Angels expect to challenge him with a big jump to high Class A Inland Empire in 2014.

Year	Club (League)	Class	W	L	ERA	G	GS	CG	SV	IP	H	HR	BB	SO	K/9	WHIP	AVG
2013	Orem (PIO)	R	1	1	6.28	9	1	0	0	14	12	2	5	12	7.5	1.19	.218
Minor League Totals			1	1	6.28	9	1	0	0	14	12	2	5	12	7.5	1.19	.218

30 REID SCOGGINS, RHP

BA GRADE
45
EXTREME

Born: July 18, 1990. **B-T:** R-R. **Ht.:** 6-3. **Wt.:** 210. **Drafted:** Howard (Texas) JC, 2012 (15th round). **Signed by:** Rudy Vasquez.

If a scout saw Scoggins on the right night as an amateur, he was in bounds to project him as a top-10 rounds talent. After all, not many amateurs can run their fastballs up to 99 mph on a regular basis. But Scoggins was tough to scout because he threw few innings (33) as a reliever for Howard (Texas) JC in 2012, and his control was frightening as times as he worked back from Tommy John surgery the year before. Most teams opted to let Scoggins head back for another year of development, allowing the Angels to nab him for $100,000 as a 15th-round pick. He has been equally electric and erratic as a pro, and the fact that he had his second Tommy John surgery in 2013 leads to serious questions about his durability. Before he injured his elbow, Scoggins pitched off a plus 90-95 mph fastball with late life. He also showed an 11-to-5 breaking ball that locked up hitters at times, and he showed the confidence to throw it at any time in the count at low Class A Burlington. His changeup was well-below-average. Scoggins never has thrown strikes consistently. If he returns to full strength in 2015, he still has a shot to be a power reliever, but his durability problems cloud his future.

Year	Club (League)	Class	W	L	ERA	G	GS	CG	SV	IP	H	HR	BB	SO	K/9	WHIP	AVG
2012	Angels (AZL)	R	1	0	4.24	15	0	0	0	17	13	0	14	34	18.0	1.59	.210
	Cedar Rapids (MWL)	LoA	0	0	5.40	3	0	0	0	3	3	0	4	7	18.9	2.10	.231
2013	Burlington (MWL)	LoA	1	4	3.46	21	17	0	0	65	53	1	35	76	10.5	1.35	.223
Minor League Totals			2	4	3.69	39	17	0	0	85	69	1	53	117	12.3	1.43	.220

Los Angeles Dodgers

BY BEN BADLER

Flush with cash in their first full season under Guggenheim Baseball Management ownership, the Dodgers arrived at spring training after having made blockbuster trades, signed expensive major league free agents and paid premium prices for international free agents.

So when a 30-42 start put them 9½ games back in the National League West, manager Don Mattingly's job appeared to be on the line. But the investments started to pay off, as they went 45-23 in the second half to finish at 92-70 and win the division.

Los Angeles defeated the Braves in an NL Division Series before losing the NL Championship Series to the Cardinals, who beat Clayton Kershaw twice. It was the only negative on the season for Kershaw, who led the majors in ERA for the third straight year.

While the Dodgers received attention for their spending, much of their success was a result of getting their evaluations right. One need only look to the neighboring Angels to see how spending sprees work when the evaluations misfire.

The Dodgers acquired Hanley Ramirez from the Marlins in July 2012 in the midst of his second straight underachieving season. Once healthy, Ramirez played like an MVP for the Dodgers. They signed Zack Greinke to a six-year, $147 million contract after the 2012 season, and Greinke's 2.63 ERA ranked fourth in the NL.

The Dodgers' most controversial signing came in June 2012, when they signed Cuban outfielder Yasiel Puig to a seven-year, $42 million deal. Puig was a talented player on the rise in Cuba, but other teams questioned the Dodgers' process—Puig had been suspended for the past year in Cuba and hadn't been seen outside of the country since June 2011, with only one light showcase in Mexico where he didn't face live pitching and wasn't in game-ready condition.

After starting 2013 in Double-A, Puig forced his way to Los Angeles, where he keyed a 42-10 spurt that changed the season. He hit .319/.391/.534 in 104 games, becoming a Dodgers fan favorite.

Another rookie, lefthander Hyun-Jin Ryu, had a stellar debut after coming over from the Korean Baseball Organization. There was more industry consensus on Ryu, but the Dodgers nailed their evaluations of both players.

Their most recent big-ticket international signing—Cuban infielder Alexander Guerrero, who signed for four years and $28 million—went against the grain. Teams had several chances to evaluate him in the Dominican Republic and came away skeptical.

The organization has more outfielders than spots to put them, and that's before considering that No. 1 prospect Joc Pederson should be ready in 2014, perhaps as soon as Opening Day. Corey Seager, a shortstop and likely future third baseman, showed a polished approach and a sweet swing at age 19.

Julio Urias, purchased from the Mexico City Red Devils in 2012, pitched effectively in the low Class A Midwest League as a 16-year-old, and opposing scouts thought he could have handled even more advanced hitters. Zach Lee pitched well in Double-A and could contribute in 2014, with mid-rotation starter upside.

JESSE SOLL

Rookie Yasiel Puig electrified fans and the Dodgers with his power/speed combination

TOP PROSPECTS OF THE DECADE

Year	Player, Pos.	2013 Org.
2004	Edwin Jackson, rhp	Cubs
2005	Joel Guzman, ss/of	Saltillo (Mexican)
2006	Chad Billingsley, rhp	Dodgers
2007	Andy LaRoche, 3b	Blue Jays
2008	Clayton Kershaw, lhp	Dodgers
2009	Andrew Lambo, of	Pirates
2010	Dee Gordon, ss	Dodgers
2011	Dee Gordon, ss	Dodgers
2012	Zach Lee, rhp	Dodgers
2013	Hyun-Jin Ryu, lhp	Dodgers

ORGANIZATION OVERVIEW

General Manager: Ned Colletti. **Farm Director:** De Jon Watson. **Scouting Director:** Logan White.

Class	Team	League	W	L	PCT	Finish	Manager
Majors	Los Angeles Dodgers	National	92	70	.568	4th (15)	Don Mattingly
Triple-A	Albuquerque Isotopes	Pacific Coast	76	68	.528	t-6th (16)	Lorenzo Bundy
Double-A	Chattanooga Lookouts	Southern	59	80	.424	10th (10)	Jody Reed
High Class A	Rancho Cucamonga Quakes	California	65	75	.464	7th (10)	Carlos Subero
Low Class A	Great Lakes Loons	Midwest	67	72	.482	10th (16)	Razor Shines
Rookie	Ogden Raptors	Pioneer	36	40	.474	5th (8)	Damon Berryhill
Rookie	AZL Dodgers	Arizona	34	22	.607	2nd (13)	P.J. Forbes
Overall 2013 Minor League Record			**337**	**357**	**.486**	**21st (30)**	

THIS YEAR'S TOP 30

No.	Player, Pos.	Grade/Risk
1.	Joc Pederson, of	60/Medium
2.	Corey Seager, ss	65/High
3.	Julio Urias, lhp	65/Extreme
4.	Zach Lee, rhp	55/Medium
5.	Chris Anderson, rhp	55/High
6.	Chris Withrow, rhp	50/Medium
7.	Alexander Guerrero, 2b	50/Medium
8.	Chris Reed, lhp	50/High
9.	Onelki Garcia, lhp	45/Low
10.	Ross Stripling, rhp	50/High
11.	Jose Dominguez, rhp	45/Medium
12.	Tom Windle, lhp	50/High
13.	Yimi Garcia, rhp	45/Medium
14.	Cody Bellinger, 1b	50/High
15.	Jacob Scavuzzo, of	55/Extreme
16.	Matt Magill, rhp	45/Medium
17.	Scott Schebler, of	45/High
18.	Justin Chigbogu, 1b	50/Extreme
19.	Pedro Baez, rhp	45/High
20.	Victor Gonzalez, lhp	50/Extreme
21.	Zach Bird, rhp	50/Extreme
22.	Jesmuel Valentin, 2b/ss	45/High
23.	Ibandel Isabel, of	50/Extreme
24.	Hector Nelo, rhp	45/High
25.	Darnell Sweeney, ss/2b	45/High
26.	Tyler Ogle, 1b/c	45/High
27.	Jon Garcia, of	45/High
28.	Ariel Sandoval, of	50/Extreme
29.	Victor Arano, rhp	50/Extreme
30.	Brandon Dixon, 3b	50/Extreme

LAST YEAR'S TOP 30

No.	Player, Pos.	Status
1.	Hyun-Jin Ryu, lhp	Majors
2.	Yasiel Puig, of	Majors
3.	Corey Seager, ss	No. 2
4.	Joc Pederson, of	No. 1
5.	Zach Lee, rhp	No. 4
6.	Chris Reed, lhp	No. 8
7.	Onelki Garcia, lhp	No. 9
8.	Paco Rodriguez, lhp	Majors
9.	Matt Magill, rhp	No. 16
10.	Ross Stripling, rhp	No. 10
11.	Alex Castellanos, 2b/3b/of	(Red Sox)
12.	Chris Withrow, rhp	No. 6
13.	Tim Federowicz, c	Majors
14.	Jesmuel Valentin, ss	No. 22
15.	Bobby Coyle, of	Dropped out
16.	Scott Van Slyke, of/1b	Majors
17.	Garrett Gould, rhp	Dropped out
18.	Scott Griggs, rhp	Dropped out
19.	Zach Bird, rhp	No. 21
20.	Josh Wall, rhp	(Angels)
21.	Steve Ames, rhp	(Marlins)
22.	James Baldwin III, of	Dropped out
23.	Alex Santana, 3b	Dropped out
24.	Scott Barlow, rhp	Dropped out
25.	Angel Sanchez, rhp	(Marlins)
26.	Brian Cavazos-Galvez, of	Dropped out
27.	Aaron Miller, lhp	Dropped out
28.	Blake Smith, of	Dropped out
29.	Jeremy Rathjen, of	Dropped out
30.	Joey Curletta, of	Dropped out

BEST TOOLS

Best Hitter for Average	Corey Seager
Best Power Hitter	Joc Pederson
Best Strike-Zone Discipline	Joc Pederson
Fastest Baserunner	James Baldwin III
Best Athlete	James Baldwin III
Best Fastball	Jose Dominguez
Best Curveball	Onelki Garcia
Best Slider	Tom Windle
Best Changeup	Zach Lee
Best Control	Julio Urias
Best Defensive Catcher	Spencer Navin
Best Defensive Infielder	Cody Bellinger
Best Infield Arm	Corey Seager
Best Defensive Outfielder	Joc Pederson
Best Outfield Arm	Noel Cuevas

TOP 15 PLAYERS 25 AND UNDER

No.	Player, Pos. (Age)	Peak Level
1.	Yasiel Puig, of (23)	Majors
2.	Joc Pederson, of (21)	Double-A
3.	Corey Seager, ss (19)	High Class A
4.	Julio Urias, lhp (17)	Low Class A
5.	Zach Lee, rhp (22)	Double-A
6.	Paco Rodriguez, lhp (22)	Majors
7.	Chris Anderson, rhp (21)	Low Class A
8.	Chris Withrow, rhp (25)	Majors
9.	Chris Reed, lhp (23)	Double-A
10.	Onelki Garcia, lhp (24)	Majors
11.	Ross Stripling, rhp (24)	Double-A
12.	Jose Dominguez, rhp (23)	Majors
13.	Tom Windle, lhp (22)	Low Class A
14.	Yimi Garcia, rhp (23)	Double-A
15.	Dee Gordon, ss (25)	Majors

MINOR LEAGUE DEPTH CHART

LOS ANGELES DODGERS

TOP 2014 ROOKIE: Joc Pederson, of. Pederson could open the year in Triple-A, but if he can crack the major league lineup, he has more upside for 2014 than anyone else in the system.

BREAKOUT PROSPECT: Cody Bellinger, 1b. One of the youngest players in the 2013 draft, Bellinger is already a stellar defender whose offensive numbers should pick up with natural physical maturity.

SLEEPER: Lucas Tirado, ss. Scouts from other teams were more skeptical, but the Dodgers paid the teenage Dominican shortstop $1 million as their top July 2 signing in 2013.

SOURCE OF TOP 30 TALENT			
Homegrown	**29**	**Acquired**	**1**
College	7	Trades	0
Junior college	1	Rule 5 draft	1
High school	11	Independent leagues	0
Nondrafted free agents	0	Free agents/waivers	0
International	10		

LF
Jacob Scavuzzo (15)
Scott Schebler (17)
Ibandel Isabel (23)

CF
Joc Pederson (1)
Ariel Sandoval (28)
Noel Cuevas
James Baldwin III

RF
Jon Garcia (27)
Joey Curletta
Michael Medina

3B
Corey Seager (2)
Brandon Dixon (30)
Alex Santana
Adam Law

SS
Miguel Rojas
Moises Perez

2B
Alexander Guerrero (7)
Jesmuel Valentin (22)
Darnell Sweeney (25)
Lucas Tirado

1B
Cody Bellinger (14)
Justin Chigbogu (18)
Angelo Songco

C
Tyler Ogle (26)
Kyle Farmer
Chris O'Brien
Spencer Navin

LHP

LHSP	LHRP
Julio Urias (3)	Onelki Garcia (9)
Chris Reed (8)	Jarret Martin
Tom Windle (12)	Michael Johnson
Victor Gonzalez (20)	

RHP

RHSP	RHRP
Zach Lee (4)	Chris Withrow (6)
Chris Anderson (5)	Jose Dominguez (11)
Ross Stripling (10)	Yimi Garcia (13)
Matt Magill (16)	Pedro Baez (19)
Zach Bird (21)	Hector Nelo (24)
Victor Arano (29)	Jacob Rhame
Jonathan Martinez	
Carlos Frias	
William Soto	
Oscar Cruz	
Garrett Gould	
J.D. Underwood	

DRAFT ANALYSIS

2013

BONUSES: $5.5 MILLION

BEST PURE HITTER: 1B Cody Bellinger (4) has a solid swing and uses the whole field. He needs to get stronger but knows his limitations and sticks to a line-drive approach, relying on his good hands.

BEST POWER HITTER: The Dodgers didn't draft a pure power bat. SS/OF Blake Hennessey (19) has the most pop now thanks to his present strength. Bellinger could outpace him as he fills out his 6-foot-4, 175-pound frame.

FASTEST RUNNER: 3B Adam Law (12) is a well above-average runner and puts his speed to good use. He stole 40 bases between two Rookie-level stops.

BEST DEFENSIVE PLAYER: Bellinger has Gold Glove potential at first base. C Spencer Navin (11) has reliable, above-average catch-and-throw skills, while SS/2B Brandon Trinkwon (7) makes up for his fringy arm with instincts, soft hands and nimble footwork.

BEST FASTBALL: RHP Chris Anderson (1) has touched 98 mph and sits 94-95. He can throw strikes at that speed and pitches downhill. RHP Jacob Rhame (6) also reaches 96-97 mph and fits in a bullpen role, while LHP Michael Johnson (14) has reached 95 mph.

BEST SECONDARY PITCH: LHP Tom Windle (2) had one of the draft's best sliders, thrown with power at 84 mph and with hard, late break. Anderson will flash a plus, power curveball but isn't consistent with it.

BEST PRO DEBUT: Anderson (3-0, 1.96, 46 IP/50 SO) and Windle (5-1, 2.68, 54 IP/51 SO) both jumped straight to the low Class A Midwest League and thrived. C Kyle Farmer (8), who converted from playing shortstop at Georgia, hit .347/.386/.533 and threw out 39.5 percent of basestealers. Trinkwon tore up Ogden (.362/.411/.587) to move up to Great Lakes and hit six homers as a pro after hitting seven in three seasons at Long Beach State.

BEST ATHLETE: Bellinger likely would be a middle infielder if he didn't throw lefthanded.

MOST INTRIGUING BACKGROUND: Bellinger's father Clay earned two World Series rings with the Yankees. Law's grandfather Vern won the 1960 NL Cy Young Award with the Pirates in a 16-year major league career, while his father Vance played 11 big league seasons, then coached the son at Brigham Young. RHP J.D. Underwood (5) is the son of ex-big leaguer Tom and nephew of ex-big leaguer Pat. Hennessey's father Scott is a Dodgers scout. 2B Tyger Pederson (33) is the older brother of Dodgers prospect Joc.

CLOSEST TO THE MAJORS: Anderson and Windle should reach Double-A, if not higher in 2014.

BEST LATE-ROUND PICK: RHP Greg Harris (17), son of the former big league reliever of the same name, signed for $175,000 to give up an Oregon scholarship. He touched 94 mph in instructional league.

THE ONE WHO GOT AWAY: The Dodgers thought they had a deal done with projectable LHP Ty Damron (13), but he wound up at Texas Tech. They also liked athletic Connecticut prep RHP Justin Dunn (37), who wound up at Boston College.

ASSESSMENT: The Dodgers were pleased by the strong debuts of Anderson and Windle, who both could move quickly. The success of the hitters will depend on Farmer's development behind the plate and Bellinger's strength catching up to his skills.

2012

BONUSES: $6.3 MILLION

LHP Paco Rodriguez (2) zipped to the majors and stuck around, joined by Cuban LHP Onelki Garcia (3). SS Corey Seager (1) had a strong first full season.

GRADE: B+

2011

BONUSES: $3.5 MILLION

The Dodgers didn't spend much, and LHP Chris Reed (1) is the best hope of a lackluster group.

GRADE: D

2010

BONUSES: $8.0 MILLION

RHP Zach Lee (1) got the attention and $5.25 million bonus, but OF Joc Pederson (11), signed for $600,000, is the system's top prospect.

GRADE: B

TOP DRAFT PICKS OF THE DECADE

Year	Player, Pos.	2013 Org.
2004	Scott Elbert, lhp	Dodgers
2005	*Luke Hochevar, rhp (1st round supp.)	Royals
2006	Clayton Kershaw, lhp	Dodgers
2007	Chris Withrow, rhp	Dodgers
2008	Ethan Martin, rhp	Phillies
2009	Aaron Miller, lhp (1st round supp.)	Dodgers
2010	Zach Lee, rhp	Dodgers
2011	Chris Reed, lhp	Dodgers
2012	Corey Seager, ss	Dodgers
2013	Chris Anderson, rhp	Dodgers

*Did not sign.

LARGEST BONUSES IN CLUB HISTORY

Yasiel Puig, 2012	$12,000,000
Alexander Guerrero, 2013	$10,000,000
Hiroki Kuroda, 2007	$7,300,000
Zach Lee, 2010	$5,250,000
Hyun-Jin Ryu, 2012	$5,000,000

1 JOC PEDERSON, OF

Born: April 21, 1992. **B-T:** L-L. **Ht.:** 6-1. **Wt.:** 185.
Drafted: HS—Palo Alto, Calif., 2010 (11th round).
Signed by: Orsino Hill.

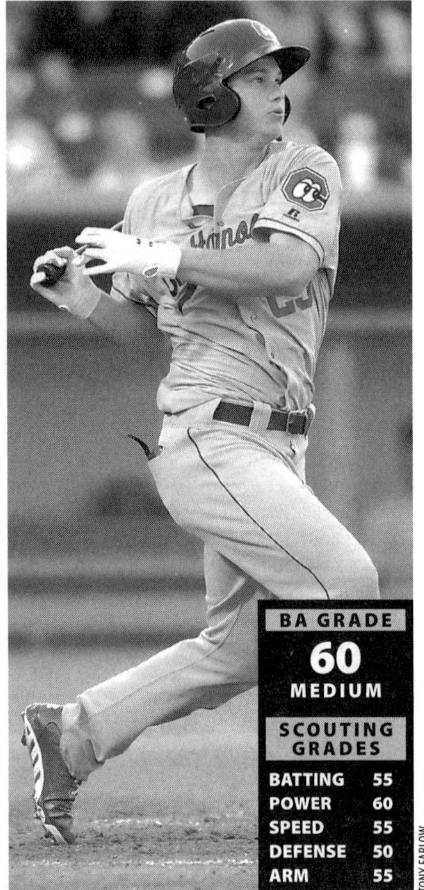

BA GRADE
60
MEDIUM
SCOUTING GRADES
BATTING 55
POWER 60
SPEED 55
DEFENSE 50
ARM 55

TONY FARLOW

Coming out of high school, Pederson had the option of playing baseball at Southern California and joining the football team as a walk-on wide receiver. Instead, he signed with the Dodgers for $600,000 at the 2010 signing deadline as an 11th-round pick. Pederson performed well in the Rookie-level Pioneer League the following year and has consistently combined strong offensive production with a well-rounded skill set at every level. After a stellar season in the Double-A Southern League where managers voted him the league's best defensive outfielder and most exciting player, Pederson became an on-base machine playing winter ball in the Venezuelan League. He should easily eclipse the career of his father Stu Pederson, who played in eight major league games with the Dodgers as an outfielder in 1985. The Dodgers drafted Joc's older brother Tyger out of Pacific in the 33rd round in 2013.

Pederson spent 2013 at Double-A Chattanooga, where he was teammates with Yasiel Puig for the first half of the season. Dodgers officials believe the competition brought out the best in both of them. Pederson is a multi-dimensional player whose tools are average to plus across the board, with comparisons ranging from Curtis Granderson and Jim Edmonds. He has a balanced hitting approach and keeps his hands back against righthanders. He's a patient hitter who ranked fifth in the Southern League in walks (70) and third in on-base percentage (.381). He also led the league in slugging (.497) and ranked second in home runs (22) thanks to his plus raw power, though sometimes that juice is more evident in batting practice than in games because he's still learning how to backspin balls. Pederson's most glaring offensive hole is against lefthanders, who turn him into a completely different player. He hit .316/.420/.609 against Double-A righthanders but lefties held him to a .200/.299/.269 line, and 20 of his 22 homers came against righties. He tends to fly off and get pull-conscious against southpaws, so he needs to do a better job staying through the baseball and using the left-center field gap. Pederson runs a tick above-average and makes good use of his wheels on the bases, with the potential for 20-30 stolen bases per year. He's not a burner, but he did a better job improving his routes and jumps in center field this season with a solid-average arm. He's solid defensively in center field but could slide over to a corner depending on which outfielders the Dodgers hold on to from their current surplus.

The Dodgers have a crowded outfield picture before even considering Pederson with Puig, Matt Kemp, Carl Crawford and Andre Ethier in Los Angeles. Despite that, he he could force his way to Los Angeles at some point in 2014, possibly by Opening Day depending on what moves the Dodgers make. With his patience, power, speed and athleticism, Pederson has the skills to contribute in all phases of the game as an above-average everyday player, with even greater potential if he can improve against lefthanders.

Year	Club (League)	Class	AVG	G	AB	R	H	2B	3B	HR	RBI	BB	SO	SB	CS	OBP	SLG
2010	Dodgers (AZL)	R	.000	3	7	1	0	0	0	0	0	4	5	0	0	.417	.000
2011	Great Lakes (MWL)	LoA	.160	16	50	4	8	0	0	0	1	7	9	2	0	.288	.160
	Ogden (PIO)	R	.353	68	266	54	94	20	2	11	64	36	54	24	5	.429	.568
2012	R. Cucamonga (CAL)	HiA	.313	110	434	96	136	26	4	18	70	51	81	26	14	.396	.516
2013	Chattanooga (SL)	AA	.278	123	439	81	122	24	3	22	58	70	114	31	8	.381	.497
Minor League Totals			.301	320	1196	236	360	70	9	51	193	168	263	83	27	.394	.503

2 COREY SEAGER, SS

Born: April 27, 1994. **B-T:** L-R. **Ht.:** 6-4. **Wt.:** 215. **Drafted:** HS—Concord, N.C., 2012 (1st round). **Signed by:** Lon Joyce.

While Kyle Seager has become an above-average third baseman for the Mariners, younger brother Corey may have a higher ceiling. The No. 18 overall pick in the 2012 draft, Seager dominated the low Class A Midwest League last year before slowing down when the Dodgers challenged him with a promotion to high Class A in August, and he appeared tired as one of the youngest players in the Arizona Fall League. Seager has a mature approach on both sides of the ball. His hand-eye coordination and smooth lefty stroke give him excellent plate coverage with good leverage, and his bat head stays in the hitting zone a long time. While he sometimes expands his strike zone and starts to dive out front, he walked in 11 percent of his plate appearances and should be an on-base threat. Seager has a line-drive approach and works gap to gap, but he can impart backspin on the ball, with the size and strength projection to have plus power in the future. While he's a shortstop now, he is headed to third base long-term and has the ingredients to be an above-average defender there. A below-average runner, he has soft hands, a good internal clock and an above-average arm. Seager will likely return to Rancho Cucamonga, but he could get to Double-A by the end of the year, with a chance to crack the majors in 2015. Seager doesn't have Joc Pederson's track record yet, but both could be future all-stars.

Year	Club (League)	Class	AVG	G	AB	R	H	2B	3B	HR	RBI	BB	SO	SB	CS	OBP	SLG
2012	Ogden (PIO)	R	.309	46	175	34	54	9	2	8	33	21	33	8	2	.383	.520
2013	Great Lakes (MWL)	LoA	.309	74	272	45	84	18	3	12	57	34	58	9	4	.389	.529
	R. Cucamonga (CAL)	HiA	.160	27	100	10	16	2	1	4	15	12	31	1	0	.246	.320
Minor League Totals			.282	147	547	89	154	29	6	24	105	67	122	18	6	.361	.488

3 JULIO URIAS, LHP

Born: Aug. 12, 1996. **B-T:** L-L. **Ht.:** 5-11. **Wt.:** 185. **Signed:** Mexico, 2012. **Signed by:** Mike Brito.

Teams considered Urias one of the better arms on the international market in 2012 but were wary of a medical condition in his left eye. He had a tumor removed from his eye when he was younger, which left a noticeable mark over his eye, but the Dodgers say it doesn't affect his vision. The Dodgers signed him in a package deal from Mexico City of the Mexican League, which owned his rights. He proved so advanced that the Dodgers sent him at age 16 to the low Class A Midwest League, where he dominated. When Urias signed, he threw 88-92 mph with a smooth delivery and advanced feel for pitching. Now his fastball ranges from 91-96 mph and the Dodgers say he touched 98, mixing a two- and four-seamer. He throws his fastball for strikes to all areas of the zone while imparting cutting, tailing and/or sinking action. He adds, subtracts and manipulates the shape of his 77-82 mph curveball, which projects as at least a plus pitch. His changeup should give him a third above-average offering but is still inconsistent. Urias is physically mature, so he has to stay on top of his conditioning. Urias has the stuff and polish to be a frontline starter and move quickly. Opposing scouts thought he could have handled an even more aggressive assignment last year. Given his age, the Dodgers are trying to carefully monitor his workload, but he could reach the big leagues when he's still a teenager.

Year	Club (League)	Class	W	L	ERA	G	GS	CG	SV	IP	H	HR	BB	SO	K/9	WHIP	AVG
2013	Great Lakes (MWL)	LoA	2	0	2.48	18	18	0	0	54	44	5	16	67	11.1	1.10	.227
Minor League Totals			2	0	2.48	18	18	0	0	54	44	5	16	67	11.1	1.10	.227

4 ZACH LEE, RHP

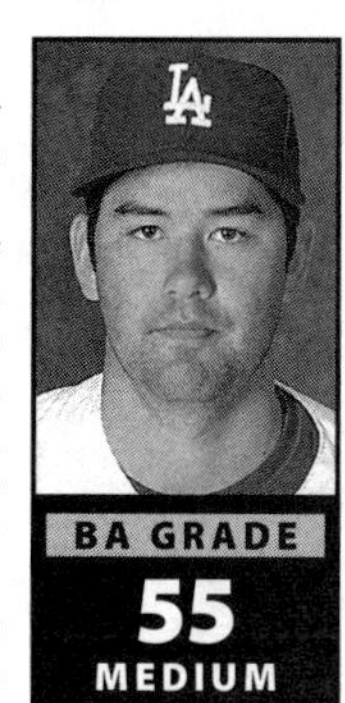

Born: Sept. 13, 1991. **B-T:** R-R. **Ht.:** 6-3. **Wt.:** 190. **Drafted:** HS—McKinney, Texas, 2010 (1st round). **Signed by:** Calvin Jones.

Lee turned down the opportunity to play quarterback and pitch at Louisiana State when he signed a heavily backloaded, two-sport deal with the Dodgers for $5.25 million as the 25th overall pick in the 2010 draft. He has proven to be a steady prospect who has moved relatively quickly through the system. Lee's stuff is solid across the board and plays up because of the improvements he's made over the last year with his command and approach. His fastball sits at 88-92 mph with good life and tops out at 95. He has the ability to sink the ball and get grounders at an above-average clip. Lee's fastball command improved, as he works down in the zone and pitches to both sides of the plate. His four-pitch mix includes an 81-85 mph slider and a low-80s changeup—both are average pitches—and a 72-75 mph curveball he'll use early in the count. He doesn't have a knockout secondary weapon, but he learned how to read swings better and attack hitters based on their strengths and weaknesses. He'll likely always rely more on his feel and command rather than being a prolific strikeout pitcher. When the Dodgers drafted Lee he appeared to have frontline starter potential, but his realistic upside now looks like more of a solid No. 3. He could open 2014 in Triple-A, but he should make his major league debut during the season.

Year	Club (League)	Class	W	L	ERA	G	GS	CG	SV	IP	H	HR	BB	SO	K/9	WHIP	AVG
2011	Great Lakes (MWL)	LoA	9	6	3.47	24	24	0	0	109	101	9	32	91	7.5	1.22	.242
2012	R. Cucamonga (CAL)	HiA	2	3	4.55	12	12	0	0	55	60	9	10	52	8.5	1.27	.270
	Chattanooga (SL)	AA	4	3	4.25	13	13	0	0	66	69	6	22	51	7.0	1.39	.272
2013	Chattanooga (SL)	AA	10	10	3.22	28	25	1	0	143	132	13	35	131	8.3	1.17	.247
Minor League Totals			25	22	3.67	77	74	1	0	373	362	37	99	325	7.8	1.24	.253

5 CHRIS ANDERSON, RHP

Born: July 29, 1992. **B-T:** R-R. **Ht.:** 6-4. **Wt.:** 215. **Drafted:** Jacksonville, 2013 (1st round). **Signed by:** Scott Hennessey.

An unsigned 35th-round pick of the Cubs out of a Wisconsin high school in 2010, Anderson closed as a Jacksonville freshman and both hit and pitched as a sophomore. The staff workhorse as a junior became Jacksonville's highest-ever draft pick when the Dodgers took him 18th overall in the 2013 draft. He signed for $1,109,900 and performed well in the low Class A Midwest League. Anderson has a big, durable frame and attacks hitters with downhill plane on a fastball that sits at 90-95 mph and peaks at 98 with the ability to hold his velocity deep into his starts. He walked too many hitters in his pro debut, but he's usually around the strike zone. His best secondary pitch is a hard, mid-80s slider that flashes above-average with late bite. His 85-87 mph changeup at times is an average offering with good arm speed and fade, but it's inconsistent. Everything Anderson throws is firm, so to give hitters another look he mixes in a high-70s curveball, which comes and goes on him. He doesn't throw with a lot of effort, but his delivery has some deception. Some Dodgers officials believe Anderson can move quickly and take off once he fine-tunes his command, with a likely assignment to high Class A Rancho Cucamonga to begin 2014. He has the potential to become a mid-rotation innings-eater.

Year	Club (League)	Class	W	L	ERA	G	GS	CG	SV	IP	H	HR	BB	SO	K/9	WHIP	AVG
2013	Great Lakes (MWL)	LoA	3	0	1.96	12	12	0	0	46	32	0	24	50	9.8	1.22	.201
Minor League Totals			3	0	1.96	12	12	0	0	46	32	0	24	50	9.8	1.22	.201

6 CHRIS WITHROW, RHP

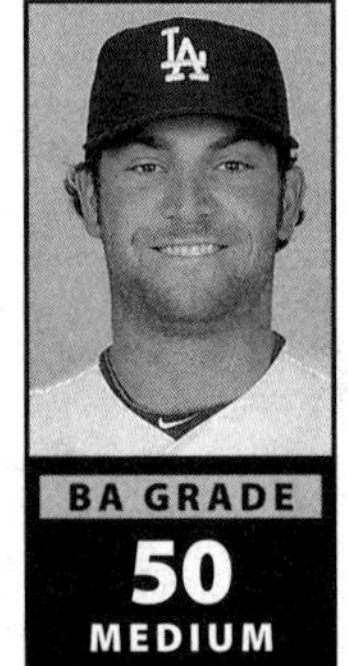

Born: April 1, 1989. **B-T:** R-R. **Ht.:** 6-4. **Wt.:** 220. **Drafted:** HS—Midland, Texas, 2007 (1st round). **Signed by:** Calvin Jones.

Withrow signed for $1.35 million as the 20th overall pick in the 2007 draft and reached Double-A two years later. His career entering the year had otherwise been a disappointment, after mediocre performance for three straight years in Double-A and a career 4.87 ERA entering the season. At the end of May 2012, the Dodgers shifted Withrow to the bullpen, where he has found a role that best suits him, and he made his major league debut in June and stayed in Los Angeles the second half of the season. Withrow's power arm plays well in relief, sitting in the mid-90s and reaching 99 mph. One of the keys for Withrow was improved fastball command, which helped him trim his walk rate and work ahead in counts more frequently to be able to get to his sharp, high-80s slider, an above-average pitch with good tilt. While some relievers tend to shelve the rest of their repertoire and stick to a two-pitch mix, Withrow started throwing his curveball more often once he got to Los Angeles than he did when he was at Triple-A Albuquerque. He also throws a firm changeup in the high 80s, but it's below-average and he rarely throws it. Withrow's time as a starter is finished, but he can be an effective reliever. He should return to the Dodgers bullpen next season to pitch in high-leverage situations.

Year	Club (League)	Class	W	L	ERA	G	GS	CG	SV	IP	H	HR	BB	SO	K/9	WHIP	AVG
2007	Dodgers (GCL)	R	0	0	5.00	6	4	0	0	9	5	0	4	13	13.0	1.00	.167
2008	Inland Empire (CAL)	HiA	0	0	4.50	4	0	0	0	4	2	0	6	1	2.3	2.00	.182
2009	Inland Empire (CAL)	HiA	6	6	4.69	19	16	0	0	86	80	3	45	105	10.9	1.45	.252
	Chattanooga (SL)	AA	2	2	3.95	6	6	0	0	27	24	2	12	26	8.6	1.32	.240
2010	Chattanooga (SL)	AA	4	9	5.97	27	27	1	0	130	146	13	69	120	8.3	1.66	.285
2011	Chattanooga (SL)	AA	6	6	4.20	25	25	1	0	129	111	8	75	130	9.1	1.45	.239
2012	Chattanooga (SL)	AA	3	3	4.65	22	7	0	2	60	52	3	36	64	9.6	1.47	.233
2013	Albuquerque (PCL)	AAA	4	0	1.71	25	0	0	0	26	25	0	13	33	11.3	1.44	.248
	Los Angeles (NL)	MAJ	3	0	2.60	26	0	0	1	35	20	5	13	43	11.2	0.95	.165
Major League Totals			3	0	2.60	26	0	0	1	35	20	5	13	43	11.2	0.95	.165
Minor League Totals			25	26	4.70	134	85	2	2	471	445	29	260	492	9.4	1.50	.253

7 ALEXANDER GUERRERO, 2B

Born: Dec. 20, 1986. **B-T:** R-R. **Ht.:** 5-10. **Wt.:** 200. **Signed:** Cuba, 2013. **Signed by:** Mike Tosar/Patrick Guerrero/Bob Engle.

Guerrero had been one of the top performers in Cuba before he left the country, hitting .290/.402/.576 with 21 homers, 39 walks and 30 strikeouts in 328 plate appearances for Las Tunas. He played sparingly on Cuba's national team, and scouts said the tools didn't match the performance. Nevertheless, Guerrero landed a four-year, $28 million deal that includes a $10 million signing bonus. While Guerrero claimed legal residency in Haiti, teams were able to evaluate him before he signed in the Dominican Republic, where he transformed his body and improved his power and speed. Above-average raw power is Guerrero's best tool, but the Dodgers were drawn to his hitting potential and ability to hit to all fields. Other scouts were skeptical, believing Guerrero has a pull-oriented approach that he will have to adjust to hit quality pitching. Some scouts called Guerrero's stroke rigid with holes that will leave him susceptible to good velocity, and he can lose his balance against breaking pitches. Guerrero was no basestealer in Cuba, but he ran above-average 60-yard times in the Dominican Republic. A shortstop in Cuba, Guerrero has solid hands but his lack of range and first-step quickness make him a better fit at second base, though he could see some time at shortstop. His arm is average. Those highest on Guerrero believe he can be an offensive-oriented second baseman, but he's far from the scouting favorite that Yoenis Cespedes was when he left Cuba. Several teams consider Guerrero to be a fringe big leaguer. The Dodgers are paying him to be their immediate second baseman in 2014.

Year	Club (League)	Class	AVG	G	AB	R	H	2B	3B	HR	RBI	BB	SO	SB	CS	OBP	SLG

Did not play—Signed 2014 contract

8 CHRIS REED, LHP

Born: May 20, 1990. **B-T:** L-L. **Ht.:** 6-4. **Wt.:** 195. **Drafted:** Stanford, 2011 (1st round). **Signed by:** Orsino Hill.

Reed made one start at Stanford but shined as the Cardinal closer in 2011, motivating the Dodgers to draft him with the No. 16 pick in the 2011 draft. After signing for $1.589 million, Reed made the conversion to starter. Blister problems slowed him in 2012, but he reached Double-A Chattanooga that season and returned there for 2013. Reed is one of the most prolific groundball pitchers in the minors, with a 2.2 groundout/airout ratio in 2013 that ranked 12th among ERA qualifiers. He throws 89-95 mph with heavy sink and run on his two-seamer. He doesn't miss many bats because he lacks a putaway pitch. Coming into the year, Reed's slider was his most advanced secondary pitch, but now scouts are mixed. It has hard downward break when it's on and can be an average pitch. His changeup improved, and its late sink contributes to his groundball tendencies. It flashes average when he maintains his arm speed. His control still needs to improve, especially since he's going to rely more on hitting his spots and working down in the zone rather than blowing hitters away. Through the first two innings of his outings, Reed had a 2.52 ERA, but his performance deteriorated once he got deeper into games. The Dodgers will likely continue to develop Reed as a starter, but his future may be as a groundball-oriented reliever, with a chance to make his big league debut in 2014 after a stop at Triple-A.

Year	Club (League)	Class	W	L	ERA	G	GS	CG	SV	IP	H	HR	BB	SO	K/9	WHIP	AVG
2011	R. Cucamonga (CAL)	HiA	0	1	7.71	3	3	0	0	7	9	1	4	9	11.6	1.86	.321
2012	R. Cucamonga (CAL)	HiA	1	4	3.09	7	6	0	0	35	25	1	14	38	9.8	1.11	.203
	Chattanooga (SL)	AA	0	4	4.84	12	11	0	0	35	31	2	20	29	7.4	1.44	.242
2013	Chattanooga (SL)	AA	4	11	3.86	29	25	1	0	138	128	9	63	106	6.9	1.39	.250
Minor League Totals			5	20	4.02	51	45	1	0	215	193	13	101	182	7.6	1.37	.244

9 ONELKI GARCIA, LHP

Born: Aug. 2, 1989. **B-T:** L-L. **Ht.:** 6-3. **Wt.:** 220. **Drafted:** Los Angeles (no school), 2012 (3rd round). **Signed by:** Dennis Moeller.

Garcia was one of the better young pitchers in Cuba when he left the island in January 2011. Less than 48 hours before the 2011 draft, MLB informed clubs that Garcia was draft eligible. Minutes before the draft, MLB changed its mind and eventually put him in the 2012 draft. Garcia stayed in shape by pitching in a Los Angeles-area adult league before the Dodgers popped him in the third round. He spent most of 2013 at Double-A Chattanooga after being slowed in the spring by knee issues, but after an August promotion to Triple-A, he made his major league debut in September. Garcia's best role is in the bullpen, where he spent the majority of 2013. His fastball sits at 92-94 mph with armside sink and touches 97, with deception that makes the pitch get on hitters quickly. He throws an above-average curveball with tight spin and good depth. He has a slider and a rudimentary changeup, but he's mostly a two-pitch guy out of the bullpen. Garcia's control is below-average, so he has to learn to command his fastball down in the zone and early in the count in order to get to his curveball to put hitters away. Garcia had arthroscopic surgery to clean out his left elbow and remove a bone spur in November. He could be ready to pitch by Opening Day, but the procedure clouds his status to start the year. He should be a solid reliever and the No. 2 lefty in the bullpen behind Paco Rodriguez.

Year	Club (League)	Class	W	L	ERA	G	GS	CG	SV	IP	H	HR	BB	SO	K/9	WHIP	AVG
2012	R. Cucamonga (CAL)	HiA	0	0	0.00	1	1	0	0	2	0	0	0	4	18.0	0.00	.000
2013	Chattanooga (SL)	AA	2	3	2.75	25	6	0	1	52	41	3	32	53	9.1	1.39	.215
	Albuquerque (PCL)	AAA	0	1	3.72	10	0	0	0	10	6	0	3	14	13.0	0.93	.176
	Los Angeles (NL)	MAJ	0	0	13.50	3	0	0	0	1	1	1	4	1	6.8	3.75	.200
Major League Totals			0	0	13.50	3	0	0	0	1	1	1	4	1	6.8	3.75	.200
Minor League Totals			2	4	2.81	36	7	0	1	64	47	3	35	71	10.0	1.28	.203

10 ROSS STRIPLING, RHP

BA GRADE **50** HIGH

Born: Nov. 23, 1989. **B-T:** R-R. **Ht.:** 6-3. **Wt.:** 190. **Drafted:** Texas A&M, 2012 (5th round). **Signed by:** Clint Bowers.

Cardinals righthander Michael Wacha was a first-round pick in 2012, then played a key role for the Cardinals in their 2013 postseason run. Stripling, Wacha's college roommate, went four rounds later and progressed quickly in his first full season. The Dodgers liked Stripling's combination of solid stuff and polish coming out of the draft, both of which were on display in 2013. He throws strikes and delivers his stuff with downhill angle, starting with an 88-94 mph fastball with sink and run that he keeps down in the zone to generate groundballs. His four-pitch mix is steady across the board, with no one standout offering but a host of average pitches. Some scouts think his best secondary pitch is his curveball, while others think it's more of a show pitch and believe his mid-80s slider is more effective with short, quick action. He throws his changeup with good arm speed and it flashes average, though it's a fairly straight pitch and still inconsistent. Stripling doesn't have Wacha's upside, but with his polish and solid arsenal of stuff, he has the talent of a back-of-the-rotation starter. He probably heads to Triple-A to open 2014, but if the Dodgers need a starter in the middle of the year, Stripling likely gets the call.

Year	Club (League)	Class	W	L	ERA	G	GS	CG	SV	IP	H	HR	BB	SO	K/9	WHIP	AVG
2012	Ogden (PIO)	R	1	0	1.24	14	12	0	0	36	26	0	6	37	9.2	0.88	.197
2013	R. Cucamonga (CAL)	HiA	2	0	2.94	6	6	0	0	34	24	1	11	34	9.1	1.04	.198
	Chattanooga (SL)	AA	6	4	2.78	21	16	0	1	94	91	4	19	83	7.9	1.17	.251
Minor League Totals			9	4	2.47	41	34	0	1	164	141	5	36	154	8.5	1.08	.229

11 JOSE DOMINGUEZ, RHP

BA GRADE **45** MEDIUM

Born: Aug. 7, 1990. **B-T:** R-R. **Ht.:** 6-0. **Wt.:** 160. **Signed:** Dominican Republic, 2007. **Signed by:** Rafael Rijo.

The Dodgers left Dominguez unprotected in the 2012 Rule 5 draft, but despite a fastball that clocks in north of 100 mph, every team in baseball passed. Some may have been wary of his history of drug-related suspensions. Dominguez was banged for 50 games after testing positive for the anabolic steroid Stanozolol (commonly sold as Winstrol) while in the Dominican Summer League in 2009, then in November 2012, Major League Baseball suspended him 25 games for an unspecified violation of the minor league drug program. The Dodgers were able to retain the righthander for 2013 and got him to the majors at the end of June, but a strained left quad ended his season. Dominguez is a pure power arm who sits at 97-100 mph and can reach 102. He has some natural life on his fastball and gets around on it sometimes, which gives it occasional cutting action. He complements his heater with a hard slider with short, quick break that comes and goes. He's learning to keep it in the bottom of the zone, and to keep it from popping out of his hand, which lets hitters see it early. He rarely throws his below-average changeup. Dominguez's fastball allows him to get away with mistakes, and he did improve his control in 2013, but it's still below-average. Even if his control remains erratic, his power arm will likely give him plenty of opportunities. He should start 2014 in the major league bullpen, where he fits as a middle reliever.

Year	Club (League)	Class	W	L	ERA	G	GS	CG	SV	IP	H	HR	BB	SO	K/9	WHIP	AVG
2008	Dodgers (DSL)	R	2	4	5.14	15	9	0	0	42	38	4	28	55	11.8	1.57	.235
2009	Dodgers (DSL)	R	4	5	3.64	15	13	0	1	59	52	1	24	57	8.6	1.28	.233
2010	Dodgers (DSL)	R	1	1	1.13	5	4	0	1	24	17	1	6	21	7.9	0.96	.191
2011	Ogden (PIO)	R	0	3	18.00	3	3	0	0	10	26	2	3	9	8.1	2.90	.464
	Dodgers (AZL)	R	4	1	3.50	10	10	0	0	44	38	3	13	43	8.9	1.17	.236
2012	Great Lakes (MWL)	LoA	4	3	5.25	33	5	0	4	72	77	4	47	78	9.8	1.72	.268
	Chattanooga (SL)	AA	0	1	1.29	5	0	0	1	7	2	0	0	9	11.6	0.29	.095
2013	Chattanooga (SL)	AA	1	0	2.60	14	0	0	5	17	8	0	8	28	14.5	0.92	.138

Year	Club (League)	Class	W	L	ERA	G	GS	CG	SV	IP	H	HR	BB	SO	K/9	WHIP	AVG
	Albuquerque (PCL)	AAA	1	0	0.00	8	0	0	0	8	1	0	5	12	13.5	0.75	.040
	Los Angeles (NL)	MAJ	0	0	2.16	9	0	0	0	8	11	0	3	4	4.3	1.68	.314
Major League Totals			0	0	2.16	9	0	0	0	8	11	0	3	4	4.3	1.68	.314
Minor League Totals			17	18	4.32	108	44	0	12	283	259	15	134	312	9.9	1.39	.239

12 TOM WINDLE, LHP

BA GRADE
50
HIGH

Born: March 10, 1992. **B-T:** L-L. **Ht.:** 6-4. **Wt.:** 215. **Drafted:** Minnesota, 2013 (2nd round). **Signed by:** Chet Sergo.

Windle spent most of his first two years at Minnesota in the bullpen, but he excelled as a starter in the Cape Cod League the summer after his sophomore year and during the 2013 college season as a junior. He threw the first nine-inning no-hitter in school history against Western Michigan in March, then in June went to the Dodgers in the second round. He signed quickly for $986,500 as the No. 56 overall pick, then pitched well in the low Class A Midwest League. Windle has a loose, lanky build and a quick arm, delivering 89-94 mph fastballs that he can cut and tail with downhill angle. His out-pitch is a hard-breaking slider in the mid-80s, a plus pitch that he will throw to lefties and righties. He'll mix an occasional curveball as well, but the slider is his primary breaking pitch. Since moving from the bullpen to the rotation, Windle has improved his changeup, but it's below-average and isn't a pitch he uses much. He throws slightly across his body, which gives him some deception, but his delivery isn't smooth and he has trouble keeping all of his long levers in sync. Stiffness and recoil in his mechanics give scouts pause about his durability and potential to develop his changeup, and he sometimes lands on his heel and spins off. He'll move through the system as a starter, but his fastball/slider mix could play well in a high-leverage relief role.

Year	Club (League)	Class	W	L	ERA	G	GS	CG	SV	IP	H	HR	BB	SO	K/9	WHIP	AVG
2013	Great Lakes (MWL)	LoA	5	1	2.68	13	12	0	0	54	50	2	20	51	8.6	1.30	.242
Minor League Totals			5	1	2.68	13	12	0	0	54	50	2	20	51	8.6	1.30	.242

13 YIMI GARCIA, RHP

BA GRADE
45
MEDIUM

Born: Aug. 18, 1990. **B-T:** R-R. **Ht.:** 6-1. **Wt.:** 175. **Signed:** Dominican Republic, 2009. **Signed by:** Bienvenido Tavarez.

Aside from a handful of starts in Rookie ball, Garcia has spent nearly his entire career as a reliever since signing with the Dodgers out of the Dominican Republic before the 2009 season. Despite generating little prospect buzz early in his career, he has maintained strong strikeout rates over the last three seasons, including a strong 2013 campaign as the closer at Double-A Chattanooga, followed by a trip to the Arizona Fall League. He can throw his 89-95 mph fastball with cutting action or late armside run. He has a full-circle arm action and gets good extension out front, which makes his fastball seem to have late hop, sneaking up on hitters faster than they expect. Garcia's tight-spinning, low-80s slider flashes average with late action but is usually a fringe-average offering, often coming in with cutter-like action on a flat plane. He added a fringy mid-80s changeup to his mix in 2013 that at times has splitter-like action, but he needs to tighten up both of his secondary weapons. Garcia lacks a true plus pitch, but he fills up the zone and finds a way to miss bats, which should allow him to be an effective set-up man. He likely opens 2014 at Triple-A Albuquerque.

Year	Club (League)	Class	W	L	ERA	G	GS	CG	SV	IP	H	HR	BB	SO	K/9	WHIP	AVG
2009	Dodgers (DSL)	R	3	2	1.67	16	5	0	0	54	37	0	15	51	8.5	0.96	.202
2010	Dodgers (AZL)	R	1	2	7.04	13	4	0	1	31	47	1	8	22	6.5	1.79	.356
2011	Ogden (PIO)	R	4	2	3.10	20	1	0	4	52	46	4	19	71	12.2	1.24	.236
2012	Great Lakes (MWL)	LoA	4	4	3.02	40	0	0	14	42	42	0	17	60	13.0	1.42	.253
	R. Cucamonga (CAL)	HiA	2	1	2.53	9	0	0	2	11	7	0	5	22	18.6	1.13	.175
2013	Chattanooga (SL)	AA	4	6	2.54	49	0	0	19	60	35	9	14	85	12.7	0.81	.164
Minor League Totals			18	17	3.10	147	10	0	40	250	214	14	78	311	11.2	1.17	.230

14 CODY BELLINGER, 1B

BA GRADE
50
HIGH

Born: July 13, 1995. **B-T:** L-L. **Ht.:** 6-4. **Wt.:** 180. **Drafted:** HS—Chandler, Ariz., 2013 (4th round). **Signed by:** Dustin Yount.

Clay Bellinger spent parts of four seasons in the majors, playing every position but pitcher for the Yankees and briefly the Angels from 1999-2002. His son Cody played in the 2007 Little League World Series and developed into one of the top Arizona high school prospects for the 2013 draft, signing for $700,000 as a Dodgers fourth-round pick. One of the youngest players in the 2013 draft, Bellinger is the rare teenage first-base prospect who makes scouts want to talk about his defense before his bat. He has Gold Glove potential with terrific actions around the bag, soft hands, good footwork and a strong arm. He runs a tick-above-average and could easily play the outfield, but his defense at first is so good that the Dodgers hesitate to move him. Bellinger combines athleticism with advanced feel for the game. Scouts like his lefthanded swing, as he loads well and has natural timing. His advanced pitch recognition and patient approach help him draw walks at a high clip. He's so gangly right now that he lacks strength, so power is the biggest question mark. He's a line-drive hitter with gap power, though he has the ability to backspin the ball. He has room to add 30 pounds to his frame, but right now he tends to jump out on his front foot trying to cheat to catch up to good fastballs because of his lack of strength. Scouts highest on Bellinger think he could develop average or better power, while others see 10-15 homers per year, which would place greater demands on his on-base skills.

Year	Club (League)	Class	AVG	G	AB	R	H	2B	3B	HR	RBI	BB	SO	SB	CS	OBP	SLG
2013	Dodgers (AZL)	R	.210	47	162	25	34	9	6	1	30	31	46	3	3	.340	.358
Minor League Totals			.210	47	162	25	34	9	6	1	30	31	46	3	3	.340	.358

15 JACOB SCAVUZZO, OF

Born: Jan. 15, 1994. **B-T:** R-R. **Ht.:** 6-4. **Wt.:** 195. **Drafted:** HS—Villa Park, Calif., 2012 (21st round). **Signed by:** Jeffrey Lachman.

The Dodgers were drawn to Scavuzzo for his combination of size and athleticism coming out of high school, where he also played football and competed in the 100 meters, triple jump and long jump in track and field. He signed as a 21st-round pick out of the 2012 draft, then looked like a raw free-swinger when he showed up to the Rookie-level Arizona League that summer. The speed of the game was too quick for Scavuzzo in his debut, but he emerged as a pleasant surprise in 2013 by leading the Rookie-level Pioneer League with 14 home runs. He made an adjustment to more fully incorporate his lower half into his swing, which helped him tap into his raw power. He's still prone to chasing pitches, but he improved his pitch selection, and he has the bat speed, swing path and hand-eye coordination to square up balls with authority. Scavuzzo has lift in his swing, but it's not a total uppercut that leaves him with glaring holes for pitchers to exploit. He's an average runner who played center and left field in 2013, but with his size he'll slow down, and his fringy arm strength make him fit best in left field, where he could be an above-average defender. Scavuzzo isn't the type of pure hitter who could move through the system in a hurry, but his 2013 production combined with his bat speed and athleticism were encouraging signs as he heads to low Class A Great Lakes in 2014.

Year	Club (League)	Class	AVG	G	AB	R	H	2B	3B	HR	RBI	BB	SO	SB	CS	OBP	SLG
2012	Dodgers (AZL)	R	.220	24	82	11	18	3	1	1	5	5	27	7	2	.281	.317
2013	Ogden (PIO)	R	.307	63	244	49	75	18	3	14	42	17	47	3	5	.350	.578
Minor League Totals			.285	87	326	60	93	21	4	15	47	22	74	10	7	.332	.512

16 MATT MAGILL, RHP

BA GRADE
45
MEDIUM

Born: Nov. 10, 1989. **B-T:** R-R. **Ht.:** 6-3. **Wt.:** 190. **Drafted:** HS—Simi Valley, Calif., 2008 (31st round). **Signed by:** Chuck Crim.

Magill had made steady progress through the Dodgers system in his first few years with the organization, with a spike in his strikeout rate in 2012 at Double-A Chattanooga that made it seem like the arrow was pointing in the right direction. He made his major league debut in 2013, but his six starts for the big league club were ugly, as his control deserted him and never returned when he went back down to Triple-A Albuquerque. Magill always had solid command throughout the minors, so his inability to throw strikes was a concern. He entered pro ball out of high school with mechanics that needed to be smoothed, and he was fairly sound with his delivery until the 2013 season, when he got out of whack with his lower half and worked to make some adjustments to separate his hands and repeat his release point. Magill needs to be around the strike zone to have success, as he lacks a put-away pitch. His fastball sits at 90-92 mph and can get up to 94. The secondary pitch he leans on the most is his solid-average slider with sharp, late break. His below-average changeup has always been a pitch he's needed to bring up to par. Magill likely returns to Triple-A in 2014, with a chance to fill in as a back-end starter or a long reliever. There's also a chance his stuff could tick up if he became a two-pitch reliever.

Year	Club (League)	Class	W	L	ERA	G	GS	CG	SV	IP	H	HR	BB	SO	K/9	WHIP	AVG
2008	Dodgers (GCL)	R	1	2	3.34	11	3	0	1	30	30	2	9	25	7.6	1.31	.265
2009	Ogden (PIO)	R	6	3	4.00	15	15	0	0	72	59	7	30	55	6.9	1.24	.224
2010	Great Lakes (MWL)	LoA	7	4	3.28	24	20	1	2	126	87	13	52	135	9.6	1.10	.194
2011	R. Cucamonga (CAL)	HiA	11	5	4.33	26	21	0	0	139	156	15	52	126	8.1	1.49	.280
2012	Chattanooga (SL)	AA	11	8	3.75	26	26	0	0	146	127	8	61	168	10.3	1.28	.232
2013	Los Angeles (NL)	MAJ	0	2	6.51	6	6	0	0	28	27	6	28	26	8.5	1.99	.257
	Dodgers (AZL)	R	0	0	0.00	1	1	0	0	3	1	0	0	3	9.0	0.33	.100
	Albuquerque (PCL)	AAA	6	2	3.47	18	16	0	0	86	72	7	50	101	10.6	1.42	.238
Major League Totals			0	2	6.51	6	6	0	0	28	27	6	28	26	8.5	1.99	.257
Minor League Totals			42	24	3.74	121	102	1	3	602	532	52	254	613	9.2	1.30	.238

17 SCOTT SCHEBLER, OF

BA GRADE
45
HIGH

Born: Oct. 6, 1990. **B-T:** L-R. **Ht.:** 6-1. **Wt.:** 208. **Drafted:** Des Moines Area CC, 2010 (26th round). **Signed by:** Scott Little.

After batting .446 with 20 home runs for Des Moines Area CC in 2010, Schebler prepared to transfer to Wichita State for the following season, that is until the Dodgers signed him for $300,000 as a 26th-round pick at the signing deadline. After a mediocre 2012 season in the low Class A Midwest League, Schebler had a breakout season in 2013 in the high Class A California League, leading the league in extra-base hits (69) while ranking second in slugging (.581) and homers (27) to become the Dodgers' minor league player of the year. He's more production than tools, and some scouts believe the hitter-friendly Cal League may have masked some of his weaknesses. Schebler sacrificed contact for power in 2013, which led to a jump in his strikeout rate (26 percent of plate appearances) along with a career-high .941 OPS. He generates surprising power and has a chance to hit 20-25 home runs in the majors, but skeptics wonder whether more advanced pitchers will be able to exploit the holes he has on the inner third of the plate. Schebler runs a tick-above-average underway, though he doesn't post correspondingly strong home-to-first times. He should steal more bases than the typical left fielder, a position he'll have to play because of his below-average arm strength, though he did spend the second half of 2013 in right field. Schebler will head to Double-A Chattanooga in 2014, where he'll get his first test against upper-level pitching.

Year	Club (League)	Class	AVG	G	AB	R	H	2B	3B	HR	RBI	BB	SO	SB	CS	OBP	SLG
2010	Dodgers (AZL)	R	.294	5	17	3	5	0	2	0	1	1	5	1	0	.333	.529
2011	Ogden (PIO)	R	.285	70	295	44	84	17	8	13	58	13	97	1	1	.324	.529
2012	Great Lakes (MWL)	LoA	.260	137	515	67	134	32	8	6	67	30	99	17	11	.312	.388
2013	R. Cucamonga (CAL)	HiA	.296	125	477	95	141	29	13	27	91	35	140	16	5	.360	.581
Minor League Totals			.279	337	1304	209	364	78	31	46	217	79	341	35	17	.333	.492

18 JUSTIN CHIGBOGU, 1B

BA GRADE
50
EXTREME

Born: July 8, 1994. **B-T:** L-L. **Ht.:** 6-1. **Wt.:** 240. **Drafted:** HS—Raytown, Mo., 2012 (4th round). **Signed by:** Scott Little.

Chigbogu was a high school football standout, earning all-state honors as a defensive end in Missouri. His athleticism and raw power attracted the Dodgers, who signed him for $250,000 as a fourth-round pick in 2012. As one of the younger players in his draft, Chigbogu turned 19 early in a 2013 season split between the Rookie-level Arizona and Pioneer leagues, where he showed outstanding power and a long way to go to reach his ceiling. Chigbogu has excellent bat speed and 70 raw power on the 20-80 scale. He can drive the ball out of the park from foul pole to foul pole, with more home runs coming to the opposite field than his pull side. Despite his ability to use the whole field, his swing and approach remain raw. He struck out in 34 percent of plate appearances in the PL, a major red flag, as he especially struggles against breaking pitches. Chigbogu is athletic and runs well for his size, but scouts say he's still working to become an adequate defender at first base. If he can close some of the holes in his swing, his raw power can carry him, but he's the type of high-risk player who might fall short of his ceiling.

Year	Club (League)	Class	AVG	G	AB	R	H	2B	3B	HR	RBI	BB	SO	SB	CS	OBP	SLG
2012	Dodgers (AZL)	R	.200	32	115	18	23	4	0	3	12	14	50	2	3	.282	.313
2013	Dodgers (AZL)	R	.326	11	46	12	15	3	1	5	19	3	18	0	0	.360	.761
	Ogden (PIO)	R	.254	49	189	34	48	9	1	9	31	22	72	2	1	.330	.455
Minor League Totals			.246	92	350	64	86	16	2	17	62	39	140	4	4	.318	.449

19 PEDRO BAEZ, RHP

BA GRADE
45
HIGH

Born: March 11, 1988. **B-T:** R-R. **Ht.:** 6-2. **Wt.:** 195. **Signed:** Dominican Republic, 2007. **Signed by:** Elvio Jimenez.

When it came to investing in Latin American amateurs, the Dodgers were the most frugal organizations in baseball for years. One exception came in 2007, when they signed Baez for $200,000 just before he turned 19. At the time, Baez was a third baseman who stood out for his plus raw power and plus arm, but he was never able to put things together at the plate, as he lacked natural hitting rhythm and succumbed to breaking pitches. After Baez stalled at Double-A Chattanooga as a hitter, the Dodgers moved him to the mound, where he made a surprisingly quick transition in 2013, his first season as a pitcher. Baez has a power arm and throws 91-96 mph with good sink. He started the year with little in the way of an offspeed pitch, but he developed a short, cutter-like slider in the mid-80s to give hitters another look, though he doesn't have a true out-pitch. Baez has a thick frame, short arm action and is understandably raw in terms of his command and keeping his delivery in sync. The Dodgers already have one hitter-turned-reliever success story in Kenley Jansen. Baez doesn't miss as many bats as Jansen did, but he could get to the big leagues as a middle reliever. The Dodgers added him to the 40-man roster in November to make sure nobody else could take him in the Rule 5 draft.

Year	Club (League)	Class	W	L	ERA	G	GS	CG	SV	IP	H	HR	BB	SO	K/9	WHIP	AVG
2013	R. Cucamonga (CAL)	HiA	2	2	3.63	32	0	0	2	35	41	3	15	32	8.3	1.62	.295
	Chattanooga (SL)	AA	1	1	4.24	16	0	0	0	23	26	3	8	23	8.9	1.46	.283
Minor League Totals			3	3	3.88	48	0	0	2	58	67	6	23	55	8.5	1.55	.290

Year	Club (League)	Class	AVG	G	AB	R	H	2B	3B	HR	RBI	BB	SO	SB	CS	OBP	SLG
2007	Dodgers (GCL)	R	.274	53	201	35	55	14	2	3	39	17	40	3	1	.341	.408
2008	Great Lakes (MWL)	LoA	.178	59	185	23	33	10	1	1	16	17	45	3	1	.244	.259
	Ogden (PIO)	R	.267	61	247	37	66	20	1	12	50	18	69	2	2	.317	.502
2009	Inland Empire (CAL)	HiA	.286	79	308	48	88	17	1	10	61	16	84	5	1	.326	.445
2010	Dodgers (AZL)	R	.000	2	7	0	0	0	0	0	1	1	1	0	0	.111	.000
	Inland Empire (CAL)	HiA	.259	75	309	41	80	10	0	6	42	17	68	4	1	.306	.350
	Chattanooga (SL)	AA	.385	7	26	2	10	1	0	0	2	2	8	1	0	.448	.423
2011	Chattanooga (SL)	AA	.210	32	105	12	22	12	0	2	15	9	28	1	2	.278	.381
2012	Chattanooga (SL)	AA	.216	78	273	41	59	13	4	4	36	33	64	5	3	.319	.337
	R. Cucamonga (CAL)	HiA	.228	50	184	19	42	14	1	7	23	14	44	2	1	.287	.429
Minor League Totals			.248	507	1850	258	458	112	10	45	286	145	452	26	12	.309	.392

20 VICTOR GONZALEZ, LHP

BA GRADE **50** EXTREME

Born: Nov. 16, 1995. **B-T:** L-L. **Ht.:** 6-0. **Wt.:** 205. **Signed:** Mexico, 2012. **Signed by:** Mike Brito.

When the Dodgers worked out a package deal in 2012 with Mexico City, the prize of the deal was Julio Urias, who was sensational in 2013, his first season with the Dodgers. Gonzalez proved to be an intriguing sleeper in his own right. When he was working out for teams in Mexico, Gonzalez threw 85-87 mph with a stocky frame but a good arm action and delivery. His velocity ticked up in 2013 and sat around 87-92 mph, and he had immediate success in the Rookie-level Arizona League as a 17-year-old, with poise beyond his years. Gonzalez throws three pitches that he'll use in any count and commands his fastball to both sides of the plate. His changeup is his most advanced offspeed pitch, flashing above-average at times. He mixes a slurvy curveball in that he will have to either tighten or eventually go with a true slider. Gonzalez has a heavy, 6-foot build that he'll have to watch as he gets older. He doesn't have the high ceiling of Urias, but he's emerged as a solid prospect whose feel for pitching could have him in the low Class A Midwest League as an 18-year-old in 2014.

Year	Club (League)	Class	W	L	ERA	G	GS	CG	SV	IP	H	HR	BB	SO	K/9	WHIP	AVG
2013	Dodgers (AZL)	R	3	2	3.79	11	10	0	0	38	31	1	12	45	10.7	1.13	.223
Minor League Totals			3	2	3.79	11	10	0	0	38	31	1	12	45	10.7	1.13	.223

21 ZACH BIRD, RHP

BA GRADE **50** EXTREME

Born: July 14, 1994. **B-T:** R-R. **Ht.:** 6-4. **Wt.:** 205. **Drafted:** HS—Jackson, Miss., 2012 (9th round). **Signed by:** Matthew Paul.

Bird's father Eugene played defensive back at Southern Mississippi from 1971-73 before the New York Jets drafted him in the 1974 draft, though he never played in the NFL. Zach also could have played at Southern Miss, but he opted instead to sign with the Dodgers for $140,000 as a ninth-round pick in the 2012 draft. One of the youngest players in his draft class, Bird opened the 2013 season as an 18-year-old in the low Class A Midwest League, but he struggled there and the Dodgers demoted him to the Rookie-level Pioneer League, where he threw more strikes but still got hit hard. Bird is a good athlete with a long, lean frame and downhill angle on a fastball that sits at 89-93 mph and maxes out at 95. He can cut and sink his fastball, helping him get plenty of groundballs. He doesn't yet have a true out-pitch among his secondary pitches, with a curveball he uses early in counts and a changeup that remains a work in progress. Bird still is learning to repeat his delivery, as he gets out of sync with his mechanics, causing his control to disappear. He made strides with his command in the second half of the 2013 season but still needs work in that regard. He should head back to the Midwest League in 2014.

Year	Club (League)	Class	W	L	ERA	G	GS	CG	SV	IP	H	HR	BB	SO	K/9	WHIP	AVG
2012	Dodgers (AZL)	R	1	2	4.54	10	10	0	0	40	36	2	17	46	10.4	1.34	.237
2013	Ogden (PIO)	R	2	4	5.77	9	9	0	0	44	43	3	19	44	9.1	1.42	.247
	Great Lakes (MWL)	LoA	2	5	5.10	19	11	0	0	60	56	5	45	50	7.5	1.68	.249
Minor League Totals			5	11	5.15	38	30	0	0	143	135	10	81	140	8.8	1.51	.245

22 JESMUEL VALENTIN, 2B/SS

BA GRADE **45** HIGH

Born: May 12, 1994. **B-T:** B-R. **Ht.:** 5-9. **Wt.:** 180. **Drafted:** HS—Gurabo, P.R., 2012 (1st round supplemental). **Signed by:** Rob Sidwell.

Scouts are drawn to Valentin's instincts and high baseball IQ, particularly on defense, which is no surprise given his background. His father is Jose Valentin, a 16-year big leaguer from 1992-2007 who was well regarded for his glove during his career with the Brewers, White Sox, Dodgers and Mets and is now the first base coach for the Padres. Jesmuel was high school teammates with Carlos Correa, who went No. 1 overall to the Astros in 2012, while Valentin signed for $984,700 as a supplemental first-round pick. With Correa at shortstop, Valentin played mostly second base in high school, and he spent the majority of 2013 at second as well. He gets better reads and reactions at the keystone than he does at shortstop, with good range and smooth hands. Scouts project Valentin's ceiling as a utility player because his bat is light. His plate discipline is solid—he's drawn nearly as many walks as strikeouts in his career—but he has minimal power and had a hard time handling the low Class A Midwest League in 2013 before being demoted to the Rookie-level Pioneer League in June. He'll get another crack with Great Lakes in 2014.

Year	Club (League)	Class	AVG	G	AB	R	H	2B	3B	HR	RBI	BB	SO	SB	CS	OBP	SLG
2012	Dodgers (AZL)	R	.211	43	152	34	32	6	2	2	18	35	24	5	2	.352	.316
2013	Great Lakes (MWL)	LoA	.212	33	99	12	21	6	1	0	5	16	28	4	3	.325	.293
	Ogden (PIO)	R	.284	62	250	53	71	10	3	4	24	33	34	11	7	.379	.396
Minor League Totals			.248	138	501	99	124	22	6	6	47	84	86	20	12	.360	.351

23 IBANDEL ISABEL, OF

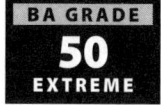

BA GRADE
50
EXTREME

Born: June 20, 1995. **B-T:** R-R. **Ht.:** 6-4. **Wt.:** 185. **Signed:** Dominican Republic, 2013. **Signed by:** Bob Engle/Patrick Guerrero.

The Dodgers signed Isabel out of the Dominican Republic one month before the 2013 Dominican Summer League season started. He quickly showed why Los Angeles was drawn to him after an outstanding pro debut in the DSL, where he ranked third in the league in slugging (.500). Isabel stands out physically for his large, projectable frame with plenty of room to add weight and strength, but he's an advanced hitter for his age and his size. He has good hitting actions, uses his hands well and has a sound, righthanded swing with good path to the ball. Isabel didn't show much over-the-fence power in 2013, but he racked up plenty of doubles (15 in 57 games) and could grow into plus power once he fills out. The power will have to come for Isabel because he doesn't offer much value beyond what he does at the plate. With speed and arm strength that both grade as below-average, Isabel is limited to left field and could end up at first base. While fellow first-year Dominican outfielder Michael Medina ranked second in the DSL in home runs, Isabel is the better prospect because he has more feel for hitting. He should make his U.S. debut in 2014, likely in the Rookie-level Arizona League.

Year	Club (League)	Class	AVG	G	AB	R	H	2B	3B	HR	RBI	BB	SO	SB	CS	OBP	SLG
2013	Dodgers (DSL)	R	.327	57	196	25	64	15	5	3	31	20	50	1	3	.398	.500
Minor League Totals			.327	57	196	25	64	15	5	3	31	20	50	1	3	.398	.500

24 HECTOR NELO, RHP

BA GRADE
45
HIGH

Born: Nov. 5, 1986. **B-T:** R-R. **Ht.:** 6-1. **Wt.:** 200. **Drafted:** St. Thomas (Fla.), 2007 (15th round). **Signed by:** Juan Alvarez (Rangers).

Nelo's career has taken a winding road, but even at 27 he's still a prospect with an intriguing fastball. A Rangers 15th-round pick in 2007, Nelo earned his release from Texas following spring training in 2011, only to be quickly signed by the Nationals. He put together a solid year for Washington in the Double-A Harrisburg bullpen in 2012, prompting the Dodgers to pick him in the minor league phase of the 2012 Rule 5 draft. He repeated Double-A in 2013, where he showed a 94-98 mph fastball with Chattanooga that peaked at 100, with heavy sink that yields an abundance of groundballs. Despite his velocity, Nelo doesn't have a big strikeout rate in part because he doesn't have much else. He telegraphs his offspeed pitches, varying his release point and slowing his arm on his below-average, mid-80s changeup. His breaking ball lacks crispness, though he can retire hitters sometimes because they have to be geared up for his fastball. Nelo can have success when he stays on top of his fastball and commands it down in the zone, but he still needs to be able to throw more strikes. If he can improve his fastball command and develop a more reliable offspeed pitch, he could be a late bloomer who works his way into a middle relief role.

Year	Club (League)	Class	W	L	ERA	G	GS	CG	SV	IP	H	HR	BB	SO	K/9	WHIP	AVG
2007	Spokane (NWL)	SS	1	2	6.55	15	0	0	0	22	20	1	21	21	8.6	1.86	.244
2008	Clinton (MWL)	LoA	1	3	2.96	17	0	0	1	24	22	1	17	19	7.0	1.60	.250
	Rangers (AZL)	R	1	4	4.04	10	8	0	0	36	40	0	19	26	6.6	1.65	.301
	Bakersfield (CAL)	HiA	0	0	3.60	2	1	0	0	5	2	1	7	6	10.8	1.80	.111
2009	Bakersfield (CAL)	HiA	0	0	5.16	19	0	0	0	30	33	1	23	27	8.2	1.89	.275
2010	Hickory (SAL)	LoA	1	2	6.82	19	0	0	1	32	40	3	11	31	8.8	1.61	.313
	Bakersfield (CAL)	HiA	0	1	5.93	20	0	0	0	27	25	5	19	32	10.5	1.61	.250
2011	Potomac (CAR)	HiA	1	0	2.40	36	0	0	18	41	32	0	16	35	7.6	1.16	.206
2012	Harrisburg (EL)	AA	1	6	2.73	47	0	0	16	53	44	4	29	63	10.8	1.39	.229
2013	Chattanooga (SL)	AA	5	2	2.67	45	0	0	3	61	51	2	29	50	7.4	1.32	.231
Minor League Totals			11	20	3.98	230	9	0	39	330	309	18	191	310	8.4	1.51	.250

25 DARNELL SWEENEY, SS/2B

BA GRADE **45** HIGH

Born: Feb. 1, 1991. **B-T:** B-R. **Ht.:** 6-1. **Wt.:** 150. **Drafted:** Central Florida, 2012 (13th round). **Signed by:** Scott Hennessey.

Sweeney has always had raw tools, but he's still trying to polish his skills in all areas of the game. Going into his junior year at Central Florida in 2012, scouts thought he had a chance to go in the top three rounds of the draft, but he didn't hit well enough to merit that type of pick and slid to the Dodgers in the 13th round, where he signed for $100,000. Sweeney is a good athlete whose best tool is his plus speed, which helped him lead the high Class A California League in triples (16) and rank third in stolen bases (48), though he needs to become more selective after getting caught a league-high 20 times. His speed gives him good range in at shortstop and he has an average arm, but he needs to improve his footwork and cut down on his mistakes after committing 36 errors. Moving to second base in August seemed to be a more natural fit. Scouts said he looked much more comfortable there and committed just two errors in 29 games. Sweeney can have success at the plate when he stays within his strike zone and works gap to gap, but he's prone to swinging and missing and struggles to catch up to good velocity. His future is at second base, with a likely assignment to Double-A Chattanooga in 2014.

Year	Club (League)	Class	AVG	G	AB	R	H	2B	3B	HR	RBI	BB	SO	SB	CS	OBP	SLG
2012	Ogden (PIO)	R	.303	16	66	12	20	1	2	0	10	9	8	10	2	.380	.379
	Great Lakes (MWL)	LoA	.291	51	199	34	58	8	4	5	23	24	41	17	4	.372	.447
2013	R. Cucamonga (CAL)	HiA	.275	134	552	79	152	34	16	11	77	43	151	48	20	.329	.455
Minor League Totals			.282	201	817	125	230	43	22	16	110	76	200	75	26	.344	.447

26 TYLER OGLE, 1B/C

BA GRADE **45** HIGH

Born: Aug. 9, 1990. **B-T:** R-R. **Ht.:** 5-10. **Wt.:** 210. **Drafted:** Oklahoma, 2011 (9th round). **Signed by:** Scott Little.

Ogle was an offensive-oriented catcher coming out of Oklahoma in 2011, when he was a third-team All-American for the Sooners and signed for $100,000 as a Dodgers ninth-round pick. He's one of the most patient hitters in the minor leagues, ranking eighth in the minors in walks (96) and leading the low Class A Midwest League in that category in 2013 while ranking third in OBP (.401). Ogle controls the strike zone and has some strength in his swing to make hard contact, though he doesn't project to have more than average power. Even though he hit just .252, he makes frequent contact and should see his batting average rise going forward, especially if he jumps to the hitter-friendly high Class A California League in 2014. The problem for Ogle is finding a position. He caught just 14 games in 2013 and is a marginal defender behind the plate with a fringy arm, so he spent the majority of his time at first base. He took to the position quickly and played good defense, though at 5-foot-10 his height doesn't give his infielders much margin for errors on throws. Ogle's power doesn't profile well at first base, but if the Dodgers allow him to develop more behind the plate he would become a much more intriguing prospect.

Year	Club (League)	Class	AVG	G	AB	R	H	2B	3B	HR	RBI	BB	SO	SB	CS	OBP	SLG
2011	Dodgers (AZL)	R	.167	6	18	4	3	0	0	0	2	0	1	0	0	.167	.167
2012	Dodgers (AZL)	R	.483	16	60	22	29	9	0	5	24	11	12	1	1	.563	.883
	Ogden (PIO)	R	.258	8	31	9	8	2	0	1	3	4	5	0	0	.351	.419
	Great Lakes (MWL)	LoA	.210	18	62	10	13	1	0	3	7	6	16	0	0	.310	.371
	Albuquerque (PCL)	AAA	1.000	1	3	0	3	0	0	0	4	1	0	0	0	1.000	1.000
2013	Great Lakes (MWL)	LoA	.252	130	437	60	110	24	0	12	57	96	76	6	7	.401	.389
Minor League Totals			.272	179	611	105	166	36	0	21	97	118	110	7	8	.403	.434

27 JON GARCIA, OF

BA GRADE **45** HIGH

Born: Nov. 11, 1991. **B-T:** R-R. **Ht.:** 5-11. **Wt.:** 175. **Drafted:** HS—Yauco, P.R., 2009 (8th round). **Signed by:** Manny Estrada.

When the Dodgers signed Garcia for $125,000 out of a Puerto Rico high school as their eighth-round pick in 2009, he was known for his impressive power displays in batting practice but still raw as a hitter. His ability to reach Double-A Chattanooga as a 21-year-old in 2013 is impressive in light of his crudeness at the plate in high school. Garcia, however, struggled with the jump in late June from the high Class A California League to more advanced pitching in Double-A, showing he still has a long way to go with his hitting approach. With a strong, stocky frame, he still generates attention for his above-average raw power, with the ability to hit the ball out of the park from his pull side to the middle of the field. Garcia can crush a fastball when he's on time, but anything offspeed throws him off balance, causing him to rack up an unhealthy number of strikeouts. He's a below-average runner with a plus arm that allows him to play right field. At 22, Garcia still is young for Double-A, where he likely will return in 2014, though because of his issues at the plate he doesn't project to move quickly to the big leagues.

Year	Club (League)	Class	AVG	G	AB	R	H	2B	3B	HR	RBI	BB	SO	SB	CS	OBP	SLG
2009	Dodgers (AZL)	R	.304	41	138	22	42	16	1	3	21	10	37	4	0	.362	.500
2010	Ogden (PIO)	R	.305	61	239	45	73	19	2	10	40	19	59	4	1	.365	.527
2011	Great Lakes (MWL)	LoA	.228	130	464	58	106	28	2	19	63	34	133	2	1	.290	.420
2012	R. Cucamonga (CAL)	HiA	.233	95	378	54	88	18	2	12	41	15	134	2	3	.266	.386
2013	R. Cucamonga (CAL)	HiA	.287	68	258	51	74	13	5	17	44	16	82	9	3	.337	.574
	Chattanooga (SL)	AA	.168	56	185	15	31	7	2	1	9	12	60	1	1	.217	.243
Minor League Totals			.249	451	1662	245	414	101	14	62	218	106	505	22	9	.301	.439

28 ARIEL SANDOVAL, OF

BA GRADE **50** EXTREME

Born: Nov. 6, 1995. **B-T:** R-R. **Ht.:** 6-2. **Wt.:** 180. **Signed:** Dominican Republic, 2012. **Signed by:** Patrick Guerrero/Bob Engle.

After the 2012 season, the Dodgers overhauled their international scouting department. First they brought in Patrick Guerrero, who had just been fired by the Mariners, to be their Latin American coordinator. Soon after, they hired Bob Engle from the Mariners to be their vice president of international scouting, reuniting the two longtime coworkers in the same roles they had in Seattle. Their first six-figure signing was Sandoval, who landed a $150,000 bonus in December 2012. Sandoval still is raw, but his combination of size, athleticism and hand-eye coordination give him a promising starter kit. He's a plus runner who projects as a center fielder, though if he gets too big his above-average arm strength should allow him to play right field. He didn't post big numbers in the Dominican Summer League in his pro debut in 2013, but he has a knack for making contact and the size to grow into more power than the occasional gap pop he shows now. Sandoval's youth and crudeness are enough to possibly warrant another year in the DSL, but it's possible he could make his U.S. debut in the Rookie-level Arizona League in 2014.

Year	Club (League)	Class	AVG	G	AB	R	H	2B	3B	HR	RBI	BB	SO	SB	CS	OBP	SLG
2013	Dodgers (DSL)	R	.255	63	243	26	62	7	2	0	16	15	39	19	12	.299	.300
Minor League Totals			.255	63	243	26	62	7	2	0	16	15	39	19	12	.299	.300

29 VICTOR ARANO, RHP

BA GRADE **50** EXTREME

Born: Feb. 7, 1995. **B-T:** R-R. **Ht.:** 6-2. **Wt.:** 200. **Signed:** Mexico, 2013. **Signed by:** Mike Brito/Pat Kelly.

After signing lefthanders Julio Urias and Victor Gonzalez out of the Mexican League in August 2012, the Dodgers went back to the same Mexico City club to purchase the rights to Arano in April 2013. Arano, who pitched for Mexico's 16U national team in 2011 at the World Championship, showed advanced feel for pitching in his 2013 debut in the Rookie-level Arizona League. He has good command for his age of an 89-94 mph fastball, with the ability to work down in the zone and keep the ball on the ground. He has good feel to spin a hard, high-70s curveball, an average pitch that he can use to finish hitters. He has a mid-80s changeup, but it's not a reliable pitch yet, and he has trouble keeping it around the strike zone. Arano has a thick, heavy build that he'll have to work to keep in check as he gets older. He could develop into a back-end starter, with a jump next year to the low Class A Midwest League possible, though the Dodgers could hold him back in extended spring training and send him to Rookie-level Ogden instead.

Year	Club (League)	Class	W	L	ERA	G	GS	CG	SV	IP	H	HR	BB	SO	K/9	WHIP	AVG
2013	Dodgers (AZL)	R	3	2	4.20	13	8	0	0	49	52	4	13	49	8.9	1.32	.255
Minor League Totals			3	2	4.20	13	8	0	0	49	52	4	13	49	8.9	1.32	.255

30 BRANDON DIXON, 3B

BA GRADE **50** EXTREME

Born: Jan. 29, 1992. **B-T:** R-R. **Ht.:** 6-2. **Wt.:** 215. **Drafted:** Arizona, 2013 (3rd round). **Signed by:** Dustin Yount.

The Rangers drafted Dixon out of a California high school with their 48th-round pick in 2010, but he didn't sign and played at Arizona instead, getting the winning hit in the 2012 College World Series. Going into his junior year, Dixon had laser eye surgery and emerged as the team's best hitter in 2013 when the Dodgers drafted him in the third round and signed him for $566,500. Dixon looked overmatched in his pro debut in the low Class A Midwest League, where he struggled to make contact and catch up to the speed of the game. He's strong, has a quick swing and shows above-average raw power in batting practice, but he doesn't project to be a huge home run hitter because his game swing doesn't have the loft or leverage for big power numbers. He runs well for his size with solid-average speed, though his feet are prone to getting tangled and his arm is below-average, so he could be destined for left field. After a rough debut, Dixon should head back to the Midwest League to try to get back on track.

Year	Club (League)	Class	AVG	G	AB	R	H	2B	3B	HR	RBI	BB	SO	SB	CS	OBP	SLG
2013	Great Lakes (MWL)	LoA	.185	59	211	28	39	11	1	1	17	11	65	6	2	.227	.261
Minor League Totals			.185	59	211	28	39	11	1	1	17	11	65	6	2	.227	.261

Miami Marlins

BY JAMES BAILEY

In late May the Marlins were looking up at the rest of the National League, practically if not mathematically eliminated at 13-41. Attendance at second-year Marlins Park was abysmal, on par with the numbers at old Sun Life Stadium. Fans took out their anger at owner Jeffrey Loria and his salary-dumping offseason deals by ignoring the team.

Then the young club suddenly showed signs of life.

After winning their final game in May, the Marlins went 15-10 in June. Mike Redmond's squad managed a respectable 51-59 mark over its final 110 games. Slowly, fans started to return, particularly on nights when rookie sensation Jose Fernandez took the hill. Yet Miami averaged just 19,584 fans per game, a figure higher than only the Rays and down 28.5 percent from 2012.

While locals were upset by the series of offseason deals that sent nearly every recognizable name out of town, the Marlins could take solace in the return they got, particularly in the 12-player blockbuster they consummated with the Blue Jays in November 2012.

Adeiny Hechavarria took over at shortstop, providing solid glovework on a team that played surprisingly tight defense. Righthander Henderson Alvarez tossed a no-hitter on the season's final day. Prospects Justin Nicolino, Anthony DeSclafani and Jake Marisnick bolstered their stock with strong showings on the farm. Additionally, lefthander Brian Flynn, acquired from the Tigers in July 2012, led the hitter-friendly Pacific Coast League in ERA.

Wave after wave of rookies washed ashore in Miami, gaining experience and giving fans a taste of the future. Seven of Miami's top 12 prospects entering the season saw big league action, including outfielder Christian Yelich, who hit a solid .288/.370/.396 in regular duty after being summoned in late July.

Unfortunately, aside from Yelich, veteran right fielder Giancarlo Stanton, and rookie Marcell Ozuna, the offensive sparks came few and far between. Miami was the only team in the majors to hit fewer than 100 home runs, finishing with 95. The Marlins were last in hits, batting (.231), on-base percentage (.293), slugging (.335) and runs (3.17 per game).

So how did they win 62 games? Pitching. The young staff ranked 11th in the major leagues with a 3.71 ERA. Fernandez, the NL rookie of the year, finished second in the bigs with a 2.19 mark with 187 strikeouts in 173 innings.

MORRIS FOSTOFF

Rookie ace Jose Fernandez was one of the few bright spots for the rebuilding Marlins

TOP PROSPECTS OF THE DECADE

Year	Player, Pos.	2013 Org.
2004	Jeremy Hermida, of	Indians
2005	Jeremy Hermida, of	Indians
2006	Jeremy Hermida, of	Indians
2007	Chris Volstad, rhp	Rockies
2008	Cameron Maybin, of	Padres
2009	Cameron Maybin, of	Padres
2010	Giancarlo Stanton, of	Marlins
2011	Matt Dominguez, 3b	Astros
2012	Christian Yelich, of	Marlins
2013	Jose Fernandez, rhp	Marlins

Longtime president of baseball operations Larry Beinfest took the fall after the season. Hired in 2002 as general manager, Beinfest was fired in the last week of the season. General manager Mike Hill was promoted to president, with vice president of player personnel Dan Jennings sliding into Hill's old job title.

The team's top 2013 pick, third baseman Colin Moran, made an immediate impact, homering in his first professional at-bat for low Class A Greensboro. However, the Marlins failed to sign supplemental first-rounder Matt Krook, a high school lefty from San Francisco, and third-rounder Ben DeLuzio, a prep shortstop from Orlando. Still, the farm system is deeper than it was a couple of years ago, with plenty of young talent already entrenched in Miami.

ORGANIZATION OVERVIEW

General Manager: Dan Jennings. **Farm Director:** Brian Chattin. **Scouting Director:** Stan Meek.

Class	Team	League	W	L	PCT	Finish	Manager
Majors	Miami Marlins	National	62	100	.383	15th (15)	Mike Redmond
Triple-A	New Orleans Zephyrs	Pacific Coast	72	72	.500	9th (16)	Ron Hassey
Double-A	Jacksonville Suns	Southern	73	63	.537	5th (10)	Andy Barkett
High A	Jupiter Hammerheads	Florida State	68	69	.496	5th (12)	Andy Haines
Low A	Greensboro Grasshoppers	South Atlantic	65	72	.474	9th (14)	Jorge Hernandez
Short-season	Batavia Muckdogs	New York-Penn	39	36	.520	6th (14)	Angel Espada
Rookie	GCL Marlins	Gulf Coast	25	34	.424	14th (16)	Julio Garcia
2013 Overall Minor League Record			**342**	**346**	**.497**	**t-13th (30)**	

THIS YEAR'S TOP 30

No.	Player, Pos.	Grade/Risk
1.	Andrew Heaney, lhp	60/Medium
2.	Colin Moran, 3b	55/Medium
3.	Jake Marisnick, of	55/High
4.	Justin Nicolino, lhp	50/Medium
5.	Anthony DeSclafani, rhp	50/Medium
6.	Brian Flynn, lhp	45/Low
7.	Jose Urena, rhp	50/High
8.	Adam Conley, lhp	50/High
9.	Avery Romero, 2b	50/High
10.	J.T. Realmuto, c	50/High
11.	Trevor Williams, rhp	50/High
12.	Arquimedes Caminero, rhp	45/Medium
13.	Jesus Solorzano, of	50/High
14.	Austin Dean, of	50/High
15.	Sam Dyson, rhp	45/Medium
16.	Angel Sanchez, rhp	50/High
17.	Colby Suggs, rhp	50/High
18.	Nick Wittgren, rhp	45/Medium
19.	Brent Keys, of	45/Medium
20.	Austin Barnes, c	45/Medium
21.	Grant Dayton, lhp	45/Medium
22.	Kyle Jensen, of	45/Medium
23.	Edgar Olmos, lhp	45/Medium
24.	Mark Canha, 1b	45/High
25.	Tyler Higgins, rhp	45/High
26.	Javier Lopez, ss	50/Extreme
27.	Austin Brice, rhp	50/Extreme
28.	Jarlin Garcia, lhp	50/Extreme
29.	Josh Hodges, rhp	45/High
30.	Michael Brady, rhp	40/Low

LAST YEAR'S TOP 30

No.	Player, Pos.	Status
1.	Jose Fernandez, rhp	Majors
2.	Christian Yelich, of	Majors
3.	Andrew Heaney, lhp	No. 1
4.	Jake Marisnick, of	No. 3
5.	Marcell Ozuna, of	Majors
6.	Justin Nicolino, lhp	No. 4
7.	Adeiny Hechavarria, ss	Majors
8.	Jose Urena, rhp	No. 7
9.	J.T. Realmuto, c	No. 10
10.	Adam Conley, lhp	No. 8
11.	Rob Brantly, c	Majors
12.	Derek Dietrich, 2b	Majors
13.	Alfredo Silverio, of	Dropped out
14.	A.J. Ramos, rhp	Majors
15.	Zack Cox, 3b	Dropped out
16.	Austin Brice, rhp	No. 27
17.	Avery Romero, 2b	No. 9
18.	Kolby Copeland, of	Dropped out
19.	Austin Dean, of	No. 14
20.	Jesus Solorzano, of	No. 13
21.	Chris Hatcher, rhp	Dropped out
22.	Raudel Lazo, lhp	Dropped out
23.	Jake Esch, rhp	Dropped out
24.	Brian Flynn, lhp	No. 6
25.	Grant Dayton, lhp	No. 21
26.	Chad James, lhp	Dropped out
27.	Jose Ceda, rhp	(Free agent)
28.	Danny Black, ss	Dropped out
29.	Austin Barnes, c/2b	No. 20
30.	Brent Keys, of	No. 19

BEST TOOLS

Best Hitter for Average	Brent Keys
Best Power Hitter	Kyle Jensen
Best Strike-Zone Discipline	Brent Keys
Fastest Baserunner	Juancito Martinez
Best Athlete	J.T. Realmuto
Best Fastball	Arquimedes Caminero
Best Curveball	Austin Brice
Best Slider	Andrew Heaney
Best Changeup	Justin Nicolino
Best Control	Justin Nicolino
Best Defensive Catcher	J.T. Realmuto
Best Defensive Infielder	Austin Nola
Best Infield Arm	Yordy Cabrera
Best Defensive Outfielder	Jake Marisnick
Best Outfield Arm	Jake Marisnick

TOP 15 PLAYERS 25 AND UNDER

No.	Player, Pos. (Age)	Peak Level
1.	Jose Fernandez, rhp (21)	Majors
2.	Giancarlo Stanton, of (24)	Majors
3.	Christian Yelich, of (22)	Majors
4.	Andrew Heaney, lhp (22)	Double-A
5.	Colin Moran, 3b (21)	Low Class A
6.	Jake Marisnick, of (23)	Majors
7.	Marcell Ozuna, of (23)	Majors
8.	Henderson Alvarez, rhp (23)	Majors
9.	Jacob Turner, rhp (22)	Majors
10.	Justin Nicolino, lhp (22)	Double-A
11.	Anthony DeSclafani, rhp (23)	Double-A
12.	Adeiny Hechavarria, ss (24)	Majors
13.	Nate Eovaldi, rhp (24)	Majors
14.	Brian Flynn, lhp (23)	Majors
15.	Brad Hand, lhp (24)	Majors

MINOR LEAGUE DEPTH CHART

MIAMI MARLINS

TOP 2014 ROOKIE: Jake Marisnick, of. He wasn't ready with the bat when called upon in 2013, but a couple hundred more at-bats at Triple-A should get him there.

BREAKOUT PROSPECT: Austin Dean, of. Corner outfielder with great bat speed gets first crack at full-season ball.

SLEEPER: Chipper Smith, lhp. The 38th-round afterthought thrived after moving to the low Class A rotation late last summer.

SOURCE OF TOP 30 TALENT

Homegrown	**24**	**Acquired**	**6**
College	11	Trades	5
Junior college	1	Rule 5 draft	0
High school	7	Independent leagues	0
Nondrafted free agents	0	Free agents/waivers	1
International	5		

LF
- Austin Dean (14)
- Brent Keys (19)
- Kyle Jensen (22)
- Kolby Copeland
- K.J. Woods
- Isaac Galloway

CF
- Jake Marisnick (3)
- Kevin Mattison
- Yefri Perez
- Ryan Aper

RF
- Jesus Solorzano (13)
- Alfredo Silverio
- Cameron Flynn

3B
- Colin Moran (2)
- Zack Cox
- Yordy Cabrera
- Ryan Fisher
- Josh Adams
- Matt Juengel

SS
- Javier Lopez (26)
- Danny Black
- Justin Bohn
- Austin Nola

2B
- Avery Romero (9)
- Anthony Gomez
- Noah Perio
- Blake Barber
- J.T. Riddle

1B
- Mark Canha (24)
- Viosergy Rosa
- Felix Munoz
- Ryan Rieger
- Matt Smith

C
- J.T. Realmuto (10)
- Austin Barnes (20)
- Kyle Skipworth
- Wilfredo Gimenez
- Chad Wallach
- Angel Reyes

LHP

LHSP	LHRP
Andrew Heaney (1)	Grant Dayton (21)
Justin Nicolino (4)	Edgar Olmos (23)
Brian Flynn (6)	Raudel Lazo
Adam Conley (8)	Charlie Lowell
Jarlin Garcia (28)	Greg Nappo
Chipper Smith	Miguel Del Pozo
Matt Milroy	
Chad James	

RHP

RHSP	RHRP
Anthony DeSclafani (5)	Arquimedes Caminero (12)
Jose Urena (7)	Sam Dyson (15)
Trevor Williams (11)	Colby Suggs (17)
Angel Sanchez (16)	Nick Wittgren (18)
Austin Brice (27)	Tyler Higgins (25)
Josh Hodges (29)	Michael Brady (30)
Domingo German	Chris Hatcher
Jake Esch	Scott McGough
Joey O'Gara	Steve Ames
Scott Lyman	Pete Andrelczyk
Robert Morey	Kevin Cravey
Ryan Newell	Frankie Reed
Mason Hope	Josh Easley
Leurys de la Rosa	Collin Cargill
	Miguel Fermin
	Brian Ellington
	Junior Rincon

DRAFT ANALYSIS

2013

BONUSES: $7.1 MILLION

BEST PURE HITTER: 3B Colin Moran (1) was on the short list of best pure hitters in the entire draft class. His hands work well and he uses the opposite field. He also controls the strike zone with a polished approach.

BEST POWER HITTER: OF K.J. Woods (4) looks like a power hitter at 6-foot-4, 215 pounds. A high school defensive end, he has to improve his feel for hitting to get to his power.

FASTEST RUNNER: The Marlins drafted a pair of burners in OFs Ryan Aper (6) and Coco Johnson (11), both capable of 6.4-second 60-yard times. Neither hit in their debuts, though. Aper batted .142/.253/.222 between two levels in 162 at-bats, while Johnson hit .172/.280/.179 for short-season Batavia.

BEST DEFENSIVE PLAYER: Aper's speed plays in center field as well. C Chad Wallach (5) has a durable frame at 6-foot-3, 220 pounds and has average catch-and-throw skills to go with consistency and baseball savvy. SS Justin Bohn (7) isn't flashy but has sound defensive tools at short.

BEST FASTBALL: RHP Colby Suggs (2s) runs his fastball up to 98 mph with heavy life out of the bullpen, sitting 92-96. RHP Trevor Williams (2) usually pitches at 90-91 mph with a two-seamer but reaches 95 with his four-seamer.

BEST SECONDARY PITCH: Suggs throws from a high arm slot that reminds some scouts of Jason Motte, delivering an over-the-top curveball that has reached 85 mph.

BEST PRO DEBUT: Area scout Joel Matthews signed two college seniors who shined: RHP Josh Easley (23), who went 5-0, 0.59 with a 43-5 strikeout-walk ratio in 31 innings between three levels; and 6-foot-7 LHP Sean Townsley (25), who touched 93 mph while posting a 41-4 strikeout-walk ratio and 1.44 ERA in 31 innings between the Rookie-level Gulf Coast League and Batavia. Moran posted a .796 OPS in 42 games with low Class A Greensboro.

BEST ATHLETE: J.T. Riddle (13) has wiry strength in his 6-foot-3, 185-pound frame and played better after shifting to shortstop after playing second base in college. He draws Ben Zobrist comparisons.

MOST INTRIGUING BACKGROUND: Moran's older brother Brian, a lefthander, has reached Triple-A with the Mariners. His uncle B.J. Surhoff was the No. 1 overall pick in the 1985 draft and a 19-year big leaguer. Wallach's dad Tim had a 17-year major league career.

CLOSEST TO THE MAJORS: Suggs pitched in the Arizona Fall League and could reach Miami in 2014. Moran shouldn't be far behind.

BEST LATE-ROUND PICK: Riddle.

THE ONE WHO GOT AWAY: LHP Matt Krook (1s) didn't sign after a postdraft physical exam raised issues that the two sides could not resolve. He's headed to Oregon. Perhaps more disappointing was 2B/OF Ben DeLuzio (3), who spurned the Marlins to attend Florida State.

ASSESSMENT: Failing to sign two of their top five selections thins the class. Yet Moran should be able to fill a big league hole quickly, and other college products could make up for the loss of Krook and DeLuzio.

2012

BONUSES: $5.8 MILLION

LHP Andrew Heaney (1) has polish and stuff, making him one of the minors' better lefties. Avery Romero (3) has earned Dan Uggla comparisons as an offensive second baseman.

GRADE: B

2011

BONUSES: $4.1 MILLION

The Marlins didn't sign their third- and fourth-round picks, or get another Top 10 prospect, but RHP Jose Fernandez (1) makes this draft on his own.

GRADE: A

2010

BONUSES: $4.4 MILLION

OF Christian Yelich (1) sped to the majors and has star potential. Converted C J.T. Realmuto (3) is the next-best hope.

GRADE: C

TOP DRAFT PICKS OF THE DECADE

Year	Player, Pos.	2013 Org.
2004	Taylor Tankersley, lhp	Out of baseball
2005	Chris Volstad, rhp	Rockies
2006	Brett Sinkbeil, rhp	Out of baseball
2007	Matt Dominguez, 3b	Astros
2008	Kyle Skipworth, c	Marlins
2009	Chad James, lhp	Marlins
2010	Christian Yelich, of	Marlins
2011	Jose Fernandez, rhp	Marlins
2012	Andrew Heaney, lhp	Marlins
2013	Colin Moran, 3b	Marlins

LARGEST BONUSES IN CLUB HISTORY

Josh Beckett, 1999	$3,625,000
Colin Moran, 2013	$3,516,500
Adrian Gonzalez, 2000	$3,000,000
Andrew Heaney, 2012	$2,600,000
Livan Hernandez, 1996	$2,500,000

1 ANDREW HEANEY, LHP

Born: June 5, 1991. **B-T:** L-L. **Ht.:** 6-2. **Wt.:** 188.
Drafted: Oklahoma State, 2012 (1st round).
Signed by: Steve Taylor.

Heaney was regarded as the top college lefthander available in the 2012 draft after he led NCAA Division I hurlers with 140 strikeouts in 118 innings as a junior. He nearly didn't come to terms with the Marlins after sometimes testy negotiations, agreeing to a $2.6 million deal just before the deadline. His first full season got off to a delayed start when he was sidelined by a strained lat muscle in a simulated game early in spring training. It took him several games to shake off the rust once he took the hill at high Class A Jupiter in May, but he soon looked dominant, going unscored upon for the entire month of July to earn a promotion to Double-A Jacksonville. He tossed six scoreless frames in his first start for the Suns, then gave up five runs his second time out—nearly a quarter of the runs he yielded all year.

Heaney makes it look simple, with easy arm action and a smooth delivery he repeats well. He gets easy velocity on his fastball, touching 95 mph regularly, particularly in two-strike counts. When he needs a little more he can push it up to 97. He has learned, however, that his command is a little crisper when he sits in the 91-93 range. There's a little deception to it and natural giddy-up at the end that gives hitters fits, even at the lower velocity. Heaney locates his fastball well down in the zone. His plus slider can be a wipeout pitch, with late, hard, sharp break that finishes outside of the hitting zone. He keeps hitters off-balance with his changeup, a valuable weapon against righthanded hitters. It's solid-average now, though there were times last year, particularly early in the season, when he telegraphed the pitch—or it came in a bit too firm without the fade it has when he turns it over right. The changeup projects as a third above-average offering. He commands all his pitches consistently and mixes them together well, though he needs to get better at reading swings and picking up on hitters' tendencies to improve his pitch selection. From early in the season to the end, his pitch management took a major step forward as he became more efficient. Heaney needs to learn to improve his tempo and control the running game after allowing 19 of 20 runners to steal against him in 2013, and it's been a notable weakness since college. He has added nearly 20 pounds to his frame since signing but could benefit from additional strength. He carries himself well on the mound and competes hard every time out.

BA GRADE
60
MEDIUM
SCOUTING GRADES
FASTBALL 65
SLIDER 65
CHANGEUP 55
COMMAND 60
DELIVERY 65

MIKE JANES

Heaney's not far away, though with just 122 pro innings he could stand more minor league time. He'll have to prove he can hold up to a full workload to fulfill his potential as a No. 2 starter, but he should join Miami's young rotation by the end of 2014.

Year	Club (League)	Class	W	L	ERA	G	GS	CG	SV	IP	H	HR	BB	SO	K/9	WHIP	AVG
2012	Marlins (GCL)	R	0	0	2.57	2	2	0	0	7	7	0	2	9	11.6	1.29	.259
	Greensboro (SAL)	LoA	1	2	4.95	4	4	0	0	20	25	0	4	21	9.5	1.45	.287
2013	Jupiter (FSL)	HiA	5	2	0.88	13	12	0	0	62	45	2	17	66	9.6	1.01	.193
	Jacksonville (SL)	AA	4	1	2.94	6	6	1	0	34	31	2	9	23	6.1	1.19	.242
Minor League Totals			10	5	2.21	25	24	1	0	122	108	4	32	119	8.8	1.14	.227

2 COLIN MORAN, 3B

GREENSBORO GRASSHOPPERS-AMANDA WILLIAMS

BA GRADE
55
MEDIUM

Born: Oct. 1, 1992. **B-T:** L-R. **Ht.:** 6-4. **Wt.:** 190. **Drafted:** North Carolina, 2013 (1st round). **Signed by:** Joel Matthews.

Moran followed his uncle B.J. Surhoff and brother Brian to North Carolina, where he was honored as BA's Freshman of the Year in 2011. He was a Golden Spikes finalist last spring after leading the nation with 91 RBIs, a school record. After the Marlins selected him sixth overall and gave him a slot bonus of $3,516,500, the second-largest in franchise history, he homered in his first pro at-bat. Scouts believe Moran will hit, but his power will determine how much impact he has in the big leagues. A pure hitter with an advanced approach at the plate, Moran controls the strike zone, has excellent hand-eye coordination and rarely chases. Though he has pull power, when he's going well he'll take what the pitcher gives him and drive it hard into the gap. He projects as a run-producing .300 hitter with the size and strong hands to put up 20 homers a year. Though not quick, he's athletic enough to stay at third, where his hands are soft and he shows average lateral range and an above-average, accurate arm. He's a below-average runner but can rev it up when digging for an extra base. The Marlins will allow Moran to set his own pace, which could be accelerated because he entered the system already polished and fits a big league need. He should claim Miami's wide-open third base job no later than 2015.

Year	Club (League)	Class	AVG	G	AB	R	H	2B	3B	HR	RBI	BB	SO	SB	CS	OBP	SLG
2013	Greensboro (SAL)	LoA	.299	42	154	19	46	8	1	4	23	15	25	1	0	.354	.442
Minor League Totals			.299	42	154	19	46	8	1	4	23	15	25	1	0	.354	.442

3 JAKE MARISNICK, OF

BA GRADE
55
HIGH

Born: March 30, 1991. **B-T:** R-R. **Ht.:** 6-3. **Wt.:** 225. **Drafted:** HS—Riverside, Calif., 2009 (3rd round). **Signed by:** Rick Ingalls (Blue Jays).

The marquee minor leaguer acquired in the Marlins' November 2012 trade with the Blue Jays, Marisnick opened 2013 on the disabled list after his left hand was broken by a pitch in spring training, and then had his season end early due to a left knee injury. He had surgery to repair a torn meniscus after the season. He and Christian Yelich were promoted to Miami the same day last July. A gifted athlete, Marisnick earns plus grades in every tool but hitting. He succeeded at Double-A Jacksonville by staying back and working the middle of the field, but big league pitchers exploited his aggressiveness and absence of a game plan. Though he exhibits good bat speed, his swing can get long at times and he lacks the hand-eye coordination of most high-average hitters. He also needs to see more breaking pitches and work himself into better counts. Marisnick has the strength and swing path to develop plus power. A plus-plus defender with an above-average arm, he's fearless in center field where he reads the ball well, runs good routes and covers a lot of ground. He's a plus runner with an eye for the extra base, though his instincts could use fine-tuning. Marisnick could use at least another half-season on the farm to refine his approach, and if his bat develops, he'll be a dynamic everyday player.

Year	Club (League)	Class	AVG	G	AB	R	H	2B	3B	HR	RBI	BB	SO	SB	CS	OBP	SLG
2010	Blue Jays (GCL)	R	.287	35	122	17	35	12	0	3	14	13	18	14	1	.373	.459
	Lansing (MWL)	LoA	.220	34	127	16	28	8	2	1	12	9	37	9	2	.298	.339
2011	Lansing (MWL)	LoA	.320	118	462	68	148	27	6	14	77	43	91	37	8	.392	.496
2012	Dunedin (FSL)	HiA	.263	65	266	41	70	18	7	6	35	26	55	10	5	.349	.451
	New Hampshire (EL)	AA	.233	55	223	25	52	11	3	2	15	11	45	14	4	.286	.336
2013	Jupiter (FSL)	HiA	.200	3	15	2	3	1	0	0	0	0	1	0	0	.200	.267
	Jacksonville (SL)	AA	.294	67	265	43	78	13	3	12	46	17	68	11	6	.358	.502
	Miami (NL)	MAJ	.183	40	109	6	20	2	1	1	5	6	27	3	1	.231	.248
Major League Totals			.183	40	109	6	20	2	1	1	5	6	27	3	1	.231	.248
Minor League Totals			.280	377	1480	212	414	90	21	38	199	119	315	95	26	.351	.446

4 JUSTIN NICOLINO, LHP

Born: Nov. 22, 1991. **B-T:** L-L. **Ht.:** 6-3. **Wt.:** 195. **Drafted:** HS—Orlando, 2010 (2nd round). **Signed by:** Carlos Rodriguez (Blue Jays).

Two years after the Blue Jays lured Nicolino away from his Virginia commitment with an above-slot $615,000 deal, they dealt him to Miami in the November 2012 blockbuster. He toyed with the high Class A Florida State League last spring, earning a July promotion to Double-A Jacksonville, where he struggled for the first time as a pro. An intelligent student of the game, Nicolino has a smooth delivery and a great feel for pitching. His fastball sits 88-92 mph, topping out at 94, with nice downhill plane and tailing movement. His best pitch is a plus straight changeup with a little diving action at the finish. He can spot his big, 1-to-7 curveball for strikes or use it as an out pitch. It's an average offering now and could develop into an above-average pitch. The key to his success is his plus control to both sides of the plate and feel for changing speeds to keep hitters off-balance. Tall and lanky, he has been handled cautiously since he was drafted and could stand to add strength to improve his durability. Intense and level-headed, he works hard at his craft and places a lot of pressure on himself to succeed. Nicolino's ceiling is a savvy No. 4-type starter whose sum will equal more than its parts. He should return to Jacksonville, where he has some unfinished business to attend to before moving on.

Year	Club (League)	Class	W	L	ERA	G	GS	CG	SV	IP	H	HR	BB	SO	K/9	WHIP	AVG
2011	Vancouver (NWL)	SS	5	1	1.03	12	9	1	0	52	28	0	11	64	11.0	0.75	.156
	Lansing (MWL)	LoA	1	1	3.12	3	3	0	0	9	11	0	2	9	9.3	1.50	.297
2012	Lansing (MWL)	LoA	10	4	2.46	28	22	0	0	124	112	6	21	119	8.6	1.07	.241
2013	Jupiter (FSL)	HiA	5	2	2.23	18	18	1	0	97	89	4	18	64	6.0	1.11	.247
	Jacksonville (SL)	AA	3	2	4.96	9	9	1	0	45	63	2	12	31	6.2	1.65	.341
Minor League Totals			24	10	2.53	70	61	3	0	327	303	12	64	287	7.9	1.12	.247

5 ANTHONY DeSCLAFANI, RHP

Born: April 18, 1990. **B-T:** R-R. **Ht.:** 6-2. **Wt.:** 195. **Drafted:** Florida, 2011 (6th round). **Signed by:** Joel Grampietro (Blue Jays).

DeSclafani worked out of the pen for much of his career at Florida, with results that never matched his stuff. Though he was overshadowed by Jake Marisnick, Justin Nicolino and Henderson Alvarez in the 12-player blockbuster that sent veterans Jose Reyes, Josh Johnson and Mark Buehrle to Toronto, he has proven to be much more than a throw-in. It all begins with attitude for DeSclafani, who burns to win and won't back down to anyone. His plus fastball has late life and sits 90-93 mph, reaching 95-96 when he needs a little extra. He gets nice downward angle on it and pounds the lower part of the zone, locating the pitch on the outside edge against righties. His best offspeed pitch is an above-average power slider, which he has tightened up to get a shorter, quicker break. He'll mix in an inconsistent curve as well, mostly for show. His straight changeup grades as average with a little fade to it and late action. He's aggressive and commands his top three pitches well, particularly the fastball. DeSclafani's ceiling is that of a durable, strike-throwing No. 3 or 4 starter, though he also has the makeup and mindset of a closer. If there's no room in Miami's rotation when he's ready, he could break in as a spot starter or long reliever.

Year	Club (League)	Class	W	L	ERA	G	GS	CG	SV	IP	H	HR	BB	SO	K/9	WHIP	AVG
2012	Lansing (MWL)	LoA	11	3	3.37	28	21	0	0	123	145	3	25	92	6.7	1.38	.307
2013	Jupiter (FSL)	HiA	4	2	1.67	12	12	0	0	54	48	3	9	53	8.8	1.06	.236
	Jacksonville (SL)	AA	5	4	3.36	13	13	0	0	75	74	7	14	62	7.4	1.17	.263
Minor League Totals			20	9	3.00	53	46	0	0	252	267	13	48	207	7.4	1.25	.279

6 BRIAN FLYNN, LHP

Born: April 19, 1990. **B-T:** L-L. **Ht.:** 6-7. **Wt.:** 240. **Drafted:** Wichita State, 2011 (7th round). **Signed by:** Chris Wimmer (Tigers).

Little more than a raw arm when the Tigers drafted him three years ago, Flynn has made tremendous strides since the Marlins acquired him, Jacob Turner and Rob Brantly in a 2012 deal for Omar Infante and Anibal Sanchez. His 2.80 ERA easily led the Triple-A Pacific Coast League in 2013. The big, physical southpaw works on a downward plane, commanding an average to above-average fastball that touches 95 mph and typically sits 88-93. His best offspeed pitch is a hard slider with nice tilt that grades as an average offering. He uses his 1-to-7 curveball as a show-me pitch most days, though he'll occasionally feature it more prominently. He has a feel for an average changeup, a pitch with good movement that he has learned to throw for strikes. A level-headed worker and great self-evaluator, Flynn has proven to be an adept student willing to try anything Marlins coaches suggest. Some mechanical adjustments in 2012 to lengthen his stride and better incorporate his entire body paid dividends last year. He's also made tremendous progress in basics like fielding his position and holding runners. Flynn uncharacteristically struggled with his control and command in four September starts. His nerves shouldn't be as much of a factor next time around. He profiles as a back-end starter with the size and stamina to eat innings.

Year	Club (League)	Class	W	L	ERA	G	GS	CG	SV	IP	H	HR	BB	SO	K/9	WHIP	AVG
2011	West Michigan (MWL)	LoA	7	2	3.46	13	13	0	0	68	58	3	23	57	7.6	1.20	.235
2012	Lakeland (FSL)	HiA	8	4	3.71	18	18	0	0	102	113	5	32	84	7.4	1.42	.280
	Erie (EL)	AA	0	1	9.00	1	1	0	0	5	8	1	2	3	5.4	2.00	.381
	Jacksonville (SL)	AA	3	0	3.80	8	8	0	0	45	48	3	13	32	6.4	1.36	.273
2013	Jacksonville (SL)	AA	1	1	1.57	4	4	0	0	23	18	2	3	25	9.8	0.91	.222
	New Orleans (PCL)	AAA	6	11	2.80	23	23	0	0	138	127	7	40	122	8.0	1.21	.246
	Miami (NL)	MAJ	0	2	8.50	4	4	0	0	18	27	4	13	15	7.5	2.22	.370
Major League Totals			0	2	8.50	4	4	0	0	18	27	4	13	15	7.5	2.22	.370
Minor League Totals			25	19	3.29	67	67	0	0	381	372	21	113	323	7.6	1.27	.257

7 JOSE URENA, RHP

Born: Sept. 12, 1991. **B-T:** R-R. **Ht.:** 6-3. **Wt.:** 190. **Signed:** Dominican Republic, 2008. **Signed by:** Albert Gonzalez/Sandy Nin.

The Marlins have brought Urena along cautiously since signing him for $52,000 in 2008. After using him in a tandem starter arrangement for much of 2012, they finally let him loose last year and he logged a career-high 150 innings at high Class A Jupiter. Urena has a loose, live arm and plus arm strength, and he pounds the zone with easy 92-94 mph heat, touching 96-97 on occasion. He'll also subtract from his fastball to keep hitters off-balance. His best pitch is his changeup, which breaks hard and down like a splitter, eliciting plenty of swings and misses. Urena's slider, while improved, is still a modest third pitch. It has good spin when it's on but lacks consistency. He has just enough funk in his delivery to add a touch of deception. His pitch selection is often poor and he has survived to this point largely on pure stuff. He also lacks the stamina to maintain his velocity deep into starts. A diligent student who works with enthusiasm, he fields his position cleanly and holds runners well. Urena will advance to Double-A Jacksonville in 2014, where he'll continue to work on his endurance and breaking stuff. How they progress could dictate his future role. Neither shortcoming would hinder him much in the bullpen, which is where many observers see him winding up.

Year	Club (League)	Class	W	L	ERA	G	GS	CG	SV	IP	H	HR	BB	SO	K/9	WHIP	AVG
2009	Marlins (DSL)	R	3	3	6.75	14	2	0	2	27	36	0	11	15	5.1	1.76	.313
2010	Marlins (DSL)	R	5	6	2.61	13	13	3	0	83	76	2	7	66	7.2	1.00	.241
2011	Jamestown (NYP)	SS	4	7	4.33	15	15	0	0	73	74	4	29	48	5.9	1.42	.264
2012	Greensboro (SAL)	LoA	9	6	3.38	27	22	1	2	138	143	13	29	101	6.6	1.24	.266
2013	Jupiter (FSL)	HiA	10	7	3.73	27	26	0	0	150	148	8	29	107	6.4	1.18	.257
Minor League Totals			31	29	3.70	96	78	4	4	470	477	27	105	337	6.5	1.24	.262

8 ADAM CONLEY, LHP

BA GRADE
50
HIGH

Born: May 24, 1990. **B-T:** L-L. **Ht.:** 6-3. **Wt.:** 210. **Drafted:** Washington State, 2011 (2nd round). **Signed by:** Gabe Sandy.

Conley moved in tandem with phenom Jose Fernandez in 2012, climbing from low Class A Greensboro to high Class A Jupiter at midseason. When Fernandez skipped over Double-A to Miami in 2013, Conley assumed the anchor role in Jacksonville's rotation and led the staff in innings, wins and strikeouts. Conley has a big arm and has reached the upper 90s on occasion, though his average fastball sat 88-92 mph last year, somewhat down from the past. That may have resulted from a conscious effort to throw strikes. He has a funky delivery that makes it hard for him to consistently command his late-tailing fastball. Conley's slider, a point of emphasis last year, breaks late with good depth. Though still inconsistent, his breaking ball has improved and has the potential to become an above-average pitch. He shows fastball arm speed on his plus changeup, which has good tail and downward break. Conley has matured every year, but he still lacks consistency inning to inning and game to game. Conley's ceiling is as a No. 3 or 4 starter, but with a young rotation in place in Miami, his opening may come in the pen, where he could be a tough matchup for lefthanded hitters. Either way, he needs more development time to establish the consistency that was missing last year.

Year	Club (League)	Class	W	L	ERA	G	GS	CG	SV	IP	H	HR	BB	SO	K/9	WHIP	AVG
2011	Marlins (GCL)	R	0	0	0.00	2	0	0	0	2	1	0	0	2	9.0	0.50	.143
2012	Greensboro (SAL)	LoA	7	3	2.78	14	14	0	0	74	58	4	24	84	10.2	1.10	.213
	Jupiter (FSL)	HiA	4	2	4.44	12	12	0	0	53	59	0	19	51	8.7	1.48	.282
2013	Jacksonville (SL)	AA	11	7	3.25	26	25	3	0	139	125	7	37	129	8.4	1.17	.236
Minor League Totals			22	12	3.33	54	51	3	0	268	243	11	80	266	8.9	1.21	.239

9 AVERY ROMERO, 2B

BA GRADE
50
HIGH

Born: May 11, 1993. **B-T:** R-R. **Ht.:** 5-11. **Wt.:** 195. **Drafted:** HS—St. Augustine, Fla., 2012 (3rd round). **Signed by:** Brian Kraft.

A shortstop in high school, Romero saw time at second and third base after signing for $700,000 just before the deadline in 2012, but he settled in at second in 2013. After drawing Dan Uggla comps for his stocky build, Romero worked hard over the winter to get leaner and improve his quickness. An above-average hitter, Romero uses a short, quick swing to square up balls, resulting in a lot of hard contact. A gap-to-gap hitter now, he projects to have average power when he matures and gains strength. Though he's a below-average runner, Romero has the instincts to surprise a battery on occasion. He also reads outfielders well and will take the extra base. His defense at second took a quantum leap forward last year. He showed good actions, soft hands and quick feet, as well as a willingness to hang in on the double play. He has plenty of arm for second or even third. He's a heady player and a hard worker whose pride was wounded by the decision to hold him back in extended spring training at the beginning of 2013. Romero will open 2014 back at low Class A Greensboro, where he finished last season. Second base is a position of need in the organization, and Romero has quickly established himself as the system's best internal option.

Year	Club (League)	Class	AVG	G	AB	R	H	2B	3B	HR	RBI	BB	SO	SB	CS	OBP	SLG
2012	Marlins (GCL)	R	.223	33	121	8	27	6	0	3	15	10	21	0	1	.309	.347
	Jamestown (NYP)	SS	.381	7	21	3	8	0	0	0	4	3	0	1	0	.458	.381
2013	Batavia (NYP)	SS	.297	56	209	27	62	18	0	2	30	15	34	3	4	.357	.411
	Greensboro (SAL)	LoA	.147	9	34	5	5	1	0	1	5	4	5	0	0	.237	.265
Minor League Totals			.265	105	385	43	102	25	0	6	54	32	60	4	5	.337	.377

10 J.T. REALMUTO, C

Born: March 18, 1991. **B-T:** R-R. **Ht.:** 6-1. **Wt.:** 206. **Drafted:** HS—Midwest City, Okla., 2010 (3rd round). **Signed by:** Steve Taylor.

A standout quarterback in high school, Realmuto spent most of his diamond time at shortstop while setting national records with 88 hits and 119 RBIs and hitting .595 with 28 homers as a senior. The Marlins converted him to catcher immediately after signing him for $600,000. A tremendous athlete, Realmuto is an above-average defender whose arm strength, footwork and release set him apart. Opponents typically stop running after seeing him throw and note his 1.8-1.85-second pop times. He receives well but tends to pick at balls he should body up and block. He handles pitchers well and calls a good game, skills that can be still fine-tuned with experience. Despite his prep résumé, Realmuto is a below-average hitter who falls into the habit of opening up too soon and pulling off the ball. When he's going well, he'll use a more athletic, line-drive swing and stay up the middle. He should develop enough power to hit 12-15 home runs a year. An average runner under way, he's a little slow out of the box due to a big follow-through. Realmuto projects as a durable catch-and-throw guy who should hit enough to hold down an everyday job. He should open 2014 at Triple-A New Orleans and be ready to help out in Miami by 2015.

Year	Club (League)	Class	AVG	G	AB	R	H	2B	3B	HR	RBI	BB	SO	SB	CS	OBP	SLG
2010	Marlins (GCL)	R	.175	12	40	2	7	0	0	0	4	7	11	0	1	.298	.175
2011	Greensboro (SAL)	LoA	.287	96	348	46	100	16	3	12	49	26	78	13	6	.347	.454
2012	Jupiter (FSL)	HiA	.256	123	446	63	114	16	0	8	46	37	64	13	5	.319	.345
2013	Jacksonville (SL)	AA	.239	106	368	41	88	21	3	5	39	36	68	9	1	.310	.353
Minor League Totals			.257	337	1202	152	309	53	6	25	138	106	221	35	13	.323	.374

11 TREVOR WILLIAMS, RHP

Born: April 25, 1992. **B-T:** R-R. **Ht.:** 6-3. **Wt.:** 228. **Drafted:** Arizona State, 2013 (2nd round). **Signed by:** Scott Stanley.

After going 12-2, 2.05 as an Arizona State sophomore, Williams tailed off to 6-6, 4.12 in 2013. The Marlins still liked him enough to pluck him in the second round and sign him for $1,261,400. They kept him on a tight pitch limit, never allowing him to work more than three innings in any start as he advanced to low Class A Greensboro. Williams is a strike-throwing workhorse who should see a much longer leash in the near future. His plus fastball sits 92-93 mph and touches 95. He'll throw a two-seamer that runs in on righthanders and away from lefties. He throws his slow changeup with a fastball grip and gets nice fade to it. It can become an average to better offering with more use. His inconsistent breaking balls prevented him from racking up big strikeout numbers in college. He struggles to throw his slider for strikes, and he also has a solid late-breaking, three-quarters curve, and neither pitch projects as more than average. Williams tends to open up too early and is working to keep his front side closed longer. A self-proclaimed perfectionist, he has an advanced feel for pitching and impressed the Marlins with his work ethic. Williams projects as a No. 3 or 4 starter capable of logging 200 innings a season.

Year	Club (League)	Class	W	L	ERA	G	GS	CG	SV	IP	H	HR	BB	SO	K/9	WHIP	AVG
2013	Marlins (GCL)	R	0	0	4.50	1	1	0	0	2	3	0	0	1	4.5	1.50	.300
	Batavia (NYP)	SS	0	2	2.48	10	10	0	0	29	26	0	8	20	6.2	1.17	.228
	Greensboro (SAL)	LoA	0	0	0.00	1	1	0	0	3	2	0	0	3	9.0	0.67	.182
Minor League Totals			0	2	2.38	12	12	0	0	34	31	0	8	24	6.4	1.15	.230

12 ARQUIMEDES CAMINERO, RHP

BA GRADE
45
MEDIUM

Born: June 16, 1987. **B-T:** R-R. **Ht.:** 6-4. **Wt.:** 255. **Signed:** Dominican Republic, 2005. **Signed by:** Fred Ferreira/Enrique Constante.

It's been a long road for Caminero, who spent three years in the Dominican Summer League and finally blossomed in 2010 before losing nearly a year and a half with an elbow injury. Back to full strength in 2013, he held Double-A Southern League hitters to a .183 average and finished the season with 13 big league appearances. Arm strength has always been Caminero's calling card, with a sinking, running fastball that touches triple digits and sits in the mid-90s. He throws a slider that gets sweepy at times and an 89-90 mph cutter that runs in on lefthanders and away from righties. His changeup is a splitter that has room to improve. Caminero's problem has been command. The Marlins suggested some mechanical adjustments in spring 2013 to keep him closed longer and maintain a more consistent arm slot, which allowed his ball to explode late. Even still, it took a stream of constant reminders from his coaches for the importance of throwing quality strikes to sink in. Caminero has matured and gained confidence and no longer lets adversity snowball on him. If he can improve his slider and throw it more consistently for strikes, he has closer stuff. Failing that, he's still got the makings of an aggressive set-up man.

Year	Club (League)	Class	W	L	ERA	G	GS	CG	SV	IP	H	HR	BB	SO	K/9	WHIP	AVG
2005	Marlins (DSL)	R	1	2	5.54	17	0	0	0	26	32	1	23	12	4.2	2.12	.299
2006	Marlins (DSL)	R	0	1	7.36	18	0	0	2	22	28	0	14	20	8.2	1.91	.322
2007	Marlins (DSL)	R	2	3	2.83	16	4	0	1	48	36	0	24	48	9.1	1.26	.209
2008	Marlins (GCL)	R	0	1	1.56	14	0	0	3	17	9	0	11	20	10.4	1.15	.158
	Greensboro (SAL)	LoA	0	0	3.00	1	0	0	0	3	2	1	0	3	9.0	0.67	.182
	Jamestown (NYP)	SS	1	0	4.91	6	0	0	0	7	8	0	3	8	9.8	1.50	.276
2009	Jupiter (FSL)	HiA	0	0	30.86	2	0	0	0	2	7	3	2	2	7.7	3.86	.500
	Jamestown (NYP)	SS	3	1	3.00	15	0	0	0	24	19	1	16	42	15.8	1.46	.218
	Greensboro (SAL)	LoA	0	0	5.65	10	0	0	0	14	16	1	8	17	10.7	1.67	.276
2010	Greensboro (SAL)	LoA	5	2	3.01	48	0	0	3	75	55	4	34	97	11.7	1.19	.200
2011	Marlins (GCL)	R	0	0	9.00	1	0	0	0	1	2	0	1	2	18.0	3.00	.400
2012	Jupiter (FSL)	HiA	1	0	0.44	19	0	0	1	21	12	0	9	27	11.8	1.02	.160
	Jacksonville (SL)	AA	0	0	3.06	12	0	0	2	18	16	0	10	17	8.7	1.47	.242
2013	Jacksonville (SL)	AA	5	2	3.61	42	0	0	5	52	34	4	21	68	11.7	1.05	.183
	New Orleans (PCL)	AAA	1	0	0.00	1	0	0	0	2	0	0	0	1	4.5	0.00	.000
	Miami (NL)	MAJ	0	0	2.77	13	0	0	0	13	10	2	3	12	8.3	1.00	.208
Major League Totals			0	0	2.77	13	0	0	0	13	10	2	3	12	8.3	1.00	.208
Minor League Totals			19	12	3.68	222	4	0	17	332	276	15	176	384	10.4	1.36	.223

13 JESUS SOLORZANO, OF

BA GRADE
50
HIGH

Born: Aug. 8, 1990. **B-T:** R-R. **Ht.:** 6-0. **Wt.:** 190. **Signed:** Venezuela, 2009. **Signed by:** Wilmer Castillo/Albert Gonzalez.

Solorzano led the short-season New York-Penn League in slugging (.519) and OPS (.894) in 2012 and followed that up with a solid campaign at low Class A Greensboro, where he finished in the league's top 10 in hits (138), doubles (29) and stolen bases (33). He remains an aggressive hitter, but he's learning to manage his at-bats, working deeper into the count instead of jumping on the first pitch. Solorzano still is prone to chase breaking balls out of the zone, but he has shown mild improvement there as well. He has the bat speed to turn around a good fastball and the raw strength to develop plus power. On the bases, he learned how to read pitchers and catchers last year, getting the most of his above-average speed by converting 33 of 37 stolen-base attempts. A solid defender, Solorzano can play all three outfield spots, though he has seen the most time in right field, where his average arm is playable. He did a better job last year of not taking poor at-bats with him out to the field and has shown more maturity in all phases of his game. Solorzano will move to high Class A Jupiter to open 2014, and at age 23, it's time for him to accelerate his progress.

Year	Club (League)	Class	AVG	G	AB	R	H	2B	3B	HR	RBI	BB	SO	SB	CS	OBP	SLG
2009	Marlins (DSL)	R	.109	23	55	6	6	0	1	1	6	5	18	2	1	.219	.200
2010	Marlins (DSL)	R	.286	51	175	22	50	7	2	0	13	11	47	12	3	.365	.349
2011	Marlins (GCL)	R	.299	51	194	34	58	13	4	3	31	13	30	18	7	.355	.454
2012	Jamestown (NYP)	SS	.314	59	210	36	66	13	3	8	27	17	49	7	6	.374	.519
2013	Greensboro (SAL)	LoA	.285	129	484	72	138	29	3	15	66	24	111	33	4	.325	.450
Minor League Totals			.284	313	1118	170	318	62	13	27	143	70	255	72	21	.341	.436

14 AUSTIN DEAN, OF

BA GRADE
50
HIGH

Born: Oct. 14, 1993. **B-T:** R-R. **Ht.:** 6-1. **Wt.:** 190. **Drafted:** HS—Spring, Texas, 2012 (4th round). **Signed by:** Ryan Wardinsky.

An infielder in high school, Dean moved to the outfield upon signing for $367,200 as a fourth-rounder in 2012. The Marlins played it conservative with him in 2013, holding him back in extended spring until short-season Batavia's season began in June. Dean swings one of the quickest bats in the organization and the ball comes off the barrel hard. Because his stance is fairly upright, he gets to balls up easier than pitches down in the zone, the latter of which can give him trouble. Dean has good bat control and is more of a line-drive hitter than a power threat, though he could develop 15-20 home run power. He's aggressive and likes to jump on the first pitch. An average runner, he was gunned out on his only two stolen base attempts in 2013 but moves well enough underway that he legged out seven triples, tops in the New York-Penn League. Dean's speed plays well enough on a corner, where his range is average. His arm is a tick-below-average but could improve with better technique, a factor of his inexperience in the outfield. He'll return to low Class A Greensboro, where he spent the final week of the 2013 campaign.

Year	Club (League)	Class	AVG	G	AB	R	H	2B	3B	HR	RBI	BB	SO	SB	CS	OBP	SLG
2012	Marlins (GCL)	R	.223	47	148	15	33	11	0	2	15	24	35	2	2	.337	.338
2013	Batavia (NYP)	SS	.268	56	213	28	57	12	7	2	19	17	47	0	2	.325	.418
	Greensboro (SAL)	LoA	.200	7	20	4	4	1	0	1	3	4	5	0	0	.346	.400
Minor League Totals			.247	110	381	47	94	24	7	5	37	45	87	2	4	.331	.386

15 SAM DYSON, RHP

BA GRADE **45** MEDIUM

Born: May 7, 1988. **B-T:** R-R. **Ht.:** 6-1. **Wt.:** 210. **Drafted:** South Carolina, 2010 (4th round). **Signed by:** John Hendricks (Blue Jays).

Drafted three times, Dyson finally signed with the Blue Jays in 2010. Tommy John surgery delayed his pro debut until two years later. Once healthy, he shot through the system, reaching the big leagues briefly in July 2012. The Marlins claimed him on waivers in January 2013. Dyson's results have yet to match his stuff, which is electric. His sinker has late run and moves so much that catchers can miss it. He excels at adding and subtracting velocity from his heater. Dyson's deceptive, fading changeup is a second plus pitch. He switches between a tight curve and biting slider. While both can be nasty, he doesn't seem to trust either and needs to utilize one or both more frequently. An easy strike-thrower, Dyson lacks the instinct to set up hitters and doesn't read their swings to gauge what's working. He needs to do a better job holding runners and speed up the tempo of his delivery. Though he started 21 games last year, Dyson is a much better fit in the bullpen, where he's capable of being a dynamic set-up man or emergency starter.

Year	Club (League)	Class	W	L	ERA	G	GS	CG	SV	IP	H	HR	BB	SO	K/9	WHIP	AVG
2012	Dunedin (FSL)	HiA	2	0	4.08	6	6	0	0	29	35	1	5	16	5.0	1.40	.297
	Toronto (AL)	MAJ	0	0	40.50	2	0	0	0	1	4	0	2	1	13.5	9.00	.667
	New Hampshire (EL)	AA	2	2	2.38	33	0	0	9	45	38	2	15	22	4.4	1.17	.233
2013	Jacksonville (SL)	AA	3	7	2.63	16	15	0	0	75	72	0	23	41	4.9	1.26	.254
	Marlins (GCL)	R	0	1	3.60	1	1	0	0	5	6	0	1	5	9.0	1.40	.316
	New Orleans (PCL)	AAA	1	3	2.61	5	5	0	0	31	23	1	12	16	4.6	1.13	.213
	Miami (NL)	MAJ	0	2	9.00	5	1	0	0	11	16	2	5	5	4.1	1.91	.348
Major League Totals			0	2	10.80	7	1	0	0	12	20	2	7	6	4.6	2.31	.385
Minor League Totals			8	13	2.82	61	27	0	9	185	174	4	56	100	4.9	1.24	.251

16 ANGEL SANCHEZ, RHP

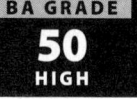

BA GRADE **50** HIGH

Born: Nov. 28, 1989. **B-T:** R-R. **Ht.:** 6-3. **Wt.:** 177. **Signed:** Dominican Republic, 2010. **Signed by:** Ezequiel Sepulveda (Dodgers).

The nephew of former major leaguer Geraldo Guzman, Sanchez signed with the Dodgers for $7,500 out of a college in Santo Domingo, Dominican Republic. After two and a half years in Class A ball, he went to the Marlins as part of the Ricky Nolasco trade in July 2013. Despite his smallish frame, he throws a live 92-95 mph fastball with a free-and-easy delivery that he repeats well. His best pitch is a plus cutter that would be more effective if he showed it less. He throws both a hard curve with medium depth and a late-breaking slider with good downward action. Sanchez's changeup could become an average pitch if he would use it more. With so many weapons, he lacks feel for when to throw which pitch. He picks at the corners and needs to work up and down to change the plane on hitters. Sanchez needs to gain strength to bolster his stamina and maintain his velocity in the later innings. Though relatively new to pitching, he is 24 and will be challenged at Double-A Jacksonville in 2014. Scouts who like him see a possible late-rotation starter.

Year	Club (League)	Class	W	L	ERA	G	GS	CG	SV	IP	H	HR	BB	SO	K/9	WHIP	AVG
2011	Great Lakes (MWL)	LoA	8	4	2.82	20	16	0	0	99	72	5	39	84	7.6	1.12	.198
2012	R. Cucamonga (CAL)	HiA	6	12	6.58	27	23	0	0	130	157	26	51	103	7.1	1.60	.300
2013	Great Lakes (MWL)	LoA	2	7	4.88	14	14	0	0	72	80	6	28	70	8.8	1.50	.273
	R. Cucamonga (CAL)	HiA	0	0	3.00	2	1	0	0	9	8	0	2	12	12.0	1.11	.235
	Jupiter (FSL)	HiA	4	3	3.22	10	10	1	0	50	45	5	21	42	7.5	1.31	.233
Minor League Totals			20	26	4.65	73	64	1	0	360	362	42	141	311	7.8	1.40	.257

17 COLBY SUGGS, RHP

BA GRADE **50** HIGH

Born: Oct. 25, 1991. **B-T:** R-R. **Ht.:** 5-11. **Wt.:** 230. **Drafted:** Arkansas, 2013 (2nd round supplemental). **Signed by:** Brian Kraft.

Suggs helped Arkansas to the College World Series as a sophomore, then set a school record with 13 saves as the Razorbacks' closer in 2013. He yielded just 44 hits in 80 innings over his college career. The flip side was the 53 walks he surrendered, which the Marlins must straighten out after signing him for $600,000. Suggs is all about power, with his plus fastball sitting in the mid-90s and touching 98 mph with good movement, particularly down in the zone. He also features a hard 85-mph curve that works as an out-pitch. His changeup is well behind his other offerings. He puts a lot of effort into an over-the-top delivery, leading to well-below-average control. He's aggressive and likes to challenge hitters. Suggs needs innings to smooth out his delivery. He'll get them at high Class A Jupiter to open 2014.

Year	Club (League)	Class	W	L	ERA	G	GS	CG	SV	IP	H	HR	BB	SO	K/9	WHIP	AVG
2013	Marlins (GCL)	R	0	0	9.00	1	0	0	0	1	1	0	2	1	9.0	3.00	.250
	Batavia (NYP)	SS	1	0	1.13	7	0	0	3	8	5	0	2	11	12.4	0.88	.200
	Jupiter (FSL)	HiA	1	3	3.93	14	0	0	0	18	9	0	14	26	12.8	1.25	.141
Minor League Totals			2	3	3.29	22	0	0	3	27	15	0	18	38	12.5	1.21	.161

18 NICK WITTGREN, RHP

Born: May 29, 1991. **B-T:** R-R. **Ht.:** 6-3. **Wt.:** 210. **Drafted:** Purdue, 2012 (9th round). **Signed by:** Kevin Ibach.

Purdue's all-time saves leader, Wittgren led the Florida State League with 25 in 2013. Wittgren's 90-93 mph fastball plays up because of natural deception in his delivery. He throws his average breaking ball down and toward the back foot of lefthanded hitters or backdoors it versus righties. Early in 2013, Wittgren's breaking ball featured a bit of hump, but it got crisper as the season progressed. His changeup can be effective, but he hasn't thrown it much as a closer. He fields his position and holds on runners well. His stuff is a little short for a big league closer, so he may fit better as a seventh- or eighth-inning bridge. He likely will move quickly through the system and could arrive in Miami in 2014.

Year	Club (League)	Class	W	L	ERA	G	GS	CG	SV	IP	H	HR	BB	SO	K/9	WHIP	AVG
2012	Jamestown (NYP)	SS	0	2	1.46	17	0	0	11	25	24	0	4	34	12.4	1.14	.250
	Greensboro (SAL)	LoA	0	0	0.00	6	0	0	2	6	1	0	1	13	19.5	0.33	.053
2013	Jupiter (FSL)	HiA	2	1	0.83	48	0	0	25	54	42	1	10	59	9.8	0.96	.211
	Jacksonville (SL)	AA	0	0	0.00	4	0	0	1	4	0	0	0	4	9.0	0.00	.000
Minor League Totals			2	3	0.91	75	0	0	39	89	67	1	15	110	11.1	0.92	.205

19 BRENT KEYS, OF

BA GRADE
45
MEDIUM

Born: July 14, 1990. **B-T:** L-R. **Ht.:** 6-1. **Wt.:** 210. **Drafted:** HS—Simi Valley, Calif., 2009 (17th round). **Signed by:** Tim McDonnell.

Keys has been hampered by hamstring issues since signing five years ago, with the latest setback coming last spring and costing him the first month of the season. He still captured his second consecutive batting crown by hitting .346 in the Florida State League. Keys uses a quiet approach, gets the barrel to the ball and rarely misses his pitch. He's a great bat-handler and accomplished bunter. He's a plus runner when his legs are healthy, though hammy issues have limited his speed to average or below. He lacks the elite range of most big league center fielders, but when healthy covers enough ground to play the position. His arm is average to a tick below and he may be a better fit in left. He should open the year at Double-A Jacksonville.

Year	Club (League)	Class	AVG	G	AB	R	H	2B	3B	HR	RBI	BB	SO	SB	CS	OBP	SLG
2009	Marlins (GCL)	R	.288	50	163	23	47	5	0	0	19	28	20	13	4	.395	.319
2010	Jamestown (NYP)	SS	.267	65	217	39	58	8	1	0	25	31	36	11	4	.360	.313
2011	Greensboro (SAL)	LoA	.208	17	53	6	11	0	0	0	5	10	14	5	1	.348	.208
	Jamestown (NYP)	SS	.340	26	106	13	36	2	0	1	12	2	9	6	2	.352	.387
2012	Greensboro (SAL)	LoA	.335	95	370	72	124	21	3	5	51	34	30	18	5	.394	.449
2013	Jupiter (FSL)	HiA	.346	95	381	57	132	14	0	2	33	46	26	13	9	.418	.399
	Jacksonville (SL)	AA	.281	8	32	3	9	0	0	0	0	5	3	1	0	.378	.281
Minor League Totals			.315	356	1322	213	417	50	4	8	145	156	138	67	25	.390	.377

20 AUSTIN BARNES, C

BA GRADE
45
MEDIUM

Born: Dec. 28, 1989. **B-T:** R-R. **Ht.:** 5-10. **Wt.:** 190. **Drafted:** Arizona State, 2011 (9th round). **Signed by:** Scott Stanley.

After spending the bulk of 2012 at second base, Barnes reversed roles last year and played 75 games behind the plate. Hitting is his most intriguing tool. He gives a quality at-bat, working counts and looking for his pitch. Barnes has below-average power but uses strong wrists and hands to pepper opposite-field liners. He's a solid receiver with good hands and moves quickly on balls in the dirt. His footwork is good and he has a quick release, but his arm is below-average. With more time at second he could become average, but his bat profiles better at catcher. A slightly below-average runner, Barnes is a hustler who plays hard. He's too small to forecast as a regular catcher, but his versatility and bat should be valuable as a reserve.

Year	Club (League)	Class	AVG	G	AB	R	H	2B	3B	HR	RBI	BB	SO	SB	CS	OBP	SLG
2011	Jamestown (NYP)	SS	.288	57	219	33	63	13	0	1	19	25	22	6	1	.369	.361
2012	Greensboro (SAL)	LoA	.318	123	478	76	152	36	3	12	65	59	61	9	2	.401	.481
2013	Jupiter (FSL)	HiA	.260	98	350	42	91	15	1	4	38	52	59	5	2	.367	.343
	Jacksonville (SL)	AA	.339	19	62	10	21	2	2	1	7	12	10	0	0	.446	.484
Minor League Totals			.295	297	1109	161	327	66	6	18	129	148	152	20	5	.386	.414

21 GRANT DAYTON, LHP

BA GRADE
45
MEDIUM

Born: Nov. 25, 1987. **B-T:** L-L. **Ht.:** 6-2. **Wt.:** 205. **Drafted:** Auburn, 2010 (11th round). **Signed by:** Mark Willoughby.

A stress fracture cost Dayton a chance to play in big league camp last spring and held him out until late May. He got stronger as the season progressed until his fastball returned to 91-93 mph. Dayton gets good depth and angle on a sharp slider, which he can drop on the back foot of righthanded hitters. He also throws a plus changeup. His command improved, especially over the second half. He's aggressive and attacks both sides of the plate with quality pitches. Though his stuff is good enough to work in a set-up role, he was particularly effective in 2013 against lefthanders, holding them to a .140 average. He'll go to spring training with a chance to impress his way onto the Miami roster, especially now that he's on the 40-man.

Year	Club (League)	Class	W	L	ERA	G	GS	CG	SV	IP	H	HR	BB	SO	K/9	WHIP	AVG
2010	Marlins (GCL)	R	0	0	0.00	1	0	0	1	1	0	0	0	1	9.0	0.00	.000
	Jamestown (NYP)	SS	1	1	1.26	17	0	0	1	29	18	0	15	23	7.2	1.15	.186
2011	Greensboro (SAL)	LoA	7	1	2.89	49	0	0	5	72	59	5	24	99	12.4	1.16	.223
2012	Jupiter (FSL)	HiA	2	5	2.10	31	6	0	2	60	48	1	18	71	10.7	1.10	.214
	Jacksonville (SL)	AA	2	1	4.15	7	0	0	0	13	12	2	4	19	13.2	1.23	.245
2013	Jacksonville (SL)	AA	4	4	2.37	30	0	0	1	38	33	4	12	56	13.3	1.18	.226
Minor League Totals			16	12	2.42	135	6	0	10	212	170	12	73	269	11.4	1.14	.217

22 KYLE JENSEN, OF

BA GRADE 45 MEDIUM

Born: May 20, 1988. **B-T:** R-L. **Ht.:** 6-3. **Wt.:** 247. **Drafted:** St. Mary's, 2009 (12th round). **Signed by:** John Hughes.

In an organization starved for power bats, Jensen stands out as a big, physical right-handed batter with the raw strength and bat speed to hit the ball out to all fields. The question is how much will he hit. He struggles to identify pitches and is tempted too frequently by breaking balls in the dirt, resulting in 306 strikeouts over the past two seasons. Though he's a below-average runner, Jensen will pick his spots to swipe a bag. Through hard work, he has turned himself into a slightly below-average corner outfielder who positions himself properly and gets good jumps. His arm strength is average with good accuracy, making him more suitable for left field but playable in right. Jensen may fit best in a platoon role.

Year	Club (League)	Class	AVG	G	AB	R	H	2B	3B	HR	RBI	BB	SO	SB	CS	OBP	SLG
2009	Jamestown (NYP)	SS	.280	55	182	24	51	10	5	4	24	18	46	3	0	.354	.456
2010	Greensboro (SAL)	LoA	.272	125	470	61	128	26	1	18	86	45	119	5	1	.342	.447
2011	Jupiter (FSL)	HiA	.309	109	391	53	121	20	1	22	66	46	114	0	0	.385	.535
	Jacksonville (SL)	AA	.250	21	80	14	20	1	1	5	10	7	23	1	0	.310	.475
2012	Jacksonville (SL)	AA	.234	132	445	70	104	21	2	24	84	69	162	1	1	.338	.452
2013	Jacksonville (SL)	AA	.237	70	245	43	58	16	0	16	42	33	73	5	3	.354	.498
	New Orleans (PCL)	AAA	.233	60	202	31	47	15	0	12	36	17	71	1	0	.293	.485
Minor League Totals			.263	572	2015	296	529	109	10	101	348	235	608	16	5	.346	.477

23 EDGAR OLMOS, LHP

BA GRADE 45 MEDIUM

Born: April 12, 1990. **B-T:** L-L. **Ht.:** 6-4. **Wt.:** 215. **Drafted:** HS—Van Nuys, Calif., 2008 (3rd round). **Signed by:** Tim McDonnell.

Shoulder problems limited Olmos to four starts his first two seasons. The Marlins shifted him to the bullpen midway through the 2012. He made his big league debut last June, then struggled to repeat his delivery after returning to Double-A Jacksonville. Olmos' boring fastball picked up velocity in his new role and now runs in the mid-90s. His breaking ball is a hard, biting slider that can be an average pitch. His average changeup features a little fade and is a true third offering. Olmos struggles to maintain his timing because of his long stride and long arms. He also tends to finish too upright. Olmos could become a situational lefthander, though he was better against righties last year. A good spring could land him in Miami.

Year	Club (League)	Class	W	L	ERA	G	GS	CG	SV	IP	H	HR	BB	SO	K/9	WHIP	AVG
2008	Marlins (GCL)	R	0	0	0.00	1	1	0	0	2	2	0	0	5	27.0	1.20	.250
2009	Marlins (GCL)	R	0	0	0.00	2	2	0	0	5	1	0	2	5	9.0	0.60	.077
	Jamestown (NYP)	SS	0	0	2.25	1	1	0	0	4	3	0	2	4	9.0	1.25	.214
2010	Greensboro (SAL)	LoA	3	9	4.37	25	25	0	0	117	122	9	59	108	8.3	1.54	.271
2011	Jupiter (FSL)	HiA	4	17	6.63	28	28	0	0	128	167	13	81	101	7.1	1.94	.318
2012	Jupiter (FSL)	HiA	1	5	4.33	24	13	0	0	89	83	5	48	78	7.9	1.47	.248
	Jacksonville (SL)	AA	0	1	0.54	9	1	0	0	17	8	0	16	13	7.0	1.44	.145
2013	Miami (NL)	MAJ	0	1	7.20	5	0	0	0	5	7	2	3	2	3.6	2.00	.350
	Jacksonville (SL)	AA	4	2	2.50	38	0	0	1	50	47	1	27	41	7.3	1.47	.244
Major League Totals			0	1	7.20	5	0	0	0	5	7	2	3	2	3.6	2.00	.350
Minor League Totals			12	34	4.59	128	71	0	1	412	433	28	235	355	7.8	1.62	.272

24 MARK CANHA, 1B

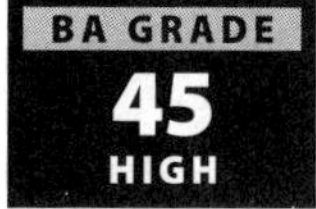

Born: Feb. 15, 1989. **B-T:** R-R. **Ht.:** 6-2. **Wt.:** 195. **Drafted:** California, 2010 (7th round). **Signed by:** John Hughes.

A two-time all-Pacific-10 Conference honoree at California, Canha signed for $300,000 in 2010. He's been a solid run producer at every stop since. Canha crushes line drives to all fields using a short stroke. He's got the strength to hit for power, particularly to his pull side, if he can maintain the adjustments he made in the second half of 2013 to use his legs more efficiently. Though his speed is below-average, Canha is a smart baserunner. While the Marlins have tried him at third base and in the outfield, he has spent most of his time at first, where he shows fringy overall defensive ability. Canha grows on scouts over time but doesn't profile well. He'll continue his march up the ladder by moving to Triple-A New Orleans in 2014.

Year	Club (League)	Class	AVG	G	AB	R	H	2B	3B	HR	RBI	BB	SO	SB	CS	OBP	SLG
2010	Marlins (GCL)	R	.176	6	17	3	3	0	0	0	1	2	1	1	1	.286	.176
	Jamestown (NYP)	SS	.264	14	53	7	14	3	1	4	9	6	13	0	0	.339	.585
2011	Greensboro (SAL)	LoA	.276	107	384	72	106	22	0	25	85	59	85	7	3	.374	.529
2012	Jupiter (FSL)	HiA	.293	114	406	65	119	24	3	6	68	54	75	1	3	.382	.411
2013	Jacksonville (SL)	AA	.273	128	425	63	116	32	2	13	58	54	102	6	1	.371	.449
Minor League Totals			.279	369	1285	210	358	81	6	48	221	175	276	15	8	.373	.463

25 TYLER HIGGINS, RHP

BA GRADE **45** HIGH

Born: April 22, 1991. **B-T:** R-R. **Ht.:** 6-3. **Wt.:** 230. **Drafted:** Lansing (Mich.) CC, 2011 (23rd round). **Signed by:** Kevin Ibach.

Higgins' radar readings might be the first thing to grab attention, but his secondary stuff also grades out well. His fastball lacks life but sits 90-93 mph and touches 95 with occasional cutting action. He also throws a two-seamer that runs to his arm side and mixes in a heavy, power curve that can look like a slider. His changeup blossomed last year into a potentially plus out-pitch. Effort in Higgins' delivery caused him to battle his command early in 2013, leading to too many balls up in the zone, but it improved in the second half. If he learns how to read hitters and attack their weaknesses his results should match his stuff, which is good enough to work in end-game situations. He may return to Jupiter to start 2014.

Year	Club (League)	Class	W	L	ERA	G	GS	CG	SV	IP	H	HR	BB	SO	K/9	WHIP	AVG
2011	Marlins (GCL)	R	0	0	27.00	2	0	0	0	1	2	1	3	1	6.8	3.75	.286
2012	Marlins (GCL)	R	1	0	3.24	7	0	0	2	8	4	0	5	8	8.6	1.08	.143
	Jupiter (FSL)	HiA	1	1	2.36	16	0	0	0	27	21	3	7	19	6.4	1.05	.210
2013	Jupiter (FSL)	HiA	2	7	4.01	45	0	0	0	58	63	5	26	64	9.9	1.53	.268
Minor League Totals			4	8	3.80	70	0	0	2	95	90	9	41	92	8.7	1.38	.243

26 JAVIER LOPEZ, SS

BA GRADE **50** EXTREME

Born: Sept. 13, 1994. **B-T:** R-R. **Ht.:** 6-3. **Wt.:** 180. **Signed:** Dominican Republic, 2011. **Signed by:** Albert Gonzalez/Alix Martinez/Sandy Nin.

The Marlins inked Lopez for $350,000, a considerable sum for an organization that doesn't spend much internationally. He struggled in the Rookie-level Dominican Summer League in 2012 but Miami pushed him to short-season Batavia in 2013, where he was the youngest player on the roster. He tantalizes with a live body and a natural feel for the game. While he struggled offensively, he showed a loose stroke and rarely looked overmatched. He makes hard contact and shows power to his pull side. He's an average runner. Lopez has smooth actions at shortstop but tends to get too flashy. He has a plus arm, though his throws were inconsistent and often rushed. The Marlins would like to give Lopez 500 at-bats in 2014, and jump him to low Class A Greensboro. More likely, he'll return to extended spring before he tackles full-season pitching.

Year	Club (League)	Class	AVG	G	AB	R	H	2B	3B	HR	RBI	BB	SO	SB	CS	OBP	SLG
2012	Marlins (DSL)	R	.208	50	207	24	43	10	0	1	13	16	47	4	7	.271	.271
2013	Batavia (NYP)	SS	.174	45	155	14	27	4	3	1	13	13	47	1	2	.243	.258
Minor League Totals			.193	95	362	38	70	14	3	2	26	29	94	5	9	.259	.265

27 AUSTIN BRICE, RHP

BA GRADE **50** EXTREME

Born: June 19, 1992. **B-T:** R-R. **Ht.:** 6-4. **Wt.:** 205. **Drafted:** HS—Pittsboro, N.C., 2010 (9th round). **Signed by:** Joel Matthews.

Brice garnered a $205,000 deal as the top-rated high school pitcher from the state of North Carolina in the 2010 draft. Though he led low Class A Greensboro with 122 strikeouts while sharing a rotation spot with Jose Urena in 2012, the Marlins returned Brice to the Grasshoppers in 2013, and his numbers slipped across the board. Long and lean, Brice throws a plus 91-93 mph fastball. He also throws a plus 11-to-5 curve. His changeup can be an average third offering, but he needs to use it more. Brice has trouble repeating his delivery and maintaining a release point, in part because of an inconsistent stride that causes him to open up. He also tends to land on a stiff front leg and leaves pitches up. The Marlins are optimistic that Brice will have solid mid-rotation stuff. He ought to move to high Class A Jupiter in 2014.

Year	Club (League)	Class	W	L	ERA	G	GS	CG	SV	IP	H	HR	BB	SO	K/9	WHIP	AVG
2010	Marlins (GCL)	R	0	1	4.32	6	0	0	0	8	7	0	7	8	8.6	1.68	.219
2011	Marlins (GCL)	R	6	0	2.96	11	9	0	0	49	32	2	33	55	10.2	1.34	.189
2012	Greensboro (SAL)	LoA	8	6	4.35	25	19	0	3	110	96	13	68	122	10.0	1.50	.237

2013	Greensboro (SAL)	LoA	8	11	5.73	26	23	0	0	113	118	11	82	111	8.8	1.77	.268
Minor League Totals			22	18	4.67	68	51	0	3	280	253	26	190	296	9.5	1.58	.242

28 JARLIN GARCIA, LHP

BA GRADE
50
EXTREME

Born: Jan. 18, 1993. **B-T:** L-L. **Ht.:** 6-2. **Wt.:** 170. **Signed:** Dominican Republic, 2010. **Signed by:** Albert Gonzalez/Sandy Nin.

Though he averaged less than five innings a start in 2013, he ranked fifth in the short-season New York-Penn League with 74 strikeouts. Garcia's arm works easy and he shows an above-average fastball that runs up to 93 mph. He also throws a plus curve, which he can get too reliant on. He's still learning how to use his changeup, which has a chance to be an above-average pitch. Garcia has the stuff to challenge hitters, but he didn't always do so. Though he doesn't issue many free passes, Garcia's command can be inconsistent. Despite his inexperience, he has shown some maturity. Garcia has a nice pitcher's build with room to fill out yet. He will vie for a job in the low Class A Greensboro rotation in 2014.

Year	Club (League)	Class	W	L	ERA	G	GS	CG	SV	IP	H	HR	BB	SO	K/9	WHIP	AVG
2011	Marlins (DSL)	R	5	5	3.29	14	8	0	1	52	47	3	12	46	8.0	1.13	.241
2012	Marlins (GCL)	R	1	3	3.60	12	4	0	0	40	38	2	14	32	7.2	1.30	.242
2013	Batavia (NYP)	SS	2	3	3.10	15	15	0	0	70	58	7	18	74	9.6	1.09	.221
Minor League Totals			8	11	3.28	41	27	0	1	162	143	12	44	152	8.5	1.16	.233

29 JOSH HODGES, RHP

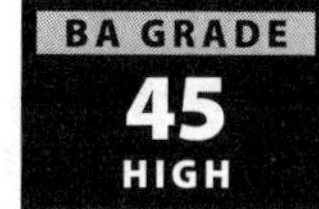

Born: June 21, 1991. **B-T:** R-R. **Ht.:** 6-7. **Wt.:** 235. **Drafted:** HS—New Albany, Miss., 2009 (7th round). **Signed by:** Mark Willoughby.

Hodges came out of high school raw, having faced little competition in a remote northern Mississippi town of 8,000. An imposing figure on the mound, Hodges gets downward plane on his heavy, sinking fastball, which sits in the low 90s. When he needs a little more he can run it up to 94 mph. His hard slider may have the makings of an average breaking pitch, though it lacks consistency. He throws two changeups, the better of which breaks down like a splitter and grades as a plus offering. Hodges' arm action is clean and his delivery smooth and repeatable. He commands all his pitches well. He projects as a back-end starter or longman. Hodgers worked briefly in relief in the first half of 2013 and saw a slight uptick in velocity to the mid-90s. He'll continue as a starter and should join the Double-A Jacksonville rotation in 2014.

Year	Club (League)	Class	W	L	ERA	G	GS	CG	SV	IP	H	HR	BB	SO	K/9	WHIP	AVG
2009	Marlins (GCL)	R	2	1	4.02	5	2	0	0	16	15	0	8	14	8.0	1.47	.238
	Jamestown (NYP)	SS	1	0	4.50	1	0	0	0	4	5	1	0	6	13.5	1.25	.294
2010	Jamestown (NYP)	SS	3	3	6.04	12	12	0	0	54	57	4	23	38	6.4	1.49	.270
2011	Jamestown (NYP)	SS	8	1	3.39	15	15	0	0	88	90	7	18	50	5.1	1.23	.272
2012	Greensboro (SAL)	LoA	8	10	3.65	27	26	1	0	148	147	14	56	98	6.0	1.37	.264
2013	Jupiter (FSL)	HiA	4	6	3.60	27	22	0	0	132	130	9	31	84	5.7	1.22	.260
Minor League Totals			26	21	3.90	87	77	1	0	441	444	35	136	290	5.9	1.31	.264

30 MICHAEL BRADY, RHP

BA GRADE
40
LOW

Born: Mar. 21, 1987. **B-T:** R-R. **Ht.:** 6-0. **Wt.:** 215. **Drafted:** California, 2009 (24th round). **Signed by:** Robby Corsaro.

Though he hit just .254 as an infielder at California, Brady's arm strength intrigued the Marlins, who converted him to the mound in 2010. He led the Double-A Southern League in saves in 2013. The key to Brady's success is uncanny command of a sinking fastball, which he typically keeps down and away, though he can paint either side of the plate. His velocity ticked up a notch in 2013 to 92-93 mph with plus movement. His out-pitch is a hard, slurvy breaking ball that is an average pitch because he can locate it. He added a forkball two years ago that's a swing-and-miss pitch when it's on. Athletic and intelligent, he fields his position well and earned a spot on the 40-man roster in November. While he has closed throughout his minor league career, his average stuff makes him more of a middle reliever.

Year	Club (League)	Class	W	L	ERA	G	GS	CG	SV	IP	H	HR	BB	SO	K/9	WHIP	AVG
2010	Jamestown (NYP)	SS	1	1	1.59	26	0	0	3	28	17	2	4	25	7.9	0.74	.173
2011	Jacksonville (SL)	AA	0	0	4.50	1	0	0	0	2	3	0	1	0	0.0	2.00	.333
	Greensboro (SAL)	LoA	7	1	1.91	48	0	0	18	61	40	4	10	81	11.9	0.82	.184
2012	Jupiter (FSL)	HiA	2	4	3.38	50	0	0	22	53	54	4	7	64	10.8	1.14	.260
2013	Jacksonville (SL)	AA	2	2	1.53	49	0	0	23	53	42	2	9	55	9.3	0.96	.216
Minor League Totals			12	8	2.18	174	0	0	66	198	156	12	31	225	10.2	0.94	.215

Year	Club (League)	Class	AVG	G	AB	R	H	2B	3B	HR	RBI	BB	SO	SB	CS	OBP	SLG
2009	Jamestown (NYP)	SS	.333	4	6	0	2	0	0	0	0	2	2	1	0	.556	.333
	Marlins (GCL)	R	.034	11	29	6	1	0	0	0	2	8	7	0	0	.256	.034
Minor League Totals			.105	51	38	6	4	1	0	0	2	10	10	1	0	.314	.132

Milwaukee Brewers

BY TOM HAUDRICOURT

When the 2013 season began, righthander Wily Peralta—the organization's No. 1 prospect for two years running—was the only rookie of note expected to see considerable time in Milwaukee. The Brewers signaled they were playing for 2013 with a week remaining in spring training when they signed free agent righthander Kyle Lohse to a lucrative three-year contract.

My, how things changed.

A series of injuries to key players as well as the steroid-related suspension of Ryan Braun created a revolving door between Triple-A Nashville and Milwaukee that never stopped spinning. Before the season was done, a dozen rookies saw action with the 74-88 Brewers, who never really challenged for a playoff spot.

Braun already was on the disabled list with a thumb injury when Major League Baseball suspended him for the balance of the season (65 games) for his connection to the infamous Biogenesis clinic. He's signed through 2020, and the organization still owes him $129 million, so the Brewers have to hope the player who led the National League with 41 homers and a .987 OPS in 2012 can contribute in similar fashion when he returns.

The Brewers were 15 games under .500 and already had plenty of holes when Braun went on the DL. First base required seven different starters, and several rookies made themselves factors for the 2014 lineup and beyond.

A power display in spring training catapulted outfielder Khris Davis onto the Opening Day roster. Braun's absence later allowed Davis to thrive in an everyday role, and he averaged a home run every 12.4 at-bats and slugging a team-best.596, forcing his way into the conversation for 2014 with a potential move of Braun to right field.

Scooter Gennett likewise went from the Milwaukee-Nashville shuttle to the starting second base job in early August when a hamstring injury shelved Rickie Weeks. Gennett raised eyebrows by batting .324/.356/.479 over 69 games while also playing better defense than advertised, potentially pushing Weeks off second. Righthander Tyler Thornburg recovered from an 0-9, 5.79 Nashville stint to turn in seven straight quality starts down the stretch, posting a 3-1, 2.03 mark in 67 innings to make a spot in the 2014 rotation likely.

Other silver linings to manager Ron Roenicke's first losing season included Jean Segura placing a firm grip on the shortstop job and earning an NL all-star berth. Center fielder Carlos Gomez also emerged as an all-star with his best season, and the duo helped the Brewers lead the NL in stolen bases. Even Peralta rebounded from a horrid start to finish 11-15, 4.37.

For the first time since 1990, the Brewers did not have a first-round pick, having forfeited the choice when they signed Lohse. That didn't help a farm system that posted a .442 domestic winning percentage, third-worst in the game. Only Rookie-level Helena posted a winning record. Outfielder Michael Ratterree, a 10th-round pick out of Rice, led Helena to the Pioneer League finals and was named league MVP.

MIKE JANES

For better or worse, the Brewers are tied to slugger Ryan Braun through the 2020 season

TOP PROSPECTS OF THE DECADE

Year	Player, Pos.	2013 Org.
2004	Rickie Weeks, 2b	Brewers
2005	Rickie Weeks, 2b	Brewers
2006	Prince Fielder, 1b	Tigers
2007	Yovani Gallardo, rhp	Brewers
2008	Matt LaPorta, of	Indians
2009	Alcides Escobar, ss	Royals
2010	Alcides Escobar, ss	Royals
2011	Mark Rogers, rhp	Brewers
2012	Wily Peralta, rhp	Brewers
2013	Wily Peralta, rhp	Brewers

ORGANIZATION OVERVIEW

General Manager: Doug Melvin. **Farm Director:** Reid Nichols. **Scouting Director:** Bruce Seid.

Class	Team	League	W	L	PCT	Finish	Manager
Majors	Milwaukee Brewers	National	74	88	.457	t-10th (15)	Ron Roenicke
Triple-A	Nashville Sounds	Pacific Coast	57	87	.396	16th (16)	Mike Guerrero
Double-A	Huntsville Stars	Southern	59	79	.428	t-8th (10)	Darnell Coles
High Class A	Brevard County Manatees	Florida State	66	68	.493	7th (12)	Joe Ayrault
Low Class A	Wisconsin Timber Rattlers	Midwest	59	76	.437	13th (16)	Matt Erickson
Rookie	Helena Brewers	Pioneer	43	33	.566	2nd (8)	Tony Diggs
Rookie	AZL Brewers	Arizona	23	33	.411	10th (13)	Nestor Corredor
2013 Overall Minor League Record			**307**	**376**	**.449**	**28th (30)**	

THIS YEAR'S TOP 30

No.	Player, Pos.	Grade
1.	Jimmy Nelson, rhp	55/Medium
2.	Tyrone Taylor, of	55/High
3.	Mitch Haniger, of	50/Medium
4.	Johnny Hellweg, rhp	55/High
5.	Victor Roache, of	55/High
6.	Taylor Jungmann, rhp	50/High
7.	Orlando Arcia, ss	50/High
8.	David Goforth, rhp	45/Medium
9.	Devin Williams, rhp	55/Extreme
10.	Hunter Morris, 1b	45/Medium
11.	Clint Coulter, c	50/High
12.	Nick Delmonico, 3b/1b	50/High
13.	Yadiel Rivera, ss	50/High
14.	Tucker Neuhaus, 3b/ss	50/High
15.	Ariel Pena, rhp	50/High
16.	Tyler Wagner, rhp	50/High
17.	Michael Blazek, rhp	45/Medium
18.	Jed Bradley, lhp	45/High
19.	Taylor Williams, rhp	50/Extreme
20.	Jason Rogers, 1b/of	45/High
21.	Kevin Shackelford, rhp	45/High
22.	Barrett Astin, rhp	45/High
23.	Damien Magnifico, rhp	50/Extreme
24.	Jorge Lopez, rhp	50/Extreme
25.	Drew Gagnon, rhp	45/High
26.	Omar Garcia, of	50/Extreme
27.	Anthony Banda, lhp	45/High
28.	Michael Ratterree, of	45/High
29.	Tyler Cravy, rhp	45/High
30.	D'Vontrey Richardson, of	50/Extreme

LAST YEAR'S TOP 30

No.	Player, Pos.	Status
1.	Wily Peralta, rhp	Majors
2.	Tyler Thornburg, rhp	Majors
3.	Taylor Jungmann, rhp	No. 6
4.	Hunter Morris, 1b	No. 10
5.	Jimmy Nelson, rhp	No. 1
6.	Johnny Hellweg, rhp	No. 4
7.	Victor Roache, of	No. 5
8.	Scooter Gennett, 2b	Majors
9.	Clint Coulter, c	No. 11
10.	Mitch Haniger, of	No. 3
11.	Mark Rogers, rhp	(Free agent)
12.	Jed Bradley, lhp	No. 18
13.	Logan Schafer, of	Majors
14.	Hiram Burgos, rhp	Dropped out
15.	Tyrone Taylor, of	No. 2
16.	Khris Davis, of	Majors
17.	Orlando Arcia, ss	No. 7
18.	Drew Gagnon, rhp	No. 25
19.	David Goforth, rhp	No. 8
20.	Nick Bucci, rhp	Dropped out
21.	Jesus Sanchez, rhp	(Marlins)
22.	Ariel Pena, rhp	No. 15
23.	Jorge Lopez, rhp	No. 24
24.	Cody Scarpetta, rhp	Dropped out
25.	Yadiel Rivera, ss	No. 13
26.	Santo Manzanillo, rhp	(Free agent)
27.	Caleb Gindl, of	Majors
28.	Kentrail Davis, of	Dropped out
29.	Kyle Heckathorn, rhp	Dropped out
30.	Josh Prince, of	Dropped out

BEST TOOLS

Best Hitter for Average	Michael Ratterree
Best Power Hitter	Victor Roache
Best Strike-Zone Discipline	Jason Rogers
Fastest Baserunner	Johnny Davis
Best Athlete	Tyrone Taylor
Best Fastball	Damien Magnifico
Best Curveball	Jorge Lopez
Best Slider	Jimmy Nelson
Best Changeup	Hiram Burgos
Best Control	Rob Wooten
Best Defensive Catcher	Adam Weisenburger
Best Defensive Infielder	Yadiel Rivera
Best Infield Arm	Orlando Arcia
Best Defensive Outfielder	Tyrone Taylor
Best Outfield Arm	Mitch Haniger

TOP 15 PLAYERS 25 AND UNDER

No.	Player, Pos. (Age)	Peak Level
1.	Jean Segura, ss (24)	Majors
2.	Wily Peralta, rhp (24)	Majors
3.	Jimmy Nelson, rhp (24)	Majors
4.	Scooter Gennett, 2b (23)	Majors
5.	Tyler Thornburg, rhp (25)	Majors
6.	Tyrone Taylor, of (20)	Low Class A
7.	Mitch Haniger, of (23)	High Class A
8.	Johnny Hellweg, rhp (25)	Majors
9.	Victor Roache, of (22)	Low Class A
10.	Taylor Jungmann, rhp (24)	Double-A
11.	Orlando Arcia, ss (19)	Low Class A
12.	David Goforth, rhp (25)	Double-A
13.	Devin Williams, rhp (19)	Rookie
14.	Caleb Gindl, of (25)	Majors
15.	Clint Coulter, c (20)	Low Class A

MINOR LEAGUE DEPTH CHART

MILWAUKEE BREWERS

TOP 2014 ROOKIE: Jimmy Nelson, rhp. With many pitching prospects knocking on the door in Milwaukee, Nelson could make the biggest impact.

BREAKOUT PROSPECT: Tyler Wagner, rhp. The former college reliever led all minor league starters in 2013 in groundball outs ratio.

SLEEPER: Michael Reed, of. Super athlete can really run, is still young (21) and is improving his pitch recognition.

SOURCE OF TOP 30 TALENT

Homegrown	**26**	**Acquired**	**4**
College	16	Trades	4
Junior college	3	Rule 5 draft	0
High school	6	Independent leagues	0
Nondrafted free agents	0	Free agents/waivers	0
International	1		

LF

Victor Roache (5)
Michael Ratterree (28)
Kentrail Davis
Ben McMahan

CF

Tyrone Taylor (2)
Omar Garcia (26)
D'Vontrey Richardson (30)
Josh Prince
Michael Reed
Johnny Davis

RF

Mitch Haniger (3)
Max Walla
Chad Stang
Jose Pena

3B

Nick Delmonico (12)
Tucker Neuhaus (14)
Michael Garza
Brandon Macias
Mike Walker

SS

Orlando Arcia (7)
Yadiel Rivera (13)
Angel Ortega
Carlos Belonis

2B

Nick Shaw
Greg Hopkins
Chris McFarland
Alfredo Rodriguez

1B

Hunter Morris (10)
Jason Rogers (20)
Sean Halton
Nick Ramirez
David Denson

C

Clint Coulter (11)
Robinzon Diaz
Adam Weisenburger
Cameron Garfield
Shawn Zarraga

LHP

LHSP	LHRP
Jed Bradley (18)	Brian Garman
Anthony Banda (27)	Alan Williams
Brent Suter	Stephen Peterson
	Michael Strong
	Taylor Wall
	Tyler Alexander
	Hobbs Johnson

RHP

RHSP	RHRP
Jimmy Nelson (1)	David Goforth (8)
Johnny Hellweg (4)	Michael Blazek (17)
Taylor Jungmann (6)	Kevin Shackelford (21)
Devin Willliams (9)	Damien Magnifico (23)
Ariel Pena (15)	Tyler Cravy (29)
Tyler Wagner (16)	Rob Wooten
Taylor Williams (19)	Michael Olmsted
Barrett Astin (22)	Greg Holle
Jorge Lopez (24)	Arcenio Leon
Drew Gagnon (25)	Tommy Toledo
Brooks Hall	Kyle Heckathorn
Hiram Burgos	Casey Medlen
Andy Moye	Eric Arnett
Jacob Barnes	Andrew Hillis
Cody Scarpetta	Josh Uhen
Chad Pierce	
Nick Bucci	

2013

BONUSES: $3.9 MILLION

BEST PURE HITTER: OF Michael Ratterree (10) seemed destined to star at Rice but hit just .248 in his final two seasons there. He has good bat speed and strength and won MVP honors in the Rookie-level Pioneer League, batting .314/.391/.585.

BEST POWER HITTER: At 6-foot-4, 240 pounds, 1B David Denson (15) has strength and massive raw power, earning Ryan Howard comparisons. He hit six homers in the Rookie-level Arizona League.

FASTEST RUNNER: The Brewers picked a pair of top-of-the-scale runners in OFs Omar Garcia (7) and Johnny Davis (22), and Garcia ranked second in the Rookie-level Pioneer League in steals with 28 in 34 attempts.

BEST DEFENSIVE PLAYER: SS/3B Tucker Neuhaus (2s) has good hands and the arm strength for the left side of the infield and might be able to handle short, though most scouts see him moving to third base. He split time between the two positions in the Rookie-level Arizona League.

BEST FASTBALL: RHPs Devin Williams (2) and Taylor Williams (4), who are not related, both throw in the mid-90s. Devin has touched 95-96 mph and has more athleticism and feel, giving him more upside and a chance to start. Taylor topped out in the upper 90s after signing. RHP Andrew Hillis (11), a 6-foot-7 behemoth, also has touched 99. He's strictly a reliever.

BEST SECONDARY PITCH: Williams' slider and changeup are inconsistent but both flash plus, and he struck out 39 in 34 AZL innings.

BEST PRO DEBUT: Ratterree nearly carried Rookie-level Helena to the Pioneer League title, going 9-for-16 with seven walks in the PL playoffs. Garcia (.305/.425/.335) and Hillis (3-1, 0.44, 5 SV; 21 IP, 23 SO) were also key Helena contributors.

BEST ATHLETE: Davis, a truly explosive runner, gave up a potential college track career for baseball. Devin Williams brings elite athleticism to the mound along with projection and arm strength.

MOST INTRIGUING BACKGROUND: RHP Josh Uhen (5) played at hometown Wisconsin-Milwaukee and became the school's highest-drafted player. Neuhaus' father Ken coached at Bethel (Minn.), and he had to overcome the death of his older brother, a junior college player, in an offseason auto accident.

CLOSEST TO THE MAJORS: LHP Hobbs Johnson (14) can sit 90-93 mph with his fastball with good life and deception, and would move rapidly as a reliever. RHP Barrett Astin (3), a power sinkerballer, also could rocket to Milwaukee as a reliever.

BEST LATE-ROUND PICK: Denson got $100,000 to give up his Hawaii commitment.

THE ONE WHO GOT AWAY: Projectable RHP Nick Eicholtz (29) is growing into his body and already has touched 93 mph and flashed three other usable pitches. He's headed to Alabama.

ASSESSMENT: The Brewers didn't have a first-round pick, but Devin Williams has first-round talent, and Neuhaus got first-round grades prior to a string of spring injuries. Milwaukee also loaded up on college pitchers with upside.

2012

BONUSES: $7.2 MILLION

The Brewers got their top three hitting prospects—OFs Victor Roache (1), Mitch Haniger (1s) and Tyrone Taylor (2)—with consecutive selections. Top choice C Clint Coulter (1) will move slowly.

GRADE: C+

2011

BONUSES: $7.5 MILLION

RHP Taylor Jungmann (1) and to a greater extent LHP Jed Bradley (1) have disappointed. If only the Brewers had signed LHP Carlos Rodon (16), the projected No. 1 pick for 2014.

GRADE: D

2010

BONUSES: $2.4 MILLION

The emergence of RHPs Jimmy Nelson (2) and Tyler Thornburg (3) relieves some of the sting of not signing RHP Dylan Covey (1).

GRADE: C

TOP DRAFT PICKS OF THE DECADE

Year	Player, Pos.	2013 Org.
2004	Mark Rogers, rhp	Brewers
2005	Ryan Braun, 3b	Brewers
2006	Jeremy Jeffress, rhp	Blue Jays
2007	Matt LaPorta, of	Indians
2008	Brett Lawrie, c/3b	Blue Jays
2009	Eric Arnett, rhp	Brewers
2010	*Dylan Covey, rhp	Athletics
2011	Taylor Jungmann, rhp	Brewers
2012	Clint Coulter, c	Brewers
2013	Devin Williams, rhp (2nd round)	Brewers

*Did not sign

LARGEST BONUSES IN CLUB HISTORY

Rickie Weeks, 2003	$3,600,000
Taylor Jungmann, 2011	$2,525,000
Ben Sheets, 1999	$2,450,000
Ryan Braun, 2005	$2,450,000
Prince Fielder, 2002	$2,400,000

1 JIMMY NELSON, RHP

Born: June 5, 1989. **B-T:** R-R. **Ht.:** 6-6. **Wt.:** 245.
Drafted: Alabama, 2010 (2nd round).
Signed by: Joe Mason.

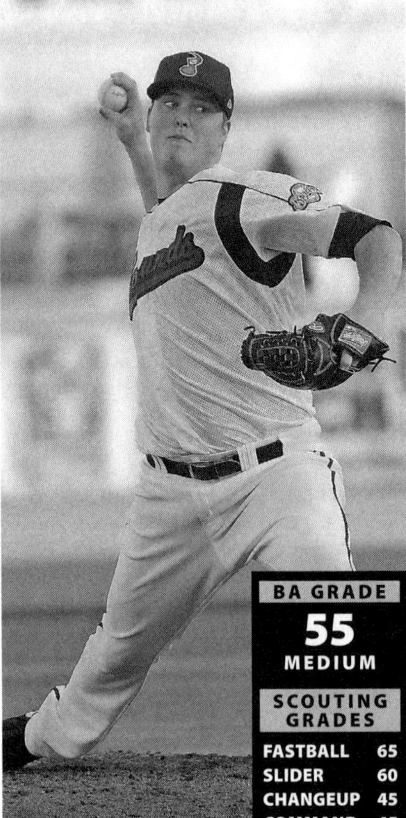

BA GRADE
55
MEDIUM
SCOUTING GRADES
FASTBALL 65
SLIDER 60
CHANGEUP 45
COMMAND 45
DELIVERY 50

MIKE STRASINGER-NASHVILLE SOUNDS

Nelson first emerged as a prospect at Niceville High in the Florida Panhandle, spurning the Reds as a 39th-round pick to attend Alabama. He has helped make up for the fact that the Brewers failed to sign 2010 first-rounder Dylan Covey, who was diagnosed with Type 1 diabetes and did not sign. A second-rounder that same year, Nelson signed for $570,600 and finished his third full season in the majors. Long considered a workhorse type who profiled as a mid-rotation starter, Nelson made a big leap in 2013, starting at Double-A Huntsville, then moving up to Triple-A Nashville at midseason and finally to Milwaukee as a September callup. His command was a bit more erratic at Nashville, but he remained tough to hit and moved to the front of the class of a developing group of pitchers who should make an impact in the big leagues soon. He ingratiated himself to the big league staff with his aggressive nature and mound presence, showing no signs of being intimidated or being in over his head. In the one start he was given, he had trouble gripping the ball and threw some very wild pitches. Nelson said the ball in the majors was slicker than in the minors and it was an adjustment he would have to make.

Nelson can overpower hitters at times with a fastball that sits at 92-94 mph but also reaches 96 when he needs it. He is very aggressive, going after hitters with hard stuff that also includes an effective two-seamer in the low 90s with good sink and movement that he uses to induce groundouts. Nelson also can be very tough on righthanded hitters with his three-quarters arm slot and power slider, which has a sharp break and registers in the 84-86 mph range. He limited righties to a .213/.295/.290 batting line and three home runs over 370 plate appearances at three levels, including 0-for-15 in his brief big league trial. He continues to work on a changeup that is improving and will be key to remaining a starter going forward. Nelson has a great build for a pitcher, maintaining the quality of his stuff deep into games. When he is throwing strikes he mows through lineups, but on other days Nelson fights his delivery and walks hitters, creating doubt about his future role. He tends to overthrow and loses his release point, resulting in an average of 4.1 walks per nine innings for his minor league career, too many for a frontline starter. He also needs to polish his defense and ability to hold runners.

Nelson likely will have to return to Nashville to open the 2014 season but could force his way into the big league picture with a strong spring. While some scouts think his iffy command will consign him to the bullpen, the Brewers see a potential No. 2 or 3 starter who misses barrels and eats innings. He appears destined for regular spot in the Milwaukee rotation before the year is done.

Year	Club (League)	Class	W	L	ERA	G	GS	CG	SV	IP	H	HR	BB	SO	K/9	WHIP	AVG
2010	Helena (PIO)	R	2	0	3.71	12	0	0	3	27	30	2	13	33	11.1	1.61	.268
2011	Wisconsin (MWL)	LoA	8	9	4.38	26	25	1	0	146	146	9	65	120	7.4	1.45	.266
2012	Brevard County (FSL)	HiA	4	4	2.21	13	13	1	0	81	63	3	25	77	8.5	1.08	.216
	Huntsville (SL)	AA	2	4	3.91	10	10	0	0	46	34	2	37	42	8.2	1.54	.206
2013	Huntsville (SL)	AA	5	4	2.74	12	12	1	0	69	63	5	15	72	9.4	1.13	.241
	Nashville (PCL)	AAA	5	6	3.67	15	15	1	0	83	74	2	50	91	9.8	1.49	.240
	Milwaukee (NL)	MAJ	0	0	0.90	4	1	0	0	10	2	0	5	8	7.2	0.70	.065
Major League Totals			0	0	0.90	4	1	0	0	10	2	0	5	8	7.2	0.70	.065
Minor League Totals			26	27	3.52	88	75	4	3	452	410	23	205	435	8.7	1.36	.243

2 TYRONE TAYLOR, OF

Born: Jan. 22, 1994. **B-T:** R-R. **Ht.:** 6-0. **Wt.:** 185. **Drafted:** HS—Torrance, Calif., 2012 (2nd round). **Signed by:** Dan Huston.

The Brewers knew they had a good athlete in Taylor, who also was a standout running back at Torrance High, and hoped he would blossom once he focused on baseball only. He impressed in Rookie ball after signing before a wrist injury cut short his season, and the Brewers jumped him to low Class A Wisconsin at age 19, where he recovered from a slow start to post a productive season. Taylor is a true center fielder with five-tool potential who figures to get better as he accumulates at-bats. He has smoothed out his mechanics at the plate and shows gap power and at times more than that. He has good bat speed and is an aggressive hitter, sometimes to his detriment. He needs to improve his plate discipline, but he doesn't strike out much and will stand in against inside offerings, which resulted in 14 hit by pitches in 2013. His above-average speed plays to his advantage in center field as well as on the bases. He shows good instincts in the field and has learned to get good jumps in stealing bases. He has an average, accurate arm and tied for third in the Midwest League with 13 assists. He adapts well to coaching and should become even stronger as he matures physically. Taylor will be tested at high Class A Brevard County, which has a tough park for righthanded hitters. He has the skill set to succeed, however, and the Brewers are excited to have a true center fielder who could hit in the top third of the order.

Year	Club (League)	Class	AVG	G	AB	R	H	2B	3B	HR	RBI	BB	SO	SB	CS	OBP	SLG
2012	Brewers (AZL)	R	.389	8	36	11	14	5	3	0	6	1	3	3	1	.395	.694
	Helena (PIO)	R	.385	10	39	11	15	4	0	2	5	5	8	3	2	.467	.641
2013	Wisconsin (MWL)	LoA	.274	122	485	69	133	33	2	8	57	35	63	19	8	.338	.400
Minor League Totals			.289	140	560	91	162	42	5	10	68	41	74	25	11	.351	.436

3 MITCH HANIGER, OF

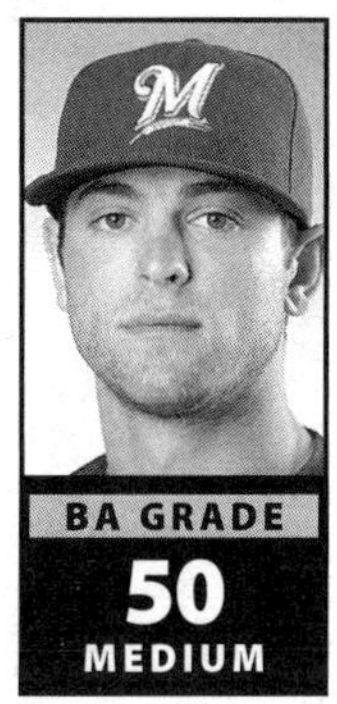

Born: Dec. 23, 1990. **B-T:** R-R. **Ht.:** 6-2. **Wt.:** 213. **Drafted:** Cal Poly, 2012 (1st round supplemental). **Signed by:** Dan Huston.

Haniger's brother Jason played college ball, and his cousins Nik (Orioles) and Alex Balog (Rockies) play pro ball. A knee injury limited Mitch, who signed for $1.2 million in 2012, to just 14 games in his pro debut. The Brewers cautiously started him at low Class A Wisconsin in 2013, then moved him to high Class A Brevard County and looked for him to survive in a pitcher's park and pitcher's league, but Haniger thrived and led the organization with 36 doubles. The Brewers like many things about Haniger, including his approach, athleticism, arm and budding power. They believe he will develop 20-homer power because of his plate discipline, pitch recognition and quick bat. He works the gaps and shows plus power to the pull side. His running is fringy at best and he is an average defender in right field. His arm is an asset because it's both strong and accurate. His solid baseball background has given him the confidence and work ethic he'll need to make adjustments. The Brewers' most advanced hitting prospect, Haniger reported to the Arizona Fall League to prepare for a 2014 jump to Double-A. If he continues to improve, he figures into Milwaukee's plans as early as 2015.

Year	Club (League)	Class	AVG	G	AB	R	H	2B	3B	HR	RBI	BB	SO	SB	CS	OBP	SLG
2012	Wisconsin (MWL)	LoA	.286	14	49	9	14	4	0	1	8	7	13	1	0	.379	.429
2013	Wisconsin (MWL)	LoA	.297	41	145	24	43	12	2	5	25	25	24	7	0	.399	.510
	Brevard County (FSL)	HiA	.250	88	328	52	82	24	3	6	43	32	68	2	2	.323	.396
Minor League Totals			.266	143	522	85	139	40	5	12	76	64	105	10	2	.351	.431

4 JOHNNY HELLWEG, RHP

Born: Oct. 29, 1988. **B-T:** R-R. **Ht.:** 6-9. **Wt.:** 215. **Drafted:** Florida CC, 2008 (16th round). **Signed by:** Tom Kotchman (Angels).

Acquired from the Angels in the July 2012 Zack Greinke trade, Hellweg had a schizophrenic season. He led the Triple-A Pacific Coast League in walks (89, which ranked fourth in the minors) and hit batters (14). Yet he also led the PCL in opponent average (.228) while ranking second in ERA (3.15) and wins (12). He won the league's pitcher of the year award but flopped in his September callup. At 6-foot-9, Hellweg can't help but throw on a downhill plane. When he's pounding the lower half of the zone with fastballs in the 92-95 mph range, he induces one groundball out after another. He's capable of reaching 98 mph whenever he wants, but because of control problems he learned to dial back his fastball and pitch more to contact, and his strikeout numbers plummeted. He has such good movement on his fastball that hitters don't square him up much, but that life, as well as Hellweg's extra-tall frame, makes the pitch hard to control. He has a lot going on with his delivery and struggles to maintain a consistent release point. His average changeup has improved and some scouts prefer it to his slurvy, below-average breaking ball. The Brewers hope Hellweg is the classic late-blooming tall pitcher, and he clearly needs more time to improve his control. With a 70-grade fastball, he's worth waiting on. He could return to the Triple-A rotation or gain big league experience in the bullpen in 2014.

Year	Club (League)	Class	W	L	ERA	G	GS	CG	SV	IP	H	HR	BB	SO	K/9	WHIP	AVG
2008	Angels (AZL)	R	1	0	4.98	14	3	0	0	22	19	1	38	25	10.4	2.63	.224
2009	Angels (AZL)	R	2	1	2.96	18	0	0	6	24	16	0	8	25	9.2	0.99	.186
	Cedar Rapids (MWL)	LoA	0	0	1.35	5	0	0	2	7	4	0	7	7	9.5	1.65	.160
2010	Cedar Rapids (MWL)	LoA	2	4	4.33	41	0	0	16	44	20	2	45	66	13.6	1.49	.133
2011	Inland Empire (CAL)	HiA	6	4	3.73	28	14	0	0	89	75	2	59	113	11.4	1.50	.229
2012	Arkansas (TL)	AA	5	10	3.38	21	21	1	0	120	105	8	60	88	6.6	1.38	.245
	Huntsville (SL)	AA	2	1	2.70	7	2	0	0	20	16	0	15	17	7.7	1.55	.222
2013	Wisconsin (MWL)	LoA	1	0	3.00	1	1	0	0	6	5	0	2	4	6.0	1.17	.217
	Nashville (PCL)	AAA	12	5	3.15	23	23	0	0	126	103	6	81	89	6.4	1.46	.228
	Milwaukee (NL)	MAJ	1	4	6.75	8	7	0	0	31	40	3	26	9	2.6	2.15	.325
Major League Totals			1	4	6.75	8	7	0	0	31	40	3	26	9	2.6	2.15	.325
Minor League Totals			31	25	3.47	158	64	1	24	457	363	19	315	434	8.5	1.48	.220

5 VICTOR ROACHE, OF

Born: Sept. 17, 1991. **B-T:** R-R. **Ht.:** 6-1. **Wt.:** 225. **Drafted:** Georgia Southern, 2012 (1st round). **Signed by:** Steve Smith.

The Brewers knew it would take some time to get Roache back on the field and swinging the bat well after he missed most of his final season at Georgia Southern with a severe wrist injury that required screws, pins and a metal plate to repair. He made his pro debut in late-April 2013 and, as might be expected, he struggled to recover his stroke at low Class A Wisconsin in the first half. He settled in during the second half, posting an .840 OPS with 16 homers in 277 at-bats. Roache has the kind of raw power that isn't easy to find. He can send pitches to far-off places, using his strength, bat speed and timing. The righty hitter struggles with breaking balls at times but crushes mistakes. He has to become more selective as a hitter to maximize his offensive potential. Roache does not project to be a high-average hitter but could hit 30 homers if he puts enough balls in play. He has fringy speed and only adequate arm strength and profiles strictly as a left fielder. The Brewers like his work habits and devotion to come back from what could have been a career-limiting injury. Roache should continue to improve as he compiles at-bats and continues to knock off the rust from missing more than a year of competition. His power stroke will be tested in 2014 as he moves up to high Class A Brevard County, which is not home-run friendly. He could move quickly if he makes consistent contact.

Year	Club (League)	Class	AVG	G	AB	R	H	2B	3B	HR	RBI	BB	SO	SB	CS	OBP	SLG
2012	Did not play—Injured																
2013	Wisconsin (MWL)	LoA	.248	119	459	62	114	14	4	22	74	46	137	6	2	.322	.440
Minor League Totals			.248	119	459	62	114	14	4	22	74	46	137	6	2	.322	.440

6 TAYLOR JUNGMANN, RHP

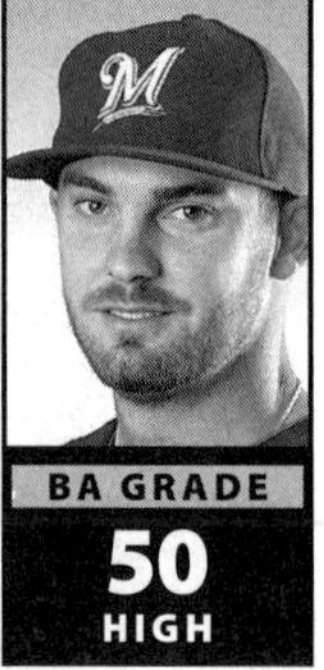

Born: Dec. 18, 1989. **B-T:** R-R. **Ht.:** 6-6. **Wt.:** 220. **Drafted:** Texas, 2011 (1st round). **Signed by:** Jeremy Booth.

After three years as ace of the Texas staff, Jungmann was attractive to clubs in the 2011 draft because he was supposed to move quickly. He seemed on the verge of living up to his $2.525 million signing bonus in the first half of 2013, when he limited hitters to a .204 average at Double-A Huntsville. But he wasn't as sharp after the break, struggling to a 5.91 ERA in nine outings. Jungmann's fastball hit 98 mph in college, but his game now is pounding a 90-92 mph sinker into the bottom of the strike zone and getting hitters to beat it into the ground. He uses his tall frame to pitch on a downhill plane and tries to get outs early in the count. He tied for second in the Southern League with 18 double plays. He has a sharp-breaking, 75-78 mph slider that is very effective against righthanders when he stays on top of it. Jungmann's fringe-average changeup can be effective if a bit firm. His command took a step backward in 2013, but scouts and the Brewers believe his delivery can be smoothed out to improve his strike-throwing capability. A groin strain ended Jungmann's Arizona Fall League stint after one start, short-circuiting his first attempt at improving his delivery. He'll head to Triple-A for 2014, likely projecting as a No. 4 starter, which would be good enough considering the difficulty the Brewers have had in developing starting pitchers.

Year	Club (League)	Class	W	L	ERA	G	GS	CG	SV	IP	H	HR	BB	SO	K/9	WHIP	AVG
2012	Brevard County (FSL)	HiA	11	6	3.53	26	26	1	0	153	159	7	46	99	5.8	1.34	.267
2013	Huntsville (SL)	AA	10	10	4.33	26	26	0	0	139	117	11	73	82	5.3	1.36	.232
Minor League Totals			21	16	3.91	52	52	1	0	292	276	18	119	181	5.6	1.35	.251

7 ORLANDO ARCIA, SS

BA GRADE **50** HIGH

Born: Aug. 4, 1994. **B-T:** R-R. **Ht.:** 6-0. **Wt.:** 165. **Signed:** Venezuela, 2010. **Signed by:** Fernando Arango.

Arcia missed the 2012 season when he broke his right ankle sliding into second base in extended spring training. Despite missing that year, the Brewers had Arcia skip Rookie ball in 2013 and assigned him to low Class A Wisconsin. His older brother Oswaldo, a power-hitting corner outfielder, reached the majors with the Twins in 2013. Unlike his big brother, the Brewers' Arcia focuses on contact ability rather than power at the plate, rarely striking out. He doesn't walk much either and has to work on his plate discipline to reach base more often. Arcia has decent pop for being so thin and figures to get stronger as he matures physically. He doesn't have great speed but is aggressive on the bases and shows good instincts there as well. In the field, Arcia can be fun to watch. He has above-average range to both sides, nimble footwork around the bag, soft hands and plenty of arm strength to stick at shortstop. Like all young players, he will make sloppy errors at times, but he has all-star potential in the field. As might be expected, Arcia had an inconsistent year at the plate but was dazzling at times in the field, showing tremendous natural instincts. His athleticism is evident and nobody doubts he will be major league ready with the glove first. He will step up to high Class A Brevard County in 2014.

Year	Club (League)	Class	AVG	G	AB	R	H	2B	3B	HR	RBI	BB	SO	SB	CS	OBP	SLG
2011	Brewers (DSL)	R	.294	64	218	47	64	16	1	6	36	30	20	13	4	.386	.459
2012	Did not play—Injured																
2013	Wisconsin (MWL)	LoA	.251	120	442	67	111	14	5	4	39	35	40	20	9	.314	.333
Minor League Totals			.265	184	660	114	175	30	6	10	75	65	60	33	13	.339	.374

8 DAVID GOFORTH, RHP

BA GRADE **45** MEDIUM

Born: Oct. 11, 1988. **B-T:** R-R. **Ht.:** 6-0. **Wt.:** 186. **Drafted:** Mississippi, 2011 (7th round). **Signed by:** Joe Mason.

The proverbial little guy with a quick arm, Goforth was in the midst of his best pro season, earning a promotion to Double-A Huntsville and tossing back-to-back, seven-inning, no-run outings in July. After the all-star break, however, the Brewers moved him to the bullpen. The organization insists he can remain a starter, but Goforth was closing in the Arizona Fall League. No one questions Goforth's ability to throw fastballs past hitters with velocity in the 93-97 mph range, and he touches higher in a bullpen role. He has improved his fastball command, locating to both sides of the plate when he's at his best, but he's more effectively wild than precise. Goforth throws a solid curveball with good shape that grades as average, but he throws more strikes with his hard, cutter-type slider, which will reach 90-91 mph. His fringe-average curve and cutter make him as effective against lefthanders (.200 average) as righthanders (.227). His pitchability and pitch selection still need polish. Many scouts have pegged Goforth as a future reliever, and the future appears to have arrived. If the Brewers do decide to pitch him strictly in relief, then he could rise quickly to the big leagues as a high-leverage reliever, perhaps as soon as 2014.

Year	Club (League)	Class	W	L	ERA	G	GS	CG	SV	IP	H	HR	BB	SO	K/9	WHIP	AVG
2011	Helena (PIO)	R	0	4	4.43	19	0	0	2	41	44	5	10	42	9.3	1.33	.277
2012	Wisconsin (MWL)	LoA	10	8	4.66	28	28	0	0	151	154	16	63	93	5.6	1.44	.269
2013	Brevard County (FSL)	HiA	7	5	3.10	14	14	0	0	78	67	4	28	58	6.7	1.21	.231
	Huntsville (SL)	AA	4	3	3.28	20	4	1	5	47	32	1	18	36	6.9	1.07	.192
Minor League Totals			21	20	4.04	81	46	1	7	316	297	26	119	229	6.5	1.32	.250

9 DEVIN WILLIAMS, RHP

BILL MITCHELL

BA GRADE
55
EXTREME

Born: Sept. 21, 1994. **B-T:** R-R. **Ht.:** 6-3. **Wt.:** 170. **Drafted:** HS—Hazelwood, Mo., 2013 (2nd round). **Signed by:** Harvey Kuenn Jr.

The Brewers didn't have a first-round pick in 2013 because they forfeited it to sign Kyle Lohse in late March. Accordingly, they were pleased to select Williams, whom they regarded as a late-first-round talent. His velocity increased dramatically the previous fall at the World Wood Bat Association World Championships, and he continued to show that heat as a West High senior. Williams pitches in the 88-92 mph range with his two-seam fastball and can hit 95 with his four-seamer. The Brewers believe his velocity will increase with time as he fills out his lanky frame. Williams can get out of whack at times with his mechanics, but when he keeps his front shoulder closed, he has a loose, easy delivery and shows a feel for three pitches. His breaking ball is a hybrid curve and slider at times, but when he stays on top of it, it has a sharp break at the knees in the low 80s. His changeup has fade and sink and keeps hitters off-balance. Both secondary pitches are inconsistent but have the potential to be plus pitches. The Brewers often used the word "upside" after drafting Williams. They coveted his athleticism and free-and-easy arm action, and they paid him $1.35 million to forgo a Missouri scholarship. He could be headed for low Class A Wisconsin if he looks good in camp.

Year	Club (League)	Class	W	L	ERA	G	GS	CG	SV	IP	H	HR	BB	SO	K/9	WHIP	AVG
2013	Brewers (AZL)	R	1	3	3.38	13	6	0	1	35	28	0	22	39	10.1	1.44	.215
Minor League Totals			1	3	3.38	13	6	0	1	35	28	0	22	39	10.1	1.44	.215

10 HUNTER MORRIS, 1B

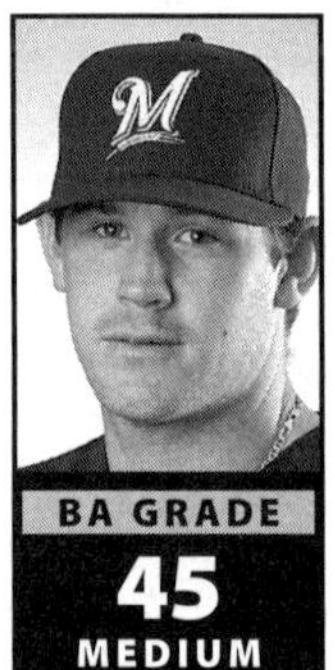

BA GRADE
45
MEDIUM

Born: Oct. 7, 1988. **B-T:** L-R. **Ht.:** 6-4. **Wt.:** 215. **Drafted:** Auburn, 2010 (4th round). **Signed by:** Joe Mason.

A second-round pick out of high school, Morris didn't sign with the Red Sox and spent three years at Auburn, then was drafted two rounds later in 2010. The Southern League's player of the year in 2012, Morris had a modest encore in 2013. The Brewers had a revolving door at the position in Milwaukee but never summoned Morris, not even in September. Morris regressed into an all-or-nothing hitter in 2013 as the improvement that Morris showed with Huntsville took a step backwards at Nashville. He struck out far too often and struggled badly against lefthanded pitchers (.211/.256/.411). Morris has middle-of-the order power potential and ranked second in the Pacific Coast League in home runs despite the inconsistent year. He has averaged 24 home runs a season in his three full years in the minors. Considered a below-average first baseman when he was drafted, Morris has worked hard to make himself a better fielder but still led the PCL with nine errors. He doesn't have great range but his hands have improved and his throwing arm is adequate for the position. Morris has below-average speed and grounds into a lot of double plays (15 in 2013). Morris could still emerge as the starter in Milwaukee if the Brewers don't find a better option before Opening Day. Whether it's later than sooner, the Brewers still believe Morris can be their starter at some point.

Year	Club (League)	Class	AVG	G	AB	R	H	2B	3B	HR	RBI	BB	SO	SB	CS	OBP	SLG
2010	Wisconsin (MWL)	LoA	.251	71	291	38	73	19	4	9	44	20	58	7	2	.306	.436
2011	Huntsville (SL)	AA	.353	4	17	6	6	1	1	1	2	0	1	0	0	.353	.706
	Brevard County (FSL)	HiA	.271	126	501	75	136	28	5	19	67	18	84	7	3	.299	.461
2012	Huntsville (SL)	AA	.303	136	522	77	158	40	6	28	113	40	117	2	1	.357	.563
2013	Nashville (PCL)	AAA	.247	134	497	61	123	26	3	24	73	43	122	3	1	.310	.457
Minor League Totals			.271	471	1828	257	496	114	19	81	299	121	382	19	7	.320	.487

11 CLINT COULTER, C

BA GRADE
50
HIGH

Born: July 30, 1993. **B-T:** R-R. **Ht.:** 6-3. **Wt.:** 210. **Drafted:** HS—Camas, Wash., 2012 (1st round). **Signed by:** Shawn Whalen.

The Brewers didn't want Coulter to sit around in extended spring training in 2013, waiting for the Rookie-level Helena season to begin, so they sent him to low Class A Wisconsin, knowing it would be a challenge for him. Accordingly, they weren't surprised when the 2012 first-rounder struggled at the plate, batting .207/.299/.345 in 33 games, to earn a ticket to Helena. Nagging injuries to Coulter's oblique muscle, knee and wrist as well as his struggles at the plate prompted him to drop a level lower to the Rookie-level Arizona League. Coulter has impressive tools. A former high school wrestling champion, he is a physical specimen with tremendous offensive upside. He gets good leverage and power from a quick bat and makes consistent contact, minimizing his strikeouts. The main question remains: Will he be able to stay behind the plate? Coulter still is a raw defensive player, though his strong arm and work ethic allowed him to show improvement in throwing out basestealers. The Brewers would like to keep him behind the plate because he shows leadership and confidence. Coulter doesn't run particularly well but shows good instincts and is aggressive on the basepaths. The 2013 season was a learning curve for Coulter in many aspects, particularly in learning how to deal with nagging injuries. He likely will return to Wisconsin to begin 2014, and the Brewers will keep him behind the plate until he proves he can't do it.

Year	Club (League)	Class	AVG	G	AB	R	H	2B	3B	HR	RBI	BB	SO	SB	CS	OBP	SLG
2012	Brewers (AZL)	R	.302	49	169	37	51	3	3	5	33	37	40	3	5	.439	.444
2013	Wisconsin (MWL)	LoA	.207	33	116	18	24	5	1	3	13	11	31	1	0	.299	.345
	Brewers (AZL)	R	.350	17	60	12	21	5	1	3	15	5	15	1	1	.409	.617
	Helena (PIO)	R	.216	20	74	8	16	4	0	1	8	4	14	1	0	.263	.311
Minor League Totals			.267	119	419	75	112	17	5	12	69	57	100	6	6	.368	.418

12 NICK DELMONICO, 3B/1B

Born: July 12, 1992. **B-T:** L-R. **Ht.:** 6-2. **Wt.:** 196. **Drafted:** HS—Knoxville, 2011 (6th round). **Signed by:** Adrian Dorsey (Orioles).

When the Brewers shopped around veteran reliever Francisco Rodriguez before the July 31 trade deadline in 2013, the Orioles showed immediate interest. The Brewers targeted Delmonico, who played a position of need in the farm system, but originally were told he was not available. When other teams joined in the bidding, Baltimore relented and offered Delmonico, whom the Brewers targeted because he bats lefthanded. However, he struggled at the plate after being assigned to high Class A Brevard County before an elbow injury stopped his season there after 21 games. The son of former Tennessee coach Rod, Delmonico has a strong, sturdy frame and shows an advanced approach and feel for hitting, working counts and recognizing breaking balls. Originally signed for $1.525 million, Delmonico has budding power but at times gets long with his swing. His offense will be his calling card, but some question whether he can stay at third base. He has had back and knee injuries, as well as missing time with a concussion in 2013. He played both first and second base during his pro debut in the Orioles system in 2012. Delmonico doesn't have the hands or footwork to play second, but the Brewers think he has enough quickness and range to stick at third, and he has the arm strength to have considered catching in high school. If he can stay healthy, which has been an issue thus far, Delmonico figures to use his bat to eventually get to the big leagues as a corner infielder.

Year	Club (League)	Class	AVG	G	AB	R	H	2B	3B	HR	RBI	BB	SO	SB	CS	OBP	SLG
2012	Delmarva (SAL)	LoA	.249	95	338	49	84	22	0	11	54	47	73	8	1	.351	.411
2013	Frederick (CAR)	HiA	.243	61	226	33	55	12	0	13	30	36	59	5	1	.350	.469
	Brevard County (FSL)	HiA	.194	21	72	8	14	4	1	0	9	12	21	2	1	.333	.278
Minor League Totals			.241	177	636	90	153	38	1	24	93	95	153	15	3	.349	.417

13 YADIEL RIVERA, SS

Born: May 1, 1992. **B-T:** R-R. **Ht.:** 6-3. **Wt.:** 180. **Drafted:** HS—Caguas, P.R., 2010 (9th round). **Signed by:** Charlie Sullivan.

If push came to shove and the Brewers needed a shortstop merely to play defense in the majors, Rivera probably could do it. That's how smooth he is in the field, with great range and instincts as well as the arm to make throws from the hole. Around the bag, Rivera shows good footwork and quickness as well as soft hands. But will Rivera hit enough to advance to the major leagues as an everyday player? He's a free swinger who doesn't work the count enough to tax a pitcher. He did make strides in 2013 at high Class A Brevard County, a pitcher-friendly environment, by cutting down his strikeout rate dramatically (15 percent of plate appearances) and raising his walk rate slightly (six percent). Rivera every now and then will juice a pitch and show more pop than expected from his lanky frame, but that generally leads to slumps because it makes him too pull-conscious and long with his swing. He sees a lot of breaking balls, especially with two strikes. Not blessed with above-average speed, Rivera improved his reads on the bases to steal 13 bases with Brevard. Still, it's his glove that makes Rivera a prospect to watch, and it'll be up to him to show he can hit enough to avoid the utility infielder tag. He will move up to Double-A Huntsville in 2014 and play every day at shortstop.

Year	Club (League)	Class	AVG	G	AB	R	H	2B	3B	HR	RBI	BB	SO	SB	CS	OBP	SLG
2010	Brewers (AZL)	R	.209	49	206	22	43	8	1	0	23	9	72	6	2	.243	.257
2011	Wisconsin (MWL)	LoA	.194	32	103	6	20	2	1	1	5	4	34	0	0	.224	.262
	Helena (PIO)	R	.248	74	330	47	82	14	7	8	38	14	91	7	3	.285	.406
2012	Wisconsin (MWL)	LoA	.247	127	465	60	115	26	5	12	49	26	119	7	3	.290	.402
2013	Brevard County (FSL)	HiA	.241	129	478	51	115	16	2	5	37	32	80	13	8	.300	.314
Minor League Totals			.237	411	1582	186	375	66	16	26	152	85	396	33	16	.282	.348

14 TUCKER NEUHAUS, 3B/SS

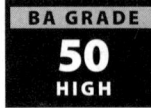

BA GRADE **50** HIGH

Born: June 18, 1995. **B-T:** L-R. **Ht.:** 6-3. **Wt.:** 190. **Drafted:** HS—Tampa, 2013 (2nd round supplemental). **Signed by:** Tim McIlvaine.

Simply put, Neuhaus' senior year at Wharton High was a nightmare. Before the season began, his older brother died in an auto accident, then a series of injuries—pulled quadriceps muscle and burst eardrum—cut into his playing time. Accordingly, the Brewers went on previous scouting reports and were thrilled when Neuhaus was still on the board in the supplemental second round of the 2013 draft. He shows all the skills and instincts you'd expect from a coach's son. His father Ken was the head coach at Division III Bethel (Minn.) and an assistant at Iowa before moving the family to Florida, where he served as a part-time scout for the Reds. Neuhaus is athletic for his size and shows soft hands and good footwork in the field. Some profile him as a future third baseman, but the Brewers want to keep giving him time at shortstop to see how he does. They believe he has the range and arm strength to stick there. Neuhaus didn't turn 18 until just after the draft and the Brewers believe he'll only get better as he accumulates playing experience. He shows decent pop from the left side and figures to get stronger as he matures. After playing third and short in the Rookie-level Arizona League in 2013, Neuhaus probably is ticketed to Rookie-level Helena in 2014.

Year	Club (League)	Class	AVG	G	AB	R	H	2B	3B	HR	RBI	BB	SO	SB	CS	OBP	SLG
2013	Brewers (AZL)	R	.231	51	195	29	45	12	1	0	24	23	56	6	3	.311	.303
Minor League Totals			.231	51	195	29	45	12	1	0	24	23	56	6	3	.311	.303

15 ARIEL PENA, RHP

Born: May 20, 1989. **B-T:** R-R. **Ht.:** 6-3. **Wt.:** 190. **Signed:** Dominican Republic, 2007. **Signed by:** Freddy Rodriguez (Angels).

The Brewers have a lot of hard-throwers in their system who have command issues and Pena is one of them. Acquired with shortstop Jean Segura and righthander Johnny Hellweg from the Angels in the Zack Greinke trade in late-July 2012, Pena has the ability to throw the ball by hitters. He throws his sinker in the 92-94 mph range and can reach 98 with his four-seamer. He also throws a hard, late-breaking slider at 82-86 mph, but he overthrows his changeup at times and that has not been an overly effective pitch for him. Much like Hellweg, Pena gets himself in trouble by not throwing strikes, resulting in a walk rate of 5.0 per nine innings at Double-A Huntsville in 2013. He struggles at times with his mechanics and long arm action, and loses his release point, but he can escape trouble via strikeout, as attested by his 8.3 strikeouts per nine innings. The Brewers have used Pena strictly as a starter to allow him to work on his command and accumulate innings, but if he doesn't harness his control soon, he'll move to the bullpen. He could be dominant in that role with his fastball-heavy approach. Pena likely will move to Triple-A Nashville in 2014, where he may move to the bullpen if he stumbles.

Year	Club (League)	Class	W	L	ERA	G	GS	CG	SV	IP	H	HR	BB	SO	K/9	WHIP	AVG
2007	Angels (DSL)	R	10	2	2.26	14	14	2	0	80	62	1	32	54	6.1	1.18	.212
2008	Angels (DSL)	R	7	3	1.86	15	15	0	0	97	73	0	26	110	10.2	1.02	.208
2009	Angels (AZL)	R	5	4	3.83	14	6	0	0	49	46	2	15	47	8.6	1.24	.247
2010	R. Cucamonga (CAL)	HiA	0	1	8.71	3	3	0	0	10	10	0	13	8	7.0	2.23	.270
	Cedar Rapids (MWL)	LoA	7	5	3.76	18	18	1	0	103	93	7	60	88	7.7	1.49	.242
2011	Inland Empire (CAL)	HiA	10	6	4.45	27	27	1	0	152	154	10	81	180	10.7	1.55	.264
	Salt Lake (PCL)	AAA	0	0	2.25	1	1	0	0	4	7	0	4	3	6.8	2.75	.389
2012	Arkansas (TL)	AA	6	6	2.99	19	19	1	0	114	95	14	42	111	8.7	1.20	.222
	Huntsville (SL)	AA	0	2	7.24	7	7	0	0	32	40	5	23	29	8.1	1.95	.336
2013	Huntsville (SL)	AA	8	9	3.73	27	27	0	0	142	115	17	79	131	8.3	1.36	.224
Minor League Totals			53	38	3.59	145	137	5	0	784	695	56	375	761	8.7	1.37	.239

16 TYLER WAGNER, RHP

BA GRADE **50** HIGH

Born: Jan. 21, 1991. **B-T:** R-R. **Ht.:** 6-4. **Wt.:** 195. **Drafted:** Utah, 2012 (4th round). **Signed by:** Jeff Scholzen.

No player in the system improved his stock in 2013 more than Wagner, who showed surprising staying power as a starter at low Class A Wisconsin. He worked as closer at Utah when the Brewers drafted him in 2012, but the club saw him as a rotation candidate. The results weren't pretty at Rookie-level Helena that same year—7.77 ERA and a 1.75 WHIP in 49 innings—but the Brewers stuck with Wagner and he bounced back in a big way at low Class A Wisconsin in 2013. His fastball features good sink and heavy life in the low- to mid-90s, touching 96. He uses it to induce groundballs, posting a 3.01 groundout/airout ratio, best among all minor league starting pitchers who qualified for their league ERA title. He induced 16 double plays, second in the Midwest League, finished third in the league in innings and eighth in ERA. Wagner has a sharp-breaking slider at 84-86 mph that is a big out-pitch against righthanded hitters. He also displayed an effective changeup that kept lefties off-balance; they posted a .652 OPS versus .629 for righthanded hitters. Wagner, who has a high leg kick in his delivery and low three-quarters release point, made strides in commanding the ball and executing clutch pitches when necessary. The mainstay of the Timber Rattlers' rotation, Wagner just might have the pitchability to profile as a starter, with a likely next step to high Class A Brevard County for 2014.

Year	Club (League)	Class	W	L	ERA	G	GS	CG	SV	IP	H	HR	BB	SO	K/9	WHIP	AVG
2012	Helena (PIO)	R	1	4	7.77	14	13	0	0	49	63	6	22	47	8.7	1.75	.304
2013	Wisconsin (MWL)	LoA	10	8	3.21	27	25	1	0	149	129	10	56	116	7.0	1.24	.236
Minor League Totals			11	12	4.33	41	38	1	0	197	192	16	78	163	7.4	1.37	.255

17 MICHAEL BLAZEK, RHP

BA GRADE **45** MEDIUM

Born: March 16, 1989. **B-T:** R-R. **Ht.:** 6-0. **Wt.:** 190. **Drafted:** HS—Las Vegas, 2007 (35th round). **Signed by:** Aaron Krawiec (Cardinals).

When the Cardinals showed interest in acquiring deposed closer John Axford before the Aug. 31 waiver trade deadline in 2013, the Brewers saw it as an opportunity to add another power arm to their system. Because Milwaukee viewed Axford as a probable non-tender candidate, they were pleased to swing a deal for Blazek, who had excelled in the St. Louis system and received a brief trial in the big leagues. A 35th-round pick in 2007, Blazek turned down an offer from Nevada to play middle infield so that he could concentrate on pitching in pro ball. He throws his fastball in the 94-97 mph range but sometimes fights his mechanics and has command issues. He'll mix in a curve in the mid-70s, a slider in the mid-80s and a changeup, all pitches that he relies on less in the bullpen than he did as a starter. When he gets his breaking stuff over, however, hitters have more to worry about. Assuming Blazek can throw enough strikes, the Brewers see him as a seventh-inning pitcher, perhaps a set-up man, at the big league level, with an ability to climb the ladder with his fastball.

Year	Club (League)	Class	W	L	ERA	G	GS	CG	SV	IP	H	HR	BB	SO	K/9	WHIP	AVG
2007	Cardinals (GCL)	R	3	3	2.60	10	3	0	0	35	33	1	13	42	10.9	1.33	.254
2008	Johnson City (APP)	R	1	4	5.05	13	9	0	0	46	49	4	16	47	9.1	1.40	.263
2009	Batavia (NYP)	SS	4	9	4.50	15	12	0	0	64	73	3	24	62	8.7	1.52	.284
2010	Palm Beach (FSL)	HiA	0	1	12.46	1	1	0	0	4	9	0	5	2	4.2	3.23	.450
	Quad Cities (MWL)	LoA	8	4	2.71	32	11	0	3	103	78	5	31	104	9.1	1.06	.210
2011	Springfield, MO (TL)	AA	11	6	5.45	24	24	0	0	134	148	25	64	128	8.6	1.59	.280
	Memphis (PCL)	AAA	2	0	3.75	2	2	0	0	12	8	1	9	6	4.5	1.42	.205
2012	Memphis (PCL)	AAA	0	1	10.80	2	1	0	0	3	6	1	2	1	2.7	2.40	.462
	Springfield, MO (TL)	AA	5	8	4.16	40	7	0	0	80	61	11	34	83	9.3	1.19	.213
2013	Springfield, MO (TL)	AA	0	0	0.92	17	0	0	7	20	11	0	10	25	11.4	1.07	.157
	Memphis (PCL)	AAA	1	2	2.77	19	0	0	2	26	17	1	16	27	9.3	1.27	.185
	St. Louis (NL)	MAJ	0	0	6.97	11	0	0	0	10	10	2	10	10	8.7	1.94	.244
	Milwaukee (NL)	MAJ	0	1	3.86	7	0	0	0	7	6	1	3	4	5.1	1.29	.222
Major League Totals			0	1	5.71	18	0	0	0	17	16	3	13	14	7.3	1.67	.235
Minor League Totals			35	38	4.13	175	70	0	12	527	493	52	224	527	9.0	1.36	.247

18 JED BRADLEY, LHP

BA GRADE **45** HIGH

Born: June 12, 1990. **B-T:** L-L. **Ht.:** 6-4. **Wt.:** 225. **Drafted:** Georgia Tech, 2011 (1st round). **Signed by:** Ryan Robinson.

As an advanced lefty coming out of Georgia Tech, Bradley profiled as a quick mover through the system when the Brewers made him the 15th pick in the 2011 draft. But the southpaw's transition to pro ball has been shaky, with injuries keeping him on the sidelines too often and mechanical issues plaguing him when he is active. Bradley made just 16 starts at high Class A Brevard County in 2013 before being shut down with shoulder issues, a disappointing conclusion to a season in which he reported to camp noticeably bigger and stronger. He also showed more life on his fastball than he had in his 2012 debut, though his velocity was below his peak as an amateur. When healthy and in control of his mechanics, Bradley throws an 89-93 mph fastball with good movement as well as a mid-80s slider, both with a loose, natural arm action. He creates deception with his low-80s changeup and will use it at any point in the count. The physical and mechanical issues have been unexpected because Bradley was a consistent power pitcher in college and was able to repeat his delivery consistently. The Brewers have a lot riding on Bradley, who will begin 2014 at Double-A Huntsville, because their system is short on lefthanders, but they expected him to be knocking on the door by now.

Year	Club (League)	Class	W	L	ERA	G	GS	CG	SV	IP	H	HR	BB	SO	K/9	WHIP	AVG
2012	Brevard County (FSL)	HiA	5	10	5.53	20	20	1	0	107	136	9	43	60	5.0	1.67	.311
2013	Brevard County (FSL)	HiA	4	4	4.14	16	16	1	0	78	81	6	39	58	6.7	1.53	.270
Minor League Totals			9	14	4.94	36	36	2	0	186	217	15	82	118	5.7	1.61	.294

19 TAYLOR WILLIAMS, RHP

BA GRADE 50 EXTREME

Born: July 21, 1991. **B-T:** S-R. **Ht.:** 5-11. **Wt.:** 180. **Drafted:** Kent State, 2013 (4th round). **Signed by:** Mike Farrell.

Sometimes, big things come in small packages. Listed at 5-foot-11, 180 pounds, Williams has a big fastball, which was one of the reasons the Brewers were glad to select him in the fourth round of the 2013 draft out of Kent State. He originally went to Washington State but didn't play much, so he transferred to Mount Hood (Ore.) CC, where he was a starter and middle infielder. He eventually followed some New England Collegiate League teammates to KSU, where as a junior he served as the most consistent starter for the Golden Flashes. Williams' draft stock rose considerably in a game against San Diego, when he struck out College Player of the Year Kris Bryant three times. He can run his fastball up to 94-95 mph with good life, but he sits mostly at 90-92. He features some effort in his delivery, but Williams also has good athleticism. He throws strikes, pounding the zone with his fastball and slider, which is a big out-pitch against righthanders. To keep lefthanders off his heater, he mixes in changeups. Because of Williams' combination of smallish stature and live fastball, many scouts project him as a reliever. For now, the Brewers plan to continue starting him, with the next step being low Class A Wisconsin in 2014.

Year	Club (League)	Class	W	L	ERA	G	GS	CG	SV	IP	H	HR	BB	SO	K/9	WHIP	AVG
2013	Helena (PIO)	R	3	1	4.25	12	6	0	0	42	42	5	17	42	8.9	1.39	.258
Minor League Totals			3	1	4.25	12	6	0	0	42	42	5	17	42	8.9	1.39	.258

20 JASON ROGERS, 1B/OF

BA GRADE 45 HIGH

Born: March 13, 1988. **B-T:** R-R. **Ht.:** 6-2. **Wt.:** 245. **Drafted:** Columbus State (Ga.), 2010 (32nd round). **Signed by:** Ryan Robinson.

As a 32nd-round pick out of Division II Columbus State (Ga.), Rogers didn't project to be a top prospect. It didn't help when he missed much of the 2011 season with a fractured hamate bone. But Rogers showed promise as a low Class A Midwest League midseason all-star in 2012 before moving up to high Class A Brevard County for the second half. Playing the 2013 season at Double-A Huntsville, Rogers led the system with 87 RBIs while belting 22 homers to place third. He performed better as the year progressed, batting .297 with a .906 OPS in the second half. Rogers has improved his plate discipline and pitch recognition, and he has a good two-strike approach, which helps him keep strikeouts in check (16 percent of plate appearances in 2013) moreso than other power hitters. Rogers is a below-average runner but has decent instincts on the bases. A stocky-but-athletic build allowed him to play left field in the Arizona Fall League, where he hit .311 but struck out 21 times in 61 at-bats. The Brewers added Rogers to the 40-man roster rather than risk losing him in the Rule 5 draft, and he will move to Triple-A Nashville in 2014, where the likely presence of first baseman Hunter Morris will necessitate that he call on his left-field experience.

Year	Club (League)	Class	AVG	G	AB	R	H	2B	3B	HR	RBI	BB	SO	SB	CS	OBP	SLG
2010	Brewers (AZL)	R	.281	42	160	31	45	7	1	3	32	20	32	5	2	.368	.394
2011	Helena (PIO)	R	.296	7	27	3	8	1	0	1	3	2	5	0	1	.345	.444
	Wisconsin (MWL)	LoA	.275	64	240	29	66	15	2	6	37	22	48	6	1	.336	.429
2012	Wisconsin (MWL)	LoA	.301	66	239	39	72	24	1	6	43	37	46	5	0	.394	.485
	Brevard County (FSL)	HiA	.300	67	233	33	70	11	0	5	23	42	42	7	1	.416	.412
2013	Huntsville (SL)	AA	.270	133	481	69	130	25	2	22	87	59	86	7	2	.346	.468
Minor League Totals			.283	379	1380	204	391	83	6	43	225	182	259	30	7	.368	.446

21 KEVIN SHACKELFORD, RHP

BA GRADE 45 HIGH

Born: April 7, 1989. **B-T:** R-R. **Ht.:** 6-5. **Wt.:** 210. **Drafted:** Marshall, 2010 (21st round). **Signed by:** Dan Nellum.

Shackelford was a catcher for two seasons at Marshall before converting to the mound and catching the eye of scouts. He made strides as a pitcher in 2013, especially after being promoted from high Class A Brevard County to Double-A Huntsville. Used to close games there, Shackelford blossomed and held opponents to a .217 average over 20 appearances. He threw his fastball in the 92-95 mph range and touched as high as 97, with a two-seamer that bore down in the strike zone and induced groundballs. His slider can be a swing-and-miss pitch, and the combination of the two power pitches makes Shackelford profile as a late-inning reliever in the majors. He's athletic with a clean delivery, but he release point can wander, causing his slider consistency. Shackelford throws on a solid downhill plane because of his 6-foot-5 height and continued his late-season success in the Arizona Fall League, striking out 13 in 12 innings. If he doesn't begin 2014 at Triple-A Nashville, he ought to arrive at that level during the season. Shackelford could see action in the Brewers bullpen before the season is out.

Year	Club (League)	Class	W	L	ERA	G	GS	CG	SV	IP	H	HR	BB	SO	K/9	WHIP	AVG
2010	Brewers (AZL)	R	1	2	5.40	13	6	1	0	40	33	6	16	25	5.6	1.23	.220
2011	Helena (PIO)	R	3	5	4.15	15	8	0	0	65	74	8	10	31	4.3	1.29	.285
2012	Wisconsin (MWL)	LoA	3	5	4.06	27	3	0	5	64	70	4	23	43	6.0	1.45	.283
2013	Brevard County (FSL)	HiA	1	3	5.06	24	0	0	2	32	39	3	4	23	6.5	1.34	.300
	Huntsville (SL)	AA	1	1	0.92	20	0	0	6	29	23	1	7	25	7.7	1.02	.217
Minor League Totals			9	16	4.06	99	17	1	13	231	239	22	60	147	5.7	1.30	.268

22 BARRETT ASTIN, RHP

BA GRADE **45** HIGH

Born: Oct. 22, 1991. **B-T:** R-R. **Ht.:** 6-1. **Wt.:** 190. **Drafted:** Arkansas, 2013 (3rd round). **Signed by:** Tim Collinsworth.

A star performer in the 2012 Arkansas bullpen, Astin closed games with aplomb and helped propel the school to the College World Series. He flashed a fastball at 94-95 mph that had heavy sink and induced groundballs regularly. Shifted to the Razorbacks rotation in 2013, Astin's fastball was less electric, sitting more at 88-92 mph under the increased workload. He throws a slider with cutting action that can be tough on lefthanders and mixes in a solid curveball with good tilt. He does a good job of pitching down in the zone, and when he misses, he usually misses down. He keeps the ball in the park and doesn't walk hitters, unafraid to throw the ball in the strike zone. Astin threw a lot of innings in 2013 and eventually wore down in his debut at Rookie-level Helena, but he finished strong with four no-hit innings in his final outing. Whether he will be durable enough to remain a starter remains to be seen, but at worst he profiles as a reliever who could move quickly. Astin likely will move up to low Class A Wisconsin in 2014.

Year	Club (League)	Class	W	L	ERA	G	GS	CG	SV	IP	H	HR	BB	SO	K/9	WHIP	AVG
2013	Helena (PIO)	R	1	1	4.30	12	8	0	0	38	41	6	11	31	7.4	1.38	.266
Minor League Totals			1	1	4.30	12	8	0	0	38	41	6	11	31	7.4	1.38	.266

23 DAMIEN MAGNIFICO, RHP

BA GRADE **50** EXTREME

Born: May 24, 1991. **B-T:** R-R. **Ht.:** 6-2. **Wt.:** 210. **Drafted:** Oklahoma, 2012 (5th round). **Signed by:** Tim Collinsworth.

Not many pitchers can throw a legitimate 100 mph fastball. Magnifico is one of them, but it's no secret as to why he lasted until the fifth round of the 2012 draft. His secondary pitches were almost non-existent at Oklahoma, and because his fastball is straight, it often got hit. Magnifico has made progress with his 83-87 mph slider in pro ball and also throws a changeup, but too often he throws them from a lower arm slot. His two-seamer has plus sinking action when he stays on top of the pitch and takes a little off the velocity. Magnifico has had elbow issues in the past, so it's imperative that he stays on top of his mechanics. His max-effort delivery may not be an innocent bystander in his injury history. Magnifico had success at low Class A Wisconsin in 2013, making the Midwest League all-star team, so the Brewers bumped him up high Class A Brevard County, where opponents batted .311 against him. Command has been an issue, as attested by his walk rate of 4.6 per nine innings at the two stops. The Brewers have used Magnfico as a starter to allow him to accumulate innings and work on his secondary pitches, but his blazing fastball and poor control mark him as a prime relief candidate.

Year	Club (League)	Class	W	L	ERA	G	GS	CG	SV	IP	H	HR	BB	SO	K/9	WHIP	AVG
2012	Helena (PIO)	R	0	3	5.82	9	1	0	0	22	21	2	15	25	10.4	1.66	.250
2013	Wisconsin (MWL)	LoA	5	1	3.83	11	8	0	0	54	51	4	24	46	7.7	1.39	.250
	Brevard County (FSL)	HiA	0	2	6.08	10	10	0	0	27	32	2	17	17	5.7	1.84	.311
Minor League Totals			5	6	4.84	30	19	0	0	102	104	8	56	88	7.7	1.56	.266

24 JORGE LOPEZ, RHP

Born: Feb. 10, 1993. **B-T:** R-R. **Ht.:** 6-4. **Wt.:** 180. **Drafted:** HS—Cayey, P.R., **2011** (2nd round). **Signed by:** Charlie Sullivan/Manolo Hernandez.

When the Brewers drafted Lopez as a raw, 18-year-old in the second round of the 2011 draft, they knew his development would feature growing pains. His 2012 season turned out to be more problematic than expected, with back issues and the a demotion from the Rookie-level Arizona League to the Dominican Summer League. But the Brewers assigned Lopez to low Class A Wisconsin in 2013 and left him there to sink or swim. He showed flashes of the talent that initially piqued the club's interest but also plenty of inconsistency. Lopez throws his fastball in the 89-93 mph range with good action. The ball comes out of his hand with ease, and his two-seamer has good sink. His curveball comes and goes, but when Lopez stays on top of the ball it has quality bite. He has good feel for his changeup, though he sometimes overthrows it. Lopez must get more consistent with his delivery and release point, as evidenced by the 13 wild pitches and nine hit batters in 117 innings at Wisconsin. Lopez still is maturing, both physically and mentally, and the Brewers believe he has mid-rotation starter potential. He likely will move up to high Class A Brevard County to begin 2014.

Year	Club (League)	Class	W	L	ERA	G	GS	CG	SV	IP	H	HR	BB	SO	K/9	WHIP	AVG
2011	Brewers (AZL)	R	0	0	2.25	4	4	0	0	12	13	0	3	10	7.5	1.33	.265
2012	Brewers (AZL)	R	1	3	5.33	7	3	0	2	25	27	2	12	20	7.1	1.54	.270
	Brewers (DSL)	R	0	1	4.76	5	3	0	0	23	22	0	10	26	10.3	1.41	.256
2013	Wisconsin (MWL)	LoA	7	8	5.23	25	22	0	2	117	120	13	48	92	7.1	1.44	.264
Minor League Totals			8	12	4.98	41	32	0	4	177	182	15	73	148	7.5	1.44	.264

25 DREW GAGNON, RHP

BA GRADE
45
HIGH

Born: June 26, 1990. **B-T:** R-R. **Ht.:** 6-4. **Wt.:** 195. **Drafted:** Long Beach State, 2011 (3rd round). **Signed by:** Josh Belovsky.

After a strong 2012 season at two levels of Class A ball in 2012, Gagnon appeared primed for good things in 2013. Instead, he struggled upon returning to high Class A Brevard, didn't fare any better after moving up to Double-A Huntsville and was plagued by command issues throughout, averaging nearly four walks per nine innings. That was unusual for Gagnon, who when at his best pounds the zone with good life on an 88-92 mph fastball. His curveball can be tough on righthanders, but he was more erratic with it in 2013. Gagnon throws his fringe-average changeup with good arm action, and he mixes in a cutter that can be effective. He doesn't have the large margin for error of a power pitcher, and more experienced Double-A hitters took advantage, lighting him up for a 5.57 ERA and 12 homers in 16 starts. The lack of plus pitch limits Gagnon's ceiling to back-of-the-rotation starter. He probably will return to Huntsville to begin 2014.

Year	Club (League)	Class	W	L	ERA	G	GS	CG	SV	IP	H	HR	BB	SO	K/9	WHIP	AVG
2011	Helena (PIO)	R	0	3	8.05	8	7	0	1	19	25	1	10	27	12.8	1.84	.321
2012	Wisconsin (MWL)	LoA	6	1	2.83	14	14	0	0	83	67	6	19	65	7.1	1.04	.219
	Brevard County (FSL)	HiA	1	2	2.82	11	11	1	0	67	56	3	18	49	6.6	1.10	.229
2013	Brevard County (FSL)	HiA	3	4	5.16	10	10	0	0	45	46	2	15	50	9.9	1.35	.263
	Huntsville (SL)	AA	4	9	5.57	16	16	1	0	84	94	12	42	58	6.2	1.62	.288
Minor League Totals			14	19	4.29	59	58	2	1	298	288	24	104	249	7.5	1.32	.255

26 OMAR GARCIA, OF

BA GRADE
50
EXTREME

Born: Aug. 1, 1993. **B-T:** R-R. **Ht.:** 5-11. **Wt.:** 170. **Drafted:** Miami Dade JC, 2013 (7th round). **Signed by:** Charlie Sullivan.

Garcia has the one dominant tool that cannot be taught—speed. An 80 runner, he had been timed at 6.3 seconds in the 60-yard dash prior to the 2013 draft. Despite batting righthanded, he's a tough out even on routine grounders to the left side of the infield. A true singles hitter with little or no power, Garcia profiles as a leadoff type who can get on base and disrupt teams with his stolen-base potential. Using that approach, he had a successful debut as a 19-year-old at Rookie-level Helena. Garcia makes consistent contact, rarely striking out, and he will wait out walks to get on base and put his speed to good use. His offensive game centers on slapping the ball on the ground and legging out infield hits. He has decent range in center field and is learning to get proper jumps on balls in the gaps. His arm is average, which won't be a deterrent. Garcia must prove his approach will work against better pitchers or adjust by learning to drive the ball. He'll get just that opportunity at low Class A Wisconsin in 2014.

Year	Club (League)	Class	AVG	G	AB	R	H	2B	3B	HR	RBI	BB	SO	SB	CS	OBP	SLG
2013	Helena (PIO)	R	.305	54	203	39	62	4	1	0	27	34	39	28	6	.425	.335
Minor League Totals			.305	54	203	39	62	4	1	0	27	34	39	28	6	.425	.335

27 ANTHONY BANDA, LHP

BA GRADE
45
HIGH

Born: Aug. 10, 1993. **B-T:** L-L. **Ht.:** 6-3. **Wt.:** 185. **Drafted:** San Jacinto (Texas) JC, 2012 (10th round). **Signed by:** Brian Sankey.

Banda helped lead San Jacinto (Texas) JC to a runner-up finish at the 2012 Junior College World Series. He struggled in the Rookie-level Arizona League following his selection in the 10th round of that year's draft, but he made strides in 2013 with Rookie-level Helena. Banda throws a fastball in the 89-92 mph range with good movement, an effective changeup and a sharp-breaking curveball that often is his best pitch. He shows good command of his fastball, keeping it down in the zone for the most part and pitching to contact. Banda's curveball was consistent throughout the season, and he showed a good feel for his changeup to keep righthanders honest. Banda did work too high in the strike zone at times and was hurt with home runs. He has a good pitcher's build and physicality. Short of lefthanders in general, the Brewers view him as a potential mid-rotation starter, and he will spend most of the 2014 as a 20-year-old at low Class A Wisconsin.

Year	Club (League)	Class	W	L	ERA	G	GS	CG	SV	IP	H	HR	BB	SO	K/9	WHIP	AVG
2012	Brewers (AZL)	R	2	3	5.83	14	4	0	0	42	54	3	24	43	9.3	1.87	.309
2013	Helena (PIO)	R	3	4	4.45	14	14	0	0	61	64	7	25	45	6.7	1.47	.274
Minor League Totals			5	7	5.01	28	18	0	0	102	118	10	49	88	7.7	1.63	.289

28 MICHAEL RATTERREE, OF

BA GRADE 45 HIGH

Born: Feb. 9, 1991. **B-T:** R-R. **Ht.:** 6-1. **Wt.:** 190. **Drafted:** Rice, 2013 (10th round). **Signed by:** Brian Sankey.

Ratterree entered 2012 as a potential high-rounds pick as a Rice junior, but he had a terrible time at the plate and went undrafted. He returned for his senior season and got off to an even slower start in 2013 before heating up in the second half and drawing the Brewers' attention. Once projected as an offensive-minded second baseman, Ratterree developed throwing problems in college and shifted to the outfield. Living up to previous expectations, he quickly made the adjustment to pro ball and led Rookie-level Helena to the Pioneer League playoffs while earning MVP honors. With good bat speed and plate discipline, Ratterree flashed raw power to all fields, accumulating home runs and extra-base hits with frequency. His confidence at the plate was apparent as he swung aggressively without worrying about drawing walks. He has good arm strength but fringy range and defensive skills, limiting him to the corner outfield. Thus, his bat will have to carry him. An early bargain as a 10th-rounder who signed for $25,000, Ratterree will move up to low Class A Wisconsin in 2014.

Year	Club (League)	Class	AVG	G	AB	R	H	2B	3B	HR	RBI	BB	SO	SB	CS	OBP	SLG
2013	Helena (PIO)	R	.314	65	258	63	81	22	6	12	58	26	72	7	3	.391	.585
Minor League Totals			.314	65	258	63	81	22	6	12	58	26	72	7	3	.391	.585

29 TYLER CRAVY, RHP

BA GRADE 45 HIGH

Born: July 13, 1989. **B-T:** R-R. **Ht.:** 6-3. **Wt.:** 198. **Drafted:** Napa Valley (Calif.) CC, 2009 (17th round). **Signed by:** Justin McCray.

Cravy made big strides in 2013 as a swingman at high Class A Brevard County, making nine starts and pitching 16 times out of the bullpen. The Brewers were so intrigued by his performance that they assigned him to the Arizona Fall League. A finesse pitcher, Cravy uses a 90-91 mph sinker to induce groundball outs. He works fast and pounds the zone, staying ahead in the count and pitching to contact. He keeps the ball in the park with his sinker, allowing only one home run during the 2013 season before giving up another in the AFL. Cravy throws a slider at 84-86 mph with good bite, and to keep hitters further off-balance, he mixes in a slower curveball at 77-78 mph with good tilt. He throws his breaking stuff with good deception, notching strikeouts despite just average velocity on all pitches. Cravy has a good feel for setting up hitters and shows confidence and poise on the mound. He could be valuable as a middle reliever also capable of filling in as a spot starter when necessary. A ticket to Double-A Huntsville awaits Cravy in 2014.

Year	Club (League)	Class	W	L	ERA	G	GS	CG	SV	IP	H	HR	BB	SO	K/9	WHIP	AVG
2009	Brewers (AZL)	R	2	1	4.45	12	4	0	0	32	28	1	12	34	9.5	1.24	.235
2010	Helena (PIO)	R	6	6	5.87	15	12	0	0	77	81	7	28	70	8.2	1.42	.269
2011	Wisconsin (MWL)	LoA	3	2	5.75	15	0	0	0	20	27	0	10	29	12.8	1.82	.307
	Helena (PIO)	R	3	4	4.76	14	11	0	0	70	70	6	19	81	10.4	1.27	.258
2012	Wisconsin (MWL)	LoA	2	5	3.38	24	0	0	3	51	45	5	15	53	9.4	1.18	.231
2013	Brevard County (FSL)	HiA	4	2	2.04	25	9	0	0	79	61	1	24	59	6.7	1.07	.210
Minor League Totals			20	20	4.18	105	36	0	3	329	312	20	108	326	8.9	1.28	.247

30 D'VONTREY RICHARDSON, OF

BA GRADE 50 EXTREME

Born: July 30, 1988. **B-T:** R-R. **Ht.:** 6-2. **Wt.:** 215. **Drafted:** Florida State, 2009 (5th round). **Signed by:** Ryan Robinson.

Richardson fell completely off the radar when he quit baseball in 2012, with the former football/baseball star at Florida State saying he was burned out. But he had a change of heart and asked the Brewers to return in 2013. Told he'd have to start over from scratch and obey every team rule, Richardson did just that, advancing from the Rookie-level Arizona League to high Class A Brevard County. With the Manatees, he began flashing the skills that had the Brewers excited when they drafted him in 2009 and convinced him to give up football. Richardson has the speed and range to play center field, while possessing the strong arm that many lack at that position. He obviously has the tools to do many things but needs to refine his all-around game. He didn't flash as much power as might be expected in 2013, but he did show improved plate discipline by cutting down his strikeouts. Because he sat out a year, Richardson turned 25 in the middle of 2013 and is behind the curve. He may move to Double-A Huntsville in 2014, where he'll continue to fight long odds to become a big league contributor.

Year	Club (League)	Class	AVG	G	AB	R	H	2B	3B	HR	RBI	BB	SO	SB	CS	OBP	SLG
2010	Wisconsin (MWL)	LoA	.243	132	522	78	127	28	8	7	51	58	164	17	15	.331	.368
2011	Brevard County (FSL)	HiA	.284	97	359	47	102	13	7	3	41	22	70	9	13	.327	.384
2012	Did not play																
2013	Brewers (AZL)	R	.292	5	24	3	7	0	0	0	3	1	6	0	0	.320	.292
	Brevard County (FSL)	HiA	.325	52	209	25	68	12	2	1	13	14	43	13	6	.372	.416
Minor League Totals			.273	286	1114	153	304	53	17	11	108	95	283	39	34	.337	.381

Minnesota Twins

BY MIKE BERARDINO

Two calendar years into his second stint as Twins general manager, Terry Ryan is still trying to right the ship.

He takes solace in the rapid turnarounds navigated in recent years by his counterparts in such places as Boston, Cleveland and Oakland, but the veteran executive also recognizes how much work remains.

Having suffered 96 or more losses for the third time in as many years, the Twins easily could have blown things up in order to appease a frustrated fan base. Instead, CEO Jim Pohlad left the decision up to Ryan, and Ryan chose to retain longtime manager Ron Gardenhire on a two-year extension along with his entire coaching staff.

Hall of Fame player Paul Molitor, often rumored as Gardenhire's eventual replacement, also was added to the big league staff after spending close to the past decade as the organization's minor league infield and baserunning coordinator. In that role Molitor worked closely with touted Twins prospects Byron Buxton and Miguel Sano.

Buxton, in his first go at full-season ball after being drafted second overall in 2012, lit up the sky at two Class A levels en route to Baseball America Minor League Player of the Year honors. The center fielder's big league ETA is probably Opening Day 2015 at the latest. Sano, who had occupied the Twins' top prospect role until Buxton's breakthrough, saw his climb reach Double-A before an issue with his throwing elbow ended his Dominican League season after just two October games. Sano, 20, could push for a big league job by midseason.

Joining Buxton and Sano in the short-term push to help in Minnesota are righthanders Alex Meyer and Trevor May, power arms Ryan was able to acquire during the 2012 offseason in separate deals that cost the Twins center fielders Denard Span and Ben Revere. Meyer missed two months at midseason with a shoulder issue, but he was able to rally after his return and was among the most impressive arms in the Arizona Fall League.

After years of relying on command-oriented starters in the Brad Radke mold, the Twins have made a philosophical shift since Ryan's return that has them scouring the landscape for power arms with the sort of strikeout potential regularly on display throughout the game.

Throughout the minors, under the supervision of new farm director Brad Steil and field coordinator

BILL MITCHELL

As a power arm who could start, Alex Meyer may be the Twins' most important prospect

TOP PROSPECTS OF THE DECADE

Year	Player, Pos.	2013 Org.
2004	Joe Mauer, c	Twins
2005	Joe Mauer, c	Twins
2006	Francisco Liriano, lhp	Pirates
2007	Matt Garza, rhp	Rangers
2008	Nick Blackburn, rhp	Twins
2009	Aaron Hicks, of	Twins
2010	Aaron Hicks, of	Twins
2011	Kyle Gibson, rhp	Twins
2012	Miguel Sano, 3b	Twins
2013	Miguel Sano, 3b	Twins

Joel Lepel, the Twins had one of their most successful seasons in 2013.Three of their top four affiliates reached the postseason, with only Double-A New Britain failing to qualify.

Twenty of the 33 players on the Twins' September roster spent at least part of the year at Triple-A Rochester under veteran skipper Gene Glynn, the former big league coach and scout. That included late-blooming catching prospect Josmil Pinto, who impressed with the bat in his September callup. In fact, Pinto is the frontrunner to replace six-time all-star Joe Mauer now that the Twins' franchise player has shifted full-time to first base in the wake of a concussion scare that wiped out his final 39 games of 2012.

ORGANIZATION OVERVIEW

General Manager: Terry Ryan. **Farm Director:** Brad Steil. **Scouting Director:** Deron Johnson.

Class	Team	League	W	L	PCT	Finish	Manager
Majors	Minnesota Twins	American	66	96	.407	13th (15)	Ron Gardenhire
Triple-A	Rochester Red Wings	International	77	67	.535	t-4th (14)	Gene Glynn
Double-A	New Britain Rock Cats	Eastern	66	76	.465	10th (12)	Jeff Smith
High Class A	Fort Myers Miracle	Florida State	79	56	.585	2nd (12)	Doug Mientkiewicz
Low Class A	Cedar Rapids Kernels	Midwest	88	50	.638	1st (16)	Jake Mauer
Rookie	Elizabethton Twins	Appalachian	37	31	.544	5th (10)	Ray Smith
Rookie	GCL Twins	Gulf Coast	28	32	.467	9th (16)	Ramon Borrego
2013 Overall Minor League Record			**375**	**312**	**.546**	**t-4th (30)**	

THIS YEAR'S TOP 30

No.	Player, Pos.	Grade/Risk
1.	Byron Buxton, of	75/Low
2.	Miguel Sano, 3b	70/Medium
3.	Alex Meyer, rhp	60/High
4.	Kohl Stewart, rhp	65/Extreme
5.	J.O. Berrios, rhp	55/High
6.	Eddie Rosario, 2b/of	55/High
7.	Lewis Thorpe, lhp	60/Extreme
8.	Trevor May, rhp	50/High
9.	Danny Santana, ss	50/High
10.	Jorge Polanco, 2b/ss	50/High
11.	Max Kepler, of/1b	50/High
12.	Fernando Romero, rhp	55/Extreme
13.	Stephen Gonsalves, lhp	50/High
14.	Josmil Pinto, c	45/Medium
15.	Mike Tonkin, rhp	45/Medium
16.	Adam Brett Walker, of	50/High
17.	Felix Jorge, rhp	50/High
18.	Mason Melotakis, lhp	50/High
19.	Taylor Rogers, lhp	45/Medium
20.	Kennys Vargas, 1b	50/High
21.	Lewin Diaz, of/1b	50/Extreme
22.	Ronny Rosario, lhp	50/Extreme
23.	Luke Bard, rhp	50/Extreme
24.	Amaurys Minier, 3b	50/Extreme
25.	Travis Harrison, 3b/of	45/High
26.	Niko Goodrum, ss/2b	45/High
27.	Tyler Jones, rhp	45/High
28.	Zack Jones, rhp	50/Extreme
29.	Roni Tapia, 3b	50/Extreme
30.	Stuart Turner, c	45/High

LAST YEAR'S TOP 30

No.	Player, Pos.	Status
1.	Miguel Sano, 3b	No. 2
2.	Byron Buxton, of	No. 1
3.	Oswaldo Arcia, of	Majors
4.	Alex Meyer, rhp	No. 3
5.	Kyle Gibson, rhp	Majors
6.	Aaron Hicks, of	Majors
7.	J.O. Berrios, rhp	No. 5
8.	Eddie Rosario, 2b/of	No. 6
9.	Trevor May, rhp	No. 8
10.	Max Kepler, of	No. 11
11.	Danny Santana, ss/2b	No. 9
12.	Luke Bard, rhp	No. 23
13.	Mason Melotakis, lhp	No. 18
14.	Jorge Polanco, 2b/ss	No. 10
15.	J.T. Chargois, rhp	Dropped out
16.	Levi Michael, 2b/ss	Dropped out
17.	Travis Harrison, 3b	No. 25
18.	Chris Herrmann, c/of	Majors
19.	Joe Benson, of	(Free agent)
20.	B.J. Hermsen, rhp	Dropped out
21.	Angel Mata, rhp	Dropped out
22.	Madison Boer, rhp	Dropped out
23.	Tyler Jones, rhp	No. 27
24.	Felix Jorge, rhp	No. 17
25.	Jason Wheeler, lhp	Dropped out
26.	Niko Goodrum, ss	No. 26
27.	Adrian Salcedo, rhp	Dropped out
28.	Mike Tonkin, rhp	No. 15
29.	Kennys Vargas, 1b	No. 20
30.	Matt Summers, rhp	Dropped out

BEST TOOLS

Best Hitter for Average	Byron Buxton
Best Power Hitter	Miguel Sano
Best Strike-Zone Discipline	Jorge Polanco
Fastest Baserunner	Byron Buxton
Best Athlete	Byron Buxton
Best Fastball	Alex Meyer
Best Curveball	Alex Meyer
Best Slider	Kohl Stewart
Best Changeup	Trevor May
Best Control	Taylor Rogers
Best Defensive Catcher	Stuart Turner
Best Defensive Infielder	Danny Santana
Best Infield Arm	Miguel Sano
Best Defensive Outfielder	Byron Buxton
Best Outfield Arm	Byron Buxton

TOP 15 PLAYERS 25 AND UNDER

No.	Player, Pos. (Age)	Peak Level
1.	Byron Buxton, of (20)	High Class A
2.	Miguel Sano, 3b (20)	Double-A
3.	Alex Meyer, rhp (24)	Double-A
4.	Oswaldo Arcia, of (22)	Majors
5.	Kohl Stewart, rhp (19)	Rookie
6.	J.O. Berrios, rhp (19)	Low Class A
7.	Eddie Rosario, 2b/of (22)	Double-A
8.	Lewis Thorpe, lhp (18)	Rookie
9.	Trevor May, rhp (24)	Double-A
10.	Aaron Hicks, of (24)	Majors
11.	Max Kepler, of/1b (21)	Low Class A
12.	Danny Santana, ss/2b (23)	Double-A
13.	Jorge Polanco, ss/2b (20)	High Class A
14.	Fernando Romero, rhp (19)	Rookie
15.	Stephen Gonsalves, lhp (19)	Rookie

MINOR LEAGUE DEPTH CHART

MINNESOTA TWINS

TOP 2014 ROOKIE: Josmil Pinto, c. After making the most of his late-season callup, this bat-first backstop is in line to replace perennial all-star Joe Mauer behind the plate.

BREAKOUT PROSPECT: Mason Melotakis, lhp. Once he stops bouncing between the bullpen and the rotation, this hard-throwing funkmeister could really take off.

SOURCE OF TOP 30 TALENT			
Homegrown	**28**	**Acquired**	**2**
College	7	Trades	2
Junior college	0	Rule 5 draft	0
High school	8	Independent leagues	0
Nondrafted free agents	1	Free agents/waivers	0
International	12		

SLEEPER: Brett Lee, lhp. Has drawn comparisons with Mark Langston with his prototype frame, heavy sinker and sweeping breaking ball. Also shows good deception and pitch-count efficiency.

LF
Travis Harrison (25)
Danny Ortiz
J.D. Williams
Zach Larson

CF
Byron Buxton (1)
Jeremias Pineda
Zach Granite

RF
Adam Brett Walker (16)
Lewin Diaz (21)
Mike Kvasnicka
Dereck Rodriguez

3B
Miguel Sano (2)
Amaurys Minier (24)
Roni Tapia (29)
Deibinson Romero
Javier Pimentel
Stephen Wickens

SS
Danny Santana (9)
Niko Goodrum (26)
Aderlin Mejia
Engelb Vielma
Ryan Walker

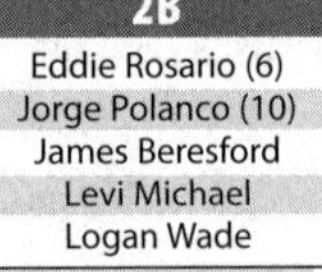

2B
Eddie Rosario (6)
Jorge Polanco (10)
James Beresford
Levi Michael
Logan Wade

1B
Max Kepler (11)
Kennys Vargas (20)
D.J. Hicks

C
Josmil Pinto (14)
Stuart Turner (30)
Brian Navarreto
Dan Rohlfing
Eric Fryer
Michael Quesada
Jorge Fernandez

LHP

LHSP	LHRP
Lewis Thorpe (7)	Kris Johnson
Stephen Gonsalves (13)	Edgar Ibarra
Mason Melotakis (18)	Matt Hoffman
Taylor Rogers (19)	Corey Williams
Randy Rosario (22)	Austin Malinowski
Brett Lee	Aaron Thompson
Logan Darnell	Steven Gruver
Miguel Sulbaran	Brandon Bixler
Jason Wheeler	Ryan O'Rourke
Hein Robb	
Pat Dean	

RHP

RHSP	RHRP
Alex Meyer (3)	Mike Tonkin (15)
Kohl Stewart (4)	Luke Bard (23)
J.O. Berrios (5)	Tyler Jones (27)
Trevor May (8)	Zach Jones (28)
Fernando Romero (12)	J.T. Chargois
Felix Jorge (17)	Madison Boer
Tyler Duffey	Deolis Guerra
Ryan Eades	A.J. Achter
Yorman Landa	Lester Oliveros
Aaron Slegers	Mark Hamburger
Hudson Boyd	Dakota Watts
D.J. Baxendale	Brian Gilbert
Matt Summers	Adrian Salcedo
Sam Gibbons	Kevin Thomas
Alex Wimmers	C.K. Irby
B.J. Hermsen	Josh Burris
Kuo Hua Lo	
Chih-Wei Hu	

2013

BONUSES: $8.1 MILLION

BEST PURE HITTER: Minnesota prioritized run prevention rather than creation, but C Mitchell Garver (10) has a line-drive stroke, doubles power and uses the whole field with an advanced approach.

Best power hitter: With a quick stroke and leverage to his swing, C Brian Navarreto (6) has average raw power and should grow into more as he adds strength to his 6-foot-3, 220-pound frame.

FASTEST RUNNER: Lefthanded-hitting OF Zack Granite (14) has well above-average speed, allowing him to get from home to first in less than 4 seconds with a swing geared toward getting out of the box quickly. OF Jason Kanzler (20) has plus or better speed.

BEST DEFENSIVE PLAYER: Minnesota, and many in the scouting community, believed C Stuart Turner (3) was the best defensive college catcher in the draft, with soft hands, advanced blocking ability and a strong, accurate arm.

BEST FASTBALL: RHP Kohl Stewart (1) put on 10 pounds after signing, and sat 93-96 mph with movement.

Best secondary pitch: Stewart has a hard, late-breaking slider that can reach the upper 80s and projects as a plus or better offering. His changeup also flashed plus this spring.

BEST PRO DEBUT: With a 93-96 mph fastball, RHP Brian Gilbert (7) posted a 0.78 ERA in 23 innings with as many strikeouts (14) as baserunners (13 H, 1 BB) across two levels. LHP Stephen Gonsalves (4), who made substantial improvement with his curveball this summer, struck out 35 percent of hitters at two levels with a 0.95 ERA in 28 innings.

BEST ATHLETE: The 6-foot-3 Stewart is a physical specimen with an ideal pitcher's build. Texas A&M recruited him as a quarterback after he scored 71 touchdowns in his junior and senior years combined.

MOST INTRIGUING BACKGROUND: 2B Tanner Vavra (30) lost sight in his right eye at the age of 3 in a fishing accident, but the son of Twins' third base coach Joe Vavra raked throughout college, with a career.331/.421/.404 line at Valparaiso. A backup quarterback at Fresno State, RHP Tyler Stirewalt (21) threw just 28 collegiate innings but was the talk of Twins instructional league, with a fastball up to 96 mph with sink from a low slot and mid-80s slider.

CLOSEST TO THE MAJORS: Gilbert could move quickly out of the bullpen.

BEST LATE-ROUND PICK: LHP Brandon Bixler (16) generated early spring buzz as a potential early-round talent, with a low-90s fastball and plus curveball, but he struggled to throw strikes. If the Twins fix his mechanics, Bixler could provide tremendous value.

THE ONE WHO GOT AWAY: RHP Logan Shore (29) picked up late helium this spring with a fastball up to 93 mph, but he headed to Florida. 3B Dustin DeMuth (8), a pure hitter with plus speed, returned to Indiana for his senior season after the Hoosiers advanced to the College World Series.

ASSESSMENT: Minnesota took the top high school hurler in the draft in Stewart, a high upside starter with power stuff. The organization loaded up on pitching and catching throughout the draft.

2012

BONUSES: $12.6 MILLION

OF Byron Buxton (1) is the game's top prospect. Injuries already have hit some power arms in this class, but not RHP J.O. Berrios (1s).

GRADE: A

2011

BONUSES: $5.9 MILLION

Two years out, the only pick from this class trending well is 3B/OF Travis Harrison (1s). Injuries have diminished SS/2B Levi Michael (1).

GRADE: D

2010

BONUSES: $3.5 MILLION

The development of 2B/OF Eddie Rosario (4), one of the system's top bats, helps mitigate the demise of RHP Alex Wimmers (1).

GRADE: D

TOP DRAFT PICKS OF THE DECADE

Year	Player, Pos.	2013 Org.
2004	Trevor Plouffe, ss	Twins
2005	Matt Garza, rhp	Rangers
2006	Chris Parmelee, 1b/of	Twins
2007	Ben Revere, of	Phillies
2008	Aaron Hicks, of	Twins
2009	Kyle Gibson, rhp	Twins
2010	Alex Wimmers, rhp	Twins
2011	Levi Michael, ss	Twins
2012	Byron Buxton, of	Twins
2013	Kohl Stewart, rhp	Twins

*Did not sign.

LARGEST BONUSES IN CLUB HISTORY

Byron Buxton, 2012	$6,000,000
Joe Mauer, 2001	$5,150,000
Kohl Stewart, 2013	$4,544,400
Miguel Sano, 2009	$3,150,000
B.J. Garbe, 1999	$2,750,000

1 BYRON BUXTON, OF

Born: Dec. 18, 1993. **B-T:** R-R. **Ht.:** 6-2. **Wt.:** 190.
Drafted: HS—Baxley, Ga., 2012 (1st round).
Signed by: Jack Powell.

In consecutive years, Buxton has been named the Baseball America High School Player of the Year and its Minor League Player of the Year. He jumped directly onto the fast track after the Twins drafted him second overall in 2012, then gave him a $6 million bonus that remains the largest in franchise history. A product of rural Georgia, Buxton led Appling County High to the Georgia state 2-A championship as a senior. Still throwing 91 mph in the seventh and final inning, he recorded an 18-strikeout complete game in the title clincher. After some early struggles in his debut in the Rookie-level Gulf Coast League, Buxton took off upon his promotion to Rookie-level Elizabethton. He helped the team win the Appalachian League title, then took his game to another level in 2013, ranking sixth in the minors in batting (.334) and seventh in on-base percentage (.424). The Twins aggressively sent him to the Arizona Fall League, where he was shut down with eight games left with a strained left shoulder. It was the same shoulder he had injured while taking a swing early in the AFL season, causing him to miss nine days. He finished with a .212 batting average and .288 on-base percentage in the AFL, but those numbers weren't much different from what Mike Trout put up at a similar age the year before exploding onto the big league scene.

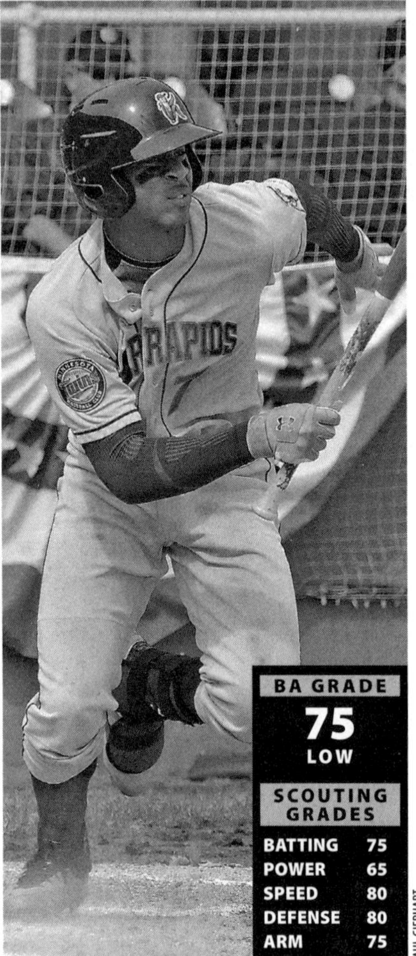

BA GRADE
75
LOW
SCOUTING GRADES
BATTING 75
POWER 65
SPEED 80
DEFENSE 80
ARM 75

PAUL GIERHART

Buxton's combination of tools and production made him the talk of the minor leagues. Blessed with quick hands and strong wrists, he generates tremendous bat speed and keeps the bat in the zone for what seems like forever. Considering his rural background, he stunned scouts with his advanced approach at the plate and shows excellent discipline for such a young player. He is learning to backspin balls and can generate easy power to all fields, and his future home run power is one of scouts' few questions about Buxton. Timed at 3.9 seconds to first from the right side, he is an 80 runner underway but is still working to improve his reads and instincts. He stole 55 bases at a 74 percent success rate that should climb as he refines his craft. Not even having a nail removed on his right big toe in late July could slow him down. He missed just five days. In the field, Buxton has tremendous arm strength and plus-plus range in center field. As his jumps and routes have improved, he habitually makes the difficult play look effortless. Quiet and still somewhat shy, Buxton is unfailingly polite and has a deep-seated work ethic that is second to none.

After the shoulder scare in Arizona, the Twins will be even more cautious than usual with Buxton. He should open the year at Double-A New Britain, where he will play for the same manager who had him in the AFL, Jeff Smith. A late-season promotion seems logical, and Buxton should have every opportunity to seize the starting center field and leadoff spots with the Twins by Opening Day 2015.

Year	Club (League)	Class	AVG	G	AB	R	H	2B	3B	HR	RBI	BB	SO	SB	CS	OBP	SLG
2012	Twins (GCL)	R	.216	27	88	17	19	4	3	4	14	11	26	4	3	.324	.466
	Elizabethton (APP)	R	.286	21	77	16	22	6	1	1	6	8	15	7	0	.368	.429
2013	Cedar Rapids (MWL)	LoA	.341	68	270	68	92	15	10	8	55	44	56	32	11	.431	.559
	Fort Myers (FSL)	HiA	.326	57	218	41	71	4	8	4	22	32	49	23	8	.415	.472
Minor League Totals			.312	173	653	142	204	29	22	17	97	95	146	66	22	.404	.502

2 MIGUEL SANO, 3B

Born: May 11, 1993. **B-T:** R-R. **Ht.:** 6-3. **Wt.:** 232. **Signed:** Dominican Republic, 2009. **Signed by:** Fred Guerrero.

How many athletes have starring roles in not one but two documentaries by age 20? That's life for Sano, who signed for $3.15 million after a long ordeal that included an age dispute, bone-density scans and sour grapes from some of the teams that fell short in the bidding. He quickly rose to No. 1 on the Twins prospect list after 2012 before ceding the top spot to Byron Buxton, whom he joined at the Futures Game in 2013. Sano was benched for four games last July by Double-A New Britain manager Jeff Smith following a 29-second home run trot against former teammate Bobby Lanigan. The report on Sano starts with the power, which earned him best power prospect in both the Florida State and Eastern leagues. He crushed a combined 35 homers in 2013, fourth-most in the minors. He also hit .330 in the FSL, where rival managers voted him best batting prospect and most exciting player. Sano's average dropped off after he was promoted to the EL on June 10, but his power played against better competition. Defensively, he worked with Hall of Famer Paul Molitor, the Twins' roving infield instructor, to improve his footwork and hands, which still need polishing. He has a plus arm and made progress in 2013, committing 23 errors and nearly halving his total in 2012. He's a below-average runner. Sano was shelved after two games in the Dominican League with a strained throwing elbow. That could cost him momentum as he heads into 2014, when he figures to open at Triple-A Rochester, but shouldn't slow his fast path to Minnesota.

Year	Club (League)	Class	AVG	G	AB	R	H	2B	3B	HR	RBI	BB	SO	SB	CS	OBP	SLG
2010	Twins (DSL)	R	.344	20	64	11	22	2	1	3	10	14	17	2	1	.463	.547
	Twins (GCL)	R	.291	41	148	23	43	14	0	4	19	10	43	2	2	.338	.466
2011	Elizabethton (APP)	R	.292	66	267	58	78	18	7	20	59	23	77	5	4	.352	.637
2012	Beloit (MWL)	LoA	.258	129	457	75	118	28	4	28	100	80	144	8	3	.373	.521
2013	Fort Myers (FSL)	HiA	.330	56	206	51	68	15	2	16	48	29	61	9	2	.424	.655
	New Britain (EL)	AA	.236	67	233	35	55	15	3	19	55	36	81	2	1	.344	.571
Minor League Totals			.279	379	1375	253	384	92	17	90	291	192	423	28	13	.373	.567

3 ALEX MEYER, RHP

Born: Jan. 3, 1990. **B-T:** R-R. **Ht.:** 6-9. **Wt. 220. Drafted:** Kentucky, 2011 (1st round). **Signed by:** Reed Dunn (Nationals)

Even Meyer was shocked when he heard he was the only piece the Nationals had to give up to get Denard Span after the 2012 season. Signed in 2011 for the same $2 million he rejected from the Red Sox out of high school, Meyer is heir to a prominent Ford dealership outside Indianapolis. He came down with a strained throwing shoulder on June 1 and missed 10 weeks. He made up for lost time at instructional league and at the Arizona Fall League. Armed with both the best fastball and best curveball in the organization, Meyer also has made significant progress with his changeup. His four-seam fastball sits at 95-96 mph and touched 100 five times in the first inning during one AFL start. He mixes in a 92-95 mph sinker with good armside run. His power knuckle-curve comes in at 84-87 mph and shows good depth and finish. His changeup has good sinking action and projects to be above-average. Meyer is 6-foot-9 and with such long levers, maintaining body control can be a challenge at times, but he continues to make progress in that area. He left instructional league more confident than ever in his overall command. Despite his stature, he holds runners and fields his position well. After waiting years to get their hands on such a powerful arm, the Twins will continue to exercise caution with Meyer. He almost certainly will open the year at Triple-A Rochester, but a first-half promotion is certainly possible, if not likely.

Year	Club (League)	Class	W	L	ERA	G	GS	CG	SV	IP	H	HR	BB	SO	K/9	WHIP	AVG
2012	Hagerstown (SAL)	LoA	7	4	3.10	18	18	1	0	90	68	4	34	107	10.7	1.13	.210
	Potomac (CAR)	HiA	3	2	2.31	7	7	0	0	39	29	2	11	32	7.4	1.03	.213
2013	Twins (GCL)	R	0	0	1.08	3	3	0	0	8	7	0	3	16	17.3	1.20	.233
	New Britain (EL)	AA	4	3	3.21	13	13	0	0	70	60	3	29	84	10.8	1.27	.226
Minor League Totals			14	9	2.91	41	41	1	0	207	164	9	77	239	10.4	1.16	.217

4 KOHL STEWART, RHP

BA GRADE 65 EXTREME

Born: Oct. 7, 1994. **B-T:** R-R. **Ht.:** 6-3. **Wt.:** 208. **Drafted:** HS—Houston, 2013 (1st round). **Signed by:** Greg Runser.

After passing for 8,803 yards and 87 touchdowns in three high school football seasons, Stewart passed up a chance to play at Texas A&M after the Twins took him fourth overall in 2013 and signed him for $4,544,400. A Type 1 diabetic, Stewart missed three weeks in the Rookie-level Gulf Coast League after stepping on a seashell and cutting his foot. The Twins then shut him down with two weeks to go in the Rookie-level Appalachian League season due to shoulder soreness and kept him off the mound at instructional league. Strong and athletic, with a clean delivery, Stewart has a fastball that sits at 92-94 mph and touches 96 with plus life and command. His putaway pitch is a mid-80s power slider with tilt. His curveball continues to improve and he has a feel for a changeup, giving him a chance to have four above-average pitches. He has competitive fire and some swagger, not unlike that of another Houston-area schoolboy pitching hero, Josh Beckett. Considering their investment in Stewart, the Twins will proceed cautiously. With his limited innings total he could start the year in extended spring training and return to the Appalachian League. If his shoulder issues are behind him, low Class A Cedar Rapids could be the call. His best-case scenario is as a No. 1 or 2 starter in the majors.

Year	Club (League)	Class	W	L	ERA	G	GS	CG	SV	IP	H	HR	BB	SO	K/9	WHIP	AVG
2013	Twins (GCL)	R	0	0	1.69	6	3	0	0	16	12	0	3	16	9.0	0.94	.188
	Elizabethton (APP)	R	0	0	0.00	1	1	0	0	4	1	0	1	8	18.0	0.50	.077
Minor League Totals			0	0	1.35	7	4	0	0	20	13	0	4	24	10.8	0.85	.169

5 J.O. BERRIOS, RHP

CEDAR RAPIDS KERNELS

BA GRADE 55 HIGH

Born: May 27, 1994. **B-T:** R-R. **Ht.:** 6-0. **Wt.:** 189. **Drafted:** HS—Bayamon, P.R., 2012 (1st round supplemental). **Signed by:** Hector Otero.

Signed for $1.55 million as the 32nd overall pick in 2012, Berrios is the highest-drafted pitcher ever from Puerto Rico. An April no-hitter that year against a Puerto Rican all-star team led by No. 1 overall pick Carlos Correa helped boost his stock. Berrios took dominant turns in two Rookie-ball stops in 2012, then opened 2013 in Puerto Rico's bullpen at the World Baseball Classic. Carrying himself with a confidence that borders on brashness, Berrios has a strong competitive streak that he typically keeps under control. He brandishes an above-average fastball at 91-93 mph that touches 95, though he needs to be more aggressive in the strike zone after walking 3.5 per nine innings at low Class A Cedar Rapids in 2013. His changeup is advanced, shows good fade and has the potential to be a plus pitch. His slider flattens out at times but can be a power breaking ball. Because of the WBC, Berrios opened the year in extended spring training as the Twins sought to stretch him back out. He received more than four days of rest between starts all season, skipping at least one turn in late June, but the Twins said injury concerns weren't the cause. After skipping winter ball at the Twins' request, Berrios should open 2014 at high Class A Fort Myers. He ultimately profiles as a No. 2 or No. 3 starter.

Year	Club (League)	Class	W	L	ERA	G	GS	CG	SV	IP	H	HR	BB	SO	K/9	WHIP	AVG
2012	Twins (GCL)	R	1	0	1.08	8	1	0	4	17	7	0	3	27	14.6	0.60	.121
	Elizabethton (APP)	R	2	0	1.29	3	3	0	0	14	8	1	1	22	14.1	0.64	.163
2013	Cedar Rapids (MWL)	LoA	7	7	3.99	19	19	0	0	104	105	6	40	100	8.7	1.40	.262
Minor League Totals			10	7	3.35	30	23	0	4	134	120	7	44	149	10.0	1.22	.236

6 EDDIE ROSARIO, 2B/OF

BA GRADE 55 HIGH

Born: Sept. 26, 1991. **B-T:** L-R. **Ht.:** 6-0. **Wt.:** 180. **Drafted:** HS—Guayama, P.R., 2010 (4th round). **Signed by:** Hector Otero.

Rosario moved to second base full-time in 2013 after starting his pro career as a center fielder. He overcame a 2012 mishap when he missed seven weeks after a line drive hit him in the face during batting practice (a plate was inserted above his lip). Former big league manager Edwin Rodriguez raved about Rosario's potential while managing him for Puerto Rico in the 2013 World Baseball Classic, where Rosario went 3-for-14. In stints in both the Arizona Fall and Puerto Rican leagues, he played both second and the outfield corners. Considered the best hitter for average in the Twins system aside from Byron Buxton, Rosario generates excellent bat speed and plate coverage. Though he holds his hands low at the set-up, he flashes them quickly through the hitting zone, generating solid gap power. He doesn't project to hit more than 15 home runs a season in the majors. After reaching Double-A New Britain, he chased more pitches than normal and got himself into some slumps. He has put in long hours on his defense and has made tremendous strides at second. He goes back on popups as well as any infielder the Twins have had in recent years, but his footwork, particularly around the bag, still needs work. His range has improved as he better understands positioning, and his arm is above-average for second. A slightly above-average runner, Rosario goes first to third well but isn't an efficient basestealer. He will give Double-A another go in 2014.

Year	Club (League)	Class	AVG	G	AB	R	H	2B	3B	HR	RBI	BB	SO	SB	CS	OBP	SLG
2010	Twins (GCL)	R	.294	51	194	34	57	9	2	5	26	16	28	22	5	.343	.438
2011	Elizabethton (APP)	R	.337	67	270	71	91	9	9	21	60	27	60	17	6	.397	.670
2012	Twins (GCL)	R	.368	5	19	2	7	3	0	1	4	1	2	0	0	.400	.684
	Beloit (MWL)	LoA	.296	95	392	60	116	32	4	12	70	31	69	11	11	.345	.490
2013	Fort Myers (FSL)	HiA	.329	52	207	40	68	13	5	6	35	17	29	3	6	.377	.527
	New Britain (EL)	AA	.284	70	289	40	82	19	3	4	38	21	67	7	4	.330	.412
Minor League Totals			.307	340	1371	247	421	85	23	49	233	113	255	60	32	.358	.510

7 LEWIS THORPE, LHP

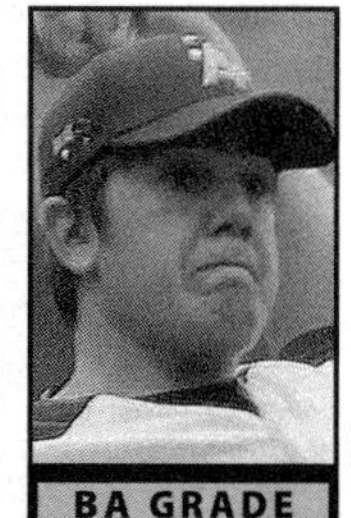

IBAF

BA GRADE
60
EXTREME

Born: Nov. 23, 1995. **B-T:** R-L. **Ht.:** 6-2. **Wt.:** 215. **Signed:** Australia, 2012. **Signed by:** Howard Norsetter.

Some international scouts considered Thorpe the best prospect in years to emerge from Australia, and the Twins signed him for $500,000 in 2012. Armed with a confidence beyond his years, he wasted little time justifying the Twins' faith and blew through the Rookie-level Gulf Coast League in 2013. Now pushing 6-foot-2, 215 pounds with long arms, Thorpe has added at least 35 pounds since signing. He shows command of all four pitches with a disdain for issuing walks. That's a change from his amateur days, when control was a problem. His fastball has jumped from the mid-80s as an amateur to 89-90 mph in the GCL, where he touched 94 mph. That velocity looks even faster thanks to the sneaky late action on his fastball. Thorpe's changeup, thrown with sink and fade, is his No. 2 pitch and has the potential to be a plus weapon. His slider tends to slice through the zone while his curveball is a classic spinner with good down action. Thorpe logged time in the Australian Baseball League as he prepares for a 2013 assignment to low Class A Cedar Rapids, where he should be among the youngest in the league. If he continues to progress, Thorpe could put himself on the fast track, even with a famously cautious organization. He projects as a mid-rotation starter.

Year	Club (League)	Class	W	L	ERA	G	GS	CG	SV	IP	H	HR	BB	SO	K/9	WHIP	AVG
2013	Twins (GCL)	R	4	1	2.05	12	8	0	0	44	32	2	6	64	13.1	0.86	.203
Minor League Totals			4	1	2.05	12	8	0	0	44	32	2	6	64	13.1	0.86	.203

8 TREVOR MAY, RHP

BA GRADE
50
HIGH

Born: Sept. 23, 1989. **B-T:** R-R. **Ht.:** 6-5. **Wt.:** 215. **Drafted:** HS—Kelso, Wash., 2008 (4th round). **Signed by:** Dave Ryles (Phillies).

Signed by the Phillies for $375,000 in 2008, May rated as the top prep prospect in Washington during his draft year. Acquired from the Phillies along with Vance Worley in a December 2012 deal for outfielder Ben Revere, May has repeated his last three league stops, spending all of 2012-13 in the Double-A Eastern League and getting better in his follow-up season. Sent to the Arizona Fall League for the first time, May missed 11 days with biceps tendinitis but pitched well in relief after his return. Considered to have the best changeup in the system, May has the proven ability to miss bats (career 10.7 strikeouts per nine innings). However, he tends to lose focus and command, as shown his career walk rate of 4.6 per nine innings. He has a 92-94 mph fastball with some run when he keeps it down in the zone, and touched 95 mph out of the bullpen in the AFL. His downer curveball had been his best secondary pitch until the changeup passed it in 2013. He also throws a slider. He worked hard to improve his conditioning, but still tends to run up high pitch counts in limited work. A pronounced flyball pitcher, he has allowed 36 homers the past two seasons. May could push for a big league spot by midseason 2014, but he figures to open the year at Triple-A Rochester and projects as a No. 4 starter unless his command improves significantly.

Year	Club (League)	Class	W	L	ERA	G	GS	CG	SV	IP	H	HR	BB	SO	K/9	WHIP	AVG
2008	Phillies (GCL)	R	1	1	3.75	5	2	0	0	12	11	0	7	11	8.3	1.50	.256
2009	Lakewood (SAL)	LoA	4	1	2.56	15	15	0	0	77	58	3	43	95	11.1	1.31	.211
2010	Clearwater (FSL)	HiA	5	5	5.01	16	14	0	0	70	53	7	61	90	11.6	1.63	.212
	Lakewood (SAL)	LoA	7	3	2.91	11	11	0	0	65	51	3	20	92	12.7	1.09	.214
2011	Clearwater (FSL)	HiA	10	8	3.63	27	27	3	0	151	121	8	67	208	12.4	1.24	.221
2012	Reading (EL)	AA	10	13	4.87	28	28	0	0	150	139	22	78	151	9.1	1.45	.249
2013	New Britain (EL)	AA	9	9	4.51	27	27	2	0	152	149	14	67	159	9.4	1.42	.256
Minor League Totals			46	40	4.05	129	124	5	0	677	582	57	343	806	10.7	1.37	.233

9 DANNY SANTANA, SS

BA GRADE
50
HIGH

Born: Nov. 7, 1990. **B-T:** B-R. **Ht.:** 5-11. **Wt.:** 174. **Signed:** Dominican Republic, 2007. **Signed by:** Fred Guerrero.

A late bloomer, Santana reestablished himself as a prospect in 2012, when he initially platooned with 2011 first-rounder Levi Michael at high Class A Fort Myers and eventually outplayed him. General manager Terry Ryan has raved about Santana's skill set, makeup and clubhouse standing. When the Twins' regional cable network televised a late-season Double-A New Britain game, Santana stole the show by going 2-for-3 with a triple, a walk and two runs scored. As he continues to add muscle to his compact frame, the switch-hitting Santana has all-around offensive ability and is making himself into more of a gap-power threat at the plate. His strikeout rate jumped last season and his two-strike approach still needs work, as does his overall patience, especially if he's going to stay in the leadoff spot. He finished the year with 32 errors, partly because of his plus range but also due to his tendency to let his mind wander in the field, but managers voted him the Eastern League's best defensive shortstop. His arm grades plus and he can move to his left or his right equally well. A plus runner, Santana continues to improve his attention to detail, stealing 30 bases for the first time in 2013. Twins incumbent Pedro Florimon shines on defense and still is two full seasons away from arbitration eligibility. That leaves Santana at Triple-A Rochester to begin 2014, where his continued progress could either push Florimon or give the Twins a much-needed trade chip in the search for starting pitchers.

Year	Club (League)	Class	AVG	G	AB	R	H	2B	3B	HR	RBI	BB	SO	SB	CS	OBP	SLG
2008	Twins (DSL)	R	.274	51	190	37	52	6	10	1	27	20	38	15	4	.343	.426
2009	Twins (GCL)	R	.265	44	170	30	45	7	5	3	25	8	27	12	1	.302	.418
2010	Elizabethton (APP)	R	.264	30	140	23	37	8	1	4	16	3	30	5	4	.285	.421
	Beloit (MWL)	LoA	.238	40	130	14	31	4	3	0	11	7	40	10	4	.289	.315
2011	Beloit (MWL)	LoA	.247	104	365	55	90	15	5	7	41	25	98	24	15	.298	.373
2012	Fort Myers (FSL)	HiA	.286	121	507	70	145	21	9	8	60	29	77	17	11	.329	.410
2013	New Britain (EL)	AA	.297	131	539	66	160	22	10	2	45	24	94	30	13	.333	.386
Minor League Totals			.274	521	2041	295	560	83	43	25	225	116	404	113	52	.318	.394

10 JORGE POLANCO, 2B/SS

CEDAR RAPIDS KERNELS

BA GRADE
50
HIGH

Born: July 5, 1993. **B-T:** B-R. **Ht.:** 5-11. **Wt. 185. Signed:** Dominican Republic, 2009. **Signed by:** Fred Guerrero.

Just two years after batting ninth most nights in the Rookie-level Appalachian League, Polanco's star is on the rise. A switch-hitter who has added 20 pounds since signing for $775,000, Polanco has the best plate discipline in the Twins system. He has struck out just 32 more times than he's walked through four pro seasons. Reminding some of a young Tony Fernandez, the switch-hitter uses the whole field, shows excellent gap power and could develop into a 15-homer threat down the road. Splitting time again at both middle-infield spots, Polanco seems more comfortable at second base, where he shows soft hands and a plus arm. Managers voted him the low Class A Midwest League's best defensive second baseman. He has slowed as he's matured physically and is just an average runner. Bothered by a groin problem for his final six weeks at low Class A Cedar Rapids, Polanco suffered the injury while rounding a base but initially tried to play through it. Quiet and intelligent, he has a strong work ethic, a grinder's mentality and is quite coachable. Selected third overall in the Dominican League's draft, he played second base for Escogido in 2013 and should do the same in 2014 at high Class A Fort Myers.

Year	Club (League)	Class	AVG	G	AB	R	H	2B	3B	HR	RBI	BB	SO	SB	CS	OBP	SLG
2010	Twins (DSL)	R	.250	18	60	5	15	2	0	0	7	6	9	1	3	.309	.283
	Twins (GCL)	R	.223	34	103	12	23	5	0	1	12	12	9	2	4	.299	.301
2011	Twins (GCL)	R	.250	51	172	21	43	8	3	1	16	15	24	6	4	.319	.349
2012	Elizabethton (APP)	R	.318	51	173	35	55	15	2	5	27	20	26	6	3	.388	.514
2013	Cedar Rapids (MWL)	LoA	.308	115	465	76	143	32	10	5	78	42	59	4	4	.362	.452
Minor League Totals			.287	269	973	149	279	62	15	12	140	95	127	19	18	.349	.418

11 MAX KEPLER, OF/1B

BA GRADE
50
HIGH

Born: Feb. 10, 1993. **B-T:** L-L. **Ht.:** 6-4. **Wt.:** 207. **Signed:** Germany, 2009. **Signed by:** Mike Radcliff.

Born to American and Polish ballet dancers, Kepler is considered the best prospect ever born and raised in Germany. Signed for $800,000 in 2009, he finished high school in Fort Myers, Fla., while attending instructional league. He has added close to 20 pounds since signing. Mature for his age, Kepler is intelligent with a pleasant personality and strong work ethic. After suffering a strained throwing elbow during spring training, he didn't make his 2013 debut until June 20 at low Class A Cedar Rapids and he never felt completely right all season. Sent to the Arizona Fall League, Kepler played first base almost exclusively, showing the soft hands and improved range to project as an above-average defender at the position. His below-average arm hurts him, but he has the athletic ability to play left field as well. At the plate, Kepler's power stroke never fully returned after the elbow injury and he struggled against lefties. His balanced swing and sound two-strike approach give him the ability to drive the ball to all fields and control the strike zone. He is a tick-above-average as a runner, especially once he gets under way. Now a member of the 40-man roster, Kepler figures to open 2014 at high Class A Fort Myers, where he will play left and first base. He must continue to add power to profile at either position.

Year	Club (League)	Class	AVG	G	AB	R	H	2B	3B	HR	RBI	BB	SO	SB	CS	OBP	SLG
2010	Twins (GCL)	R	.286	37	140	15	40	6	1	0	11	13	27	6	1	.346	.343
2011	Elizabethton (APP)	R	.262	50	191	29	50	11	3	1	24	23	54	1	1	.347	.366
2012	Elizabethton (APP)	R	.297	59	232	40	69	16	5	10	49	27	33	7	0	.387	.539
2013	Cedar Rapids (MWL)	LoA	.237	61	236	35	56	11	3	9	40	24	43	2	0	.312	.424
Minor League Totals			.269	207	799	119	215	44	12	20	124	87	157	16	2	.348	.429

12 FERNANDO ROMERO, RHP

BA GRADE
55
EXTREME

Born: Dec. 24, 1994. **B-T:** R-R. **Ht.:** 6-0. **Wt.:** 228. **Signed:** Dominican Republic, 2011. **Signed by:** Fred Guerrero.

Signed for $220,000 in November 2011 at age 16, Romero made the jump to the Rookie-level Gulf Coast League in 2013. Though it was Australian lefty Lewis Thorpe who headlined the staff, Romero quietly experienced a quantum leap of his own. Over his final month he struck out 21 and walked three, and he still has yet to allow a professional home run. Featuring a loose, powerful arm and a sturdy frame, his fastball sits at 92-94 mph and touches 97. It's already a 70 on the 20-80 scouting scale. Romero's power curveball has impressive down action at 78-81 mph, and his changeup shows signs of being a plus pitch as well. His low-effort delivery has required no substantial tweaks since signing, and his improved powers of concentration helped him repeat his delivery and reach peak efficiency. He split his workload evenly between starting and relieving and could continue to keep a hand in both as he likely heads to a low Class A Cedar Rapids staff in 2014 that should include Kohl Stewart, Felix Jorge and lefties Thorpe and Stephen Gonsalves. With the pitch mix and ceiling Romero has, the Twins figure to get him as many innings as possible.

Year	Club (League)	Class	W	L	ERA	G	GS	CG	SV	IP	H	HR	BB	SO	K/9	WHIP	AVG
2012	Twins (DSL)	R	1	4	4.65	14	6	0	0	31	26	0	14	28	8.1	1.29	.224
2013	Twins (GCL)	R	2	0	1.60	12	6	0	0	45	32	0	13	47	9.4	1.00	.196
Minor League Totals			3	4	2.84	26	12	0	0	76	58	0	27	75	8.9	1.12	.208

13 STEPHEN GONSALVES, LHP

BA GRADE
50
HIGH

Born: July 8, 1994. **B-T:** L-L. **Ht.:** 6-5. **Wt.:** 195. **Drafted:** HS—San Diego, 2013 (4th round). **Signed By:** John Leavitt.

Suspended for eight games during his senior year at San Diego's Cathedral Catholic High, Gonsalves dropped out of a possible spot in the first round after lying to the school's dean about a roommate's drug usage during USA Baseball's National High School Invitational. The preseason All-American fell to the Twins in the fourth round, where they relied heavily on the recommendation of veteran area scout John Leavitt. They signed Gonsalves for $700,000, well above the slot figure of $468,200, and were pleased to see him register 12.4 strikeouts per nine innings at two Rookie-level stops. Lanky and athletic at 6-foot-5 and more than his listed 195 pounds, Gonsalves is an accomplished surfer who still has plenty of projection. His fastball sits at 88-91 mph and will occasionally touch 93, though he needs to command to his glove-side better. His spike curveball showed improvement during his first pro summer, and his split-changeup remains average at best. Intelligent with a quiet competitive streak, Gonsalves should open the year in the rotation at low Class A Cedar Rapids and projects as a future No. 3 starter as he adds strength and polishes his secondary pitches.

Year	Club (League)	Class	W	L	ERA	G	GS	CG	SV	IP	H	HR	BB	SO	K/9	WHIP	AVG
2013	Twins (GCL)	R	1	0	0.63	5	2	0	0	14	8	0	7	18	11.3	1.05	.163
	Elizabethton (APP)	R	1	1	1.29	3	3	0	0	14	10	0	4	21	13.5	1.00	.200
Minor League Totals			2	1	0.95	8	5	0	0	28	18	0	11	39	12.4	1.02	.182

14 JOSMIL PINTO, C

BA GRADE
45
MEDIUM

Born: March 31, 1989. **B-T:** R-R. **Ht.:** 5-11. **Wt.:** 210. **Signed:** Venezuela, 2006. **Signed by:** Jose Leon.

Talk about your late-blooming revelations. Pinto, who signed six weeks before his 17th birthday, spent seven seasons in the Twins system before being added to the 40-man roster for the first time after the 2012 season. His bat had long been considered his best tool, but Pinto's offense really took off in 2013, a season in which he rocketed from Double-A New Britain to his first September callup. Getting the bulk of late-season playing time while Joe Mauer recovered from a concussion, Pinto showed the ability to hit for power and average to all fields. His footwork, receiving and game-calling still need improvement, but he showed the willingness to accept daily coaching from former all-star catcher Terry Steinbach, now the Twins' bench coach. Pinto throws well enough, gunning down 26 percent of basestealers in the minors in 2013, but shoulder fatigue limited him to DH duties for two weeks at midseason in Double-A. Considering his age and modest pedigree, Pinto is probably close to his ceiling, but his attitude and hustling style greatly impressed big league manager Ron Gardenhire. Mauer's move to first base opens the catcher spot for Pinto, who was sidelined again in November by shoulder soreness during winter ball in Venezuela. If he's healthy, he's in line to share time behind the plate in Minnesota.

Year	Club (League)	Class	AVG	G	AB	R	H	2B	3B	HR	RBI	BB	SO	SB	CS	OBP	SLG
2006	Twins/Blue Jays (VSL)	R	.251	53	195	25	49	7	1	3	30	25	27	3	3	.336	.344
2007	Twins (DSL)	R	.193	54	171	18	33	8	1	1	23	29	23	3	1	.327	.269
2008	Twins (GCL)	R	.329	24	85	14	28	9	3	1	14	9	14	1	0	.394	.541
2009	Elizabethton (APP)	R	.332	53	205	34	68	14	2	13	55	19	39	0	1	.387	.610
2010	Beloit (MWL)	LoA	.225	100	347	60	78	21	1	10	54	32	67	2	3	.295	.378
2011	Beloit (MWL)	LoA	.250	9	32	4	8	3	0	1	9	2	10	0	0	.278	.438
	Fort Myers (FSL)	HiA	.262	64	221	21	58	11	1	5	32	12	36	1	0	.305	.389
2012	Fort Myers (FSL)	HiA	.295	93	349	45	103	22	2	12	51	39	63	0	0	.361	.473
	New Britain (EL)	AA	.298	12	47	8	14	4	1	2	9	4	10	0	0	.365	.553
2013	New Britain (EL)	AA	.308	107	386	59	119	23	1	14	68	64	71	0	2	.411	.482
	Rochester (IL)	AAA	.314	19	70	6	22	9	0	1	6	2	12	0	0	.333	.486
	Minnesota (AL)	MAJ	.342	21	76	10	26	5	0	4	12	6	22	0	0	.398	.566
Major League Totals			.342	21	76	10	26	5	0	4	12	6	22	0	0	.398	.566
Minor League Totals			.275	588	2108	294	580	131	13	63	351	237	372	10	10	.351	.439

15 MIKE TONKIN, RHP

BA GRADE **45** MEDIUM

Born: Nov. 19, 1989. **B-T:** R-R. **Ht.:** 6-7. **Wt.:** 220. **Drafted:** HS—Palmdale, Calif., 2008 (30th round). **Signed by:** Dan Cox.

Tall and wiry strong, Tonkin made 83 appearances across three seasons at low Class A Beloit before finally getting to pitch above Class A in 2013, his sixth professional season. Once the light went on for the lanky righty, however, he moved quickly through the system. The brother-in-law of big league outfielder Jason Kubel, Tonkin passed up Southern California and signed for $230,000 in 2008. He converted 21 of 25 save opportunities at the top two minor league levels in 2013, and he handled himself well in three separate big league auditions. He throws a heavy two-seamer at 92-94 mph and has a riding fastball he can pump past the likes of Evan Longoria (his first strikeout victim) at 94-96 mph. They key to Tonkin's emergence, however, has been his sharp-breaking slider. When he remembers to use it, especially early in the count, he has more than enough stuff to become a key part of the Twins bullpen in 2014. He could improve at holding runners and his long levers keep him from being quick to the plate, but the Twins are intrigued with what Tonkin has shown them thus far.

Year	Club (League)	Class	W	L	ERA	G	GS	CG	SV	IP	H	HR	BB	SO	K/9	WHIP	AVG
2008	Twins (GCL)	R	0	1	3.27	6	1	0	0	11	10	0	3	8	6.5	1.18	.244
2009	Twins (GCL)	R	3	4	3.62	11	9	0	0	55	55	2	9	60	9.9	1.17	.258
2010	Beloit (MWL)	LoA	3	6	4.29	13	12	0	0	65	76	7	18	40	5.5	1.45	.287
	Elizabethton (APP)	R	1	0	1.08	10	0	0	1	25	18	1	4	26	9.4	0.88	.196
2011	Beloit (MWL)	LoA	4	3	3.87	48	3	0	2	77	82	3	24	69	8.1	1.38	.271
2012	Beloit (MWL)	LoA	3	0	1.38	22	0	0	6	39	29	1	9	53	12.2	0.97	.206
	Fort Myers (FSL)	HiA	1	1	2.97	22	0	0	6	30	24	2	11	44	13.1	1.15	.212
2013	New Britain (EL)	AA	1	2	2.22	22	0	0	7	24	21	0	8	30	11.1	1.19	.216
	Rochester (IL)	AAA	1	2	4.41	30	0	0	14	33	33	3	8	36	9.9	1.26	.256
	Minnesota (AL)	MAJ	0	0	0.79	9	0	0	0	11	9	0	3	10	7.9	1.06	.205
Major League Totals			0	0	0.79	9	0	0	0	11	9	0	3	10	7.9	1.06	.205
Minor League Totals			17	19	3.29	184	25	0	36	359	348	19	94	366	9.2	1.23	.250

16 ADAM BRETT WALKER, OF

BA GRADE **50** HIGH

Born: Oct. 18, 1991. **B-T:** R-R. **Ht.:** 6-4. **Wt.:** 225. **Drafted:** Jacksonville, 2012 (3rd round). **Signed by:** Billy Corrigan.

Walker put on a power show during his pre-draft workout at Target Field and signed for $490,400. A Wisconsin native, Walker has a father who played for the Minnesota Vikings as a replacement player in 1987 and a mother who was a college high jumper and volleyball player. The Atlantic Sun Conference player of the year in 2011, Walker's stock dropped when he struck out 56 times in 134 at-bats in the Cape Cod League that summer. Walker has slugged .516 in pro ball, showing raw power the equal of Miguel Sano along with a flair for the dramatic. His two-out, three-run blast lifted Rookie-level Elizabethton to the Appalachian League title in the 2012 playoff finale, and Walker ranked third in the organization with 27 homers in 2013 at low Class A Cedar

Rapids. Midwest League managers rated him the league's best power prospect. A streaky hitter, Walker showed better plate discipline but still has a tendency to chase breaking pitches. Walker is a tick-above-average as a runner, but he has yet to be caught in 14 career stolen base attempts. Mostly a first baseman in college, Walker made strides while spending most of his time in right field in 2013. His arm strength and accuracy are inconsistent, but he has the athletic ability to handle the corner outfield. Having earned comparisons with Astros slugger Chris Carter, Walker is headed to high Class A Fort Myers in 2014.

Year	Club (League)	Class	AVG	G	AB	R	H	2B	3B	HR	RBI	BB	SO	SB	CS	OBP	SLG
2012	Elizabethton (APP)	R	.250	58	232	44	58	7	4	14	45	19	76	4	0	.310	.496
2013	Cedar Rapids (MWL)	LoA	.278	129	508	83	141	31	7	27	109	31	115	10	0	.319	.526
Minor League Totals			.269	187	740	127	199	38	11	41	154	50	191	14	0	.316	.516

17 FELIX JORGE, RHP

BA GRADE
50
HIGH

Born: Jan. 2, 1994. **B-T:** R-R. **Ht.:** 6-2. **Wt.:** 170. **Signed:** Dominican Republic, 2011. **Signed by:** Fred Guerrero.

Borderline dominant atop the Rookie-level Elizabethton rotation in 2013, Jorge ranked as the No. 14 prospect in the Appalachian League after posting a 4.0 SO/BB ratio. Lanky and athletic with a lean lower half, Jorge signed for $400,000 in 2011 and still has plenty of upside as he projects to add strength to his wiry frame. Equipped with long arms and large hands, he sits at 90-92 mph with his fastball, showing solid run and sink. He touches 94 mph and also features an atypical slider that slices through the zone, making a hard left turn and dropping fast and late. His changeup is clearly his No. 3 pitch at this point but it shows potential. He holds runners well enough, helps himself with his fielding ability and is extremely coachable. Jorge has progressed well in learning to speak English, a key emphasis in the Twins system. He has a quiet personality overall but flashes a competitive streak on the mound. He projects as a mid- to late-rotation starter, but he could wind up in the bullpen down the road if he doesn't smooth out his delivery. He'll make his full-season debut as part of a loaded low Class A Cedar Rapids rotation in 2014.

Year	Club (League)	Class	W	L	ERA	G	GS	CG	SV	IP	H	HR	BB	SO	K/9	WHIP	AVG
2011	Twins (DSL)	R	2	1	2.67	9	5	0	1	27	19	0	9	26	8.7	1.04	.192
2012	Twins (GCL)	R	0	3	2.34	12	7	0	1	35	30	0	12	37	9.6	1.21	.221
2013	Elizabethton (APP)	R	2	2	2.95	12	12	0	0	61	56	2	18	72	10.6	1.21	.245
Minor League Totals			4	6	2.71	33	24	0	2	123	105	2	39	135	9.9	1.17	.226

18 MASON MELOTAKIS, LHP

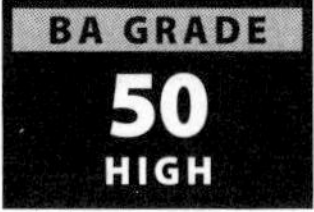

Born: June 28, 1991. **B-T:** R-L. **Ht.:** 6-2. **Wt.:** 204. **Drafted:** Northwestern State, 2012 (2nd round). **Signed by:** Greg Runser.

Like Twins reliever Ryan Pressly, Melotakis spent a good portion of his youth taking pitching lessons from former big league pitcher (and current Rangers TV voice) Steve Busby. In his first full pro season, Melotakis made a successful transition to the rotation at low Class A Cedar Rapids after making just nine college starts in the previous four seasons. As a starter his fastball sits at 88-92 mph and touches 94. His spinning slider comes in at 81-84 mph and can be a put-away pitch for him, though his strikeout rate dropped considerably (to 6.8 strikeouts per nine innings) with the move out of the bullpen. At the same time, his walk rate spiked, narrowing his SO/BB ratio from more than 6.0 in 2012 to barely 2.0. Melotakis' changeup has improved enough that he handles righthanded hitters just fine. He throws from a high three-quarters arm slot, and the ball gets on hitters in a hurry. His short arm action and unconventional delivery has prompted some scouts to project him as a bullpen piece, where his fastball has jumped up to 97 mph. Melotakis' stuff plays up due to the funk in his delivery, and he's difficult for hitters to handle upon first look. For now the Twins will keep him in the rotation as he heads to high Class A Fort Myers in 2014.

Year	Club (League)	Class	W	L	ERA	G	GS	CG	SV	IP	H	HR	BB	SO	K/9	WHIP	AVG
2012	Elizabethton (APP)	R	1	1	1.35	7	0	0	0	7	2	0	2	10	13.5	0.60	.091
	Beloit (MWL)	LoA	3	1	2.08	13	0	0	1	17	15	3	4	24	12.5	1.10	.221
2013	Cedar Rapids (MWL)	LoA	11	4	3.16	24	18	0	1	111	106	6	39	84	6.8	1.31	.249
Minor League Totals			15	6	2.93	44	18	0	2	135	123	9	45	118	7.9	1.24	.238

19 TAYLOR ROGERS, LHP

BA GRADE
45
MEDIUM

Born: Dec. 17, 1990. **B-T:** L-L. **Ht.:** 6-3. **Wt.:** 173. **Drafted:** Kentucky, 2012 (11th round). **Signed by:** Rick Sellers.

Signed for $100,000 as an 11th-round pick in 2012, Rogers' younger brother Tyler is a submarining reliever in the Giants system. Taylor's fastball touches 93 mph and is solid average at 90-92 with late movement. His breaking ball is more of a slurve and needs to get sharper, though it helped him issue strike out nearly one-third (42 of 140) of lefthanders in 2013 at two Class A levels. Equipped with a wiry build and a deep competitive streak, Rogers is an aggressive strike-thrower who just needs to refine his changeup in order to make that next leap. His changeup improved late in 2013, helping him post a 0.89 ERA in 40 August innings, but too often he throws it without enough separation from his fastball. He threw nine shutout innings (with nine strikeouts and one walk) for high Class A Fort Myers in the Florida State League playoffs. He showed his durability by lasting at least six innings in eight of his last 10 starts, including the playoffs. Rogers is a back-end starter if it all works and will be tested at Double-A New Britain in 2014.

Year	Club (League)	Class	W	L	ERA	G	GS	CG	SV	IP	H	HR	BB	SO	K/9	WHIP	AVG
2012	Elizabethton (APP)	R	2	1	1.80	6	6	0	0	30	20	2	5	39	11.7	0.83	.187
	Beloit (MWL)	LoA	2	2	2.70	9	4	0	0	33	33	5	12	35	9.5	1.35	.248
2013	Cedar Rapids (MWL)	LoA	0	1	7.20	3	3	0	0	10	14	1	4	10	9.0	1.80	.304
	Fort Myers (FSL)	HiA	11	6	2.55	22	21	3	0	131	119	5	32	83	5.7	1.16	.248
Minor League Totals			15	10	2.69	40	34	3	0	204	186	13	53	167	7.4	1.17	.243

20 KENNYS VARGAS, 1B

BA GRADE
50
HIGH

Born: Aug. 1, 1990. **B-T:** B-R. **Ht:** 6-5. **Wt.:** 272. **Signed:** HS—Canovanas, P.R., 2009 (NDFA). **Signed by:** Hector Otero.

Signed as a 215-pound third baseman for $90,000, Vargas has ballooned as high as 285 pounds as he struggles to maintain his conditioning and improve his diet. Suspended for 50 games late in 2011 after testing positive for a weight-loss product, Vargas has overcome that stigma with a gregarious clubhouse presence and light-tower power that has attracted the attention of Red Sox slugger David Ortiz, his favorite player and someone with whom Vargas has become friendly. Strictly a first baseman/DH at this point, Vargas crushed a number of majestic homers off the batter's eye at high Class A Fort Myers' Hammond Stadium. His raw power ranks behind only that of Miguel Sano and Adam Brett Walker in the organization, and his advanced plate discipline has helped him build a career .370 on-base percentage. Vargas got his weight back to 270 pounds by the end of the 2013 season. His arm strength is slightly-above-average, but he is a below-average defender and well-below-average runner who improves the latter grade somewhat when underway. Lateral movement remains a challenge despite extra work with the Twins conditioning staff. If he keeps hitting for prodigious power, Vargas' defense may not matter. He's headed for Double-A New Britain in 2014.

Year	Club (League)	Class	AVG	G	AB	R	H	2B	3B	HR	RBI	BB	SO	SB	CS	OBP	SLG
2009	Twins (GCL)	R	.257	35	109	12	28	7	0	3	18	17	34	2	0	.369	.404
2010	Twins (GCL)	R	.324	39	142	24	46	15	1	3	26	13	40	1	0	.388	.507
2011	Elizabethton (APP)	R	.322	44	174	27	56	11	0	6	33	15	50	0	0	.377	.489
2012	Beloit (MWL)	LoA	.318	41	154	22	49	10	1	11	36	28	41	0	0	.419	.610
2013	Fort Myers (FSL)	HiA	.267	125	457	68	122	33	1	19	93	50	105	0	0	.344	.468
Minor League Totals			.291	284	1036	153	301	76	3	42	206	123	270	3	0	.370	.491

21 LEWIN DIAZ, OF/1B

BA GRADE
50
EXTREME

Born: Sept. 19, 1996. **B-T:** L-L. **Ht.:** 6-4. **Wt.:** 210. **Signed:** Dominican Republic, 2013. **Signed by:** Fred Guerrero.

More than a decade has passed since the Twins let David Ortiz escape their grasp. If everything breaks right, they might finally have found a legitimate heir in Lewin Diaz. Signed for $1.4 million at the start of the 2013 international signing period, Diaz is more than a one-dimensional slugger. Like Ortiz, he shows the ability to hit the ball where it's pitched along with impressive raw power. Diaz has plus bat speed and an advanced feel for hitting, but at times he settled for too many singles as an amateur in the Dominican Prospect League. Before signing he showed a tendency toward pre-pitch movement in his swing and could get tied up inside. Already 6-foot-4 and approaching 230 pounds, Diaz is close to outgrowing right field, but the Twins will let him continue to bounce between the outfield and first base. Few thought Miguel Sano would be able to stay at third base as long as he has, so perhaps Diaz, who turned 17 in September, will do the same with his outfield skills. He has a plus arm but projects as a first baseman as he matures. A below-average runner, Diaz reminds some Twins officials of 2006 first-rounder Chris Parmelee, albeit with more athletic ability. The Twins like Diaz's makeup and will bring him to the U.S. for his pro debut in 2014, likely in the Rookie-level Gulf Coast League.

Year	Club (League)	Class	AVG	G	AB	R	H	2B	3B	HR	RBI	BB	SO	SB	CS	OBP	SLG
2013	Did not play—Signed 2014 contract																

22 RANDY ROSARIO, LHP

BA GRADE
50
EXTREME

Born: May 18, 1994. **B-T:** L-L. **Ht.:** 6-0. **Wt.:** 198. **Signed:** Dominican Republic, 2010. **Signed by:** Fred Guerrero.

Signed for $220,000 at age 16, Rosario already was touching 90 mph at the time of his signing in 2010. He has since bumped that up to 95 mph, pitching at 88-92 with a smooth, easy delivery when he is starting. As a reliever, he has touched 96 mph and usually sits in the 92-94 range, though he started exclusively in 2013 for Rookie-level Elizabethton. Rosario's slider has plus potential and his changeup shows signs of being an above-average pitch if he would trust it more. For now it's a clear third pitch. He has worked hard to eliminate the command issues that plagued him early in his pro career, cutting his walk rate by nearly one per nine innings (down to 3.6). However, his strikeout rate also dropped by more than two batters per nine innings (down to 7.5) from 2012. Rosario throws a heavy ball and has yet to allow a home run in 118 pro innings. He shows good mound presence and solid makeup, working hard after hours to improve his English. A move up the ladder to low Class A Cedar Rapids is next, but with a crowded rotation he could be pushed back into a swing role similar to the one fellow lefty Mason Melotakis handled for the Kernels in 2013.

Year	Club (League)	Class	W	L	ERA	G	GS	CG	SV	IP	H	HR	BB	SO	K/9	WHIP	AVG
2011	Twins (DSL)	R	2	4	3.86	13	8	0	0	35	28	0	19	26	6.7	1.34	.212
2012	Twins (GCL)	R	2	1	1.64	10	7	0	0	38	19	0	19	42	9.9	0.99	.147
2013	Elizabethton (APP)	R	4	3	2.82	9	9	0	0	45	42	0	18	37	7.5	1.34	.251
Minor League Totals			8	8	2.75	32	24	0	0	118	89	0	56	105	8.0	1.23	.208

23 LUKE BARD, RHP

BA GRADE
50
EXTREME

Born: Nov. 13, 1990. **B-T:** R-R. **Ht. 6-3. Wt.:** 195. **Drafted:** Georgia Tech, 2012 (1st round supplemental). **Signed by:** Jack Powell.

The Twins still aren't sure exactly what they have in Bard—younger brother of former Red Sox reliever Daniel—as nagging injuries have limited him to 19 innings through his first two professional seasons. Drafted 42nd overall out of Georgia Tech in 2012, Bard signed for $1.227 million despite a torn lat muscle that cut short his junior season. He aggravated the injury during instructional league and then struggled with biceps tendinitis and a sore throwing shoulder last spring, so he had to wait until late July to get back on the mound. Command remains an issue for Bard, who walked 7.5 batters per nine innings in limited time, but he did finish 2013 with seven straight scoreless outings. When he's healthy, Bard has some of the best pure stuff in the organization. He flashed an above-average fastball that touched 97 mph as a reliever in college and sat at 93-95 as a starter in 2012. His slider also grades out as a plus pitch at its best, showing good depth and late bite in the low 80s. His changeup is clearly a third pitch, but it has the potential to be an average offering. Despite a frustrating start to his career, Bard still displays strong makeup and the type of smooth arm action and delivery that makes him a starting candidate. That, however, would require him to prove he can hold up to the physical burden.

Year	Club (League)	Class	W	L	ERA	G	GS	CG	SV	IP	H	HR	BB	SO	K/9	WHIP	AVG
2012	Twins (GCL)	R	0	0	6.75	3	1	0	0	4	3	0	5	3	6.8	2.00	.231
	Elizabethton (APP)	R	0	0	0.00	4	0	0	1	3	2	0	2	4	12.0	1.33	.200
2013	Twins (GCL)	R	0	0	12.00	4	0	0	0	3	5	0	3	1	3.0	2.67	.333
	Elizabethton (APP)	R	1	0	1.08	7	0	0	0	8	2	0	6	6	6.5	0.96	.091
	Fort Myers (FSL)	HiA	0	0	0.00	1	0	0	0	1	0	0	0	2	18.0	0.00	.000
Minor League Totals			1	0	3.72	19	1	0	1	19	12	0	16	16	7.4	1.45	.190

24 AMAURYS MINIER, 3B

Born: Jan. 30, 1996. **B-T:** B-R. **Ht.:** 6-2. **Wt.:** 217. **Signed:** Dominican Republic, 2012. **Signed by:** Fred Guerrero.

The jewel of the Twins' 2012 international signings, Minier signed for $1.4 million and wasted little time showing why. Reporting to the Rookie-level Gulf Coast League for the first time in 2013, the switch-hitter flashed some of the best raw power in the organization. Witnesses are still buzzing about the low laser he sent over the wall in left field only to have the disbelieving umpire rule it a ground-rule double due to its odd trajectory. Minier's overall hitting approach still needs work from both sides, and he doesn't make nearly enough contact at this point, as shown by his 26 percent strikeout rate. However, his batting-practice swing features a crispness that produces line drives to all fields and natural backspin. Listed at 6-foot-2, 217 pounds, he already has added nearly 20 pounds since signing. His build is reminiscent of Miguel Sano's at a similar stage. Like Sano, Minier didn't last long at shortstop, and he still has room to pack on more muscle as he eventually settles in at a corner infield spot or even right field, where his strong arm would play well. He remains extremely raw and has poor instincts in the field and on the bases, where he is a below-average runner. Minier will try to play catch-up in 2014 in extended spring training, then move up to the Rookie-level Appalachian League.

Year	Club (League)	Class	AVG	G	AB	R	H	2B	3B	HR	RBI	BB	SO	SB	CS	OBP	SLG
2013	Twins (GCL)	R	.214	31	112	10	24	5	2	6	17	6	29	1	1	.252	.455
Minor League Totals			.214	31	112	10	24	5	2	6	17	6	29	1	1	.252	.455

25 TRAVIS HARRISON, 3B/OF

BA GRADE
45
HIGH

Born: Oct. 17, 1992. **B-T:** R-R. **Ht.:** 6-2. **Wt.:** 215. **Drafted:** HS—Tustin, Calif., 2011 (1st round supplemental). **Signed by:** John Leavitt.

Signed for $1.05 million as the 50th overall pick in 2011, Harrison is doing his part to make up for the struggles of first-round shortstop Levi Michael. After averaging 25 errors his first two seasons at third base, Harrison spent much of his instructional league learning to play left field. He predictably struggled with his reads and routes but showed more than enough arm and instincts to make the move. He will probably split time in 2014 at high Class A Fort Myers between left and third base, where he has a tendency to be too mechanical and lacks the requisite first-step quickness and agility. Better going to his left with an average third-base arm, Harrison is a below-average runner who will go as far as his bat takes him. His 15 homers ranked second at low Class A Cedar Rapids to Adam Brett Walker, but Harrison led the way with 68 walks and 125 strikeouts, many of them on breaking pitches out of the zone. He tends to get too pull-conscious at times and his swing can get closed-off, but he has good bat speed and a short swing that generates solid power to all fields. Harrison's overall athleticism improved after he devoted himself to the organization's agility program.

Year	Club (League)	Class	AVG	G	AB	R	H	2B	3B	HR	RBI	BB	SO	SB	CS	OBP	SLG
2012	Elizabethton (APP)	R	.301	60	219	39	66	12	4	5	27	24	51	3	0	.383	.461
2013	Cedar Rapids (MWL)	LoA	.253	129	450	66	114	28	0	15	59	68	125	2	4	.366	.416
Minor League Totals			.269	189	669	105	180	40	4	20	86	92	176	5	4	.372	.430

26 NIKO GOODRUM, SS/2B

BA GRADE **45** HIGH

Born: Feb. 28, 1992. **B-T:** B-R. **Ht.:** 6-4. **Wt.:** 190. **Drafted:** HS—Fayetteville, Ga., 2010 (2nd round). **Signed by:** Jack Powell.

Signed for $514,800 as a second-round pick in 2010, Goodrum finally made it to full-season ball at low Class A Cedar Rapids in 2013, his fourth pro year. Injured in a home-plate collision in early June, he missed two weeks with a concussion that sent him to the hospital, then suffered through a difficult July (.195 average). The switch-hitting Goodrum's numbers were almost identical from both sides of the plate, where he showed fast hands, decent gap power and continued to improve his patience (60 walks). Tall and lanky with a high waist, some believe he will have to move off shortstop, eventually landing at a corner infield or outfield spot. He made 27 errors in 2013, many of them because he fails to follow through on his throws. For now he will stay put because he shows plus arm strength and surprisingly good range for his body type, thanks to excellent first-step quickness. He's an average runner and doesn't project as a true stolen-base threat at the higher levels. Goodrum shows leadership qualities and brings good energy to the ballpark each day. He figures to open 2014 as the starting shortstop at high Class A Fort Myers.

Year	Club (League)	Class	AVG	G	AB	R	H	2B	3B	HR	RBI	BB	SO	SB	CS	OBP	SLG
2010	Twins (GCL)	R	.161	36	118	10	19	4	0	0	5	9	34	4	2	.219	.195
2011	Elizabethton (APP)	R	.275	59	204	39	56	10	3	2	20	21	56	8	1	.352	.382
2012	Elizabethton (APP)	R	.242	58	227	38	55	12	8	4	38	38	56	6	3	.349	.419
2013	Cedar Rapids (MWL)	LoA	.260	103	385	62	100	22	4	4	45	60	105	20	4	.364	.369
Minor League Totals			.246	256	934	149	230	48	15	10	108	128	251	38	10	.340	.362

27 TYLER JONES, RHP

BA GRADE **45** HIGH

Born: Sept. 5, 1989. **B-T:** R-R. **Ht.:** 6-4. **Wt.:** 247. **Drafted:** Louisiana State, 2011 (11th round). **Signed by:** Greg Runser.

Jones distinguished himself in 2013 by making the full-time move to the bullpen. Splitting his year between two Class A levels, the big-bodied righty showed a renewed commitment to fitness and saw the quality of his repertoire improve considerably. Signed for $105,000, Jones' stock may have dropped after a misdemeanor shoplifting charge cost him a rotation spot in his lone season at Louisiana State. The former Madison (Wis.) JC standout saw his fastball jump from 88-91 mph during a frigid April to 93-95 by August, with cut and sink that rates a 70 on the 20-80 scouting scale. He was touching 97 mph by season's end. Jones' hard, heavy slider has good downward action in the upper 80s and approaches plus status at times. He also throws a curve and changeup. The change, which he uses rarely out of the bullpen, has some late drop and has become his third pitch. Jones missed most of May with a right elbow strain, but he threw well upon his return, earning a promotion to high Class A Fort Myers. The Twins see his frame and repertoire as suitable for starting, though his stabbing arm action hinders his command and breaking ball consistency.

Year	Club (League)	Class	W	L	ERA	G	GS	CG	SV	IP	H	HR	BB	SO	K/9	WHIP	AVG
2011	Elizabethton (APP)	R	0	0	12.86	4	1	0	0	7	16	2	2	8	10.3	2.57	.432
2012	Beloit (MWL)	LoA	5	5	4.67	18	16	0	0	87	90	5	35	102	10.6	1.44	.263
2013	Cedar Rapids (MWL)	LoA	4	3	1.93	24	0	0	9	37	19	0	16	44	10.6	0.94	.146
	Fort Myers (FSL)	HiA	1	3	4.20	12	0	0	4	15	18	0	4	22	13.2	1.47	.305
Minor League Totals			10	11	4.32	58	17	0	13	146	143	7	57	176	10.8	1.37	.252

28 ZACK JONES, RHP

Born: Dec. 4, 1990. **B-T:** R-R. **Ht.:** 6-1. **Wt.:** 205. **Drafted:** San Jose State, 2012 (4th round). **Signed by:** Elliott Strankman.

Armed with one of the biggest fastballs in the organization, the 2012 fourth-rounder out of San Jose State has moved rapidly since signing for $356,700. He converted 14 of 18 save chances at high Class A Fort Myers in 2013, fanning 13 batters per nine innings. Sitting at 96-97 mph most nights, he has touched 99 but doesn't often command the fastball. Jones issued 5.2 walks per nine innings and has failed thus far to develop a reliable breaking ball. He has experimented with different types since coming to the Twins, with the slider showing the most upside. Like many relievers he needs to do a better job holding runners, but he is a good athlete who fields his position well. Jones struggled in the Arizona Fall League, walking nine batters in just six innings before missing the final two weeks with a finger issue on his pitching hand. The issue wasn't serious and didn't come as a result of an angry outburst, but still was shrouded in some mystery. Jones should get a chance to close at Double-A New Britain in 2014. If he improves his command and sharpens his slider, he could climb the ladder fast.

Year	Club (League)	Class	W	L	ERA	G	GS	CG	SV	IP	H	HR	BB	SO	K/9	WHIP	AVG
2012	Elizabethton (APP)	R	0	0	0.00	6	0	0	0	6	2	0	4	9	13.5	1.00	.100
	Beloit (MWL)	LoA	0	0	3.21	12	0	0	4	14	9	1	7	25	16.1	1.14	.184
2013	Fort Myers (FSL)	HiA	4	3	1.85	39	0	0	14	49	28	2	28	70	12.9	1.15	.172
Minor League Totals			4	3	1.97	57	0	0	18	69	39	3	39	104	13.6	1.14	.168

29 RONI TAPIA, 3B

BA GRADE **50** EXTREME

Born: April 3, 1997. **B-T:** R-R. **Ht.:** 6-3. **Wt.:** 170. **Signed:** Dominican Republic, 2013. **Signed by:** Fred Guerrero.

Signed for $550,000 in July 2013, Tapia has a sleeker build than the typical young Dominican third baseman. Some see a young Aramis Ramirez in the angular Tapia, who quickly grew an inch to 6-foot-4 in the first three months after signing. Though just an average runner, he has a plus arm and enough agility to convince the Twins he could yet turn into a strong defender at third. Others believe he might need to change positions, with a switch to corner outfield a distinct possibility. Another product of the Dominican Prospect League, Tapia has solid makeup and maintains a sharp focus on his game. He displays easy power with a righthanded swing that has some finish and length. The Twins already have Miguel Sano playing third base at the top of their prospect food chain. Tapia may contend with Amaurys Minier to see if one can become a worthy heir in the coming years. He may start his pro career in the Dominican Summer League with a chance to earn a jump to the Rookie-level Gulf Coast League.

Year	Club (League)	Class	AVG	G	AB	R	H	2B	3B	HR	RBI	BB	SO	SB	CS	OBP	SLG
2013	Did not play—Signed 2014 contract																

30 STUART TURNER, C

BA GRADE **45** HIGH

Born: Dec. 27, 1991. **B-T:** R-R. **Ht.:** 6-3. **Wt.:** 215. **Drafted:** Mississippi, 2013 (3rd round). **Signed by:** Alan Sandberg.

Signed for $550,000 out of the third round, Turner was the second college catcher drafted in 2013. A first-team All-American his only season at Mississippi, Turner earned tournament MVP honors in 2012 when he helped Louisiana State-Eunice JC win the Division II NJCAA World Series. His advanced receiving skills, leadership traits and competitive fire impressed Rookie-level Appalachian League managers, as he ranked as the league's No. 18 prospect. He still needs to refine his game-calling, but he had no problem handling an Elizabethton staff that at various times featured five other top 30 prospects, including Kohl Stewart, Luke Bard and Felix Jorge. When a mound visit was required, Turner often handled the honors on his own. He has soft, reliable hands, is flexible enough to block balls in the dirt and shows a plus arm with outstanding accuracy. In college he threw out more than 50 percent of basestealers and flashed consistent pop times of 1.9 seconds to second base. He frames pitches well and has quick feet and quiet movements. Strong with a solid frame, Turner could hit for average power in time. For now he has a line-drive swing that has some stiffness and length. He can get too pull-conscious and is a below-average runner, but the defensive skills trump all at this stage. He'll head to full-season ball in 2014, probably at a low Class A Cedar Rapids.

Year	Club (League)	Class	AVG	G	AB	R	H	2B	3B	HR	RBI	BB	SO	SB	CS	OBP	SLG
2013	Elizabethton (APP)	R	.264	34	121	15	32	5	0	3	19	12	22	0	1	.340	.380
	New Britain (EL)	AA	.500	1	4	1	2	0	0	0	0	0	1	0	0	.500	.500
Minor League Totals			.272	35	125	16	34	5	0	3	19	12	23	0	1	.345	.384

New York Mets

BY MATT EDDY

On the heels of their fifth straight losing season—and second consecutive 88-loss effort—the Mets received some *really* bad news. Ace righthander Matt Harvey will miss the 2014 season as he rehabs from Tommy John surgery.

The seventh pick in the 2010 draft, Harvey electrified the baseball world with a power arsenal that got power results in 2013. He went 9-5, 2.27 in 26 starts and struck out 191 batters in 178 innings.

Harvey even started the All-Star Game in front of a hometown crowd at Citi Field, but his season ended on a sour note after he allowed a career-high 13 hits to the Tigers on Aug. 24. An MRI revealed a torn ulnar collateral ligament in his elbow, and after the 24-year-old initially tried rest and rehab, he gave in to the inevitable and had surgery in October.

While the Mets drafted Harvey after a 92-loss disaster in 2009, they went the trade route to acquire their other two prized young righthanders, 2013 rookie Zack Wheeler and current No. 1 prospect Noah Syndergaard. The former is a product of the Carlos Beltran trade with the Giants in 2011, while the latter arrived from the Blue Jays in December 2012 as part of the prospect haul for R.A. Dickey.

The 23-year-old Wheeler made his big league debut on June 18. After initial growing pains, he reeled off a string of quality outings in July and August, going 6-2, 2.96 in those 11 starts with 7.9 strikeouts and 3.2 walks per nine innings. He finished the year as one of five rookie starters to pitch 100 innings with an average fastball velocity of 94 mph or higher.

Syndergaard, meanwhile, ranked as the top pitching prospect in both the high Class A Florida State and Double-A Eastern leagues, and he appears poised to follow Wheeler's path to the big leagues in 2014.

The Mets believe they have as much pitching depth as anybody. For proof, they can point to the fact that their pitchers at the full-season levels finished with a collective 2.79 SO/BB ratio, better than any of the other 29 organizations. They handed out the second-fewest unintentional walks (7.6 percent of batters) and struck out the third-most (21.3 percent).

Outside of Travis d'Arnaud and Wilmer Flores, who made their big league debuts in 2013, all the Mets' brightest position-player prospects spent the season in the low minors. That list includes catcher Kevin Plawecki, shortstop Amed Rosario and the club's three successive high school first-rounders from 2011-13: outfielder Brandon Nimmo, shortstop Gavin Cecchini and first baseman Dominic Smith.

The Mets would benefit from the offensive reinforcements sooner rather than later after scoring 619 runs in 2013, their lowest output for a full season since 1992. Only franchise cornerstone David Wright fits the profile of a championship-caliber starter on the current roster.

On the international front, the Mets traded with the Angels to acquire bonus pool space, giving them a budget of more than $3 million. They invested nearly $2.5 million to sign five international players in 2013, headlined by Dominican outfielder Ricardo Cespedes ($725,000), Venezuelan catcher Ali Sanchez ($690,000) and Venezuelan shortstop Luis Carpio ($300,000).

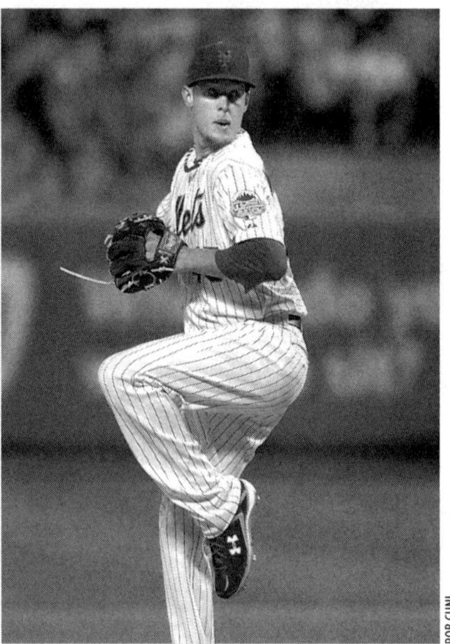

ROB CUNI

Zack Wheeler thrived at times as a Mets rookie, averaging 94 mph on his fastball

TOP PROSPECTS OF THE DECADE

Year	Player, Pos	2013 Org
2004	Kazuo Matsui, ss	Rakuten (Japan)
2005	Lastings Milledge, of	Yakult (Japan)
2006	Lastings Milledge, of	Yakult (Japan)
2007	Mike Pelfrey, rhp	Twins
2008	Fernando Martinez, of	Yankees
2009	Fernando Martinez, of	Yankees
2010	Jenrry Mejia, rhp	Mets
2011	Jenrry Mejia, rhp	Mets
2012	Zack Wheeler, rhp	Mets
2013	Zack Wheeler, rhp	Mets

ORGANIZATION OVERVIEW

General Manager: Sandy Alderson. **Farm Director:** Paul DePodesta. **Scouting Director:** Tommy Tanous.

Class	Team	League	W	L	PCT	Finish	Manager
Majors	New York Mets	National	74	88	.457	12th (15)	Terry Collins
Triple-A	Las Vegas 51s	Pacific Coast	81	63	.563	2nd (16)	Wally Backman
Double-A	Binghamton Mets	Eastern	86	55	.610	1st (12)	Pedro Lopez
High Class A	St. Lucie Mets	Florida State	71	60	.542	3rd (12)	Ryan Ellis
Low Class A	Savannah Sand Gnats	South Atlantic	77	61	.558	4th (14)	Luis Rojas
Short-season	Brooklyn Cyclones	New York-Penn	38	37	.507	7th (14)	Rich Donnelly
Rookie	Kingsport Mets	Appalachian	40	27	.597	3rd (10)	Jose Leger
Rookie	GCL Mets	Gulf Coast	20	40	.333	16th (16)	Jose Carreno
2013 Overall Minor League Record			**413**	**343**	**.546**	**t-4th (30)**	

THIS YEAR'S TOP 30

No.	Player, Pos.	Grade
1.	Noah Syndergaard, rhp	65/Medium
2.	Travis d'Arnaud, c	60/High
3.	Rafael Montero, rhp	55/Medium
4.	Dominic Smith, 1b	60/High
5.	Kevin Plawecki, c/1b	50/Medium
6.	Wilmer Flores, 2b/3b	50/Medium
7.	Amed Rosario, ss	60/Extreme
8.	Brandon Nimmo, of	50/High
9.	Gavin Cecchini, ss	50/High
10.	Jake deGrom, rhp	50/High
11.	Cesar Puello, of	50/High
12.	Steve Matz, lhp	60/Extreme
13.	Dilson Herrera, 2b	50/High
14.	Michael Fulmer, rhp	50/High
15.	Gabriel Ynoa, rhp	50/High
16.	Cory Mazzoni, rhp	45/Medium
17.	Vic Black, rhp	45/Medium
18.	Jeurys Familia, rhp	45/Medium
19.	Domingo Tapia, rhp	50/Extreme
20.	Logan Verrett, rhp	45/Medium
21.	Gonzalez Germen, rhp	40/Low
22.	Luis Mateo, rhp	55/Extreme
23.	Jack Leathersich, lhp	45/High
24.	Matt Koch, rhp	50/Extreme
25.	Matt den Dekker, of	40/Low
26.	Dustin Lawley, of/3b	45/High
27.	Rob Whalen, rhp	50/Extreme
28.	Juan Centeno, c	40/Low
29.	Wilfredo Tovar, ss	40/Low
30.	Jayce Boyd, 1b	45/High

LAST YEAR'S TOP 30

No.	Player, Pos.	Status
1.	Zack Wheeler, rhp	Majors
2.	Gavin Cecchini, ss	No. 9
3.	Brandon Nimmo, of	No. 8
4.	Luis Mateo, rhp	No. 22
5.	Rafael Montero, rhp	No. 3
6.	Wilmer Flores, 3b/2b	No. 6
7.	Michael Fulmer, rhp	No. 14
8.	Jeurys Familia, rhp	No. 18
9.	Domingo Tapia, rhp	No. 19
10.	Cory Mazzoni, rhp	No. 16
11.	Jake deGrom, rhp	No. 10
12.	Hansel Robles, rhp	Dropped out
13.	Wilfredo Tovar, ss	No. 29
14.	Cory Vaughn, of	Dropped out
15.	Matt den Dekker, of	No. 25
16.	Phillip Evans, ss	Dropped out
17.	Robert Carson, lhp	(Angels)
18.	Cesar Puello, of	No. 11
19.	Aderlin Rodriguez, 3b/1b	Dropped out
20.	Gabriel Ynoa, rhp	No. 15
21.	Kevin Plawecki, c	No. 5
22.	Jack Leathersich, lhp	No. 23
23.	Matt Reynolds, ss	Dropped out
24.	Collin McHugh	(Rockies)
25.	Tyler Pill, rhp	Dropped out
26.	Logan Verrett, rhp	No. 20
27.	Darrell Ceciliani, of	Dropped out
28.	Amed Rosario, ss	No. 7
29.	Steve Matz, lhp	No. 12
30.	Cam Maron, c	Dropped out

BEST TOOLS

Best Hitter for Average	Kevin Plawecki
Best Power Hitter	Dustin Lawley
Best Strike-Zone Discipline	Brandon Nimmo
Fastest Baserunner	Champ Stuart
Best Athlete	Amed Rosario
Best Fastball	Noah Syndergaard
Best Curveball	Rob Whalen
Best Slider	Logan Verrett
Best Changeup	Gonzalez Germen
Best Control	Rafael Montero
Best Defensive Catcher	Juan Centeno
Best Defensive Infielder	Wilfredo Tovar
Best Infield Arm	Aderlin Rodriguez
Best Defensive Outfielder	Matt den Dekker
Best Outfield Arm	Cesar Puello

TOP 15 PLAYERS 25 AND UNDER

No.	Player, Pos. (Age)	Peak Level
1.	Matt Harvey, rhp (25)	Majors
2.	Zack Wheeler, rhp (23)	Majors
3.	Noah Syndergaard, rhp (21)	Double-A
4.	Travis d'Arnaud, c (25)	Majors
5.	Rafael Montero, rhp (23)	Triple-A
6.	Jenrry Mejia, rhp (24)	Majors
7.	Dominic Smith, 1b (18)	Rookie
8.	Ruben Tejada, ss (24)	Majors
9.	Kevin Plawecki, c (23)	High Class A
10.	Wilmer Flores, 2b (22)	Majors
11.	Amed Rosario, ss (18)	Rookie
12.	Brandon Nimmo, of (21)	Low Class A
13.	Gavin Cecchini, ss (20)	Short-season
14.	Jake deGrom, rhp (25)	Triple-A
15.	Cesar Puello, of (23)	Double-A

MINOR LEAGUE DEPTH CHART

NEW YORK METS

TOP 2014 ROOKIE: Noah Syndergaard, rhp. The Mets unveil a third power righty in three years as Syndergaard follows Matt Harvey (2012) and Zack Wheeler (2013) to Flushing.

BREAKOUT PROSPECT: Rob Whalen, rhp. A live fastball and plus curveball combine with advanced pitchability to make for a sterling full-season debut at low Class A Savannah.

SOURCE OF TOP 30 TALENT			
Homegrown	**26**	**Acquired**	**4**
College	9	Trades	4
Junior college	0	Rule 5 draft	0
High school	7	Independent leagues	0
Nondrafted free agents	0	Free agents/waivers	0
International	10		

SLEEPER: Miller Diaz, rhp. The 21-year-old converted catcher already throws a mid-90s sinker and power slider, and he enters 2014 as the reigning strikeout champ of the New York-Penn League.

LF
Brandon Nimmo (8)
Dustin Lawley (26)
Vicente Lupo
Jared King

CF
Matt den Dekker (25)
Darrell Ceciliani
Ivan Wilson
Champ Stuart
Ricardo Cespedes

RF
Cesar Puello (11)
Cory Vaughn
Travis Taijeron
Kyle Johnson
Wuilmer Becerra

3B
Zach Lutz
Jhoan Urena

SS
Amed Rosario (7)
Gavin Cecchini (9)
Wilfredo Tovar (29)
Matt Reynolds
Luis Guillorme
Luis Carpio

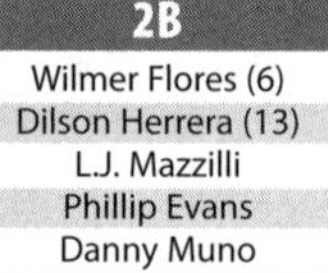

2B
Wilmer Flores (6)
Dilson Herrera (13)
L.J. Mazzilli
Phillip Evans
Danny Muno

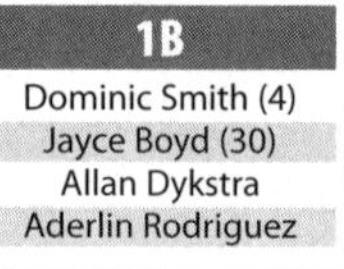

1B
Dominic Smith (4)
Jayce Boyd (30)
Allan Dykstra
Aderlin Rodriguez

C
Travis d'Arnaud (2)
Kevin Plawecki (5)
Juan Centeno (28)
Cam Maron
Albert Cordero
Jose Garcia
Ali Sanchez

LHP

LHSP	LHRP
Steve Matz (12)	Jack Leathersich (23)
	Chase Huchingson
	Darin Gorski

RHP

RHSP	RHRP
Noah Syndergaard (1)	Vic Black (17)
Rafael Montero (3)	Jeurys Familia (18)
Jake deGrom (10)	Domingo Tapia (19)
Michael Fulmer (14)	Gonzalez Germen (21)
Gabriel Ynoa (15)	Erik Goeddel
Cory Mazzoni (16)	Jeff Walters
Logan Verrett (20)	Chase Bradford
Luis Mateo (22)	Greg Peavey
Matt Koch (24)	Akeel Morris
Rob Whalen (27)	Beck Wheeler
Robert Gsellman	Tyler Bashlor
Miller Diaz	Johnny Magliozzi
Chris Flexen	
Rainy Lara	
Hansel Robles	
Andrew Church	
Luis Cessa	
Matt Bowman	
Tyler Pill	
Casey Meisner	

DRAFT ANALYSIS

2013

BONUSES: $6.9 MILLION

BEST PURE HITTER: The Mets weren't the only club that considered 1B Dominic Smith (1) the best pure hitter in the entire draft. He controls the strike zone, recognizes breaking balls well and combines excellent hand-eye coordination with bat speed.

BEST POWER HITTER: The Mets believe in OF Ivan Wilson's (3) raw power and approach, faith that wasn't shaken by a .219/.321/.300 debut in the Rookie-level Gulf Coast League.

FASTEST RUNNER: OF Champ Stuart (6) covered 60 yards in 6.3 seconds in a predraft workout and stole 11 bases in 43 games in his debut.

BEST DEFENSIVE PLAYER: Smith earns well above-average grades at first base and has Gold Glove potential with the hands of a shortstop. SS Luis Guillorme (10), one of the top defenders in the draft, has soft hands and tremendous footwork.

BEST FASTBALL: RHP Tyler Bashlor (11) signed for $500,000 because of his heater. A junior college outfielder who hit third, then closed late, he has a quick arm that generates easy velocity, sitting 93-94 and reaching 97 mph consistently.

BEST SECONDARY PITCH: RHPs Andrew Church (2) and Johnny Magliozzi (17) both spin good curveballs. Church's is advanced for a high school pitcher as he controls it well. Magliozzi's is more of a 12-to-6 hammer.

BEST PRO DEBUT: Smith finished strong, finishing with a .301/.398/.439 line and a trip to the Rookie-level Appalachian League playoffs with Kingsport. RHPs Ricky Jacquez (25) and Robby Coles (28) shared closer duties at Kingsport, with Jacquez (2-0, 1.74, 21 IP/33 SO) and Coles (4-1, 1.83, 20 IP/20 SO) saving six games apiece.

BEST ATHLETE: Wilson has impressed the Mets with his play in center field and above-average speed as well as his prodigious strength. Stuart has wiry strength to go with his speed and an above-average arm as well.

MOST INTRIGUING BACKGROUND: 2B L.J. Mazzilli (4) is the son of outfielder Lee, the Mets' first-round pick 40 years prior. Lee, who played 10 years with the Mets, grew up in Brooklyn, where L.J. hit .278/.329/.381 this summer. OF Jared King (6) played with his brother Jason, a 2011 fourth-round pick who is now in the Tigers system, at Kansas State. RHP Ricky Knapp (8) is the son of Dodgers minor league pitching coach Rick Knapp.

CLOSEST TO THE MAJORS: Mazzilli should move quickly as a middle infielder with solid tools.

BEST LATE-ROUND PICK: Bashlor got his bonus for a reason, and the Mets also like 1B/C Brandon Brosher (36) for his plus raw power. It's not clear he has the defensive chops to remain behind the plate.

THE ONE WHO GOT AWAY: Projectable RHP Morgan Earman (21), whose fastball has scraped 93-94 mph, wasn't committed to college when the Mets drafted him, but they couldn't get a deal done and he headed to Arizona.

ASSESSMENT: Smith has star potential and would fill a need in New York if he moves as quickly as anticipated. The Mets' first four selections were all preps, so the rest of the class may take a while to shake out.

2012

BONUSES: $7.0 MILLION

C/1B Kevin Plawacki (1s) has outshined SS Gavin Cecchini (1) to this point. RHP Matt Koch (3) and 1B Jayce Boyd (6) earned Top 30 spots as well.

GRADE: C

2011

BONUSES: $6.8 MILLION

Raw OF Brandon Nimmo (1), like Cecchini, will need time. The Mets have high hopes for RHPs Michael Fulmer (1s) and Cory Mazzoni (2) and OF Dustin Lawley (19).

GRADE: C

2010

BONUSES: $4.7 MILLION

RHP Matt Harvey (1) started the 2013 All-Star Game at Citi Field but needed Tommy John surgery. RHP Jake deGrom (9) still has some ceiling.

GRADE: B+

TOP DRAFT PICKS OF THE DECADE

Year	Player, Pos.	2013 Org
2004	Phil Humber, rhp	Astros
2005	Mike Pelfrey, rhp	Twins
2006	Kevin Mulvey, rhp (2nd round)	Out of baseball
2007	Eddie Kunz, rhp (1st round supp.)	Out of baseball
2008	Ike Davis, 1b	Mets
2009	Steve Matz, lhp (2nd round)	Mets
2010	Matt Harvey, rhp	Mets
2011	Brandon Nimmo, of	Mets
2012	Gavin Cecchini, ss	Mets
2013	Dominic Smith, 1b	Mets

LARGEST BONUSES IN CLUB HISTORY

Mike Pelfrey, 2005	$3,550,000
Philip Humber, 2004	$3,000,000
Dominic Smith, 2013	$2,600,000
Matt Harvey, 2010	$2,525,000
Gavin Cecchini, 2012	$2,300,000

1 NOAH SYNDERGAARD, RHP

Born: Aug. 29, 1992. **B-T:** L-R. **Ht.:** 6-6. **Wt.:** 240. **Drafted:** HS—Mansfield, Texas, 2010 (1st round supplemental). **Signed by:** Steve Miller (Blue Jays).

The Blue Jays correctly gauged Syndergaard's potential and signability when they nabbed the Dallas Baptist commit with the 38th pick in the 2010 draft. He flew up Toronto's draft board that spring as area scout Steve Miller watched the 17-year-old righthander's velocity climb from the high 80s to a steady 92-94 mph. Syndergaard struck out 39 batters in his final three starts for Legacy High in the Texas 4-A playoffs, then wasted no time in signing with the Blue Jays for a below-slot $600,000 bonus. He breezed through two short-season levels in 2011, then starred in a prospect-studded Lansing rotation in 2012 that also featured Justin Nicolino and Aaron Sanchez. That offseason, Syndergaard (and catcher Travis d'Arnaud) joined the Mets in the trade that sent reigning Cy Young Award winner R.A. Dickey to the Blue Jays. He started the 2013 Futures Game for the U.S. team at New York's Citi Field, then jumped on the fast track with a second-half promotion to Double-A Binghamton. He ranked as the top pitching prospect in both the Florida State and Eastern leagues.

Overpowering fastball velocity and sharp control have always been Syndergaard's hallmarks. He throws his fastball at 94-98 mph with vicious armside run that saws off righthanders, who hit .196/.240/.294 with four homers in 251 plate appearances against him in 2013. Just six starters who qualified for the minor league ERA title struck out batters at a higher rate than Syndergaard (28.2 percent), and his 4.75 SO/BB ratio surpassed anyone in the top 10. A repeatable delivery and clean arm action help him pitch downhill and throw consistent strikes, and he averaged a tick more than one walk per start in 2013. His secondary stuff grades more as average in most starts, though his 12-to-6 curveball features more power and spin than it did when he first turned pro. Pitching coordinator Ron Romanick encouraged Syndegaard to visualize throwing his breaking ball with a fastball mentality and arm speed, rather than casting the pitch and trying to drop the perfect curve in the zone. He throws a firm changeup that sits in the high 80s, a pitch he must refine after allowing lefties to hit .296 and slug .471 against him in 2013. He still has yet to throw more than 120 innings in a season.

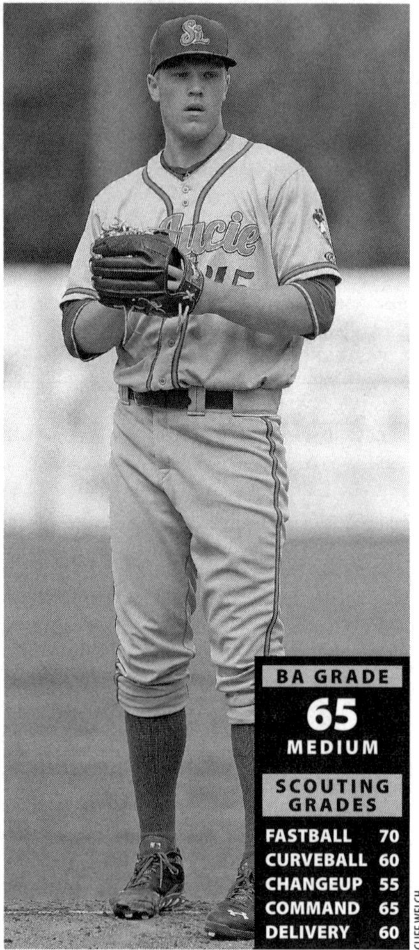

BA GRADE
65
MEDIUM
SCOUTING GRADES
FASTBALL 70
CURVEBALL 60
CHANGEUP 55
COMMAND 65
DELIVERY 60

CLIFF WELCH

With a typical development track at Triple-A Las Vegas, Syndergaard stands poised to make his big league debut around midseason in 2014, a la Matt Harvey in 2012 and Zack Wheeler in 2013. With the stuff he has now Syndegaard would profile as a No. 3 starter, but if one of his secondary pitches becomes a consistent plus, then he becomes a prototype No. 2 because scouts have no questions about his mound presence or command.

Year	Club (League)	Class	W	L	ERA	G	GS	CG	SV	IP	H	HR	BB	SO	K/9	WHIP	AVG
2010	Blue Jays (GCL)	R	0	1	2.70	5	5	0	0	13	11	0	4	6	4.1	1.13	.229
2011	Bluefield (APP)	R	4	0	1.41	7	5	0	0	32	23	1	11	37	10.4	1.06	.198
	Vancouver (NWL)	SS	1	2	2.00	4	4	0	0	18	15	0	5	22	11.0	1.11	.221
	Lansing (MWL)	LoA	0	0	3.00	2	2	0	0	9	8	0	2	9	9.0	1.11	.235
2012	Lansing (MWL)	LoA	8	5	2.60	27	19	0	1	104	81	3	31	122	10.6	1.08	.212
2013	St. Lucie (FSL)	HiA	3	3	3.11	12	12	0	0	64	61	3	16	64	9.0	1.21	.255
	Binghamton (EL)	AA	6	1	3.00	11	11	0	0	54	46	8	12	69	11.5	1.07	.228
Minor League Totals			22	12	2.64	68	58	0	1	294	245	15	81	329	10.1	1.11	.225

2 TRAVIS D'ARNAUD, C

Born: Feb. 10, 1989. **B-T:** R-R. **Ht.:** 6-2. **Wt.:** 195. **Drafted:** HS—Lakewood, Calif., 2007 (1st round supplemental). **Signed by:** Tim Kissner (Phillies).

D'Arnaud has twice been included in December trades for Cy Young Award winners. He went from the Phillies to the Blue Jays for Roy Halladay in 2009, and then to the Mets for R.A. Dickey in 2012. D'Arnaud spent much of the first half of 2013 on the disabled list after taking a foul ball off his left foot on April 17 and breaking a bone. He finished 2012 on the DL with a torn posterior cruciate ligament in his left knee. D'Arnaud's offensive potential made him an attractive trade target, but he's a strong fundamental catcher with average to plus tools across the board. Pitchers trust him because he frames and blocks pitches with aplomb, while also working with his charges to execute game plans. He used solid-average arm strength to gun down 11 of 23 basestealers in an abbreviated minor league season and five of 24 in the big leagues. D'Arnaud mashed 21 homers at Double-A in 2011 to win the Eastern League MVP award, and his short, powerful stroke should translate in the big leagues. Good feel for the barrel and a willingness to use the middle of the field should allow him to hit for average, too, with some seeing him as a .280 hitter with 15-20 homers a year. D'Arnaud would have made his big league debut much earlier than August if not for his foot injury. He's the organization's catcher of the future, and barring a significant offseason move, nobody stands in his way for the starting job in 2014.

Year	Club (League)	Class	AVG	G	AB	R	H	2B	3B	HR	RBI	BB	SO	SB	CS	OBP	SLG
2007	Phillies (GCL)	R	.241	41	141	18	34	3	0	4	20	4	23	4	2	.278	.348
2008	Williamsport (NYP)	SS	.309	48	175	21	54	13	1	4	25	18	29	1	2	.371	.463
	Lakewood (SAL)	LoA	.297	16	64	12	19	5	0	2	5	5	10	0	0	.357	.469
2009	Lakewood (SAL)	LoA	.255	126	482	71	123	38	1	13	71	41	75	8	4	.319	.419
2010	Dunedin (FSL)	HiA	.259	71	263	36	68	20	1	6	38	20	63	3	1	.315	.411
2011	New Hampshire (EL)	AA	.311	114	424	72	132	33	1	21	78	33	100	4	2	.371	.542
2012	Las Vegas (PCL)	AAA	.333	67	279	45	93	21	2	16	52	19	59	1	1	.380	.595
2013	Mets (GCL)	R	.318	6	22	4	7	3	0	0	5	1	2	0	0	.348	.455
	Binghamton (EL)	AA	.222	7	27	2	6	2	1	1	3	3	9	0	0	.300	.481
	Las Vegas (PCL)	AAA	.304	19	56	19	17	8	0	2	12	21	12	0	0	.487	.554
	New York (NL)	MAJ	.202	31	99	4	20	3	0	1	5	12	21	0	0	.286	.263
Major League Totals			.202	31	99	4	20	3	0	1	5	12	21	0	0	.286	.263
Minor League Totals			.286	515	1933	300	553	146	7	69	309	165	382	21	12	.347	.476

3 RAFAEL MONTERO, RHP

Born: Oct. 17, 1990. **B-T:** R-R. **Ht.:** 6-0. **Wt.:** 170. **Signed:** Dominican Republic, 2011. **Signed by:** Rafael Perez/Ismael Cruz/Gerardo Cabrera.

Few of the system's top prospects signed with less fanfare than Montero, who turned pro in 2011 as an undersized 20-year-old. Three years later, he's knocking on the door of the big leagues after mastering Double-A and Triple-A. He ranked among the top 30 qualified minor league starters in 2013 in terms of SO/BB ratio (4.29) and home run rate (0.35 per nine innings) despite pitching his home games at the hitter's haven that is Las Vegas in the second half—where he logged a 2.87 ERA a 1.11 WHIP in nine home starts. Montero's work ethic and mound presence stand out as much as his stuff. With long arms and loose limbs, he pounds the zone with fastballs, changeups and sliders delivered from a three-quarters arm slot. Montero sits in the low 90s, works the black on both sides of the plate and keeps enough in reserve to touch 95 mph in a pinch. A solid-average changeup fades away from the barrel of lefthanders. While his low-80s slider can be good at times, it would benefit from tighter rotation and greater depth. Montero's small frame puts off some evaluators, though his plus-plus command and poise are such assets that he defies convention. Montero expects to pitch in the big leagues, and he'll do just that in 2014. In time, he could profile as a good No. 3 starter.

Year	Club (League)	Class	W	L	ERA	G	GS	CG	SV	IP	H	HR	BB	SO	K/9	WHIP	AVG
2011	Mets1 (DSL)	R	1	1	1.00	4	4	0	0	18	7	1	0	20	10.0	0.39	.119
	Mets (GCL)	R	1	2	1.45	7	4	0	1	31	28	0	6	32	9.3	1.10	.228
	Kingsport (APP)	R	2	1	4.24	4	4	0	0	17	17	2	6	9	4.8	1.35	.258
	Brooklyn (NYP)	SS	1	0	3.60	2	0	0	0	5	3	1	1	5	9.0	0.80	.176
2012	Savannah (SAL)	LoA	6	3	2.52	12	12	0	0	71	61	4	8	54	6.8	0.97	.223
	St. Lucie (FSL)	HiA	5	2	2.13	8	8	1	0	51	35	2	11	56	9.9	0.91	.196
2013	Binghamton (EL)	AA	7	3	2.43	11	11	0	0	67	51	2	10	72	9.7	0.92	.204
	Las Vegas (PCL)	AAA	5	4	3.05	16	16	0	0	89	85	4	25	78	7.9	1.24	.254
Minor League Totals			28	16	2.51	64	59	1	1	348	287	16	67	326	8.4	1.02	.220

4 DOMINIC SMITH, 1B

Born: June 15, 1995. **B-T:** L-L. **Ht.:** 6-0. **Wt.:** 185. **Drafted:** HS—Gardena, Calif., 2013 (1st round). **Signed by:** Drew Touissaint.

The Mets drafted a high school position player in the first round for the third straight year in 2013, tabbing Smith with the 11th pick and signing him for $2.6 million, their largest expenditure ever for a prep product. After hitting .196 through his first 51 pro at-bats, Smith batted .328/.424/.448 in his final 33 games in the Rookie-level Gulf Coast League to earn a late bump to Rookie-level Kingsport. Southern California area scouts turned in favorable reviews of Smith's bat and defense at first base throughout his high school career. A sweet lefthanded swing combined with hand-eye coordination and sound pitch recognition all indicate that he will hit for average while posting a high on-base percentage. He hits with authority to his pull side and straight away, and he could mature into a steady 20-homer threat. Smith gets in trouble when his hips drift and he tries to yank everything to right field, so the Mets have worked with him to stay down and through the ball. Though he doesn't run well, he has quick feet, solid arm strength and soft hands, and many see him as a Gold Glove-caliber defender at first base. The Mets love Smith's quick bat and say he's much more athletic than he appears, so he could jump to low Class A Savannah to begin the 2014 season. He has the ingredients to develop into a first-division first baseman.

Year	Club (League)	Class	AVG	G	AB	R	H	2B	3B	HR	RBI	BB	SO	SB	CS	OBP	SLG
2013	Mets (GCL)	R	.287	48	167	23	48	9	1	3	22	24	37	2	4	.384	.407
	Kingsport (APP)	R	.667	3	6	2	4	4	0	0	4	2	0	0	0	.750	1.333
Minor League Totals			.301	51	173	25	52	13	1	3	26	26	37	2	4	.398	.439

5 KEVIN PLAWECKI, C/1B

Born: Feb. 26, 1991. **B-T:** R-R. **Ht.:** 6-2. **Wt.:** 205. **Drafted:** Purdue, 2012 (1st round supplemental). **Signed by:** Scott Trcka.

Plawecki struck out just 29 times in three seasons at Purdue, and he continued to show fine bat control after signing for $1.4 million as the 35th pick in the 2012 draft. He walked more often than he whiffed in his pro debut, then hit .305/.390/.448 at two Class A stops in 2013. Plawecki can drive the ball to his pull side or take breaking balls the other way, and he seldom strikes out. He's a safe bet to hit .280 with a dozen homers at his peak. Plawecki receives the ball well and despite a large frame has enough agility to have allowed just five passed balls in 88 games behind the plate. His arm earns fringe-average to average grades, and he threw out 29 percent of basestealers, an average rate. He needs to do a better job of reading opposing batters to help his pitchers get through tough spots, but he has good hands and sets a nice target. If he can handle the demands of catching 100 games a year, then Plawecki has the bat to profile as a starting catcher. It not, he could be a valuable part-timer behind the plate and at first base, especially if he continues to crush lefthanders as he did in 2013 (.981 OPS). He'll begin the 2014 season at Double-A and might make his Mets debut the following season.

Year	Club (League)	Class	AVG	G	AB	R	H	2B	3B	HR	RBI	BB	SO	SB	CS	OBP	SLG
2012	Brooklyn (NYP)	SS	.250	61	216	26	54	8	0	7	27	25	24	0	0	.345	.384
2013	Savannah (SAL)	LoA	.314	65	245	35	77	24	1	6	43	23	32	1	0	.390	.494
	St. Lucie (FSL)	HiA	.294	60	204	25	60	14	0	2	37	19	21	0	0	.391	.392
Minor League Totals			.287	186	665	86	191	46	1	15	107	67	77	1	0	.376	.427

6 WILMER FLORES, 2B/3B

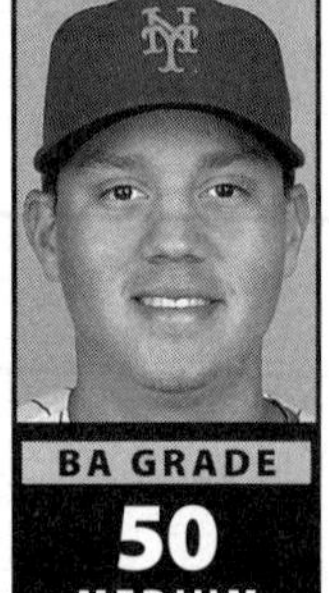

Born: Aug. 6, 1991. **B-T:** R-R. **Ht.:** 6-3. **Wt.:** 190. **Signed:** Venezuela, 2007. **Signed by:** Sandy Johnson/Ismael Cruz/Robert Alfonzo.

Flores has been the standard bearer for the Mets' international program since he signed for $750,000 in 2007. He continued to raise the bar on his offensive production in 2013, posting career bests for OPS (.887) and extra-base hits (55). The Mets called him up on Aug. 6 to fill in for injured third baseman David Wright. Flores began turning on the inside pitch for home run power in 2012, though his natural power stroke carries the ball to right-center field. While he still doesn't work many deep counts, he has impressive bat control and the hand-eye coordination to hit different pitch types to all fields. Flores has spent the bulk of the past two seasons at third (2012) and second (2013) base as the Mets try to find him a defensive home. A bottom-of-the-scale runner, he lacks any semblance of first-step quickness, though his hands are sure and his arm strong enough for any infield post. Big league pitchers, particularly lefties, had success expanding Flores' strike zone, but his minor league track record suggests he will hit for at least fringe-average power. He may begin 2014 back at Triple-A Las Vegas, but if he hits then the Mets will find playing-time opportunities for him.

Year	Club (League)	Class	AVG	G	AB	R	H	2B	3B	HR	RBI	BB	SO	SB	CS	OBP	SLG
2008	Kingsport (APP)	R	.310	59	245	36	76	12	4	8	41	12	28	2	1	.352	.490
	Savannah (SAL)	LoA	.400	1	5	1	2	0	0	0	0	0	2	0	0	.400	.400
	Brooklyn (NYP)	SS	.267	8	30	3	8	1	0	0	1	1	7	0	0	.290	.300
2009	Savannah (SAL)	LoA	.264	125	488	44	129	20	2	3	36	22	72	3	3	.305	.332
2010	Savannah (SAL)	LoA	.278	66	277	30	77	18	2	7	44	23	37	2	1	.342	.433
	St. Lucie (FSL)	HiA	.300	67	277	32	83	18	1	4	40	9	40	2	4	.324	.415
2011	St. Lucie (FSL)	HiA	.269	133	516	52	139	26	2	9	81	27	68	2	2	.309	.380
2012	St. Lucie (FSL)	HiA	.289	64	242	31	70	12	0	10	42	18	30	3	2	.336	.463
	Binghamton (EL)	AA	.311	66	251	37	78	18	2	8	33	20	30	0	0	.361	.494
2013	Las Vegas (PCL)	AAA	.321	107	424	69	136	36	4	15	86	25	63	1	3	.357	.531
	New York (NL)	MAJ	.211	27	95	8	20	5	0	1	13	5	23	0	0	.248	.295
Major League Totals			.211	27	95	8	20	5	0	1	13	5	23	0	0	.248	.295
Minor League Totals			.290	696	2755	335	798	161	17	64	404	157	377	15	16	.331	.430

7 AMED ROSARIO, SS

Born: Nov. 20, 1995. **B-T:** R-R. **Ht.:** 6-2. **Wt.:** 170. **Signed:** Dominican Republic, 2012. **Signed by:** Chris Becerra/Gerardo Cabrera.

Rosario's tools and makeup prompted the Mets to sign him for $1.75 million, the largest international signing bonus in franchise history. He wowed the Mets during instructional league in 2012 and then played so well in spring training that the 17-year-old earned a ticket straight to Rookie-level Kingsport, where he ranked as the circuit's top prospect. Fluid actions, supreme body control and above-average speed and quickness could allow Rosario to remain at shortstop if he can gain consistency. He makes strong throws from all angles, so he could handle third base if needed. Rosario whips the bat through the hitting zone and already drives the ball with authority from his pull side to right-center field, so more power will come as he fills out his lean frame. Like most young hitters, he must learn to shorten his swing and improve his pitch selection and discipline. He runs well, so he could add stolen bases to his portfolio, but it won't dictate his future value. Rosario offers a more exciting package of tools than 2012 first-round shortstop Gavin Cecchini, though he may have to play one level behind him as they progress through the system. If the Mets follow recent precedent, then Rosario will be bound for short-season Brooklyn in 2014.

Year	Club (League)	Class	AVG	G	AB	R	H	2B	3B	HR	RBI	BB	SO	SB	CS	OBP	SLG
2013	Kingsport (APP)	R	.241	58	212	22	51	8	4	3	23	11	43	2	6	.279	.358
Minor League Totals			.241	58	212	22	51	8	4	3	23	11	43	2	6	.279	.358

8 BRANDON NIMMO, OF

Born: March 27, 1993. **B-T:** L-R. **Ht.:** 6-3. **Wt.:** 185. **Drafted:** HS—Cheyenne, Wyo., 2011 (1st round). **Signed by:** Jim Reeves.

Wyoming high schools don't field baseball teams, so when Nimmo entered pro ball as the first-ever first-rounder from the Cowboy State, he had much less game experience than many in his draft class. Yet Nimmo's game is surprisingly refined, and he ranked third in the low Class A South Atlantic League with 71 walks and fourth with a .397 on-base percentage in 2013 while making his full-season debut. Nimmo does a little bit of everything well but may lack a carrying tool that would make him an unquestioned first-division regular. He played center field at Savannah, though scouts envision him settling in at a corner because he's an average runner. They like his strong lefthanded stroke, and given his plate discipline, expect him to hit for a solid average even though he struck out more than a quarter of the time in 2013. His current approach is geared more toward rifling balls to the gaps, but his physicality and patience give him home run potential. He went deep just twice for the Sand Gnats, however, thanks to a bruised left hand that bothered him for much of the first half and a spacious home park in Savannah, where Sand Gnats lefty hitters combined to hit three home runs all year. Some scouts see Nimmo as a left fielder who will reach base, rack up doubles and pop 15 or so homers a year. He's probably three full years away from New York and will likely begin 2014 at high Class A St. Lucie.

Year	Club (League)	Class	AVG	G	AB	R	H	2B	3B	HR	RBI	BB	SO	SB	CS	OBP	SLG
2011	Mets (GCL)	R	.241	7	29	5	7	0	0	2	4	3	9	0	0	.313	.448
	Kingsport (APP)	R	.111	3	9	0	1	0	0	0	0	3	5	0	0	.333	.111
2012	Brooklyn (NYP)	SS	.248	69	266	41	66	20	2	6	40	46	78	1	5	.372	.406
2013	Savannah (SAL)	LoA	.273	110	395	62	108	16	6	2	40	71	131	10	7	.397	.359
Minor League Totals			.260	189	699	108	182	36	8	10	84	123	223	11	12	.383	.378

9 GAVIN CECCHINI, SS

BA GRADE **50** HIGH

Born: Dec. 22, 1993. **B-T:** R-R. **Ht.:** 6-1. **Wt.:** 180. **Drafted:** HS—Lake Charles, La., 2012 (1st round). **Signed by:** Tommy Jackson.

Cecchini charted a similar course as older brother Garin, a third baseman in the Red Sox system, when he reported to the short-season New York-Penn League one year after signing. For the second straight season, an injury cut into Cecchini's playing time. After missing time with a broken finger in 2012, he missed most of July 2013 after badly spraining his left ankle on a slide into second base. He hit .324/.378/.370 in 28 August games after returning from the disabled list. More of a slap hitter who serves the ball the other way now, Cecchini projects to add strength and hit with more authority to his pull side. If he does so, he can become an above-average hitter with below-average power. Despite being no more than an average runner, he has room to grow as a basestealer. Cecchini's defensive play, instincts and competitiveness are his calling cards. He converts all the plays at shortstop—slow rollers, hard shots to his backhand—making use of solid-average range, fluid actions, quick hands and a strong arm. Cecchini's ticket to the big leagues will be his ability to play shortstop, but he's likely four full years away from reaching that ceiling. He'll suit up for low Class A Savannah to begin 2014, watching Amed Rosario chase him up the organizational ladder.

Year	Club (League)	Class	AVG	G	AB	R	H	2B	3B	HR	RBI	BB	SO	SB	CS	OBP	SLG
2012	Kingsport (APP)	R	.246	53	191	21	47	9	2	1	22	18	43	5	4	.311	.330
	Brooklyn (NYP)	SS	.000	5	5	2	0	0	0	0	0	0	1	0	0	.167	.000
2013	Brooklyn (NYP)	SS	.273	51	194	18	53	8	0	0	14	14	30	2	3	.319	.314
Minor League Totals			.256	109	390	41	100	17	2	1	36	32	74	7	7	.313	.318

10 JAKE DEGROM, RHP

BA GRADE **50** HIGH

Born: June 19, 1988. **B-T:** L-R. **Ht.:** 6-4. **Wt.:** 185. **Drafted:** Stetson, 2010 (9th round). **Signed by:** Steve Nichols.

DeGrom began his college career as the starting shortstop for Stetson before transitioning to the mound as a junior, first serving as closer before moving into the rotation down the stretch in 2010. He has completed four levels of the full-season minors in two years, after missing the entire 2011 season while rehabbing from Tommy John surgery he had the previous fall. DeGrom succeeds by pounding the zone and showing a clean arm action and bulldog mentality. He threw nearly two-thirds of his pitches for strikes in 2013, though he would benefit form expanding the zone and getting batters to chase when he gets ahead in the count. He sits at 92-94 mph with plus sinking life, and he can rear back for 98 when he needs it. DeGrom made progress with a straight changeup this season, giving him a good weapon against lefties, though he misses more bats against righties with a fastball and slurvy breaking ball. He's working on improving the rotation and bite of his breaking ball. After logging a combined 148 innings in 2013, deGrom has put his surgery completely behind him. An offseason addition to the 40-man roster, he likely will begin 2014 at Triple-A Las Vegas, flying standby for the big league rotation. He has a ceiling as a No. 4 starter or better.

Year	Club (League)	Class	W	L	ERA	G	GS	CG	SV	IP	H	HR	BB	SO	K/9	WHIP	AVG
2010	Kingsport (APP)	R	1	1	5.19	6	6	0	0	26	35	2	6	22	7.6	1.58	.324
2011	Did not play—Injured																
2012	Savannah (SAL)	LoA	6	3	2.51	15	15	0	0	90	77	3	14	78	7.8	1.01	.225
	St. Lucie (FSL)	HiA	3	0	2.08	4	4	0	0	22	14	1	6	18	7.5	0.92	.177
2013	St. Lucie (FSL)	HiA	1	0	3.00	2	2	0	0	12	12	1	2	13	9.8	1.17	.261
	Binghamton (EL)	AA	2	5	4.80	10	10	0	0	60	69	4	20	44	6.6	1.48	.295
	Las Vegas (PCL)	AAA	4	2	4.52	14	14	0	0	76	87	6	24	63	7.5	1.47	.288
Minor League Totals			17	11	3.76	51	51	0	0	285	294	17	72	238	7.5	1.28	.265

11 CESAR PUELLO, OF

BA GRADE **50** HIGH

Born: April 1, 1991. **B-T:** R-R. **Ht.:** 6-2. **Wt.:** 195. **Signed:** Dominican Republic, 2007. **Signed by:** Ismael Cruz/Marciano Alvarez.

Myriad bumps and bruises have sidetracked Puello's development since he signed for $400,000 six years ago, but the biggest disruptor yet came down the pike last Aug. 5 when he accepted a 50-game suspension for violating the joint drug agreement. His name—and 16 others—surfaced in MLB's investigation of the Miami-based Biogenesis clinic that supplied performance-enhancers to athletes, most notably Ryan Braun and Alex Rodriguez. In a statement, Puello admitted to "errors in judgment" during the 2012 season, a year in which he was plagued by hamstring trouble and a fractured hamate bone in his left wrist. Prior to his suspension, Puello had enjoyed a breakthrough season at the plate in his first go at Double-A Binghamton. Scouts have long projected him to hit for corner-profile power because the ball explodes off his bat, and as proof the righthanded hitter slammed eight of 16 Eastern League homers to either center or right field. Puello takes a big, aggressive hack, but he showed improved pitch recognition in 2013, laying off breaking balls he would have swung at before. He improved the load in his swing by moving his hands away from his body during setup, and it paid off when he won the EL batting (.326) and slugging (.547) titles. Puello runs well enough to steal double-digit bases, has good range and a strong arm in right field. He returned to play in the Dominican League, though he struggled there. His suspension behind him, Puello has one option year remaining to prove to the Mets his 2013 performance was no fluke, chemically-induced or otherwise.

Year	Club (League)	Class	AVG	G	AB	R	H	2B	3B	HR	RBI	BB	SO	SB	CS	OBP	SLG
2008	Mets (GCL)	R	.305	40	151	24	46	6	0	1	17	5	32	13	5	.350	.364
2009	Kingsport (APP)	R	.296	49	196	37	58	10	0	5	23	10	51	15	5	.373	.423
2010	Savannah (SAL)	LoA	.292	109	404	80	118	22	1	1	34	32	82	45	10	.375	.359
2011	St. Lucie (FSL)	HiA	.259	117	441	67	114	21	5	10	50	18	103	19	9	.313	.397
2012	St. Lucie (FSL)	HiA	.260	66	227	36	59	17	4	4	21	7	58	19	2	.328	.423
2013	Binghamton (EL)	AA	.326	91	331	63	108	21	2	16	73	28	82	24	7	.403	.547
Minor League Totals			.287	472	1750	307	503	97	12	37	218	100	408	135	38	.357	.420

12 STEVE MATZ, LHP

BA GRADE
60
EXTREME

Born: May 29, 1991. **B-T:** R-L. **Ht.:** 6-2. **Wt.:** 192. **Drafted:** HS—East Setauket, N.Y., 2009 (2nd round). **Signed by:** Larry Izzo Jr.

Matz offers a power arm worth waiting for, which is good because that's exactly what the Mets have been forced to do. Four years after being drafted, he finally reached low Class A Savannah, where he made 23 starts including the playoffs. The top Northeast pitching prospect for the 2009 draft, Matz signed for $895,000 as the Mets' top pick (second round) but then had Tommy John surgery in May 2010 that knocked him out for two entire seasons. He made his pro debut in 2012 by making six mostly-electric starts for Rookie-level Kingsport. Scouts reported seeing three plus pitches in some of Matz's best 2013 starts. He sits 93-94 mph and tops out near 96 with his riding four-seamer, while also sinking his fastball at about 90 with a two-seam grip he added in 2013. He sells a plus circle changeup with terrific arm speed, while taking to a buzzsaw curve in 2013 that sits 78-80 mph and breaks straight down. He doesn't always repeat the rotation on the breaking ball, but it could be a plus pitch in time. Matz pitches with a long stride that helps him leverage the ball down in the zone, and scouts regard his delivery and arm action as positive attributes. Despite a lengthy injury history, Matz unleashes uncommonly good stuff with late life from the left side. He could mature into a No. 2 or 3 starter if he stays healthy, making him the ultimate lottery ticket. He'll move to high Class A St. Lucie in 2014.

Year	Club (League)	Class	W	L	ERA	G	GS	CG	SV	IP	H	HR	BB	SO	K/9	WHIP	AVG
2010	Did not play—Injured																
2011	Did not play—Injured																
2012	Kingsport (APP)	R	2	1	1.55	6	6	0	0	29	16	1	17	34	10.6	1.14	.158
2013	Savannah (SAL)	LoA	5	6	2.62	21	21	1	0	106	86	4	38	121	10.2	1.17	.225
Minor League Totals			7	7	2.39	27	27	1	0	135	102	5	55	155	10.3	1.16	.211

13 DILSON HERRERA, 2B

BA GRADE
50
HIGH

Born: March 3, 1994. **B-T:** R-R. **Ht.:** 5-10. **Wt.:** 150. **Signed:** Colombia, 2010. **Signed by:** Rene Gayo/Orlando Covo (Pirates).

The Pirates had scouted Herrera in his native Colombia since he was 12 years old, finally signing him for $220,000 in 2010. He made a boisterous U.S. debut in 2012 by hitting .281 and leading the Rookie-level Gulf Coast League with 22 extra-base hits, and then he represented the Pirates at the 2013 Future Game. A late-August trade landed Herrera and reliever Vic Black with the Mets and Marlon Byrd and John Buck with the Pirates. A high-energy player who endeared himself right away to his new teammates, Herrera could develop into an offensive-minded second baseman. He's worked hard to clean up his actions at the keystone, and though some South Atlantic League managers didn't like his stiff actions or transfer, most evaluators think he's quick enough and throws well enough to profile at the position. Herrera really shines in the batter's box, where a balanced, all-fields hitting approach and lots of hard contact enable him to hit for a solid average. He gets in trouble when he enters pull mode and expands his zone, but he has enough juice for average power. He runs well despite a stocky frame. Herrera sports many 50 grades on his report card and could be major league ready by 2016, but first he'll take on the high Class A Florida State League in 2014.

Year	Club (League)	Class	AVG	G	AB	R	H	2B	3B	HR	RBI	BB	SO	SB	CS	OBP	SLG
2011	Pirates (VSL)	R	.308	65	214	42	66	19	5	2	27	32	40	16	8	.413	.472
2012	Pirates (GCL)	R	.281	53	199	41	56	11	4	7	27	18	41	11	4	.341	.482
	State College (NYP)	SS	.321	7	28	7	9	1	1	1	2	1	6	1	0	.345	.536
2013	West Virginia (SAL)	LoA	.265	109	423	69	112	27	3	11	56	37	110	11	6	.330	.421
	Savannah (SAL)	LoA	.316	7	19	6	6	0	0	0	4	3	6	3	0	.417	.316
Minor League Totals			.282	241	883	165	249	58	13	21	116	91	203	42	18	.356	.448

14 MICHAEL FULMER, RHP

Born: March 15, 1993. **B-T:** R-R. **Ht.:** 6-3. **Wt.:** 200. **Drafted:** HS—Edmond, Okla., 2011 (1st round supplemental). **Signed by:** Steve Gossett.

Many pitchers endure a lost year on their climb up the minor league ladder, and Fulmer got his out of the way in 2013. He had surgery on his right knee during spring training to repair a torn meniscus, and the procedure sidelined him for the first three months of the season. After a pair of rehab outings, Fulmer debuted with high Class A St. Lucie on July 7, but he didn't have his legs under him initially, showing reduced velocity. He recovered his stuff in August, topping out near 95 mph with running action and sinking the ball at 92-93 low in the zone. He reinjured his knee after just seven starts, however, and didn't return to the mound. A mid-80s slider with reliable two-plane tilt is Fulmer's preferred secondary weapon, and when it's on, righties can't touch it. Scouts see enough promise with his changeup to project it to future average, though they don't universally like his direction to the plate or soft-bodied physique. For that reason, many see him as a future reliever, but potentially an effective one. With good health, he'll reach Double-A Binghamton by the end of the 2014 season.

Year	Club (League)	Class	W	L	ERA	G	GS	CG	SV	IP	H	HR	BB	SO	K/9	WHIP	AVG
2011	Mets (GCL)	R	0	1	10.13	4	3	0	0	5	9	0	4	10	16.9	2.44	.346
2012	Savannah (SAL)	LoA	7	6	2.74	21	21	1	0	108	92	6	38	101	8.4	1.20	.227
2013	Mets (GCL)	R	1	1	3.00	2	2	0	0	12	9	0	1	13	9.8	0.83	.205
	St. Lucie (FSL)	HiA	2	2	3.44	7	7	0	0	34	24	1	18	29	7.7	1.24	.198
Minor League Totals			10	10	3.16	34	33	1	0	160	134	7	61	153	8.6	1.22	.225

15 GABRIEL YNOA, RHP

Born: May 26, 1993. **B-T:** R-R. **Ht.:** 6-2. **Wt.:** 160. **Signed:** Dominican Republic, 2009. **Signed by:** Rafael Perez/Ismael Cruz/Modesto Abreu.

The low Class A Savannah pitching staff led the full-season minors with 4.3 strikeouts for every walk in 2013, and Ynoa was a major reason for that gaudy ratio. He issued fewer walks per nine innings (1.1) than any qualified minor league starter in 2013, pulling down the South Atlantic League's pitcher of the year award. Tall and lean, Ynoa has a quiet delivery and a quiet demeanor that sees him through good times and bad. His two-seam fastball sits in the low 90s with sink, and he can bump his four-seamer up to 94 mph with riding life to his arm side. Ynoa's go-to secondary pitch is a double-plus changeup that batters struggle to read because of textbook arm action for the pitch. Scouts want to see a firmer breaking ball before pegging him as more than back-end starter, but some believe he can improve his low-80s slider by simply slowing down his delivery and staying on top of the pitch. He's headed for high Class A St. Lucie in 2014.

Year	Club (League)	Class	W	L	ERA	G	GS	CG	SV	IP	H	HR	BB	SO	K/9	WHIP	AVG
2010	Mets2 (DSL)	R	5	3	1.99	14	12	1	0	72	63	1	8	35	4.4	0.98	.243
2011	Mets (GCL)	R	2	3	3.00	10	7	0	0	48	51	1	4	21	3.9	1.15	.277
	Kingsport (APP)	R	0	0	4.50	2	0	0	1	8	6	4	0	6	6.8	0.75	.207
2012	Brooklyn (NYP)	SS	5	2	2.23	13	13	0	0	77	61	1	10	64	7.5	0.93	.213
2013	Savannah (SAL)	LoA	15	4	2.72	22	22	1	0	136	123	9	16	106	7.0	1.02	.238
Minor League Totals			27	12	2.54	61	54	2	1	341	304	16	38	232	6.1	1.00	.239

16 CORY MAZZONI, RHP

BA GRADE
45
MEDIUM

Born: Oct. 19, 1989. **B-T:** R-R. **Ht.:** 6-1. **Wt.:** 190. **Drafted:** North Carolina State, 2011 (2nd round). **Signed by:** Marlin MacPhail.

Mazzoni's rapid transit from the second round of the 2011 draft to the big leagues took a detour in 2013, when he dealt with problems in his right knee that knocked him out of action in April, July and then for good in early August when he had surgery to repair a torn meniscus. He fires low-90s sinkers and low-80s sliders in quick succession from a three-quarters arm slot, though he can dial his heater up to 95 mph with cutting action as necessary. His slider features depth and late break when it's working. Mazzoni gained confidence in a low-80s splitter that sinks as it nears the plate. Many scouts have pegged him as a bullpen candidate because of a long, hooking arm action and because his stuff tends to lose crispness late in his starts. He also tends to emphasize his fastball at the expense of developing his secondary pitches, which could further indicate a future role change. The Mets expect Mazzoni to be at full strength during spring training, and if that's the case then he could begin at Triple-A Las Vegas and make his big league debut during the season. He could be a No. 4 type starter or a late-inning reliever.

Year	Club (League)	Class	W	L	ERA	G	GS	CG	SV	IP	H	HR	BB	SO	K/9	WHIP	AVG
2011	Brooklyn (NYP)	SS	1	0	0.00	6	1	0	0	6	5	0	2	10	15.0	1.17	.238
	St. Lucie (FSL)	HiA	1	1	2.57	6	0	0	0	7	7	1	1	8	10.3	1.14	.250
2012	St. Lucie (FSL)	HiA	5	1	3.25	12	12	0	0	64	64	3	16	48	6.8	1.26	.264
	Binghamton (EL)	AA	5	5	4.46	14	14	2	0	81	90	9	20	56	6.2	1.36	.281
2013	Binghamton (EL)	AA	5	3	4.36	13	12	0	0	66	70	4	19	74	10.1	1.35	.275
Minor League Totals			17	10	3.91	51	39	2	0	223	236	17	58	196	7.9	1.32	.273

17 VIC BLACK, RHP

BA GRADE **45** MEDIUM

Born: May 23, 1988. **B-T:** R-R. **Ht.:** 6-4. **Wt.:** 215. **Drafted:** Dallas Baptist, 2009 (1st round supplemental). **Signed by:** Mike Leuzinger (Pirates).

Mets general manager Sandy Alderson has excelled at maximizing the value of veterans on expiring contracts, exchanging them at peak value for prospects. He famously acquired Zack Wheeler for Carlos Beltran in 2011, both Noah Syndergaard and Travis d'Arnaud for R.A. Dickey in 2012 and, most recently, Dilson Herrera and Black for veterans Marlon Byrd and John Buck in 2013. Black pitched erratically and sporadically in the Pirates system until talking flight in 2012, when he led Double-A Eastern League relievers in opponent average (.189) and strikeouts per nine innings (12.8). Black has two plus weapons at his disposal that both generate swings and misses in great volume. He pitches at 95 mph with plus armside life, and he can rear back for 97 in tight spots. His mid-80s curveball features so much depth and power when it's sharp that neither righties nor lefties can touch it. Black's control is below-average, but that won't be much of a hindrance in a late-inning relief role so long as he continues to miss bats. After making 15 September appearances for the Mets in 2013, he's ready for a full-time role.

Year	Club (League)	Class	W	L	ERA	G	GS	CG	SV	IP	H	HR	BB	SO	K/9	WHIP	AVG
2009	State College (NYP)	SS	1	2	3.45	13	7	0	1	31	26	0	15	33	9.5	1.31	.213
2010	West Virginia (SAL)	LoA	0	0	9.64	2	2	0	0	5	3	1	5	8	15.4	1.71	.176
2011	West Virginia (SAL)	LoA	2	1	5.28	22	0	0	1	29	30	0	16	23	7.1	1.59	.268
	Bradenton (FSL)	HiA	1	0	4.05	5	0	0	0	7	8	1	4	5	6.8	1.80	.333
2012	Altoona (EL)	AA	2	3	1.65	51	0	0	13	60	40	2	29	85	12.8	1.15	.189
2013	Pittsburgh (NL)	MAJ	0	0	4.50	3	0	0	0	4	6	0	2	3	6.8	2.00	.333
	Indianapolis (IL)	AAA	5	3	2.51	38	0	0	17	47	28	2	21	63	12.2	1.05	.169
	New York (NL)	MAJ	3	0	3.46	15	0	0	1	13	11	1	4	12	8.3	1.15	.224
Major League Totals			3	0	3.71	18	0	0	1	17	17	1	6	15	7.9	1.35	.254
Minor League Totals			11	9	3.08	131	9	0	32	178	135	6	90	217	11.0	1.26	.207

18 JEURYS FAMILIA, RHP

BA GRADE **45** MEDIUM

Born: Oct. 10, 1989. **B-T:** R-R. **Ht.:** 6-4. **Wt.:** 230. **Signed:** Dominican Republic, 2007. **Signed by:** Ismael Cruz/Marcelino Vallejo.

Following Familia's powerful-but-wild year in the Triple-A Buffalo rotation in 2012, the Mets shifted him to the bullpen and expected him to blossom in 2013. He looked sharp at Triple-A Las Vegas initially, but elbow soreness cropped up in May while in the big leagues and he ultimately succumbed to surgery to remove bone chips. Familia missed June, July and August, then made just three September appearances, though he headed to the Arizona Fall League to recover innings. He still shows the same tantalizing attributes that made him the organization's pitcher of the year in 2009: mid-90s velocity with power sink, a strong work ethic and a pair of interesting secondary pitches. Everything Familia throws features late, crisp action, including his live 94-96 mph fastball that touched 99 in the AFL and a high-80s slider that often behaves like a cutter. He's getting better at commanding a spread-finger changeup that behaves like a splitter. A physical righthander with hard-to-repeat mechanics and slow times to the plate, Familia could see a lot of big league time in 2014, though he has one option remaining if more minor league seasoning is required.

Year	Club (League)	Class	W	L	ERA	G	GS	CG	SV	IP	H	HR	BB	SO	K/9	WHIP	AVG
2008	Mets (GCL)	R	2	2	2.79	11	11	0	0	52	46	2	13	38	6.6	1.14	.232
2009	Savannah (SAL)	LoA	10	6	2.69	24	23	0	0	134	109	3	46	109	7.3	1.16	.221
2010	St. Lucie (FSL)	HiA	6	9	5.58	24	24	0	0	121	117	7	74	137	10.2	1.58	.257
2011	St. Lucie (FSL)	HiA	1	1	1.49	6	6	0	0	36	21	1	8	36	8.9	0.80	.171
	Binghamton (EL)	AA	4	4	3.49	17	17	0	0	88	85	10	35	96	9.9	1.37	.249
2012	Buffalo (IL)	AAA	9	9	4.73	28	28	1	0	137	145	8	73	128	8.4	1.59	.267
	New York (NL)	MAJ	0	0	5.84	8	1	0	0	12	10	0	9	10	7.3	1.54	.233
2013	Las Vegas (PCL)	AAA	0	0	0.00	4	0	0	1	5	5	0	1	4	7.2	1.20	.278
	St. Lucie (FSL)	HiA	0	1	3.00	3	1	0	0	3	2	0	2	3	9.0	1.33	.182
	Brooklyn (NYP)	SS	0	0	0.00	1	1	0	0	1	1	0	0	0	0.0	1.00	.250
	New York (NL)	MAJ	0	0	4.22	9	0	0	1	11	12	2	9	8	6.8	1.97	.293
Major League Totals			0	0	5.09	17	1	0	1	23	22	2	18	18	7.0	1.74	.262
Minor League Totals			32	32	3.81	118	111	1	1	577	531	31	252	551	8.6	1.36	.243

19 DOMINGO TAPIA, RHP

BA GRADE **50** EXTREME

Born: Dec. 16, 1991. **B-T:** R-R. **Ht.:** 6-4. **Wt.:** 186. **Signed:** Dominican Republic, 2009. **Signed by:** Rafael Perez/Ismael Cruz/Camilo Pina/Sandy Rosario.

Because he's 6-foot-4 and tops out at 98 mph with plus sinking life, Tapia could have a higher ceiling than any prospect outside the top 10. However, he struggled badly with his command in 2013, finishing with 5.6 walks per nine innings and a career-worst SO/BB ratio (1.4). Tapia tended to speed up his mechanics and miss up and away, and as the walks piled up he tried to throw harder to escape jams. Add to that the fact that 24 of 30 basestealers succeeded on their attempts and Tapia frequently lost focus and confidence. On the positive side, he pitches at 93-95 mph with long, loose arms, and his high-80s slider also showed more power and depth than it had in the past, while his changeup continued to be a reliable No. 2 offering. Many scouts see Tapia's future in the bullpen, and they saw no reason to alter that evaluation in 2013.

Year	Club (League)	Class	W	L	ERA	G	GS	CG	SV	IP	H	HR	BB	SO	K/9	WHIP	AVG
2009	Did not play																
2010	Mets1 (DSL)	R	0	1	3.09	3	3	0	0	12	8	0	5	5	3.9	1.11	.195
	Mets (GCL)	R	4	3	3.45	10	10	0	0	47	49	0	10	29	5.6	1.26	.269
2011	Kingsport (APP)	R	5	5	3.78	11	11	0	0	50	50	3	16	30	5.4	1.32	.258
	Brooklyn (NYP)	SS	1	0	0.00	1	1	0	0	6	5	0	0	6	9.0	0.83	.227
2012	Savannah (SAL)	LoA	6	5	3.98	20	19	0	0	109	92	2	32	101	8.4	1.14	.227
2013	St. Lucie (FSL)	HiA	3	9	4.62	23	22	0	0	101	87	3	63	89	7.9	1.48	.231
Minor League Totals			19	23	3.96	68	66	0	0	325	291	8	126	260	7.2	1.28	.238

20 LOGAN VERRETT, RHP

BA GRADE **45** MEDIUM

Born: June 19, 1990. **B-T:** R-R. **Ht.:** 6-2. **Wt.:** 180. **Drafted:** Baylor, 2011 (3rd round). **Signed by:** Max Semler.

Drafted in successive rounds in 2011, Verrett and Cory Mazzoni share many traits in common. Both are tall, lean college righthanders who sport exemplary control. Verrett attacks the zone with a four-pitch mix where each offering grades out near average, with scouts favoring his slider due to its late three-quarters break at 83-85 mph. His low-80s changeup often features late fade to his arm side, though his typical 89-91 mph fastball velocity affords batters time to foul off the heater if they're sitting offspeed. Verrett can dial up his fastball a few ticks out of the bullpen, and given that he throws across his body and gets hit hard by lefties (.453 slugging in 2013) a role change could be in his future. On the other hand, he also drops in a low-80s curve and proved his durability by working 146 innings in 2013. Verrett is ready for Triple-A, though he would have to leapfrog the system's higher-ceiling prospects at Las Vegas to get more than a cursory look in New York in 2014.

Year	Club (League)	Class	W	L	ERA	G	GS	CG	SV	IP	H	HR	BB	SO	K/9	WHIP	AVG
2012	Savannah (SAL)	LoA	3	2	3.06	11	11	1	0	65	57	7	9	67	9.3	1.02	.228
	St. Lucie (FSL)	HiA	2	0	2.09	6	6	1	0	39	30	4	4	26	6.1	0.88	.205
2013	Binghamton (EL)	AA	12	6	4.25	24	24	0	0	146	136	21	31	132	8.1	1.14	.249
Minor League Totals			17	8	3.61	41	41	2	0	249	223	32	44	225	8.1	1.07	.237

21 GONZALEZ GERMEN, RHP

BA GRADE **40** LOW

Born: Sept. 23, 1987. **B-T:** R-R. **Ht.:** 6-2. **Wt.:** 200. **Signed:** Dominican Republic, 2007. **Signed by:** Ismael Cruz/Ramon Pena/Sandy Rosario.

The Mets signed both Germen (age 20) and Jeurys Familia (17) as passed-over players out of the Dominican Republic in 2007, and they eventually got both to the big leagues. Germen moved to the bullpen in 2013 at Triple-A Las Vegas and made his big league debut in mid-July. He brandishes two plus pitches and great control, giving him a strong relief profile. His low-80s changeup, the best in the system, dives and evades bats as it nears the plate. Batters try to make early-count contact so they don't have to contend with the double-plus pitch. In a relief role, Germen sits comfortably at 93-94 mph with tailing, two-seam life. He was uncharacteristically wild in the big leagues until September, when he brandished a 13/3 SO/BB ratio in 10 appearances. Germen could pitch middle relief in the big leagues, and he could be ready to do so in 2014.

Year	Club (League)	Class	W	L	ERA	G	GS	CG	SV	IP	H	HR	BB	SO	K/9	WHIP	AVG
2008	Mets (DSL)	R	5	2	1.34	15	14	0	0	74	41	0	15	70	8.5	0.76	.159
2009	Mets (DSL)	R	5	0	1.80	8	8	0	0	45	31	1	3	54	10.8	0.76	.189
	Mets (GCL)	R	0	1	6.00	2	1	0	0	6	6	1	0	7	10.5	1.00	.250
2010	Kingsport (APP)	R	2	5	3.69	10	10	0	0	61	64	3	11	54	8.0	1.23	.274
	Savannah (SAL)	LoA	1	0	2.77	2	2	1	0	13	11	1	1	10	6.9	0.92	.220
2011	Savannah (SAL)	LoA	7	7	3.93	26	21	0	0	119	126	9	35	111	8.4	1.35	.271
2012	St. Lucie (FSL)	HiA	3	0	3.04	5	4	0	0	27	25	3	8	21	7.1	1.24	.255
	Buffalo (IL)	AAA	1	0	5.14	1	1	0	0	7	7	0	2	3	3.9	1.29	.259
	Binghamton (EL)	AA	8	12	4.59	20	19	0	0	120	127	11	33	97	7.3	1.34	.272
2013	Las Vegas (PCL)	AAA	3	3	5.52	35	0	0	4	44	47	7	11	51	10.4	1.32	.270
	New York (NL)	MAJ	1	2	3.93	29	0	0	1	34	32	1	16	33	8.7	1.40	.241
Major League Totals			1	2	3.93	29	0	0	1	34	32	1	16	33	8.7	1.40	.241
Minor League Totals			35	30	3.60	124	80	1	4	515	485	36	119	478	8.3	1.17	.247

22 LUIS MATEO, RHP

BA GRADE **55** EXTREME

Born: March 22, 1990. **B-T:** R-R. **Ht.:** 6-3. **Wt.:** 185. **Signed:** Dominican Republic, 2011. **Signed by:** Rafael Perez/Ismael Cruz/Sandy Rosario.

Mateo appeared to be a $150,000 bargain in 2012 when he carved up the short-season

New York-Penn League. The reason he came cheaply was because he had contracts with the Giants ($625,000) and Padres ($300,000) dissolved in 2008, and he signed with the Mets on the heels of a one-year suspension received for falsifying his age by two years. The 23-year-old Mateo jumped to high Class A St. Lucie to begin 2013, but elbow pain limited him to four appearances spread over two months. He ultimately had Tommy John surgery in June and won't step back on a mound until late in 2014. Prior to his injury, Mateo had two plus weapons at his disposal: a 92-95 mph fastball and a high-80s power slider that draws some 70 grades from scouts for its tight, late break. Incredible arm strength and sharp control point to a future as a mid-rotation starter or wipeout closer.

Year	Club (League)	Class	W	L	ERA	G	GS	CG	SV	IP	H	HR	BB	SO	K/9	WHIP	AVG
2011	Mets1 (DSL)	R	6	1	2.00	13	13	0	0	63	44	1	5	80	11.4	0.78	.194
2012	Brooklyn (NYP)	SS	4	5	2.45	12	12	0	0	73	57	2	9	85	10.4	0.90	.210
2013	Binghamton (EL)	AA	0	1	12.00	1	1	0	0	3	6	1	3	2	6.0	3.00	.400
	St. Lucie (FSL)	HiA	1	1	4.15	3	1	0	0	9	10	1	3	11	11.4	1.50	.303
Minor League Totals			11	8	2.55	29	27	0	0	148	117	5	20	178	10.8	0.93	.214

23 JACK LEATHERSICH, LHP

BA GRADE
45
HIGH

Born: July 14, 1990. **B-T:** R-L. **Ht.:** 5-11. **Wt.:** 205. **Drafted:** Massachusetts-Lowell, 2011 (5th round). **Signed by:** Art Pontarelli.

Few pitchers revel in missing bats quite like Leathersich, who notched 14.1 strikeouts per nine innings as a reliever across two Class A levels in 2012 before upping the ante in 2013 with 15.7 whiffs per nine at Double-A and Triple-A. That rate that topped all qualified minor league relievers. Unfortunately, Leathersich also walked 6.9 per nine. Batters struggle to pick up—or square up—Leathersich's 92-94 mph tailing fastball, though Triple-A batters did a better job fouling it off while waiting for the southpaw to throw four wide ones. His breaking ball can feature wicked depth at times, but he could improve its consistency by staying back in his delivery. He also mixes in the occasional fringe changeup. Leathersich has the ideal reliever's mentality in that he never backs off, even when he's getting hit. Now he needs to throw more strikes. Remarkably, Leathersich has held righthanded batters to a .170 average in his two years in full-season ball, striking out 40 percent of them.

Year	Club (League)	Class	W	L	ERA	G	GS	CG	SV	IP	H	HR	BB	SO	K/9	WHIP	AVG
2011	Brooklyn (NYP)	SS	0	0	0.71	9	0	0	1	13	6	0	3	26	18.5	0.71	.136
2012	Savannah (SAL)	LoA	0	1	0.75	12	0	0	1	24	10	0	8	37	13.9	0.75	.132
	St. Lucie (FSL)	HiA	2	5	4.13	26	0	0	1	48	41	3	24	76	14.3	1.35	.224
2013	Binghamton (EL)	AA	2	0	1.53	24	0	0	3	29	19	1	16	55	16.9	1.19	.181
	Las Vegas (PCL)	AAA	2	0	7.76	28	0	0	0	29	32	2	29	47	14.6	2.10	.278
Minor League Totals			6	6	3.46	99	0	0	6	143	108	6	80	241	15.2	1.31	.207

24 MATT KOCH, RHP

Born: Nov. 2, 1990. **B-T:** L-R. **Ht.:** 6-3. **Wt.:** 185. **Drafted:** Louisville, 2012 (3rd round). **Signed by:** Jarrett England.

A third-round pick out of Louisville in 2012, Koch signed with the Mets for $425,000 and made 13 appearances for short-season Brooklyn, mostly in relief. Koch joined low Class A Savannah's six-man rotation in 2013 and produced an incredible 17.0 SO/BB ratio before being struck in the head by a comebacker in his Aug. 2 start. He brings an aggressive, reliever-type mentality to the mound, pounding the zone and throwing predominately fastballs with some cutters and sliders mixed in. Koch shows above-average command of a plus 93-95 mph four-seamer and a low-90s two-seamer with good sink. He'll need to add depth to a slurvy breaking ball to generate more swings and misses, though his high-80s cutter is good more often than not. He's still learning the finer points of throwing a changeup. Koch has an ideal pitcher's frame, plus athleticism and he repeats his mechanics with a clean arm action, so scouts who like him see him as a potential mid-rotation arm.

Year	Club (League)	Class	W	L	ERA	G	GS	CG	SV	IP	H	HR	BB	SO	K/9	WHIP	AVG
2012	Brooklyn (NYP)	SS	0	2	5.01	13	2	0	0	23	25	1	7	19	7.3	1.37	.278
2013	Savannah (SAL)	LoA	6	4	4.70	18	15	1	0	82	100	7	4	68	7.4	1.26	.295
Minor League Totals			6	6	4.77	31	17	1	0	106	125	8	11	87	7.4	1.29	.291

25 MATT DEN DEKKER, OF

BA GRADE
40
LOW

Born: Aug. 10, 1987. **B-T:** L-L. **Ht.:** 6-1. **Wt.:** 205. **Drafted:** Florida, 2010 (5th round). **Signed by:** Les Parker.

Den Dekker lost his place in line on the center-field depth chart in 2013 when he injured his left wrist while attempting a diving catch during spring training. Had he not been on the disabled list for the first two and a half months, then he, and not Juan Lagares, probably would have received the callup in late April. A graceful athlete, den Dekker has above-average speed and plays a plus center field, which could be his ticket to a big league reserve role. A fringy offensive player because he strikes out a lot—more than a third of the time during a September callup—he offers value in the form of walks and power, though probably not enough of the latter to start on a good team. Den Dekker will be 26 on Opening Day and he does enough things well to earn an extended look with the rebuilding Mets during the 2014 season.

Year	Club (League)	Class	AVG	G	AB	R	H	2B	3B	HR	RBI	BB	SO	SB	CS	OBP	SLG
2010	Mets (GCL)	R	.278	5	18	2	5	2	0	0	5	2	5	0	0	.350	.389
	Savannah (SAL)	LoA	.346	27	104	21	36	13	0	0	15	9	28	3	0	.404	.471
2011	St. Lucie (FSL)	HiA	.296	67	267	54	79	19	8	6	36	24	65	12	5	.362	.494
	Binghamton (EL)	AA	.235	72	272	49	64	13	3	11	32	27	91	12	5	.312	.426
2012	Binghamton (EL)	AA	.340	58	238	47	81	21	4	8	29	20	64	10	7	.397	.563
	Buffalo (IL)	AAA	.220	77	295	37	65	10	4	9	47	14	90	11	2	.256	.373
2013	St. Lucie (FSL)	HiA	.276	14	58	8	16	2	0	0	4	3	6	1	0	.306	.310
	Las Vegas (PCL)	AAA	.296	53	179	34	53	8	4	6	38	20	46	8	1	.366	.486
	New York (NL)	MAJ	.207	27	58	7	12	1	0	1	6	4	23	4	1	.270	.276
Major League Totals			.207	27	58	7	12	1	0	1	6	4	23	4	1	.270	.276
Minor League Totals			.279	373	1431	252	399	88	23	40	206	119	395	57	20	.338	.456

26 DUSTIN LAWLEY, OF/3B

BA GRADE 45 HIGH

Born: April 11, 1989. **B-T:** R-R. **Ht.:** 6-1. **Wt.:** 195. **Drafted:** West Florida, 2011 (19th round). **Signed by:** Tommy Jackson.

Despite spending just two years at Division II West Florida, Lawley ranks inside the program's top 10 in career home runs (sixth), doubles (eighth) and RBIs (ninth). A 19th-round pick in 2011, he put himself on the map with a loud 2013 season, leading the high Class A Florida State League with 25 homers and a .512 slugging percentage to win the circuit's MVP award. He led the organization in 26 home runs and 96 RBIs. Lawley takes a big swing and can crush mistakes a long way to his pull side, generating well-above-average carry and loft when he barrels the ball. Some scouts give him little chance to hit for average based on his trouble reading breaking-ball spin and foibles versus righthanders (.244/.301/.474 with 24 percent strikeouts in 2013). He's a fringe runner with tick-below-average range and solid arm strength suitable for either left or right field. He's athletic enough to have spotted at third base 17 times in 2013. With 60-grade power, Lawley has a carrying tool to be at least a part-time corner bat. Now he must prove he can hit, a test he'll take at Double-A in 2014.

Year	Club (League)	Class	AVG	G	AB	R	H	2B	3B	HR	RBI	BB	SO	SB	CS	OBP	SLG
2011	Kingsport (APP)	R	.284	57	232	37	66	17	3	9	43	14	48	5	5	.325	.500
	Savannah (SAL)	LoA	.273	3	11	2	3	2	0	1	1	0	4	0	0	.273	.727
2012	Savannah (SAL)	LoA	.261	129	482	77	126	35	3	14	66	50	122	14	4	.333	.434
2013	St. Lucie (FSL)	HiA	.260	122	469	69	122	33	5	25	92	36	111	6	3	.313	.512
	Las Vegas (PCL)	AAA	.300	6	20	3	6	2	0	1	4	0	2	0	0	.333	.550
Minor League Totals			.266	317	1214	188	323	89	11	50	206	100	287	25	12	.324	.481

27 ROB WHALEN, RHP

Born: Jan. 31, 1994. **B-T:** R-R. **Ht.:** 6-2. **Wt.:** 200. **Drafted:** HS—Haines City, Fla., 2012 (12th round). **Signed by:** Mike Silvestri.

The Mets loved Whalen's pitchability when they scouted him as an amateur at Haines City High, so much so that they signed the 12th-rounder for $100,000 even as his velocity dipped as a senior when he pitched through a dead arm. Scouts don't believe he has much projection left because of his maxed-out 6-foot-2 frame, though the Mets say he has the best curveball in the system, a high-70s pitch with three-quarters tilt that will be a consistent plus eventually. He sits 91-92 mph and bumps 94 with above-average life, and a two-seamer he learned in 2013 helped him rack up more than twice as many groundouts as airouts at Rookie-level Kingsport. Whalen commands his fastball well for a teenager, and his secondary pitches play up as a result. He's also working to polish a changeup and slider to round out his repertoire. Whalen is a prime candidate to head to low Class A Savannah in 2014.

Year	Club (League)	Class	W	L	ERA	G	GS	CG	SV	IP	H	HR	BB	SO	K/9	WHIP	AVG
2012	Kingsport (APP)	R	0	0	0.00	1	0	0	0	1	1	0	0	1	9.0	1.00	.333
2013	Kingsport (APP)	R	3	2	1.87	12	12	0	0	72	50	1	17	76	9.5	0.93	.187
Minor League Totals			3	2	1.84	13	12	0	0	73	51	1	17	77	9.5	0.93	.188

28 JUAN CENTENO, C

BA GRADE 40 LOW

Born: Nov. 16, 1989. **B-T:** L-R. **Ht.:** 5-10. **Wt.:** 170. **Drafted:** HS—Arecibo, P.R., 2007 (32nd round). **Signed by:** Junior Roman.

When the Mets needed a third catcher for their expanded September roster, they turned to Centeno, the system's best defender at the position who gunned down 56 percent of basestealers in 2013. He became the answer to a trivia question when on Sept. 25 he became the first (and so far only) big league catcher to throw out Reds speedster Billy Hamilton. On the Hamilton caught stealing, Centeno turned in a pop time between 1.7 to 1.8 seconds, which is well-above-average. Pitchers like throwing to him because he's an agile receiver with good hands and a strong, accurate arm. Because he has a contact-oriented lefty bat, he could be a backup in the big leagues for a long time, though he generates practically no power from his lean, 5-foot-9 frame. Centeno has thrown out 42 percent of basestealers in the minors and could one day be a nice backup complement to Travis d'Arnaud.

Year	Club (League)	Class	AVG	G	AB	R	H	2B	3B	HR	RBI	BB	SO	SB	CS	OBP	SLG
2007	Mets (GCL)	R	.146	12	41	4	6	0	0	0	2	3	6	0	0	.222	.146
2008	Mets (GCL)	R	.220	23	59	10	13	1	0	0	1	8	8	0	0	.333	.237
2009	Brooklyn (NYP)	SS	.164	32	110	8	18	2	1	0	9	5	18	1	1	.212	.200
2010	St. Lucie (FSL)	HiA	.200	11	35	1	7	0	0	0	1	3	7	1	0	.256	.200
	Binghamton (EL)	AA	.000	1	1	0	0	0	0	0	0	0	0	0	0	.000	.000
	Brooklyn (NYP)	SS	.371	32	89	17	33	8	1	1	10	6	8	1	0	.417	.517
2011	St. Lucie (FSL)	HiA	.318	52	157	22	50	5	1	1	11	12	22	3	1	.368	.382
2012	Binghamton (EL)	AA	.285	79	281	29	80	12	2	0	35	23	43	1	1	.337	.342
2013	Binghamton (EL)	AA	.261	6	23	4	6	1	1	0	3	0	5	0	0	.261	.391
	Las Vegas (PCL)	AAA	.305	67	213	25	65	10	2	0	28	12	24	1	1	.346	.371
	New York (NL)	MAJ	.300	4	10	0	3	0	0	0	1	0	1	0	0	.300	.300
Major League Totals			.300	4	10	0	3	0	0	0	1	0	1	0	0	.300	.300
Minor League Totals			.276	315	1009	120	278	39	8	2	100	72	141	8	4	.328	.336

29 WILFREDO TOVAR, SS

BA GRADE
40
LOW

Born: Aug. 11, 1991. **B-T:** R-R. **Ht.:** 5-10. **Wt.:** 160. **Signed:** Venezuela, 2007. **Signed by:** Ismael Cruz/Robert Alfonzo.

The four-times-running best defensive infielder in the system, Tovar made his big league debut in September, joining catcher Juan Centeno and center fielder Matt den Dekker as possible members of the franchise's future B-team. For his part, Tovar has a utility-infielder profile because of his strong defensive skills, including plus range, sure hands and a strong, accurate arm. He has played second base only sporadically in the minors, but he has the quickness to man the keystone and the arm strength to fill in at third as well. A team starting Tovar will be looking for an offensive upgrade. He's a below-average hitter with practically zero power who will get the bat knocked out of his hands by the pitching elite. He's also a below-average runner. Tovar has a low ceiling, but a high floor because teams need multi-positional infielders, particularly in the National League.

Year	Club (League)	Class	AVG	G	AB	R	H	2B	3B	HR	RBI	BB	SO	SB	CS	OBP	SLG
2008	Mets (VSL)	R	.203	49	153	16	31	7	1	2	11	12	23	7	4	.269	.301
2009	Mets (VSL)	R	.289	12	38	3	11	3	1	0	2	5	3	1	1	.364	.421
	Mets (GCL)	R	.243	38	148	21	36	5	3	0	14	8	19	16	8	.294	.318
2010	St. Lucie (FSL)	HiA	.246	30	118	14	29	5	1	0	6	3	22	4	3	.276	.305
	Savannah (SAL)	LoA	.281	44	160	12	45	10	0	0	17	8	12	4	5	.327	.344
	Brooklyn (NYP)	SS	.265	18	68	11	18	2	1	0	6	2	9	4	3	.311	.324
2011	Savannah (SAL)	LoA	.251	131	491	70	123	21	3	2	41	44	53	15	9	.318	.318
2012	St. Lucie (FSL)	HiA	.284	65	218	31	62	17	1	1	23	29	17	12	7	.377	.385
	Binghamton (EL)	AA	.254	57	193	20	49	11	2	0	27	11	22	2	1	.308	.332
2013	Binghamton (EL)	AA	.263	133	441	70	116	14	4	4	36	33	49	12	7	.323	.340
	New York (NL)	MAJ	.200	7	15	1	3	0	0	0	2	1	3	1	0	.294	.200
Major League Totals			.200	7	15	1	3	0	0	0	2	1	3	1	0	.294	.200
Minor League Totals			.256	577	2028	268	520	95	17	9	183	155	229	77	48	.319	.333

30 JAYCE BOYD, 1B

BA GRADE
45
HIGH

Born: Dec. 30, 1990. **B-T:** R-R. **Ht.:** 6-3. **Wt.:** 185. **Drafted:** Florida State, 2012 (6th round). **Signed by:** Jim Bryant.

Boyd hit .376 as a Florida State junior in 2012, but because of his right/right profile at first base and the four home runs he hit in his draft year, he slipped to the sixth round, where the Mets signed him for $150,000. That looked like money well spent in 2013 when he hit .330/.410/.461 in 123 games at two Class A levels to lead the system in average and rank ninth in the minors in that category. Though he hit just nine homers, Boyd walked as often as he struck out (61) and ranked as the low Class A South Atlantic League's best defensive first baseman. He emphasizes contact, doing an expert job of working pitchers for a fastball he can hammer to the gaps. He played through a sore shoulder in 2013, which forced him to DH the last two months of the season. Improved health combined with the plus power displays he shows in batting practice suggest future average power. He'll spend the bulk of 2014 at Double-A and could force his way into the big league picture the following year.

Year	Club (League)	Class	AVG	G	AB	R	H	2B	3B	HR	RBI	BB	SO	SB	CS	OBP	SLG
2012	Brooklyn (NYP)	SS	.239	54	201	18	48	9	1	5	19	25	30	1	3	.320	.368
2013	Savannah (SAL)	LoA	.361	65	249	40	90	16	1	5	46	35	32	0	4	.441	.494
	St. Lucie (FSL)	HiA	.292	58	209	28	61	13	1	4	37	26	29	2	0	.372	.421
Minor League Totals			.302	177	659	86	199	38	3	14	102	86	91	3	7	.383	.432

New York Yankees

BY JOSH NORRIS

When the Yankees missed the playoffs in 2008, they spent $423 million on free agents A.J. Burnett, C.C. Sabathia and Mark Teixeira in the next offseason and won the 2009 World Series.

The offseason following the team's 2013 playoff miss began similarly, with the team doling out $283 million for catcher Brian McCann and outfielders Jacoby Ellsbury and Carlos Beltran. That free agent trio will attempt to make up for the offense lost when Robinson Cano bolted for the Mariners and Curtis Granderson reached a deal with the Mets.

And although injuries to key pieces played a major role in the team's worst season since 1992, the second surge was needed because of the massive deficiencies at the upper levels of the minor league system, evident even though Double-A Trenton won the Eastern League title.

Without internal options, the Yankees were forced to turn to retreads like Mark Reynolds, Chris Nelson, Luis Cruz and Vernon Wells to fill their voids. Alfonso Soriano, acquired at midseason for hard-throwing righty Corey Black, did provide a jolt of punch down the stretch, however, while the team clung to flickering playoff hopes.

The Yankees haven't produced an everyday player since the 2005 draft, which yielded Brett Gardner and Austin Jackson, and the players who got a shot in 2013, such as outfielder Zoilo Almonte, third baseman David Adams and catcher Austin Romine, proved inadequate. The Yankees' recent success with pitching prospects didn't extend to righthander Dellin Betances, relegated to the bullpen, and lefty Manny Banuelos, whose Tommy John surgery put him on the sidelines with injured Mariners acquisition Michael Pineda.

Nearly all of the Yankees' potential impact prospects took a step back. Outfielder Mason Williams struggled with weight gain and poor performance. Outfielder Slade Heathcott was just getting going before knee tendinitis ended his season. Outfielder Tyler Austin missed significant time at Double-A with a wrist injury.

Righthander Jose Campos, already on a strict innings limit after missing most of 2012 with a fractured elbow, plodded along at low Class A. Second baseman Angelo Gumbs was demoted from high Class A Tampa to low Class A Charleston. Righty Ty Hensley, the team's first-rounder in 2012, missed the entire season with surgeries to both hips.

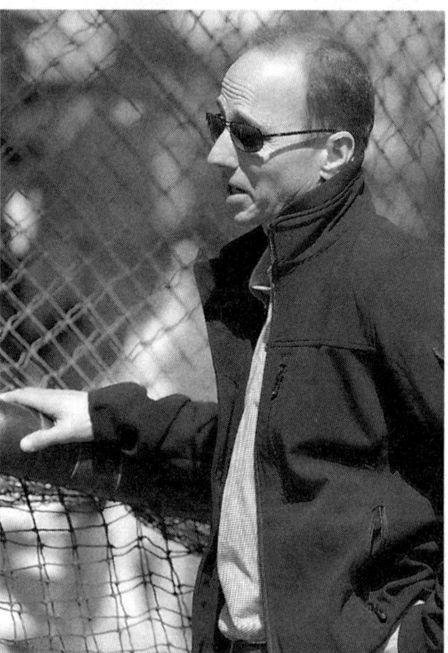

CLIFF WELCH

When injuries struck, GM Brian Cashman turned to veterans instead of farm products

TOP PROSPECTS OF THE DECADE

Year	Player, Pos.	2013 Org.
2004	Dioner Navarro, c	Cubs
2005	Eric Duncan, 3b	Out of baseball
2006	Phil Hughes, rhp	Yankees
2007	Phil Hughes, rhp	Yankees
2008	Joba Chamberlain, rhp	Yankees
2009	Austin Jackson, cf	Tigers
2010	Jesus Montero, c	Mariners
2011	Jesus Montero, c	Mariners
2012	Jesus Montero, c	Mariners
2013	Mason Williams, of	Yankees

The Yankees restocked with three first-round picks in the 2013 draft—Eric Jagielo, Ian Clarkin, Aaron Judge—but even they missed time with injuries. Still, that trio and offensive second baseman Gosuke Katoh give the system a jolt of potential impact talent, and there were other bright spots, most notably catcher Gary Sanchez reaching Double-A while improving defensively.

The front office made also made procedural changes to the team's scouting system, added former Cubs manager Mike Quade as a roving outfield coordinator and hired former Yankees minor league manager Trey Hillman as a special assistant for player development and pro scouting.

ORGANIZATION OVERVIEW

General Manager: Brian Cashman. **Farm Director:** Mark Newman. **Scouting Director:** Damon Oppenheimer.

Class	Team	League	W	L	PCT	Finish	Manager
Majors	New York Yankees	American	85	77	.525	9th (15)	Joe Girardi
Triple-A	Scranton/Wilkes-Barre RailRiders	International	68	76	.472	10th (14)	Dave Miley
Double-A	Trenton Thunder	Eastern	74	67	.525	4th (12)	Tony Franklin
High Class A	Tampa Yankees	Florida State	58	78	.426	11th (12)	Luis Sojo
Low Class A	Charleston RiverDogs	South Atlantic	75	63	.543	6th (14)	Al Pedrique
Short-season	Staten Island Yankees	New York-Penn	34	41	.453	10th (14)	Justin Pope
Rookie	GCL Yankees 1	Gulf Coast	28	32	.467	10th (16)	Tom Nieto
Rookie	GCL Yankees 2	Gulf Coast	36	24	.600	2nd (16)	Mario Garza
2013 Overall Minor League Record			**373**	**381**	**.495**	**17th (30)**	

THIS YEAR'S TOP 30

No.	Player, Pos.	Grade/Risk
1.	Gary Sanchez, c	60/Medium
2.	Slade Heathcott, of	55/High
3.	Mason Williams, of	55/High
4.	J.R. Murphy, c	50/Medium
5.	Eric Jagielo, 3b	55/High
6.	Aaron Judge, of	55/High
7.	Ian Clarkin, lhp	55/High
8.	Greg Bird, 1b	50/High
9.	Luis Severino, rhp	55/Extreme
10.	Gosuke Katoh, 2b	50/High
11.	Manny Banuelos, lhp	50/High
12.	Abiatal Avelino, ss	55/Extreme
13.	Jose Ramirez, rhp	50/High
14.	Jose Campos, rhp	50/High
15.	Rafael De Paula, rhp	50/High
16.	Shane Greene, rhp	45/Medium
17.	Tyler Austin, of	50/High
18.	Miguel Andujar, 3b	55/Extreme
19.	Luis Torrens, c	55/Extreme
20.	Ramon Flores, of	45/Medium
21.	Bryan Mitchell, rhp	55/Extreme
22.	Jake Cave, of	50/High
23.	Peter O'Brien, c/3b	45/Medium
24.	Ty Hensley, rhp	55/Extreme
25.	Angelo Gumbs, 2b	50/Extreme
26.	Dellin Betances, rhp	45/High
27.	Brett Marshall, rhp	45/High
28.	Robert Refsnyder, 2b/of	45/High
29.	Thairo Estrada, ss	50/Extreme
30.	Vidal Nuno, lhp	40/Low

LAST YEAR'S TOP 30

No.	Player, Pos.	Status
1.	Mason Williams, of	No. 3
2.	Slade Heathcott, of	No. 2
3.	Gary Sanchez, c	No. 1
4.	Tyler Austin, of	No. 17
5.	Jose Campos, rhp	No. 14
6.	Brett Marshall, rhp	No. 27
7.	Angelo Gumbs, 2b	No. 25
8.	Manny Banuelos, lhp	No. 11
9.	Ty Hensley, rhp	No. 24
10.	Rafael De Paula, rhp	No. 15
11.	Mark Montgomery, rhp	Dropped out
12.	Ramon Flores, of	No. 20
13.	Bryan Mitchell, rhp	No. 21
14.	Nik Turley, lhp	Dropped out
15.	J.R. Murphy, c	No. 4
16.	Jose Ramirez, rhp	No. 13
17.	Austin Romine, c	Majors
18.	Melky Mesa, of	(Released)
19.	Dellin Betances, rhp	No. 26
20.	Austin Aune, ss	Dropped out
21.	Dante Bichette Jr., 3b	Dropped out
22.	Greg Bird, 1b	No. 8
23.	David Adams, 2b/3b	(Free agent)
24.	Adam Warren, rhp	Majors
25.	Corey Black, rhp	(Cubs)
26.	Matt Tracy, lhp	Dropped out
27.	Corban Joseph, 2b	Dropped out
28.	Tommy Kahnle, rhp	Dropped out
29.	Cito Culver, ss	Dropped out
30.	Gabe Encinas, rhp	Dropped out

BEST TOOLS

Best Hitter for Average	Greg Bird
Best Power Hitter	Gary Sanchez
Best Strike-Zone Discipline	Greg Bird
Fastest Baserunner	Mason Williams
Best Athlete	Mason Williams
Best Fastball	Jose Ramirez
Best Curveball	Nik Turley
Best Slider	Mark Montgomery
Best Changeup	Jose Ramirez
Best Control	Vidal Nuno
Best Defensive Catcher	J.R. Murphy
Best Defensive Infielder	Cito Culver
Best Infield Arm	Cito Culver
Best Defensive Outfielder	Mason Williams
Best Outfield Arm	Slade Heathcott

TOP 15 PLAYERS 25 AND UNDER

No.	Player, Pos. (Age)	Peak Level
1.	Gary Sanchez, c (21)	Double-A
2.	Slade Heathcott, of (23)	Double-A
3.	Mason Williams, of (22)	Double-A
4.	J.R. Murphy, c (22)	Majors
5.	Michael Pineda, rhp (25)	Majors
6.	Eric Jagielo, 3b (21)	Short-season
7.	Aaron Judge, of (21)	Did not play
8.	Ian Clarkin, lhp (19)	Rookie
9.	Greg Bird, 1b (21)	Low Class A
10.	Luis Severino, rhp (19)	Low Class A
11.	Gosuke Katoh, 2b (19)	Rookie
12.	Manny Banuelos, lhp (23)	Triple-A
13.	Abiatal Avelino, ss (19)	Rookie
14.	Jose Ramirez, rhp (24)	Triple-A
15.	Jose Campos, rhp (21)	Low Class A

MINOR LEAGUE DEPTH CHART

NEW YORK YANKEES

TOP 2014 ROOKIE: J.R. Murphy, c. A solid bat and improved defense gives him a chance to enter catcher rotation in 2014.

BREAKOUT PROSPECT: Abiatal Avelino, ss: The 18-year-old showed all five tools in his U.S. debut in the Gulf Coast League in 2013.

SLEEPER: Dustin Fowler, of: The Yankees gave him $278,000 in the 18th round of the 2013 draft and he's shown 80 speed in his young career.

SOURCE OF TOP 30 TALENT

Homegrown	**28**	**Acquired**	**2**
College	4	Trades	1
Junior college	1	Rule 5 draft	0
High school	13	Independent leagues	1
Nondrafted free agents	0	Free agents/waivers	0
International	10		

LF
Ramon Flores (20)
Ben Gamel
Brandon Thomas
Taylor Dugas

CF
Slade Heathcott (2)
Mason Williams (3)
Jake Cave (22)
Leonardo Molina

RF
Aaron Judge (6)
Tyler Austin (17)
Zoilo Almonte
Adonis Garcia
Yeicok Calderon

3B
Eric Jagielo (5)
Miguel Andujar (18)
Dante Bichette Jr.
Rob Segedin

SS
Abiatal Avelino (12)
Thairo Estrada (29)
Addison Maruszak
Cito Culver
Carmen Angelini
Dan Fiorito

2B
Angelo Gumbs (25)
Rob Refsnyder (28)
Corban Joseph
Jose Pirela

1B
Greg Bird (8)
Peter O'Brien (23)

C
Gary Sanchez (1)
J.R. Murphy (4)
Luis Torrens (19)

LHP

LHSP	LHRP
Ian Clarkin (7)	James Pazos
Manny Banuelos (11)	Matt Tracy
Vidal Nuno (30)	Francisco Rondon
Nik Turley	Cesar Cabral
Rony Bautista	Freddy Lewis
Daniel Camarena	
Omar Luis	
Evan Rutckyj	
Caleb Frare	

RHP

RHSP	RHRP
Luis Severino (9)	Dellin Betances (26)
Jose Ramirez (13)	Mark Montgomery
Jose Campos (14)	Danny Burawa
Rafael De Paula (15)	Tommy Kahnle
Shane Greene (16)	Chase Whitley
Bryan Mitchell (21)	Nick Goody
Ty Hensley (24)	Nick Rumbelow
Brett Marshall (27)	Zach Nuding
Mikey O'Brien	Stefan Lopez
Rookie Davis	Branden Pinder
Brady Lail	
Giovany Gallegos	
David Palladino	

DRAFT ANALYSIS

2013

BONUSES: $8.1 MILLION

BEST PURE HITTER: 3B Eric Jagielo (1), who had a late start to his summer because of a strained quad from the spring, has a smooth stroke with loft to all fields, a disciplined approach and the ability to make consistent hard contact.

BEST POWER HITTER: Six-foot-7 OF Aaron Judge (1) has raw power that rates at least 70 on the 20-80 scale, and he can put on a show in batting practice. He has tremendous natural strength in his extra-large frame. Judge injured his quad before he could appear in a game.

FASTEST RUNNER: OF Michael O'Neill (3) has well above-average speed and could profile in center field. But 2B Gosuke Katoh (2), a plus runner, might get to first base faster because of his first-step quickness. OF Jordan Barnes (15) and 2B Derek Toadvine (22) can both run the 60-yard dash in 6.5 seconds.

BEST DEFENSIVE PLAYER: SS Tyler Wade (4), who could hit for average, is a good athlete with above-average speed, good actions, steady hands and an above-average arm.

BEST FASTBALL: The Yankees took four college RHPs who touch 96 mph or better: David Palladino (5), Nick Rumbelow (7), Cale Coshow (13) and Phillip Walby (12), who was up to 98. LHP Tyler Webb (10) pitches with average velocity, but his fastball plays up because of his command and deception.

BEST SECONDARY PITCH: LHP Ian Clarkin (1) has the makings of a plus curveball. Palladino's curveball and Rumbelow's slider are plus at their best.

BEST PRO DEBUT: Double-play partners Katoh and Wade had big summers in the Rookie-level Gulf Coast League. Katoh led the GCL with six home runs and ranked second in slugging at .310/.402/.522. Wade batted .309/.429/.370 with 11 steals. LHP Caleb Smith (14) struck out nearly 10 per nine while registering a 1.89 ERA at short-season Staten Island.

BEST ATHLETE: Judge was one of the best athletes in the draft, a physical specimen with light-tower power, plus arm strength and average speed. OF Brandon Thomas (8) is a switch-hitting center fielder with power and speed.

MOST INTRIGUING BACKGROUND: O'Neill is the nephew of former Yankees right fielder Paul. C Trent Garrison (28) was drafted by the Yankees a year after his twin brother, RHP Tyler, was selected in the seventh round. Unsigned LHP Josh Pettitte (37), now at Baylor, is the son of LHP Andy Pettitte.

CLOSEST TO THE MAJORS: Jagielo is an advanced hitter.

BEST LATE-ROUND PICK: Smith has a potentially plus changeup and fastball up to 94. OF Dustin Fowler, who received $278,000, is a good athlete with a simple lefthanded swing and above-average speed.

THE ONE WHO GOT AWAY: Canadian RHP Cal Quantrill (26), the son of ex-big leaguer Paul, is a good athlete with a fastball up to 94 mph and an emerging slider. He is attending Stanford.

ASSESSMENT: With three first-rounders, New York came away with a good haul of talent. After five of the first six picks were position players, the Yankees emphasized pitching depth in rounds five-15.

2012

BONUSES: $4.9 MILLION

RHP Ty Hensley (1) hardly has pitched and had hip surgery in 2013. C/3B Peter O'Brien (2) and 2B/OF Rob Refsnyder (5) can hit but have defensive issues. RHP Corey Black (4) was traded to the Cubs.

GRADE: C

2011

BONUSES: $6.3 MILLION

The Yankees lament not signing RHP Jonathan Gray (10). 3B Dante Bichette Jr. (1s) hasn't hit, leaving 1B Greg Bird (5) and OF Jake Cave (6) as the class' best hopes.

GRADE: D

2010

BONUSES: $6.7 MILLION

The reach for SS Cito Culver (1) hasn't panned out, and OFs Tyler Austin (13) and Mason Williams (4) and 2B Angelo Gumbs (2) backed up in 2013.

GRADE: D

TOP DRAFT PICKS OF THE DECADE

Year	Player, Pos.	2013 Org.
2004	Phil Hughes, rhp	Yankees
2005	C.J. Henry, ss	Out of baseball
2006	Ian Kennedy, rhp	Padres
2007	Andrew Brackman, rhp	White Sox
2008	Gerrit Cole, rhp*	Pirates
2009	Slade Heathcott, of	Yankees
2010	Cito Culver, ss	Yankees
2011	Dante Bichette Jr., 3b (1st round supp.)	Yankees
2012	Ty Hensley, rhp	Yankees
2013	Eric Jagielo, 3b	Yankees

* Did not sign

LARGEST BONUSES IN CLUB HISTORY

Hideki Irabu, 1997	$8,500,000
Jose Contreras, 2002	$6,000,000
Andrew Brackman, 2007	$3,350,000
Gary Sanchez, 2009	$3,000,000
Wily Mo Pena, 1999	$2,440,000

1 GARY SANCHEZ, C

Born: Dec. 2, 1992. **B-T:** R-R. **Ht.:** 6-2. **Wt.:** 220. **Signed:** Dominican Republic, 2009. **Signed by:** Victor Mata/Raymon Sanchez.

Sanchez either is the last member of the Yankees' wave of catching prospects, or the beginning of their next wave. Jesus Montero got a taste of the Bronx before being spun to the Mariners for Michael Pineda. Austin Romine has struggled through back problems and concussions, and his progress has stalled. Homegrown products Francisco Cervelli and J.R. Murphy also saw time behind the plate in New York in 2013, but the Yankees have yet to develop a replacement for Jorge Posada, whose final year as the club's regular catcher was 2010. Sanchez signed in 2009 for a $3 million bonus, large even by Yankees standards, and sported a career .286/.350/.496 batting line with 43 home runs entering 2013, but questions about his conditioning and maturity lingered. His attitude was problematic enough to earn an internal suspension while at low Class A Charleston in 2011. By all accounts, those problems dissipated by 2013, which ended with Sanchez beneath a raucous dogpile while he and his teammates with Double-A Trenton celebrated an Eastern League championship.

Sanchez's bat still rates as the best in the system by a long shot, thanks to effortless, well above-average raw power and an above-average hit tool. Scouts see his floor as being a .260-.270 hitter with at least 20 home runs annually, which would be all-star-caliber production for a catcher. Sanchez can shoot line drives to all fields and has sock to the opposite field as well. His defense has gotten better and he's quieter behind the plate. He still needs to work on blocking balls, specifically when it comes to pitches in the dirt to his right or left, when he tends to try to use his hands to pick the ball rather than blocking with his getting his body in front of it. He led the Florida State League with 11 passed balls during his time at high Class A Tampa. Sanchez's arm has been rated as high as an 80 by some scouts, and he led the FSL by throwing out 46 percent of basestealers. He spent the season in better shape and had a better attitude than in the past, and scouts noticed. Sanchez took charge behind the plate and was handling staffs with much more authority than in years past.

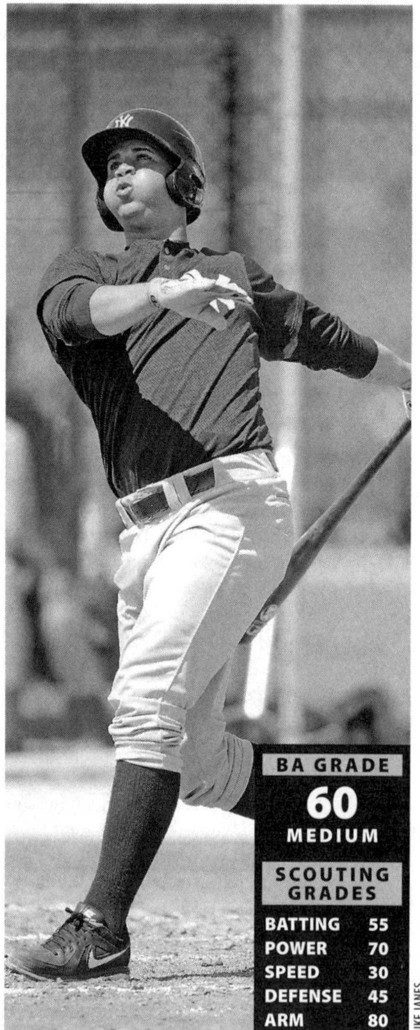

MIKE JANES

BA GRADE
60
MEDIUM

SCOUTING GRADES

BATTING	55
POWER	70
SPEED	30
DEFENSE	45
ARM	80

The Yankees threw a roadblock into Sanchez's path by signing free agent Brian McCann for five years and $80 million. While McCann could mix in time at DH and first base—where Mark Teixeira is signed through 2016—it's difficult to imagine a full-time spot for Sanchez in New York in the near future. For now, he's ticketed for a return trip to Double-A for 2014, and he gives the Yankees a key trade chip at a premium position.

Year	Club (League)	Class	AVG	G	AB	R	H	2B	3B	HR	RBI	BB	SO	SB	CS	OBP	SLG
2010	Yankees (GCL)	R	.353	31	119	25	42	11	0	6	36	11	28	1	1	.419	.597
	Staten Island (NYP)	SS	.278	16	54	8	15	2	0	2	7	3	16	1	1	.333	.426
2011	Charleston, SC (SAL)	LoA	.256	82	301	49	77	16	1	17	52	36	93	2	1	.335	.485
2012	Charleston, SC (SAL)	LoA	.297	68	263	44	78	19	0	13	56	22	65	11	4	.353	.517
	Tampa (FSL)	HiA	.279	48	172	21	48	10	1	5	29	10	41	4	0	.330	.436
2013	Tampa (FSL)	HiA	.254	94	362	38	92	21	0	13	61	28	71	3	1	.313	.420
	Trenton (EL)	AA	.250	23	92	12	23	6	0	2	10	13	16	0	0	.364	.380
Minor League Totals			.275	362	1363	197	375	85	2	58	251	123	330	22	8	.342	.468

2 SLADE HEATHCOTT, OF

BA GRADE
55
HIGH

Born: Sept. 28, 1990. **B-T:** L-L. **Ht.:** 6-0. **Wt.:** 195. **Drafted:** HS—Texarkana, Texas, 2009 (1st round). **Signed by:** Mark Batchko/Tim Kelly.

Littered with run-ins with alcohol, guns and family drama, Heathcott's past is well documented. He's not shy about the mistakes he's made, though, and has worked diligently to become a better man as he's grown up. More directly relevant is his extensive injury history. He's had surgeries on both shoulders, missed time in spring 2013 with patellar tendinitis, and sat out the last 40 games, including Double-A Trenton's postseason run, with the same issue. After the season, he had surgery on his right knee to repair the damage. With a max-effort playing style Heathcott at his best is a speedy slash-hitter who uses the whole field. He does have significant issues with plate discipline, especially when it comes to the recognition of breaking balls. He'd heated up (hitting .306 in July) before the knee problems cropped up in August. He's a plus defender in center field whose arm remains above-average, even after the operations. He's a better-than-average runner but needs to learn to better pick his spots when going for steals. The Yankees' signing of Jacoby Ellsbury means that Heathcott may have to move to right field to be a regular in New York. He'll have to stay healthy first. He could force way to Triple-A to begin 2014.

Year	Club (League)	Class	AVG	G	AB	R	H	2B	3B	HR	RBI	BB	SO	SB	CS	OBP	SLG
2009	Yankees (GCL)	R	.100	3	10	0	1	0	0	0	0	1	2	0	0	.182	.100
2010	Charleston (SAL)	LoA	.258	76	298	48	77	16	3	2	30	42	101	15	10	.359	.352
2011	Charleston (SAL)	LoA	.271	52	210	36	57	11	4	4	16	19	57	6	7	.342	.419
	Tampa (FSL)	HiA	.600	1	5	2	3	0	0	1	1	0	1	0	0	.600	1.200
2012	Yankees (GCL)	R	.235	5	17	3	4	2	0	0	2	5	4	2	0	.409	.353
	Tampa (FSL)	HiA	.307	60	215	38	66	16	2	5	27	20	66	17	4	.378	.470
2013	Trenton (EL)	AA	.261	103	399	59	104	22	7	8	49	36	107	15	8	.327	.411
Minor League Totals			.270	300	1154	186	312	67	16	20	125	123	338	55	29	.349	.408

3 MASON WILLIAMS, OF

BA GRADE
55
HIGH

Born: Aug. 21, 1991. **B-T:** L-R. **Ht.:** 6-1. **Wt.:** 180. **Drafted:** HS—Winter Garden, Fla., 2010 (4th round). **Signed by:** Jeff Deardorff.

The son of former Patriots wide receiver Derwin Williams, Mason's grandfather Walt "No Neck" Williams finished his 10-year big league career with the Yankees. Coming off surgery to repair a torn labrum in his left shoulder that ended his 2012 season early, Williams entered the 2013 season as the system's No. 1 prospect but had a rough season from the start, with a DUI arrest in April. When he was on the field, Williams didn't show the same tools he had in 2012, particularly at the plate, where he rarely made hard contact and adopted an Ichiro-style slapping approach. Scouts thought Williams had gained weight—most evident in his inability to catch up to quality fastballs—and lost speed. He didn't turn in good times to first base, either, because of less effort. Williams' well-above-average defense didn't suffer as much. Evaluators uniformly praise his range, instincts and routes. Williams got a scenery change in August when he was moved to Double-A Trenton, where he struggled at the plate. Williams ought to start the 2014 season back in Trenton if Slade Heathcott graduates to Triple-A. Much like Heathcott, Williams' future in pinstripes is muddled by the team's acquisition of Jacoby Ellsbury.

Year	Club (League)	Class	AVG	G	AB	R	H	2B	3B	HR	RBI	BB	SO	SB	CS	OBP	SLG
2010	Yankees (GCL)	R	.222	5	18	0	4	0	0	0	0	1	4	1	2	.263	.222
2011	Staten Island (NYP)	SS	.349	68	269	42	94	11	6	3	31	20	41	28	12	.395	.468
2012	Charleston (SAL)	LoA	.304	69	276	55	84	19	4	8	28	21	33	19	9	.359	.489
	Tampa (FSL)	HiA	.277	22	83	13	23	3	0	3	7	3	14	1	4	.302	.422
2013	Tampa (FSL)	HiA	.261	100	406	56	106	21	3	3	24	39	61	15	9	.327	.350
	Trenton (EL)	AA	.153	17	72	7	11	3	1	1	4	1	18	0	0	.164	.264
Minor League Totals			.286	281	1124	173	322	57	14	18	94	85	171	64	36	.338	.410

4 J.R. MURPHY, C

Born: May 13, 1991. **B-T:** R-R. **Ht.:** 5-11. **Wt.:** 195. **Drafted:** HS—Bradenton, Fla., 2009 (2nd round). **Signed by:** Jeff Deardorff/Brian Barber.

Signed for $1.25 million in 2009, Murphy played both catcher and third base early in his career and has become a durable option behind the plate. He caught a minor league-leading 105 games in 2013 while having his best offensive season, and he made his major league debut in September. He was behind the plate at Yankee Stadium for Mariano Rivera's final major league pitch. Murphy doesn't have a plus tool, but he has sharpened his skills in the minors. After years of hard work, he improved his footwork and his release and gunned down 37 percent of basestealers at Double-A Trenton and Triple-A Scranton/Wilkes-Barre. He has become a much better, quieter receiver, though he can get a little stabby behind the plate at times. His line-drive bat produces consistent solid contact to the gaps with fringe-average power. He'll compete with Francisco Cervelli and Austin Romine for the right to be Brian McCann's backup in New York in 2014, but McCann ahead and Gary Sanchez coming up behind put the squeeze on Murphy's chances to be a regular in New York.

Year	Club (League)	Class	AVG	G	AB	R	H	2B	3B	HR	RBI	BB	SO	SB	CS	OBP	SLG
2009	Yankees (GCL)	R	.333	9	33	4	11	2	0	1	7	3	8	0	0	.405	.485
2010	Charleston (SAL)	LoA	.255	87	330	46	84	15	2	7	54	36	64	4	5	.327	.376
2011	Charleston (SAL)	LoA	.297	63	256	31	76	23	0	6	32	19	38	2	0	.343	.457
	Tampa (FSL)	HiA	.259	23	85	8	22	6	0	1	14	2	9	0	0	.270	.365
2012	Tampa (FSL)	HiA	.257	67	265	39	68	14	1	5	28	26	41	4	3	.322	.374
	Trenton (EL)	AA	.231	43	147	23	34	12	1	4	16	16	32	0	0	.306	.408
2013	Trenton (EL)	AA	.268	49	183	34	49	10	0	6	25	24	32	1	0	.352	.421
	Scranton/W-B (IL)	AAA	.270	59	230	26	62	19	0	6	21	23	41	0	1	.342	.430
	New York (AL)	MAJ	.154	16	26	3	4	1	0	0	1	1	9	0	0	.185	.192
Major League Totals			.154	16	26	3	4	1	0	0	1	1	9	0	0	.185	.192
Minor League Totals			.266	400	1529	211	406	101	4	36	197	149	265	11	9	.331	.407

5 ERIC JAGIELO, 3B

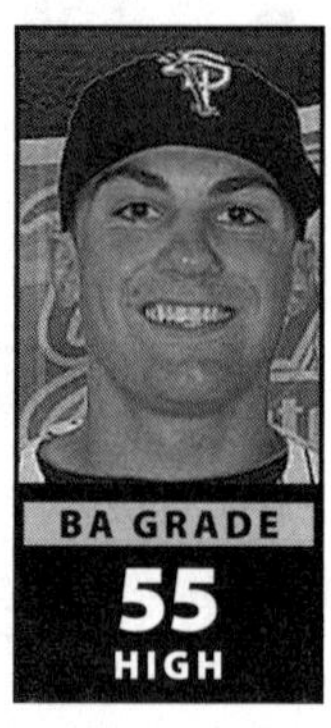

Born: May 17, 1992. **B-T:** L-R. **Ht.:** 6-2. **Wt.:** 195. **Drafted:** Notre Dame, 2013 (1st round). **Signed by:** Mike Gibbons.

Jagielo started for three seasons at Notre Dame, slamming 13 homers as a sophomore and 13 more in the Cape Cod League before ranking sixth in the nation in on-base percentage (.500) as a junior. A late-season strained quad muscle meant that as soon as the Yankees signed him for $1.875 million with the first of three first-round selections, he went on the disabled list. He debuted on June 27 in the Rookie-level Gulf Coast League before heading north to short-season Staten Island. Jagielo is a polished hitter with above-average vision that allows him to turn on fastballs and stay back on breaking pitches. He has the ability to make hard contact to all fields, as well as above-average power that projects to 20-25 homers a year. Most of the questions about Jagielo center on defense. He's a below-average runner with fair agility and footwork, but most scouts think he has the hands, actions and arm strength for third base. He figures to start 2014 at low Class A Charleston but could battle with Dante Bichette Jr. for a spot at high Class A Tampa. As a polished college bat, he should move past Bichette sooner rather than later.

Year	Club (League)	Class	AVG	G	AB	R	H	2B	3B	HR	RBI	BB	SO	SB	CS	OBP	SLG
2013	Yankees1 (GCL)	R	.000	1	2	1	0	0	0	0	0	0	0	0	0	.333	.000
	Yankees2 (GCL)	R	.286	3	7	2	2	2	0	0	0	1	2	0	0	.375	.571
	Staten Island (NYP)	SS	.266	51	184	19	49	14	1	6	27	26	54	0	0	.376	.451
Minor League Totals			.264	55	193	22	51	16	1	6	27	27	56	0	0	.376	.451

6 AARON JUDGE, OF

LARRY GOREN

Born: April 26, 1992. **B-T:** R-R. **Ht.:** 6-7. **Wt.:** 255. **Drafted:** Fresno State, 2013 (1st round). **Signed by:** Troy Afenir.

Judge's physicality earned him football scholarship offers out of high school in 2010, when he was also a 31st-round pick of the Athletics, as well as comparisons to NBA star Blake Griffin. Instead he headed to Fresno State for baseball, where he hit just six home runs in his first two seasons before bopping 12 and slugging .655 as a junior. The Yankees took him 32nd overall and signed him for $1.8 million, though a torn quad muscle in his right leg delayed his pro debut. If his 6-foot-7 frame didn't make it obvious, Judge is a physical beast and has earned comparisions to Marlins slugger Giancarlo Stanton. He shows impressive batting-practice power thanks to his strength and leverage, though some scouts are worried about how well it will translate into games. At his height, it's hard for his swing path to be short, and he's not expected to be more than a .260 hitter. He has slightly above-average speed and a strong arm, and while he can play center field, he profiles better on a corner. The Yankees had not spent a first-round pick on a college hitter since 2001 (John-Ford Griffin) before taking Eric Jagielo and Judge in 2013. A healthy Judge ought to join Jagielo at low Class A Charleston to open the season, and while Jagielo is more polished, Judge offers more upside.

Year	Club (League)	Class	AVG	G	AB	R	H	2B	3B	HR	RBI	BB	SO	SB	CS	OBP	SLG
2013	Did Not Play—Injured																

7 IAN CLARKIN, LHP

Born: Feb. 14, 1995. **B-T:** L-L. **Ht.:** 6-2. **Wt.:** 186. **Drafted:** HS—San Diego, 2013 (1st round). **Signed by:** Dave Keith.

Clarkin helped USA Baseball's 18U national team win gold at the 2012 IBAF World Championship in South Korea, spinning six strong innings in the final to beat Canada. His strong spring pushed him into first-round consideration, and the Yankees took him with the third of their three first-rounders. He made waves for saying he "couldn't stand" the Yankees while growing up, but a $1,650,100 bonus offer made that moot. He's the first prep lefty the Yankees have drafted in the first round since taking Brien Taylor No. 1 overall in 1991. At his best, Clarkin shows three average to above-average pitches. His fastball sits 90-92 mph and touches 94. He flashes a plus curveball with sharp bite and downer action, and he located it well to both sides of the plate as an amateur. He spent time sharpening an inconsistent changeup in the instructional league, but the pitch has shown fading action, and he sells it with good arm speed. He's shown willingness to pitch inside. Clarkin missed time after twisting his right ankle slipping on a baseball in Tampa but returned in late August to pitch in the Rookie-level Gulf Coast League. An assignment to low Class A Charleston in 2014 isn't out of the question for Clarkin, but a more likely path is extended spring training and a trip to short-season Staten Island.

Year	Club (League)	Class	W	L	ERA	G	GS	CG	SV	IP	H	HR	BB	SO	K/9	WHIP	AVG
2013	Yankees1 (GCL)	R	0	2	10.80	3	3	0	0	5	5	2	4	4	7.2	1.80	.263
Minor League Totals			0	2	10.80	3	3	0	0	5	5	2	4	4	7.2	1.80	.263

8 GREG BIRD, 1B

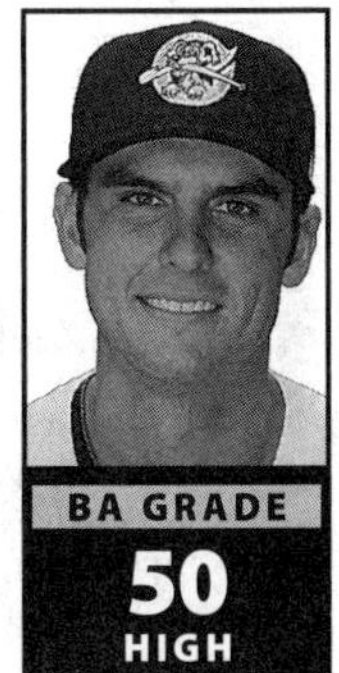

Born: Nov. 9, 1992. **B-T:** L-R. **Ht.:** 6-3. **Wt.:** 215. **Drafted:** HS—Aurora, Colo., 2011 (5th round). **Signed by:** Steve Kmetko.

Bird spent his prep days catching future Orioles first-rounder Kevin Gausman, but he was not long for the position. The Yankees bought him out of his Arkansas commitment for $1.1 million in 2011, gave him a brief look at catcher and quickly converted him to first base in 2013. He became the first lefthanded hitter for low Class A Charleston to reach 20 home runs since it became a Yankees affiliate, while also leading the minors with 107 walks. Bird was the Yankees' breakout prospect and has a mature offensive approach. He led the South Atlantic League with a .428 on-base percentage, remembers pitch sequences and learned which pitches he could drive, hitting 13 of his 20 homers in the second half. Bird's hit tool is more advanced than his power, and some scouts and managers noted that his swing has little loft and lacks premium bat speed. Back problems helped prompt his move to first base and limit his athleticism and defensive ability. He has limited range but adequate arm strength. He's a below-average runner. Bird draws comparisons with the Yankees' primary first baseman in 2013, Lyle Overbay. He's slated for high Class A Tampa in 2014.

Year	Club (League)	Class	AVG	G	AB	R	H	2B	3B	HR	RBI	BB	SO	SB	CS	OBP	SLG
2011	Yankees (GCL)	R	.083	4	12	0	1	0	0	0	0	1	4	0	0	.154	.083
2012	Yankees (GCL)	R	.286	17	49	9	14	2	1	0	5	11	13	0	0	.419	.367
	Staten Island (NYP)	SS	.400	11	40	4	16	4	0	2	8	6	10	0	0	.489	.650
2013	Charleston (SAL)	LoA	.288	130	458	84	132	36	3	20	84	107	132	1	1	.428	.511
Minor League Totals			.292	162	559	97	163	42	4	22	97	125	159	1	1	.426	.499

9 LUIS SEVERINO, RHP

BA GRADE **55** EXTREME

Born: Feb. 20, 1994. **B-T:** R-R. **Ht.:** 6-0. **Wt.:** 195. **Signed:** Dominican Republic, 2011. **Signed by:** Juan Rosario.

Severino, who didn't sign until he was 17, received a $225,000 bonus and pitched in the Dominican Summer League in 2012. The Yankees put him on the fast track in 2013, promoting him to low Class A Charleston after he shined in the Rookie-level Gulf Coast League. Equipped with a loose arm, Severino has raw stuff that is as good as any Yankees farmhand, and he has shown the ability to throw strikes with three pitches. His fastball sits between 93-95 mph and touches the upper 90s often. He has shown a tendency to fall in love with radar-gun readings and overthrow, and he's better working down in the zone and inducing groundballs. While Severino's slider was his top secondary pitch before he signed, he has developed a solid changeup since signing, and it's presently the better of the two. His slider still flashes plus but remains inconsistent. Severino provided a bright spot in a bleak season for Yankees pitching prospects. His three-pitch mix and strike-throwing ability allow him to profile as a starter. After spending his final four starts with the RiverDogs, he's slated to return there to start 2014.

Year	Club (League)	Class	W	L	ERA	G	GS	CG	SV	IP	H	HR	BB	SO	K/9	WHIP	AVG
2012	Yankees 1 (DSL)	R	4	2	1.68	14	14	0	0	64	46	2	17	45	6.3	0.98	.205
2013	Yankees1 (GCL)	R	3	1	1.37	6	4	0	0	26	16	0	6	32	10.9	0.84	.172
	Charleston (SAL)	LoA	1	1	4.08	4	4	0	0	18	21	1	4	21	10.7	1.42	.292
Minor League Totals			8	4	1.99	24	22	0	0	108	83	3	27	98	8.1	1.02	.213

CLIFF WELCH

10 GOSUKE KATOH, 2B

BA GRADE **50** HIGH

Born: Oct. **8, 1994. B-T:** L-R. **Ht.:** 6-2. **Wt.:** 180. **Drafted:** HS—San Diego, 2013 (2nd round). **Signed by:** Dave Keith.

A UCLA signee and friend of Yankees first-rounder Ian Clarkin growing up in San Diego, Katoh elevated his draft stock with an outstanding performance at the Area Code Games in 2012. He followed that with a strong senior year at Rancho Bernardo High, posting a .451 average and eight homers. The Yankees took him in the second round and quickly inked him for $845,700. Katoh continued to rake in pro ball, tying for the Rookie-level Gulf Coast League home run lead (six) while pacing the circuit in triples (five) and ranking second in slugging (.522). Katoh is lean and strong, with plenty of strength in his forearms. He generates his thump despite choking up on the bat, and he has average power potential. He's a slick, graceful defender around the bag at second base, to the point that the Yankees may try him at shortstop in the future despite his below-average arm. He's a plus runner who's learning to translate his speed into steals. Katoh has patience at the plate, leading to both walks and strikeouts, and he was vulnerable to chasing the high fastball. The Yankees' last wave of middle infielders, 2010 draftees Cito Culver and Angelo Gumbs, hasn't progressed, so Katoh will face few obstacles if he produces. He will jump to low Class A Charleston for his full-season debut.

Year	Club (League)	Class	AVG	G	AB	R	H	2B	3B	HR	RBI	BB	SO	SB	CS	OBP	SLG
2013	Yankees1 (GCL)	R	.310	50	184	28	57	11	5	6	25	27	44	4	2	.402	.522
Minor League Totals			.310	50	184	28	57	11	5	6	25	27	44	4	2	.402	.522

11 MANNY BANUELOS, LHP

BA GRADE **50** HIGH

Born: March 13, 1991. **B-T:** L-L. **Ht.:** 5-10. **Wt.:** 155. **Signed:** Mexico, 2008. **Signed by:** Lee Sigman.

Banuelos already was a top prospect when he tore up big league camp during spring training 2011, looking big league ready. He has struggled since then, however, losing his command in 2011, then having a back problem and later elbow pain that ended his 2012 season in May. He had Tommy John surgery in October 2012 and missed all of 2013. At his best, Banuelos sports a low- to mid-90s fastball that has touched as high as 97 mph. Reports had him at 93-94 in simulated games last fall. He couples the fastball with a plus changeup with tumbling action and a sharp curveball in the mid-70s. He had control issues at the upper levels, which the Yankees had explained by his youth and by the jump in his velocity. He has yet to command the strike zone above Class A, and he broke down the only year that he pitched more than 110 innings, so durability is a real question. Banuelos didn't pitch in winter ball, so he's slated to start the 2014 season in Triple-A Scranton/Wilkes-Barre with a closely monitored workload. Now 23 and three years removed from that scintillating spring showing, he needs to prove he can throw strikes and stay healthy, but he's got time.

Year	Club (League)	Class	W	L	ERA	G	GS	CG	SV	IP	H	HR	BB	SO	K/9	WHIP	AVG
2008	Yankees (GCL)	R	4	1	2.57	12	3	0	0	42	32	3	13	37	7.9	1.07	.208
2009	Charleston (SAL)	LoA	9	5	2.67	25	19	0	0	108	88	4	28	104	8.7	1.07	.219
	Tampa (FSL)	HiA	0	0	0.00	1	0	0	0	1	0	0	0	2	18.0	0.00	.000
2010	Yankees (GCL)	R	0	0	1.80	2	2	0	0	5	1	0	3	6	10.8	0.80	.063
	Tampa (FSL)	HiA	0	3	2.23	10	10	0	0	44	38	1	14	62	12.6	1.17	.230
	Trenton (EL)	AA	0	1	3.52	3	3	0	0	15	15	2	8	17	10.0	1.50	.273
2011	Trenton (EL)	AA	4	5	3.59	20	20	0	0	95	94	7	52	94	8.9	1.53	.263
	Scranton/W-B (IL)	AAA	2	2	4.19	7	7	1	0	34	36	2	19	31	8.1	1.60	.277
2012	Scranton/W-B (IL)	AAA	0	2	4.50	6	6	0	0	24	29	2	10	22	8.3	1.63	.299
2013	Did not play—Injured																
Minor League Totals			19	19	3.12	86	70	1	0	369	333	21	147	375	9.1	1.30	.241

12 ABIATAL AVELINO, SS

BA GRADE 55 EXTREME

Born: Feb. 14, 1995. **B-T:** R-R. **Ht.:** 5-11. **Wt.:** 200. **Signed:** Dominican Republic, 2011. **Signed by:** Jose Sabino.

Though preceded by less hype, Avelino stood out to evaluators as one of the two best shortstops in the Rookie-level Gulf Coast League in 2013, along with Phillies first-rounder J.P. Crawford. Signed by the Yankees for $300,000 the day after Christmas in 2011, Avelino stood out with his bat, basestealing and glove in his first season in the U.S. He has a body that has drawn comparisons with Brewers shortstop Jean Segura—short, stocky and strong—and showed the ability to hit to all fields. He gets to every ball on the infield, has an arm that already grades as plus and possesses impressive baseball instincts for an 18-year-old. While he's not a burner, Avelino's baserunning aptitude helped him lead the GCL with 26 steals despite being promoted to short-season Staten Island in mid-August. He also led all Yankees farmhands. The late-season promotion hinted that Avelino is at the front of the line for the organization's young shortstops, and that he could begin 2014 back under the lights at Staten Island or, if the Yankees choose to be aggressive, low Class A Charleston.

Year	Club (League)	Class	AVG	G	AB	R	H	2B	3B	HR	RBI	BB	SO	SB	CS	OBP	SLG
2012	Yankees 1 (DSL)	R	.302	57	222	46	67	11	1	1	25	27	34	20	2	.398	.374
2013	Yankees1 (GCL)	R	.259	17	58	14	15	2	1	0	4	7	7	9	3	.348	.328
	Yankees2 (GCL)	R	.400	17	70	21	28	5	4	0	13	9	4	17	1	.481	.586
	Staten Island (NYP)	SS	.243	17	70	10	17	2	0	0	6	4	6	2	0	.303	.271
Minor League Totals			.302	108	420	91	127	20	6	1	48	47	51	48	6	.390	.386

13 JOSE RAMIREZ, RHP

Born: Jan. 21, 1990. **B-T:** R-R. **Ht.:** 6-3. **Wt.:** 190. **Signed:** Dominican Republic, 2007. **Signed by:** Victor Mata.

Ramirez jumped into the Yankees' Top 30 after pitching in the Rookie-level Gulf Coast League in 2009 but has progressed slowly from there, spending three seasons in Class A. The quality of his fastball and changeup rivals anyone in the system. A rail-thin righty, he brings an explosive fastball in the mid- to upper 90s and backs it up with a tumbling changeup that often gets mistaken for a splitter. The change easily rates as a 60 pitch on the 20-80 scouting scale. Ramirez's slider has its moments, but due to a long arm stroke during takeaway, his command and his breaking ball remain inconsistent, and most scouts project him as a reliever. He also remains slight of build and injury prone. He missed most of April after starting the year on Double-A Trenton's disabled list with tendinitis, then had his season end in July with Triple-A Scranton/Wilkes-Barre due to an oblique strain. He also showed a tendency to let mistakes snowball, and his body language worsened when a break didn't go his way or a play wasn't made behind him. Now 24, Ramirez never has thrown more than 115 innings in a season. Headed back to Triple-A, he could be one injury away from being moved to the bullpen, where his fastball/changeup combination should play well.

Year	Club (League)	Class	W	L	ERA	G	GS	CG	SV	IP	H	HR	BB	SO	K/9	WHIP	AVG
2008	Yankees 2 (DSL)	R	0	3	4.15	12	10	0	0	39	35	2	18	39	9.0	1.36	.238
2009	Yankees (GCL)	R	6	0	1.48	11	10	0	0	61	33	5	16	53	7.8	0.80	.159
	Tampa (FSL)	HiA	0	0	0.00	1	0	0	0	3	1	0	0	2	6.0	0.33	.100
2010	Charleston (SAL)	LoA	6	5	3.60	22	21	0	0	115	106	3	42	105	8.2	1.29	.239
2011	Tampa (FSL)	HiA	0	5	8.14	6	6	0	0	24	35	3	11	25	9.2	1.89	.337
	Charleston (SAL)	LoA	5	7	4.90	15	15	0	0	79	84	9	32	74	8.4	1.47	.276
2012	Tampa (FSL)	HiA	7	6	3.19	21	18	0	0	99	92	7	30	94	8.6	1.24	.239
2013	Trenton (EL)	AA	1	3	2.76	9	8	0	1	42	28	7	15	50	10.6	1.02	.192
	Scranton/W-B (IL)	AAA	1	3	4.88	8	8	0	0	31	29	3	21	28	8.0	1.60	.259
Minor League Totals			26	32	3.72	105	96	0	1	494	443	39	185	470	8.6	1.27	.238

14 JOSE CAMPOS, RHP

BA GRADE 50 HIGH

Born: March 24, 1991. **B-T:** R-R. **Ht.:** 6-4. **Wt.:** 200. **Signed:** Venezuela, 2009. **Signed by:** Emilio Carrasquel/Patrick Guerrero (Mariners).

Neither the Yankees nor the Mariners have gotten much out of the four-player trade prior to the 2012 season that brought righthanders Michael Pineda and Jose Campos to the Yankees for top prospect Jesus Montero and righty Hector Noesi. Not one player in the deal has lived up to expectations. For his part, Campos missed the final five months of 2012 with a small fracture in his pitching elbow, but he showed promising results in 2013 at low Class A Charleston despite being on an extremely short leash. At his best, Campos' fastball, which showcases average sink and tail, sat between 91-93 mph and touched as high as 95. He backs it up with a curveball that comes and goes and occasionally acts like a slider. His third pitch is an inconsistent but deceptive 82-84 mph changeup. He repeats his clean delivery and has an excellent pitcher's body at 6-foot-4, 200 pounds, so he should be able to handle a heavier workload in 2014. The jury is out on whether he's a starter or a reliever in the future. The Yankees thought enough of Campos to protect him on the 40-man roster rather than risk losing him in the Rule 5 draft and hope to get a longer look at him in 2014 at high Class A Tampa.

Year	Club (League)	Class	W	L	ERA	G	GS	CG	SV	IP	H	HR	BB	SO	K/9	WHIP	AVG
2009	Mariners (VSL)	R	1	3	5.73	13	4	0	1	33	38	3	16	23	6.3	1.64	.297
2010	Mariners (VSL)	R	8	2	3.16	13	12	1	0	57	49	0	19	59	9.3	1.19	.231
2011	Everett (NWL)	SS	5	5	2.32	14	14	0	0	81	66	4	13	85	9.4	0.97	.214
2012	Charleston (SAL)	LoA	3	0	4.01	5	5	0	0	25	20	2	8	26	9.5	1.14	.213
2013	Charleston (SAL)	LoA	4	2	3.41	26	19	0	2	87	82	5	16	77	8.0	1.13	.249
Minor League Totals			21	12	3.37	71	54	1	3	283	255	14	72	270	8.6	1.16	.238

15 RAFAEL DE PAULA, RHP

BA GRADE 50 HIGH

Born: March 24, 1991. **B-T:** R-R. **Ht.:** 6-2. **Wt.:** 212. **Signed:** Dominican Republic, 2010. **Signed by:** Arturo Pena.

After identity snafus led to a one-year suspension and a 16-month layoff before Major League Baseball approved his $500,000 deal with the Yankees, De Paula spent his first year laying waste to much younger hitters in the Dominican Summer Leagues, building anticipation for his U.S. debut in 2013. He started in the low Class A South Atlantic League and treated hitters there much the same. The problem was, he relied on a fastball that could regularly reach into the mid- to upper 90s with hard, late sink. That all changed once De Paula got high Class A Tampa, where hitters promptly taught him that he'd need to rely more on his slider and changeup, which are both works in progress. De Paula's delivery gets out of sync easily, making it hard for him to throw either secondary offering for strikes. Moreover, evaluators thought he seemed hesitant to go to those pitches when necessary, instead choosing to throw his fastball as hard as he could in the hopes of blowing it past hitters as he'd done previously. His fastball is good enough that if even one of his offspeed pitches can touch average, he could be a quality reliever down the road. De Paula will require significant improvement to project as a starter in the long term, and he'll begin 2014 back at Tampa.

Year	Club (League)	Class	W	L	ERA	G	GS	CG	SV	IP	H	HR	BB	SO	K/9	WHIP	AVG
2011	Did not play—Restricted																
2012	Yankees 1 (DSL)	R	8	2	1.46	14	14	1	0	62	35	2	18	85	12.4	0.86	.162
2013	Charleston (SAL)	LoA	6	2	2.94	13	13	0	0	64	43	3	23	96	13.4	1.03	.189
	Tampa (FSL)	HiA	1	3	6.06	11	10	0	0	49	54	5	30	50	9.2	1.71	.283
Minor League Totals			15	7	3.29	38	37	1	0	175	132	10	71	231	11.9	1.16	.208

16 SHANE GREENE, RHP

BA GRADE 45 MEDIUM

Born: Nov. 17, 1988. **B-T:** R-R. **Ht.:** 6-3. **Wt.:** 200. **Drafted:** Daytona Beach (Fla.) JC, 2009 (15th round). **Signed by:** Jeff Deardorff.

The system's biggest jump on the mound in 2013 came from Greene, who's trying to become the first big leaguer out of Florida's Daytona Beach JC (now Daytona State JC). He had Tommy John surgery as a freshman at Division II West Florida in 2008 and transferred to the junior college, where the Yankees scouted him, drafted him and signed him for $100,000 in 2009. Greene had his first real pro success in 2013, a year after being sent back to extended spring training. He has made mechanical adjustments that got him more on-line to the plate, and mental adjustments to pitch more to the middle of the plate and let his stuff take over. Those changes made a world of difference and helped Greene lower his walk rate from 5.1 per nine innings in 2012 to 1.7 across two levels in 2013. He features a three-pitch mix that includes a 90-94 mph fastball with good angle from his crossfire delivery, a plus slider that ranges between 82-88 and a developing changeup. He's a quick worker with some inherent deception in his delivery that makes it difficult for hitters to pick up the ball. Added to the 40-man roster following the 2013 season, Greene projects as a reliever in the eyes of many scouts due to his fastball/slider combo. He could contend for such a role in New York in 2014, or move up a level as a starter at Triple-A Scranton/Wilkes-Barre.

Year	Club (League)	Class	W	L	ERA	G	GS	CG	SV	IP	H	HR	BB	SO	K/9	WHIP	AVG
2009	Yankees (GCL)	R	1	2	5.87	13	0	0	0	23	30	2	6	20	7.8	1.57	.297
2010	Staten Island (NYP)	SS	2	6	4.59	10	10	0	0	49	57	1	21	44	8.1	1.59	.289
	Charleston (SAL)	LoA	0	2	4.58	4	4	0	0	20	14	1	8	22	10.1	1.12	.206
2011	Charleston (SAL)	LoA	5	14	4.37	27	27	0	0	138	141	9	68	128	8.3	1.51	.265
2012	Tampa (FSL)	HiA	4	7	5.22	24	23	0	0	112	113	5	63	101	8.1	1.57	.265
2013	Tampa (FSL)	HiA	4	6	3.60	13	13	0	0	75	83	4	10	69	8.3	1.24	.279
	Trenton (EL)	AA	8	4	3.18	14	13	1	0	79	92	6	20	68	7.7	1.41	.289
Minor League Totals			24	41	4.35	105	90	1	0	496	530	28	196	452	8.2	1.46	.273

17 TYLER AUSTIN, OF

BA GRADE 45 MEDIUM

Born: Sept. 16, 1991. **B-T:** R-R. **Ht.:** 6-2. **Wt.:** 200. **Drafted:** HS—Conyers, Ga., 2010 (13th round). **Signed by:** Darryl Monroe.

The Yankees looked for big things from Double-A Trenton's outfield of Austin, Ramon Flores and Slade Heathcott, but injuries again frustrated Heathcott, while Flores and Austin had modest seasons. Austin slugged .373 with just 23 extra-base hits in 366 plate appearances, with the caveat being that he missed a month and a half with a wrist injury that he may have been playing with long before he told anyone. Austin looked rejuvenated down the stretch, hitting .304 in the Eastern League playoffs to help the Thunder win their third league title. He played just four games in the Arizona Fall League, however, before the wrist started barking again and he had to be shut down. He received a cortisone shot, and the wrist will bear watching, especially as it pertains to his future power potential. When healthy, Austin has showcased a quick, compact swing with power potential, though it was negated by his early struggles with breaking pitches, especially sliders from righties. Austin was to play first base in the AFL and may get more time there in 2014, though the Yankees say they still view him as a profile corner outfielder. He's slated to return to Trenton in 2014.

Year	Club (League)	Class	AVG	G	AB	R	H	2B	3B	HR	RBI	BB	SO	SB	CS	OBP	SLG
2010	Yankees (GCL)	R	.000	2	2	0	0	0	0	0	0	0	1	0	0	.500	.000
2011	Yankees (GCL)	R	.390	20	82	13	32	8	1	3	22	5	16	11	0	.438	.622
	Staten Island (NYP)	SS	.323	27	96	16	31	10	1	3	14	10	23	7	0	.402	.542
2012	Charleston (SAL)	LoA	.320	70	266	69	85	22	5	14	54	37	68	17	2	.405	.598
	Yankees (GCL)	R	.500	2	6	1	3	0	0	1	2	1	1	0	0	.571	1.000
	Tampa (FSL)	HiA	.321	36	134	20	43	13	1	2	23	12	28	6	0	.385	.478
	Trenton (EL)	AA	.286	2	7	2	2	0	0	0	1	1	1	0	0	.375	.286
2013	Yankees2 (GCL)	R	.667	2	6	1	4	0	0	0	0	1	0	0	0	.714	.667
	Trenton (EL)	AA	.257	83	319	43	82	17	1	6	40	41	79	4	0	.344	.373
Minor League Totals			.307	244	918	165	282	70	9	29	156	108	217	45	2	.387	.498

18 MIGUEL ANDUJAR, 3B

BA GRADE 55 EXTREME

Born: March 2, 1995. **B-T:** R-R. **Ht.:** 6-0. **Wt.:** 200. **Signed:** Dominican Republic, 2011. **Signed by:** Victor Mata/Coanabo Cosme.

Andujar worked with the same Dominican trainer, Basilio Vizcaino (known as "Cachaza"), who delivered Gary Sanchez to the Yankees. Andujar signed in July 2011 for $750,000, the largest in the Yankees' international class that year, and he jumped straight to the Rookie-level Gulf Coast League and struggled to adjust in 2012. The Yankees kept Andujar in the same league in 2013, and he broke out. As far as tools, Andujar has it all but speed. He can hit for average and has plus raw power thanks to his bat speed and sound swing. Defensively, he fits the third-base profile with above-average range and a good arm, though his inexperience led to 11 errors in just 26 games. His manager in the GCL, Mario Garza, said that if Andujar concentrated on base hits and sacrificed power, he could hit .400. And while that might be hyperbolic, it highlights Andujar's chops at the plate. He needs to be a little more selective to realize his future and is just a fringe-average runner, but he has the ingredients to zoom up this list. Andujar likely will begin 2014 in extended spring training with a June assignment to short-season Staten Island.

Year	Club (League)	Class	AVG	G	AB	R	H	2B	3B	HR	RBI	BB	SO	SB	CS	OBP	SLG
2012	Yankees (GCL)	R	.232	50	177	21	41	9	0	1	19	13	37	1	3	.288	.299
2013	Yankees2 (GCL)	R	.323	34	133	18	43	11	0	4	25	7	21	4	1	.368	.496
Minor League Totals			.271	84	310	39	84	20	0	5	44	20	58	5	4	.322	.384

19 LUIS TORRENS, C

BA GRADE 55 EXTREME

Born: May 2, 1996. **B-T:** R-R. **Ht.:** 6-0. **Wt.:** 185. **Signed:** Venezuela, 2012. **Signed by:** Alan Atacho/Darwin Bracho/Ricardo Finol.

Torrens trained with Carlos Rios, the Yankees' former international scouting director, and played for Rios' team in Panama's winter league when he was just 15. He signed for $1.3 million in 2012, and even though he's fairly new to catching, he might be the best defender in the current line of Yankees catching prospects. He used an incredibly quick release to throw out an eye-popping 45 percent of basestealers in the Rookie-level Gulf Coast League in 2013. The finer points of the position—blocking, game-calling, receiving—are in development, but the signs are good for the 17-year-old. Despite his inexperience, Torrens held his own when catching high-velocity arms like Luis Severino, Omar Luis and Rony Bautista in the GCL. His bat produces both power and average and projects to be similar to that of fellow Yankees prospect J.R. Murphy down the line, possibly with more home run power. Torrens tired toward the end of the 2013 season, and he probably will start 2014 in extended spring training with a chance to move up to short-season Staten Island in June.

Year	Club (League)	Class	AVG	G	AB	R	H	2B	3B	HR	RBI	BB	SO	SB	CS	OBP	SLG
2013	Yankees2 (GCL)	R	.241	48	174	17	42	7	0	1	14	27	40	2	0	.348	.299
Minor League Totals			.241	48	174	17	42	7	0	1	14	27	40	2	0	.348	.299

20 RAMON FLORES, OF

BA GRADE
45
MEDIUM

Born: March 26, 1992. **B-T:** L-L. **Ht.:** 5-10. **Wt.:** 150. **Signed:** Venezuela, 2008. **Signed by:** Ricardo Finol.

Scouts have liked Flores' offensive game for years while waiting for more production, a trend that continued in 2013. They saw much the same Flores at Double-A Trenton, a tweener who can play center field but fits better on a corner, with one of the lowest slugging percentages (.363) among Eastern Leaguers who played primarily corner outfield. Flores, one of just six players who played the entire season in the EL at 21 or younger, remains comfortable working deep counts and ranked sixth in the league in walks (77). The lefthanded hitter's line-drive power was to his pull side only. He spent a good part of the winter at the Yankees' Tampa complex working to put on weight and add strength. If his power doesn't develop, Flores will be no more than a fourth outfielder. A member of the 40-man roster, he could head to Triple-A Scranton/Wilkes-Barre in 2014, but a return to Trenton isn't out of the picture, either.

Year	Club (League)	Class	AVG	G	AB	R	H	2B	3B	HR	RBI	BB	SO	SB	CS	OBP	SLG
2009	Yankees 2 (DSL)	R	.256	11	39	8	10	0	3	1	5	11	5	0	1	.423	.487
	Yankees (GCL)	R	.196	51	158	14	31	5	1	0	14	22	35	7	5	.303	.241
2010	Tampa (FSL)	HiA	.250	8	28	0	7	0	0	0	2	0	5	0	0	.250	.250
	Yankees (GCL)	R	.329	43	158	33	52	10	4	2	22	28	22	4	1	.436	.481
	Charleston (SAL)	LoA	.250	14	48	3	12	3	0	0	2	3	15	1	0	.294	.313
2011	Charleston (SAL)	LoA	.265	125	468	59	124	26	2	11	59	61	93	13	2	.353	.400
2012	Tampa (FSL)	HiA	.302	131	517	83	156	29	7	6	39	54	85	24	9	.370	.420
	Trenton (EL)	AA	.400	1	5	2	2	0	0	1	2	0	0	0	0	.400	1.000
2013	Trenton (EL)	AA	.260	136	534	79	139	25	6	6	55	77	98	7	6	.353	.363
Minor League Totals			.273	520	1955	281	533	98	23	27	200	256	358	56	24	.360	.388

21 BRYAN MITCHELL, RHP

BA GRADE
55
EXTREME

Born: April 19, 1991. **B-T:** R-R. **Ht.:** 6-3. **Wt.:** 205. **Drafted:** HS—Hamlet, N.C., 2009 (16th round). **Signed by:** Scott Lovekamp.

Mitchell may be the system's biggest tease, with tremendous stuff paired with mediocre results. His 5.12 ERA was one of the worst in the high Class A Florida State League among qualifiers, and he led the league with 23 wild pitches. He still earned a late-season promotion to Double-A Trenton, where he thrived in three starts before walking 11 in 10 playoff innings. Mitchell invites questions about his mental toughness and wrinkles that need to be ironed out in his delivery, namely finding a more consistent release point. Like Rafael De Paula, he has a tendency to respond to adversity by trying to throw his fastball—which sits between 91-94 mph and has touched 97 in the past—through the catcher's mitt. Unlike De Paula, however, Mitchell has good enough offspeed stuff that he shouldn't have to. His curveball can be a true wipeout pitch with power, as he'll touch 85 mph with it, and his overall package has drawn comparisons with A.J. Burnett's. His changeup is still in its developmental stages. Added to the 40-man roster following the 2013 season, he's far from ready to help in New York, and he's headed back to Trenton to open 2014.

Year	Club (League)	Class	W	L	ERA	G	GS	CG	SV	IP	H	HR	BB	SO	K/9	WHIP	AVG
2010	Yankees (GCL)	R	2	1	3.67	10	9	0	0	42	28	2	22	36	7.8	1.20	.190
	Staten Island (NYP)	SS	0	1	6.75	1	1	0	0	4	7	0	1	3	6.8	2.00	.368
2011	Staten Island (NYP)	SS	1	3	4.09	14	14	0	0	62	65	5	31	59	8.6	1.56	.275
2012	Charleston (SAL)	LoA	9	11	4.58	27	26	0	0	120	107	7	72	121	9.1	1.49	.240
2013	Tampa (FSL)	HiA	4	11	5.12	24	23	1	0	127	144	5	53	104	7.4	1.56	.289
	Trenton (EL)	AA	0	0	1.93	3	3	0	0	19	14	0	5	16	7.7	1.02	.206
Minor League Totals			16	27	4.47	79	76	1	0	373	365	19	184	339	8.2	1.47	.258

22 JAKE CAVE, OF

Born: Dec. 7, 1992. **B-T:** L-L. **Ht.:** 6-0. **Wt.:** 179. **Drafted:** HS—Hampton, Va., 2011 (6th round). **Signed by:** Scott Lovekamp.

Despite having only one pro at-bat after missing the entire 2012 season recovering from a right knee injury, Cave wasn't fazed by an assignment to low Class A Charleston, holding his own in a tough hitter's park. He opened the 2013 season in extended spring training but hit his way onto the RiverDogs roster, then tied for third in the South Atlantic League in doubles and grinded his way through a full season, a good sign considering his youth and injury history. As everyday center fielder for Charleston, Cave provided professional at-bats and showed a solid lefthanded swing with a good feel for the barrel. His dirtbag approach and instincts to stay in center field further endear him to scouts. A former high school pitcher who reached 94 mph from the left side, he has the raw arm strength for right field and runs well. Cave still is growing and adding strength, so some of those doubles could become homers a few years down the line. He's an intense player who also earns solid marks for his makeup. After last season's success, Cave will head to high Class A Tampa in 2014. He looks like at least a fourth outfielder, and more if his bat continues to develop.

Year	Club (League)	Class	AVG	G	AB	R	H	2B	3B	HR	RBI	BB	SO	SB	CS	OBP	SLG
2011	Yankees (GCL)	R	.000	1	1	0	0	0	0	0	0	1	0	0	0	.500	.000
2012	Did not play—Injured																
2013	Charleston (SAL)	LoA	.282	115	464	69	131	37	6	2	31	40	110	18	9	.347	.401
Minor League Totals			.282	116	465	69	131	37	6	2	31	41	110	18	9	.347	.400

23 PETER O'BRIEN, C/3B

BA GRADE **45** MEDIUM

Born: July 15, 1990. **B-T:** R-R. **Ht.:** 6-3. **Wt.:** 215. **Drafted:** Miami, 2011 (2nd round). **Signed by:** Carlos Marti.

O'Brien was two of the organization's better developments in an otherwise down year on the farm in 2013. A senior sign out of Miami, O'Brien led the system in home runs (22) and RBIs (96) and ranked second to Robert Refsnyder in batting (.291). He generates the most usable power of anyone in the organization except for Gary Sanchez and hit a 455-foot homer that ranked as the longest in the Arizona Fall League. Despite the high average, scouts grade O'Brien as a modest hitter thanks to a long, one-plane swing and lack of fluidity. He's strong enough to hit for power if he shortens up, and he has shown signs of making adjustments. Defense is a bigger question, and he grades out as a below-average defender either behind the plate or on the infield corners. He hadn't played third base since high school until 2013 and lacks mobility and agility. His plus arm does give him value as a catcher, but he's a limited receiver and struggles blocking balls in the dirt. His well below-average speed may preclude a move to the outfield. O'Brien will move to Double-A Trenton in 2014 and could wind up as a Jim Leyritz type who catches and sees time at the corners at the big league level.

Year	Club (League)	Class	AVG	G	AB	R	H	2B	3B	HR	RBI	BB	SO	SB	CS	OBP	SLG
2012	Yankees (GCL)	R	.357	4	14	2	5	2	0	0	2	0	1	0	0	.357	.500
	Staten Island (NYP)	SS	.202	48	198	27	40	8	0	10	32	10	61	0	1	.249	.394
2013	Charleston (SAL)	LoA	.325	53	194	47	63	22	1	11	41	22	58	0	0	.394	.619
	Tampa (FSL)	HiA	.265	66	253	31	67	17	3	11	55	19	76	0	1	.314	.486
Minor League Totals			.266	171	659	107	175	49	4	32	130	51	196	0	2	.321	.498

24 TY HENSLEY, RHP

BA GRADE **55** EXTREME

Born: July 30, 1993. **B-T:** B-R. **Ht.:** 6-5. **Wt.:** 220. **Drafted:** HS—Edmond, Okla., 2012 (1st round). **Signed by:** Lloyd Simmons/Dennis Woody.

The Yankees hadn't drafted and signed a prep righthander in the first round since Phil Hughes in 2004 when they took Hensley in 2012. He originally agreed to terms for $1.6 million but had his bonus reduced to $1.2 million after a physical revealed shoulder abnormalities. His injury news worsened in 2013 when abdominal pain that sidelined him in spring training turned out to be tied to a hip impingement that required surgery. The procedure cost Hensley the entire season, which means he'll have just 12 pro innings under his belt when the 2014 season gets under way. At his best, he couples a 92-95 mph fastball with a 12-to-6 curveball reminiscent of the one Phillies righty Ethan Martin employs. Hensley hasn't gotten many pro innings to work on his nascent changeup. His health will be closely monitored, and the Yankees are eager to see what their first-rounder can do if he's ever healthy. They hope to find out in 2014 at low Class A Charleston.

Year	Club (League)	Class	W	L	ERA	G	GS	CG	SV	IP	H	HR	BB	SO	K/9	WHIP	AVG
2012	Yankees (GCL)	R	1	2	3.00	5	4	0	0	12	8	1	7	14	10.5	1.25	.174
2013	Did not play—Injured																
Minor League Totals			1	2	3.00	5	4	0	0	12	8	1	7	14	10.5	1.25	.174

25 ANGELO GUMBS, 2B

BA GRADE **50** EXTREME

Born: Oct. 13, 1992. **B-T:** R-R. **Ht.:** 6-0. **Wt.:** 175. **Drafted:** HS—Torrance, Calif., 2010 (2nd round). **Signed by:** Dave Keith.

Gumbs was having a breakout season in 2012 at low Class A Charleston when a torn ligament in his left elbow cut it short. He didn't need surgery, and the Yankees aggressively assigned him to high Class A Tampa to start the 2013 season. He had three hits in his first two games, then didn't get another hit the rest of April. He missed a month with a bruised middle finger and never got going, forcing a late-June demotion back to Charleston. Gumbs still has plenty of bat speed, with a compact but unorthodox swing that he has made work with his high-level hand-eye coordination. He's sound defensively at second base and has shown the ability to hang in on double-play pivots. An average runner out of the box and a tick better once he gets going, he is capable of stealing 15-20 bases. Robert Refsnyder emerged and is a level higher in the system, but Gumbs is younger and has more tools. He will return to Tampa for 2014.

Year	Club (League)	Class	AVG	G	AB	R	H	2B	3B	HR	RBI	BB	SO	SB	CS	OBP	SLG
2010	Yankees (GCL)	R	.192	7	26	1	5	1	0	0	0	1	3	3	0	.222	.231
2011	Staten Island (NYP)	SS	.264	51	197	32	52	11	4	3	29	20	57	11	7	.332	.406
2012	Charleston (SAL)	LoA	.272	67	257	40	70	14	3	7	36	18	60	26	3	.320	.432
2013	Tampa (FSL)	HiA	.214	39	159	16	34	10	2	0	11	8	31	6	1	.265	.302
	Charleston (SAL)	LoA	.213	52	202	20	43	10	3	4	26	13	55	10	5	.261	.351
Minor League Totals			.243	216	841	109	204	46	12	14	102	60	206	56	16	.296	.376

26 DELLIN BETANCES, RHP

BA GRADE 45 HIGH

Born: March 23, 1988. **B-T:** R-R. **Ht.:** 6-8. **Wt.:** 260. **Drafted:** HS—Brooklyn, 2006 (8th round). **Signed by:** Cesar Presbott/Brian Barber.

Betances made six Triple-A starts to open 2013, posting a 6.00 ERA, before shifting to relief full-time. In 42 games out of the pen, he posted a 1.35 ERA and allowed just 33 hits in 60 innings to go with 83 strikeouts. His fastball touched 99 mph out of the pen, and he backed it up with a power curve and a changeup. Mechanical adjustments made with new pitching coordinator Gil Patterson helped him stay in his delivery longer, which in turn improved Betances' command. Being in the bullpen also helped him flush his bad outings more quickly. Control always will be an issue for Betances, who qualifies for a fourth minor league option in 2014, giving the Yankees another long look at his two-pitch mix.

Year	Club (League)	Class	W	L	ERA	G	GS	CG	SV	IP	H	HR	BB	SO	K/9	WHIP	AVG
2006	Yankees (GCL)	R	0	1	1.16	7	7	0	0	23	14	1	7	27	10.4	0.90	.173
2007	Staten Island (NYP)	SS	1	2	3.60	6	6	0	0	25	24	0	17	29	10.4	1.64	.255
2008	Yankees (GCL)	R	0	1	8.53	3	2	0	0	6	13	0	3	6	8.5	2.53	.406
	Charleston (SAL)	LoA	9	4	3.67	22	22	0	0	115	87	9	59	135	10.5	1.27	.208
2009	Tampa (FSL)	HiA	2	5	5.48	11	11	0	0	44	48	2	27	44	8.9	1.69	.277
2010	Tampa (FSL)	HiA	8	1	1.77	14	14	0	0	71	43	1	19	88	11.2	0.87	.169
	Trenton (EL)	AA	0	0	3.77	3	3	0	0	14	10	3	3	20	12.6	0.91	.200
2011	Trenton (EL)	AA	4	6	3.42	21	21	0	0	105	86	7	55	115	9.8	1.34	.219
	Scranton/W-B (IL)	AAA	0	3	5.14	4	4	1	0	21	16	2	15	27	11.6	1.48	.208
	New York (AL)	MAJ	0	0	6.75	2	1	0	0	3	1	0	6	2	6.8	2.63	.125
2012	Scranton/W-B (IL)	AAA	3	5	6.39	16	16	0	0	75	71	9	69	71	8.6	1.88	.250
	Trenton (EL)	AA	3	4	6.51	11	10	0	0	57	73	4	30	53	8.4	1.82	.319
2013	Scranton/W-B (IL)	AAA	6	4	2.68	38	6	0	5	84	52	2	42	108	11.6	1.12	.178
	New York (AL)	MAJ	0	0	10.80	6	0	0	0	5	9	1	2	10	18.0	2.20	.375
Major League Totals			0	0	9.39	8	1	0	0	8	10	1	8	12	14.1	2.35	.312
Minor League Totals			36	36	3.99	156	122	1	5	641	537	40	346	723	10.1	1.38	.226

27 BRETT MARSHALL, RHP

BA GRADE 45 HIGH

Born: March 22, 1990. **B-T:** R-R. **Ht.:** 6-1. **Wt.:** 195. **Drafted:** HS—Baytown, Texas, 2008 (6th round). **Signed by:** Steve Boros.

Marshall made his big league debut in 2013, but overall had his worst season since he had Tommy John surgery in 2009. He missed up in the zone too much in 2013, giving up the most home runs (17) of his career while also issuing a career high in walks (4.4 per nine innings). Still, Marshall has the makings of an innings-eater who brings a four-pitch arsenal of fastball, slider, changeup and little-used curveball to the table. His fastball, which sits between 87-92 mph with occasional flickers of 93 and 94, features strong tail. His changeup has similar tail and sink as his fastball, but he didn't command the pitch as well in 2013. Marshall's long arm action always has inhibited command of his breaking ball, but he went more to the slider in 2013, which is fringe-average. He has a tenuous hold on a 40-man roster spot, and should return to Triple-A in 2014.

Year	Club (League)	Class	W	L	ERA	G	GS	CG	SV	IP	H	HR	BB	SO	K/9	WHIP	AVG
2008	Yankees (GCL)	R	0	0	0.00	3	3	0	0	6	2	0	2	8	12.0	0.67	.087
2009	Charleston (SAL)	LoA	3	6	5.56	17	17	0	0	87	98	7	37	60	6.2	1.55	.290
2010	Yankees (GCL)	R	0	0	2.25	2	1	0	0	8	6	0	4	8	9.0	1.25	.194
	Charleston (SAL)	LoA	4	2	2.50	13	13	1	0	72	52	2	22	56	7.0	1.03	.199
	Tampa (FSL)	HiA	0	0	4.50	1	1	0	0	4	5	0	0	6	13.5	1.25	.294
2011	Tampa (FSL)	HiA	9	7	3.78	27	26	0	0	140	142	6	48	114	7.3	1.35	.271
2012	Trenton (EL)	AA	13	7	3.52	27	27	0	0	158	151	15	53	120	6.8	1.29	.255
2013	Scranton/W-B (IL)	AAA	7	10	5.13	25	25	0	0	139	144	17	68	120	7.8	1.53	.271
	New York (AL)	MAJ	0	0	4.50	3	0	0	0	12	13	3	7	7	5.3	1.67	.283
Major League Totals			0	0	4.50	3	0	0	0	12	13	3	7	7	5.3	1.67	.283
Minor League Totals			36	32	4.07	115	113	1	0	615	600	47	234	492	7.2	1.36	.259

28 THAIRO ESTRADA, SS

BA GRADE
50
EXTREME

Born: Feb. 22, 1996. **B-T:** R-R. **Ht.:** 5-10. **Wt.:** 155. **Signed:** Venezuela, 2012. **Signed by:** Alan Atacho/Ricardo Finol.

The Yankees fielded two Rookie-level Gulf Coast League teams in 2013 for the first time, often shifting players back and forth between the two rosters. Estrada was the regular shortstop on GCL Yankees 2, sliding to second base when Abiatal Avelino joined the team for 15 games. Signed in July 2012 for a bonus just shy of $50,000, Estrada impresses with skills and tools. His swing is short and flat with a good feel for the barrel and the ability to go to the opposite field. He's a plus runner with a plus arm who has shown the ability to play at both second base and shortstop. He uses his quick hands and quick feet to make the play on every ball he gets to. The system's lower levels are crowded with middle-infield options, so Estrada could be headed back to the GCL in 2014. He may profile best as a utility infielder in the long term.

Year	Club (League)	Class	AVG	G	AB	R	H	2B	3B	HR	RBI	BB	SO	SB	CS	OBP	SLG
2013	Yankees2 (GCL)	R	.278	50	176	28	49	11	5	2	17	12	30	7	5	.350	.432
Minor League Totals			.278	50	176	28	49	11	5	2	17	12	30	7	5	.350	.432

29 ROBERT REFSNYDER, 2B/OF

BA GRADE
45
HIGH

Born: March 26, 1991. **B-T:** R-R. **Ht.:** 6-1. **Wt.:** 205. **Drafted:** Arizona, 2012 (5th round). **Signed by:** Steve Kmetko.

Much like Peter O'Brien, Refsnyder is man without a position. He played right field at Arizona, but the Yankees shifted him from outfield to second base in 2013, and he received mixed reviews for his work. Refsnyder has enough athleticism to become an average defender at the position in time, but he needs plenty of repetitions. He's a smart, above-average runner, but not a burner, who led Yankees full-season players in stolen bases (23). He's an extremely patient hitter, as evinced by his 84 walks against 82 strikeouts, who recognizes spin well and knows when and how to go with a pitch. Refsnyder sprays line drives all over the field and has the ability to keep the head of the bat in the zone for a long time. He doesn't get much lift, so he's not going to hit more than 10-12 home runs going forth. Refnsyder's modest power fits the second base profile better than the corner-outfield profile, so taking root at the keystone is crucial. He's headed for Double-A Trenton in 2014.

Year	Club (League)	Class	AVG	G	AB	R	H	2B	3B	HR	RBI	BB	SO	SB	CS	OBP	SLG
2012	Charleston (SAL)	LoA	.241	46	162	22	39	8	0	4	22	16	25	11	1	.319	.364
2013	Charleston (SAL)	LoA	.370	13	54	9	20	4	1	0	6	6	12	7	0	.452	.481
	Tampa (FSL)	HiA	.283	117	413	66	117	28	2	6	51	78	70	16	6	.408	.404
Minor League Totals			.280	176	629	97	176	40	3	10	79	100	107	34	7	.390	.401

30 VIDAL NUNO, LHP

Born: July 26, 1987. **B-T:** L-L. **Ht.:** 5-11. **Wt.:** 195. **Drafted:** Baker (Kan.), 2009 (48th round). **Signed by:** Steve Abney (Indians).

After being dumped by the Indians and biding his time in the independent Frontier League, the Yankees signed Nuno in June 2011. Two years later, he was pitching in Yankee Stadium. Nuno had the best control in the organization coming into 2013 and threw quality strikes in the majors as well before a left groin strain ended his campaign in June. Nuno returned in the Arizona Fall League and carved up hitters with fringy stuff and plus command. He relies on a sinker/slider combination, with a fastball in the 87-90 mph range. He has a knack for pitching, and can locate his curveball and changeup. Nuno will compete for a starting role but could wind up in the bullpen, or back at Triple-A Scranton/Wilkes-Barre

Year	Club (League)	Class	W	L	ERA	G	GS	CG	SV	IP	H	HR	BB	SO	K/9	WHIP	AVG
2009	Indians (AZL)	R	0	0	5.14	4	0	0	1	7	10	0	1	11	14.1	1.57	.333
	Mahoning Valley (NYP)	SS	5	0	2.05	13	8	0	0	57	43	3	14	48	7.6	1.00	.207
2010	Lake County (MWL)	LoA	6	8	4.96	21	16	0	0	94	104	13	14	94	9.0	1.25	--
2011	Washington (FRN)	IND	2	3	2.83	6	6	1	0	41	35	2	12	34	7.4	1.14	--
	Staten Island (NYP)	SS	5	0	0.72	8	0	0	1	25	14	0	3	29	10.4	0.68	.161
	Charleston (SAL)	LoA	2	1	1.80	7	7	0	0	40	37	4	2	37	8.3	0.98	.248
2012	Tampa (FSL)	HiA	1	1	2.96	11	1	0	0	24	22	2	6	26	9.6	1.15	.232
	Trenton (EL)	AA	9	5	2.45	20	20	0	0	114	109	10	27	100	7.9	1.19	.252
2013	New York (AL)	MAJ	1	2	2.25	5	3	0	0	20	16	2	6	9	4.1	1.10	.213
	Scranton/W-B (IL)	AAA	2	0	1.44	5	5	0	0	25	14	2	2	30	10.8	0.64	.157
Major League Totals			1	2	2.25	5	3	0	0	20	16	2	6	9	4.1	1.10	.213
Minor League Totals			30	15	2.84	89	57	0	2	387	353	34	69	375	8.7	1.09	.242

Oakland Athletics

BY JIM SHONERD

The Athletics proved their 2012 resurgence was no fluke, taking home their second straight American League West division title in 2013. They followed it with yet another Division Series exit, but the franchise appears set to keep competing with its bigger-spending division rivals for the next few seasons.

General manager Billy Beane won the Baseball America Executive of the Year award as the A's embraced the use of platoons as a means of generating offense on a tight budget. (Oakland ranked 27th out of 30 teams in Opening Day payroll in 2013 at $60.7 million.) The A's used platoons at four positions in the lineup and had four outfielders share three jobs. To get to that point, the organization found some new homes for several current or former big-name prospects.

Having young, cost-controlled players on hand will continue to be vital to the Athletics' success. Still, that hasn't stopped them from using prospects as moveable assets to help the big league team, and they did in 2013 to further their use of platoons.

The A's made a pair of key prospects-for-big leaguer deals following the 2012 season in which they surrendered their two highest-ranked pitching prospects at the time, righthanders A.J. Cole and Brad Peacock.

Oakland traded Cole to the Nationals in January 2013 in a three-team deal that also involved the Mariners and brought John Jaso to the A's to be part of their catching rotation. A few weeks later, Oakland brought in shortstop Jed Lowrie from the Astros, giving up Peacock, first baseman Chris Carter and catcher Max Stassi.

The A's dealt another former top prospect at the July trade deadline, when they dispatched 2009 first-round pick Grant Green to the Angels for Alberto Callaspo, whom they paired in a platoon with Eric Sogard at second base.

Even minus Cole and Peacock, the A's didn't lack for young pitching in 2013. Four-fifths of Oakland's rotation was age 26 or younger, save for 40-year-old Bartolo Colon.

Righthander Dan Straily, the organization's breakout prospect in 2012, had a solid first full year in Oakland, going 10-8, 3.86 in 27 starts. The A's also got vital contributions from righty Sonny Gray, their 2011 first-round pick, who made his major league debut in July and went on to join the rotation down the stretch. Gray went 5-3, 2.67 in 64 big league innings during the regular season and made two playoff starts, including an electrifying performance in which he threw eight shutout innings against the Tigers in Game Two of the ALDS.

Between their assorted trades, the graduations of Gray and Straily and a couple of thin drafts in 2010 and 2011, the upper levels of Oakland's system have been largely cleaned out. Just three of Oakland's top 10 prospects—Addison Russell, Michael Choice and Max Muncy—are expected to open the season at Double-A or above. While the A's have already gotten Gray to the majors out of the 2011 draft and did well to find A.J. Griffin in the 13th round in 2010, that leaves just four players from those two classes to rank among the system's top 30 prospects.

BILL NICHOLS

Sonny Gray became the latest young arm to join Oakland's major league rotation

TOP PROSPECTS OF THE DECADE

Year	Player, Pos.	2013 Org.
2004	Bobby Crosby, ss	Out of baseball
2005	Nick Swisher, of	Indians
2006	Daric Barton, 1b	Athletics
2007	Travis Buck, of	Padres
2008	Daric Barton, 1b	Athletics
2009	Brett Anderson, lhp	Athletics
2010	Chris Carter, 1b/of	Astros
2011	Grant Green, ss	Angels
2012	Jarrod Parker, rhp	Athletics
2013	Addison Russell, ss	Athletics

ORGANIZATION OVERVIEW

General Manager: Billy Beane. **Farm Director:** Keith Lieppman. **Scouting Director:** Eric Kubota.

Class	Team	League	W	L	PCT	Finish	Manager
Majors	Oakland Athletics	American	96	66	.593	2nd (15)	Bob Melvin
Triple-A	Sacramento	Pacific Coast	79	65	.549	3rd (16)	Steve Scarsone
Double-A	Midland Rockhounds	Texas	62	78	.443	7th (8)	Aaron Nieckula
High Class A	Stockton Ports	California	69	71	.493	t-5th (10)	Webster Garrison
Low Class A	Beloit Snappers	Midwest	77	62	.554	5th (16)	Ryan Christenson
Short-season	Vermont Lake Monsters	New York-Penn	33	43	.434	12th (14)	Rick Magnante
Rookie	AZL Athletics	Arizona	25	30	.455	9th (13)	Marcus Jensen
Overall 2013 Minor League Record			**345**	**349**	**.497**	**t-13th (30)**	

THIS YEAR'S TOP 30

No.	Player, Pos.	Grade/Risk
1.	Addison Russell, ss	65/Medium
2.	Billy McKinney, of	55/High
3.	Michael Choice, of	50/Medium
4.	Raul Alcantara, rhp	55/High
5.	Michael Ynoa, rhp	55/Extreme
6.	Renato Nunez, 3b	55/Extreme
7.	Max Muncy, 1b	50/High
8.	Dylan Covey, rhp	50/High
9.	Bobby Wahl, rhp	50/High
10.	Daniel Robertson, ss	50/High
11.	Nolan Sanburn, rhp	50/High
12.	Matt Olson, 1b	50/High
13.	Ryon Healy, 3b/1b	50/High
14.	Dillon Overton, lhp	55/Extreme
15.	Chad Pinder, ss	50/High
16.	Kyle Finnegan, rhp	50/High
17.	Ronald Herrera, rhp	50/High
18.	Chris Bostick, 2b	50/High
19.	Chris Kohler, lhp	50/High
20.	B.J. Boyd, of	50/High
21.	Arnold Leon, rhp	45/Medium
22.	Miles Head, 3b/1b	45/High
23.	Anthony Aliotti, 1b	45/High
24.	Aaron Shipman, of	45/High
25.	Seth Streich, rhp	45/High
26.	Dustin Driver, rhp	50/Extreme
27.	Michael Taylor, of	40/Low
28.	Bruce Maxwell, c	45/High
29.	Tanner Peters, rhp	45/High
30.	Iolana Akau, c	45/High

LAST YEAR'S TOP 30

No.	Player, Pos.	Status
1.	Addison Russell, ss	No. 1
2.	Michael Choice, of	No. 3
3.	A.J. Cole, rhp	(Nationals)
4.	Brad Peacock, rhp	(Astros)
5.	Sonny Gray, rhp	Majors
6.	Dan Straily, rhp	Majors
7.	Miles Head, 3b/1b	No. 22
8.	Grant Green, 2b/of	(Angels)
9.	Daniel Robertson, ss/3b	No. 10
10.	Matt Olson, 1b	No. 12
11.	Nolan Sanburn, rhp	No. 11
12.	Renato Nunez, 3b	No. 6
13.	Pedro Figueroa, lhp	Dropped out
14.	Max Stassi, c	(Astros)
15.	Michael Taylor, of	No. 27
16.	Max Muncy, 1b	No. 7
17.	B.A. Vollmuth, 3b/1b	Dropped out
18.	Michael Ynoa, rhp	No. 5
19.	Beau Taylor, c	Dropped out
20.	Chris Bostick, 2b/ss	No. 18
21.	Seth Streich, rhp	No. 25
22.	B.J. Boyd, of	No. 20
23.	Bruce Maxwell, c	No. 28
24.	Aaron Shipman, of	No. 24
25.	Bobby Crocker, of	Dropped out
26.	Raul Alcantara, rhp	No. 4
27.	Steve Parker, 3b	(Brewers)
28.	Andrew Carignan, rhp	(Free agent)
29.	Arnold Leon, rhp	No. 21
30.	Josh Bowman, rhp	Dropped out

BEST TOOLS

Best Hitter for Average	Addison Russell
Best Power Hitter	Michael Choice
Best Strike-Zone Discipline	Max Muncy
Fastest Baserunner	Aaron Shipman
Best Athlete	Addison Russell
Best Fastball	Michael Ynoa
Best Curveball	Dylan Covey
Best Slider	Bobby Wahl
Best Changeup	Raul Alcantara
Best Control	Raul Alcantara
Best Defensive Catcher	Iolana Akau
Best Defensive Infielder	Addison Russell
Best Infield Arm	Chad Pinder
Best Defensive Outfielder	Billy McKinney
Best Outfield Arm	Michael Taylor

TOP 15 PLAYERS 25 AND UNDER

No.	Player, Pos. (Age)	Peak Level
1.	Addison Russell, ss (20)	Triple-A
2.	Jarrod Parker, rhp (25)	Majors
3.	Sonny Gray, rhp (24)	Majors
4.	Billy McKinney, of (19)	Short-season
5.	Michael Choice, of (24)	Majors
6.	Dan Straily, rhp (25)	Majors
7.	Raul Alcantara, rhp (21)	High Class A
8.	Michael Ynoa, rhp (22)	High Class A
9.	Derek Norris, c (25)	Majors
10.	Renato Nunez, 3b (19)	Low Class A
11.	Dylan Covey, rhp (22)	Low Class A
12.	Bobby Wahl, rhp (22)	Short-season
13.	Max Muncy, 1b (23)	Double-A
14.	Daniel Robertson, ss (20)	Low Class A
15.	Nolan Sanburn, rhp (22)	Low Class A

MINOR LEAGUE DEPTH CHART

OAKLAND ATHLETICS

TOP 2014 ROOKIE: Michael Choice, of. If he can elbow his way into Oakland's outfield, Choice's bat can make an immediate impact.

BREAKOUT PROSPECT: Ronald Herrera, rhp. The previously unheralded Venezuelan teenager has projection and advanced feel for pitching.

SLEEPER: Boog Powell, of. A 20th-round pick in 2012, Powell's athleticism stands out and his hitting made strides in 2013 at short-season Vermont.

SOURCE OF TOP 30 TALENT

Homegrown	**27**	**Acquired**	**3**
College	13	Trades	3
Junior college	0	Rule 5 draft	0
High school	10	Independent leagues	0
Nondrafted free agents	0	Free agents/waivers	0
International	4		

LF
Bobby Crocker
Shane Peterson
Luis Barrera
Conner Crumbliss
Josh Whitaker

CF
Billy McKinney (2)
B.J. Boyd (20)
Aaron Shipman (24)
Boog Powell

RF
Michael Choice (3)
Michael Taylor (27)
Jaycob Brugman
Tyler Marincov

3B
Renato Nunez (6)
B.A. Vollmuth
Vinnie Catricala

SS
Addison Russell (1)
Daniel Robertson (10)
Chad Pinder (15)
Carlos Hiciano

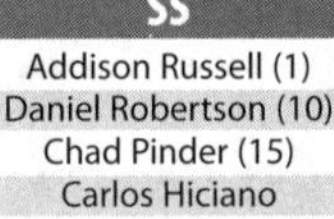

2B
Chris Bostick (18)
Jesus Lopez
Edwin Diaz

1B
Max Muncy (7)
Matt Olson (12)
Ryon Healy (13)
Miles Head (22)
Anthony Aliotti (23)

C
Bruce Maxwell (28)
Iolana Akau (30)
Beau Taylor
David Freitas

LHP

LHSP	LHRP
Dillon Overton (14)	Pedro Figueroa
Chris Kohler (19)	Jeff Urlaub
Jose Torres	Omar Duran

RHP

RHSP	RHRP
Raul Alcantara (4)	Arnold Leon (21)
Michael Ynoa (5)	Blake Hassebrock
Dylan Covey (8)	Seth Frankoff
Bobby Wahl (9)	Ryan Dull
Nolan Sanburn (11)	Kris Hall
Kyle Finnegan (16)	Stuart Pudenz
Ronald Herrera (17)	
Seth Streich (25)	
Dustin Driver (26)	
Tanner Peters (29)	
Drew Granier	
Josh Bowman	
Sean Murphy	
Lou Trivino	

DRAFT ANALYSIS

2013

BONUSES: $5.9 MILLION

BEST PURE HITTER: OF Billy McKinney (1) combines a good feel for the strike zone with excellent barrel control. Throw in excellent bat speed and he has all the makings of an above-average hitter. While he didn't show it in his pro debut, 1B Ryon Healy (3) also projects to be an above-average hitter.

BEST POWER HITTER: Healy hasn't translated the raw power he shows in batting practice into games on a regular basis, but he has the potential to be a 25-home run hitter.

FASTEST RUNNER: OF Justin Higley (13) turned in sub-6.4-second 60-yard dash times during workouts, which makes him a top-of-the-scale speedster. But Higley is a long strider, so it's arguable that OF Ben McQuown (30) has as much usable speed. He led NCAA Division I with 54 steals in 61 attempts at Campbell in the spring and added 10 in 12 tries as a pro this summer.

BEST DEFENSIVE PLAYER: C Iolana Akau (20) is advanced for a high school catcher. He shows a plus arm, good footwork and excellent agility. SS Chad Pinder (2s) showed better than expected defense in his pro debut, silencing concerns that he might need to move off the position.

BEST FASTBALL: RHP Bobby Wahl (5) was touching 95-96 mph in his short stints as a starter this summer. He might touch higher than that down the road if ends up moving to the bullpen. RHP Dylan Covey (4) was consistently 90-92 mph, touching 94 as a starter after turning pro.

BEST SECONDARY PITCH: Covey can break off a plus breaking ball on a regular basis. LHP Dillon Overton (2) will have to wait until late next year to throw in a game as he recovers from Tommy John surgery, but he previously showed an excellent changeup.

BEST PRO DEBUT: McKinney hit .320/.383/.414 in the Rookie-level Arizona League, then posted an even better .353/.405/.559 line after a late promotion to short-season Vermont. RHP Sam Bragg (19) went 1-2, 1.24 while allowing earned runs in only two of his 19 appearances between three stops.

BEST ATHLETE: In addition to having blazing speed, Higley has size (6-foot-4) and athleticism.

MOST INTRIGUING BACKGROUND: Akau played on Hawaii's 2008 Little League World Series championship team, making a diving catch in left field and hitting a home run in the championship game against Mexico.

CLOSEST TO THE MAJORS: Wahl and Covey are both polished college pitchers, and their paths could be even quicker if they move to the bullpen.

BEST LATE-ROUND PICK: Akau fell to the 20th round because of questions about how much it would cost to buy him out of his Hawaii commitment, but the A's were able to sign him for $375,000.

THE ONE WHO GOT AWAY: Oakland wasn't able to get injured RHP A.J. Vanegas (19) to give up his senior year with Stanford. The A's made a run at signing C Francis Christy (38), now at Palomar (Calif.) JC.

ASSESSMENT: McKinney's value is tied to his bat, but it could be a special bat. After him, Oakland added accomplished college arms in Overton, Covey and Wahl. Overton's reduced bonus due to injury allowed the club to add Akau as well.

2012

BONUSES: $8.3 MILLION

Top prospect SS Addison Russell (1) highlights a prep-heavy class. SS/3B Daniel Robertson (1s), 1B Matt Olson (1s) also show promise.

GRADE: B+

2011

BONUSES: $3.1 MILLION

RHP Sonny Gray (1) struggled a bit in his first full season but was the Athletics' playoff ace in 2013. 2B Chris Bostick (44) was a nice late find.

GRADE: B

2010

BONUSES: $5.0 MILLION

OF Michael Choice (1) looks like a solid regular if not a star. RHP A.J. Griffin (13) has surprised in the majors. Oakland couldn't sign OF Aaron Judge (31).

GRADE: C

TOP DRAFT PICKS OF THE DECADE

Year	Player, Pos.	2013 Org.
2004	Landon Powell, c	Mets
2005	Cliff Pennington, ss	Diamondbacks
2006	Trevor Cahill, rhp (2nd round)	Diamondbacks
2007	James Simmons, rhp	Athletics
2008	Jemile Weeks, 2b	Athletics
2009	Grant Green, ss	Angels
2010	Michael Choice, of	Athletics
2011	Sonny Gray, rhp	Athletics
2012	Addison Russell, ss	Athletics
2013	Billy McKinney, of	Athletics

LARGEST BONUSES IN CLUB HISTORY

Michael Ynoa, 2008	$4,250,000
Mark Mulder, 1998	$3,200,000
Grant Green, 2009	$2,750,000
Addison Russell, 2012	$2,625,000
Renato Nunez, 2010	$2,200,000

1 ADDISON RUSSELL, SS

Born: Jan. 23, 1994. **B-T:** R-R. **Ht.:** 6-0. **Wt.:** 195.
Drafted: HS—Pace, Fla., 2012 (1st round).
Signed by: Kelcey Mucker.

A prominent amateur player, Russell was one of just two underclassmen to play in the 2010 Under Armour All-America Game. Athletics scouts were impressed at how he stood out playing with USA Baseball's 18U team, where he hit a grand slam in the gold-medal win against Canada in the 2011 Pan Am Championship in Colombia. In 2012, Oakland made him its first first-round pick out of high school since Jeremy Bonderman in 2001. The 11th overall pick, Russell signed for $2.625 million. After tearing up three levels in his pro debut in 2012, he earned an invitation to big league spring training in 2013, even though it wasn't stipulated in his contract. The A's gave him an aggressive assignment to high Class A Stockton, where he was the youngest player on a California League Opening Day roster by six months. Russell took some time to catch up with the speed of the league but responded to hit .305/.424/.555 in the second half, followed by a solid .282/.361/.435 showing in the Arizona Fall League.

One of the game's premier shortstop prospects, Russell can do everything on the field while showing polish beyond his years. His swing hasn't required much tinkering since he entered pro ball, as he generates explosive bat speed and has the bat-to-ball skills to make consistent contact. During Russell's time in big league camp, A's manager Bob Melvin noted the quality of the shortstop's at-bats. He uses the whole field and stays inside the ball well. He already had a mature approach, but he chased fewer pitches and controlled the strike zone even better as the 2013 season went along. His 61 walks were the second most of any Stockton player, and he drew 34 free passes over 52 games in the second half. Russell has plenty of power for a shortstop, though he'll rate closer to average overall as he projects to continue producing 15-20 homers a season after clubbing 17 in 2013. Russell tried bulking up in high school to become more of a power hitter, but the extra muscle mass did little more than relegate him to third base with Team USA. As a result, he refocused his efforts on ensuring he could stay at shortstop, and few question his defensive future now. Russell has solid fundamentals and takes good angles to balls. His lower half works well, and he has the range and athleticism to make plenty of highlight-quality plays. He doesn't have a cannon for an arm, but it's strong enough for the position and plays up thanks to his quick transfer and accuracy. He runs well and steals bases efficiently.

27
BA GRADE
65
MEDIUM
SCOUTING GRADES
BATTING 65
POWER 50
SPEED 60
DEFENSE 60
ARM 55

LARRY GOREN

The question isn't if Russell will become the A's everyday shortstop, but when. Jed Lowrie and Nick Punto will hold down the position in 2014, but neither should stand in Russell's way when he's ready. Slated to open 2014 at Double-A Midland, he should debut in Oakland at some point in 2014 and be the regular shortstop in 2015.

Year	Club (League)	Class	AVG	G	AB	R	H	2B	3B	HR	RBI	BB	SO	SB	CS	OBP	SLG
2012	Athletics (AZL)	R	.415	26	106	29	44	4	5	6	29	14	23	9	1	.488	.717
	Vermont (NYP)	SS	.340	13	53	9	18	2	2	1	7	4	13	2	0	.386	.509
	Burlington (MWL)	LoA	.310	16	58	8	18	4	2	0	9	5	12	5	1	.369	.448
2013	Stockton (CAL)	HiA	.275	107	429	85	118	29	10	17	60	61	116	21	3	.377	.508
	Sacramento (PCL)	AAA	.077	3	13	1	1	0	0	0	0	0	9	0	0	.077	.077
Minor League Totals			.302	165	659	132	199	39	19	24	105	84	173	37	5	.389	.528

2 BILLY McKINNEY, OF

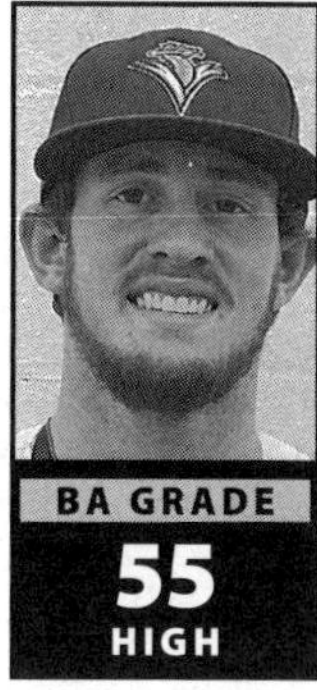

Born: Aug. 23, 1994. **B-T:** L-L. **Ht.:** 6-1. **Wt.:** 195. **Drafted:** HS—Plano, Texas, 2013 (1st round). **Signed by:** Armann Brown.

The Athletics had not selected a prep hitter in the first round since Eric Chavez in 1996, but they went to that demographic in successive drafts by taking Addison Russell in 2012 and McKinney in 2013, signing the latter for $1.8 million. McKinney played through a dislocated shoulder his junior year while starring on the showcase circuit, then showed his offensive polish by hitting a combined .326/.387/.437 at two levels in his 2013 debut spent mostly in the Rookie-level Arizona League. It didn't take long for observers in pro ball to fall in love with his baseball aptitude and picturesque lefthanded swing. He shows advanced instincts both at the plate and in the field, with his tool set drawing Mark Kotsay comparisons. McKinney gets around on good fastballs but also has the bat control to handle offspeed stuff, and he hits balls hard from line to line. Scouts forecast his power to show up more down the road, projecting him for 15-20 homers. He doesn't have premium speed, but he's a good athlete and average runner. He gets good jumps and takes quality routes in the outfield, giving him a chance to stick in center field, though the pre-draft consensus was he'd have to move to a corner. His average could give him a chance in right if he can't stick in center, though many scouts see him as a left fielder. Though McKinney isn't bursting with elite tools, he doesn't have any real holes, either, and his quality work ethic helps his tools play. He starts the climb to Oakland at low Class A Beloit in 2014.

Year	Club (League)	Class	AVG	G	AB	R	H	2B	3B	HR	RBI	BB	SO	SB	CS	OBP	SLG
2013	Athletics (AZL)	R	.320	46	181	31	58	7	2	2	20	17	29	7	0	.383	.414
	Vermont (NYP)	SS	.353	9	34	5	12	2	1	1	6	3	4	1	1	.405	.559
Minor League Totals			.326	55	215	36	70	9	3	3	26	20	33	8	1	.387	.437

3 MICHAEL CHOICE, OF

Born: Nov. 10, 1989. **B-T:** R-R. **Ht.:** 6-0. **Wt.:** 215. **Drafted:** Texas-Arlington, 2010 (1st round). **Signed by:** Armann Brown.

The Athletics took Choice 10th overall in 2010 on the strength of his power bat and signed him for $2 million. Since hitting 30 home runs in the high Class A California League in 2011, he hit just 24 the next two seasons combined. Choice hit a career-best .302 at Triple-A Sacramento in 2013 and made his big league debut in September. He has worked diligently to simplify his swing in pro ball, toning down the moving parts, a la Gary Sheffield, to give him a more direct path to the ball. The drop off in his homer production notwithstanding, Choice has plus raw power, with the bat speed and strength to hit balls out of any part of the park. He does take big hacks and will accumulate strikeouts, but he has good plate coverage and has sliced his strikeout rate from 25 percent in 2011 to 19 percent in 2013. Choice can play passable defense in center field but most likely ends up on a corner. His solid-average speed and arm strength make right field a good fit. He has the upside to be an impact bat at the major league level, even if he lands in a corner. Though he performed well in Sacramento in 2013, he has no obvious place in Oakland's outfield with Yoenis Cespedes, Coco Crisp and Josh Reddick from left to right. He faces a return to Triple-A in 2014.

Year	Club (League)	Class	AVG	G	AB	R	H	2B	3B	HR	RBI	BB	SO	SB	CS	OBP	SLG
2010	Athletics (AZL)	R	.000	3	7	1	0	0	0	0	0	2	2	0	0	.222	.000
	Vancouver (NWL)	SS	.284	27	102	20	29	10	2	7	26	15	43	6	1	.388	.627
2011	Stockton (CAL)	HiA	.285	118	467	79	133	28	1	30	82	61	134	9	5	.376	.542
2012	Midland (TL)	AA	.287	91	359	59	103	15	2	10	58	33	88	5	1	.356	.423
2013	Sacramento (PCL)	AAA	.302	132	510	90	154	29	1	14	89	69	115	1	2	.390	.445
	Oakland (AL)	MAJ	.278	9	18	2	5	1	0	0	0	1	6	0	0	.316	.333
Major League Totals			.278	9	18	2	5	1	0	0	0	1	6	0	0	.316	.333
Minor League Totals			.290	371	1445	249	419	82	6	61	255	180	382	21	9	.376	.482

4 RAUL ALCANTARA, RHP

Born: Dec. 4, 1992. **B-T:** R-R. **Ht.:** 6-3. **Wt.:** 180. **Signed:** Dominican Republic, 2009. **Signed by:** Manny Nanita (Red Sox).

The lowest-profile component of the three-player package the Athletics received from the Red Sox for Andrew Bailey in December 2011, joining the organization along with Josh Reddick and Miles Head, Alcantara now stands as Oakland's best pitching prospect after a big 2013. Hit hard in 2012, he dominated at low Class A Beloit in a followup. The A's attribute much of Alcantara's improvement to staying more on line to the plate and finishing his pitches better. He now throws with a smooth, repeatable delivery and commands the zone with fastballs that sit 92-93 mph and top out at 95. He sells his plus changeup with fading action well. He was able to turn his slider and curveball into distinct offerings last season, with the slider the more promising of the two, flashing plus at times. Scouts also noted a difference in Alcantara's mound presence, another issue in 2012. The A's added Alcantara to the 40-man roster after 2013, and he'll probably begin 2014 back at high Class A Stockton but could reach Double-A Midland at some point. He has the makings of a possible mid-rotation starter and could be ready for Oakland by mid-2015.

Year	Club (League)	Class	W	L	ERA	G	GS	CG	SV	IP	H	HR	BB	SO	K/9	WHIP	AVG
2010	Red Sox (DSL)	R	5	3	3.28	13	13	1	0	60	61	1	8	34	5.1	1.14	.260
2011	Red Sox (GCL)	R	1	1	0.75	9	9	0	0	48	23	0	6	36	6.8	0.60	.147
	Lowell (NYP)	SS	0	3	6.23	4	4	0	0	17	25	0	6	14	7.3	1.79	.333
2012	Burlington (MWL)	LoA	6	11	5.08	27	17	0	0	103	119	12	38	57	5.0	1.53	.304
2013	Beloit (MWL)	LoA	7	1	2.44	13	13	1	0	77	84	3	7	58	6.8	1.18	.272
	Stockton (CAL)	HiA	5	5	3.76	14	14	0	0	79	73	8	17	66	7.5	1.14	.243
Minor League Totals			24	24	3.51	80	70	2	0	385	385	24	82	265	6.2	1.21	.263

5 MICHAEL YNOA, RHP

Born: Sept. 24, 1991. **B-T:** R-R. **Ht.:** 6-7. **Wt.:** 210. **Signed:** Dominican Republic, 2008. **Signed by:** Trevor Schaffer.

Injuries knocked Ynoa's career off the rails for the better part of three years, but he's finally regained most of his prospect luster. The star of the 2008 international class, he signed with the Athletics for a then-Latin American amateur record $4.25 million, but he lost all of the 2009 and 2011 seasons to injury, most notably Tommy John surgery. He didn't make his full-season debut until 2013 at low Class A Beloit. The A's monitored Ynoa's workload closely, limiting him to 55 pitches early in the season and maxing him out at 90 late, yet he managed to more than double his single-season total for innings. Scouts worry about some uprightness to his delivery, but he gets good downhill plane from his 6-foot-7 frame, throwing fastballs at 93-95 mph and peaking at 97. His changeup and inconsistent curveball both rate as solid-average and show the makings of being plus in the future. Ynoa's curve drops straight down with hard velocity in the low 80s when it's on, while the changeup shows some sink to the arm side. After losing so much development time, he still must enhance his feel and mound presence. With a healthy season and a trip to the Futures Game, Ynoa's stock rebounded in 2013, but his injury history is long. The A's will try to add another 30-40 innings to his workload 2014, which he'll open back at high Class A Stockton.

Year	Club (League)	Class	W	L	ERA	G	GS	CG	SV	IP	H	HR	BB	SO	K/9	WHIP	AVG
2009	Did not play—Injured																
2010	Athletics (AZL)	R	0	1	5.00	3	3	0	0	9	6	1	4	11	11.0	1.11	.188
2011	Did not play—Injured																
2012	Athletics (AZL)	R	0	1	5.40	6	6	0	0	10	11	1	9	6	5.4	2.00	.282
	Vermont (NYP)	SS	1	3	6.97	8	6	0	0	21	20	2	16	19	8.3	1.74	.247
2013	Beloit (MWL)	LoA	2	1	2.14	15	15	0	0	55	45	3	18	48	7.9	1.15	.221
	Stockton (CAL)	HiA	1	2	7.71	7	6	0	1	21	23	2	17	20	8.6	1.90	.274
Minor League Totals			4	8	4.53	39	36	0	1	115	105	9	64	104	8.1	1.47	.239

6 RENATO NUNEZ, 3B

BA GRADE 55 EXTREME

Born: April 4, 1994. **B-T:** R-R. **Ht.:** 6-1. **Wt.:** 185. **Signed:** Venezuela, 2010. **Signed by:** Julio Franco.

Nunez got onto scouts' radars in August 2009 when he hit .333/.385/.583 for Venezuela at the World Youth Championship. The Athletics were already onto him, however, and signed him the following July for $2.2 million. Nunez made his full-season debut as a 19-year-old in 2013, part of a youthful, talented low Class A Beloit infield, and he hit .278/.327/.496 with 13 homers in the first half before tailing off. His power potential started turning into game power in 2013, when his 19 homers more than doubled his career total (nine) from two years in Rookie ball. Nunez has as pure a swing as any hitter in the organization. He can cover all parts of the plate and hit balls hard to all fields. He has the ingredients to hit for high averages, but right now he's overly aggressive and too often gets himself in bad counts. Scouts have doubted Nunez's glove going back to his amateur days, and it remains an issue after he made 39 errors in 2013, the most among Midwest League third basemen. He does have a strong enough arm, but his hands and footwork are rough and his throwing accuracy erratic. A below-average runner, he's not a great athlete either, so Nunez's bat will have to carry him. He'll step up to high Class A Stockton in 2014.

Year	Club (League)	Class	AVG	G	AB	R	H	2B	3B	HR	RBI	BB	SO	SB	CS	OBP	SLG
2011	Athletics (DSL)	R	.268	53	194	20	52	12	0	5	28	6	42	1	2	.301	.407
2012	Athletics (AZL)	R	.325	42	160	31	52	18	3	4	42	17	32	4	0	.403	.550
2013	Beloit (MWL)	LoA	.258	128	508	69	131	27	0	19	85	28	136	2	2	.301	.423
Minor League Totals			.273	223	862	120	235	57	3	28	155	51	210	7	4	.322	.443

7 MAX MUNCY, 1B

BA GRADE 50 MEDIUM

Born: Aug. 25, 1990. **B-T:** L-R. **Ht.:** 6-0. **Wt.:** 190. **Drafted:** Baylor, 2012 (5th round). **Signed by:** Armann Brown.

The Indians tried drafting Muncy as a catcher out of high school in 2009, but he opted to attend Baylor instead, where he was a two-time all-Big 12 Conference selection as a first baseman. Signed for $240,000 in the fifth round in 2012, he had a banner first full season in 2013, leading the Athletics system in homers (25) and RBIs (100) while reaching Double-A Midland. A lack of power always has been the knock on Muncy, and while he hit 21 home runs at high Class A Stockton, he connected for 15 of those in home games in a park that favors lefthanders. Scouts view his hit tool more favorably, because his pitch-recognition skills are second-to-none in the system and his short swing allows him to stay inside the ball. Muncy struggled at Double-A Midland initially after his July promotion but improved steadily, hitting .296/.386/.490 in August. A playable defender at first base, he's a below-average runner who's fairly nimble around the bag and has enough arm strength that some scouts can envision left field as an option. The A's have shown no inclination to move him. After he finished the 2013 season in the Arizona Fall League, where he hit .224/.350/.265, Muncy will return to Double-A in 2014.

Year	Club (League)	Class	AVG	G	AB	R	H	2B	3B	HR	RBI	BB	SO	SB	CS	OBP	SLG
2012	Burlington (MWL)	LoA	.275	64	229	34	63	20	2	4	23	41	37	3	1	.383	.432
2013	Stockton (CAL)	HiA	.285	93	351	67	100	13	1	21	76	64	68	1	1	.400	.507
	Midland (TL)	AA	.250	47	172	22	43	12	2	4	24	24	34	0	1	.340	.413
Minor League Totals			.274	204	752	123	206	45	5	29	123	129	139	4	3	.382	.463

8 DYLAN COVEY, RHP

BA GRADE 50 HIGH

Born: Aug. 14, 1991. **B-T:** R-R. **Ht.:** 6-2. **Wt.:** 195. **Drafted:** San Diego, 2013 (4th round). **Signed by:** Eric Martins.

The Brewers drafted Covey with the 14th pick in the 2010 draft but failed to sign him when he decided to attend San Diego after an August physical revealed he had Type 1 Diabetes. He had an inconsistent three-year run with the Toreros, posting a 5.05 ERA as a junior before landing with the Athletics in the 2013 draft and signing for $370,000. The A's believe they got a first-round caliber arm in the fourth round. Covey throws four quality pitches, led by a 90-95 mph fastball he throws with nice downhill angle. He has a power curveball with hard top-to-bottom break, and he can use it either as a put-away pitch or take a little off if he needs to get one over. His low- to mid-80s slider can be another strikeout pitch, and his changeup shows promise with the arm speed and fading action he generates. Covey throws with a smooth, easy motion and pounds the strike zone, though he does need to throw more quality strikes. Scouts felt he didn't always trust his stuff in college, but he pitched with more confidence against wood bats. Covey didn't execute as consistently with low Class A Beloit after signing and could head back there in 2014. The A's believe they got a big league starter and one of the 2013 draft's steals.

Year	Club (League)	Class	W	L	ERA	G	GS	CG	SV	IP	H	HR	BB	SO	K/9	WHIP	AVG
2013	Vermont (NYP)	SS	0	0	0.00	4	4	0	0	12	9	0	1	15	11.3	0.83	.205
	Beloit (MWL)	LoA	1	1	4.75	10	10	0	0	47	64	4	17	31	5.9	1.71	.327
Minor League Totals			1	1	3.79	14	14	0	0	59	73	4	18	46	7.0	1.53	.304

9 BOBBY WAHL, RHP

BA GRADE **50** HIGH

Born: March 21, 1992. **B-T:** R-R. **Ht.:** 6-2. **Wt.:** 210. **Drafted:** Mississippi, 2013 (5th round). **Signed by:** Kelcey Mucker.

The Indians pushed hard to sign Wahl as a 39th-round pick out of high school but couldn't keep him from going to Mississippi. Entering spring 2013 as a potential first-round pick, he dealt with persistent blister issues on his right middle finger and pitched with diminished stuff. He still dominated nonetheless, going 10-0, 2.03 for the Rebels, though he lasted until the fifth round and signed with Oakland for $500,000. The Athletics limited Wahl to shorter stints after signing him and worked on shortening his delivery, and his stuff seemed to rebound. He demonstrated the arm strength to hit 97 mph in college, but he often worked at 89-92 for Ole Miss in 2013. He reverted back to the mid-90s over the summer, though, while his slider, the main culprit behind his blister problems, showed hard, late break. He also has a quality changeup with depth. Wahl uses both sides of the plate and generally keeps the ball down. Scouts see some effort in his delivery, though it does give him deception. Wahl has the three-pitch repertoire to be a starter, not to mention a successful track record as an ace in the Southeastern Conference. However, he shined as a closer for USA Baseball's Collegiate National Team in 2012 with just his fastball and slider, and he could reach the majors fairly quickly as a reliever. He'll probably open 2014 at low Class A Beloit.

Year	Club (League)	Class	W	L	ERA	G	GS	CG	SV	IP	H	HR	BB	SO	K/9	WHIP	AVG
2013	Athletics (AZL)	R	0	0	9.00	1	1	0	0	1	0	0	2	1	9.0	2.00	.000
	Vermont (NYP)	SS	0	0	3.92	9	4	0	2	21	20	3	6	27	11.8	1.26	.241
Minor League Totals			0	0	4.15	10	5	0	2	22	20	3	8	28	11.6	1.29	.235

10 DANIEL ROBERTSON, SS

BA GRADE **50** HIGH

Born: March 22, 1994. **B-T:** R-R. **Ht.:** 6-1. **Wt.:** 185. **Drafted:** HS—Upland, Calif., 2012 (1st round supplemental). **Signed by:** Eric Martins.

After taking Addison Russell in the first round in 2012, the Athletics continued their splurge on high school players by taking Robertson and first baseman Matt Olson in the sandwich round. Signed for $1.5 million, Robertson went to low Class A Beloit in 2013 and steadily picked up his production as the season went along, batting .314/.381/.495 with five homers in August. Robertson brings an advanced plate approach for his age. He takes short swings and is willing to hit balls to all fields. Projections on his power have varied going back to his high school days, but he has the physicality, bat speed and swing path to suggest he'll hit for quality power down the road. Robertson's skeptics don't believe he can stick at shortstop, though the A's believe he has a chance. He's a below-average runner but not a bad athlete. He has good hands and can make the throws on balls he gets to. Range is a question, but he compensates with his anticipation skills, instincts and internal clock. The A's laud Robertson's work ethic. A move to third base may be inevitable with Addison Russell ahead of him in the organization, and whether he will profile at third base depends on his power development. He moves to high Class A Stockton for 2014.

Year	Club (League)	Class	AVG	G	AB	R	H	2B	3B	HR	RBI	BB	SO	SB	CS	OBP	SLG
2012	Athletics (AZL)	R	.297	29	101	25	30	10	2	4	22	16	15	2	0	.405	.554
	Vermont (NYP)	SS	.181	26	94	9	17	2	0	1	8	7	31	1	1	.238	.234
2013	Beloit (MWL)	LoA	.277	101	401	59	111	21	1	9	46	41	79	1	7	.353	.401
Minor League Totals			.265	156	596	93	158	33	3	14	76	64	125	4	8	.345	.401

11 NOLAN SANBURN, RHP

BA GRADE **50** HIGH

Born: July 21, 1991. **B-T:** R-R. **Ht.:** 6-1. **Wt.:** 205. **Drafted:** Arkansas, 2012 (2nd round). **Signed by:** Yancy Ayres.

Sanburn has the potential to be one of the Athletics' most exciting pitching prospects, but he hasn't had many chances to show it. Used as a reliever at Arkansas, he threw just 73 innings in two seasons before he signed for $710,000 as a draft-eligible sophomore in 2012. A shoulder strain in 2013 prevented him from joining low Class A Beloit until mid-July. The A's kept him on a regular schedule of working two innings every four days, then built him up to three-inning outings in instructional league. Sanburn remains inexperienced on the mound but has the four-pitch mix to be a starter with two plusses. His fastball is electric at 93-94 mph and touches 96 with riding life, and his curveball shows impressive depth while coming in hard in the high 70s. He'll also flash a quality sinking changeup at times and has some feel for using it. Even his fourth pitch, a slider, features promising tight spin. Sanburn has the athleticism and delivery to hold up as a starter, but after years as a reliever, he's still learning to pace himself and develop a starter's routine. His upside is immense if everything comes together. The A's will keep building up Sanburn's innings in 2014 at high Class A Stockton.

Year	Club (League)	Class	W	L	ERA	G	GS	CG	SV	IP	H	HR	BB	SO	K/9	WHIP	AVG
2012	Vermont (NYP)	SS	0	1	3.86	7	7	0	0	19	23	2	6	19	9.2	1.55	.299
2013	Athletics (AZL)	R	0	0	2.25	2	1	0	0	4	3	0	1	6	13.5	1.00	.200
	Beloit (MWL)	LoA	1	3	1.38	14	1	0	0	26	17	1	9	20	6.9	1.00	.191
Minor League Totals			1	4	2.40	23	9	0	0	49	43	3	16	45	8.3	1.21	.238

12 MATT OLSON, 1B

BA GRADE **50** HIGH

Born: March 29, 1994. **B-T:** L-R. **Ht.:** 6-4. **Wt.:** 235. **Drafted:** HS—Lilburn, Ga., 2012 (1st round supplemental). **Signed by:** Matt Ranson.

Olson put together a lengthy, impressive résumé in high school. He hit a home run off Max Fried, the No. 7 pick in the 2012 draft, and starred both at the plate and on the mound as his Parkview High squad finished the 2012 season ranked No. 1 in the country. The third of the Athletics' trio of premium high-school picks in 2012, along with Addison Russell and Daniel Robertson, Olson went 47th overall and signed for $1,079,700. Playing alongside fellow teenagers Robertson and Renato Nunez at low Class A Beloit in 2013, Olson's first full season was a mixed bag. He finished second in the Midwest League in homers (23) and fifth in walks (72) but also second in strikeouts (148). With his big frame, Olson has evident raw power. He generates good leverage and hits balls hard to all parts of the park. Singled out for his natural feel for hitting in high school, he tended to get too pull-conscious in 2013, working plenty of deep counts and causing his strikeouts to spike. Olson doesn't have much foot speed, but he's a solid defender at first base and has a strong arm for the position. He has the upside to be a middle-of-the-order presence, but he'll have to address his contact issues as he moves up. He'll team with Nunez and Robertson again at high Class A Stockton in 2014.

Year	Club (League)	Class	AVG	G	AB	R	H	2B	3B	HR	RBI	BB	SO	SB	CS	OBP	SLG
2012	Athletics (AZL)	R	.282	46	177	29	50	16	1	8	41	16	46	0	0	.345	.520
	Vermont (NYP)	SS	.273	4	11	3	3	0	0	1	4	3	4	0	0	.438	.545
2013	Beloit (MWL)	LoA	.225	134	481	69	108	32	0	23	93	72	148	4	3	.326	.435
Minor League Totals			.241	184	669	101	161	48	1	32	138	91	198	4	3	.333	.459

13 RYON HEALY, 3B/1B

BA GRADE **50** HIGH

Born: Jan. 10, 1992. **B-T:** R-R. **Ht.:** 6-5. **Wt.:** 205. **Drafted:** Oregon, 2013 (3rd round). **Signed by:** Jim Coffman.

Healy's seven-figure asking price caused him to go undrafted out of high school in 2010, though he got considerable buzz by tearing up the California Collegiate League the summer before his freshman season at Oregon. He also drew interest as a pitching prospect in high school, though he focused on hitting with the Ducks. After hitting just eight homers over his first two seasons, Healy belted 11 as a junior while batting .333/.408/.566, and the Athletics signed him for $500,000 out of the third round of the 2013 draft. He struggled in his pro debut at short-season Vermont in 2013, but he has a quick bat and the loft in his swing to be a power threat, potentially settling in with 20-plus homers. He's got a big, physical frame that still has some room to add more muscle. There are promising signs in his feel for hitting and willingness to use the whole field, though he got out of sync over the summer. Oregon used Healy primarily at first base, but the A's are going to try him at third. He's a below-average runner, and his range is a question at third, as is his arm. Wherever he winds up defensively, Healy's bat will be what carries him through the system. With Renato Nunez and Matt Olson slated to man the infield corners at high Class A Stockton, Healy likely will begin 2014 at low Class A Beloit.

Year	Club (League)	Class	AVG	G	AB	R	H	2B	3B	HR	RBI	BB	SO	SB	CS	OBP	SLG
2013	Athletics (AZL)	R	.214	11	28	4	6	0	1	2	8	3	4	0	0	.273	.500
	Vermont (NYP)	SS	.233	36	146	12	34	10	0	4	21	2	24	2	1	.252	.384
Minor League Totals			.230	47	174	16	40	10	1	6	29	5	28	2	1	.255	.402

14 DILLON OVERTON, LHP

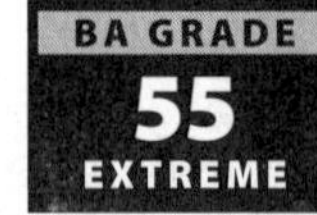

Born: Aug. 17, 1991. **B-T:** L-L. **Ht.:** 6-2. **Wt.:** 172. **Drafted:** Oklahoma, 2013 (2nd round). **Signed by:** Yancy Ayres.

Overton and No. 3 overall pick Jonathan Gray formed a dominant one-two punch atop the Oklahoma rotation in 2013, though it was Overton who ranked higher on draft boards entering the season. While Gray surged, Overton had a solid junior year, going 9-3, 3.02, but he had to deal with a forearm strain in the middle of the season. That strain turned out to be the tip of the iceberg and Overton needed Tommy John surgery after signing for $400,000, the smallest bonus of any second-round pick in 2013. Overton showed first-round-caliber stuff at points during his college career. Though he has a skinny frame, he was able to run his fastball up to 95 mph at times. He pitched more often at 88-90 mph in 2013. His 78-80 mph changeup is a legitimate plus pitch with fading movement. He also broke out a much-improved curveball in 2013, featuring late, tight break in the mid-70s. Overton pitches with some crossfire to his delivery, though scouts like his loose arm action and he has no trouble pounding the zone. His motion does give him some deception, which along with his advanced feel for pitching allowed him to succeed despite diminished velocity. If Overton's velocity comes all the way back and he has no further health problems, he has the components to be a frontline starter. He won't make his professional debut until June 2014 at the earliest and the Athletics will be careful with him.

Year	Club (League)	Class	W	L	ERA	G	GS	CG	SV	IP	H	HR	BB	SO	K/9	WHIP	AVG
2013	Did not play—Injured																

15 CHAD PINDER, SS

BA GRADE
50
HIGH

Born: March 29, 1992. **B-T:** R-R. **Ht.:** 6-2. **Wt.:** 192. **Drafted:** Virginia Tech, 2013 (2nd round supplemental). **Signed by:** Neil Avent.

Pinder, the 71st overall pick in 2013, became the highest-drafted Virginia Tech position player since Franklin Stubbs went 19th overall in 1982. A .321 career hitter in college, Pinder was a first-team all-Atlantic Coast Conference pick in 2013 after hitting .321/.404/.483 with eight homers, and he signed for $750,000 out of the supplemental second round. His father Chris was a pitcher for four seasons in the Orioles and Indians systems from 1987-90. Pinder played the bulk of his college career at third base, but he did make 17 starts at shortstop as a junior, and the Athletics are giving him a chance to play the position as a pro. He has a chance to stick there due to solid hands, a good transfer and a strong, accurate arm. His fringy range could push him to second base if shortstop doesn't work out. Pinder's bat profiles better as a middle infielder because he lacks profile corner power to fit at third base. He does generate good bat speed and has a nice path to the ball, but the A's would like to see him use a little better load in his swing. He's shown a feel for hitting in the past, but he struggled to adjust to the speed of pro ball at short-season Vermont in 2013. Shoulder and oblique injuries that cost him a month didn't help. The A's hope to see Pinder's offense show up more frequently in 2014, probably at low Class A Beloit.

Year	Club (League)	Class	AVG	G	AB	R	H	2B	3B	HR	RBI	BB	SO	SB	CS	OBP	SLG
2013	Vermont (NYP)	SS	.200	42	140	14	28	4	0	3	8	12	41	1	0	.286	.293
Minor League Totals			.200	42	140	14	28	4	0	3	8	12	41	1	0	.286	.293

16 KYLE FINNEGAN, RHP

BA GRADE
50
HIGH

Born: Sept. 4, 1991. **B-T:** R-R. **Ht.:** 6-2. **Wt.:** 170. **Drafted:** Texas State, 2013 (6th round). **Signed by:** Armann Brown.

Finnegan's arm strength made him a prominent attraction for scouts heading into 2013, but he struggled to find consistent success and even lost his place in Texas State's weekend rotation, finishing the college season 5-3, 4.66. Getting Finnegan into pro ball after signing him for $200,000 in the sixth round, the Athletics turned him around quickly, and he posted a strong summer at short-season Vermont. He took too long a stride in his delivery, which made it hard for him to finish and hurt his command, so Oakland shortened him up and he started throwing more strikes. His fastball remains his best pitch, showing late run to go with 92-93 mph velocity, and he can top out at 97. The A's continued the overhaul by turning his slurvy breaking ball into more of a true curveball with downward movement. It's a solid-average breaking ball now and shows plus at times. Finnegan hardly threw his changeup in college, but the A's had him focus on it as well and it's become a useable weapon. His athleticism and body type draw comparisons with Tim Hudson. The A's were excited about how he embraced the concepts they were teaching him, and he'll open 2014 at low Class A Beloit but could move up quickly if he performs.

Year	Club (League)	Class	W	L	ERA	G	GS	CG	SV	IP	H	HR	BB	SO	K/9	WHIP	AVG
2013	Vermont (NYP)	SS	3	3	2.70	11	11	0	0	50	43	0	12	35	6.3	1.10	.231
	Beloit (MWL)	LoA	1	1	9.82	2	2	0	0	7	12	1	6	5	6.1	2.45	.375
Minor League Totals			4	4	3.61	13	13	0	0	57	55	1	18	40	6.3	1.27	.252

17 RONALD HERRERA, RHP

Born: May 3, 1995. **B-T:** R-R. **Ht.:** 5-10. **Wt.:** 170. **Signed:** Venezuela, 2011. **Signed by:** Julio Franco/Juan Carlos Villanueva.

The Athletics haven't shied away from spending big money on Latin American amateurs, dropping millions on players like Renato Nunez and Michael Ynoa, but they might have found a bargain in Herrera. The righthander cost just $20,000 to sign out of Venezuela in December 2011 and has become one of Oakland's more intriguing young arms after showing advanced stuff in his U.S. debut in the Rookie-level Arizona League in 2013. Herrera's not particularly physical, standing only 5-foot-10, but he's athletic and has some room to add strength. His fastball already sits at 90-91 mph and can hit 94. The velocity he has plays up because of his ability to sink the ball and command it to both sides of the plate. He showed exceptional control for his age and experience level. Herrera's secondary pitches, a curveball and changeup, both rate as solid-average for now. The changeup flashes plus potential at times, and the A's believe his curve can become a putaway weapon in the future. Herrera has solid, repeatable mechanics and draws praise for his composure on the mound. He has the makings of a solid big league starter and should have a chance to open 2014 at low Class A Beloit, with a return to short-season Vermont a fallback option.

Year	Club (League)	Class	W	L	ERA	G	GS	CG	SV	IP	H	HR	BB	SO	K/9	WHIP	AVG
2012	Athletics (DSL)	R	2	4	2.47	14	14	1	0	58	66	1	20	44	6.8	1.47	.292
2013	Athletics (AZL)	R	6	4	3.82	14	9	0	0	71	76	3	11	58	7.4	1.23	.272
	Vermont (NYP)	SS	1	0	5.87	2	1	0	0	8	10	0	2	8	9.4	1.57	.303
Minor League Totals			9	8	3.36	30	24	1	0	137	152	4	33	110	7.2	1.35	.283

18 CHRIS BOSTICK, 2B

BA GRADE
50
HIGH

Born: March 24, 1993. **B-T:** R-R. **Ht.:** 5-10. **Wt.:** 175. **Drafted:** HS—Rochester, N.Y., 2011 (44th round). **Signed by:** Matt Higginson.

Signed for $125,000 in the 44th round in 2011, Bostick was the old man of the low Class A Beloit infield in 2013, playing beside teenagers Renato Nunez, Matt Olson and Daniel Robertson. The Athletics love the energy he brings to the park, and his hitting garners comparisons with former big leaguer Junior Spivey. Bostick has a simple, sound swing with good plate coverage and the ability to hit line drives all over the field. He has legitimate bat speed and enough sneaky pop to keep pitchers honest. Beloit plays in one of the Midwest League's more homer-friendly parks, and 12 of his 14 long balls came at home. He's a good athlete with solid-average speed and basestealing instincts who led the A's system with 25 stolen bases. Drafted as a shortstop, Bostick moved to second base as a pro and has the raw tools, including adequate arm strength, to play the middle infield, but his defense is rough. He tied for the most errors among Midwest League second basemen in 2013 with 22. He may not have the consistency to play shortstop well enough even in a utility role. He'll move up to high Class A in 2014.

Year	Club (League)	Class	AVG	G	AB	R	H	2B	3B	HR	RBI	BB	SO	SB	CS	OBP	SLG
2011	Athletics (AZL)	R	.442	14	52	13	23	6	1	1	5	3	12	4	0	.482	.654
2012	Vermont (NYP)	SS	.251	70	279	41	70	16	4	3	29	27	66	12	5	.325	.369
2013	Beloit (MWL)	LoA	.282	129	489	75	138	25	8	14	89	51	122	25	8	.354	.452
Minor League Totals			.282	213	820	129	231	47	13	18	123	81	200	41	13	.352	.437

19 CHRIS KOHLER, LHP

BA GRADE
50
HIGH

Born: May 4, 1995. **B-T:** L-L. **Ht.:** 6-3. **Wt.:** 190. **Drafted:** HS—Rancho Cucamonga, Calif., 2013 (3rd round supplemental). **Signed by:** Eric Martins.

Kohler spent most of his time growing up as a position player. By his own admission, he didn't start thinking of himself as more of a pitcher than hitter until his junior year of high school. His future is most certainly on the mound, though. The Athletics used the compensation pick they received for not signing 2012 third-rounder Kyle Twomey to take Kohler 106th overall in 2013, then signed him away from an Oklahoma commitment for $486,600. He pitches with a 90-92 mph fastball, touching 93, and has room to add strength to his frame and velocity. What he lacks in power he makes up for with aptitude and his secondary stuff. His 1-to-7 curveball has the potential to be a plus pitch down the road, and he has good feel for his changeup. Kohler has a polished delivery and a level of pitchability well beyond his years. He has confidence in all his pitches and will use them in any count. He already shows he can fill the zone and could develop true plus command. If Kohler does add some velocity, he could have a very high ceiling. The A's won't rush him, but he looks advanced enough to handle an assignment to low Class A Beloit in 2014.

Year	Club (League)	Class	W	L	ERA	G	GS	CG	SV	IP	H	HR	BB	SO	K/9	WHIP	AVG
2013	Athletics (AZL)	R	1	2	2.78	13	4	0	1	23	19	0	9	32	12.7	1.24	.224
Minor League Totals			1	2	2.78	13	4	0	1	23	19	0	9	32	12.7	1.24	.224

20 B.J. BOYD, OF

BA GRADE **50** HIGH

Born: July 16, 1993. **B-T:** L-R. **Ht.:** 5-10. **Wt.:** 190. **Drafted:** HS—Palo Alto, Calif., 2012 (4th round). **Signed by:** Jermaine Clark.

Boyd was more raw than the Athletics' other high-profile 2012 high school draft picks, having also been a football recruit as a running back/wide receiver at Palo Alto High. Baseball was his first choice, however, and he signed with Oakland as a fourth-rounder for $300,000. Given his relative inexperience, Boyd stayed behind in extended spring training in 2013 before joining short-season Vermont. The youngest regular in the Lake Monsters' lineup, he hit .331/.399/.531 through the end of July before tailing off. Boyd struggled to maintain his swing mechanics at times at Vermont, but when he was going well he showed a balanced swing with nice wrist action. He has some feel for hitting and is willing to use the whole field, though he'll lapse into getting pull happy like most young hitters. Boyd does have some physicality and sneaky power. With above-average speed, he profiles as a table-setting center fielder, though he primarily played left field in 2013. His routes in center need refinement and his arm grades below-average. Boyd should move to center and up to low Class A Beloit in 2014.

Year	Club (League)	Class	AVG	G	AB	R	H	2B	3B	HR	RBI	BB	SO	SB	CS	OBP	SLG
2012	Athletics (AZL)	R	.301	39	143	37	43	8	4	1	20	23	36	16	4	.401	.434
2013	Vermont (NYP)	SS	.285	71	260	39	74	13	2	8	32	35	66	8	6	.375	.442
Minor League Totals			.290	110	403	76	117	21	6	9	52	58	102	24	10	.384	.439

21 ARNOLD LEON, RHP

BA GRADE **45** MEDIUM

Born: Sept. 6, 1988. **B-T:** R-R. **Ht.:** 6-1. **Wt.:** 205. **Signed:** Mexico, 2008. **Signed by:** Randy Johnson/Craig Weissmann.

Leon began 2013 by touching off a veritable international incident. Pitching for Mexico in the World Baseball Classic, his plunking of Canada's Rene Tosoni in the late innings of a blowout loss for the Mexicans led to a nasty benches-clearing brawl. Despite that ignominious beginning, Leon had a strong season, converting to starting three years removed from Tommy John surgery and throwing a lot of quality strikes. Leon has the weapons to pitch in a rotation with three usable pitches. His 92-93 mph fastball, which hit 96 out of the bullpen, could use more movement, but he can command it to both sides of the plate. He gets good arm speed and fading action on his changeup, his best secondary pitch. He uses a cutter-type slider as his primary breaking ball. He can also mix in the occasional slow, loopy curveball that he throws for strikes. The Athletics like Leon's smooth delivery, and he works with a good tempo on the mound. He'll sometimes open up too early in his motion, costing him deception especially against lefthanders, who torched him for a .348 average in 2013. A member of the Oakland 40-man roster, Leon's strong finish at Triple-A Sacramento in 2013 (3-1, 2.95 in August) has him positioned to make his big league debut in 2014.

Year	Club (League)	Class	W	L	ERA	G	GS	CG	SV	IP	H	HR	BB	SO	K/9	WHIP	AVG
2006	Saltillo (MEX)	AAA	0	0	2.70	4	0	0	0	3	2	0	2	2	5.4	1.20	.167
2007	Saltillo (MEX)	AAA	3	0	1.94	35	0	0	1	42	31	2	24	38	8.2	1.32	.217
2008	Stockton (CAL)	HiA	0	0	2.86	20	0	0	2	28	25	1	9	28	8.9	1.20	.238
	Saltillo (MEX)	AAA	2	1	4.30	13	0	0	0	15	12	0	2	21	12.9	0.95	.235
2009	Midland (TL)	AA	2	3	3.51	33	7	0	1	74	71	3	28	63	7.6	1.33	.247
2010	Midland (TL)	AA	0	0	6.23	3	0	0	0	4	6	1	3	1	2.1	2.08	.333
2011	Athletics (AZL)	R	0	1	8.53	5	5	0	0	6	6	0	4	8	11.4	1.58	.273
2012	Stockton (CAL)	HiA	0	1	5.28	12	0	0	0	15	26	1	5	25	14.7	2.02	.366
	Midland (TL)	AA	1	0	2.30	10	0	0	1	16	17	0	3	18	10.3	1.28	.288
	Sacramento (PCL)	AAA	3	0	1.77	22	0	0	0	36	26	4	15	31	7.8	1.15	.208
2013	Midland (TL)	AA	4	5	3.84	13	13	0	0	73	87	9	11	48	5.9	1.35	.295
	Sacramento (PCL)	AAA	5	3	4.42	12	11	0	0	71	81	4	13	49	6.2	1.32	.287
Minor League Totals			20	14	3.52	182	36	0	5	384	390	25	119	332	7.8	1.33	.273

22 MILES HEAD, 3B

BA GRADE **45** HIGH

Born: May 2, 1991. **B-T:** R-R. **Ht.:** 6-0. **Wt.:** 215. **Drafted:** HS—Fayetteville, Ga., 2009 (26th round). **Signed by:** Tim Hyers (Red Sox).

The Athletics have unquestionably come out ahead on the December 2011 deal that sent Andrew Bailey to the Red Sox for Head, Josh Reddick and Raul Alcantara, but Head had a lost season in 2013. Signed by Boston for an above-slot $335,000 in 2009, Head was a smashing success in his first full season with the A's in 2012, winning the organization's minor league player of the year award after hitting .333/.391/.577 across two levels. Not the most athletic player to begin with, he came into camp in 2013 out of shape, and shoulder problems limited him to 40 games for Double-A Midland. Despite the setback, Head has undeniable natural hitting ability. He has a calm presence at the plate and takes short, compact swings. He can barrel up balls in all parts of the strike zone with the strength to be a 20-homer hitter. His contact skills worked against him at times last year, as he needs to show more patience and learn what pitches he can drive. The Red

Sox played Head at first base, where his subpar athleticism is less of a factor, but the A's are trying to have him make a go of it at third thanks to his plus arm. Head will return to Midland in 2014.

Year	Club (League)	Class	AVG	G	AB	R	H	2B	3B	HR	RBI	BB	SO	SB	CS	OBP	SLG
2009	Red Sox (GCL)	R	.103	10	29	1	3	0	0	0	0	3	8	0	0	.188	.103
2010	Lowell (NYP)	SS	.240	65	229	21	55	16	2	1	35	30	36	1	1	.328	.341
2011	Greenville (SAL)	LoA	.338	66	263	61	89	25	1	15	53	30	53	4	2	.409	.612
	Salem (CAR)	HiA	.254	63	232	27	59	12	1	7	29	20	56	0	2	.328	.405
2012	Stockton (CAL)	HiA	.382	67	267	57	102	23	6	18	56	23	55	3	0	.433	.715
	Midland (TL)	AA	.272	57	213	25	58	9	2	5	28	16	75	0	1	.338	.404
2013	Midland (TL)	AA	.196	40	148	13	29	4	0	2	8	12	42	0	1	.264	.264
Minor League Totals			.286	368	1381	205	395	89	12	48	209	134	325	8	7	.355	.472

23 ANTHONY ALIOTTI, 1B

Born: July 16, 1987. **B-T:** L-L. **Ht.:** 6-0. **Wt.:** 204. **Drafted:** St. Mary's, 2009 (15th round). **Signed by:** Jermaine Clark.

Aliotti comes from a football family. His father Joe is an assistant coach at California prep power De La Salle High, and his uncle Nick is the University of Oregon's defensive coordinator. Anthony stuck to baseball, and he's slowly built up his prospect status. He hit a combined .318/.432/.403 in three years at St. Mary's, but the lack of sock in his bat—he hit just seven homers in his entire college career—caused him to last until the 15th round of the 2009 draft. He's made strides toward addressing that deficiency, and the results showed in his combined 14 homers at Double-A Midland and Triple-A Sacramento in 2013. Aliotti always has possessed the ability to control the strike zone and a feel to hit, but he's added some loft to his stroke and now takes authoritative swings more often, rather than settling for singles. Though he's a below-average runner, he's an outstanding fielder and has been voted his league's best defensive first baseman by managers each of the last three years. Though he was left off the 40-man roster, Aliotti might one day fit into Oakland's platoon-friendly approach to the lineup. He hit .360/.444/.540 against righthanders at Double-A and Triple-A in 2013.

Year	Club (League)	Class	AVG	G	AB	R	H	2B	3B	HR	RBI	BB	SO	SB	CS	OBP	SLG
2009	Vancouver (NWL)	SS	.239	60	218	19	52	8	0	0	25	36	63	6	1	.351	.275
2010	Kane County (MWL)	LoA	.278	133	478	75	133	29	2	5	77	92	132	14	4	.397	.379
2011	Stockton (CAL)	HiA	.276	127	457	73	126	20	1	11	66	80	123	2	1	.392	.396
2012	Midland (TL)	AA	.292	123	455	72	133	29	1	10	76	68	129	0	0	.385	.426
2013	Midland (TL)	AA	.350	91	340	49	119	29	0	12	51	66	83	3	2	.452	.541
	Sacramento (PCL)	AAA	.266	42	154	17	41	4	1	2	20	15	44	0	0	.329	.344
Minor League Totals			.287	576	2102	305	604	119	5	40	315	357	574	25	8	.393	.406

24 AARON SHIPMAN, OF

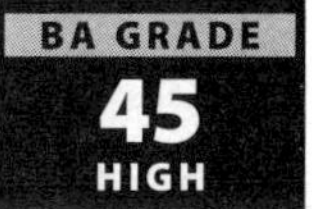

Born: Jan. 27, 1992. **B-T:** L-L. **Ht.:** 6-2. **Wt.:** 185. **Drafted:** HS—Quitman, Ga., 2010 (3rd round). **Signed by:** Matt Ranson.

Shipman was viewed as too physically immature to garner much attention for most of his high school career, but he took off as a senior and landed a $500,000 bonus. Shipman entered the system offering a promising array of tools, but he's battled injuries the last couple years and has yet to really take off. He missed much of the first half of 2013 with low Class A Beloit due to a shoulder problem but did come back to hit .314/.417/.361 after returning in late June. Shipman has a sweet lefthanded swing with an up-the-middle approach. He's always been able to control the strike zone, posting consistently strong walk-to-strikeout rates, but it's been a constant battle for the A's as they try to turn up his aggressiveness. He hasn't homered as a pro and has succeeded on just 61 percent of stolen base attempts the last two seasons. He played left field primarily in 2013 but is capable of playing all three spots with above-average speed and arm strength. The A's hope the offensive environment at high Class A Stockton encourages Shipman to start unlocking his top-of-the-order potential.

Year	Club (League)	Class	AVG	G	AB	R	H	2B	3B	HR	RBI	BB	SO	SB	CS	OBP	SLG
2010	Athletics (AZL)	R	.118	4	17	2	2	0	0	0	2	0	6	3	0	.118	.118
2011	Vermont (NYP)	SS	.254	63	201	34	51	8	1	0	19	42	39	17	3	.385	.303
2012	Burlington (MWL)	LoA	.206	108	360	40	74	12	4	0	32	60	86	11	11	.319	.261
2013	Athletics (AZL)	R	.421	6	19	7	8	1	1	0	3	4	0	2	0	.542	.579
	Beloit (MWL)	LoA	.279	68	244	44	68	7	2	0	16	47	50	17	8	.397	.324
Minor League Totals			.241	249	841	127	203	28	8	0	72	153	181	50	22	.360	.294

25 SETH STREICH, RHP

BA GRADE
45
HIGH

Born: Feb. 19, 1991. **B-T:** L-R. **Ht.:** 6-3. **Wt.:** 210. **Drafted:** Ohio, 2012 (6th round). **Signed by:** Rich Sparks.

A two-way player at Ohio, Streich was more successful as a college hitter but a better prospect on the mound. The Athletics signed him for $183,500 as a 2012 sixth-rounder, and he struggled in the first half of 2013 before finishing strong until he was shut down to control his innings. He throws a solid three-pitch mix, beginning with a low-90s sinking fastball he throws with good plane and easy effort. He has an average changeup that flashes plus at times with cutting action, but most of his improvement in 2013 came from the strides he made with his curveball. As the season went on, Streich did a better job of staying on line and getting over his front side in his delivery, helping him drive the ball down, all of which added up to a better curve. The improved breaking ball should help boost his modest strikeout totals. He doesn't have any problems throwing strikes, particularly with the fastball and changeup. The A's will look for Streich to maintain the consistency of his delivery and pitches as he moves up to high Class A Stockton in 2014.

Year	Club (League)	Class	W	L	ERA	G	GS	CG	SV	IP	H	HR	BB	SO	K/9	WHIP	AVG
2012	Athletics (AZL)	R	0	0	3.38	2	0	0	0	3	1	0	1	6	20.3	0.75	.111
	Vermont (NYP)	SS	4	1	2.60	15	4	0	0	35	26	1	17	42	10.9	1.24	.206
2013	Beloit (MWL)	LoA	10	6	3.82	21	21	1	0	111	114	2	41	82	6.7	1.40	.268
Minor League Totals			14	7	3.53	38	25	1	0	148	141	3	59	130	7.9	1.35	.252

26 DUSTIN DRIVER, RHP

BA GRADE **50** EXTREME

Born: Oct. 11, 1994. **B-T:** R-R. **Ht.:** 6-2. **Wt.:** 210. **Drafted:** HS—Wenatchee, Wash., 2013 (7th round). **Signed by:** Jim Coffman.

Driver gave up football to focus solely on pitching after his sophomore year at Wenatchee High, and he looked poised to be one of the elite high school arms in the 2013 draft class after a strong showing at the 2012 Area Code Games. His stock dropped in the spring leading up to the draft, though, and he wasn't taken until the seventh round by the Athletics. Oakland still had to spend $500,000 to keep Driver from going to UCLA, his bonus matching Ryon Healy's and Bobby Wahl's as the third-largest in the A's draft class. Driver has physicality and a short arm action that helps his plus fastball jump on hitters. His heater sits in the low 90s and touches 96-97. His secondary stuff involves plenty of projection. He has focused on a curveball as a pro, shelving his slider, and both his curve and changeup are inconsistent, flashing average. The A's worked on straightening out his delivery after signing him, treating his stint in the Rookie-level Arizona League as a sort of spring training after he'd had a seven-week layoff before signing. Driver has solid upside, but he needs a lot of innings. He'll stay in extended spring training to start 2014, followed by an assignment to short-season Vermont.

Year	Club (League)	Class	W	L	ERA	G	GS	CG	SV	IP	H	HR	BB	SO	K/9	WHIP	AVG
2013	Athletics (AZL)	R	0	2	7.15	7	4	0	0	11	18	0	11	4	3.2	2.56	.367
Minor League Totals			0	2	7.15	7	4	0	0	11	18	0	11	4	3.2	2.56	.367

27 MICHAEL TAYLOR, OF

BA GRADE **40** LOW

Born: Dec. 19, 1985. **B-T:** R-R. **Ht.:** 6-5. **Wt.:** 255. **Drafted:** Stanford, 2007 (5th round). **Signed by:** Joey Davis (Phillies).

Taylor has been a fixture of Athletics prospects lists ever since coming to the organization in December 2009, when the Phillies sent him to the Blue Jays with Kyle Drabek and Travis d'Arnaud for Roy Halladay, with Toronto then flipping him to Oakland for Brett Wallace. In 2013, Taylor put up another solid season with Triple-A Sacramento, with his 18 homers his best total since 2009, but he was only given a couple brief callups in April and May, and Oakland opted not to bring him up in September during the playoff race. Taylor remains much the same hitter he's always been, with tantalizing raw power but a line-drive approach that doesn't maximize it. He has a physical, imposing 6-foot-5 frame and gets good bat speed and leverage in his stroke. Yet he continues to frustrate scouts, as he always has, by taking passive swings and not looking to drive more balls. His defense is good enough to be an asset in right field, where he has a strong arm and gets good enough jumps on balls to make up for a lack of above-average speed. Taylor still possesses the potential to be a serviceable major league outfielder, but it looks increasingly doubtful that opportunity will come in Oakland. He remains on the club's 40-man roster but is out of minor league options as he heads into 2014 spring training.

Year	Club (League)	Class	AVG	G	AB	R	H	2B	3B	HR	RBI	BB	SO	SB	CS	OBP	SLG
2007	Williamsport (NYP)	SS	.227	66	233	30	53	14	0	6	33	23	53	8	2	.300	.365
2008	Lakewood (SAL)	LoA	.361	67	249	40	90	12	3	10	50	31	43	10	3	.441	.554
	Clearwater (FSL)	HiA	.329	65	243	36	80	27	1	9	38	19	46	5	6	.380	.560
2009	Reading (EL)	AA	.333	86	318	59	106	22	4	15	65	35	51	18	4	.408	.569
	Lehigh Valley (IL)	AAA	.282	30	110	15	31	6	1	5	19	13	19	3	1	.359	.491
2010	Sacramento (PCL)	AAA	.272	127	464	79	126	26	6	6	78	51	92	16	5	.348	.392
2011	Sacramento (PCL)	AAA	.272	93	349	51	95	16	0	16	64	46	80	14	5	.360	.456
	Oakland (AL)	MAJ	.200	11	30	4	6	0	0	1	1	5	11	0	0	.314	.300
2012	Oakland (AL)	MAJ	.143	6	21	2	3	1	0	0	0	0	10	0	0	.143	.190
	Sacramento (PCL)	AAA	.287	120	449	81	129	31	1	12	67	86	105	18	3	.405	.441
2013	Oakland (AL)	MAJ	.043	9	23	0	1	0	0	0	0	2	5	0	0	.120	.043
	Sacramento (PCL)	AAA	.281	112	420	54	118	25	1	18	85	50	88	5	2	.360	.474
Major League Totals			.135	26	74	6	10	1	0	1	1	7	26	0	0	.210	.189
Minor League Totals			.292	766	2835	445	828	179	17	97	499	354	577	97	31	.375	.470

28 BRUCE MAXWELL, C

BA GRADE **45** HIGH

Born: Dec. 20, 1990. **B-T:** L-R. **Ht.:** 6-2. **Wt.:** 235. **Drafted:** Birmingham-Southern, 2012 (2nd round). **Signed by:** Kelcey Mucker.

Maxwell dominated NCAA Division III competition, and the Athletics made him the highest-drafted D-III player since Jason Hirsh in 2003 when they chose him 62nd overall in 2012. Primarily a first baseman in college, Maxwell was drafted as a catcher, but his receiving isn't pretty. His 17 passed balls in 83 games in 2013 were a vast improvement on 18 in just 38 games in 2012. His hands and agility have improved, and he's embraced the work it takes to get better. Opponents ran on him because a hitch in his throwing motion mitigates his average arm strength, and he caught just 16 percent of the 103 basestealers who tested him last year at low Class A Beloit and high Class A Stockton. Maxwell's swing takes a good plane through the zone, and he has the physicality and bat speed to produce solid power numbers. He controls the plate well, and the A's believe all his work on his defense detracted a bit from his offense. If his catching works out, Maxwell offers outstanding value as a capable lefty-hitting catcher. He may start 2014 back at Stockton but could move quicker considering the organization's lack of catching depth.

Year	Club (League)	Class	AVG	G	AB	R	H	2B	3B	HR	RBI	BB	SO	SB	CS	OBP	SLG
2012	Athletics (AZL)	R	.524	6	21	8	11	4	0	0	4	5	3	0	0	.615	.714
	Vermont (NYP)	SS	.254	61	228	22	58	14	0	0	22	26	35	1	0	.329	.316
2013	Beloit (MWL)	LoA	.286	57	199	25	57	14	0	2	28	24	29	0	0	.360	.387
	Stockton (CAL)	HiA	.263	47	175	19	46	8	0	5	21	19	34	0	0	.335	.394
Minor League Totals			.276	171	623	74	172	40	0	7	75	74	101	1	0	.351	.374

29 TANNER PETERS, RHP

BA GRADE **45** HIGH

Born: Aug. 6, 1990. **B-T:** R-R. **Ht.:** 6-0. **Wt.:** 155. **Drafted:** Nevada-Las Vegas, 2011 (16th round). **Signed by:** Rick Magnante.

Peters broke out as a junior for Nevada-Las Vegas in 2011, going 9-4, 1.50 as the Mountain West Conference pitcher of the year. Spending all of 2013 in the high Class A Stockton rotation, he was a workhorse, logging the most innings of any California League pitcher (166) and ranking second in strikeouts (159). While he's undersized and doesn't have huge upside, Peters gives himself a chance with four solid-average pitches and feel for his craft. His fastball sits at 88-91 mph, sometimes touching 92, and he gets good sink on it to pound the bottom half of the zone. When he misses up, he's homer-prone. His changeup is the closest thing he has to a plus pitch, and with its deception and good fading action it does garner a few plus grades from scouts. He throws his curveball for strikes but realized he needed a quicker breaking ball and added a slider during the season. The Athletics laud Peters for being a quick learner and good self-evaluator. He repeats his delivery and added some deception in 2013 when the team moved him to the third-base side of the rubber. He will move up to Double-A Midland in 2014 and projects as a back-end starter or middle reliever.

Year	Club (League)	Class	W	L	ERA	G	GS	CG	SV	IP	H	HR	BB	SO	K/9	WHIP	AVG
2011	Vermont (NYP)	SS	1	1	1.35	21	0	0	11	27	12	1	8	33	11.1	0.75	.135
2012	Vermont (NYP)	SS	0	0	6.00	2	0	0	0	3	2	0	2	7	21.0	1.33	.182
	Burlington (MWL)	LoA	2	6	3.16	14	12	0	0	68	58	8	18	66	8.7	1.11	.233
2013	Stockton (CAL)	HiA	12	8	4.07	28	28	0	0	166	167	24	27	159	8.6	1.17	.261
Minor League Totals			15	15	3.58	65	40	0	11	264	239	33	55	265	9.0	1.12	.241

30 IOLANA AKAU, C

BA GRADE **45** HIGH

Born: Aug. 31, 1995. **B-T:** R-R. **Ht.:** 5-11. **Wt.:** 180. **Drafted:** HS—Honolulu, 2013 (20th round). **Signed by:** J.T. Stotts.

Akau already has excelled in the face of big-time pressure. He helped lead his team from Waipio, Hawaii, to the 2008 Little League World Series title, homering in the championship game against Mexico. He went on to play his prep baseball at St. Louis High in Honolulu, the same school that produced Dodgers righthander Brandon League, and was committed to the University of Hawaii before the Athletics signed him for an above-slot $375,000 in the 20th round of the 2013 draft. The A's see in Akau shades of another Hawaiian catcher who came through their system, Kurt Suzuki. He's best known for his defense, while his offensive upside looks fairly limited. He's highly agile behind the plate and an advanced receiver, and the A's like how he takes charge of games. His arm strength and transfer on his throws are solid as well. Offensively, he has a sound fundamental swing with limited power potential. The A's would like him to get stronger, but even then he'll likely always have below-average power. Akau profiles as a catch-and-throw backup, and will compete for a spot at low Class A Beloit in 2014.

Year	Club (League)	Class	AVG	G	AB	R	H	2B	3B	HR	RBI	BB	SO	SB	CS	OBP	SLG
2013	Athletics (AZL)	R	.133	11	30	2	4	1	0	0	1	2	10	0	0	.182	.167
Minor League Totals			.133	11	30	2	4	1	0	0	1	2	10	0	0	.182	.167

Philadelphia Phillies

BY JOSH NORRIS

After years of reaching into their farm system to replenish the big league club, the Phillies have a system that's a bit threadbare. And for the second straight season, the lack of prospects was not offset by October baseball at Citizens Bank Park.

The 2013 season was supposed to be a transition year, when entering-their-prime holdovers such as Domonic Brown and rookies like Darin Ruf would help kickstart Philly toward a playoff run.

That never came together. The Phillies' first losing record since 2000 cost manager Charlie Manuel his job. The same fate befell pitching coach Rich Dubee. Hall of Famer Ryne Sandberg, who was serving as third-base coach, replaced Manuel, at first on an interim basis and then on a three-year contract.

The season went bad fast. Roy Halladay was startlingly ineffective and gave up nine home runs in his first seven starts before having shoulder surgery in May. He returned for a few late-season starts before getting shut down with "arm fatigue" and has thrown his last pitch for the Phillies. The back of the rotation was a continual source of frustration, as was the bullpen, and closer Jonathan Papelbon blew seven save opportunities in 36 tries, drawing plenty of boobirds at Pattison and Broad.

The offense nearly matched the pitching staff in its struggles, due in part to injuries to Ryan Howard (now a recurring theme) and new center fielder Ben Revere, the inevitable decline of shortstop Jimmy Rollins and a roster that lacked depth.

Unlike 2012, however, when Philadelphia flipped Hunter Pence, Joe Blanton and Shane Victorino to contenders for prospects, general manager Ruben Amaro Jr. held on to his veteran players at the trade deadline. Amaro then watched the Phillies lose eight in a row in July's final week, sinking any playoff hopes they had.

Sandberg inherits a roster that had few bright spots in 2013, but foremost among them was Brown, who finally broke out in his third full season. The former organization top prospect made the all-star team and hit 27 homers, 12 of them during a torrid May stretch. Rookie righthander Jonathan Pettibone brought stability to the back of the rotation, while rookie Ruf swatted 14 home runs, ranking third on the team. Third baseman Cody Asche rushed to the majors just two years after being a fourth-round pick, and he did a creditable job at the hot corner.

The farm system can't be counted on to provide immediate help for 2014, particularly on the mound, where the system's futility cost pitching coordinator Gorman Heimueller his job. Phillies full-season pitchers walked 9.8 percent of batters faced and posted a composite 1.90 SO/BB ratio, ranking 29th out of 30 organizations. Their 1.48 WHIP was the worst in the minors.

Despite the bleak overall picture, the system does have bright spots. Third baseman Maikel Franco swatted 31 homers across two levels in 2013, and lefty Jesse Biddle overcame two ailments to rank third in the Eastern League in strikeouts. First-round pick J.P. Crawford won the Rookie-level Gulf Coast League batting crown, heading what could be a strong draft class.

TOMASSO DeROSA

Domonic Brown broke out in 2013, giving the Phillies a rare young regular in the lineup

TOP PROSPECTS OF THE DECADE

Year	Player, Pos.	2013 Org.
2004	Cole Hamels, lhp	Phillies
2005	Ryan Howard, 1b	Phillies
2006	Cole Hamels, lhp	Phillies
2007	Carlos Carrasco, rhp	Indians
2008	Carlos Carrasco, rhp	Indians
2009	Domonic Brown, of	Phillies
2010	Domonic Brown, of	Phillies
2011	Domonic Brown, of	Phillies
2012	Trevor May, rhp	Twins
2013	Jesse Biddle, lhp	Phillies

ORGANIZATION OVERVIEW

General Manager: Ruben Amaro Jr. **Farm Director:** Joe Jordan. **Scouting Director:** Marti Wolever.

Class	Team	League	W	L	PCT	Finish	Manager(s)
Majors	Philadelphia Phillies	National	73	89	.451	13th (15)	C. Manuel/R. Sandberg
Triple-A	Lehigh Valley IronPigs	International	72	72	.500	7th (14)	Dave Brundage
Double-A	Reading Fightin' Phils	Eastern	62	80	.437	12th (12)	Dusty Wathan
High Class A	Clearwater Threshers	Florida State	67	68	.496	6th (12)	Chris Truby
Low Class A	Lakewood BlueClaws	South Atlantic	56	80	.412	12th (14)	Mickey Morandini
Short-season	Williamsport Crosscutters	New York-Penn	37	38	.493	9th (14)	Nelson Prada
Rookie	GCL Phillies	Gulf Coast	30	30	.500	7th (16)	Roly DeArmas
Overall 2013 Minor League Record			**324**	**368**	**.468**	**26th (30)**	

THIS YEAR'S TOP 30

No.	Player, Pos.	Grade/Risk
1.	Maikel Franco, 3b	65/Medium
2.	Jesse Biddle, lhp	55/Medium
3.	J.P. Crawford, ss	60/High
4.	Miguel Gonzalez, rhp	50/Medium
5.	Carlos Tocci, of	55/Extreme
6.	Ethan Martin, rhp	50/Medium
7.	Cesar Hernandez, 2b/of	45/Low
8.	Aaron Altherr, of	50/High
9.	Severino Gonzalez, rhp	50/High
10.	Roman Quinn, ss	55/Extreme
11.	Adam Morgan, lhp	50/High
12.	Cameron Perkins, of	50/High
13.	Luis Encarnacion, 3b	55/Extreme
14.	Deivi Grullon, c	55/Extreme
15.	Zach Green, 3b	50/High
16.	Cameron Rupp, c	45/Low
17.	Kelly Dugan, of	50/High
18.	Shane Watson, rhp	50/High
19.	Jose Pujols, of	50/Extreme
20.	Kenny Giles, rhp	50/Extreme
21.	Tommy Joseph, c	50/Extreme
22.	Dylan Cozens, of	50/Extreme
23.	Yoel Mecias, lhp	50/Extreme
24.	Andrew Knapp, c	45/High
25.	Cord Sandberg, of	50/Extreme
26.	Jan Hernandez, 3b	50/Extreme
27.	Zach Collier, of	45/High
28.	Malquin Canelo, ss	45/High
29.	Austin Wright, lhp	45/High
30.	Dan Child, rhp	45/High

LAST YEAR'S TOP 30

No.	Player, Pos.	Status
1.	Jesse Biddle, lhp	No. 2
2.	Roman Quinn, ss	No. 10
3.	Tommy Joseph, c/1b	No. 21
4.	Jonathan Pettibone, rhp	Majors
5.	Adam Morgan, lhp	No. 11
6.	Ethan Martin, rhp	No. 6
7.	Cody Asche, 3b	Majors
8.	Maikel Franco, 3b	No. 1
9.	Darin Ruf, 1b/of	Majors
10.	Carlos Tocci, of	No. 5
11.	Larry Greene, of	Dropped out
12.	Shane Watson, rhp	No. 18
13.	Phillippe Aumont, rhp	Majors
14.	Sebastian Valle, c	Dropped out
15.	Cesar Hernandez, 2b	No. 7
16.	Mitchell Walding, 3b	Dropped out
17.	Mitch Gueller, rhp	Dropped out
18.	Austin Wright, lhp	No. 29
19.	Kenny Giles, rhp	No. 20
20.	Justin DeFratus, rhp	Majors
21.	Tyler Cloyd, rhp	(Indians)
22.	Cameron Rupp, c	No. 16
23.	Brody Colvin, rhp	Dropped out
24.	Zach Collier, of	No. 27
25.	Aaron Altherr, of	No. 8
26.	Tyson Gillies, of	Dropped out
27.	Dylan Cozens, of	No. 22
28.	Andrew Pullin, of/2b	Dropped out
29.	Kyrell Hudson, of	Dropped out
30.	Kyle Simon, rhp	Dropped out

BEST TOOLS

Best Hitter for Average	J.P. Crawford
Best Power Hitter	Maikel Franco
Best Strike-Zone Discipline	J.P. Crawford
Fastest Baserunner	Roman Quinn
Best Athlete	Roman Quinn
Best Fastball	Kenny Giles
Best Curveball	Jesse Biddle
Best Slider	Adam Morgan
Best Changeup	Hoby Milner
Best Control	Severino Gonzalez
Best Defensive Catcher	Cameron Rupp
Best Defensive Infielder	J.P. Crawford
Best Infield Arm	Maikel Franco
Best Defensive Outfielder	Aaron Altherr
Best Outfield Arm	Jose Pujols

TOP 15 PLAYERS 25 AND UNDER

No.	Player, Pos. (Age)	Peak Level
1.	Maikel Franco, 3b (21)	Double-A
2.	Jesse Biddle, lhp (22)	Double-A
3.	J.P. Crawford, ss (19)	Low Class A
4.	Ben Revere, of (25)	Majors
5.	Cody Asche, 3b (23)	Majors
6.	Jonathan Pettibone, rhp (23)	Majors
7.	Roman Quinn, ss (20)	Low Class A
8.	Carlos Tocci, of (18)	Low Class A
9.	Ethan Martin, rhp (24)	Majors
10.	Freddy Galvis, ss (24)	Majors
11.	Cesar Hernandez, 2b/of (23)	Majors
12.	Aaron Altherr, of (23)	High Class A
13.	Severino Gonzalez, rhp (21)	Double-A
14.	Zach Collier, of (23)	Double-A
15.	Andrew Knapp, c (22)	Short-season

MINOR LEAGUE DEPTH CHART

PHILADELPHIA PHILLIES

TOP 2014 ROOKIE: Miguel Gonzalez, rhp. The Cuban defector should have an immediate impact in the back of the rotation.

BREAKOUT PROSPECT: Zach Green, 3b. High school shortstop has incredible raw power, which he actualized in the New York-Penn League.

SLEEPER: Andrew Pullin, 2b. Former prep switch-pitcher who converted from outfielder to second base has impressed Phillies with makeup.

SOURCE OF TOP 30 TALENT

Homegrown	**28**	**Acquired**	**2**
College	6	Trades	2
Junior college	0	Rule 5 draft	0
High school	12	Independent leagues	0
Nondrafted free agents	0	Free agents/waivers	0
International	10		

LF
- Cord Sandberg (25)
- Larry Greene
- Leandro Castro
- Jiandido Tromp

CF
- Carlos Tocci (5)
- Aaron Altherr (8)
- Zach Collier (27)
- Jiwan James

RF
- Cameron Perkins (12)
- Kelly Dugan (17)
- Jose Pujols (19)

3B
- Maikel Franco (1)
- Luis Encarnacion (13)
- Zach Green (15)
- Jan Hernandez (26)
- Mitch Walding
- Harold Martinez

SS
- J.P. Crawford (3)
- Roman Quinn (10)
- Malquin Canelo (28)

2B
- Cesar Hernandez (7)
- Andrew Pullin
- Albert Cartwright
- Angelo Mora
- Alejandro Villalobos

1B
- Dylan Cozens (22)
- Trey Williams
- Jim Murphy
- Wilmer Oberto

C
- Deivi Grullon (14)
- Cameron Rupp (16)
- Tommy Joseph (21)
- Andrew Knapp (24)
- Sebastian Valle
- Gabriel Lino
- Jake Sweaney

LHP

LHSP	LHRP
Jesse Biddle (2)	Austin Wright (29)
Adam Morgan (11)	Nick Hernandez
Mario Hollands	Chris O'Hare
Ethan Stewart	
Mitch Gueller	
Hoby Milner	

RHP

RHSP	RHRP
Miguel Gonzalez (4)	Kenny Giles (20)
Ethan Martin (6)	Daniel Child (30)
Severino Gonzalez (9)	Mike Nesseth
Shane Watson (18)	Tyler Knigge
Yoel Mecias (23)	Colby Shreve
Mitch Gueller	Kyle Simon
Percy Garner	Steven Inch
Brody Colvin	Ryan O'Sullivan
Tyler Viza	
Seth Rosin	
Miguel Nunez	
Mark Leiter Jr.	

DRAFT ANALYSIS

2013

BONUSES: $5.6 MILLION

BEST PURE HITTER: SS J.P. Crawford (1) exceeded the Phillies' expectations when he won the batting title in the Rookie-level Gulf Coast League and jumped to low Class A Lakewood. C Andrew Knapp (2) was drafted for his offensive upside.

BEST POWER HITTER: Knapp combines athleticism, strength at 6-foot-1, 192 pounds and a sound swing for above-average power. He tied for the short-season New York-Penn League lead with 20 doubles.

FASTEST RUNNER: OF Justin Parr (8) is a grinder with above-average speed, edging out Crawford.

BEST DEFENSIVE PLAYER: Crawford laps this draft class, as he's a smooth defender with above-average footwork and hands to go with baseball instincts and a good internal clock.

BEST FASTBALL: RHP Dan Child (18) has effort in his delivery and his arm action is less than ideal, but he can sit 92-95 mph in relief outings and was an effective bullpen piece for USA Baseball's college national team in 2012.

BEST SECONDARY PITCH: RHP Tyler Buckley (27) struggled at Arkansas-Little Rock, posting a 6.70 ERA in 48 innings over two seasons. The Phillies saw the ability to spin a breaking ball, though, and that plus curveball helped him post a 2.22 ERA at short-season Williamsport.

BEST PRO DEBUT: Crawford, who hit .308/.405/.400 overall while adding 14 stolen bases. RHP Tyler Viza (32) gave up just five runs and posted a 1.41 ERA in 32 innings in the GCL.

BEST ATHLETE: OF Cord Sandberg (3) was committed to Mississippi State to play quarterback and has some stiffness to work out. But he has strength, speed and explosiveness. The Phillies like his swing and power potential.

MOST INTRIGUING BACKGROUND: Sandberg, as well as Crawford, whose father played pro football in Canada and who is a cousin of Dodgers outfielder Carl Crawford. Parr has two brothers, Jordan and Josh, who are infielders in the Diamondbacks system. Unsigned 2B Cavan Biggio (29) is the son of 3,000-hit big leaguer Craig. RHP Mark Leiter Jr. (22), son of the former big leaguer of the same name, had a strong debut, going 4-0, 1.20 with 50 strikeouts in 45 innings, including 16 scoreless at Lakeland.

CLOSEST TO THE MAJORS: Child may get there first as a reliever, but Crawford will challenge him, even as a high school infielder.

BEST LATE-ROUND PICK: Viza and LHP Denton Keys (11), who signed for $350,000. Like many successful Colorado prep pitchers, Keys has a projectable frame (6-foot-4, 200 pounds) and clean delivery, and he has bumped 91 mph.

THE ONE WHO GOT AWAY: The Phillies failed to sign college LHP Ben Wetzler (5, Oregon State) and OF Jason Monda (6, Washington State), who both returned for their senior seasons. They made a hard run at Biggio, a potentially special hitter if not the same all-around talent as his father.

ASSESSMENT: The Phillies signed an exciting class of hitters, though Knapp had to have Tommy John surgery this fall, which may slow his progress. Their pitching class offers less upside after Keys and Viza.

2012

BONUSES: $4.8 MILLION

The Phillies started with high-risk, high-reward preps in RHP Shane Watson (1) and OF Dylan Cozens (2). OF Cam Perkins (6) is a sleeper.

GRADE: C

2011

BONUSES: $4.7 MILLION

3B Cody Asche (4) zoomed to the majors, helping save a class that had a bad 2013. OF Larry Greene (1s), the top pick, is approaching bust status.

GRADE: C

2010

BONUSES: $3.9 MILLION

Top pick LHP Jesse Biddle (1) misses bats but also lost his command in 2013. C Cameron Rupp (3) reached the majors and may be a solid backup.

GRADE: D

TOP DRAFT PICKS OF THE DECADE

Year	Player, Pos.	2013 Org.
2004	Greg Golson, of	Braves
2005	Mike Costanzo, 3b (2nd round)	Reds
2006	Kyle Drabek, rhp	Blue Jays
2007	Joe Savery, lhp	Phillies
2008	Anthony Hewitt, 3b/of	Phillies
2009	Kelly Dugan, of (2nd round)	Phillies
2010	Jesse Biddle, lhp	Phillies
2011	Larry Greene, of (1st round supp.)	Phillies
2012	Shane Watson, lhp (1st round supp.)	Phillies
2013	J.P. Crawford, ss	Phillies

LARGEST BONUSES IN CLUB HISTORY

Gavin Floyd, 2001	$4,200,000
Pat Burrell, 1998	$3,150,000
J.P. Crawford, 2013	$2,299,300
Brett Myers, 1999	$2,050,000
Cole Hamels, 2002	$2,000,000

1 MAIKEL FRANCO, 3B

Born: Aug 26, 1992. **B-T:** R-R. **Ht.:** 6-1. **Wt.:** 180.
Signed: Dominican Republic, 2010.
Signed by: Koby Perez.

Signed for just $100,000 out of the Dominican Republic, Franco stood out as an amateur for his power bat, throwing arm and 7.7-second time in the 60-yard dash. That lack of speed had the Phillies consider a move to catcher, but that's no longer the case. Franco showed enough offensive polish to jump to the Rookie-level Gulf Coast League as a 17-year-old and reached low Class A Lakewood in late 2011 at age 18. Back at Lakewood in 2012, he dealt with a serious case of over-aggression, leading to a .207/.269/.338 line over his first 64 games in full-season ball. Once the weather in the Northeast warmed up, however, so did Franco (.346/.395/.530), and he hasn't stopped hitting. Franco followed up with a 31-homer season in 2013, earning himself a spot on the Florida State League all-star team in the first half, as well as his second Futures Game nod and a promotion to Double-A. He was the organization's player of the year after leading it in batting (.320), homers (31) and RBIs (103).

Franco offers premium bat speed that produces 70 power on the 20-80 scale. He's still too aggressive at times, but he has significantly cut down on his strikeouts and increased his walk rate. He doesn't walk much but makes such hard, consistent contact that he rarely goes into slumps. His swing gets out of control at times, and he has shown a vulnerability to breaking pitches down and in. Even with those dings and despite his top-shelf power, he struck out just 70 times in 581 plate appearances in 2013, or just 12 percent of the time. At third base, Franco showed good hands and actions, along with an above-average arm while making 15 errors. He moves left to right well and has the footwork to stick at third despite his poor running speed. The Phillies see him as a true middle-of-the-order bat who can hit for average and produce something on the order of 30 homers annually. They moved Franco to first base for the last week or so of the season, a move designed to make him more comfortable with a new position rather than an abandonment of the hot corner.

Rookie third baseman Cody Asche jumped to Philadelphia in August, and while his promotion was a factor in Franco's late stint at first base, Franco's ceiling is higher. His time at first provides Ryan Howard insurance for Philly, which intends to send Franco to Triple-A Lehigh Valley to open the 2014 season. He could challenge for a spot at Citizens Bank Park sometime toward the end of the season. Once he gets there, Philadelphia should have a power righthanded bat to complement Howard, Chase Utley and Domonic Brown in the middle of the lineup.

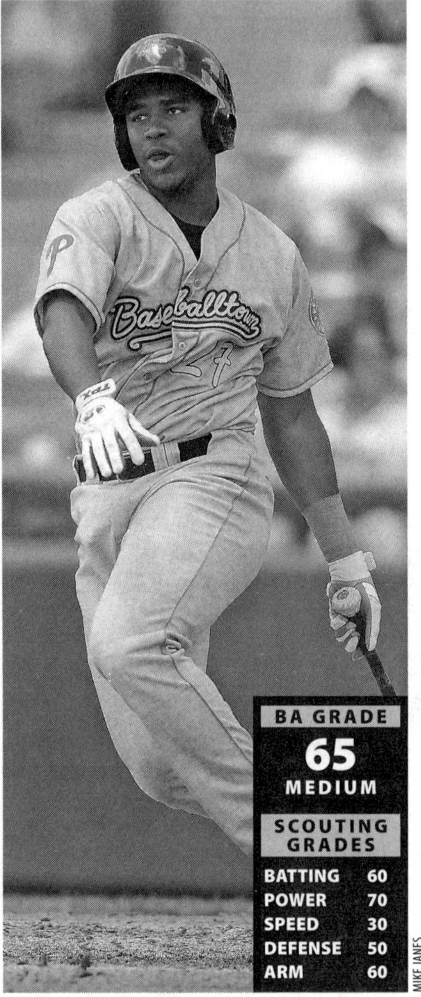

Baseballtown
BA GRADE
65
MEDIUM
SCOUTING GRADES
BATTING 60
POWER 70
SPEED 30
DEFENSE 50
ARM 60

MIKE JANES

Year	Club (League)	Class	AVG	G	AB	R	H	2B	3B	HR	RBI	BB	SO	SB	CS	OBP	SLG
2010	Phillies (GCL)	R	.222	51	194	23	43	11	2	2	29	16	46	0	0	.292	.330
2011	Lakewood (SAL)	LoA	.123	17	65	6	8	2	0	1	6	1	15	0	0	.149	.200
	Williamsport (NYP)	SS	.287	54	202	19	58	17	1	2	38	25	30	0	0	.367	.411
2012	Lakewood (SAL)	LoA	.280	132	503	70	141	32	3	14	84	38	80	3	1	.336	.439
2013	Clearwater (FSL)	HiA	.299	65	264	42	79	23	1	16	52	20	39	0	0	.349	.576
	Reading (EL)	AA	.339	69	277	47	94	13	2	15	51	10	31	1	2	.363	.563
Minor League Totals			.281	388	1505	207	423	98	9	50	260	110	241	4	3	.334	.458

2 JESSE BIDDLE, LHP

DAVID SCHOFIELD

BA GRADE
55
MEDIUM

Born: Oct. 22, 1991. **B-T:** L-L. **Ht.:** 6-4. **Wt.:** 225. **Drafted:** HS—Philadelphia, 2010 (1st round). **Signed by:** Eric Valent.

In his third full pro season, Biddle ranked third in the Double-A Eastern League in strikeouts (154) while ranking first among starters in opponent average (.210), and he struck out Maikel Franco in his one-inning stint in the Futures Game. He dealt with a bout of whooping cough that sapped his energy and had a bout of plantar fasciitis late in the season, though he never missed a start. Biddle has excellent size and athleticism, and he runs his fastball up to 94 mph and sits comfortably in the low 90s when he's at full strength. His dynamic curveball has reminded some evaluators of Barry Zito's offering and rates as the system's best. He also features a slider, which he threw in high school and then initially shelved in pro ball, and a changeup. The latter is average now and has a chance to be plus in the future. Biddle's spotty fastball command and a tendency to come out of his delivery when throwing his curveball led to a walk rate of 5.3 per nine innings, and he led the EL in walks (82). Biddle will have to pitch more efficiently in order to remain a starter. The Phillies believe that he will, giving him the stuff and frame to be a middle-of-the-rotation workhorse for years. If not, he'll still have a spot in the majors, most likely toward the back end of a rotation. He should start 2014 in Triple-A.

Year	Club (League)	Class	W	L	ERA	G	GS	CG	SV	IP	H	HR	BB	SO	K/9	WHIP	AVG
2010	Phillies (GCL)	R	3	1	4.32	9	9	1	0	33	35	2	9	41	11.1	1.32	.263
	Williamsport (NYP)	SS	1	0	2.61	3	3	0	0	10	5	0	11	9	7.8	1.55	.152
2011	Lakewood (SAL)	LoA	7	8	2.98	25	24	0	0	133	104	5	66	124	8.4	1.28	.219
2012	Clearwater (FSL)	HiA	10	6	3.22	26	26	1	0	143	129	10	54	151	9.5	1.28	.237
2013	Reading (EL)	AA	5	14	3.64	27	27	2	0	138	104	10	82	154	10.0	1.34	.210
Minor League Totals			26	29	3.34	90	89	4	0	458	377	27	222	479	9.4	1.31	.224

3 J.P. CRAWFORD, SS

DAVID SCHOFIELD

BA GRADE
60
HIGH

Born: Jan. 11, 1995. **B-T:** L-R. **Ht.:** 6-2. **Wt.:** 180. **Drafted:** HS—Lakewood, Calif., 2013 (1st round). **Signed by:** Demerius Pittman.

Crawford clearly comes from premium stock. He's the cousin of Dodgers outfielder Carl Crawford, and his father played football at Iowa State and in the Canadian Football League. The Phillies first saw Crawford as a high school junior when they were scouting his teammate, 2012 first-rounder Shane Watson. (They also drafted Travis d'Arnaud from the school in 2007.) Crawford won the Rookie-level Gulf Coast League batting title after signing and finished the year with low Class A Lakewood. Crawford combines athleticism with Southern California polish and has drawn rave reviews in his brief foray in pro ball. He gets plus marks for his play at shortstop, where he has soft hands, an above-average arm and a good knack for the game. Although his lefthanded swing can get long at times, he has a good feel to hit, hand-eye coordination and plenty of bat speed to make evaluators believe he will hit for average. He'll have to get stronger to hit for any kind of home run power. He'll return to Lakewood to open the season.

Year	Club (League)	Class	AVG	G	AB	R	H	2B	3B	HR	RBI	BB	SO	SB	CS	OBP	SLG
2013	Phillies (GCL)	R	.345	39	142	24	49	8	3	1	19	25	25	12	5	.443	.465
	Lakewood (SAL)	LoA	.208	14	53	10	11	1	0	0	2	7	10	2	1	.300	.226
Minor League Totals			.308	53	195	34	60	9	3	1	21	32	35	14	6	.405	.400

4 MIGUEL GONZALEZ, RHP

EZIO RATTI-IBAF

BA GRADE
50
MEDIUM

Born: Sept. 23, 1986. **B-T:** R-R. **Ht.:** 6-3. **Wt.:** 195. **Signed:** Cuba, 2013. **Signed by:** Sal Agostinelli.

Gonzalez pitched in front of major league scouts in several significant international events as the ace of Cuba's national team. The biggest feather in his cap came in Taiwan in 2010, when he struck out 14 against Team USA in a 151-pitch epic in the gold-medal game of the World University Championship. He defected to Mexico in 2012 and initially agreed with the Phillies on a six-year, $48 million contract. After a physical, however, he signed a reworked three-year, $12 million deal in August. Gonzalez works with a fastball that typically sits between 90-94 mph and has been known to touch 96 on occasion. He sometimes has issues commanding the heater. He complements his fastball with an above-average splitter and solid-average changeup that make him effective against lefthanded hitters. His 75-79 mph hybrid breaking ball has flashed average, but more often than not it acts as a way to vary the looks hitters get. He has added a cutter in the last year. He can throw uphill at times, which flattens out his pitches. Gonzalez hasn't pitched much since 2011 thanks to a suspension in Cuba due to his defection attempts and then his subsequent flight from the island. He also didn't pitch in instructional league, but assuming he's healthy in spring training, the Phillies expect him to compete for a spot in the big league rotation.

Year	Club (League)	Class	W	L	ERA	G	GS	CG	SV	IP	H	HR	BB	SO	K/9	WHIP	AVG
Did Not Play—Signed 2014 contract																	

5 CARLOS TOCCI, OF

Born: Aug. 23, 1995. **B-T:** R-R. **Ht.:** 6-2. **Wt.:** 170. **Signed:** Venezuela, 2011. **Signed by:** Jesus Mendez.

After signing him on his 16th birthday for $759,000, the Phillies assigned Tocci to their Rookie-level Gulf Coast League affiliate in 2012, where he was the youngest player on his team by nearly a full year. They skipped him over short-season Williamsport in 2013 and instead opted to send the 17-year-old to the low Class A South Atlantic League, where only Royals shortstop Raul Adalberto Mondesi was younger. One look at Tocci makes it apparent that he needs to add at least 20 pounds to his rail-thin frame. Even as currently constructed, though, he shows flashes of why the Phillies gambled on his projection. He wasn't overmatched in the SAL thanks to good pitch recognition and the ability to get the barrel on the ball. Problem is, his lack of strength means his well-struck balls often die in outfielders' gloves. He has good instincts in center field, an arm that projects as above-average, and a combination of solid-average speed and long strides that allow him to glide to balls all around him. When Tocci reported to instructional league, he was already 10 pounds heavier than his listed weight entering this year. As he bulks up, he'll add more sock to his swing and be able to better withstand the rigors of a 140-game season. He should begin 2014 back at Lakewood.

Year	Club (League)	Class	AVG	G	AB	R	H	2B	3B	HR	RBI	BB	SO	SB	CS	OBP	SLG
2012	Phillies (GCL)	R	.278	38	97	13	27	2	0	0	9	6	18	9	2	.330	.299
2013	Lakewood (SAL)	LoA	.209	118	421	40	88	17	0	0	26	22	77	6	7	.261	.249
Minor League Totals			.222	156	518	53	115	19	0	0	35	28	95	15	9	.274	.259

6 ETHAN MARTIN, RHP

Born: June 6, 1989. **B-T:** R-R. **Ht.:** 6-2. **Wt.:** 195. **Drafted:** HS—Toccoa, Ga., 2008 (1st round). **Signed by:** Lon Joyce (Dodgers).

BA's 2008 High School Player of the Year has endured a lot in his pro career, struggling significantly with control issues early in his career with the Dodgers. The Phillies acquired him for Shane Victorino in 2012, and Martin made his big league debut in 2013. He was hammered as a starter before moving to the bullpen in September. Armed with a live arm and clean delivery, Martin has a four-pitch repertoire that includes a fastball that sits at 92-93 mph and touches 95 as a starter. His fastball plays up to 97 in shorter stints. He throws both a downer curveball that he struggles to command consistently, as well as a slider that flashes plus and a straight changeup. While his curve tends to be in the low 70s, his slider at times features cutter action and reaches 87 mph. Martin has below-average command that regressed in 2013, and he has averaged 5.5 walks per nine innings as a professional. With the big league rotation in flux, particularly from the right side, Martin has a great chance to start in Philadelphia. His main challenge will be throwing strikes consistently. If he succeeds, Martin could find himself in the back end of the rotation. If not, he'll still probably be a weapon out of the bullpen.

Year	Club (League)	Class	W	L	ERA	G	GS	CG	SV	IP	H	HR	BB	SO	K/9	WHIP	AVG
2009	Great Lakes (MWL)	LoA	6	8	3.87	27	19	0	1	100	85	4	61	120	10.8	1.46	.232
2010	Inland Empire (CAL)	HiA	9	14	6.35	25	22	1	0	113	120	10	81	105	8.3	1.77	.279
2011	R. Cucamonga (CAL)	HiA	4	4	7.36	16	9	0	0	55	65	8	37	61	10.0	1.85	.291
	Chattanooga (SL)	AA	5	3	4.02	21	3	0	2	40	31	3	29	43	9.6	1.49	.215
2012	Chattanooga (SL)	AA	8	6	3.58	20	20	0	0	118	89	5	61	112	8.5	1.27	.214
	Reading (EL)	AA	5	0	3.18	7	7	0	0	40	29	3	18	35	7.9	1.18	.206
2013	Lehigh Valley (IL)	AAA	11	5	4.12	21	21	1	0	116	94	11	67	107	8.3	1.39	.229
	Philadelphia (NL)	MAJ	2	5	6.08	15	8	0	0	40	42	9	26	47	10.6	1.70	.261
Major League Totals			2	5	6.08	15	8	0	0	40	42	9	26	47	10.6	1.70	.261
Minor League Totals			48	40	4.64	137	101	2	3	582	513	44	354	583	9.0	1.49	.241

7 CESAR HERNANDEZ, 2B/OF

BA GRADE
45
LOW

Born: May 23, 1990. **B-T:** B-R. **Ht.:** 5-10. **Wt.:** 160. **Signed:** Venezuela, 2006. **Signed by:** Sal Agostinelli/Jesus Mendez.

Rated as the best defensive second baseman in both the Eastern and International leagues over the past two seasons, Hernandez has earned all-star nods in three different leagues in his career. Shifted to center field in July, he earned a September callup and played virtually every day for the Phillies in the season's final month. Much like countryman and system-mate Freddy Galvis, Hernandez's slight frame oozes with athleticism, which came in handy with his shift to center field. He wasn't a natural at his new position, but he showed enough progress to make his employers believe he's a legitimate option there. He's a plus runner with the smarts to make his legs a weapon on the basepaths, and they play in center. He's also sure-handed when focused at second, with an average arm makes him merely an emergency option at shortstop, which he's played sparingly. At the plate he showcases a line-drive swing with gap-to-gap power but can get beat with good velocity up in the zone. Hernandez will head to the Venezuelan League to keep himself sharp at both second and in center. The Phillies' infield remains crowded, with veterans like Jimmy Rollins and Chase Utley, as well as Freddy Galvis, so Hernandez fits better in the short-term in a utility role, putting his new outfield experience to work.

Year	Club (League)	Class	AVG	G	AB	R	H	2B	3B	HR	RBI	BB	SO	SB	CS	OBP	SLG
2007	Phillies (VSL)	R	.276	54	181	32	50	7	8	2	21	11	30	6	4	.328	.436
2008	Phillies (VSL)	R	.315	60	197	31	62	7	6	1	24	33	22	19	7	.412	.426
2009	Phillies (GCL)	R	.267	41	150	21	40	5	1	0	18	17	20	13	5	.351	.313
2010	Williamsport (NYP)	SS	.325	65	255	36	83	13	2	0	23	26	27	32	6	.390	.392
2011	Clearwater (FSL)	HiA	.268	119	421	47	113	7	4	4	37	23	80	23	10	.306	.333
2012	Reading (EL)	AA	.304	103	411	50	125	26	11	2	51	27	67	16	12	.345	.436
	Lehigh Valley (IL)	AAA	.248	30	121	13	30	4	1	0	6	4	11	5	3	.270	.298
2013	Reading (EL)	AA	.500	3	10	2	5	1	0	0	3	1	1	1	0	.500	.600
	Lehigh Valley (IL)	AAA	.309	104	391	59	121	12	9	2	34	41	81	32	8	.375	.402
	Philadelphia (NL)	MAJ	.289	34	121	17	35	5	0	0	10	9	26	0	3	.344	.331
Major League Totals			.289	34	121	17	35	5	0	0	10	9	26	0	3	.344	.331
Minor League Totals			.294	579	2137	291	629	82	42	11	217	183	339	147	55	.351	.387

8 AARON ALTHERR, OF

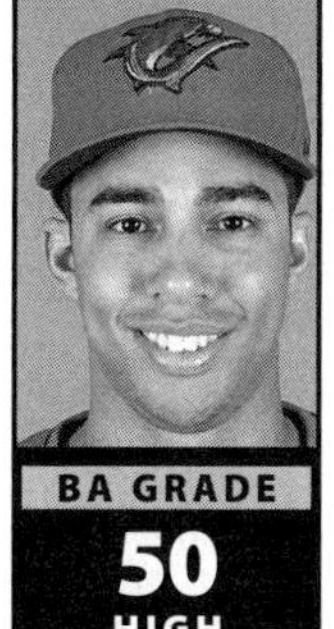

BA GRADE
50
HIGH

Born: Jan. 14, 1991. **B-T:** R-R. **Ht.:** 6-5. **Wt.:** 190. **Drafted:** HS—Avondale, Ariz., 2009 (9th round). **Signed by:** Brad Holland

Altherr is a prime example of the Phillies' style of gambling draft picks on toolsy players that require a lot of projection. Born in Germany, his mother was a U.S. service member and his father a former German soccer player. He played for the Germans in the World Baseball Classic qualification round in 2012 and went 6-for-11 with two homers, including one off future big leaguer Andrew Albers. With one of the most athletic bodies in the system, Altherr is just beginning to tap into his impressive tools. He honed his swing in 2013, though he still has a tendency to collapse on the back side, and established career bests in hits (128), walks (45), home runs (12) and slugging percentage (.455). He also had the most strikeouts in his short career, fanning nearly 27 percent of the time, due mostly to a long stroke that leaves him vulnerable to pitches on the inner half. He's a true center fielder with sneaky speed and enough arm to play in a corner if he's pushed there. He ranked second in the high Class A Florida State League with 17 assists. The Phillies assigned Altherr to the Arizona Fall League to get him more at-bats, and he's headed to Double-A Reading in 2014 to see if he can maintain his improved power while making more consistent contact. If he does, he profiles as a major league regular in center field.

Year	Club (League)	Class	AVG	G	AB	R	H	2B	3B	HR	RBI	BB	SO	SB	CS	OBP	SLG
2009	Phillies (GCL)	R	.214	28	84	10	18	3	0	1	11	8	15	6	1	.283	.286
2010	Phillies (GCL)	R	.304	27	115	12	35	6	1	1	15	3	22	10	3	.331	.400
	Williamsport (NYP)	SS	.287	28	94	11	27	7	3	0	10	8	13	2	3	.350	.426
2011	Lakewood (SAL)	LoA	.211	41	147	20	31	6	0	1	15	11	47	12	0	.272	.272
	Williamsport (NYP)	SS	.260	71	269	41	70	12	2	5	31	13	52	25	4	.302	.375
2012	Lakewood (SAL)	LoA	.252	110	420	65	106	27	6	8	50	38	102	25	8	.319	.402
2013	Clearwater (FSL)	HiA	.275	123	466	57	128	36	6	12	69	45	140	23	5	.337	.455
Minor League Totals			.260	428	1595	216	415	97	18	28	201	126	391	103	24	.318	.396

9 SEVERINO GONZALEZ, RHP

DAVID SCHOFIELD

BA GRADE
50
HIGH

Born: Sept. 28, 1992. **B-T:** R-R. **Ht.:** 6-1. **Wt.:** 153. **Signed:** Panama, 2011. **Signed by:** Allen Lewis.

The biggest surprise in the organization, Gonzalez didn't sign until he was 18 but made up for lost time in 2013. Making his U.S. debut after having starred in the Rookie-level Venezuelan Summer League for two seasons, he took advantage of what was supposed to be a two-start fill-in role at high Class A Clearwater and never went back to low Class A Lakewood. Gonzalez's command elevates an otherwise average arsenal. He showcases near elite-level control of a three-pitch mix, which is predicated on a low-90s heater that features both cut and sink. He has added nearly 10 mph to his fastball since signing and commands the pitch well. His curveball and slider both project to be average as he throws both for strikes, and he's been toying with a changeup as well. He varies the velocity on his breaking balls to keep hitters off balance, but he'll need the changeup after allowing lefthanded hitters to bat .309/.380/.404 against him in the FSL. His slight frame prompts questions about whether he can handle a starter's workload. Gonzalez finished the year with a flourish, fanning six in 6 2/3 frames in Double-A Reading's season finale, with Twins prospect Miguel Sano as his final strikeout victim. Gonzalez figures to return to Reading to start 2014.

Year	Club (League)	Class	W	L	ERA	G	GS	CG	SV	IP	H	HR	BB	SO	K/9	WHIP	AVG
2011	Phillies (VSL)	R	1	1	2.11	17	0	0	1	43	36	0	3	29	6.1	0.91	.228
2012	Phillies (VSL)	R	7	3	1.65	14	14	2	0	93	59	4	6	86	8.4	0.70	.179
2013	Lakewood (SAL)	LoA	3	0	1.69	4	4	0	0	21	10	1	3	31	13.1	0.61	.137
	Clearwater (FSL)	HiA	3	5	2.02	20	9	0	0	76	66	4	19	82	9.8	1.12	.239
	Reading (EL)	AA	1	0	2.70	1	1	0	0	7	8	0	0	6	8.1	1.20	.308
Minor League Totals			15	9	1.88	56	28	2	1	239	179	9	31	234	8.8	0.88	.208

10 ROMAN QUINN, SS

DAVID SCHOFIELD

BA GRADE
55
EXTREME

Born: May 14, 1993. **B-T:** B-R. **Ht.:** 5-10. **Wt.:** 170. **Drafted:** HS—Port St. Joe, Fla., 2011 (2nd round). **Signed by:** Aaron Jersild.

When he was in high school, Quinn was neither a shortstop nor a switch-hitter. He has become both in pro ball, which speaks both to his athleticism and his coachability. He was an effective running prep quarterback, earning scholarship offers from football programs including Florida State. Instead he signed for $775,000 with the Phillies. His first full season was cut short on June 24, when a pitch struck and broke his right wrist. Quinn's calling card is his blazing speed, which rates at the top of the scouting scale and is just a tick below Reds burner Billy Hamilton's. He was clocked this season at 14 seconds flat on an inside-the-park home run. He is still learning to switch-hit but should be a solid hitter from both sides. Despite his size, he has enough pop to keep pitchers honest. He's raw at shortstop, as shown by his 31 errors in 66 games last year. Most came on throws, and the Phillies have worked with Quinn to correct flaws in his motion and iron out that part of his game. The presence of 2013 first-rounder J.P. Crawford and a postseason injury cloud Quinn's future. Crawford might have pushed him off shortstop anyway, and in November, Quinn ruptured the Achilles tendon in his right leg. The injury and rehabilitation could sideline him most or all of 2014, costing him valuable development time and perhaps hastening his move to center field or second base.

Year	Club (League)	Class	AVG	G	AB	R	H	2B	3B	HR	RBI	BB	SO	SB	CS	OBP	SLG
2012	Williamsport (NYP)	SS	.281	66	267	56	75	9	11	1	23	28	61	30	6	.370	.408
2013	Lakewood (SAL)	LoA	.238	67	260	37	62	7	3	5	21	27	64	32	9	.323	.346
Minor League Totals			.260	133	527	93	137	16	14	6	44	55	125	62	15	.347	.378

11 ADAM MORGAN, LHP

BA GRADE
50
HIGH

Born: Feb. 27, 1990. **B-T:** L-L. **Ht.:** 6-1. **Wt.:** 195. **Drafted:** Alabama, 2011 (3rd round). **Signed by:** Mike Stauffer.

In mid-2012, some evaluators were calling Morgan the best arm in the Phillies system. He finished his first full season at Double-A Reading, and he threw well in big league camp in spring training 2013. It looked like the southpaw would be on the Citizens Bank Park mound at some point in 2013, but instead, Morgan suffered a small tear in his left shoulder that limited him to just 78 innings in the minors. He escaped the scalpel through a rehab program, which provides a silver lining. He went down for two months in May, then returned to the Triple-A Lehigh Valley rotation in late July and threw well down the stretch, posting a 2.73 ERA in his final 30 innings. When at full strength in 2013, Morgan sported a fastball that sat between 88-91 mph and touched 93. He backed it up with a mid-80s slider that is plus now and has a chance to be double-plus in the future, as well as an above-average changeup. He also has a curveball, but it lags well behind his other three offerings. He had a tendency in 2013 to rush himself through his delivery and fall off line, costing him his formerly above-average command. If healthy in 2014, Morgan should return to the Lehigh Valley rotation.

Year	Club (League)	Class	W	L	ERA	G	GS	CG	SV	IP	H	HR	BB	SO	K/9	WHIP	AVG
2011	Williamsport (NYP)	SS	3	3	2.01	11	11	0	0	54	42	2	14	43	7.2	1.04	.206
2012	Clearwater (FSL)	HiA	4	10	3.29	21	20	1	0	123	103	7	28	140	10.2	1.07	.227
	Reading (EL)	AA	4	1	3.53	6	6	0	0	36	34	2	11	29	7.3	1.26	.260
2013	Phillies (GCL)	R	0	1	2.57	2	2	0	0	7	6	0	0	8	10.3	0.86	.231
	Lehigh Valley (IL)	AAA	2	7	4.04	16	16	0	0	71	84	10	26	49	6.2	1.54	.296
Minor League Totals			13	22	3.25	56	55	1	0	291	269	21	79	269	8.3	1.20	.245

12 CAMERON PERKINS, OF

BA GRADE 50 HIGH

Born: Sept. 27, 1990. **B-T:** R-R. **Ht.:** 6-5. **Wt.:** 205. **Drafted:** Purdue, 2012 (6th round). **Signed by:** Nate Dion.

A first-team all-conference third baseman at Purdue, Perkins helped the Boilermakers win their first Big Ten Conference title since 1907, then moved quickly in his first full pro season. When Kelly Dugan went down with an injury early, Perkins moved to high Class A Clearwater as his replacement and earned a midseason all-star spot in the Florida State League. A pitch broke his left wrist and prompted him to miss the exhibition and the month of June, but Perkins returned and wound up finishing third in the FSL batting race at .295. His body, which draws comparisons with Hunter Pence, isn't done maturing. The doubles he produces at present have to potential to turn into home runs once he adds muscle, giving him average power potential. Like Pence, Perkins' swing isn't the prettiest, but he's got a good feel for the barrel and can put it on just about any pitch. As a right fielder, he's athletic and uses his long strides to have average range, and he has average arm strength. His speed is just average but is a tick better when he gets going. Perkins hasn't hit for corner-profile power yet, but his bat is intriguing. He's headed for Double-A Reading in 2014.

Year	Club (League)	Class	AVG	G	AB	R	H	2B	3B	HR	RBI	BB	SO	SB	CS	OBP	SLG
2012	Phillies (GCL)	R	.158	5	19	0	3	0	0	0	3	0	2	0	0	.150	.158
	Williamsport (NYP)	SS	.304	67	270	31	82	23	1	1	38	14	41	5	2	.352	.407
2013	Phillies (GCL)	R	.571	2	7	1	4	1	0	1	1	1	0	0	0	.625	1.143
	Clearwater (FSL)	HiA	.295	103	387	54	114	30	5	6	53	25	57	4	5	.346	.444
Minor League Totals			.297	177	683	86	203	54	6	8	95	40	100	9	7	.346	.429

13 LUIS ENCARNACION, 3B

BA GRADE 55 EXTREME

Born: Aug. 9, 1997. **B-T:** R-R. **Ht.:** 6-3. **Wt.:** 215. **Signed:** Dominican Republic, 2013. **Signed by:** Koby Perez.

Encarnacion, who signed last Aug. 29, mere weeks after turning 16, solidified his reputation among scouts by collecting four hits at MLB's international showcase in January 2013, and he then notched two more hits against the Canadian national team five months later. The Phillies liked what they saw and in July 2013 responded with a $1 million bonus, the largest outlay the organization ever has given to a Latin American teen. (Korean righty Seung Lee got a $1.2 million back in 2001 to set the franchise record.) Encarnacion is an extremely powerful hitter who also has the tools to hit for average. The knock on him right now is his lack of a defensive home. The Phillies worked with him at instructional league to help build his instincts and range at third base, but there a lot more work remains. He doesn't run particularly well, which even further limits his overall potential. If Encarnacion does have to move across the diamond (or to left field)—even as a righthanded hitter—he projects to produce enough power to land gracefully at either spot. Because he's so young, Encarnacion will play in extended spring training in 2014 before heading to the Rookie-level Gulf Coast League as a 16-year-old.

Year	Club (League)	Class	AVG	G	AB	R	H	2B	3B	HR	RBI	BB	SO	SB	CS	OBP	SLG
2013	Did not play—Signed 2014 contract																

14 DEIVI GRULLON, C

BA GRADE 55 EXTREME

Born: Feb. 17, 1996. **B-T:** R-R. **Ht.:** 6-1. **Wt.:** 180. **Signed:** Dominican Republic, 2012. **Signed by:** Koby Perez.

Signed for $575,000, Grullon earned the top bonus handed out by the Phillies to an international amateur in 2012. The organization intends to invest more heavily in Latin America, and they believed the expenditure for Grullon was money well spent. He's the rare teen catcher whose defense appears to have the early lead on his offensive potential. He comes with a broad, durable body, and he has already proved himself adept at blocking balls. Grullon's lateral movement needs improvement at the moment, but not enough to be a worry. His arm rates as a 70 on the 20-80 scale right now, and he threw out 28 percent of basestealers in the Rookie-level Gulf Coast League in 2013. Grullon's offensive tools are understandably raw, but he made progress in the GCL. The length of his swing concerned scouts who believed it would cause him to swing-and-miss excessively, so his low strikeout rate in the GCL (about 13 percent of plate appearances) was a pleasant surprise. The Phillies project Grullon as a 10-15 homer threat eventually if he can get his average to the .250 range. He should start 2014 in extended spring training, where he'll work on adding strength in his lower half, and he likely will repeat the GCL.

Year	Club (League)	Class	AVG	G	AB	R	H	2B	3B	HR	RBI	BB	SO	SB	CS	OBP	SLG
2013	Phillies (GCL)	R	.273	41	121	13	33	8	0	1	14	10	18	0	0	.333	.364
Minor League Totals			.273	41	121	13	33	8	0	1	14	10	18	0	0	.333	.364

15 ZACH GREEN, 3B

BA GRADE **50** HIGH

Born: March 7, 1994. **B-T:** R-R. **Ht.:** 6-3. **Wt.:** 210. **Drafted:** HS—Sacramento, 2012 (3rd round). **Signed by:** Joey Davis

Green signed for $420,000 in 2012 out of Sacramento's Jesuit High, which has produced recent big leaguers such as J.P. Howell and Lars Anderson. His ability to put a charge in a ball is not in question. Green led the short-season New York-Penn League in homers (13), was tied for the top in doubles (20) and finished second in slugging percentage (.476). Whether he'll hit for average, however, is a different story entirely. Green led the NYP with 91 strikeouts in 311 plate appearances, and opposing managers noted he had particular trouble with breaking pitches. He's also a bit pull-happy at this point, and he will have to learn to adjust as he moves up the ladder. Evaluators are split as Green's defensive value at third base. None sees him as a definite candidate to move off the position, but nearly all see areas he'll need to clean up. He sometimes fails to finish the play, and he needs to complete his arm action more consistently. A big, broad-shouldered guy, Green will have to work to maintain his agility. He's not a baseclogger, but speed won't be a part of his game. After his success at Williamsport, he'll move up to low Class A Lakewood, where he and J.P. Crawford will form a talented left side of the infield.

Year	Club (League)	Class	AVG	G	AB	R	H	2B	3B	HR	RBI	BB	SO	SB	CS	OBP	SLG
2012	Phillies (GCL)	R	.284	47	169	20	48	13	1	3	21	8	43	2	2	.333	.426
2013	Williamsport (NYP)	SS	.252	74	270	52	68	20	1	13	41	31	91	8	5	.344	.478
Minor League Totals			.264	121	439	72	116	33	2	16	62	39	134	10	7	.340	.458

16 CAMERON RUPP, C

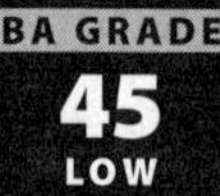

BA GRADE **45** LOW

Born: Sept. 28, 1988. **B-T:** R-R. **Ht.:** 6-2. **Wt.:** 230. **Drafted:** Texas, 2010 (3rd round). **Signed by:** Steve Cohen.

When the Phillies acquired Tommy Joseph as the key to the 2012 Hunter Pence trade, they appeared to have found their catcher of the future, and to have relegated Rupp to a backup role. A year later, Joseph's stock has tumbled as he's dealt with concussion-related problems, while Rupp reached a career-high in homers (14) and finished the season in the major leagues. A durable Texan with huge hands and great makeup, Rupp has the physicality to hold up as an everyday catcher. Pitchers love throwing to him, and he has improved his receiving and game-calling to the point where he can be at least a serviceable backup. His plus, accurate arm rates as his best tool and helped him throw out 34 percent of basestealers in the minors in 2013. Rupp's swing is powerful but long, so he probably won't ever hit for a high average or avoid strikeouts. He has the power to punish mistakes. Rupp's lack of speed makes him a baseclogger despite his consistent best efforts. The Phillies re-signed veteran Carlos Ruiz in November, so Rupp's best bet is to compete for the backup job in spring training. More likely, he'll be the starter at Triple-A Lehigh Valley in 2014.

Year	Club (League)	Class	AVG	G	AB	R	H	2B	3B	HR	RBI	BB	SO	SB	CS	OBP	SLG
2010	Williamsport (NYP)	SS	.218	55	193	20	42	16	0	5	28	25	51	0	0	.318	.378
2011	Lakewood (SAL)	LoA	.272	99	324	33	88	19	1	4	44	31	96	0	0	.346	.373
2012	Clearwater (FSL)	HiA	.267	104	344	32	92	22	1	10	49	40	77	0	0	.345	.424
2013	Reading (EL)	AA	.245	41	143	18	35	6	0	8	21	14	36	0	0	.329	.455
	Lehigh Valley (IL)	AAA	.269	53	182	18	49	10	0	6	24	10	55	1	1	.309	.423
	Philadelphia (NL)	MAJ	.308	4	13	1	4	1	0	0	2	1	4	0	0	.357	.385
Major League Totals			.308	4	13	1	4	1	0	0	2	1	4	0	0	.357	.385
Minor League Totals			.258	352	1186	121	306	73	2	33	166	120	315	1	1	.334	.406

17 KELLY DUGAN, OF

BA GRADE **50** HIGH

Born: Sept. 18, 1990. **B-T:** L-R. **Ht.:** 6-3. **Wt.:** 195. **Drafted:** HS—Sherman Oaks, Calif., 2009 (2nd round). **Signed by:** Shane Bowers.

The son of Dennis Dugan, best known as the director of Adam Sandler's early comedy movies, Kelly played at the same high school as Giancarlo Stanton. He started making a name for himself in 2013, his best pro season, and earned a spot on the 40-man roster as a result. The Phillies' first pick in the

2009 draft (in the second round), Dugan signed for $485,000 as the 75th overall pick. He has the body of a power hitter, with a chiseled frame and long, looping, lefthanded swing that helps produce an impressive batting practice power display. He started translating his raw pop into actual home runs in 2013. He'd hit 15 homers in his career previously, then hit 20 between high Class A Clearwater and Double-A Reading despite missing most of April with a case of turf toe. Mainly a pull hitter with occasional opposite-field sock, Dugan holds his hands low, crowds the plate and has a hitch in his load. As is to be expected from someone with those traits, he's vulnerable to breaking pitches and doesn't project to hit for much average. He's also too aggressive and was exposed to a degree by Double-A pitchers. He's just a fair athlete and defender, though he has an average arm, and has played more left field as he's moved up the ladder after playing primarily right field at Class A. Dugan will start 2014 back at Reading.

Year	Club (League)	Class	AVG	G	AB	R	H	2B	3B	HR	RBI	BB	SO	SB	CS	OBP	SLG
2009	Phillies (GCL)	R	.233	45	150	18	35	8	1	0	8	12	30	9	5	.297	.300
2010	Phillies (GCL)	R	.576	9	33	12	19	4	1	1	4	4	4	2	2	.650	.848
	Williamsport (NYP)	SS	.250	19	60	6	15	6	0	0	4	5	17	0	0	.343	.350
2011	Williamsport (NYP)	SS	.284	47	176	25	50	4	4	2	21	14	34	6	0	.343	.386
2012	Lakewood (SAL)	LoA	.300	117	430	83	129	33	2	12	60	48	122	5	1	.387	.470
2013	Clearwater (FSL)	HiA	.318	56	217	37	69	12	3	10	36	24	60	1	3	.401	.539
	Reading (EL)	AA	.264	56	212	25	56	12	1	10	23	5	54	0	1	.299	.472
Minor League Totals			.292	349	1278	206	373	79	12	35	156	112	321	23	12	.365	.455

18 SHANE WATSON, RHP

BA GRADE **50** HIGH

Born: Aug. 13, 1993. **B-T:** R-R. **Ht.:** 6-4. **Wt.:** 200. **Drafted:** HS—Lakewood, Calif., 2012 (1st round supplemental). **Signed by:** Demerius Pittman.

A high school teammate of J.P. Crawford at Lakewood (Calif.) High, Watson lost about 30 pounds after signing with the Phillies before he learned that he had Type 1 diabetes. Once that was under control, he rebuilt his prototype pitcher's frame and showed flashes in 2013 of the pitcher the Phillies liked enough to pop in the sandwich round in 2012. He signed for $1,291,300 At his best, Watson sports a fastball that gets up to 95 mph and rates as a 60 on the 20-80 scale. He complements it with a big overhand curveball that flashes above-average. He's learning a changeup to go with those pitches, and got into trouble in 2013 when he went to the pitch too many times. Shoulder tendinitis and elbow inflammation limited him to just 72 innings at low Class A Lakewood—none after July 4—which raises red flags going forward. Watson's stuff and command came and went, and he appeared to run out of gas prior to being shut down. He has the stuff to pitch in the middle of a big league rotation, but he'll have to learn to maintain his stuff and hold up physically over the course of a full season. Watson needs innings and most likely will head back to Lakewood, but he could graduate to high Class A Clearwater during the season.

Year	Club (League)	Class	W	L	ERA	G	GS	CG	SV	IP	H	HR	BB	SO	K/9	WHIP	AVG
2012	Phillies (GCL)	R	0	1	1.29	5	3	0	0	7	5	0	1	8	10.3	0.86	.200
2013	Lakewood (SAL)	LoA	4	6	4.75	16	16	0	0	72	63	12	28	53	6.6	1.26	.230
Minor League Totals			4	7	4.44	21	19	0	0	79	68	12	29	61	6.9	1.23	.227

19 JOSE PUJOLS, OF

BA GRADE **50** EXTREME

Born: Sept. 29, 1995. **B-T:** R-R. **Ht.:** 6-3. **Wt.:** 195. **Signed:** Dominican Republic, 2012. **Signed by:** Koby Perez.

Much like Carlos Tocci at low Class A Lakewood and the since-traded Domingo Santana, Jose Pujols is a lottery ticket waiting to be scratched. The Phillies signed him during the 2012 international signing period for $540,000, a bonus second only to Dominican catcher Deivi Grullon in his class. Built with a tall, lean and powerful frame, Pujols' calling card is prodigious raw power, which some scouts have projected to an 80 on the 20-80 scale, borne from his premium, righthanded bat speed. His six home runs in 2013 tied for the Rookie-level Gulf Coast League lead with a quartet of other players, including teammate Wilmer Oberto. To get to that power, Pujols hit just .188 and struck out nearly a third of the time due to a lack of hitting polish. Right now, his power is exclusively to the pull side, but age and maturity should help him gain a better approach at the plate, which in turn will allow him to tap into his strength more evenly and more often. He's an average runner right now, but his long legs and strides help magnify that tool a bit. Pujols, whose body has earned comparisons with John Mayberry Jr., has an average arm and fits the right-field profile. He will begin 2014 back in the GCL.

Year	Club (League)	Class	AVG	G	AB	R	H	2B	3B	HR	RBI	BB	SO	SB	CS	OBP	SLG
2013	Phillies (GCL)	R	.188	45	160	27	30	7	2	6	18	19	56	1	3	.278	.369
Minor League Totals			.188	45	160	27	30	7	2	6	18	19	56	1	3	.278	.369

20 KENNY GILES, RHP

BA GRADE 50 EXTREME

Born: Sept. 20, 1990. **B-T:** R-R. **Ht.:** 6-2. **Wt.:** 188. **Drafted:** Yavapai (Ariz.) JC, 2011 (7th round). **Signed by:** Brad Holland.

A classic reliever if there ever were one, Giles was drafted out of a New Mexico high school by the Marlins in 2009 but didn't sign, then attended New Mexico JC for a year, then took off at Yavapai (Ariz.) JC in 2011, moving up 37 rounds and signing for $250,000. He has the power arsenal that profiles well for the back of the bullpen. When healthy, Giles brings his heat in the upper-90s with ease and couples it with a tight, mid-80s slider. The fastball, which was clocked as high as 101 mph in the Arizona Fall League, does have a tendency to be a little flat, and he has been much more hittable than someone with that kind of velocity should be. Because major league hitters can catch up with any velocity, Giles must hone his control to make the pitch play to its potential. In a year that was supposed to present his first real test, Giles missed a significant chunk of the season with an oblique strain that he later reinjured. He has the stuff to be successful, but he needs to stay in his delivery and harness his adrenaline to throw more strikes. He'll head to Double-A Reading to begin 2014 and should be on the fast track toward the major league pen.

Year	Club (League)	Class	W	L	ERA	G	GS	CG	SV	IP	H	HR	BB	SO	K/9	WHIP	AVG
2011	Phillies (GCL)	R	1	1	5.79	3	0	0	0	5	6	1	3	7	13.5	1.93	.333
2012	Lakewood (SAL)	LoA	3	3	3.61	29	6	0	5	67	54	5	44	86	11.5	1.46	.215
	Clearwater (FSL)	HiA	1	0	3.07	10	0	0	3	15	10	1	6	25	15.3	1.09	.182
2013	Clearwater (FSL)	HiA	2	2	6.31	24	0	0	6	26	23	4	19	34	11.9	1.64	.237
Minor League Totals			7	6	4.25	66	6	0	14	112	93	11	72	152	12.2	1.47	.221

21 TOMMY JOSEPH, C

BA GRADE 50 EXTREME

Born: July 16, 1991. **B-T:** R-R. **Ht.:** 6-1. **Wt.:** 215. **Drafted:** HS—Scottsdale, Ariz., 2009 (2nd round). **Signed by:** Chuck Hensley (Giants).

A pair of concussions laid waste to Joseph's 2013 season and put his future as a catcher, if not in baseball, in question. He had a strong spring, making a positive impression in big league camp, and started the season at Triple-A Lehigh Valley before he took a foul ball off the mask on May 4 that sidelined him the rest of the month with a concussion. Joseph tried to come back in June with high Class A Clearwater and struggled badly, and while he moved up to Double-A Reading, he never shook the concussion symptoms. He didn't play in the regular season after July 11 and was shut down in early August. Joseph caught for much of November in the Dominican League but didn't hit anywhere in 2013, posting a .179/.229/.285 line with three home runs, then hitting .192 in winter ball. At his best, Joseph, the centerpiece of the Hunter Pence trade with the Giants in 2012, is a thick, offense-first catcher with plus raw power to all fields. He has a strong arm behind the plate, as evinced by his 40 percent caught stealing rate two seasons ago. He still needs to polish the finer points of catching, namely receiving and blocking, obviously missing out on development time due to his injury. The first concern for Joseph is his health, which will determine his 2014 assignment and position.

Year	Club (League)	Class	AVG	G	AB	R	H	2B	3B	HR	RBI	BB	SO	SB	CS	OBP	SLG
2010	Augusta (SAL)	LoA	.236	117	436	46	103	22	1	16	68	26	116	0	0	.290	.401
2011	San Jose (CAL)	HiA	.270	127	514	80	139	33	2	22	95	29	102	1	0	.317	.471
2012	Richmond (EL)	AA	.260	80	304	32	79	16	0	8	38	25	64	0	3	.313	.391
	Reading (EL)	AA	.250	28	100	12	25	8	0	3	10	9	32	0	1	.327	.420
2013	Lehigh Valley (IL)	AAA	.209	21	67	6	14	1	0	3	14	4	15	0	1	.264	.358
	Phillies (GCL)	R	.333	1	3	0	1	0	0	0	0	2	1	0	0	.600	.333
	Clearwater (FSL)	HiA	.095	11	42	0	4	2	0	0	1	0	13	0	0	.095	.143
	Reading (EL)	AA	.273	3	11	0	3	1	0	0	1	1	1	0	0	.333	.364
Minor League Totals			.249	388	1477	176	368	83	3	52	227	96	344	1	5	.302	.415

22 DYLAN COZENS, OF

BA GRADE 50 EXTREME

Born: May 31, 1994. **B-T:** L-L. **Ht.:** 6-6. **Wt.:** 235. **Drafted:** HS—Scottsdale, Ariz., 2012 (2nd round). **Signed by:** Brad Holland.

As befitting a one-time Pacific-12 Conference defensive-end recruit, Cozens stands out for his physicality and strength. That strength translated into what most evaluators believed was among the best raw power in the 2013 short-season New York-Penn League, not to mention the entire Phillies system. Cozens' power comes not just from his size but also a quick swing with natural leverage and lift. With that power-oriented approach and long-limbed, 6-foot-6 frame has come a lot of swing and miss. Evaluators who watched with at Williamsport noted that he was particularly vulnerable to offspeed pitches and had trouble recognizing the spin on breaking pitches, both of which could be attributable to his youth and relative inexperience after spending so much time as an amateur focusing on football. Cozens runs well for his size and ranked second on the Crosscutters with 11 stolen bases. He's an adequate-at-best defender with enough arm for right field, but he may lose too much speed as he matures and land at first base. Cozens' value lies in his bat anyway. He'll play an outfield corner with low Class A Lakewood in 2014.

Year	Club (League)	Class	AVG	G	AB	R	H	2B	3B	HR	RBI	BB	SO	SB	CS	OBP	SLG
2012	Phillies (GCL)	R	.255	50	161	24	41	11	2	5	24	21	44	8	2	.341	.441
2013	Williamsport (NYP)	SS	.265	68	245	50	65	19	2	9	35	28	64	11	6	.343	.469
Minor League Totals			.261	118	406	74	106	30	4	14	59	49	108	19	8	.342	.458

23 YOEL MECIAS, LHP

BA GRADE **50** EXTREME

Born: Oct. 11, 1993. **B-T:** L-L. **Ht.:** 6-2. **Wt.:** 160. **Signed:** Venezuela, 2010. **Signed by:** Jesus Mendez.

After signing with the Phillies in December 2010, Mecias spent 2011 on the restricted list before debuting in the Rookie-level Gulf Coast League as a 19-year-old in 2012. He moved up to low Class A Lakewood in 2013 and began to deliver. At his best, Mecias showcased a fastball that sat between 85-92 mph, and he backs it up with a curveball and slider that both range between the high 70s and low 80s. His main off-speed weapon, however, is a 79-80 mph changeup that features late tail and sink. Mecias' fastball, curveball and slider have the potential to bump average in the future, while his changeup has a chance to be above-average. His delivery is sound, but he does have a tendency to fall to the side after following through. Phillies fans will have to wait a little longer to see Mecias again, however, because he had Tommy John surgery in the middle of 2013. If he does pitch in 2014, it will be in the second half and mostly at the Class A level.

Year	Club (League)	Class	W	L	ERA	G	GS	CG	SV	IP	H	HR	BB	SO	K/9	WHIP	AVG
2011	Did not play—Restricted																
2012	Phillies (GCL)	R	0	2	2.16	14	4	0	2	42	32	4	11	34	7.3	1.03	.206
2013	Lakewood (SAL)	LoA	4	3	3.79	13	11	0	1	57	53	3	25	70	11.1	1.37	.244
Minor League Totals			4	5	3.10	27	15	0	3	99	85	7	36	104	9.5	1.23	.228

24 ANDREW KNAPP, C

BA GRADE **45** HIGH

Born: Nov. 9, 1991. **B-T:** B-R. **Ht.:** 6-1. **Wt.:** 195. **Drafted:** California, 2013 (2nd round). **Signed by:** Joey Davis.

After starting the 2013 draft with prep shortstop J.P. Crawford, Phillies scouting director Marti Wolever scooped up Knapp, a switch-hitting, bat-first backstop with an above-average arm and a chance to improve behind the plate. Evaluators in the short-season New York-Penn League liked Knapp's chances to hit long-term but weren't as sold on his power potential. He caught just 21 of his 62 games with the Crosscutters, and his bat is far ahead of his glove. That's a bit of a surprise considering Knapp's father Mike also was a catcher, first at California like Knapp, then in pro ball for 11 years. Knapp felt something pop in his elbow while in instructional league and had Tommy John surgery in October, which obviously will slow his development. The rehab for TJ is quicker for position players, and Knapp likely will be ready to play when extended spring training begins in 2014. He'll get at-bats as a DH before gradually easing back behind the plate. Knapp played first base and right field at California but has the athleticism, hands and above-average arm strength to make catching work, if he puts in the time and hard work. Knapp's pro career got off to a rocky start, but he should be able to play most of next season at low Class A Lakewood.

Year	Club (League)	Class	AVG	G	AB	R	H	2B	3B	HR	RBI	BB	SO	SB	CS	OBP	SLG
2013	Williamsport (NYP)	SS	.253	62	217	30	55	20	0	4	23	22	57	7	5	.340	.401
Minor League Totals			.253	62	217	30	55	20	0	4	23	22	57	7	5	.340	.401

25 CORD SANDBERG, OF

BA GRADE **50** EXTREME

Born: Jan. 2, 1995. **B-T:** L-L. **Ht.:** 6-3. **Wt.:** 215. **Drafted:** HS—Bradenton, Fla., 2013 (3rd round). **Signed by:** Alan Marr.

The Phillies wooed Sandberg, a two-sport star at Bradenton's Manatee High, away from a scholarship to play quarterback at Mississippi State with an over-slot bonus of $775,000. He was the first of the franchise's two third-round selections in 2013. Sandberg's father Chuck played three seasons in the minors for the Red Sox, who took him in the ninth round in 1979. Big, physical, speedy and lefthanded, Sandberg drew comparisons with Tim Tebow as he navigated football's recruiting trail. Those same qualities will serve him well in center field. He spent the 2013 season learning what it's like to play every day and getting into baseball shape. For now, Sandberg sports power potential, signs of aptitude with his hitting approach and plenty of quickness, though his reads in center need work. Though the Phillies have shown a willingness to push younger players up to low Class A Lakewood for a trial by fire, Sandberg's rawness likely means he'll begin 2014 in extended spring training before moving to short-season Williamsport come June.

Year	Club (League)	Class	AVG	G	AB	R	H	2B	3B	HR	RBI	BB	SO	SB	CS	OBP	SLG
2013	Phillies (GCL)	R	.207	48	169	23	35	3	1	2	14	24	36	4	3	.313	.272
Minor League Totals			.207	48	169	23	35	3	1	2	14	24	36	4	3	.313	.272

26 JAN HERNANDEZ, 3B

BA GRADE **50** EXTREME

Born: Jan. 3, 1995. **B-T:** R-R. **Ht.:** 6-1. **Wt.:** 195. **Drafted:** HS—Florida, P.R., 2013 (3rd round). **Signed by:** Alan Marr.

When the Phillies popped him in the 2013 draft's third round, Hernandez made a history as the first drafted player from the Carlos Beltran Baseball Academy in Puerto Rico, which the major league all-star established in 2011. Hernandez signed for $550,000. A shortstop in high school, he's been converted to third base as a pro because of his below-average speed. He does, however, have good hands and a better-than-average arm. Hernandez has a quick swing from the right side, which the Phillies see as capable of producing power to all fields in the future. Opposing scouts aren't as sold on his power, but they believe he will hit for average in the future. And though he didn't make a ton of contact in his pro debut in the Rookie-level Gulf Coast League, the most important part of his initial experience was getting used to the speed of the game. He'll begin 2014 in extended spring before likely returning to the GCL.

Year	Club (League)	Class	AVG	G	AB	R	H	2B	3B	HR	RBI	BB	SO	SB	CS	OBP	SLG
2013	Phillies (GCL)	R	.210	39	124	16	26	6	1	3	14	12	50	7	2	.291	.347
Minor League Totals			.210	39	124	16	26	6	1	3	14	12	50	7	2	.291	.347

27 ZACH COLLIER, OF

BA GRADE **45** HIGH

Born: Sept. 8, 1990. **B-T:** L-L. **Ht.:** 6-2. **Wt.:** 185. **Drafted:** HS—Chino Hills, Calif., 2008 (1st round supplemental). **Signed by:** Darrell Conner.

Collier was having a miserable 2013 season until August, when everything seemed to click. During that final month, he hit .327/.433/.485 with three doubles, five triples and a home run. Before that, however, he had cobbled together a .191 average, the worst among all players in the Double-A Eastern League. The Phillies attributed Collier's poor season to his not being in a strong position to hit at the outset of his swing. They worked on that throughout the year and saw the benefits toward the end. He also has injuries in his background, including a pair of hand injuries that cost him all of the 2010 season. Collier also served a 50-game suspension at the outset of 2012 after testing positive for the stimulant Adderall, and he has never put it all together for a full season. If everything clicks, he projects to be an average hitter with below-average power. His eight home runs this year matched his previous career total. He has plenty of strength, but it hasn't translated into a slugging percentage of better than .400 in any of his five professional seasons. Collier shows terrific range in center field and has the arm strength and accuracy to be an acceptable defender in either corner. He likely will head back to Double-A Reading in 2014 to build on his strong August and fulfill his potential as a backup outfielder in the big leagues.

Year	Club (League)	Class	AVG	G	AB	R	H	2B	3B	HR	RBI	BB	SO	SB	CS	OBP	SLG
2008	Phillies (GCL)	R	.271	37	129	15	35	9	1	0	19	17	28	5	0	.347	.357
2009	Lakewood (SAL)	LoA	.218	82	298	40	65	16	7	0	32	23	80	13	7	.275	.319
	Williamsport (NYP)	SS	.226	34	137	21	31	10	1	1	13	9	42	7	0	.280	.336
2010	Did not play—Injured																
2011	Lakewood (SAL)	LoA	.255	112	416	50	106	24	6	1	36	40	99	35	13	.328	.349
2012	Clearwater (FSL)	HiA	.269	78	283	39	76	13	3	6	32	26	60	11	3	.333	.399
2013	Reading (EL)	AA	.222	123	446	57	99	14	9	8	36	47	129	17	6	.310	.348
Minor League Totals			.241	466	1709	222	412	86	27	16	168	162	438	88	29	.313	.351

28 MALQUIN CANELO, SS

BA GRADE **45** HIGH

Born: Sept. 5, 1994. **B-T:** R-R. **Ht.:** 5-10. **Wt.:** 156. **Signed:** Dominican Republic, 2012. **Signed by:** Koby Perez.

A defensive wizard in the mold of Adeiny Hechavarria, Canelo signed with the Phillies out of the Dominican Republic in April 2012. He faces the same looming question as many of his predecessors: Will he ever hit enough to get his glove into the lineup on an everyday basis? Canelo made progress in 2013 as an 18-year-old in the short-season New York-Penn League, making more hard contact and swatting more line drives overall, even if his final line doesn't necessarily reflect it. He's quick and light on his feet, carries a plus arm and can make every play scouts want to see at shortstop. Canelo also is versatile enough to move over to third base in a pinch, so he could be a candidate for a super utility role down the line. He's a solid-average runner who was a skilled-enough baserunner in 2013 to swipe 10 bags in 13 tries. With J.P. Crawford entrenched as low Class A Lakewood shortstop in 2014, Canelo likely will head to extended spring training before taking another go at short-season Williamsport.

Year	Club (League)	Class	AVG	G	AB	R	H	2B	3B	HR	RBI	BB	SO	SB	CS	OBP	SLG
2012	Phillies (DSL)	R	.167	54	162	23	27	5	2	0	9	15	50	9	4	.251	.222
2013	Phillies (GCL)	R	.235	4	17	1	4	1	0	0	2	0	1	0	1	.235	.294
	Williamsport (NYP)	SS	.220	57	182	22	40	9	1	1	13	17	47	10	2	.291	.297
Minor League Totals			.197	115	361	46	71	15	3	1	24	32	98	19	7	.271	.263

29 AUSTIN WRIGHT, LHP

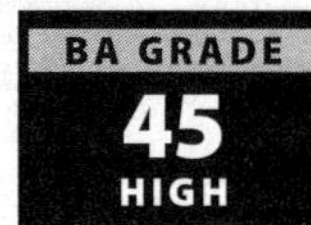

Born: Sept. 26, 1989. **B-T:** L-L. **Ht.:** 6-4. **Wt.:** 235. **Drafted:** Mississippi, 2011 (8th round). **Signed by:** Mike Stauffer.

After a strong 2012, Wright took enough of a tumble in 2013 for the Phillies to cut the cord on his future as a starter and instead take their chances on him as a lefty reliever. His results out of the bullpen were modest (4.96 ERA, 1.7 SO/BB ratio) but better than his rotation work (6.06 ERA, 1.2 SO/BB) at Double-Reading. The results weren't much better in the Arizona Fall League, where Wright surrendered 16 hits and six walks in 11 frames with Peoria. He utilizes a max-effort delivery and throws across his body, sporting a 90-93 mph fastball that has sink and tail. He failed to command it as his walk rate skyrocketed, and when he fell behind, hitters teed off. Wright gave up more home runs (13) in 94 innings than he did (11) in 148 innings in 2012. The Phillies like his slurvy, three-quarters curveball, which should serve him well in relief. His changeup, which sits between 78-80 mph, features sinking action but lags behind his heater and hook. In need of a rebound year, Wright's spring training in 2014 will determine whether he head back to Reading or moves up to Triple-A Lehigh Valley.

Year	Club (League)	Class	W	L	ERA	G	GS	CG	SV	IP	H	HR	BB	SO	K/9	WHIP	AVG
2011	Williamsport (NYP)	SS	3	1	3.38	8	7	1	0	35	30	1	13	44	11.4	1.24	.231
	Lakewood (SAL)	LoA	1	2	2.67	7	7	0	0	34	29	2	9	41	11.0	1.13	.238
2012	Clearwater (FSL)	HiA	11	5	3.47	27	25	0	0	148	147	11	60	133	8.1	1.40	.259
2013	Reading (EL)	AA	6	5	5.92	27	16	0	0	94	91	13	59	77	7.3	1.59	.253
Minor League Totals			21	13	4.12	69	55	1	0	310	297	27	141	295	8.6	1.41	.252

30 DAN CHILD, RHP

BA GRADE
45
HIGH

Born: July 24, 1992. **B-T:** R-R. **Ht.:** 6-4. **Wt.:** 200. **Drafted:** Oregon State, 2013 (18th round). **Signed by:** Rick Jaques.

A member of USA Baseball's 16U national team, Child was drafted by the Padres in the 48th round in 2010 but did not sign. He instead opted for Oregon State, where he served as a midweek starter and again got the chance to represent his country as a member of the 2012 Collegiate National Team. Because of his funky and effort-filled delivery, Child was shifted to the bullpen immediately after the Phillies signed him for $100,000. Philadelphia pushed him aggressively as he finished the season in the high Class A Florida State League. He throws two pitches: a fastball that can reach as high 95 mph and a slider that flashes plus at times and has a chance to stay that way in the future. Child has a chance to move quickly if he can harness his arsenal, but the effort in his delivery makes it tough for him to repeat and throw consistent strikes. He appears headed for a return engagement in the high Class A Clearwater bullpen to begin 2014.

Year	Club (League)	Class	W	L	ERA	G	GS	CG	SV	IP	H	HR	BB	SO	K/9	WHIP	AVG
2013	Phillies (GCL)	R	0	0	1.59	4	0	0	0	6	4	0	3	8	12.7	1.24	.190
	Clearwater (FSL)	HiA	0	0	1.38	11	0	0	2	13	9	0	5	4	2.8	1.08	.209
Minor League Totals			0	0	1.45	15	0	0	2	19	13	0	8	12	5.8	1.13	.203

Pittsburgh Pirates

BY JOHN PERROTTO

Neal Huntington never put a timetable on how long it would take to make the Pirates competitive when he replaced Dave Littlefield as general manager late in the 2007 season.

However, Huntington said he had a definitive plan for what it would take to transform the once-proud franchise back to its winning ways: build through scouting and player development. He also vowed he would not deviate from that plan, even if quick fixes might appease the fans and media, and perhaps even save his job.

The commitment to that plan finally paid off in 2013 as the Pirates not only broke a string of 20 consecutive losing seasons, which is the record for major North American professional team sports, but also reached the postseason for the first time since 1992. The Pirates went 94-68, beat the Reds in the Wild Card Game at a raucous PNC Park, then took the eventual pennant-winning Cardinals a full five games before falling in the National League Division Series.

The Pirates won with a roster primarily filled with players Huntington acquired from outside the organization or those drafted or signed as international free agents during Littlefield's tenure.

However, four of Huntington's draft picks made significant contributions: third baseman Pedro Alvarez (No. 2 overall, 2008), righthander Gerrit Cole (No. 1 overall, 2011), shortstop Jordy Mercer (third round, '08) and lefthanded reliever Justin Wilson (fifth, '08). Alvarez hit 36 home runs to tie for the NL lead with Arizona's Paul Goldschmidt, Cole was the NL rookie pitcher of the month in September, Mercer posted a .772 OPS as a part-time starter, and Wilson had a 2.08 ERA in 58 games and 74 innings.

While owner Bob Nutting often has been criticized for being a spendthrift, he was willing to give Huntington the money necessary to routinely go over slot to sign draft picks and also to become a bigger player in Latin America. Nutting has started to see the payoff with the performances of Alvarez and Cole, and there should be more soon. Top prospects such as outfielder Gregory Polanco and righthanders Jameson Taillon and Nick Kingham appear close to big league-ready.

The Pirates also have a wave of talent at the lower levels, such as outfielders Josh Bell and Harold Ramirez and righthander Luis Heredia. And after failing to sign their first-rounder in 2012, they had two selections among the first 14 picks in 2013 and landed a pair of blue-chip high school players in outfielder Austin Meadows and catcher Reese McGuire. Justifiably, the Pirates believe their farm system ranks with anyone's in the game.

Huntington inherited one of the least-talented organizations in baseball. The Pirates lacked quality players at the major league level and also had a weak farm system.

He took on a major rebuilding job, and Nutting showed a great amount of patience in his GM as he allowed Huntington to survive a 105-loss season in 2010, his third full year on the job.

However, despite having his skeptics in the fan base and media, Huntington proved his plan was the right one to return the Pirates to respectability and beyond.

GEORGE GOJKOVICH

Homegrown stars like Pedro Alvarez helped drive the Pirates back to the postseason

TOP PROSPECTS OF THE DECADE

Year	Player, Pos.	2013 Org.
2004	John Van Benschoten, rhp	Out of baseball
2005	Zach Duke, lhp	Reds
2006	Neil Walker, c	Pirates
2007	Andrew McCutchen, of	Pirates
2008	Andrew McCutchen, of	Pirates
2009	Pedro Alvarez, 3b	Pirates
2010	Pedro Alvarez, 3b	Pirates
2011	Jameson Taillon, rhp	Pirates
2012	Gerrit Cole, rhp	Pirates
2013	Gerrit Cole, rhp	Pirates

ORGANIZATION OVERVIEW

General Manager: Neal Huntington. **Farm Director:** Larry Broadway. **Scouting Director:** Joe Delli Carri

Class	Team	League	W	L	PCT	Finish	Manager
Majors	Pittsburgh Pirates	National	94	68	.580	3rd (15)	Clint Hurdle
Triple-A	Indianapolis Indians	International	80	64	.556	3rd (14)	Dean Treanor
Double-A	Altoona Curve	Eastern	63	79	.444	11th (12)	Carlos Garcia
High Class A	Bradenton Marauders	Florida State	57	77	.425	12th (12)	Frank Kremblas
Low Class A	West Virginia Power	South Atlantic	82	58	.586	2nd (14)	Michael Ryan
Short-season	Jamestown Jammers	New York-Penn	43	32	.573	3rd (14)	Dave Turgeon
Rookie	GCL Pirates	Gulf Coast	33	27	.550	4th (16)	Milver Reyes
Overall 2013 Minor League Record			**358**	**337**	**.515**	**8th (30)**	

THIS YEAR'S TOP 30

No.	Player, Pos.	Grade/Risk
1.	Gregory Polanco, of	65/Medium
2.	Jameson Taillon, rhp	65/Medium
3.	Tyler Glasnow, rhp	65/High
4.	Austin Meadows, of	60/High
5.	Nick Kingham, rhp	55/Medium
6.	Alen Hanson, ss	55/Medium
7.	Josh Bell, of	55/High
8.	Reese McGuire, c	60/Extreme
9.	Harold Ramirez, of	55/High
10.	Luis Heredia, rhp	55/Extreme
11.	Brandon Cumpton, rhp	45/Safe
12.	Wyatt Mathisen, c	50/High
13.	Barrett Barnes, of	50/High
14.	Willy Garcia, of	50/High
15.	Tony Sanchez, c	45/Low
16.	Stolmy Pimentel, rhp	45/Medium
17.	Clay Holmes, rhp	50/High
18.	Blake Taylor, lhp	50/High
19.	JaCoby Jones, of/ss	55/Extreme
20.	Cody Dickson, lhp	50/High
21.	Andrew Lambo, of	45/Medium
22.	Jaff Decker, of	45/Medium
23.	Stetson Allie, 1b	50/Extreme
24.	Jin-De Jhang, c	50/Extreme
25.	Elvis Escobar, of	50/Extreme
26.	Wei-Chung Wang, lhp	50/Extreme
27.	Adrian Sampson, rhp	45/High
28.	Jon Sandfort, rhp	50/Extreme
29.	Gift Ngoepe, ss	45/High
30.	Joely Rodriguez, lhp	45/High

LAST YEAR'S TOP 30

No.	Player, Pos.	Status
1.	Gerrit Cole, rhp	Majors
2.	Jameson Taillon, rhp	No. 2
3.	Luis Heredia, rhp	No. 10
4.	Gregory Polanco, of	No. 1
5.	Alen Hanson, ss	No. 6
6.	Josh Bell, of	No. 7
7.	Kyle McPherson, rhp	Dropped out
8.	Justin Wilson, lhp	Majors
9.	Barrett Barnes, of	No. 13
10.	Clay Holmes, rhp	No. 17
11.	Alex Dickerson, 1b	(Padres)
12.	Tony Sanchez, c	No. 15
13.	Andy Oliver, lhp	Dropped out
14.	Bryan Morris, rhp	Majors
15.	Wyatt Mathisen, c	No. 12
16.	Vic Black, rhp	(Mets)
17.	Nick Kingham, rhp	No. 5
18.	Willy Garcia, of	No. 14
19.	Tyler Glasnow, rhp	No. 3
20.	Dilson Herrera, 2b	(Mets)
21.	Adrian Sampson, rhp	No. 27
22.	Brock Holt, ss/2b	(Red Sox)
23.	Matt Curry, 1b	Dropped out
24.	Jose Osuna, 1b	Dropped out
25.	Brandon Cumpton, rhp	No. 11
26.	Duke Welker, rhp	Dropped out
27.	Jin-De Jhang, c	No. 24
28.	Harold Ramirez, of	No. 9
29.	Clint Robinson, 1b	(Dodgers)
30.	Gift Ngoepe, ss	No. 29

BEST TOOLS

Best Hitter for Average	Gregory Polanco
Best Power Hitter	Andrew Lambo
Best Strike-Zone Discipline	Austin Meadows
Fastest Baserunner	Gregory Polanco
Best Athlete	Gregory Polanco
Best Fastball	Tyler Glanow
Best Curveball	Jameson Taillon
Best Slider	Stolmy Pimentel
Best Changeup	Nick Kingham
Best Control	Nick Kingham
Best Defensive Catcher	Reese McGuire
Best Defensive Infielder	Gift Ngoepe
Best Infield Arm	Edwin Espinal
Best Defensive Outfielder	Gregory Polanco
Best Outfield Arm	Willy Garcia

TOP 15 PLAYERS 25 AND UNDER

No.	Player, Pos. (Age)	Peak Level
1.	Gerrit Cole, rhp (23)	Majors
2.	Gregory Polanco, of (22)	Triple-A
3.	Starling Marte, of (25)	Majors
4.	Jameson Taillon, rhp (22)	Triple-A
5.	Tyler Glasnow, rhp (20)	Low Class A
6.	Austin Meadows, of (18)	Short-season
7.	Nick Kingham, rhp (22)	Double-A
8.	Alen Hanson, ss (21)	Double-A
9.	Josh Bell, of (21)	Low Class A
10.	Reese McGuire, c (19)	Short-season
11.	Harold Ramirez, of (19)	Short-season
12.	Luis Heredia, rhp (19)	Low Class A
13.	Tony Sanchez, c (25)	Majors
14.	Wyatt Mathisen, c (20)	Short-season
15.	Barrett Barnes, of (22)	Low Class A

MINOR LEAGUE DEPTH CHART

PITTSBURGH PIRATES

TOP 2014 ROOKIE: Gregory Polanco, of. If he hits the ground running at Triple-A, he could ascend quickly to right field, giving the Pirates perhaps the fastest outfield in the majors.

BREAKOUT PROSPECT: Wei-Chung Wang, lhp. His curveball and overall command are an interesting combination.

SLEEPER: Casey Sadler, rhp. From 25th-round pick to the 40-man roster, he has three average-to-above pitches required to start.

SOURCE OF TOP 30 TALENT

Homegrown	27	Acquired	3
College	5	Trades	3
Junior college	1	Rule 5 draft	0
High school	11	Independent leagues	0
Nondrafted free agents	0	Free agents/waivers	0
International	10		

LF
- Andrew Lambo (21)
- Adalberto Santos

CF
- Gregory Polanco (1)
- Austin Meadows (4)
- Harold Ramirez (9)
- Barrett Barnes (13)
- JaCoby Jones (19)
- Elvis Escobar (25)
- Mel Rojas Jr.

RF
- Josh Bell (7)
- Willy Garcia (14)
- Jaff Decker

3B
- Erich Weiss
- Eric Wood

SS
- Alen Hanson (6)
- Gift Ngoepe (29)
- Max Moroff
- Adam Frazier
- Trae Arbet

2B
- Jarek Cunningham
- Dan Gamache
- Ulises Montilla

1B
- Stetson Allie (23)
- Jose Osuna
- Edwin Espinal
- Matt Hague

C
- Reese McGuire (8)
- Wyatt Mathisen (12)
- Tony Sanchez (15)
- Jin-De Jhang (24)
- Elias Diaz
- Daniel Arribas

LHP

LHSP
- Blake Taylor (18)
- Cody Dickson (20)
- Wei-Chung Wang (26)
- Joely Rodriguez (30)
- Andy Oliver
- Zack Dodson

LHRP
- Orlando Castro
- Robert Kilcrease
- Thomas Harlan

RHP

RHSP
- Jameson Taillon (2)
- Tyler Glasnow (3)
- Nick Kingham (5)
- Luis Heredia (10)
- Brandon Cumpton (11)
- Stolmy Pimentel (16)
- Clay Holmes (17)
- Adrian Sampson (27)
- Jon Sandfort (28)
- Dovydas Neverauskas
- Casey Sadler
- Jason Creasey
- Chad Kuhl
- Isaac Sanchez
- Billy Roth
- Neil Kozikowski
- Phil Irwin
- Tyler Waldron

RHRP
- Miles Mikolas
- Ryan Hafner
- Ryan Reid
- Duke Welker
- Zach Thornton
- Quinton Miller
- Jhondaniel Medina
- Kyle Haynes
- Matt Benedict

DRAFT ANALYSIS

2013

BONUSES: $9.0 MILLION

BEST PURE HITTER: OF Austin Meadows (1) can make hitting look easy, with a smooth, loose swing, strength and good hand speed through the hitting zone. The ball came off his bat better as a pro than it did during the spring, when heavy draft scrutiny may have weighed on him.

BEST POWER HITTER: SS/OF JaCoby Jones (3) has prodigious power/speed tools. He has tremendous bat speed and raw pop, though he hit just 14 homers in three seasons with Louisiana State. Meadows hit eight in his pro debut.

FASTEST RUNNER: Jones, Meadows and OF Jeff Roy (19) all are consistent above-average or better runners, with Meadows turning in well above-average times to first after signing.

BEST DEFENSIVE PLAYER: C Reese McGuire (1) hopes to buck the rough history for first-round prep catchers. He has above-average catch-and-throw tools and blocks well. What stood out for Pirates scouts was his natural feel for the game. He reads hitters' swings, understands game situations and has baseball savvy.

BEST FASTBALL: RHP Buddy Borden (7) works at 90-93 mph, and his heater plays up due to good sink and command. Several college products throw harder and top out at 95-96, including RHPs Chad Kuhl (9), Justin Topa (17), Brett McKinney (19) and Henry Hirsch (22).

BEST SECONDARY PITCH: LHP Cody Dickson (4) has both a curveball and a changeup that can be above-average pitches. RHP Neil Kozikowski (8) can spin a breaking ball and throws a good changeup.

BEST PRO DEBUT: Most of the Pirates' top picks performed, but none as well as Meadows, the Rookie-level Gulf Coast League's top prospect. He hit .316/.424/.554 overall with 23 extra-base hits, and McGuire followed him to short-season Jamestown after hitting .330/.388/.392 in the GCL. SS Adam Frazier (5) hit .321/.399/.362 for Jamestown.

BEST ATHLETE: Jones was one of the best athletes in the draft but will have to recover from a knee injury that ended his debut early.

MOST INTRIGUING BACKGROUND: Gary Weiss, father of 3B Erich Weiss (11), played pro ball and spent parts of two seasons with the Dodgers. McKinney's father Chuck was an eighth-round pick in 1978 and played three minor league seasons.

CLOSEST TO THE MAJORS: Meadows' boffo start may have accelerated his timetable. Frazier's combination of polish at the plate and reliability in the field make him a prime candidate.

BEST LATE-ROUND PICK: RHP Billy Roth (16) was more of a hitter as an amateur, but the Pirates like his fresh, loose arm and hand speed. He has touched the low 90s and has flashed an above-average breaking ball. Hirsch had success and hit a lot of 96s.

THE ONE WHO GOT AWAY: The Pirates will keep a close eye on RHP Bryan Baker (40), a projectable, athletic righty who headed for North Florida.

ASSESSMENT: After failing to sign Mark Appel last year, the Pirates took Meadows with the compensatory pick and McGuire as their regular first-rounder. If Jones develops, this draft could yield three impact bats.

2012

BONUSES: $3.8 MILLION

Not signing RHP Mark Appel (1) helped set up a banner 2013 draft but hurt this class. C Wyatt Mathisen (2) and OF Barrett Barnes (1s) are the top prospects the club signed.

GRADE: C

2011

BONUSES: $17.0 MILLION

No. 1 overall pick Gerrit Cole (1) pitched up to his $8 million bonus in 2013. RHP Tyler Glasnow (5), OF Josh Bell (2) have star upside.

GRADE: A

2010

BONUSES: $11.9 MILLION

RHPs Jameson Taillon (1), Nick Kingham (4) look like future rotation-mates. RHP Brandon Cumpton (9) was solid in his MLB debut.

GRADE: B

TOP DRAFT PICKS OF THE DECADE

Year	Player, Pos.	2013 Org.
2004	Neil Walker, c	Pirates
2005	Andrew McCutchen, of	Pirates
2006	Brad Lincoln, rhp	Blue Jays
2007	Daniel Moskos, lhp	White Sox
2008	Pedro Alvarez, 3b	Pirates
2009	Tony Sanchez, c	Pirates
2010	Jameson Taillon, rhp	Pirates
2011	Gerrit Cole, rhp	Pirates
2012	*Mark Appel, rhp	Astros
2013	Austin Meadows, of	Pirates

*Did not sign.

LARGEST BONUSES IN CLUB HISTORY

Gerrit Cole, 2011	$8,000,000
Jameson Taillon, 2010	$6,500,000
Pedro Alvarez, 2008	$6,000,000
Josh Bell, 2011	$5,000,000
Bryan Bullington, 2001	$4,000,000

1 GREGORY POLANCO, OF

Born: Sept, 14, 1991. **B-T:** L-L. **Ht.:** 6-4. **Wt.:** 170.
Signed: Dominican Republic, 2009.
Signed by: Rene Gayo/Ellis Pena.

When Pirates Latin American scouting director Rene Gayo first laid eyes on Polanco as a 17-year-old amateur pitcher in the Dominican Republic, he said was reminded of a sick giraffe. Polanco still has giraffe-like qualities. His long legs make him appear taller than his listed height of 6-foot-4, and he has the frame to pack on more than his listed 170 pounds. Gayo's second thought about Polanco was that he wouldn't make it as a pitcher in professional baseball, but his long frame made him an intriguing outfield prospect. So Gayo offered Polanco a $150,000 bonus if he would give up pitching, and he hasn't stepped on a mound since. Polanco's lack of hitting experience showed in his first two seasons in the United States as he hit a combined .218/.288/.322 in the Rookie-level Gulf Coast League. Polanco broke out in 2012 at low Class A West Virginia, winning the South Atlantic League player of the year award as he hit .325/.388/.522 with 16 home runs and 40 stolen bases. While Polanco didn't match that performance in 2013, he hit .285/.356/.434 over three levels, advancing from high Class A Bradenton to finish the season as part of Triple-A Indianapolis' playoff team. He also wowed scouts with his batting practice before the Futures Game at spacious Citi Field in New York by driving a number of balls deep into the right-field stands.

Polanco is an athletic five-tool talent with the ability to hit for power and average, run, throw and play superior defense in center field. The area in which Polanco needs the most work is hitting. Though he has exceptional bat speed and fast hands, his swing tends to get long, and he also has trouble laying off breaking pitches outside the zone. At his size, Polanco always will have some holes in his swing, and some scouts question whether he will hit for plus power because of the lengthy swing. Others are convinced his improved plate discipline and growing feel for hitting will translate into an all-star power/speed combination. Polanco's long, gliding strides enable him to cover tons of ground, especially laterally, as he can track down flyballs from gap to gap, and his plus arm would allow him to play right field. His route-running, especially on balls over his head, needs polish but should improve with experience. His above-average speed also makes him a threat on the bases, and he continues to hone his baserunning instincts.

While face-of-the-franchise Andrew McCutchen patrols center, right field is open in Pittsburgh, and Polanco is so talented that he almost certainly will force his way into the major league lineup at some point in 2014, most likely in right. He would join McCutchen and Starling Marte to give the Pirates one of the most dynamic outfields in the business, but he still needs some finishing touches, so he will start the 2014 season back at Indianapolis. He should be in the major leagues before long and figures to be an impact player for many years to come.

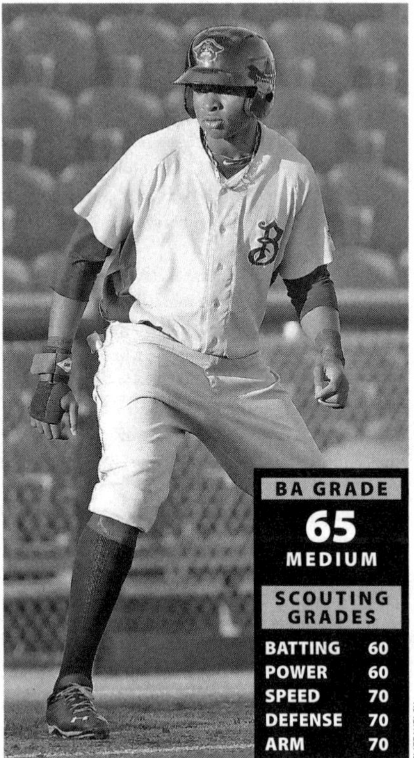

BA GRADE
65
MEDIUM
SCOUTING GRADES
BATTING 60
POWER 60
SPEED 70
DEFENSE 70
ARM 70

CLIFF WELCH

Year	Club (League)	Class	AVG	G	AB	R	H	2B	3B	HR	RBI	BB	SO	SB	CS	OBP	SLG
2009	Pirates (DSL)	R	.267	63	221	34	59	8	6	0	24	33	50	12	4	.370	.357
2010	Pirates (GCL)	R	.202	53	188	21	38	5	1	3	23	9	41	19	2	.245	.287
2011	Pirates (GCL)	R	.237	48	169	34	40	4	4	3	34	24	33	18	0	.333	.361
	State College (NYP)	SS	.100	3	10	0	1	0	0	0	1	0	2	0	0	.100	.100
2012	West Virginia (SAL)	LoA	.325	116	437	84	142	26	6	16	85	44	64	40	15	.388	.522
2013	Bradenton (FSL)	HiA	.312	57	218	29	68	17	0	6	30	16	37	24	4	.364	.472
	Altoona (EL)	AA	.263	68	243	36	64	13	2	6	41	36	36	13	7	.354	.407
	Indianapolis (IL)	AAA	.222	2	9	1	2	0	0	0	0	0	0	1	0	.222	.222
Minor League Totals			.277	410	1495	239	414	73	19	34	238	162	263	127	32	.350	.419

2 JAMESON TAILLON, RHP

Born: Nov. 18, 1991. **B-T:** R-R. **Ht.:** 6-6. **Wt.:** 235. **Drafted:** HS—The Woodlands, Texas, 2010 (1st round). **Signed by:** Trevor Haley.

The Pirates chose Taillon over Miami prep shortstop Manny Machado with the second overall pick in the 2010 draft and signed him to what was then a club-record $6.5 million bonus. While Machado played in the All-Star Game last season, Taillon finished at Triple-A Indianapolis, then had to withdraw from the Arizona Fall League with a groin strain. He impressed in the World Baseball Classic last March while pitching for Canada (his parents are both natives) when he held the United States to two runs in four innings of a start at Chase Field in Phoenix. Taillon has two plus pitches, starting with a fastball that has reached triple digits and routinely sits in the 92-96 mph range. At times his fastball has heavy sink. His best secondary pitch is his hard curveball that reaches the low 80s and features big break and power, but at times he casts the pitch. He has learned to consistently command the fastball to both sides of the plate as he has gotten older. Taillon began throwing his changeup more last season and it improved, though he still needs to trust it more in big situations. He also throws a fringe-average hard slider at times. He's very mature for his age and does not rattle easily. After reaching Triple-A last season, Taillon is close to a big league shot. He likely will begin 2014 back at Indianapolis but should be in Pittsburgh by September, if not earlier.

Year	Club (League)	Class	W	L	ERA	G	GS	CG	SV	IP	H	HR	BB	SO	K/9	WHIP	AVG
2011	West Virginia (SAL)	LoA	2	3	3.98	23	23	0	0	93	89	9	22	97	9.4	1.20	.249
2012	Bradenton (FSL)	HiA	6	8	3.82	23	23	2	0	125	109	10	37	98	7.1	1.17	.230
	Altoona (EL)	AA	3	0	1.59	3	3	0	0	17	11	0	1	18	9.5	0.71	.183
2013	Altoona (EL)	AA	4	7	3.67	20	19	0	0	110	112	8	36	106	8.6	1.34	.257
	Indianapolis (IL)	AAA	1	3	3.89	6	6	0	0	37	31	1	16	37	9.0	1.27	.223
Minor League Totals			16	21	3.72	75	74	2	0	382	352	28	112	356	8.4	1.21	.240

3 TYLER GLASNOW, RHP

Born: Aug. 23, 1993. **B-T:** L-R. **Ht.:** 6-7. **Wt.:** 195. **Drafted:** HS—Santa Clarita, Calif., 2011 (5th round). **Signed by:** Rick Allen.

The lanky Glasnow was relatively unknown going into his senior year at Hart High, which also produced future big leaguers Bob Walk, James Shields and Trevor Bauer. He comes from an athletic family. His mother was a gymnast while his brother Ted is a track-and-field athlete at Notre Dame. The youngest Glasnow grew a foot in high school, coming on as a senior to earn an over-slot $600,000 bonus from the Pirates. He dominated much of his first full season, leading the low Class A South Atlantic League in strikeouts while allowing only one hit in his final three starts, spanning 14 innings. Exceptionally raw when he signed, Glasnow made significant progress in 2013 harnessing his big, athletic body and delivery. He pitches off a plus fastball that reaches 97-99 mph at times but normally sits in the 93-95 range. When he threw strikes with the heater, he overpowered SAL hitters. He also can induce empty swings with his inconsistent but at times plus curve in the upper 70s, which for now is a chase pitch he throws out of the zone. He made progress finding a comfortable changeup grip as the season progressed and used the pitch more, locating it better than his curve, which he rarely throws for a strike. At his size, Glasnow still has trouble keeping his delivery together and overthrows at times, costing him control. Glasnow will need time to develop, which the Pirates plan to give him. He'll start 2014 at high Class A Bradenton. When his control improves, Glasnow will move quickly.

Year	Club (League)	Class	W	L	ERA	G	GS	CG	SV	IP	H	HR	BB	SO	K/9	WHIP	AVG
2012	Pirates (GCL)	R	0	3	2.10	11	10	0	0	34	19	3	16	40	10.5	1.02	.156
	State College (NYP)	SS	0	0	0.00	1	1	0	0	4	4	0	1	4	9.0	1.25	.267
2013	West Virginia (SAL)	LoA	9	3	2.18	24	24	0	0	111	54	9	61	164	13.3	1.03	.142
Minor League Totals			9	6	2.10	36	35	0	0	150	77	12	78	208	12.5	1.04	.149

4 AUSTIN MEADOWS, OF

Born: May 3, 1995. **B-T:** L-L. **Ht.:** 6-3. **Wt.:** 200. **Drafted:** HS—Loganville, Ga., 2013 (1st round). **Signed by:** Jerry Jordan.

Meadows' father Kenny played baseball and football at Morehead State, and his mother Staci played softball at Georgia State. He entered the spring as one of nation's top high school players but had a fairly ordinary spring. The Pirates used the No. 9 overall pick—compensation for not signing 2012 first-rounder Mark Appel—on Meadows, signing him for $3.025 million. He dominated in his pro debut, hitting eight home runs (counting the playoffs) after hitting just four in the spring. Meadows draws comparisons to Reds right fielder Jay Bruce as a lefthanded hitter with power and athleticism. He repeats his easy, fluid swing, has present strength, good plate discipline and the ability to hit the ball hard to all fields. He will need to add some loft to his swing but has started making that adjustment already. He is a good defensive center fielder with decent range and ran better after signing, flashing plus to double-plus times to first base. His arm is below-average, likely limiting him to left field in the future if he can't stay in center. Meadows' defensive home and power projection are the biggest keys to his development.

Year	Club (League)	Class	AVG	G	AB	R	H	2B	3B	HR	RBI	BB	SO	SB	CS	OBP	SLG
2013	Pirates (GCL)	R	.294	43	160	29	47	11	5	5	20	24	42	3	2	.399	.519
	Jamestown (NYP)	SS	.529	5	17	8	9	0	0	2	2	5	4	0	0	.636	.882
Minor League Totals			.316	48	177	37	56	11	5	7	22	29	46	3	2	.424	.554

5 NICK KINGHAM, RHP

Born: Nov. 8, 1991. **B-T:** R-R. **Ht.:** 6-5. **Wt.:** 220. **Drafted:** HS—Las Vegas, 2010 (4th round). **Signed by:** Larry Broadway.

Kingham was the third of seven pitchers the Pirates selected in the first 10 rounds of the 2010 draft. They signed him away from an Oregon commitment for $480,000, which was $225,300 over the recommended slot bonus. Kingham, who grew up playing against Nationals left fielder Bryce Harper in Las Vegas, broke out in 2013, earning a midseason promotion to Double-A Altoona. Kingham features an enviable combination of velocity, command and control. He throws downhill with a fastball that usually sits at 91-93 mph and can reach 95, and he can throw it for strikes to all four quadrants of the zone. His hybrid curveball stands out for his ability to locate it with good power at up to 85 mph. He knows how to use his changeup, which helped him limit lefthanded hitters to just two home runs in 229 plate appearances. Kingham has a good feel for pitching and has been adept at pitch sequencing and attacking hitters' weaknesses. He also repeats his mechanics well. Kingham raised his stock in 2013 with a fine season, and GM Neal Huntington said other teams bring him up frequently in trade talks. He'll return to Double-A to start 2014 and profiles as a mid-rotation workhorse, slotting into a future rotation alongside Gerrit Cole, Jameson Taillon and Tyler Glasnow.

Year	Club (League)	Class	W	L	ERA	G	GS	CG	SV	IP	H	HR	BB	SO	K/9	WHIP	AVG
2010	Pirates (GCL)	R	0	0	0.00	2	0	0	0	3	3	0	0	2	6.0	1.00	.273
2011	State College (NYP)	SS	6	2	2.15	15	15	0	0	71	63	5	15	47	6.0	1.10	.238
2012	West Virginia (SAL)	LoA	6	8	4.39	27	27	0	0	127	115	15	36	117	8.3	1.19	.243
2013	Bradenton (FSL)	HiA	6	3	3.09	13	13	0	0	70	55	6	14	75	9.6	0.99	.212
	Altoona (EL)	AA	3	3	2.70	14	12	0	0	73	70	1	30	69	8.5	1.36	.253
Minor League Totals			21	16	3.27	71	67	0	0	344	306	27	95	310	8.1	1.16	.238

6 ALEN HANSON, SS

Born: Oct. 22, 1992. **B-T:** B-R. **Ht.:** 5-11. **Wt.:** 152. **Signed:** Dominican Republic, 2009. **Signed by:** Rene Gayo/Ellis Pena.

The days of teams signing a future star out of Latin America for $1,000 are over, but the Pirates might have gotten a pretty good bargain when they signed Hanson for $90,000 out of the Dominican Republic in 2009. Following a breakout season at low Class A West Virginia in 2012, Hanson struggled immensely early in 2013 at high Class A Bradenton, committing 10 errors in his first 10 games. After being benched for three straight games, Hanson responded well and eventually earned a promotion to Double-A Altoona. Hanson is very athletic and stronger than his slight build would suggest, and he has enough power to consistently hit balls into the gaps and, occasionally, over the fence. Scouts like his loose swing and fast hands. He has above-average speed and is an aggressive baserunner. Hanson is willing to take a walk but needs to cut down on his strikeouts and make a little bit more consistent contact. Hanson has the range to play shortstop, especially going into the hole. However, his arm is fringe-average, which may eventually force a move to second base. Hanson will start the season back at Altoona. He has the talent to be an everyday middle infielder; whether that's at shortstop or second base is to be determined. The Pirates plan to keep him at shortstop unless or until he proves he cannot handle the position.

Year	Club (League)	Class	AVG	G	AB	R	H	2B	3B	HR	RBI	BB	SO	SB	CS	OBP	SLG
2010	Pirates (DSL)	R	.324	68	244	48	79	10	7	2	28	22	37	20	8	.383	.447
2011	Pirates (GCL)	R	.263	52	198	42	52	13	7	2	35	21	34	24	6	.352	.429
	State College (NYP)	SS	.200	3	10	1	2	0	0	0	0	1	2	0	0	.273	.200
2012	West Virginia (SAL)	LoA	.309	124	489	99	151	33	13	16	62	55	105	35	19	.381	.528
2013	Bradenton (FSL)	HiA	.281	92	367	51	103	23	8	7	48	33	70	24	14	.339	.444
	Altoona (EL)	AA	.255	35	137	13	35	4	5	1	10	8	26	6	2	.299	.380
Minor League Totals			.292	374	1445	254	422	83	40	28	183	140	274	109	49	.359	.463

7 JOSH BELL, OF

BA GRADE
55
HIGH

Born: Aug. 14, 1992. **B-T:** B-R. **Ht.:** 6-3. **Wt.:** 213. **Drafted:** HS—Dallas, 2011 (2nd round). **Signed by:** Mike Leuzinger.

The Pirates signed Bell for a $5 million bonus to forgo playing collegiately at Texas, even though he had written all 30 clubs asking not to be drafted. It is the largest bonus ever given to a player selected after the first round, a record likely to stand for a long time because of the draft bonus-pool rules that went into effect in 2012. Bell's first professional season in 2012 ended after just 15 games with low Class A West Virginia when he tore the meniscus in his left knee while running the bases and required surgery. Bell is a switch-hitter with the potential to hit for average and power from both sides of the plate. Scouts report his righthanded swing is geared more toward contact with a flatter swing plane, while he turns it loose and has more leverage from the left side. True to the reports, he hit home runs about twice as frequently batting lefthanded while also striking out about twice as often. Bell finished third in the South Atlantic League in doubles last season and is likely to turn some of those two-base hits into home runs as he gains experience and his knee gets stronger. He has decent range for a corner outfielder, and his above-average arm should enable him to stick in right field. Bell will begin the season at high Class A Bradenton, and he has breakout potential as he puts more distance between himself and his knee injury. He may have to in order to keep up with a crowded Pirates outfield picture.

Year	Club (League)	Class	AVG	G	AB	R	H	2B	3B	HR	RBI	BB	SO	SB	CS	OBP	SLG
2012	West Virginia (SAL)	LoA	.274	15	62	6	17	5	0	1	11	2	21	1	0	.288	.403
2013	West Virginia (SAL)	LoA	.279	119	459	75	128	37	2	13	76	52	90	1	2	.353	.453
Minor League Totals			.278	134	521	81	145	42	2	14	87	54	111	2	2	.345	.447

8 REESE McGUIRE, C

BA GRADE
60
EXTREME

Born: March 2, 1995. **B-T:** L-R. **Ht.:** 6-0. **Wt.:** 181. **Drafted:** HS—Covington, Wash., 2013 (1st round). **Signed by:** Greg Hopkins.

The Pirates used the second of their two first-round picks in 2013 (14th overall) to select McGuire. They signed him away from a full scholarship offer from San Diego for a $2.369 million bonus. McGuire became the highest-drafted high school catcher since the Marlins took Kyle Skipworth at No. 6 in 2008. He began playing exclusively behind the plate when he was 10, and he comes from a baseball background. His grandfather John McGuire played at Duke with Dick Groat, who won the National League MVP award in 1960 while playing shortstop for the Pirates. McGuire is an above-average defensive catcher who consistently produces pop times below 1.8 seconds on throws to second, and he has the arm strength to throw out runners from his knees. He also works well with pitchers and was entrusted with calling pitches at Kentwood High. The Pirates feel McGuire will develop into an above-average hitter with gap power. He showcased a smooth lefthanded stroke with good bat speed and feel for the barrel in his professional debut, ranking third in the Rookie-level Gulf Coast League with a .330 average. He runs well for a catcher. McGuire will begin 2014 at low Class A West Virginia. Though he is young, he could potentially move through the system quickly if his physical tools catch up to his baseball aptitude.

Year	Club (League)	Class	AVG	G	AB	R	H	2B	3B	HR	RBI	BB	SO	SB	CS	OBP	SLG
2013	Pirates (GCL)	R	.330	46	176	30	58	11	0	0	21	15	18	5	1	.388	.392
	Jamestown (NYP)	SS	.250	4	16	3	4	0	0	0	0	1	1	1	0	.294	.250
Minor League Totals			.323	50	192	33	62	11	0	0	21	16	19	6	1	.380	.380

9 HAROLD RAMIREZ, OF

MIKE JANES

BA GRADE
55
HIGH

Born: Sept. 6, 1994. **B-T:** R-R. **Ht.:** 5-11. **Wt.:** 175. **Signed:** Colombia, 2011. **Signed by:** Rene Gayo/Orlando Covo.

When the Pirates signed Ramirez out of Colombia for $1.05 million, Latin American scouting director Rene Gayo threw out a Willie Mays comparison. That is obviously a bit of a stretch, but Ramirez wowed Pirates scouts as an amateur and has performed well since coming to the United States. He ranked as the No. 1 prospect in the short-season New York-Penn League in 2013 while playing at Jamestown. Ramirez has an exciting package of tools, first and foremost his ability to hit for average and consistently get on base. He has exceptionally large and strong hands that foreshadow a power increase as he gains more experience against professional pitching. Ramirez has above-average speed despite thick legs and good baserunning instincts. He possesses good range in center field. The only tool that is not plus is a fringe-average arm, more than enough for center field. Opposing managers in the NY-P thought he had some growing up to do, which is fairly normal for a player his age. Ramirez gives the Pirates yet another potential impact outfielder. He will join Austin Meadows in the low Class A West Virginia outfield in 2014. He has plenty of raw ability, and some members of the front office believe he has as much upside as any player in the system.

Year	Club (League)	Class	AVG	G	AB	R	H	2B	3B	HR	RBI	BB	SO	SB	CS	OBP	SLG
2012	Pirates (GCL)	R	.259	39	135	18	35	5	1	1	12	6	20	9	5	.310	.333
2013	Jamestown (NYP)	SS	.285	71	274	42	78	11	4	5	40	23	52	23	11	.354	.409
Minor League Totals			.276	110	409	60	113	16	5	6	52	29	72	32	16	.340	.384

10 LUIS HEREDIA, RHP

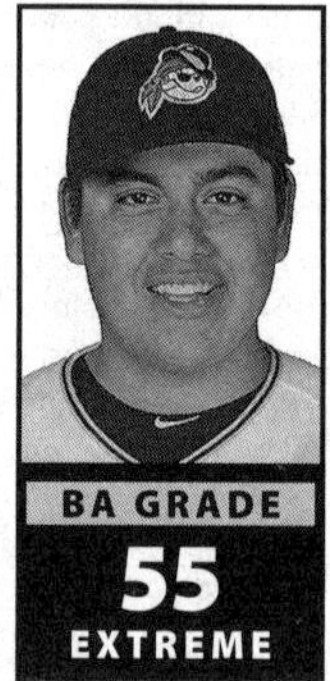

BA GRADE
55
EXTREME

Born: Aug. 10, 1994. **B-T:** R-R. **Ht.:** 6-6. **Wt.:** 205. **Signed:** Mexico, 2010. **Signed by:** Rene Gayo/Chino Valdez.

Heredia signed with Veracruz of the Mexican League when he was 15 years old and then had his contract sold to the Pirates a week after his 16th birthday for $2.6 million. That is easily the most money the Pirates ever have spent on an international player. Heredia was scheduled to open the season with low Class A West Virginia but was held back in extended spring training after reporting to camp overweight. Heredia's weight gain made his fastball go backward. While he hit 95 mph in 2013, he usually sat 89-91 and touched some 92s. The bigger version of Heredia lost arm speed and crispness on all his stuff, but he still survived the South Atlantic League with a solid four-pitch mix. His best pitch this year was his changeup, and he stymied lefthanded hitters, who hit .207 and slugged .298. Heredia's curveball, which at its best shows the most promise among his secondary pitches, and slider have their moments but need more power that he simply didn't have in 2013. The Pirates are hopeful Heredia's velocity will increase as he becomes more consistent with his mechanics and gets his weight under control. Heredia set himself back in 2013, and because he threw just 65 innings, the Pirates will monitor his innings closely in 2014. First, he has to get in shape in the offseason, then he can head back to West Virginia to get his career back on track.

Year	Club (League)	Class	W	L	ERA	G	GS	CG	SV	IP	H	HR	BB	SO	K/9	WHIP	AVG
2011	Pirates (GCL)	R	1	2	4.75	12	11	0	0	30	28	3	19	23	6.8	1.55	.257
2012	State College (NYP)	SS	4	2	2.71	14	14	0	0	66	53	2	20	40	5.4	1.10	.224
2013	West Virginia (SAL)	LoA	7	3	3.05	14	13	0	0	65	52	5	37	55	7.6	1.37	.224
Minor League Totals			12	7	3.23	40	38	0	0	162	133	10	76	118	6.6	1.29	.230

11 BRANDON CUMPTON, RHP

BA GRADE
45
SAFE

Born: Nov. 16, 1988. **B-T:** R-R. **Ht.:** 6-2. **Wt.:** 210. **Drafted:** Georgia Tech, 2010 (9th round). **Signed by:** Greg Schilz.

The Pirates have been undecided about Cumpton's role, starter or reliever, ever since drafting him in 2010. He reached the big leagues as a starter in 2013 and did well in spot usage, which included seven shutout innings versus the eventual National League-champion Cardinals. Cumpton does not overpower batters, especially as a starter, as his fastball sits in the 91-92 mph rage. He complements it with a good, low-80s slider that is particularly tough on righthanders. His changeup comes and goes. Cumpton still needs to be more consistent with his control and command, but he showed good mound presence in Pittsburgh, not to mention a pronounced groundball tilt. Just five minor league pitchers who qualified for the ERA title in 2013 had a higher groundout/airout ratio than Cumpton (2.4). Yet some Pirates officials believe he would fit better as a set-up man, owing to his peak velocity of 96 mph during short stints in spring training. If Cumpton can master the changeup, he could wind up as a strike-throwing, mid-rotation starter.

Year	Club (League)	Class	W	L	ERA	G	GS	CG	SV	IP	H	HR	BB	SO	K/9	WHIP	AVG
2010	State College (NYP)	SS	0	1	2.53	4	3	0	0	11	8	0	5	6	5.1	1.22	.200
2011	West Virginia (SAL)	LoA	7	4	4.30	13	12	0	0	67	60	6	18	48	6.4	1.16	.240
	Bradenton (FSL)	HiA	3	3	3.66	13	12	0	0	66	73	6	12	42	5.7	1.28	.280
2012	Altoona (EL)	AA	12	11	3.84	27	27	0	0	152	149	9	46	88	5.2	1.28	.261
2013	Altoona (EL)	AA	0	1	7.45	2	2	0	0	10	11	0	5	7	6.5	1.66	.282
	Indianapolis (IL)	AAA	6	7	3.32	21	19	1	0	122	115	6	44	90	6.6	1.30	.253
	Pittsburgh (NL)	MAJ	2	1	2.05	6	5	0	0	31	26	1	5	22	6.5	1.01	.226
Major League Totals			2	1	2.05	6	5	0	0	31	26	1	5	22	6.5	1.01	.226
Minor League Totals			28	27	3.79	80	75	1	0	428	416	27	130	281	5.9	1.28	.257

12 WYATT MATHISEN, C

BA GRADE **50** HIGH

Born: Dec. 30, 1993. **B-T:** R-R. **Ht.:** 6-1. **Wt.:** 210. **Drafted:** HS—Corpus Christi, Texas, 2012 (2nd round). **Signed by:** Trevor Haley.

The Pirates were happy that Mathisen was still on the board at pick No. 69 in the 2012 draft, and the Texas recruit quickly signed for slot value at $746,300. He played multiple positions as an amateur, including pitcher and shortstop, but the Pirates and many other teams were convinced he could become an above-average catcher and follow a similar career path as Brandon Inge. Pittsburgh assigned Mathisen to low Class A West Virginia at the outset of 2013 and he struggled offensively before having surgery in late May to repair a torn labrum in his right shoulder. He came back to join short-season Jamestown in mid-August, and the Pirates were especially happy that he looked good on defense. Mathisen receives the ball well and gets rid of the ball quickly with plus arm strength. The organization believes he eventually will hit for a bit of average and power—though still probably at below-average rates—because he has shown decent plate discipline in his young career. He's a fringe-average runner. Mathisen will begin 2014 at West Virginia, and the Pirates will take things a bit slower this time.

Year	Club (League)	Class	AVG	G	AB	R	H	2B	3B	HR	RBI	BB	SO	SB	CS	OBP	SLG
2012	Pirates (GCL)	R	.295	45	139	24	41	8	0	1	15	16	19	10	8	.388	.374
2013	West Virginia (SAL)	LoA	.185	32	119	13	22	3	0	0	9	9	22	1	0	.256	.210
	Pirates (GCL)	R	.409	8	22	5	9	1	0	0	3	7	2	0	0	.552	.455
	Jamestown (NYP)	SS	.269	8	26	4	7	0	0	0	3	5	7	1	0	.394	.269
Minor League Totals			.258	93	306	46	79	12	0	1	30	37	50	12	8	.353	.307

13 BARRETT BARNES, OF

BA GRADE **50** HIGH

Born: July 29, 1991. **B-T:** R-R. **Ht.:** 6-1. **Wt.:** 195. **Drafted:** Texas Tech, 2012 (1st round supplemental). **Signed by:** Mike Leuzinger.

Taken 45th overall in the 2012 draft, Barnes became the highest-drafted player in Texas Tech history and then signed for $1 million, a bonus that was $136,400 under the recommended slot. Scouts like a lot of things about Barnes, primarily that he has plus speed and range to remain in center field, along with a quick bat that ought to provide at least average power for the position. Barnes may not hit for a high average, but he offsets that liability by taking walks and getting on base at a good clip. His biggest problem has been staying healthy. He missed the final month of 2012 at short-season State College because of a stress-related shin injury, then was limited to 46 games in 2013 at low Class A West Virginia because of lower back stiffness and a severely strained right hamstring. Barnes will likely begin 2014 at high Class A Bradenton. He's an intriguing prospect and has the tools, including an average arm, to move quickly through the system, but his durability is obviously in question.

Year	Club (League)	Class	AVG	G	AB	R	H	2B	3B	HR	RBI	BB	SO	SB	CS	OBP	SLG
2012	State College (NYP)	SS	.288	38	125	16	36	6	0	5	24	17	21	10	6	.401	.456
2013	West Virginia (SAL)	LoA	.268	46	183	26	49	9	0	5	24	17	48	10	3	.338	.399
Minor League Totals			.276	84	308	42	85	15	0	10	48	34	69	20	9	.365	.422

14 WILLY GARCIA, OF

BA GRADE **50** HIGH

Born: Sept. 4, 1992. **B-T:** R-R. **Ht.:** 6-3. **Wt.:** 180. **Signed:** Dominican Republic, 2010. **Signed by:** Rene Gayo/Marino Tejeda.

The Pirates signed Garcia from the Dominican Republic for $280,000 in April 2010, a few months prior to signing Mexican righthander Luis Heredia for $2.6 million. Garcia has plenty of tools, the loudest of which is power. He hit a combined 34 home runs during his first two years in full-season ball, including 16 in the pitcher-friendly high Class A Florida State League in 2013 at age 20. He also has good range for a corner outfielder and a strong arm—he logged 20 assists in 2013—that will play in right. He's a tick-above-average runner, though he needs to improve his stolen-base efficiency. What has kept Garcia from blossoming into a frontline prospect is his complete lack of plate discipline—he takes a swing-first mentality that hasn't changed in three seasons in the U.S. He will begin 2014 at Double-A Altoona, the level where many free-swingers begin to be exploited by advanced pitchers.

Year	Club (League)	Class	AVG	G	AB	R	H	2B	3B	HR	RBI	BB	SO	SB	CS	OBP	SLG
2010	Pirates (DSL)	R	.250	51	168	27	42	11	0	1	22	14	29	8	5	.333	.333
2011	Pirates (GCL)	R	.266	47	177	26	47	9	4	5	35	11	49	7	5	.323	.446
	State College (NYP)	SS	.286	3	7	1	2	0	0	0	0	0	0	0	0	.286	.286
2012	West Virginia (SAL)	LoA	.240	122	459	57	110	17	2	18	77	32	131	10	8	.286	.403
2013	Bradenton (FSL)	HiA	.256	118	449	51	115	21	6	16	60	23	154	13	6	.294	.437
Minor League Totals			.251	341	1260	162	316	58	12	40	194	80	363	38	24	.301	.411

15 TONY SANCHEZ, C

BA GRADE **45** LOW

Born: May 20, 1988. **B-T:** R-R. **Ht.:** 5-11. **Wt.:** 230. **Drafted:** Boston College, 2009 (1st round). **Signed by:** Chris Kline.

The Pirates pulled a surprise in the 2009 draft when they selected Sanchez, a consensus late-first-round talent, with the No. 4 overall pick. He finally rewarded the organization's faith by getting to the major leagues in 2013 and sticking with the club for good after backup catcher Mike McKenry suffered a season-ending knee injury in late July. The book on Sanchez when he was drafted was that he was nearly ready for the major leagues defensively—the Pirates compared him with the Cardinals' Yadier Molina—but that his hitting would need time to develop. While Sanchez has turned into an offensive threat with power and decent plate discipline, his defense has regressed because he has developed throwing problems. The Pirates and Sanchez won't go as far as to say he has the yips, but manager Clint Hurdle tried to limit his starts against running teams. The Pirates are optimistic he can overcome his problems. Sanchez has a good feel for the game and if he can overcome the throwing demons he could become a first-division catcher.

Year	Club (League)	Class	AVG	G	AB	R	H	2B	3B	HR	RBI	BB	SO	SB	CS	OBP	SLG
2009	State College (NYP)	SS	.308	4	13	2	4	1	0	0	1	1	2	0	0	.357	.385
	West Virginia (SAL)	LoA	.316	41	155	29	49	15	1	7	46	21	34	1	0	.415	.561
	Lynchburg (CAR)	HiA	.200	3	10	2	2	2	0	0	1	1	4	0	0	.385	.400
2010	Bradenton (FSL)	HiA	.314	59	207	31	65	17	0	4	35	28	41	2	1	.416	.454
2011	Altoona (EL)	AA	.241	118	402	46	97	14	1	5	44	47	76	5	5	.340	.318
2012	Altoona (EL)	AA	.277	40	141	22	39	14	1	0	17	18	33	1	1	.370	.390
	Indianapolis (IL)	AAA	.233	62	206	21	48	12	0	8	26	23	46	0	0	.316	.408
2013	Indianapolis (IL)	AAA	.288	76	260	35	75	26	0	10	42	28	60	0	0	.368	.504
	Altoona (EL)	AA	.176	4	17	2	3	1	0	0	0	0	3	0	0	.176	.235
	Pittsburgh (NL)	MAJ	.233	22	60	9	14	4	0	2	5	3	14	0	0	.288	.400
Major League Totals			.233	22	60	9	14	4	0	2	5	3	14	0	0	.288	.400
Minor League Totals			.271	407	1411	190	382	102	3	34	212	167	299	9	7	.364	.420

16 STOLMY PIMENTEL, RHP

BA GRADE **45** MEDIUM

Born: Feb. 1, 1990. **B-T:** R-R. **Ht.:** 6-3. **Wt.:** 235. **Signed:** Dominican Republic, 2006. **Signed by:** Luis Scheker (Red Sox).

Pimentel's prospect status had dimmed in the Red Sox organization when he stalled at the Double-A level. He got a fresh start in 2013 after an offseason trade to the Pirates that shipped closer Joel Hanrahan to Boston. Pimentel began 2013 at Double-A Altoona but finished the season with the big league club. His fastball sits at 92-94 mph and has added velocity as he has gotten older and stronger, topping out near 95. He offsets his fastball with an excellent, mid-80s split-changeup that nets him a fair share of strikeouts. His slider and curveball flash plus at times but are inconsistent. The Pirates would prefer Pimentel remain in the rotation, but they may be forced to move him to the bullpen in 2014. He will stick with Pittsburgh, regardless, because he's out of minor league options, and the club won't risk losing him on waivers. Because he's probably not quite ready for prime time, Pimentel may have to earn his stripes in low-leverage work. With a good showing, he could earn a look in the rotation.

Year	Club (League)	Class	W	L	ERA	G	GS	CG	SV	IP	H	HR	BB	SO	K/9	WHIP	AVG
2007	Red Sox (DSL)	R	3	1	2.90	14	13	0	0	62	44	2	22	60	8.7	1.06	.202
2008	Lowell (NYP)	SS	5	2	3.14	13	11	0	0	63	51	7	17	61	8.7	1.08	.224
2009	Greenville (SAL)	LoA	10	7	3.82	24	23	1	0	118	135	12	29	103	7.9	1.39	.290
2010	Salem (CAR)	HiA	9	11	4.06	26	26	0	0	129	120	11	42	102	7.1	1.26	.248
2011	Portland (EL)	AA	0	9	9.12	15	15	0	0	50	75	8	23	30	5.4	1.95	.352
	Salem (CAR)	HiA	6	4	4.53	11	10	0	0	52	50	8	16	35	6.1	1.28	.259
2012	Portland (EL)	AA	6	7	4.59	22	22	1	0	116	115	9	42	86	6.7	1.36	.259
2013	Altoona (EL)	AA	4	3	3.61	13	13	1	0	77	74	8	35	61	7.1	1.41	.252
	Indianapolis (IL)	AAA	2	6	3.13	14	14	1	0	92	76	6	21	62	6.1	1.05	.224
	Pittsburgh (NL)	MAJ	0	0	1.93	5	0	0	0	9	6	0	2	9	8.7	0.86	.171
Major League Totals			0	0	1.93	5	0	0	0	9	6	0	2	9	8.7	0.86	.171
Minor League Totals			45	50	4.14	152	147	4	0	758	740	71	247	600	7.1	1.30	.257

17 CLAY HOLMES, RHP

Born: March 27, 1993. **B-T:** R-R. **Ht.:** 6-5. **Wt.:** 230. **Drafted:** HS—Slocomb, Ala., 2011 (9th round). **Signed by:** Darren Mazeroski.

The valedictorian of his Slocomb High class, Holmes had a strong commitment to Auburn. However, the Pirates went over slot and signed him for $1.2 million, even though he was considered a bit of a project because of inconsistent, maximum-effort mechanics. Holmes' fastball sits at 90-92 mph, but his best pitch is a sharp-breaking slider that he has a hard time throwing consistently for strikes. His changeup still is in the rudimentary stages. While Holmes appeared to take a step backward in 2013—he issued 5.2 walks per nine innings—he was not quite as bad as he looked. Opposing hitters batted .240 and slugged just .339. The Pirates knew Holmes was a project when they drafted him, but they will challenge him in 2014 with an assignment to high Class A Bradenton.

Year	Club (League)	Class	W	L	ERA	G	GS	CG	SV	IP	H	HR	BB	SO	K/9	WHIP	AVG
2012	State College (NYP)	SS	5	3	2.28	13	13	0	0	59	35	1	29	34	5.2	1.08	.176
2013	West Virginia (SAL)	LoA	5	6	4.08	26	25	0	0	119	106	7	69	90	6.8	1.47	.240
Minor League Totals			10	9	3.48	39	38	0	0	178	141	8	98	124	6.3	1.34	.220

18 BLAKE TAYLOR, LHP

Born: Aug. 17, 1995. **B-T:** L-L. **Ht.:** 6-3. **Wt.:** 220. **Drafted:** HS—Dana Point, Calif., 2013 (2nd round). **Signed by:** Brian Tracy.

Taylor projected as a second-round pick in the 2013 draft, yet he accepted a well-below-slot $750,000 to forgo a scholarship to Hawaii. The suggested bonus for the 51st pick was $1,065,400. Taylor throws from a three-quarters arm slot, which makes it difficult for lefthanders to pick up his pitches. He also has the projectable frame that ought to allow him to increase his velocity as his body fills out. Taylor's fastball sits at 89-91 mph, though he topped out at 94. He throws a big-breaking curveball that will likely become his out-pitch as he gains experience. His changeup, though, needs quite a bit of work. While Taylor has a relatively clean delivery, his biggest problem is command and control. He's young for his draft class and did not turn 18 until two months after he graduated from Dana Hills High. The Pirates will take things slowly with Taylor and he will probably begin 2014 in extended spring training, then go to short-season Jamestown in mid-June.

Year	Club (League)	Class	W	L	ERA	G	GS	CG	SV	IP	H	HR	BB	SO	K/9	WHIP	AVG
2013	Pirates (GCL)	R	0	2	2.57	8	7	0	0	21	7	0	9	13	5.6	0.76	.104
Minor League Totals			0	2	2.57	8	7	0	0	21	7	0	9	13	5.6	0.76	.104

19 JACOBY JONES, OF/SS

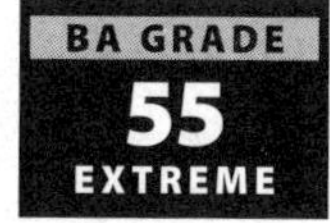

Born: May 10, 1992. **B-T:** R-R. **Ht.:** 6-3. **Wt.:** 200. **Drafted:** Louisiana State, 2013 (3rd round). **Signed by:** Jerome Cochran.

Jones played all over the diamond at Louisiana State, including both middle-infield positions. The Pirates selected him as a center fielder in the third round of the 2013 draft, but he also saw five games at shortstop before suffering a season-ending knee injury at short-season Jamestown. Jones has all five tools but has yet to see his production match his raw talent. He hit .253 with a .672 OPS as an LSU sophomore in 2012 before improving to .283/.382/.417 in 187 at-bats for the Tigers in 2013. Jones won the Cape Cod League home run derby in 2012, yet hit just 13 bombs in 627 collegiate at-bats then went deep only once in first 67 pro plate appearances. Most scouts feel Jones eventually will settle in center to take advantage of his speed and range. Despite a shortened debut season, Jones figures to begin 2014 at high Class A Bradenton, though it remains to be seen if his knee gives him any long-term problems.

Year	Club (League)	Class	AVG	G	AB	R	H	2B	3B	HR	RBI	BB	SO	SB	CS	OBP	SLG
2013	Jamestown (NYP)	SS	.311	15	61	14	19	2	2	1	10	3	14	3	2	.358	.459
Minor League Totals			.311	15	61	14	19	2	2	1	10	3	14	3	2	.358	.459

20 CODY DICKSON, LHP

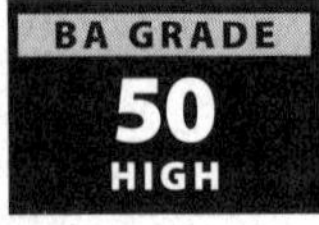

Born: April 27, 1992. **B-T:** L-L. **Ht.:** 6-3. **Wt.:** 180. **Drafted:** Sam Houston State, 2013 (4th round). **Signed by:** Trevor Haley.

The Pirates have lacked lefthanded pitching prospects in recent years and attempted to try rectify that in the 2013 draft by selecting high schooler Blake Taylor in the second round and Dickson in the fourth. They signed Dickson for $375,000 after he bounced between the rotation and bullpen at Sam Houston State during an inconsistent junior season. His fastball usually sits in the 91-93 mph range and tops out of 95. Unlike most college pitchers, he still has projection remaining and could add a tick or two to his fastball as his body fills out. Dickson's curveball and changeup also flash plus at times, but his biggest problem is control. He will go through spells where he almost completely loses the strike zone—he walked 5.2 batters per nine innings over three college seasons. Though Dickson had a few control glitches, he pitched well in his pro debut at short-season Jamestown in 2013 and did not allow an earned run in seven of his last eight starts. The Pirates likely will push him to high Class A Bradenton in 2014, and as a three-pitch lefty he has the potential to be a mid-rotation starter if he can cut down on the walks.

Year	Club (League)	Class	W	L	ERA	G	GS	CG	SV	IP	H	HR	BB	SO	K/9	WHIP	AVG
2013	Jamestown (NYP)	SS	2	0	2.37	14	14	0	0	57	42	3	24	59	9.3	1.16	.209
Minor League Totals			2	0	2.37	14	14	0	0	57	42	3	24	59	9.3	1.16	.209

21 ANDREW LAMBO, OF

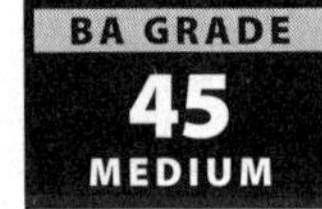

Born: Aug. 11, 1988. **B-T:** L-L. **Ht.:** 6-3. **Wt.:** 220. **Drafted:** HS—Newbury Park, Calif., 2007 (4th round). **Signed by:** Chuck Crim (Dodgers).

If such an award existed, Lambo might have been the minor league comeback player of the year. Traded by the Dodgers, for whom he ranked as No. 1 prospect in 2009, to the Pirates for veteran reliever Octavio Dotel in July 2010, Lambo's stock had fallen so far that Pittsburgh left him unprotected in the 2012 Rule 5 draft. All 29 other teams passed and him, on the heels of an injury-wracked campaign, and he went on to lead all Pirates minor leaguers with 32 home runs and 99 RBIs in 2013, while receiving his first callup to the big leagues. Power is Lambo's only plus tool, though he does have an average arm. He's a fringe-average runner and defender in either outfield corner. Like many power hitters, he's prone to strikeouts, which will cut into his ability to hit for average. Lambo did not get much playing time in Pittsburgh, but he opened plenty of eyes and will get a chance to make the club, perhaps as the starting right fielder, in 2014.

Year	Club (League)	Class	AVG	G	AB	R	H	2B	3B	HR	RBI	BB	SO	SB	CS	OBP	SLG
2007	Dodgers (GCL)	R	.343	54	181	38	62	15	1	5	32	29	34	1	2	.440	.519
2008	Great Lakes (MWL)	LoA	.288	123	472	58	136	33	2	15	79	41	110	5	2	.346	.462
	Jacksonville (SL)	AA	.389	8	36	7	14	2	1	3	12	2	9	0	0	.421	.750
2009	Chattanooga (SL)	AA	.256	130	492	70	126	39	1	11	61	39	95	4	3	.311	.407
2010	Chattanooga (SL)	AA	.271	47	181	26	49	11	2	4	25	15	39	1	1	.325	.420
	Altoona (EL)	AA	.275	26	91	12	25	1	0	2	10	9	30	0	0	.353	.352
2011	Indianapolis (IL)	AAA	.184	60	185	19	34	11	0	3	17	17	48	1	0	.257	.292
	Altoona (EL)	AA	.274	69	252	35	69	17	0	8	41	26	59	4	3	.345	.437
2012	Pirates (GCL)	R	.485	9	33	10	16	4	0	1	6	5	5	1	0	.550	.697
	Altoona (EL)	AA	.250	26	92	13	23	3	1	4	16	14	19	0	1	.346	.435
2013	Altoona (EL)	AA	.291	58	220	35	64	9	4	14	46	20	60	6	1	.351	.559
	Indianapolis (IL)	AAA	.272	62	224	32	61	15	1	18	53	24	67	1	0	.344	.589
	Pittsburgh (NL)	MAJ	.233	18	30	4	7	2	0	1	2	3	11	0	1	.303	.400
Major League Totals			.233	18	30	4	7	2	0	1	2	3	11	0	1	.303	.400
Minor League Totals			.276	672	2459	355	679	160	13	88	398	241	575	24	13	.343	.459

22 JAFF DECKER, OF

BA GRADE
45
MEDIUM

Born: Feb. 23, 1990. **B-T:** L-L. **Ht.:** 5-10. **Wt.:** 190. **Drafted:** HS—Peoria, Ariz., 2008 (1st round supplemental). **Signed by:** Dave Lottsfeldt (Padres).

The Pirates acquired Decker plus righthanded reliever Miles Mikolas from the Padres in a late-November trade for first baseman Alex Dickerson. Both players had been designated for assignment by San Diego. Ranked as the Padres' No. 3 prospect heading into 2009, Decker's luster steadily dimmed from his star. His best attribute is plate discipline. He's willing to work a walk and has a .402 career on-base percentage in six minor league seasons. However, Decker has yet to develop much power and can be too passive at the plate, letting hittable pitches go by for strikes. At Triple-A Tucson last season, he played mainly center field, but he does not possess the range necessary to play the position in the major leagues and also has below-average speed. His arm is strong enough for right field. Decker will get a chance to become the lefthanded half of a platoon in right field with Jose Tabata to begin the 2014 season, though No. 1 prospect Gregory Polanco figures seize the full-time job before too long.

Year	Club (League)	Class	AVG	G	AB	R	H	2B	3B	HR	RBI	BB	SO	SB	CS	OBP	SLG
2008	Padres (AZL)	R	.352	49	159	51	56	11	2	5	34	55	36	9	1	.523	.541
	Eugene (NWL)	SS	.200	3	10	2	2	0	0	0	0	2	5	0	0	.333	.200
2009	Fort Wayne (MWL)	LoA	.299	104	358	78	107	25	2	16	64	85	92	10	6	.442	.514
2010	Lake Elsinore (CAL)	HiA	.262	79	290	53	76	14	2	17	58	47	80	5	4	.374	.500
2011	San Antonio (TL)	AA	.236	133	496	90	117	29	2	19	92	103	145	15	5	.373	.417
2012	San Antonio (TL)	AA	.184	47	147	30	27	3	2	3	9	40	37	6	2	.365	.293
	Padres (AZL)	R	.296	9	27	5	8	1	2	1	7	4	3	0	0	.394	.593
2013	San Diego (NL)	MAJ	.154	13	26	3	4	0	0	1	2	3	4	0	1	.233	.269
	Tucson (PCL)	AAA	.286	105	350	63	100	23	1	10	40	55	94	4	6	.381	.443
Major League Totals			.154	13	26	3	4	0	0	1	2	3	4	0	1	.233	.269
Minor League Totals			.268	529	1837	372	493	106	13	71	304	391	492	49	24	.402	.456

23 STETSON ALLIE, 1B

BA GRADE 50 EXTREME

Born: March 13, 1991. **B-T:** R-R. **Ht.:** 6-2. **Wt.:** 238. **Drafted:** HS—Lakewood, Ohio, 2010 (2nd round). **Signed by:** Brian Tracy.

The Pirates signed Allie for $2.25 million following a senior year at St. Edward High in which he reached 100 mph multiple times with his fastball and 90 mph with his slider in the Ohio state championship game. His pro pitching career, however, lasted just 27 innings over two seasons as he developed severe control problems. Allie walked 37 batters, hit 10 others and gave up 10 wild pitches while compiling a 7.76 ERA. He reinvented himself as a power-hitting first baseman, mashing 17 home runs in 66 games at low Class A West Virginia during the first half of 2013. He struggled following a promotion to high Class A Bradenton, and while not adjusting more quickly to the Florida State League was disappointing, the Pirates have not written off Allie. He has big-time power potential, and that overshadows his otherwise lacking tools, including below-average speed, range and arm strength. Unless he tones down his pull-happy, uppercut stroke, he may never hit more than about .250, but given how far he came in a year, the organization will settle with a lottery ticket rather than a bust.

Year	Club (League)	Class	W	L	ERA	G	GS	CG	SV	IP	H	HR	BB	SO	K/9	WHIP	AVG
2011	State College (NYP)	SS	0	2	6.58	15	7	0	0	26	20	1	29	28	9.7	1.88	.208
2012	West Virginia (SAL)	LoA	0	1	54.00	2	1	0	0	1	1	0	8	1	13.5	13.50	.333
Minor League Totals			0	3	7.76	17	8	0	0	27	21	1	37	29	9.8	2.18	.212

Year	Club (League)	Class	AVG	G	AB	R	H	2B	3B	HR	RBI	BB	SO	SB	CS	OBP	SLG
2012	Pirates (GCL)	R	.213	42	150	23	32	6	2	3	19	21	50	2	0	.314	.340
2013	West Virginia (SAL)	LoA	.324	66	244	42	79	16	1	17	61	36	79	6	1	.414	.607
	Bradenton (FSL)	HiA	.229	66	236	28	54	18	0	4	25	41	82	2	3	.342	.356
Minor League Totals			.262	174	630	93	165	40	3	24	105	98	211	10	4	.363	.449

24 JIN-DE JHANG, C

BA GRADE 50 EXTREME

Born: May 17, 1993. **B-T:** L-R. **Ht.:** 5-11. **Wt.:** 220. **Signed:** Taiwan, 2011. **Signed by:** Fu-Chun Chiang.

The Pirates made their biggest investment in the Asian amateur free agent market by signing Jhang for $250,000 in 2011. Also known as Chin-De Jhang before signing, he impressed Pirates scouts with a quick lefthanded bat and strong arm behind the plate. He has had little trouble adjusting to pitching in the lower levels of the minors, hitting for both average and power. Jhang will probably develop more power as he gains a better sense for when he can turn on pitches. He did not play behind the plate much in Taiwan but is showing signs of becoming a strong defensive catcher. His arm is not only strong but accurate, and his footwork and pitch-blocking ability are improving. Jhang has made great strides during his first two seasons in the U.S., but he could wind up back at short-season Jamestown because the Pirates have a glut of young catching prospects, including 2013 first-rounder Reese McGuire and 2012 second-rounder Wyatt Mathisen. Jhang has a chance to be an everyday catcher in the major leagues, but he also could eventually become trade bait because of the Pirates' depth at a position where the demand seems to always outstrip the supply.

Year	Club (League)	Class	AVG	G	AB	R	H	2B	3B	HR	RBI	BB	SO	SB	CS	OBP	SLG
2011	Played in Australian Summer League																
2012	Pirates (GCL)	R	.305	43	128	12	39	5	2	1	23	14	16	1	1	.382	.398
2013	Jamestown (NYP)	SS	.277	53	184	22	51	8	1	5	34	17	24	0	1	.338	.413
Minor League Totals			.288	96	312	34	90	13	3	6	57	31	40	1	2	.356	.407

25 ELVIS ESCOBAR, OF

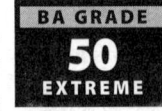

BA GRADE 50 EXTREME

Born: Sept. 6, 1994. **B-T:** L-L. **Ht.:** 5-10. **Wt.:** 180. **Signed:** Venezuela, 2011. **Signed by:** Rene Gayo/Rodolfo Petit/Marc DelPiano.

Escobar and Colombian outfielder Harold Ramirez were the Pirates' top international signings in 2011. Coincidentally, they have the same birthday. While Ramirez has become one of the top prospects in the organization, Escobar did not match his production at short-season Jamestown in 2013. Signed for $570,000, Escobar has an intriguing blend of above-average speed, ample range in center field and arm strength to spare. He could become a leadoff threat if he develops better contact skills and plate discipline to improve his on-base percentage. While the Pirates may advance Escobar to low Class A West Virginia in 2014, some in the organization feel he would be better served by beginning in extended spring training and repeating the New York-Penn League.

Year	Club (League)	Class	AVG	G	AB	R	H	2B	3B	HR	RBI	BB	SO	SB	CS	OBP	SLG
2012	Pirates (GCL)	R	.274	54	190	29	52	5	4	2	18	18	46	6	5	.338	.374
2013	Jamestown (NYP)	SS	.268	56	183	25	49	8	2	1	23	9	47	9	4	.293	.350
Minor League Totals			.271	110	373	54	101	13	6	3	41	27	93	15	9	.316	.362

26 WEI-CHUNG WANG, LHP

BA GRADE 50 EXTREME

Born: April 25, 1992. **B-T:** L-L. **Ht.:** 6-1. **Wt.:** 160. **Signed:** Taiwan, 2011. **Signed by:** Fu-Chun Chiang.

The Pirates and Wang originally agreed to terms on a $350,000 bonus in 2011, a deal that got scuttled when a physical turned up a torn elbow ligament. Wang signed for a lower figure, had Tommy John surgery, then made a fine pro debut in the Rookie-level Gulf Coast League in 2013. Because he signed a new deal, the Pirates either had to protect him on the 40-man roster or expose him to the Rule 5 draft, and they chose not to protect him. He showed exceptional command of a three-pitch mix, effectively mixing his fastball, curveball and changeup. Wang's fastball gained velocity last season, going from 87-89 mph to 91-93 by his final start. His curveball is his preferred go-to weapon, and it flashes plus, giving both lefthanders and righthanders fits. Spring training will determine whether Wang moves to low Class A West Virginia or stays back in extended spring training and heads to short-season Jamestown.

Year	Club (League)	Class	W	L	ERA	G	GS	CG	SV	IP	H	HR	BB	SO	K/9	WHIP	AVG
2013	Pirates (GCL)	R	1	3	3.23	12	11	0	0	47	37	2	4	42	8.0	0.87	.209
Minor League Totals			1	3	3.23	12	11	0	0	47	37	2	4	42	8.0	0.87	.209

27 ADRIAN SAMPSON, RHP

BA GRADE 45 HIGH

Born: Oct. 7, 1991. **B-T:** R-R. **Ht.:** 6-3. **Wt.:** 200. **Drafted:** Bellevue (Wash.) CC, 2012 (5th round). **Signed by:** Greg Hopkins.

Sampson committed to play collegiately at Oregon twice but never made it to Eugene. He had Tommy John surgery in 2010, during his senior year at Skyline High in Sammamish, Wash., and decided to attend Bellevue (Wash.) CC after graduation. Drafted in the 16th round by the Marlins in 2011, Sampson declined to sign, though he did recommit to Oregon. The Pirates enticed him to turn pro the following year with a $250,000 bonus for the fifth-rounder. Sampson's fastball sits in the 89-91 mph range, topping out at 94, but his out-pitch is a drop-off-the-table curveball. His changeup also is becoming a solid-average pitch, giving him the diversified arsenal needed to remain a starter. The Pirates jumped Sampson to high Class A Bradenton in 2013, but he had a tough time adjusting to the better level of competition. He fared better as the season went on, though he might begin 2014 back at Bradenton before moving up to Double-A Altoona.

Year	Club (League)	Class	W	L	ERA	G	GS	CG	SV	IP	H	HR	BB	SO	K/9	WHIP	AVG
2012	State College (NYP)	SS	0	1	2.95	11	9	0	0	43	38	2	17	44	9.3	1.29	.241
2013	Bradenton (FSL)	HiA	5	8	5.14	25	24	1	0	140	177	18	22	85	5.5	1.42	.310
Minor League Totals			5	9	4.63	36	33	1	0	183	215	20	39	129	6.4	1.39	.295

28 JON SANDFORT, RHP

BA GRADE 50 EXTREME

Born: Aug. 27, 1994. **B-T:** B-R. **Ht.:** 6-6. **Wt.:** 215. **Drafted:** HS—Winter Springs, Fla., 2012 (3rd round). **Signed by:** Nick Presto.

Sandfort boosted his draft stock with a strong senior year Winter Springs High in 2012, then signed with the Pirates as a third-rounder for the recommended slot bonus of $462,900 rather than play collegiately at Florida. The long and lanky Sandfort is the type of pitcher scouts dream on because of his projectable body. His fastball usually sits in the 88-91 mph range and reaches as high as 94, but the Pirates believe he will throw harder as he adds muscle. He also has a very good curveball that he can throw consistently for strikes. His changeup, though, is still in the rudimentary stages. Sandfort has yet to make it out of the Rookie-level Gulf Coast League in his first two pro seasons, and his performance has been poor. The Pirates, however, knew Sandfort was raw and would require time to move through the system. He has the upside of a No. 2 starter or power reliever, though he's lined up for extended spring training followed by an assignment to short-season Jamestown in 2014.

Year	Club (League)	Class	W	L	ERA	G	GS	CG	SV	IP	H	HR	BB	SO	K/9	WHIP	AVG
2012	Pirates (GCL)	R	0	1	4.80	8	8	0	0	15	11	1	10	7	4.2	1.40	.204
2013	Pirates (GCL)	R	2	2	4.95	10	9	0	0	36	39	3	14	35	8.7	1.46	.281
Minor League Totals			2	3	4.91	18	17	0	0	51	50	4	24	42	7.4	1.44	.259

29 GIFT NGOEPE, SS

BA GRADE
45
HIGH

Born: Jan. 18, 1990. **B-T:** B-R. **Ht.:** 5-10. **Wt.:** 165. **Signed:** South Africa, 2008. **Signed by:** Tom Randolph.

Ngoepe became the first black South African to sign a contract with an affiliated club when he caught the Pirates' eye at a tournament in Italy in 2008. Ngoepe's story has been well-chronicled. He was literally raised in the clubhouse of an amateur baseball team in Randburg, a suburb of Johannesburg, during apartheid while his mother Maureen worked as the team's cleaning woman and groundskeeper. Ngoepe has the tools to be an above-average shortstop, with good range and instincts along with a strong arm. He is also an above-average runner and a threat on the bases. While Ngoepe is willing to take walks, his offensive game has been sabotaged by his inability to lay off breaking pitches out of the zone, which has led to plenty of strikeouts. He began 2013 at Double-A Altoona, then missed a month after heading home to attend his mother's funeral. Ngoepe headed for high Class A Bradenton once he returned to the U.S., and he hit well, leading to hopes he will do better in 2014 in his second taste of Double-A.

Year	Club (League)	Class	AVG	G	AB	R	H	2B	3B	HR	RBI	BB	SO	SB	CS	OBP	SLG
2009	Pirates (GCL)	R	.238	47	160	24	38	4	0	1	9	21	52	13	9	.341	.281
2010	Bradenton (FSL)	HiA	.250	2	4	0	1	0	0	0	0	1	2	0	0	.400	.250
	State College (NYP)	SS	.205	64	229	30	47	13	5	1	20	36	68	11	7	.315	.319
2011	West Virginia (SAL)	LoA	.306	25	85	14	26	5	1	2	5	7	14	3	3	.359	.459
	Pirates (GCL)	R	.167	2	6	0	1	0	0	0	0	0	1	0	0	.286	.167
2012	Bradenton (FSL)	HiA	.232	124	456	66	106	11	5	9	36	63	131	22	14	.330	.338
2013	Altoona (EL)	AA	.177	72	220	29	39	10	2	3	16	28	82	10	3	.278	.282
	Bradenton (FSL)	HiA	.292	28	96	17	28	7	3	0	6	21	35	7	1	.424	.427
Minor League Totals			.228	364	1256	180	286	50	16	16	92	177	385	66	37	.329	.331

30 JOELY RODRIGUEZ, LHP

BA GRADE
45
HIGH

Born: Nov. 14, 1991. **B-T:** L-L. **Ht.:** 6-1. **Wt.:** 175. **Signed:** Dominican Republic, 2009. **Signed by:** Rene Gayo/Ellis Pena.

Rodriguez has been slow to develop since being signed in 2009, but he took a big step forward in 2013 and made the 40-man roster in November. Extremely raw when signed, Rodriguez is capable of throwing his fastball at 95 mph, but he has only a rudimentary curveball and changeup. Command was a problem for him at the start of his career, but he has learned to sink his fastball, which now sits at 91-93 mph, to both sides of the plate while learning to take something off the pitch to generate more movement. The curve and change are now serviceable pitches, but he will need to continue refining both in order to remain a starter. Rodriguez has become a groundball pitcher over the last two years, and that fits with the organizational philosophy of frequently employing defensive shifts. He was limited to two starts at short-season State College in 2011 because of a strained elbow but has been durable since that injury. Rodriguez figures to make the jump to Double-A Altoona in 2014 to see if he can build on the momentum he generated last year.

Year	Club (League)	Class	W	L	ERA	G	GS	CG	SV	IP	H	HR	BB	SO	K/9	WHIP	AVG
2009	Pirates (DSL)	R	2	5	4.60	12	12	0	0	47	53	1	24	24	4.6	1.64	.291
2010	Pirates (GCL)	R	2	2	3.99	12	9	0	1	47	44	10	7	26	4.9	1.08	.240
	State College (NYP)	SS	0	0	6.75	2	0	0	0	4	6	0	2	2	4.5	2.00	.333
2011	State College (NYP)	SS	0	1	5.40	2	1	0	0	5	12	0	1	3	5.4	2.60	.444
2012	State College (NYP)	SS	3	4	4.50	14	14	0	0	64	74	2	15	32	4.5	1.39	.298
2013	West Virginia (SAL)	LoA	5	5	2.72	14	14	0	0	73	79	4	20	57	7.1	1.36	.280
	Bradenton (FSL)	HiA	4	3	2.67	12	12	0	0	67	63	4	19	44	5.9	1.22	.251
Minor League Totals			16	20	3.66	68	62	0	1	307	331	21	88	188	5.5	1.36	.278

St. Louis Cardinals

BY DERRICK GOOLD

When second-year manager Mike Matheny gathered his flock for their first official team meeting of spring training 2013, the expectation he set for them was four words long and easier said than done: "Win the World Series."

Looking around the Cardinals clubhouse he not only saw the weight of history—Willie McGee, Red Schoendienst and Jim Edmonds, all World Series winners, sat nearby—but the lift of the present. Talent harvested from the best farm system in baseball populated the room. Matheny believed this group should aim for championships, plural.

The Cardinals, who grew increasingly younger as a roster through October, tied for the best record in baseball (97-65), won the National League pennant and appeared in the organization's fourth World Series in 10 years. They came two wins shy of the franchise's 12th World Series championship, but in their Game Six loss to the Red Sox they started a 22-year-old phenom, had a 25-year-old first baseman and closed with a 23-year-old flamethrower.

"To have our minor league system be able to produce and really sort of define this club, I think it said a lot about the organization," general manager John Mozeliak said. "When you think about creating that sustained model to always be competitive, year in and year out, it really does start with how you procure the talent and how you develop it."

Injuries to closer Jason Motte, shortstop Rafael Furcal, and ace Chris Carpenter at the start of the year helped clear the pipeline for a gush of rookies. After the Cardinals debuted nine players in 2012—not including manager Matheny, himself a prospect of sorts—the Cardinals had a tops-in-baseball 20 rookies reach the majors in 2013.

The Cardinals received 36 wins from rookie pitchers and 109 of the 162 regular-season games were started by pitchers age 26 or younger. By the playoffs, nearly 70 percent of the club's innings were thrown by pitchers 26 or younger.

Rookie righthander Michael Wacha, less than 18 months removed from Texas A&M, led the way with 30⅔ innings, four wins and the NL Championship Series MVP. Shelby Miller, another rookie righty, won 15 games but threw only one inning in October partially because of Wacha's ascension and in an aim to conserve innings.

The roster churn at the major league level created ripples in the minor leagues. Of the 100 players who started the year on full-season rosters, 63 moved up. Outfielder James Ramsey, Piscotty and lefty Tim Cooney—three 2012 draft picks from the college ranks—asserted themselves in early promotions to Double-A and are poised for Triple-A in 2014.

Pitching remains the wealth of the organization, while the graduations of second baseman Kolten Wong and first baseman Matt Adams to the majors creates opportunity for hitters after Taveras and Piscotty. The Cardinals may have to reach into their purse of pitchers to fill another hole in the majors: shortstop, where they made due with Pete Kozma and Daniel Descalso in 2013. They have the depth to do that and still contend—for years to come.

KEN BABBITT

Michael Wacha fell to the 19th pick in 2012 but was a playoff ace barely a year later

TOP PROSPECTS OF THE DECADE

Year	Player, Pos.	2013 Org.
2004	Blake Hawksworth, rhp	Out of baseball
2005	Anthony Reyes, rhp	Out of baseball
2006	Anthony Reyes, rhp	Out of baseball
2007	Colby Rasmus, of	Blue Jays
2008	Colby Rasmus, of	Blue Jays
2009	Colby Rasmus, of	Blue Jays
2010	Shelby Miller, rhp	Cardinals
2011	Shelby Miller, rhp	Cardinals
2012	Shelby Miller, rhp	Cardinals
2013	Oscar Taveras, of	Cardinals

ORGANIZATION OVERVIEW

General Manager: John Mozeliak. **Farm Director:** Gary LaRocque. **Scouting Director:** Dan Kantrovitz.

Class	Team	League	W	L	PCT	Finish	Manager
Majors	St. Louis Cardinals	National	97	65	.599	1st (15)	Mike Matheny
Triple-A	Memphis Redbirds	Pacific Coast	69	75	.486	11th (16)	Ron Warner
Double-A	Springfield Cardinals	Texas	64	74	.464	6th (8)	Mike Shildt
High A	Palm Beach Cardinals	Florida State	64	71	.474	10th (12)	Johnny Rodriguez
Low A	Peoria Chiefs	Midwest	68	69	.496	t-7th (16)	Dann Bilardello
Short-season	State College Spikes	New York-Penn	48	27	.640	1st (14)	Oliver Marmol
Rookie	Johnson City Cardinals	Appalachian	36	31	.480	6th (10)	Joe Kruzel
Rookie	GCL Cardinals	Gulf Coast	24	35	.407	15th (16)	Steve Turco
Overall 2013 Minor League Record			**373**	**382**	**.494**	**18th (30)**	

THIS YEAR'S TOP 30

No.	Player, Pos.	Grade/Risk
1.	Oscar Taveras, of	70/Low
2.	Carlos Martinez, rhp	60/Low
3.	Kolten Wong, 2b	55/Medium
4.	Stephen Piscotty, of	55/High
5.	Marco Gonzales, lhp	55/High
6.	Tim Cooney, lhp	50/Medium
7.	Alex Reyes, rhp	60/Extreme
8.	James Ramsey, of	50/Medium
9.	Rob Kaminsky, lhp	55/High
10.	Randal Grichuk, of	50/High
11.	Carson Kelly, 3b/c	50/High
12.	Charlie Tilson, of	50/High
13.	Patrick Wisdom, 3b	50/High
14.	Greg Garcia, ss	45/Medium
15.	Zach Petrick, rhp	50/High
16.	Mike O'Neill, of	45/Medium
17.	Tyrell Jenkins, rhp	55/Extreme
18.	Kenny Peoples-Walls, ss/of	50/Extreme
19.	Oscar Mercado, ss	50/Extreme
20.	Juan Herrera, ss	45/High
21.	Keith Butler, rhp	40/Low
22.	Lee Stoppelman, lhp	40/Low
23.	Tommy Pham, of	45/High
24.	C.J. McElroy, of	50/Extreme
25.	Edmundo Sosa, ss	50/Extreme
26.	Boone Whiting, rhp	40/Medium
27.	John Gast, lhp	45/High
28.	Steve Bean, c	50/Extreme
29.	Jacob Wilson, 2b	45/High
30.	Xavier Scruggs, 1b	45/Extreme

LAST YEAR'S TOP 30

No.	Player, Pos.	Status
1.	Oscar Tavares, of	No. 1
2.	Shelby Miller, rhp	Majors
3.	Carlos Martinez, rhp	No. 2
4.	Trevor Rosenthal, rhp	Majors
5.	Kolten Wong, 2b	No. 3
6.	Michael Wacha, rhp	Majors
7.	Matt Adams, 1b	Majors
8.	Tyrell Jenkins, rhp	No. 17
9.	Carson Kelly, 3b	No. 11
10.	Stephen Piscotty, of/3b	No. 4
11.	Patrick Wisdom, 3b	No. 13
12.	James Ramsey, of	No. 8
13.	Pete Kozma, ss/2b	Majors
14.	Kevin Siegrist, lhp	Majors
15.	Ryan Jackson, ss/2b	(Astros)
16.	Victor DeLeon, rhp	Dropped out
17.	C.J. McElroy, of	No. 24
18.	Jordan Swagerty, rhp	Dropped out
19.	Charlie Tilson, of	No. 12
20.	Steve Bean, c	No. 28
21.	Eric Fornataro, rhp	Dropped out
22.	Sam Freeman, lhp	Dropped out
23.	Seth Maness, rhp	Dropped out
24.	Jorge Rondon, rhp	Dropped out
25.	Tim Cooney, lhp	No. 6
26.	John Gast, lhp	No. 27
27.	Maikel Cleto, rhp	(Royals)
28.	Mike O'Neill, of	No. 16
29.	Keith Butler, rhp	No. 21
30.	Seth Blair, rhp	Dropped out

BEST TOOLS

Best Hitter for Average	Oscar Taveras
Best Power Hitter	Xavier Scruggs
Best Strike-Zone Discipline	Mike O'Neill
Fastest Baserunner	Charlie Tilson
Best Athlete	C.J. McElroy
Best Fastball	Carlos Martinez
Best Curveball	Rob Kaminsky
Best Slider	Carlos Martinez
Best Changeup	Marco Gonzales
Best Control	Tim Cooney
Best Defensive Catcher	Audry Perez
Best Defensive Infielder	Patrick Wisdom
Best Infield Arm	Patrick Wisdom
Best Defensive Outfielder	Tommy Pham
Best Outfield Arm	Stephen Piscotty

TOP 15 PLAYERS 25 AND UNDER

No.	Player, Pos. (Age)	Level
1.	Michael Wacha, rhp (22)	Majors
2.	Oscar Taveras, of (21)	Triple-A
3.	Shelby Miller, rhp (23)	Majors
4.	Trevor Rosenthal, rhp (23)	Majors
5.	Carlos Martinez, rhp (22)	Majors
6.	Kolten Wong, 2b (23)	Majors
7.	Matt Adams, rhp (25)	Majors
8.	Stephen Piscotty, of (23)	Double-A
9.	Marco Gonzales, lhp (22)	High Class A
10.	Tim Cooney, lhp (23)	Majors
11.	Alex Reyes, rhp (19)	Rookie
12.	Joe Kelly, rhp (25)	Majors
13.	James Ramsey, of (24)	Triple-A
14.	Rob Kaminsky, lhp (19)	Rookie
15.	Kevin Siegrist, lhp (24)	Majors

MINOR LEAGUE DEPTH CHART

ST. LOUIS CARDINALS

TOP 2014 ROOKIE: Kolten Wong, 2b. The Cardinals cleared room in the lineup and shifted all-star Matt Carpenter back to third base to make room for the Hawaiian infielder.

BREAKOUT PROSPECT: Patrick Wisdom, 3b. A gifted fielder, he has the swing for opposite-field success, more power yet to reveal, and the possibility to unlock it when he reaches the Texas League.

SOURCE OF TOP 30 TALENT			
Homegrown	**28**	**Acquired**	**2**
College	13	Trades	2
Junior college	1	Rule 5 draft	0
High school	9	Independent leagues	0
Nondrafted free agents	1	Free agents/waivers	0
International	4		

SLEEPER: Nick Petree, rhp. The 2013 ninth-rounder out of Missouri State has exceptional command with movement on every pitch, and some scouts believe he'll begin a quick ascent.

LF	CF	RF
Mike O'Neill (16)	James Ramsey (8)	Oscar Taveras (1)
Anthony Garcia	Charlie Tilson (12)	Stephen Piscotty (4)
David Popkins	Tommy Pham (23)	Randal Grichuk (10)
Starlin Rodriguez	C.J. McElroy (24)	Kenny Peoples-Walls (18)
Luis Perez	Vaughn Bryan	Rowan Wick
Colin Walsh	DeAndre Asbury-Heath	Chris Swauger

3B	SS	2B	1B
Patrick Wisdom (13)	Greg Garcia (14)	Kolten Wong (3)	Xavier Scruggs (30)
Jermaine Curtis	Oscar Mercado (19)	Jacob Wilson (29)	Jonathan Rodriguez
Rafael Medina	Juan Herrera (20)	Breyvic Valera	David Washington
Leobaldo Pina	Edmundo Sosa (25)	Mason Katz	
	Cesar Valera	Malik Collymore	
	Alex Mejia		

C
Carson Kelly (11)
Steve Bean (28)
Audry Perez
Cody Stanley
Adam Ehrlich
Ed Easley

LHP	
LHSP	**LHRP**
Marco Gonzales (5)	Lee Stoppelman (22)
Tim Cooney (6)	Nick Greenwood
Rob Kaminsky (9)	Dean Kiekhefer
John Gast (27)	Justin Wright
Anthony Ferrara	Danny Miranda
Ian McKinney	Iden Nazario
Ryan Sherriff	
Dewin Perez	

RHP	
RHSP	**RHRP**
Carlos Martinez (2)	Keith Butler (21)
Alex Reyes (7)	Victor De Leon
Zack Petrick (15)	Jordan Swagerty
Tyler Jenkins (17)	Jose Almarante
Boone Whiting (26)	Sam Tuivailala
Nick Petree	Dixon Llorens
Mike Mayers	Jordon Rondon
Sam Gaviglio	Eric Fornataro
Kurt Heyer	Ronnie Shaban
Cory Jones	Fernando Baez
Andrew Pierce	Heath Wyatt

2013 — BONUSES: $7.2 MILLION

BEST PURE HITTER: The Cardinals have had great success with college seniors of late, from Allen Craig to Matt Carpenter. It's hard to expect 2B Mason Katz (4) to reach those standards, but he hit .370 with more walks than strikeouts as a senior at Louisiana State. His pro debut was more modest (.249, 49 strikeouts in 197 at-bats).

BEST POWER HITTER: Lefthanded-hitting OF Ricardo Bautista (12) intrigues the Cardinals with his pure stroke and loft power. He's just 17 and didn't homer in his debut in the Rookie-level Gulf Coast League. Katz also has above-average power.

FASTEST RUNNER: Acquiring speed and athleticism was a key to this draft class. Canadian SS Malik Collymore (10) stands out in a deep crowd of above-average runners, including OFs De'Andre Asbury (15), D'Vante Lacy (24) and Vaughn Bryan (35).

BEST DEFENSIVE PLAYER: SS Oscar Mercado (2) got a $1.5 million bonus for his smooth, fluid defense that features good feet, soft hands and a plus arm.

BEST FASTBALL: RHP Nick Petree (9) had the best 89-90 mph fastball in the draft, a pitch that's rarely straight and that plays up due to good command. RHP Blake Higgins (16) throws harder when healthy; the Michigan junior-college product made just two starts this spring before needing Tommy John surgery, but Cardinals scouts saw him hit 94-95 mph.

BEST SECONDARY PITCH: The Cardinals got two of the best in the draft from LHPs Marco Gonzales (1) and Rob Kaminsky (1). Gonzales's changeup helped him limit righthanded hitters to a .212 average in his debut; Kaminsky has a hard, late curveball he controls well.

BEST PRO DEBUT: Kaminsky struck out 28 in 22 innings in the Rookie-level Gulf Coast League. Bryan hit .280/.341/.394 with 13 steals and five triples for Rookie-level Johnson City.

BEST ATHLETE: Bryan, Collymore and Asbury combine power with their wheels. Asbury was an all-state wideout in South Carolina, while Bryan showed surprising polish defensively and as a switch-hitter.

MOST INTRIGUING BACKGROUND: RHP Blake McKnight (38) didn't play high school baseball, as he was home schooled. He worked his way up from the junior-varsity team at Evangel (Mo.) to become the NAIA school's first drafted player. SS J.J. Altobelli (18) is the son of John, coach at Orange Coast (Calif.) JC.

CLOSEST TO THE MAJORS: Gonzales has an outside shot to get to St. Louis by the end of 2014. Petree's fastball command should also speed his ascent.

BEST LATE-ROUND PICK: McKnight has an 87-93 mph sinker and pounds the strike zone. Bryan and RHP Artie Reyes (40), who has an average fastball and slider, are also legitimate prospects.

THE ONE WHO GOT AWAY: St. Louis signed 38 of its 41 picks. Missouri prep OF/RHP Calvin Munson (31) considered signing but chose football and is playing at San Diego State as a linebacker.

ASSESSMENT: The Cardinals have had success with college bats of late, but took just two in the first 16 rounds in a draft that favored pitching. They came up with impact lefties led by Gonzales and Kaminsky.

2012 — BONUSES: $9.9 MILLION

RHP Michael Wacha (1) makes the class alone, but St. Lous also is high on LHP Tim Cooney (3) and OFs Stephen Piscotty (1s) and James Ramsey (1), among others.

GRADE: A

2011 — BONUSES: $4.6 MILLION

2B Kolten Wong (1) and RHP Seth Maness (11) were on the World Series roster. Toolsy OFs such as Charlie Tilson (2) highlight the rest of the class.

GRADE: C

2010 — BONUSES: $6.7 MILLION

The Cardinals wisely flipped 3B Zack Cox (1) for Edward Mujica. LHPs John Gast (6) and Tyler Lyons (9) have reached St. Louis but have lower upside.

GRADE: D

TOP DRAFT PICKS OF THE DECADE

Year	Player, Pos.	2013 Org.
2004	Chris Lambert, rhp	Out of baseball
2005	Colby Rasmus, of	Blue Jays
2006	Adam Ottavino, rhp	Rockies
2007	Pete Kozma, ss	Cardinals
2008	Brett Wallace, 3b	Astros
2009	Shelby Miller, rhp	Cardinals
2010	Zack Cox, 3b	Marlins
2011	Kolten Wong, 2b	Cardinals
2012	Michael Wacha, rhp	Cardinals
2013	Marco Gonzales, lhp	Cardinals

LARGEST BONUSES IN CLUB HISTORY

J.D. Drew, 1998	$3,000,000
Shelby Miller, 2009	$2,875,000
Rick Ankiel, 1999	$2,500,000
Chad Hutchinson, 1998	$2,300,000
Zack Cox, 2010	$2,000,000

1 OSCAR TAVERAS, OF

Born: June 19, 1992. **B-T:** L-L. **Ht.:** 6-2. **Wt.:** 185.
Signed: Dominican Republic, 2008.
Signed by: Juan Mercado.

As if the hesitancy of Taveras' steps rounding second base in May wasn't enough, the slam of his batting helmet as he got to dugout revealed just as much any MRI could. The top hitting prospect developed by the Cardinals since Albert Pujols lost a majority of the 2013 season because of an ankle sprain that three times knocked him off the field and eventually required high-ankle surgery. The lefthanded-hitting Taveras was limited to 173 at-bats and 46 games at Triple-A Memphis, but general manager John Mozeliak became fond of repeating, "When he played, he hit." Taveras always has. Signed for $145,000 from the Dominican Republic in 2008, Taveras has a .320/.377/.518 batting line in five professional seasons. In his first three seasons with a domestic affiliate he won a league MVP, a low Class A Midwest League batting title and three championships at three different levels. He was a comet streaking toward the majors with a scheduled debut in 2013 until his ankle gave out and chronic discomfort slowed his trip around the bases—and his arrival.

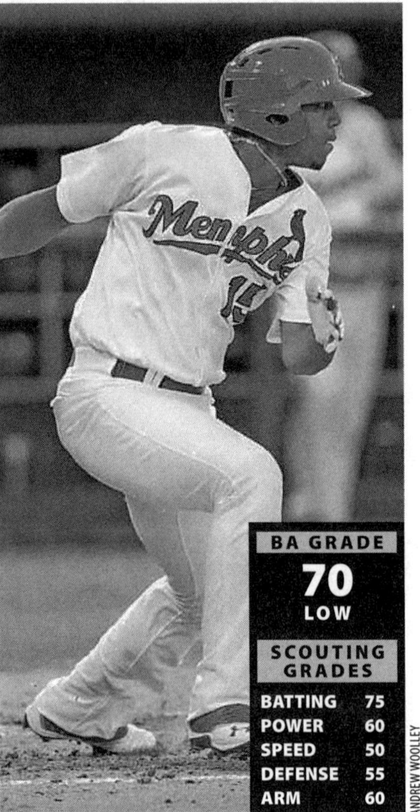

Memphis
BA GRADE
70
LOW
SCOUTING GRADES
BATTING 75
POWER 60
SPEED 50
DEFENSE 55
ARM 60

ANDREW WOOLLEY

Taveras has a preternatural gift for hitting, one honed by trying to hit the caps of water jugs spun fast to veer like a Frisbee, and thousands of swings against a tire lashed to a fence. He has electron-quick bat speed. He barrels pitches in the zone, and he can drive any pitch he can reach, sometimes going outside the zone to do so. He's a bad-ball hitter who doesn't strike out often, and whose 57 extra-base hits at Double-A show the power ahead. He displayed his knack during spring training against big league pitchers and had some staff members arguing he was ready to open the season in the majors. The other elements of his game, including attention to detail and constant effort, are catching up to his hitting. Taveras' zest is at the plate, and his game can wander away from it. His best position is right field, where his plus arm and range play, but the Cardinals believe his athleticism is a fit for center. The high-ankle injury cost him valuable experience in center, where he played well at times in 2013 and drifted at other times. Mozeliak said the big question because of the lost time "is where he can play defensively and how confident we are with him in center."

Taveras had a turbulent 2013, one buffeted by the injury, fickle changes to his representation, two off-field matters that required returns to the Dominican and other instances that reminded the organization he's young and still adapting. He will have to mature on the job. Taveras would have been on the postseason roster in 2013 and perhaps the starting center fielder if not for injury. He will arrive in spring training with a chance to win a spot on the major league roster, and if he can prove reliable in center, an everyday job awaits him. The Cardinals want his bat in the lineup and believe that given health and given playing time he's a Rookie of the Year candidate and all-star in the making.

Year	Club (League)	Class	AVG	G	AB	R	H	2B	3B	HR	RBI	BB	SO	SB	CS	OBP	SLG
2009	Cardinals (DSL)	R	.257	65	237	35	61	13	8	1	42	28	36	9	4	.338	.392
2010	Cardinals (GCL)	R	.167	7	30	1	5	1	0	0	2	1	5	1	0	.194	.200
	Johnson City (APP)	R	.322	53	211	39	68	13	3	8	43	12	41	8	5	.362	.526
2011	Quad Cities (MWL)	LoA	.386	78	308	52	119	27	5	8	62	32	52	1	4	.444	.584
2012	Springfield, MO (TL)	AA	.321	124	477	83	153	37	7	23	94	42	56	10	1	.380	.572
2013	Memphis (PCL)	AAA	.306	46	173	25	53	12	0	5	32	9	22	5	1	.341	.462
	Cardinals (GCL)	R	1.000	1	1	0	1	1	0	0	0	1	0	0	0	1.000	2.000
Minor League Totals			.320	374	1437	235	460	104	23	45	275	125	212	34	15	.377	.518

2 CARLOS MARTINEZ, RHP

Born: Sept. 21, 1991. **B-T:** R-R. **Ht.:** 6-0. **Wt.:** 165. **Signed:** Dominican Republic, 2010. **Signed by:** Juan Mercado.

A delay in securing a work visa cost Martinez all of 2013 spring training but didn't slow his accelerated arrival to the majors. He leapfrogged from Double-A Springfield to his big league debut, rode the St. Louis-to-Triple-A Memphis shuttle, and by the World Series was the club's eighth-inning flamethrower. Known as Carlos Matias when he originally signed with the Red Sox in 2009, Martinez was suspended a year when his paperwork couldn't be verified. The Cardinals spent a year gathering a 40-page binder, shepherding him through an investigation and to a $1.5 million bonus. The lithe righty draws comparisons with Pedro Martinez for his build. From the small frame, Martinez unleashes an action fastball at 97-101 mph. Of his first 117 pitches in the postseason, 10 were 100 mph or faster and 21 were sinkers at about 96. He abandoned his curveball in 2013 for a hard slider, one that he could throw with the same delivery as his fastball and gave him something in the 80s to offset the power. A former shortstop, Martinez is flamboyant—bordering on frenetic—on the field, eager to field any grounder he can reach, but also has learned to control and repeat his delivery for greater consistency. He won't need a changeup if he remains in the bullpen. Martinez drew a lot of interest from other teams at the trade deadline and will continue to do so. He'll come to big league spring training as a starter, ready to compete for the rotation, but his high-voltage stuff will assure him a late-inning role in the bullpen for 2014.

Year	Club (League)	Class	W	L	ERA	G	GS	CG	SV	IP	H	HR	BB	SO	K/9	WHIP	AVG
2010	Cardinals (DSL)	R	3	2	0.76	12	12	1	0	59	28	1	14	78	11.9	0.71	.144
2011	Quad Cities (MWL)	LoA	3	2	2.33	8	8	0	0	39	27	1	14	50	11.6	1.06	.196
	Palm Beach (FSL)	HiA	3	3	5.28	10	10	0	0	46	49	2	30	48	9.4	1.72	.269
2012	Palm Beach (FSL)	HiA	2	2	3.00	7	7	0	0	33	29	0	10	34	9.3	1.18	.236
	Springfield (TL)	AA	4	3	2.90	15	14	0	0	71	62	6	22	58	7.3	1.18	.237
2013	Springfield (TL)	AA	1	0	2.31	3	3	0	0	12	11	1	1	9	6.9	1.03	.239
	Memphis (PCL)	AAA	5	3	2.51	13	13	0	0	68	54	3	27	63	8.3	1.19	.213
	St. Louis (NL)	MAJ	2	1	5.08	21	1	0	1	28	31	1	9	24	7.6	1.41	.282
Major League Totals			2	1	5.08	21	1	0	1	28	31	1	9	24	7.6	1.41	.282
Minor League Totals			21	15	2.69	68	67	1	0	328	260	14	118	340	9.3	1.15	.217

3 KOLTEN WONG, 2B

Born: Oct. 10, 1990. **B-T:** L-R. **Ht.:** 5-9. **Wt.:** 190. **Drafted:** Hawaii, 2011 (1st round). **Signed by:** Matt Swanson.

For a decade, the Cardinals had a carousel at second base, twice converting players—outfielder Skip Schumaker, third baseman Matt Carpenter—to handle the pivot. Wong was drafted to bring an end to the merry-go-round. The first second baseman taken in the first round in 25 years by the Cardinals, Wong signed for $1.3 million in 2011 and advanced rapidly, reaching the majors in 2013 but struggling in his first swing at big league pitching. He earned a spot on the World Series roster for his baserunning and improved feel at second base. Wong uncoils from a compact stance for a balanced, lefty swing that sprays line drives and hints at the high average and gap power that will be his hallmark. Wong made strides as a fielder and base thief at Triple-A Memphis in 2013, two priorities for him. He improved his footwork and instincts to become above-average at second, though his arm is fringy. He picked the brains of Willie McGee and Lou Brock for baserunning advice, and he got sharper at his jumps and reads to go 23-for-24 in steal attempts. Wong comes to spring training with a range of options, ranging from Triple-A to starter at second. His immediate role is tied to the club's decision with Carpenter, who could move to third, creating an opening for Wong at second as soon as this summer or next.

Year	Club (League)	Class	AVG	G	AB	R	H	2B	3B	HR	RBI	BB	SO	SB	CS	OBP	SLG
2011	Quad Cities (MWL)	LoA	.335	47	194	39	65	15	2	5	25	21	24	9	5	.401	.510
2012	Springfield (TL)	AA	.287	126	523	79	150	23	6	9	52	44	74	21	11	.348	.405
2013	Memphis (PCL)	AAA	.303	107	412	68	125	21	8	10	45	41	60	20	1	.369	.466
	St. Louis (NL)	MAJ	.153	32	59	6	9	1	0	0	0	3	12	3	0	.194	.169
Major League Totals			.153	32	59	6	9	1	0	0	0	3	12	3	0	.194	.169
Minor League Totals			.301	280	1129	186	340	59	16	24	122	106	158	50	17	.365	.446

4 STEPHEN PISCOTTY, OF

SCOTT ROVAK-ST. LOUIS CARDINALS

BA GRADE
55
HIGH

Born: Jan. 14, 1991. **B-T:** R-R. **Ht.:** 6-3. **Wt.:** 210. **Drafted:** Stanford, 2012 (1st round supplemental). **Signed by:** Matt Swanson.

The Cardinals used the two compensation picks they got for Albert Pujols on Michael Wacha and Piscotty, a polished college bat. Piscotty sped to Double-A early in 2013 while shifting from third base to right field, where his skills were a better fit. He responded well to the new position and continued to hit above his level after getting experience. He recovered from a midseason hamstring injury to hit .330 with 18 RBIs in August. Piscotty has a mature feel for the strike zone and profiles as a hitter for average, batting right around .300 at every level. He keeps both hands on the bat and maintains an ability to drive the ball the opposite way. He teases at hitting for more power. His frame and his swing say he will. An official described how he hits mistakes hard, but that 20-homer power may not manifest until he's in the majors. Piscotty's range improved in right field, and he sports the organization's best outfield arm. He will get time during big league spring training before reporting to Triple-A Memphis as the everyday right fielder and middle-of-the-order hitter. Some in the organization believe he'll debut in 2014 as an injury replacement or young bat off the bench.

Year	Club (League)	Class	AVG	G	AB	R	H	2B	3B	HR	RBI	BB	SO	SB	CS	OBP	SLG
2012	Quad Cities (MWL)	LoA	.295	55	210	29	62	18	1	4	27	18	25	3	0	.376	.448
2013	Palm Beach (FSL)	HiA	.292	63	243	30	71	14	2	9	35	18	27	4	5	.348	.477
	Springfield (TL)	AA	.299	49	184	17	55	9	0	6	24	19	19	7	3	.364	.446
Minor League Totals			.295	167	637	76	188	41	3	19	86	55	71	14	8	.362	.458

5 MARCO GONZALES, LHP

Born: Feb. 16, 1992. **B-T:** L-L. **Ht.:** 6-0. **Wt.:** 185. **Drafted:** Gonzaga, 2013 (1st round). **Signed by:** Matt Swanson.

With the 19th pick in the 2013 draft, the Cardinals followed a familiar formula, taking a college pitcher who had a winning pedigree, athleticism and a plus changeup. That profile fit Michael Wacha in 2012 and Gonzales in 2013. The Gonzaga lefty is the son of Rockies short-season pitching coach Frank Gonzales. Marco checked all the boxes—including the character ones—the Cardinals use for evaluation, and he signed quickly for $1.85 million. With Wacha's promotion, Gonzales has the best changeup in the system. The lefty pitches with purpose, starting with a fastball that hums in the 88-91 mph range with late tail. He's improving two breaking pitches to give him something else to play off the command of his fastball, flashing an average curve with depth. Gonzales has an easy, refined, metronome-like delivery that he can repeat, adding to above-average command of his pitches. Gonzales threw and 106 innings for Gonzaga in 2013, so the Cardinals used him sparingly in his pro debut to manage his workload. He'll have a chance to start 2014 in the rotation at Double-A or higher, and the Cardinals expect him to move rapidly and arrive as a mid-rotation starter.

Year	Club (League)	Class	W	L	ERA	G	GS	CG	SV	IP	H	HR	BB	SO	K/9	WHIP	AVG
2013	Cardinals (GCL)	R	0	0	5.40	4	2	0	0	7	8	0	3	10	13.5	1.65	.276
	Palm Beach (FSL)	HiA	0	0	1.62	4	4	0	0	17	10	1	5	13	7.0	0.90	.179
Minor League Totals			0	0	2.70	8	6	0	0	23	18	1	8	23	8.9	1.11	.212

6 TIM COONEY, LHP

SCOTT ROVAK-ST. LOUIS CARDINALS

BA GRADE
50
MEDIUM

Born: Dec. 19, 1990. **B-T:** L-L. **Ht.:** 6-3. **Wt.:** 195. **Drafted:** Wake Forest, 2012 (3rd round). **Signed by:** Matt Blood.

Cooney first earned attention as a prospect with a strong turn in the Cape Cod League in 2011. That gave way to an erratic junior year and a slip in the draft. After signing for $404,400, he's been the pitcher envisioned on the Cape. The trickle-down effect of injuries at the upper levels forced Cooney to Double-A Springfield earlier than planned in his 2013 full-season debut. Cooney thrived in the challenging Texas League because of a seasoned approach and four accessible pitches. He had 12 quality starts out of 20 and did not miss a scheduled outing. The tall, angular lefty has a fastball that sits at 90-92 mph and has late, natural movement. He has a workable curve in the 75-76 mph range and continues to improve his above-average changeup to go with a burgeoning cutter. A scout described how Cooney adds and subtracts velocity well to upset timing, and he doesn't shy from challenging righthanded or lefthanded hitters with strikes. He is constantly around the zone and was one of the stingiest with walks in the whole organization. The Cardinals like Cooney's pitchability and durability. His consistency and pitch mix puts him in the Triple-A Memphis rotation and near the big league conversation as a potential No. 4 starter less than 24 months after his draft.

Year	Club (League)	Class	W	L	ERA	G	GS	CG	SV	IP	H	HR	BB	SO	K/9	WHIP	AVG
2012	Batavia (NYP)	SS	3	3	3.40	13	11	1	0	56	56	4	8	43	7.0	1.15	.268
2013	Palm Beach (FSL)	HiA	3	3	2.75	6	6	1	0	36	38	1	4	23	5.8	1.17	.273
	Springfield (TL)	AA	7	10	3.80	20	20	0	0	118	132	8	18	125	9.5	1.27	.284
Minor League Totals			13	16	3.51	39	37	2	0	210	226	13	30	191	8.2	1.22	.278

7 ALEX REYES, RHP

Born: Aug. 29, 1994. **B-T:** R-R. **Ht.:** 6-3. **Wt.:** 185. **Signed:** Dominican Republic, 2012. **Signed by:** Rodny Jimenez/Angel Ovalles.

A high school standout in New Jersey, Reyes circumnavigated the draft by moving to the Dominican and living there with family until becoming eligible as an amateur free agent. Born and raised in the United States, he received a $950,000 bonus on the international market. Like Carlos Martinez, the last Dominican youth to receive that kind of coin from the Cardinals, Reyes had the athleticism and power arm to attract scouts. Reyes is the raw clay that the Cardinals covet. He has two plus pitches and a third in development, scouts say. He starts with a fastball at 92-95 mph that will consistently hit 97. His frame and long arms project power, and he has a sharp plane to his fastball as it cuts through the strike zone. With a more consistent delivery, he'll have better command and some deception. Reyes has a hard curveball with two-plane break and precocious feel for a changeup, but he's only now learning to "pitch soft," as one scout said. Reyes shined as the top righthander in the Rookie-level Appalachian League, striking out 27 percent of batters faced. The Cardinals will keep him on a deliberate path, advancing to full-season ball at some point in 2014, when he won't turn 20 until August. If the Cardinals are right, he could reach the majors by the end of 2016.

Year	Club (League)	Class	W	L	ERA	G	GS	CG	SV	IP	H	HR	BB	SO	K/9	WHIP	AVG
2013	Johnson City (APP)	R	6	4	3.39	12	12	0	0	58	54	1	28	68	10.5	1.41	.249
Minor League Totals			6	4	3.39	12	12	0	0	58	54	1	28	68	10.5	1.41	.249

8 JAMES RAMSEY, OF

SCOTT ROVAK-ST. LOUIS CARDINALS

Born: Dec. 19, 1989. **B-T:** L-R. **Ht.:** 6-0. **Wt.:** 190. **Drafted:** Florida State, 2012 (1st round). **Signed by:** Rob Fidler.

The descriptions of Ramsey continue to trend more toward his character and constitution than his tools and production, but he brought them more in synch with a superb first full pro season. Ramsey's reputation for leadership, charisma and his Christian faith preceded him into pro ball. He was the first Florida State player to wear a "C" on his jersey and was a Rhodes Scholar nominee. Scouts call Ramsey a gamer with great makeup, while others don't see a standout tool. He doesn't have a glaring weakness, however, grading out at least average across the board. Ramsey proved adept in center field with improved instincts, above-average closing speed, smart range and a solid-average arm. He took advantage of Double-A Springfield's comfy home park and hit 15 homers but doesn't project for that kind of power. Rather, he's a gap hitter who will turn singles into doubles thanks to his above-average speed. His strike-zone discipline improved in 2013, but his 108 strikeouts in 347 at-bats at Double-A speak to the adjustments in store. The Cardinals love Ramsey's intangibles and will give him the chance to earn the center field job at Triple-A Memphis, with the majors on deck.

Year	Club (League)	Class	AVG	G	AB	R	H	2B	3B	HR	RBI	BB	SO	SB	CS	OBP	SLG
2012	Palm Beach (FSL)	HiA	.229	56	210	36	48	9	3	1	14	33	59	10	2	.333	.314
2013	Palm Beach (FSL)	HiA	.361	18	61	17	22	5	2	1	7	12	12	1	0	.481	.557
	Springfield (TL)	AA	.251	93	347	61	87	11	2	15	44	53	108	8	4	.356	.424
	Memphis (PCL)	AAA	.000	1	3	0	0	0	0	0	0	0	1	0	0	.000	.000
Minor League Totals			.253	168	621	114	157	25	7	17	65	98	180	19	6	.360	.398

9 ROB KAMINSKY, LHP

SCOTT ROVAK-ST. LOUIS CARDINALS

BA GRADE
55
HIGH

Born: Sept. 2, 1994. **B-T:** R-L. **Ht.:** 5-11. **Wt.:** 191. **Drafted:** HS—Montvale, N.J., 2013 (1st round). **Signed by:** Sean Moran.

A strong frame, big hands and a huge curveball belie Kaminsky's frame and made him the 28th overall pick in 2013. He turned down a commitment to North Carolina to sign for $1.785 million. He ended his senior season at St. Joseph Regional High with a 0.10 ERA, 126 strikeouts and the chip on his shoulder that comes with being called undersized his entire career. Kaminsky has a lively fastball that touches 94 mph and ranges from 88-92. He has the makings of an above-average changeup, but it's his sharp curve that ranked No. 1 among high schoolers entering the draft and also tops in the Cardinals system. It misses bats. He can get curveball-happy because of its deceptive, downward break, and he'll have to gain confidence in his fastball, said two evaluators. He throws from a consistent high-three-quarters slot that gives him better success against righties. Kaminsky pitched just 22 innings in his pro debut to save his arm. He'll come into 2014 with an innings limit, but the Cardinals will give him a chance to win a spot in the low Class A Peoria rotation.

Year	Club (League)	Class	W	L	ERA	G	GS	CG	SV	IP	H	HR	BB	SO	K/9	WHIP	AVG
2013	Cardinals (GCL)	R	0	3	3.68	8	5	0	0	22	23	1	9	28	11.5	1.45	.261
Minor League Totals			0	3	3.68	8	5	0	0	22	23	1	9	28	11.5	1.45	.261

10 RANDAL GRICHUK, OF

BA GRADE
50
HIGH

Born: Aug. 13, 1991. **B-T:** R-R. **Ht.:** 6-1. **Wt.:** 195. **Drafted:** HS—Rosenburg, Texas, 2009 (1st round). **Signed by:** Kevin Ham (Angels).

Grichuk always will be the guy the Angels took one spot ahead of Mike Trout in the 2009 draft, but he started making his own pro legacy in 2013, first with a career-high 22 home runs in his first crack at Double-A, then in the offseason, when he was traded to the Cardinals. St. Louis insisted on Grichuk's inclusion in the trade that brought Peter Bourjos to St. Louis and sent David Freese to Anaheim. Grichuk's calling card has been power since he hit four home runs during the 2004 Little League World Series, and he led the Texas League in extra-base hits (57) in 2013. The biggest key for Grichuk's success was health. He'd missed time in 2010 and 2011 with thumb, wrist and knee injuries, which limited him to just 117 games in those two seasons combined. He has wiry strength and excellent bat speed that helps him catch up to good fastballs, and while he's aggressive, he's made contact at an acceptable rate for a power hitter. Grichuk could use a bit more patience at the plate and more polish defensively, where he's solid and profiles as an average right fielder with a solid-average arm. He runs enough to man an outfield corner but won't steal many bases. Power is Grichuk's game. Triple-A Memphis should be his first assignment as a Cardinal.

Year	Club (League)	Class	AVG	G	AB	R	H	2B	3B	HR	RBI	BB	SO	SB	CS	OBP	SLG
2009	Angels (AZL)	R	.322	53	236	47	76	13	10	7	53	9	64	6	4	.352	.551
2010	Angels (AZL)	R	.327	12	49	7	16	3	2	4	10	3	9	0	0	.365	.714
	Cedar Rapids (MWL)	LoA	.292	52	202	41	59	19	4	7	36	9	50	4	0	.327	.530
2011	Angels (AZL)	R	.333	7	24	2	8	1	1	0	6	2	4	0	0	.357	.458
	Cedar Rapids (MWL)	LoA	.230	32	122	12	28	7	4	2	13	6	29	0	1	.267	.402
	Inland Empire (CAL)	HiA	.283	14	53	13	15	4	2	1	6	0	13	0	0	.316	.491
2012	Inland Empire (CAL)	HiA	.298	135	537	79	160	30	9	18	71	23	92	16	6	.335	.488
2013	Arkansas (TL)	AA	.256	128	500	85	128	27	8	22	64	28	92	9	5	.306	.474
Minor League Totals			.284	433	1723	286	490	104	40	61	259	80	353	35	16	.324	.497

11 CARSON KELLY, 3B/C

BA GRADE
50
HIGH

Born: July 14,1994. **B-T:** R-R. **Ht.:** 6-2. **Wt.:** 200. **Drafted:** HS—Portland, Ore., 2012 (2nd round). **Signed by:** Matt Swanson.

The Cardinals pushed the then-18 Kelly to a full-season club to start 2013, an aggressive move that needed a correction when he moved down a peg to short-season State College in June. There, he took off. A second-round pick in 2012, Kelly was the highest-drafted Oregon prep player in 15 years and received the highest bonus ($1.6 million) in his round that year. He has a sturdy frame that has started to add muscle with maturity. He has a calm, quiet approach at the plate with a furious, balanced swing. He gets the barrel to pitches in the zone and does not strike out often for a player with his latent power. As Kelly ages and gains strength, the Cardinals expect the power will come, and the eye for a high on-base percentage should remain. At third base, Kelly's best tool is his arm. He moves forward well and handles routine grounders, but his range is limited, which prompted the Cardinals to try a conversion to catcher during instructional league. Kelly will report to spring training to gain more experience behind the plate. In limited game exposure, he appeared comfortable and agile enough for the position. If his bat develops and his move behind the plate takes, he could grow into a top-ranked prospect.

Year	Club (League)	Class	AVG	G	AB	R	H	2B	3B	HR	RBI	BB	SO	SB	CS	OBP	SLG
2012	Johnson City (APP)	R	.225	56	213	24	48	10	0	9	25	10	33	0	0	.263	.399
2013	Peoria (MWL)	LoA	.219	43	146	18	32	6	0	2	13	13	25	0	0	.288	.301
	State College (NYP)	SS	.277	70	271	35	75	16	1	4	32	20	31	1	0	.340	.387
Minor League Totals			.246	169	630	77	155	32	1	15	70	43	89	1	0	.303	.371

12 CHARLIE TILSON, OF

BA GRADE 50 HIGH

Born: Dec. 2, 1992. **B-T:** L-L. **Ht.:** 5-11. **Wt.:** 175. **Drafted:** HS—Winnetka, Ill., 2011 (2nd round). **Signed by:** Kris Gross.

Back from a season-stealing shoulder that wiped out his 2012, the lefthanded-hitting Tilson surged at low Class A Peoria in 2013, batting .303/.349/.388 in 100 games after a slow start. During extended spring training 2012, Tilson attempted to make a diving catch and tore the labrum in his right (non-throwing) shoulder. Surgery followed. What was supposed to be his first full pro season was spent recovering. In 2013, Tilson played every day, showed durability and shook any rust off his swing. The Chicagoland high school star first caught teams' attention with a sublime showing at the 2010 Area Code Games. The Cardinals signed him for $1.275 million after making him a second-round pick in 2011. The question that followed him into the pros was whether the Area Code jubilee was his peak or a peek. Given health, Tilson proved it was the latter. He improved his plate discipline and was able to use his speed to raise his average. He runs from home to first base in 4.1 seconds, and using that plus speed to conjure extra bases will be necessary unless power develops beyond 20 extra-base hits in 410 at-bats he showed in 2013. Tilson will receive priority playing time in center field, where's he's a plus defender, with a likely assignment to high Class A Palm Beach in 2014.

Year	Club (League)	Class	AVG	G	AB	R	H	2B	3B	HR	RBI	BB	SO	SB	CS	OBP	SLG
2011	Cardinals (GCL)	R	.167	4	12	2	2	0	0	0	1	2	3	1	0	.286	.167
	Johnson City (APP)	R	.467	4	15	2	7	2	0	0	4	1	1	0	0	.500	.600
2012	Did not play—Injured																
2013	Peoria (MWL)	LoA	.303	100	376	49	114	8	6	4	30	25	58	15	6	.349	.388
	Palm Beach (FSL)	HiA	.294	9	34	1	10	1	1	0	0	5	6	0	0	.385	.382
Minor League Totals			.304	117	437	54	133	11	7	4	35	33	68	16	6	.355	.389

13 PATRICK WISDOM, 3B

BA GRADE 50 HIGH

Born: Aug. 27, 1991. **B-T:** R-R. **Ht.:** 6-2. **Wt.:** 210. **Drafted:** St. Mary's, 2012 (1st round supplemental). **Signed by:** Matt Swanson.

One of three third basemen the Cardinals took early in the 2012 draft, Wisdom is the fielder who has remained at the position—and the one with the skills necessary to advance at the position. Taken 52th overall, Wisdom was bookended by Stephen Piscotty and Carson Kelly, both of whom have gravitated toward other positions and into the organization's top 11. Wisdom is the best fielder of the trio, with a strong, true arm that earns 70 grades and exceptional instincts at the position. His above-average range is predicated on a swift first step. One official called him the best defensive prospect the Cardinals have had at third base in at least a decade. Wisdom compiled a .925 OPS in the wood-bat Alaska League during college, but his junior-year slump allowed the Cardinals to nab him for a $678,790 bonus. His success with a wood bat revealed a swing and future pop that will translate to the pros. Wisdom hit 13 homers in low Class A Peoria but had hiccups because he struck out 114 times, chewing into his productivity. He undermines his swing when he tries to pull for power. But he has the ingredients of hitters before him who have thrived at Double-A Springfield once he harnesses the ability to drive the ball the ball to right field. A profile third baseman if he hits, Wisdom is slated to report to high Class A Palm Beach in 2014.

Year	Club (League)	Class	AVG	G	AB	R	H	2B	3B	HR	RBI	BB	SO	SB	CS	OBP	SLG
2012	Batavia (NYP)	SS	.282	65	241	40	68	16	5	6	32	31	58	2	1	.373	.465
2013	Peoria (MWL)	LoA	.231	104	372	54	86	20	4	13	62	42	114	4	1	.312	.411
	Palm Beach (FSL)	HiA	.250	25	92	8	23	4	0	2	11	9	23	1	0	.317	.359
Minor League Totals			.251	194	705	102	177	40	9	21	105	82	195	7	2	.334	.423

14 GREG GARCIA, SS

BA GRADE 45 MEDIUM

Born: Aug. 8, 1989. **B-T:** L-R. **Ht.:** 6-0. **Wt.:** 190. **Drafted:** Hawaii, 2010 (7th round). **Signed by:** Matt Swanson.

A Western Athletic Conference first-team selection at shortstop, Garcia came to the Cardinals with a solid defensive reputation—including a strong arm and good feet—at several positions and an on-base-centric approach at the plate that needed refining. He broke out in 2012, leading the organization with 80 walks, seizing the shortstop job, batting .284/.408/.420 and teaming with former Hawaii teammate Kolten

Wong to boost Double-A Springfield to the Texas League title in 2012. The Cardinals have had a carousel at shortstop—in 2014, Jhonny Peralta figures to be the eighth different Opening Day shortstop in eight years—and Garcia's performance at Double-A brought him to spring training where, amidst the scramble, he asserted himself. "He opened a lot of eyes," an official said. But after earning a starting job at Triple-A Memphis, he hit just .235 in the first half. He had to hit his way back into the conversation and onto the 40-man roster with a brilliant finish, hitting .368/.471/.529 in August and pushing past Ryan Jackson on the organizational depth chart. Garcia is a lefty hitter at shortstop who, during Peralta's contract, could emerge as a versatile complement as soon as 2014. He has an average arm some scouts see as better suited for second baes, and he maximizes his average speed, which augments his utility profile.

Year	Club (League)	Class	AVG	G	AB	R	H	2B	3B	HR	RBI	BB	SO	SB	CS	OBP	SLG
2010	Johnson City (APP)	R	.286	58	220	49	63	15	1	4	24	18	36	7	5	.363	.418
2011	Quad Cities (MWL)	LoA	.273	46	150	20	41	10	1	0	10	17	24	4	2	.360	.353
	Palm Beach (FSL)	HiA	.290	59	210	36	61	11	5	2	16	31	42	4	4	.400	.419
2012	Springfield (TL)	AA	.284	124	412	81	117	20	3	10	51	80	83	10	5	.408	.420
2013	Memphis (PCL)	AAA	.271	116	354	50	96	23	4	3	35	49	70	14	2	.377	.384
Minor League Totals			.281	403	1346	236	378	79	14	19	136	195	255	39	18	.386	.403

15 ZACH PETRICK, RHP

BA GRADE
50
HIGH

Born: July 29, 1989. **B-T:** R-R. **Ht.:** 6-3. **Wt.:** 195. **Signed:** Northwestern Ohio, 2012 (NDFA). **Signed by:** Brian Hopkins.

As he waited with friends through the third day of the 2012 draft, Petrick passed the time surfing the Internet and trying to avoid a creeping dread. When the name of the 1,238th selection was announced, it was official. Not one of the names was his. Less than 18 months later, Petrick learned he was the Cardinals' minor league pitcher of the year. Signed as a nondrafted free agent out of Northwestern Ohio in 2012, he zoomed through three levels in 2013 with mature command of three pitches and enough velocity to excel. The angular righty with an easy, repeatable delivery touched 91 mph in college. A move to relief untapped some additional speed—up to 94 mph—and he maintained it with a move back to the rotation. Petrick's sinking fastball sets up his slider and an above-average changeup. His command, based on reliable mechanics, is keen. He had more strikeouts (122) in 113 innings in 2013 than hits and walks combined (116). Petrick might receive an invitation to major league camp and exposure to the coaches there before returning to his audition for the Triple-A Memphis rotation.

Year	Club (League)	Class	W	L	ERA	G	GS	CG	SV	IP	H	HR	BB	SO	K/9	WHIP	AVG
2012	Johnson City (APP)	R	5	0	2.17	13	7	0	0	46	33	2	9	50	9.9	0.92	.195
2013	Peoria (MWL)	LoA	1	0	0.83	16	0	0	7	33	24	1	8	46	12.7	0.98	.200
	Palm Beach (FSL)	HiA	3	0	0.27	9	4	0	1	33	21	0	4	32	8.6	0.75	.176
	Springfield (TL)	AA	3	3	3.99	9	9	0	0	47	44	3	15	44	8.4	1.25	.247
Minor League Totals			12	3	2.04	47	20	0	8	159	122	6	36	172	9.7	0.99	.208

16 MIKE O'NEILL, OF

BA GRADE
45
MEDIUM

Born: Feb. 12, 1988. **B-T:** L-L. **Ht.:** 5-9. **Wt.:** 170. **Drafted:** Southern California, 2010 (31st round). **Signed by:** Jamal Strong.

A fourth outfielder in the making, O'Neill is an on-base monster who has mastered the crafty art of working a walk. He led the minors with a .458 OBP in 2012, led the minors with a 2.4 BB/SO ratio in 2013 and sports a career OBP of .435 through four seasons. He hit .320 at Double-A Springfield in 2013 to finish second in the Texas League in batting. In a 32-game exposure to Triple-A Memphis, O'Neill continued to have a better feel for the strike zone than anyone other than the umpire, walking his way to a .402 OBP. Signed for $1,000 as a 31st-round senior pick in 2010, O'Neill embraces the role of table-setter and is eager to test his eye at the big league level. He has built a lefthanded swing for contact and average, not for power. That lack of pop makes him a tough fit for an everyday role. But sharp, fundamental instincts in the field, average speed and a fringy arm have allowed him to play all three spots in the outfield. Scouts laud his energy but acknowledge his unique profile. O'Neill earned a spot on the 40-man roster in the offseason and has positioned himself for a chance to be an extra outfielder when the Cardinals inevitably call on the minors for depth.

Year	Club (League)	Class	AVG	G	AB	R	H	2B	3B	HR	RBI	BB	SO	SB	CS	OBP	SLG
2010	Batavia (NYP)	SS	.283	40	92	23	26	5	2	0	9	18	13	5	1	.393	.380
2011	Batavia (NYP)	SS	.290	25	93	18	27	9	0	1	8	22	10	3	1	.432	.419
	Quad Cities (MWL)	LoA	.338	25	80	15	27	8	0	0	10	13	13	1	0	.430	.438
2012	Palm Beach (FSL)	HiA	.342	108	386	56	132	19	5	0	35	70	24	12	10	.442	.417
	Springfield (TL)	AA	.563	13	32	8	18	5	0	0	5	8	2	3	0	.643	.719
2013	Springfield (TL)	AA	.320	98	359	66	115	13	2	2	35	71	26	18	4	.431	.384
	Memphis (PCL)	AAA	.295	32	112	16	33	3	0	0	3	20	11	1	0	.402	.321
Minor League Totals			.328	341	1154	202	378	62	9	3	105	222	99	43	16	.435	.405

17 TYRELL JENKINS, RHP

BA GRADE 55 EXTREME

Born: July 20, 1992. **B-T:** R-R. **Ht.:** 6-4. **Wt.:** 200. **Drafted:** HS—Henderson, Texas, 2010 (1st round supplemental). **Signed by:** Ralph Garr Jr.

What set up to be the season the hyper-athletic Jenkins would affirm his prospect status became corrupted by an injury that had slowed him for several years. Jenkins surrendered to shoulder surgery in August 2013 to patch the latissimus muscle in his right (throwing) shoulder. The Cardinals expect recovery from the injury to take at least six months, but the result of the repair and the rehab should be an end to the shoulder discomfort that nagged at the talented righty. Jenkins has been limited to less than 85 innings in each of his first three full pro seasons, and each of the past two seasons have ended with a shoulder injury. The abbreviated seasons have given a staccato feel to his development since signing for $1.3 million with the Cardinals in 2010 and leaving behind a football scholarship to Baylor. The soreness in his shoulder could be a reason for inconsistent mechanics that hampered his control. When healthy, Jenkins showed a 93-96 mph fastball and can touch higher registers. His curveball has improved with more velocity, and he had gained movement on his fastball. The Cardinals knew they would have to be patient with Jenkins. He has the frame, power, and raw athleticism of a top-shelf starting pitcher. Once he finally has health, he may connect it all at high Class A Palm Beach.

Year	Club (League)	Class	W	L	ERA	G	GS	CG	SV	IP	H	HR	BB	SO	K/9	WHIP	AVG
2010	Johnson City (APP)	R	0	0	0.00	2	2	0	0	3	2	0	2	2	6.0	1.33	.200
2011	Johnson City (APP)	R	4	2	3.86	11	11	0	0	56	63	3	13	55	8.8	1.36	.296
2012	Quad Cities (MWL)	LoA	4	4	5.14	19	19	0	0	82	84	5	36	80	8.7	1.46	.267
2013	Peoria (MWL)	LoA	4	4	4.74	10	10	2	0	49	51	4	24	34	6.2	1.52	.267
	Palm Beach (FSL)	HiA	0	0	4.50	3	3	0	0	10	13	0	1	6	5.4	1.40	.310
Minor League Totals			12	10	4.57	45	45	2	0	201	213	12	76	177	7.9	1.44	.276

18 KENNY PEOPLES-WALLS, SS/OF

BA GRADE 50 EXTREME

Born: Aug. 16, 1993. **B-T:** R-R. **Ht.:** 6-1. **Wt.:** 180. **Drafted:** HS—Los Angeles, 2011 (4th round). **Signed by:** Jamal Strong.

The electric athleticism that first drew Cardinals scouts to Peoples-Walls when he was a Los Angeles-area youth started to translate into production with Rookie-level Johnson City in 2013. One of the Appalachian League's top athletes, Peoples-Walls finished in the top 10 in average (.300), slugging (.468) and OPS (.820). The righthanded hitter connects with authority but had some stretches where his swing lengthened and his strikeout rate soared. He has worked to achieve better balance, a more level swing and to do so without limiting any power potential. Peoples-Walls doesn't project to hit many home runs but should have solid gap power. He played shortstop through the season until a change during instructional league, when the Cardinals shifted him to center field. His arm plays there, and given experience his strides and speed should excel at the free-range position. He'll have to prove his offensive upswing will continue at a rate that meets the higher demands of the new position. He'll vie in the spring for a chance to play center field for a full-season club.

Year	Club (League)	Class	AVG	G	AB	R	H	2B	3B	HR	RBI	BB	SO	SB	CS	OBP	SLG
2011	Cardinals (GCL)	R	.239	28	88	8	21	1	0	0	7	9	24	4	4	.313	.250
2012	Cardinals (GCL)	R	.260	43	150	19	39	4	3	2	21	7	35	4	5	.317	.367
2013	Johnson City (APP)	R	.300	59	237	41	71	11	4	7	35	15	73	9	3	.352	.468
Minor League Totals			.276	130	475	68	131	16	7	9	63	31	132	17	12	.333	.396

19 OSCAR MERCADO, SS

BA GRADE 50 EXTREME

Born: Dec. 16, 1994. **B-T:** R-R. **Ht.:** 6-2. **Wt.:** 175. **Drafted:** HS—Tampa, 2013 (2nd round). **Signed by:** Charlie Gonzalez.

Less than a decade after his family left Colombia to move to the U.S., Mercado had established himself as the finest-fielding high school shortstop available in the draft. Six years after moving from his homeland at 8, he had become the starter at Tampa's Gaither High. He was considered one of the few surefire shortstops in the 2013 draft class, one with the defensive agility and plus arm strength to remain at the position while the Cardinals work on the bat. Mercado hit .370 as a junior at Gaither but struggled in his senior year as draft hype took hold. He had a .286 average with just five extra-base hits all season. His commitment to Florida State further clouded his signability. The Cardinals went above slot ($1.5 million) based on their need for the position and his potential. A disconnect exists between Mercado's results and his approach. He has a sound right-handed swing, level control of the bat, and the backspin for gap power. However, he hit just .209 in an extended look in the Rookie-level Gulf Coast League. He is an average runner, but his astute baseball savvy makes him a standout baserunner who stole 12 bases in his debut. Mercado is a project for extended spring training who could play his way to a full-season appearance at some point in 2014.

Year	Club (League)	Class	AVG	G	AB	R	H	2B	3B	HR	RBI	BB	SO	SB	CS	OBP	SLG
2013	Cardinals (GCL)	R	.209	42	163	18	34	5	4	1	14	17	39	12	4	.290	.307
Minor League Totals			.209	42	163	18	34	5	4	1	14	17	39	12	4	.290	.307

20 JUAN HERRERA, SS

BA GRADE **45** HIGH

Born: June 28, 1993. **B-T:** R-R. **Ht.:** 5-11. **Wt.:** 165. **Signed:** Dominican Republic, 2010. **Signed by:** Ramon Pena/Claudio Brito (Indians).

The Cardinals' search for a shortstop extended far beyond the major league level. They traded two big leaguers in 12 months for shortstops, drafted six shortstops in the first 20 picks of the 2013 draft and went the trade route. Herrera made the best first impression among the imports. Acquired from the Indians at the 2013 trade deadline in exchange for lefty Marc Rzepczynski, Herrera had been overshadowed in the Cleveland system but blossomed with a quick promotion from the Cardinals. He has a career .370 on-base percentage and had flashes of reliable offense at low Class A Peoria. He doesn't hit for power and will have to continue to find ways to get on base, and his swing can get big, but he has shown some bat speed and feel for the barrel. A scout called Herrera one of the best pure shortstop prospects in the short-season New York-Penn League, citing sure hands and body control, and the Cardinals believe his footwork, arm strength and feel for fielding are a good fit for the position. Upon joining the organization, he immediately challenged for the title of top fielding prospect at shortstop. Herrera has a chance to jump to high Class A Palm Beach for 2014.

Year	Club (League)	Class	AVG	G	AB	R	H	2B	3B	HR	RBI	BB	SO	SB	CS	OBP	SLG
2011	Indians (DSL)	R	.297	58	192	30	57	11	2	1	20	22	27	7	5	.384	.391
2012	Indians (AZL)	R	.283	39	138	28	39	11	2	0	15	26	35	8	2	.395	.391
2013	Mahoning Valley (NYP)	SS	.275	39	149	20	41	9	1	1	11	16	30	2	1	.366	.369
	State College (NYP)	SS	.067	4	15	1	1	0	0	0	0	2	1	0	0	.176	.067
	Peoria (MWL)	LoA	.271	23	85	5	23	4	0	0	3	7	22	2	0	.333	.318
Minor League Totals			.278	163	579	84	161	35	5	2	49	73	115	19	8	.370	.366

21 KEITH BUTLER, RHP

BA GRADE **40** LOW

Born: Jan. 30, 1989. **B-T:** R-R. **Ht.:** 6-0. **Wt.:** 170. **Drafted:** Wabash Valley (Ill.) CC, 2009 (24th round). **Signed by:** Rob Fidler.

Part of the parade of rookies who made their debuts in 2013 with the Cardinals, Butler showed in the majors what he has in the minors: stinginess with hits coupled with a need for better command to be successful. Another one of the Cardinals' late-round, small-college picks to reach the majors, Butler has a breaking ball that some call a slider, others say is a curve and sometimes acts as a slurve. He can throw it at different paces, from a Frisbee pitch with horizontal break to a harder-biting variety. In 20 big league innings, Butler averaged 74 mph on his curve, featured an improved changeup, and still sat at 91 mph with a lively fastball. In five pro seasons, opponents are hitting .201 against him, but his walk rate (3.6 per nine innings in the minors) remains too high for more than a set-up role. Butler is not an imposing figure on the mound, but he has a quick, snappy delivery and delivers the ball from a low angle that can confound. He's positioned to compete for a spot in a crowded major league bullpen, but will likely open as a depth option assigned to Triple-A Memphis.

Year	Club (League)	Class	W	L	ERA	G	GS	CG	SV	IP	H	HR	BB	SO	K/9	WHIP	AVG
2009	Cardinals (GCL)	R	1	1	2.22	21	0	0	6	28	18	0	12	34	10.8	1.06	.182
	Johnson City (APP)	R	0	0	0.00	2	0	0	0	2	0	0	1	4	18.0	0.50	.000
2010	Batavia (NYP)	SS	0	3	2.93	27	0	0	5	31	29	1	15	50	14.7	1.43	.242
2011	Quad Cities (MWL)	LoA	0	1	1.17	12	0	0	5	15	7	0	5	16	9.4	0.78	.135
	Palm Beach (FSL)	HiA	1	0	1.25	34	0	0	12	36	19	1	18	52	13.0	1.03	.151
2012	Springfield (TL)	AA	5	1	2.76	53	0	0	25	59	53	5	23	59	9.1	1.30	.242
2013	Springfield (TL)	AA	0	0	0.66	13	0	0	7	14	8	1	2	21	13.8	0.73	.163
	St. Louis (NL)	MAJ	0	0	4.05	16	0	0	0	20	13	0	11	16	7.2	1.20	.181
	Memphis (PCL)	AAA	3	2	3.62	20	1	0	2	27	21	3	9	28	9.2	1.10	.210
Major League Totals			0	0	4.05	16	0	0	0	20	13	0	11	16	7.2	1.20	.181
Minor League Totals			10	8	2.29	182	1	0	62	212	155	11	85	264	11.2	1.13	.201

22 LEE STOPPELMAN, LHP

BA GRADE **40** LOW

Born: May 24, 1990. **B-T:** L-L. **Ht.:** 6-2. **Wt.:** 210. **Drafted:** Central Missouri, 2012 (24th round). **Signed by:** Dirk Kinney.

Stoppelman earned an invite to big league camp in 2013 and put boosted his prospect status with a strong spring. Stoppelman had the frame and handedness of another spring sensation, major league-bound Kevin Siegrist. Stoppelman doesn't have Siegrist's velocity—he's more in the low 90s, not the upper 90s—but works with a sharp breaking ball that lefties have difficulty reading and a funky delivery that adds to its deception. In his first full pro season, the 2012 24th-round pick advanced through three levels, finishing at Triple-A Memphis. In an August split between Double-A Springfield and Memphis, Stoppelman limited batters to a .140 average and logged 21 strikeouts in 14 innings. He fits the mold of the Cardinals' other late-round, small-college picks, having gone 8-0, 1.25 with 75 strikeouts and nine walks in 65 innings as a senior at Division II Central Missouri in 2012. That control has translated to relief success and a meteoric rise that will put him in the Triple-A bullpen in 2014 and on the cusp of being the first lefty promoted when needed.

Year	Club (League)	Class	W	L	ERA	G	GS	CG	SV	IP	H	HR	BB	SO	K/9	WHIP	AVG
2012	Batavia (NYP)	SS	2	1	0.79	22	0	0	7	34	23	0	7	49	12.8	0.87	.183
2013	Palm Beach (FSL)	HiA	2	1	1.50	15	0	0	0	24	16	0	10	26	9.8	1.08	.184
	Springfield (TL)	AA	3	1	1.35	37	0	0	6	40	20	3	14	50	11.3	0.85	.150
	Memphis (PCL)	AAA	1	1	4.50	3	0	0	0	2	4	0	2	2	9.0	3.00	.400
Minor League Totals			8	4	1.26	77	0	0	13	100	63	3	33	127	11.4	0.96	.177

23 TOMMY PHAM, OF

Born: March 8, 1988. **B-T:** R-R. **Ht.:** 6-1. **Wt.:** 185. **Drafted:** HS—Las Vegas, 2006 (16th round). **Signed by:** Manny Guerra.

A collection of desirable tools, Pham hasn't had any trouble sending off sparks of potential every time he's on the field. It's just getting on the field that has been difficult. He has the arm and range for center field, the speed to steal bases and occasional bursts of hitting ability. The skill he hasn't shown is health. In his pro career, Pham has missed time with a wrist injury, several shoulder maladies and the eye disorder keratoconus that requires him to wear special contacts to correct his vision. He had shoulder surgery to end his 2013 season just as he surged toward September callup consideration. Originally a shortstop with an untamed arm, Pham has found center to be a better fit for his live-wire athleticism. He finally earned a promotion to Triple-A Memphis in 2013 with a .301/.388/.521 turn at Double-A Springfield, his fourth season there, and he clobbered lefties for a .328/.392/.522 line. He avoided free agency by signing a two-year deal with the Cardinals for 2013 and 2014. Injuries have kept him in the organization even though he has been exposed to the Rule 5 draft. But injuries have also kept him from securing his place in the Triple-A outfield, until now.

Year	Club (League)	Class	AVG	G	AB	R	H	2B	3B	HR	RBI	BB	SO	SB	CS	OBP	SLG
2006	Johnson City (APP)	R	.231	54	182	26	42	8	3	1	19	26	42	12	3	.340	.324
2007	Quad Cities (MWL)	LoA	.063	14	32	3	2	0	0	0	1	3	9	3	0	.189	.063
	Batavia (NYP)	SS	.205	67	239	33	49	8	5	2	16	25	60	14	6	.283	.305
2008	Palm Beach (FSL)	HiA	.146	27	82	9	12	3	0	1	7	7	30	1	1	.222	.220
	Quad Cities (MWL)	LoA	.218	86	312	51	68	11	4	17	49	27	126	17	4	.285	.442
2009	Palm Beach (FSL)	HiA	.232	114	336	47	78	15	5	8	44	36	102	18	6	.313	.378
2010	Palm Beach (FSL)	HiA	.262	68	237	42	62	14	4	3	27	42	59	13	4	.377	.392
	Springfield (TL)	AA	.339	38	121	19	41	13	1	3	18	18	28	4	2	.429	.537
2011	Springfield (TL)	AA	.294	40	143	31	42	11	3	5	16	18	40	3	3	.372	.517
2012	Springfield (TL)	AA	.154	12	39	3	6	2	0	1	3	4	19	0	0	.233	.282
2013	Springfield (TL)	AA	.301	45	163	27	49	6	6	6	28	20	42	6	3	.388	.521
	Memphis (PCL)	AAA	.264	30	106	6	28	6	1	1	13	7	25	2	1	.310	.368
Minor League Totals			.240	595	1992	297	479	97	32	48	241	233	582	93	33	.326	.394

24 C.J. McELROY, OF

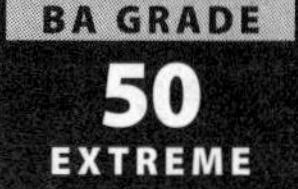

Born: May 29, 1993. **B-T:** R-R. **Ht.:** 5-10. **Wt.:** 180. **Drafted:** HS—League City, Texas, 2011 (3rd round). **Signed by:** Ralph Garr Jr.

The speedy McElroy began the 2013 season working on switch-hitting to better feature his biggest asset, but five games into his low Class A debut, McElroy injured his foot. He spent most of the next two months trying to regain health, and he had to go to instructional league in order to make up for lost at-bats. The injury interrupted what was poised to be the breakout year for McElroy. The son of former big league reliever Chuck McElroy and nephew to all-star Cecil Cooper, C.J. was two years removed from dodging a football career at the University of Houston for a $510,000 bonus to play baseball. "It's in my blood," he said. He reached the pros with 80-grade speed on the 20-80 scale. The idea to have him switch-hit was intended to get him one stride closer to first base from the left side. He had to abandon the experiment early in 2013, though the Cardinals hope he revisits it. With little power, McElroy has to focus on walks, gap power and baserunning. He's got the goods to be a basestealer and has improved his instincts. Back up to speed this spring, McElroy will compete for a starting center field job at high Class A Palm Beach.

Year	Club (League)	Class	AVG	G	AB	R	H	2B	3B	HR	RBI	BB	SO	SB	CS	OBP	SLG
2011	Cardinals (GCL)	R	.228	23	79	10	18	2	1	0	7	7	15	8	2	.303	.278
2012	Johnson City (APP)	R	.271	61	247	40	67	11	2	0	22	15	42	24	5	.314	.332
2013	Cardinals (GCL)	R	.300	3	10	0	3	1	0	0	0	0	2	1	1	.364	.400
	Peoria (MWL)	LoA	.240	58	242	24	58	9	3	0	23	17	40	8	8	.288	.302
Minor League Totals			.253	145	578	74	146	23	6	0	52	39	99	41	16	.303	.313

25 EDMUNDO SOSA, SS

BA GRADE
50
EXTREME

Born: March 6, 1996. **B-T:** R-R. **Ht.:** 5-11. **Wt.:** 170. **Signed:** Panama, 2012. **Signed by:** Arquimedes Nieto.

On the first day they could sign international amateur free agents in 2012, the Cardinals announced a pact with a 16-year-old Sosa. He received a $425,000 bonus, the largest for a Panamanian that year, and he was described as the best true shortstop available in his age bracket. In his 2013 pro debut, Sosa didn't disappoint. He led all Dominican Summer League shortstops with an .846 OPS. On raw ability, he hit beyond the level. Sosa has a frenetic style of fielding that is part athleticism, part improvisation. His fringe arm strength has some evaluators believing he's a better fit for second base, but he's too young to pigeonhole before he gains strength with age. Sosa is in the larval stage as a prospect and that comes with all the caveats of youth. He fits behind Oscar Mercado on the depth chart but shares a lot of the same traits. The sign of his place in the organization wasn't just his numbers but the Cardinals' reaction. They invited Sosa to instructional league to get a head start on the domestic assignment that could be a revealing test in 2014.

Year	Club (League)	Class	AVG	G	AB	R	H	2B	3B	HR	RBI	BB	SO	SB	CS	OBP	SLG
2013	Cardinals (DSL)	R	.314	47	169	33	53	8	3	3	27	22	15	7	5	.396	.450
Minor League Totals			.314	47	169	33	53	8	3	3	27	22	15	7	5	.396	.450

26 BOONE WHITING, RHP

BA GRADE **40** MEDIUM

Born: Aug. 20, 1989. **B-T:** R-R. **Ht.:** 6-1. **Wt.:** 175. **Drafted:** Centenary, 2010 (18th round). **Signed by:** Matt Blood.

The steady, innings-eating Whiting is a pitcher out of his time. Less than a decade ago, before teams favored power to the exclusion of pitchability, the righthander would have ranked among the best in the Cardinals organization. Whiting made 27 starts in 2013, logged a team-high 21 at Triple-A Memphis, and averaged five innings per start. He had nine quality starts, seven at Triple-A. The workload helped answer questions of shoulder durability. Whiting pitches taller than his 6-foot-1 height and creates deception with a high arm slot. He's a detail-oriented pitcher, maximizing his ability and command with precise delivery. Whiting throws a fringe-average fastball that sits between 89-91 mph, and he builds off a quality sinker and a solid changeup. He's able to exploit the mix against both lefties and righties and for telling swings and misses. He misses bats despite fringy stuff and continues to average more than four strikeouts for every walk thanks to solid command. The Cardinals left Whiting unprotected in the Rule 5 draft despite four open spots on the 40-man roster, and he's ticketed to return to the Triple-A rotation.

Year	Club (League)	Class	W	L	ERA	G	GS	CG	SV	IP	H	HR	BB	SO	K/9	WHIP	AVG
2010	Johnson City (APP)	R	5	3	3.50	13	9	0	0	54	54	6	5	68	11.3	1.09	.250
2011	Quad Cities (MWL)	LoA	5	2	2.41	30	14	0	4	120	82	8	24	122	9.2	0.89	.191
2012	Cardinals (GCL)	R	0	0	7.71	4	1	0	0	7	10	1	1	11	14.1	1.57	.323
	Quad Cities (MWL)	LoA	1	0	0.56	3	3	0	0	16	7	0	1	14	7.9	0.50	.130
	Springfield (TL)	AA	0	0	1.50	2	2	0	0	12	11	0	3	9	6.8	1.17	.268
2013	Springfield (TL)	AA	3	2	2.93	6	6	0	0	31	28	2	7	34	10.0	1.14	.237
	Memphis (PCL)	AAA	5	5	4.09	21	21	1	0	106	107	11	40	99	8.4	1.39	.261
Minor League Totals			19	12	3.13	79	56	1	4	345	299	28	81	357	9.3	1.10	.230

27 JOHN GAST, LHP

BA GRADE **45** HIGH

Born: Feb. 16, 1989. **B-T:** L-L. **Ht.:** 6-1. **Wt.:** 195. **Drafted:** Florida State, 2010 (6th round). **Signed by:** Mike Elias.

When the Cardinals needed a starter because of an injury, it wasn't Michael Wacha who got the first call or even Carlos Martinez or Tyler Lyons. Crafty lefty Gast did. The Florida State alum had a 1.16 ERA and 35 strikeouts in his first 39 innings (seven starts) at Triple-A Memphis, and he brought that changeup-based success with him to the majors. He also brought his tricky shoulder. Gast got through two games without incident, both wins, and then couldn't throw a second inning in his third start because of shoulder soreness he didn't tell the team about. The shoulder troubles that put him on the disabled list in 2012 also ended his 2013, and they could erase his 2014. Gast had surgery in July to have a muscle in his left shoulder reattached after it had torn loose. Understandably, his recovery could take a full year. At his best, Gast has a deceptive, slinging delivery that contributes to the organization's best pickoff and improves his stuff. He further challenges hitters with changes in speeds, averaging 10 mph difference between his 88-91 mph sinking fastball and changeup, and another 6-10 mph on his work-in-progress curve. He'll spend most of 2014 rehabbing.

Year	Club (League)	Class	W	L	ERA	G	GS	CG	SV	IP	H	HR	BB	SO	K/9	WHIP	AVG
2010	Batavia (NYP)	SS	6	0	1.54	8	6	0	0	35	27	1	8	36	9.3	1.00	.227
2011	Palm Beach (FSL)	HiA	5	4	3.95	13	12	1	0	82	85	7	28	59	6.5	1.38	.272
	Springfield (TL)	AA	4	4	4.08	13	13	1	0	79	80	9	33	54	6.1	1.42	.266
2012	Springfield (TL)	AA	4	2	1.93	8	8	0	0	51	38	5	13	41	7.2	0.99	.211
	Memphis (PCL)	AAA	9	5	5.10	20	20	0	0	109	124	10	42	86	7.1	1.52	.286
2013	Memphis (PCL)	AAA	3	1	1.16	7	7	0	0	39	28	0	13	35	8.1	1.06	.214
	St. Louis (NL)	MAJ	2	0	5.11	3	3	0	0	12	11	1	5	8	5.8	1.30	.234
Major League Totals			2	0	5.11	3	3	0	0	12	11	1	5	8	5.8	1.30	.234
Minor League Totals			31	16	3.55	69	66	2	0	396	382	32	137	311	7.1	1.31	.259

28 STEVE BEAN, C

Born: Sept. 15, 1993. **B-T:** L-R. **Ht.:** 6-2. **Wt.:** 190. **Drafted:** HS—Rockwall, Texas, 2012 (1st round supplemental). **Signed by:** Aaron Looper.

Though the Cardinals' attempt to push him up a level early may have contributed to a sink in offense, Bean remained the organization's top defensive catcher, a complete-package prospect behind the plate. St. Louis selected Bean 66th overall in 2012 and lured him away from a committee to Texas with a $700,000 bonus. He hit .125/.263/.213 when pressed to Rookie-level Johnson City for a debut, so while he didn't hit great in his return, he did improve, taming some of the movement at the plate to help steady his lefthanded swing. He projects for more power as he gains strength with age. Bean's arm grades as a 65 on the 20-80 scale, and he has above-average accuracy on his throws and a quick transfer after receiving the pitch. He's thrown out 41 percent of basestealers at Johnson City in two seasons. He plays with more athleticism and energy than most catchers, and has merged his nimbleness with fundamentals. He'll get some tutelage in spring training and is earmarked for another push, his full-season debut at low Class A Peoria in 2014. He's talented enough behind the plate to advance while he works at becoming more potent at the plate.

Year	Club (League)	Class	AVG	G	AB	R	H	2B	3B	HR	RBI	BB	SO	SB	CS	OBP	SLG
2012	Johnson City (APP)	R	.125	24	80	6	10	4	0	1	5	15	32	2	0	.263	.213
	Cardinals (GCL)	R	.320	15	50	8	16	4	0	0	7	8	11	0	0	.424	.400
2013	Johnson City (APP)	R	.229	32	118	15	27	4	0	2	14	11	44	0	0	.303	.314
Minor League Totals			.214	71	248	29	53	12	0	3	26	34	87	2	0	.315	.298

29 JACOB WILSON, 2B

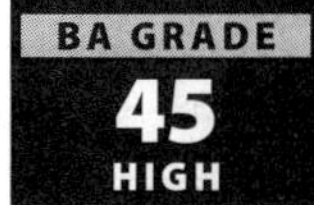

Born: July 29, 1990. **B-T:** R-R. **Ht.:** 5-11. **Wt.:** 180. **Drafted:** Memphis, 2012 (10th round). **Signed by:** Jay Catalano

The Conference USA Player of the Year in 2012, Wilson had the trappings for college hitters the Cardinals like: His offensive production satisfied the analytics, his approach assured the scouts, and his athleticism said that because he could hit they'd eventually find him a position. Like Allen Craig and Matt Carpenter—also seniors when drafted—Wilson entered pro ball with little leverage and less fanfare, signing for $125,00. His breakout came in 2013. Showing plus power for his position with 18 homers and 47 extra-base hits at two levels, Wilson has a swing for damage while controlling the strike zone. A college third baseman, Wilson took his arm strength and below-average speed and relocated to second base, where his footwork and range could improve to average with work. His bat earned him an invite to the Arizona Fall League, where he worked at second and in spot duty hit (.304/.373/.413). He should reach Double-A in 2014, which will test his bat.

Year	Club (League)	Class	AVG	G	AB	R	H	2B	3B	HR	RBI	BB	SO	SB	CS	OBP	SLG
2012	Batavia (NYP)	SS	.275	46	160	28	44	7	1	6	25	13	33	2	1	.341	.444
2013	Peoria (MWL)	LoA	.264	97	348	63	92	24	1	15	72	40	54	6	5	.350	.468
	Palm Beach (FSL)	HiA	.179	32	117	12	21	4	0	3	10	17	20	0	1	.294	.291
Minor League Totals			.251	175	625	103	157	35	2	24	107	70	107	8	7	.337	.429

30 XAVIER SCRUGGS, 1B

BA GRADE
45
EXTREME

Born: Sept. 23, 1987. **B-T:** R-R. **Ht.:** 6-1. **Wt.:** 210. **Drafted:** Nevada-Las Vegas, 2008 (19th round). **Signed by:** Aaron Krawiec.

Throughout his minor league career, Scruggs has provided a commodity that is always in high demand: big-time power. He slugged 29 home runs at Double-A Springfield in 2013—a total last seen there from Matt Adams and Colby Rasmus, though both hit lefthanded. Scruggs did his damage at age 25, and the Cardinals opted to go with journeyman Brock Peterson at first base in Triple-A Memphis rather than promote Scruggs. The gregarious "X-Man" has hit at least 20 home runs in three consecutive seasons. He has the high strikeout rates to go with the power and a three-true-outcome approach: 52.6 percent of his plate appearances end with a walk, a strikeout or a homer. His increased selectivity in 2013 (a career-high 81 walks) helped lessen the swings of his signature streakiness. He has that strong base and uppercut swing that launches mistakes. The Cardinals have thrice left him unprotected in the Rule 5 draft, and he's due to test his power at Triple-A in 2014.

Year	Club (League)	Class	AVG	G	AB	R	H	2B	3B	HR	RBI	BB	SO	SB	CS	OBP	SLG
2008	Batavia (NYP)	SS	.219	61	215	23	47	17	0	6	33	19	68	0	1	.295	.381
2009	Batavia (NYP)	SS	.234	41	145	21	34	7	0	7	26	21	48	1	1	.345	.428
	Quad Cities (MWL)	LoA	.295	34	129	17	38	7	1	7	33	23	43	2	1	.409	.527
2010	Palm Beach (FSL)	HiA	.269	87	316	42	85	18	1	13	53	30	107	3	0	.345	.456
	Springfield (TL)	AA	.245	33	110	16	27	6	0	8	21	10	36	0	0	.320	.518
2011	Palm Beach (FSL)	HiA	.260	117	411	57	107	27	3	21	63	40	125	4	1	.340	.494
2012	Springfield (TL)	AA	.235	130	452	64	106	26	1	22	91	58	150	8	4	.331	.442
2013	Springfield (TL)	AA	.248	133	448	67	111	18	1	29	81	82	177	11	7	.376	.487
Minor League Totals			.249	636	2226	307	555	126	7	113	401	283	754	29	15	.346	.465

San Diego Padres

BY MATT EDDY

The Padres played their best baseball in May and June, going 30-26 and pulling to within two games of the National League West leaders on June 20. From that point, however, a slow slide to irrelevance, a second straight 86-loss season and a fifth losing year out of the last six left the organization with more questions than answers.

What if three-fifths of the projected rotation—lefthander Cory Luebke and righties Casey Kelly and Joe Wieland—hadn't been sidelined all season while recovering from Tommy John surgery? The loss of Kelly in spring training hurt most, as he'd pitched well enough when healthy to earn a 2012 September callup and enter 2013 as the system's top prospect.

What if sophomore first baseman Yonder Alonso, center fielder Cameron Maybin and left fielder Carlos Quentin had not been hobbled by injuries?

What if the season had not been bookended by 50-game suspensions to starting catcher Yasmani Grandal and starting shortstop Everth Cabrera? Both received their penalties for their involvement with the Biogenesis clinic, which supplied performance-enhancers to at least 17 players.

Grandal returned to action in late May and hit .266/.402/.422 in 81 plate appearances in June before a gruesome collision at home plate on July 6 knocked him out for the season. He had reconstructive surgery to repair a torn anterior cruciate ligament in his right knee and could miss the first half of 2014.

Amid the chaos, two young Padres stepped up. Jedd Gyorko, a 25-year-old rookie, held down second base after playing a total of 51 games there in three minor league seasons. He became just the fifth rookie keystone sacker in history to hit 20 home runs, joining the likes of Dan Uggla (2006), Alexei Ramirez (2008) and Danny Espinosa (2011).

Righthander Andrew Cashner missed a large chunk of 2012 with a lat muscle strain, but the 27-year-old shined in 2013, his second season with the Padres after coming over in the deal that sent first baseman Anthony Rizzo to the Cubs. Cashner, whose average fastball velocity of 94.6 mph trailed just three other ERA qualifiers, put an exclamation point on his best season by one-hitting the Pirates on Sept. 27. Overall he went 10-9, 3.09 in 31 appearances while notching 6.6 strikeouts per nine innings and a 1.13 WHIP.

Down on the farm, the Padres have one of the top catching prospects in the game (Austin Hedges), one of the top lefthanders (Max Fried) and one of the most unheralded righties (Matt Wisler). Hedges and Wisler lead the next wave of talent headed for San Diego after helping push Double-A San Antonio to the Texas League title. The Missions have won the TL three times in seven seasons as a Padres affiliate, including two out of the last three years.

The system doesn't feature as much upper-level depth as it did two years ago, when Alonso, lefty Robbie Erlin, Grandal, Gyorko and Rizzo all qualified for this list. All but Gyorko had been acquired in a trio of trades in which the Padres parted with veterans Mike Adams, Adrian Gonzalez and Mat Latos. San Diego also acquired prospects Kelly, Reymond Fuentes and Wieland in those deals, but the bulk of the Top 30 consists of players signed by the Padres.

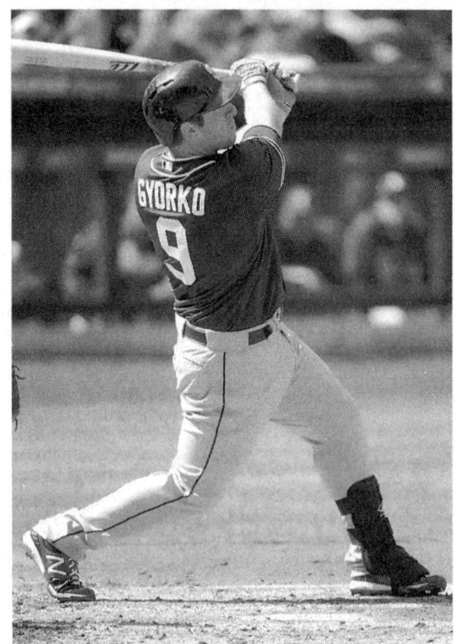

TOMASSO DeROSA

Jedd Gyorko became the fifth rookie second basemen in history to top 20 home runs

TOP PROSPECTS OF THE DECADE

Year	Player, Pos.	2013 Org.
2004	Josh Barfield, 2b	Out of baseball
2005	Josh Barfield, 2b	Out of baseball
2006	Cesar Carrillo, rhp	Tigers
2007	Cedric Hunter, of	Indians
2008	Chase Headley, 3b	Padres
2009	Kyle Blanks, 1b	Padres
2010	Donavan Tate, of	Padres
2011	Casey Kelly, rhp	Padres
2012	Anthony Rizzo, 1b	Cubs
2013	Casey Kelly, rhp	Padres

ORGANIZATION OVERVIEW

General Manager: Josh Byrnes. **Farm Director:** Randy Smith. **Scouting Director:** Billy Gasparino.

Class	Team	League	W	L	PCT	Finish	Manager
Majors	San Diego Padres	National	76	86	.469	8th (15)	Bud Black
Triple-A	*Tucson Padres	Pacific Coast	77	67	.535	5th (16)	Pat Murphy
Double-A	San Antonio Missions	Texas League	78	61	.561	2nd (8)	Rich Dauer
High Class A	Lake Elsinore Storm	California	61	79	.436	9th (10)	Shawn Wooten
Low Class A	Fort Wayne Tincaps	Midwest	72	69	.511	6th (16)	Jose Valentin
Short-season	Eugene Emeralds	Northwest	27	49	.365	8th (8)	Jim Gabella
Rookie	AZL Padres	Arizona	28	26	.519	5th (13)	Michael Collins
Overall 2013 Minor League Record			**343**	**349**	**.436**	**16th (30)**	

*Franchise moves to El Paso (Pacific Coast) in 2014

THIS YEAR'S TOP 30

No.	Player, Pos.	Grade/Risk
1.	Austin Hedges, c	60/Medium
2.	Matt Wisler, rhp	60/Medium
3.	Max Fried, lhp	60/High
4.	Hunter Renfroe, of	60/High
5.	Casey Kelly, rhp	55/High
6.	Rymer Liriano, of	50/Medium
7.	Jace Peterson, ss	50/Medium
8.	Burch Smith, rhp	50/High
9.	Keyvius Sampson, rhp	50/High
10.	Joe Ross, rhp	50/High
11.	Cory Spangenberg, 2b	50/High
12.	Franchy Cordero, ss	55/Extreme
13.	Joe Wieland, rhp	50/High
14.	Zach Eflin, rhp	50/High
15.	Matt Andriese, rhp	50/High
16.	Gabriel Quintana, 3b	50/High
17.	Travis Jankowski, of	50/High
18.	Juan Oramas, lhp	50/High
19.	Walker Weickel, rhp	50/High
20.	Reymond Fuentes, of	45/Medium
21.	Leonel Campos, rhp	50/High
22.	Dustin Peterson, 3b	50/High
23.	Tommy Medica, 1b	45/Medium
24.	Yeison Asencio, of	45/Medium
25.	Alex Dickerson, of/1b	45/Medium
26.	Donn Roach, rhp	45/High
27.	Kevin Quackenbush, rhp	45/High
28.	Adys Portillo, rhp	45/High
29.	Jose Urena, of	50/Extreme
30.	Johnny Barbato, rhp	45/High

LAST YEAR'S TOP 30

No.	Player, Pos.	Status
1.	Casey Kelly, rhp	No. 5
2.	Max Fried, lhp	No. 3
3.	Jedd Gyorko, 3b/2b	Majors
4.	Austin Hedges, c	No. 1
5.	Rymer Liriano, of	No. 6
6.	Matt Wisler, rhp	No. 2
7.	Cory Spangenberg, 2b	No. 11
8.	Joe Wieland, rhp	No. 13
9.	Adys Portillo, rhp	No. 28
10.	Robbie Erlin, lhp	Majors
11.	Jace Peterson, ss	No. 7
12.	Walker Weickel, rhp	No. 19
13.	Keyvius Sampson, rhp	No. 9
14.	Joe Ross, rhp	No. 10
15.	Brad Boxberger, rhp	Majors
16.	Zach Eflin, rhp	No. 14
17.	Fernando Perez, 3b	Dropped out
18.	James Darnell, 3b/of	(Released)
19.	Donn Roach, rhp	No. 26
20.	Matt Andriese, rhp	No. 15
21.	Travis Jankowski, of	No. 17
22.	Burch Smith, rhp	No. 8
23.	Jaff Decker, of	(Pirates)
24.	Yeison Asencio, of	No. 24
25.	Miles Mikolas, rhp	(Pirates)
26.	Juan Oramas, lhp	No. 18
27.	Matt Stites, rhp	(Diamondbacks)
28.	Mallex Smith, of	Dropped out
29.	Kevin Quackenbush, rhp	No. 27
30.	Johnny Barbato, rhp	No. 30

BEST TOOLS

Best Hitter for Average	Jace Peterson
Best Power Hitter	Hunter Renfroe
Best Strike-Zone Discipline	Jace Peterson
Fastest Baserunner	Mallex Smith
Best Athlete	Jace Peterson
Best Fastball	Matt Wisler
Best Curveball	Max Fried
Best Slider	Leonel Campos
Best Changeup	Zach Eflin
Best Control	Matt Wisler
Best Defensive Catcher	Austin Hedges
Best Defensive Infielder	Jace Peterson
Best Infield Arm	Carlos Belen
Best Defensive Outfielder	Rico Noel
Best Outfield Arm	Yeison Asencio

TOP 15 PLAYERS 25 AND UNDER

No.	Player, Pos. (Age)	Level
1.	Austin Hedges, c (21)	Double-A
2.	Matt Wisler, rhp (21)	Double-A
3.	Max Fried, lhp (20)	Low Class A
4.	Jedd Gyorko, 2b (25)	Majors
5.	Yasmani Grandal, c (25)	Majors
6.	Hunter Renfroe, of (22)	Low Class A
7.	Casey Kelly, rhp (24)	Majors
8.	Rymer Liriano, of (22)	Double-A
9.	Jace Peterson, ss (23)	High Class A
10.	Burch Smith, rhp (23)	Majors
11.	Robbie Erlin, lhp (23)	Majors
12.	Keyvius Sampson, rhp (23)	Triple-A
13.	Joe Ross, rhp (20)	Low Class A
14.	Cory Spangenberg, 2b (23)	Double-A
15.	Joe Wieland, rhp (24)	Majors

MINOR LEAGUE DEPTH CHART

SAN DIEGO PADRES

TOP 2014 ROOKIE: Burch Smith, rhp. He took his lumps in San Diego in 2013 but has shown fine control in the minors (2.1 BB/9) and swing-and-miss stuff in the majors during September callup (31 SO in 24 IP).

BREAKOUT PROSPECT: Franchy Cordero, ss. Rare lefty-hitting Dominican infielder shows quick-twitch athleticism and strong tools across the board.

SOURCE OF TOP 30 TALENT			
Homegrown	**25**	**Acquired**	**5**
College	7	Trades	5
Junior college	1	Rule 5 draft	0
High school	9	Independent leagues	0
Nondrafted free agents	0	Free agents/waivers	0
International	8		

SLEEPER: Walker Lockett, rhp. The 2012 fourth-rounder has thrown just 21 pro innings (all in the Arizona League), but after clearing up blister problem in 2013 he showed exciting upside with plus sinker/slider mix and picturesque delivery.

LF
Jeremy Baltz
Everett Williams
Luis Domoromo
Donavan Tate

CF
Travis Jankowski (17)
Reymond Fuentes (20)
Rico Noel
Mallex Smith
Mason Smith

RF
Hunter Renfroe (4)
Rymer Liriano (6)
Yeison Asencio (24)
Jose Urena (29)

3B
Gabriel Quintana (16)
Dustin Peterson (22)
Fernando Perez
Carlos Belen

SS
Jace Peterson (7)
Franchy Cordero (12)
Stephen Carmon
Beamer Weems

2B
Cory Spangenberg (11)
Josh VanMeter
Jonathan Galvez

1B
Tommy Medica (23)
Alex Dickerson (25)
Cody Decker
Lee Orr

C
Austin Hedges (1)
Rodney Daal
Dane Phillips
Jose Ruiz

LHP

LHSP	LHRP
Max Fried (3)	Chris Rearick
Juan Oramas (18)	Frank Garces

RHP

RHSP	RHRP
Matt Wisler (2)	Leonel Campos (21)
Casey Kelly (5)	Kevin Quackenbush (27)
Burch Smith (8)	Adys Portillo (28)
Keyvius Sampson (9)	Johnny Barbato (30)
Joe Ross (10)	Matt Lollis
Joe Wieland (13)	Mike Kelly
Zach Eflin (14)	Roman Madrid
Matt Andriese (15)	
Walker Weickel (19)	
Donn Roach (26)	
Adrian De Horta	
Walker Lockett	
Justin Hancock	
Tayron Guerrero	
Matt Shepherd	

DRAFT ANALYSIS

2013 BONUSES: $6.8 MILLION

BEST PURE HITTER: 3B Dustin Peterson (2) has tremendous natural rhythm, his hands work well from his load through the hitting zone, and he's a baseball rat who loves to work on his swing.

BEST POWER HITTER: OF Hunter Renfroe (1) has well above-average raw power thanks to his tremendous strength and bat speed. The Padres hope to simplify his swing so he gets to his power more often.

FASTEST RUNNER: OF Rod Boykin (12) turns in plus-plus times from the right side of the plate.

BEST DEFENSIVE PLAYER: Boykin's speed plays in center field, where he makes it look easy. He also hit better than expected in his debut, belying his limited baseball background by hitting .279/.358/.312 with 11 stolen bases in the Rookie-level Arizona League.

BEST FASTBALL: RHP Bryan Verbitsky (3) is a 6-foot righty who was a two-way player at Hofstra. The Padres like his arm strength, with a fastball that sits at 92-93 mph, and see more velocity to come as he focuses full-time on pitching. RHP Justin Livengood (10) sits 92-94 mph in short relief bursts.

BEST SECONDARY PITCH: RHP Trevor Gott (6) throws an 80-82 mph breaking ball that has two-plane break, depth and good shape. It's a hybrid pitch that is usually described as a slurve.

BEST PRO DEBUT: Padres instructors have raved about 2B Josh VanMeter (5), and his savvy and good hands helped him hit .278/.378/.348 with nearly as many walks (24) as strikeouts (25) in the AZL. LHP Erik Schoenrock (11) went 2-3, 2.51 at short-season Eugene with 52 strikeouts and 15 walks in 57 innings.

BEST ATHLETE: OF Jordan Paroubeck (2s) has five-tool ability and athleticism. His total package resembles that of Marlins outfielder Jake Marisnick.

MOST INTRIGUING BACKGROUND: Peterson's older brother D.J. was the Mariners' first-round pick. Barry Bonds was a childhood friend of Paroubeck's father and has given Paroubeck private hitting lessons. Livengood gave up baseball for three years before walking on at UNC Wilmington and emerging as a live-armed reliever. Schoenrock's father Daron was his head coach at Memphis. RHP Max Beatty (32) overcame a bout with testicular cancer that caused him to miss the 2012 college season.

CLOSEST TO THE MAJORS: Renfroe.

BEST LATE-ROUND PICK: RHP Tony Rizzotti (25) signed for $175,000; he appeared set for much more early in the spring, when he flashed first-round stuff. At his best he pitches with a plus fastball up to 96 mph and a hard, power slider. Teams worried about his signability and his injury history.

THE ONE WHO GOT AWAY: The Padres took several highly regarded high schoolers who were tough signs, led by RHP Connor Jones (21, now at Virginia) and including C Chris Okey (31, Clemson) and LHP Garrett Williams (33, Oklahoma State).

ASSESSMENT: San Diego started with hitters with present tools then branched out, seeking upside from such players as Verbistky, VanMeter and Idaho prep slugger Mason Smith (4). Their development could determine the class' depth.

2012 BONUSES: $11.0 MILLION

The low Class A Fort Wayne rotation in 2013 featured LHP Max Fried (1) and RHPs Zach Eflin (1s) and Walker Weickel (1s), keys to this class. OFs Travis Jankowski (1s) and Mallex Smith (6) both can fly.i

GRADE: B

2011 BONUSES: $11.0 MILLION

RHP Burch Smith (14) rocketed to San Diego. RHP Matt Wisler (7) looks like a steal, while C Austin Hedges (2) and SS Jace Peterson (1s) look like future up-the-middle regulars.

GRADE: B+

2010 BONUSES: $4.3 MILLION

2B Jedd Gyorko (2) may have to carry this class, which lost unsigned RHP Karsten Whitson (1). 1B Tommy Medica (14) is the best of the rest.

GRADE: D

TOP DRAFT PICKS OF THE DECADE

Year	Player, Pos.	2013 Org
2004	Matt Bush, ss	Out of baseball
2005	Cesar Carrillo, rhp	Tigers
2006	Matt Antonelli, 3b	Indians
2007	Nick Schmidt, lhp	Rockies
2008	Allan Dykstra, 1b	Mets
2009	Donavan Tate, of	Padres
2010	*Karsten Whitson, rhp	University of Florida
2011	Cory Spangenberg, 2b	Padres
2012	Max Fried, lhp	Padres
2013	Hunter Renfroe, of	Padres

* Did not sign

LARGEST BONUSES IN CLUB HISTORY

Donavan Tate, 2009	$6,250,000
Matt Bush, 2004	$3,150,000
Austin Hedges, 2011	$3,000,000
Max Fried, 2012	$3,000,000
Joe Ross, 2011	$2,750,000

1 AUSTIN HEDGES, C

Born: Aug. 18, 1992. **B-T:** R-R. **Ht.:** 6-1. **Wt.:** 190. **Drafted:** HS—San Juan Capistrano, Calif., 2011 (2nd round). **Signed by:** Josh Emmerick.

MISSIONS
21
BA GRADE
60
MEDIUM
SCOUTING GRADES
BATTING 50
POWER 50
SPEED 40
DEFENSE 65
ARM 60

ANDREW WOOLLEY

Hedges knows how to stand out from a crowd. Southern California area scouts regarded him as one of the finest defensive catchers they had seen at the high school level, the product of six years under the wing of JSerra High coach Brett Kay, a former catcher at Cal State Fullerton and in the Mets system. The Padres nabbed Hedges with the 82nd pick (second round) in the 2011 draft and lured the strong student away from a UCLA commitment with a $3 million bonus. Evaluators have singled him out as best defensive catcher and one of the top handful of position prospects in the low Class A Midwest (2012) and high Class A California (2013) leagues in successive years. Hedges finished 2013 at Double-A San Antonio as the Missions barreled toward the Texas League title. He started eight of 10 playoff games, including two shutouts against Arkansas in the finals. He might have reached Double-A even sooner had he not missed most of May with a deep bone bruise on his left hand, the result of being hit by a pitch.

Hedges impressed the Padres by launching home runs during batting practice at Petco Park the summer after he signed. While he has strength and explosiveness to his swing, his ticket to the All-Star Game will be equal parts power and defensive prowess. Strong technique and abundant confidence are apparent in the way he sets targets for his pitchers, receives the ball and shifts his feet while blocking balls in the dirt or firing missiles to second base. He records consistent 1.8-second pop times and has thrown out more than one-third of basestealers in each of the past two seasons. His plus arm plays up due to accuracy and a quick release. Being ahead of the curve defensively has allowed Hedges to study the art of game-calling and refine his hitting technique at a stage where most catchers are grinding through fundamentals. Scouts almost uniformly view Hedges as a good bet to hit and an even better one to deliver extra-base power. He strikes the ball with a quick, balanced swing, hitting enough line drives to keep his average in the black while not striking out excessively. Hedges can pull the ball for power, but he's most effective against all pitch types when using the whole field. An energetic presence on the field, Hedges has a durable frame, though he won't beat out many infield hits with below-average speed.

The Padres have Hedges on the express train to San Diego, and when he reaches his destination they envision him as a first-division catcher who can impact the game on both sides of the ball. He made quick work of Class A, then spent his offseason in the Arizona Fall League, where he threw out 12 of 22 basestealers, and he will begin his age-21 season back at Double-A in 2014. Despite the defensive demands of his position, he may not require much more than another season of development before he's ready for the big leagues, putting him on target for a 2015 arrival.

Year	Club (League)	Class	AVG	G	AB	R	H	2B	3B	HR	RBI	BB	SO	SB	CS	OBP	SLG
2011	Padres (AZL)	R	.313	5	16	3	5	0	0	1	4	5	1	1	0	.500	.500
	Eugene (NWL)	SS	.100	4	10	0	1	1	0	0	0	2	3	0	0	.250	.200
2012	Fort Wayne (MWL)	LoA	.279	96	337	44	94	28	0	10	56	23	62	14	9	.334	.451
2013	Lake Elsinore (CAL)	HiA	.270	66	233	34	63	22	1	4	30	22	45	5	4	.343	.425
	San Antonio (TL)	AA	.224	20	67	4	15	3	0	0	8	6	9	3	1	.297	.269
Minor League Totals			.268	191	663	85	178	54	1	15	98	58	120	23	14	.337	.421

2 MATT WISLER, RHP

Born: Sept. 12, 1992. **B-T:** R-R. **Ht.:** 6-3. **Wt.:** 195. **Drafted:** HS—Bryan, Ohio, 2011 (7th round). **Signed by:** Mark Conner.

The Padres drafted five righthanders before calling Wisler's name in 2011, but the seventh-rounder has rocketed to the head of the class after forgoing an Ohio State commitment to signing for $500,000. Following a six-start tuneup at high Class A Lake Elsinore in 2013, he advanced to the Double-A San Antonio rotation and thrived as a 20-year-old, especially in the Texas League playoffs when he allowed one run in 16 innings, striking out 13. Wisler pounds both sides of the plate with a 92-93 mph heater that features plus life and solid sinking action. He can dial his fastball up to 95 mph when he needs it, though he just as effectively deploys an assortment of quality secondary pitches, including a low-80s slider that grades as plus. Just when opposing hitters begin looking for the hard stuff, Wisler will drop in an average changeup or, later in the game, a fringy mid-70s curveball. With a career walk rate of 2.3 per nine innings, he shows exceptional control for a young power pitcher, and for the second straight season he decimated righthanded batters, holding them to a .184 average and striking out one-third of them. He'll need to tighten his secondary pitches to combat lefties, who made considerably more contact while hitting .254 and slugging .421. Wisler's mental toughness, competitive streak and poise put him on the fast track, and the Padres won't back off now that he's ready for Triple-A El Paso. He has No. 2 starter upside and might be a callup candidate to San Diego in the second half of 2014.

Year	Club (League)	Class	W	L	ERA	G	GS	CG	SV	IP	H	HR	BB	SO	K/9	WHIP	AVG
2011	Padres (AZL)	R	0	0	—	1	0	0	0	0	2	0	2	0	—	—	1.000
2012	Fort Wayne (MWL)	LoA	5	4	2.53	24	23	1	0	114	95	1	28	113	8.9	1.08	.227
2013	Lake Elsinore (CAL)	HiA	2	1	2.03	6	6	0	0	31	22	1	6	28	8.1	0.90	.196
	San Antonio (TL)	AA	8	5	3.00	20	20	0	0	105	85	7	27	103	8.8	1.07	.223
Minor League Totals			15	10	2.81	51	49	1	0	250	204	9	63	244	8.8	1.07	.223

3 MAX FRIED, LHP

Born: Jan. 18, 1994. **B-T:** L-L. **Ht.:** 6-4. **Wt.:** 185. **Drafted:** HS—Studio City, Calif., 2012 (1st round). **Signed by:** Brent Mayne.

The seventh overall pick in 2012, Fried paired with fellow Harvard-Westlake School product Lucas Giolito, now the Nationals' No. 1 prospect, to become the seventh pair of high school teammates selected in the first round of the same draft. Signed for $3 million, Fried advanced to low Class A Fort Wayne in 2013 and made all 23 of his starts in a six-man rotation. His strikeout (7.6 per nine innings) and walk (4.2) rates ranked among the highest in the Midwest League for ERA qualifiers. Fried can spin a plus curveball and has two other pitches that scouts grade favorably, but what enhances his ceiling is the projection remaining in his lean 6-foot-4 frame. He fires 90-91 mph fastballs and tops out at 95 in each start—doing so from a textbook delivery and clean arm action—and scouts project a future plus fastball once he's done filling out. Fried's power curve turns the most heads for its tight rotation and top-to-bottom spin, and it was responsible for claiming the most strikeout victims. His changeup came a long way in 2013 as he began incorporating into his everyday repertoire. The Padres believe Fried's walk rate will drop once he challenges hitters more frequently in the zone. A three-pitch lefty who misses bats and has a good pickoff move, Fried will zoom through the minors if he throws more strikes. He has No. 2 starter upside, with a chance to jump quickly to Double-A San Antonio if he excels early at high Class A Lake Elsinore in 2014.

Year	Club (League)	Class	W	L	ERA	G	GS	CG	SV	IP	H	HR	BB	SO	K/9	WHIP	AVG
2012	Padres (AZL)	R	0	1	3.57	10	9	0	0	18	14	1	6	17	8.7	1.13	.215
2013	Fort Wayne (MWL)	LoA	6	7	3.49	23	23	0	0	119	107	7	56	100	7.6	1.37	.249
Minor League Totals			6	8	3.50	33	32	0	0	136	121	8	62	117	7.7	1.34	.245

4 HUNTER RENFROE, OF

BA GRADE **60** HIGH

Born: Jan. 28, 1992. **B-T:** R-R. **Ht.:** 6-1. **Wt.:** 200. **Drafted:** Mississippi State, 2013 (1st round). **Signed by:** Andrew Salvo.

A 31st-round pick by the Red Sox out of high school in 2010, Renfroe headed to Mississippi State rather than turn pro after establishing the Magnolia State's single-season prep record with 20 home runs. After two shaky years at MSU, he blossomed as a junior, tying for the Southeastern Conference lead with 16 homers while driving the Bulldogs to the College World Series finals. The Padres evaluated Renfroe as one of the top power bats available in the 2013 draft and signed him for $2.678 million after taking him 13th overall. His value will be tied to how often he unleashes his well-above-average raw power in games. He has tremendous strength and bat speed but needs to simplify his swing in order to shorten his bat path and not get under the ball so frequently. He'll also need to polish his strike-zone discipline after fanning five times as often as he walked in 2013, though he tracks the ball well out of the pitcher's hand. A plus athlete who caught and pitched in high school, Renfroe is an average runner—but plus underway—who has above-average range and instincts in the outfield. His arm compares favorably with those of Rymer Liriano and Yeison Asencio, two other strong-armed right fielders in the system. Renfroe will begin 2014 at high Class A Lake Elsinore. Scouts who like him see him as a future .270 hitter with 25-home run potential.

Year	Club (League)	Class	AVG	G	AB	R	H	2B	3B	HR	RBI	BB	SO	SB	CS	OBP	SLG
2013	Eugene (NWL)	SS	.308	25	104	20	32	9	0	4	18	5	26	2	0	.333	.510
	Fort Wayne (MWL)	LoA	.212	18	66	6	14	5	0	2	7	4	23	0	0	.268	.379
Minor League Totals			.271	43	170	26	46	14	0	6	25	9	49	2	0	.308	.459

5 CASEY KELLY, RHP

BA GRADE **55** HIGH

Born: Oct. 4, 1989. **B-T:** R-R. **Ht.:** 6-3. **Wt.:** 210. **Drafted:** HS—Sarasota, Fla., 2008 (1st round). **Signed by:** Anthony Turco (Red Sox).

Just when he appeared ready to deliver on the promise that made him the 30th overall pick by the Red Sox in 2008 and the centerpiece of the Adrian Gonzalez trade two years later, Kelly missed half the 2012 season with a strained elbow ligament and then all of 2013 after having Tommy John surgery in April. He shook a reputation for projection over production with his injury-abbreviated performance at Double-A and Triple-A in 2012, which included a 32/3 SO/BB ratio and 0.91 WHIP over 29 innings. He owed much of his enhanced strikeout rate to improved fastball location and finish on a curveball that had only teased plus in the past. Kelly wears out the bottom of the zone with a low-90s sinking fastball that features consistent armside run, and generating groundballs is one of his strong suits. Just when batters get used to seeing the fastball he mixes in a changeup, though he could improve his results by adding more separation on the pitch between either his fastball or curveball. An exceptional athlete who played both ways in high school and his first year as a pro, Kelly repeats his delivery, so further improvement of his secondary pitches is possible. Assuming a full recovery, he has mid-rotation upside. In a best-case scenario Kelly could be on regular schedule by May and in the big league rotation near the all-star break.

Year	Club (League)	Class	W	L	ERA	G	GS	CG	SV	IP	H	HR	BB	SO	K/9	WHIP	AVG
2009	Salem (CAR)	HiA	1	4	3.09	8	8	0	0	47	33	4	7	35	6.8	0.86	.196
	Greenville (SAL)	LoA	6	1	1.12	9	9	0	0	48	32	0	9	39	7.3	0.85	.184
2010	Portland (EL)	AA	3	5	5.31	21	21	0	0	95	118	10	35	81	7.7	1.61	.307
2011	San Antonio (TL)	AA	11	6	3.98	27	27	0	0	142	153	8	46	105	6.6	1.40	.278
2012	Tucson (PCL)	AAA	0	0	2.25	2	2	0	0	12	12	0	0	14	10.5	1.00	.261
	Padres (AZL)	R	0	1	4.00	3	3	0	0	9	10	0	0	7	7.0	1.11	.250
	San Antonio (TL)	AA	0	1	3.78	3	3	0	0	17	11	1	3	18	9.7	0.84	.190
	San Diego (NL)	MAJ	2	3	6.21	6	6	0	0	29	39	5	10	26	8.1	1.69	.322
2013	Did not play—Injured																
Major League Totals			2	3	6.21	6	6	0	0	29	39	5	10	26	8.1	1.69	.322
Minor League Totals			21	18	3.77	73	73	0	0	370	369	23	100	299	7.3	1.27	.260

6 RYMER LIRIANO, OF

BA GRADE
50
MEDIUM

Born: June 20, 1991. **B-T:** R-R. **Ht.:** 6-0. **Wt.:** 225. **Signed:** Dominican Republic, 2007. **Signed by:** Randy Smith/Felix Francisco.

Liriano developed soreness in his right elbow in December 2012 during the Dominican League season, then blew it out in spring training while long-tossing in the outfield. He had Tommy John surgery in mid-February 2013 and missed the entire season. Liriano flashes all five tools, highlighted by plus raw power to all fields, arm strength and range in right field. His power will play better in games if he makes more contact and once he plays in a more favorable park for power. Shaky pitch recognition, though, may mean Liriano never hits for a high average. A solid runner, he chooses his spots well and has swiped 30 bases in each season from 2010-12. Scouts expect him to fill out and lose a tick of speed, though that won't prevent him from being a strong defender. Liriano started taking batting practice in August, then hit in games during Dominican instructional league. The Padres expect him to return at full strength to Double-A San Antonio, where he finished 2012.

Year	Club (League)	Class	AVG	G	AB	R	H	2B	3B	HR	RBI	BB	SO	SB	CS	OBP	SLG
2008	Padres (DSL)	R	.198	67	232	34	46	13	1	9	37	28	106	9	5	.296	.379
2009	Padres (AZL)	R	.350	50	197	44	69	8	1	8	44	15	52	14	5	.398	.523
2010	Fort Wayne (MWL)	LoA	.191	50	188	21	36	11	1	2	20	10	54	11	6	.234	.293
	Eugene (NWL)	SS	.271	53	203	35	55	13	6	0	12	17	53	17	7	.335	.394
	Lake Elsinore (CAL)	HiA	.220	14	50	3	11	2	0	1	6	5	12	3	0	.291	.320
2011	Lake Elsinore (CAL)	HiA	.127	15	55	8	7	1	1	0	6	6	13	1	1	.213	.182
	Fort Wayne (MWL)	LoA	.319	116	455	81	145	30	8	12	62	47	95	65	20	.383	.499
2012	Lake Elsinore (CAL)	HiA	.298	74	282	41	84	22	2	5	41	21	69	22	7	.360	.443
	San Antonio (TL)	AA	.251	53	183	24	46	10	2	3	20	20	50	10	1	.335	.377
2013	Did not play—Injured																
Minor League Totals			.270	492	1845	291	499	110	22	40	248	169	504	152	52	.338	.419

7 JACE PETERSON, SS

BA GRADE
50
MEDIUM

Born: May 9, 1990. **B-T:** L-R. **Ht.:** 6-0. **Wt.:** 205. **Drafted:** McNeese State, 2011 (1st round supplemental). **Signed by:** Kevin Ellis.

At McNeese State, Peterson starred on the diamond and as a cornerback on the football team, but he made the right decision in pursuing baseball. He spent all of 2013 as shortstop at high Class A Lake Elsinore, ranking among the California League leaders in average (.303), stolen bases (42) and triples (13). Peterson has no single plus tool, but he adeptly combines athleticism, skill and instincts, so his average tools play. He shows average range and arm strength at shortstop to go with throwing accuracy and first-step quickness. That quickness, combined with his ability to read pitchers, makes up for his average run times, and he boasts a career 80 percent stolen-base success rate. Peterson shows no give in left-on-left matchups and sprays line drives where the ball is pitched. Though he has below-average power, he can turn on the inside pitch when he's geared to do so. If he reaches his ceiling, Peterson will be a table-setting starter at shortstop.

Year	Club (League)	Class	AVG	G	AB	R	H	2B	3B	HR	RBI	BB	SO	SB	CS	OBP	SLG
2011	Eugene (NWL)	SS	.243	73	276	48	67	9	5	2	27	50	53	39	10	.360	.333
2012	Fort Wayne (MWL)	LoA	.286	117	444	78	127	23	9	2	48	62	63	51	13	.378	.392
2013	Lake Elsinore (CAL)	HiA	.303	113	423	78	128	17	13	7	66	54	58	42	10	.382	.454
Minor League Totals			.282	303	1143	204	322	49	27	11	141	166	174	132	33	.375	.401

8 BURCH SMITH, RHP

BA GRADE
50
HIGH

Born: April 12, 1990. **B-T:** R-R. **Ht.:** 6-4. **Wt.:** 215. **Drafted:** Oklahoma, 2011 (14th round). **Signed by:** Lane Decker.

Smith led the high Class A California League with 5.1 SO/BB ratio in 2012 and continued in that vein with a 4.4 ratio at Double-A and Triple-A in 2013. Called on as an emergency starter after just six starts at Double-A San Antonio, Smith received three different callups to San Diego in 2013. His physicality, clean arm action, up-tempo delivery and above-average fastball stand out immediately. He sits 92-93 mph and can run his fastball up to about 97, often with natural cutting action. Getting bushwhacked by big league hitters taught him that he'll need more than his fastball to succeed. Smith threw his changeup about one in five pitches for San Diego and it's his go-to secondary weapon, which he sells with good arm speed. Finding conviction in his curveball has been more of a challenge, though the Padres say it should be an average pitch once he uses it with more power and learns to better sync his delivery when throwing it. Smith seemed to get his feet under him in September, going 1-2, 3.80 with 31 strikeouts in 24 innings over four starts. He might be ready to claim a permanent rotation spot in spring training and has mid-rotation potential.

Year	Club (League)	Class	W	L	ERA	G	GS	CG	SV	IP	H	HR	BB	SO	K/9	WHIP	AVG
2011	Padres (AZL)	R	0	0	4.50	2	0	0	1	2	3	0	1	4	18.0	2.00	.300
2012	Lake Elsinore (CAL)	HiA	9	6	3.85	26	26	0	0	129	127	11	27	137	9.6	1.20	.256
2013	San Antonio (TL)	AA	1	2	1.15	6	6	0	0	31	17	1	6	37	10.6	0.73	.155
	Tucson (PCL)	AAA	5	1	3.39	12	12	0	0	61	56	4	17	65	9.6	1.20	.246
	San Diego (NL)	MAJ	1	3	6.44	10	7	0	0	36	39	9	21	46	11.4	1.65	.269
Major League Totals			1	3	6.44	10	7	0	0	36	39	9	21	46	11.4	1.65	.269
Minor League Totals			15	9	3.35	46	44	0	1	223	203	16	51	243	9.8	1.14	.241

9 KEYVIUS SAMPSON, RHP

BA GRADE
50
HIGH

Born: Jan. 6, 1991. **B-T:** R-R. **Ht.:** 6-0. **Wt.:** 185. **Drafted:** HS—Ocala, Fla., 2009 (4th round). **Signed by:** Rob Sidwell.

Signing Sampson for $600,000 in 2009 signaled a shift in the Padres' preference from college to prep arms at the top of the draft. He overcame a disastrous four-start opening at Triple-A Tucson to thrive in 2013 at Double-A San Antonio, overhauling his approach, improving his velocity and leading the organization with 135 strikeouts. Sampson went 8-0, 1.57 through his final 12 appearances at San Antonio before a return trip to Tucson, owing his dominance to improved fastball velocity and the substitution of a slider for his below-average curveball. Scouts clocked Sampson's heater at a consistent 93-95 mph in 2013, while his slider gave him the weapon and aggressive mindset to retire righthanders on a consistent basis. He still throws a quality changeup that he sells with the same arm slot and speed as his fastball. Below-average command remains an issue for Sampson, who tends to catch too much of the plate. His near 1.0 SO/BB ratio and 1.71 WHIP with Tucson in August indicate he still has work to do. Sampson worked as a reliever in the Arizona Fall League, and his newfound power arsenal means a career in that role could still be a productive one.

Year	Club (League)	Class	W	L	ERA	G	GS	CG	SV	IP	H	HR	BB	SO	K/9	WHIP	AVG
2009	Padres (AZL)	R	0	0	3.00	2	1	0	0	3	1	0	0	3	9.0	0.33	.111
	Eugene (NWL)	SS	0	0	3.60	2	1	0	0	5	3	0	3	5	9.0	1.20	.176
2010	Eugene (NWL)	SS	3	3	3.56	10	10	0	0	43	35	4	17	58	12.1	1.21	.226
2011	Fort Wayne (MWL)	LoA	12	3	2.90	24	24	0	0	118	81	8	49	143	10.9	1.10	.192
2012	San Antonio (TL)	AA	8	11	5.00	26	25	0	0	122	108	11	57	122	9.0	1.35	.233
2013	San Antonio (TL)	AA	10	4	2.26	19	18	0	0	103	74	9	33	110	9.6	1.04	.199
	Tucson (PCL)	AAA	2	3	7.11	9	9	0	0	38	44	5	29	25	5.9	1.92	.306
Minor League Totals			35	24	3.79	92	88	0	0	433	346	37	188	466	9.7	1.23	.219

10 JOE ROSS, RHP

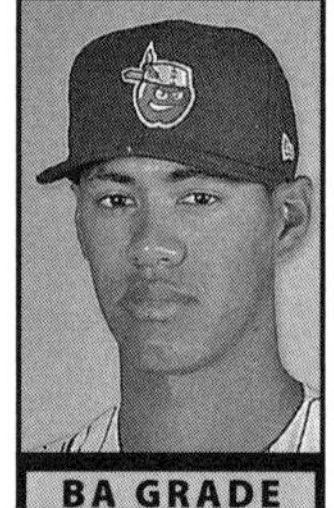

BA GRADE
50
HIGH

Born: May 21, 1993. **B-T:** R-R. **Ht.:** 6-3. **Wt.:** 185. **Drafted:** HS—Oakland, 2011 (1st round). **Signed by:** Noah Jackson.

Though the results haven't indicated as much, Ross may have more arm speed than any of the projectable pitchers the Padres drafted in 2011 or 2012, a list headed by Matt Wisler and Max Fried. Ross signed for $2.75 million as the 25th overall pick in 2011, but shoulder tendinitis dented his full-season debut in 2012. His brother Tyson turned in a career-best performance for the big league Padres in 2013. Ross remained healthy in 2013 and made all 23 starts in low Class A Fort Wayne's six-man rotation. He shows two plus pitches with consistency, though his changeup still has a long way to go for scouts to confidently peg him as a quality starter. Ross pitches at 93-94 mph and tops out at 97 with above-average riding life, which helps him keep the ball on the ground and home runs off the board. He can alter batters' eye level with a power slider that darts out of the zone and flashes plus potential. He loses velocity in later innings and doesn't have the best feel for mixing his pitches. The Padres believe his changeup can be an average pitch because he's athletic and is refining his delivery and feel for pitching. Some scouts see Ross as a mid-rotation starter, while others see a power reliever. He is right where he needs to be on the development cycle, on target for high Class A Lake Elsinore in 2014.

Year	Club (League)	Class	W	L	ERA	G	GS	CG	SV	IP	H	HR	BB	SO	K/9	WHIP	AVG
2011	Padres (AZL)	R	0	0	0.00	1	0	0	0	1	2	0	0	0	0.0	2.00	.400
2012	Fort Wayne (MWL)	LoA	0	2	6.26	6	6	0	0	27	33	2	11	27	8.9	1.61	.297
	Padres (AZL)	R	0	0	13.50	1	1	0	0	1	2	0	2	1	13.5	6.00	.500
	Eugene (NWL)	SS	0	2	2.03	8	8	0	0	27	16	1	9	28	9.5	0.94	.178
2013	Fort Wayne (MWL)	LoA	5	8	3.75	23	23	0	0	122	124	7	40	79	5.8	1.34	.267
Minor League Totals			5	12	3.89	39	38	0	0	178	177	10	62	135	6.8	1.34	.262

11 CORY SPANGENBERG, 2B

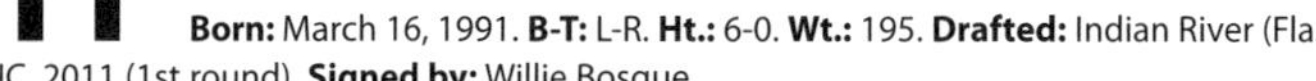

Born: March 16, 1991. **B-T:** L-R. **Ht.:** 6-0. **Wt.:** 195. **Drafted:** Indian River (Fla.) JC, 2011 (1st round). **Signed by:** Willie Bosque.

The 10th overall pick in the 2011 draft, Spangenberg's production tailed off in the second half of 2012 following a concussion he endured when struck in the head by a ball during batting practice. He advanced to Double-A San Antonio at midseason 2013, and he still turns in double-plus run times and has the above-average range to play second base. Scouts, however, don't see eye to eye about his overall potential. Because Spangenberg still is ironing out the finer points of his swing and defensive technique, the most charitable explanation proffered may be that he's a good athlete who's learning to refine his baseball skills. The high Class A Lake Elsinore coaching staff succeeded in getting Spangenberg to tone down his stride and square himself off at the plate in 2013 so that the lefty hitter could pull the inside pitch instead of flicking everything to left field or rolling over for 4-3 groundouts. With a flat swing plane, he won't elevate many pitches for home runs, but he can shoot balls into the gaps. He's an excellent runner and good basestealer who only will get more efficient. Spangenberg worked with San Antonio manager and 10-year big league second sacker Rich Dauer to smooth out his defensive actions at the keystone, touching on the backhand play, the double-play pivot and throwing accuracy. Reports from scouts outside the organization indicate that Spangenberg could be an average defender with a fringe arm. If he hits, he can be a starter at second base. If not, his speed and lefty bat could make him an attractive utility option at second and third base and perhaps in center field.

Year	Club (League)	Class	AVG	G	AB	R	H	2B	3B	HR	RBI	BB	SO	SB	CS	OBP	SLG
2011	Eugene (NWL)	SS	.384	25	86	20	33	10	0	1	20	31	15	10	4	.545	.535
	Fort Wayne (MWL)	LoA	.286	47	189	35	54	7	1	2	24	14	42	15	4	.345	.365
2012	Lake Elsinore (CAL)	HiA	.271	98	384	53	104	12	8	1	40	26	72	27	9	.324	.352
2013	Lake Elsinore (CAL)	HiA	.296	54	226	33	67	13	6	4	31	23	51	17	3	.364	.460
	San Antonio (TL)	AA	.289	76	287	35	83	10	3	2	20	17	61	19	11	.331	.366
Minor League Totals			.291	300	1172	176	341	52	18	10	135	111	241	88	31	.357	.392

12 FRANCHY CORDERO, SS

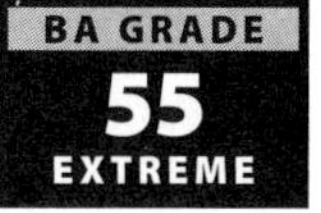

Born: Sept. 2, 1994. **B-T:** L-R. **Ht.:** 6-3. **Wt.:** 175. **Signed:** Dominican Republic, 2011. **Signed by:** Felix Feliz/Jose Salado/Randy Smith.

Trainer Antonio Arias presented Cordero to teams as a third baseman, but when the Padres signed him for $175,000 in November 2011 they determined that his athleticism would allow him to play shortstop. While the lean, 6-foot-3 Cordero might one day outgrow the position, he has the first-step quickness, range, sure hands and above-average arm to stay there for the foreseeable future. In his U.S. debut in 2013, he tied for the Rookie-level Arizona League lead in slugging (.511) while also finishing among the leaders in average (.333) and OPS (.891). The rare lefthanded hitter from the Dominican Republic, Cordero has exciting offensive potential thanks to plus bat speed and an innate feel to hit. When he barrels the ball it travels a long way with big-time carry, leading some to project above-average power to go with a strong batting average. He's also an above-average runner who went a perfect 11-for-11 on steals in the AZL and will leg out his share of doubles and triples. Like many young shortstops, Cordero suffers from occasional lapses in focus, but overall he has five-tool talent with the luxury of having time on his side to hone his skills. No lefty-hitting Dominican shortstop ever has played in the major leagues—and the number of second and third basemen totals just four players—so Cordero is fighting history as he advances to low Class A Fort Wayne.

Year	Club (League)	Class	AVG	G	AB	R	H	2B	3B	HR	RBI	BB	SO	SB	CS	OBP	SLG
2012	Padres (DSL)	R	.270	61	230	39	62	9	6	1	38	37	73	14	4	.372	.374
2013	Padres (AZL)	R	.333	35	141	23	47	4	6	3	17	10	33	11	0	.381	.511
Minor League Totals			.294	96	371	62	109	13	12	4	55	47	106	25	4	.375	.426

13 JOE WIELAND, RHP

BA GRADE
50
HIGH

Born: Jan. 21, 1990. **B-T:** R-R. **Ht.:** 6-3. **Wt.:** 205. **Drafted:** HS—Reno, Nev., 2008 (4th round). **Signed by:** Butch Metzger (Rangers).

The Padres acquired Wieland and lefthander Robbie Erlin when they dealt reliever Mike Adams to the Rangers at the 2011 trade deadline. Wieland had Tommy John surgery a year after joining San Diego, but not before making five big league starts early in 2012. His rehab from elbow surgery stretched to 15 months, due to setbacks, before he took the mound again in the 2013 Arizona Fall League. Wieland's stuff will play against major league hitters, though he doesn't have a large margin for error given that he relies on precision over power. His fastball sits at about 91 mph and can bump 94 with late life. He favors a big-breaking curveball that sits in the high 70s and a low-80s changeup that fades away from the barrels of lefthanders. Wieland had success incorporating a fringy slider into his repertoire after joining the Padres, and he goes to it when he needs to throw a strike. Add it all up and he profiles as a strike-throwing No. 4 starter. Erlin made nine starts and logged 55 innings for San Diego in 2013, losing his prospect eligibility, and Wieland ought to follow suit in 2014.

Year	Club (League)	Class	W	L	ERA	G	GS	CG	SV	IP	H	HR	BB	SO	K/9	WHIP	AVG
2008	Rangers (AZL)	R	5	1	1.44	13	7	0	0	44	32	2	8	41	8.5	0.92	.200
2009	Hickory (SAL)	LoA	4	6	5.31	19	18	0	0	83	102	7	24	73	7.9	1.52	.299
2010	Hickory (SAL)	LoA	7	4	3.34	15	15	2	0	89	84	4	15	71	7.2	1.11	.251
	Bakersfield (CAL)	HiA	4	3	5.19	11	10	0	0	59	67	6	10	62	9.5	1.31	.283
2011	Myrtle Beach (CAR)	HiA	6	3	2.10	14	13	1	0	86	78	7	4	96	10.1	0.96	.240
	Frisco (TL)	AA	4	0	1.23	7	7	1	0	44	35	2	11	36	7.4	1.05	.217
	San Antonio (TL)	AA	3	1	2.77	5	5	0	0	26	23	0	6	18	6.2	1.12	.240
2012	Tucson (PCL)	AAA	0	1	3.52	2	2	0	0	8	10	0	2	11	12.9	1.57	.313
	San Diego (NL)	MAJ	0	4	4.55	5	5	0	0	28	26	5	9	24	7.8	1.27	.245
Major League Totals			0	4	4.55	5	5	0	0	28	26	5	9	24	7.8	1.27	.245
Minor League Totals			33	19	3.29	86	77	4	0	438	431	28	80	408	8.4	1.17	.255

14 ZACH EFLIN, RHP

BA GRADE 50 HIGH

Born: April 8, 1994. **B-T:** R-R. **Ht.:** 6-4. **Wt.:** 200. **Drafted:** HS—Oviedo, Fla., 2012 (1st round supplemental). **Signed by:** Willie Bosque.

The Padres hit the state of Florida hard in the 2012 draft, selecting three prep righthanders in the first four rounds. Eflin, taken 33rd overall and signed for $1.2 million, appears to be a safer bet to reach his ceiling than either Walker Weickel (sandwich round) or Walker Lockett (fourth). After all, he won the low Class A Midwest League ERA title (2.73) in 2013 while also placing fifth with a 1.19 WHIP, throwing three average-to-above pitches but no wipeout offering. Eflin touched the mid-90s in high school but sits more comfortably at 90-92 mph with sink in a pro rotation. He threw one of the top changeups in the MWL, showing advanced arm speed, and he throws the above-average pitch in any count. Eflin scrapped the fringy curveball he threw as an amateur to pick up a slider, and he succeeded in throwing it as a chase pitch, though it will require further power and precision to be a consistent average pitch. A physical 6-foot-4, Eflin tends to stay tall and rigid in his delivery, preventing him from getting ideal extension and plane on his pitches. Scouts see him as a potential No. 4 starter in the big leagues if he can refine his command, and he's ready for high Class A Lake Elsinore.

Year	Club (League)	Class	W	L	ERA	G	GS	CG	SV	IP	H	HR	BB	SO	K/9	WHIP	AVG
2012	Padres (AZL)	R	0	1	7.71	4	3	0	0	7	9	0	3	4	5.1	1.71	.300
2013	Fort Wayne (MWL)	LoA	7	6	2.73	22	22	0	0	119	110	7	31	86	6.5	1.19	.239
Minor League Totals			7	7	3.01	26	25	0	0	126	119	7	34	90	6.4	1.22	.243

15 MATT ANDRIESE, RHP

BA GRADE 50 HIGH

Born: Aug. 28, 1989. **B-T:** R-R. **Ht.:** 6-3. **Wt.:** 210. **Drafted:** UC Riverside, 2011 (3rd round). **Signed by:** Josh Emmerick.

Andriese spent the second half of 2013 at Triple-A Tucson and showed a strong blend of command (3.6 SO/BB ratio) and ability to keep the ball on the ground (1.8 groundout/airout ratio). Both ratios placed him within the top 60 for qualified minor league starters. While he gets results, Andriese doesn't do it pretty, nor does he have knockout stuff. He unleashes low-90s sinkers that run in on the hands of righthanders, doing so with a long, hooking arm action and closed-off delivery that force him to pull the ball across his body. This appears to have no effect on his control because his career walk rate is 2.1 per nine innings. Andriese worked in more four-seamers at 93-94 mph in 2013 to change eye levels and set up an average high-70s curveball and mid-80s changeup. His curve often features vicious downward break, and he'll sometimes try to spot a slider/cutter or a splitter. Andriese could be a mid-rotation starter if he can improve his performance against lefthanders. They've hit .280/.335/.408 in full-season ball, so he'll try to improve upon that at Triple-A El Paso in 2014.

Year	Club (League)	Class	W	L	ERA	G	GS	CG	SV	IP	H	HR	BB	SO	K/9	WHIP	AVG
2011	Eugene (NWL)	SS	5	1	1.51	12	8	0	0	42	29	0	10	42	9.1	0.94	.197
2012	Lake Elsinore (CAL)	HiA	10	8	3.58	27	26	0	0	146	140	9	38	131	8.1	1.22	.252
2013	San Antonio (TL)	AA	8	2	2.37	15	15	0	0	76	71	3	17	63	7.5	1.16	.242
	Tucson (PCL)	AAA	3	5	4.45	12	10	0	0	59	64	2	12	42	6.4	1.30	.287
Minor League Totals			26	16	3.18	66	59	0	0	322	304	14	77	278	7.8	1.18	.250

16 GABRIEL QUINTANA, 3B

BA GRADE 50 HIGH

Born: Sept. 7, 1992. **B-T:** R-R. **Ht.:** 6-2. **Wt.:** 190. **Signed:** Dominican Republic, 2009. **Signed by:** Randy Smith/Felix Feliz/Jose Salido.

Signed at age 16 out of the Dominican Republic in 2009, Quintana didn't blow away the Padres during his tryout, though he did have evident leverage in his swing and a sturdy frame with room to add muscle mass. He began to show San Diego the player they had envisioned with his play in the Rookie-level Arizona League in 2012, batting .291/.337/.483 with 17 extra-base hits in 37 games. That showing earned Quintana a ticket to low Class A Fort Wayne for 2013, and he quickly earned admirers with his plus bat speed, loose actions and propensity for loud contact. He missed a month and a half at midseason with a broken hand after being hit with a pitch, but when he returned, Quintana hit .344 with 11 extra-base hits over his final 35 games. He has impact potential with the bat, profiling as a third baseman who can hit for average and power, but his over-anxiousness at the plate was apparent with nine times as many strikeouts as walks. Though he has present strength, he's not quite done filling out yet. Quintana throws well, but he probably won't win any Gold Gloves with fringe-average range and fielding ability. The Padres want him to use his legs while fielding grounders, not simply bend at the waist. Quinatana could be a breakout star in 2014 when he tackles high Class A Lake Elsinore.

Year	Club (League)	Class	AVG	G	AB	R	H	2B	3B	HR	RBI	BB	SO	SB	CS	OBP	SLG
2010	Padres (DSL)	R	.194	61	211	30	41	14	0	1	24	19	56	6	4	.279	.275
2011	Padres (DSL)	R	.284	60	211	35	60	16	0	7	34	18	55	3	3	.363	.460
	Padres (AZL)	R	.267	8	30	3	8	1	0	1	3	3	6	0	1	.333	.400
2012	Padres (AZL)	R	.291	37	151	25	44	10	2	5	36	6	37	2	1	.337	.483
	Eugene (NWL)	SS	.230	16	61	2	14	2	0	1	8	1	18	0	0	.234	.311
2013	Padres (AZL)	R	.333	6	21	4	7	2	0	0	3	1	4	0	0	.417	.429
	Fort Wayne (MWL)	LoA	.305	88	347	50	106	20	1	9	44	11	91	6	2	.334	.447
Minor League Totals			.271	276	1032	149	280	65	3	24	152	59	267	17	11	.325	.410

17 TRAVIS JANKOWSKI, OF

Born: June 15, 1991. **B-T:** L-R. **Ht.:** 6-2. **Wt.:** 190. **Drafted:** Stony Brook, 2012 (1st round supplemental). **Signed by:** Jim Bretz.

Evaluators in the high Class A California League in 2013 singled out Jankowski as fastest baserunner, best baserunner and best defensive outfielder in a survey of best tools. Those attributes will be his ticket to the big leagues. Batters seldom hit the ball over Jankowski's head in center field, with some scouts throwing 70 grades on his defensive ability. His below-average arm would not play in right field. Jankowski went 71-for-85 (84 percent) on the bases for Lake Elsinore and led the Cal League in steals, showcasing double-plus run times to first base. He improved his stealing efficiency in 2013, but he'll need to take another step forward with the bat to profile as an everyday player. Jankowski must add heft to his frame and authority to his swing to keep defenses honest, though adding loft to his swing would be fruitless given well below-average power potential. Jankowski profiles as a table-setter, one who has relied on line drives, ground balls, speed and the occasional bunt to reach base. A season at Double-A San Antonio in 2014 will tell the Padres a lot about his future potential.

Year	Club (League)	Class	AVG	G	AB	R	H	2B	3B	HR	RBI	BB	SO	SB	CS	OBP	SLG
2012	Padres (AZL)	R	.250	2	8	1	2	0	0	0	4	0	1	0	0	.222	.250
	Fort Wayne (MWL)	LoA	.282	59	238	32	67	10	4	1	23	13	44	17	7	.318	.370
2013	Lake Elsinore (CAL)	HiA	.286	122	493	89	141	19	6	1	38	54	96	71	14	.356	.355
Minor League Totals			.284	183	739	122	210	29	10	2	65	67	141	88	21	.343	.359

18 JUAN ORAMAS, LHP

BA GRADE
50
HIGH

Born: May 11, 1990. **B-T:** L-L. **Ht.:** 5-10. **Wt.:** 215. **Signed:** Mexico, 2006. **Signed by:** Robert Rowley.

Oramas pitched for Double-A San Antonio's Texas League champions in both 2011 and 2013, sandwiching those playoff runs around Tommy John surgery in 2012. He announced his return to full health by making 12 starts for the Missions in 2013 and going 3-2, 3.07 with a 4.0 SO/BB ratio, then dealing 12 scoreless innings in the playoffs. The Padres non-tendered Oramas following the 2012 season to make room for other players on the 40-man roster, though they subsequently re-signed him to a minor league deal for 2013. The reason San Diego has made such a great effort to retain Oramas is because he projects to have three major league pitches with a feel to deploy them for maximum impact. Short and stout, he locates an 89-92 mph fastball all over the strike zone with a fearless demeanor, hiding the ball until the last instant and varying his arm angle. His curveball features tight rotation and average power, while he doesn't hesitate to lean on his fading changeup when he has feel for it. Oramas returned to the familiar surroundings of the Mexican Pacific League in October 2013 as he prepares to audition for the big league club. Making or not making the rotation might have more to do with inventory than ability, seeing as Oramas will be competing for innings with veterans such as Andrew Cashner, Josh Johnson, Ian Kennedy, Cory Luebke, Tyson Ross and a host of prospect hopefuls.

Year	Club (League)	Class	W	L	ERA	G	GS	CG	SV	IP	H	HR	BB	SO	K/9	WHIP	AVG
2007	Padres (DSL)	R	2	3	3.81	16	5	0	0	54	39	1	20	63	10.4	1.09	.196
2008	Padres (DSL)	R	3	2	1.02	19	5	0	3	53	23	0	24	70	11.9	0.89	.125
2009	Mexico City (MEX)	AAA	9	1	2.31	25	14	0	0	90	72	4	44	89	8.9	1.29	--
2010	Fort Wayne (MWL)	LoA	0	1	1.20	5	0	0	0	15	9	0	3	25	15.0	0.80	.176
	Lake Elsinore (CAL)	HiA	7	3	3.00	24	21	0	0	84	64	10	26	90	9.6	1.07	.209
2011	Tucson (PCL)	AAA	0	1	14.73	1	1	0	0	4	7	3	1	4	9.8	2.18	.389
	San Antonio (TL)	AA	10	5	3.10	19	18	0	0	105	99	10	28	102	8.8	1.21	.249
2012	San Antonio (TL)	AA	3	4	6.37	8	8	0	0	35	39	5	16	33	8.4	1.56	.267
2013	Padres (AZL)	R	0	0	1.29	2	2	0	0	7	6	0	2	15	19.3	1.14	.214
	San Antonio (TL)	AA	3	2	3.07	12	12	0	0	56	52	4	16	64	10.3	1.22	.249
Minor League Totals			37	22	3.03	131	86	0	3	502	410	37	180	555	9.9	1.17	.220

19 WALKER WEICKEL, RHP

BA GRADE
50
HIGH

Born: Nov. 14, 1993. **B-T:** R-R. **Ht.:** 6-6. **Wt.:** 195. **Drafted:** HS—Orlando, 2012 (1st round supplemental). **Signed by:** Willie Bosque.

Among players drafted by the Padres in 2012, only seventh overall pick Max Fried received a higher bonus than Weickel, who signed for $2 million as the 55th selection. Lean, 6-foot-6 and broad-shouldered, he tantalizes scouts with his frame, clean arm action and potential for two plus pitches. Weickel made the low Class A Fort Wayne rotation in 2013, though he stumbled to the most bloated ERA (5.04) and WHIP (1.52) among the club's primary starters. Pro scouts still like his arm strength and projectability but question his feel to pitch. Weickel sits 91-92 mph with vicious sink at times and has topped out at 95, but he struggles to maintain rhythm in his delivery, particularly from the stretch. He snaps off plus mid-70s curveballs early in starts, but he can lose feel and rotation on the pitch when his arm angle creeps too high. Weickel has shown a developing feel for a changeup, though it's a third pitch now. His overall profile suggests a ceiling along the lines of a No. 4 starter if he can iron out his command.

Year	Club (League)	Class	W	L	ERA	G	GS	CG	SV	IP	H	HR	BB	SO	K/9	WHIP	AVG
2012	Padres (AZL)	R	1	3	4.50	9	6	0	0	14	16	0	6	12	7.7	1.57	.262
2013	Fort Wayne (MWL)	LoA	3	6	5.04	24	23	0	0	111	125	8	43	82	6.7	1.52	.283
Minor League Totals			4	9	4.98	33	29	0	0	125	141	8	49	94	6.8	1.52	.281

20 REYMOND FUENTES, OF

BA GRADE
45
MEDIUM

Born: Feb. 12, 1991. **B-T:** L-L. **Ht.:** 6-0. **Wt.:** 160. **Drafted:** HS—Manati, P.R., 2009 (1st round). **Signed by:** Edgar Perez (Red Sox).

The Padres rewarded Fuentes, a Red Sox first-round pick in 2009 and part of the Adrian Gonzalez deal, for his improved maturity, plate discipline and effort level in 2013 by calling him up on Aug. 26. He didn't play much in San Diego, but he hit .330/.413/.448 with 35 stolen bases in 107 games in the minors, mostly at Double-A San Antonio. Thanks to a career-high walk rate of 11 percent, his on-base percentage ranked 19th in the minors. Missions batting coach Jacque Jones had Fuentes spread out his stance at the plate, and he made more hard contact and hit to the middle of the field unlike he ever had before. If he doesn't keep up that pace, he still has supporting tools that will make him an attractive reserve, including plus speed and range. His arm is fringy and not suited to regular play in right field. A wiry athlete, Fuentes has very little power potential but should be able to leg out the occasional double. He could better utilize his speed by bunting more often. Fuentes appears destined for Triple-A El Paso in 2014, but he's not far away.

Year	Club (League)	Class	AVG	G	AB	R	H	2B	3B	HR	RBI	BB	SO	SB	CS	OBP	SLG
2009	Red Sox (GCL)	R	.290	40	145	16	42	6	2	1	14	7	24	9	5	.331	.379
2010	Greenville (SAL)	LoA	.270	104	374	59	101	15	5	5	41	25	87	42	5	.328	.377
2011	Lake Elsinore (CAL)	HiA	.275	124	510	84	140	15	9	5	45	44	117	41	14	.342	.369
2012	San Antonio (TL)	AA	.218	136	473	53	103	20	4	4	34	52	133	35	9	.301	.302
2013	San Antonio (TL)	AA	.316	93	345	56	109	21	2	6	35	41	71	29	10	.396	.441
	Tucson (PCL)	AAA	.418	14	55	17	23	4	0	0	8	10	10	6	1	.515	.491
	San Diego (NL)	MAJ	.152	23	33	4	5	0	0	0	1	3	16	3	0	.222	.152
Major League Totals			.152	23	33	4	5	0	0	0	1	3	16	3	0	.222	.152
Minor League Totals			.272	511	1902	285	518	81	22	21	177	179	442	162	44	.344	.371

21 LEONEL CAMPOS, RHP

BA GRADE
50
HIGH

Born: July 17, 1987. **B-T:** R-R. **Ht.:** 6-3. **Wt.:** 185. **Signed:** Venezuela, 2010. **Signed by:** Yfrain Linares.

Campos injured his elbow and required Tommy John surgery after his first pro appearance for short-season Eugene in 2011. Because he signed out of Venezuela at age 23 after pursuing soccer as a youth, his elbow surgery effectively put off his debut season until 2013, which he finished as a 26 year old at Double-A San Antonio. Few in the system can out-stuff Campos, however. He sits 93-95 mph with a double-plus fastball that tops out at 98 and saws off righthanders with sinking, boring action. Same-sided batters went just 16-for-137 (.117) with strikeouts nearly 44 percent of the time in 2013. Campos throws a low-80s curveball that features late, tight breaking action, and he sometimes toys with a fringy changeup. Despite his inexperience, he throws from an athletic, repeatable delivery, and he ought to throw more strikes once he stops overthrowing as much as he does now. That will be a crucial task for Campos after he walked 5.1 batters per nine innings in 2013. The Padres expect him to contribute to the 2014 bullpen, perhaps in the second half.

Year	Club (League)	Class	W	L	ERA	G	GS	CG	SV	IP	H	HR	BB	SO	K/9	WHIP	AVG
2011	Eugene (NWL)	SS	0	0	18.00	1	1	0	0	2	5	1	0	4	18.0	2.50	.455
2012	Did not play—Injured																
2013	Fort Wayne (MWL)	LoA	2	1	2.23	28	0	0	5	36	19	2	22	63	15.6	1.13	.150
	San Antonio (TL)	AA	1	0	0.88	26	0	0	2	31	14	0	16	43	12.6	0.98	.137
Minor League Totals			3	1	2.09	55	1	0	7	69	38	3	38	110	14.3	1.10	.158

22 DUSTIN PETERSON, 3B

Born: Sept. 10, 1994. **B-T:** R-R. **Ht.:** 6-2. **Wt.:** 180. **Drafted:** HS—Gilbert, Ariz., 2013 (2nd round). **Signed by:** Dave Lottsfeldt.

Not wanting to miss the boat on another Peterson brother, area scouts zeroed in on Dustin at Gilbert High in 2013 after letting big brother D.J. slip to the 33rd round three years earlier. While D.J. blossomed at New Mexico and eventually went 12th overall to the Mariners in 2013, Dustin slipped to the second round (50th overall) of the same draft and pulled down $1.4 million from the Padres to forgo a commitment Arizona State. San Diego regarded Peterson as one of the best bats in the draft thanks to his quick hips, natural rhythm and electric bat speed. He creates enough loft and backspin to hit for average power one day while also hitting for a high average because he uses the whole ballpark. A prep shortstop and an average runner, Peterson shifted to third base in the Rookie-level Arizona League, but many scouts don't view him as a fit for the left side of the infield because of an unconventional throwing motion and fringy arm. Opinion on future position varies from second base to first base to left field. Peterson will head to low Class A Fort Wayne in 2014.

Year	Club (League)	Class	AVG	G	AB	R	H	2B	3B	HR	RBI	BB	SO	SB	CS	OBP	SLG
2013	Padres (AZL)	R	.293	38	157	20	46	8	0	0	18	9	33	3	0	.337	.344
Minor League Totals			.293	38	157	20	46	8	0	0	18	9	33	3	0	.337	.344

23 TOMMY MEDICA, 1B

BA GRADE
45
MEDIUM

Born: April 9, 1988. **B-T:** R-R. **Ht.:** 6-1. **Wt.:** 190. **Drafted:** Santa Clara, 2010 (14th round). **Signed by:** Noah Jackson.

A shoulder injury at Santa Clara cost Medica virtually all of 2009 and forced him out from behind the plate to the outfield when he returned as a redshirt junior in 2010. A 14th-round pick by the Padres that year, he hasn't fared much better at avoiding the injury bug in pro ball, averaging about 90 games a season from 2011-13 as he has dealt with shoulder surgery (his second after having one in college) and a strained muscle in his ribcage. The organization received a pleasant surprise when a 25-year-old Medica, now a first baseman, put up a .954 OPS at Double-A San Antonio in 2013 while leading the system with 20 homers to receive a September callup. At high Class A Lake Elsinore the year before he led the system with a .330 average. That is to say, he has a track record for hitting whenever he's been on the field. Scouts like Medica's approach at the plate even if he doesn't have elite bat speed. He looks to hit the ball to all fields, recognizes spin on breaking balls early and hits with authority to right-center field with a strong righthanded stroke. He doesn't lift the ball all that well, so he'll probably be limited to below-average home run output. An ordinary defender at first base, Medica would enhance his attractiveness to the big club if he could play left field or possibly spot at his college position of catcher. He could be an early callup from Triple-A El Paso in 2014 if he hits.

Year	Club (League)	Class	AVG	G	AB	R	H	2B	3B	HR	RBI	BB	SO	SB	CS	OBP	SLG
2010	Eugene (NWL)	SS	.176	34	102	7	18	4	0	0	9	18	18	0	2	.318	.216
2011	Fort Wayne (MWL)	LoA	.268	44	142	22	38	19	0	3	21	17	33	0	1	.366	.465
	Padres (AZL)	R	.391	6	23	8	9	2	0	1	6	4	3	0	0	.464	.609
	Lake Elsinore (CAL)	HiA	.302	42	139	21	42	10	0	6	17	25	32	0	1	.440	.504
2012	Lake Elsinore (CAL)	HiA	.330	93	355	65	117	37	5	19	87	41	86	1	1	.406	.623
2013	Padres (AZL)	R	.294	5	17	6	5	2	0	2	8	1	7	0	0	.333	.765
	San Antonio (TL)	AA	.296	76	280	48	83	20	3	18	57	28	67	4	2	.372	.582
	San Diego (NL)	MAJ	.290	19	69	9	20	2	0	3	10	10	23	0	0	.380	.449
Major League Totals			.290	19	69	9	20	2	0	3	10	10	23	0	0	.380	.449
Minor League Totals			.295	300	1058	177	312	94	8	49	205	134	246	5	7	.388	.538

24 YEISON ASENCIO, OF

BA GRADE
45
MEDIUM

Born: Nov. 14, 1989. **B-T:** R-R. **Ht.:** 6-1. **Wt.:** 225. **Signed:** Dominican Republic, 2009. **Signed by:** Randy Smith/Felix Feliz/Martin Jose.

Asencio won the low Class A Midwest League batting title in 2012 and ranked as the No. 1 prospect in the Rookie-level Arizona League the year before that. However, the latter feat he accomplished while playing as Yoan Alcantara, the identity he assumed to take three years off his age when he signed in 2009. Nevertheless, he played at two levels in 2013, reaching Double-A San Antonio in June. At the plate, Asencio leaves nothing in reserve, swinging at the first pitch he can handle and frequently hitting the ball hard. The definition of a bad-ball hitter, he carries a .295 average in full-season ball while striking out only once out of every 10 trips to the plate. He puts on a show with long drives to his pull side during batting practice, but in games Asencio is susceptible to pitches on the outer half because he pulls off the ball. For this reason, he may never hit for a consistently high average. An average defender in right field, Asencio has one of the strongest arms in the system and sports perhaps the quickest release in the minors. He recorded 16 assists in 2013 and 21 the year before. He's a below-average runner, with no chance to handle center field if he doesn't hit it off in right. A return engagement at Double-A awaits Asencio in 2014.

Year	Club (League)	Class	AVG	G	AB	R	H	2B	3B	HR	RBI	BB	SO	SB	CS	OBP	SLG
2010	Padres (DSL)	R	.241	66	228	43	55	14	3	5	37	27	40	12	5	.332	.395
2011	Padres (AZL)	R	.348	50	210	50	73	13	8	7	46	4	25	8	2	.367	.586
2012	Fort Wayne (MWL)	LoA	.323	92	350	47	113	21	4	8	61	16	38	7	6	.353	.474
2013	Lake Elsinore (CAL)	HiA	.296	57	243	34	72	20	2	5	44	10	29	1	1	.319	.457
	San Antonio (TL)	AA	.261	74	291	25	76	15	3	2	32	13	29	3	2	.298	.354
Minor League Totals			.294	339	1322	199	389	83	20	27	220	70	161	31	16	.333	.449

25 ALEX DICKERSON, OF/1B

BA GRADE 45 MEDIUM

Born: May 26, 1990. **B-T:** L-L. **Ht.:** 6-3. **Wt.:** 235. **Drafted:** Indiana, 2011 (3rd round). **Signed by:** Jerry Jordan (Pirates).

Dickerson won the Big Ten Conference triple crown as a sophomore at Indiana in 2010. He tailed off as a junior, however, as he dealt with a back injury and fell to the third round of the draft. The Padres acquired him in a November 2013 trade with the Pirates in which they parted with Jaff Decker and Miles Mikolas. Dickerson has a good hitting approach, using the whole field and showing good bat-to-ball skills. A line-drive hitter, he does not generate the power typically expected from a corner player, particularly one with his physicality. At Double-A Altoona in 2013, he went on a power binge in June and July, mashing 11 home runs. The Pirates converted Dickerson to first base immediately after signing him after he played the outfield in college, but he played primarily right field in the Eastern and Arizona Fall leagues in 2013. He has below-average range and speed, though, and many scouts believe his future lies at first base. Dickerson will begin 2014 at Triple-A El Paso as he attempts to chase down Yonder Alonso and Tommy Medica on the depth chart.

Year	Club (League)	Class	AVG	G	AB	R	H	2B	3B	HR	RBI	BB	SO	SB	CS	OBP	SLG
2011	State College (NYP)	SS	.313	41	150	25	47	16	1	3	19	16	28	0	0	.393	.493
2012	Bradenton (FSL)	HiA	.295	129	488	65	144	31	3	13	90	39	93	12	7	.353	.451
2013	Altoona (EL)	AA	.288	126	451	61	130	36	3	17	68	27	89	10	7	.337	.494
Minor League Totals			.295	296	1089	151	321	83	7	33	177	82	210	22	14	.352	.475

26 DONN ROACH, RHP

BA GRADE 45 HIGH

Born: Dec. 14, 1989. **B-T:** R-R. **Ht.:** 6-1. **Wt.:** 200. **Drafted:** JC of Southern Nevada, 2010 (3rd round supplemental). **Signed by:** Jeff Scholzen (Angels).

A junior-college teammate of Bryce Harper, Roach toned down his delivery after signing with the Angels and has ranked as one of the more extreme groundball pitchers in the minors. He ranked seventh among minor league ERA title qualifiers with a groundout/airout ratio of 2.4 in 2013, his first extended exposure at Double-A San Antonio. Roach throws his sinker with below-average velocity at 87-89 mph but with 100 percent conviction and solid-average life. He throws an average, mid-80s splitter that helps him evade bats, but not nearly so many as he had at high Class A Lake Elsinore in 2012. His strikeout rate dropped from 7.4 per nine innings to 4.9 between 2012 and 2013. Roach throws consistent strikes with an easy arm action—especially in the second half, when he walked 13 batters in 14 starts—and his fringy, mid-70s slurve gives him a different look the second time through the order. If everything breaks right for him, Roach could be a groundball-oriented No. 5 starter or middle reliever.

Year	Club (League)	Class	W	L	ERA	G	GS	CG	SV	IP	H	HR	BB	SO	K/9	WHIP	AVG
2010	Orem (PIO)	R	4	1	6.04	16	10	0	0	54	64	6	16	59	9.9	1.49	.294
2011	Cedar Rapids (MWL)	LoA	5	5	3.45	45	0	0	2	70	73	1	20	68	8.7	1.32	.266
2012	Inland Empire (CAL)	HiA	5	0	2.16	6	6	0	0	42	36	1	3	29	6.3	0.94	.228
	Lake Elsinore (CAL)	HiA	5	1	1.74	8	7	0	0	47	41	1	11	44	8.5	1.11	.233
	San Antonio (TL)	AA	1	1	1.59	4	3	0	0	17	9	0	8	5	2.6	1.00	.155
2013	San Antonio (TL)	AA	8	12	3.53	28	28	0	0	143	138	7	40	77	4.9	1.25	.252
Minor League Totals			28	20	3.41	107	54	0	2	372	361	16	98	282	6.8	1.23	.252

27 KEVIN QUACKENBUSH, RHP

BA GRADE 45 HIGH

Born: Nov. 28, 1988. **B-T:** R-R. **Ht.:** 6-3. **Wt.:** 220. **Drafted:** South Florida, 2011 (8th round). **Signed by:** Willie Bosque.

Quackenbush has closed games for every Padres affiliate from short-season Eugene up through Triple-A Tucson, where he spent the second half of 2013. He creates deception with a short arm action, hiding the ball to the last instant, which enables his 91-93 mph fastball to play up to plus. Quackenbush creates excellent plane from a high three-quarters slot, making the heater tough for batters to lift, and he's allowed just two home runs in 144 appearances. Quackenbush throws a loopy high-70s curveball, but he picked up a splitter in 2013 that could function as a second go-to pitch to pair with his fastball. He struck out nearly 40 percent of righthanded batters in 2013, while holding lefties to a .200 average, but some scouts are hesitant to buy into Quackenbush's fastball-heavy approach due to a lack of premium velocity. After walking 5.0 batters per nine innings at Triple-A in 2013, he'll attempt to put his typical strong control on display at El Paso in 2014.

Year	Club (League)	Class	W	L	ERA	G	GS	CG	SV	IP	H	HR	BB	SO	K/9	WHIP	AVG
2011	Eugene (NWL)	SS	1	0	0.44	17	0	0	9	21	13	0	6	33	14.4	0.92	.188
	Fort Wayne (MWL)	LoA	1	1	0.84	18	0	0	9	21	12	0	6	38	16.0	0.84	.158
2012	Lake Elsinore (CAL)	HiA	3	2	0.94	52	0	0	27	58	42	1	22	70	10.9	1.11	.205
2013	San Antonio (TL)	AA	2	0	0.29	29	0	0	13	31	16	1	10	46	13.4	0.84	.151
	Tucson (PCL)	AAA	8	2	2.91	28	0	0	4	34	33	0	19	38	10.1	1.53	.256
Minor League Totals			15	5	1.15	144	0	0	62	165	116	2	63	225	12.3	1.09	.198

28 ADYS PORTILLO, RHP

BA GRADE **45** HIGH

Born: Dec. 20, 1991. **B-T:** R-R. **Ht.:** 6-2. **Wt.:** 235. **Signed:** Venezuela, 2008. **Signed by:** Yfrain Linares/Felix Feliz/Randy Smith.

Portillo's career has been a series of peaks and valleys since he signed with the Padres for $2 million in July 2008, and in 2013 he dealt with his first extended bout with injuries. He suffered a lat injury at the end of spring training that cost him the entire season, save for three rehab starts at low Class A Fort Wayne in June. The Padres assigned him to the Arizona Fall League to get more work. Portillo sat at 94-96 mph with sinking action during the 2012 season, but he pitched a few ticks lower in the AFL as he eased back into a routine. Feel to pitch never has been his strong point, though his high-70s slider has become an average pitch for him. Portillo can throw a good changeup when he stays on top of the ball, though organization consensus is beginning to coalesce around the idea that his future lies in the bullpen, owing to a career walk rate of 5.3 per nine innings. If he makes the bullpen home in 2014, then Portillo could begin at Triple-A El Paso.

Year	Club (League)	Class	W	L	ERA	G	GS	CG	SV	IP	H	HR	BB	SO	K/9	WHIP	AVG
2009	Padres (AZL)	R	1	9	5.13	13	12	0	0	53	67	2	28	44	7.5	1.80	.321
2010	Eugene (NWL)	SS	2	6	4.79	14	14	0	0	62	55	2	40	62	9.0	1.53	.241
	Fort Wayne (MWL)	LoA	0	0	4.50	1	0	0	0	2	2	1	1	1	4.5	1.50	.286
2011	Fort Wayne (MWL)	LoA	3	11	7.11	23	20	0	0	82	89	10	55	97	10.6	1.75	.278
2012	Fort Wayne (MWL)	LoA	6	6	1.87	18	18	0	0	92	54	3	45	81	8.0	1.08	.169
	San Antonio (TL)	AA	2	5	7.20	8	8	0	0	35	34	4	25	26	6.7	1.69	.250
2013	Fort Wayne (MWL)	LoA	0	1	4.82	3	3	0	0	9	14	0	4	10	9.6	1.93	.350
Minor League Totals			14	38	4.86	80	75	0	0	335	315	22	198	321	8.6	1.53	.250

29 JOSE URENA, OF

BA GRADE **50** EXTREME

Born: Jan. 14, 1995. **B-T:** R-R. **Ht.:** 6-3. **Wt.:** 200. **Signed:** Mexico, 2011. **Signed by:** Robert Rowley/Juan Lara/Randy Smith.

The Padres purchased the rights of the 17-year-old Urena from the Mexican League in August 2011, sending $550,000 to Mexico City for the strong-framed, righthanded hitter. He led the Rookie-level Arizona League with nine home runs in 2013, and among the system's lower-level prospects he may have the most power, owing to quick hands, above-average present strength and high rate of hard contact. Scouts give him a chance to hit for average because he can drive the ball to the off field. Urena played a lot of left field in the AZL, though the Padres view him as a right fielder long term, based on average range and solid-average arm strength. A slow release negatively affects how his arm plays, and he's a below-average runner. Urena will bat in the middle of the order at low Class A Fort Wayne in 2014.

Year	Club (League)	Class	AVG	G	AB	R	H	2B	3B	HR	RBI	BB	SO	SB	CS	OBP	SLG
2012	Padres (DSL)	R	.285	57	214	37	61	13	3	6	33	28	58	3	6	.382	.458
2013	Padres (AZL)	R	.257	49	191	32	49	11	5	9	34	22	54	1	2	.341	.508
Minor League Totals			.272	106	405	69	110	24	8	15	67	50	112	4	8	.363	.481

30 JOHNNY BARBATO, RHP

BA GRADE **45** HIGH

Born: July 11, 1992. **B-T:** R-R. **Ht.:** 6-2. **Wt.:** 185. **Drafted:** HS—Miami, 2010 (6th round). **Signed by:** Rob Sidwell/Bob Filotei.

Barbato played dual roles at high Class A Lake Elsinore in 2013, closing games for the first four months before shifting to the rotation for seven starts down the stretch. In a relief role he sits at about 94 mph while dialing up to 97 with explosive life. He also generates swings and misses with a big, high-rotation, high-70s knuckle-curveball, though the Padres would like to see him refine or learn a slurvy breaking ball, something that won't be as recognizable out of his hand. Barbato shows the potential for three pitches—he also shows feel for a decent changeup as a starter—but sometimes his rigid delivery prevents him from throwing quality strikes. If he returns to the bullpen, Barbato could one day surface in the big leagues as a set-up man.

Year	Club (League)	Class	W	L	ERA	G	GS	CG	SV	IP	H	HR	BB	SO	K/9	WHIP	AVG
2011	Eugene (NWL)	SS	1	4	4.89	15	13	0	0	57	52	4	31	50	7.9	1.46	.248
2012	Fort Wayne (MWL)	LoA	6	1	1.84	48	0	0	3	73	52	4	31	84	10.3	1.13	.195
2013	Lake Elsinore (CAL)	HiA	3	6	5.01	49	7	0	14	88	90	8	33	89	9.1	1.40	.269
Minor League Totals			10	11	3.92	112	20	0	17	218	194	16	95	223	9.2	1.32	.240

San Francisco Giants

BY ANDREW BAGGARLY

In one respect, the Giants had a tremendous year on the farm. Their domestic affiliates combined for a 391-302 record, when only the Astros posted a better winning percentage among major league organizations.

But in a more significant respect, the season was a colossal disappointment. For the second time in three years, the Giants went from World Series champions to entirely shut out of postseason play. This time, they needed a strong finish in September just to avoid joining the 1998 Marlins as the only defending champions to finish in last place.

And when the Giants needed it most, their farm system was a major letdown.

When center fielder and leadoff man Angel Pagan was lost to hamstring surgery, 2010 first-round pick Gary Brown wasn't ready to handle major league pitchers. When righthanded set-up man Santiago Casilla had leg surgery, power-armed righty Heath Hembree was still working on a dependable offspeed pitch at Triple-A Fresno.

Most critically, when the Giants' stalwart rotation showed some deep cracks, the pitchers they hoped to provide upper-level depth—lefthanders Mike Kickham and Eric Surkamp and righty Chris Heston—weren't made of major league timber.

"I think it's pretty simple," Giants general manager Brian Sabean said. "We didn't have enough depth. (In 2012), we seemingly were able to overcome injury and lack of performance. We didn't do that this year. We didn't get any kind of life from the minor leagues, whether that was the fifth starter or what we went through in center and left field."

The Giants won those two World Series championships with astute draft picks such as Buster Posey (2008), Madison Bumgarner (2007), Matt Cain (2002) and Tim Lincecum (2006). They have a few intriguing arms in the system now, a list headed by 2011 supplemental first-round righthander Kyle Crick. But too many of their recent high draft picks either don't wow scouts with their tools or have moved through the minor leagues slowly as they struggle to make adjustments.

Sabean is the longest-tenured GM in baseball and his job just got tougher now that the archrival Dodgers have the game's most expensive payroll. The Giants might have learned a lesson from Los Angeles' success with international stars like Yasiel Puig and Hyun-Jin Ryu. Similarly, the Athletics, the Giants' counterparts across the San Francisco Bay, scored big with Yoenis Cespedes.

If the Giants are to reclaim their place atop the National League West, they'll have to do it with improved pitching and defense. Knowing they wouldn't be blown away by the choices on the free agent market, the Giants made preemptive strikes by committing $90 million to Hunter Pence (for five years) and $35 million to a declining Tim Lincecum (for two years). They also made a low-risk pact with former Braves righthander Tim Hudson for two years and $23 million on the free agent market.

And until the next wave of pitchers arrives, the Giants will have to keep their frontline players on the field. They don't have the depth to compete otherwise.

LARRY GOREN

The farm system bare, Giants GM Brian Sabean had nowhere to turn in 2013

TOP PROSPECTS OF THE DECADE

Year	Player, Pos.	2013 Org.
2004	Merkin Valdez, rhp	Out of baseball
2005	Matt Cain, rhp	Giants
2006	Matt Cain, rhp	Giants
2007	Tim Lincecum, rhp	Giants
2008	Angel Villalona, 1b	Giants
2009	Madison Bumgarner, lhp	Giants
2010	Buster Posey, c	Giants
2011	Brandon Belt, 1b	Giants
2012	Gary Brown, of	Giants
2013	Kyle Crick, rhp	Giants

ORGANIZATION OVERVIEW

General Manager: Brian Sabean. **Farm Director:** Fred Stanley. **Scouting Director:** John Barr.

Class	Team	League	W	L	PCT	Finish	Manager(s)
Majors	San Francisco Giants	National	76	86	.469	9th (15)	Bruce Bochy
Triple-A	Fresno Giants	Pacific Coast	68	75	.476	12th (16)	Bob Mariano
Double-A	Richmond Flying Squirrels	Eastern	70	72	.493	6th (12)	Dave Machemer
High Class A	San Jose Giants	California	83	57	.593	1st (10)	Andy Skeels
Low Class A	Augusta Greenjackets	South Atlantic	82	55	.599	1st (14)	Mike Goff
Short-season	Salem-Keizer Volcanoes	Northwest	47	29	.618	1st (8)	Gary Davenport
Rookie	AZL Giants	Arizona	41	15	.745	1st (13)	D. McMains/N. Rojas
Overall 2013 Minor League Record			**391**	**302**	**.564**	**2nd (30)**	

THIS YEAR'S TOP 30

No.	Player, Pos.	Grade/Risk
1.	Kyle Crick, rhp	65/High
2.	Edwin Escobar, lhp	60/Medium
3.	Chris Stratton, rhp	55/High
4.	Adalberto Mejia, lhp	55/High
5.	Mac Williamson, of	55/High
6.	Christian Arroyo, ss	55/High
7.	Heath Hembree, rhp	50/High
8.	Ty Blach, lhp	50/High
9.	Joe Panik, 2b	45/Medium
10.	Clayton Blackburn, rhp	50/High
11.	Andrew Susac, c	50/High
12.	Derek Law, rhp	45/Medium
13.	Keury Mella, rhp	55/Extreme
14.	Kendry Flores, rhp	50/High
15.	Ryder Jones, 3b	50/High
16.	Angel Villalona, 1b	45/High
17.	Joan Gregorio, rhp	45/High
18.	Ehire Adrianza, ss	40/Low
19.	Gary Brown, of	50/Extreme
20.	Mike Kickham, lhp	45/High
21.	Martin Agosta, rhp	45/High
22.	Juan Perez, of	40/Low
23.	Josh Osich, lhp	45/High
24.	Steven Okert, lhp	45/High
25.	Chase Johnson, rhp	45/High
26.	Jose DePaula, lhp	45/High
27.	Cody Hall, rhp	45/High
28.	Stephen Johnson, rhp	50/Extreme
29.	Roger Kieschnick, of	40/Medium
30.	Erik Cordier, rhp	45/Extreme

LAST YEAR'S TOP 30

No.	Player, Pos.	Status
1.	Kyle Crick, rhp	No. 1
2.	Joe Panik, 2b	No. 9
3.	Chris Stratton, rhp	No. 3
4.	Gary Brown, of	No. 19
5.	Mike Kickham, lhp	No. 20
6.	Clayton Blackburn, rhp	No. 10
7.	Heath Hembree, rhp	No. 7
8.	Francisco Peguero, of	(Free agent)
9.	Roger Kieschnick, of	No. 29
10.	Adalberto Mejia, lhp	No. 4
11.	Adam Duvall, 3b	Dropped out
12.	Gustavo Cabrera, of	Dropped out
13.	Andrew Susac, c	No. 11
14.	Edwin Escobar, lhp	No. 2
15.	Martin Agosta, rhp	No. 21
16.	Mac Williamson, of	No. 5
17.	Chris Heston, rhp	Dropped out
18.	Steven Okert, lhp	No. 24
19.	Chris Marlowe, rhp	Dropped out
20.	Josh Osich, lhp	No. 23
21.	Stephen Johnson, rhp	No. 28
22.	Juan Perez, of	No. 22
23.	Nick Noonan, ss/3b	Dropped out
24.	Ehire Adrianza, ss	No. 18
25.	Eric Surkamp, lhp	Dropped out
26.	Cody Hall, rhp	No. 27
27.	Ricky Oropesa, 1b	Dropped out
28.	Jacob Dunnington, rhp	Dropped out
29.	Shawn Payne, of	Dropped out
30.	Brett Bochy, rhp	Dropped out

BEST TOOLS

Best Hitter for Average	Christian Arroyo
Best Power Hitter	Angel Villalona
Best Strike-Zone Discipline	Joe Panik
Fastest Baserunner	Gary Brown
Best Athlete	Gary Brown
Best Fastball	Kyle Crick
Best Curveball	Kyle Crick
Best Slider	Derek Law
Best Changeup	Clayton Blackburn
Best Control	Ty Blach
Best Defensive Catcher	Jeff Arnold
Best Defensive Infielder	Ehire Adrianza
Best Infield Arm	Chris Dominguez
Best Defensive Outfielder	Juan Perez
Best Outfield Arm	Juan Perez

TOP 15 PLAYERS 25 AND UNDER

No.	Player, Pos. (Age)	Peak Level
1.	Madison Bumgarner, lhp (24)	Majors
2.	Brandon Belt, 1b (25)	Majors
3.	Kyle Crick, rhp (21)	High Class A
4.	Edwin Escobar, lhp (21)	Double-A
5.	Chris Stratton, rhp (23)	Low Class A
6.	Adalberto Mejia, lhp (20)	Triple-A
7.	Mac Williamson, of (23)	High Class A
8.	Christian Arroyo, ss (18)	Rookie
9.	Heath Hembree, rhp (25)	Majors
10.	Ty Blach, lhp (23)	High Class A
11.	Joe Panik, 2b (23)	Double-A
12.	Andrew Susac, c (24)	Double-A
13.	Hector Sanchez, c (24)	Majors
14.	Clayton Blackburn, rhp (21)	High Class A
15.	Kendry Flores, rhp (22)	Low Class A

MINOR LEAGUE DEPTH CHART

SAN FRANCISCO GIANTS

TOP 2014 ROOKIE: Heath Hembree, rhp. He showed he had the stuff and temperament to get big league hitters out in a September glimpse, and he could inherit save opps should anything befall Sergio Romo.

BREAKOUT PROSPECT: Keury Mella, rhp. He combines youth, strength, stuff and a sunny temperament that has Giants officials convinced he'll be game for tougher competition.

SLEEPER: Ian Gardeck, rhp. A 16th-rounder out of Alabama in 2012, Gardeck had little idea where his 96 mph fastball and slider were going before a mechanical adjustment in instructional league improved his delivery.

SOURCE OF TOP 30 TALENT

Homegrown	**27**	**Acquired**	**3**
College	15	Trades	1
Junior college	2	Rule 5 draft	0
High school	4	Independent leagues	0
Nondrafted free agents	0	Free agents/waivers	2
International	6		

LF
Juan Perez (22)
Roger Kieschnick (29)
Devin Harris
Shilo McCall
Shawn Payne

CF
Gary Brown (19)
Gustavo Cabrera
Jesus Galindo
Johneshwy Fargas

RF
Mac Williamson (5)
Jarrett Parker

3B
Ryder Jones (15)
Adam Duvall
Jonah Arenado

SS
Christian Arroyo (6)
Ehire Adrianza (18)
Matt Duffy
Brandon Bednar

2B
Joe Panik (9)
Nick Noonan
Ryan Cavan

1B
Angel Villalona (16)
Brian Ragira
Ricky Oropesa
Mark Minicozzi

C
Andrew Susac (11)
John Riley
Jeff Arnold

LHP

LHSP	LHRP
Edwin Escobar (2)	Josh Osich (23)
Adalberto Mejia (4)	Steven Okert (24)
Ty Blach (8)	Bryce Bandilla
Mike Kickham (20)	Mason McVay
Jose DePaula (26)	
Eric Surkamp	

RHP

RHSP	RHRP
Kyle Crick (1)	Heath Hembree (7)
Chris Stratton (3)	Derek Law (12)
Clayton Blackburn (10)	Joan Gregorio (17)
Keury Mella (13)	Cody Hall (27)
Kendry Flores (14)	Stephen Johnson (28)
Martin Agosta (21)	Erik Cordier (30)
Chase Johnson (25)	Jake Dunning
Chris Heston	Jose Casilla
	Daniel Slania
	Chris Marlowe
	Ian Gardeck
	Tyler Mizenko
	Jorge Bucardo
	Brett Bochy

DRAFT ANALYSIS

2013

BONUSES: $4.9 MILLION

BEST PURE HITTER: The Giants considered SS Christian Arroyo (1) one of the best pure hitters in the class, which pushed him up their draft board. He has a knack for getting the barrel on the ball.

BEST POWER HITTER: 3B Ryder Jones (2) has present strength and room to get bigger and stronger, and there's leverage in his swing. OF Tyler Horan (8) matched the Cape Cod League single-season home run record with 16 in 2012, the year of juiced balls in summer leagues.

FASTEST RUNNER: Puerto Rican OF Joneshway Fargas (11) is a 70 runner on the 20-80 scale with a wiry 6-foot-2, 160-pound build.

BEST DEFENSIVE PLAYER: C Ty Ross (12) handled a staff with plenty of velocity and different looks at Louisiana State and has solid catch-and-throw skills. Some in the organization like Arroyo's arm strength, internal clock and good hands at second base.

BEST FASTBALL: RHP Chase Johnson (3) was a college reliever who has hit 97 mph. He sits in the low 90s as a starter but still touches 95-96 mph.

BEST SECONDARY PITCH: The Giants drafted several pitchers who have breaking balls with potential, starting with RHP Dan Slania (5), who throws both a curve and slider. LHP Nick Gonzalez (24) and RHP Dusten Knight (28) also have good breaking balls.

BEST PRO DEBUT: Arroyo earned Rookie-level Arizona League MVP honors after hitting .326/.388/.511 with 18 doubles. RHP Pat Young (13) went 4-1, 1.22 in 44 innings, then finished with an emergency callup to high Class A San Jose in the playoffs and threw well.

BEST ATHLETE: Some scouts wanted Arroyo to move behind the plate, but the Giants believe in his athletic ability and body control, even if his speed is modest.

MOST INTRIGUING BACKGROUND: Arroyo was MVP of the gold-medal winning USA Baseball 18U team in 2012. Jones' father Billy is Appalachian State's head coach. 3B Jonah Arendado (16) is the younger brother of Rockies third baseman Nolan.

CLOSEST TO THE MAJORS: Johnson or IF Brooks Bednar (7), a versatile defender with no glaring weakness or true plus tool.

BEST LATE-ROUND PICK: The Giants' local appeal and a $450,000 bonus lured C John Riley (31) away from a California commitment. He's a developing defender with good bat speed, and the Giants had inside dope on his makeup via big league pitching coach Dave Righetti, whose brother Steve coaches at Riley's high school in San Jose.

THE ONE WHO GOT AWAY: OF Ryan Kirby (40) is a fine hitter who batted .316 this summer in the West Coast League; he's at San Diego. The Giants also took a run at 6-foot-9 RHP Chris Viali (39), who's at Stanford.

ASSESSMENT: The Giants' belief in the bats of Arroyo and Jones was stronger than that of other clubs. So far, so good. The organization's pitching track record means at least one of these arms will help in San Francisco as well.

2012

BONUSES: $4.6 MILLION

RHP Chris Stratton (1) got off to a slow start, but the Giants believe in his arm. LHP Ty Blach (9) has more polish with less upside. OF Mac Williamson (3) is a key power bat in a system in need. .

GRADE: C

2011

BONUSES: $6.3 MILLION

RHP Kyle Crick (1s) fits the Giants mold. 2B Joe Panik (1) and C Andrew Susac (2) still have a shot to be regulars. RHP Derek Law (9) is a nice sleeper. .

GRADE: B

2010

BONUSES: $4.1 MILLION

The Giants hoped for more from OFs Gary Brown (1), Jarrett Parker (2). RHP Heath Hembree (5), LHP Mike Kickham (6) are the best hopes left.

GRADE: D

TOP DRAFT PICKS OF THE DECADE

Year	Player, Pos.	2013 Org.
2004	Eddy Martinez-Esteve, of (2nd round)	Somerset (Atlantic)
2005	Ben Copeland, of (4th round)	Out of baseball
2006	Tim Lincecum, rhp	Giants
2007	Madison Bumgarner, lhp	Giants
2008	Buster Posey, c	Giants
2009	Zack Wheeler, rhp	Mets
2010	Gary Brown, of	Giants
2011	Joe Panik, ss	Giants
2012	Chris Stratton, rhp	Giants
2013	Christian Arroyo, ss	Giants

LARGEST BONUSES IN CLUB HISTORY

Buster Posey, 2008	$6,200,000
Zack Wheeler, 2009	$3,300,000
Rafael Rodriguez, 2008	$2,550,000
Angel Villalona, 2006	$2,100,000
Tim Lincecum, 2006	$2,025,000

1 KYLE CRICK, RHP

Born: November 30, 1992. **B-T:** L-R. **Ht.:** 6-4. **Wt.:** 225. **Drafted:** HS—Sherman, Texas, 2011 (1st round supplemental). **Signed by:** Todd Thomas.

The Giants have a lot more invested in Crick than just the $900,000 he received as the 49th overall pick in 2011. He has the highest ceiling among a wave of pitching prospects the Giants must rely upon to create a foundation for future success in the National League West. Crick has a low-mileage arm because he mostly played first base in high school and didn't concentrate on pitching until he hit 94 mph on the showcase circuit. The Giants loved his size, competitiveness, arm speed and the life on his pitches, and weren't concerned that his mechanics needed to be cleaned up. He has made the transition from a short-arm delivery to smoother, more repeatable mechanics, but his progress was interrupted when he strained an oblique in his third start of the season for high Class A San Jose in 2013 and missed two months. When he got healthy, he more than made up for lost time. In his first start back on June 21, the 20-year-old struck out 10 in four shutout innings and kept on pumping his power stuff the rest of the season and into the Arizona Fall League.

Crick's fastball is a 70 pitch that is as lively as it is hard. He draws natural comparisons with Matt Cain from coaches who saw the Giants ace when he was a teenager. Crick ran his fastball up to 98 mph at times, but it's his ability to maintain mid-90s velocity past 80 pitches that sets him apart from so many other live arms. Crick's strong and athletic build reminds some coaches of 1999 first-rounder Kurt Ainsworth. He drops his arms as he starts from the windup and separates his hands late, making up for it with tremendous arm speed. That gives him a bit of deception to go along with power stuff that seemingly explodes out of his hand. Crick threw a slider in high school, but his curveball became a better breaking pitch. Managers in the low Class A South Atlantic League in 2012 voted it best breaking pitch, even though he basically used it as a show-me offering while learning to throw it dependably for strikes. Crick didn't throw the curve nearly as often as coaches would have preferred, because his fastball was too overpowering. Scouts project him to have a solid-average changeup. His stuff is so live, he's unlikely to ever have great command, but scouts project him to have average control as he gains experience.

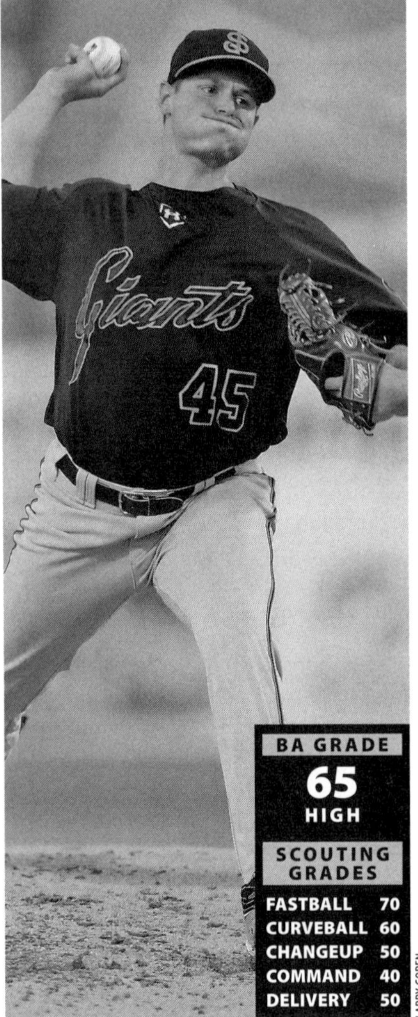

Giants
45
BA GRADE
65
HIGH
SCOUTING GRADES
FASTBALL 70
CURVEBALL 60
CHANGEUP 50
COMMAND 40
DELIVERY 50

LARRY GOREN

Cain reached the big leagues before his 21st birthday, but it's difficult to imagine Crick being ready so soon—especially after the oblique injury limited him to just 69 innings at San Jose. He has only 187 professional innings under his belt and has issued 5.5 walks per nine innings, so Crick has to work on throwing quality strikes and trusting his offspeed pitches. The Giants sent him to the AFL to log additional innings, and after initial struggles, he struck out 24 in 16 innings. He's ready to move up to Double-A Richmond in 2014.

Year	Club (League)	Class	W	L	ERA	G	GS	CG	SV	IP	H	HR	BB	SO	K/9	WHIP	AVG
2011	Giants (AZL)	R	1	0	6.43	7	0	0	0	7	9	0	8	8	10.3	2.43	.321
2012	Augusta (SAL)	LoA	7	6	2.51	23	22	0	0	111	75	1	67	128	10.3	1.28	.193
2013	San Jose (CAL)	HiA	3	1	1.57	14	14	0	0	69	48	1	39	95	12.5	1.27	.201
Minor League Totals			11	7	2.31	44	36	0	0	187	132	2	114	231	11.1	1.32	.202

2 EDWIN ESCOBAR, LHP

BA GRADE
60
MEDIUM

Born: April 22, 1992. **B-T:** L-L. **Ht.:** 6-1. **Wt.:** 195. **Signed:** Venezuela, 2008. **Signed by:** Wilmer Becerra/Rafic Saab (Rangers).

Escobar has multiple cousins and relatives in professional baseball, from Kelvim and Alcides Escobar to Yankees farmhand Jose Campos. The Giants tried to sign Escobar as a teenager out of Venezuela, but his family had connections to the Rangers and he signed with them. The Giants finally got Escobar when the Rangers picked Giants lefty Ben Snyder in the Rule 5 draft, then traded Escobar to the Giants to keep Snyder in the spring of 2010. He was the only member of high Class A San Jose's prospect-laden rotation to earn a promotion to Double-A Richmond in 2013, and his numbers only got better from there. Escobar always had size and strength, but he got himself in better condition and made an adjustment to raise his elbow in his delivery, allowing him to locate his 92-93 mph fastball, and for the first time, throw a dependable breaking ball. He gained confidence in his slider and it's a plus offering at times that he can throw early in the count or as a put-away pitch. His changeup also ranges from average to plus, and he held righthanded hitters to a .222 average. Escobar has a durable arm and likes to throw a lot between starts, so a bullpen role isn't out of the question. He was pitching in that role in the Venezuelan League, but his three-pitch mix offers too much potential as a starter. He figures to start 2014 at Triple-A Fresno.

Year	Club (League)	Class	W	L	ERA	G	GS	CG	SV	IP	H	HR	BB	SO	K/9	WHIP	AVG
2009	Rangers (AZL)	R	2	5	5.00	13	12	0	0	45	53	1	16	48	9.6	1.53	.279
2010	Salem-Keizer (NWL)	SS	2	4	4.86	14	14	0	0	63	64	6	40	69	9.9	1.65	.270
2011	Augusta (SAL)	LoA	1	3	18.00	4	2	0	0	6	15	0	5	5	7.5	3.33	.455
	Giants gy(AZL)	R	2	4	5.09	15	12	0	0	46	51	2	17	42	8.2	1.48	.293
2012	Augusta (SAL)	LoA	7	8	2.96	22	22	0	0	131	121	7	32	122	8.4	1.17	.241
2013	San Jose (CAL)	HiA	3	4	2.89	16	14	0	0	75	68	3	17	92	11.1	1.14	.234
	Richmond (EL)	AA	5	4	2.67	10	10	0	0	54	44	2	13	54	9.0	1.06	.219
Minor League Totals			22	32	3.86	94	86	0	0	419	416	21	140	432	9.3	1.33	.256

3 CHRIS STRATTON, RHP

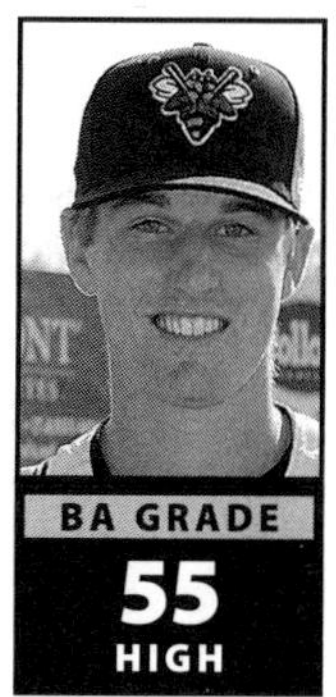

BA GRADE
55
HIGH

Born: Aug. 22, 1990. **B-T:** R-R. **Ht.:** 6-3. **Wt.:** 186. **Drafted:** Mississippi State, 2012 (1st round). **Signed by:** Hugh Walker.

The Giants had their eye on two college pitchers as their 21st overall selection neared in the 2012 draft. Stratton was one. Michael Wacha, who went 19th overall to the Cardinals, was the other. While Wacha was winning NLCS MVP honors, Stratton was resting up following his first full professional season at low Class A Augusta, a year after sustaining a concussion when he was struck by a line drive during batting practice at short-season Salem-Keizer. Stratton's fastball ranges anywhere from 89-93 mph and he has the ability to touch 95, but it's the downward movement of his two-seamer that makes him effective. He used a short slider as a strikeout pitch in college—he fanned 17 Louisiana State batters on the day Giants scouting director John Barr saw him—and it's gotten better as he had plenty of righthanded hitters lunging at it in the South Atlantic League. Stratton is a good athlete who doesn't have a lot of effort in his delivery. His curve and changeup will be priorities to improve as he advances. Stratton's combination of stuff and ability to pitch probably merited him a higher assignment, but the high Class A San Jose rotation was loaded, and Stratton didn't blow the doors off the SAL anyway. He'll start 2014 at San Jose to see if he can be a bit more consistently crisp with his stuff.

Year	Club (League)	Class	W	L	ERA	G	GS	CG	SV	IP	H	HR	BB	SO	K/9	WHIP	AVG
2012	Salem-Keizer (NWL)	SS	0	1	2.76	8	5	0	0	16	14	1	10	16	8.8	1.47	.237
2013	Augusta (SAL)	LoA	9	3	3.27	22	22	1	0	132	128	5	47	123	8.4	1.33	.258
Minor League Totals			9	4	3.22	30	27	1	0	148	142	6	57	139	8.4	1.34	.256

4 ADALBERTO MEJIA, LHP

BA GRADE
55
HIGH

Born: June 20, 1993. **B-T:** L-L. **Ht.:** 6-3. **Wt.:** 205. **Signed:** Dominican Republic, 2011. **Signed by:** Pablo Peguero.

The Giants have to like what their $350,000 investment in Mejia could bring them. Not only was he the youngest member of high Class A San Jose's prospect-studded rotation, but at 19, he ranked as the youngest starter in the Cal League. He added 2-3 mph to his fastball—something club officials thought he could do as he matured into his body—but it's his ability to pitch that most excites them. Mejia has a loose arm and shows the ability to throw three plus pitches for strikes. He'll pitch to contact with his two-seamer, his slider has plus tilt and depth and he effectively sells his changeup. His fastball, which reaches 92-93 mph, has natural cut that sometimes causes it to veer over the plate, leaving him a bit homer-prone. Mejia improved his delivery in 2013 but at times spins off and misses arm-side. The San Jose pitching staff led the Cal League in ERA for the eighth time in 10 seasons even though the Giants lost Mejia (lat strain) and Kyle Crick (oblique) in the first week of May. They rehabbed together and pitched together in the Arizona Fall League as well. They should' form a right-left complement again at Double-A Richmond, but Mejia's advanced command and feel could allow him to reach the big leagues first.

Year	Club (League)	Class	W	L	ERA	G	GS	CG	SV	IP	H	HR	BB	SO	K/9	WHIP	AVG
2011	Giants (DSL)	R	5	2	1.42	13	13	0	0	76	58	0	8	71	8.4	0.87	.209
2012	Augusta (SAL)	LoA	10	7	3.97	30	14	1	0	107	122	4	21	79	6.7	1.34	.284
2013	Fresno (PCL)	AAA	0	0	3.60	1	1	0	0	5	5	2	2	2	3.6	1.40	.250
	San Jose (CAL)	HiA	7	4	3.31	16	16	0	0	87	75	11	23	89	9.2	1.13	.228
Minor League Totals			22	13	3.05	60	44	1	0	275	260	17	54	241	7.9	1.14	.246

5 MAC WILLIAMSON, OF

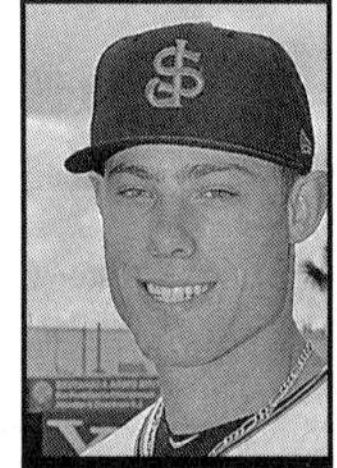

BA GRADE
55
HIGH

Born: July 15, 1990. **B-T:** R-R. **Ht.:** 6-4. **Wt.:** 245. **Drafted:** Wake Forest, 2012 (3rd round). **Signed by:** Jeremy Cleveland.

Williamson easily had the most impressive season of any Giants hitting prospect at a full-season affiliate, leading the organization in home runs (25) and RBIs (89). He started his banner year by blasting three homers in a spring training scrimmage and kept making hard contact while tying for third in the Cal League in bombs. A prep catcher and pitcher who had labrum surgery as a college freshman, Williamson is making up for lost time with a max-effort approach, desire and a good work ethic. Williamson's righthanded power is his best tool, but he's shown an improved approach, leading high Class A San Jose in walks. Breaking balls can still vex him, but he has the strength to hit his pitch out of the park to all fields. Williamson combines imposing size with solid athleticism. He's an above-average athlete who runs average underway, and he was caught stealing only once in 11 attempts. His range is average and his arm is strong enough for right field, if not always accurate. His pitch recognition skills will be tested as he moves up to face more advanced competition in the pitching-rich Double-A Eastern League.

Year	Club (League)	Class	AVG	G	AB	R	H	2B	3B	HR	RBI	BB	SO	SB	CS	OBP	SLG
2012	Giants (AZL)	R	.176	4	17	4	3	0	0	2	7	2	5	0	0	.263	.529
	Salem-Keizer (NWL)	SS	.342	29	114	22	39	8	0	7	25	6	19	0	0	.392	.596
2013	San Jose (CAL)	HiA	.292	136	520	94	152	31	2	25	89	51	132	10	1	.375	.504
Minor League Totals			.298	169	651	120	194	39	2	34	121	59	156	10	1	.375	.521

6 CHRISTIAN ARROYO, SS

BILL MITCHELL

BA GRADE
55
HIGH

Born: May 30, 1995. **B-T:** R-R. **Ht.:** 6-1. **Wt.:** 180. **Drafted:** HS—Brooksville, Fla., 2013 (1st round). **Signed by:** Mike Metcalf.

Arroyo hit .341 to win MVP honors for USA Baseball's 18-and-under team that won the World Championships in South Korea in 2012, and the Giants went off most experts' draft boards to take him in the first round in 2013. A smart competitor who was salutatorian of his high school class and lists AP Calculus as his favorite subject, Arroyo put up some advanced numbers in the Rookie-level Arizona League, leading the circuit in doubles (18), RBIs (39) and slugging (.511) to add another MVP award to his collection. Some scouts had Arroyo pegged as a catcher because he's an average athlete and below-average runner. But the Giants fell in love with his pure hitting ability, and for now he'll continue to develop as a shortstop. He faces a likely move to second base in the future because of his average range and speed, though he probably has enough arm strength to play third. Arroyo profiles to be a gap hitter with occasional power, but many scouts said the same thing about Buster Posey. Arroyo generates plenty of bat speed and doesn't get beaten by quality fastballs. The Giants will have an interesting decision to make this spring. They could be justified in skipping Arroyo one level to high Class A San Jose. More likely, he'll start out at low Class A Augusta, along with second-round pick Ryder Jones.

Year	Club (League)	Class	AVG	G	AB	R	H	2B	3B	HR	RBI	BB	SO	SB	CS	OBP	SLG
2013	Giants (AZL)	R	.326	45	184	47	60	18	5	2	39	19	32	3	2	.388	.511
Minor League Totals			.326	45	184	47	60	18	5	2	39	19	32	3	2	.388	.511

7 HEATH HEMBREE, RHP

BA GRADE
50
HIGH

Born: Jan. 13, 1989. **B-T:** R-R. **Ht.:** 6-4. **Wt.:** 205. **Drafted:** College of Charleston, 2010 (5th round). **Signed by:** Jeremy Cleveland.

Expected to be the club's closer of the future, Hembree wasn't ready for any relief role when the Giants badly needed help in May and June. Instead, he gave up 17 runs in 21 innings to Triple-A Pacific Coast League hitters. Though Hembree had recovered from the forearm strain that bothered him a year earlier, his lack of a dependable secondary pitch kept him at Fresno. He improved in the second half and kept it up into September, when he was unscored upon in nine big league appearances. A seldom-used college closer, Hembree vaulted up the prospect rankings because of his 98 mph fastball and power slider. He pitched more effectively in the 92-94 mph range in 2013, but has addressed past issues of wildness within the strike zone and shows more ability to dial back and locate. Hembree's slider was the key to his second-half turnaround. He developed the ability to shape it to steal strikes or sweep it when he wants a strikeout. Hembree saved 31 games for Fresno and will be given every opportunity to win a job in the Giants bullpen this spring as a set-up man. Even if he never gets back that 98 mph heat, his size and stuff compare well with former Giant Bob Howry, who had a long career in late relief.

Year	Club (League)	Class	W	L	ERA	G	GS	CG	SV	IP	H	HR	BB	SO	K/9	WHIP	AVG
2010	Giants (AZL)	R	0	0	0.82	12	0	0	3	11	9	0	0	22	18.0	0.82	.220
2011	San Jose (CAL)	HiA	0	0	0.73	26	0	0	21	25	16	1	12	44	16.1	1.14	.182
	Richmond (EL)	AA	1	1	2.83	28	0	0	17	29	20	1	13	34	10.7	1.15	.194
2012	San Jose (CAL)	HiA	0	0	0.00	5	0	0	0	5	0	0	1	7	12.6	0.20	.000
	Fresno (PCL)	AAA	1	1	4.74	39	0	0	15	38	29	2	20	36	8.5	1.29	.207
2013	Fresno (PCL)	AAA	1	4	4.07	54	0	0	31	55	54	7	16	63	10.2	1.27	.248
	San Francisco (NL)	MAJ	0	0	0.00	9	0	0	0	8	4	0	2	12	14.1	0.78	.148
Major League Totals			0	0	0.00	9	0	0	0	8	4	0	2	12	14.1	0.78	.148
Minor League Totals			3	6	3.15	164	0	0	87	163	128	11	62	206	11.4	1.17	.211

8 TY BLACH, LHP

BA GRADE
50
HIGH

Born: Oct. 20, 1990. **B-T:** R-L. **Ht.:** 6-2. **Wt.:** 200. **Drafted:** Creighton, 2012 (5th round). **Signed by:** Lou Colletti.

A Colorado high school product, Blach spent three years in Creighton's rotation, shouldering a heavy load in 2012 when he led the nation with 21 starts and ranked 12th with 120 innings pitched. The Giants signed him for $224,500, then gave him the rest of the year off. He jumped to high Class A San Jose for his pro debut and led the California League in ERA en route to pitcher of the year honors. Blach has a true four-pitch mix and is a perfectionist when it comes to location, often expressing dissatisfaction with a pitch even when he gets a good result. He led the Cal League with 1.2 walks per nine innings and profiles as a command lefty. He can spot both sides of the plate with both his two-seamer as well as a four-seamer that sits at 89-90 mph and tops out at 94. He likes to throw his backfoot slider to righthanded hitters and can bury a solid-average curve with two strikes, but his changeup is his best offspeed pitch. It has some fade and his herky-jerky motion adds deception. Blach was the oldest and least heralded of the five prospects who began the season in the rotation at San Jose but quickly became the ace. He doesn't profile as a top-of-the-rotation pitcher, but his combination of smarts and command should work at higher levels, starting at Double-A Richmond in 2014.

Year	Club (League)	Class	W	L	ERA	G	GS	CG	SV	IP	H	HR	BB	SO	K/9	WHIP	AVG
2013	San Jose (CAL)	HiA	12	4	2.90	22	20	0	0	130	124	8	18	117	8.1	1.09	.248
Minor League Totals			12	4	2.90	22	20	0	0	130	124	8	18	117	8.1	1.09	.248

9 JOE PANIK, 2B

REAL LIFE STUDIOS

BA GRADE
45
MEDIUM

Born: Oct. 30, 1990. **B-T:** L-R. **Ht.:** 6-1. **Wt.:** 195. **Drafted:** St. John's, 2011 (1st round). **Signed by:** John DiCarlo.

An all-Big East Conference shortstop at St. John's, Panik hit .341 in his pro debut and was the short-season Northwest League MVP in 2011. He hasn't quite been able to replicate his early success, however. He injured his hamstring to spoil his first invitation to big league spring training, and the injury continued to affect him at Double-A Richmond, where he went through a horrific slump in June and July and struggled with his approach at times against lefthanders. Panik doesn't have standout tools, but he works deep counts, turns around quality fastballs and has some gap power. While he won't hit it over the fence, he's an unselfish hitter who has a knack for getting a runner home with less than two outs. He'll steal a base when you forget about him but is a fringe-average runner. Moving from shortstop to second base, he showed improved range and a better backhand. He has enough arm to turn double plays and solid infield actions. While some scouts think a Nick Punto-type utility role will be in his future, the Giants see a smart, contact-oriented No. 2 hitter in the mold of Marco Scutaro or Freddy Sanchez. Panik ought to get off to a cleaner start at Triple-A Fresno, and he could be in the big leagues in 2014 if the 38-year-old Scutaro needs relief.

Year	Club (League)	Class	AVG	G	AB	R	H	2B	3B	HR	RBI	BB	SO	SB	CS	OBP	SLG
2011	Salem-Keizer (NWL)	SS	.341	69	270	49	92	10	3	6	54	28	25	13	5	.401	.467
2012	San Jose (CAL)	HiA	.297	130	535	93	159	27	4	7	76	58	54	10	4	.368	.402
2013	Richmond (EL)	AA	.257	137	522	64	134	27	4	4	57	58	68	10	5	.333	.347
Minor League Totals			.290	336	1327	206	385	64	11	17	187	144	147	33	14	.361	.393

10 CLAYTON BLACKBURN, RHP

Born: Jan. 6, 1993. **B-T:** L-R. **Ht.:** 6-3. **Wt.:** 220. **Drafted:** HS—Edmond, Okla., 2011 (16th round). **Signed by:** Daniel Murray.

The Giants bought Blackburn out of his commitment to Oklahoma for $150,000, then watched him pitch with the maturity and finesse of a college senior. He led the low Class A South Atlantic League in WHIP (1.02) and strikeouts (143) in 2012 but struggled to replicate his success at high Class A San Jose in 2013. In one nine-start stretch in May and June, he allowed 33 earned runs in 49 innings. Blackburn struggled with command for the first time, and several nagging injuries probably were to blame for inconsistent mechanics and pitches that rode up in the zone. He's a big-bodied presence on the mound in the mold of Rick Reuschel and when healthy, his command of four pitches draws comparisons with a young Joe Blanton. He's a better athlete than his size would indicate, though coaches have to stay on him about his conditioning work. Blackburn can pitch at 89-93 mph with his fastball but is more comfortable sitting 87-90 with the ability to throw his curve, changeup and slider for strikes in any count. His curveball has some power at up to 77 mph and earns some plus grades. Although Blackburn had some growing pains, he still had a near-4.0 SO/BB ratio and finished strong, particularly after taking a perfect game into the seventh inning on July 25 at Lancaster. He profiles as a rotation workhorse and heads to Double-A in 2014.

Year	Club (League)	Class	W	L	ERA	G	GS	CG	SV	IP	H	HR	BB	SO	K/9	WHIP	AVG
2011	Giants (AZL)	R	3	1	1.08	12	6	0	0	33	16	2	3	30	8.1	0.57	.140
2012	Augusta (SAL)	LoA	8	4	2.54	22	22	0	0	131	116	3	18	143	9.8	1.02	.232
2013	San Jose (CAL)	HiA	7	5	3.65	23	23	0	0	133	111	12	35	138	9.3	1.10	.224
Minor League Totals			18	10	2.87	57	51	0	0	298	243	17	56	311	9.4	1.00	.219

11 ANDREW SUSAC, C

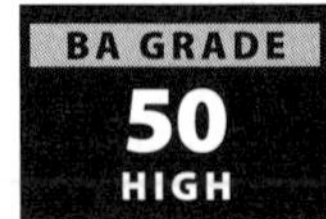

Born: March 22, 1990. **B-T:** R-R. **Ht.:** 6-1. **Wt.:** 200. **Drafted:** Oregon State, 2011 (2nd round). **Signed by:** Matt Woodward.

A hamate fracture in his wrist ended Susac's college career a month before the 2011 draft and probably caused him to slide to the second round. The Giants were excited to take him, signing for an over-slot $1.1 million bonus, feeling that his bat would be ready long before his receiving skills were. It turned out Susac was challenged in both areas in a humbling debut at high Class A San Jose in 2012. He got back on track at Double-A Richmond in 2013 before a thumb injury took him out of action. Susac has above-average raw power, and his natural stroke gives him more power to right-center field than anywhere else. He made adjustments to keep his swing from getting too long, and he made harder, more consistent contact. Susac still is learning to pull the ball with authority as he gains experience, and his patient approach helps. He led the Arizona Fall League with a .507 on-base percentage. He also earned plaudits for the progress he made with game-calling.

Susac has all the tools to be an above-average defensive catcher, including a quick release and strong arm. He threw out 40 percent of Eastern League basestealers in 2013. Scouts, however, point out that Susac still has plenty of work to do when it comes to receiving and blocking. His bat remains his ticket to the big leagues and his AFL performance opened eyes. Susac will begin 2014 at Triple-A Fresno, and one day he might move Buster Posey to a less-stressful position.

Year	Club (League)	Class	AVG	G	AB	R	H	2B	3B	HR	RBI	BB	SO	SB	CS	OBP	SLG
2012	San Jose (CAL)	HiA	.244	102	361	58	88	16	3	9	52	55	100	1	1	.351	.380
2013	Richmond (EL)	AA	.256	84	262	32	67	17	0	12	46	42	68	1	0	.362	.458
Minor League Totals			.249	186	623	90	155	33	3	21	98	97	168	2	1	.356	.413

12 DEREK LAW, RHP

BA GRADE
45
MEDIUM

Born: Sept. 14, 1990. **B-T:** R-R. **Ht.:** 6-3. **Wt.:** 218. **Drafted:** Miami Dade JC, 2011 (9th round). **Signed by:** Michael Metcalf.

Law's father Joe pitched nine seasons in the Athletics system and once spent four days on Oakland's major league roster, but he never appeared in the majors. The junior Law certainly doesn't have the textbook delivery that would suggest baseball bloodlines, perhaps explaining how a power arm was able to slide in the draft both out of high school (28th-round pick by the Rangers in 2009) and out of junior college (ninth round, Giants, 2011). Law turns his back to the hitter, stabs with his takeaway arm action and throws over the top, giving him deception along with perhaps the best breaking ball in the Giants system. It's a hard curve that breaks sharply down, and his fastball has good downward plane as well. Law boosted his velocity, threw consistently in the low 90s and was a dynamic force after being promoted to high Class A San Jose, where he posted an unreal 45-to-1 strikeout-to-walk ratio in 28 innings. The Giants sent Law to the Arizona Fall League for some additional exposure, and he was among the most dominant relievers on the circuit with a 16/6 SO/BB ratio. His electric stuff and ability to neutralize righthanders could allow him to move rapidly through the system.

Year	Club (League)	Class	W	L	ERA	G	GS	CG	SV	IP	H	HR	BB	SO	K/9	WHIP	AVG
2011	Giants (AZL)	R	0	0	2.50	15	0	0	4	18	16	0	2	19	9.5	1.00	.232
2012	Augusta (SAL)	LoA	5	2	2.91	32	0	0	2	56	45	6	23	67	10.8	1.22	.216
2013	Augusta (SAL)	LoA	0	3	2.31	19	0	0	3	35	27	1	10	48	12.3	1.06	.206
	Giants (AZL)	R	1	0	3.18	5	0	0	0	6	4	0	1	9	14.3	0.88	.200
	San Jose (CAL)	HiA	4	0	2.10	22	0	0	11	26	20	1	1	45	15.8	0.82	.208
Minor League Totals			10	5	2.57	93	0	0	20	140	112	8	37	188	12.1	1.06	.214

13 KEURY MELLA, RHP

BA GRADE
55
EXTREME

Born: Aug. 2, 1993. **B-T:** R-R. **Ht.:** 6-2. **Wt.:** 190. **Signed:** Dominican Republic, 2011. **Signed by:** Pablo Peguero.

It's always a big deal when a Giants pitcher can shut down the Dodgers with a season on the line, even if it's only the championship game in the Rookie-level Arizona League. Mella was the right man for the assignment, holding the Dodgers scoreless over five innings to cap a season in which he emerged as a staff ace and one of the most promising arms in the system. Signed for $275,000 in 2011, Mella throws a heavy, above-average fastball that sits 93-95 mph with sinking action. He is learning to harness a power curve that has plus movement, and his changeup is functional even if he throws it infrequently. He goes to his fastball when he's in trouble and is better at climbing the ladder than throwing to both sides of the plate. Mella has a strong body and big, strong hands. His stuff would play up in relief, but the Giants expect to continue developing him as a starter. A high-energy personality, Mella is a favorite with teammates because he wants the ball and clearly enjoys being on the mound—especially in a big situation. Expect him to begin 2014 in low Class A Augusta's rotation.

Year	Club (League)	Class	W	L	ERA	G	GS	CG	SV	IP	H	HR	BB	SO	K/9	WHIP	AVG
2012	Giants (DSL)	R	3	3	2.47	14	14	0	0	69	59	3	28	75	9.7	1.25	.225
2013	Giants (AZL)	R	3	2	2.25	10	9	0	0	36	34	0	11	41	10.3	1.25	.252
Minor League Totals			6	5	2.39	24	23	0	0	105	93	3	39	116	9.9	1.25	.234

14 KENDRY FLORES, RHP

BA GRADE
50
HIGH

Born: Nov. 24, 1991. **B-T:** R-R. **Ht.:** 6-2. **Wt.:** 175. **Signed:** Dominican Republic, 2009. **Signed by:** Pablo Peguero.

Flores was well regarded as a hard-throwing teenager but wasn't able to maintain his velocity. His stuff didn't miss bats in two years at short-season Salem-Keizer and few thought he'd be much better at low Class A Augusta in 2013, his fifth pro season. But Flores turned out to be the biggest surprise in the system, posting an unreal 8.1 SO/BB ratio that topped all minor league ERA qualifiers. In an Aug. 21 start at Lexington he struck out 15 (with no walks), and he consistently outperformed 2012 first-rounder Chris Stratton atop Augusta's rotation. Flores never had a problem throwing strikes from a deliberate delivery. Getting his unremarkable, 87-90 mph fastball past hitters was the bigger issue. He doesn't have much projection, but he reliably hits the outside corner and has excellent feel for his changeup. For that reason, he actually was more effective against lefthanders. His curveball has the makings of a plus pitch but it isn't consistent. Flores still has youth on his side and coaches noted he carried himself with more confidence as he strung together one good starter after another. Even if he doesn't add any velocity, Flores will need to get more movement on his two-seamer since his flyball tendencies might not translate so well to the high Class A Cal League in 2104.

Year	Club (League)	Class	W	L	ERA	G	GS	CG	SV	IP	H	HR	BB	SO	K/9	WHIP	AVG
2009	Giants (DSL)	R	7	2	2.18	13	13	0	0	66	45	1	24	57	7.8	1.05	.200
2010	Giants (AZL)	R	5	4	3.60	13	11	0	0	55	49	2	13	56	9.2	1.13	.241
2011	Salem-Keizer (NWL)	SS	4	3	5.06	12	11	0	0	48	59	5	14	47	8.8	1.52	.304
2012	Salem-Keizer (NWL)	SS	1	3	4.46	10	8	0	0	42	44	4	11	34	7.2	1.30	.257
2013	Augusta (SAL)	LoA	10	6	2.73	22	22	1	0	142	113	11	17	137	8.7	0.92	.216
Minor League Totals			27	18	3.29	70	65	1	0	353	310	23	79	331	8.4	1.10	.236

15 RYDER JONES, 3B

BA GRADE **50** HIGH

Born: June 7, 1994. **B-T:** L-R. **Ht.:** 6-3. **Wt.:** 185. **Drafted:** HS—Boone, N.C., 2013 (2nd round). **Signed by:** Donnie Jones.

The son of Appalachian State baseball coach Billy Jones, Ryder must possess more than baseball smarts. He was committed to Stanford, but the Giants had a good read on his signability and the Cardinal ended up losing their first recruit since 2007. Every scout the Giants sent to watch Jones came away impressed with his contact skills and projectable power. A two-way star in high school who threw 92 mph off the mound, Jones moved from shortstop to third base and had a solid debut alongside fellow 2013 draftee Christian Arroyo in the Rookie-level Arizona League. In fact, he and Arroyo collected their first pro home runs by going back to back on July 19. Jones is solidly built, a below-average runner likely destined for an infield corner. He struggled at times while learning third base, and those sun-scorched, concrete-hard infields in the AZL didn't help. He's a pure hitter with an upright stance who has excellent barrel accuracy, a good feel for the strike zone and the chance to get stronger. Figure on Jones and Arroyo continuing to move up the ranks together, possibly at low Class A Augusta in 2014.

Year	Club (League)	Class	AVG	G	AB	R	H	2B	3B	HR	RBI	BB	SO	SB	CS	OBP	SLG
2013	Giants (AZL)	R	.317	37	145	29	46	9	0	1	18	14	38	0	0	.394	.400
Minor League Totals			.317	37	145	29	46	9	0	1	18	14	38	0	0	.394	.400

16 ANGEL VILLALONA, 1B

BA GRADE **45** HIGH

Born: Aug. 13, 1990. **B-T:** R-R. **Ht.:** 6-3. **Wt.:** 257. **Signed:** Dominican Republic, 2006. **Signed by:** Pablo Peguero.

The list of Giants' No. 1 prospects from 2006-11 includes Matt Cain, Tm Lincecum, Madison Bumgarner, Buster Posey and Brandon Belt. It also includes Villalona, who held more promise than anyone in the organization in 2008. Then came the murder charge in the Dominican Republic, nearly a year of house arrest, a lawsuit alleging the Giants with breach of contract and a two-year saga to reestablish his U.S. work visa. The Giants still aren't sure what to make of Villalona, who has some major deficiencies in his game as well as ongoing weight issues. But there's no denying his power is for real. Despite hitting just .229/.278/.433 at high Class A San Jose through June, the Giants swapped him with Double-A first baseman Ricky Oropesa in July. Villalona wasn't overmatched at Richmond and hit 22 homers combined, but his overall .276 on-base percentage was an issue. Villalona has smooth actions at first base, even if he isn't a good athlete. The Giants still hope he can put the rest of his game together, allowing his power to play in the big leagues.

Year	Club (League)	Class	AVG	G	AB	R	H	2B	3B	HR	RBI	BB	SO	SB	CS	OBP	SLG
2007	Giants (AZL)	R	.285	52	200	40	57	12	3	5	37	15	42	1	1	.344	.450
	Salem-Keizer (NWL)	SS	.167	5	12	1	2	0	0	0	1	0	2	1	0	.231	.167
2008	Augusta (SAL)	LoA	.263	123	464	64	122	29	0	17	64	18	118	1	2	.312	.435
2009	San Jose (CAL)	HiA	.267	74	292	47	78	11	0	9	42	9	73	0	1	.306	.397
2010	Did not play—Restricted																
2011	Did not play—Restricted																
2012	Giants (DSL)	R	.303	44	155	32	47	9	0	7	34	23	40	0	0	.430	.497
2013	San Jose (CAL)	HiA	.229	73	284	37	65	16	0	14	42	15	76	0	0	.278	.433
	Richmond (EL)	AA	.235	52	196	23	46	11	0	8	28	8	60	0	0	.273	.413
Minor League Totals			.260	423	1603	244	417	88	3	60	248	88	411	3	4	.317	.431

17 JOAN GREGORIO, RHP

BA GRADE 45 HIGH

Born: Jan. 12, 1992. **B-T:** R-R. **Ht.:** 6-7. **Wt.:** 180. **Signed:** Dominican Republic, 2010. **Signed by:** Pablo Peguero.

Gregorio could be Ubaldo Jimenez's mirror image. They're both tall, impossibly skinny and all of those long levers in their delivery seldom appear under control. Gregorio might not have the 99 mph fastball that Jimenez brought to the big leagues, but his power arm has few peers in the Giants system. After a couple of rough years in short-season ball when he struggled to maintain consistent mechanics, Gregorio showed enough flashes at low Class A Augusta in 2013 to firm up his prospect status. Limited to 14 games because of an oblique injury and a recurring blister issue, he nevertheless struck out 84 and walked just 17 in 70 innings for the GreenJackets. Despite pitching from different arm slots, he managed to stay around the strike zone with a 92-94 mph fastball and show good feel for a changeup.His sweeping slider is his best offspeed pitch and is particularly uncomfortable for righthanders. Gregorio gives you a unique look, and he's not an easy at-bat.Combine that with his health issues and he's a better bet to contribute as a reliever in the big leagues.

Year	Club (League)	Class	W	L	ERA	G	GS	CG	SV	IP	H	HR	BB	SO	K/9	WHIP	AVG
2010	Giants (DSL)	R	6	3	2.80	14	14	0	0	74	65	1	17	41	5.0	1.11	.242
2011	Giants (AZL)	R	3	0	2.32	12	12	0	0	50	43	1	16	43	7.7	1.17	.235
2012	Salem-Keizer (NWL)	SS	7	7	5.54	16	16	0	0	76	85	9	23	69	8.1	1.41	.272
2013	Augusta (SAL)	LoA	6	3	4.00	14	13	0	0	70	65	3	17	84	10.9	1.18	.243
Minor League Totals			22	13	3.80	56	55	0	0	270	258	14	73	237	7.9	1.22	.250

18 EHIRE ADRIANZA, SS

BA GRADE 40 MEDIUM

Born: Aug. 21, 1989. **B-T:** B-R. **Ht.:** 6-0. **Wt.:** 168. **Signed:** Venezuela, 2006. **Signed by:** Ciro Villalobos.

Adrianza has been one of the Giants' more intriguing prospects for the better part of a decade because of his smooth hands, quick actions and Gold Glove ability at shortstop. But it wasn't his glove that a sold-out crowd noticed at Yankee Stadium on Sept. 22. A September callup in his eighth professional season, he hit his first home run off Andy Pettitte in the lefthander's final start in the Bronx. While the longball isn't often part of Adrianza's game, its rare appearance is another hint at the he made offensive strides he took after a midseason promotion to Triple-A Fresno in 2013. He ended the year in San Francisco with a 7-for-17 stretch that included two triples. Always a decent hitter from his natural right side, Adrianza has worked with coaches to make adjustments to his lefthanded swing. Now his bat stays in the zone a little longer, improving his contact rate. He should make the Giants' Opening Day roster in a utility role, since he'll be out of minor league options.

Year	Club (League)	Class	AVG	G	AB	R	H	2B	3B	HR	RBI	BB	SO	SB	CS	OBP	SLG
2006	Giants (DSL)	R	.156	44	122	17	19	2	1	0	7	24	31	3	2	.311	.189
2007	Giants (DSL)	R	.241	66	249	44	60	17	2	0	30	41	31	23	6	.351	.325
2008	Fresno (PCL)	AAA	.500	2	6	2	3	1	0	0	0	2	1	0	0	.625	.667
	Giants (AZL)	R	.255	15	55	13	14	4	0	1	6	7	4	0	1	.349	.382
	Salem-Keizer (NWL)	SS	.400	1	5	3	2	0	0	0	0	0	1	0	0	.400	.400
2009	Augusta (SAL)	LoA	.258	117	388	54	100	15	3	2	46	42	66	7	1	.333	.327
2010	San Jose (CAL)	HiA	.256	124	445	70	114	22	5	3	35	47	87	33	15	.333	.348
2011	Augusta (SAL)	LoA	.231	38	143	18	33	10	1	3	17	18	32	3	2	.315	.378
	San Jose (CAL)	HiA	.300	56	230	34	69	24	3	3	27	23	46	5	1	.375	.470
2012	Richmond (EL)	AA	.220	127	451	52	99	22	5	3	32	41	90	16	4	.289	.310
2013	Richmond (EL)	AA	.240	73	250	31	60	12	0	2	23	31	45	11	6	.331	.312
	Fresno (PCL)	AAA	.310	45	145	23	45	7	6	0	12	23	31	6	2	.409	.441
	San Francisco (NL)	MAJ	.222	9	18	3	4	1	0	1	3	1	5	0	0	.263	.444
Major League Totals			.222	9	18	3	4	1	0	1	3	1	5	0	0	.263	.444
Minor League Totals			.248	708	2489	361	618	136	26	17	235	299	465	107	40	.335	.344

19 GARY BROWN, OF

BA GRADE 50 EXTREME

Born: Sept. 28, 1988. **B-T:** R-R. **Ht.:** 6-1. **Wt.:** 190. **Drafted:** Cal State Fullerton, 2010 (1st round). **Signed by:** Brad Cameron.

A gifted athlete with premium speed, Brown was an apparent lock to become the club's future center fielder after he tore up the high Class A California League in 2011 and set a San Jose franchise record with 188 hits. But scouts had concerns about his unorthodox swing, in which he pins his hands to his chest as he begins to load. Sure enough, Brown had myriad issues against righthanders at Double-A Richmond in 2012 and his struggles became acute at Triple-A Fresno last year, when he hit .231/.286/.375 and struck out 135 times in 137 games. Brown is not a lost cause, though. He still has bat speed and all the physical tools to succeed if he is willing to overhaul his approach. Though the Giants drafted him as a future leadoff hitter, he doesn't draw walks and is woefully inefficient on the bases, having succeeded on 68 percent of steal attempts over four seasons, including 61 percent at Fresno. A favorite with teammates because of his upbeat and quirky personality, Brown should at least have a better idea of what awaits him when he returns to the Pacific Coast League in 2014.

Year	Club (League)	Class	AVG	G	AB	R	H	2B	3B	HR	RBI	BB	SO	SB	CS	OBP	SLG
2010	Giants (AZL)	R	.182	6	22	6	4	1	0	0	0	4	5	2	0	.333	.227
	Salem-Keizer (NWL)	SS	.136	6	22	2	3	0	1	0	2	2	7	0	1	.259	.227
2011	San Jose (CAL)	HiA	.336	131	559	115	188	34	13	14	80	46	77	53	19	.407	.519
2012	Richmond (EL)	AA	.279	134	538	73	150	32	2	7	42	40	87	33	18	.347	.385
2013	Fresno (PCL)	AAA	.231	137	558	79	129	29	6	13	50	33	135	17	11	.286	.375
Minor League Totals			.279	414	1699	275	474	96	22	34	174	125	311	105	49	.346	.421

20 MIKE KICKHAM, LHP

BA GRADE **45** HIGH

Born: Dec. 12, 1988. **B-T:** L-L. **Ht.:** 6-4. **Wt.:** 210. **Drafted:** Missouri State, 2010 (6th round). **Signed by:** Hugh Walker.

When they won the World Series in 2012, the Giants had five pitchers start 160 of their 162 regular-season games. They weren't blessed with the same health or effectiveness last year, but they figured that Kickham would provide a solid alternative. It didn't turn out that way, as he got hit hard in three starts and ended up with a 10.16 ERA. The block appeared to be more mental than anything, because Kickham's stuff has few peers in the system. He has a plus fastball that touches 95 mph, and he has shown a knack for making his breaking ball harder or tighter as the situation warrants. But he is not pitch-efficient. His walk totals have been higher than desired at every minor league stop, and he'll find it tougher to be "effectively wild" against big league hitters. In each of his three big league starts, Kickham turned in a perfect first inning before struggling—perhaps a clue that he could be more effective in relief. He isn't expected to compete for a big league rotation spot at the outset of 2014, but the Giants hope he'll be ready the next time they need to call upon him.

Year	Club (League)	Class	W	L	ERA	G	GS	CG	SV	IP	H	HR	BB	SO	K/9	WHIP	AVG
2010	Giants (AZL)	R	0	0	11.57	3	0	0	0	2	4	0	2	3	11.6	2.57	.400
2011	Augusta (SAL)	LoA	5	10	4.11	21	21	0	0	112	112	9	37	103	8.3	1.33	.261
2012	Richmond (EL)	AA	11	10	3.05	28	27	1	0	151	119	8	75	137	8.2	1.29	.219
2013	Fresno (PCL)	AAA	7	7	4.31	20	20	0	0	111	105	9	49	90	7.3	1.39	.250
	San Francisco (NL)	MAJ	0	3	10.16	12	3	0	0	28	46	8	10	29	9.2	1.98	.351
Major League Totals			0	3	10.16	12	3	0	0	28	46	8	10	29	9.2	1.98	.351
Minor League Totals			23	27	3.79	72	68	1	0	375	340	26	163	333	8.0	1.34	.243

21 MARTIN AGOSTA, RHP

BA GRADE **45** HIGH

Born: April 7, 1991. **B-T:** R-R. **Ht.:** 6-1. **Wt.:** 180. **Drafted:** St. Mary's, 2012 (2nd round). **Signed by:** Keith Snider.

Agosta's solid numbers at low Class A Augusta in 2013—including a 2.06 ERA and 10.7 strikeouts per nine innings—obscured what otherwise was a difficult season in which he battled a dead arm and dealt with a blister issue. Worn down at the end of his first full season, he competed well despite a fastball that dipped to the upper 80s. But a few weeks of rest did him good and he was throwing crisper again during instructional league. Agosta's fatigue issues lend credence to scouts who pegged him as a reliever out of St. Mary's. His fastball and plus slider were enough to succeed against South Atlantic League hitters, but he'll need better command of his low-90s heat. He'll also need to find a changeup grip to his liking if he wants to continue developing as a starter. He has tried using a cutter grip to change speeds, but the blister forced him to tinker most of the season. Agosta, who threw to Giants Double-A catcher Andrew Susac when both attended Sacramento's Jesuit High, figures to open 2014 in the high Class A San Jose rotation.

Year	Club (League)	Class	W	L	ERA	G	GS	CG	SV	IP	H	HR	BB	SO	K/9	WHIP	AVG
2012	Giants (AZL)	R	0	0	4.22	5	5	0	0	11	8	0	9	19	16.0	1.59	.205
2013	Augusta (SAL)	LoA	9	3	2.06	18	18	0	0	92	57	4	43	109	10.7	1.09	.180
Minor League Totals			9	3	2.29	23	23	0	0	102	65	4	52	128	11.3	1.14	.183

22 JUAN PEREZ, OF

BA GRADE **40** LOW

Born: Nov. 13, 1986. **B-T:** R-R. **Ht.:** 5-11. **Wt.:** 185. **Drafted:** Western Oklahoma State JC, 2008 (13th round). **Signed by:** Todd Thomas.

The Giants had a mostly forgettable 2013 season, but Perez's defense was a sight to behold. His first big league chance was a wall-crashing catch in center field in Phoenix, and the Bronx native kept making plays from there. In fact, he led Giants outfielders with eight assists despite playing just 218 innings. Undrafted out of high school, Perez worked for his father as a plumber's apprentice and played in the Bronx's El Caribe men's league before winding up at Western Oklahoma State JC, where he set a junior-college home run record. He's a plus-plus runner with surprising power, but he gets overmatched at times and probably strikes out too often to profile as an everyday player. Perez lived a dream when the Giants spent a week in New York in September, getting three hits at Citi Field one day and two at Yankee Stadium the next. Given the importance of outfield defense at AT&T Park, there's a good chance he sticks with the Giants as a fifth outfielder to open the 2014 season.

Year	Club (League)	Class	AVG	G	AB	R	H	2B	3B	HR	RBI	BB	SO	SB	CS	OBP	SLG
2009	Augusta (SAL)	LoA	.244	123	447	56	109	29	3	9	54	23	101	18	4	.283	.383
2010	San Jose (CAL)	HiA	.298	131	551	83	164	37	10	13	63	31	116	17	15	.337	.472
2011	Richmond (EL)	AA	.256	131	457	58	117	25	10	4	40	28	95	22	6	.303	.381
2012	Richmond (EL)	AA	.302	126	483	65	146	26	4	11	53	22	85	18	15	.341	.441
2013	Fresno (PCL)	AAA	.291	101	382	52	111	27	5	10	50	15	75	18	6	.323	.466
	San Francisco (NL)	MAJ	.258	34	89	8	23	5	0	1	8	6	21	2	0	.302	.348
Major League Totals			.258	34	89	8	23	5	0	1	8	6	21	2	0	.302	.348
Minor League Totals			.279	612	2320	314	647	144	32	47	260	119	472	93	46	.318	.429

23 JOSH OSICH, LHP

BA GRADE 45 HIGH

Born: Sept. 3, 1988. **B-T:** L-L. **Ht.:** 6-3. **Wt.:** 230. **Drafted:** Oregon State, 2011 (6th round). **Signed by:** Matt Woodward.

Osich will forever be remembered by Oregon State fans for the no-hitter he threw in 2011 to beat Trevor Bauer and UCLA. Health has been the issue for Osich, who signed for second-round money despite a Tommy John surgery in his past and arm soreness in the weeks leading up to the 2011 draft. He worked to lower his arm angle while logging 32 innings over 27 appearances at high Class A San Jose in 2012, and the changes appeared to help, as he combined to throw 70 innings over 56 appearances at high Class A San Jose and Double-A Richmond in 2013. Osich has a big league arm when healthy, touching 98 mph with a solid-average slider and a functional changeup. He has a big, strong body and generates a ton of late life on his fastball. He struggled against lefthanders early, and his first experience in big league spring training didn't go well, but he moved to the other side of the rubber and that helped him locate the fastball away. Though Osich has the potential to start, the Giants plan to build his innings incrementally.

Year	Club (League)	Class	W	L	ERA	G	GS	CG	SV	IP	H	HR	BB	SO	K/9	WHIP	AVG
2012	San Jose (CAL)	HiA	0	2	3.62	27	2	0	1	32	34	1	11	34	9.5	1.39	.272
2013	San Jose (CAL)	HiA	3	1	2.45	34	0	0	12	40	32	1	10	48	10.7	1.04	.213
	Richmond (EL)	AA	2	3	4.85	22	0	0	3	30	26	2	12	28	8.5	1.28	.241
Minor League Totals			5	6	3.52	83	2	0	16	102	92	4	33	110	9.7	1.22	.240

24 STEVEN OKERT, LHP

BA GRADE 45 HIGH

Born: July 9, 1991. **B-T:** L-L. **Ht.:** 6-2. **Wt.:** 210. **Drafted:** Oklahoma, 2012 (4th round). **Signed by:** Daniel Murray.

The Giants considered assigning Okert to high Class A San Jose to begin the 2013 season, or perhaps using him as the closer at low Class A Augusta. But his fastball wasn't impressive in the spring and he ended up pitching mostly middle relief out of what turned out to be a surprisingly stout GreenJackets bullpen. Okert began to throw harder toward the end of the year, showing the low-90s fastball and hard slider that encouraged the Brewers to draft him twice out of Grayson County (Texas) CC, before the Giants signed him in 2012 after he transferred to Oklahoma. The Giants have challenged Okert to improve his conditioning. He's athletic enough to repeat his delivery despite stepping over his front leg and throwing crossfire to the plate. A good competitor who wants the ball, he's capable of throwing multiple innings, but short stints and effectiveness against lefties are his likely tickets to the big leagues. Okert could move quickly if he can fill up the strike zone.

Year	Club (League)	Class	W	L	ERA	G	GS	CG	SV	IP	H	HR	BB	SO	K/9	WHIP	AVG
2012	Giants (AZL)	R	0	0	0.00	2	0	0	0	2	2	0	1	6	27.0	1.50	.250
	Salem-Keizer (NWL)	SS	2	0	2.36	15	0	0	0	27	26	0	11	22	7.4	1.39	.255
2013	Augusta (SAL)	LoA	2	2	2.97	44	0	0	2	61	55	3	24	59	8.8	1.30	.244
Minor League Totals			4	2	2.72	61	0	0	2	89	83	3	36	87	8.8	1.33	.248

25 CHASE JOHNSON, RHP

BA GRADE 45 HIGH

Born: Jan. 9, 1992. **B-T:** R-R. **Ht.:** 6-3. **Wt.:** 200. **Drafted:** Cal Poly, 2013 (3rd round). **Signed by:** Gil Kubski.

Johnson wasn't used much as a Cal Poly junior in 2013, when he struggled early in the year with control issues and ended up logging just 17 innings over 10 appearances, mostly in low-leverage situations. The Giants had strong reports on him from his sophomore year and loved his arm strength, however, so he ended up being the first pitcher they took in the 2013 draft. Johnson has hit 97 mph but pitches with little effort at 92-94. He's flashed an average changeup at times and has some feel for a curveball, but he doesn't yet have a dependable secondary pitch. His mechanics are robotic and he isn't particularly athletic or agile, but the arm strength is genuine. Johnson pitched exclusively from the stretch in college, but the Giants want him to gain comfort using a windup because they want to try him as a starting pitcher. After three relief appearances in the Rookie-level Arizona League, he logged a 4.17 ERA in 10 starts at short-season Salem-Keizer. The Giants just hope to get him a healthy amount of innings at low Class A Augusta in 2014.

Year	Club (League)	Class	W	L	ERA	G	GS	CG	SV	IP	H	HR	BB	SO	K/9	WHIP	AVG
2013	Giants (AZL)	R	1	0	1.69	3	0	0	0	5	5	0	1	7	11.8	1.13	.263
	Salem-Keizer (NWL)	SS	3	2	4.17	10	10	0	0	41	36	3	12	37	8.1	1.17	.240
Minor League Totals			4	2	3.88	13	10	0	0	46	41	3	13	44	8.5	1.17	.243

26 JOSE DePAULA, LHP

BA GRADE **45** HIGH

Born: March 4, 1990. **B-T:** L-L. **Ht.:** 6-1. **Wt.:** 170. **Signed:** Dominican Republic, 2006. **Signed by:** Felix Francisco (Padres).

The Giants claimed DePaula on waivers in November when the Padres designated him for assignment to make room on their 40-man roster. He spent all of 2012 on the restricted list when a background investigation during spring training revealed that he was one year older than San Diego had previously believed. He resolved the issues in time to play in 2013, cruising through 14 starts at Double-A San Antonio prior to coming down with shoulder tendinitis that sidelined him from mid-June through the end of the year. DePaula works at 90-91 mph with an easy arm action and plenty of late tailing, sinking action, topping out near 95. Control never has been an issue, and scouts regard his secondary pitches as average to a tick above. He throws a mid-70s curveball with plus rotation and big vertical break. He has gained feel for his changeup in recent years, and the mid-80s pitch shows enough fade to be effective. DePaula may not out-stuff his competition for the rotation, but he has good feel and a low boiling point, which could work in any number of roles. In terms of upside, he could be a back-end starter. If healthy he probably will head to Triple-A Fresno in 2014.

Year	Club (League)	Class	W	L	ERA	G	GS	CG	SV	IP	H	HR	BB	SO	K/9	WHIP	AVG
2007	Padres (DSL)	R	2	5	2.44	14	13	0	0	66	52	0	21	78	10.6	1.10	.208
2008	Padres (AZL)	R	4	3	3.57	13	13	0	0	53	61	2	9	56	9.5	1.32	.288
2009	Eugene (NWL)	SS	1	0	2.79	2	2	0	0	10	9	0	2	10	9.3	1.14	.243
2010	Fort Wayne (MWL)	LoA	8	5	3.27	20	14	0	0	85	71	7	20	69	7.3	1.07	.222
2011	Lake Elsinore (CAL)	HiA	10	5	5.22	26	23	0	0	112	129	4	37	87	7.0	1.48	.282
2012	Did not play—Restricted																
2013	San Antonio (TL)	AA	4	6	3.86	14	14	0	0	75	84	3	11	57	6.9	1.27	.284
Minor League Totals			29	24	3.82	89	79	0	0	401	406	16	100	357	8.0	1.26	.258

27 CODY HALL, RHP

BA GRADE **45** HIGH

Born: Jan. 6, 1988. **B-T:** R-R. **Ht.:** 6-4. **Wt.:** 220. **Drafted:** Southern, 2011 (19th round). **Signed by:** Hugh Walker.

Hall has compiled some incredible statistics in two-plus professional seasons, including a combined 1.80 ERA and 0.78 WHIP between high Class A San Jose and Double-A Richmond in 2013, but the Giants never know quite what they'll get from him. That was never more evident than Aug. 29, when he threw the first pitch of an intentional walk over the head of Richmond catcher Tyler LaTorre for a walkoff wild pitch against Reading. Hall has prototype closer stuff and mentality. He's physically imposing with aggressive body language on the mound, and his fastball ranges anywhere from 92-97 mph. But he didn't play baseball in high school and barely had any formal pitching instruction before arriving at Southern in 2010. He doesn't have much consistency with his slider and he's still learning his delivery. He tends to muscle up in big situations, and thus far he's had enough fastball to escape most of them. The Giants made some changes to Hall's mechanics before sending him to the Arizona Fall League, where he worked on establishing a better breaking ball and a more consistent release point. He probably return to Richmond to open the season.

Year	Club (League)	Class	W	L	ERA	G	GS	CG	SV	IP	H	HR	BB	SO	K/9	WHIP	AVG
2011	Salem-Keizer (NWL)	SS	3	1	2.63	23	0	0	4	27	21	1	19	42	13.8	1.46	.210
2012	Augusta (SAL)	LoA	3	0	1.60	36	0	0	20	39	36	0	12	54	12.4	1.22	.247
	San Jose (CAL)	HiA	1	1	3.24	9	0	0	1	8	12	0	4	10	10.8	1.92	.333
2013	San Jose (CAL)	HiA	2	0	1.34	26	0	0	2	34	15	2	7	48	12.8	0.65	.130
	Richmond (EL)	AA	2	2	2.39	20	0	0	8	26	17	4	8	27	9.2	0.95	.181
Minor League Totals			11	4	2.00	114	0	0	35	135	101	7	50	181	12.1	1.12	.206

28 STEPHEN JOHNSON, RHP

BA GRADE **50** EXTREME

Born: Feb. 21, 1991. **B-T:** R-R. **Ht.:** 6-4. **Wt.:** 205. **Drafted:** St. Edward's (Texas), 2012 (6th round). **Signed by:** Todd Thomas.

Johnson is as filthy as any reliever in the Giants system, and he rallied back from shoulder soreness to strike out 71 in 52 innings while working in a set-up role at low Class A Augusta in 2013. Widely regarded as the best college draft prospect outside NCAA Division I in 2012, Johnson is a late bloomer who didn't make his Colorado high school varsity team until his senior year. He recovered from a partially torn elbow ligament to flash 100 mph velocity while striking out 63 in 36 innings and holding opponents to a .131 average as a junior in 2011. Johnson throws a power curve that acts more like a slider and was a plus-plus pitch against South Atlantic League hitters. He isn't efficient, which limits his ability to pitch on consecutive days and might continue to be an issue because of irregular mechanics in which he stabs as he loads. Johnson and Derek Law give the Giants two power righthanders with plenty of funk, but Johnson has a long way to go to approach Law's control and consistency. Johnson could get a look as a starter, but health will play a key role in that decision.

Year	Club (League)	Class	W	L	ERA	G	GS	CG	SV	IP	H	HR	BB	SO	K/9	WHIP	AVG
2012	Giants (AZL)	R	0	0	4.50	2	0	0	0	2	1	0	2	2	9.0	1.50	.167
	Salem-Keizer (NWL)	SS	0	2	4.66	17	0	0	2	19	19	2	12	19	8.8	1.60	.257
2013	Augusta (SAL)	LoA	5	1	3.61	45	0	0	8	52	41	2	30	71	12.2	1.36	.215
Minor League Totals			5	3	3.91	64	0	0	10	74	61	4	44	92	11.2	1.43	.225

29 ROGER KIESCHNICK, OF

BA GRADE 40 MEDIUM

Born: Jan. 21, 1987. **B-T:** L-R. **Ht.:** 6-3. **Wt.:** 229. **Drafted:** Texas Tech, 2008 (3rd round). **Signed by:** Todd Thomas.

Kieschnick was the last to reach the majors among a celebrated 2008 Giants draft quartet of college bats that also included Buster Posey, Brandon Crawford and Conor Gillaspie. It's safe to say the Giants haven't seen the best of Kieschnick, though. He looked bewildered by major league pitchers in 2013 while hitting a soft .202 following a July 31 call-up. Worse still, he connected for only one extra-base hit, a triple—not what the Giants expected from a strapping outfielder for whom they had projected 30 home runs a season. Kieschnick also failed to make a good impression in the spring, spoiling chances of making the Opening Day roster. He's a good athlete whose arm plays in right field, but he often finds himself in-between pitches and battles a swing that gets long at times. At least he managed to stay healthy after missing chunks of development time with a recurring back issue, followed by a stress fracture in his shoulder when he collided with a wall in 2012. He'll have to be more confident and aggressive whenever he gets another recall from Triple-A Fresno.

Year	Club (League)	Class	AVG	G	AB	R	H	2B	3B	HR	RBI	BB	SO	SB	CS	OBP	SLG
2009	San Jose (CAL)	HiA	.296	131	517	86	153	37	8	23	110	36	130	9	1	.345	.532
2010	Richmond (EL)	AA	.251	60	223	21	56	8	3	4	23	18	55	2	3	.305	.368
2011	Richmond (EL)	AA	.255	126	459	71	117	22	5	16	65	34	121	13	7	.307	.429
2012	Giants (AZL)	R	.083	3	12	0	1	1	0	0	4	0	5	0	0	.077	.167
	Fresno (PCL)	AAA	.306	55	222	49	68	13	4	15	40	24	68	0	2	.376	.604
2013	Fresno (PCL)	AAA	.273	101	374	50	102	27	9	13	56	40	102	4	1	.339	.497
	San Francisco (NL)	MAJ	.202	38	84	6	17	0	1	0	5	11	29	0	0	.295	.226
Major League Totals			.202	38	84	6	17	0	1	0	5	11	29	0	0	.295	.226
Minor League Totals			.275	476	1807	277	497	108	29	71	298	152	481	28	14	.331	.485

30 ERIK CORDIER, RHP

BA GRADE 45 EXTREME

Born: Feb. 25, 1986. **B-T:** R-R. **Ht.:** 6-4. **Wt.:** 245. **Drafted:** HS—Southern Door, Wis., 2004 (2nd round). **Signed by:** Phil Huttmann (Royals).

It's not often that a club hands a major league contract to a minor league free agent with no big league service time. But Cordier drew sufficient interest from multiple clubs, and the Giants liked his upside and power stuff enough to carve out space on the 40-man roster. He is on his fourth organization after failing to stay healthy with the Royals, Braves and Pirates. He missed all of 2005 with a knee injury, lost 2007 to Tommy John surgery, then had another elbow operation prior to the 2011 season to remove a bone spur. He transitioned to relief in 2013 for the Pirates' Triple-A club and was inconsistent, but he also struck out 65 in 53 innings with a lively, two-seam fastball that played up at 96-99 mph. His slider has plenty of break from his three-quarters arm slot and rates as a plus pitch. He showed a fringy changeup as a starter, but its development won't be as important in late relief, which is how the Giants intend to use him. Cordier has one minor league option remaining, so he's expected to begin in the bullpen at Triple-A Fresno.

Year	Club (League)	Class	W	L	ERA	G	GS	CG	SV	IP	H	HR	BB	SO	K/9	WHIP	AVG
2004	Royals (AZL)	R	2	4	5.19	11	11	0	0	35	38	1	21	22	5.7	1.70	.279
2005	Did not play—Injured																
2006	Idaho Falls (PIO)	R	1	0	3.38	3	3	0	0	16	11	0	3	19	10.7	0.88	.186
	Burlington (MWL)	LoA	3	1	2.70	7	7	0	0	37	27	3	14	23	5.6	1.12	.203
2007	Did not play—Injured																
2008	Braves (GCL)	R	0	0	0.00	3	2	0	0	5	4	0	1	5	9.0	1.00	.211
	Rome (SAL)	LoA	1	2	5.18	9	9	0	0	40	51	3	21	31	7.0	1.80	.317
2009	Myrtle Beach (CAR)	HiA	7	8	3.87	25	25	1	0	121	115	13	74	88	6.5	1.56	.257
2010	Mississippi (SL)	AA	11	7	3.71	25	21	0	0	136	116	3	69	113	7.5	1.36	.236
	Gwinnett (IL)	AAA	1	1	5.63	2	2	0	0	8	7	0	7	4	4.5	1.75	.233
2011	Mississippi (SL)	AA	0	1	5.40	1	1	0	0	5	6	1	0	4	7.2	1.20	.286
	Gwinnett (IL)	AAA	5	8	5.13	19	19	0	0	86	88	9	51	61	6.4	1.62	.267
2012	Gwinnett (IL)	AAA	1	1	4.38	8	4	0	0	25	27	1	21	15	5.5	1.95	.297
	Braves (GCL)	R	0	0	0.00	4	1	0	0	4	0	0	6	6	14.7	1.64	.000
	Mississippi (SL)	AA	0	2	20.25	5	0	0	0	4	8	0	5	6	13.5	3.25	.421
2013	Indianapolis (IL)	AAA	4	2	4.58	44	0	0	4	53	51	3	28	65	11.0	1.49	.256
Minor League Totals			36	37	4.29	166	105	1	4	573	549	37	321	462	7.3	1.52	.256

Seattle Mariners

BY JOHN PERROTTO

The weekend of Dec. 6-8 contained an offseason's worth of drama in just three days.

On Dec. 6, the Mariners stunned the baseball world by agreeing to terms with free agent second baseman Robinson Cano on a 10-year, $240 million contract, surprising many who had assumed Cano and his agents, Jay-Z and CAA, would steer the negotiation toward New York and staying with the Yankees. The next day saw the Mariners take their share of criticism from media leading into the Winter Meetings as the magnitude of the contract set in, as did the realization Seattle was committed to Cano until he is 40.

Another bombshell hit Dec. 8 when the Seattle Times published a well-sourced look inside the Mariners front office. Former special assistant to the general manager Tony Blengino made various allegations about his old boss, GM Jack Zduriencik, stating that Zduriencik inflated his knowledge of statistical analysis when applying for the job. Manager Eric Wedge, who resigned at the end of the 2013 season, talked about how Mariners CEO Howard Lincoln and club president Chuck Armstrong would come to his office and berate him and his players.

Regardless of the bad publicity, Zduriencik and the Mariners believe they are now at a stage where they are ready to make some noise in the American League West despite losing an average of nearly 94 games a year in the four seasons since 2010.

"We have been putting a core of young players in place at the major league level for the last few years and we've always said when the time was right we would augment that group," said Zduriencik, who quietly received a one-year contract extension in 2013. "We felt now was the time."

Since going a surprising 85-77 in 2009 in Zduriencik's first year on the job, the Mariners haven't sniffed contention. Seattle, however, almost certainly will have to be competitive this season in order for Zdurienick to keep his job.

Zduriencik has put his faith in Lloyd McClendon, hiring him to help engineer a turnaround as he replaces Wedge as manager. McClendon spent the past eight years with the Tigers on Jim Leyland's coaching staff. He had a five-year stint as the Pirates' manager from 2001-05 and compiled a 330-440 record with some awful teams. He's the fourth manager in Zduriencik's GM tenure.

Cano and ace Felix Hernandez—who is signed through 2019—are strong building blocks, but the Mariners need young players to mature into competent complementary pieces. Catcher/DH Jesus Montero, second baseman-turned-outfielder Dustin Ackley, first baseman Justin Smoak and outfielder Michael Saunders have failed to live up to their lofty billing to this point. Seattle hopes three of its 2013 rookies, second baseman Nick Franklin, shortstop Brad Miller and catcher Mike Zunino, turn out better than Ackley, Montero and Smoak have.

The farm system is not deep, but Taijuan Walker gives the Mariners one of the top young righthanders in the game. However, lefthander Danny Hultzen, the No. 2 overall pick in 2011 and last year's No. 3 prospect, had a disastrous year that ended with shoulder surgery that clouds his future.

LARRY GOREN

The Mariners keep collecting power bats with defensive questions like D.J. Peterson

TOP PROSPECTS OF THE DECADE

Year	Player, Pos.	2013 Org.
2004	Felix Hernandez, rhp	Mariners
2005	Felix Hernandez, rhp	Mariners
2006	Jeff Clement, c	Twins
2007	Adam Jones, of	Orioles
2008	Jeff Clement, c	Twins
2009	Greg Halman, of	Deceased
2010	Dustin Ackley, of/1b	Mariners
2011	Dustin Ackley, 2b	Mariners
2012	Taijuan Walker, rhp	Mariners
2013	Mike Zunino, c	Mariners

ORGANIZATION OVERVIEW

General Manager: Jack Zduriencik. **Farm Director:** Chris Gwynn. **Scouting Director:** Tom McNamara.

Class	Team	League	W	L	PCT	Finish	Manager(s)
Majors	Seattle Mariners	American	71	91	.438	12th (15)	Eric Wedge
Triple-A	Tacoma Rainiers	Pacific Coast	73	68	.518	t-6th (16)	Daren Brown/John Stearns
Double-A	Jackson Generals	Southern	62	73	.459	7th (10)	Jim Pankovits
High Class A	High Desert Mavericks	California	64	76	.457	8th (10)	Jim Horner
Low Class A	Clinton Lumber Kings	Midwest	67	72	.482	9th (16)	Eddie Menchaca
Short-season	Everett Aquasox	Northwest	44	32	.579	2nd (8)	Rob Mummau
Rookie	Pulaski Mariners	Appalachian	41	27	.603	1st (10)	Chris Prieto
Rookie	AZL Mariners	Arizona	22	32	.407	11th (13)	Darrin Garner
Overall 2013 Minor League Record			**376**	**380**	**.497**	**t-13th (30)**	

THIS YEAR'S TOP 30

No.	Player, Pos.	Grade
1.	Taijuan Walker, rhp	65/Medium
2.	D.J. Peterson, 3b	60/High
3.	James Paxton, lhp	55/High
4.	Luiz Gohara, lhp	60/Extreme
5.	Edwin Diaz, rhp	55/Extreme
6.	Austin Wilson, of	55/Extreme
7.	Victor Sanchez, rhp	50/High
8.	Tyler Marlette, c	50/High
9.	Chris Taylor, ss	45/Medium
10.	Danny Hultzen, lhp	55/Extreme
11.	Julio Morban, of	50/High
12.	Patrick Kivlehan, 3b	50/High
13.	Gabriel Guerrero, of	55/Extreme
14.	Carson Smith, rhp	45/Medium
15.	Stefen Romero, of/2b	45/Medium
16.	Tyler Pike, lhp	50/High
17.	Abraham Almonte, of	45/Medium
18.	Tyler O'Neill, of	50/Extreme
19.	Jabari Blash, of	50/Extreme
20.	Ketel Marte, ss/2b	45/High
21.	Wilton Martinez, of	50/Extreme
22.	Dominic Leone, rhp	45/High
23.	John Hicks, c	45/High
24.	Timmy Lopes, 2b	45/High
25.	Ji-Man Choi, 1b	45/High
26.	Jack Reinheimer, ss	45/High
27.	James Jones, of	45/High
28.	Lars Huijer, rhp	45/Extreme
29.	Guillermo Pimentel, of	45/Extreme
30.	Dylan Unsworth, rhp	45/Extreme

LAST YEAR'S TOP 30

No.	Player, Pos.	Status
1.	Mike Zunino, c	Majors
2.	Taijuan Walker, rhp	No. 1
3.	Danny Hultzen, lhp	No. 10
4.	James Paxton, lhp	No. 5
5.	Nick Franklin ss/2b	Majors
6.	Brandon Maurer, rhp	Majors
7.	Carter Capps, rhp	Majors
8.	Stefen Romero, 2b	No. 15
9.	Brad Miller, ss	Majors
10.	Victor Sanchez, rhp	No. 7
11.	Stephen Pryor, rhp	Majors
12.	Luiz Gohara, lhp	No. 4
13.	Joe DeCarlo, 3b	Dropped out
14.	Tyler Pike, lhp	No. 16
15.	Gabriel Guerrero, of	No. 13
16.	Carson Smith, rhp	No. 14
17.	Leon Landry, of	Dropped out
18.	Patrick Kivlehan, 3b	No. 12
19.	Edwin Diaz, rhp	No. 5
20.	Jack Marder, 2b/c/of	Dropped out
21.	John Hicks, c	No. 23
22.	Francisco Martinez, 3b/of	(Tigers)
23.	Julio Morban, of	No. 11
24.	Jabari Blash, of	No. 19
25.	Timmy Lopes, 2b	No. 24
26.	Vinnie Catricala, 3b/of	(Athletics)
27.	Chance Ruffin, rhp	Dropped out
28.	Chris Taylor, ss	No. 9
29.	Ramor Morla, 3b	Dropped out
30.	Anthony Fernandez, lhp	Dropped out

BEST TOOLS

Best Hitter for Average	D.J. Peterson
Best Power Hitter	D.J. Peterson
Best Strike-Zone Discipline	Ty Smith
Fastest Baserunner	Ketel Marte
Best Athlete	Gabriel Guerrero
Best Fastball	Taijuan Walker
Best Curveball	James Paxton
Best Slider	Taijuan Walker
Best Changeup	Tyler Pike
Best Control	Dylan Unsworth
Best Defensive Catcher	John Hicks
Best Defensive Infielder	Gabriel Noriega
Best Infield Arm	Carlos Triunfel
Best Defensive Outfielder	Leon Landry
Best Outfield Arm	Gabriel Guerrero

TOP 15 PLAYERS 25 AND UNDER

No.	Player, Pos. (Age)	Peak Level
1.	Taijuan Walker, rhp (21)	Majors
2.	Mike Zunino, c (23)	Majors
3.	D.J. Peterson, 3b (22)	Low Class A
4.	Brad Miller, ss (24)	Majors
5.	James Paxton, lhp (25)	Majors
6.	Nick Franklin 2b (23)	Majors
7.	Jesus Montero, dh/c (24)	Majors
8.	Luiz Gohara, rhp (17)	Rookie
9.	Edwin Diaz, rhp (20)	Rookie
10.	Austin Wilson, of (22)	Short-season
11.	Erasmo Ramirez, rhp (23)	Majors
12.	Carter Capps, rhp (23)	Majors
13.	Victor Sanchez, rhp (19)	High Class A
14.	Brandon Maurer, rhp (23)	Majors
15.	Tyler Marlette, c (21)	Low Class A

MINOR LEAGUE DEPTH CHART

SEATTLE MARINERS

TOP 2014 ROOKIE: Taijuan Walker, rhp. Though just 21, he has nothing left to prove in the minor leagues.

BREAKOUT PROSPECT: Gabriel Guerrero, of. All the tools are there to become a star, but he has to temper his aggressive approach.

SLEEPER: Kevin Rivers, of. Power is intriguing despite being 25 and at Double-A Jackson, and he could fit the right-field profile.

SOURCE OF TOP 30 TALENT

Homegrown	**29**	**Acquired**	**1**
College	12	Trades	1
Junior college	1	Rule 5 draft	0
High school	5	Independent leagues	0
Nondrafted free agents	0	Free agents/waivers	0
International	11		

LF
- Stefen Romero (15)
- Tyler O'Neill (18)
- Guillermo Pimentel (29)
- Darlo Pizzano

CF
- Abraham Almonte (17)
- Xavier Avery
- Travis Witherspoon
- Jabari Henry
- Aaron Barbosa

RF
- Austin Wilson (6)
- Julio Morban (11)
- Gabriel Guerrero (13)
- Jabari Blash (19)
- Wilton Martinez (21)
- James Jones (27)
- Kevin Rivers

3B
- Patrick Kivlehan (12)

SS
- Chris Taylor (9)
- Jack Reinheimer (26)
- Carlos Triunfel
- Tyler Smith

2B
- Ketel Marte (20)
- Timmy Lopes (24)
- Ty Kelly

1B
- D.J. Peterson (2)
- Ji-Man Choi (25)
- Rich Poythress
- Steven Proscia

C
- Tyler Marlette (8)
- John Hicks (23)
- Jesus Sucre
- Marcus Littlewood
- Steve Baron

LHP

LHSP	LHRP
James Paxton (3)	Bobby LaFramboise
Luiz Gohara (4)	Jordan Shipers
Danny Hultzen (10)	Kyle Hunter
Tyler Pike (16)	
Anthony Fernandez	
Roenis Elias	
Ryan Horstman	
Tyler Olson	

RHP

RHSP	RHRP
Taijuan Walker (1)	Carson Smith (14)
Edwin Diaz (5)	Dominic Leone (22)
Victor Sanchez (7)	Logan Bawcom
Lars Huijer (28)	Forrest Snow
Dylan Unsworth (30)	Stephen Kohlscheen
Brett Shankin	Jochi Ogando
Stephen Landazuri	Chance Ruffin
Trevor Miller	David Colvin
Thyago Vieira	Jonathan Arias
Rigoberto Garcia	Emilio Pagan
David Holman	

DRAFT ANALYSIS

2013

BONUSES: $6.4 MILLION

BEST PURE HITTER: 3B D.J. Peterson (1) was considered one of the best pure hitters in the 2013 draft class. He has short arms, a short stroke and enough bat speed to lace line drives all over the park. He does need to get less pull-happy and use the whole field more.

BEST POWER HITTER: Peterson has the most usable pop and projects to have above-average power, although OF Austin Wilson (2) may have more raw power. He needs to more consistently turn the shows he puts on in batting practice into home runs and doubles in games.

FASTEST RUNNER: OF Ian Miller (14) is a well above-average runner, turning in 4.0-second times from home to first from the left side. Nondrafted free agent Aaron Barbosa, signed after a solid summer in the Cape Cod League, is a true top-of-the-scale runner who stole 19 bases in 22 tries after signing.

BEST DEFENSIVE PLAYER: SS Jack Reinheimer (5) has soft hands, excellent instincts and an accurate arm. He's more reliable than flashy, but he has a solid chance to stick at shortstop long-term.

BEST FASTBALL: LHP Ryan Horstman (4) sat at 92-93 mph in the spring at Seton Hall and touched 93-94 as a pro. RHP Kevin McCoy (24) has more pure velocity, as he'll touch 96, but Horstman's fastball has more life.

BEST SECONDARY PITCH: LHP Jake Zokan (9) throws a tight, late-breaking curveball that he can locate in the zone and out. It has a chance to be an above-average major league pitch. LHP Eddie Campbell's (15) breaking ball is a little harder than Zokan's, but he doesn't command it as well.

BEST PRO DEBUT: RHP Emilio Pagan (10) didn't allow a run in 15 appearances at Rookie-level Pulaski and struck out 27 in 20 innings. He struggled more at short-season Everett, but still finished with 1-1, 1.03 numbers in 26 innings. Peterson hit .303/.365/.553 between stops at Everett and low Class A Clinton.

BEST ATHLETE: Wilson is a potential five-tool player. Horstman might rival Wilson's athleticism, as he was approached by the St. John's basketball team about walking on in addition to pitching for the baseball team.

MOST INTRIGUING BACKGROUND: 1B Justin Seager (12) is the middle Seager between Mariners 3B Kyle and Dodgers SS prospect Corey. Miller is the godson of former Pirates manager Danny Murtaugh.

CLOSEST TO THE MAJORS: Peterson will have to establish a defensive home, as most scouts think he'll eventually end up in an outfielder corner or at first base, but his polished bat should allow him to move quickly.

BEST LATE-ROUND PICK: Campbell has solid stuff for a lefthander, with a fastball that touches 90-92 mph and a solid curveball.

THE ONE WHO GOT AWAY: Toolsy OF Corey Ray (33) impressed the Mariners at a predraft workout and the club made a run at him, but he opted to go to Louisville.

ASSESSMENT: While most teams preferred the pitching in the 2013 draft class, the Mariners were happy to go hitter-heavy in the first five rounds. Peterson, Wilson and OF Tyler O'Neill (3) provide a trio of potential impact bats.

2012

BONUSES: $9.3 MILLION

C Mike Zunino (1) rushed to the majors. RHP Edwin Diaz (3) is a ways away but flashes tantalizing upside. SS Chris Taylor (5) has surprised with the bat.

GRADE: B

2011

BONUSES: $11.3 MILLION

SS Brad Miller (2) rocketed to Seattle and has exceeded expectations, as has RHP Carter Capps (3s). But LHP Danny Hultzen (1), he of the $8 million contract, had major shoulder surgery.

GRADE: B

2010

BONUSES: $4.9 MILLION

RHP Taijuan Walker (1s) and LHP James Paxton (4) have reached Seattle and rank first and third on the Top 30. RHP Stephen Pryor (5) is in Seattle's bullpen.

GRADE: B

TOP DRAFT PICKS OF THE DECADE

Year	Player, Pos.	2013 Org.
2004	Matt Tuiasosopo, 3b (3rd round)	Tigers
2005	Jeff Clement, c	Twins
2006	Brandon Morrow, rhp	Blue Jays
2007	Phillippe Aumont, rhp	Phillies
2008	Josh Fields, rhp	Astros
2009	Dustin Ackley, of	Mariners
2010	Taijuan Walker, rhp (1st round supp.)	Mariners
2011	Danny Hultzen, lhp	Mariners
2012	Mike Zunino, c	Mariners
2013	D.J. Peterson, 3b	Mariners

LARGEST BONUSES IN CLUB HISTORY

Player	Bonus
Danny Hultzen, 2009	$6,350,000
Dustin Ackley, 2011	$6,000,000
Ichiro Suzuki, 2000	$5,000,000
Mike Zunino, 2012	$4,000,000
Jeff Clement, 2005	$3,400,000

1 TAIJUAN WALKER, RHP

Born: Aug. 13, 1992. **B-T:** R-R. **Ht.:** 6-4. **Wt.:** 210. **Drafted:** HS—Yucaipa, Calif., 2010 (first round supplemental). **Signed by:** John Ramey.

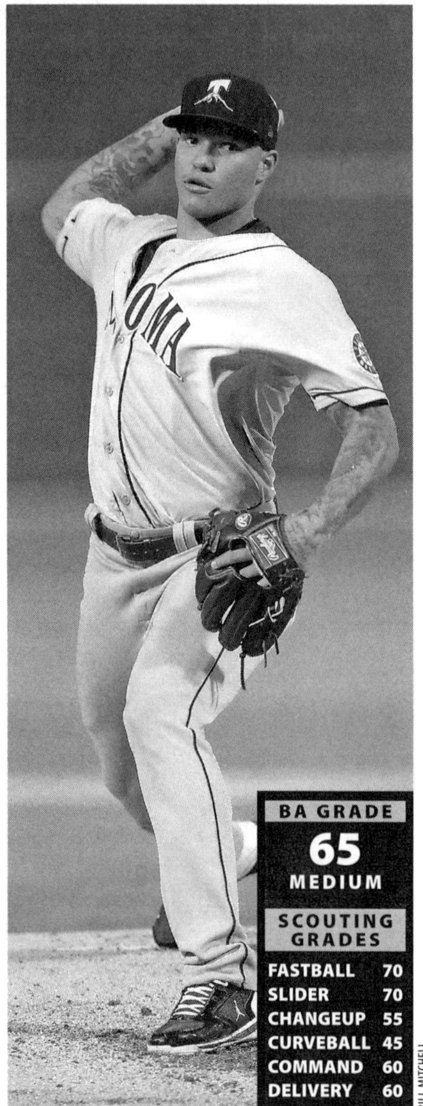

BA GRADE
65
MEDIUM
SCOUTING GRADES
FASTBALL 70
SLIDER 70
CHANGEUP 55
CURVEBALL 45
COMMAND 60
DELIVERY 60

BILL MITCHELL

Walker returns to the Mariners' No. 1 prospect ranking after dropping to No. 2 for one season, 2013, behind catcher Mike Zunino. He concentrated more on basketball at Yucaipa High, when he had the nickname "Sky Walker" and averaged 21 points and 15 rebounds as a senior. But he also played baseball for coach Jeff Stout, who has worked with big leaguers such as Mark Teahen, Corky Miller, Matt Carson and Walker's former prep teammate, Diamondbacks prospect third baseman Matt Davidson. The Mariners made Walker their first pick in the 2010 draft, selecting him 43rd overall, then signing him for $800,000. He's a quick learner and hard worker, which combined with his outstanding athletic ability has allowed him to become one of baseball's top pitching prospects. Walker turned heads at the Futures Game in both 2012 and 2013. The latter was particularly special because it marked the first time Walker's father had a chance to see his son play in a professional game.

Walker has two plus pitches, a fastball with plus armside action and a slider/cutter hybrid. The fastball ranges from 93-98 mph and usually sits at 95-96, while the slider is in the 88-92 range and has good, late break. Scouts consider his slider his best pitch, even over his fastball. Walker also throws a curveball and changeup. The latter has a chance to be an above-average pitch if he can learn to throw it for strikes more often and subtract more velocity to add differentiation from his fastball. He has a hard time commanding his mid-70s curveball, which can be a sharp pitch but is his fourth offering. All of Walker's pitches tend to catch a little bit too much of the plate at times, and he needs to work on honing his command, which has improved quite a bit since he first entered pro ball. As one would expect from a former basketball star, Walker is agile. That not only helps him repeat his delivery but has enabled him to improve his pickoff move and defense.

Walker made his major league debut in September 2013, getting three starts before being shut down after reaching 156 innings for the season. The Mariners were so impressed by how he handled his first taste of the big leagues that he figures to slot in near the back of their rotation to begin 2014. He has the raw ability to be a No.1 starter and at least settle in as a fine wing man for Felix Hernandez.

Year	Club (League)	Class	W	L	ERA	G	GS	CG	SV	IP	H	HR	BB	SO	K/9	WHIP	AVG
2010	Mariners (AZL)	R	1	1	1.29	4	0	0	0	7	2	0	3	9	11.6	0.71	.087
2011	Clinton (MWL)	LoA	6	5	2.89	18	18	1	0	97	69	4	39	113	10.5	1.12	.202
2012	Jackson (SL)	AA	7	10	4.69	25	25	0	0	127	124	12	50	118	8.4	1.37	.258
2013	Jackson (SL)	AA	4	7	2.46	14	14	0	0	84	58	6	30	96	10.3	1.05	.195
	Tacoma (PCL)	AAA	5	3	3.61	11	11	0	0	57	54	5	27	64	10.0	1.41	.249
	Seattle (AL)	MAJ	1	0	3.60	3	3	0	0	15	11	0	4	12	7.2	1.00	.204
Major League Totals			1	0	3.60	3	3	0	0	15	11	0	4	12	7.2	1.00	.204
Minor League Totals			23	26	3.49	72	68	1	0	372	307	27	149	400	9.7	1.23	.226

2 D.J. PETERSON, 3B

BA GRADE **60** HIGH

Born: Dec. 31, 1991. **B-T:** R-R. **Ht.:** 6-1. **Wt.:** 190. **Drafted:** New Mexico, 2013 (1st round). **Signed by:** Lee Pelekoudas.

The Mariners drafted Peterson in the 33rd round in 2010 out of Gilbert (Ariz.) High, but he went to New Mexico instead and hit .414 with 35 homers in his final two seasons,prompting the Mariners to take him 12th overall last year. He quickly signed for the slot value of $2,759,100. His younger brother Dustin signed with the Padres as a second-round pick out of high school in 2013. Peterson was considered by many to be the best power bat available in the draft, and that is where his value lies. He can drive the ball to all fields with his big swing, but he keeps it under control well enough that he may not strike out as much as most sluggers. Peterson most likely will shift across the diamond to first base at some point, as he did at New Mexico in 2013. His arm is strong enough to play third base, but he lacks the range and footwork necessary for the position. He is a below-average runner. Peterson was thriving in his debut until Aug. 22, when a pitch hit him in the jaw, breaking it and requiring two surgeries. The Mariners expect him to be ready for spring training, with a probable 2014 assignment to high Class A High Desert, putting Peterson on course to reach Seattle by late 2015.

Year	Club (League)	Class	AVG	G	AB	R	H	2B	3B	HR	RBI	BB	SO	SB	CS	OBP	SLG
2013	Everett (NWL)	SS	.312	29	109	20	34	6	0	6	27	13	18	0	1	.382	.532
	Clinton (MWL)	LoA	.293	26	99	16	29	5	1	7	20	7	24	1	0	.346	.576
Minor League Totals			.303	55	208	36	63	11	1	13	47	20	42	1	1	.365	.553

3 JAMES PAXTON, LHP

BA GRADE **55** HIGH

Born: Nov. 6, 1988. **B-T:** L-L. **Ht.:** 6-4. **Wt.:** 220. **Drafted:** Grand Prairie (American Association), 2010 (4th round). **Signed by:** Brian Williams/Jesse Kapellusch

Paxton took the long road to Seattle, the team he grew up rooting for in British Columbia. A supplemental first-round pick in 2009 by the Blue Jays, he didn't sign and didn't return to college after Jays president Paul Beeston told a Toronto newspaper he had negotiated with Paxton's agent Scott Boras, effectively ending Paxton's eligibility. He went on to play independent ball, and the Mariners drafted him in 2010, finally signing him for $942,500 in March 2011. Paxton's fastball runs anywhere from 91-98 mph, though his velocity fluctuates because the long-limbed lefty can have trouble repeating his mechanics. His hammer curveball is a plus pitch, sitting in the low 80s at its best, but Paxton also has trouble throwing it for strikes consistently. His cutter and changeup lag behind the other two pitches. Paxton tightened his delivery considerably late in 2013, which allowed him to pitch well when he was called up to the major leagues for the first time in September. Paxton will get a chance to win a spot in the big league rotation in spring training. If he throws enough strikes, he could be a mid-rotation starter. If he moves to the bullpen, he has the stuff to pitch high-leverage innings.

Year	Club (League)	Class	W	L	ERA	G	GS	CG	SV	IP	H	HR	BB	SO	K/9	WHIP	AVG
2010	Grand Prairie (A-A)	IND	1	2	4.24	4	4	0	0	17	15	1	7	18	9.5	1.29	—
2011	Clinton (MWL)	LoA	3	3	2.73	10	10	0	0	56	45	1	30	80	12.9	1.34	.225
	Jackson (SL)	AA	3	0	1.85	7	7	0	0	39	28	2	13	51	11.8	1.05	.201
2012	Jackson (SL)	AA	9	4	3.05	21	21	0	0	106	96	5	54	110	9.3	1.41	.244
2013	Tacoma (PCL)	AAA	8	11	4.45	28	26	2	0	146	158	10	58	131	8.1	1.48	.277
	Seattle (AL)	MAJ	3	0	1.50	4	4	0	0	24	15	2	7	21	7.9	0.92	.172
Major League Totals			3	0	1.50	4	4	0	0	24	15	2	7	21	7.9	0.92	.172
Minor League Totals			23	18	3.45	66	64	2	0	347	327	18	155	372	9.6	1.39	.251

4 LUIZ GOHARA, LHP

Born: July 31, 1996. **B-T:** L-L. **Ht.:** 6-3. **Wt.:** 210. **Signed:** Brazil, 2012. **Signed by:** Emilio Carrasquel/Hide Sueyoshi.

Gohara was a baseball rat from the time he was young and began playing in national tournaments in Brazil by age 10. The Mariners signed him for $800,000 in 2012 and, in a rare move, had him skip the complex leagues and assigned him to Rookie-level Pulaski as a 16-year-old in 2013. He held his own again older competition, though he was slowed by a sore shoulder. The big-bodied Gohara has good stuff, but he must refine his secondary pitches. His fastball sits at 92-93 mph, occasionally reaches 96, and probably will sit more consistently at the upper range with more experience and strength. He throws a curveball and slider and both are inconsistent. Gohara's command of the changeup is also erratic but it has a chance to be a plus pitch because of its late fade. His delivery is sound and advanced for his age. However, Gohara tends to put on weight despite still being a teenager, and some scouts see a body type along the lines of a shorter version of C.C. Sabathia. He pitched just 22 innings in 2013 because of the balky shoulder. The Mariners don't want to greatly increase his workload in 2014, so he probably will be held back at extended spring training before a return trip to Pulaski. Based on his velocity and clean mechanics, Gohara has a chance to be at least a mid-rotation starter, and maybe more.

Year	Club (League)	Class	W	L	ERA	G	GS	CG	SV	IP	H	HR	BB	SO	K/9	WHIP	AVG
2013	Pulaski (APP)	R	1	2	4.15	6	6	0	0	22	22	1	9	27	11.2	1.43	.256
Minor League Totals			1	2	4.15	6	6	0	0	22	22	1	9	27	11.2	1.43	.256

5 EDWIN DIAZ, RHP

Born: March 22, 1994. **B-T:** R-R. **Ht.:** 6-2. **Wt.:** 165. **Drafted:** HS—Caguas, P.R., 2012 (3rd round). **Signed by:** Noel Sevilla.

The Mariners signed Diaz for $300,000 as their third-round pick in 2012. Pitching is in his bloodlines. His cousin Jose Melendez was a reliever with the Mariners, Padres and Red Sox from 1990-94. Diaz grew up idolizing Pedro Martinez and wears No. 45 in his honor. He has two above-average pitches in his fastball and slider. The fastball had sneaky velocity, usually sitting 90-94 mph, and he'll occasionally ramp it up to 96. Diaz has strong command for such a young pitcher, locating his fastball to both sides of the plate. The slider became a plus pitch when the Mariners had him raise his three-quarters arm slot, which allowed him to throw on more of a downhill plane. Like most young pitchers, Diaz needs to work on his changeup because he still is learning how to throw it at the same arm speed as his fastball. Diaz is on the thin side, even though he has gained 20 pounds since signing, and he tired at the end of 2013 at Rookie-level Pulaski. Diaz has a ceiling to rival any pitcher in the organization other than Taijuan Walker. He profiles as at least a potential mid-rotation starter or a strong late-inning reliever if stamina becomes a long-term issue. He should be ready for a jump to low Class A Clinton.

Year	Club (League)	Class	W	L	ERA	G	GS	CG	SV	IP	H	HR	BB	SO	K/9	WHIP	AVG
2012	Mariners (AZL)	R	2	1	5.21	9	1	0	0	19	12	2	17	20	9.5	1.53	.176
2013	Pulaski (APP)	R	5	2	1.43	13	13	0	0	69	45	5	18	79	10.3	0.91	.191
Minor League Totals			7	3	2.25	22	14	0	0	88	57	7	35	99	10.1	1.05	.188

6 AUSTIN WILSON, OF

Born: Feb. 7, 1992. **B-T:** R-R. **Ht.:** 6-4. **Wt.:** 210. **Drafted:** Stanford, 2013 (2nd round). **Signed by:** Stacey Pettis.

The Mariners needed to go well over the recommended slot value for the 49th overall pick in 2013 to sign Wilson and keep him from returning to Stanford for his senior season. He missed half the college season with a stress reaction in his right elbow and wound up singing for $1.7 million, which was $590,000 over slot. Wilson is a physical specimen and has the raw tools to match. The most intriguing tool is the one that hasn't fully developed yet—power. He hit 20 homers total in college but worked to add loft in his swing after signing with Seattle and hit five of his six home runs at short-season Everett in August. A poor bet to hit for a high average, Wilson has the type of raw power to make that tradeoff acceptable. He has a very strong arm and is an above-average runner, making him a natural for right field. He would need to tighten his route-taking to be able play center. The Mariners will take it slowly with Wilson and have him begin 2014 at low Class A Clinton with an eye on an in-season promotion to high Class A High Desert. Wilson is still somewhat raw for a college player, but his tools, intelligence and work ethic give him a chance to potentially become a first-division regular.

Year	Club (League)	Class	AVG	G	AB	R	H	2B	3B	HR	RBI	BB	SO	SB	CS	OBP	SLG
2013	Everett (NWL)	SS	.241	56	203	22	49	11	3	6	27	17	42	2	4	.319	.414
Minor League Totals			.241	56	203	22	49	11	3	6	27	17	42	2	4	.319	.414

7 VICTOR SANCHEZ, RHP

BA GRADE
50
HIGH

Born: Jan. 30, 1995. **B-T:** R-R. **Ht.:** 6-0. **Wt.:** 255. **Signed:** Venezuela, 2011. **Signed by:** Luis Martinez/Emilio Carrasquel/Bob Engle.

Sanchez began making his mark when was 12 while playing for Venezuela in international play, and the Mariners signed him for $2.5 million in 2011. He got a late start at low Class A Clinton in 2013 as he returned from offseason appendicitis, but he recovered to throw a nine-inning no-hitter on July 18 against Lansing. Sanchez's wife and mother witnessed the gem as they had flown in from Venezuela the day before. What stands out most about Sanchez is his thick, barrel-chested body. However, he is much more muscular than overweight, and one scout compared him physically to former NFL linebacker Ray Lewis, a nickname his short-season Everett teammates hung on him in 2012. Sanchez pitched well with less stuff in 2013, pitching off an 88-91 mph fastball that touched 94. His changeup, which flashes above-average, and curveball also were ordinary. What makes his three pitches play up, though, is pinpoint control. He pounds the bottom half of the zone and throws them all on a downhill angle. Sanchez will move up to high Class A High Desert in 2014, a difficult environment for even the best of pitching prospects. He'll have to tighten up his secondary stuff to achieve his mid-rotation ceiling, but he has the pitchability to move quickly if he does.

Year	Club (League)	Class	W	L	ERA	G	GS	CG	SV	IP	H	HR	BB	SO	K/9	WHIP	AVG
2012	Everett (NWL)	SS	6	2	3.18	15	15	0	0	85	69	5	27	69	7.3	1.13	.223
2013	Clinton (MWL)	LoA	6	6	2.78	20	20	1	0	113	106	4	18	79	6.3	1.09	.241
Minor League Totals			12	8	2.95	35	35	1	0	198	175	9	45	148	6.7	1.11	.233

8 TYLER MARLETTE, C

BA GRADE
50
HIGH

Born: Jan. 23, 1993. **B-T:** R-R. **Ht.:** 5-11. **Wt.:** 195. **Drafted:** HS—Oviedo, Fla., 2011 (5th round). **Signed by:** Rob Mummau.

Marlette had a strong amateur career, including a home run at Petco Park in the 2010 Aflac All-American Game in San Diego. The Mariners' $650,000 over-slot bonus in 2011 convinced him to pass up a scholarship to Central Florida. Marlette is a bat-first catching prospect at this stage of his career. He has a good approach at the plate with a relatively good eye and a willingness to hit the ball the other way. He showed very good raw power as an amateur, which started to manifest more as doubles power with low Class A Clinton in 2013, where he also made good strides defensively. Marlette shows signs of being a potentially plus player behind the plate because his receiving skills are improving. However, his throws tend to sail at times because of improper footwork. He has a strong arm, though, and threw out 38 percent of basestealers, third in the Midwest League in 2013. With a squat body and thick lower half, Marlette will have to work hard to monitor his conditioning and avoid becoming a baseclogger. The Mariners will move him to high Class A High Desert in 2014, where he'll try to increase his workload while maintaining his offensive production.

Year	Club (League)	Class	AVG	G	AB	R	H	2B	3B	HR	RBI	BB	SO	SB	CS	OBP	SLG
2011	Pulaski (APP)	R	.156	12	45	4	7	2	0	0	2	0	13	0	0	.156	.200
2012	Pulaski (APP)	R	.284	56	208	23	59	14	0	5	23	6	46	3	1	.304	.423
	Everett (NWL)	SS	.400	2	5	0	2	1	0	0	0	0	1	0	1	.400	.600
2013	Clinton (MWL)	LoA	.304	75	270	36	82	17	2	6	37	24	53	10	4	.367	.448
Minor League Totals			.284	145	528	63	150	34	2	11	62	30	113	13	6	.326	.419

9 CHRIS TAYLOR, SS

BA GRADE **45** MEDIUM

Born: Aug. 29, 1990. **B-T:** R-R. **Ht.:** 6-0. **Wt.:** 170. **Drafted:** Virginia 2012 (5th round). **Signed by:** Mike Moriarty.

Taylor signed for $500,000 in 2012 following his junior season at Virginia, almost double the recommended slot of $264,000. His father Chris Sr. and uncle Armand both wrestled at Virginia Tech, and the former held the school record for fastest pin, while the latter was a three-time conference wrestler of the year. Taylor was considered a glove-first prospect when he entered pro ball, but he hit his way to Double-A Jackson in 2013. He handles the bat well, sprays line drives to all fields and also is willing to be patient and take walks. However, he does not possess over-the-fence power, and his willingness to go deep in counts also results in a lot of strikeouts for someone with minimal power. He can be induced to chase two-strike pitches out of the zone. A stolen-base threat despite being just a tick-above-average runner, he has good instincts on the bases as well as in the field. He plays a good shortstop because of his range and hands, but some scouts question whether his fringe arm strength will force him to second base. Taylor has a chance to begin 2014 at Triple-A Tacoma with a good spring training. Seattle's middle-infield depth makes Taylor a better fit for them as a utility player.

Year	Club (League)	Class	AVG	G	AB	R	H	2B	3B	HR	RBI	BB	SO	SB	CS	OBP	SLG
2012	Everett (NWL)	SS	.328	37	137	26	45	12	1	2	18	21	18	13	5	.430	.474
	Clinton (MWL)	LoA	.304	12	46	5	14	0	0	0	4	2	4	4	1	.373	.304
2013	High Desert (CAL)	HiA	.335	67	269	62	90	16	7	7	44	44	62	20	2	.426	.524
	Jackson (SL)	AA	.293	67	256	46	75	12	4	1	16	40	55	18	3	.391	.383
Minor League Totals			.316	183	708	139	224	40	12	10	82	107	139	55	11	.411	.449

10 DANNY HULTZEN, LHP

BA GRADE **55** EXTREME

Born: Nov. 28, 1989. **B-T:** L-L. **Ht.:** 6-3. **Wt.:** 200. **Drafted:** Virginia, 2011 (1st round). **Signed by:** Mike Moriarty.

Hultzen's parents are both doctors—his father is a neonatologist and his mother a psychiatrist. He saw too much of doctors in 2013, however, after being shut down twice and eventually needing surgery in October to repair a torn rotator cuff in his left shoulder. His pre-surgery stuff played up because he had outstanding deception in his delivery. However, that deception was created by severely throwing across his body, a motion that many other teams felt could lead to injury eventually. It remains to be seen how much Hultzen will need to change his delivery once he recovers. His best pitch is an outstanding changeup that he throws with the same arm action as his fastball, which sat 90-92 mph and touched 95 when healthy. He also has a curveball and a slider, which he uses primarily against lefthanders. The Mariners didn't get a star with Dustin Ackley as the No. 2 overall pick in 2009, and Hultzen could be another No. 2 overall miss if he struggles to come back from his surgery. Seattle expects him to miss the 2014 season, and their lofty investment—including an $8.5 million major league contract and team-record $6.35 million signing bonus—could be in jeopardy.

Year	Club (League)	Class	W	L	ERA	G	GS	CG	SV	IP	H	HR	BB	SO	K/9	WHIP	AVG
2012	Jackson (SL)	AA	8	3	1.19	13	13	0	0	75	38	2	32	79	9.4	0.93	.151
	Tacoma (PCL)	AAA	1	4	5.92	12	12	0	0	49	49	2	43	57	10.5	1.89	.258
2013	Mariners (AZL)	R	1	0	1.80	1	1	0	0	5	3	0	0	8	14.4	0.60	.167
	Tacoma (PCL)	AAA	4	1	2.05	6	6	0	0	31	19	1	7	34	10.0	0.85	.168
Minor League Totals			14	8	2.82	32	32	0	0	160	109	5	82	178	10.0	1.20	.190

11 JULIO MORBAN, OF

BA GRADE **50** HIGH

Born: Feb. 13, 1992. **B-T:** L-L. **Ht.:** 6-1. **Wt.:** 205. **Signed:** Dominican Republic, 2008. **Signed by:** Patrick Guerrero/Bob Engle.

The Mariners have long sought the next Ken Griffey, but with Morban they might have to settle for production more along the lines of Griffey senior than junior. Viewed by scouts as the top hitter available on the international amateur market in 2008, Morban signed with the Mariners for $1.1 million, and his level, lefthanded swing produces power, though not necessarily the loft to profile as a top-end home run threat. He generates above-average power with a wide-open stance and should be a threat to annually hit 15-plus home runs as a major league regular. Improved selectivity could help Morban hit for a consistently high average and improve his walk total. He's aggressive to a fault, especially against lefthanders, batting .241/.310/.329 against them at Double-A Jackson in 2013. After the first four years of his career were marked by injury and inconsistency, Morban started putting things together in 2012 at high Class A High Desert and had another strong year at Jackson in 2013 before breaking the fibula in his right calf in mid-August on a slide into second base. His below-average speed and range limits him to a corner-outfield spot, perhaps left field even though his arm is good enough for right. A member of the 40-man roster, Morban will start 2014 at Triple-A Tacoma.

Year	Club (League)	Class	AVG	G	AB	R	H	2B	3B	HR	RBI	BB	SO	SB	CS	OBP	SLG
2009	Pulaski (APP)	R	.333	4	9	3	3	1	0	0	0	0	3	0	0	.400	.444
	Mariners (AZL)	R	.266	42	154	28	41	9	7	5	23	7	49	8	3	.303	.513
2010	Pulaski (APP)	R	.100	4	10	1	1	0	0	0	0	4	3	0	0	.357	.100
	Mariners (AZL)	R	.400	3	5	0	2	0	0	0	1	0	1	0	0	.400	.400
	High Desert (CAL)	HiA	.333	2	6	0	2	0	0	0	1	0	2	0	0	.333	.333
	Everett (NWL)	SS	.250	1	4	0	1	0	0	0	0	0	2	0	0	.250	.250
2011	Clinton (MWL)	LoA	.256	80	301	44	77	12	7	4	28	26	99	10	5	.315	.382
2012	Mariners (AZL)	R	.238	6	21	2	5	0	0	0	3	0	3	0	0	.227	.238
	High Desert (CAL)	HiA	.313	76	300	56	94	16	2	17	52	21	67	5	1	.361	.550
2013	Jackson (SL)	AA	.295	86	295	46	87	20	5	7	44	28	95	7	2	.362	.468
Minor League Totals			.283	304	1105	180	313	58	21	33	152	86	324	30	11	.338	.463

12 PATRICK KIVLEHAN, 3B

BA GRADE
50
HIGH

Born: Dec. 22, 1989. **B-T:** R-R. **Ht.:** 6-2. **Wt.:** 210. **Drafted:** Rutgers, 2012 (4th round). **Signed by:** Mike Moriarty.

Kivlehan did not play baseball at Rutgers until his senior year, stepping away from the sport for three years while concentrating on playing safety for the Scarlet Knights football team. He has certainly made up for lost time, winning Big East Conference player of the year honors in 2012, his lone college season on the diamond, and quickly working his way into prospect status as a pro. Kivlehan surprised scouts by hitting for more average than power in 2013, while making fairly consistent contact by using an all-fields approach. He hasn't learned to pull the ball for power yet, but most coaches consider that easier to teach, and he has as much power to the opposite field as the pull side. Kivlehan has had his struggles at third base because he lacks first-step quickness and his arm is erratic. However, the Mariners like his work ethic and want to give him every chance to succeed at the hot corner before moving him to first base. He's a fringy runner but will steal an occasional base. Kivlehan struggled in the Arizona Fall League, going 10-for-61 (.164), but likely will be ticketed for Double-A Jackson in 2014.

Year	Club (League)	Class	AVG	G	AB	R	H	2B	3B	HR	RBI	BB	SO	SB	CS	OBP	SLG
2012	Everett (NWL)	SS	.301	72	282	46	85	17	3	12	52	19	93	14	1	.373	.511
2013	Clinton (MWL)	LoA	.283	60	223	26	63	12	1	3	31	17	42	5	3	.344	.386
	High Desert (CAL)	HiA	.320	68	266	48	85	13	2	13	59	26	65	10	3	.384	.530
Minor League Totals			.302	200	771	120	233	42	6	28	142	62	200	29	7	.368	.481

13 GABRIEL GUERRERO, OF

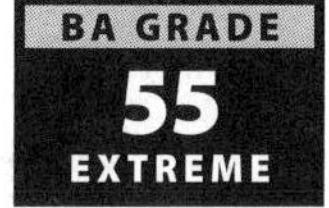

Born: Dec. 11, 1993. **B-T:** R-R. **Ht.:** 6-3. **Wt.:** 190. **Signed:** Dominican Republic, 2011. **Signed by:** Patrick Guerrero/Bob Engle/Franklin Taveras Jr.

The comparisons between Gabriel Guerrero and his uncle, nine-time all-star outfielder Vladimir, were inevitable from the moment Gabriel signed for $400,000 in 2011. While he isn't quite as toolsy at Uncle Vlad, he's pretty close. They both have very similar hitting styles, including not wearing batting gloves. Gabriel is a free-swinger who is adept at hitting pitches out of the zone, and yet he doesn't strike out copiously because he can handle breaking pitches fairly well. He has an outstanding arm, earning 70 grades on the 20-80 scouting scale, and that gives him a chance to be an above-average right fielder. He also runs well. The Mariners aggressively promoted Guerrero in 2013, assigning him to low Class A Clinton, and he survived even though his raw power didn't play. He puts on batting practice displays, but his lack of discipline keeps him from getting to his power in games. A probable assignment to high Class A High Desert is in store for 2014.

Year	Club (League)	Class	AVG	G	AB	R	H	2B	3B	HR	RBI	BB	SO	SB	CS	OBP	SLG
2011	Mariners (DSL)	R	.236	57	191	24	45	9	0	1	14	14	29	4	3	.288	.298
2012	Mariners (DSL)	R	.355	50	200	38	71	9	4	11	54	21	28	4	6	.409	.605
	Mariners (AZL)	R	.333	18	75	17	25	5	0	4	18	3	13	0	0	.350	.560
2013	Clinton (MWL)	LoA	.271	125	469	60	127	23	3	4	50	21	113	12	3	.303	.358
Minor League Totals			.287	250	935	139	268	46	7	20	136	59	183	20	12	.327	.415

14 CARSON SMITH, RHP

BA GRADE
45
MEDIUM

Born: Oct. 19, 1989. **B-T:** R-R. **Ht.:** 6-6. **Wt.:** 215. **Drafted:** Texas State, 2011 (8th round). **Signed by:** Kyle Van Hook.

Smith thrived as a starter at Texas State, going 19-7, 2.52 in two seasons, but his slinging, low-slot delivery prompted the Mariners to make him a reliever once he signed for $215,000 as an eight-round pick in 2011. He's succeeded in the role, and Seattle selected him as its minor league relief pitcher of the year for 2013. Smith works off a hard sinker/slider combination. The fastball usually parks in the 91-93 mph range, which is nothing special for a reliever, but what makes it a plus pitch is its outstanding movement. The slider sits 84-88 mph, and Smith sometimes has a hard time controlling the break on it. He consistently forces hitters to beat the ball into the ground, however, as evidenced by a well-above-average 4.13 groundout/airout ratio at Double-A Jackson in 2013. The biggest concern about Smith is his delivery, because his max-effort mechanics are difficult to repeat and often find him slinging the ball more than throwing it. He continues to work on smoothing out his motion, and he walked just 3.1 per nine innings in 2013. Smith likely will begin 2014 at Triple-A Tacoma and should graduate to the big league bullpen at some point during the season.

Year	Club (League)	Class	W	L	ERA	G	GS	CG	SV	IP	H	HR	BB	SO	K/9	WHIP	AVG
2012	High Desert (CAL)	HiA	5	1	2.90	49	0	0	15	62	54	2	28	77	11.2	1.32	.234
2013	Jackson (SL)	AA	1	3	1.98	44	0	0	15	50	33	1	17	71	12.8	1.00	.183
Minor League Totals			6	4	2.49	93	0	0	30	112	87	3	45	148	11.9	1.18	.212

15 STEFEN ROMERO, OF/2B

BA GRADE
45
MEDIUM

Born: Oct. 17, 1988. **B-T:** R-R. **Ht.:** 6-2. **Wt.:** 220. **Drafted:** Oregon State, 2010 (12th round). **Signed by:** Joe Rossi.

Romero broke through in 2012 when he earned the Mariners' minor league player of the year honor, batting .352/.391/.599 with 23 homers between high Class A High Desert and Double-A Jackson. His production went backward in 2013, but he still earned a spot on the club's 40-man roster. Romero suffered a strained left oblique muscle when he swung at and missed a breaking pitch during 2013 spring training, an injury that caused him to miss the last four weeks. A second and third baseman previously, he shifted to left field at Triple-A Tacoma in 2013, though he still played two games at the keystone. Romero can hit for average and has average power, but his speed and arm are just adequate. He draws high marks for his makeup and work ethic. He will go back to Triple-A Tacoma in 2014 to try to hit his way into a crowded Mariners outfield picture.

Year	Club (League)	Class	AVG	G	AB	R	H	2B	3B	HR	RBI	BB	SO	SB	CS	OBP	SLG
2011	Clinton (MWL)	LoA	.280	116	429	62	120	22	4	16	65	32	69	16	9	.342	.462
2012	High Desert (CAL)	HiA	.357	60	258	47	92	19	3	11	51	13	35	6	2	.391	.581
	Jackson (SL)	AA	.347	56	216	38	75	15	4	12	50	14	37	6	3	.392	.620
2013	High Desert (CAL)	HiA	.278	5	18	1	5	1	0	0	2	2	1	0	0	.381	.333
	Tacoma (PCL)	AAA	.277	93	375	51	104	23	4	11	74	28	87	8	4	.331	.448
Minor League Totals			.306	330	1296	199	396	80	15	50	242	89	229	36	18	.357	.506

16 TYLER PIKE, LHP

Born: Jan. 26, 1994. **B-T:** L-L. **Ht.:** 6-0. **Wt.:** 180. **Drafted:** HS—Winter Haven, Fla., 2012 (3rd round supplemental). **Signed by:** Rob Mummau.

The Mariners went nearly half a million dollars over slot to convince Pike to forego a scholarship to Florida State, signing him for $850,000 in 2012 as a supplemental third-round pick. He has met expectations and then some to this point, falling just four outs short of having enough innings to lead the low Class A Midwest League in ERA (2.37) in 2013. Pike's fastball sits in the 88-91 mph range, and he has good feel for his changeup at a young age, as well as decent deception in his delivery. However, his slow curveball is erratic and he will need that pitch in order to have a varied enough arsenal to be a major league starter. Pike tends to throw everything to the outer third of the plate and is hesitant to pitch inside or to contact. That approach to pitching works against lesser competition, but most scouts believe Pike is going to need to learn to use the inner half of the plate. The hitting environment of high Class A High Desert will be a difficult proving ground. Some Mariners officials see the athletic Pike as a future No. 4 starter, but he's far from reaching that ceiling.

Year	Club (League)	Class	W	L	ERA	G	GS	CG	SV	IP	H	HR	BB	SO	K/9	WHIP	AVG
2012	Mariners (AZL)	R	2	1	1.78	11	11	0	0	51	34	1	21	57	10.1	1.09	.193
2013	Clinton (MWL)	LoA	7	4	2.37	22	22	0	0	110	73	5	57	90	7.3	1.18	.194
Minor League Totals			9	5	2.18	33	33	0	0	161	107	6	78	147	8.2	1.15	.193

17 ABRAHAM ALMONTE, OF

BA GRADE
45
MEDIUM

Born: June 27, 1989. **B-T:** B-R. **Ht.:** 5-9. **Wt.:** 205. **Signed:** Dominican Republic, 2005. **Signed by:** Hector Luna (Yankees).

Acquired from the Yankees for reliever Shawn Kelley on the eve of spring training 2013, Almonte benefitted from the change in scenery. He made his major league debut on Aug. 30 and started 18 times over the season's final month. Managers voted Almonte as the Double-A Eastern League's fastest baserunner in 2012, and he swiped 20 bases in 27 attempts at Triple-A Tacoma in 2013. The switch-hitter plays with energy, hits for solid average and shows some pop from the left side, and with 11 home runs in 2013 he more than doubled his previous single-season high. Almonte can be too aggressive both at the plate and in the field, where he generally runs good routes in center field and has a strong arm. His best tool is 60 speed, and he's an excellent, if inefficient, basestealer. Almonte will have a chance to win a bench job with the Mariners this spring, but he has the look of a late-bloomer who could work his way into a part-regular role.

Year	Club (League)	Class	AVG	G	AB	R	H	2B	3B	HR	RBI	BB	SO	SB	CS	OBP	SLG
2006	Yankees1 (DSL)	R	.254	63	209	51	53	11	3	8	26	55	45	36	14	.409	.450
2007	Yankees (GCL)	R	.288	49	160	29	46	4	3	3	16	21	34	8	9	.372	.406
2008	Charleston, SC (SAL)	LoA	.228	115	443	61	101	20	7	8	46	47	101	29	10	.303	.359
2009	Charleston, SC (SAL)	LoA	.280	115	440	63	123	14	10	5	56	35	81	36	5	.333	.391
2010	Tampa (FSL)	HiA	.263	15	57	9	15	3	1	0	3	6	16	5	3	.333	.351
2011	Tampa (FSL)	HiA	.268	131	537	92	144	27	11	4	52	52	100	30	11	.333	.382
2012	Yankees (GCL)	R	.222	7	18	2	4	2	0	0	0	2	4	2	0	.300	.333
	Trenton (EL)	AA	.276	78	319	47	88	17	4	4	25	37	59	30	5	.350	.392
2013	Jackson (SL)	AA	.255	29	102	18	26	6	1	4	18	18	28	6	1	.367	.451
	Tacoma (PCL)	AAA	.314	94	338	63	106	17	5	11	50	49	66	20	7	.403	.491
	Seattle (AL)	MAJ	.264	25	72	10	19	4	0	2	9	6	21	1	0	.313	.403
Major League Totals			.264	25	72	10	19	4	0	2	9	6	21	1	0	.313	.403
Minor League Totals			.269	696	2623	435	706	121	45	47	292	322	534	202	65	.350	.403

18 TYLER O'NEILL, OF

BA GRADE
50
EXTREME

Born: June 22, 1995. **B-T:** R-R. **Ht.:** 5-11. **Wt.:** 205. **Drafted:** HS—Maple Ridge, B.C., 2013 (3rd round). **Signed by:** Wayne Norton.

The son of former Mr. Canada bodybuilder Terry O'Neill, Tyler carries the nickname "Tank" for his sturdy physique. The Mariners liked him enough to give him a $600,000 bonus as their third-round pick in 2013. Though he hit only one home run in his first 100 at-bats in the Rookie-level Arizona League in 2013, O'Neill has the strong hands and arms to become a power hitter as he matures and learns to put a little more loft into what is currently a pretty—but level—righthanded swing. While he has plenty of muscle, O'Neill is not a one-dimensional player. He is anaverage runner and a good enough athlete to have played shortstop in high school in British Columbia. Short of range and with an average arm, O'Neill's long-term position figures to be left field or perhaps first base. Though he grew up in Maple Ridge, the same town as all-star outfielder Larry Walker, he reminds many scouts of another B.C. native, Blue Jays third baseman Brett Lawrie. He will begin 2014 at low Class A Clinton.

Year	Club (League)	Class	AVG	G	AB	R	H	2B	3B	HR	RBI	BB	SO	SB	CS	OBP	SLG
2013	Mariners (AZL)	R	.310	28	100	12	31	5	3	1	15	12	27	2	4	.405	.450
Minor League Totals			.310	28	100	12	31	5	3	1	15	12	27	2	4	.405	.450

19 JABARI BLASH, OF

Born: July 4, 1989. **B-T:** R-R. **Ht.:** 6-5. **Wt.:** 224. **Drafted:** Miami-Dade CC, 2010 (8th round). **Signed by:** Mike Tosar.

Despite playing little baseball while growing up in the Virgin Islands, Blash was drafted three times as an amateur, first by the White Sox out of high school in 2007. Following a year at Alcorn State, where he was ineligible, he was drafted in each of his years at Miami-Dade CC, finally signing with the Mariners for $140,000 as a 2010 eight-rounder after being kicked off the junior-college team in mid-April. Scouts can dream on Blash because he has an athletic build—he draws comparisons with Eric Davis—along with plenty of tools. He has big-time power potential, runs well and has a plus arm, though at times his throws lack accuracy. However, Blash has yet to have his production match his tools. He's streaky at the plate, has a hole in his swing middle-in and gets caught cheating on fastballs by savvy pitchers. The Mariners have been patient with Blash because athletic righthanded power hitters are hard to find. He likely will begin 2014 back at Double-A Jackson, where ended 2013. Left off the 40-man roster, Blash has profile right fielder upside but remains raw more than 1,200 at-bats into his pro career.

Year	Club (League)	Class	AVG	G	AB	R	H	2B	3B	HR	RBI	BB	SO	SB	CS	OBP	SLG
2010	Pulaski (APP)	R	.266	32	109	21	29	6	1	5	20	13	44	1	1	.362	.477
2011	Clinton (MWL)	LoA	.218	42	124	13	27	5	1	3	13	38	43	5	2	.401	.347
	Everett (NWL)	SS	.292	57	195	26	57	16	3	11	43	28	65	10	3	.393	.574
2012	Clinton (MWL)	LoA	.245	113	400	71	98	20	5	15	50	60	134	13	7	.355	.433
2013	High Desert (CAL)	HiA	.258	80	283	42	73	16	3	16	53	40	85	14	8	.358	.505
	Jackson (SL)	AA	.309	29	97	13	30	3	0	9	21	20	28	1	1	.442	.619
Minor League Totals			.260	353	1208	186	314	66	13	59	200	199	399	44	22	.375	.483

20 KETEL MARTE, SS/2B

BA GRADE 45 HIGH

Born: Oct. 12, 1993. **B-T:** B-R. **Ht.:** 6-1. **Wt.:** 180. **Signed:** Dominican Republic, 2010. **Signed by:** Patrick Guerrero/Bob Engle/Franklin Taveras Jr.

Signed for $100,000 in 2010, Marte made his full-season league debut in 2013 by playing both middle infield positions at low Class A Clinton. His best attributes at this stage are speed and defense. He is a well-above-average runner who grades as a 60 on the 20-80 scouting scale. Marte also is a good defender with plus range and a strong arm, though he appears more comfortable at second base, where he turns the double play well, than shortstop. The biggest question about Marte is the hit tool. He consistently puts the bat on the ball and does not strike out much for a young player. However, he also draws few walks and swings at too many bad pitches. Marte will begin 2014 at high Class A High Desert. He could develop into a prototype No. 2 hitter capable of playing either middle-infield position or, more likely, a utility player and pinch-runner.

Year	Club (League)	Class	AVG	G	AB	R	H	2B	3B	HR	RBI	BB	SO	SB	CS	OBP	SLG
2011	Mariners (DSL)	R	.259	62	220	44	57	5	3	2	22	26	35	16	6	.341	.336
2012	Clinton (MWL)	LoA	.286	4	14	3	4	0	0	0	2	2	3	1	0	.375	.286
	Everett (NWL)	SS	.247	65	251	36	62	4	2	0	22	12	35	14	4	.281	.279
2013	Clinton (MWL)	LoA	.304	98	378	61	115	15	5	0	29	15	39	16	8	.330	.370
	High Desert (CAL)	HiA	.256	19	86	18	22	0	2	1	8	4	11	4	3	.289	.337
Minor League Totals			.274	248	949	162	260	24	12	3	83	59	123	51	21	.317	.334

21 WILTON MARTINEZ, OF

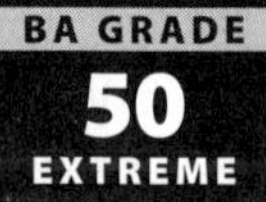

BA GRADE 50 EXTREME

Born: Dec. 11, 1993. **B-T:** R-R. **Ht.:** 6-4. **Wt.:** 195. **Signed:** Dominican Republic, 2011. **Signed by:** Patrick Guerrero/Franklin Taveras Jr./Bob Engle.

After playing his first two seasons in the Dominican Summer League, Martinez made a big splash in his domestic debut in 2013, leading the Rookie-level Appalachian League with 12 home runs. He has the power to hit tape-measure shots and figures to get even stronger once his body completely fills out. Most of Martinez's power is to the pull side at this stage, and his righthanded swing tends to get long at times. Like most young hitters, he needs to work on his plate discipline, but the Mariners are willing to trade off some strikeouts for home runs. Power isn't Martinez's only tool as he has above-average speed and a plus arm. Though he may lose a step as he matures, he should remain a plus runner, and his arm makes him a natural fit for right field. Martinez took a big step forward in his development in 2013 and he will get his first taste of full-season ball in 2014 at low Class A Clinton.

Year	Club (League)	Class	AVG	G	AB	R	H	2B	3B	HR	RBI	BB	SO	SB	CS	OBP	SLG
2011	Mariners (DSL)	R	.170	49	147	14	25	6	1	1	13	14	29	2	2	.262	.245
2012	Mariners (DSL)	R	.251	66	243	30	61	9	1	10	37	20	36	9	1	.321	.420
2013	Pulaski (APP)	R	.209	53	201	29	42	9	1	12	33	12	65	3	2	.261	.443
Minor League Totals			.217	168	591	73	128	24	3	23	83	46	130	14	5	.286	.384

22 DOMINIC LEONE, RHP

BA GRADE 45 HIGH

Born: Oct. 26, 1991. **B-T:** R-R. **Ht.:** 5-11. **Wt.:** 185. **Drafted:** Clemson, 2012 (16th round). **Signed by:** Garrett Ball.

Leone has proven to be a late-round find for the Mariners, reaching Double-A Jackson in 2013 only a year after being a 16th-round draft pick. In three seasons at Clemson, Leone started and relieved, helping the Tigers reach the College World Series once and regionals two other times. Passed over for 15 rounds primarily because of his slight stature and 5.25 ERA as a junior, Leone nonetheless throws his fastball in the 89-94 mph range and also has an effective slider up to 85 mph and a cutter that can break bats. He thrived in the Arizona Fall League, leading the circuit with six saves but more importantly posting a 15/1 SO/BB ratio. His above-average control separates him from other relief candidates in the organization. Leone will begin the 2014 season at Triple-A Tacoma but likely will make his major league debut in season. His stuff may be just a tad short for closing, but he has a chance of being an effective set-up man.

Year	Club (League)	Class	W	L	ERA	G	GS	CG	SV	IP	H	HR	BB	SO	K/9	WHIP	AVG
2012	Everett (NWL)	SS	3	0	1.36	19	0	0	5	33	20	0	19	39	10.6	1.18	.177
2013	Clinton (MWL)	LoA	0	0	0.00	3	0	0	0	6	6	0	4	10	14.2	1.58	.250
	High Desert (CAL)	HiA	0	1	2.50	29	0	0	12	40	31	2	9	37	8.4	1.01	.220
	Jackson (SL)	AA	1	2	2.50	16	0	0	4	18	12	2	5	17	8.5	0.94	.182
Minor League Totals			4	3	1.95	67	0	0	21	97	69	4	37	103	9.6	1.09	.201

23 JOHN HICKS, C

BA GRADE 45 HIGH

Born: Aug. 31, 1989. **B-T:** R-R. **Ht.:** 6-2. **Wt.:** 210. **Drafted:** Virginia, 2011 (4th round). **Signed by:** Mike Moriarty.

Hicks was Danny Hultzen's catcher at Virginia and one of three Cavaliers the Mariners drafted in 2011, along with first baseman Steve Proscia. Noted primarily for his defense, Hicks wasn't even a full-time catcher until pro ball. The Mariners see him as a strong catch-and-throw receiver, and he led the Double-A Southern League in percentage of basestealers caught (47 percent) but also in passed balls (19). He needs reps to improve his blocking skills. Hicks draws high marks for his ability to work with pitchers, his work ethic and his personality. While his intangibles are off the chart, one tangible aspect of the game he must work on is his hitting. He has bat speed and has shown the ability to make adjustments, but he lacks power and expands his strike zone too often. Hicks profiles comfortably as a backup catcher with more polished receiving and blocking. He could report back to Jackson for 2014.

Year	Club (League)	Class	AVG	G	AB	R	H	2B	3B	HR	RBI	BB	SO	SB	CS	OBP	SLG
2011	Clinton (MWL)	LoA	.309	38	139	21	43	9	2	2	26	5	17	2	3	.331	.446
2012	High Desert (CAL)	HiA	.312	121	506	87	158	32	2	15	79	28	73	22	8	.351	.472
2013	Jackson (SL)	AA	.236	80	296	40	70	14	1	4	29	22	62	13	4	.301	.331
Minor League Totals			.288	239	941	148	271	55	5	21	134	55	152	37	15	.332	.424

24 TIMMY LOPES, 2B

BA GRADE 45 HIGH

Born: June 24, 1994. **B-T:** R-R. **Ht.:** 5-11. **Wt.:** 180. **Drafted:** HS—Huntington Beach, Calif., 2012 (6th round). **Signed by:** John Ramey.

Lopes seemed rock-solid in his commitment to play collegiately at UC Irvine before the Mariners went far over slot to sign him for $550,000 as a sixth-round pick in 2012. His older brother Christian plays second base in the Blue Jays system. Timmy is less physical than Christian and has a lower ceiling, but he plays the game with savvy and skill. He has a mature hitting approach, looking to make contact and use the entire field. He has a decent batting eye for a young player, though it could still use some improvement. His power is fringe-average at best, though, and home runs won't be a part of his game. Lopes has seamlessly made the transition from shortstop to second base as a pro, where his average arm plays better, and has above-average range and defensive ability. He's an average runner. Nagging injuries cut into his playing time at low Class A Clinton in 2013, and shoulder soreness ended his season two weeks early. Lopes still has youth on his side, and he will be 19 when the 2014 season opens, so the Mariners might have him repeat Clinton.

Year	Club (League)	Class	AVG	G	AB	R	H	2B	3B	HR	RBI	BB	SO	SB	CS	OBP	SLG
2012	Mariners (AZL)	R	.316	53	215	42	68	11	12	0	32	24	29	7	3	.381	.479
	High Desert (CAL)	HiA	.250	4	12	2	3	0	1	0	1	0	1	0	0	.250	.417
2013	Clinton (MWL)	LoA	.272	92	334	40	91	15	3	1	36	20	46	10	7	.315	.344
Minor League Totals			.289	149	561	84	162	26	16	1	69	44	76	17	10	.340	.398

25 JI-MAN CHOI, 1B

BA GRADE 45 HIGH

Born: May 19, 1991. **B-T:** L-R. **Ht.:** 6-1. **Wt.:** 195. **Signed:** South Korea, 2009. **Signed by:** Jamey Storvick/Pat Kelly.

Choi had a breakout season in 2013, starting at high Class A High Desert, making stops at Double-A Jackson and the Futures Game along the way. He ended the year at Triple-A Tacoma. All of that happened while he was making the conversion from catcher to first baseman, and he wound up being protected on the 40-man roster in November. Choi made a splash in 2010 when was the MVP of the Rookie-level Arizona League, but his career stagnated until he became a full-time first baseman and also put together a better plan of attack in the batter's box. Already possessing a good eye, Choi has become even more selective and laid off the pitches he could not drive. He struggles with lefthanders and lacks profile power for a first baseman, instead spraying line drives to the gaps at his best. Choi fits the second-division regular description and is in an organization that continues to chase power at first base. He'll likely man the position at Tacoma in 2014 unless he's needed in Seattle.

Year	Club (League)	Class	AVG	G	AB	R	H	2B	3B	HR	RBI	BB	SO	SB	CS	OBP	SLG
2010	Mariners (AZL)	R	.378	39	135	23	51	15	2	1	23	21	30	10	1	.459	.541
	High Desert (CAL)	HiA	.302	11	43	7	13	1	1	1	7	6	9	0	0	.380	.442
2011	Did not play—Injured																
2012	Clinton (MWL)	LoA	.298	66	242	43	72	14	1	8	43	39	55	0	2	.420	.463
2013	High Desert (CAL)	HiA	.337	48	181	34	61	24	3	7	40	27	33	0	1	.427	.619
	Jackson (SL)	AA	.268	61	198	21	53	10	3	9	39	32	28	2	2	.377	.485
	Tacoma (PCL)	AAA	.244	13	45	9	11	2	0	2	6	4	7	0	0	.333	.422
Minor League Totals			.309	238	844	137	261	66	10	28	158	129	162	12	6	.411	.511

26 JACK REINHEIMER, SS

BA GRADE 45 HIGH

Born: July 19, 1992. **B-T:** R-R. **Ht.:** 6-0. **Wt.:** 165. **Drafted:** East Carolina, 2013 (5th round). **Signed by:** Devitt Moore.

The Mariners seem to have a production line of scrappy middle infielders with middling power who draw raves for their baseball IQ. Reinheimer is the latest in that line after being drafted in the fifth round in 2013 and signing for $327,600. The shortstop doesn't have one clearly above-average tool, though he opened eyes by stealing 18 bases in 66 games last season at short-season Everett. However, the stolen bases are more a result of instincts than pure speed, because he is just a tick-above-average runner. Reinheimer also is a solid defender at shortstop despite having average range, hands and arm. He makes all the routine plays and has an accurate arm as well as a good internal clock. The big question is whether he will hit enough to play in the major leagues. He doesn't have a lot of pop or make consistent contact, though he does show a willingness to take a walk. Reinheimer will spend 2014 at low Class A Clinton.

Year	Club (League)	Class	AVG	G	AB	R	H	2B	3B	HR	RBI	BB	SO	SB	CS	OBP	SLG
2013	Everett (NWL)	SS	.269	66	249	39	67	6	1	2	30	32	51	18	5	.359	.325
Minor League Totals			.269	66	249	39	67	6	1	2	30	32	51	18	5	.359	.325

27 JAMES JONES, OF

BA GRADE 45 HIGH

Born: Sept. 24, 1988. **B-T:** L-L. **Ht.:** 6-4. **Wt.:** 195. **Drafted:** Long Island, 2009 (4th round). **Signed by:** David May.

A draft prospect as both a pitcher and hitter in college, Jones signed for $267,300 after a poor junior season in 2009 at Long Island dropped his stock on the mound. He still looks the part more than he produces, but he did enough to earn a spot on the 40-man roster in November. Jones has good raw power, but a stiff, lefthanded swing leads to more soft contact than over-the-fence power. He does offer plus speed, having hit 10 triples with Double-A Jackson in 2013 to lead the Southern League, and has learned the short game, improving his basestealing and bunting ability. Jones' arm has backed up since college, when he threw 94-95 mph off the mound, and he missed time in August with a triceps injury. He still has enough arm to play right field and played all three spots in 2013. Jones has an infectious, positive personality that managers want in a reserve and fits the fourth outfielder profile well. He should progress to Triple-A Tacoma in 2014.

Year	Club (League)	Class	AVG	G	AB	R	H	2B	3B	HR	RBI	BB	SO	SB	CS	OBP	SLG
2009	Everett (NWL)	SS	.311	45	164	28	51	12	2	3	24	19	40	0	3	.392	.463
2010	Clinton (MWL)	LoA	.269	132	491	87	132	24	10	12	65	62	122	24	10	.356	.432
2011	High Desert (CAL)	HiA	.247	83	296	42	73	16	4	5	29	42	92	16	3	.347	.378
2012	High Desert (CAL)	HiA	.306	126	493	109	151	28	12	14	76	54	124	26	17	.378	.497
2013	Jackson (SL)	AA	.275	101	363	44	100	14	10	6	45	40	72	28	9	.347	.419
	Tacoma (PCL)	AAA	.333	4	15	2	5	2	0	0	1	2	2	0	0	.412	.467
Minor League Totals			.281	491	1822	312	512	96	38	40	240	219	452	94	42	.362	.441

28 LARS HUIJER, RHP

BA GRADE 45 EXTREME

Born: Sept. 22, 1993. **B-T:** R-R. **Ht.:** 6-4. **Wt.:** 183. **Signed:** Netherlands, 2011. **Signed by:** Wayne Norton/Peter VanDalen.

The Mariners signed Huijer for $170,000 in 2011 after he served as the top pitcher on the Dutch junior national team. He spent his two first years in Rookie leagues before acquitting himself well at short-season Everett in 2013, showing three effective pitches that all have a chance to be average to a tick above as he continues to develop. His fastball ranges from 85-90 mph now, and he does a good job keeping it in the bottom half of the zone, making it difficult for hitters to square up. Huijer also figures to add a little more velocity as his body fills out. He has good feel and deception on his changeup and a slow curveball that he is able to throw consistently for strikes. Though he showed some signs of fatigue late in 2013, Huijer has the poise and polish to make the jump to low Class A Clinton in 2014. He projects as a back-end starter now, but he has the potential to be more than that.

Year	Club (League)	Class	W	L	ERA	G	GS	CG	SV	IP	H	HR	BB	SO	K/9	WHIP	AVG
2011	Mariners (AZL)	R	0	1	5.40	5	3	0	0	15	19	2	2	9	5.4	1.40	.317
2012	Pulaski (APP)	R	1	2	3.86	21	0	0	2	33	39	1	14	21	5.8	1.62	.302
2013	Everett (NWL)	SS	8	2	3.03	14	13	0	0	71	57	2	23	61	7.7	1.12	.218
Minor League Totals			9	5	3.55	40	16	0	2	119	115	5	39	91	6.9	1.29	.256

29 GUILLERMO PIMENTEL, OF

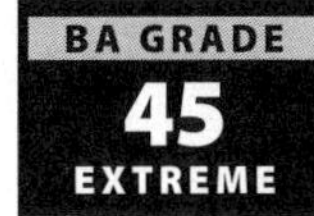

Born: Oct. 5, 1992. **B-T:** L-L. **Ht. 6-1. Wt.:** 206. **Signed:** Dominican Republic, 2009. **Signed by:** Patrick Guerrero/Bob Engle.

Despite signing for $2 million in 2009 and ranking as the No. 1 prospect in the Rookie-level Arizona League the following year, Pimentel has been passed by a multitude of other young prospects in the Mariners system. He has yet to deliver on his power potential, primarily because he lacks plate discipline and struggles to recognize pitches. Making matters worse, Pimentel takes his struggles to heart, which can result in sulking and ultimately putting more pressure on himself. His value is wrapped up in his power because below-average arm strength and range consign him to left field, and he also is a below-average runner. Pimentel provided a glimmer of hope late in 2013, when he homered in his first three games after being promoted to high Class A High Desert. Granted, High Desert's home ballpark is the best hitting environments in the domestic minors, but it was a small sign of progress. The Mariners hope a full season at High Desert will give Pimentel the confidence to unlock his prodigious power.

Year	Club (League)	Class	AVG	G	AB	R	H	2B	3B	HR	RBI	BB	SO	SB	CS	OBP	SLG
2010	Mariners (AZL)	R	.250	51	184	20	46	7	6	6	31	5	58	5	1	.276	.451
2011	Pulaski (APP)	R	.265	65	245	33	65	10	0	11	46	15	73	4	1	.308	.441
2012	Clinton (MWL)	LoA	.245	105	372	37	91	18	0	9	51	19	115	5	2	.289	.366
2013	Clinton (MWL)	LoA	.257	55	202	24	52	10	2	6	30	20	68	4	3	.330	.416
	Mariners (AZL)	R	.300	6	20	1	6	2	0	0	2	0	6	0	0	.300	.400
	High Desert (CAL)	HiA	.333	15	63	10	21	3	1	4	14	2	18	0	0	.358	.603
Minor League Totals			.259	297	1086	125	281	50	9	36	174	61	338	18	7	.303	.421

30 DYLAN UNSWORTH, RHP

BA GRADE
45
EXTREME

Born: Sept. 23, 1992. **B-T:** R-R. **Ht.:** 6-1. **Wt.:** 175. **Signed:** South Africa, 2009. **Signed by:** Wayne Norton/Phillip Biersteker.

Unsworth took command to a new level in 2013 with 28 SO/BB ratio, striking out 56 and walking just two in 72 innings. Though none of those innings were logged above the low Class A level, it shows how far he has come since signing in 2009 after spending time at MLB's International European Academy in Italy. Unsworth gained confidence by pitching six strong innings for South Africa against Israel in a 2012 World Baseball Classic qualifier, a game in which he struck out six and allowing five hits, including a solo homer to big leaguer Nate Freiman. The slightly-built Unsworth doesn't overpower hitters, as his fastball usually sits 85-88 mph and tops out at 90. However, he spots it to all four quadrants of the strike zone, and he also is developing a changeup and curveball. Considering he did not face strong competition growing up in South Africa, Unsworth has made considerable strides since signing with the Mariners. While he won't light up any radar guns, his command at least gives him a chance to reach the high minors, and possibly pitch his way to a big league trial.

Year	Club (League)	Class	W	L	ERA	G	GS	CG	SV	IP	H	HR	BB	SO	K/9	WHIP	AVG
2010	Mariners (AZL)	R	2	5	3.93	11	10	0	0	50	71	1	1	44	7.9	1.43	.340
2011	Pulaski (APP)	R	6	5	5.16	12	12	0	0	61	73	7	10	46	6.8	1.36	.294
2012	Everett (NWL)	SS	7	2	3.90	14	14	0	0	85	76	9	19	67	7.1	1.11	.235
2013	Mariners (AZL)	R	0	0	4.50	3	3	0	0	6	4	1	0	10	15.0	0.67	.190
	Clinton (MWL)	LoA	4	1	2.32	11	11	1	0	66	58	2	2	46	6.3	0.91	.237
Minor League Totals			19	13	3.82	51	50	1	0	269	282	20	32	213	7.1	1.17	.270

Tampa Bay Rays

BY BILL BALLEW

No small-revenue team in any sport does more with less better than the Rays. The 2013 campaign proved that once again.

Tampa Bay entered the season having made one major move over the winter, but once again the front office made it count. The Rays traded righthanders James Shields and Wade Davis to the Royals in December 2012 for four prospects, including outfielder Wil Myers and righthander Jake Odorizzi.

While that deal helped make the Royals more relevant, the Rays got back to the playoffs as one of the American League's streakiest teams. With manager Joe Maddon operating his lineup like a mad scientist, the Rays remained in the playoff hunt and wound up advancing to the AL Division Series by taking a trio of must-win road games against three teams—the Blue Jays, Rangers and Indians—in four days to close the season.

The achievement helped clinch the Rays' fourth trip to the postseason in six years, including five seasons with at least 90 wins.

The trade with Kansas City not only saved Tampa Bay nearly $14 million in payroll for 2013—keeping it at $57.5 million, 28th in the majors—but it also provided immediate impact. Myers emerged as the AL rookie of the year after he received the call in mid-June. The 22-year-old hit .293/.354/.478 with 13 homers and 53 RBIs in 88 games. Odorizzi didn't provide the same immediate payoff, but he did make impressive strides at Triple-A Durham and emerged as the organization's top prospect.

The rotation found another long-term answer when righthander Chris Archer showed up in early June. He finished runner-up to Myers in the AL rookie race and was the key piece in the deal that sent Matt Garza to the Cubs in 2011. Four other prospects received their first cups of coffee, including lefthander Enny Romero and righty Alex Colome, shortstop Tim Beckham and outfielder Kevin Kiermaier.

General manager Andrew Friedman has been able to keep the Rays competitive by trading veteran talent for prospects, whom Maddon incorporates into his ever-changing lineup and pitching staff. The constant replenishing of talent from the minor leagues is the key to the Rays' continued success. The greatest amount of current talent is found on the mound, though the Rays also are deep in position players up the middle—including such prospects as shortstops Hak-Ju Lee and Tim Beckham, center fielder Andrew Toles, catcher Nick Ciuffo and second baseman Ryan Brett—thanks in part to extra draft picks garnered as free agent compensation earlier in the decade.

If there is a flaw to the Tampa Bay farm system, however, it centers on the lack of development by several high draft picks, particularly the unprecedented seven supplemental first-rounders from 2011. The organization also has been hit hard with character and makeup issues, including eight minor leaguers receiving 50-game suspensions over the past two years for use of recreational drugs or stimulants. That list includes a trio of first-rounders: Beckham from 2008, outfielder Josh Sale from 2010 and righthander Taylor Guerrieri from 2011. Sale headlines that motley crew after missing all of 2013 due to a pair of suspensions.

CLIFF WELCH

The Rays acquired AL Rookie of the Year Wil Myers in a trade, epitomizing their model

TOP PROSPECTS OF THE DECADE

Year	Player, Pos.	2013 Org.
2004	B.J. Upton, ss	Braves
2005	Delmon Young, of	Rays
2006	Delmon Young, of	Rays
2007	Delmon Young, of	Rays
2008	Evan Longoria, 3b	Rays
2009	David Price, lhp	Rays
2010	Desmond Jennings, of	Rays
2011	Matt Moore, lhp	Rays
2012	Matt Moore, lhp	Rays
2013	Wil Myers, of/3b	Rays

ORGANIZATION OVERVIEW

General Manager: Andrew Friedman. **Farm Director:** Mitch Lukevics. **Scouting Director:** R.J. Harrison

Class	Team	League	W	L	PCT	Finish	Manager
Majors	Tampa Bay Rays	American	92	71	.564	5th (15)	Joe Maddon
Triple-A	Durham Bulls	International	87	57	.604	1st (14)	Charlie Montoyo
Double-A	Montgomery Biscuits	Southern	71	69	.507	6th (10)	Billy Gardner Jr.
High Class A	Charlotte Stone Crabs	Florida State	67	65	.508	4th (12)	Brady Williams
Low Class A	Bowling Green Hot Rods	Midwest	82	56	.594	2nd (14)	Jared Sandberg
Short-season	Hudson Valley Renegades	New York-Penn	38	37	.507	8th (14)	Michael Johns
Rookie	Princeton Rays	Appalachian	25	43	.368	9th (10)	Danny Sheaffer
Rookie	GCL Rays	Gulf Coast	27	33	.450	12th (16)	Jim Morrison
Overall 2013 Minor League Record			**358**	**337**	**.524**	**7th (30)**	

THIS YEAR'S TOP 30

No.	Player, Pos.	Grade
1.	Jake Odorizzi, rhp	50/Safe
2.	Hak-Ju Lee, ss	55/High
3.	Taylor Guerrieri, rhp	60/Extreme
4.	Enny Romero, lhp	55/High
5.	Alex Colome, rhp	55/High
6.	Andrew Toles, of	55/High
7.	Nick Ciuffo, c	55/High
8.	Ryan Brett, 2b	50/High
9.	Tim Beckham, ss/2b	45/Medium
10.	Kevin Kiermaier, of	45/Medium
11.	Ryan Stanek, rhp	55/Extreme
12.	Justin O'Conner, c	50/High
13.	Richie Shaffer, 1b/3b	50/High
14.	Blake Snell, lhp	55/Extreme
15.	Jesse Hahn, rhp	55/Extreme
16.	Grayson Garvin, lhp	50/High
17.	Felipe Rivero, lhp	50/High
18.	Jake Hager, ss	50/High
19.	Riley Unroe, ss	50/High
20.	Drew Vettleson, of	45/High
21.	Jose Mujica, rhp	50/Extreme
22.	Tyler Goeddel, 3b	45/High
23.	C.J. Riefenhauser, lhp	45/High
24.	Oscar Hernandez, c	50/Extreme
25.	Mikie Mahtook, of	45/High
26.	Dylan Floro, rhp	45/High
27.	Thomas Milone, of	50/Extreme
28.	Jose Castillo, lhp	50/Extreme
29.	Curt Casali, c	45/High
30.	Jeff Ames, rhp	45/High

LAST YEAR'S TOP 30

No.	Player, Pos.	Status
1.	Wil Myers, of/3b	Majors
2.	Chris Archer, rhp	Majors
3.	Taylor Guerrieri, rhp	No. 3
4.	Hak-Ju Lee, ss	No. 2
5.	Jake Odorizzi, rhp	No. 1
6.	Alex Colome, rhp	No. 5
7.	Richie Shaffer, 3b	No. 13
8.	Enny Romero, lhp	No. 4
9.	Blake Snell, lhp	No. 14
10.	Tim Beckham, ss/2b	No. 9
11.	Drew Vettleson, of	No. 20
12.	Mikie Mahtook, of	No. 25
13.	Jeff Ames, rhp	No. 30
14.	Jesse Hahn, rhp	No. 15
15.	Mike Montgomery, lhp	Dropped out
16.	Tyler Goeddel, 3b	No. 22
17.	Brandon Martin, ss	Dropped out
18.	Jake Hager, ss	No. 18
19.	Andrew Toles, of	No. 6
20.	Felipe Rivero, lhp	No. 17
21.	Todd Glaesmann, of	Dropped out
22.	Ryan Brett, 2b	No. 8
23.	Jose Mujica, rhp	No. 21
24.	Josh Sale, of	Dropped out
25.	Parker Markel, rhp	Dropped out
26.	Patrick Leonard, 3b	Dropped out
27.	Bralin Jackson, of	Dropped out
28.	Ty Morrison, of	Dropped out
29.	Spencer Edwards, ss	Dropped out
30.	Nick Sawyer, rhp	Dropped out

BEST TOOLS

Best Hitter for Average	Andrew Toles
Best Power Hitter	Jeff Malm
Best Strike-Zone Discipline	Vince Belnome
Fastest Baserunner	Andrew Toles
Best Athlete	Andrew Toles
Best Fastball	Ryne Stanek
Best Curveball	Taylor Guerrieri
Best Slider	Enny Romero
Best Changeup	Mike Montgomery
Best Control	Dylan Floro
Best Defensive Catcher	Justin O'Conner
Best Defensive Infielder	Hak-Ju Lee
Best Infield Arm	Tim Beckham
Best Defensive Outfielder	Kevin Kiermaier
Best Outfield Arm	Kevin Kiermaier

TOP 15 PLAYERS 25 AND UNDER

No.	Player, Pos. (Age)	Peak Level
1.	Wil Myers, of (23)	Majors
2.	Matt Moore, lhp (24)	Majors
3.	Chris Archer, rhp (25)	Majors
4.	Jake Odorizzi, rhp (24)	Majors
5.	Hak-Ju Lee, ss (23)	Triple-A
6.	Tyler Guerreri, rhp (21)	Low Class A
7.	Enny Romero, lhp (23)	Majors
8.	Alex Colome, rhp (25)	Majors
9.	Andrew Toles, of (21)	Low Class A
10.	Nick Ciuffo, c (19)	Rookie
11.	Ryan Brett, 2b (22)	Double-A
12.	Tim Beckham, ss/2b (24)	Majors
13.	Kevin Kiermaier, of (23)	Majors
14.	Ryne Stanek, rhp (22)	Did not play
15.	Justin O'Conner, c (22)	Low Class A

MINOR LEAGUE DEPTH CHART

TAMPA BAY RAYS

TOP 2014 ROOKIE: Jake Odorizzi, rhp. Part of the haul obtained from the Royals last year, Odorizzi appears ready to step into the big league rotation after an impressive 2013 at Triple-A Durham.

BREAKOUT PROSPECT: Jose Mujica, rhp. One of the younger pitchers in the organization, Mujica is making rapid progress on his secondary pitches while showing advanced poise with a live arm.

SLEEPER: German Marquez, rhp. Another product of the Rays' scouting efforts in Venezuela, the 19-year-old Marquez has an easy delivery and live arm that could blossom with experience.

SOURCE OF TOP 30 TALENT

Homegrown	27	Acquired	3
College	6	Trades	3
Junior college	4	Rule 5 draft	0
High school	11	Independent leagues	0
Nondrafted free agents	0	Free agents/waivers	0
International	6		

LF
Mikie Mahtook (25)
Willie Argo
Ty Morrison
Todd Glaesmann
Granden Goetzman

CF
Andrew Toles (6)
Kevin Kiermaier (10)
Thomas Milone (27)
Bralin Jackson

RF
Drew Vettleson (20)
Brandon Guyer
Johnny Field

3B
Tyler Goeddel (22)
Patrick Leonard
Ty Young

SS
Hak-Ju Lee (2)
Jake Hager (18)
Riley Unroe (19)
Brandon Martin

2B
Ryan Brett (8)
Tim Beckham (9)
Kean Wong
Tommy Coyle
Robby Price

1B
Richie Shaffer (13)
Vince Belnome
Jeff Malm

C
Nick Ciuffo (7)
Justin O'Conner (12)
Oscar Hernandez (24)
Curt Casali (29)
Luke Maile
Armando Araiza
David Rodriguez

LHP

LHSP	LHRP
Enny Romero (4)	Felipe Rivero (17)
Blake Snell (14)	C.J. Riefenhauser (23)
Grayson Garvin (16)	
Jose Castillo (28)	

RHP

RHSP	RHRP
Jake Odorizzi (1)	Alex Colome (5)
Taylor Guerreri (3)	Dylan Floro (26)
Ryan Stanek (11)	Kirby Yates
Jesse Hahn (15)	Merrill Kelly
Jose Mujica (21)	Parker Markel
Jeff Ames (30)	Roel Ramirez
German Marquez	
Mike Montgomery	
Jacob Faria	

DRAFT ANALYSIS

2013 — BONUSES: $6.3 MILLION

BEST PURE HITTER: Like his older brother, Cardinals 2B and 2011 first-rounder Kolten, 2B Kean Wong (4) is a natural hitter. The lefthanded hitter has a quick, compact swing conducive to hard line drives, an advanced approach and gap power. Switch-hitting SS Riley Unroe (2) uses the whole field.

BEST POWER HITTER: With a 6-foot-1, 205-pound frame and natural strength, C Nick Ciuffo (1) has above-average raw power, especially to his pull side, that should only improve. OF Hunter Lockwood (11) has plus power potential from a strong build and led the Appalachian League in extra-base hits (25).

FASTEST RUNNER: OF Tom Milone (3) and Unroe are both plus runners with athleticism. Wong is an above-average runner, as is 2B Coty Blanchard (15), who is a good athlete with good actions.

BEST DEFENSIVE PLAYER: The Rays say Ciuffo, Unroe and Milone all have the ability to stay at premium defensive positions. Ciuffo has an above-average arm and leadership ability. Unroe has soft hands, good quickness and an average arm. Milone could be an above-average center fielder.

BEST FASTBALL: RHP Ryne Stanek (1) can sit 92-95 mph and touch 98 with downhill plane and sink. He was shut down after signing but was pitching at instructional league. RHP Jaime Schultz (14) can touch 97 mph with late life through the zone.

BEST SECONDARY PITCH: Stanek offers a plus breaking ball. RHP Austin Pruitt (9) has a plus changeup to pair with good fastball command and a solid breaking ball.

BEST PRO DEBUT: Wong hit .328/.377/.390 in the Rookie-level Gulf Coast League. Pruitt, a $5,000 senior sign, had a 1.44 ERA across two levels. LHP Ben Griset (13) piled up 55 SO/10 BB in 66 IP for short-season Hudson Valley, and RHP Aaron Griffin (10) was right behind him with 54 SO/8 BB in 76 IP.

BEST ATHLETE: Milone, who was a football standout in high school and generated college recruiting interest on the gridiron.

MOST INTRIGUING BACKGROUND: Unroe's father is former major league infielder Tim. Griffin is the younger brother of A's righthander A.J. Unsigned C David Sheaffer (38) is the son of former big league catcher Danny, who is the manager of the Rays' Appy League affiliate. Blanchard played both baseball and football (quarterback, punter) at Jacksonville State.

CLOSEST TO THE MAJORS: Stanek, with his electric fastball/breaking ball combo.

BEST LATE-ROUND PICK: Lockwood, who received an over slot $247,500, and Schultz among those who signed for slot money. OF Julian Ridings (18) is a good power-speed athlete in center field.

THE ONE WHO GOT AWAY: 2B Willie Calhoun (17), who stood out because of his bat, went to Arizona. RHP Stephen Woods (6) has a fastball up to 93 mph and will attend Albany.

ASSESSMENT: The Rays drafted a nice core of up-the-middle high school players in the first four rounds and grabbed one of the biggest power arms in the draft with their second first-rounder by taking Stanek.

2012 — BONUSES: $4.4 MILLION

Top pick 3B Richie Shaffer (1) hasn't hit as hoped while tinkering with his hitting load. OF Andrew Toles (3) has passed him as a prospect. RHP Dylan Floro (13) led the minors in ERA in 2013.

GRADE: C

2011 — BONUSES: $11.5 MILLION

Tampa had 10 of the first 60 picks, but none has broken out yet. RHP Tyler Guerreri (1) had Tommy John surgery and a drug suspension. Preps such as SS Jake Hager (1s) are more projection than production.

GRADE: D

2010 — BONUSES: $7.2 MILLION

OF Josh Sale (1) missed the year with two suspensions. 2B Ryan Brett (2) and OF Kevin Kiermaier (31) have become the top products of the class.

GRADE: D

TOP DRAFT PICKS OF THE DECADE

Year	Player, Pos.	2013 Org.
2004	Jeff Niemann, rhp	Rays
2005	Wade Townsend, rhp	Out of baseball
2006	Evan Longoria, 3b	Rays
2007	David Price, lhp	Rays
2008	Tim Beckham, ss	Rays
2009	*LeVon Washington, of	Indians
2010	Josh Sale, of	Rays
2011	Taylor Guerrieri, rhp	Rays
2012	Richie Shaffer, 3b	Rays
2013	Nick Ciuffo, c	Rays

* Did not sign

LARGEST BONUSES IN CLUB HISTORY

Matt White, 1996	$10,200,000
Rolando Arrojo, 1997	$7,000,000
Tim Beckham, 2008	$6,150,000
David Price, 2007	$5,600,000
B.J. Upton, 2002	$4,600,000

1 JAKE ODORIZZI, RHP

Born: March 27, 1990. **B-T:** R-R. **Ht.:** 6-2. **Wt.:** 180. **Drafted:** HS—Highland, Ill., 2008 (1st round supplemental). **Signed by:** Harvey Kuenn Jr. (Brewers).

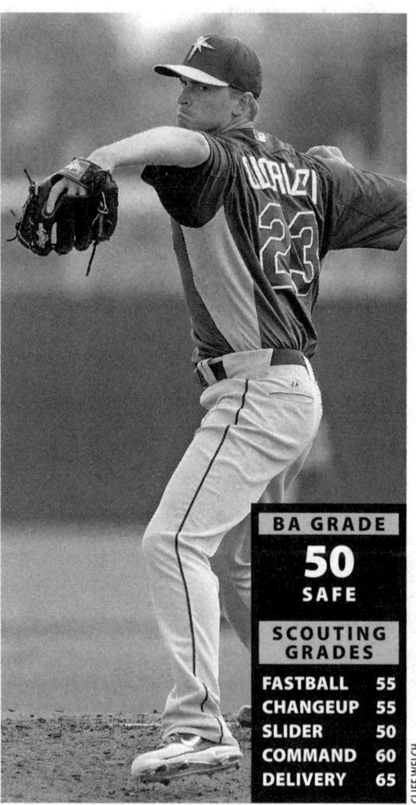

BA GRADE
50
SAFE
SCOUTING GRADES
FASTBALL 55
CHANGEUP 55
SLIDER 50
COMMAND 60
DELIVERY 65

CLIFF WELCH

Considered to be one of the top high school pitchers available in the 2008 draft, Odorizzi has been part of two major trades since signing with the Brewers as the 32nd overall pick for $1.06 million. At the end of 2010, shortly after ranking as Milwaukee's No. 1 prospect, Odorizzi was part of the four-player package the Brewers sent to the Royals for Zack Greinke. The Royals in December 2012 packaged Odorizzi with outfielder Wil Myers as part of the trade that sent James Shields to Kansas City. Odorizzi spent most of the 2013 season at Triple-A Durham and ranked third in the International League in strikeouts (124) and WHIP (1.13), second in opponent average (.225) and eighth in ERA (3.33). He concluded the minor league slate with 28 consecutive scoreless innings, with 14 coming in the IL playoffs for the Governors' Cup champion Bulls.

Improved fastball command helped Odorizzi take the next big step in his development during the 2013 campaign. By working off his low-90s fastball with solid sinking action and armside run and using both sides of the plate, he was able to mix his three average-to-above secondary offerings to his advantage. He also upgraded his low-80s changeup to keep hitters off-balance while displaying better command of his low-80s slurvy slider and decent curveball. His slider is his best secondary offering, which borders on being an above-average pitch. He has added deception to his changeup by increasing his arm speed to make it closer to his fastball delivery. An excellent athlete who garnered attention as a high school shortstop and wide receiver, Odorizzi repeats his clean delivery with consistency. The ball comes out of his hand easily and makes his fastball appear even quicker. He is an excellent fielder with soft hands who moves well around the mound. Odorizzi has quick feet on his pickoff move but has struggled at times during his career to keep runners at bay. He has been able to maintain his velocity throughout his starts since signing and has held up well over the course of his first six professional seasons.

Odorizzi has spent time in the big leagues in each of the past two seasons, and he made four spot starts for the Rays in 2013. With opportunity often right around the corner for deserving starters in Tampa Bay, he could see significant time in the major leagues in 2014. Based on the adjustments and the ongoing improvements with his secondary pitches he makes at the game's top level, Odorizzi could be a strong mid-rotation starter. Once he establishes himself in the big leagues, he should fit nicely in a Rays' long-term rotation behind Matt Moore, Chris Archer and Alex Cobb.

Year	Club (League)	Class	W	L	ERA	G	GS	CG	SV	IP	H	HR	BB	SO	K/9	WHIP	AVG
2008	Brewers (AZL)	R	1	2	3.48	11	4	0	0	21	18	2	9	19	8.3	1.31	.220
2009	Helena (PIO)	R	1	4	4.40	12	10	0	0	47	55	3	9	43	8.2	1.36	.296
2010	Wisconsin (MWL)	LoA	7	3	3.43	23	20	0	1	121	99	7	40	135	10.1	1.15	.220
2011	Wilmington (CAR)	HiA	5	4	2.87	15	15	0	0	78	68	4	22	103	11.8	1.15	.235
	NW Arkansas (TL)	AA	5	3	4.72	12	12	0	0	69	66	13	22	54	7.1	1.28	.254
2012	NW Arkansas (TL)	AA	4	2	3.32	7	7	0	0	38	27	2	10	47	11.1	0.97	.191
	Omaha (PCL)	AAA	11	3	2.93	19	18	0	0	107	105	12	40	88	7.4	1.35	.254
	Kansas City (AL)	MAJ	0	1	4.91	2	2	0	0	7	8	1	4	4	4.9	1.64	.267
2013	Durham (IL)	AAA	9	6	3.33	22	22	0	0	124	101	12	40	124	9.0	1.13	.225
	Tampa Bay (AL)	MAJ	0	1	3.94	7	4	0	1	30	28	3	8	22	6.7	1.21	.252
Major League Totals			0	2	4.14	9	6	0	1	37	36	4	12	26	6.3	1.30	.255
Minor League Totals			43	27	3.47	121	108	0	1	605	539	55	192	613	9.1	1.21	.238

2 HAK-JU LEE, SS

Born: Nov. 4, 1990. **B-T:** L-R. **Ht.:** 6-2. **Wt.:** 170. **Signed:** South Korea, 2008. **Signed by:** Steve Wilson (Cubs).

A key component in the Matt Garza deal with the Cubs in January 2011, Lee got off to a great start at Triple-A Durham in 2013 before tearing ligaments in his left knee in a collision while covering second base. A two-time Futures Game participant, he had surgery in late April and missed the remainder of the season, but he should be ready for 2014. A quick-twitch athlete with great defensive instincts, he possesses soft hands and a strong, accurate arm with a quick release. He handles the speed of the game with aplomb, producing highlight-reel plays. His offensive production had leveled off during two stints at Double-A Montgomery before he showed the ability to drive the ball to the opposite field at Durham. He still tends to slap at pitches in order to use his plus speed to get on base. He has improved his ability to work counts and recognize pitches he can drive. He also has become an aggressive baserunner who should steal at least 30 bases annually if his plus speed returns in full. With Yunel Escobar holding down shortstop in the big leagues, Lee should spend 2014 honing his skills at Durham and could emerge as the Rays' shortstop as soon as 2015.

Year	Club (League)	Class	AVG	G	AB	R	H	2B	3B	HR	RBI	BB	SO	SB	CS	OBP	SLG
2009	Boise (NWL)	SS	.330	68	264	56	87	14	2	2	33	31	50	25	8	.399	.420
2010	Peoria (MWL)	LoA	.282	122	485	85	137	22	4	1	40	49	86	32	7	.354	.351
2011	Charlotte (FSL)	HiA	.318	97	400	82	127	16	11	4	23	42	72	28	14	.389	.443
	Montgomery (SL)	AA	.190	24	100	16	19	1	4	1	7	11	22	5	2	.272	.310
2012	Montgomery (SL)	AA	.261	116	475	68	124	15	10	4	37	51	102	37	9	.336	.360
2013	Durham (IL)	AAA	.422	15	45	13	19	3	1	1	7	11	9	6	2	.536	.600
Minor League Totals			.290	442	1769	320	513	71	32	13	147	195	341	133	42	.364	.388

3 TAYLOR GUERRIERI, RHP

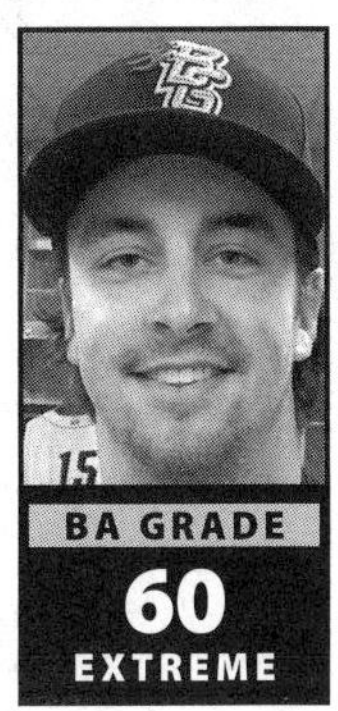

Born: Dec. 1, 1992. **B-T:** R-R. **Ht.:** 6-3. **Wt.:** 195. **Drafted:** HS—Columbia, S.C., 2011 (1st round). **Signed by:** Brad Matthews.

The 24th overall pick in the 2011 draft, Guerrieri appeared to hit his stride in the low Class A Midwest League in June when he put together a 22-ininng scoreless stretch. In July, however, the Rays pulled him from the Futures Game with elbow soreness, and he had Tommy John surgery in late July. Adding insult to injury, he was suspended 50 games for testing positive for a drug of abuse in late September. Guerrieri has an electric arm and an ideal pitcher's frame. Clocked as high as 98 mph in high school, his fastball has resided in the 91-93 mph range while touching 95 in pro ball, with hard, late sink and good armside run. His above-average curveball has a sharp drop, making it a swing-and-miss offering. His changeup should be at least a solid-average pitch. He works both sides of the plate and is not afraid to pitch inside, as evidenced by his 10 hit batters in 2013. Worries about Guerrieri's makeup dropped him in the draft, and the drug suspension reinforces those concerns. He will miss most if not all of the 2014 season due to his injury. He will be 22 when he returns to the mound in 2015 and should remain on course to develop into a potential No. 2 or 3 starter.

Year	Club (League)	Class	W	L	ERA	G	GS	CG	SV	IP	H	HR	BB	SO	K/9	WHIP	AVG
2012	Hudson Valley (NYP)	SS	1	2	1.04	12	12	0	0	52	35	0	5	45	7.8	0.77	.186
2013	Bowling Green (MWL)	LoA	6	2	2.01	14	14	0	0	67	54	5	12	51	6.9	0.99	.225
Minor League Totals			7	4	1.59	26	26	0	0	119	89	5	17	96	7.3	0.89	.208

4 ENNY ROMERO, LHP

Born: Jan. 24, 1991. **B-T:** L-L. **Ht.:** 6-3. **Wt.:** 165. **Signed:** Dominican Republic, 2008. **Signed by:** Eddy Toledo.

Romero tied for second in the Double-A Southern League in opponent average (.215) and fifth in ERA (2.76) last year but also tied for third in walks (73). That follows a career trend, as he's been both stingy with hits (.217 average) and generous with walks (4.6 per nine innings). More consistent in 2013, Romero dominated in mid-May when he did not allow an earned run over four starts, covering nearly 25 innings. He has a live arm that generates a tailing 92-94 mph fastball that touches 96. He shows a plus breaking ball, a slurve with hard-breaking, two-plane action. The problem has been finding a consistent release point from his three-quarters arm slot, which affects his control and the sharpness of the pitch. He has a fringy, firm changeup that needs to improve if he hopes to be a starter in the big leagues. The Rays say that once Romero conquers his mechanics, he will be an elite pitcher, and his development will determine whether he is a mid-rotation starter or a reliever in the big leagues. He likely will spend most of 2014 at Triple-A Durham.

Year	Club (League)	Class	W	L	ERA	G	GS	CG	SV	IP	H	HR	BB	SO	K/9	WHIP	AVG
2008	Rays (DSL)	R	1	0	2.76	10	0	0	0	16	11	0	8	20	11.0	1.16	.175
2009	Rays (GCL)	R	2	4	4.81	11	4	0	0	39	38	2	21	33	7.6	1.50	.255
2010	Princeton (APP)	R	4	1	1.95	13	13	0	0	69	51	2	14	72	9.3	0.94	.204
	Hudson Valley (NYP)	SS	1	0	1.80	1	1	0	0	5	1	0	5	4	7.2	1.20	.071
2011	Bowling Green (MWL)	LoA	5	5	4.26	26	26	0	0	114	104	9	68	140	11.1	1.51	.245
2012	Charlotte (FSL)	HiA	5	7	3.93	25	23	1	0	126	89	5	76	107	7.6	1.31	.201
2013	Montgomery (SL)	AA	11	7	2.76	27	27	0	0	140	110	9	73	110	7.1	1.30	.215
	Durham (IL)	AAA	0	0	0.00	1	1	0	0	8	4	0	2	2	2.3	0.75	.154
	Tampa Bay (AL)	MAJ	0	0	0.00	1	1	0	0	5	1	0	4	0	0.0	1.07	.071
Major League Totals			0	0	0.00	1	1	0	0	5	1	0	4	0	0.0	1.07	.071
Minor League Totals			29	24	3.37	114	95	1	0	518	408	27	267	488	8.5	1.30	.217

5 ALEX COLOME, RHP

BA GRADE **55** HIGH

Born: Dec. 31, 1988. **B-T:** L-R. **Ht.:** 6-2. **Wt.:** 185. **Signed:** Dominican Republic, 2007. **Signed by:** Eddy Toledo.

Colome made his big league debut at midseason 2013, following in the footsteps of his uncle Jesus, a 10-year major league veteran. Unfortunately, for the second time in as many seasons, he missed the latter part of the season, this time due to an elbow strain. He opted for rest and rehab instead of surgery and figures to be ready for 2014. Colome has made impressive strides over the past two years in his development as a pitcher after being a thrower early in his career. He has a plus fastball in the 93-95 mph range that touches 97 with decent sinking action and armside run, though at times it can be too true. He mixes in a tight power curveball and a hard slider. His changeup has improved, though it remains his fourth pitch. Colome's command and feel for pitching also have taken big steps forward, making him more effective at getting ahead in the count and generating groundball outs. His durability has become his biggest question mark, and it could land Colome in the bullpen on a permanent basis. Regardless of role, he has the arm and the ability to pitch in the major leagues, which is where he should find himself again at some point in 2014.

Year	Club (League)	Class	W	L	ERA	G	GS	CG	SV	IP	H	HR	BB	SO	K/9	WHIP	AVG
2007	Devil Rays (DSL)	R	1	6	2.97	14	11	0	0	39	30	1	31	50	11.4	1.55	.208
2008	Princeton (APP)	R	0	5	6.80	12	11	0	0	46	50	5	26	52	10.1	1.64	.272
2009	Hudson Valley (NYP)	SS	7	4	1.66	15	15	2	0	76	46	0	32	94	11.1	1.03	.174
2010	Bowling Green (MWL)	LoA	6	6	3.95	22	22	1	0	114	98	14	45	118	9.3	1.25	—
	Charlotte (FSL)	HiA	0	0	2.25	1	1	0	0	4	5	0	0	8	18.0	1.25	.333
2011	Charlotte (FSL)	HiA	9	5	3.66	19	19	1	0	106	78	8	44	92	7.8	1.15	.214
	Montgomery (SL)	AA	3	4	4.15	9	9	1	0	52	41	5	28	31	5.4	1.33	.219
2012	Montgomery (SL)	AA	8	3	3.48	14	14	1	0	75	69	2	34	75	9.0	1.37	.252
	Durham (IL)	AAA	0	1	3.24	3	3	0	0	17	12	1	9	15	8.1	1.26	.207
2013	Durham (IL)	AAA	4	6	3.07	14	14	0	0	70	63	5	29	72	9.2	1.31	.236
	Tampa Bay (AL)	MAJ	1	1	2.25	3	3	0	0	16	14	2	9	12	6.8	1.44	.230
Major League Totals			1	1	2.25	3	3	0	0	16	14	2	9	12	6.8	1.44	.230
Minor League Totals			38	40	3.59	123	119	6	0	599	492	41	278	607	9.1	1.28	.226

6 ANDREW TOLES, OF

BA GRADE **55** HIGH

Born: May 24, 1992. **B-T:** L-R. **Ht.:** 5-10. **Wt.:** 185. **Drafted:** Chipola (Fla.) JC, 2012 (3rd round). **Signed by:** Milt Hill.

Drafted by the Marlins in the fourth round in 2010, Toles opted to attend Tennessee, where his father Alvin and uncle Johnnie Jones played football. Dismissed from the program after a year, he wound up at Chipola (Fla.) JC, where he was benched and suspended. The Rays loved his athletic ability and signed him for $394,200 as a third-rounder in 2012, then watched him put together a breakout season in 2013. The Rays named Toles their minor league player of the year and best baserunner. Toles inspires Michael Bourn comparisons as a speed-oriented center fielder who has the strength and ability to drive the ball. Considered a 70 runner on the 20-80 scouting scale, he runs down balls in the gaps and led the organization with 62 stolen bases, a total that ranked second in the low Class A Midwest League. He also ranked second in the minors in triples (16) and fourth in the MWL with 53 extra-base hits while using the entire field. Despite winning the MWL batting title at .326, his pitch recognition and strike-zone discipline need work. His below-avearage arm strength is playable in center and accurate. Several parts of Toles' game remain raw, which should mean the best is yet to come for this blossoming athlete. He has the ability to develop into a starting center fielder in the major leagues, and he should make the jump to high Class A Charlotte this spring.

Year	Club (League)	Class	AVG	G	AB	R	H	2B	3B	HR	RBI	BB	SO	SB	CS	OBP	SLG
2012	Princeton (APP)	R	.281	51	199	31	56	13	3	7	33	12	36	14	5	.327	.482
2013	Bowling Green (MWL)	LoA	.326	121	519	79	169	35	16	2	57	22	105	62	17	.359	.466
Minor League Totals			.313	172	718	110	225	48	19	9	90	34	141	76	22	.350	.471

7 NICK CIUFFO, C

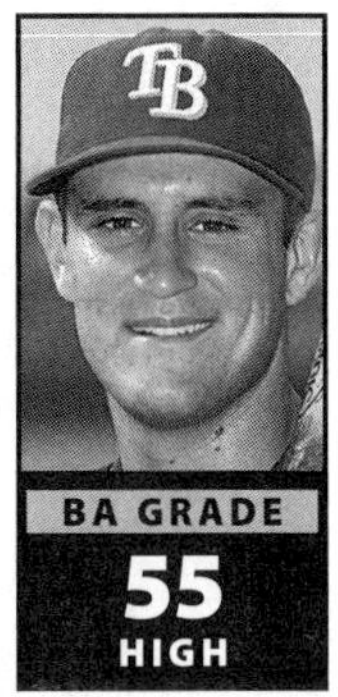

BA GRADE
55
HIGH

Born: March 7, 1995. **B-T:** L-R. **Ht.:** 6-1. **Wt.:** 205. **Drafted:** HS—Lexington, S.C., 2013 (1st round). **Signed by:** Brian Hickman.

The Rays have spent big on prep catchers, investing $750,000 in Luke Bailey (2009) and $1.025 million in Justin O'Conner (2010). They did it again in 2013 with Ciuffo, who signed for $1,972,200. He made a seamless move to pro ball in the Rookie-level Gulf Coast League, though he tired late in the season. As a lefthanded-hitting receiver who has a chance to produce for power and average, Ciuffo has the traits scouts long for in a catcher. He has above-average bat speed with a solid up-the-middle approach, and his power should become more prominent as he learns to incorporate his lower half into his swing more consistently. He has wide shoulders and a strong, solid build with good athleticism. He displays above-average arm strength with a quick release and above-average accuracy on his throws. An intense, fiery player with a take-charge attitude, Ciuffo leads by example with his hustle and by blocking balls in the dirt and guiding the pitching staff. The Rays tend to move pitchers and catchers slowly, but Ciuffo could make the organization reconsider because he has all the tools. He's expected to open 2014 in extended spring training before drawing a short-season assignment.

Year	Club (League)	Class	AVG	G	AB	R	H	2B	3B	HR	RBI	BB	SO	SB	CS	OBP	SLG
2013	Rays (GCL)	R	.258	43	159	11	41	6	1	0	25	9	40	0	0	.296	.308
Minor League Totals			.258	43	159	11	41	6	1	0	25	9	40	0	0	.296	.308

8 RYAN BRETT, 2B

MIKE JANES

BA GRADE
50
HIGH

Born: Oct. 9, 1991. **B-T:** R-R. **Ht.:** 5-9. **Wt.:** 180. **Drafted:** HS—Burien, Wash., 2010 (3rd round). **Signed by:** Paul Kirsch.

Brett began his 2013 season on the shelf, completing a 50-game suspension after failing a test for amphetamine use in 2012. He jumped to the high Class A Florida State League upon his return in mid-May and ranked among the league leaders in batting until his promotion to Double-A Montgomery in early August. While many focus on Brett's short stature, he gets as much out of his ability as anyone in the organization. He employs a hustling, blue-collar approach, though his Pete Rose intensity can work against him at times and his standout season came in part from a more relaxed approach on the field. He has an excellent feel for the strike zone and drives the ball consistently with strong, quick hands and a compact swing. His power is more to the gaps than over the fence. He has above-average speed and first-step quickness and displays solid instincts on the bases that could make him a leadoff hitter at the major league level. Defensively, Brett has plus range at second base with average arm strength, but he does not have soft hands and committed 11 errors in 73 games at second in 2013. While the Rays expect him to open 2014 back at Montgomery, he could push for a role in the big leagues by 2015.

Year	Club (League)	Class	AVG	G	AB	R	H	2B	3B	HR	RBI	BB	SO	SB	CS	OBP	SLG
2010	Rays (GCL)	R	.303	27	89	8	27	5	2	0	9	8	17	12	3	.364	.404
2011	Princeton (APP)	R	.300	61	240	42	72	22	5	3	24	26	24	21	3	.370	.471
2012	Bowling Green (MWL)	LoA	.285	100	410	77	117	20	3	6	35	37	73	48	8	.348	.393
2013	Rays (GCL)	R	.000	1	4	0	0	0	0	0	0	0	2	0	0	.000	.000
	Charlotte (FSL)	HiA	.340	51	206	38	70	11	4	4	22	15	27	22	7	.396	.490
	Montgomery (SL)	AA	.238	25	105	19	25	6	1	3	16	8	14	4	0	.289	.400
Minor League Totals			.295	265	1054	184	311	64	15	16	106	94	157	107	21	.357	.430

9 TIM BECKHAM, SS/2B

BA GRADE
45
MEDIUM

Born: Jan. 27, 1990. **B-T:** R-R. **Ht.:** 6-0. **Wt.:** 190. **Drafted:** HS—Griffin, Ga., 2008 (1st round). **Signed by:** Milt Hill.

Beckham made his major league debut last September, more than five years after being the No. 1 overall pick in the 2008 draft and signing for $6.15 million. But his 2014 season was put in jeopardy when he tore the ACL in his right knee during an offseason workout. Along the way he has peformed modestly and earned a 50-game suspension in 2012 for testing positive for marijuana for the second time. Beckham hit a career-best .276 during his third stint at Triple-A Durham, sliding to shortstop after Hak-Ju Lee's knee injury. He continued to display above-average bat speed and raw power to all fields, but that hasn't translated to home runs. He tends to overswing and has difficulty with pitch recognition, leading to low walk totals and more than 100 strikeouts in four of his five full seasons. He has also played second base and seems better suited for that position, despite above-average arm strength, given his average speed and range. The Rays say Beckham can be a starting shortstop in the big leagues, but that's complicated by Yunel Escobar and Lee. He may break in as a backup infielder, though the first task at hand will be rehabbing his knee.

Year	Club (League)	Class	AVG	G	AB	R	H	2B	3B	HR	RBI	BB	SO	SB	CS	OBP	SLG
2008	Princeton (APP)	R	.243	46	177	30	43	12	0	2	14	13	43	5	1	.297	.345
	Hudson Valley (NYP)	SS	.333	2	6	5	2	1	0	0	0	2	1	1	0	.556	.500
2009	Bowling Green (SAL)	LoA	.275	125	491	58	135	33	4	5	63	34	116	13	10	.328	.389
2010	Charlotte (FSL)	HiA	.256	123	465	68	119	23	5	5	57	62	119	22	14	.346	.359
2011	Montgomery (SL)	AA	.275	107	418	82	115	25	2	7	57	39	91	15	4	.339	.395
	Durham (IL)	AAA	.255	24	106	12	27	3	2	5	13	3	29	2	1	.282	.462
2012	Durham (IL)	AAA	.256	72	285	40	73	10	1	6	28	29	71	6	0	.325	.361
2013	Durham (IL)	AAA	.276	122	460	71	127	25	7	4	51	44	108	17	7	.342	.387
	Tampa Bay (AL)	MAJ	.429	5	7	1	3	0	0	0	1	0	0	0	0	.375	.429
Major League Totals			.429	5	7	1	3	0	0	0	1	0	0	0	0	.375	.429
Minor League Totals			.266	621	2408	366	641	132	21	34	283	226	578	81	37	.332	.381

10 KEVIN KIERMAIER, OF

BA GRADE
45
MEDIUM

Born: April 22, 1990. **B-T:** L-R. **Ht.:** 6-1. **Wt.:** 200. **Drafted:** Parkland (Ill.) JC, 2010 (31st round). **Signed by:** Tom Couston.

The MVP of the 2009 Division II Junior College World Series, Kiermaier is the organization's latest Cinderella story after he reached the big leagues in his fourth pro season. He got the call in late September and served as a defensive replacement in Game No. 163 against the Rangers. That capped a year when Kiermaier led all regular, full-season minor league center fielders with 2.85 putouts per game, was the Double-A Montgomery MVP and helped Triple-A Durham win the International League title. Tabbed by the Rays as the organization's best defensive outfielder the past two seasons, Kiermaier is one of the premier flycatchers in pro ball. He shows outstanding instincts with great first-step quickness and has a plus arm with above-average accuracy and carry. He also has above-average speed, though he doesn't use it to his full advantage on the basepaths. At the plate, he has a quick, short swing that allows him to stay on the ball. He uses the entire field and can drive pitches, though power is not a big part of his game. Kiermaier is knocking on the door of the big leagues and could be a starter down the road, but first he must continue to improve his consistency at the plate. He'll return to Durham to open the 2014 season.

Year	Club (League)	Class	AVG	G	AB	R	H	2B	3B	HR	RBI	BB	SO	SB	CS	OBP	SLG
2010	Princeton (APP)	R	.303	57	218	44	66	8	7	2	16	24	54	17	5	.380	.431
2011	Bowling Green (MWL)	LoA	.241	120	402	54	97	11	8	4	39	37	99	27	10	.316	.338
2012	Rays (GCL)	R	.167	2	6	0	1	0	0	0	0	0	2	0	0	.167	.167
	Charlotte (FSL)	HiA	.260	57	177	16	46	7	6	0	12	26	38	10	4	.361	.367
	Durham (IL)	AAA	.333	4	9	2	3	0	0	0	1	3	1	0	0	.500	.333
2013	Montgomery (SL)	AA	.307	97	371	65	114	14	9	5	28	31	61	14	11	.370	.434
	Durham (IL)	AAA	.263	39	137	24	36	7	6	1	13	14	26	7	1	.338	.423
	Tampa Bay (AL)	MAJ	—	1	0	0	0	0	0	0	0	0	0	0	0	—	—
Major League Totals			—	1	0	0	0	0	0	0	0	0	0	0	0	—	—
Minor League Totals			.275	376	1320	205	363	47	36	12	109	135	281	75	31	.351	.392

11 RYNE STANEK, RHP

Born: July 26, 1991. **B-T:** R-R. **Ht.:** 6-4. **Wt.:** 190. **Drafted:** Arkansas, 2013 (1st round). **Signed by:** Rickey Drexler.

A Mariners third-round pick in 2010 out of a Kansas high school, Stanek opted to attend Arkansas, where as a sophomore he led the Razorbacks to the College World Series and as a junior earned second-team All-America recognition. The Rays took him with the 29th overall pick following a college career when he went 22-8, 2.55, including a stellar 10-2, 1.39 showing in 16 starts in 2013. After signing for $1,755,800, Stanek did not pitch due to a lingering hip injury, which required mid-December surgery and clouds his availability for 2014. When healthy, Stanek is a true power pitcher with poise and mound presence who generates plus arm speed. His fastball sits in the 92-98 mph range, and he mixes it with a plus, hard slider that sits at 84-87 mph. He also flashed a curveball and changeup in college, displaying good feel for the latter offering. Stanek throws from a three-quarters arm slot but needs to stay on top of the ball in order to maximize his pitches. Scouts said he may need to tweak his mechanics in order to accomplish that goal. While some think he might be a back-end reliever down the road, Stanek should begin the 2014 campaign in the rotation of either low Class A Bowling Green or high Class A Charlotte.

Year	Club (League)	Class	W	L	ERA	G	GS	CG	SV	IP	H	HR	BB	SO	K/9	WHIP	AVG
2013	Did not play—Injured																

12 JUSTIN O'CONNER, C

Born: March 31, 1992. **B-T:** R-R. **Ht.:** 6-2. **Wt.:** 190. **Drafted:** HS—Muncie, Ind., 2010 (1st round). **Signed by:** James Bonnici.

The first catcher the Rays ever drafted in the first round, O'Conner went 31st overall in 2010 and spent three years in short-season ball before graduating to low Class A Bowling Green in 2013. An offensive force in high school who split his time between shortstop, third base and the mound, he moved behind the plate as a senior and emerged as one of the top prep catchers in the country. A career .199 hitter entering the 2013 campaign, he displayed plus raw power during batting practice but failed to show that same thump during games. That trend started to change at Bowling Green, where one-third of his hits went for extra bases, including 14 home runs. O'Conner admits he used to fret about his stats, which affected his approach. He has learned to relax while focusing on making solid contact. He may not hit for a high average, but he should be a solid run producer, owing to his power. Defensively, he has plus-plus arm strength with good athleticism behind the plate that helped him throw out 25 of 45 basestealers in 2013. He has the necessary leadership traits and soft hands to be a premium receiver, and he is still learning the nuances of calling a game. Given his short time at the position, O'Conner has the defensive tools to be a starting receiver in the big leagues. His next step is the high Class A Florida State League.

Year	Club (League)	Class	AVG	G	AB	R	H	2B	3B	HR	RBI	BB	SO	SB	CS	OBP	SLG
2010	Rays (GCL)	R	.211	48	161	18	34	13	0	3	29	18	46	1	0	.301	.348
2011	Princeton (APP)	R	.157	48	178	18	28	8	0	9	29	17	78	4	1	.234	.354
2012	Hudson Valley (NYP)	SS	.223	59	238	39	53	18	1	5	29	18	73	2	0	.276	.370
2013	Bowling Green (MWL)	LoA	.233	102	399	49	93	17	0	14	56	31	111	5	0	.290	.381
Minor League Totals			.213	257	976	124	208	56	1	31	143	84	308	12	1	.278	.368

13 RICHIE SHAFFER, 1B/3B

BA GRADE
50
HIGH

Born: March 15, 1991. **B-T:** R-R. **Ht.:** 6-3. **Wt.:** 210. **Drafted:** Clemson, 2012 (1st round). **Signed by:** Brian Hickman.

After ranking as the No. 4 prospect in the short-season New York-Penn League after being drafted in 2012, Shaffer received a two-step promotion to the high Class A Florida State League to open the 2013 campaign and had an eye-opening experience. He struggled with the speed of the game, particularly with his lateral range at third base, and put excessive pressure on himself. To his credit, he worked hard to improve and made significant progress during the second half of the season. Shaffer possesses above-average bat speed and generates power to all fields. He has a good approach at the plate and solid strike-zone discipline, though he tends to chase breaking balls when he gets behind in the count. He has solid athleticism with fringe-average speed. Defensively, he has a plus arm, which is strong enough for third and possibly right field, but he needs to become crisper at the hot corner in order to remain there. A move to first base would mitigate his defensive struggles and fill an organizational need. Shaffer is a potential run-producer at the major league level, and the Rays will be looking for a spike in power in 2014 when he opens the slate at Double-A Montgomery.

Year	Club (League)	Class	AVG	G	AB	R	H	2B	3B	HR	RBI	BB	SO	SB	CS	OBP	SLG
2012	Hudson Valley (NYP)	SS	.308	33	117	25	36	5	2	4	26	16	31	0	0	.406	.487
2013	Charlotte (FSL)	HiA	.254	122	469	55	119	33	1	11	73	35	106	6	0	.308	.399
Minor League Totals			.265	155	586	80	155	38	3	15	99	51	137	6	0	.329	.416

14 BLAKE SNELL, LHP

BA GRADE
55
EXTREME

Born: Dec. 4, 1992. **B-T:** L-L. **Ht.:** 6-4. **Wt.:** 180. **Drafted:** HS—Shoreline, Wash., 2011 (1st round supplemental). **Signed by:** Paul Kirsch.

The Rays have been patient with Snell since drafting him with the 52nd overall pick in 2011. One of several Tampa Bay prospects from the Pacific Northwest, he has projection to spare but still is learning how to pitch while growing into his body. The Rays shut him down in mid-August 2012, just seven innings shy of qualifying for the Rookie-level Appalachian League ERA title, and then kept him under 100 innings in 2013 at low Class A Bowling Green. Snell has an above-average fastball with good sink that touches 94 mph. He mixes his heater with a low-80s slider that flashes plus to limit lefthanders in the Midwest League to a .200 average. He also has a good changeup that could become a plus offering, and a curveball that continues to improve. Snell struggled with his control and ranked third in the MWL in walks (73) last year, but scouts believe he should be able to reduce that number as he repeats his delivery more consistently. He has done a better job of focusing on getting outs early in the count and should register a more groundball outs at higher levels due to the solid sinking action of all his offerings. Snell could be a solid No. 3 starter if he refines all of his pitches, and he should make the move to high Class A Charlotte in 2014.

Year	Club (League)	Class	W	L	ERA	G	GS	CG	SV	IP	H	HR	BB	SO	K/9	WHIP	AVG
2011	Rays (GCL)	R	1	2	3.08	11	8	0	0	26	30	0	11	26	8.9	1.56	.291
2012	Princeton (APP)	R	5	1	2.09	11	11	1	0	47	34	4	17	53	10.1	1.08	.202
2013	Bowling Green (MWL)	LoA	4	9	4.27	23	23	0	0	99	90	8	73	106	9.6	1.65	.245
Minor League Totals			10	12	3.49	45	42	1	0	173	154	12	101	185	9.6	1.48	.241

15 JESSE HAHN, RHP

BA GRADE
55
EXTREME

Born: July 30, 1989. **B-T:** R-R. **Ht.:** 6-5. **Wt.:** 185. **Drafted:** Virginia Tech, 2010 (6th round). **Signed by:** Lou Wieben.

The Rays are beginning to see the potential Hahn showed in college before he tore the ulnar collateral ligament in his right elbow two days prior to the 2010 draft. Realizing Hahn would need Tommy John surgery, Tampa Bay gambled and guided him through a rehab that included missing the entire 2011 season. He pitched well during his pro debut in the short-season New York-Penn League in 2012 and earned all-star recognition in the high Class A Florida State League in 2013. The Rays limited Hahn to three-inning starts to open the season and never allowed him to go more than five innings before he was shut down for a month in late July. His fastball sits in the 90-93 mph range and touches 97 with plus life. He also throws a heavy two-seamer in the low 90s with impressive sink, an overhand curveball with a sharp drop and a changeup that has the potential to be above-average. Hahn worked hard with the organization's coaches to rework and fine-tune his mechanics, improving his overall command. Scouts also are impressed with his feel for pitching and believe he could start moving more quickly now that he's nearing full health. Should he continue to hone all four pitches, Hahn could emerge as a strong mid-rotation starter or possible closer, a role he filled at Virginia Tech, but his durability is a significant question. His next stint will come as a member of the Double-A Montgomery rotation.

Year	Club (League)	Class	W	L	ERA	G	GS	CG	SV	IP	H	HR	BB	SO	K/9	WHIP	AVG
2010	Did not play—Injured																
2011	Did not play—Injured																
2012	Hudson Valley (NYP)	SS	2	2	2.77	14	14	0	0	52	38	0	15	55	9.5	1.02	.199
2013	Rays (GCL)	R	0	0	0.00	1	1	0	0	2	4	0	0	4	18.0	2.00	.364
	Charlotte (FSL)	HiA	2	1	2.15	19	19	0	0	67	55	1	18	63	8.5	1.09	.218
Minor League Totals			4	3	2.38	34	34	0	0	121	97	1	33	122	9.1	1.07	.214

16 GRAYSON GARVIN, LHP

BA GRADE
50
HIGH

Born: Oct. 27, 1989. **B-T:** L-L. **Ht.:** 6-6. **Wt.:** 225. **Drafted:** Vanderbilt, 2011 (1st round supplemental). **Signed by:** James Bonnici.

Garvin considered having Tommy John surgery as far back as 2009 at Vanderbilt, but he opted instead for rest and rehab. He wound up pacing the Cape Cod League in ERA in 2010 and garnering Southeastern Conference pitcher of the year accolades after an 11-1, 2.08 mark in 2011, leading to his selection by the Rays with the 59th overall pick that year. But he could not escape the sugery, finally having it in 2012 to clear up his lingering elbow problemafter 11 inconsistent outings at high Class A Charlotte. He returned to the mound last July and split the final two months between the Rookie-level Gulf Coast League and Charlotte before seeing more activity in the Arizona Fall League, showing greater strength with every outing in the AFL. Garvin has good stuff, but his makeup and intelligence are separators. He has a tremendous mound presence and uses his 6-foot-6 frame to his advantage by throwing downhill. He repeated his delivery with consistency and little effort last year, generating a 91-93 mph fastball that touches 95. He also has a good changeup and throws a cutter in the 85-88 mph range. The Rays believe Garvin could move quickly once he regains his strength. A potential back-end starter or situational reliever, he should move up to Double-A Montgomery in 2014.

Year	Club (League)	Class	W	L	ERA	G	GS	CG	SV	IP	H	HR	BB	SO	K/9	WHIP	AVG
2012	Charlotte (FSL)	HiA	2	4	5.05	11	10	0	0	46	45	0	19	37	7.2	1.38	.259
2013	Rays (GCL)	R	0	1	2.31	6	6	0	0	12	11	1	4	12	9.3	1.29	.244
	Charlotte (FSL)	HiA	0	1	1.08	5	5	0	0	17	8	0	4	12	6.5	0.72	.138
Minor League Totals			2	6	3.74	22	21	0	0	75	64	1	27	61	7.4	1.22	.231

17 FELIPE RIVERO, LHP

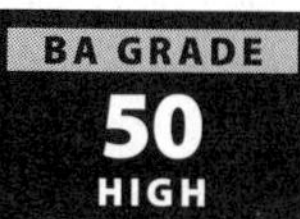

Born: July 5, 1991. **B-T:** L-L. **Ht.:** 6-0. **Wt.:** 170. **Signed:** Venezuela, 2008. **Signed by:** Ronnie Blanco.

A Futures Game participant in 2012, Rivero has one of the liveliest arms in the organization and is making strides against higher levels of competition as his body matures. He concluded the 2013 season on a strong note in the high Class A Florida State League by allowing a combined five earned runs over his last six starts. Rivero works off a 91-94 mph fastball with late, tailing movement that generates a healthy percentage of groundball outs. He also uses a curveball that has a hard, vertical drop and shows good feel for a changeup that he unleashes with the same arm speed as his fastball. Considered small when he signed with the Rays out of Venezuela, Rivero has grown two inches over the past five years and developed a stronger and thicker lower half that he employs in his delivery. He throws the ball from an upright delivery with a three-quarters arm slot that helps him keep pitches down in the zone. Control and endurance are the keys to his future. He tends to lose velocity over the course of his starts and could end up in the bullpen if he fails to improve in that area. Either way, the Rays are looking forward to seeing how he competes as a 22-year-old at Double-A Montgomery in 2014.

Year	Club (League)	Class	W	L	ERA	G	GS	CG	SV	IP	H	HR	BB	SO	K/9	WHIP	AVG
2009	Rays (VSL)	R	6	4	3.74	16	0	0	1	34	38	0	12	25	6.7	1.49	.286
2010	Rays (VSL)	R	3	3	2.09	14	9	0	2	52	46	1	10	44	7.7	1.08	.243
2011	Princeton (APP)	R	3	3	4.62	14	12	0	0	60	64	7	13	57	8.5	1.28	.264
2012	Bowling Green (MWL)	LoA	8	8	3.41	27	21	0	0	113	115	5	29	98	7.8	1.27	.266
2013	Charlotte (FSL)	HiA	9	7	3.40	25	23	2	0	127	122	7	52	91	6.4	1.37	.257
Minor League Totals			29	25	3.45	96	65	2	3	386	385	20	116	315	7.3	1.30	.262

18 JAKE HAGER, SS

Born: March 4, 1993. **B-T:** R-R. **Ht.:** 6-1. **Wt.:** 170. **Drafted:** HS—Las Vegas, 2011 (1st round). **Signed by:** Jayson Durocher.

Hager lacks a standout tool, yet he also has few weaknesses. Since joining the organization as the 32nd overall pick in the 2011 draft, he has meshed his skills with an uncanny focus and work ethic and should be ready for Double-A at age 21. Hager is a solid, reliable defensive shortstop who makes all of the routine plays. He has good instincts in the field along with soft hands, and he does an exceptional job on relays and turning double plays. His arm strength is average, but his throws are accurate with enough zip that he should be able to remain at the position at higher levels. Hager found high Class A Florida State League pitching challenging, hitting .228 during the second half, but made adjustments that the Rays think will pay off in future seasons. He is quick to the ball with good hands, which should allow him to move runners as a No. 2 or bottom-of-the-order hitter. His power is limited to occasional pop to his pull side, but that could increase as he gains strength and experience. Hager will not receive the attention of more flashy shortstops, but his skills and approach should allow him to play regularly in the major leagues, perhaps as a second-division starter or utility player. His next stop will be Double-A Montgomery.

Year	Club (League)	Class	AVG	G	AB	R	H	2B	3B	HR	RBI	BB	SO	SB	CS	OBP	SLG
2011	Princeton (APP)	R	.269	47	193	29	52	11	1	4	17	9	26	5	7	.305	.399
2012	Bowling Green (MWL)	LoA	.281	114	442	63	124	22	3	10	72	40	60	17	11	.345	.412
2013	Rays (GCL)	R	.500	1	4	1	2	1	0	0	1	0	0	0	0	.500	.750
	Charlotte (FSL)	HiA	.258	113	449	56	116	15	3	0	33	38	81	12	8	.318	.305
Minor League Totals			.270	275	1088	149	294	49	7	14	123	87	167	34	26	.328	.367

19 RILEY UNROE, SS

Born: Aug. 3, 1995. **B-T:** B-R. **Ht.:** 5-10. **Wt.:** 180. **Drafted:** HS—Mesa, Ariz., 2013 (2nd round). **Signed by:** Jayson Durocher.

The 60th overall pick in the 2013 draft, Unroe is the son of Tim Unroe, a corner infielder who had a long minor league career and several cups of coffee in the big leagues. Riley put together an impressive amateur career, including stints with Team USA's 14-and-under and 18-and-under teams. His draft stock rose last spring as he showed the ability to remain at shortstop in pro ball. Unroe has an impressive feel for the game, and he does a great job of positioning himself at short, which allows him to make plays others might miss. He has soft hands, excellent range and above-average arm strength, completing plays deep in the hole with relative ease. A switch-hitter throughout his amateur days, Unroe generates plus bat speed and barrels the ball consistently from both sides of the plate. He has an advanced feel for the strike zone and his pitch recognition allows him to drive balls to all fields. He possesses both quickness and foot speed, making him an above-average to plus runner. What scouts liked most about Unroe, however, were his makeup and heady play on the field, which should allow him to make adjustments as he climbs the ladder. He could land in a full-season Class A league sooner than most players drafted by the Rays out of high school.

Year	Club (League)	Class	AVG	G	AB	R	H	2B	3B	HR	RBI	BB	SO	SB	CS	OBP	SLG
2013	Rays (GCL)	R	.246	46	167	34	41	7	3	1	15	33	43	7	2	.376	.341
Minor League Totals			.246	46	167	34	41	7	3	1	15	33	43	7	2	.376	.341

20 DREW VETTLESON, OF

BA GRADE **45** HIGH

Born: July 19, 1991. **B-T:** L-R. **Ht.:** 6-1. **Wt.:** 185. **Drafted:** HS—Silverdale, Wash., 2010 (1st round supplemental). **Signed by:** Paul Kirsch.

Vettleson has lived up to his billing as a hitter since being selected with the 42nd overall pick in the 2010 draft. He established the low Class A Bowling Green franchise mark for hits (139) in 2012 and tied for fifth in hits (128) in the high Class A Florida State League in 2013. Noted as a switch-pitcher during his high school days in the Pacific Northwest, Vettleson gave that up and has used his short, quick swing that produces plus bat speed from the left side to find holes in the defense. After hitting 15 home runs in the South Atlantic League in 2012, he had just four in the pitcher-friendly FSL but should be able to post at least average power numbers as he gains experience. He needs to do a better job of being patient and swinging at pitches he can drive, rather than expanding the strike zone. Defensively, Vettleson has above-average arm strength with excellent accuracy and carry in right field, allowing him to register 13 assists in 2013. However, he also committed 14 errors due to poor footwork and a lack of focus. Much like Richie Shaffer, Vettleson has the potential to be a regular, but the Rays want to see his power output increase in 2014 at Double-A Montgomery.

Year	Club (League)	Class	AVG	G	AB	R	H	2B	3B	HR	RBI	BB	SO	SB	CS	OBP	SLG
2011	Princeton (APP)	R	.282	61	234	33	66	13	4	7	40	27	53	20	6	.357	.462
2012	Bowling Green (MWL)	LoA	.275	132	505	80	139	24	5	15	69	51	117	20	11	.340	.432
2013	Charlotte (FSL)	HiA	.274	121	467	50	128	29	6	4	62	40	78	5	7	.331	.388
Minor League Totals			.276	314	1206	163	333	66	15	26	171	118	248	45	24	.340	.420

21 JOSE MUJICA, RHP

BA GRADE **50** EXTREME

Born: June 29, 1996. **B-T:** R-R. **Ht.:** 6-2. **Wt.:** 180. **Signed:** Venezuela, 2012. **Signed by:** Ronnie Blanco.

Deemed by many scouts to be the best international pitching prospect available in 2012, Mujica signed with the Rays for $1 million out of Carlos Guillen's academy in Venezuela and has made rapid progress despite being one of the youngest players in the organization. Expected to spend 2013 in the Dominican Summer League, Mujica showed enough maturity and development to make the jump to the Rookie-level Gulf Coast League, where he ranked as the circuit's No. 16 prospect. He's the classic teen pitching prospect, with loose actions, a live arm, a durable frame and a clean, compact delivery. He repeats his mechanics with consistency and pounds the strike zone while using both sides of the plate. His four-seam fastball sits in the low 90s and touched 94 mph in 2013, while his two-seamer is a heavy pitch that generates groundball outs. The Rays believe he has a chance to boost his velocity as he gains experience and strength. His changeup has the makings of becoming a plus pitch, and he creates deception by using the same arm speed as his fastball. Mujica also made strides in adding a more consistent curveball to his repertoire, and it shows tight spin and break. He has the potential to skyrocket on this list, but first he'll pitch for Rookie-level Princeton in 2014.

Year	Club (League)	Class	W	L	ERA	G	GS	CG	SV	IP	H	HR	BB	SO	K/9	WHIP	AVG
2013	Rays (GCL)	R	3	2	3.09	12	5	0	1	32	32	0	3	20	5.6	1.09	.244
Minor League Totals			3	2	3.09	12	5	0	1	32	32	0	3	20	5.6	1.09	.244

22 TYLER GOEDDEL, 3B

BA GRADE **45** HIGH

Born: Oct. 20, 1992. **B-T:** R-R. **Ht.:** 6-4. **Wt.:** 185. **Drafted:** HS—Mountain View, Calif., 2011 (1st round supplemental). **Signed by:** Brian Morrison.

Goeddel made the nearly unprecedented organizational move (for a high school draft pick) of skipping over short-season ball and beginning his pro career at low Class A Bowling Green in 2012. The results suggest why the Rays prefer a more conservative approach. The 41st overall pick in the 2011 draft, Goeddel received the largest bonus ($1.5 million) of the Rays' seven early picks that year. He didn't put up great numbers in his two seasons in the Midwest League but finally started showing progress at the plate during the last several weeks of last year. Tall and lanky with above-average athleticism, he has solid bat speed, but his swing tends to get long. He showed a better ability to drive the ball last year, which should increase as he adds strength. Goeddel has above-average speed and puts it to use on the basepaths with solid instincts. On defense he has a strong arm and good hands but has been error-prone, committing 64 miscues in 205 games (.896 fielding percentage). While he has played exclusively at third base in his first two seasons, the Rays believe he could man any of the four corner positions down the road. The Rays sent Goeddel to play winter ball in Australia following the season to gain more experience, and the organization is confident that he has the tools and makeup to become a contributor at the big league level. A promotion to the high Class A Florida State League is next on the agenda.

Year	Club (League)	Class	AVG	G	AB	R	H	2B	3B	HR	RBI	BB	SO	SB	CS	OBP	SLG
2012	Bowling Green (MWL)	LoA	.246	103	329	52	81	19	2	6	46	38	94	30	5	.335	.371
2013	Bowling Green (MWL)	LoA	.249	112	450	63	112	18	12	7	65	40	98	30	5	.313	.389
Minor League Totals			.248	215	779	115	193	37	14	13	111	78	192	60	10	.322	.381

23 C.J. RIEFENHAUSER, LHP

Born: Jan. 30, 1990. **B-T:** L-L. **Ht.:** 6-0. **Wt.:** 180. **Drafted:** Chipola (Fla.) JC, 2010 (20th round). **Signed by:** Milt Hill.

After playing at three colleges, Riefenhauser was unheralded coming into the organization but has since blossomed into one of the system's bigger surprises. He earned all-star recognition in the low Class A Midwest and high Class A Florida State leagues in 2011 and 2012 as a starter, then shifted to the bullpen in 2013 and wound up pitching in the Futures Game and making Baseball America's year-end Minor League All-Star Team. Among relievers who qualified for the ERA title, he allowed the fifth-fewest baserunners per inning (0.83 WHIP) in the minor leagues. Riefenhauser shuts down lefthanders with a plus fastball and slider. His heater sits at 91-93 mph with above-average movement, and he's not afraid to challenge hitters with it. His slider has solid, tight spin and a good late break. He also has made strides with a changeup that shows good fade and depth. Riefenhauser works down in the zone and repeats his simple mechanics well. The Rays rave about his work ethic and competitiveness. Riefenhauser should emerge as a situational reliever at the major league level, and he will compete for a spot in the Tampa Bay bullpen now that he's on the 40-man roster.

Year	Club (League)	Class	W	L	ERA	G	GS	CG	SV	IP	H	HR	BB	SO	K/9	WHIP	AVG
2010	Princeton (APP)	R	1	0	2.84	11	0	0	1	19	14	1	6	16	7.6	1.05	.203
	Bowling Green (MWL)	LoA	1	0	1.00	2	2	0	0	9	7	0	1	4	4.0	0.89	.200
2011	Bowling Green (MWL)	LoA	6	5	2.31	18	18	1	0	101	77	7	25	99	8.8	1.01	.212
	Charlotte (FSL)	HiA	1	3	4.14	8	7	0	0	37	35	3	11	24	5.8	1.24	.252
2012	Charlotte (FSL)	HiA	7	8	4.76	23	14	0	1	96	98	11	32	103	9.6	1.35	.264
	Montgomery (SL)	AA	1	1	3.44	9	1	0	0	18	15	4	8	15	7.4	1.25	.224
2013	Montgomery (SL)	AA	4	0	0.51	34	0	0	11	53	28	3	11	48	8.2	0.74	.153
	Durham (IL)	AAA	2	1	3.05	17	0	0	0	21	14	2	8	22	9.6	1.06	.189
Minor League Totals			23	18	2.99	122	42	1	13	355	288	31	102	331	8.4	1.10	.221

24 OSCAR HERNANDEZ, C

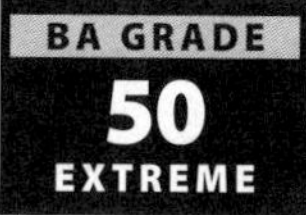

Born: July 9, 1993. **B-T:** R-R. **Ht.:** 6-0. **Wt.:** 195. **Signed:** Venezuela, 2009. **Signed by:** Ronnie Blanco.

Hernandez won the Venezuelan Summer League MVP award in 2011, capturing the triple crown and establishing league records for average (.402), home runs (21) and RBIs (66). He made his U.S. debut in the Rookie-level Appalachian League in 2012, throwing out 38 percent of basestealers, and jumped to the short-season New York-Penn League in 2013, where he ranked as the circuit's No. 2 prospect. After impressing with his bat early in his career, Hernandez has improved immensely with the glove and could prove to be a top-of-the-line receiver. He can shut down running games with plus arm strength and above-average footwork and athleticism, and he threw out 57 percent of basestealers last year. He receives and blocks the ball cleanly and does an excellent job of working with pitchers. Hernandez shows solid bat speed with a good approach but tends to get pull-happy. The Rays want him to use the middle of the field more consistently and concentrate on hitting line drives. Given the strides he has made over the past three seasons, Hernandez could make a big move up this list in 2014 if he hits. He'll start by returning to low Class A Bowling Green.

Year	Club (League)	Class	AVG	G	AB	R	H	2B	3B	HR	RBI	BB	SO	SB	CS	OBP	SLG
2010	Rays (VSL)	R	.223	34	103	17	23	6	0	4	14	11	19	0	0	.319	.398
2011	Rays (VSL)	R	.402	69	239	56	96	14	1	21	66	37	44	3	5	.503	.732
2012	Princeton (APP)	R	.231	49	160	25	37	9	1	5	24	23	31	0	1	.349	.394
2013	Hudson Valley (NYP)	SS	.228	43	167	22	38	6	0	6	33	11	24	9	1	.282	.371
	Bowling Green (MWL)	LoA	.222	3	9	1	2	0	0	0	1	2	1	0	0	.364	.222
Minor League Totals			.289	198	678	121	196	35	2	36	138	84	119	12	7	.386	.506

25 MIKIE MAHTOOK, OF

BA GRADE
45
HIGH

Born: Nov. 30, 1989. **B-T:** R-R. **Ht.:** 6-1. **Wt.:** 200. **Drafted:** Louisiana State, 2011 (1st round). **Signed by:** Rickey Drexler.

A two-time All-American at Louisiana State who helped lead the Tigers to a College World Series title in 2009, Mahtook was the 31st overall pick in the 2011 draft and signed with the Rays for

$1.15 million. A hard-nosed player who plays the game at full throttle, Mahtook does most things well, leading to solid all-around production. He lacks a defining tool but does offer above-average speed. A center fielder in college, he moved to right in 2012 and spent the first four months of 2013 on the corner before returning to the middle garden the last six weeks, and he profiles better there. He gets good jumps and takes great angles on fly balls. He also has good arm strength and accuracy on his throws, but his arm is fringy for a right fielder. He uses a deep crouch at the plate and has a short stroke that generates good carry to all fields and fringe-average power. His pitch recognition needs fine-tuning. Good instincts could allow him to steal 20 bases annually in the big leagues. Mahtook profiles as a second-division regular or extra outfielder on a contender, with a chance to play regularly if he refines his approach. He will open the 2014 season at Triple-A Durham.

Year	Club (League)	Class	AVG	G	AB	R	H	2B	3B	HR	RBI	BB	SO	SB	CS	OBP	SLG
2012	Charlotte (FSL)	HiA	.290	92	341	44	99	15	7	5	37	29	71	19	6	.358	.419
	Montgomery (SL)	AA	.248	39	153	17	38	10	1	4	25	11	31	4	3	.308	.405
2013	Montgomery (SL)	AA	.254	132	511	71	130	30	8	7	68	43	102	25	8	.322	.386
Minor League Totals			.266	263	1005	132	267	55	16	16	130	83	204	48	17	.332	.400

26 DYLAN FLORO, RHP

BA GRADE
45
HIGH

Born: Dec. 27, 1990. **B-T:** L-R. **Ht.:** 6-2. **Wt.:** 180. **Drafted:** Cal State Fullerton, 2012 (13th round). **Signed by:** Brian Morrison.

The Rays took Floro in the 20th round of the 2009 draft coming out of high school in Atwater, Calif., but he headed to Cal State Fullerton. After three successful seasons with the Titans, he again was drafted by Tampa Bay in 2012 and signed for $100,000. He worked in relief after being drafted, then returned to the rotation in 2013 and performed exceptionally well, winning the minor league ERA title and finishing fifth among qualifiers with a groundout/airout ratio of 2.5. Most scouts agreed that Floro's stuff and mechanics regressed during his time in college. His fastball went from 91-93 mph to 88-91, and his slider lost much of its bite. More notable were his mechanics, which now feature an extreme coil and crow-hop finish, though his unorthodox delivery does create deception and movement. He also has excellent control and combines it with an advanced feel for pitching and a competitive streak. He pitches off his fringe-average fastball and mixes it well with a decent slider and improving changeup. Scouts project him as a reliever in the big leagues, but the Rays will continue to deploy him as a starter for now. Spring training will determine whether he returns to Charlotte to open the 2014 season or moves up to Double-A Montgomery.

Year	Club (League)	Class	W	L	ERA	G	GS	CG	SV	IP	H	HR	BB	SO	K/9	WHIP	AVG
2012	Hudson Valley (NYP)	SS	4	1	2.40	18	0	0	2	30	26	0	4	21	6.3	1.00	.228
2013	Bowling Green (MWL)	LoA	9	2	1.81	19	19	0	0	109	103	4	19	85	7.0	1.12	.251
	Charlotte (FSL)	HiA	2	0	1.61	4	4	2	0	28	20	0	2	14	4.5	0.79	.206
Minor League Totals			15	3	1.88	41	23	2	2	167	149	4	25	120	6.5	1.04	.240

27 THOMAS MILONE, OF

Born: Jan. 26, 1995. **B-T:** L-L. **Ht.:** 5-11. **Wt.:** 190. **Drafted:** HS—Monroe, Conn., 2013 (4th round). **Signed by:** Tim Alexander.

The Rays have a history of drafting athletic high school players with raw skills, and Milone is the latest after Tampa Bay took him 97th overall in June and signed him for $528,100. He played more football than baseball growing up, but he batted .471 during his senior season and stole 28 bases in 29 attempts to earn Connecticut state player of the year honors. He also became the highest-drafted player from a Connecticut public school since the Braves took Charlie Morton 95th overall in 2002. He had up-and-down results in his professional debut before putting together an impressive showing during instructional league. Milone has above-average strength with strong hands, and he is working on making his swing smoother and more consistent. He has plus speed with good aggressiveness and instincts on the bases. His speed plays well in center field, but he needs to improve his routes and get better reads off the bat. His arm strength is fringe-average, but he has good accuracy on his throws. The Rays knew Milone would require development time, but he has already made strides during his short time in the organization. He appears destined for short-season ball in 2014.

Year	Club (League)	Class	AVG	G	AB	R	H	2B	3B	HR	RBI	BB	SO	SB	CS	OBP	SLG
2013	Rays (GCL)	R	.190	40	142	18	27	2	4	0	4	7	38	5	1	.243	.261
	Hudson Valley (NYP)	SS	.667	2	6	3	4	0	0	1	2	0	1	1	0	.714	1.167
Minor League Totals			.209	42	148	21	31	2	4	1	6	7	39	6	1	.264	.297

28 JOSE CASTILLO, LHP

BA GRADE
50
EXTREME

Born: Jan. 10, 1996. **B-T:** L-L. **Ht.:** 6-4. **Wt.:** 200. **Signed:** Venezuela, 2012. **Signed by:** Marlon Roche/Ronnie Blanco.

Castillo has raw tools that leave scouts drooling. The 18-year-old combines youth with size and arm strength, a package that enticed the Rays to sign him for $1.55 million, the second-largest bonus of the 2012 international signing period and the most ever given to a Venezuelan southpaw. Castillo's value escalated during the first six months of 2012 along with his velocity. He continued to show an above-average fastball during his initial pro exposure in the Rookie-level Gulf Coast League in 2013, sitting in the low 90s and touching 95 mph on numerous occasions. Castillo also throws a slurvy breaking ball that shows a hard, sharp break on occasion, as well as a firm changeup that is in the early phases of its development. The Rays have been encouraged with the adjustments he has made to his delivery since signing. He initially threw over the top before the Rays lowered his arm angle to three-quarters. He tends to rush his mechanics, causing him to fly open in his delivery, but his control has been adequate even with the ongoing adjustments. The Rays are always cautious with young pitchers and will likely have Castillo spent the 2014 season at Rookie-level Princeton. Provided he masters all three pitches, he could be a mid-rotation starter or better down the road.

Year	Club (League)	Class	W	L	ERA	G	GS	CG	SV	IP	H	HR	BB	SO	K/9	WHIP	AVG
2013	Rays (GCL)	R	2	2	5.87	12	3	0	0	31	34	1	8	25	7.3	1.37	.288
Minor League Totals			2	2	5.87	12	3	0	0	31	34	1	8	25	7.3	1.37	.288

29 CURT CASALI, C

BA GRADE **45** HIGH

Born: Nov. 9, 1988. **B-T:** R-R. **Ht.:** 6-2. **Wt.:** 220. **Drafted:** Vanderbilt, 2011 (10th round). **Signed by:** Harold Zonder (Tigers).

The Rays acquired Casali at the end of spring training 2013 when the Tigers traded him to Tampa Bay to keep major league Rule 5 drdaft pickup Kyle Lobstein. Casali stood out immediately in an organization that has lacked quality catching depth. He made solid strides with his defensive work and drove the ball consistently while making the jump from high Class A Charlotte to Double-A Montgomery. Casali had Tommy John surgery at Vanderbilt and lost much of his plus arm strength. He has regained some of the snap on his throws, however, and his release quickened and his footwork improved considerably after working with Rays minor league coaches. Casali threw out just 25 percent of basestealers last year, and he needs to improve his technique and success rate to be an everyday catcher in the big leagues. He has above-average receiving skills with soft hands, and he does a good job of working with pitchers. Prior to 2013, his polished approach at the plate, including a discerning eye, had led to decent gap power, but he started to drive the ball more consistently in 2013, popping 10 homers and slugging .488. He has an ideal frame for a catcher, and the overall skill set to be at least a backup catcher in the big league.

Year	Club (League)	Class	AVG	G	AB	R	H	2B	3B	HR	RBI	BB	SO	SB	CS	OBP	SLG
2011	Connecticut (NYP)	SS	.278	10	36	7	10	2	0	1	2	6	5	0	0	.409	.417
	West Michigan (MWL)	LoA	.227	25	75	10	17	7	0	2	14	13	9	0	0	.344	.400
2012	West Michigan (MWL)	LoA	.288	48	170	25	49	12	0	8	25	27	18	2	1	.402	.500
	Lakeland (FSL)	HiA	.250	46	160	18	40	13	0	1	18	11	28	0	0	.322	.350
2013	Charlotte (FSL)	HiA	.267	46	165	15	44	6	1	5	22	18	31	1	0	.342	.406
	Montgomery (SL)	AA	.383	35	120	25	46	11	0	5	31	21	18	0	0	.483	.600
Minor League Totals			.284	210	726	100	206	51	1	22	112	96	109	3	1	.380	.448

30 JEFF AMES, RHP

BA GRADE **45** HIGH

Born: Jan. 31, 1991. **B-T:** R-R. **Ht.:** 6-4. **Wt.:** 225. **Drafted:** Lower Columbia (Wash.) CC, 2011 (1st round supplemental). **Signed by:** Paul Kirsch.

The 42nd overall selection in the 2011 draft, Ames had an unimpressive pro debut at Rookie-level Princeton but has made rapid adjustments while making the move from thrower to pitcher over the past two seasons. In the short-season New York-Penn League in 2012, he ranked third in ERA (1.96) and fourth in strikeouts (70) before pacing the low Class A Midwest League in opponent average (.210) and finishing second in WHIP (1.09) in 2013. Ames owes his success to his ability to command an above-average four-seam fastball that sits at 93-95 mph. He also throws a two-seam fastball in the 88-90 mph range, and a plus slider in the mid-80s, with all three offerings complementing each other. He continues to work on his changeup, which shows promise and could give him a strong four-pitch repertoire. The key to Ames' future success is continuing to work down in the zone by keeping his delivery tight and over his front leg. He also needs to trust his stuff and avoid overthrowing, which tends to flatten both of his fastballs.A candidate to be a mid-rotation starter, Ames should make the jump to high Class A Charlotte to open the 2014 campaign.

Year	Club (League)	Class	W	L	ERA	G	GS	CG	SV	IP	H	HR	BB	SO	K/9	WHIP	AVG
2011	Princeton (APP)	R	4	2	7.12	11	5	0	1	30	40	4	7	39	11.6	1.55	.317
2012	Hudson Valley (NYP)	SS	6	1	1.96	14	13	0	0	64	44	1	20	70	9.8	0.99	.195
2013	Bowling Green (MWL)	LoA	9	4	2.98	23	23	0	0	115	87	10	38	83	6.5	1.09	.210
Minor League Totals			19	7	3.27	48	41	0	1	209	171	15	65	192	8.3	1.13	.223

Texas Rangers

BY BEN BADLER

Few teams have had a more impressive four-year run than the Rangers. In each season from 2010-13, the Rangers have won at least 90 games, and they're tied with the Braves for the second-best record during that stretch, trailing only the Yankees.

Yet a 91-win season in 2013 still ended on a sour note. After the Rangers ended August in first place in the American League West, a 12-16 September dropped them into a three-way tie for the wild card. A 5-2 loss to the Rays in the Game No. 163 tiebreaker ended their season without a trip to the playoffs.

Despite the bitter aftertaste, the Rangers have still positioned themselves to be among the game's better teams going forward. The offseason trade that sent Ian Kinsler to the Tigers for Prince Fielder should provide a major upgrade for the Rangers at first base while clearing the way for Jurickson Profar to play every day at second base.

Entering his age-21 season, Profar has breakout potential to be a perennial all-star, giving Texas one of the best infields in baseball with Fielder at first, Elvis Andrus at shortstop and Adrian Beltre at third base.

While the farm system still is in solid shape, it's no longer elite, in part because some of that young talent has started to matriculate to the major leagues. Yet the team's inability to develop position players from the draft is a cause for concern. Since stumbling into Kinsler in the 17th round in 2003, the Rangers' only draft to deliver an impact position player was 2006, when they drafted Chris Davis (who only blossomed following a trade to the Orioles) and outfielder Craig Gentry, along with lefthander Derek Holland.

The Rangers hope their 2012 draft can reverse that trend, with a trio of hitters in third baseman Joey Gallo and outfielders Lewis Brinson and Nick Williams who teamed up in 2013 on a fascinating low Class A Hickory team filled with toolsy, high-risk players. The system would have been deeper had the Rangers not made the July 23 trade with the Cubs for Matt Garza that cost them prized righthander C.J. Edwards, along with third baseman Mike Olt and righthanders Justin Grimm and Neil Ramirez.

The international program led by A.J. Preller and Mike Daly is one of the most productive in baseball, yielding both high-end talent and depth, with most of their success coming outside the usual talent hotbed of the Dominican Republic. Yu Darvish has been the ace the Rangers expected, while Profar (Curacao), Leonys Martin (Cuba) and Martin Perez (Venezuela) have made their way to the majors.

ANDREW WOOLLEY

Trading Ian Kinsler clears the way for Jurickson Profar to take over at second base

TOP PROSPECTS OF THE DECADE

Year	Player, Pos.	2013 Org.
2004	Adrian Gonzalez, 1b	Dodgers
2005	Thomas Diamond, rhp	Out of baseball
2006	Edinson Volquez, rhp	Dodgers
2007	John Danks, lhp	White Sox
2008	Elvis Andrus, ss	Rangers
2009	Neftali Feliz, rhp	Rangers
2010	Neftali Feliz, rhp	Rangers
2011	Martin Perez, lhp	Rangers
2012	Jurickson Profar, ss	Rangers
2013	Jurickson Profar, ss	Rangers

Venezuelan second baseman Rougned Odor is the system's No. 1 prospect, and he, Profar and Perez have made it four straight years that a Rangers international signing takes the top spot. Colombian catcher Jorge Alfaro and Venezuelan shortstop Luis Sardinas also rank among the team's best prospects.

As soon as the 2013-14 international signing period opened, the Rangers blew past their bonus pool, landing Dominican righthander Marcos Diplan for $1.3 million and Dominican shortstop Yeyson Yrizarri for $1.35 million. Dominican outfielder Jose Almonte landed the team's biggest bonus ($1.8 million), though he was not a consensus top prospect.

ORGANIZATION OVERVIEW

General Manager: Jon Daniels. **Farm Director:** Tim Purpura. **Scouting Director:** A.J. Preller.

Class	Team	League	W	L	PCT	Finish	Manager
Majors	Texas Rangers	American	91	72	.558	6th (15)	Ron Washington
Triple-A	Round Rock Express	Pacific Coast	73	71	.507	8th (16)	Bobby Jones
Double-A	Frisco RoughRiders	Texas	70	70	.500	4th (8)	Steve Buechele
High Class A	Myrtle Beach Pelicans	Carolina	77	62	.554	2nd (8)	Jason Wood
Low Class A	Hickory Crawdads	South Atlantic	76	63	.547	5th (14)	Corey Ragsdale
Short-season	Spokane Indians	Northwest	38	38	.500	5th (8)	Tim Hulett
Rookie	AZL Rangers	Arizona	32	23	.582	3rd (13)	Kenny Holmberg
Overall 2013 Minor League Record			**366**	**327**	**.528**	**6th (30)**	

THIS YEAR'S TOP 30

No.	Player, Pos.	Grade
1.	Rougned Odor, 2b	60/Medium
2.	Jorge Alfaro, c	60/High
3.	Nick Williams, of	60/Extreme
4.	Joey Gallo, 3b	60/Extreme
5.	Alex Gonzalez, rhp	55/High
6.	Luis Sardinas, ss	50/Medium
7.	Luke Jackson, rhp	50/Medium
8.	Travis Demeritte, ss/3b	55/High
9.	Ronald Guzman, 1b	55/High
10.	Marcos Diplan, rhp	55/Extreme
11.	Akeem Bostick, rhp	55/Extreme
12.	Nick Martinez, rhp	50/Medium
13.	Yeyson Yrizarri, ss	55/Extreme
14.	Alec Asher, rhp	50/High
15.	Lewis Brinson, of	55/Extreme
16.	Jose Leclerc	50/High
17.	Jairo Beras, of	55/Extreme
18.	Keone Kela	45/Medium
19.	David Ledbetter, rhp	50/High
20.	Lisalverto Bonilla	45/Medium
21.	Drew Robinson, 3b	45/Medium
22.	Ryan Rua, 2b/3b	45/High
23.	Ben Rowen, rhp	40/Low
24.	Nomar Mazara, of	50/Extreme
25.	Engel Beltre, of	40/Low
26.	Wilmer Font, rhp	40/Low
27.	Alexander Claudio, lhp	40/Medium
28.	Kellin Deglan, c	45/High
29.	Roman Mendez, rhp	45/High
30.	Kelvin Vasquez, rhp	45/High

LAST YEAR'S TOP 30

No.	Player, Pos.	Grade
1.	Jurickson Profar, ss/2b	Majors
2.	Mike Olt, 3b/1b	(Cubs)
3.	Martin Perez, lhp	Majors
4.	Leonys Martin, of	Majors
5.	Justin Grimm, rhp	Majors
6.	Luke Jackson, rhp	No. 7
7.	Luis Sardinas, ss/2b	No. 6
8.	Cody Buckel, rhp	Dropped out
9.	Jorge Alfaro, c/1b	No. 2
10.	Joey Gallo, 3b	No. 4
11.	Rougned Odor, 2b/ss	No. 1
12.	Lewis Brinson, of	No. 15
13.	Roman Mendez, rhp	No. 29
14.	C.J. Edwards, rhp	(Cubs)
15.	Hanser Alberto, ss/3b	Dropped out
16.	Nomar Mazara, of	No. 24
17.	Ronald Guzman, 1b	No. 9
18.	Jairo Beras, of	No. 17
19.	Nick Tepesch, rhp	Majors
20.	Leury Garcia, 2b/ss	(White Sox)
21.	Drew Robinson, 3b/2b	No. 21
22.	Wilmer Font, rhp	No. 26
23.	Neil Ramirez, rhp	(Cubs)
24.	Zach Cone, of	Dropped out
25.	Nick Williams, of	No. 3
26.	Keone Kela, rhp	No. 18
27.	Nick Martinez, rhp	No. 12
28.	Matt West, rhp	Dropped out
29.	Randy Henry, rhp	Dropped out
30.	Joe Ortiz, lhp	Majors

BEST TOOLS

Best Hitter for Average	Rougned Odor
Best Power Hitter	Joey Gallo
Best Strike-Zone Discipline	Drew Robinson
Fastest Baserunner	Chris Garia
Best Athlete	Lewis Brinson
Best Fastball	Keone Kela
Best Curveball	Nick Martinez
Best Slider	Alex Gonzalez
Best Changeup	Alexander Claudio
Best Control	Alex Gonzalez
Best Defensive Catcher	Pat Cantwell
Best Defensive Infielder	Luis Sardinas
Best Infield Arm	Joey Gallo
Best Defensive Outfielder	Lewis Brinson
Best Outfield Arm	Preston Beck

TOP 15 PLAYERS 25 AND UNDER

No.	Player, Pos. (Age)	Peak Level
1.	Jurickson Profar, ss (21)	Majors
2.	Elvis Andrus, ss (25)	Majors
3.	Rougned Odor, 2b (20)	Double-A
4.	Martin Perez, lhp (22)	Majors
5.	Neftali Feliz, rhp (25)	Majors
6.	Jorge Alfaro, c (20)	High Class A
7.	Nick Williams, of (20)	Low Class A
8.	Joey Gallo, 3b (20)	Low Class A
9.	Alex Gonzalez, rhp (22)	High Class A
10.	Robbie Ross, lhp (24)	Majors
11.	Luis Sardinas, ss (20)	Double-A
12.	Luke Jackson, rhp (22)	Double-A
13.	Nick Tepesch, rhp (25)	Majors
14.	Travis Demeritte, ss (19)	Rookie
15.	Ronald Guzman, 1b (19)	Low Class A

MINOR LEAGUE DEPTH CHART

TEXAS RANGERS

TOP 2014 ROOKIE: Lisalverto Bonilla, rhp: He ran into trouble in Triple-A in 2013, but his fastball/changeup combination gives him a pair of plus pitches to miss bats and get groundballs out of the bullpen.

BREAKOUT PROSPECT: Jose Leclerc, rhp: The Rangers have developed Leclerc as a reliever, but they are toying with the idea of giving him a chance to start, as some scouts think he has mid-rotation potential.

SLEEPER: Michael de Leon, ss. A Dominican shortstop signed in July 2013 for $550,000, de Leon projects as a middle infielder with good bat-to-ball skills.

SOURCE OF TOP 30 TALENT			
Homegrown	**27**	**Acquired**	**3**
College	5	Trades	3
Junior college	2	Rule 5 draft	0
High school	9	Independent leagues	0
Nondrafted free agents	0	Free agents/waivers	0
International	11		

LF

Nick Williams (3)
Jim Adduci
Eduard Pinto

CF

Lewis Brinson (15)
Engel Beltre (25)
Rafael Ortega
Todd McDonald
Chris Garia
Zach Cone
Jake Skole

RF

Jairo Beras (17)
Nomar Mazara (24)
Jose Almonte
Ronny Carvajal
Preston Beck
Ryan Cordell

3B

Joey Gallo (4)
Yeyson Yrizarri (13)
Drew Robinson (21)
Juremi Profar

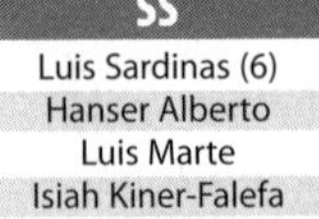

SS

Luis Sardinas (6)
Hanser Alberto
Luis Marte
Isiah Kiner-Falefa

2B

Rougned Odor (1)
Travis Demeritte (8)
Ryan Rua (22)
Michael de Leon
Odubel Herrera
Brallan Perez

1B

Ronald Guzman (9)
Chris McGuiness
Brett Nicholas

C

Jorge Alfaro (2)
Kellin Deglan (28)
Pat Cantwell
Tomas Telis
Joe Jackson
Carlos Garay

LHP

LHSP	LHRP
Victor Payano	Alexander Claudio (27)
Yohander Mendez	Jimmy Reyes
Luis Parra	

RHP

RHSP	RHRP
Alex Gonzalez (5)	Jose Leclerc (16)
Luke Jackson (7)	Keone Kela (18)
Marcos Diplan (10)	Lisalverto Bonilla (20)
Akeem Bostick (11)	Ben Rowen (23)
Nick Martinez (12)	Wilmer Font (26)
Alec Asher (14)	Roman Mendez (29)
David Ledbetter (19)	Kelvin Vasquez (30)
Cody Buckel	Cole Wiper
Ariel Jurado	Ryan Harvey
Omarlin Lopez	Sam Wolff
David Perez	Cory Burns
Collin Wiles	Matt West
Kevin Sosa	Chaz Roe
Luke Lanphere	
Edgar Arredondo	
Cole Wiper	
Jerad Eickhoff	
Connor Sadzeck	

DRAFT ANALYSIS

2013

BONUSES: $6.8 MILLION

BEST PURE HITTER: In a pitching-heavy draft, the Rangers were able to land a potentially premium bat in SS Travis Demeritte (1). Demeritte has above-average bat speed and an understanding of how to set up pitchers. 2B Evan Van Hoosier (8) is limited defensively, but it's hard to sneak a fastball by him.

BEST POWER HITTER: Demeritte has a chance to hit 20 or more home runs thanks to his bat speed and hands that whip the bat through the zone.

FASTEST RUNNER: Van Hoosier is an above-average runner at his best. OF Ryan Cordell (11) probably would lose a footrace to Van Hoosier, but his speed plays better on the basepaths.

BEST DEFENSIVE PLAYER: SS Isiah Kiner-Falefa (4) should be able to stay at the position thanks to excellent all-around skills. He makes all the routine plays, displays soft hands and good footwork, shows an accurate arm and has an excellent internal clock.

BEST FASTBALL: RHP Sam Wolff (6) touched 100 mph coming out of the bullpen this summer. RHP Alex Gonzalez (1) flashed 96 mph as a starter. RHP Akeem Bostic already touches 94 mph with some projection left in his arm.

BEST SECONDARY PITCH: Gonzalez's slider almost seems like two different pitches at times, as he can throw a harder 88-90 mph pitch with cutting action and a bigger-breaking 84-86 mph ball with more depth. RHP David Ledbetter (3) has the best curveball among the draft class.

BEST PRO DEBUT: Wolff went 4-0, 0.60 with five saves in 30 innings between short-season Spokane and low Class A Hickory. Demeritte finished second in the Rookie-level Arizona League with a .411 OBP.

BEST ATHLETE: Bostic played football, basketball and baseball in high school and would have had opportunities to play football in college if he had not made it clear that baseball was his primary sport.

MOST INTRIGUING BACKGROUND: C Joe Jackson (5) is the great-great-great nephew of Shoeless Joe Jackson. RHPs David (3) and Ryan Ledbetter (19) are identical twins who became the first players ever drafted from Ohio's Cedarville College.

CLOSEST TO THE MAJORS: Both Gonzalez and Wolff could fly through the system as relievers, but both will be given chances to start.

BEST LATE-ROUND PICK: The Rangers drafted late-blooming RHP Lucas Lanphere (21) on area scout Steve Flores' recommendation, then signed him for $400,000 after a post-draft workout. His velocity jumped 5 mph in the past year, giving him a 90-92 mph fastball with a projectable 6-foot-2 frame.

THE ONE WHO GOT AWAY: As an all-state basketball player, 6-foot-7 RHP Jackson Lamb (20) already shows a low-90s fastball at his best, and he has lots of projection. He and the Rangers never came close to a deal, so he headed to Michigan.

ASSESSMENT: Scouting director Kip Fagg has never been shy about taking chances to try to land impact players. After loading up on toolsy position players in 2011 and 2012, the Rangers loaded up on arms this time around.

2012

BONUSES: $7.4 MILLION

Watch this fascinating boom-or-bust class. So far, OF Nick Williams (3) and minor league home run king Joey Gallo (1s) stand out. RHPs Alec Asher (4), Keone Kela (12) have upside on the mound

GRADE: B+

2011

BONUSES: $4.2 MILLION

Texas found three solid RHPs, dealing two to the Cubs: C.J. Edwards (48) and Kyle Hendricks (8). Nick Martinez (18) broke out for the Rangers.

GRADE: C

2010

BONUSES: $8.5 MILLION

Three picks have reached the majors, with 3B Mike Olt (1s) and RHP Justin Grimm (5) now Cubs. RHP Nick Tepesch (14) pitched 93 innings as a 2013 rookie. RHP Luke Jackson (1s) is refining his power stuff.

GRADE: A

TOP DRAFT PICKS OF THE DECADE

Year	Player, Pos.	2013 Org.
2004	Thomas Diamond, rhp	Out of baseball
2005	John Mayberry Jr., of	Phillies
2006	Kasey Kiker, lhp	Out of baseball
2007	Blake Beavan, rhp	Mariners
2008	Justin Smoak, 1b	Mariners
2009	*Matt Purke, lhp	Nationals
2010	Jake Skole, of	Rangers
2011	Kevin Matthews, lhp	Rangers
2012	Lewis Brinson, of	Rangers
2013	Alex Gonzalez, rhp	Rangers

*Did not sign

LARGEST BONUSES IN CLUB HISTORY

Leonys Martin, 2011	$5,000,000
Nomar Mazara, 2011	$4,950,000
Mark Teixeira, 2001	$4,500,000
Jairo Beras, 2012	$4,500,000
Justin Smoak, 2008	$3,500,000

1 ROUGNED ODOR, 2B

Born: Feb. 3, 1994. **B-T:** L-R. **Ht.:** 5-11. **Wt.:** 170.
Signed: Venezuela, 2011.
Signed by: Rafic Saab/Mike Daly.

RIDERS
BA GRADE
60
MEDIUM
SCOUTING GRADES
BATTING 70
POWER 50
SPEED 50
DEFENSE 50
ARM 50

ANDREW WOOLLEY

Before becoming eligible to sign on July 2, 2010, Odor had already demonstrated his advanced offensive ability while representing Venezuela at international tournaments. He spent time in Florida training with Miguel Nava, the former Diamondbacks scout who signed Venezuelan outfielders Carlos Gonzalez and Gerardo Parra when he was with Arizona. While Odor stood out for his sweet swing, game performance and baseball savvy, his small stature, ordinary-at-best speed and the consensus that he would have to move off shortstop turned off some teams. Those who liked him balked at his seven-figure asking price, which kept Odor unsigned months after the international signing period opened. Mike Daly, who at the time was the Rangers' international scouting director, went to Florida in December 2010 to see Odor again. After he showed he had shaved his 60-yard dash time down to 6.7 seconds, the Rangers signed him for $425,000 in January 2011. Odor has rocketed through the system, reaching Double-A Frisco in August 2013 and hitting .306 with six homers in 30 games as a 19-year-old.

The nephew of Indians high Class A Carolina hitting coach Rouglas Odor, Rougned has the swing, quiet hitting approach and instincts to develop into an all-star second baseman. His lefty swing is easy, compact and fluid, with quick hands and plenty of bat speed to catch up to premium velocity. He has good hand-eye coordination and can manipulate the bat head, which helps him drive breaking pitches. Odor has surprising power for his size with the ability to drive the ball to all fields. He'll likely top out at slightly-above-average power, with the potential for 15 home runs or more per year. Focusing on nutrition and strength helped keep him strong toward the end of the 2013 season despite his youth, helping him to flourish when he got to Double-A. Odor is an average runner who reads pitchers well, which makes him a more prolific basestealer than his raw speed would suggest. He isn't an average defender yet but should become one in time. He's adept at turning the double play, with a quick exchange, average arm strength and a fearless attitude with runners barreling in on him. He's still smoothing out his footwork and learning to cut down on mental lapses—often stemming from pre-pitch preparation—that will make him better at making the routine play. Rangers officials frequently talk about the hard-nosed Odor playing with a chip on his shoulder.

With Elvis Andrus cemented at shortstop and Jurickson Profar expected to take over at second base, Odor's path to the majors isn't clear. The offseason trade that sent Ian Kinsler to the Tigers for Prince Fielder helped alleviate some of the congestion, but with two young impact middle infielders ahead of him, Odor's future could be with another organization. He likely will open 2014 back in Frisco, with a chance to move up to Triple-A Round Rock quickly.

Year	Club (League)	Class	AVG	G	AB	R	H	2B	3B	HR	RBI	BB	SO	SB	CS	OBP	SLG
2011	Spokane (NWL)	SS	.262	58	233	33	61	9	3	2	29	13	37	10	4	.323	.352
2012	Hickory (SAL)	LoA	.259	109	432	60	112	23	4	10	47	25	65	19	10	.313	.400
2013	Myrtle Beach (CAR)	HiA	.305	100	377	65	115	33	4	5	59	26	67	27	8	.369	.454
	Frisco (TL)	AA	.306	30	134	20	41	8	2	6	19	9	24	5	2	.354	.530
Minor League Totals			.280	297	1176	178	329	73	13	23	154	73	193	61	24	.338	.423

2 JORGE ALFARO, C

Born: June 11, 1993. **B-T:** R-R. **Ht.:** 6-2. **Wt.:** 185. **Signed:** Colombia, 2010. **Signed by:** Rodolfo Rosario/Don Welke.

Alfaro worked out for teams as a shortstop and third baseman in Colombia, but he moved behind the plate and started training in the Dominican Republic before signing with Texas for $1.3 million in January 2010. Alfaro caught just 29 games in 2012 due to hamstring and shoulder issues, but he spent most of 2013 behind the plate while repeating at low Class A Hickory, though he did miss about a month in July with a broken left hand. He has a 70 arm and is an outstanding athlete for a catcher, producing pop times as low as 1.8 seconds. Alfaro's blocking and receiving remain raw. His footwork and lateral movement improved last season, as did his in-game focus, but they still need work after allowing 28 passed balls in 86 games. He doesn't have a prototype catcher's body and is one of the fastest catchers in baseball, a legitimate 50 runner. Alfaro has good bat speed and plus power, though he's a free-swinger whose stroke can get long, resulting in low contact and walk rates. He has the upside to be a low on-base, power-hitting catcher with the arm strength to shut down a running game, and he thrived in the Arizona Fall League. He'll head back to high Class A Myrtle Beach in 2014.

Year	Club (League)	Class	AVG	G	AB	R	H	2B	3B	HR	RBI	BB	SO	SB	CS	OBP	SLG
2010	Rangers (DSL)	R	.221	48	172	18	38	5	2	1	23	5	48	1	4	.278	.291
2011	Spokane (NWL)	SS	.300	45	160	18	48	9	1	6	23	4	54	1	0	.345	.481
2012	Hickory (SAL)	LoA	.261	74	272	40	71	21	5	5	34	16	84	7	3	.320	.430
2013	Rangers (AZL)	R	.429	6	21	5	w9	2	0	2	8	2	6	2	0	.500	.810
	Hickory (SAL)	LoA	.258	104	372	63	96	22	1	16	53	28	111	16	3	.338	.452
	Myrtle Beach (CAR)	HiA	.182	3	11	4	2	0	0	0	0	2	5	0	0	.308	.182
Minor League Totals			.262	280	1008	148	264	59	9	30	141	57	308	27	10	.328	.428

3 NICK WILLIAMS, OF

Born: Sept. 8, 1993. **B-T:** L-L. **Ht.:** 6-3. **Wt.:** 195. **Drafted:** HS—Galveston, Texas, 2012 (2nd round). **Signed by:** Jay Heafner.

Williams slid to the second round of the 2012 draft after an inconsistent senior season. After missing a month early in 2013 when he hurt his shoulder making a diving catch, Williams finished third in the low Class A South Atlantic League in slugging (.543). He has natural hitting actions, an easy lefthanded swing and lightning hand speed. While his swing doesn't generate a ton of loft, Williams produces above-average raw power with his strength and bat speed, clubbing an equal number of home runs to left and right field. He seldom pops up a ball and makes consistently hard contact when he connects, but he has a high strikeout rate and rarely walks. He's a free-swinger easily fooled by soft stuff, which throws off his balance and causes his swing to get long. Williams' home-to-first times don't reflect it, but he's a plus runner and led the SAL with 12 triples. With Lewis Brinson in center field, he played left and will probably stay there, though the Rangers could experiment with him in center. He has an average arm. Williams has the physical gifts to be an everyday corner outfielder, but he'll have to become a more selective hitter. He'll jump to high Class A Myrtle Beach in 2014.

Year	Club (League)	Class	AVG	G	AB	R	H	2B	3B	HR	RBI	BB	SO	SB	CS	OBP	SLG
2012	Rangers (AZL)	R	.313	48	201	34	63	9	6	2	27	16	50	15	2	.375	.448
2013	Hickory (SAL)	LoA	.293	95	376	70	110	19	12	17	60	15	110	8	5	.337	.543
Minor League Totals			.300	143	577	104	173	28	18	19	87	31	160	23	7	.350	.510

4 JOEY GALLO, 3B

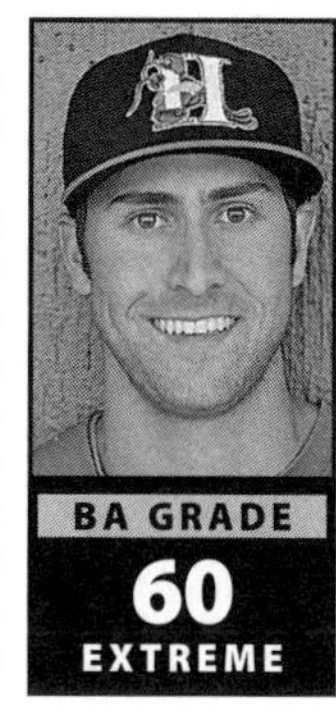

Born: Nov. 19, 1993. **B-T:** L-R. **Ht.:** 6-5. **Wt.:** 205. **Drafted:** HS—Las Vegas, 2012 (1st round supplemental). **Signed by:** Todd Guggiana.

After Gallo set a Nevada high school record with 65 career home runs, the Rangers drafted him with the No. 39 pick in 2012 and signed him for $2.25 million. In his pro debut, he set a Rookie-level Arizona League record with 18 homers and was named its MVP. In his first full season in 2013, Gallo led the minors with 40 home runs despite missing most of July with a groin injury. He has one of the most extreme skill sets in baseball. Scouts gush about him having the best raw power in the minors, with veteran scouts and managers consistently remarking that Gallo hits balls unlike anyone they've seen at his age, with tremendous backspin, loft, leverage and quick-twitch bat speed. He has the potential for another 40-homer season, but the question is whether that's going to come in the majors or in Japan. Gallo struck out in an alarming 37 percent of his plate appearances at low Class A Hickory, with long arms and a long swing that create serious contact issues, especially against high heat or soft stuff off the plate. He walked in 11 percent of his trips to the plate, so he's not a total hacker. Despite below-average speed, Gallo is a smart baserunner who goes well from first to third. He has a plus arm and solid hands, so the Rangers want to keep him at third base. But with his lack of range, first-step quickness and footwork issues, his future more likely is in an outfield corner or first base. Gallo could become anything from Mike Hessman to Russ Branyan to Chris Davis, with a high-risk, high-reward skill set that makes him one of the game's most fascinating prospects. He'll continue at high Class A Myrtle Beach in 2014.

Year	Club (League)	Class	AVG	G	AB	R	H	2B	3B	HR	RBI	BB	SO	SB	CS	OBP	SLG
2012	Rangers (AZL)	R	.293	43	150	44	44	10	1	18	43	37	52	6	0	.435	.733
	Spokane (NWL)	SS	.214	16	56	9	12	2	0	4	9	11	26	0	0	.343	.464
2013	Rangers (AZL)	R	.368	5	19	4	7	4	0	2	10	2	7	1	0	.429	.895
	Hickory (SAL)	LoA	.245	106	392	82	96	19	5	38	78	48	165	14	1	.334	.610
Minor League Totals			.258	170	617	139	159	35	6	62	140	98	250	21	1	.365	.635

5 ALEX GONZALEZ, RHP

BA GRADE
55
HIGH

Born: Jan. 15, 1992. **B-T:** R-R. **Ht.:** 6-2. **Wt.:** 195. **Drafted:** Oral Roberts, 2013 (1st round). **Signed by:** Jay Eddings.

An unsigned Orioles 11th-round pick out of high school in 2010, Gonzalez's draft stock jumped after a dominant junior season at Oral Roberts, becoming the school's best prospect since righthander Mike Moore went No. 1 overall to the Mariners in 1981. With two first-round picks in 2013, the Rangers' used their top selection (No. 23 overall) on Gonzalez, who signed for $2.215 million. He reached high Class A Myrtle Beach in his pro debut, though he looked a little run down at the end of the year. Gonzalez is a strike-thrower with a sound delivery who uses both sides of the plate with two above-average pitches, including a lively 90-94 mph fastball. He can cut and sink his fastball, resulting in an abundance of groundballs. Once Gonzalez gets to two strikes, he uses his plus slider as a put-away pitch. He can manipulate the speed of his slider, cranking it up to 87 mph with sharp bite to finish hitters or dialing it down for a strike earlier in the count. His changeup has improved, flashing average at times, and he'll sprinkle in an occasional show-me curveball as well. Gonzalez has the makings of a potential No. 3 starter who shouldn't need too much time in the minors. He'll likely start 2014 at high Class A Myrtle Beach, but he has a chance to be in Double-A quickly and reach Texas by 2015.

Year	Club (League)	Class	W	L	ERA	G	GS	CG	SV	IP	H	HR	BB	SO	K/9	WHIP	AVG
2013	Spokane (NWL)	SS	0	4	4.56	9	9	0	0	24	30	1	7	20	7.6	1.56	.313
	Myrtle Beach (CAR)	HiA	0	0	2.84	5	5	0	0	19	15	1	9	15	7.1	1.26	.221
Minor League Totals			0	4	3.80	14	14	0	0	43	45	2	16	35	7.4	1.43	.274

6 LUIS SARDINAS, SS

BA GRADE
50
MEDIUM

Born: May 16, 1993. **B-T:** B-R. **Ht.:** 6-1. **Wt.:** 170. **Signed:** Venezuela, 2009. **Signed by:** Mike Daly/Rafic Saab/Pedro Avila.

The Rangers signed Jurickson Profar from Curacao and Sardinas from Venezuela on July 2, 2009, with Sardinas commanding a $1.2 million bonus. While Profar zipped through the system, a slew of injuries cut Sardinas' 2010-12 seasons short. After adding strength to his skinny frame, Sardinas stayed healthy in 2013 and reached Double-A Frisco in August as a 20-year-old. He has spent the last two seasons moving through the system with double-play partner Rougned Odor. While Odor has more offensive upside, Sardinas is the superior defender. A 70 runner with good range and an above-average arm, he's light on his feet and is adept at charging balls and making the instinctive play. He has all the tools to be an above-average defender, though like many young shortstops he still tends to lose focus and make errors on routine plays. Sardinas has minimal power, so he plays a contact-oriented game at the plate, hitting line drives to all fields and keeping the ball on the ground. He has good bat-to-ball skills and solid plate discipline, so he could hit for a high average. Sardinas was in over his head when he got to Double-A, so he should return to Frisco to start 2014. He has the defense and contact skills to be an everyday shortstop, but the development of his plate patience and strength will determine whether he hits at the top or bottom of the lineup, or whether he fits better as a utility man.

Year	Club (League)	Class	AVG	G	AB	R	H	2B	3B	HR	RBI	BB	SO	SB	CS	OBP	SLG
2010	Rangers (AZL)	R	.311	26	103	22	32	4	0	0	8	7	15	8	2	.363	.350
2011	Rangers (AZL)	R	.308	14	52	11	16	2	1	0	7	4	10	2	1	.367	.385
2012	Hickory (SAL)	LoA	.291	96	374	65	109	14	2	2	30	29	52	32	9	.346	.356
2013	Myrtle Beach (CAR)	HiA	.298	97	383	69	114	15	3	1	31	32	54	27	8	.358	.360
	Frisco (TL)	AA	.259	29	135	12	35	4	0	1	15	4	21	5	2	.286	.311
Minor League Totals			.292	262	1047	179	306	39	6	4	91	76	152	74	22	.346	.352

7 LUKE JACKSON, RHP

Born: Aug. 24, 1991. **B-T:** R-R. **Ht.:** 6-2. **Wt.:** 185. **Drafted:** HS—Fort Lauderdale, 2010 (1st round supplemental). **Signed by:** Juan Alvarez.

The Rangers tend to be aggressive with their prospect assignments, but Jackson has moved along at a steady pace since signing out of high school in 2010 as the No. 45 overall pick. He didn't log an ERA under 4.00 in either of his first two seasons, but he broke out in 2013, reaching Double-A Frisco in August shortly before his 22nd birthday. Jackson challenges hitters aggressively with his best pitch, a fastball that sits at 90-95 mph and reaches 97 with downhill angle. He throws a hard curveball that is inconsistent but got better toward the end of the season. His gets short with his breaking ball at times, and when he overthrows it can come out looking like a slider. His changeup was a point of emphasis this season, as it's still his No. 3 pitch and usually below-average, though it will flash average at times. Jackson has long arm action, which hinders his secondary pitches and his control, evident in his walk rate of 4.1 per nine innings in 2013. Jackson likely will return to Double-A to open 2014, where he'll focus on bringing along his offspeed stuff and throwing more strikes to reach his potential as a back-end starter, though some scouts see him better suited for bullpen work.

Year	Club (League)	Class	W	L	ERA	G	GS	CG	SV	IP	H	HR	BB	SO	K/9	WHIP	AVG
2011	Hickory (SAL)	LoA	5	6	5.64	19	19	0	0	75	83	9	48	78	9.4	1.75	.276
2012	Hickory (SAL)	LoA	5	5	4.92	13	13	1	0	64	63	4	33	72	10.1	1.50	.259
	Myrtle Beach (CAR)	HiA	5	2	4.39	13	13	0	0	66	67	2	32	74	10.1	1.51	.273
2013	Myrtle Beach (CAR)	HiA	9	4	2.41	19	19	0	0	101	79	6	47	104	9.3	1.25	.216
	Frisco (TL)	AA	2	0	0.67	6	4	0	0	27	13	0	12	30	10.0	0.93	.144
Minor League Totals			26	17	3.87	70	68	1	0	333	305	21	172	358	9.7	1.43	.245

8 TRAVIS DEMERITTE, SS/3B

Born: Sept. 30, 1994. **B-T:** R-R. **Ht.:** 6-0. **Wt.:** 178. **Drafted:** HS—Winder, Ga., 2013 (1st round). **Signed by:** Derrick Tucker.

The Rangers had two first-round picks in the 2013 draft, including the No. 30 overall pick as compensation for losing free agent Josh Hamilton to the Angels. Texas used that pick on Demeritte, who pitched and played shortstop for his Georgia high school team, and signed him for $1.9 million. His bat is his calling card, with extremely quick hands that enable him to buggy-whip the bat through the zone. He's a quick-twitch athlete with excellent bat speed, so he could grow into average or better power once he gets stronger, though for now he mostly stays gap to gap. Demeritte draws plenty of walks, though for a player whose bat is supposed to be his carrying tool, he struck out at a surprising 28 percent clip in his debut. A shortstop in high school, Demeritte also played third base in about one-third of his games in the Rookie-level Arizona League. He doesn't profile as a true shortstop, so during instructional league the Rangers had him focus on second base. He's an average runner with an above-average arm. The Rangers like to give their infielders the opportunity to move around the diamond, but Demeritte probably will take most of his reps at second in 2014. He's in the mix to open the year at low Class A Hickory.

Year	Club (League)	Class	AVG	G	AB	R	H	2B	3B	HR	RBI	BB	SO	SB	CS	OBP	SLG
2013	Rangers (AZL)	R	.285	39	144	31	41	5	3	4	20	29	49	5	1	.411	.444
Minor League Totals			.285	39	144	31	41	5	3	4	20	29	49	5	1	.411	.444

9 RONALD GUZMAN, 1B

Born: Oct. 20, 1994. **B-T:** L-L. **Ht.:** 6-5. **Wt.:** 205. **Signed:** Dominican Republic, 2011. **Signed by:** Willy Espinal/Mike Daly.

When the Rangers signed Guzman for $3.45 million on July 2, 2011, several teams had him as either the top prospect or the top hitter available that year in Latin America. Surgery in March 2013 to repair a torn right meniscus in his knee delayed his low Class A Hickory debut for two months, and a pitch that struck him on the right hand ended his season on July 30. Guzman has a polished hitting approach for his age. Despite his long arms, he stays inside the ball well with a simple approach and minimal unnecessary movement in his setup. His head stays locked in, which helps him recognize pitches and stay within his strike zone. He has good hand-eye coordination and a direct, line-drive swing to all fields, which leads to a high contact rate. Guzman can take the ball over the fence in batting practice, but he's more content with a hit-first, power-second approach in games. More strength should lead to a power increase, though he's not a quick-twitch guy and doesn't have the bat speed some scouts would like from a first baseman. Signed as a lead-footed outfielder, Guzman immediately moved to first base, where his size gives infielders greater margin for error. He's limber and flexible, with the ability to pick balls in the dirt. He earns rave reviews for his makeup, aptitude and intelligence. If Guzman can grow into above-average game power, he has the potential to be a middle-of-the-order force given his contact and on-base skills. Due to the time he missed, Guzman probably will return to Hickory in 2014.

Year	Club (League)	Class	AVG	G	AB	R	H	2B	3B	HR	RBI	BB	SO	SB	CS	OBP	SLG
2012	Rangers (AZL)	R	.321	52	212	29	68	15	3	1	33	19	42	7	1	.374	.434
2013	Hickory (SAL)	LoA	.272	49	173	17	47	8	0	4	26	11	27	0	0	.325	.387
Minor League Totals			.299	101	385	46	115	23	3	5	59	30	69	7	1	.352	.413

10 MARCOS DIPLAN, RHP

BA GRADE **55** EXTREME

Born: Sept. 18, 1996. **B-T:** R-R. **Ht.:** 5-10. **Wt.:** 160. **Signed:** Dominican Republic, 2013. **Signed by:** Willy Espinal/Mike Daly.

Diplan trained with Luis Polonia in the Dominican Republic, where he separated himself as the top pitcher on the international market for 2013 after throwing two perfect innings with three strikeouts at an MLB showcase in January. When he became eligible to sign on July 2, the Rangers signed him for $1.3 million. At 17, Diplan already flashes three average or better pitches. Before signing, he sat at 89-92 mph and peaked at 94, then at instructional league he hit 96. While Diplan has a small 5-foot-10 frame, he has terrific arm speed, so there could be more velocity coming. His curveball has good depth and rotation, giving him another potentially above-average pitch. He hasn't needed to use his changeup much, but it's flashed average at times. Diplan has some effort and herky-jerky action in his delivery, which leads him to lose his release point and causes inconsistent control. His size leads some teams to question whether he may fit better in the bullpen, but he has the arsenal to remain a starter. He earns praise from scouts for his hard-nosed, competitive attitude. Diplan is the most exciting Latin American pitcher the Rangers have signed since Martin Perez. They expect him to make his pro debut in 2014 in the Rookie-level Arizona League.

Year	Club (League)	Class	W	L	ERA	G	GS	CG	SV	IP	H	HR	BB	SO	K/9	WHIP	AVG
2013	Did not play—Signed 2014 contract																

11 AKEEM BOSTICK, RHP

BA GRADE **55** EXTREME

Born: May 4, 1995. **B-T:** R-R. **Ht.:** 6-4. **Wt.:** 180. **Drafted:** HS—West Florence, S.C., 2013 (2nd round). **Signed by:** Chris Kemp.

A three-sport athlete in high school with athletic bloodlines, Bostick's cousin Brandon plays tight end for the Green Bay Packers. Scouts considered Bostick a raw project coming out of high school, but he had a strong pro debut in the Rookie-level Arizona League after signing with the Rangers for $520,600 in the second round (62nd overall) of the 2013 draft. His athleticism and long, lanky frame offer plenty of physical projection, with a fastball that sat at 90-94 mph before the draft and tickled 96 in the AZL. Bostick is fairly polished mechanically with good balance in his delivery, which contributes to him having good control of his fastball. He delivers the ball with downhill angle and has deception, making it a challenge for hitters to square up his fastball. The key for Bostick will be the development of his secondary pitches. He's shown improved ability to spin a breaking ball over the past year and he'll snap off some average ones at times, but he's still working to define the pitch. He never threw his changeup much in high school, so it's still a work in progress. Bostick should graduate to low Class A Hickory in 2014.

Year	Club (League)	Class	W	L	ERA	G	GS	CG	SV	IP	H	HR	BB	SO	K/9	WHIP	AVG
2013	Rangers (AZL)	R	4	1	2.83	14	6	0	1	41	42	0	12	33	7.2	1.31	.264
Minor League Totals			4	1	2.83	14	6	0	1	41	42	0	12	33	7.2	1.31	.264

12 NICK MARTINEZ, RHP

BA GRADE **50** MEDIUM

Born: Aug. 5, 1990. **B-T:** L-R. **Ht.:** 6-1. **Wt.:** 175. **Drafted:** Fordham, 2011 (18th round). **Signed by:** Jay Heafner.

Primarily a shortstop during his three years at Fordham, Martinez pitched just 26 relief innings in college, but the Rangers saw a future on the mound when they took an 18th-round flier on him in 2011. After showing inconsistent velocity early in 2013, Martinez sat 89-94 mph by the summer and touched 95 with sneaky life, as it runs in on righthanders. He throws a solid-average curveball from 76-80 mph with 12-to-6 action, and his high arm slot makes it challenging for hitters to recognize the pitch out of his hand. Martinez entered the season with a fringy changeup but showed more feel for it in 2013, developing it into an average pitch with good sink and deception to become a swing-and-miss pitch at times at 82-84 mph. Martinez has a short stride and his delivery isn't the smoothest, but it's repeatable and he's a good athlete who fills up the zone with plenty of strikes. His solid three-pitch mix and knack for generating groundballs could make him a No. 4 starter with an outside chance to reach Texas in 2014, though he's probably destined for Double-A Frisco to begin the year.

Year	Club (League)	Class	W	L	ERA	G	GS	CG	SV	IP	H	HR	BB	SO	K/9	WHIP	AVG
2011	Rangers (AZL)	R	2	1	1.83	6	4	0	0	20	21	0	2	19	8.7	1.17	.266
	Spokane (NWL)	SS	1	2	2.54	9	7	0	0	39	37	0	16	37	8.5	1.36	.252
2012	Hickory (SAL)	LoA	8	6	4.83	31	20	0	1	117	121	8	37	109	8.4	1.35	.265
2013	Myrtle Beach (CAR)	HiA	10	7	2.87	22	21	1	0	119	106	5	38	105	7.9	1.21	.236
	Frisco (TL)	AA	2	0	1.13	5	4	0	0	32	11	1	7	23	6.5	0.56	.107
Minor League Totals			23	16	3.30	73	56	1	1	327	296	14	100	293	8.1	1.21	.239

13 YEYSON YRIZARRI, SS

BA GRADE **55** EXTREME

Born: Feb. 2, 1997. **B-T:** R-R. **Ht.:** 6-0. **Wt.:** 175. **Signed:** Dominican Republic, 2013. **Signed by:** Roberto Aquino/Gil Kim.

Though Yrizarri was born in Venezuela, he was raised in the Dominican Republic, where he trained before signing with the Rangers for $1.35 million on July 2, 2013. His uncle is Deivi Cruz, who served as regular shortstop for four different teams in a nine-year big league career, and his aunt played on the Dominican national softball team. Yrizarri's older brother Deibi is a righthander in the Nationals system. Coming into 2013, Yrizarri wasn't expected to be one of the premium prospects available, but his stock shot up after a handful of teams took strong interest in him. Yrizarri sets his hands up a little lower than most players and has a quick, loose swing with good bat path. Scouts highest on him saw him hit in games and use the middle of the field with a solid approach. He has big hands, strong forearms and puts the ball in play with gap power and occasional home run pop to his pull side, though that can get him in trouble at times when he gets to his front side too early and becomes pull-oriented. Yrizari has a wide, athletic physique and lacks the first-step quickness for shortstop, though he'll probably start his career there. He has a 70 arm and he's an average runner. He could fit at either second or third base, with a pro debut likely to come in the Rookie-level Arizona League in 2014.

Year	Club (League)	Class	AVG	G	AB	R	H	2B	3B	HR	RBI	BB	SO	SB	CS	OBP	SLG
2013	Did not play—Signed 2014 contract																

14 ALEC ASHER, RHP

BA GRADE **50** HIGH

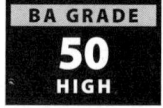

Born: Oct. 4, 1991. **B-T:** R-R. **Ht.:** 6-4. **Wt.:** 218. **Drafted:** Polk County (Fla.) JC, 2012 (4th round). **Signed by:** Cliff Terracuso.

The Giants selected Asher out of high school in the 23rd round of the 2010 draft and had him signed for $80,000 before voiding his contract due to a bone chip in his elbow. So he went to Santa Fe (Fla.) JC in 2011 and transferred in-state to Polk County JC in 2012, where he helped the school to its first Junior College World Series appearance before signing with the Rangers for $150,000 as a fourth-round pick. Asher's full-season debut at high Class A Myrtle Beach in 2013 was a success, as he led the Carolina League in strikeouts (139) and ranked fourth in ERA (2.90). He has the repertoire of a starter, with a 90-96 mph fastball he throws for strikes and can drive downhill to both sides of the plate. His secondary pitches coming out of college were a work in progress, but his mid-80s slider has developed into an out-pitch and he's shown feel for an average changeup with solid sink. Asher has a fair delivery, a big, durable frame and is equally effective against righties and lefties, but his medical history, which includes Tommy John surgery when he was 14, is a concern. He has a ceiling as a No. 4 starter and will move up to Double-A Frisco in 2014.

Year	Club (League)	Class	W	L	ERA	G	GS	CG	SV	IP	H	HR	BB	SO	K/9	WHIP	AVG
2012	Spokane (NWL)	SS	2	3	3.09	20	0	0	5	35	29	4	11	50	12.9	1.14	.221
2013	Myrtle Beach (CAR)	HiA	9	7	2.90	26	25	0	0	133	120	10	40	139	9.4	1.20	.235
Minor League Totals			11	10	2.94	46	25	0	5	168	149	14	51	189	10.1	1.19	.232

15 LEWIS BRINSON, OF

BA GRADE **55** EXTREME

Born: May 8, 1994. **B-T:** R-R. **Ht.:** 6-3. **Wt.:** 170. **Drafted:** HS—Coral Springs, Fla., 2012 (1st round). **Signed by:** Frankie Thon.

Brinson didn't have a great senior season, but the Rangers were so drawn to his tools and athleticism that they took him with the No. 29 pick in the 2012 draft and signed him for $1.625 million. His raw tools are as good as anyone's in the system, but his baseball skills remain unrefined. He has outstanding bat speed and plus raw power to all fields, and he beat out Byron Buxton in the finals of the home run derby of the 2011 Under Armour All-America Game. Brinson came into pro ball as merely an adequate defensive center fielder, but the Rangers felt he improved significantly in the second half at low Class A Hickory in 2013 to take advantage of his plus speed and above-average arm. There's still a long ways for Brinson to go at the plate. He struck out 191 times in 2013, finishing one behind the minor league leader in that category, with a whiff in 38 percent of his trips to the plate and a .209/.292/.374 batting line away from hitter-friendly Hickory. Brinson hit home runs to right field in games, but he doesn't cover the outer half of the plate or use the opposite field like he should, becoming extremely pull-conscious with an uphill swing. His awkward hitting mechanics, which by the end of the year had him in a crouched position and nearly standing over the plate, cause him to lose his balance, and he lacks the pitch recognition or plate discipline to resist chasing breaking pitches off the plate. Nevertheless, Brinson should move up to high Class A Myrtle Beach in 2014.

Year	Club (League)	Class	AVG	G	AB	R	H	2B	3B	HR	RBI	BB	SO	SB	CS	OBP	SLG
2012	Rangers (AZL)	R	.283	54	237	54	67	22	7	7	42	21	74	14	2	.345	.523
2013	Hickory (SAL)	LoA	.237	122	447	64	106	18	2	21	52	48	191	24	7	.322	.427
Minor League Totals			.253	176	684	118	173	40	9	28	94	69	265	38	9	.330	.461

16 JOSE LECLERC, RHP

BA GRADE 50 HIGH

Born: Dec. 19, 1993. **B-T:** R-R. **Ht.:** 6-0. **Wt.:** 180. **Signed:** Dominican Republic, 2010. **Signed by:** Willy Espinal.

In June 2010 the Rangers signed Leclerc's older brother Angelo, who pitched for the organization's Rookie-level Arizona League affiliate the last two seasons. In December that same year, the Rangers signed Jose, who at the time was throwing 88-90 mph but with good arm action that made the Rangers think there was more velocity coming. His fastball crept up to 90-93 mph in 2012, when he spent his second season in the Dominican Summer League, and has continued to climb while pitching exclusively in relief. Pushed to low Class A Hickory in 2013, Leclerc's strikeout rate jumped along with his fastball, which parked at 94-97 mph with late life that can miss bats or get grounders at a high rate. He came to the U.S. with a good slider that's continued to improve to a plus pitch at 85-87 mph with sharp bite that he uses to finish hitters. His changeup and curveball can both occasionally flash average and gives hitters another look, though in the bullpen he often sticks to a two-pitch mix. Some scouts wonder whether Leclerc has the repertoire to transition to the rotation, and the Rangers have debated whether to let him start in 2014 or fast-track him in the bullpen. His next step will be high Class A Myrtle Beach.

Year	Club (League)	Class	W	L	ERA	G	GS	CG	SV	IP	H	HR	BB	SO	K/9	WHIP	AVG
2011	Rangers (DSL)	R	3	1	2.36	20	1	0	1	34	25	1	18	27	7.1	1.25	.203
2012	Rangers (DSL)	R	3	1	1.54	19	0	0	1	47	32	1	18	41	7.9	1.07	.193
2013	Hickory (SAL)	LoA	3	4	3.36	39	0	0	5	59	53	2	21	77	11.7	1.25	.240
Minor League Totals			9	6	2.51	78	1	0	7	140	110	4	57	145	9.3	1.19	.216

17 JAIRO BERAS, OF

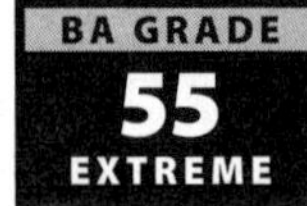

Born: Dec. 25, 1994. **B-T:** R-R. **Ht.:** 6-6. **Wt.:** 190. **Signed:** Dominican Republic, 2012. **Signed by:** Danilo Troncoso/Roberto Aquino/Paul Kruger/Mike Daly.

Beras was at the center of one of the biggest controversies in international baseball when he signed with the Rangers for $4.5 million in 2012. Following news that massive signing restrictions for international amateurs were coming down the pike in the next Collective Bargaining Agreement, Beras and his representatives presented teams with a new birthdate, making Beras one year older than previously advertised. That made him 17 and thus eligible to sign in February before the new $2.9 million bonus pools for international signings went into effect in July. MLB ruled that Beras' age was undetermined and made the unusual decision to suspend him for one year for lying about his age while allowing his contract to stand. After missing the first week of the Rookie-level Arizona League season in 2013 while on suspension, he played for just a few weeks before a broken hamate bone ended his season in July. The 6-foot-6 Beras shows plus raw power when he gets his long arms extended, though he's also an aggressive hitter prone to getting tied up inside and is still learning to get more lift and use the whole field. He runs well for someone his size, and his strong arm fits well in right field, though the Rangers may try him in center field in 2014. Much is still unknown about Beras, and the injury only adds to his high-risk, high-reward profile. The Rangers' recent track record with toolsy outfielders suggests he's destined for low Class A Hickory.

Year	Club (League)	Class	AVG	G	AB	R	H	2B	3B	HR	RBI	BB	SO	SB	CS	OBP	SLG
2013	Rangers (AZL)	R	.250	17	64	11	16	2	2	2	15	5	19	1	0	.314	.438
Minor League Totals			.250	17	64	11	16	2	2	2	15	5	19	1	0	.314	.438

18 KEONE KELA

BA GRADE 45 MEDIUM

Born: April 16, 1993. **B-T:** R-R. **Ht.:** 6-1. **Wt.:** 190. **Drafted:** Everett (Wash.) CC, 2012 (12th round). **Signed by:** Gary McGraw.

Kela spent his first three years of high school in California before moving to Seattle for his senior season. Rather than sign with the Mariners as a 29th-round pick in 2011, Kela went to nearby Everett (Wash.) CC, where he saw his fastball jump from 88-91 mph to 91-93 and touching 95. After signing with the Rangers for $100,000 as a 12th-rounder in 2012, Kela's velocity continued to climb. He's now one of the hardest throwers in the minors, sitting at 96-99 mph and touching 101 out of the bullpen. It's a fastball with both premium velocity and late life, which helps him rack up strikeouts and groundballs at an above-average rate. His breaking ball is inconsistent, with hard, slurve-like break. He hasn't used his changeup much, so it's still raw, but if his slider continues to mature he should be able to have success as a two-pitch reliever. Kela came into pro ball with a lot of effort in his mechanics, but he's done a nice job of smoothing his delivery to some degree, which has helped improve his controls. Kela, who missed a month in 2013 with arm tightness in the spring, has peaked at low Class A Hickory, but some promising outings in the Arizona Fall League and Venezuelan League could help accelerate his timetable.

Year	Club (League)	Class	W	L	ERA	G	GS	CG	SV	IP	H	HR	BB	SO	K/9	WHIP	AVG
2012	Rangers (AZL)	R	0	1	1.59	9	0	0	0	11	4	0	4	15	11.9	0.71	.105
2013	Hickory (SAL)	LoA	2	2	2.41	12	0	0	1	19	18	0	6	20	9.6	1.29	.250
	Rangers (AZL)	R	2	0	7.36	3	0	0	0	4	8	0	3	6	14.7	3.00	.421
	Spokane (NWL)	SS	1	2	3.78	12	0	0	2	17	17	1	6	26	14.0	1.38	.250
Minor League Totals			5	5	3.04	36	0	0	3	50	47	1	19	67	12.0	1.31	.239

19 DAVID LEDBETTER, RHP

BA GRADE **50** HIGH

Born: Feb. 13, 1992. **B-T:** L-R. **Ht.:** 5-11. **Wt.:** 188. **Drafted:** Cedarville (Ohio), 2013 (3rd round). **Signed by:** Roger Coryell.

Ledbetter became the first player ever drafted out of Division II Cedarville (Ohio) when the Rangers used their third-round pick (No. 99 overall) on him in 2013 and signed him for $350,000. The Rangers also drafted Ledbetter's identical twin brother Ryan, who also is a righthander, in the 19th round from the same program. The transition to pro ball didn't faze Ledbetter, who pounded the strike zone in his debut with short-season Spokane. He has sound, repeatable mechanics, which helps him throw strikes consistently with a 90-94 mph fastball. His heater has heavy sink that leads to a high groundball rate. He throws a hard, late-breaking curveball that's an average pitch, a sinking changeup that can be effective at times along with an occasional slider. Ledbetter is a good athlete who also played right field and DH in college. Despite his small college background, he has the command and savvy to move fairly quickly through the system, with his next step coming at one of the Rangers' Class A affiliates in 2014.

Year	Club (League)	Class	W	L	ERA	G	GS	CG	SV	IP	H	HR	BB	SO	K/9	WHIP	AVG
2013	Spokane (NWL)	SS	3	3	2.93	13	13	0	0	58	53	3	19	51	7.9	1.23	.243
Minor League Totals			3	3	2.93	13	13	0	0	58	53	3	19	51	7.9	1.23	.243

20 LISALVERTO BONILLA, RHP

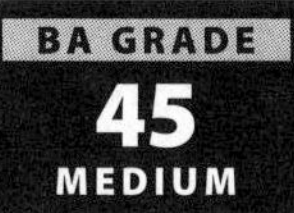

Born: June 18, 1990. **B-T:** R-R. **Ht.:** 6-0. **Wt.:** 175. **Signed:** Dominican Republic, 2008. **Signed by:** Sal Agostinelli (Phillies).

The Phillies signed Bonilla as an 18-year-old in December 2008, putting him on the older end of the spectrum for a Dominican signing. He moved steadily through the system, reaching Double-A as a reliever in 2012 before Philadelphia traded him and righthander Josh Lindblom to the Rangers in exchange for Michael Young and cash after the season. In his first year with the Rangers in 2013, Bonilla was nearly unhittable the first half at Double-A Frisco, but when he got to Triple-A Round Rock his command deserted him and he made too many mistakes, which he paid for in the hitter-friendly Pacific Coast League. Despite his second-half struggles, Bonilla has the attributes to be a high-leverage reliever, as he averaged 13.0 strikeouts per nine innings in 2013 and generates grounders at a high clip. Bonilla pitches off his 92-96 mph fastball and misses plenty of bats with a plus changeup, though his slider remains below-average. The deception in his delivery keeps hitters uncomfortable, though his mechanics have some effort and he finishes with a head whack, while his long arm action can impede his command. Bonilla most likely returns to Round Rock to open 2014, but he should make his major league debut at some point during the season.

Year	Club (League)	Class	W	L	ERA	G	GS	CG	SV	IP	H	HR	BB	SO	K/9	WHIP	AVG
2009	Phillies (DSL)	R	6	2	1.41	11	11	2	0	70	48	2	16	76	9.8	0.91	.189
2010	Phillies (GCL)	R	2	1	1.95	6	6	0	0	32	32	3	5	38	10.6	1.14	.246
	Williamsport (NYP)	SS	1	3	6.49	10	3	0	0	26	33	5	12	18	6.2	1.71	.308
2011	Lakewood (SAL)	LoA	4	5	2.80	26	15	1	4	106	91	8	29	95	8.1	1.13	.229
2012	Clearwater (FSL)	HiA	1	1	1.35	10	0	0	1	13	9	0	4	18	12.2	0.98	.188
	Reading (EL)	AA	2	1	1.64	21	0	0	3	33	22	1	17	46	12.5	1.18	.193
2013	Round Rock (PCL)	AAA	5	5	7.95	26	2	0	0	43	52	8	24	56	11.7	1.77	.299
	Frisco (TL)	AA	2	0	0.30	21	0	0	6	30	16	0	9	50	14.8	0.82	.152
Minor League Totals			23	18	2.97	131	37	3	14	354	303	27	116	397	10.1	1.18	.228

21 DREW ROBINSON, 3B

Born: April 20, 1992. **B-T:** L-R. **Ht.:** 6-1. **Wt.:** 185. **Drafted:** HS—Las Vegas, 2010 (4th round). **Signed by:** Todd Guggiana.

When the Rangers signed Robinson for $198,000 out of high school in 2010, they thought they were getting one of the more advanced prep bats in the draft, but he floundered in short-season Spokane the next season. He rebounded with a solid season in 2012 and another steady campaign in 2013 at high Class A Myrtle Beach after a slow start. He rebounded to hit .275/.398/.454 in the second half while cutting his strikeout rate. Robinson has a sweet, compact stroke from the left side and a keen eye at the plate. He's a patient hitter—to the point of being passive in the view of some scouts—whose game is more about getting on base than hitting for power. He uses the whole field, though he'll still fall into the trap of pulling off the ball and rolling over for a grounder to second base. Robinson's power is below-average with some over-the-fence pop to his pull side, but some think he could grow into 15-20 homers in his prime. His position once was in question, but he made the biggest strides in the field in 2013. He started the year playing very tall and upright at third base, but he worked hard to get down into a more athletic fielding position, which helped his lateral range and his ability to charge the slow rollers. He's a below-average runner with a solid-average arm. He should reach Double-A Frisco in 2014.

Year	Club (League)	Class	AVG	G	AB	R	H	2B	3B	HR	RBI	BB	SO	SB	CS	OBP	SLG
2010	Rangers (AZL)	R	.286	44	140	26	40	6	2	0	11	26	41	6	3	.406	.357
2011	Rangers (AZL)	R	.500	6	18	9	9	2	0	1	5	6	4	4	1	.640	.778
	Spokane (NWL)	SS	.163	45	147	18	24	6	0	3	25	22	46	3	1	.266	.265
2012	Hickory (SAL)	LoA	.273	123	410	72	112	23	4	13	67	86	123	10	7	.409	.444
2013	Myrtle Beach (CAR)	HiA	.257	122	436	62	112	26	7	8	70	72	124	10	2	.369	.404
Minor League Totals			.258	340	1151	187	297	63	13	25	178	212	338	33	14	.380	.401

22 RYAN RUA, 2B/3B

BA GRADE
45
HIGH

Born: March 11, 1990. **B-T:** R-R. **Ht.:** 6-2. **Wt.:** 205. **Drafted:** Lake Erie (Ohio), 2011 (17th round). **Signed by:** Roger Coryell.

Assigned to a low Class A Hickory team loaded with toolsy, swing-happy hitters in 2013, Rua stood out for his mature hitting approach, which should be expected from a 23-year-old in the South Atlantic League. Even with a hitter-friendly park in Hickory, Rua's breakout performance and 29 home runs there were a surprise, so the Rangers jumped him to Double-A Frisco in August. Added weight and strength in the offseason helped Rua, who showed plus raw power and hit home runs to all fields. He has solid plate discipline and did a better job last year of staying back and using his hands in his swing, though he still gets long to the ball sometimes. After playing primarily third base his first two seasons, Rua transitioned well to second base at Hickory before sliding back to third at the end of the year with Rougned Odor at second in Frisco. Rua is a below-average runner and doesn't have much range, but he's reliable when a ball is hit to him and has an average arm. His path to the majors may require him to spend time at second, third, the corner outfield spots and perhaps first base in an offensive-oriented utility role. He's headed back to Frisco for 2014.

Year	Club (League)	Class	AVG	G	AB	R	H	2B	3B	HR	RBI	BB	SO	SB	CS	OBP	SLG
2011	Spokane (NWL)	SS	.192	7	26	2	5	0	0	1	3	1	6	0	0	.250	.308
	Rangers (AZL)	R	.321	45	162	41	52	12	5	3	34	20	34	10	0	.395	.512
2012	Spokane (NWL)	SS	.293	74	280	40	82	16	1	7	43	29	64	4	1	.368	.432
2013	Hickory (SAL)	LoA	.251	104	367	70	92	24	1	29	82	49	91	13	2	.356	.559
	Frisco (TL)	AA	.233	23	86	19	20	2	1	3	9	7	24	1	0	.305	.384
Minor League Totals			.273	253	921	172	251	54	8	43	171	106	219	28	3	.359	.489

23 BEN ROWEN, RHP

Born: Nov. 15, 1988. **B-T:** R-R. **Ht.:** 6-4. **Wt.:** 190. **Drafted:** Virginia Tech, 2010 (22nd round). **Signed by:** Rick Matsko.

Rowen's pure stuff might be the worst in the Prospect Handbook, but because of his submarine delivery, the raw stuff doesn't need to be there for him to make hitters top the ball into the ground. A reliever his entire minor league career, he has had success at every level, including at Triple-A Round Rock in 2013, because of his ability to throw strikes and get quick groundball outs. Rowen throws only in the low 80s, but the angle and sink he delivers the ball with make him one of the most extreme groundball machines in baseball. In fact, just five qualified minor league relievers bettered his 3.4 groundout/airout ratio in 2013. Rowen throws a frisbee breaking ball in the low 70s that grades out below-average, though with his delivery it's effective enough for him to give hitters a second look when needed. In November, the Rangers added Rowen to the 40-man roster to shield him from the Rule 5 draft. While his ceiling and future role are limited, he could very well carve out a career along the lines of former Ranger Darren O'Day or Brad Ziegler, with a chance to crack the big league bullpen in 2014.

Year	Club (League)	Class	W	L	ERA	G	GS	CG	SV	IP	H	HR	BB	SO	K/9	WHIP	AVG
2010	Spokane (NWL)	SS	2	0	1.09	21	0	0	1	33	18	0	14	30	8.2	0.97	.155
2011	Hickory (SAL)	LoA	5	4	1.98	33	0	0	2	59	55	1	18	43	6.6	1.24	.246
2012	Myrtle Beach (CAR)	HiA	5	0	1.57	38	0	0	19	57	41	2	3	52	8.2	0.77	.201
2013	Frisco (TL)	AA	3	0	0.53	31	0	0	10	34	23	1	11	28	7.5	1.01	.198
	Round Rock (PCL)	AAA	3	1	0.84	20	0	0	3	32	18	0	6	30	8.4	0.75	.157
Minor League Totals			18	5	1.34	143	0	0	35	215	155	4	52	183	7.7	0.96	.200

24 NOMAR MAZARA, OF

Born: April 26, 1995. **B-T:** L-L. **Ht.:** 6-4. **Wt.:** 200. **Signed:** Dominican Republic, 2011. **Signed by:** Rodolfo Rosario/Mike Daly.

The Rangers raised eyebrows around the industry on July 2, 2011, when they lavished a $4.95 million bonus on Mazara, in addition to $650,000 for righthander Pedro Payano and $200,000 for shortstop Crisford Adames, a $5.8 million package deal for three players from Dominican trainer Ivan Noboa. Mazara's bonus set a record for an international amateur player, but the move was seen throughout the industry as an overpay for a player no other team seemed to have as the top player available. Scouts' concerns—particularly about his hit tool—have been justified thus far. Mazara entered pro ball with an exaggerated leg kick that he's worked to tone down, but he still has a lot of movement in his setup and holes in his lefthanded swing that contribute to his tendency to swing and miss in the strike zone. Power was Mazara's calling card as an amateur and his swing still generates loft, but now most scouts give him average raw power with the ability to take balls over the fence to his pull side. The Rangers still consider his power plus. Though he has below-average speed, Mazara's biggest strides have come on defense, where he's gone from raw to adequate in right field and improved his arm strength to a tick-above-average tool. Just 18 at low Class A Hickory in 2013, he could stand to repeat the level in 2014.

Year	Club (League)	Class	AVG	G	AB	R	H	2B	3B	HR	RBI	BB	SO	SB	CS	OBP	SLG
2012	Rangers (AZL)	R	.264	54	201	40	53	13	3	6	39	37	70	5	2	.383	.448
2013	Hickory (SAL)	LoA	.236	126	453	48	107	23	2	13	62	44	131	1	2	.310	.382
Minor League Totals			.245	180	654	88	160	36	5	19	101	81	201	6	4	.334	.402

25 ENGEL BELTRE, OF

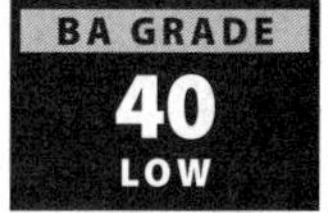

Born: Nov. 1, 1989. **B-T:** L-L. **Ht.:** 6-2. **Wt.:** 180. **Signed:** Dominican Republic, 2006. **Signed by:** Pablo Lantigua (Red Sox).

Beltre signed with the Red Sox for $600,000 when the 2006 international signing period opened in 2006, then one year later went to the Rangers along with outfielder David Murphy and lefthander Kason Gabbard in the trade-deadline deal that sent reliever Eric Gagne to Boston. More known for his immaturity than his talent (he was suspended 15 games in 2011 after throwing a trash can into the stands while at Double-A Frisco), Beltre made his major league debut in June, bouncing between Texas and Triple-A Round Rock the rest of the 2013 season. His best tools show up in center field, where his plus speed gives him good range and his plus arm gives him another weapon. He's not as adept at using his speed on the basepaths, as he was only successful on 53 percent of stolen base attempts in 2013. Beltre lacks the bat to be an everyday player. He has a lefthanded stroke and occasional home run power to his pull side, but his swing path leads to a lot of balls on the ground, so he's not a power threat. He has a big leg kick, a long swing and impatient hitting approach, which cuts into his on-base ability. With an iffy bat and good defense, Beltre has a chance to stick around as an extra outfielder. He's on the 40-man roster and out of options, so if the Rangers don't keep him in the majors, he could end up in another organization.

Year	Club (League)	Class	AVG	G	AB	R	H	2B	3B	HR	RBI	BB	SO	SB	CS	OBP	SLG
2007	Red Sox (GCL)	R	.208	34	125	20	26	3	3	5	13	12	44	6	3	.310	.400
	Rangers (AZL)	R	.310	22	84	19	26	3	4	4	15	8	21	3	2	.388	.583
	Spokane (NWL)	SS	.211	9	38	3	8	0	0	0	1	2	10	2	1	.250	.211
2008	Clinton (MWL)	LoA	.283	130	566	87	160	26	9	8	47	15	105	31	11	.308	.403
2009	Bakersfield (CAL)	HiA	.227	84	357	44	81	13	5	3	23	17	77	17	7	.281	.317
	Rangers (AZL)	R	.300	3	10	4	3	1	1	0	0	0	3	2	0	.364	.600
	Frisco (TL)	AA	.071	4	14	1	1	1	0	0	1	0	2	1	0	.133	.143
2010	Bakersfield (CAL)	HiA	.331	68	263	38	87	11	4	5	35	11	34	10	7	.376	.460
	Frisco (TL)	AA	.254	47	181	14	46	4	4	1	14	10	24	8	2	.301	.337
2011	Frisco (TL)	AA	.231	118	437	64	101	15	6	1	28	28	103	16	6	.285	.300
2012	Frisco (TL)	AA	.261	133	564	80	147	17	17	13	55	26	118	36	10	.307	.420
2013	Round Rock (PCL)	AAA	.292	94	394	58	115	19	1	7	34	28	84	15	12	.340	.398
	Texas (AL)	MAJ	.250	22	40	7	10	1	0	0	2	0	5	1	2	.268	.275
Major League Totals			.250	22	40	7	10	1	0	0	2	0	5	1	2	.268	.275
Minor League Totals			.264	746	3033	432	801	113	54	47	266	157	625	147	61	.312	.383

26 WILMER FONT, RHP

BA GRADE
40
LOW

Born: May 24, 1990. **B-T:** R-R. **Ht.:** 6-4. **Wt.:** 230. **Signed:** Venezuela, 2006. **Signed by:** Manny Batista/Andres Espinosa.

When Font showed up in the Rookie-level Arizona League as a 17-year-old in 2007, his 98 mph fastball generated buzz, but injuries have sidetracked his career. After Tommy John surgery erased his 2011 season, Font became a full-time reliever and made his major league debut in 2012 with three appearances. He had a strong 2013 campaign split mostly between Double-A Frisco and Triple-A Round Rock, with a pair of major league relief outings in July. He went to Caracas to pitch in the Venezuelan League after the season. With an imposing, extra-large frame, Font leans heavily on a power fastball that he runs anywhere from 92-98 mph. His 80-84 mph slider has short, slurvy break that flashes as an average pitch, as does his changeup, but they're usually below-average. Font has a loose arm but his long arm action hampers his slider and his fastball command, as his arm tends to lag behind when he gets to his balance point and causes timing issues. The development of a more consistent offspeed pitch and better fastball location will be two keys for him going forward. Font will have a chance to compete for a bullpen job in 2014 as a middle reliever or else return to Triple-A.

Year	Club (League)	Class	W	L	ERA	G	GS	CG	SV	IP	H	HR	BB	SO	K/9	WHIP	AVG
2007	Rangers (AZL)	R	2	3	4.53	14	10	0	0	46	41	2	24	61	12.0	1.42	.238
2008	Rangers (AZL)	R	1	0	10.38	3	0	0	0	4	1	1	1	6	12.5	0.46	.071
2009	Hickory (SAL)	LoA	8	3	3.49	29	24	0	0	108	93	4	59	105	8.7	1.40	.231
2010	Hickory (SAL)	LoA	4	1	5.16	7	7	0	0	30	35	3	13	33	10.0	1.62	.294
	Bakersfield (CAL)	HiA	1	2	3.86	9	9	0	0	49	38	5	32	52	9.6	1.43	.217
2011	Did not play—Injured																
2012	Myrtle Beach (CAR)	HiA	2	5	4.21	23	19	0	0	83	58	10	37	109	11.8	1.14	.198
	Frisco (TL)	AA	2	0	3.00	10	0	0	1	15	9	1	7	29	17.4	1.07	.170
	Texas (AL)	MAJ	0	0	9.00	3	0	0	0	2	0	0	4	1	4.5	2.00	.000
2013	Frisco (TL)	AA	1	2	1.41	26	0	0	10	32	14	2	24	45	12.7	1.19	.132
	Texas (AL)	MAJ	0	0	0.00	2	0	0	0	1	1	0	2	0	0.0	2.25	.200
	Round Rock (PCL)	AAA	1	0	0.45	16	0	0	4	20	8	0	10	26	11.7	0.90	.119
Major League Totals			0	0	5.40	5	0	0	0	3	1	0	6	1	2.7	2.10	.091
Minor League Totals			22	16	3.67	137	69	0	15	387	297	28	207	466	10.8	1.30	.212

27 ALEXANDER CLAUDIO, LHP

BA GRADE
40
MEDIUM

Born: Jan. 31, 1992. **B-T:** L-L. **Ht.:** 6-3. **Wt.:** 160. **Drafted:** HS—Juncos, P.R., 2010 (27th round). **Signed by:** Frankie Thon.

When Claudio signed with the Rangers as a 27th-round flier out of high school in 2010, he was a long-limbed, extremely skinny lefty with a fastball that maxed out at 87 mph. While the velocity hasn't ramped up, he's changed his arm slot and developed a Bugs Bunny changeup to become a legitimate prospect. A pure reliever, Claudio made his full-season debut in 2013 at low Class A Hickory and pitched so well that the Rangers skipped him in the second half to Double-A Frisco, where he didn't miss a beat. He throws just 82-87 mph with good tail, and he's now a siderarmer with plenty of deception caused by arms and legs flying at the hitter. Claudio's high-60s changeup is a devastating pitch, a plus-plus weapon with sink, fade and screwball-type action that gets hitters caught out in front routinely. He maintains his arm speed on his changeup and gets tremendous separation from his fastball, which plays up because hitters have to stay back for his changeup. Claudio's slurvy 72-76 mph slider gives hitters another look, but his changeup is his bread and butter. It's a repertoire that leads to plenty of strikeouts and a near 3-to-1 groundout/airout rate. Claudio's ceiling is low and his fastball leaves little margin for error, but he has a chance to work as a middle reliever.

Year	Club (League)	Class	W	L	ERA	G	GS	CG	SV	IP	H	HR	BB	SO	K/9	WHIP	AVG
2010	Rangers (AZL)	R	0	1	6.60	12	1	0	0	15	19	1	6	13	7.8	1.67	.311
2011	Rangers (AZL)	R	4	0	2.13	15	0	0	1	25	20	1	9	29	10.3	1.14	.222
	Spokane (NWL)	SS	1	0	0.00	1	0	0	0	3	2	0	1	2	6.0	1.00	.200
2012	Rangers (AZL)	R	4	0	1.79	14	3	0	1	45	36	1	5	54	10.7	0.90	.222
2013	Hickory (SAL)	LoA	3	1	1.15	24	0	0	11	47	22	2	7	62	11.9	0.62	.139
	Frisco (TL)	AA	1	5	2.84	21	0	0	0	32	28	2	11	29	8.2	1.23	.243
Minor League Totals			13	7	2.26	87	4	0	13	167	127	7	39	189	10.2	0.99	.213

28 KELLIN DEGLAN, C

BA GRADE
45
HIGH

Born: May 3, 1992. **B-T:** L-R. **Ht.:** 6-2. **Wt.:** 195. **Drafted:** HS—Langley, B.C., 2010 (1st round). **Signed by:** Gary McGraw.

Deglan's high school in British Columbia didn't have a baseball team, but scouts evaluated him on Canada's junior national team and saw him play well in spring-training exhibitions against pro players, which vaulted him into the first round in 2010. Since signing for $1 million as the 22nd pick that year, Deglan has flashed promising tools but without the performance to match. With a quick, lefthanded bat and above-average raw power, Deglan can hit home runs to any part of the park. He's not a total free-swinger, but he's still learning the strike zone and becomes pull-happy in games. He has a long swing, a low contact rate and tends to tinker by trying to make adjustments on the fly, never settling into a consistent approach. Deglan has a plus arm and good footwork that help him get rid of the ball quickly, but his throws can be erratic and he's never been great at throwing out basestealers, catching just 21 percent in 2013. His blocking and receiving remain works in progress. A big man who sets up more upright than most catchers, Deglan doesn't move well laterally. He can get careless at times with his receiving, but he earns consistent high marks for his work ethic and dedication.

Year	Club (League)	Class	AVG	G	AB	R	H	2B	3B	HR	RBI	BB	SO	SB	CS	OBP	SLG
2010	Rangers (AZL)	R	.286	10	28	5	8	0	1	0	5	2	7	0	0	.355	.357
	Spokane (NWL)	SS	.159	22	82	7	13	2	0	1	4	7	21	0	0	.222	.220
2011	Hickory (SAL)	LoA	.227	89	291	39	66	15	1	6	39	34	91	2	0	.320	.347
2012	Hickory (SAL)	LoA	.234	92	320	46	75	25	2	12	41	32	96	4	4	.310	.438
2013	Myrtle Beach (CAR)	HiA	.231	89	308	37	71	10	2	12	49	33	94	0	0	.331	.393
Minor League Totals			.226	302	1029	134	233	52	6	31	138	108	309	6	4	.314	.379

29 ROMAN MENDEZ, RHP

BA GRADE 45 HIGH

Born: July 25, 1990. **B-T:** R-R. **Ht.:** 6-2. **Wt.:** 190. **Signed:** Dominican Republic, 2007. **Signed by:** Luciano del Rosario (Red Sox).

Mendez originally signed with the Red Sox for $125,000 in 2007 and developed into one of the organization's best young international pitchers. When the Rangers traded Jarrod Saltalamacchia to Boston at the trade deadline in 2010, Mendez was the best prospect the Rangers received in return, along with first baseman Chris McGuiness and catcher Michael Thomas. After climbing through the minors as a starter, Mendez pitched exclusively in relief in 2013, but he lasted just two months before having surgery to repair a stress fracture in his right elbow, ending his season. When healthy, he pitches off a 93-96 mph fastball that he can crank even higher at times. His best secondary pitch is an inconsistent slider that's average at times, while his below-average changeup doesn't get much use out of the bullpen. Mendez is a solid strike-thrower, though he does have a hook in his arm action that sometimes makes it tricky for him to repeat his release point. His delivery has a lot of torque and shoulder rotation that keeps hitters off-balance but may have contributed to his arm problems. Durability is less of a concern now that Mendez is no longer starting, and he projects as a middle reliever.

Year	Club (League)	Class	W	L	ERA	G	GS	CG	SV	IP	H	HR	BB	SO	K/9	WHIP	AVG
2008	Red Sox (DSL)	R	3	1	2.65	11	11	0	0	51	43	1	16	46	8.1	1.16	.222
2009	Red Sox (GCL)	R	2	3	1.99	12	10	0	0	50	33	1	8	47	8.5	0.83	.184
2010	Greenville (SAL)	LoA	0	2	11.40	6	6	0	0	15	29	5	10	18	10.8	2.60	.392
	Lowell (NYP)	SS	2	3	4.36	8	8	0	0	33	31	5	19	35	9.5	1.52	.240
	Spokane (NWL)	SS	1	1	2.31	3	3	0	0	12	19	2	3	13	10.0	1.89	.373
2011	Hickory (SAL)	LoA	9	1	3.31	26	20	0	1	117	117	7	45	130	10.0	1.38	.259
2012	Rangers (AZL)	R	0	1	3.00	3	3	0	0	9	7	1	1	7	7.0	0.89	.219
	Myrtle Beach (CAR)	HiA	4	6	5.14	18	12	0	1	70	69	7	25	71	9.1	1.34	.260
	Frisco (TL)	AA	2	0	1.46	5	0	0	1	12	8	2	4	9	6.6	0.97	.174
2013	Frisco (TL)	AA	2	0	1.82	16	0	0	2	25	12	1	11	24	8.8	0.93	.146
Minor League Totals			25	18	3.59	108	73	0	5	393	368	32	142	400	9.2	1.30	.245

30 KELVIN VASQUEZ, RHP

Born: April 6, 1993. **B-T:** R-R. **Ht.:** 6-5. **Wt.:** 191. **Signed:** Dominican Republic, 2011. **Signed by:** Roberto Aquino.

One month before the Rangers lavished seven-figure bonuses on Dominican outfielders Nomar Mazara and Ronald Guzman, they watched Vasquez, a converted outfielder, throw a bullpen session in the Dominican Republic and signed him for $30,000 as an 18-year-old. After Vasquez spent two seasons in the Dominican Summer League, the Rangers threw him into the low Class A South Atlantic League to open 2013, but he was in over his head. By mid-May he had been sent back to extended spring training before he rebounded at short-season Spokane, where he led the Northwest League in ERA (2.13). Vasquez has a long, lanky frame, and his pitchability is understandably raw given his lack of mound experience, but he gets swings and misses from his lively 90-94 mph fastball with solid sink. He's still developing his secondary pitches, the most advanced of which is a slider that's average at times. He focused on throwing his changeup more often when he was demoted to Spokane, but it's still below-average. Vasquez generates his velocity fairly easily and has some deception in his delivery, but he needs to throw more strikes. He'll jump back to Hickory in 2014, with his future likely in middle relief.

Year	Club (League)	Class	W	L	ERA	G	GS	CG	SV	IP	H	HR	BB	SO	K/9	WHIP	AVG
2011	Rangers (DSL)	R	0	1	3.24	9	1	0	0	17	20	0	7	10	5.4	1.62	.299
2012	Rangers (DSL)	R	2	3	3.42	16	13	0	0	55	56	1	15	51	8.3	1.28	.256
2013	Hickory (SAL)	LoA	2	2	6.49	8	7	0	0	26	31	4	18	19	6.5	1.86	.292
	Spokane (NWL)	SS	2	2	2.13	14	13	0	0	63	46	3	34	72	10.2	1.26	.199
Minor League Totals			6	8	3.40	47	34	0	0	162	153	8	74	152	8.5	1.40	.246

Toronto Blue Jays

BY CLINT LONGENECKER

The Blue Jays' 2013 season was as disappointing as the prior offseason was exciting.

Toronto considered the winter following a moribund 73-89 season in 2012 a transformative period for the organization, which seemingly had been working with a more long-term time horizon.

For three years, general manager Alex Anthopoulos and his crew worked to purge onerous long-term contracts (such as Vernon Wells and Alex Rios), acquire cost-controlled position players with impact potential (Brett Lawrie and Colby Rasmus) and spent heavily to acquire amateur talent, both domestic and international. Toronto invested its resources toward building internal assets.

Then the organization, with one of the game's best farm systems, traded from considerable depth to acquire a cadre of veteran talent, led by 2012 National League Cy Young Award winner R.A. Dickey (acquired from the Mets) and shortstop Jose Reyes (acquired from the Marlins). Those trades, which also added Mark Buehrle and Josh Johnson, helped increase payroll by 42 percent.

But the Blue Jays never took flight in 2013 as nothing went right. After losing Reyes to an ankle injury, the team finished April seven games under .500. The Jays had only one winning month on the year, June, when they climbed up to .500 on the strength of an 11-game winning streak—only to lose 19 of their next 26. Toronto, outscored by 44 runs on the season, ultimately finished last in the American League East.

Although the Blue Jays employed a league-average offensive attack, an improvement over the past two seasons, the pitching was a disaster. The problems began with the rotation, marred by injuries (Johnson and Brandon Morrow) and ineffectiveness. The rotation had the second-highest ERA in the AL (4.81), and threw the second-fewest innings (899). In their search for reliable starters, the Jays used 13 different starters, the second-highest figure in MLB. Buoyed by frequent waiver claims, they used the most pitchers (31) in the majors for the third year in a row.

The farm system still has high-ceiling arms, but after the wave of trades, the talent is concentrated at the lower levels of the system. Those left at the upper levels were long in the tooth. The pitching staffs for Triple-A Buffalo, high Class A Dunedin and short-season Vancouver were the oldest in their leagues. A single staff, Rookie-level Bluefield, was young for its level, and four pitchers from that club are among the system's top 15 prospects (Alberto Tirado, Chase DeJong and Jairo Labourt).

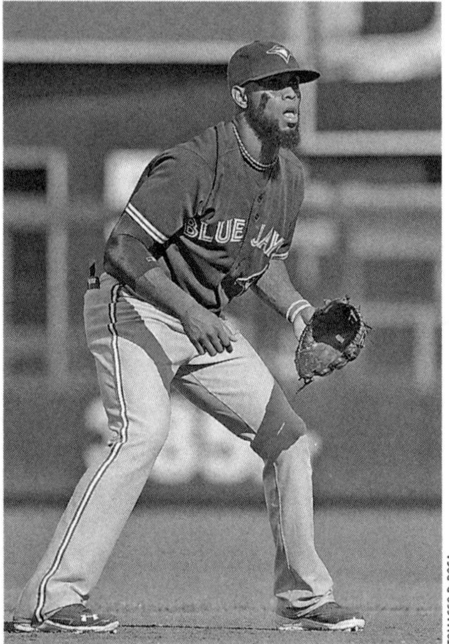

TOMASSO DeROSA

Big-money acquisitions like Jose Reyes did not pay dividends in Toronto in 2013

TOP PROSPECTS OF THE DECADE

Year	Player, Pos.	2013 Org.
2004	Alex Rios, of	Rangers
2005	Brandon League, rhp	Dodgers
2006	Dustin McGowan, rhp	Blue Jays
2007	Adam Lind, of	Blue Jays
2008	Travis Snider, of	Pirates
2009	Travis Snider, of	Pirates
2010	Zach Stewart, rhp	White Sox
2011	Kyle Drabek, rhp	Blue Jays
2012	Travis d'Arnaud, c	Mets
2013	Aaron Sanchez, rhp	Blue Jays

The Blue Jays are arguably as deep and as talented as any organization at the lower levels, with a strong contingent of Latin American pitchers and infielders and early-round draft picks from 2012 and 2013. That's even after failing to sign 2013 first-round pick Phil Bickford, a California prep righthander. Toronto also failed to sign 2011 first-rounder Tyler Beede.

The current regime continues to invest in building pitching depth. In the past four drafts, Toronto has used 74 percent of its top-five-round picks on arms, versus a league-wide average of 49.7 percent. Toronto will have two-first round picks, Nos. 9 and 11, in the 2014 draft after failing to sign Bickford.

ORGANIZATION OVERVIEW

General Manager: Alex Anthopoulos. **Farm Director:** Charlie Wilson. **Scouting Director:** Brian Parker.

Class	Team	League	W	L	PCT	Finish	Manager
Majors	Toronto Blue Jays	American	74	88	.457	11th (15)	John Gibbons
Triple-A	Buffalo Bisons	International	74	70	.514	6th (14)	Marty Brown
Double-A	New Hampshire Fisher Cats	Eastern	68	72	.486	7th (10)	Gary Allenson
High A	Dunedin Blue Jays	Florida State	63	68	.481	9th (12)	Bobby Meachem
Low A	Lansing Lugnuts	Midwest	61	78	.439	12th (16)	John Tamargo
Short-season	Vancouver Canadians	Northwest	39	37	.513	4th (8)	Clayton McCullough
Rookie	Bluefield Blue Jays	Appalachian	40	27	.597	2nd (10)	Dennis Holmberg
Rookie	GCL Blue Jays	Gulf Coast	28	32	.467	8th (16)	John Schneider
Overall 2013 Minor League Record			**373**	**384**	**.493**	**19th (30)**	

THIS YEAR'S TOP 30

No.	Player, Pos.	Grade/Risk
1.	Aaron Sanchez, rhp	65/High
2.	Marcus Stroman, rhp	55/Medium
3.	D.J. Davis, of	60/Extreme
4.	Mitch Nay, 3b	55/High
5.	Franklin Barreto, ss	60/Extreme
6.	Daniel Norris, lhp	55/High
7.	Roberto Osuna, rhp	55/High
8.	Alberto Tirado, rhp	60/Extreme
9.	Dawel Lugo, ss	55/Extreme
10.	Sean Nolin, lhp	45/Low
11.	Chase DeJong, rhp	55/Extreme
12.	Jairo Labourt, lhp	55/Extreme
13.	Matt Smoral, lhp	55/Extreme
14.	A.J. Jimenez, c	50/Medium
15.	Clinton Hollon, rhp	55/Extreme
16.	Tom Robson, rhp	50/High
17.	Dalton Pompey, of	50/High
18.	Rowdy Tellez, 1b	55/Extreme
19.	Andy Burns, 3b/2b	50/High
20.	Kevin Pillar, of	45/Low
21.	John Stilson, rhp	45/Medium
22.	Kenny Wilson, of	45/High
23.	Santiago Nessy, c	50/Extreme
24.	Richard Urena, ss	50/Extreme
25.	Matt Dean, 1b	50/Extreme
26.	Miguel Castro, rhp	50/Extreme
27.	Dwight Smith Jr., of	45/High
28.	Jake Brentz, lhp	50/Extreme
29.	Ryan Goins, 2b/ss	40/Low
30.	Yeltsin Gudino, ss	50/Extreme

LAST YEAR'S TOP 30

No.	Player, Pos.	Status
1.	Travis d'Arnaud, c	(Mets)
2.	Noah Syndergaard, rhp	(Mets)
3.	Aaron Sanchez, rhp	No. 1
4.	Roberto Osuna, rhp	No. 7
5.	Marcus Stroman, rhp	No. 2
6.	D.J. Davis, of	No. 3
7.	John Stilson, rhp	No. 21
8.	Daniel Norris, lhp	No. 6
9.	Matt Smoral, lhp	No. 13
10.	Anthony Alford	Dropped out
11.	A.J. Jimenez, c	No. 14
12.	Tyler Gonzales, rhp	Dropped out
13.	Franklin Barreto, ss/of	No. 5
14.	Santiago Nessy, c	No. 23
15.	Alberto Tirado, rhp	No. 8
16.	Dwight Smith Jr., of	No. 27
17.	Matt Dean, 3b	No. 25
18.	Chad Jenkins, rhp	Dropped out
19.	Sean Nolin, lhp	No. 10
20.	Deck McGuire, rhp	Dropped out
21.	Kevin Pillar, of	No. 20
22.	Chase DeJong, rhp	No. 11
23.	Christian Lopes, 2b/ss	Dropped out
24.	Mitch Nay, 3b	No. 4
25.	Wuilmer Becerra, of	(Mets)
26.	Dawel Lugo, ss	No. 9
27.	Dickie Joe Thon, ss	Dropped out
28.	Jairo Labourt, lhp	No. 12
29.	Yeyfry del Rosario, rhp	Dropped out
30.	Chris Hawkins, of	Dropped out

BEST TOOLS

Best Hitter for Average	Kevin Pillar
Best Power Hitter	Rowdy Tellez
Best Strike-Zone Discipline	Mitch Nay
Fastest Baserunner	D.J. Davis
Best Athlete	D.J. Davis
Best Fastball	Aaron Sanchez
Best Curveball	Aaron Sanchez
Best Slider	Marcus Stroman
Best Changeup	Sean Nolin
Best Control	Roberto Osuna
Best Defensive Catcher	A.J. Jimenez
Best Defensive Infielder	Jonathan Berti
Best Infield Arm	Dawel Lugo
Best Defensive Outfielder	Kenny Wilson
Best Outfield Arm	Jesus Gonzalez

TOP 15 PLAYERS 25 AND UNDER

No.	Player, Pos. (Age)	Peak Level
1.	Aaron Sanchez, rhp (21)	High Class A
2.	Marcus Stroman, rhp (22)	Double-A
3.	Brett Lawrie, 3b (24)	Majors
4.	Drew Hutchison, rhp (23)	Majors
5.	D.J. Davis, of (19)	Short-season
6.	Mitch Nay, 3b (20)	Rookie
7.	Franklin Barreto, ss (18)	Rookie
8.	Anthony Gose, of (23)	Majors
9.	Daniel Norris, lhp (20)	High Class A
10.	Roberto Osuna, rhp (19)	Low Class A
11.	Alberto Tirado, rhp (19)	Rookie
12.	Dawel Lugo, ss (19)	Short-season
13.	Sean Nolin, lhp (24)	Majors
14.	Chase DeJong, rhp (20)	Rookie
15.	Jairo Labourt, lhp (20)	Rookie

MINOR LEAGUE DEPTH CHART

TORONTO BLUE JAYS

TOP 2014 ROOKIE: John Stilson, rhp. His mid-90s fastball and two plus offspeed pitches will enable his success out of the bullpen.

BREAKOUT PROSPECT: Miguel Castro, rhp. Big, projectable arm with mid-90s velocity, sink and developing offspeed stuff that could jump into next year's top 10.

SLEEPER: Patrick Murphy, rhp. A 2013 third-round pick, Murphy missed his senior year with Tommy John surgery but had a 90-93 mph fastball as a junior and a projectable body.

SOURCE OF TOP 30 TALENT

Homegrown	**30**	**Acquired**	**0**
College	5	Trades	0
Junior college	1	Rule 5 draft	0
High school	15	Independent leagues	0
Nondrafted free agents	0	Free agents/waivers	0
International	9		

LF
Kevin Pillar (20)
Dwight Smith (27)
Marcus Knecht

CF
D.J. Davis (3)
Dalton Pompey (17)
Kenny Wilson (22)
Anthony Alford
Freddy Rodriguez

RF
Jacob Anderson
Jesus Gonzalez
Mike Crouse

3B
Mitch Nay (4)
Andy Burns (19)
Kellen Sweeney

SS
Franklin Barreto (5)
Dawel Lugo (9)
Richard Urena (24)
Yeltsin Gudino (30)
Emilio Guerrero
Kevin Nolan

2B
Ryan Goins (29)
Christian Lopes
Jonathan Berti
Tim Locastro

1B
Rowdy Tellez (18)
Matt Dean (25)

C
A.J. Jimenez (14)
Santiago Nessy (23)
Derrick Chung
Jorge Saez
Mike Reeves

LHP

LHSP	LHRP
Daniel Norris (6)	Tyler Ybarra
Sean Nolin (10)	John Anderson
Jairo Labourt (12)	
Matt Smoral (13)	
Jake Brentz (28)	
Shane Dawson	
Evan Smith	
Ryan Borucki	
Daniel Lietz	
Matt Boyd	

RHP

RHSP	RHRP
Aaron Sanchez (1)	John Stilson (21)
Marcus Stroman (2)	Justin Jackson
Roberto Osuna (7)	Dustin Antolin
Alberto Tirado (8)	Tucker Donahue
Chase DeJong (11)	Wil Browning
Clinton Hollon (15)	
Tom Robson (16)	
Miguel Castro (26)	
Adonys Cardona	
Deck McGuire	
Jesus Tinoco	
Yeyfry del Rosario	
Javier Avendano	

DRAFT ANALYSIS

2013

BONUSES: $3.1 MILLION

BEST PURE HITTER: 1B Rowdy Tellez (30) has the ability to become an above-average hitter because of his sound approach, ability to drive the ball to all fields and strong hand-eye coordination.

BEST POWER HITTER: The lefthanded-hitting Tellez could become an above-average power hitter at the major league level and has unparalleled raw power in this class, especially to his pull side.

FASTEST RUNNER: OF Jonathan Davis (15) and SS/2B Tim Locastro (13), who went 40-for-41 in stolen base attempts at Ithaca (N.Y.) last spring, both have well above-average speed.

BEST DEFENSIVE PLAYER: With Davis' speed and quickness, he could become an above-average defensive center fielder. He has a fringy arm.

BEST FASTBALL: RHP Clint Hollon (2) has a quick arm that produces fastballs up to 95 mph with downhill plane and above-average life and sink. LHP Jake Brentz (11) shows inconsistent velocity but touches 97 at his best. LHP Matt Boyd (6) worked at 88-92 mph in the Oregon State rotation as a senior but hit 96 on the Cape the summer prior out of the bullpen.

BEST SECONDARY PITCH: Hollon has a plus slider to go with a developing changeup and curveball.

BEST PRO DEBUT: 1B L.B. Dantzler (14) led short-season Vancouver to the Northwest League title and was league MVP after leading the league with 20 doubles and nine home runs and batting .302/.385/.504. LHP Matt Dermody (28) had a 1.77 ERA in 41 NWL innings.

BEST ATHLETE: Locastro and Davis among position players. Hollon has rare athleticism for a pitcher.

MOST INTRIGUING BACKGROUND: Boyd is a distant relative of Hall of Fame pitcher Bob Feller and former first lady Dolly Madison. RHP Patrick Murphy (3) had Tommy John surgery last summer but touched 93 mph as a junior and offers athleticism and projection.

CLOSEST TO THE MAJORS: Boyd, who finished at high Class A, could move quickly because of his command and the tough looks he gives same-side hitters.

BEST LATE-ROUND PICK: Though he was a 30th-rounder, Tellez received the most money of any Jays pick ($850,000). Danzler, Dermody and C Mike Reeves (21), a lefthanded hitting catcher who grew up in Canada before attending Florida Gulf Coast, stand out among those who signed more conventional deals.

THE ONE WHO GOT AWAY: The only unsigned first-round pick in this year's draft was RHP Phil Bickford, who went No. 10 overall but ended up at Cal State Fullerton. Toronto never came that close to signing him, and it's still not clear exactly why. The Jays get the No. 11 pick in 2014 as compensation.

ASSESSMENT: Toronto took pitchers with its first nine picks. Losing Bickford hurt, but the Jays continued to load up on high school hurlers with fastball velocity and athleticism such as Hollon and Brentz.

2012

BONUSES: $10.5 MILLION

Toronto loaded up on toolsy preps in the first three rounds, leavened by college RHP Marcus Stroman (1). Two-sport OF Anthony Alford (3) has given the Jays just 40 at-bats for his $750,000.

GRADE: C

2011

BONUSES: $11.0 MILLION

The Blue Jays failed to sign three potential 2014 first-round RHPs in Tyler Beede (1), Luke Weaver (19) and Aaron Nola (22). OF Kevin Pillar (32) has overachieved. LHP Daniel Norris (2) remains a tease.

GRADE: D

2010

BONUSES: $11.6 MILLION

This class stands out for arms. Toronto kept RHP Aaron Sanchez (1s) and LHP Sean Nolin (6) but traded RHPs Noah Snydergaard (1s), Asher Wojciechowski (1s) and Sam Dyson (4) and LHP Justin Nicolino (2).

GRADE: A

TOP DRAFT PICKS OF THE DECADE

Year	Player, Pos.	2013 Org.
2004	David Purcey, lhp	White Sox
2005	Ricky Romero, lhp	Blue Jays
2006	Travis Snider, of	Pirates
2007	Kevin Ahrens, 3b	Blue Jays
2008	David Cooper, 1b	Indians
2009	Chad Jenkins, rhp	Blue Jays
2010	Deck McGuire, rhp	Blue Jays
2011	*Tyler Beede, rhp	Vanderbilt
2012	D.J. Davis, of	Blue Jays
2013	*Phil Bickford, rhp	Cal State Fullerton

* Did not sign

LARGEST BONUSES IN CLUB HISTORY

Adeiny Hechavarria, 2010	$4,000,000
Adonys Cardona, 2010	$2,800,000
Ricky Romero, 2005	$2,400,000
Felipe Lopez, 1998	$2,000,000
Deck McGuire, 2010	$2,000,000
Daniel Norris, 2011	$2,000,000
Matt Smoral, 2012	$2,000,000

1 AARON SANCHEZ, RHP

Born: July 1, 1992. **B-T:** R-R. **Ht.:** 6-4. **Wt.:** 190.
Drafted: HS—Barstow, Calif., 2010
(1st round supplemental). **Signed by:** Blake Crosby.

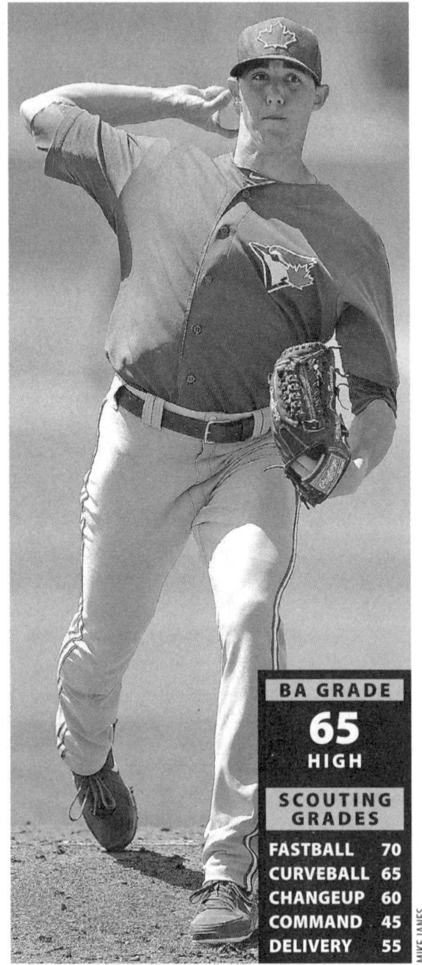

BA GRADE
65
HIGH
SCOUTING GRADES
FASTBALL 70
CURVEBALL 65
CHANGEUP 60
COMMAND 45
DELIVERY 55

MIKE JANES

One of the youngest players in the 2010 draft, Sanchez was the 34th overall pick and signed for a below-slot $775,000 bonus. He paid immediate dividends, as just months after the draft in instructional league, his velocity jumped from 93-94 mph to 97. An above-average athlete, the 6-foot-4 Sanchez has long limbs and a wiry, angular build that will accommodate additional strength gains. Toronto has been careful with his workload, and Sanchez was limited to 22 games and 86 innings in the 2013 regular season after missing more than a month with shoulder discomfort. He started six times in the Arizona Fall League and had the second-highest strikeout rate (24 percent) of any pitcher with more than 20 innings, showcasing his potential.

Sanchez has standout stuff and is lauded as an intelligent student of the game with a quiet aggression on the mound. His heavy fastball can sit 93-98 mph with plus life. It explodes out of his hand with smooth and effortless arm action. He throws a four-seamer with above-average cutting action to his glove side and increased the use of a two-seamer to his arm side. Sanchez induces groundballs at a high rate, as his 2.34 groundout/airout ratio was the second-best mark of any high Class A Florida State League pitcher with 80 or more innings. His curveball has plus potential with tilt and depth. TrackMan data from the AFL indicated his breaker's spin rate is 21 percent higher than the major league average. Sanchez has a tendency to get on the side on the pitch, creating slider tilt and a large velocity discrepancy. His changeup is currently an average offering but has plus potential with late tumble and fade. Despite his easy arm action, Sanchez has posted below-average control numbers. His delivery underwent a transformation this season, as he had a tendency to miss up and arm side, getting under his pitches. The organization shortened his stride length in order to have him work over the ball more with greater downhill plane. This made his arm action more compact and consistent. If he can maintain his plane to the plate, Sanchez could increase his stride length. He cut his walk rate (11.1 percent) in 2013, but it was still 31 percent higher than the FSL average. He walked more hitters (14.3 percent) out of the stretch than he struck out (13.6 percent) in 2013. In his 20 healthy regular season starts, he averaged just more than four innings per outing.

To reach his ceiling as a No. 2 starter, Sanchez will have to improve his control and increase his workload. But few pitchers in the minors can match his ceiling and pure talent. If he can't show the control to start, he has the stuff to become a high-leverage reliever. He likely will start 2014 at Double-A New Hampshire.

Year	Club (League)	Class	W	L	ERA	G	GS	CG	SV	IP	H	HR	BB	SO	K/9	WHIP	AVG
2010	Blue Jays (GCL)	R	0	2	1.42	8	8	0	0	19	19	1	12	28	13.3	1.63	.271
	Auburn (NYP)	SS	0	1	4.50	2	2	0	0	6	4	0	5	9	13.5	1.50	.182
2011	Bluefield (APP)	R	3	2	5.48	11	6	0	1	43	45	4	18	43	9.1	1.48	.269
	Vancouver (NWL)	SS	0	1	4.63	3	3	0	0	12	8	0	8	13	10.0	1.37	.195
2012	Lansing (MWL)	LoA	8	5	2.49	25	18	0	0	90	64	3	51	97	9.7	1.27	.204
2013	Dunedin (FSL)	HiA	4	5	3.34	22	20	0	0	86	63	4	40	75	7.8	1.19	.202
Minor League Totals			15	16	3.34	71	57	0	1	256	203	12	134	265	9.3	1.32	.219

2 MARCUS STROMAN, RHP

Born: May 1, 1991. **B-T:** R-R. **Ht.:** 5-9. **Wt.:** 185. **Drafted:** Duke, 2012 (1st round). **Signed by:** John Hendricks.

A premium athlete, Stroman became Duke's first-ever first-round pick in 2012, signing for $1.8 million. He tested positive for an amphetamine in August 2012, and his 50-game suspension stretched into the 2013 season. He fell one out short of qualifying for the ERA title in the Double-A Eastern League, which he would have led in strikeout percentage (28.1 percent) while finishing second in SO/BB ratio (4.80). With a strong, compact build and quick-twitch athleticism, Stroman maintains plus stuff. He brandishes a heavy fastball at 92-95 mph with above-average movement. He has an out-pitch in his plus upper-80s slider, a plus cutter that can touch the low 90s and an average changeup that flashes plus potential. He varies the shape of his offspeed offerings. Staying on top of the baseball has been key to getting better downhill plane, and so has softening his landing, which allows him to get over his front side better and limits him spinning off to the first-base side. He shuts down the opposition's running game and is an exceptional defender. Stroman likely will begin 2014 at Triple-A Buffalo but could reach Toronto during the season. Since 1960, just two righthanders 5-foot-9 or shorter (Tom Phoebus and Tom Gordon) have more than 30 career major league starts. If Stroman does not defy the odds and become at least a No. 3 starter, then he could be a high-end late-game reliever.

Year	Club (League)	Class	W	L	ERA	G	GS	CG	SV	IP	H	HR	BB	SO	K/9	WHIP	AVG
2012	Vancouver (NWL)	SS	1	0	3.18	7	0	0	0	11	8	0	3	15	11.9	0.97	.190
	New Hampshire (EL)	AA	2	0	3.38	8	0	0	0	8	8	1	6	8	9.0	1.75	.258
2013	New Hampshire (EL)	AA	9	5	3.30	20	20	0	0	112	99	13	27	129	10.4	1.13	.234
Minor League Totals			12	5	3.30	35	20	0	0	131	115	14	36	152	10.4	1.15	.232

3 D.J. DAVIS, OF

Born: July 25, 1994. **B-T:** L-R. **Ht.:** 6-1. **Wt.:** 180. **Drafted:** HS—Wiggins, Miss., 2012 (1st round). **Signed by:** Brian Johnston.

One of the youngest players in the 2012 draft, Davis was the first of five picks the Blue Jays made before the second round. His father Wayne, also an outfielder, played in the organization from 1985-88. Davis has the highest ceiling of any position player in the system, offering impact potential at a premium position. Davis has a lean, wiry build with good strength in his hands and forearms, quick-twitch athleticism and top-of-the-scale speed. He has plus range in center field and could become a plus defender. He has natural strength and leverage in his swing, producing plus raw power from the left side. He has above-average bat speed, and Davis could hit 15-20 home runs at his peak. His hit tool and overall game remain raw, however, and he has struggled to make consistent contact. His aggressive approach and limited breaking ball recognition led to strikeouts in nearly 30 percent of plate appearances at Rookie-level Bluefield. Davis, who has a below-average arm, will need to improve his outfield reads and game awareness, and learn to use his speed on the bases more efficiently, as he stole bases at a below-average rate of 62 percent. Davis is a high-ceiling talent who will take time to develop. He should get his first taste of full-season ball in 2014 at low Class A Lansing.

Year	Club (League)	Class	AVG	G	AB	R	H	2B	3B	HR	RBI	BB	SO	SB	CS	OBP	SLG
2012	Blue Jays (GCL)	R	.233	43	163	30	38	7	2	4	12	18	54	18	7	.339	.374
	Bluefield (APP)	R	.340	12	47	9	16	3	1	1	6	4	10	6	2	.415	.511
	Vancouver (NWL)	SS	.167	5	18	3	3	0	0	0	0	5	6	1	1	.348	.167
2013	Bluefield (APP)	R	.240	58	225	35	54	8	7	6	25	26	76	13	8	.323	.418
Minor League Totals			.245	118	453	77	111	18	10	11	43	53	146	38	18	.339	.402

4 MITCH NAY, 3B

Born: Sept. 20, 1993. **B-T:** R-R. **Ht.:** 6-3. **Wt.:** 195. **Drafted:** HS—Chandler, Ariz., 2012 (1st round supplemental). **Signed by:** Blake Crosby.

The grandson of Lou Klimchock, who played in the big leagues over parts of 12 seasons, Nay signed for $1 million in 2012 but broke his foot before playing that summer. He showed above-average hitting and power potential in 2013 and was MVP of the short-season Northwest League playoffs. With a large frame and strong build, Nay has the potential to be a middle-of-the-order hitter with power and on-base ability. In extended spring training, he raised his hitting load, got rid of his bat waggle and shortened his stride, shortening his swing path. Nay has bat speed and quick hands and makes hard contact to all fields. Scouts praise his contact ability, up-the-middle approach and ability to drive the ball to right field. He could be an above-average hitter to go with his 70-grade raw power. Nay, who has a plus arm, is a below-average runner with adequate range but good hands at third base. He led Rookie-level Appalachian League third basemen with 17 errors, and improving his lateral quickness and pre-pitch setup will be key for him to remain at the position. Nay's advanced approach should earn him a spot at low Class A Lansing for 2014. If he moves off third, he moves well enough to try right field.

Year	Club (League)	Class	AVG	G	AB	R	H	2B	3B	HR	RBI	BB	SO	SB	CS	OBP	SLG
2012	Did not play—Injured																
2013	Bluefield (APP)	R	.300	64	230	41	69	11	0	6	42	25	35	0	1	.364	.426
Minor League Totals			.300	64	230	41	69	11	0	6	42	25	35	0	1	.364	.426

5 FRANKLIN BARRETO, SS

Born: Feb. 27, 1996. **B-T:** R-R. **Ht.:** 5-9. **Wt.:** 175. **Signed:** Venezuela, 2012. **Signed by:** Ismael Cruz/Luis Marquez.

With a track record of performance in international tournaments, Barreto was one of the most decorated Venezuelan players ever and one of the top international talents available in 2012. He signed for $1.45 million and made his stateside debut in 2013, earning a promotion to the Rookie-level Appalachian League for 15 games. Barreto has the tools to be an above-average hitter, with above-average bat speed, quick hands and a line-drive stroke. He is an aggressive, righthanded hitter with good pitch recognition and drives the ball to right field well. He has natural strength, a physical upper body and good natural leverage in his swing that could allow him to hit double-digit home runs and plenty of doubles. With athleticism, plus speed and a plus arm, Barreto is an up-the-middle player, though his long-term defensive destination is not determined. Currently a shortstop, he lacks elite defensive actions and footwork, but he will be given every opportunity to stay at short. Barreto has the potential to hit at the top of a lineup and become an impact regular. He likely will start 2014 in extended spring training, then return to the Appy League as an 18-year-old. He may wind up at second base or in center field if he moves out of the infield.

Year	Club (League)	Class	AVG	G	AB	R	H	2B	3B	HR	RBI	BB	SO	SB	CS	OBP	SLG
2013	Blue Jays (GCL)	R	.299	44	174	30	52	16	6	4	19	13	42	10	4	.368	.529
	Bluefield (APP)	R	.204	15	54	4	11	5	1	0	7	2	14	0	2	.259	.333
Minor League Totals			.276	59	228	34	63	21	7	4	26	15	56	10	6	.343	.482

6 DANIEL NORRIS, LHP

Born: April 25, 1993. **B-T:** L-L. **Ht.:** 6-2. **Wt.:** 180. **Drafted:** HS—Johnson City, Tenn., 2011 (2nd round). **Signed by:** Nate Murrie.

The Blue Jays had seven of the first 78 picks in the 2011 draft, and while Norris was the sixth selection, he got the largest signing bonus at $2 million, which also was the most for any prep lefthander that year. He has moved slowly due to mechanical alterations and missed much of June 2013 with forearm tightness, then was substantially better after his return as the changes took hold. Norris' strong second half at low Class A Lansing in 2013 is a testament to his plus athleticism. He made several alterations to his stride that made his arm slot more consistent and improved his direction to the plate, whereas in the past he threw severely across his body and had a very stiff front leg. The differences were dramatic to scouts and his stat line, as he doubled his SO/BB ratio (3.4) in the second half. His release point became more consistent and his 91-95 mph fastball with above-average movement got greater downhill plane. His changeup became a more consistent plus offering to complement his plus mid-80s slider. His curveball, which had a large velocity separation, added power, flashing above-average. He still throws across his body some, and his command will have to improve. Norris, who should open 2014 at high Class A Dunedin, needs to show he can go deeper into games with imroved strike-throwing ability to reach his No. 3 starter ceiling.

Year	Club (League)	Class	W	L	ERA	G	GS	CG	SV	IP	H	HR	BB	SO	K/9	WHIP	AVG
2012	Bluefield (APP)	R	2	3	7.97	11	10	0	0	35	44	4	13	38	9.8	1.63	.301
	Vancouver (NWL)	SS	0	1	10.57	2	2	0	0	8	14	0	5	5	5.9	2.48	.400
2013	Lansing (MWL)	LoA	1	7	4.20	23	22	0	0	86	84	6	44	99	10.4	1.49	.255
	Dunedin (FSL)	HiA	1	0	0.00	1	1	0	0	5	1	0	2	1	1.8	0.60	.063
Minor League Totals			4	11	5.40	37	35	0	0	133	143	10	64	143	9.7	1.55	.271

7 ROBERTO OSUNA, RHP

BA GRADE **55** HIGH

Born: Feb. 7, 1995. **B-T:** R-R. **Ht.:** 6-2. **Wt.:** 230. **Signed:** Mexico, 2011. **Signed by:** Marco Paddy.

A heralded amateur who starred at international tournaments and showed mid-90s velocity as a 15-year-old, Osuna signed with the Blue Jays for $1.5 million in 2011. The nephew of former big league reliever Antonio Osuna, Roberto entered 2013 as the youngest player in the low Class A Midwest League and got off to a tremendous start, striking out 35 percent of hitters with a 7.8 SO/BB ratio, before missing a month with a torn ulnar collateral ligament. He returned to make five starts but had Tommy John surgery in July. Osuna showed a 92-96 mph fastball featuring plus life from a quick, loose arm action with minimal effort. He has feel for a plus changeup. His slider, which has heavy two-plane break, has been inconsistent but shows plus potential. He has an advanced feel for pitching and showed the potential for plus control. With a large frame and burly build, Osuna's physique warrants monitoring, but he has responded well to instruction, shedding a significant amount of weight entering the 2013 season and getting significantly stronger in his lower half and core. In the wake of Tommy John surgery, Osuna's age buoys his prospect status. He could see some 2014 action, but it would be limited. Osuna, who profiles as a No. 3 starter, should be healthy for 2015, when he will be 20.

Year	Club (League)	Class	W	L	ERA	G	GS	CG	SV	IP	H	HR	BB	SO	K/9	WHIP	AVG
2011	Mexico City (MEX)	AAA	0	1	5.49	13	2	0	0	20	25	3	11	12	5.5	1.83	—
2012	Bluefield (APP)	R	1	0	1.50	7	4	0	0	24	18	1	6	24	9.0	1.00	.209
	Vancouver (NWL)	SS	1	0	3.20	5	5	0	0	20	14	1	9	25	11.4	1.17	.192
2013	Lansing (MWL)	LoA	3	5	5.53	10	10	0	0	42	39	6	11	51	10.8	1.18	.242
Minor League Totals			5	6	4.17	35	21	0	0	106	96	11	37	112	9.5	1.26	.222

8 ALBERTO TIRADO, RHP

BA GRADE **60** EXTREME

Born: Dec. 10, 1994. **B-T:** R-R. **Ht.:** 6-1. **Wt.:** 177. **Signed:** Dominican Republic, 2011. **Signed by:** Marco Paddy/Domingo Toribio.

The Jays signed Tirado for $300,000 in 2011 as part of a deep international crop. He had the highest upside of any pitcher on a deep Rookie-level Bluefield pitching staff in 2013, and he helped pitch the club to the Appalachian League playoffs. The athletic Tirado is an unrefined pitcher whom scouts can dream on because he has some of the most electric stuff in the lower minors. He has a thin, wiry build, long limbs and a loose arm that is lightning quick, and the ball explodes out his hand. His fastball sat 92-96 mph with late life and touched 98, and he is working a sinker into game action. Tirado has two sliders, the harder of which (high 80s) could become a true swing-and-miss offering that is at least plus. He can get around on his sliders, causing them to flatten. His changeup is ahead of his breaking ball, which some believe has the higher long-term ceiling and plus potential. Both offspeed pitches improved substantially in 2013. Tirado has below-average command, with a tendency to overthrow, and has trouble staying on line to the plate, rushing his delivery and lacking balance at release. Tirado has No. 2 starter upside if he can maintain his electric stuff over extended innings and refine his delivery. He has a chance to earn a spot in the low Class A Lansing rotation in 2014.

Year	Club (League)	Class	W	L	ERA	G	GS	CG	SV	IP	H	HR	BB	SO	K/9	WHIP	AVG
2012	Blue Jays (GCL)	R	1	2	2.68	11	11	0	0	37	28	0	12	34	8.3	1.08	.217
	Bluefield (APP)	R	2	0	2.45	3	3	0	0	11	4	0	5	5	4.1	0.82	.121
2013	Bluefield (APP)	R	3	0	1.68	12	8	0	0	48	41	1	20	44	8.2	1.26	.236
Minor League Totals			6	2	2.15	26	22	0	0	96	73	1	37	83	7.8	1.14	.217

9 DAWEL LUGO, SS

BA GRADE
55
EXTREME

Born: Dec. 13, 1994. **B-T:** R-R. **Ht.:** 6-0. **Wt.:** 188. **Signed:** Dominican Republic, 2011. **Signed by:** Marco Paddy/Hilario Soriano.

The Jays had the second-largest expenditure ($7.57 million) during the 2011 international signing period, and Lugo was one of three seven-figure signings ($1.3 million). He led Rookie-level Bluefield in home runs (six), hitting .297/.317/.469 to earn a promotion to short-season Vancouver. An above-average athlete, Lugo is a natural, pure hitter with supreme hand-eye coordination, feel for the barrel and the ability to drive the ball to all fields. He had the third-lowest strikeout rate of any Appalachian League teenager (13.9) in 2013, which leads scouts to project him to be an above-average hitter. Lugo has surprising power that could enable him to hit more than 20 home runs annually. His see-ball, hit-ball approach leaves him impatient, walking in 2.2 percent of plate appearances in 2013. Lugo excels at driving balls on the inner half but has struggled at times with pitches on the outer half. Defensively, he has good, dependable hands with smooth actions at shortstop. His arm is plus, but he's a fringy runner. While he has worked diligently to improve his lateral quickness and range, Lugo may fit better at third base long-term than at short. He will compete for a spot at low Class A Lansing but could return to Vancouver in 2014.

Year	Club (League)	Class	AVG	G	AB	R	H	2B	3B	HR	RBI	BB	SO	SB	CS	OBP	SLG
2012	Blue Jays (GCL)	R	.224	47	170	20	38	2	5	2	20	7	25	5	1	.275	.329
2013	Bluefield (APP)	R	.297	51	192	28	57	11	2	6	36	5	28	1	0	.317	.469
	Vancouver (NWL)	SS	.246	16	69	6	17	4	0	1	8	1	13	0	0	.257	.348
Minor League Totals			.260	114	431	54	112	17	7	9	64	13	66	6	1	.291	.394

10 SEAN NOLIN, LHP

BA GRADE
45
LOW

Born: Dec. 26, 1989. **B-T:** L-L. **Ht.:** 6-5. **Wt.:** 235. **Drafted:** San Jacinto (Texas) JC, 2010 (6th round). **Signed by:** Aaron Jersild.

In the first draft for the current regime, Toronto got good value in the sixth round, signing Nolin for $175,000. He has lost bad weight, especially from his lower half and core, since signing and has moved quickly. After starting the 2013 season late with a groin injury, he made an unsuccessful spot start in the majors in May, returned to Double-A New Hampshire and earned a late promotion to Triple-A Buffalo. Nolin offers a true four-pitch mix with above-average command, and he's capable of locating to all quadrants of the zone. He pitches with average fastball velocity, although can he reach back for a 95 mph four-seamer. Nolin creates deception, hides the ball well and gets downhill plane from a high three-quarters arm slot, and he uses a two-seamer to get sink. His changeup with late tumble is a plus offering. He entered the system with a curveball, which is now an average offering, and picked up an average, mid-80s slider with sharp bite. With his high arm slot, Nolin's fastball can have below-average life and he likely will be an extreme flyball pitcher. Nolin is close to a finished product, and his above-average command could allow him to contribute in Toronto if called upon in 2014. He fits a No. 4 starter profile.

Year	Club (League)	Class	W	L	ERA	G	GS	CG	SV	IP	H	HR	BB	SO	K/9	WHIP	AVG
2010	Blue Jays (GCL)	R	0	0	0.00	1	1	0	0	2	1	0	1	4	18.0	1.00	.167
	Auburn (NYP)	SS	0	2	6.05	6	6	0	0	19	25	0	9	22	10.2	1.76	.313
2011	Lansing (MWL)	LoA	4	4	3.49	25	21	0	1	108	102	9	31	113	9.4	1.23	.253
2012	Dunedin (FSL)	HiA	9	0	2.19	17	15	0	0	86	72	7	21	90	9.4	1.08	.226
	New Hampshire (EL)	AA	1	0	1.20	3	3	0	0	15	9	0	6	18	10.8	1.00	.170
2013	Toronto (AL)	MAJ	0	1	40.50	1	1	0	0	1	7	1	1	0	0.0	6.00	.700
	New Hampshire (EL)	AA	8	3	3.01	17	17	1	0	93	89	6	25	103	10.0	1.23	.251
	Buffalo (IL)	AAA	1	1	1.53	3	3	0	0	18	13	1	10	13	6.6	1.30	.232
Major League Totals			0	1	40.50	1	1	0	0	1	7	1	1	0	0.0	6.00	.700
Minor League Totals			23	10	2.95	72	66	1	1	341	311	23	103	363	9.6	1.21	.245

11 CHASE DEJONG, RHP

BA GRADE
55
EXTREME

Born: Dec. 29, 1993. **B-T:** L-R. **Ht.:** 6-4. **Wt.:** 185. **Drafted:** HS—Long Beach, 2012 (2nd round). **Signed by:** Joe Aversa.

DeJong was the third righthander the Blue Jays selected in the 2012 draft. After pitching 12 innings in 2012, he had a standout season in the Rookie-level Appalachian League, finishing fifth in strikeout rate (28 percent) and second in strikeout-walk ratio (6.6). DeJong, who gets downhill plane from a high three-quarters slot, relies almost exclusively on a four-seam fastball. Though his fastball sat 88-92 mph last summer, evaluators project him to pitch at 90-94 or better because of his arm action and physical projection. He has a large frame with a lean, angular build that should allow him to carry significantly more weight. He has a plus curveball with 12-to-6 action, but can be inconsistent. He gained greater feel for his changeup last summer, and it flashes plus. He has a repeatable delivery that could give him plus command, and he finished with the Appy League's fourth-lowest walk rate (4 percent). The Blue Jays have worked with him to make his lower half more athletic, lengthen his stride and maintain better direction to the plate, although his stride length remains below-average. He will likely to be a fly-ball pitcher as his slot occasionally leaves his pitches flat. DeJong should make the Lansing rotation this season and projects as a No. 3 starter long-term.

Year	Club (League)	Class	W	L	ERA	G	GS	CG	SV	IP	H	HR	BB	SO	K/9	WHIP	AVG
2012	Blue Jays (GCL)	R	1	0	1.50	6	0	0	0	12	7	0	1	15	11.3	0.67	.171
2013	Bluefield (APP)	R	2	3	3.05	13	10	1	0	56	58	2	10	66	10.6	1.21	.261
Minor League Totals			3	3	2.78	19	10	1	0	68	65	2	11	81	10.7	1.12	.247

12 JAIRO LABOURT, LHP

Born: March 7, 1994. **B-T:** L-L. **Ht.:** 6-4. **Wt.:** 204. **Signed:** Dominican Republic, 2011. **Signed by:** Marco Paddy/Hilario Soriano.

Labourt, who signed for $350,000 as a 17-year-old in 2011, has improved as much as any pitcher in the system since he signed, giving him the chance to fulfill a rare profile, as there have just been four Dominican lefthanders 6-foot-4 or taller in major league history, and none with more than 20 major league starts. Labourt, who had a mid-80s fastball when he signed, has a quick arm and now sits 90-93 mph with his fastball, touching 95. He gets good extension out front, downhill plane and above-average sink, projecting to produce ground balls at an above-average rate. He has a large frame and strong build to handle innings, repeats his delivery well and projects to have above-average control. He has firmed up his body and improved his mechanics since signing. He has advanced feel for a changeup that he can throw to lefthanded hitters and projects as plus. His 82-85 mph slider is inconsistent, as he tends to get on the side of it and throw it too hard, but it shows plus potential. Labourt, who has the ceiling of a No. 3 starter, will likely pitch at Lansing in 2014.

Year	Club (League)	Class	W	L	ERA	G	GS	CG	SV	IP	H	HR	BB	SO	K/9	WHIP	AVG
2011	Blue Jays (DSL)	R	0	4	2.23	12	12	0	0	36	29	0	14	29	7.2	1.18	.220
2012	Blue Jays (GCL)	R	0	3	3.79	12	12	0	0	38	38	2	23	39	9.2	1.61	.253
2013	Bluefield (APP)	R	2	2	1.92	12	8	0	0	52	39	3	14	45	7.8	1.03	.204
Minor League Totals			2	9	2.57	36	32	0	0	126	106	5	51	113	8.1	1.25	.224

13 MATT SMORAL, LHP

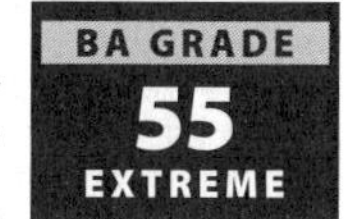

Born: March 18, 1994. **B-T:** L-L. **Ht.:** 6-8. **Wt.:** 220. **Drafted:** HS—Solon, Ohio, 2012 (1st round supplemental). **Signed by:** Coulson Barbiche.

Some scouts viewed Smoral as one of the top prep lefthanders heading into the 2012 draft, but then he registered only one regular season start his senior year because of a stress fracture in his right foot. Doctors posited that a seven-inch growth spurt between his sophomore and junior years contributed to the injury. Uncertainty about his health allowed the Jays to grab Smoral with the 50th overall pick and sign him for $2 million. He did not pitch in 2012 after signing, and was limited to 25 innings last year due to a cracked fingernail. Now 6-foot-8, Smoral uses his extra-large frame and long levers to generate a 91-96 mph fastball with above-average life. His slider has at least plus potential, and his developing changeup has average potential. Smoral has worked on accelerating his arm out of his glove, reducing the length of his arm stroke in the back and getting on top of the ball from a higher slot than in high school. He shed the weight he put on during his injury layoff. If he improves his control, he has front-half-of-the-rotation potential, but that's a rare profile, as only one 6-foot-8 or taller prep lefthander has started a major league game (Sean West, 22). So Smoral, who will likely begin 2014 with another short-season assignment, could profile as a dynamic late-game reliever.

Year	Club (League)	Class	W	L	ERA	G	GS	CG	SV	IP	H	HR	BB	SO	K/9	WHIP	AVG
2013	Blue Jays (GCL)	R	0	2	7.01	15	5	0	0	26	22	1	26	27	9.5	1.87	.237
Minor League Totals			0	2	7.01	15	5	0	0	26	22	1	26	27	9.5	1.87	.237

14 A.J. JIMENEZ, C

Born: May 1, 1990. **B-T:** R-R. **Ht.:** 6-0. **Wt.:** 210. **Drafted:** HS—Bayamon, P.R., 2008 (9th round). **Signed by:** Jorge Rivera.

Jimenez went in the ninth round of the 2008 draft due to concerns about his elbow, and injuries have delayed his development, including Tommy John surgery in 2012. When healthy, however, Jimenez profiles as an everyday catcher who excels in every aspect defensively. His accurate, plus arm shuts down running games. Of the 157 catchers who played at Triple-A in 2013, just six had a higher career caught stealing percentage than Jimenez's 43 percent. Not only does he nail baserunners at a high clip, Jimenez severly limits stolen base attempts, as runners have attempted steals at nearly half the league average rate with Jimenez catching.

With quick feet and athleticism, he blocks well, and his strong, steady hands give him good receiving and framing skills. Jimenez has above-average bat speed, and he has lowered his hands and reduced his stride to make his line-drive swing more compact. He should be a fringe-average hitter, and despite above-average raw power, his swing is geared more for gap power and his home run ceiling is likely 8-12 a year with plenty of doubles. He is a below-average runner. Jimenez, who will likely open the season in Triple-A, could make his major league debut in 2014.

Year	Club (League)	Class	AVG	G	AB	R	H	2B	3B	HR	RBI	BB	SO	SB	CS	OBP	SLG
2008	Blue Jays (GCL)	R	.191	19	47	5	9	2	0	0	5	3	16	5	2	.255	.234
2009	Lansing (MWL)	LoA	.263	80	278	30	73	15	1	3	31	7	72	5	2	.280	.356
2010	Lansing (MWL)	LoA	.305	70	262	35	80	22	0	4	54	18	56	17	4	.347	.435
	Dunedin (FSL)	HiA	.111	2	9	1	1	0	0	1	1	0	5	0	0	.111	.444
2011	Dunedin (FSL)	HiA	.303	102	379	49	115	29	1	4	52	28	60	11	2	.353	.417
2012	New Hampshire (EL)	AA	.257	27	105	14	27	4	1	2	10	5	14	2	3	.295	.371
2013	Dunedin (FSL)	HiA	.429	9	28	5	12	3	0	1	9	1	3	0	0	.448	.643
	New Hampshire (EL)	AA	.276	50	203	28	56	15	0	3	29	16	37	1	2	.327	.394
	Buffalo (IL)	AAA	.233	8	30	0	7	1	0	0	0	1	2	0	1	.258	.267
Minor League Totals			.283	367	1341	167	380	91	3	18	191	79	265	41	16	.324	.396

15 CLINTON HOLLON, RHP

BA GRADE
55
EXTREME

Born: Dec. 24, 1994. **B-T:** R-R. **Ht.:** 6-1. **Wt.:** 195. **Drafted:** HS—Versailles, Ky., 2013 (2nd round). **Signed by:** Nate Murrie.

Scouts keyed in on Hollon after he touched 95 mph as an underclassman, and the Jays grabbed him in the second round last June. His bonus ($467,280) was reduced to 40 percent of slot value after a post-draft physical raised questions about a ligament in his right elbow, but he showed he was healthy during a brief summer debut. A plus athlete, Hollon has broad shoulders, a strong build and powerful lower half that produces a power arsenal. With a loose, quick arm, he throws a 90-94 mph fastball that touches 95 with life and sink and should produce groundballs at an above-average clip. His 82-85 mph slider is a plus pitch with late tilt. His curveball and changeup could be above-average offerings but need development. Hollon has worked on maintaining direction to the plate, keeping his front shoulder closed and limiting his spinoffs to the first-base side. He projects to have average or better control and a delivery that will hold up in the rotation. With athleticism, a deep repertoire and strike-throwing ability, Hollon profiles as at least a No. 3 starter and will likely begin 2014 in Bluefield.

Year	Club (League)	Class	W	L	ERA	G	GS	CG	SV	IP	H	HR	BB	SO	K/9	WHIP	AVG
2013	Blue Jays (GCL)	R	1	0	0.00	4	2	0	0	12	2	0	3	10	7.5	0.42	.056
	Bluefield (APP)	R	0	1	10.13	2	1	0	0	5	6	1	3	5	8.4	1.69	.261
Minor League Totals			1	1	3.12	6	3	0	0	17	8	1	6	15	7.8	0.81	.136

16 TOM ROBSON, RHP

Born: June 27, 1993. **B-T:** R-R. **Ht.:** 6-4. **Wt.:** 200. **Drafted:** HS—Ladner, B.C., 2011 (4th round). **Signed by:** Jamie Lehman.

Robson, the top Canadian in the 2011 draft, had a forgettable debut in 2012, pitching in the mid- to high 80s with a slow, deliberate delivery. But he improved as much as any pitcher in the organization last season and profiles as a No. 4 starter with a chance to develop into a No. 3. Robson began to work more on line to the plate, maintained better balance throughout his delivery and sped up his arm significantly, now working with 91-95 mph fastball featuring plus life and downhill plane from a high three-quarters arm slot. His fastball was somewhat straight in high school, but he has added a two-seamer with plus sink and produced a 3.5 groundout/airout ratio in 2013 that was nearly twice league average across two levels. His changeup projects to be a plus offering. His curveball plays as solid-average with the potential to be better, but he has trouble commanding it. He has a repeatable delivery and the potential for at least average control. Robson will likely begin 2014 in Lansing and profiles as a durable, innings-eating starter as long as his offspeed stuff continues to progress.

Year	Club (League)	Class	W	L	ERA	G	GS	CG	SV	IP	H	HR	BB	SO	K/9	WHIP	AVG
2012	Bluefield (APP)	R	0	2	4.09	3	3	0	0	11	10	2	0	7	5.7	0.91	.238
2013	Bluefield (APP)	R	3	0	1.38	6	5	0	0	26	15	1	5	18	6.2	0.77	.172
	Vancouver (NWL)	SS	3	0	0.94	7	7	0	0	38	28	0	11	29	6.8	1.02	.212
Minor League Totals			6	2	1.55	16	15	0	0	75	53	3	16	54	6.5	0.92	.203

17 DALTON POMPEY, OF

BA GRADE
50
HIGH

Born: Dec. 11, 1992. **B-T:** B-R. **Ht.:** 6-1. **Wt.:** 180. **Drafted:** HS—Mississauga, Ontario, 2010 (16th round). **Signed by:** Jamie Lehman.

The Ontario native wasn't yet 17 years and six months old when the Jays drafted him in 2010, and was likely the youngest player selected in the draft. A plus athlete, he has started to turn his tools into baseball skills. His carrying tool is his potentially-plus center-field defense, and he won the minor league Gold

Glove Award for center fielders last season. He's an above-average runner with gliding strides who ranges well into the gaps and has good instincts, and his arm has improved to a plus after grading as below-average as an amateur. Pompey has an athletic, sleek and defined physique and is growing into his natural strength, and his speed could allow him to steal 25-30 bases a year. While the switch-hitter continues to improve his bat, he'll probably be no better than an average hitter, though his strike zone knowledge and discipline could boost his on-base skills, as he walked in 12 percent of his plate appearances. He has gap power and could hit 30 or more doubles annually, but his swing path will likely produce below-average home run power. Pompey, who will likely begin 2014 at Dunedin, has the athleticism, makeup and tools to be an everyday big leaguer at a premium position.

Year	Club (League)	Class	AVG	G	AB	R	H	2B	3B	HR	RBI	BB	SO	SB	CS	OBP	SLG
2010	Blue Jays (GCL)	R	.191	11	47	4	9	0	0	2	5	3	10	4	1	.255	.319
2011	Blue Jays (GCL)	R	.259	42	158	34	41	7	2	4	12	24	35	19	0	.361	.405
	Bluefield (APP)	R	.191	18	68	15	13	3	0	1	5	14	23	4	1	.353	.279
2012	Vancouver (NWL)	SS	.294	11	34	11	10	3	1	0	4	9	7	3	0	.442	.441
	Bluefield (APP)	R	.357	4	14	2	5	1	1	0	1	0	2	1	0	.357	.571
	Lansing (MWL)	LoA	.227	5	22	1	5	0	1	0	3	1	5	1	1	.261	.318
2013	Lansing (MWL)	LoA	.261	115	437	68	114	22	9	6	40	63	106	38	10	.358	.394
Minor League Totals			.253	206	780	135	197	36	14	13	70	114	188	70	13	.354	.385

18 ROWDY TELLEZ, 1B

BA GRADE **55** EXTREME

Born: March 16, 1995. **B-T:** L-L. **Ht.:** 6-4. **Wt.:** 220. **Drafted:** HS—Elk Grove, Calif., 2013 (30th round). **Signed by:** Darold Brown.

Although he was selected in the 30th round, Tellez signed for an $850,000 bonus in last year's draft, commensurate to late second-round money and the highest bonus in the Jays draft. With some of the best lefthanded power in last year's draft class, Tellez has the potential to become an impact middle-of-the order hitter. He has an extra-large frame, broad shoulders and a powerful lower half. With natural loft in his swing, Tellez has plus-plus raw power, can drive the ball out to all fields and displays stunning power to his pull side. His quick hands, above-average bat speed and strong hand-eye coordination give him a chance to reach that power in games with a potentially above-average hit tool. He excels at driving balls to the opposite field and has a patient approach that should give him above-average walk rates. Tellez, a well-below average runner with an average arm, could become an average defensive first baseman with adequate range. He has worked hard to get in good shape but will always have to focus on conditioning. Tellez is a bat-first player who will have to hit to provide value and he will likely begin doing that in 2014 at Rookie-level Bluefield.

Year	Club (League)	Class	AVG	G	AB	R	H	2B	3B	HR	RBI	BB	SO	SB	CS	OBP	SLG
2013	Blue Jays (GCL)	R	.234	34	124	10	29	5	3	2	20	15	26	1	0	.319	.371
Minor League Totals			.234	34	124	10	29	5	3	2	20	15	26	1	0	.319	.371

19 ANDY BURNS, 3B/2B

BA GRADE **50** HIGH

Born: Aug. 7, 1990. **B-T:** R-R. **Ht.:** 6-2. **Wt.:** 190. **Drafted:** Arizona, 2011 (11th round). **Signed by:** Blake Crosby.

Burns had to sit out his draft-eligible season after transferring to Arizona from Kentucky, but the Jays grabbed him in the 11th round in 2011. Burns had a breakout campaign across two levels in 2013. A college shortstop with an above-average arm, Burns is an above-average defender with first-step quickness, soft hands and agility. He should be an average hitter and excels at driving middle-away fastballs and stays on breaking balls well. He has bat-to-ball skills and a good idea of the strike zone. With present gap power, he has the strength for at least average power. Despite average speed, Burns is an aggressive, instinctive baserunner who stole 33 bases last year, though he will have to be more efficient, as his success rate was 70 percent in 2013. Opinions of Burns' major league role differ as much as any player in the organization. Supporters believe he can be a regular at third base with above-average defense, 15-20-home run potential and a broad skill set bolstered by plus instincts. His more realistic role is a utility player with the athleticism and versatility to play third, second and the outfield in the mold of Mark DeRosa. Burns will likely begin the season at Double-A, and his versatility could help him reach Toronto this year.

Year	Club (League)	Class	AVG	G	AB	R	H	2B	3B	HR	RBI	BB	SO	SB	CS	OBP	SLG
2011	Blue Jays (GCL)	R	.625	5	16	5	10	0	0	1	7	2	0	0	1	.650	.813
	Vancouver (NWL)	SS	.179	23	84	10	15	4	0	2	7	6	14	2	1	.233	.298
2012	Lansing (MWL)	LoA	.248	78	278	57	69	25	4	9	37	38	75	15	2	.351	.464
2013	Dunedin (FSL)	HiA	.327	64	248	45	81	15	5	8	53	25	38	21	9	.383	.524
	New Hampshire (EL)	AA	.253	64	265	40	67	19	2	7	32	23	55	12	5	.309	.419
Minor League Totals			.272	234	891	157	242	63	11	27	136	94	182	50	18	.343	.458

20 KEVIN PILLAR, OF

BA GRADE 45 LOW

Born: Jan. 4, 1989. **B-T:** R-R. **Ht.:** 6-0. **Wt.:** 200. **Drafted:** Cal State Dominguez Hills, 2011 (32nd round). **Signed by:** Kevin Fox.

A $1,000 senior sign in 2011, Pillar has already exceeded expectations and made his major league debut in 2013. Pillar fits a tough profile as a righthanded-hitting outfielder without a plus tool or loud secondary skills, but his overall hitting skills and versatility give him a fourth outfielder profile, and his plus instincts and makeup could help him outstrip even those expectations. Pillar has one of the most direct, compact swings in the minors, and he makes consistent hard contact and hits to all fields. He has the strength for pull-side home runs and could hit 10-12 annually with 30-35 doubles. With average speed and an above-average arm, he can play all three outfield spots. He likely won't be a plus defensive center fielder, but he has first-step quickness and covers enough ground to play there for some clubs. His career walk rate (6 percent) is below-average, and he has struggled against breaking stuff at the higher levels, with a much higher strikeout rate at Triple-A (18 percent) and in the majors (26 percent), so that could limit his utility. In a small sample at the major league level, Pillar often chased out of the zone. Pillar is close to a finished product and could exhaust his prospect eligibility.

Year	Club (League)	Class	AVG	G	AB	R	H	2B	3B	HR	RBI	BB	SO	SB	CS	OBP	SLG
2011	Bluefield (APP)	R	.347	60	236	44	82	17	3	7	37	10	36	8	4	.377	.534
2012	Lansing (MWL)	LoA	.322	86	335	49	108	20	4	5	57	35	53	35	6	.390	.451
	Dunedin (FSL)	HiA	.323	42	164	16	53	8	2	1	34	5	17	16	3	.339	.415
2013	New Hampshire (EL)	AA	.313	71	304	44	95	20	2	5	30	19	31	15	8	.361	.441
	Buffalo (IL)	AAA	.299	52	201	30	60	19	4	4	27	12	39	8	5	.341	.493
	Toronto (AL)	MAJ	.206	36	102	11	21	4	0	3	13	4	29	0	1	.250	.333
Major League Totals			.206	36	102	11	21	4	0	3	13	4	29	0	1	.250	.333
Minor League Totals			.321	311	1240	183	398	84	15	22	185	81	176	82	26	.366	.466

21 JOHN STILSON, RHP

BA GRADE 45 MEDIUM

Born: July 28, 1990. **B-T:** R-R. **Ht.:** 6-3. **Wt.:** 200. **Drafted:** Texas A&M, 2011 (3rd round). **Signed by:** C.J. Ebarb.

Stilson led NCAA Division I with a 0.80 ERA while striking out 13 hitters per nine as a sophomore reliever in 2010, then moved to the rotation for his draft-eligible season. Doctors diagnosed a torn labrum in his shoulder in the spring before the draft, though subsequent exams revealed surgery could be avoided through rest and rehab. The Jays grabbed Stilson in the third round in 2011 and signed him for a $500,000 bonus. He pitched in the rotation his during his pro debut, but his high-effort, energy-packed delivery and command that is average at best—to say nothing of his shoulder—led most evaluators to project him as a reliever. Stilson moved to relieving full time in 2013 after he started the season on the disabled list with a rib cage injury. His stuff plays up in short stints and allows him to maintain his velocity. His 93-97 mph fastball explodes out of his hand and gets downhill plane. He has multiple offspeed weapons, with a changeup and sharp-breaking slider that are both plus offerings. With more control than command, an aggressive mentality and plus raw stuff, Stilson projects to be at least a high-end set-up man, and he will likely get his first opportunity to contribute in Toronto's bullpen in 2014.

Year	Club (League)	Class	W	L	ERA	G	GS	CG	SV	IP	H	HR	BB	SO	K/9	WHIP	AVG
2012	Dunedin (FSL)	HiA	3	0	2.82	13	13	0	0	54	56	2	19	47	7.8	1.38	.265
	New Hampshire (EL)	AA	2	4	5.04	17	9	0	1	50	54	6	23	44	7.9	1.54	.277
2013	New Hampshire (EL)	AA	0	0	3.86	2	0	0	1	2	3	0	0	6	23.1	1.29	.333
	Buffalo (IL)	AAA	6	2	2.09	33	0	0	4	47	36	3	15	47	8.9	1.08	.211
Minor League Totals			11	6	3.33	65	22	0	6	154	149	11	57	144	8.4	1.34	.254

22 KENNY WILSON, OF

BA GRADE 45 HIGH

Born: Jan. 30, 1990. **B-T:** R-R. **Ht.:** 6-0. **Wt.:** 185. **Drafted:** HS—Tampa, 2008 (2nd round). **Signed by:** Joel Grampietro.

Wilson has developed at a slow pace but began to turn his tools into baseball skills in his fifth full pro season. He had a strong Arizona Fall League after a regular season shortened by a stress fracture and was added to the 40-man roster. Wilson is an electric athlete who is a plus center-field defender. A plus-plus runner, Wilson has a quick first step, gap-closing speed and plus range. While his arm was below-average as an amateur, it is now plus. Wilson, who switch-hit earlier in his career, is now hitting only righthanded, his natural side, and his bat has improved enough that he could be a fringe-average hitter with continued development. He has natural bat speed, and altering his hitting load and shortening his stride have helped him make more contact. Despite a high career walk rate, he has a naturally aggressive approach, has been prone to expanding the strike zone and has struggled with breaking stuff, though his pitch recognition has improved. Wilson has an athletic frame and is growing into strength that could allow him to hit 8-10 home runs a year. He has the glove to be a defense-first outfield reserve and could be an everyday center fielder if his bat continues to improve.

Year	Club (League)	Class	AVG	G	AB	R	H	2B	3B	HR	RBI	BB	SO	SB	CS	OBP	SLG
2008	Blue Jays (GCL)	R	.210	51	162	25	34	6	2	0	12	20	60	25	3	.319	.272
2009	Blue Jays (GCL)	R	.200	8	25	6	5	2	1	0	0	3	8	3	1	.310	.360
	Lansing (MWL)	LoA	.212	87	321	51	68	12	3	4	27	35	99	37	12	.306	.305
2010	Lansing (MWL)	LoA	.216	95	361	54	78	10	4	0	22	51	112	35	11	.326	.266
	Dunedin (FSL)	HiA	.138	18	58	5	8	1	0	0	4	8	15	5	0	.242	.155
2011	Dunedin (FSL)	HiA	.201	48	164	21	33	8	2	0	10	16	52	17	4	.296	.274
2012	Lansing (MWL)	LoA	.252	94	349	68	88	13	6	4	40	44	75	41	8	.360	.358
	Dunedin (FSL)	HiA	.282	29	117	24	33	6	0	1	13	14	22	14	4	.368	.359
2013	Blue Jays (GCL)	R	.222	3	9	2	2	0	0	0	1	2	2	0	1	.364	.222
	Dunedin (FSL)	HiA	.625	2	8	4	5	2	0	0	1	2	1	1	0	.700	.875
	New Hampshire (EL)	AA	.259	55	216	31	56	14	1	3	11	19	56	16	6	.333	.375
Minor League Totals			.229	490	1790	291	410	74	19	12	141	214	502	194	50	.329	.312

23 SANTIAGO NESSY, C

BA GRADE 50 EXTREME

Born: Dec. 8, 1992. **B-T:** R-R. **Ht.:** 6-2. **Wt.:** 220. **Signed:** Venezuela, 2009. **Signed by:** Rafael Moncada.

Nessy spent three years in short-season ball and had a lost year in his full-season debut because of a hamstring injury and concussion in April. Still, he has the ceiling of an offense-first everyday catcher. With a large frame and strong build, Nessy has plus raw power and can hit home runs to the opposite field. He has above-average bat speed and the ball jumps off his bat. His power is ahed of his hit tool, and he has struck out in 25 percent of his career plate appearances. His swing can get long as he searches for pull-side power, and he has inconsistent swing mechanics. He has an aggressive approach and walked at a below-average rate (5.4 percent). With a plus arm, solid receiving skills and strong leadership ability, Nessy has the tools to be at least an average defender. After rating as the best defensive catcher in the Appalachian League in 2012, his defense regressed in 2013, which can mainly be attributed to his concussion. Nessy should open 2014 at high Class A Dunedin, and a healthy 2014 could significantly bolster his value.

Year	Club (League)	Class	AVG	G	AB	R	H	2B	3B	HR	RBI	BB	SO	SB	CS	OBP	SLG
2010	Blue Jays (DSL)	R	.248	44	141	15	35	12	0	2	17	14	44	4	0	.327	.376
2011	Blue Jays (GCL)	R	.306	35	134	12	41	7	0	3	19	8	29	0	2	.347	.425
2012	Bluefield (APP)	R	.256	45	160	26	41	8	0	8	23	13	47	0	0	.320	.456
	Vancouver (NWL)	SS	.091	6	22	4	2	1	0	1	3	3	7	0	0	.200	.273
2013	Lansing (MWL)	LoA	.241	61	224	23	54	15	0	5	23	13	59	0	0	.293	.375
Minor League Totals			.254	191	681	80	173	43	0	19	85	51	186	4	2	.314	.401

24 RICHARD URENA, SS

Born: Feb. 26, 1996. **B-T:** L-R. **Ht.:** 6-1. **Wt.:** 170. **Signed:** Dominican Republic, 2012. **Signed by:** Ismael Cruz/Sandi Rosario/Luciano del Rosario.

Urena signed out of the Dominican for $725,000 in 2012, had a strong showing in the Dominican Summer League and made a brief debut stateside in the Rookie-level Gulf Coast League last year. With quick-twitch athleticism, smooth actions, above-average range and soft hands, Urena coule be an above-average defensive shortstop. He has above-average arm strength, a quick release and can throw from any angle. Naturally quicker than fast, he has average straight-line speed and could steal 10 or more bases annually. He has a long, lean and athletic physique with strong legs and a tapered waist. While Urena's glove is his carrying tool, he has the chance to contribute offensively. He has an unusual set-up, as his hands load very low (about halfway between his shoulders and waist), but he has natural feel for the barrel. He has a good feel for the strike zone. Urena has a tendency to open his hips early, which leaves him susceptible to offspeed stuff away. He has below-average raw power but can drive the ball to the gaps, especially to left-center. Urena will likely open 2014 in extended spring training before reporting to a Rookie-level club.

Year	Club (League)	Class	AVG	G	AB	R	H	2B	3B	HR	RBI	BB	SO	SB	CS	OBP	SLG
2013	Blue Jays (DSL)	R	.296	64	243	45	72	19	2	1	35	30	43	9	5	.381	.403
	Blue Jays (GCL)	R	.333	7	27	3	9	2	0	0	3	3	6	0	0	.400	.407
Minor League Totals			.300	71	270	48	81	21	2	1	38	33	49	9	5	.383	.404

25 MATT DEAN, 1B

BA GRADE 50 EXTREME

Born: Dec. 22, 1992. **B-T:** R-R. **Ht.:** 6-3. **Wt.:** 190. **Drafted:** HS—The Colony, Texas, 2011 (13th round). **Signed by:** Michael Wagner.

Dean signed for a well over-slot $737,500 bonus in 2011, the equivalent of supplemental first-round money. He had a lackluster professional debut at Rookie-level Bluefield in 2012, striking out in one-third of his plate appearances while struggling defensively at third base. He made significant offensive alterations, moved to first base and had a strong bounceback season in a repeat of Bluefield, and he led the Appalachian League in batting. Dean previously committed to swinging early, making him susceptible to breaking stuff. He widened his hitting base and stopped striding, which quieted his head, helped him lay off breaking pitches and drive the ball to all fields. He showed his commitment to improving by keeping a journal tracking every pitch he saw on the season. He has plus raw power to all fields and an athletic, strong build, and he could have plus power production if he makes more contact. His swing still has some length, however, and his batting average was propped up by an unsustainable average on balls in play (.436), so he projects as an average hitter. A good athlete with fluid actions, average speed and a plus arm, Dean could be an above-average defender with plus range at first. He'll make his full-season debut at low Class A Lansing.

Year	Club (League)	Class	AVG	G	AB	R	H	2B	3B	HR	RBI	BB	SO	SB	CS	OBP	SLG
2012	Bluefield (APP)	R	.222	49	167	22	37	8	4	2	24	12	60	3	2	.282	.353
2013	Bluefield (APP)	R	.338	63	210	37	71	14	3	6	35	14	57	8	5	.390	.519
Minor League Totals			.286	112	377	59	108	22	7	8	59	26	117	11	7	.342	.446

26 MIGUEL CASTRO, RHP

BA GRADE **50** EXTREME

Born: Dec. 24, 1994. **B-T:** R-R. **Ht.:** 6-5. **Wt.:** 190. **Drafted:** Dominican Republic, 2012. **Signed by:** Ismael Cruz/Sandi Rosario.

Castro's stateside debut was delayed by visa issues, but he dominated the Dominican Summer League. He struck out more than one-third of the hitters he faced, and had he qualified his ERA (1.36) would have been fourth-best in the league. The 6-foot-5 Castro is a physical specimen with one of the most projectable bodies in the minors, and has the potential to become a front-half-of-the-rotation starter. He has a lean, wiry build, a tapered waist and long limbs. He threw 91-92 mph before signing, and last year sat 93-96 and touched 99. He throws from a low three-quarters arm slot and gets above-average sink. His long stride and long arms give him good extension, and the ball explodes out of his hand. His velocity, sink, angle and release distance should make him tough on righthanded hitters. His arm slot allows him to turn over a changeup with above-average potential, and he has a developing slider with sweepy action and pronounced lateral tilt. Increased weight and strength have helped his body control and strike-throwing ability and will continue to be a priority for his development for the lithe Castro. Castro will probably return to Rookie-level Bluefield to open the season.

Year	Club (League)	Class	W	L	ERA	G	GS	CG	SV	IP	H	HR	BB	SO	K/9	WHIP	AVG
2012	Blue Jays (DSL)	R	3	2	4.87	8	3	0	0	20	16	1	11	20	8.9	1.33	.232
2013	Blue Jays (DSL)	R	5	2	1.36	11	10	0	0	53	40	0	12	71	12.1	0.98	.208
	Blue Jays (GCL)	R	1	0	2.40	3	2	0	1	15	11	0	2	14	8.4	0.87	.212
	Bluefield (APP)	R	0	0	0.00	1	0	0	0	2	1	0	0	3	13.5	0.50	.111
Minor League Totals			9	4	2.29	23	15	0	1	90	68	1	25	108	10.8	1.03	.211

27 DWIGHT SMITH JR., OF

BA GRADE **45** HIGH

Born: Oct. 26, 1992. **B-T:** L-R. **Ht.:** 5-11. **Wt.:** 180. **Drafted:** HS—McIntosh, Ga., 2011 (1st round supplemental). **Signed by:** Eric McQueen.

Smith, whose father of the same name had an eight-year big league career, faces a tough profile as a corner outfielder without plus power, but his natural feel to hit, potentially above-average hit tool and plate discipline could give him high walk rates that overcome his lack of over-the-fence power. The lefthanded hitter has supreme hand-eye coordination and the most consistent swing in the organization. His compact swing produces hard contact and line drives to all fields. He commands the strike zone and has advanced pitch recognition. Although he has a strong, compact build, Smith's line-drive oriented swing path limits his power potential, which likely tops out around 10-12 home runs a year, but he projects to hit 30 or more doubles. His average speed and instincts could allow him to play center in a pinch, but he really fits better in a corner. His arm, which was below-average as an amateur, has improved to average and will work best in left at the highest levels. His speed should enable double-digit steals annually, and he stole bases efficiently (83 percent success rate) in 2013. Smith, who will likely start 2014 at high Class A Dunedin, will have to hit at every level but could become an everyday regular.

Year	Club (League)	Class	AVG	G	AB	R	H	2B	3B	HR	RBI	BB	SO	SB	CS	OBP	SLG
2012	Bluefield (APP)	R	.226	41	159	20	36	6	0	4	21	11	22	1	1	.289	.340
	Vancouver (NWL)	SS	.175	18	63	5	11	3	1	0	8	6	11	0	0	.254	.254
2013	Lansing (MWL)	LoA	.284	109	423	57	120	17	3	7	46	52	82	25	5	.365	.388
Minor League Totals			.259	168	645	82	167	26	4	11	75	69	115	26	6	.336	.363

28 JAKE BRENTZ, LHP

BA GRADE **50** EXTREME

Born: Sept. 14, 1994. **B-T:** L-L. **Ht.:** 6-2. **Wt.:** 195. **Drafted:** HS—Manchester, Mo., 2013 (11th round). **Signed by:** Darin Vaughn.

Scouts viewed Brentz as a potential top-five-rounds pick as an outfielder heading into the 2013 season, but his path to the draft changed when he touched 96 mph off the mound in the fall. His lack of experience on the mound and Missouri commitment made him a wild card, and the Jays took him in the 11th round. Brentz received a $700,000 signing bonus that was commensurate with third-round money. He has the upside to pitch in the front half of a major league rotation, but his inexperience will put him on a slow developmental track. He has an athletic, muscular and projectable build, with a loose, quick arm. The ball explodes out of his hand and he has a 90-95 mph fastball that can touch 97 with average movement. He has surprising feel for a changeup, a testament to his athleticism, and it's his best secondary offering. He needs to add power to his curveball, which flashes average, because it can get loopy. The priority for his development is learning to repeat his delivery so he can throw strikes consistently, which will include a smaller leg kick, not collapsing his back leg and getting on top of his fastball. Brentz will likely open 2014 in extended spring training before getting a short-season assignment.

Year	Club (League)	Class	W	L	ERA	G	GS	CG	SV	IP	H	HR	BB	SO	K/9	WHIP	AVG
2013	Blue Jays (GCL)	R	0	0	10.57	9	0	0	0	8	5	1	12	8	9.4	2.22	.192
Minor League Totals			0	0	10.57	9	0	0	0	8	5	1	12	8	9.4	2.22	.192

29 RYAN GOINS, 2B/SS

BA GRADE
40
LOW

Born: Feb. 13, 1988. **B-T:** L-R. **Ht.:** 5-10. **Wt.:** 170. **Drafted:** Dallas Baptist, 2009 (4th round). **Signed by:** Aaron Jersild.

Goins made steady progress through the system and made his major league debut in 2013. A minor league shortstop, he profiles as a utility player at the major league level but could be pressed into duty as a defense-first second baseman. He has athletic, polished defensive actions, defensive instincts and steady hands, and his best tool is his accurate, average arm. He played above-average defense in his major league stint. Goins profiles as a bottom-of-the-order hitter with well below-average power and a below-average hit tool. With a long stride and length to his swing, he is susceptible to breaking stuff and posted a 14-1 strikeout-walk ratio in a small major league sample, though he has posted acceptable strikeout rates for his career (17 percent). He swung at pitches out of the zone and struggled with pitches on the outer third of the plate. Goins is also a below-average runner and has been a run-erasing basestealer, with a 51 percent career success rate stealing bases. His reliable defense should allow Goins to see additional time with Toronto in 2014.

Year	Club (League)	Class	AVG	G	AB	R	H	2B	3B	HR	RBI	BB	SO	SB	CS	OBP	SLG
2009	Blue Jays (GCL)	R	.111	3	9	1	1	0	0	0	0	0	2	0	0	.111	.111
	Auburn (NYP)	SS	.297	24	101	15	30	5	1	0	8	8	23	2	2	.349	.366
	Lansing (MWL)	LoA	.198	19	81	6	16	4	0	0	9	7	23	1	2	.258	.247
2010	Lansing (MWL)	LoA	.308	77	295	49	91	19	2	3	35	35	60	6	7	.380	.417
	Dunedin (FSL)	HiA	.205	47	166	8	34	9	0	0	18	11	33	1	1	.251	.259
2011	Blue Jays (GCL)	R	.000	1	3	0	0	0	0	0	0	0	1	0	0	.000	.000
	Dunedin (FSL)	HiA	.286	101	353	50	101	24	5	3	52	32	67	2	2	.343	.408
2012	New Hampshire (EL)	AA	.289	136	546	66	158	33	4	7	61	47	78	15	9	.342	.403
2013	Buffalo (IL)	AAA	.257	111	377	42	97	22	1	6	46	29	85	3	5	.311	.369
	Toronto (AL)	MAJ	.252	34	119	11	30	5	0	2	8	2	28	0	0	.264	.345
Major League Totals			.252	34	119	11	30	5	0	2	8	2	28	0	0	.264	.345
Minor League Totals			.273	519	1931	237	528	116	13	19	229	169	372	30	28	.330	.376

30 YELTSIN GUDINO, SS

Born: Jan. 17, 1997. **B-T:** R-R. **Ht.:** 6-0. **Wt.:** 165. **Signed:** Venezuela, 2013. **Signed by:** Ismael Cruz/Luis Marquez/Jose Contreras.

A year after signing Franklin Barreto, the Jays continued to extract top-flight middle infield talent from Venezuela by signing Gudino for $1.29 million. A well-rounded player with a broad skill set, Gudino has the potential to be an everyday shortstop who excels on both sides of the ball. He is a polished, smooth defender with fluid actions, soft hands and a good internal clock. He has significant physical projection remaining as he fills out his frame and should have an above-average arm. He has put on 15 pounds since signing, and additional strength should make him an average runner and enhance his lateral quickness. With strong hand-eye coordination and a feel for the barrel, Gudino has the potential to be an average hitter. He has a good swing path, stays inside the ball well and hit consistently at international amateur tournaments, and he has narrowed his stance and reduced his stride as a pro. His offensive potential reminds some evaluators of Wilmer Flores, though Gudino is more athletic. Power is likely his fifth tool, but Gudino can drive the ball to the gaps. His tools play up because of his game awareness, intelligence and leadership qualities. Gudino will likely make his domestic debut in 2014.

Year	Club (League)	Class	AVG	G	AB	R	H	2B	3B	HR	RBI	BB	SO	SB	CS	OBP	SLG
Did not play—Signed 2014 contract																	

Washington Nationals

BY AARON FITT

After snapping the franchise's 31-year postseason drought in 2012, the Nationals headed into 2013 as a popular pick to win the World Series. But Washington scuffled out of the gate and played .500 ball for the season's first three months, then went into a tailspin in July. The low point came on Aug. 7, when Washington found itself six games below .500 and 15½ games out of first place.

For much of the season, the Nats were too reliant upon home runs to score, but they evolved into a more efficient offense down the stretch and finished 32-16. Core players Ian Desmond, Ryan Zimmerman and Jayson Werth all finished with strong seasons, while sophomore Bryce Harper turned in a historically good season for a 20-year-old despite a nagging hip injury.

Washington still has one of the best young cores in baseball, and a strong case can be made that they landed the best player available in four consecutive drafts. Having the No. 1 pick in back-to-back seasons helped, as Stephen Strasburg and Harper have thus far lived up to their lofty billing. Anthony Rendon was rated as the top prospect for the 2011 draft but slipped to the Nats at No. 6 because of injury concerns. Rendon finally stayed healthy in 2013 and turned in an impressive rookie season despite learning to play second base on the fly.

In 2012, Washington once again pounced on an elite talent who slid in the draft because of injury and signability issues. Righthander Lucas Giolito had Tommy John surgery shortly after signing for a $2.9 million bonus as the 16th pick, but he returned to action in 2013 and showed the kind of dazzling stuff that gives him a Strasburg-esque ceiling.

Opportunistic drafting clearly has played a big role in Washington's surge, but the player-development staff also deserves credit for developing homegrown talents like Desmond, Ross Detwiler and Taylor Jordan, who turned in an encouraging nine-start run in his big league debut.

After sending numerous young stars to the big leagues in recent years, Washington's farm system has been left somewhat depleted. The return of righthander A.J. Cole—traded away in the Gio Gonzalez deal but re-acquired from the Athletics last offseason in the three-team Michael Morse trade—helped immensely. Cole thrived in his return to the organization and established himself as one of Washington's top prospects.

ED WOLFSTEIN

Anthony Rendon put together a solid rookie season while learning second base on the fly

TOP PROSPECTS OF THE DECADE

Year	Player, Pos.	2013 Org.
2004	Clint Everts, rhp	Sugar Land (Atlantic)
2005	Mike Hinckley, lhp	Out of baseball
2006	Ryan Zimmerman, 3b	Nationals
2007	Collin Balester, rhp	Rangers
2008	Chris Marrero, 1b	Nationals
2009	Jordan Zimmermann, rhp	Nationals
2010	Stephen Strasburg, rhp	Nationals
2011	Bryce Harper, of	Nationals
2012	Bryce Harper, of	Nationals
2013	Anthony Rendon, 3b	Nationals

The Nationals are also starting to reap rewards from their rejuvenated Latin American program. Exciting young talents like Jefry Rodriguez and Rafael Bautista had sterling U.S. debuts, helping the Rookie-level Gulf Coast League Nationals put together an incredible 49-9 season.

After essentially starting over from scratch three and a half years ago, Washington is now spending money again in Latin America, highlighted by the $900,000 bonus it doled out for 16-year-old Dominican third baseman Anderson Franco in August. It has been a long time since Washington has been a player on the market for pricy international free agents, so this development is one more sign that the franchise is healthier than ever.

ORGANIZATION OVERVIEW

General Manager: Mike Rizzo. **Farm Director:** Bob Boone. **Scouting Director:** Kris Kline.

Class	Team	League	W	L	PCT	Finish	Manager
Majors	Washington Nationals	National	86	76	.531	6th (15)	Davey Johnson
Triple-A	Syracuse Chiefs	International	66	78	.458	11th (14)	Tony Beasley
Double-A	Harrisburg Senators	Eastern	77	65	.542	2nd (12)	Matt LeCroy
High Class A	Potomac Nationals	Carolina	84	55	.604	1st (8)	Brian Daubach
Low Class A	Hagerstown Suns	South Atlantic	80	57	.584	3rd (14)	Tripp Keister
Short-season	Auburn Doubledays	New York-Penn	26	49	.347	14th (14)	Gary Cathcart
Rookie	GCL Nationals	Gulf Coast	49	9	.845	1st (16)	Patrick Anderson
Overall 2013 Minor League Record			**382**	**313**	**.550**	**3rd (30)**	

THIS YEAR'S TOP 30

No.	Player, Pos.	Grade
1.	Lucas Giolito, rhp	70/High
2.	A.J. Cole, rhp	55/High
3.	Brian Goodwin, of	55/High
4.	Matt Skole, 1b/3b	50/Medium
5.	Robbie Ray, lhp	55/High
6.	Sammy Solis, lhp	50/High
7.	Michael Taylor, of	55/Extreme
8.	Jake Johansen, rhp	55/Extreme
9.	Nate Karns, rhp	45/Medium
10.	Steven Souza, of	50/High
11.	Matt Purke, lhp	50/High
12.	Billy Burns, of	45/Medium
13.	Tony Renda, 2b	50/High
14.	Zach Walters, ss/3b	45/Medium
15.	Austin Voth, rhp	50/High
16.	Pedro Severino, c	50/Extreme
17.	Drew Ward, 3b/1b	50/Extreme
18.	Aaron Barrett, rhp	45/Medium
19.	Jeff Kobernus, 2b/of	45/Medium
20.	Eury Perez, of	45/Medium
21.	Jefry Rodriguez, rhp	50/Extreme
22.	Nick Pivetta, rhp	50/Extreme
23.	Blake Treinen, rhp	45/Medium
24.	Christian Garcia, rhp	45/Medium
25.	Brett Mooneyham, lhp	45/High
26.	Nick Lee, lhp	45/High
27.	Robert Benincasa, rhp	45/High
28.	Rafael Bautista, of	45/Extreme
29.	Erik Davis, rhp	40/Safe
30.	Adrian Nieto, c	45/Extreme

LAST YEAR'S TOP 30

No.	Player, Pos.	Status
1.	Anthony Rendon, 3b	Majors
2.	Lucas Giolito, rhp	No. 1
3.	Brian Goodwin, of	No. 3
4.	Matt Skole, 3b	No. 4
5.	Nate Karns, rhp	No. 9
6.	Christian Garcia, rhp	No. 24
7.	Eury Perez, of	No. 20
8.	Sammy Solis, lhp	No. 6
9.	Matt Purke, lhp	No. 11
10.	Zach Walters, ss	No. 14
11.	Michael Taylor, of	No. 7
12.	Tony Renda, 2b	No. 13
13.	Taylor Jordan, rhp	Majors
14.	Jason Martinson, ss	Dropped out
15.	Sandy Leon, c	Dropped out
16.	Rick Hague, 2b	Dropped out
17.	Destin Hood, of	Dropped out
18.	Robbie Ray, lhp	No. 5
19.	Brett Mooneyham, lhp	No. 25
20.	Corey Brown, of	Dropped out
21.	Estarlin Martinez, of	Dropped out
22.	Brandon Miller, of	Dropped out
23.	Chris Marrero, 1b	(Free agent)
24.	Carlos Rivero, 3b/ss	(Free agent)
25.	Steven Souza, of	No. 10
26.	Billy Burns, of	No. 12
27.	Ivan Pineyro, rhp	(Cubs)
28.	Paul Demny, rhp	Dropped out
29.	Wirkin Estevez, rhp	Dropped out
30.	Jhonatan Solano, c	Dropped out

BEST TOOLS

Best Hitter for Average	Tony Renda
Best Power Hitter	Matt Skole
Best Strike-Zone Discipline	Billy Burns
Fastest Baserunner	Billy Burns
Best Athlete	Michael Taylor
Best Fastball	Lucas Giolito
Best Curveball	Lucas Giolito
Best Slider	Aaron Barrett
Best Changeup	Christian Garcia
Best Control	Taylor Hill
Best Defensive Catcher	Pedro Severino
Best Defensive Infielder	Stephen Perez
Best Infield Arm	Zach Walters
Best Defensive Outfielder	Michael Taylor
Best Outfield Arm	Narciso Mesa

TOP 15 PLAYERS 25 AND UNDER

No.	Player, Pos. (Age)	Peak Level
1.	Bryce Harper, of (21)	Majors
2.	Stephen Strasburg, rhp (24)	Majors
3.	Anthony Rendon, 2b (23)	Majors
4.	Lucas Giolito, rhp (18)	Short-season
5.	A.J. Cole, rhp (22)	Double-A
6.	Taylor Jordan, rhp (25)	Majors
7.	Brian Goodwin, of (23)	Double-A
8.	Matt Skole, 1b/3b (24)	Double-A
9.	Robbie Ray, lhp (22)	Double-A
10.	Sammy Solis, lhp (25)	High Class A
11.	Steven Lombardozzi, 2b/of (25)	Majors
12.	Ian Krol, lhp (22)	Majors
13.	Michael Taylor, of (23)	High Class A
14.	Jake Johansen, rhp (23)	Low Class A
15.	Steven Souza, of (24)	Double-A

MINOR LEAGUE DEPTH CHART

WASHINGTON NATIONALS

TOP 2014 ROOKIE: Nate Karns, rhp. He struggled in three big league starts in 2013, but Karns has the power stuff and experience to succeed in the big league bullpen now, or provide rotation depth.

BREAKOUT PROSPECT: Jefry Rodriguez, rhp. Lean, loose and projectable, Rodriguez already flashes 97 mph heat and the makings of a plus curveball, and he handled the Gulf Coast League with aplomb.

SOURCE OF TOP 30 TALENT			
Homegrown	**25**	**Acquired**	**5**
College	12	Trades	4
Junior college	3	Rule 5 draft	0
High school	6	Independent leagues	0
Nondrafted free agents	0	Free agents/waivers	1
International	4		

SLEEPER: Anderson Franco, 3b. Signed for $900,000 in July, Franco has a plus arm and intriguing leverage in his swing, but some scouts in the Dominican Republic weren't sold on his unorthodox swing, which leads to high strikeout totals.

LF
- Estarlin Martinez
- Destin Hood
- Wander Ramos

CF
- Brian Goodwin (3)
- Michael Taylor (7)
- Billy Burns (12)
- Eury Perez (20)
- Rafael Bautista (28)
- Narciso Mesa
- Corey Brown
- Isaac Ballou

RF
- Steven Souza (10)
- Brandon Miller

3B
- Drew Ward (17)
- Anderson Franco
- Cody Gunter

SS
- Zach Walters (14)
- Jason Martinson
- Stephen Perez
- Osvaldo Abreu
- David Masters

2B
- Tony Renda (13)
- Jeff Kobernus (19)
- Rick Hague
- Cutter Dykstra

1B
- Matt Skole (4)
- Shawn Pleffner
- Jimmy Yezzo

C
- Pedro Severino (16)
- Adrian Nieto (30)
- Jhonatan Solano
- Sandy Leon
- Raudy Read

LHP	
LHSP	**LHRP**
Robbie Ray (5)	Nick Lee (26)
Sammy Solis (6)	David Napoli
Matt Purke (11)	Hector Silvestre
Brett Mooneyham (25)	
Daniel Rosenbaum	
Kylin Turnbull	

RHP	
RHSP	**RHRP**
Lucas Giolito (1)	Aaron Barrett (18)
A.J. Cole (2)	Blake Treinen (23)
Jake Johansen (8)	Christian Garcia (24)
Nate Karns (9)	Robert Benincasa (27)
Austin Voth (15)	Erik Davis (29)
Jefry Rodriguez (21)	Taylor Hill
Nick Pivetta (22)	Dakota Bacus
Blake Schwartz	Ronaldo Pena
Paul Demny	Pedro Encarnacion
Dixon Anderson	Luis Reyes
	Reynaldo Abreu
	Wander Suero

DRAFT ANALYSIS

2013 — BONUSES: $2.7 MILLION

BEST PURE HITTER: 3B Drew Ward (3), the first position player the Nationals drafted, adjusted quickly to pro pitching even though he faced modest prep competition in rural Oklahoma and advanced his timeline by reclassifying from a high school junior to a senior last year so he could enter the '13 draft. He batted third most of the summer in the Rookie-level Gulf Coast League and hit .299.

BEST POWER HITTER: Ward's hit tool is ahead of his power, but he has strength and leverage in his 6-foot-4, 210-pound frame, and the Nationals expect him to come into average or better power. 1B Jimmy Yezzo (7) has plus raw power but must improve his aggressive approach to get to it more consistently.

FASTEST RUNNER: OF Isaac Ballou (15) is an above-average runner with above-average range in center field.

BEST DEFENSIVE PLAYER: SS David Masters (14) is a slick defender with excellent hands, above-average arm strength and easy infield actions. His total package earns comparisons to Paul Janish.

BEST FASTBALL: The Nationals' top selection, RHP Jake Johansen (2) touched 99 mph in the spring and did it again after signing, including in instructional league. He generally sits in the 94-96 mph range. RHPs Nic Pivetta (4) and Austin Voth (5) both run their fastballs up to 95 mph as well, with Voth usually holding his velocity deeper into starts.

BEST SECONDARY PITCH: Pivetta throws both a hard, downer curveball at 78-80 mph and a slower slurve. The Nats believe his harder breaking ball will play up when he stops throwing the slurve.

BEST PRO DEBUT: Voth and Johansen both dominated with short-season Auburn and earned promotions to low Class A Hagerstown. Voth was 3-0, 1.74 overall with 55 strikeouts and just six walks in 41 innings. Johansen posted a 1.92 ERA with 51 strikeouts in 52 innings.

BEST ATHLETE: Ballou, who reminds some scouts of ex-big leaguer Fred Lewis for his athleticism, speed and late development path.

MOST INTRIGUING BACKGROUND: RHP Andrew Cooper (12) is the nephew of NHL coach Joe Quenneville of the Stanley Cup champion Chicago Blackhawks. Masters' second cousin is "Mad Men" star John Hamm. IF Cody Dent (22) is the son of former big leaguer Bucky. Unsigned RHP Lukas Schiraldi (35) is the son of former big leaguer Calvin.

CLOSEST TO THE MAJORS: Johansen will race Voth, who has better control.

BEST LATE-ROUND PICK: Ballou and Masters have the chance to be big league contributors.

THE ONE WHO GOT AWAY: The Nats made runs at SS Garrett Hampson (26, Long Beach State) and hard-throwing RHP Andrew Dunlap (33, Rice). They had talks with Schiraldi (Texas) and injured RHP Karsten Whitson (37), an unsigned 2010 first-rounder who chose to return to Florida.

ASSESSMENT: Despite not having a first-round pick, Washington found power arms in Johansen, Pivetta and Voth. Ward may have to carry an otherwise thin class of position players on his own.

2012 — BONUSES: $4.9 MILLION

RHP Lucas Giolito (1) has regained No. 1-starter stuff since Tommy John surgery. 2B Tony Renda (2) and LHP Brett Mooneyham (3) provide depth.

GRADE: C

2011 — BONUSES: $15.0 MILLION

Injuries allowed the Nats to snag IF Anthony Rendon (1) sixth overall, and money allowed them to sign RHP Alex Meyer (1; traded to Twins) and OF Brian Goodwin (1s) for a combined $5 million.

GRADE: B+

2010 — BONUSES: $11.9 MILLION

OF Bryce Harper (1) keeps getting better. Washington also got pitching depth in LHPs Robbie Ray (12) and Sammy Solis (2) and RHP A.J. Cole (4).

GRADE: A

TOP DRAFT PICKS OF THE DECADE

Year	Player, Pos.	2013 Org.
2004	Bill Bray, lhp	Nationals
2005	Ryan Zimmerman, 3b	Nationals
2006	Chris Marrero, of	Nationals
2007	Ross Detwiler, lhp	Nationals
2008	*Aaron Crow, rhp	Royals
2009	Stephen Strasburg, rhp	Nationals
2010	Bryce Harper, of	Nationals
2011	Anthony Rendon, 3b	Nationals
2012	Lucas Giolito, rhp	Nationals
2013	Jake Johansen, rhp (2nd round)	Nationals

*Did not sign.

LARGEST BONUSES IN CLUB HISTORY

Stephen Strasburg, 2009	$7,500,000
Bryce Harper, 2010	$6,250,000
Anthony Rendon, 2011	$6,000,000
Brian Goodwin, 2011	$3,000,000
Ryan Zimmerman, 2006	$2,975,000

1 LUCAS GIOLITO, RHP

Born: July 14, 1994. **B-T:** R-R. **Ht.:** 6-6. **Wt.:** 225. **Drafted:** HS—Studio City, Calif., 2012 (1st round). **Signed by:** Mark Baca.

After establishing himself as a big-name prep prospect years ago, Giolito dazzled in the fall and winter of his senior year at Harvard-Westlake High, prompting some scouts to suggest he had a chance to be the best high school righthander in draft history. He regularly ran his fastball up to 99 mph that January and February, but he sprained the ulnar collateral ligament in his elbow in early March, ending his season and transforming him into a draft wild card. The son of Hollywood actors Lindsay Frost and Rick Giolito, Lucas made it clear a hefty bonus would be required to sign him away from a UCLA commitment. The price tag, coupled with the injury, caused Giolito to fall to the Nationals at No. 16, and they signed him for $2,925,000, exceeding his assigned pick value by $800,000. He made one pro appearance in 2012 before having Tommy John surgery on Aug. 31, but he returned to game action about 10 months later in the Rookie-level Gulf Coast League, where his stuff was as electric as ever. He continued dominating in three August outings in the short-season New York-Penn League.

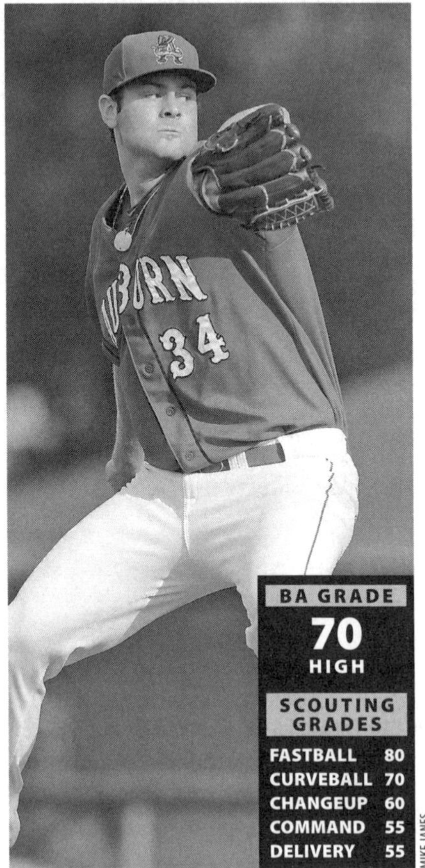

BA GRADE
70
HIGH
SCOUTING GRADES
FASTBALL 80
CURVEBALL 70
CHANGEUP 60
COMMAND 55
DELIVERY 55

MIKE JANES

The first three pitches out of Giolito's hand in his 2013 GCL debut were 100 mph fastballs. His fastball routinely ranges from 93-100 with exceptional downhill angle, and he learned by the end of the summer that he was more comfortable and had better command when he sat at 95-97, rather than reaching back for triple digits all the time. Between his velocity and his angle, Giolito's fastball rates as a true 80 pitch on the 20-80 scouting scale, and he does it with minimal effort. He also throws a 12-to-6 power curveball in the 84-86 range that Nationals pitching coordinator Spin Williams has called one of the best curves he's ever seen when Giolito throws a good one. It has late bite and excellent depth, projecting as a plus-plus pitch with a chance to be a second 80 offering. Giolito is still learning to control his 6-foot-6 body, and his delivery is not always in sync. When he does not repeat his delivery, his curveball is not as good, and neither is his fastball command. When he throws his 82-83 mph changeup with conviction, it flashes plus, but it remains a work in progress. Giolito also stands out for his competitive mound demeanor and tireless work ethic, and he spent his rehab learning bunt defenses and working on his fielding, which helped him make big strides holding runners and fielding his position this summer.

Giolito has a real chance to become a No. 1 starter in the big leagues, because his repertoire is electrifying and his feel for pitching is fairly advanced for his age. The Nationals have a great track record with building pitchers back up after Tommy John surgery—former No. 1 prospects Jordan Zimmermann and Stephen Strasburg both overcame the procedure to become stars—which allays concerns about Giolito's long-term health. The next step is proving he can handle a full-season workload. He figures to start 2014 at low Class A Hagerstown, and if he dominates as expected, he could move quickly. A big league debut by the end of 2015 is within the realm of possibility, though 2016 is a safer bet.

Year	Club (League)	Class	W	L	ERA	G	GS	CG	SV	IP	H	HR	BB	SO	K/9	WHIP	AVG
2012	Nationals (GCL)	R	0	0	4.50	1	1	0	0	2	2	0	0	1	4.5	1.00	.286
2013	Nationals (GCL)	R	1	1	2.78	8	8	0	0	23	19	0	10	25	9.9	1.28	.232
	Auburn (NYP)	SS	1	0	0.64	3	3	0	0	14	9	1	4	14	9.0	0.93	.191
Minor League Totals			2	1	2.09	12	12	0	0	39	30	1	14	40	9.3	1.14	.221

2 A.J. COLE, RHP

Born: Jan. 5, 1992. **B-T:** R-R. **Ht.:** 6-4. **Wt.:** 180. **Drafted:** HS—Oviedo, Fla., 2010 (4th round). **Signed by:** Paul Tinnell.

The Nationals signed Cole for a fourth-round-record $2 million bonus in 2010, then traded him to Oakland in the Gio Gonzalez deal after the 2011 season. He spent one year with the Athletics, then returned to the Nationals in the March 2013 Michael Morse deal. Cole pitches predominantly off his explosive fastball, which sits at 94-95 mph and regularly touches 97. His two-seamer has plus sink, and his four-seamer has riding life. His fastball command is solid, but it remains better to his arm side than his glove side. His second pitch is a fringe-average changeup that flashes plus when he maintains his arm speed. The biggest knock on Cole is his lack of a wipeout breaking ball, but he worked hard to tighten it up and add some power to it this year. The shape and depth of the pitch are inconsistent, and so is the velocity, which ranges from 75-82 mph. Whether it winds up as a curve or a slider, it has a chance to be fringy to average in time. Cole should get a shot in Triple-A in 2014. He could get a big league callup by season's end and projects as a mid-rotation starter.

Year	Club (League)	Class	W	L	ERA	G	GS	CG	SV	IP	H	HR	BB	SO	K/9	WHIP	AVG
2010	Vermont (NYP)	SS	0	0	0.00	1	0	0	0	1	1	0	1	1	9.0	2.00	.333
2011	Hagerstown (SAL)	LoA	4	7	4.04	20	18	0	0	89	87	6	24	108	10.9	1.25	.251
2012	Stockton (CAL)	HiA	0	7	7.82	8	8	0	0	38	60	7	10	31	7.3	1.84	.364
	Burlington (MWL)	LoA	6	3	2.07	19	19	0	0	96	78	7	19	102	9.6	1.01	.222
2013	Potomac (CAR)	HiA	6	3	4.25	18	18	0	0	97	96	12	23	102	9.4	1.22	.257
	Harrisburg (EL)	AA	4	2	2.18	7	7	0	0	45	31	3	10	49	9.7	0.90	.188
Minor League Totals			20	22	3.73	73	70	0	0	366	353	35	87	393	9.7	1.20	.252

3 BRIAN GOODWIN, OF

WILL BENTZEL-HARRISBURG SENATORS

Born: Nov. 2, 1990. **B-T:** L-L. **Ht.:** 6-1. **Wt.:** 195. **Drafted:** Miami Dade JC, 2011 (1st round supplemental). **Signed by:** Alex Morales.

After signing for $3 million in 2011, Goodwin reached Double-A by the second half of 2012, but he has struggled at that level for the last year and a half. He hit just .204 against Double-A lefties in 2013, but he showed a more disciplined approach in the final month. Goodwin has tantalizing five-tool ability. His best tool is his speed, which rates as a 65 on the 20-80 scale, but he still needs to refine his routes in center field and his basestealing acumen. He has at least a chance to be a solid-average to above-average defender with an average arm. Goodwin has plenty of bat speed and average power potential, but he still has work to do at the plate. His approach can still be segmented, causing his swing to be late. If he can get himself into better hitting position more consistently and learn to chase fewer lefthanded breaking balls, he could become a slightly above-average hitter. Some evaluators think Goodwin has all-star potential, while others view him as a borderline regular or even an extra outfielder. He figures to reach Triple-A in 2014 and could compete for a big league job by 2015.

Year	Club (League)	Class	AVG	G	AB	R	H	2B	3B	HR	RBI	BB	SO	SB	CS	OBP	SLG
2012	Hagerstown (SAL)	LoA	.324	58	216	47	70	18	1	9	38	43	39	15	4	.438	.542
	Harrisburg (EL)	AA	.223	42	166	17	37	8	1	5	14	18	50	3	3	.306	.373
2013	Harrisburg (EL)	AA	.252	122	457	82	115	19	11	10	40	66	121	19	11	.355	.407
Minor League Totals			.265	222	839	146	222	45	13	24	92	127	210	37	18	.368	.435

4 MATT SKOLE, 1B/3B

WILL BENTZEL-HARRISBURG SENATORS

Born: July 30, 1989. **B-T:** L-R. **Ht.:** 6-4. **Wt.:** 220. **Drafted:** Georgia Tech, 2011 (5th round). **Signed by:** Eric Robinson.

Skole won South Atlantic League MVP honors and was named Washington's minor league hitter of the year in 2012. His 2013 season was cut short in his second game when he collided with a runner while playing first base, causing a microfracture in his wrist and severing the ulnar collateral ligament in his non-throwing elbow. He had Tommy John surgery and wrist surgery but returned to action in the Arizona Fall League, where he homered twice in his first four games. Skole's calling card is his plus lefthanded power, primarily to the pull side. He has a flicker with his bat head right before letting loose on the baseball, and he generates serious bat speed. The Nationals helped him get more out of his huge frame by minimizing his leg kick, solidifying his base and improving his balance. He showed an improved ability to stay back and drive breaking pitches the other way in his last healthy season. Skole also has an advanced feel for the strike zone, giving him a chance to be an average or slightly better hitter. He has good hands at either infield corner and a solid arm, but he lacks the range at the hot corner, so he figures to focus on first base going forward. Skole will return to Harrisburg to start 2014, and he could push for a big league callup by season's end. He is the best power prospect in the system and could be the organization's first baseman of the future.

Year	Club (League)	Class	AVG	G	AB	R	H	2B	3B	HR	RBI	BB	SO	SB	CS	OBP	SLG
2011	Auburn (NYP)	SS	.290	72	272	43	79	23	1	5	48	42	52	2	1	.382	.438
2012	Hagerstown (SAL)	LoA	.286	101	343	73	98	18	0	27	92	94	116	10	0	.438	.574
	Potomac (CAR)	HiA	.314	18	70	11	22	10	1	0	12	5	17	1	0	.355	.486
2013	Harrisburg (EL)	AA	.200	2	5	1	1	1	0	0	2	2	2	0	0	.429	.400
Minor League Totals			.290	193	690	128	200	52	2	32	154	143	187	13	1	.410	.510

5 ROBBIE RAY, LHP

WILL BENTZEL-HARRISBURG SENATORS

BA GRADE
55
HIGH

Born: Oct. 1, 1991. **B-T:** L-L. **Ht.:** 6-2. **Wt.:** 170. **Drafted:** HS—Brentwood, Tenn., 2010 (12th round). **Signed by:** Paul Faulk.

Ray first made a name for himself by flashing mid-90s heat on the high school showcase circuit, but he pitched mostly in the 87-91 mph range and topped out at 93 over his first three pro seasons. His velocity jumped in 2013, and his prospect status jumped with it. He ranked as the No. 16 prospect in the high Class A Carolina League, and he more than held his own as a 21-year-old in the Double-A Eastern League following a midseason promotion. In their 2012 instructional league, the Nationals made an adjustment with Ray's lower half to maximize his deception, and hitters struggle to pick up his fastball. He attacks hitters primarily with his heater, which ranges from 91-96 mph, averaging about 93. His arm still drags at times, causing his release point and command to be inconsistent, but he is a good athlete with a loose arm, prompting scouts to project his command as at least average. His changeup came along nicely in 2013, showing flashes of being a slightly above-average pitch in the low 80s. The biggest question about Ray is whether he has enough feel to spin an effective breaking ball. He throws a short slurve that ranges from 74-79 mph, and too many of them are tumblers with loose spin, rating as 35 pitches. His best ones are average, but the pitch still has a long way to go. Ray's plus fastball, athleticism and durable frame give him a chance to be a mid-rotation starter if he can develop his breaking ball. He'll continue to work on the pitch as a 22-year-old in Double-A next year.

Year	Club (League)	Class	W	L	ERA	G	GS	CG	SV	IP	H	HR	BB	SO	K/9	WHIP	AVG
2010	Vermont (NYP)	SS	0	0	0.00	1	0	0	0	1	0	0	0	2	18.0	0.00	.000
2011	Hagerstown (SAL)	LoA	2	3	3.13	20	20	0	0	89	71	3	38	95	9.6	1.22	.221
2012	Potomac (CAR)	HiA	4	12	6.56	22	21	0	0	106	122	14	49	86	7.3	1.62	.292
2013	Potomac (CAR)	HiA	6	3	3.11	16	16	3	0	84	60	9	41	100	10.7	1.20	.205
	Harrisburg (EL)	AA	5	2	3.72	11	11	1	0	58	56	4	21	60	9.3	1.33	.247
Minor League Totals			17	20	4.29	70	68	4	0	338	309	30	149	343	9.1	1.36	.245

6 SAMMY SOLIS, LHP

BA GRADE
50
HIGH

Born: Aug. 10, 1988. **B-T:** R-L. **Ht.:** 6-5. **Wt.:** 230. **Drafted:** San Diego, 2010 (2nd round). **Signed by:** Tim Reynolds.

Staying healthy has been an issue for Solis since his college days, but his body and stuff tantalize when he is on the mound. He missed almost all of 2009 at San Diego with a herniated disc in his back, then saw his first full pro season in 2011 delayed by a quadriceps injury. He missed all of 2012 after having Tommy John surgery, but he returned to action in May and looked stronger than ever. Right before he injured his elbow, Solis had touched 96-97 mph, but his comfort zone this year was 89-93, touching 95 early in games. His fastball has natural tail and run, and he has solid command of it. His No. 2 pitch is usually his changeup, which projects as a slightly above-average to plus offering, but there are days his slurvy breaking ball can be the more effective pitch. The three-quarters breaking ball is still somewhat inconsistent, sometimes flashing solid-average but other times rating as a slightly below-average pitch. Solis has a good delivery, a physical frame and an unflappable demeanor on the mound. With a chance for three average to plus pitches from the left side, Solis has a chance to be a No. 4 starter in the majors, if he can stay healthy. He's already 25 and has not yet reached Double-A, so the Nationals figure to push him in 2014, starting with an assignment to Harrisburg. He could reach Washington by season's end.

Year	Club (League)	Class	W	L	ERA	G	GS	CG	SV	IP	H	HR	BB	SO	K/9	WHIP	AVG
2010	Hagerstown (SAL)	LoA	0	0	0.00	2	2	0	0	4	2	0	0	3	6.8	0.50	.143
2011	Hagerstown (SAL)	LoA	2	1	4.02	7	7	0	0	40	39	3	12	40	8.9	1.26	.253
	Potomac (CAR)	HiA	6	2	2.72	10	10	0	0	56	61	5	11	53	8.5	1.28	.279
2013	Nationals (GCL)	R	0	0	0.00	1	1	0	0	2	1	0	0	3	13.5	0.50	.167
	Potomac (CAR)	HiA	2	1	3.43	13	12	0	0	58	58	3	19	40	6.2	1.34	.270
Minor League Totals			10	4	3.20	33	32	0	0	160	161	11	42	139	7.8	1.27	.265

7 MICHAEL TAYLOR, OF

Born: March 26, 1991. **B-T:** R-R. **Ht.:** 6-4. **Wt.:** 205. **Drafted:** HS—Fort Lauderdale, 2009 (6th round). **Signed by:** Tony Arango.

Drafted as a shortstop, Taylor took to center field in a hurry and made himself into a legitimate prospect based primarily on his spectacular defense. After struggling offensively in high Class A in 2012, he repeated the level in 2013 and made major gains. The wiry, quick-twitch Taylor earns frequent physical comparisons to Mike Cameron and Adam Jones. He's a plus runner with plus-plus range thanks to his outstanding reads and jumps, and his plus arm is accurate. He made huge strides with his baserunning, demonstrating good leads, reads and jumps. Taylor also has above-average raw power, but scouts have reservations about whether he'll ever hit enough to unlock it. He has a choppy, disjointed swing and a tendency to get very aggressive with his stride, though he made progress toning it down in instructional league. He still struggles mightily against offspeed stuff, but he can punish fastballs in or over the plate. If Taylor can become even a below-average hitter, his other tools could give him significant big league value. If he can mature into a fringy or average hitter, he can be an all-star. Next year will be a big test, as he'll get his first taste of upper-level pitching in Double-A.

Year	Club (League)	Class	AVG	G	AB	R	H	2B	3B	HR	RBI	BB	SO	SB	CS	OBP	SLG
2010	Nationals (GCL)	R	.195	38	128	14	25	4	3	1	12	14	31	1	2	.270	.297
	Hagerstown (SAL)	LoA	.231	5	13	0	3	1	0	0	1	1	2	0	0	.333	.308
2011	Hagerstown (SAL)	LoA	.253	126	442	64	112	26	7	13	68	32	120	23	12	.310	.432
2012	Potomac (CAR)	HiA	.242	109	384	51	93	33	2	3	37	40	113	19	9	.318	.362
2013	Potomac (CAR)	HiA	.263	133	509	79	134	41	6	10	87	55	131	51	7	.340	.426
Minor League Totals			.249	411	1476	208	367	105	18	27	205	142	397	94	30	.319	.399

8 JAKE JOHANSEN, RHP

RODGER WOOD

Born: Jan. 23, 1991. **B-T:** R-R. **Ht.:** 6-6. **Wt.:** 235. **Drafted:** Dallas Baptist, 2013 (2nd round). **Signed by:** Ed Gustafson.

Johansen never harnessed his potential at Dallas Baptist, where he went 7-6, 5.40 in 15 starts as a fourth-year junior in 2013. The Nationals were pleased to land a player with Johansen's arm strength with their top pick (No. 68 overall), and his pro debut in the New York-Penn League was very encouraging. Though his command and his secondary stuff remain works in progress, Johansen dominated the NY-P with a premium fastball that sat at 94-96 mph with heavy sink and topped out at 99. He arrived in pro ball with a poor 74-77 mph curveball, but he threw it with more power as the summer progressed, coming in at 77-83 with tighter rotation at its best. He also made progress with his 86-90 cutter/slider and showed improving feel for his changeup, but all of his secondary stuff needs refinement. The Nats think Johansen is a late-bloomer who is still growing into his huge frame, but when he maintains a quick tempo, he can throw strikes and succeed. The Nats will keep Johansen in a starting role as long as possible, and if everything clicks, he has No. 3 starter upside, though many scouts see him as a better fit in the back of a bullpen.

Year	Club (League)	Class	W	L	ERA	G	GS	CG	SV	IP	H	HR	BB	SO	K/9	WHIP	AVG
2013	Auburn (NYP)	SS	1	1	1.06	10	10	0	0	42	22	1	18	44	9.4	0.94	.147
	Hagerstown (SAL)	LoA	0	2	5.79	2	2	0	0	9	13	1	5	7	6.8	1.93	.317
Minor League Totals			1	3	1.92	12	12	0	0	52	35	2	23	51	8.9	1.12	.183

9 NATE KARNS, RHP

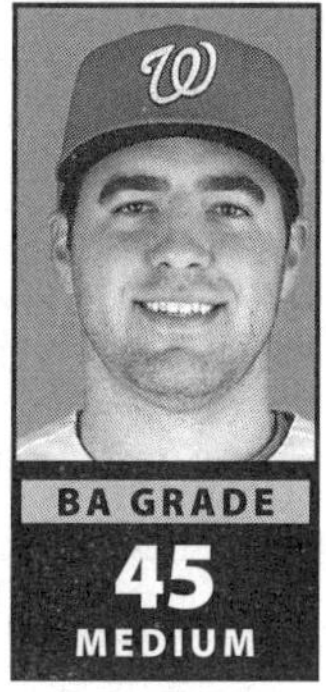

Born: Nov. 25, 1987. **B-T:** R-R. **Ht.:** 6-3. **Wt.:** 230. **Drafted:** Texas Tech, 2009 (12th round). **Signed by:** Jimmy Gonzales.

Karns recovered from a torn labrum to jump back onto the prospect landscape in 2012, leading the minor leagues in opponent average (.174) in his full-season debut. He followed that up with a strong season in the Double-A Eastern League. Karns made his big league debut in May but was sent back down to Harrisburg after struggling in three starts. He really found his groove upon his return to the EL, posting a 2.57 ERA the rest of the way. Physical and aggressive, Karns attacks hitters with a 91-95 mph power sinker, peaking at 98 on occasion. He has a second plus pitch in his wipeout hammer curveball, which ranges from 82-85 mph. He's still learning to throw the curve for strikes, but he excels at getting hitters to chase it. Karns also has a below-average changeup at 83-85 mph, but his feel for it increased marginally in 2013. He has a long arm action and a stiff front leg, leading to just fair command, though he does throw strikes with his fastball. Unless Karns can make significant strides with his command and his third pitch, he profiles best as a big league set-up man. He'll enter 2014 as a 26-year-old in Triple-A, where he will continue to work as a starter.

Year	Club (League)	Class	W	L	ERA	G	GS	CG	SV	IP	H	HR	BB	SO	K/9	WHIP	AVG
2010	Did not play—Injured																
2011	Nationals (GCL)	R	0	0	0.00	5	5	0	0	19	2	0	6	26	12.5	0.43	.035
	Auburn (NYP)	SS	3	2	3.44	8	8	0	0	37	27	1	27	33	8.1	1.47	.211
2012	Hagerstown (SAL)	LoA	3	0	2.03	11	5	1	2	44	23	1	21	61	12.4	0.99	.148
	Potomac (CAR)	HiA	8	4	2.26	13	13	1	0	72	47	1	26	87	10.9	1.02	.190
2013	Washington (NL)	MAJ	0	1	7.50	3	3	0	0	12	17	5	6	11	8.3	1.92	.321
	Harrisburg (EL)	AA	10	6	3.26	23	23	3	0	133	109	14	48	155	10.5	1.18	.224
Major League Totals			0	1	7.50	3	3	0	0	12	17	5	6	11	8.3	1.92	.321
Minor League Totals			24	12	2.66	60	54	5	2	304	208	17	128	362	10.7	1.11	.194

10 STEVEN SOUZA, OF

WILL BENTZEL-HARRISBURG SENATORS

BA GRADE
50
HIGH

Born: April 24, 1989. **B-T:** R-R. **Ht.:** 6-3. **Wt.:** 220. **Drafted:** HS—Everett, Wash., 2007 (3rd round). **Signed by:** Doug McMillan.

Maturity issues undermined Souza's ability to maximize his tantalizing raw talent for the first few years of his career. As he grew up, he rejuvenated his career with a breakout 2012 campaign, then performed well in Double-A in 2013, though he missed time with an oblique injury. Souza is a physical specimen with multiple loud tools. He has 65 raw power and is capable of hitting home runs from pole to pole. A former third baseman, Souza has found a home as a corner outfielder, where he is a solid-average defender with a plus arm. He's also a slightly above-average runner with good baserunning instincts. If Souza hits, he has the tool set to be an everyday right fielder. He has done a better job staying in his legs and maintaining a balanced swing, helping him drive the ball to all fields. Souza can hit premium velocity, but his swing still has some length, making him vulnerable against offspeed stuff. He couples his high strikeout totals with an improving walk rate, though he remains a fringe-average hitter. He should advance to Triple-A in 2014. Washington retained Souza by adding him to the 40-man roster this fall, preventing him from becoming a minor league free agent.

Year	Club (League)	Class	AVG	G	AB	R	H	2B	3B	HR	RBI	BB	SO	SB	CS	OBP	SLG
2007	Nationals (GCL)	R	.194	44	144	17	28	9	0	4	19	18	46	4	1	.299	.340
2008	Hagerstown (SAL)	LoA	.266	23	79	14	21	4	0	2	10	8	26	8	2	.348	.392
	Vermont (NYP)	SS	.189	48	175	27	33	7	0	5	25	24	54	14	7	.296	.314
2009	Hagerstown (SAL)	LoA	.237	126	447	52	106	18	3	4	47	54	116	25	10	.325	.318
2010	Hagerstown (SAL)	LoA	.231	81	303	49	70	16	6	11	56	27	85	18	4	.306	.432
2011	Potomac (CAR)	HiA	.228	122	390	58	89	17	2	11	56	75	131	25	9	.360	.367
2012	Hagerstown (SAL)	LoA	.290	70	262	48	76	20	2	17	72	22	49	7	7	.346	.576
	Potomac (CAR)	HiA	.319	27	91	16	29	2	1	6	13	13	25	7	1	.421	.560
2013	Nationals (GCL)	R	.200	4	10	3	2	1	0	0	2	3	4	2	0	.400	.300
	Harrisburg (EL)	AA	.300	77	273	54	82	23	1	15	44	41	76	20	6	.396	.557
Minor League Totals			.247	622	2174	338	536	117	15	75	344	285	612	130	47	.342	.418

11 MATT PURKE, LHP

BA GRADE
50
HIGH

Born: July 17, 1990. **B-T:** L-L. **Ht.:** 6-4. **Wt.:** 205. **Drafted:** Texas Christian, 2011 (3rd round). **Signed by:** Ed Gustafson.

Purke has lost prospect luster since the Rangers drafted him 14th overall out of high school in 2009. After a deal with Texas fell apart, he wound up at Texas Christian, where he went 16-0 to earn BA Freshman of the Year honors in 2010. Injuries torpedoed Purke's sophomore season, but the Nationals nevertheless signed their third-rounder for a $2.75 million bonus and $4.15 million total guaranteed. He pitched just 15 innings in his 2012 pro debut before having surgery in August to relieve bursitis and clean out scar tissue in his shoulder. When he returned to action in 2013, Purke's stuff was rather pedestrian, as he worked mostly at 88-91 mph with inconsistent secondary stuff. He was better in the Arizona Fall League, working at 90-93 mph and flashing a plus changeup in the 82-84 range. Purke's changeup projects as an above-average to plus offering that enables him to get swings-and-misses. His slurvy breaking ball sometimes looks more like a show-me curveball in the mid-70s and sometimes like an average 11-to-5 pitch at 78-80 mph. His fastball has decent arm-side run and sink, helping him get groundball outs. Purke's breaking ball should be effective enough against lefties to give him a floor as a middle reliever, but he still has a chance to become a back-end starter if he can harness his command, because he has the makings of three average or better pitches. He'll advance to Double-A Harrisburg in 2014.

Year	Club (League)	Class	W	L	ERA	G	GS	CG	SV	IP	H	HR	BB	SO	K/9	WHIP	AVG
2012	Hagerstown (SAL)	LoA	0	2	5.87	3	3	0	0	15	15	1	12	14	8.2	1.76	.263
2013	Hagerstown (SAL)	LoA	1	1	2.48	6	6	0	0	29	25	3	7	41	12.7	1.10	.229
	Potomac (CAR)	HiA	5	3	4.43	12	12	0	0	61	67	3	18	41	6.0	1.39	.284
Minor League Totals			6	6	4.10	21	21	0	0	105	107	7	37	96	8.2	1.37	.266

12 BILLY BURNS, OF

Born: Aug. 30, 1989. **B-T:** B-R. **Ht.:** 5-9. **Wt.:** 180. **Drafted:** Mercer, 2011 (32nd round). **Signed by:** Eric Robinson.

The son of former New York Jets running back Bob Burns, Billy is a premium athlete who has made himself into a prospect despite his lack of size. A switch-hitter in high school, he hit solely from the right side in college, and the Nationals reintroduced the lefthanded swing in 2011 instructional league. Burns has a slap-and-dash approach from the left side and a little more strength from the right side, but he has no power and does not try to hit home runs. His game is completely built around his 80 speed, which allows him to beat out infield hits and bunt his way on base regularly. Burns has walked more than he's struck out in his pro career, and his patient approach makes him a perfect table-setter. His reads and jumps on the basepaths improved immensely in 2013, helping him rank third in the minors with 74 steals in 81 attempts between high Class A and Double-A. He also cuts bases extremely well. Burns is capable of making dazzling plays in center field and left, but he is actually a better defender in the latter. His arm is below-average, but he worked on improving it in instructional league. Burns plays with intensity and savvy, and he knows his strengths and weaknesses better than any player in the system. A lack of impact offensive ability causes many scouts to view him as a fourth outfielder, but he might begin winning converts if he continues hitting at Double-A to start 2014.

Year	Club (League)	Class	AVG	G	AB	R	H	2B	3B	HR	RBI	BB	SO	SB	CS	OBP	SLG
2011	Auburn (NYP)	SS	.262	32	107	21	28	3	2	1	18	12	22	13	1	.367	.355
2012	Hagerstown (SAL)	LoA	.322	113	398	83	128	14	5	0	41	65	68	38	9	.432	.382
2013	Potomac (CAR)	HiA	.312	91	330	70	103	8	9	0	29	52	37	54	5	.422	.391
	Harrisburg (EL)	AA	.325	30	114	26	37	4	0	0	8	20	17	20	2	.434	.360
Minor League Totals			.312	266	949	200	296	29	16	1	96	149	144	125	17	.421	.379

13 TONY RENDA, 2B

Born: Jan. 24,1991. **B-T:** R-R. **Ht.:** 5-10. **Wt.:** 170. **Drafted:** California, 2012 (2nd round). **Signed by:** Fred Costello.

A career .347 hitter during a standout three-year career at California, Renda stands out for his pure hitting ability and his makeup. He had a solid but unspectacular pro debut after signing for $500,000 as a second-round pick in 2012, and then he ranked second in the minors with 43 doubles in his first full season in 2013. Generously listed at 5-foot-10, Renda will never be a home run hitter, but he is strong enough to drive the gaps, and he makes consistently hard, line-drive contact with a slight uppercut stroke. He controls the strike zone well and never gives away an at-bat, and he has a chance to be an above-average hitter. None of his other tools rate as above-average, but the sum may be greater than the parts. Renda has average speed, but he is an efficient, aggressive basestealer, helping him swipe 45 bags in 54 tries in his pro career. He was an unpolished, mechanical defender at second base when the Nationals drafted him, and scouts who saw him early last year said his hands were stiff and his instincts were questionable. But he made progress improving his hands, footwork, reads and pivots in 2013, giving him a chance to become a fringy to average defender with an average arm. Renda needs to be seen in large doses to be appreciated, and scouts who like him invoke the names Freddy Sanchez or Ryan Theriot. He lacks the defensive versatility to carve out a career as a utilityman, so he'll need to hit. Renda will advance to high Class A Potomac to begin 2014 but could push his way to Double-A by midseason.

Year	Club (League)	Class	AVG	G	AB	R	H	2B	3B	HR	RBI	BB	SO	SB	CS	OBP	SLG
2012	Auburn (NYP)	SS	.264	71	295	47	78	9	0	0	32	31	33	15	3	.341	.295
2013	Hagerstown (SAL)	LoA	.294	135	521	99	153	43	3	3	51	68	65	30	6	.380	.405
Minor League Totals			.283	206	816	146	231	52	3	3	83	99	98	45	9	.366	.365

14 ZACH WALTERS, SS/3B

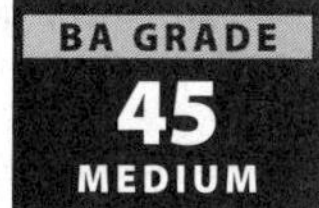

Born: Sept. 5, 1989. **B-T:** B-R. **Ht.:** 6-2. **Wt.:** 220. **Drafted:** San Diego, 2010 (9th round). **Signed by:** Jeffrey Mousser (Diamondbacks).

A ninth-round pick by the Diamondbacks, Walters was traded for Jason Marquis in 2011. A broken hamate bone sapped his power in 2012, but he stayed healthy at Triple-A Syracuse in 2013 and saw his power numbers jump, tying for the International League lead with 29 home runs and earning him a September callup. Walters has good extension and leverage in his swing, particularly from the left side (he hit 25 of 29 homers in 2013 against righties). He has above-average raw power and the ability to drive the ball to all fields, but he is a free swinger who must learn to control the strike zone and take more walks. He has a tendency to get out on his front side and chase pitches. Walters is a good athlete with a plus arm that plays at shortstop, but he has stiff hands and he tends to make too many careless throwing errors. If he can improve his defensive instincts and actions, he could become an adequate defensive shortstop with offensive upside. Walters, however, profiles better as a utilityman who can fill in all around the infield or on an outfield corner. He's a fringe-average runner who lacks exceptional first-step quickness but is better underway. Walters could compete for a backup job in the majors in 2104, but he would benefit from more time at Triple-A to refine all aspects of his game.

Year	Club (League)	Class	AVG	G	AB	R	H	2B	3B	HR	RBI	BB	SO	SB	CS	OBP	SLG
2010	Yakima (NWL)	SS	.302	69	275	44	83	18	4	4	43	16	59	14	4	.338	.440
2011	South Bend (MWL)	LoA	.302	97	361	69	109	27	6	9	56	42	96	12	10	.377	.485
	Potomac (CAR)	HiA	.293	30	116	15	34	7	1	0	11	8	33	7	1	.336	.371
2012	Potomac (CAR)	HiA	.269	54	193	24	52	8	1	5	24	10	43	6	3	.304	.399
	Harrisburg (EL)	AA	.293	43	164	23	48	11	4	6	19	8	38	1	0	.326	.518
	Syracuse (IL)	AAA	.214	29	98	9	21	4	0	1	6	6	28	0	0	.260	.286
2013	Syracuse (IL)	AAA	.253	134	487	69	123	32	5	29	77	20	134	4	3	.286	.517
	Washington (NL)	MAJ	.375	8	8	2	3	0	1	0	1	1	0	0	0	.444	.625
Major League Totals			.375	8	8	2	3	0	1	0	1	1	0	0	0	.444	.625
Minor League Totals			.277	456	1694	253	470	107	21	54	236	110	431	44	21	.322	.461

15 AUSTIN VOTH, RHP

BA GRADE 50 HIGH

Born: June 26, 1992. **B-T:** R-R. **Ht.:** 6-1. **Wt.:** 190. **Drafted:** Washington, 2013 (5th round). **Signed by:** Fred Costello.

Voth had a solid but unspectacular three-year career at Washington, highlighted by his 7-6, 2.99 junior season in 2013. He spent two summers in the Cape Cod League, where he ditched his "bendy" curveball, as he called it, for a slider in 2012. His slider has developed into a promising pitch, a short, 83-85 mph offering that currently rates as fringe-average but projects as solid-average. Voth's bread and butter is his fastball, which tends to sit in the 89-92 mph range for the first five innings of his outings, then starts bumping 95 in the middle innings. He commands the pitch well to both sides of the plate, and his ability to hide the ball and work downhill helps induce swing-throughs. He also has an average changeup that flashes plus, with late sinking action. Voth is a gritty competitor who impressed the Nationals with his ability to control opposing running games by mixing up his times to the plate. He's a good athlete who fields his position well. The Nationals believe they got a fifth-round steal in Voth, who has back-of-the-rotation potential, and perhaps a bit more. Though he made just two appearances in low Class A in 2013, he ought to force his way to high Class A to start 2014.

Year	Club (League)	Class	W	L	ERA	G	GS	CG	SV	IP	H	HR	BB	SO	K/9	WHIP	AVG
2013	Nationals (GCL)	R	0	0	0.00	2	2	0	0	5	4	0	0	4	7.2	0.80	.235
	Auburn (NYP)	SS	2	0	1.47	7	7	0	0	31	21	0	4	42	12.3	0.82	.193
	Hagerstown (SAL)	LoA	1	0	3.38	2	2	0	0	11	8	0	2	9	7.6	0.94	.195
Minor League Totals			3	0	1.75	11	11	0	0	46	33	0	6	55	10.7	0.84	.198

16 PEDRO SEVERINO, C

Born: July 20, 1993. **B-T:** R-R. **Ht.:** 6-1. **Wt.:** 180. **Signed:** Dominican Republic, 2010. **Signed by:** Johnny DiPuglia/Moises de la Mota.

As a pull-happy hitter with a big leg kick, Severino struggled offensively for two years in the GCL, but he still put himself on the prospect radar because of his defensive prowess. The Nationals worked with him to simplify his hitting mechanics and get him to use the middle of the field more often, and they challenged him with an assignment to low Class A Hagerstown in 2013. Severino's calling card is his well-above-average arm, which is deadly accurate and helped him throw out 40 percent of basestealers in 2013. His hands are strong and soft, making him a good receiver who blocks well, and his quick feet help him get out in front of the plate to field bunts adeptly. To wit, he led all minor league catchers with 71 non-caught stealing assists in 82 games last year. He projects as an above-average defender, and the Nationals rave about his ability to call games and handle pitchers, thanks in part to his magnetic personality and good ear for the English language. He's a good athlete who even flashes average running times. At the plate, Severino became more consistent with his approach in the second half of the season, and the Nats think he has a chance to hit enough down the road to become an everyday big leaguer. Scouts aren't yet convinced, saying that he often looks overmatched at the plate. But even his skeptics are intrigued by his batting practice displays, suggesting he could grow into occasional pop. He could return to Hagerstown in 2014, though the Nats might push him again to high Class A Potomac.

Year	Club (League)	Class	AVG	G	AB	R	H	2B	3B	HR	RBI	BB	SO	SB	CS	OBP	SLG
2011	Nationals (GCL)	R	.183	32	115	16	21	4	1	2	9	10	27	0	0	.260	.287
2012	Nationals (GCL)	R	.220	38	109	9	24	3	1	0	8	9	9	0	0	.301	.266
2013	Hagerstown (SAL)	LoA	.241	84	282	28	68	19	2	1	45	13	54	1	0	.274	.333
Minor League Totals			.223	154	506	53	113	26	4	3	62	32	90	1	0	.277	.308

17 DREW WARD, 3B/1B

BA GRADE 50 EXTREME

Born: Nov. 25, 1994. **B-T:** L-R. **Ht.:** 6-4. **Wt.:** 210. **Drafted:** HS—Leedey, Okla., 2013 (3rd round). **Signed by:** Ed Gustafson.

Ward graduated high school a year early and successfully lobbied Major League Baseball to make him eligible for the 2013 draft. Area scouts in Oklahoma had a difficult time getting a handle on him because his high school competition was exceedingly weak. Still, the Nationals bought him out of an

Oklahoma commitment with an $850,000 bonus as a third-round pick, and he had a strong debut in the Rookie-level Gulf Coast League. A high school shortstop, Ward shifted to third base in pro ball, and he showed soft hands and good instincts at the position, though his footwork needs plenty of refinement. Like Matt Skole, Ward has the arm strength for the hot corner and has at least a chance to stick at the position, but like Skole he seems destined for first base as he grows into his big frame. He impressed the Nationals in 2013 with his simple offensive approach and ability to control the strike zone as an 18-year-old. He showed he can hit good velocity and hold his own against breaking balls, giving him at least a chance to be a plus hitter down the road. He has a doubles-oriented approach currently, but he has plus raw power and time on his side. Ward has the potential to be a quality everyday player at an infield corner or perhaps an outfield corner. The next step figures to be the short-season New York-Penn League, though he could push his way to low Class A Hagerstown in 2014.

Year	Club (League)	Class	AVG	G	AB	R	H	2B	3B	HR	RBI	BB	SO	SB	CS	OBP	SLG
2013	Nationals (GCL)	R	.292	49	168	24	49	13	0	1	28	25	44	2	4	.402	.387
Minor League Totals			.292	49	168	24	49	13	0	1	28	25	44	2	4	.402	.387

18 AARON BARRETT, RHP

BA GRADE 45 MEDIUM

Born: Jan. 2, 1988. **B-T:** R-R. **Ht.:** 6-4. **Wt.:** 215. **Drafted:** Mississippi, 2010 (9th round). **Signed by:** Eric Robinson.

Drafted three times prior to signing with the Nationals in 2010, Barrett ranked as a top-200 draft prospect as a Wabash Valley (Ill.) CC sophomore in 2008 but elected to attend Mississippi instead of signing. His stock dropped somewhat over two seasons in Oxford, as he struggled with his command, but the Nationals took Barrett in the ninth round in 2010 as a money-saving senior sign, inking him for $35,000. He spent his senior year as a starter, but he has found a home in the bullpen in pro ball. He ranked second in the Double-A Eastern League with 26 saves in 2013, and the Nationals added him to the 40-man roster in November. Barrett's calling card is his wipeout slider, an 85-86 mph offering with sharp, late three-quarters tilt. The pitch rates as a 65 or 70 on the 20-80 scale. He also has developed fringy to average command of his 92-94 mph fastball despite a violent delivery, which adds some deception. Barrett's ultra-aggressive, competitive mentality is a good fit for the bullpen, but he needs to harness his emotions and do a little less barking at hitters. He lacks big-time upside, but he is just about big league-ready as a middle reliever or set-up candidate. He will compete for a major league job in spring training.

Year	Club (League)	Class	W	L	ERA	G	GS	CG	SV	IP	H	HR	BB	SO	K/9	WHIP	AVG
2010	Vermont (NYP)	SS	0	5	9.43	10	4	0	0	21	26	3	22	25	10.7	2.29	.299
2011	Auburn (NYP)	SS	1	2	4.05	19	0	0	9	27	16	2	20	32	10.8	1.35	.172
2012	Hagerstown (SAL)	LoA	3	2	2.60	31	0	0	16	35	25	2	11	52	13.5	1.04	.197
	Potomac (CAR)	HiA	0	0	1.06	11	0	0	1	17	9	0	3	21	11.1	0.71	.153
2013	Harrisburg (EL)	AA	1	1	2.15	51	0	0	26	50	40	2	15	69	12.3	1.09	.215
Minor League Totals			5	10	3.49	122	4	0	52	150	116	9	71	199	12.0	1.25	.210

19 JEFF KOBERNUS, 2B/OF

BA GRADE 45 MEDIUM

Born: June 30, 1988. **B-T:** R-R. **Ht.:** 6-2. **Wt.:** 210. **Drafted:** California, 2009 (2nd round). **Signed by:** Ryan Fox.

Nagging injuries hindered Kobernus' development over his first four seasons, and the Nats left him off the 40-man roster following the 2012 campaign. The Red Sox selected him in the Rule 5 draft and traded him to the Tigers for Justin Henry, but Kobernus returned to Washington in March and went on to put together his best pro season. He posted a career-high .754 OPS at Triple-A Syracuse and spent most of June and September in the big leagues as a reserve. Kobernus started his collegiate career at third base before moving to second, and he handled himself adequately at both positions plus left and center field in 2013, boosting his stock as potential utilityman. He's a fringy defender at all four spots, and his below-average arm is a liability. Kobernus' plus-plus speed gives him value as a pinch-runner and a chance to become an average defensive outfielder as he gets more comfortable tracking down fly balls. His premium speed really plays on the basepaths, where he is instinctive and aggressive, helping him swipe 140 bases in 170 tries (82 percent) over the last three years. Kobernus lacks the strength to be an impact hitter—his power is well-below-average—but his contact-oriented approach works for him. He does not draw enough walks to thrive as a table-setter. Kobernus is close to reaching his ceiling as a versatile speedster off the bench, and he will compete for a big league reserve spot in 2014.

Year	Club (League)	Class	AVG	G	AB	R	H	2B	3B	HR	RBI	BB	SO	SB	CS	OBP	SLG
2009	Vermont (NYP)	SS	.220	10	41	8	9	1	0	0	2	2	5	4	0	.273	.244
2010	Hagerstown (SAL)	LoA	.279	74	312	40	87	18	0	1	42	17	58	21	10	.316	.346
2011	Potomac (CAR)	HiA	.282	124	489	67	138	22	4	7	52	21	87	53	8	.313	.387
2012	Harrisburg (EL)	AA	.282	82	330	41	93	10	2	1	19	19	57	42	11	.325	.333
2013	Syracuse (IL)	AAA	.318	95	371	59	118	19	2	1	36	28	59	42	9	.366	.388
	Washington (NL)	MAJ	.167	24	30	8	5	0	0	1	1	5	6	3	2	.306	.267
Major League Totals			.167	24	30	8	5	0	0	1	1	5	6	3	2	.306	.267
Minor League Totals			.288	385	1543	215	445	70	8	10	151	87	266	162	38	.328	.364

20 EURY PEREZ, OF

BA GRADE **45** MEDIUM

Born: May 30, 1990. **B-T:** R-R. **Ht.:** 6-0. **Wt.:** 180. **Signed:** Dominican Republic, 2007. **Signed by:** Dana Brown/Moises de la Mota.

Perez has consistently hit for average and stolen bases throughout his career. He set career highs for doubles and home runs last year in Triple-A, while his stolen-base rate declined, but his game still is built around double-plus speed, a tool that sometimes draws 80 grades. His speed gives him excellent range in center field, where he is a plus defender. He also played left and right field well last year, and his 55 arm is an asset. Perez has a quick righthanded swing, and he hit the ball with more authority in 2013, but his power still rates as well-below-average. He has a chance to be a solid-average hitter, but he's a free-swinger with a career walk rate of just 6 percent, limiting his value as a table-setter. Scouts say he'll need to maximize his on-base ability by racking up infield hits. At this stage of his development, Perez seems unlikely to suddenly start taking more walks, so most evaluators view him as an extra outfielder. He'll be in the mix for a big league roster spot in 2014.

Year	Club (League)	Class	AVG	G	AB	R	H	2B	3B	HR	RBI	BB	SO	SB	CS	OBP	SLG
2007	Nationals1 (DSL)	R	.253	51	158	41	40	5	1	0	14	32	39	15	5	.399	.297
2008	Nationals 1 (DSL)	R	.324	60	213	51	69	9	2	4	44	32	36	28	6	.428	.441
2009	Nationals (GCL)	R	.381	47	181	38	69	3	5	3	24	15	20	16	8	.443	.503
2010	Hagerstown (SAL)	LoA	.299	131	438	88	131	17	5	3	42	23	74	64	13	.345	.381
2011	Potomac (CAR)	HiA	.283	119	424	54	120	9	2	1	41	22	63	45	15	.319	.321
2012	Nationals (GCL)	R	.409	5	22	4	9	1	0	0	2	1	0	5	0	.435	.455
	Harrisburg (EL)	AA	.299	82	351	34	105	11	2	0	30	7	53	26	10	.325	.342
	Syracuse (IL)	AAA	.333	40	159	21	53	7	1	0	10	8	26	20	5	.373	.390
	Washington (NL)	MAJ	.200	13	5	3	1	0	0	0	0	0	0	3	0	.200	.200
2013	Syracuse (IL)	AAA	.300	96	403	55	121	18	5	7	28	13	64	23	8	.336	.422
	Washington (NL)	MAJ	.125	9	8	1	1	0	0	0	0	0	3	1	0	.125	.125
Major League Totals			.154	22	13	4	2	0	0	0	0	0	3	4	0	.154	.154
Minor League Totals			.305	631	2349	386	717	80	23	18	235	153	375	242	70	.359	.382

21 JEFRY RODRIGUEZ, RHP

BA GRADE **50** EXTREME

Born: July 26, 1993. **B-T:** R-R. **Ht.:** 6-5. **Wt.:** 185. **Signed:** Dominican Republic, 2012. **Signed by:** Johnny DiPuglia/Moises de la Mota.

The Nationals converted Rodriguez from infielder to pitcher after signing him in January 2012. He had a solid first year on the mound in the Dominican Summer League, then was even better in the Rookie-level Gulf Coast League in 2013. Rodriguez continued to make progress with his command and his changeup in instructional league. Long, lanky and projectable, Rodriguez needs to strengthen his legs to improve his endurance and help him repeat his mechanics more consistently. But he has the foundation of a good delivery, and he has a lightning-fast arm, helping him sit in the 93-95 mph range and touch 97 on occasion. He improved his strike-throwing ability last year but still needs to learn how to command the zone. Rodriguez has the makings of a plus curveball in the low 80s that is a true swing-and-miss pitch when he throws it right. His changeup is still in its nascent stage, but he started to gain some confidence in the pitch in instructs. Rodriguez quickly has put himself on the prospect map, and his stock could soar if he proves himself at low Class A Hagerstown in 2014.

Year	Club (League)	Class	W	L	ERA	G	GS	CG	SV	IP	H	HR	BB	SO	K/9	WHIP	AVG
2012	Nationals (DSL)	R	0	2	2.93	10	9	0	0	43	28	2	33	35	7.3	1.42	.185
2013	Nationals (GCL)	R	3	0	2.45	12	12	0	0	48	40	1	20	43	8.1	1.26	.229
Minor League Totals			3	2	2.68	22	21	0	0	91	68	3	53	78	7.7	1.33	.209

22 NICK PIVETTA, RHP

BA GRADE **50** EXTREME

Born: Feb. 14, 1993. **B-T:** R-R. **Ht.:** 6-5. **Wt.:** 220. **Drafted:** New Mexico JC, 2012 (4th round). **Signed by:** Mitch Sokol

A native of British Columbia, Pivetta played for the Canadian Junior National Team in 2009 and 2010. He made a name for himself at New Mexico JC, and the Nationals took him in the fourth round of the 2012 draft, signing him away from a commitment to New Mexico for $364,300. Pivetta signed on June 18 and debuted a month later after securing a visa, and it took him some time to build his arm strength back up after the downtime. He works in the 90-93 mph range and touches 95, and his fastball could become even firmer as he fills out his lanky 6-foot-5 frame. The Nats want him to focus on refining the better breaking ball and scrap the lazy sweeper. He also has the makings of a solid changeup, but it is inconsistent at this stage. His delivery has no major red flags, though he is a bit of a short strider with a low three-quarters slot. Pivetta has a lot to learn, but he has big league starter upside. He figures to spend the bulk of 2014 at low Class A Hagerstown.

Year	Club (League)	Class	W	L	ERA	G	GS	CG	SV	IP	H	HR	BB	SO	K/9	WHIP	AVG
2013	Nationals (GCL)	R	1	0	2.13	4	3	0	0	13	11	0	2	8	5.7	1.03	.234
	Auburn (NYP)	SS	0	1	3.38	5	5	0	0	21	19	1	11	17	7.2	1.41	.238
Minor League Totals			1	1	2.91	9	8	0	0	34	30	1	13	25	6.6	1.26	.236

23 BLAKE TREINEN, RHP

Born: June 30, 1988. **B-T:** R-R. **Ht.:** 6-4. **Wt.:** 215. **Drafted:** South Dakota State, 2011 (7th round). **Signed by:** Kevin Mello (Athletics).

Treinen started his college career in 2007 on the junior varsity at NAIA Baker (Kan.), then spent 2008 at Arkansas (where he did not play) before transferring to South Dakota State (where he sat out 2009 due to NCAA transfer rules). His arm strength got him drafted by the Marlins in 2010 (23rd round) despite a 6.09 ERA, but he returned to post a 3.00 ERA as the SDSU ace in 2011, leaving as the program's highest-drafted player since 1985. The A's traded Treinen along with A.J. Cole to the Nationals in the Michael Morse deal before the 2013 season, and he turned in a solid year in Double-A. He works predominantly off his plus fastball, which sits in the 91-95 mph range and tops out at 97 with power sink at times. He has a durable 6-foot-4 frame and works downhill effectively. His secondary stuff is inconsistent, but he has the makings of a four-pitch repertoire. His curveball flashes plus at times but is below-average at other times, projecting as an average offering with more refinement. He also works in a below-average, short slider in the 81-84 mph range and a fringy changeup in the low 80s with decent arm speed and sink. Treinen is a strike-thrower, but scouts question the quality of his strikes, and most evaluators project him as a middle reliever. The Nationals could leave him in a starting role and move him to Triple-A in 2014, but he could push for a bullpen job during the season.

Year	Club (League)	Class	W	L	ERA	G	GS	CG	SV	IP	H	HR	BB	SO	K/9	WHIP	AVG
2011	Athletics (AZL)	R	0	0	0.00	3	0	0	0	3	3	0	1	7	21.0	1.33	.250
	Burlington (MWL)	LoA	1	1	3.67	18	0	0	2	27	20	1	7	29	9.7	1.00	.202
2012	Stockton (CAL)	HiA	7	7	4.37	24	15	1	0	103	116	11	23	92	8.0	1.35	.278
2013	Auburn (NYP)	SS	0	0	0.00	2	2	0	0	6	1	0	0	7	10.5	0.17	.056
	Harrisburg (EL)	AA	6	7	3.64	21	20	0	0	119	125	9	33	86	6.5	1.33	.269
Minor League Totals			14	15	3.81	68	37	1	2	258	265	21	64	221	7.7	1.28	.262

24 CHRISTIAN GARCIA, RHP

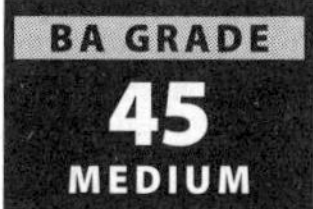

Born: Aug. 24, 1985. **B-T:** R-R. **Ht.:** 6-5. **Wt.:** 230. **Drafted:** HS—Miami, 2004 (3rd round). **Signed by:** Dan Radison (Yankees).

Garcia's career has been plagued by injuries. Two separate Tommy John surgeries cost him all of 2007 and nearly all of 2010, and the Nationals signed him as a minor league free agent after the latter season. Washington moved Garcia from a starting role to the bullpen, and he thrived in the new role in 2012, reaching the majors and earning a spot on the postseason roster. But a forearm injury derailed him again in spring training 2013, and by the time he recovered from that, a nagging hamstring injury kept him on the shelf. When healthy, Garcia's stuff remains electric. His fastball sits in the mid-90s and tops out at 97 mph with good life, and his plus changeup is effective against both righties and lefties. His hard-biting curveball has tight spin and good power in the low 80s, and it flashes plus at times. Garcia's command is fringy, but he throws enough strikes to carve out a role as a middle reliever if he can stay healthy—but that's a big "if." He remains on the 40-man roster and is ready to stick in the big leagues, but he's 28 years old, and he has yet to make a major league impact.

Year	Club (League)	Class	W	L	ERA	G	GS	CG	SV	IP	H	HR	BB	SO	K/9	WHIP	AVG
2004	Yankees (GCL)	R	3	4	2.84	13	6	0	0	38	26	1	17	47	11.1	1.13	.188
2005	Yankees (GCL)	R	0	0	4.50	2	1	0	0	6	4	0	5	7	10.5	1.50	.200
	Charleston, SC (SAL)	LoA	5	6	3.91	21	20	0	0	106	102	3	53	103	8.7	1.46	.249
2006	Yankees (GCL)	R	0	1	9.53	5	3	0	0	11	15	1	4	15	11.9	1.68	.313
	Charleston, SC (SAL)	LoA	2	3	3.46	7	7	0	0	42	37	2	12	45	9.7	1.18	.243
2007	Did not play—Injured																
2008	Yankees (GCL)	R	0	2	14.73	3	3	0	0	7	19	3	2	9	11.0	2.86	.487
	Tampa (FSL)	HiA	4	2	2.90	10	10	0	0	50	45	2	17	60	10.9	1.25	.241
	Trenton (EL)	AA	0	0	3.38	1	0	0	0	5	4	0	6	5	8.4	1.88	.211
2009	Trenton (EL)	AA	2	0	0.71	5	5	0	0	25	15	1	17	24	8.5	1.26	.172
2010	Trenton (EL)	AA	1	0	0.00	1	1	0	0	6	2	0	1	3	4.8	0.53	.111
2011	Auburn (NYP)	SS	3	1	2.95	10	0	0	1	18	17	1	2	28	13.7	1.04	.239
	Syracuse (IL)	AAA	0	0	0.00	1	0	0	0	2	0	0	1	2	9.0	0.50	.000
2012	Harrisburg (EL)	AA	1	0	1.35	18	0	0	7	20	13	0	6	28	12.6	0.95	.181
	Syracuse (IL)	AAA	1	1	0.56	27	0	0	14	32	18	0	11	38	10.6	0.90	.157
	Washington (NL)	MAJ	0	0	2.13	13	0	0	0	13	8	2	2	15	10.7	0.79	.186
2013	Harrisburg (EL)	AA	0	1	2.25	3	2	0	0	4	5	0	2	4	9.0	1.75	.294
	Syracuse (IL)	AAA	1	0	3.24	7	2	0	0	8	5	0	6	10	10.8	1.32	.172
	Auburn (NYP)	SS	0	0	0.00	1	0	0	0	1	0	0	0	2	18.0	0.00	.000
Major League Totals			0	0	2.13	13	0	0	0	13	8	2	2	15	10.7	0.79	.186
Minor League Totals			23	21	3.20	135	60	0	22	382	327	14	162	430	10.1	1.28	.229

25 BRETT MOONEYHAM, LHP

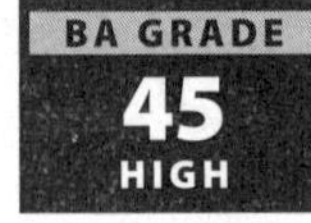

Born: Jan. 24, 1990. **B-T:** L-L. **Ht.:** 6-5. **Wt.:** 235. **Drafted:** Stanford, 2012 (3rd round). **Signed by:** Fred Costello.

Erratic control kept Mooneyham from living up to lofty expectations at Stanford. He thrived in low Class A last year in his first full pro season, though his walk rate was still on the high side. Mooneyham has a tendency to tinker with his mechanics from outing to outing, and his command is poor because his arm tends to drag and disrupt his timing. He no longer flashes the high-90s heat he showed when he was younger, but he did run his fastball up to 94 mph last year, pitching at 90-91 with decent sink and run. His secondary stuff is erratic, but when he has good feel, his 79-82 mph slurvy breaking ball is solid-average to a tick above, and his 79-81 fading changeup is average. Other times, both pitches are below-average. Mooneyham's physical build and three-pitch repertoire give him a chance to be a back-end starter, but most evaluators think his lack of consistent command will consign him to the bullpen. Mooneyham figures to open 2014 in high Class A.

Year	Club (League)	Class	W	L	ERA	G	GS	CG	SV	IP	H	HR	BB	SO	K/9	WHIP	AVG
2012	Auburn (NYP)	SS	2	2	2.55	10	9	0	0	42	36	2	16	29	6.2	1.23	.225
2013	Hagerstown (SAL)	LoA	10	3	1.94	17	17	0	0	93	50	5	41	79	7.6	0.98	.161
	Potomac (CAR)	HiA	0	3	13.50	3	3	0	0	11	17	2	13	6	4.8	2.65	.354
Minor League Totals			12	8	3.01	30	29	0	0	147	103	9	70	114	7.0	1.18	.199

26 NICK LEE, LHP

BA GRADE
45
HIGH

Born: Jan. 13, 1991. **B-T:** L-L. **Ht.:** 5-11. **Wt.:** 185. **Drafted:** Weatherford (Texas) JC, 2011 (18th round). **Signed by:** Ed Gustafson.

The Nationals drafted Lee in the 38th round after his freshman year in 2010, then signed him as an 18th-rounder a year later. Lee struck out more than a batter per inning in 2013 at low Class A Hagerstown, where he made progress learning to repeat his delivery and command the strike zone. Smallish but strong and athletic, he has a quick arm and a competitive demeanor. He attacks hitters with an 88-92 mph fastball that bumps 95, and his 77-80 mph downer curveball is a wipeout pitch with good depth when it's on. He was more of a fastball/changeup pitcher in junior college, but the development of his curveball gives Lee a potential future as a lefthanded reliever. His low-80s changeup has decent sink and projects as an average third pitch. He also throws a below-average 82-84 mph slider. Lee's lack of fine command, his high-effort delivery and his size suggest his future is in the bullpen, but the Nats will keep him in a starting role in high Class A in 2014.

Year	Club (League)	Class	W	L	ERA	G	GS	CG	SV	IP	H	HR	BB	SO	K/9	WHIP	AVG
2011	Nationals (GCL)	R	1	0	4.05	10	0	0	0	13	16	1	15	15	10.1	2.33	.302
2012	Auburn (NYP)	SS	3	1	3.77	13	11	0	0	62	63	2	21	62	9.0	1.35	.267
2013	Hagerstown (SAL)	LoA	6	4	3.96	19	17	0	0	91	83	7	43	102	10.1	1.38	.249
Minor League Totals			10	5	3.90	42	28	0	0	166	162	10	79	179	9.7	1.45	.260

27 ROBERT BENINCASA, RHP

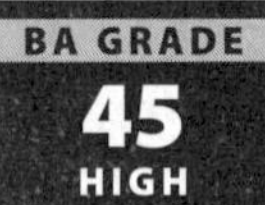

Born: Sept. 5, 1990. **B-T:** R-R. **Ht.:** 6-2. **Wt.:** 180. **Drafted:** Florida State, 2012 (7th round). **Signed by:** Paul Tinnell.

A first-team All-America closer during his 2012 junior year at Florida State, Benincasa saved 27 games between low Class A and high A in 2013, but his stuff fell off down the stretch as he wore down physically, partially a result of poor nutritional habits. At his best, Benincasa works in the 92-94 mph range and touches 96 with slightly above-average sink, but he sat around 89-92 late in the season. At full strength, his low-80s slider has good depth and rates as a 55 pitch on the 20-80 scale, but it was not as sharp late in the year. Benincasa has a solid third pitch in his split-changeup, giving him another weapon against lefties. He is a good athlete with plenty of poise in tight spots and promising feel for pitching, giving him a chance to reach the big leagues as a middle reliever. He'll need to do a better job putting on weight—and keeping it on—for him to reach that ceiling. Benincasa figures to advance to Double-A Harrisburg in 2014 and might not be far from the majors.

Year	Club (League)	Class	W	L	ERA	G	GS	CG	SV	IP	H	HR	BB	SO	K/9	WHIP	AVG
2012	Auburn (NYP)	SS	2	0	3.09	16	0	0	3	23	27	0	3	32	12.3	1.29	.278
2013	Hagerstown (SAL)	LoA	0	1	2.57	20	0	0	10	21	17	2	5	30	12.9	1.05	.213
	Potomac (CAR)	HiA	0	4	3.30	25	0	0	17	30	28	2	9	34	10.2	1.23	.243
Minor League Totals			2	5	3.03	61	0	0	30	74	72	4	17	96	11.6	1.20	.247

28 RAFAEL BAUTISTA, OF

BA GRADE
45
EXTREME

Born: March 8, 1993. **B-T:** R-R. **Ht.:** 6-2. **Wt.:** 165. **Signed:** Dominican Republic, 2012. **Signed by:** Johnny DiPuglia/Moises De La Mota.

Bautista impressed organization officials with his makeup in his first two seasons, quickly picking up on new drills and then showing teammates how to do them. Bautista's best tool is his double-plus speed, and he knows how to use it. He is an instinctive baserunner who gets excellent reads and jumps in center field, where his arm is average. He also has an intelligent approach at the plate, working counts and grinding out at-bats. He has a short, quick righthanded swing and some gap power, though he doesn't figure to ever be a home-run hitter. Bautista's aptitude and athleticism give him a chance to become a big league center fielder or fourth outfielder, but he still has a lot to prove. He might be ready to jump to low Class A in 2014.

Year	Club (League)	Class	AVG	G	AB	R	H	2B	3B	HR	RBI	BB	SO	SB	CS	OBP	SLG
2012	Nationals (DSL)	R	.329	67	210	38	69	8	3	0	25	27	39	47	7	.419	.395
2013	Nationals (GCL)	R	.322	52	202	44	65	7	2	1	27	18	34	26	7	.400	.391
Minor League Totals			.325	119	412	82	134	15	5	1	52	45	73	73	14	.410	.393

29 ERIK DAVIS, RHP

BA GRADE
40
SAFE

Born: Oct. 8, 1986. **B-T:** R-R. **Ht.:** 6-2. **Wt.:** 190. **Drafted:** Stanford, 2008 (13th round). **Signed by:** Rich Bordi (Padres).

In the summer of 2006, Davis was struck in the face by a line drive in the Cape Cod League, nearly causing him to lose an eye. The injury required two surgeries and the insertion of a titanium plate in his face, but he recovered and emerged as the ace of Stanford's staff as a senior. San Diego traded him to Washington for Alberto Gonzalez in March 2011, and he proved himself in the high minors for two seasons, earning a June 2013 callup to Washington. He has some funk in his delivery, helping his fastball play up. He sits in the 88-92 mph range but can reach 94 when he really needs to. His best pitch is an above-average 82-83 mph sinking changeup that he can throw in any count and use as an out-pitch. He also flashes an average curveball in the mid-70s, but it rates as a below-average. At age 27, Davis has essentially reached his ceiling, but he should continue to provide useful bullpen innings between Triple-A Syracuse and the majors.

Year	Club (League)	Class	W	L	ERA	G	GS	CG	SV	IP	H	HR	BB	SO	K/9	WHIP	AVG
2008	Eugene (NWL)	SS	2	0	2.70	14	5	0	0	27	19	2	7	39	13.2	0.98	.200
2009	Fort Wayne (MWL)	LoA	16	6	3.64	32	19	0	0	124	111	5	44	106	7.7	1.25	.240
2010	Portland (PCL)	AAA	1	0	3.60	1	1	0	0	5	3	1	2	7	12.6	1.00	.176
	Lake Elsinore (CAL)	HiA	9	3	3.82	19	19	0	0	99	102	5	34	91	8.3	1.37	.266
	San Antonio (TL)	AA	4	0	2.75	7	7	0	0	39	29	1	12	35	8.0	1.04	.210
2011	Harrisburg (EL)	AA	5	7	4.79	19	18	1	0	94	110	9	41	93	8.9	1.61	.289
	Potomac (CAR)	HiA	0	5	6.75	6	6	1	0	33	37	2	16	24	6.5	1.59	.289
2012	Harrisburg (EL)	AA	7	3	2.52	40	0	0	5	64	61	5	18	69	9.7	1.23	.253
	Syracuse (IL)	AAA	1	0	4.15	8	0	0	0	9	10	1	2	5	5.2	1.38	.278
2013	Syracuse (IL)	AAA	3	7	3.10	45	0	0	15	52	55	4	20	54	9.3	1.43	.267
	Washington (NL)	MAJ	1	0	3.12	10	0	0	0	9	10	0	1	12	12.5	1.27	.278
Major League Totals			1	0	3.12	10	0	0	0	9	10	0	1	12	12.5	1.27	.278
Minor League Totals			48	31	3.77	191	75	2	20	546	537	35	196	523	8.6	1.34	.257

30 ADRIAN NIETO, C

BA GRADE
45
EXTREME

Born: Nov. 12, 1989. **B-T:** B-R. **Ht.:** 6-0. **Wt.:** 200. **Drafted:** HS—Plantation, Fla., 2008 (5th round). **Signed by:** Tony Arango.

Nieto emigrated from Cuba when he was 8 and made a name for himself while playing alongside Eric Hosmer in travel ball and at American Heritage High. Injuries and immaturity derailed his pro career, which bottomed out when he was suspended 50 games at the start of the 2011 season after testing positive for a performance-enhancing substance. Nieto put himself back on the prospect landscape with a strong 2013 campaign in high Class A. He made big strides simplifying his offensive approach, reducing the big leg kick he once employed and showing a more direct swing path. The switch-hitter is a better hitter with more power from the left side—he hit .300 with 10 homers against righties, but just .203 in 74 homer-less at-bats versus lefties. Nieto's bat speed and doubles-oriented approach give him a chance to be an offensive backup catcher in the big leagues. His footwork behind the plate also has improved, but his receiving and blocking remain works in progress. He projects as an average defensive catcher with a slightly-above-average to plus arm. Nieto will have to work to keep his weight in check, and he is a poor runner. He is ready to tackle Double-A as a 24-year-old in 2014.

Year	Club (League)	Class	AVG	G	AB	R	H	2B	3B	HR	RBI	BB	SO	SB	CS	OBP	SLG
2008	Nationals (GCL)	R	.217	8	23	1	5	3	0	0	3	2	7	0	0	.308	.348
2009	Nationals (GCL)	R	.228	42	136	22	31	6	1	0	17	20	30	1	2	.337	.287
2010	Hagerstown (SAL)	LoA	.195	60	174	23	34	4	0	2	14	23	44	1	0	.291	.253
2011	Auburn (NYP)	SS	.302	30	106	20	32	5	0	4	22	17	34	2	0	.397	.462
	Potomac (CAR)	HiA	.200	2	5	1	1	0	0	0	0	1	2	0	0	.333	.200
	Hagerstown (SAL)	LoA	.255	27	98	17	25	8	1	3	12	9	31	0	0	.318	.449
2012	Nationals (GCL)	R	.154	8	26	3	4	1	0	1	3	5	7	0	0	.290	.308
	Hagerstown (SAL)	LoA	.257	70	257	32	66	17	0	6	39	35	64	4	2	.346	.393
2013	— (WBC)	INT	.000	2	6	0	0	0	0	0	0	0	2	0	0	.000	.000
	Potomac (CAR)	HiA	.285	110	390	68	111	29	1	11	53	53	82	4	2	.373	.449
Minor League Totals			.254	357	1215	187	309	73	3	27	163	165	301	12	6	.346	.386

APPENDIX

MASAHIRO TANAKA

Born: Nov. 1, 1988. **Ht.:** 6-2. **Wt.:** 205. **B-T:** R-R.

Tanaka earned national fame in Japan when he broke Daisuke Matsuzaka's career record for strikeouts by a high school pitcher in 2006, then the next year pitched a full season in the Rakuten Eagles rotation as an 18-year-old. Tanaka soon became one of the top pitchers in Japan, winning the 2011 Sawamura Award, the Japanese equivalent of the Cy Young. When Yu Darvish left Japan after the 2011 season, Tanaka became the undisputed No. 1 pitcher in Nippon Professional Baseball. In 2013 he won his second Sawamura Award and the Pacific League MVP en route to leading Rakuten to an NPB championship. Tanaka has the stuff and polish to become a No. 2 starter in the major leagues immediately. He pitches off a fastball that sits at 90-94 mph and touches 96 while making one start a week. He mixes a two-seamer to get quick groundball outs and a four-seamer when he needs extra velocity. Tanaka has a plus fastball but he sinks on the backside of his delivery, which causes his fastball to come in on a flat plane, making the pitch more hittable than the pure velocity would suggest. Tanaka's 84-89 mph splitter alleviates some of the concern about his fastball angle, as it's a wipeout pitch that hitters have trouble distinguishing from his fastball. It's arguably the best splitter on the planet, earning 70 grades with late downward tumble, starting at the hitter's thighs and looking like a juicy fastball before dropping beneath the bottom of the zone. Tanaka's 82-85 mph slider has flashed as a third plus pitch, though he had some trouble snapping it off consistently last year and got hurt when he hung them, but it's another swing-and-miss pitch when it's on point. Tanaka also mixes a 71-76 mph curveball that he'll use early in the count on occasion. Tanaka does wrap his wrist in the back of his arm action, but he has a repeatable delivery and a track record of throwing strikes. Facing Japanese hitters, Tanaka is known to cruise against hitters at the bottom of the lineup, then ramp up his stuff against the better hitters or when pitching out of a jam. Tanaka doesn't have the upside of Darvish when he left Japan, but several teams project him as a frontline starter.

RUSNEY CASTILLO, OF

Born: June 9, 1987. **B-T:** R-R. **Ht.:** 5-9. **Wt.:** 185.

When Yoenis Cespedes was in Cuba, he was the star center fielder on the country's national team, with Leonys Martin the young backup on the rise. When both players left the country, Castillo took over as the team's national center fielder. His most notable performance came at the 2011 World Cup in Panama, where in 10 games he hit .512/.523/.854. But Castillo wasn't allowed to participate in the 2013 World Baseball Classic and was suspended for the 2013-14 Cuban season for what's believed to be an attempted defection. With Castillo now successfully out of Cuba, he offers speed, athleticism and intriguing versatility wrapped in a small frame. Castillo is a plus runner and one of the more prolific basestealers in Cuba. Castillo has a track record of strong performance both in Cuba and in international tournaments, but his swing can get long and he's prone to chasing out of the strike zone. His strength helps him put a surprising charge into the ball for a little guy, but he's more of a line-drive hitter than a power threat. Castillo was primarily a center fielder in Cuba, though he has experience at second and third base too. He earns praise for his aggressive, high-energy style. Scouts are mixed on whether he's an everyday player, though if he can play multiple positions that would enhance his value. He could go straight to the majors, though given his time away from the field he could also get time in Triple-A first.

BARBARO ERISBEL ARRUEBARRUENA, SS

BA GRADE
50
EXTREME

Born: March 25, 1990. **B-T:** R-R. **Ht.:** 6-0. **Wt.:** 198.

Three of the best defensive shortstops on the planet were born in Cuba within a one-year span. While Jose Iglesias and Adeiny Hechavarria both left Cuba before they established themselves in Serie Nacional, Arruebarruena only left in 2013 after cementing himself as the regular shortstop on the Cuban national team at a young age. Arruebarruena is equally spectacular in the field, with the tools and instincts to be a well above-average defender. Despite below-average speed, Arruebarruena's quick first step and reads off the bat give him good range. He has clean hands, quick actions and good body control. He has a 70 arm with a quick release and accuracy, which allows him to make plays deep in the hole, throwing from any angle or turning the back end of a double play. Arruebarruena will never hit higher than the bottom of a lineup, and scouts question whether he'll hit enough for his defense to carry him. His swing is long, his pitch recognition is poor, he expands the strike zone too often and swings through too many pitches in the zone, without much power to speak of. A team that believes Arruebarruena can be at least an adequate hitter will sign him, though he will probably need time in Double-A or Triple-A first.

RAISEL IGLESIAS, RHP

BA GRADE
45
MEDIUM

Born: April 1, 1990. **B-T:** R-R. **Ht.:** 5-11. **Wt.:** 165.

Iglesias pitched for Cuba in the 2013 World Baseball Classic, but he jumped out more in July 2013, when he pitched well at the World Port Tournament in the Netherlands and later that month in a friendship series in the United States against USA Baseball's Collegiate National Team. After throwing around 88-92 mph in the WBC, Iglesias showed a 92-95 mph fastball over the summer. Iglesias also throws a 76-81 mph breaking ball with sweepy action that generates a surprising number of swings and misses. Like a lot of Cuban pitchers, Iglesias will add and subtract from his breaking ball, varying his arm angle to give pitch a different shape. Iglesias was primarily used as a reliever in Cuba, a role he will likely end up in if he gets to the major leagues, though the team that signs him might opt to develop him as a starter to help him get more experience and try to develop a third pitch. He showed solid control this summer, though he does have a history of issuing too many walks in Cuba. Once Iglesias signs, he would likely report to a Double-A affiliate.

SIGNING BONUSES

2013 DRAFT BONUS SPENDING BY TEAM

Teams combined to spend $219.3 million on draft bonuses in 2013, the second-highest total ever. The record was set in 2011, the final year of the previous Collective Bargaining Agreement, when the clubs spent $228 million on bonuses and another $8.1 million on guaranteed salaries that were part of major league contracts.

The current CBA took effect in 2012 and drastically changed the draft rules. Rather than having the freedom to spend whatever they wanted on the draft as in the past, clubs now are assigned bonus pools for the first 10 rounds and lose draft picks if they exceed their allocations by more than 5 percent. In the first year under the new rules, teams spent $207.9 million on bonuses.

Teams at the top of the draft get more money in their pools, so it's no surprise that the clubs selecting second (Cubs, $11,724,900), first (Astros, $11,441,000) and third (Rockies, $10,368,200) led the industry in spending. The Angels ($3,168,200) and Nationals ($3,176,200) brought up the rear after forfeiting their first-round picks to sign free agents.

Team	2013	2012	2011
Cubs	$11,724,900	$9,164,700	$11,994,550
Astros	$11,441,000	$12,074,200	$5,545,800
Rockies	$10,368,200	$6,978,700	$3,967,900
Pirates	$9,887,400	$3,830,700	$17,005,700
Royals	$9,581,900	$7,573,000	$14,066,000
Yankees	$9,197,400	$4,898,400	$6,324,500
Twins	$8,776,400	$12,602,400	$5,902,300
Cardinals	$8,526,400	$9,909,490	$4,554,000
Diamondbacks	$8,049,100	$4,594,800	$11,930,000
Marlins	$7,951,000	$5,755,700	$4,135,000
Padres	$7,895,000	$10,993,000	$11,020,600
Mets	$7,854,400	$7,007,400	$6,782,500
Rangers	$7,696,500	$7,394,400	$4,193,000
Mariners	$7,376,700	$9,325,200	$11,330,500
Orioles	$7,235,000	$7,433,200	$8,432,100
Red Sox	$7,210,900	$7,908,000	$10,978,700
Rays	$7,147,000	$4,427,300	$11,482,900
Tigers	$6,839,100	$3,172,300	$2,878,700
Reds	$6,757,800	$7,450,400	$6,378,900
Indians	$6,713,600	$5,330,000	$8,225,000
Athletics	$6,506,100	$8,301,600	$3,067,300
Dodgers	$6,366,100	$6,277,300	$3,509,300
Phillies	$6,186,900	$4,787,800	$4,689,800
Giants	$6,063,800	$4,630,500	$6,266,000
White Sox	$5,810,800	$6,452,100	$2,786,300
Braves	$5,410,500	$4,758,000	$3,735,700
Brewers	$4,637,300	$7,200,100	$7,509,300
Blue Jays	$3,747,280	$10,486,000	$10,996,500
Nationals	$3,176,200	$4,880,500	$15,002,100
Angels	$3,168,200	$2,289,800	$3,318,100
Total	**$219,302,880**	**$207,886,990**	**$228,009,050**
Average	**$7,310,096**	**$6,929,566**	**$7,600,302**

TOP 50 BONUSES VS. PICK VALUES

Just as they did last year in the first draft under the revamped rules, the signing bonuses and the assigned pick values tracked each other nicely.

To give the worst teams extra spending power, the values for the selections at the top of the draft were set higher than the perceived market value. As a result, only four of the top 11 choices received their full pick value, and only three of the 33 first-rounders exceeded theirs.

But all told, the top 50 bonuses added up to $110.5 million, while the first 50 pick values totaled $114.5 million. By comparison, when MLB unilaterally determined slot recommendations in the last year of the previous Collective Bargaining Agreement (2011), the total of the first 50 bonuses ($120.5 million) dwarfed that of the top 50 slots ($70 million).

Fifty-one players turned pro for a seven-figure bonus in 2013. The top 50 bonuses are below, and Cubs outfielder Jacob Hannemann (third round/No. 75 overall) signed for $1 million.

Player, Pos., Team (Round/Overall Pick)	Bonus	Pick Value
1. Kris Bryant, 3b, Cubs (1st round/No. 2)	$6,708,400	$7,790,400
2. Mark Appel, rhp, Astros (1st round/No. 1)	$6,350,000	$6,708,400
3. Jonathan Gray, rhp, Rockies (1st round/No. 3)	$4,800,000	$5,626,400
4. Kohl Stewart, rhp, Twins (1st round/No. 4)	$4,544,400	$4,544,400
5. Sean Manaea, lhp, Royals (supp. 1st round/No. 34)	$3,550,000	$3,787,000
6. Colin Moran, 3b, Marlins (1st round/No. 6)	$3,516,500	$3,516,500
7. Clint Frazier, of, Indians (1st round/No. 5)	$3,500,000	$3,246,000
8. Austin Meadows, of, Pirates (1st round/No. 9)	$3,029,600	$3,137,800
9. D.J. Peterson, 3b, Mariners (1st round/No. 12)	$2,759,100	$3,029,600
10. Trey Ball, lhp, Red Sox (1st round/No. 7)	$2,750,000	$2,921,400
11. Hunter Renfroe, of, Padres (1st round/No. 13)	$2,678,000	$2,840,300
12. Dominic Smith, 1b, Mets (1st round/No. 11)	$2,600,000	$2,759,100
13. Reese McGuire, c, Pirates (1st round/No. 14)	$2,369,800	$2,678,000
14. J.P. Crawford, ss, Phillies (1st round/No. 16)	$2,299,300	$2,569,800
15. Braden Shipley, rhp, Diamondbacks (1st round/No. 15)	$2,250,000	$2,434,500
16. Alex Gonzalez, rhp, Rangers (1st round/No. 23)	$2,215,000	$2,299,300
17. Hunter Dozier, 3b, Royals (1st round/No. 8)	$2,200,000	$2,164,000
18. Tim Anderson, ss, White Sox (1st round/No. 17)	$2,164,000	$2,109,900
19. Chris Anderson, rhp, Dodgers (1st round/No. 18)	$2,109,900	$2,055,800
20. Jonathon Crawford, rhp, Tigers (1st round/No. 20)	$2,001,700	$2,001,700
21. Nick Ciuffo, c, Rays (1st round/No. 21)	$1,972,200	$1,974,700
22. Hunter Harvey, rhp, Orioles (1st round/No. 22)	$1,947,600	$1,947,600
23. Travis Demeritte, ss, Rangers (1st round/No. 30)	$1,900,000	$1,920,600
24. Christian Arroyo, ss, Giants (1st round/No. 25)	$1,866,500	$1,893,500
25. Marco Gonzales, lhp, Cardinals (1st round/No. 19)	$1,850,000	$1,866,500
26. Eric Jagielo, 3b, Yankees (1st round/No. 26)	$1,839,400	$1,839,400
27. Phillip Ervin, of, Reds (1st round/No. 27)	$1,812,400	$1,812,400
28. Billy McKinney, of, Athletics (1st round/No. 24)	$1,800,000	$1,785,300
Aaron Judge, of, Yankees (1st round/No. 32)	$1,800,000	$1,758,300
30. Rob Kaminsky, lhp, Cardinals (1st round/No. 28)	$1,785,300	$1,731,200
31. Ryne Stanek, rhp, Rays (1st round/No. 29)	$1,755,800	$1,704,200
32. Jason Hursh, rhp, Braves (1st round/No. 31)	$1,704,200	$1,677,100
33. Austin Wilson, of, Mariners (2nd round/No. 49)	$1,700,000	$1,650,100
34. Ian Clarkin, lhp, Yankees (1st round/No. 33)	$1,650,100	$1,623,000
35. Michael Lorenzen, rhp/of, Reds (supp. 1st round/No. 38)	$1,500,000	$1,587,700
Oscar Mercado, ss, Cardinals (2nd round/No. 57)	$1,500,000	$1,547,700
37. Josh Hart, of, Orioles (supp. 1st round/No. 37)	$1,450,000	$1,508,600
38. Aaron Blair, rhp, Diamondbacks (supp. 1st round/No. 36)	$1,435,000	$1,470,500
39. Corey Knebel, rhp, Tigers (supp. 1st round/No. 39)	$1,433,400	$1,433,400
40. Dustin Peterson, ss, Padres (2nd round/No. 50)	$1,400,000	$1,397,200
41. Andrew Thurman, rhp, Astros (2nd round/No. 40)	$1,397,200	$1,361,900
42. Devin Williams, rhp, Brewers (2nd round/No. 54)	$1,350,000	$1,327,600
43. Ryan McMahon, 3b, Rockies (2nd round/No. 42)	$1,327,600	$1,294,100
44. Ryan Eades, rhp, Twins (2nd round/No. 43)	$1,294,100	$1,261,400
45. Trevor Williams, rhp, Marlins (2nd round/No. 44)	$1,261,400	$1,229,600
46. Cody Reed, lhp, Royals (2nd round/No. 46)	$1,198,500	$1,198,500
47. Rob Zastryzny, lhp, Cubs (2nd round/No. 41)	$1,100,000	$1,168,200
48. Justin Williams, of, Diamondbacks (2nd round/No. 52)	$1,050,000	$1,138,800
49. Andrew Knapp, c, Phillies (2nd round/No. 53)	$1,033,100	$1,110,000
50. Tyler Danish, rhp, White Sox (2nd round/No. 55)	$1,001,800	$1,082,000
Total	**$110,511,300**	**$114,521,400**

SIGNING BONUSES

2012 DRAFT

TOP 100 PICKS

These are the bonuses and assigned pick values for the first 100 picks of the 2012 draft. New draft rules that went into effect in 2012 establish assigned values for every pick in the first 10 rounds. The aggregate of all of a team's pick values constitute its draft signing budget. Teams are not required to adhere to the assigned value of any particular pick, but if they exceed their aggregate budget they face penalties that range from fines to lost draft picks.

FIRST ROUND

Pick. Team: Player, Pos.	Pick Value	Bonus
1. Hou: Carlos Correa, ss	$7,200,000	$4,800,000
2. Min: Byron Buxton, of	$6,200,000	$6,000,000
3. Sea: Mike Zunino, c	$5,200,000	$4,000,000
4. Bal: Kevin Gausman, rhp	$4,200,000	$4,320,000
5. KC: Kyle Zimmer, rhp	$3,500,000	$3,000,000
6. ChC: Albert Almora, of	$3,250,000	$3,900,000
7. SD: Max Fried, lhp	$3,000,000	$3,000,000
8. Pit: Mark Appel, rhp	$2,900,000	Did Not Sign
9. Mia: Andrew Heaney, lhp	$2,800,000	$2,600,000
10. Col: David Dahl, of	$2,700,000	$2,600,000
11. Oak: Addison Russell, ss	$2,625,000	$2,625,000
12. NYM: Gavin Cecchini, ss	$2,550,000	$2,300,000
13. CWS: Courtney Hawkins, of	$2,475,000	$2,475,000
14. Cin: Nick Travieso, rhp	$2,375,000	$2,000,000
15. Cle: Tyler Naquin, of	$2,250,000	$1,750,000
16. Was: Lucas Giolito, rhp	$2,125,000	$2,925,000
17. Tor: D.J. Davis, of	$2,000,000	$1,750,000
18. LAD: Corey Seager, 3b	$1,950,000	$2,350,000
19. StL: Michael Wacha, rhp	$1,900,000	$1,900,000
20. SF: Chris Stratton, rhp	$1,850,000	$1,850,000
21. Atl: Lucas Sims, rhp	$1,825,000	$1,650,000
22. Tor: Marcus Stroman, rhp	$1,800,000	$1,800,000
23. StL: James Ramsey, of	$1,775,000	$1,600,000
24. Bos: Deven Marrero, ss	$1,750,000	$2,050,000
25. TB: Richie Shaffer, 3b	$1,725,000	$1,710,000
26. Ari: Stryker Trahan, c/of	$1,700,000	$1,700,000
27. Mil: Clint Coulter, c	$1,675,000	$1,675,000
28. Mil: Victor Roache, of	$1,650,000	$1,525,000
29. Tex: Lewis Brinson, of	$1,625,000	$1,625,000
30. NYY: Ty Hensley, rhp	$1,600,000	$1,200,000
31. Bos: Brian Johnson, lhp	$1,575,000	$1,575,000

SUPPLEMENTAL FIRST ROUND

Pick. Team: Player, Pos.	Pick Value	Bonus
32. Min: J.O. Berrios, rhp	$1,550,000	$1,550,000
33. SD: Zach Eflin, rhp	$1,525,000	$1,200,000
34. Oak: Daniel Robertson, 3b	$1,500,000	$1,500,000
35. NYM: Kevin Plawecki, c	$1,467,400	$1,400,000
36. StL: Stephen Piscotty, of/3b	$1,430,400	$1,430,400
37. Bos: Pat Light, rhp	$1,394,300	$1,000,000
38. Mil: Mitch Haniger, of	$1,359,100	$1,200,000
39. Tex: Joey Gallo, 3b/rhp	$1,324,800	$2,250,000
40. Phi: Shane Watson, rhp	$1,291,300	$1,291,300
41. Hou: Lance McCullers, rhp	$1,258,700	$2,500,000
42. Min: Luke Bard, rhp	$1,227,000	$1,227,000
43. ChC: Pierce Johnson, rhp	$1,196,000	$1,196,000
44. SD: Travis Jankowski, of	$1,165,800	$975,000
45. Pit: Barrett Barnes, of	$1,136,400	$1,000,000
46. Col: Eddie Butler, rhp	$1,107,700	$1,000,000
47. Oak: Matt Olson, 1b	$1,079,700	$1,079,700
48. CWS: Keon Barnum, 1b	$1,052,500	$950,000
49. Cin: Jesse Winker, of	$1,025,900	$1,000,000
50. Tor: Matt Smoral, lhp	$1,000,000	$2,000,000
51. LAD: Jesmuel Valentin, 2b	$984,700	$984,700
52. StL: Patrick Wisdom, 3b	$969,700	$678,790
53. Tex: Collin Wiles, rhp	$954,800	$975,000
54. Phi: Mitch Gueller, rhp	$940,200	$940,200
55. SD: Walker Weickel, rhp	$925,900	$2,000,000
56. ChC: Paul Blackburn, rhp	$911,700	$911,700
57. Cin: Jeff Gelalich, of	$897,800	$825,000
58. Tor: Mitch Nay, 3b	$884,100	$1,000,000
59. StL: Steve Bean, c	$870,600	$700,000
60. Tor: Tyler Gonzales, rhp	$857,200	$750,000

SECOND ROUND

Pick. Team: Player, Pos.	Pick Value	Bonus
61. Hou: Nolan Fontana, ss	$844,100	$875,000
62. Oak: Bruce Maxwell, c/1b	$831,200	$700,000
63. Min: Mason Melotakis, lhp	$818,500	$750,000
64. Sea: Joe DeCarlo, 3b	$806,000	$1,300,000
65. Bal: Branden Kline, rhp	$793,700	$793,700
66. KC: Sam Selman, lhp	$781,600	$750,000
67. ChC: Duane Underwood, rhp	$769,600	$1,050,000
68. SD: Jeremy Baltz, of	$757,900	$625,000
69. Pit: Wyatt Mathisen, c	$746,300	$746,300
70. SD: Dane Phillips, c/1b	$734,900	$450,000
71. NYM: Matt Reynolds, 3b	$723,600	$525,000
72. Min: J.T. Chargois, rhp	$712,600	$712,600
73. Col: Max White, of	$701,700	$1,000,000
74. Oak: Nolan Sanburn, rhp	$691,000	$710,000
75. NYM: Teddy Stankiewicz, rhp	$680,400	Did Not Sign
76. CWS: Chris Beck, rhp	$670,000	$600,000
77. Phi: Dylan Cozens, of	$659,800	$659,800
78. Cin: Tanner Rahier, ss	$649,700	$649,700
79. Cle: Mitch Brown, rhp	$639,700	$800,000
80. Was: Tony Renda, 2b	$630,000	$500,000
81. Tor: Chase DeJong, rhp	$620,300	$860,000
82. LAD: Paco Rodriguez, lhp	$610,800	$610,800
83. Tex: Jamie Jarmon, of	$601,500	$601,500
84. SF: Martin Agosta, rhp	$592,300	$612,500
85. Atl: Alex Wood, lhp	$583,300	$700,000
86. StL: Carson Kelly, 3b/rhp	$574,300	$1,600,000
87. Bos: Jamie Callahan, rhp	$565,600	$600,000
88. TB: Spencer Edwards, of	$556,900	$554,400
89. NYY: Austin Aune, of	$548,400	$1,000,000
90. Ari: Joe Munoz, 3b	$540,000	$520,500
91. Det: Jake Thompson, rhp	$531,800	$531,800
92. Mil: Tyrone Taylor, of	$523,600	$750,000
93. Tex: Nick Williams, of	$515,600	$500,000
94. NYY: Peter O'Brien, c	$507,800	$460,000
95. Phi: Alec Rash, rhp	$500,000	Did Not Sign

THIRD ROUND

Pick. Team: Player, Pos.	Pick Value	Bonus
96. Hou: Brady Rodgers, rhp	$495,200	$495,200
97. Min: Adam Brett Walker, 1b	$490,400	$490,400
98. Sea: Edwin Diaz, rhp	$485,700	$300,000
99. Bal: Adrian Marin, ss	$481,100	$481,100
100. KC: Colin Rodgers, lhp	$476,500	$700,000

2011 DRAFT

TOP 100 PICKS

Bonuses and estimated slot recommendations by Major League Baseball for the first 100 selections of the 2011 draft. Asterisks indicate bonuses that were part of a major league contract, and crosses signify a two-sport contract, which allows the club to spread the bonus over as many as five years.

FIRST ROUND

Pick. Team: Player, Pos.	'11 Bonus	'11 Slot
1. Pit: Gerrit Cole, rhp	$8,000,000	$4,000,000
2. Sea: Danny Hultzen, lhp	*$6,350,000	$3,250,000
3. Ari: Trevor Bauer, rhp	*$3,400,000	$3,000,000
4. Bal: Dylan Bundy, rhp	*$4,000,000	$2,750,000
5. KC: Bubba Starling, of	+$7,500,000	$2,520,000
6. Was: Anthony Rendon, 3b	*$6,000,000	$2,340,000
7. Ari: Archie Bradley, rhp	+$5,000,000	$2,178,000
8. Cle: Francisco Lindor, ss	$2,900,000	$2,043,000
9. ChC: Javier Baez, ss	$2,625,000	$1,962,000
10. SD: Cory Spangenberg, 2b	$1,863,000	$1,863,000
11. Hou: George Springer, of	$2,525,000	$1,791,000
12. Mil: Taylor Jungmann, rhp	$2,525,000	$1,719,000
13. NYM: Brandon Nimmo, of	$2,100,000	$1,656,000
14. Fla: Jose Fernandez, rhp	$2,000,000	$1,602,000
15. Mil: Jed Bradley, lhp	$2,000,000	$1,557,000
16. LAD: Chris Reed, lhp	$1,589,000	$1,512,000
17. LAA: C.J. Cron, 1b	$1,467,000	$1,467,000
18. Oak: Sonny Gray, rhp	$1,540,000	$1,422,000
19. Bos: Matt Barnes, rhp	$1,500,000	$1,386,000
20. Col: Tyler Anderson, lhp	$1,400,000	$1,359,000
21. Tor: Tyler Beede, rhp	Did Not Sign	$1,332,000
22. StL: Kolten Wong, 2b	$1,300,000	$1,287,000
23. Was: Alex Meyer, rhp	$2,000,000	$1,260,000
24. TB: Taylor Guerrieri, rhp	$1,600,000	$1,242,000
25. SD: Joe Ross, rhp	$2,750,000	$1,215,000
26. Bos: Blake Swihart, c	$2,500,000	$1,197,000
27. Cin: Robert Stephenson, rhp	$2,000,000	$1,161,000
28. Atl: Sean Gilmartin, lhp	$1,134,000	$1,134,000
29. SF: Joe Panik, ss	$1,116,000	$1,116,000
30. Min: Levi Michael, ss	$1,175,000	$1,089,000
31. TB: Mikie Mahtook, of	$1,150,000	$972,000
32. TB: Jake Hager, ss	$963,000	$954,000
33. Tex: Kevin Matthews, lhp	$936,000	$936,000

SUPPLEMENTAL FIRST ROUND

Pick. Team: Player, Pos.	'11 Bonus	'11 Slot
34. Was: Brian Goodwin, of	$3,000,000	$918,000
35. Tor: Jacob Anderson, of	$990,000	$900,000
36. Bos: Henry Owens, lhp	$1,550,000	$889,200
37. Tex: Zach Cone, of	$873,000	$873,000
38. TB: Brandon Martin, ss	$860,000	$858,600
39. Phi: Larry Greene, of	$1,000,000	$844,200
40. Bos: Jackie Bradley, of	$1,100,000	$829,800
41. TB: Tyler Goeddel, 3b	$1,500,000	$815,400
42. TB: Jeff Ames, rhp	$650,000	$802,800
43. Ari: Andrew Chafin, lhp	$875,000	$789,300
44. NYM: Michael Fulmer, rhp	$937,500	$776,700
45. Col: Trevor Story, ss	$915,000	$764,100
46. Tor: Joe Musgrove, rhp	$500,000	$751,500
47. CWS: Keenyn Walker, of	$795,000	$739,800
48. SD: Michael Kelly, rhp	$718,000	$728,100
49. SF: Kyle Crick, rhp	$900,000	$717,300
50. Min: Travis Harrison, 3b	$1,050,000	$705,600
51. NYY: Dante Bichette Jr., 3b	$750,000	$694,800
52. TB: Blake Snell, lhp	$684,000	$684,000
53. Tor: Dwight Smith Jr., of	$800,000	$674,100
54. SD: Brett Austin, c	Did Not Sign	$663,300
55. Min: Hudson Boyd, rhp	$1,000,000	$653,400
56. TB: Kes Carter, of	$625,000	$643,500
57. Tor: Kevin Comer, rhp	$1,650,000	$634,500
58. SD: Jace Peterson, ss	$624,600	$624,600
59. TB: Grayson Garvin, lhp	$370,000	$614,700
60. TB: James Harris, of	$490,000	$605,700

SECOND ROUND

Pick. Team: Player, Pos.	'11 Bonus	'11 Slot
61. Pit: Josh Bell, of	$5,000,000	$596,700
62. Sea: Brad Miller, ss	$750,000	$587,700
63. Ari: Anthony Meo, rhp	$625,000	$579,600
64. Bal: Jason Esposito, 3b	$600,000	$570,600
65. KC: Cam Gallahager, c	$750,000	$562,500
66. Phi: Roman Quinn, ss	$775,000	$555,000
67. Cle: Dillon Howard, rhp	$1,850,000	$545,400
68. ChC: Dan Vogelbach, 1b	$1,600,000	$537,300
69. Hou: Adrian Houser, rhp	$530,100	$530,100
70. Mil: Jorge Lopez, rhp	$690,000	$522,000
71. NYM: Cory Mazzoni, rhp	$437,500	$514,800
72. Fla: Adam Conley, lhp	$625,000	$506,700
73. LAD: Alex Santana, 3b	$499,500	$499,500
74. Tor: Daniel Norris, lhp	$2,000,000	$492,300
75. TB: Granden Goetzman, of	$490,000	$485,100
76. Det: James McCann, c	$577,900	$477,900
77. Col: Carl Thomore, of	$480,000	$470,700
78. Tor: J. Gabryszwski, rhp	$575,000	$463,500
79. StL: Charlie Tilson, of	$1,275,000	$457,200
80. CWS: Erik Johnson, rhp	$450,000	$450,000
81. Bos: Williams Jerez, of	$443,700	$443,700
82. SD: Austin Hedges, c	$3,000,000	$436,500
83. Tex: Will Lamb, lhp	$430,200	$430,200
84. Cin: Gabriel Rosa, of	$500,000	$423,900
85. Atl: Nick Ahmed, ss	$417,600	$417,600
86. SF: Andrew Susac, c	$1,100,000	$411,300
87. Min: Madison Boer, rhp	$405,000	$405,000
88. NYY: Sam Stafford, lhp	Did Not Sign	$398,700
89. TB: Leonard Linsky, rhp	$392,400	$392,400
90. Phi: Harold Martinez, 3b	$387,000	$387,000

THIRD ROUND

Pick. Team: Player, Pos.	'11 Bonus	'11 Slot
91. Pit: Alex Dickerson, 1b	$380,700	$380,700
92. Sea: Kevin Cron, 1b	Did Not Sign	$375,300
93. Ari: Justin Bianco, of	$369,000	$369,000
94. Bal: Mike Wright, rhp	$363,600	$363,600
95. KC: Bryan Brickhouse, rhp	$1,500,000	$358,200
96. Was: Matt Purke, lhp	*$2,750,000	$351,900
97. Cle: Jake Sisco, rhp	$325,000	$346,500
98. ChC: Zeke DeVoss, of	$500,000	$341,100
99. Hou: Jack Armstrong Jr., rhp	$750,000	$335,700
100. Mil: Drew Gagnon, rhp	$340,000	$330,300

2014 DRAFT PROSPECTS

COLLEGE TOP 100

Rank	Name, Pos., School	B-T	Ht.	Wt.	Previously Drafted
1.	Carlos Rodon, lhp, North Carolina State	L-L	6-3	234	Brewers '11 (16)
2.	Jeff Hoffman, rhp, East Carolina	R-R	6-4	192	Never
3.	Trea Turner, ss, North Carolina State	R-R	6-1	171	Pirates '11 (20)
4.	Tyler Beede, rhp, Vanderbilt	R-R	6-4	215	Blue Jays '11 (1)
5.	Aaron Nola, rhp, Louisiana State	R-R	6-1	183	Blue Jays '11 (22)
6.	Luke Weaver, rhp, Florida State	R-R	6-2	170	Blue Jays '11 (19)
7.	Michael Conforto, of, Oregon State	L-R	6-1	215	Never
8.	Bradley Zimmer, of, San Francisco	L-R	6-5	205	Cubs '11 (23)
9.	Kyle Freeland, lhp, Evansville	L-L	6-3	170	Phillies '11 (35)
10.	Derek Fisher, of, Virginia	L-R	6-3	210	Rangers '11 (6)
11.	Michael Cederoth, rhp, San Diego State	R-R	6-6	210	Diamondbacks '11 (41)
12.	Nick Burdi, rhp, Louisville	R-R	6-4	218	Twins '11 (24)
13.	Brandon Finnegan, lhp, Texas Christian	L-L	5-11	184	Rangers '11 (45)
14.	Matt Chapman, 3b/rhp, Cal State Fullerton	R-R	6-2	215	Never
15.	Sean Newcomb, lhp, Hartford	L-L	6-5	240	Never
16.	Kyle Schwarber, c/1b, Indiana	L-L	6-0	235	Never
17.	Erick Fedde, rhp, UNLV	R-R	6-4	165	Padres '11 (24)
18.	Max Pentecost, c, Kennesaw State	R-R	6-1	190	Rangers '11 (7)
19.	Taylor Sparks, 3b/1b, UC Irvine	R-R	6-4	215	Indians '11 (24)
20.	J.D. Davis, 1b/3b/rhp, Cal State Fullerton	R-R	6-3	215	Rays '11 (5)
21.	Dylan Davis, of/rhp, Oregon State	R-R	6-0	210	Never
22.	Matt Imhof, lhp, Cal Poly	L-L	6-5	220	Never
23.	Andrew Suarez, lhp, Miami	L-L	6-0	205	Blue Jays '11 (9)
24.	Grayson Greiner, c, South Carolina	R-R	6-5	210	Never
25.	Jordan Brink, rhp, Fresno State	L-R	6-1	180	Never
26.	Scott Heineman, of, Oregon	R-R	6-1	190	Never
27.	Chris Oliver, rhp, Arkansas	R-R	6-4	180	Orioles '11 (27)
28.	Casey Gillaspie, 1b, Wichita State	B-L	6-4	238	Never
29.	Alex Blandino, 3b, Stanford	R-R	6-0	190	Athletics '11 (38)
30.	Dillon Peters, lhp, Texas	L-L	5-11	200	Indians '11 (20)
31.	Zech Lemond, rhp, Rice	R-R	6-4	195	Pirates '11 (50)
32.	Brian Anderson, 2b/3b/of, Arkansas	R-R	6-3	185	Twins '11 (20)
33.	Brandon Woodruff, rhp, Mississippi State	L-R	6-2	225	Rangers '11 (5)
34.	Pat Connaughton, rhp, Notre Dame	R-R	6-5	205	Padres '11 (38)
35.	Sam Coonrod, rhp, Southern Illinois	R-R	6-1	205	Never
36.	Chad Sobotka, rhp, South Carolina-Upstate	R-R	6-6	195	Never
37.	Jordan Foley, rhp, Central Michigan	R-R	6-3	214	Yankees '11 (26)
38.	Greg Allen, of, San Diego State	B-R	6-0	165	Never
39.	Mike Papi, of/1b, Virginia	L-R	6-3	210	Angels '11 (30)
40.	Joey Pankake, 3b/rhp, South Carolina	R-R	6-1	200	Rangers '11 (42)
41.	Ross Kivett, 2b, Kansas State	R-R	6-1	200	Indians '13 (10)
42.	Austin Byler, 3b/1b, Nevada	L-R	6-3	225	Never
43.	Nick Howard, 3b/rhp, Virginia	R-R	6-4	215	Never
44.	Aramis Garcia, c, Florida International	R-R	6-2	220	Cardinals '11 (20)
45.	Daniel Mengden, rhp, Texas A&M	R-R	6-1	215	Never
46.	Parker French, rhp, Texas	L-R	6-2	210	Never
47.	Branden Cogswell, ss, Virginia	L-R	6-2	180	Never
48.	Ben Smith, lhp, Coastal Carolina	L-L	6-2	190	Never
49.	Jace Fry, lhp, Oregon State	L-L	6-0	194	Athletics '11 (9)
50.	Sam Travis, 1b, Indiana	R-R	6-0	205	Never

Rank	Name, Pos., School	B-T	Ht.	Wt.	Previously Drafted
51.	Michael Suchy, of, Florida Gulf Coast	R-R	6-4	230	Never
52.	Wyatt Strahan, rhp, Southern California	R-R	6-3	195	Diamondbacks '11 (27)
53.	Brandon Downes, of, Virginia	R-R	6-3	200	Red Sox '11 (43)
54.	Scott Squier, lhp, Hawaii	L-L	6-5	190	Tigers '11 (21)
55.	Spencer Turnbull, rhp, Alabama	R-R	6-3	220	Never
56.	Jake Reed, rhp, Oregon	R-R	6-2	190	White Sox '11 (40)
57.	Lukas Schiraldi, rhp, Texas	R-R	6-4	197	Nationals '13 (35)
58.	Colin Welmon, rhp, Loyola Marymount	L-R	6-3	190	Never
59.	Connor Joe, c/1b, San Diego	R-R	6-0	205	Never
60.	Chris Marconcini, 1b/of, Duke	L-L	6-5	230	Never
61.	James Norwood, rhp, Saint Louis	R-R	6-2	200	Never
62.	Jacob Lindgren, lhp, Mississippi State	R-L	5-11	206	Cubs '11 (12)
63.	A.J. Vanegas, rhp, Stanford	R-R	6-3	215	Athletics '13 (19)
64.	John Curtiss, rhp, Texas	R-R	6-4	200	Rockies '11 (30)
65.	*Mark Laird, of, Louisiana State	L-L	6-1	172	Never
66.	Ben Wetzler, lhp, Oregon State	L-L	6-1	209	Phillies '13 (5)
67.	Boo Vazquez, of, Pittsburgh	L-R	6-4	215	Rockies '11 (38)
68.	Rhys Hoskins, of, Sacramento State	R-R	6-4	225	Never
69.	Benton Moss, rhp, North Carolina	R-R	6-2	174	Never
70.	Chandler Shepherd, rhp, Kentucky	R-R	6-2	185	White Sox '11 (41)
71.	Logan Jernigan, rhp, North Carolina State	R-R	6-3	201	Never
72.	Sam Howard, lhp, Georgia Southern	L-L	6-3	170	Cubs '11 (48)
73.	Jalen Beeks, lhp, Arkansas	L-L	5-11	180	Never
74.	Adam Ravenelle, rhp, Vanderbilt	R-R	6-2	190	Yankees '11 (44)
75.	Jordan Ramsey, rhp, UNC Wilmington	L-R	6-4	205	Royals '11 (28)
76.	Matt Troupe, rhp, Arizona	R-R	6-2	195	Yankees '11 (17)
77.	Daniel Gossett, rhp, Clemson	R-R	6-0	180	Red Sox '11 (16)
78.	Hunter Cole, of, Georgia	R-R	6-1	186	Nationals '11 (49)
79.	Nick Torres, of, Cal Poly	R-R	6-1	210	Never
80.	David Lucroy, rhp, East Carolina	R-R	6-2	220	Brewers '11 (29)
81.	Dante Flores, 2b/of, Southern California	L-R	5-10	160	Padres '11 (41)
82.	Mason Robbins, of, Southern Mississippi	L-L	6-0	205	Mets '11 (20)
83.	Austin Davis, lhp, Cal State Bakersfield	L-L	6-5	240	Never
84.	Chris Ellis, rhp, Mississippi	L-R	6-5	205	Dodgers '11 (50)
85.	A.J. Reed, lhp/1b, Kentucky	L-L	6-4	245	Mets '11 (25)
86.	Austin Robichaux, rhp, Louisiana-Lafayette	R-R	6-6	170	Reds '11 (50)
87.	Jared Miller, lhp, Vanderbilt	L-L	6-6	235	Never
88.	Brett Austin, c, North Carolina State	B-R	6-1	190	Padres '11 (1s)
89.	Kevin Kramer, ss/3b, UCLA	L-R	6-0	194	Indians '11 (25)
90.	Chris Mariscal, ss, Fresno State	R-R	5-11	175	Orioles '11 (41)
91.	Evan Beal, rhp, South Carolina	R-R	6-4	190	Royals '11 (8)
92.	Daniel Savas, rhp, Illinois State	R-R	6-5	220	Never
93.	Aaron Brown, lhp/of, Pepperdine	L-L	6-1	222	Pirates '11 (17)
94.	Zach Thompson, rhp, Texas-Arlington	R-R	6-6	210	Pirates '11 (48)
95.	Nigel Nootbaar, rhp, Southern California	B-R	6-1	185	Never
96.	Dustin DeMuth, 3b, Indiana	L-R	6-3	205	Twins '11 (8)
97.	Austin Cousino, of, Kentucky	L-L	5-10	180	Never
98.	Jonathan Holder, rhp, Mississippi State	R-R	6-2	229	Never
99.	Ashton Perritt, rhp/of, Liberty	R-R	6-3	195	Never
100.	Jose Lopez, rhp, Seton Hall	R-R	6-1	180	Never

FOR UPDATES AND MORE SCOUTING REPORTS, GO TO BASEBALLAMERICA.COM

2014 DRAFT PROSPECTS

HIGH SCHOOL TOP 100

Rk.	Player	Position	B/T	Ht.	Weight	School	Commitment
1.	Tyler Kolek	RHP	R/R	6-6	250	Shepherd (Texas) HS	Texas Christian
2.	Alex Jackson	C/OF	R/R	6-2	210	Rancho Bernardo, Escondido, Calif.	Oregon
3.	Jacob Gatewood	SS/3B	R/R	6-4	190	Clovis (Calif.) High	Southern California
4.	Brady Aiken	LHP	L/L	6-4	205	Cathedral Catholic, San Diego	UCLA
5.	Touki Toussaint	RHP	R/R	6-2	195	Coral Springs (Florida) Academy	Vanderbilt
6.	Luis Ortiz	RHP	R/R	6-2	210	Sanger (Calif.) High	Fresno State
7.	Kodi Medeiros	LHP	L/L	6-1	190	Waiakea HS, Hilo, Hawaii	Pepperdine
8.	Cobi Johnson	RHP	R/R	6-4	180	Mitchell HS, Holiday, Fla.	Florida State
9.	Sean Reid-Foley	RHP	R/R	6-3	220	Sandalwood High, Jacksonville	Florida State
10.	Braxton Davidson	1B/OF	L/L	6-1	220	Roberson High, Asheville, N.C.	North Carolina
11.	Alex Verdugo	LHP/OF	L/L	6-0	190	Sahuaro, Tucson, Ariz.	Arizona State
12.	Nick Gordon	SS/RHP	L/R	6-2	170	Olympia High, Orlando, Fla.	Florida State
13.	Grant Holmes	RHP	L/R	6-2	220	Conway (S.C.) HS	Florida
14.	Scott Blewett	RHP	R/R	6-6	235	Baker HS, Baldwinsville, N.Y.	St. Johns
15.	Michael Gettys	OF/RHP	R/R	6-2	205	Gainesville (Ga.) HS	Georgia
16.	Mac Marshall	LHP	R/L	6-1	185	Parkview HS, Lilburn, Ga.	Louisiana State
17.	Michael Chavis	3B/2B	R/R	5-11	190	Sprayberry HS, Marietta, Ga.	Clemson
18.	Derek Hill	OF	R/R	6-1	170	Elk Grove (Calif.) High	Oregon
19.	Forrest Wall	2B	L/R	6-0	170	Orangewood Christian HS, Winter Park, Fla.	North Carolina
20.	Justus Sheffield	LHP	L/L	6-0	195	Tullahoma (Tenn.) HS	Vanderbilt
21.	Spencer Adams	RHP	R/R	6-3	190	White County, Cleveland, Ga.	Georgia
22.	Monte Harrison	OF	R/R	6-2	195	Lee's Summit West (Mo.)	Nebraska
23.	Ti'Quan Forbes	SS/3B	R/R	6-4	175	Columbia (Miss.) HS	Mississippi
24.	Marcus Wilson	OF	R/R	6-3	175	Junipero Serra HS, Los Angeles	Arizona State
25.	Milton Ramos	SS	R/R	6-1	165	American Heritage, Hialeah Gardens, Fla.	Florida Atlantic
26.	Cameron Varga	RHP	R/R	6-3	205	Cincinatti Hills Academy, Loveland, Ohio	North Carolina
27.	Josh Morgan	SS	R/R	6-0	185	Orange County Lutheran, Corona, Calif.	UCLA
28.	Dylan Cease	RHP	R/R	6-2	180	Milton (Ga.) HS	Vanderbilt
29.	Joseph Gatto	RHP	R/R	6-5	215	St. Augustine Prep, Hammonton, N.J.	North Carolina
30.	Sean Bouchard	3B	R/R	6-3	195	Cathedral Catholic, San Diego	UCLA
31.	Keaton McKinney	RHP	R/R	6-5	215	Ankeny (Iowa) HS	Arkansas
32.	Keith Weisenberg	RHP	R/R	6-4	195	Osceola HS, Seminole, Fla.	Stanford
33.	Jakson Reetz	C/OF	R/R	6-1	195	Norris HS, Hickman, Neb.	Nebraska
34.	Jeren Kendall	OF	L/R	5-10	175	Holmen (Wisc.) HS	Vanderbilt
35.	Michael Kopech	RHP	R/R	6-3	190	Mount Pleasant (Texas) HS	Arizona
36.	Adam Haseley	LHP/OF	L/L	6-1	185	The First Academy, Orlando	Virginia
37.	Shane Benes	3B/RHP	R/R	6-3	200	Westminster Academy, Town and Country, Mo.	Missouri
38.	J.J. Schwarz	C	R/R	6-2	190	Palm Beach (Fla.) Gardens	Florida
39.	Scott Hurst	OF	L/R	6-0	175	Bishop Amat, La Puente., Calif.	Cal State Fullerton
40.	Clay Casey	OF	R/R	6-3	205	Desoto Central, Southhaven, Miss.	Mississippi
41.	Jake Godfrey	RHP	R/R	6-2	215	Providence Catholic, New Lenox, Ill.	Notre Dame
42.	Matthew Railey	OF	L/L	5-11	195	North Florida Christian, Tallahassee, Fla.	Florida State
43.	Justin Smith	OF	R/R	6-2	205	Bartram Trail, St. Johns, Fla.	Miami
44.	Blake Bivens	RHP	R/R	6-2	205	George Washington, Sutherlin, Va.	Liberty
45.	Gareth Morgan	OF	R/R	6-4	215	North Toronto (Ont.) Collegiate	Uncommitted
46.	Trenton Kemp	OF	R/R	6-1	190	Buchanan HS, Clovis, Calif.	Fresno State
47.	Evan Skoug	C	L/R	5-11	205	Libertyvile (Ill.) HS	Texas Christian
48.	Alex Faedo	RHP	R/R	6-4	210	Alonso HS, Tampa	Florida
49.	Jack Flaherty	3B/RHP	R/R	6-4	205	Harvard-Westlake, Burbank, Calif.	North Carolina
50.	Trace Loehr	2B	L/R	5-11	195	Putnam HS, Milwaukie, Ore.	Oregon State

Rk.	Player	Position	B/T	Ht.	Weight	School	Commitment
51.	Roberto Gonzalez	OF	R/R	6-1	195	University HS, Orlando, Fla.	Uncommitted
52.	Lane Thomas	OF	R/R	6-0	180	Bearden HS, Knoxville, Tenn.	"Tennessee
53.	Foster Griffin	LHP	R/L	6-5	190	The First Academy, Orlando	Mississippi
54.	Turner Larkins	RHP	R/R	6-3	215	Martin HS, Arlington	Texas A&M
55.	Isan Diaz	2B/SS	L/R	6-0	180	Springfield (Mass.) Central HS	Vanderbilt
56.	David Peterson	LHP	L/L	6-6	220	Regis Jesuit, Denver	Oregon
57.	Raphael Ramirez	OF	L/L	5-11	175	Pace Academy, Atlanta	North Carolina State
58.	Tim Susnara	C	L/R	6-0	195	St. Francis HS, Redwood City, Calif.	Oregon
59.	Alex Lange	RHP	R/R	6-2	210	Lee's Summit West (Mo.)	Louisiana State
60.	Stone Garrett	OF	R/R	6-2	195	George Ranch HS, Sugarland, Texas	Rice
61.	Reese Cooley	OF	R/R	6-1	200	Fleming Island, Orange Park, Fla.	Chipola College
62.	Bryce Montes de Oca	RHP	R/R	6-8	265	Lawrence (Kan.) HS	Missouri
63.	Zach Shannon	RHP/OF	R/R	6-2	220	Anderson HS, Cincinnati, Ohio	Ohio State
64.	Kyle Marsh	RHP	R/R	6-2	177	Spruce Creek HS, Port Orange, Fla.	Central Florida
65.	Kel Johnson	1B/OF	R/R	6-4	215	Homeschooled, Palmetto, Ga.	Georgia Tech
66.	D.J. Peters	OF/1B	R/R	6-6	220	Glendora (Calif.) HS	Cal State Fullerton
67.	Jake Jarvis	3B/RHP	R/R	6-0	180	Klein Collins HS, Spring, Texas	Texas A&M
68.	Alex Destino	LHP/OF	L/L	6-3	220	North Buncombe, Weaverville, N.C.	South Carolina
69.	Carl Chester	OF	R/R	6-0	175	Lake Brantley, Longwood, Fla.	Miami
70.	Todd Isaacs Jr.	OF	R/R	6-1	175	American Heritage, Hialeah Gardens, Fla.	Uncommitted
71.	K.J. Bryant	OF	R/R	6-1	185	Hampton HS, Taylors, S.C.	Clemson
72.	Willie Rios	LHP/OF	S/L	6-0	185	IMG Academy, Bradenton, Fla.	Maryland
73.	Devon Fisher	C	R/R	6-1	200	Western Branch HS, Portsmouth, Va.	Virginia
74.	Jacob Nix	RHP	R/R	6-4	205	Los Alamitos (Calif.) HS	UCLA
75.	Chandler Avant	2B	R/R	6-0	175	Pike Liberty, Troy, Ala.	Alabama
76.	Carson Sands	LHP	L/L	6-3	205	North Florida Christian, Tallahassee, Fla.	Florida State
77.	Austin Murphy	OF	L/L	6-2	210	Episcopal HS, Jacksonville	Auburn
78.	Christian Martinek	LHP	L/L	6-4	225	Jesuit HS, Beaverton, Ore.	Oregon State
79.	Mitch Hart	RHP	R/R	6-4	190	Granite Bay (Calif.) HS	Southern California
80.	Garrett Fulenchek	RHP	R/R	6-3	190	Howe (Texas) HS	Dallas Baptist
81.	Derek Casey	RHP	R/R	6-1	185	Hanover HS, Mechanicsville, Va.	Virginia
82.	Travis Jones	OF	R/R	6-5	205	Atascocita HS, Humble, Texas	Texas
83.	Payton Squier	2B/SS	L/R	6-1	190	Greenway HS, Glendale, Ariz.	UNLV
84.	Gabe Gonzalez	RHP	R/R	6-3	200	Arbor View HS, Las Vegas	UNLV
85.	Branden Kelliher	RHP	R/R	5-11	170	Lake Stevens (Wash.) HS	Oregon
86.	Austin DeCarr	RHP	R/R	6-3	215	Salisbury (Conn.) School	Vanderbilt
87.	Shane Mardirosian	2B	L/R	5-10	175	Martin Luther King HS, Riverside, Calif.	UC Santa Barbara
88.	Justin Twine	2B/SS	R/R	5-10	195	Falls City HS, Hemphill, Texas	Texas Christian
89.	Greg Deichmann	2B/SS	L/R	6-2	180	Brothers Martin, Metairie, La.	Louisiana State
90.	Benito Santiago	C	L/R	5-10	175	Coral Springs (Florida) Academy	Tennessee
91.	Erik Manoah Jr.	RHP	R/R	6-2	210	South Dade HS, Homestead, Fla.	Florida International
92.	Tucker Baca	LHP	L/L	6-3	195	North Gwinett HS, Suwanee, Ga.	Arizona State
93.	Luke Dykstra	2B/3B	R/R	6-1	190	Westlake HS, Thousands Oaks, Calif.	Fresno State
94.	Zach Sullivan	OF	R/R	6-3	175	Corning (N.Y.) Painted Post East	Stony Brook
95.	Quinn Brodey	LHP/OF	L/L	6-1	195	Loyola HS, Los Angeles	Stanford
96.	Cre Finfrock	RHP	S/L	6-0	170	Martin County HS, Jensen Beach, Fla.	Central Florida
97.	Weston Davis	RHP	R/R	6-4	175	Manatee HS, Bradenton, Fla.	Florida
98.	Brandon Murray	RHP	R/R	6-3	200	Hobert (Ind.) High	South Carolina
99.	Tate Blackman	2B/3B	R/R	6-1	190	Lake Brantley, Longwood, Fla.	Mississippi
100.	Devin Smeltzer	LHP	R/L	6-2	170	Bishop Eustace Prep, Voorhees, N.J.	Florida Gulf Coast

TOP 20 PROSPECTS

FROM EVERY MINOR LEAGUE

As a complement to the organization prospect rankings, Baseball America also ranks prospects in all the minor leagues at the end of their seasons. Like the organization lists, they place more weight on potential than performance and should not be regarded as all-star teams. Unlike the organization lists, which are from more of a scouting perspective, the minor league lists reflect the views of minor league managers, who give more weight to what a player does on the field now. We think both perspectives are useful, so we give you both, even though they don't always match up. For a player to qualify for a league prospect list, he must have spent at least one-third of the season in a league. Also unlike the organization lists, players can make the league lists even if they exhausted their rookie eligibility during the 2013 season.

TRIPLE-A

INTERNATIONAL LEAGUE

1. Xander Bogaerts, ss, Pawtucket (Red Sox)
2. Wil Myers, of, Durham (Rays)
3. Gerrit Cole, rhp, Indianapolis (Pirates)
4. Chris Archer, rhp, Durham (Rays)
5. Nick Castellanos, of, Toledo (Tigers)
6. Danny Salazar, rhp, Columbus (Indians)
7. Avisail Garcia, of, Toledo (Tigers)/Charlotte (White Sox)
8. Jackie Bradley, of, Pawtucket (Red Sox)
9. Cody Asche, 3b, Lehigh Valley (Phillies)
10. Billy Hamilton, of, Louisville (Reds)
11. Erik Johnson, rhp, Charlotte (White Sox)
12. Oswaldo Arcia, of, Rochester (Twins)
13. Allen Webster, rhp, Pawtucket (Red Sox)
14. Jonathan Schoop, 2b/ss, Norfolk (Orioles)
15. Jake Odorizzi, rhp, Durham (Rays)
16. Trevor Bauer, rhp, Columbus (Indians)
17. Darin Ruf, of/1b, Lehigh Valley (Phillies)
18. Carlos Sanchez, 2b/ss, Charlotte (White Sox)
19. Kevin Pillar, of, Buffalo (Blue Jays)
20. Joey Terdoslavich, of, Gwinnett (Braves)

PACIFIC COAST LEAGUE

1. Oscar Taveras, of, Memphis (Cardinals)
2. Jurickson Profar, ss, Round Rock (Rangers)
3. George Springer, of, Oklahoma City (Astros)
4. Zack Wheeler, rhp, Las Vegas (Mets)
5. Michael Wacha, rhp, Memphis (Cardinals)
6. Taijuan Walker, rhp, Tacoma (Mariners)
7. Carlos Martinez, rhp, Memphis (Cardinals)
8. Chris Owings, ss, Reno (Diamondbacks)
9. Nick Franklin, 2b/ss, Tacoma (Mariners)
10. Yordano Ventura, rhp, Omaha (Royals)
11. Jarred Cosart, rhp, Oklahoma City (Astros)
12. Sonny Gray, rhp, Sacramento (Athletics)
13. Jonathan Singleton, 1b, Oklahoma City (Astros)
14. Matt Davidson, 3b, Reno (Diamondbacks)
15. Wilmer Flores, 2b/1b, Las Vegas (Mets)
16. Kolten Wong, 2b, Memphis (Cardinals)
17. Tyler Skaggs, lhp, Reno (Diamondbacks)
18. Rafael Montero, rhp, Las Vegas (Mets)
19. Jonathan Villar, ss, Oklahoma City (Astros)
20. Michael Choice, of, Sacramento (Athletics)

DOUBLE-A

EASTERN LEAGUE

1. Xander Bogaerts, ss, Portland (Red Sox)
2. Miguel Sano, 3b, New Britain (Twins)
3. Noah Syndergaard, rhp, Binghamton (Mets)
4. Maikel Franco, 3b, Reading (Phillies)
5. Alex Meyer, rhp, New Britain (Twins)
6. Jameson Taillon, rhp, Altoona (Pirates)
7. Gregory Polanco, of, Altoona (Pirates)
8. Anthony Rendon, 3b, Harrisburg (Nationals)
9. Eduardo Rodriguez, lhp, Bowie (Orioles)
10. Marcus Stroman, rhp, New Hampshire (Blue Jays)
11. Jesse Biddle, lhp, Reading (Phillies)
12. Taylor Jordan, rhp, Harrisburg (Nationals)
13. Rafael Montero, rhp, Binghamton (Mets)
14. Garin Cecchini, 3b, Portland (Red Sox)
15. Nick Kingham, rhp, Altoona (Pirates)
16. Anthony Ranaudo, rhp, Portland (Red Sox)
17. Jose Ramirez, 2b/ss, Akron (Indians)
18. J.R. Murphy, c, Trenton (Yankees)
19. Brandon Workman, rhp, Portland (Red Sox)
20. Josmil Pinto, c, New Britain (Twins)

SOUTHERN LEAGUE

1. Yasiel Puig, of, Chattanooga (Dodgers)
2. Archie Bradley, rhp, Mobile (Diamondbacks)
3. Javier Baez, ss, Tennessee (Cubs)
4. Taijuan Walker, rhp, Jackson (Mariners)
5. Chistian Yelich, of, Jacksonville (Marlins)
6. Alex Wood, lhp, Mississippi (Braves)
7. Joc Pederson, of, Chattanooga (Dodgers)
8. Christian Bethencourt, c, Mississippi (Braves)
9. Arismendy Alcantara, ss/2b, Tennessee (Cubs)
10. Jake Marisnick, of, Jacksonville (Marlins)
11. Erik Johnson, rhp, Birmingham (White Sox)
12. Enny Romero, lhp, Montgomery (Rays)
13. Brad Miller, ss, Jackson (Mariners)
14. Marcus Semien, ss/2b, Birmingham (White Sox)
15. Zach Lee, rhp, Chattanooga (Dodgers)
16. Tommy La Stella, 2b, Mississippi (Braves)
17. Julio Morban, of, Jackson (Mariners)
18. Jimmy Nelson, rhp, Huntsville (Brewers)
19. Edward Salcedo, 3b, Mississippi (Braves)
20. Yorman Rodriguez, Pensacola (Reds)

TEXAS LEAGUE

1. George Springer, of, Corpus Christi (Astros)
2. Mike Foltynewicz, rhp, Corpus Christi (Astros)
3. Yordano Ventura, rhp, Northwest Arkansas (Royals)
4. Rougned Odor, 2b, Frisco (Rangers)
5. Matt Wisler, rhp, San Antonio (Padres)
6. Domingo Santana, of, Corpus Christi (Astros)
7. Keyvius Sampson, rhp, San Antonio (Padres)
8. Jason Adam, rhp, Northwest Arkansas (Royals)
9. Stephen Piscotty, of, Springfield (Cardinals)
10. Taylor Lindsey, 2b, Arkansas (Angels)
11. Luis Sardinas, ss, Frisco (Rangers)
12. Tim Cooney, lhp, Springfield (Cardinals)
13. Kyle Parker, of/1b, Tulsa (Rockies)
14. Chad Bettis, rhp, Tulsa (Rockies)

15. Matt Andriese, rhp, San Antonio (Padres)
16. Max Stassi, c, Corpus Christi (Astros)
17. Randal Grichuk, of, Arkansas (Angels)
18. Orlando Calixte, ss/3b, Northwest Arkansas (Royals)
19. Reymond Fuentes, of, San Antonio (Padres)
20. Cheslor Cuthbert, 3b, Northwest Arkansas (Royals)

HIGH CLASS A

CALIFORNIA LEAGUE

1. Addison Russell, ss, Stockton (Athletics)
2. Eddie Butler, rhp, Modesto (Rockies)
3. Kyle Crick, rhp, San Jose (Giants)
4. Delino DeShields Jr., 2b, Lancaster (Astros)
5. Austin Hedges, c, Lake Elsinore (Padres)
6. Edwin Escobar, lhp, San Jose (Giants)
7. Patrick Kivlehan, 3b, High Desert (Mariners)
8. Jace Peterson, ss, Lake Elsinore (Padres)
9. Alex Yarbrough, 2b, Inland Empire (Angels)
10. Adalberto Mejia, lhp, San Jose (Giants)
11. Chris Taylor, ss, High Desert (Mariners).
12. Travis Jankowski, of, Lake Elsinore (Padres).
13. Yorman Rodriguez, of, Bakersfield (Reds).
14. Max Muncy, 1b, Stockton (Athletics).
15. Ty Blach, lhp, San Jose (Giants).
16. Mark Sappington, rhp, Inland Empire (Angels).
17. R.J. Alvarez, rhp, Inland Empire (Angels).
18. Mac Williamson, of, San Jose (Giants).
19. Trevor Story, ss, Modesto (Rockies).
20. Clayton Blackburn, rhp, San Jose (Giants).

CAROLINA LEAGUE

1. Francisco Lindor, ss, Carolina (Indians)
2. Kyle Zimmer, rhp, Wilmington (Royals)
3. Rougned Odor, 2b, Myrtle Beach (Rangers)
4. Henry Owens, lhp, Salem (Red Sox)
5. Blake Swihart, c, Salem (Red Sox)
6. Garin Cecchini, 3b, Salem (Red Sox)
7. Mookie Betts, 2b, Salem (Red Sox)
8. Eduardo Rodriguez, lhp, Frederick (Orioles)
9. Luke Jackson, rhp, Myrtle Beach (Rangers)
10. A.J. Cole, rhp, Potomac (Nationals)
11. Jorge Bonifacio, of, Wilmington (Royals)
12. Michael Taylor, of, Potomac (Nationals)
13. Deven Marrero, ss, Salem (Red Sox)
14. Luis Sardinas, ss, Myrtle Beach (Rangers)
15. Courtney Hawkins, of, Winston-Salem (White Sox)
16. Robbie Ray, lhp, Potomac (Nationals)
17. Robby Hefflinger, of, Lynchburg (Braves)
18. Michael Ohlman, c, Frederick (Orioles)
19. Billy Burns, of, Potomac (Nationals)
20. Cody Anderson, rhp, Carolina (Indians)

FLORIDA STATE LEAGUE

1. Byron Buxton, of, Fort Myers (Twins)
2. Miguel Sano, 3b, Fort Myers (Twins)
3. Javier Baez, ss, Daytona (Cubs)
4. Gregory Polanco, of, Bradenton (Pirates)
5. Maikel Franco, 3b, Clearwater (Phillies)
6. Noah Syndergaard, rhp, St. Lucie (Mets)
7. Gary Sanchez, c, Tampa (Yankees)
8. Jorge Soler, of, Daytona (Cubs)
9. Andrew Heaney, lhp, Jupiter (Marlins)
10. Aaron Sanchez, rhp, Dunedin (Blue Jays)
11. Nick Kingham, rhp, Bradenton (Pirates)
12. Eddie Rosario, 2b, Fort Myers (Twins)
13. Alen Hanson, ss, Bradenton (Pirates)
14. Stephen Piscotty, of, Palm Beach (Cardinals)
15. Pierce Johnson, rhp, Daytona (Cubs)
16. Justin Nicolino, lhp, Jupiter (Marlins)
17. Devon Travis, 2b, Lakeland (Tigers)
18. Anthony DeSclafani, rhp, Jupiter (Marlins)
19. Mason Williams, of, Tampa (Yankees)
20. Aaron Altherr, of, Clearwater (Phillies)

LOW CLASS A

MIDWEST LEAGUE

1. Byron Buxton, of, Cedar Rapids (Twins)
2. Carlos Correa, ss, Quad Cities (Astros)
3. Robert Stephenson, rhp, Dayton (Reds)
4. Corey Seager, ss, Great Lakes (Dodgers)
5. Lance McCullers Jr, rhp, Quad Cities (Astros)
6. Albert Almora, of, Kane County (Cubs)
7. Julio Urias, lhp, Great Lakes (Dodgers)
8. Max Fried, lhp, Fort Wayne (Padres)
9. Jesse Winker, of, Dayton (Reds)
10. Pierce Johnson, rhp, Kane County (Cubs)
11. Zach Eflin, rhp, Fort Wayne (Padres)
12. Vince Velasquez, rhp, Quad Cities (Astros)
13. Jose Berrios, rhp, Cedar Rapids (Twins)
14. Joe Ross, rhp, Fort Wayne (Padres)
15. Adam Brett Walker, of, Cedar Rapids (Twins)
16. Brandon Drury, 3b, South Bend (Diamondbacks)
17. Dan Vogelbach, 1b, Kane County (Cubs)
18. Taylor Guerrieri, rhp, Bowling Green (Rays)
19. Andrew Toles, of, Bowling Green (Rays)
20. Jorge Polanco, 2b/ss, Cedar Rapids (Twins)

SOUTH ATLANTIC LEAGUE

1. Eddie Butler, rhp, Asheville (Rockies)
2. Tyler Glasnow, rhp, West Virginia (Pirates)
3. C.J. Edwards, rhp, Hickory (Rangers/Cubs)
4. Raul Adalberto Mondesi, ss, Lexington (Royals)
5. Rosell Herrera, ss, Asheville (Rockies)
6. Miguel Almonte, rhp, Lexington (Royals)
7. Colin Moran, 3b, Greensboro (Marlins)
8. Mookie Betts, 2b, Greenville (Red Sox)
9. Lucas Sims, rhp, Rome (Braves)
10. Mauricio Cabrera, rhp, Rome (Braves)
11. Lewis Brinson, of, Hickory (Rangers)
12. Joey Gallo, 3b, Hickory (Rangers)
13. Nick Williams, of, Hickory (Rangers)
14. Jorge Alfaro, c, Hickory (Rangers)
15. Nomar Mazara, of, Hickory (Rangers)
16. Jose Peraza, ss, Rome (Braves)
17. Rafael De Paula, rhp, Charleston (Yankees)
18. Carlos Tocci, of, Lakewood (Phillies)
19. Bubba Starling, of, Lexington (Royals)
20. Steve Matz, lhp, Savannah (Mets)

SHORT-SEASON

NEW YORK-PENN LEAGUE

1. Harold Ramirez, of, Jamestown (Pirates)
2. Oscar Hernandez, c, Hudson Valley (Rays)
3. Michael Feliz, rhp, Tri-City (Astros)
4. Zach Green, 3b, Williamsport (Phillies)
5. Carson Kelly, 3b, State College (Cardinals)
6. Eric Jagielo, 3b, Staten Island (Yankees)
7. Manuel Margot, of, Lowell (Red Sox)
8. Avery Romero, 2b, Batavia (Marlins)
9. Dylan Cozens, of, Williamsport (Phillies)
10. Simon Mercedes, rhp, Lowell (Red Sox)

11. Gavin Cecchini, ss, Brooklyn (Mets)
12. B.J. Boyd, of, Vermont (Athletics)
13. Jake Johansen, rhp, Auburn (Nationals)
14. Trevor Williams, rhp, Batavia (Marlins)
15. Jamie Callahan, rhp, Lowell (Red Sox)
16. Steven Brault, lhp, Aberdeen (Orioles)
17. Zac Reininger, rhp, Connecticut (Tigers)
18. Robert Gsellman, rhp, Brooklyn (Mets)
19. Juan Herrera, ss, Mahoning Valley (Indians)/State College (Cardinals)
20. Miller Diaz, rhp, Brooklyn (Mets)

NORTHWEST LEAGUE

1. Kris Bryant, 3b, Boise (Cubs)
2. Hunter Renfroe, of, Eugene (Padres)
3. D.J. Peterson, 3b, Everett (Mariners)
4. Aaron Blair, rhp, Hillsboro (Diamondbacks)
5. Austin Wilson, of, Everett (Mariners)
6. Kelvin Vasquez, rhp, Spokane (Rangers)
7. Paul Blackburn, rhp, Boise (Cubs)
8. Chase Johnson, rhp, Salem-Keizer (Giants)
9. Yasiel Balaguert, of, Boise (Cubs)
10. Dillon Maples, rhp, Boise (Cubs)
11. David Ledbetter, rhp, Spokane (Rangers)
12. Shawon Dunston Jr., of, Boise (Cubs)
13. Tom Robson, rhp, Vancouver (Blue Jays)
14. Jack Reinheimer, ss, Everett (Mariners)
15. Daniel Gibson, lhp, Hillsboro (Diamondbacks)
16. Ryan Warner, rhp, Tri-City (Rockies)
17. Kevin Encarnacion, of, Boise (Cubs)
18. Lars Huijer, rhp, Everett (Mariners)
19. L.B. Dantzler, 1b, Vancouver (Blue Jays)
20. Jose Martinez, rhp, Hillsboro (Diamondbacks)

ROOKIE

APPALACHIAN LEAGUE

1. Amed Rosario, ss, Kingsport (Mets)
2. D.J. Davis, of, Bluefield (Blue Jays)
3. Victor Caratini, 3b, Danville (Braves)
4. Mitch Nay, 3b, Bluefield (Blue Jays)
5. Dawel Lugo, ss, Bluefield (Blue Jays)
6. Chase DeJong, rhp, Bluefield (Blue Jays)
7. Alex Reyes, rhp, Johnson City (Cardinals)
8. Alberto Tirado, rhp, Bluefield (Blue Jays)
9. Edwin Diaz, rhp, Pulaski (Mariners)
10. Tyler Danish, rhp, Bristol (White Sox)
11. Johan Camargo, ss, Danville (Braves)
12. Jairo Labourt, lhp, Bluefield (Blue Jays)
13. Wilton Martinez, of, Pulaski (Mariners)
14. Felix Jorge, rhp, Elizabethton (Twins)
15. Rob Whalen, rhp, Kinsport (Mets)
16. Adonys Cardona, rhp, Bluefield (Blue Jays)
17. Kenny Peoples, ss, Johnson City (Cardinals)
18. Stuart Turner, c, Elizabethton (Twins)
19. Chris Flexen, rhp, Kingsport (Mets)
20. Steve Bean, c, Johnson City (Cardinals)

PIONEER LEAGUE

1. Hunter Dozier, 3b, Idaho Falls (Royals)
2. Phillip Ervin, of, Billings (Reds)
3. Raimel Tapia, of, Grand Junction (Rockies)
4. Ryan McMahon, 3b, Grand Junction (Rockies)
5. Emerson Jimenez, ss, Grand Junction (Rockies)
6. Ben Lively, rhp, Billings (Reds)
7. Zach Bird, rhp, Ogden (Dodgers)
8. Stryker Trahan, c, Missoula (Diamondbacks)
9. Jacob Scavuzzo, of, Ogden (Dodgers)
10. Jose Briceno, c, Grand Junction (Rockies)
11. Elier Hernandez, of Idaho Falls (Royals)
12. Adam Engel, of, Great Falls (White Sox)
13. Zane Evans, c, Idaho Falls (Royals)
14. Cody Reed, lhp, Idaho Falls (Royals)
15. Jose Rondon, ss, Orem (Angels)
16. Michael Ratterree, of, Helena (Brewers)
17. Barrett Astin, rhp, Helena (Brewers)
18. Geordy Parra, rhp, Missoula (Diamondbacks)
19. Dustin Houle, c, Helena (Brewers)
20. Scott Barlow, rhp, Ogden (Dodgers)

ARIZONA LEAGUE

1. Clint Frazier, of, Indians
2. Christian Arroyo, ss, Giants
3. Franchy Cordero, ss, Padres
4. Sergio Alcantara, ss, Diamondbacks
5. Jose Urena, of, Padres
6. Akeem Bostick, rhp, Rangers
7. Francisco Mejia, c, Indians
8. Billy McKinney, of, Athletics
9. Travis Demeritte, ss/3b, Rangers
10. Jairo Beras, of, Rangers
11. Justin Williams, of, Diamondbacks
12. Devin Williams, rhp, Brewers
13. Natanael Delgado, of, Angels
14. Keury Mella, rhp, Giants
15. Dustin Peterson, 3b, Padres
16. Samir Duenez, 1b, Royals
17. Adrian De Horta, rhp, Padres
18. Ryder Jones, 3b, Giants
19. Brad Keller, rhp, Diamondbacks
20. Cole Wiper, rhp, Rangers

GULF COAST LEAGUE

1. Austin Meadows, of, Pirates
2. Lucas Giolito, rhp, Nationals
3. Reese McGuire, c, Pirates
4. Dominic Smith, 1b, Mets
5. Franklin Barreto, ss, Blue Jays
6. J.P. Crawford, ss, Phillies
7. Lewis Thorpe, lhp, Twins
8. Rob Kaminsky, lhp, Cardinals
9. Wendell Rijo, 2b, Red Sox
10. Luis Torrens, c, Yankees
11. Miguel Andujar, 3b, Yankees
12. Nick Ciuffo, c, Rays
13. Abiatal Avelino, ss, Yankees
14. Victor Reyes, of, Braves
15. Gosuke Katoh, 2b, Yankees
16. Jose Mujica, rhp, Rays
17. Luis Severino, rhp, Yankees
18. Javier Betancourt, ss, Tigers
19. Jose Castillo, lhp, Rays
20. Thairo Estrada, ss, Yankees

INDEX

D

E

F

G

H

I

J

K

L

M

N

O

P

Q

R

S

T